Baseball america®
PROSPECT
HANDBOOK

2004

Durham, N.C.

EDITORS
Jim Callis, Will Lingo

ASSOCIATE EDITORS
Josh Boyd, Allan Simpson

CONTRIBUTING WRITERS
Bill Ballew, Mike Berardino, Pat Caputo, J.J. Cooper, Tom Haudricourt,
Jim Ingraham, Will Kimmey, Michael Levesque, John Manuel,
John Perrotto, Tracy Ringolsby, Phil Rogers, Casey Tefertiller

PHOTO EDITOR
Alan Matthews

EDITORIAL ASSISTANT
Gary Martin

DESIGN & PRODUCTION
Phillip Daquila, Matthew Eddy, Linwood Webb

COVER PHOTO
Joe Mauer by David Schofield

COVER DESIGN
Linwood Webb

STATISTICAL CONSULTANT
SportsTicker
Boston

BaseBall america

President/CEO: Catherine Silver
Vice President/Publisher: Lee Folger
Editor In Chief: Allan Simpson
Managing Editor: Will Lingo
Executive Editor: Jim Callis
Design & Production Director: Phillip Daquila

BaseballAmerica.com

CONTENTS

Foreword by Pat Gillick	5
Introduction	6
Profiling Prospects	7
Explanation of Minor League Depth Charts	8
Organization Talent Rankings	9
Top 50 Prospects	10
Anaheim Angels	14
Arizona Diamondbacks	30
Atlanta Braves	46
Baltimore Orioles	62
Boston Red Sox	78
Chicago Cubs	94
Chicago White Sox	110
Cincinnati Reds	126
Cleveland Indians	142
Colorado Rockies	158
Detroit Tigers	174
Florida Marlins	190
Houston Astros	206
Kansas City Royals	222
Los Angeles Dodgers	238
Milwaukee Brewers	254
Minnesota Twins	270
Montreal Expos	286
New York Mets	302
New York Yankees	318
Oakland Athletics	334
Philadelphia Phillies	350
Pittsburgh Pirates	366
St. Louis Cardinals	382
San Diego Padres	398
San Francisco Giants	414
Seattle Mariners	430
Tampa Bay Devil Rays	446
Texas Rangers	462
Toronto Blue Jays	478
Draft Bonus History	494
2003 Draft Prospects	498
Minor League Top Prospects	502
Index	505

FOREWORD

When I ran the Toronto Blue Jays from 1977–94, we didn't have a lot of rules when it came to scouting. We were fortunate enough to have hard-working people like Al LaMacchia, Bobby Mattick, Moose Johnson, Ellis Dungan, Bob Engle and Epy Guerrero.

We did have a rule regarding Baseball America, which was reiterated at each of our organizational meetings: The rule was that none of our scouts was allowed to speak to a Baseball America employee. Why? Because they did too good a job at rating our prospects and our minor league system. Looking back now, it was a backhanded compliment for the job Allan Simpson and his staff have done over the years.

The thing about the magazine was that from the very start until today, it always has recognized the importance of the personal aspects of scouting and has never lost sight of those all-important values. Baseball America always has had its finger on the pulse of the game and the hard-working scouts who cover it from the high school sandlot park without lights, to the college game, to the minors from Rookie ball to Triple-A, and then to the majors.

A lot of these men spent more time at the ballpark—from Key West, Fla., to St. Cloud, Minn., or from San Diego to Bangor, Maine—than they did at home, not because of a high salary but because of a love of the game. These scouts recognize that projectability, athleticism and makeup, as well as raw statistical analysis, play an important role in making decisions on players.

Properly analyzing and ranking prospects is not an easy job, as any general manager will tell you. But any GM also will tell you that he has a Baseball America Prospect Handbook in his office. Why? Because they do an excellent job and put out a fine product.

Growing up in Chico, Calif., and later at the University of Southern California and in the minors, my friends and I would rush to read The Sporting News. Now that I'm older—and speaking to Baseball America—I rush to read Baseball America the magazine and Baseball America publications like this one.

Pat Gillick
Consultant
Seattle Mariners

INTRODUCTION

Drew Henson struck out hundreds of times before finally giving up baseball to try his hand at the NFL. Josh Hamilton has battled personal issues and injuries to try to stay on the field and fulfill his promise. Injuries have so damaged Ryan Anderson's and Matt White's arms that they were taken off 40-man rosters this offseason.

Major league teams spent millions of dollars on these players, and Baseball America touted them as top prospects—repeatedly. If they can fail so miserably, what is the point of trying to pick out the best prospects at all?

The point is Mark Teixeira, Rocco Baldelli, Jose Reyes, Miguel Cabrera, Jeremy Bonderman, Rich Harden, Rafael Soriano, Francisco Rodriguez, Mike MacDougal and Dontrelle Willis, to name just a few of the players who were in last year's Prospect Handbook and made contributions in the big leagues in 2003. And those are just the guys who were the cream of the crop. Players from up and down the 30 top 30 lists that follow will make themselves heard in the big leagues in the coming years.

But really, the point is even bigger than that. As you read about the 900 players in this book—the players who are considered the best in the minors—you know that a significant number of them won't make it at all, or won't have extended major league careers. You know it, but you devour all the information anyway. Because you want to know what the future holds for your favorite team. Because you love the feeling when one of the players you decide is going to be a star actually becomes a star. Because you simply love the game and love to follow it in this way.

That's why we're here, and why this book returns for the fourth year. Even after just four editions, the Prospect Handbook has clearly established itself as the best book of its kind. What sets our prospect analysis apart is the work that goes into each organization's top 30 list and accompanying information. It's really the culmination of work we do year-round. We talk to general managers, scouting directors, farm directors, scouts, managers, coaches and other people in the game. Then we spend hours researching, writing, editing and proof-reading.

The Prospect Handbook was a massive undertaking made possible only by the great work of our editorial staff and correspondents, as well as our crack production team. It also represents the last major contribution from our national writer Josh Boyd, better known simply as our prospect maven. He's going to work as a scout for the Padres, which is a loss for us but a great opportunity for him (and the Padres). He's one of the reasons this book is so good and has gotten better each year.

Remember that for the purposes of this book, a prospect is anyone who is still rookie-eligible under Major League Baseball guidelines (no more than 50 innings pitched or 130 at-bats), without regard to service time. Players are listed with the organizations they were with on Feb. 1.

You'll also notice several grades in each team section. Boyd graded each organization's impact potential—players who are potential all-stars or frontline players—and depth—the number of players who could become at least big league contributors. Those grades give you an idea of why organizations rank where they do in our minor league talent ratings.

Also, Jim Callis graded each team's drafts from 1999–2002. The grades are based solely on the quality of the players signed, with no consideration given to whom they were traded for or how many first-round picks the club had or lost.

The fourth Prospect Handbook is the best yet, so plow through our lists and see which players you think will pan out—and which ones won't. It's all part of the fun.

Will Lingo
Managing Editor

PROFILING **PROSPECTS**

Among all the scouting lingo you'll come across in this book, perhaps no terms are more telling and prevalent than "profile" and "projection."

When scouts evaluate a player, their main objective is to identify—or project—what the player's future role will be in the major leagues. Each organization has its own philosophy when it comes to grading players, so we talked to scouts from several teams to provide general guidelines.

The first thing to know is what scouts are looking for. In short, tools. These refer to the physical skills a player needs to be successful in the major leagues. For a position player, the five basic tools are hitting, hitting for power, fielding, arm strength and speed. For a pitcher, the tools are based on the pitches he throws. Each pitch is graded, as well as a pitcher's control, delivery and durability.

For most teams, the profiling system has gone through massive changes in recent years because of the offensive explosion in baseball. Where arm strength and defense used to be a must in the middle of the diamond, there has been an obvious swing toward finding players who can rake, regardless of their gloves. In the past, players like Jeff Kent and Alfonso Soriano wouldn't have been accepted as second basemen, but now they are the standard for offensive-minded second basemen.

While more emphasis is placed on hitting—which also covers getting on base—fielding and speed are still at a premium up the middle. As teams sacrifice defense at the corner outfield slots, they look for a speedy center fielder to make up ground in the alleys. Most scouts prefer at least a 55 runner (on the 20-80 scouting scale; see chart) at short and center field, but as power increases at those two positions, running comes down (see Rich Aurilia, Jim Edmonds). Shortstops need range and at least average arm strength, and second basemen need to be quick on the pivot. Teams are more willing to put up with an immobile corner infielder if he can mash.

The Scouting Scale

When grading a player's tools, scouts use a standard 20-80 scale. When you read that a pitcher throws an above-average slider, it can be interpreted as a 60 pitch, or a plus pitch. Plus-plus is 70, or well-above-average, and so on. Scouts don't throw 80s around very freely. Here's what each grade means:

80	Outstanding
70	Well-above-average
60	Above-average
50	Major league average
40	Below-average
30	Well-below-average
20	Poor

Arm strength is the one tool moving way down preference lists. For a catcher, it was always the No. 1 tool, but with fewer players stealing and the slide step helping to shut down running games, scouts are looking for more offensive production from the position. Receiving skills, including game-calling, blocking pitches and release times, can make up for the lack of a plus arm.

On the mound, it doesn't just come down to pure stuff. While a true No. 1 starter on a first-division team should have a couple of 70 or 80 pitches in his repertoire, like Josh Beckett and Mark Prior, they also need to produce 250-plus innings, 35 starts and 15-plus wins.

A player's overall future potential is also graded on the 20-80 scale, though some teams use a letter grade. This number is not just the sum of his tools, but rather a profiling system and a scout's ultimate opinion of the player.

70-80 (A): This category is reserved for the elite players in baseball. This player will be a perennial all-star, the best player at his position, one of the top five starters in the game or a frontline closer. Alex Rodriguez, Barry Bonds and Pedro Martinez reside here.

60-69 (B) You'll find all-star-caliber players here: No. 2 starters on a championship club and first-division players. See Mike Mussina, Miguel Tejada and Alfonso Soriano.

55-59 (C+) The majority of first-division starters are found in this range, including quality No. 2 and 3 starters, frontline set-up men and second-tier closers.

50-54 (C) Solid-average everyday major leaguers. Most are not first-division regulars. This group also includes No. 4 and 5 starters.

45-49 (D+) Fringe everyday players, backups, some No. 5 starters, middle relievers, pinch-hitters and one-tool players.

40-44 (D) Up-and-down roster fillers, situational relievers and 25th players.

38-39 (O) Organizational players who provide depth for the minor leagues but are not considered future major leaguers.

20-37 (NP) Not a prospect.

MINOR LEAGUE
DEPTH CHART

AN OVERVIEW

Another feature of the Prospect Handbook is a depth chart of every organization's minor league talent. This shows you at a glance where a system's strengths and weaknesses lie and provides even more prospects beyond an organization's top 30. Each depth chart is accompanied by analysis of the system's impact players and depth, as well as where it ranks in baseball (see facing page for the complete list). The rankings are based on our judgment of the quality and quantity of talent in each system, with higher marks to organizations that have more high-ceiling prospects or a deep system. The best systems have both.

To help you better understand why players are slotted at particular positions, we show you here what scouts look for in the ideal candidate at each spot, with individual tools ranked in descending order.

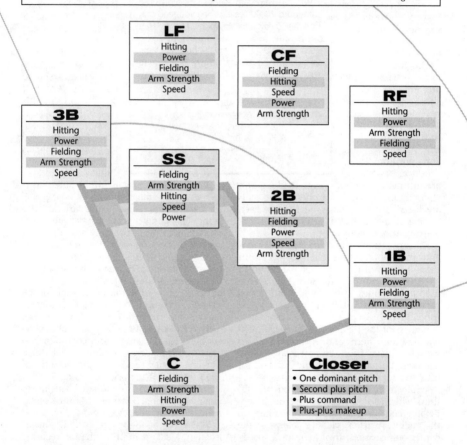

LF
- Hitting
- Power
- Fielding
- Arm Strength
- Speed

CF
- Fielding
- Hitting
- Speed
- Power
- Arm Strength

RF
- Hitting
- Power
- Arm Strength
- Fielding
- Speed

3B
- Hitting
- Power
- Fielding
- Arm Strength
- Speed

SS
- Fielding
- Arm Strength
- Hitting
- Speed
- Power

2B
- Hitting
- Fielding
- Power
- Speed
- Arm Strength

1B
- Hitting
- Power
- Fielding
- Arm Strength
- Speed

C
- Fielding
- Arm Strength
- Hitting
- Power
- Speed

Closer
- One dominant pitch
- Second plus pitch
- Plus command
- Plus-plus makeup

Starting Pitchers

No. 1 starter	No. 2 starter	No. 3 starter	No. 4-5 starters
• Two plus pitches	• Two plus pitches	• One plus pitch	• Command of two major league pitches
• Average third pitch	• Average third pitch	• Two average pitches	
• Plus-plus command	• Average command	• Average command	• Average velocity
• Plus makeup	• Average makeup	• Average makeup	• Consistent breaking ball
			• Decent changeup

TALENT RANKINGS

	2003	2002	2001	2000	1999
1 Milwaukee Brewers	16	26	30	30	27
If fans can wait a little bit longer and Brewers can stay the course, major help is on the way.					
2 Los Angeles Dodgers	14	25	28	23	24
Ownership change has front office in flux, but the farm is loaded with high-ceiling talent.					
3 Anaheim Angels	5	17	25	29	30
Former scouting director Donny Rowland's drafts will be appreciated long after his departure.					
4 Atlanta Braves	2	7	5	4	1
It's no accident that Braves' run of high rankings has coincided with run of division titles.					
5 Minnesota Twins	4	6	15	10	10
Deep system will graduate its best player, Minor League Player of the Year Joe Mauer.					
6 Cleveland Indians	1	20	26	19	4
Even after sending numerous players to the big leagues last year, system still has depth.					
7 Chicago Cubs	3	1	2	16	26
Big league success came sooner than expected, and now young talent will build upon it.					
8 Toronto Blue Jays	6	13	17	8	4
Competing on a budget in the American League East is easier with this kind of talent.					
9 Tampa Bay Devil Rays	10	15	6	13	29
Premium prospects at the top of the organization take a back seat to no one.					
10 New York Mets	13	27	20	22	23
Signing of Kazuo Matsui highlights a system on the upswing.					
11 Pittsburgh Pirates	18	22	19	14	15
Front office has built good depth, winning attitude in minors, but Pirates lack impact players.					
12 Seattle Mariners	9	2	4	24	20
Mariners have made up for spotty recent draft history with key international signings.					
13 Arizona Diamondbacks	21	23	29	12	18
Player development becomes essential as the franchise looks to cut its big league payroll.					
14 Florida Marlins	8	10	9	2	2
Minor league talent was key to Marlins' unlikely run to World Series title.					
15 Colorado Rockies	25	24	16	26	25
In spite of run of losing seasons, ownership says stability in front office is key to turnaround.					
16 Texas Rangers	19	8	13	7	8
Texas might end up being better off with the Alex Rodriguez trade not going through.					
17 Oakland Athletics	22	19	11	3	6
Bobby Crosby will be next youngster to step in as exodus of major league talent continues.					
18 Baltimore Orioles	30	29	27	18	19
Move from the bottom to middle of the pack shows major infusion of talent Orioles received.					
19 Kansas City Royals	26	21	14	5	13
Surprise contention in the big leagues paralleled by turnaround in the minor leagues.					
20 Chicago White Sox	15	9	1	6	12
Trades to bolster team in unsuccessful playoff run further sapped once-plentiful talent base.					
21 Philadelphia Phillies	7	11	12	17	21
Trades, injuries, disappointing performances leave little depth behind premium pitchers.					
22 Detroit Tigers	12	18	18	25	16
Disappointments in minor leagues accompanied disaster in the big leagues.					
23 Boston Red Sox	27	28	24	21	17
New administration's commitment to turning the system around shows early signs of progress.					
24 San Francisco Giants	11	12	22	28	22
Unconventional (but successful) approach to player development aims at short-term success.					
25 San Diego Padres	20	4	8	11	5
Big league team is primed for a leap forward, but minor league talent has been drained.					
26 Cincinnati Reds	24	14	3	20	28
New GM Dan O'Brien finds plenty of work to do at the major and minor league levels.					
27 New York Yankees	17	5	7	1	3
Drew Henson's failure adds to a growing list of disappointments among Yankees prospects.					
28 St. Louis Cardinals	28	30	23	27	9
Shakeup in the scouting department indicates dissatisfaction with talent that was coming in.					
29 Houston Astros	23	3	10	9	11
With major league payroll maxed out, Astros need minor leagues to be productive again.					
30 Montreal Expos	29	16	21	15	7
If anyone ever buys the team, they'll have to start over in the majors as well as the minors.					

TOP 50
PROSPECTS

f nothing else, a collection of top 50 lists proves that reasonable people can disagree. These are the personal top 50s for the four people who oversee Baseball America's prospect rankings, giving you a glimpse at each person's preferences.

There was no question about the top two players this year: Joe Mauer and B.J. Upton ranked 1-2 on all four lists. Delmon Young was also a near-unanimous pick for No. 3, but after that the lists start to diverge. The wild card this year was Kazuo Matsui, who meets the requirements of rookie eligibility (and thus inclusion in the book) but has a proven track record of success in Japan. He's as

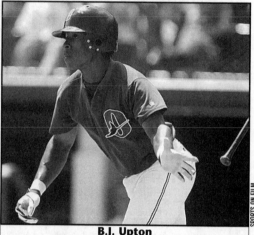

B.J. Upton

SPORTS ON FILM

safe a bet as anyone on these lists, but the question is how long he'll be a contributor for the Mets.

These lists are snapshots after the end of winter ball and before spring training, and they would almost certainly change the next time we put them together. From lists like these (except longer), we assemble a consensus list, argue about it, run it by more people in the industry and argue about it more. That ends up as our annual Top 100 Prospects list, which we consider the best compilation of prospects in the game.

Allan Simpson

1. Joe Mauer, c, Twins
2. B.J. Upton, ss, Devil Rays
3. Delmon Young, of, Devil Rays
4. Rickie Weeks, 2b, Brewers
5. Edwin Jackson, rhp, Dodgers
6. Kazuo Matsui, ss, Mets
7. Scott Kazmir, lhp, Mets
8. Alexis Rios, of, Blue Jays
9. Zack Greinke, rhp, Royals
10. Greg Miller, lhp, Dodgers
11. Adam Loewen, lhp, Orioles
12. Cole Hamels, lhp, Phillies
13. Grady Sizemore, of, Indians
14. Justin Morneau, 1b, Twins
15. Gavin Floyd, rhp, Phillies
16. Andy Marte, 3b, Braves
17. Prince Fielder, 1b, Brewers
18. John VanBenschoten, rhp, Pirates
19. Josh Barfield, 2b, Padres
20. Chin-Hui Tsao, rhp, Rockies
21. J.J. Hardy, ss, Brewers
22. Casey Kotchman, 1b, Angels
23. Adam Wainwright, rhp, Cardinals
24. Franklin Gutierrez, of, Dodgers
25. Angel Guzman, rhp, Cubs
26. Jeff Mathis, c, Angels
27. Ervin Santana, rhp, Angels
28. Felix Hernandez, rhp, Mariners
29. Kyle Sleeth, rhp, Tigers
30. Dustin McGowan, rhp, Blue Jays
31. David Wright, 3b, Mets
32. James Loney, 1b, Dodgers
33. Jeremy Reed, of, White Sox
34. Guillermo Quiroz, c, Blue Jays
35. Scott Hairston, 2b, Diamondbacks
36. Jeff Francoeur, of, Braves
37. Taylor Buchholz, rhp, Astros
38. Bobby Crosby, ss, Athletics
39. Adrian Gonzalez, 1b, Rangers
40. Jeremy Hermida, of, Marlins
41. Dioner Navarro, c, Yankees
42. Hanley Ramirez, ss, Red Sox
43. Dallas McPherson, 3b, Angels
44. Jason Stokes, 1b, Marlins
45. Jeff Allison, rhp, Marlins
46. Joe Blanton, rhp, Athletics
47. Ryan Wagner, rhp, Reds
48. Sean Burnett, lhp, Pirates
49. Jeremy Guthrie, rhp, Indians
50. Merkin Valdez, rhp, Giants

Will Lingo

1. Joe Mauer, c, Twins
2. B.J. Upton, ss, Devil Rays
3. Grady Sizemore, of, Indians
4. Andy Marte, 3b, Braves
5. Edwin Jackson, rhp, Dodgers
6. Rickie Weeks, 2b, Brewers
7. Kazuo Matsui, ss, Mets
8. Delmon Young, of, Devil Rays
9. Alexis Rios, of, Blue Jays
10. Chin-Hui Tsao, rhp, Rockies
11. Greg Miller, lhp, Dodgers
12. Prince Fielder, 1b, Brewers
13. Blake Hawksworth, rhp, Cardinals
14. Josh Barfield, 2b, Padres
15. Merkin Valdez, rhp, Giants
16. Ryan Wagner, rhp, Reds
17. Bobby Crosby, ss, Athletics
18. Felix Hernandez, rhp, Mariners
19. Dustin McGowan, rhp, Blue Jays
20. Adam Loewen, lhp, Orioles
21. Gavin Floyd, rhp, Phillies
22. Jeremy Hermida, of, Marlins
23. Zack Greinke, rhp, Royals
24. Justin Morneau, 1b, Twins
25. Jeff Mathis, c, Angels
26. Jeremy Reed, of, White Sox
27. Kyle Sleeth, rhp, Tigers
28. Scott Kazmir, lhp, Mets
29. Cole Hamels, lhp, Phillies
30. Casey Kotchman, 1b, Angels
31. Sergio Santos, ss, Diamondbacks
32. Jeff Francoeur, of, Braves
33. J.J. Hardy, ss, Brewers
34. Dallas McPherson, 3b, Angels
35. Hanley Ramirez, ss, Red Sox
36. Angel Guzman, rhp, Cubs
37. Ervin Santana, rhp, Angels
38. John Maine, rhp, Orioles
39. Jason Stokes, 1b, Marlins
40. David Wright, 3b, Mets
41. Joe Blanton, rhp, Athletics
42. Adam Wainwright, rhp, Cardinals
43. Khalil Greene, ss, Padres
44. Scott Hairston, 2b, Diamondbacks
45. Clint Nageotte, rhp, Mariners
46. Guillermo Quiroz, c, Blue Jays
47. Jeremy Guthrie, rhp, Indians
48. John VanBenschoten, rhp, Pirates
49. Kris Honel, rhp, White Sox
50. Clint Everts, rhp, Expos

Kazuo Matsui

Rickie Weeks, Anthony Gwynn and Prince Fielder

Grady Sizemore

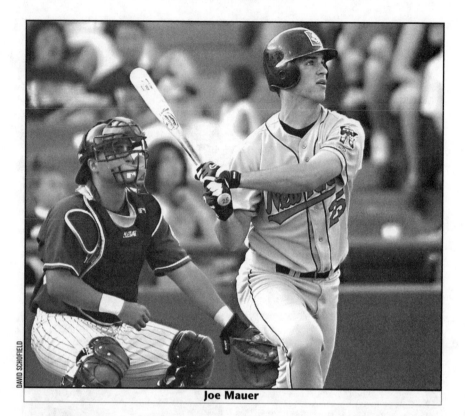

Joe Mauer

Jim Callis

1. Joe Mauer, c, Twins
2. B.J. Upton, ss, Devil Rays
3. Delmon Young, of, Devil Rays
4. Rickie Weeks, 2b, Brewers
5. Prince Fielder, 1b, Brewers
6. Edwin Jackson, rhp, Dodgers
7. Kazuo Matsui, ss, Mets
8. Greg Miller, lhp, Dodgers
9. Grady Sizemore, of, Indians
10. Alexis Rios, of, Blue Jays
11. Andy Marte, 3b, Braves
12. Casey Kotchman, 1b, Angels
13. David Wright, 3b, Mets
14. Justin Morneau, 1b, Twins
15. J.J. Hardy, ss, Brewers
16. Zack Greinke, rhp, Royals
17. Dustin McGowan, rhp, Blue Jays
18. Jeff Mathis, c, Angels
19. Scott Kazmir, lhp, Mets
20. Cole Hamels, lhp, Phillies
21. Angel Guzman, rhp, Cubs
22. Adam Loewen, lhp, Orioles
23. Ervin Santana, rhp, Angels
24. Josh Barfield, 2b, Padres
25. Scott Hairston, 2b, Diamondbacks

26. Gavin Floyd, rhp, Phillies
27. Jeremy Reed, of, White Sox
28. Bobby Crosby, ss, Athletics
29. Jeremy Hermida, of, Marlins
30. Dallas McPherson, 3b, Angels
31. Chin-Hui Tsao, rhp, Rockies
32. Felix Hernandez, rhp, Mariners
33. Brad Nelson, of, Brewers
34. Kyle Sleeth, rhp, Tigers
35. Franklin Gutierrez, of, Dodgers
36. Jeff Allison, rhp, Marlins
37. Hanley Ramirez, ss, Red Sox
38. James Loney, 1b, Dodgers
39. Clint Nageotte, rhp, Mariners
40. Sergio Santos, ss, Diamondbacks
41. Guillermo Quiroz, c, Blue Jays
42. Justin Jones, lhp, Cubs
43. Blake Hawksworth, rhp, Cardinals
44. Joe Blanton, rhp, Athletics
45. Dioner Navarro, c, Yankees
46. Merkin Valdez, rhp, Giants
47. Jeff Francoeur, of, Braves
48. John Maine, rhp, Orioles
49. Ryan Wagner, rhp, Reds
50. Adam Wainwright, rhp, Cardinals

Josh Boyd

1. Joe Mauer, c, Twins
2. B.J. Upton, ss, Devil Rays
3. Delmon Young, of, Devil Rays
4. Edwin Jackson, rhp, Dodgers
5. Alexis Rios, of, Blue Jays
6. Greg Miller, lhp, Dodgers
7. Prince Fielder, 1b, Brewers
8. Rickie Weeks, 2b, Brewers
9. Grady Sizemore, of, Indians
10. Andy Marte, 3b, Braves
11. Kazuo Matsui, ss, Mets
12. Justin Morneau, 1b, Twins
13. Casey Kotchman, 1b, Angels
14. Scott Kazmir, lhp, Mets
15. David Wright, 3b, Mets
16. Jeff Mathis, c, Angels
17. Adam Loewen, lhp, Orioles
18. Zack Greinke, rhp, Royals
19. Dallas McPherson, 3b, Angels
20. Jeff Francoeur, of, Braves
21. Gavin Floyd, rhp, Phillies
22. Franklin Gutierrez, of, Dodgers
23. Ervin Santana, rhp, Angels
24. Cole Hamels, lhp, Phillies
25. J.J. Hardy, ss, Brewers
26. Jeremy Hermida, of, Marlins
27. Dustin McGowan, rhp, Blue Jays
28. Josh Barfield, 2b, Padres
29. James Loney, 1b, Dodgers
30. Brad Nelson, of, Brewers
31. Merkin Valdez, rhp, Giants
32. Jeremy Reed, of, White Sox
33. Bobby Jenks, rhp, Angels
34. Chin-Hui Tsao, rhp, Rockies
35. Guillermo Quiroz, c, Blue Jays
36. Sergio Santos, ss, Diamondbacks
37. Ian Stewart, 3b, Rockies
38. Angel Guzman, rhp, Cubs
39. Felix Hernandez, rhp, Mariners
40. Dioner Navarro, c, Yankees
41. Hanley Ramirez, ss, Red Sox
42. Kyle Sleeth, rhp, Tigers
43. Jeff Allison, rhp, Marlins
44. Scott Olsen, lhp, Marlins
45. Chris Lubanski, of, Royals
46. John VanBenschoten, rhp, Pirates
47. Mike Hinckley, lhp, Expos
48. Justin Jones, lhp, Cubs
49. Matt Moses, 3b, Twins
50. Denny Bautista, rhp, Orioles

Edwin Jackson

Delmon Young

Greg Miller

ANAHEIM
ANGELS

TOP 30 PROSPECTS

1. Casey Kotchman, 1b
2. Jeff Mathis, c
3. Dallas McPherson, 3b
4. Ervin Santana, rhp
5. Bobby Jenks, rhp
6. Alberto Callaspo, 2b
7. Brandon Wood, ss
8. Erick Aybar, ss
9. Rafael Rodriguez, rhp
10. Steven Shell, rhp
11. Joe Saunders, lhp
12. Kevin Jepsen, rhp
13. Jake Woods, lhp
14. Howie Kendrick, 2b
15. Anthony Whittington, lhp
16. Warner Madrigal, of
17. Bobby Wilson, c
18. Nick Gorneault, of
19. Chris Bootcheck, rhp
20. Rich Fischer, rhp
21. Tim Bittner, lhp
22. Quan Cosby, of
23. Carlos Morban, rhp
24. Sean Rodriguez, ss/2b
25. Jared Abruzzo, c
26. Bob Zimmermann, rhp
27. Richard Thompson, rhp
28. Kyle Pawelczyk, lhp
29. Blake Balkcom, of
30. Stephen Andrade, rhp

By Josh Boyd

The Walt Disney Co. capped its four-year ownership of the Angels with a World Series championship in 2002 and made way for new owner Arte Moreno last May. Moreno's first year was like most non-2002 seasons in Anaheim: lackluster.

The Angels became just the second team in the wild-card era to fail to reach the playoffs the year after winning the World Series. But Moreno didn't allow the excitement to die down. Shortly after taking over the club, he lowered beer prices. Then he lowered the cost of some tickets. While they were a disappointment on the field, the Angels did top the 3 million barrier in attendance for the first time. Most significant, Moreno allowed general manager Bill Stoneman to be aggressive during the offseason.

During their 2002 run, the Angels' only significant move was to add Alex Ochoa. After the World Series, they did almost nothing to upgrade the club. And when Anaheim slumped last year, its only move was to trade swingman Scott Schoeneweis to the White Sox for three young pitchers.

Compare that with this offseason. The Angels struck quickly to add two of the best starters on the free-agent market, Bartolo Colon (four years, $51 million) and Kelvim Escobar (three years, $18.75 million). After already bolstering their outfield with Jose Guillen (two years, $6 million), they came out of nowhere in January to get the biggest prize of all in Vladimir Guerrero (five years, $70 million).

Not only did Moreno shell out $145.75 million for four players, but baseball's first Hispanic owner signed four Hispanic stars. It's the first real attempt the team has made to reach out to its region's growing Latin American community. If Moreno's first nine months with the club show anything, it's that the Angels won't take a back seat to the Dodgers in Southern California any longer. The new acquisitions don't guarantee a turnaround but provide reason for optimism in a softening AL West.

So too does the farm system, which is in better shape than it ever has been. Elite prospects Casey Kotchman, Jeff Mathis, Dallas McPherson and Ervin Santana are about a year from being ready to make an impact in Anaheim.

In August, however, Stoneman fired scouting director Donny Rowland. Rowland and his staff built a destitute system into one of the top three in baseball. Rowland was instructed to pursue high-ceiling talent, and he delivered. The decision to relieve him along with national crosscheckers Hank Sargent and Guy Mader came as a shock to many in the industry. A rift between Rowland and Stoneman led to his downfall, and Stoneman replaced him with former Devil Rays special assistant Eddie Bane.

ORGANIZATION OVERVIEW

General manager: Bill Stoneman. **Farm director:** Tony Reagins. **Scouting director:** Eddie Bane.

2003 PERFORMANCE

Class	Team	League	W	L	Pct.	Finish*	Manager
Majors	Anaheim	American	77	85	.475	9th (14)	Mike Scioscia
Triple-A	Salt Lake Stingers	Pacific Coast	68	75	.476	13th (16)	Mike Brumley
Double-A	Arkansas Travelers	Texas	70	70	.500	5th (8)	Tyrone Boykin
High A	Rancho Cucamonga Quakes	California	74	66	.529	t-5th (10)	Bobby Meacham
Low A	Cedar Rapids Kernels	Midwest	66	72	.478	9th (14)	Todd Claus
Rookie	Provo Angels	Pioneer	54	22	.710	1st (8)	Tom Kotchman
Rookie	AZL Angels	Arizona	20	29	.408	7th (9)	Brian Harper
OVERALL 2003 MINOR LEAGUE RECORD			352	334	.513	9th (30)	

*Finish in overall standings (No. of teams in league)

ORGANIZATION LEADERS

BATTING
*Minimum 250 At-Bats
*AVG	Warner Madrigal, Provo	.369
R	Jeff Mathis, Arkansas/Rancho Cucamonga	93
H	Alberto Callaspo, Cedar Rapids	168
TB	Nick Gorneault, Arkansas/Rancho Cuca.	260
2B	Nick Gorneault, Arkansas/Rancho Cuca.	42
3B	Chone Figgins, Salt Lake	15
HR	Dallas McPherson, Arkansas/Rancho Cuca.	23
RBI	Nick Gorneault, Arkansas/Rancho Cuca.	91
BB	Mike O'Keefe, Arkansas	62
SO	Tommy Murphy, Rancho Cucamonga	138
SB	Trent Durrington, Salt Lake	35
*OBP	Dallas McPherson, Arkansas/Rancho Cuca.	.410
*SLG	Dallas McPherson, Arkansas/Rancho Cuca.	.596

PITCHING
#Minimum 75 Innings
W	Jean Toledo, Cedar Rapids	12
	Jake Woods, Rancho Cucamonga	12
L	Billy Stokley, Salt Lake/Arkansas	14
#ERA	Bobby Jenks, Arkansas/AZL Angels	2.07
G	Richard Thompson, Rancho Cuca./Cedar Rapids	55
CG	Chris Bootcheck, Salt Lake	3
SV	Jonathon Rouwenhorst, RC	20
	Joel Peralta, Salt Lake/Arkansas	20
IP	Jake Woods, Rancho Cucamonga	171
	Chris Bootcheck, Salt Lake	171
BB	Rafael Rodriguez, Cedar Rapids	59
SO	Ervin Santana, Arkansas/Rancho Cuca.	153

BEST TOOLS

Best Hitter for Average	Casey Kotchman
Best Power Hitter	Dallas McPherson
Fastest Baserunner	Quan Cosby
Best Athlete	Quan Cosby
Best Fastball	Bobby Jenks
Best Curveball	Bobby Jenks
Best Slider	Ervin Santana
Best Changeup	Abel Moreno
Best Control	Steven Shell
Best Defensive Catcher	Jeff Mathis
Best Defensive Infielder	Erick Aybar
Best Infield Arm	Tommy Murphy
Best Defensive Outfielder	Nick Kimpton
Best Outfield Arm	Warner Madrigal

PROJECTED 2007 LINEUP

Catcher	Jeff Mathis
First Base	Casey Kotchman
Second Base	Alberto Callaspo
Third Base	Troy Glaus
Shortstop	Erick Aybar
Left Field	Garret Anderson
Center Field	Darin Erstad
Right Field	Vladimir Guerrero
Designated Hitter	Dallas McPherson
No. 1 Starter	Bartolo Colon
No. 2 Starter	Ervin Santana
No. 3 Starter	Jarrod Washburn
No. 4 Starter	Kelvim Escobar
No. 5 Starter	Bobby Jenks
Closer	Francisco Rodriguez

LAST YEAR'S TOP 20 PROSPECTS

1. Francisco Rodriguez, rhp
2. Casey Kotchman, 1b
3. Bobby Jenks, rhp
4. Jeff Mathis, c
5. Johan Santana, rhp
6. Dallas McPherson, 3b
7. Joe Saunders, lhp
8. Rich Fischer, rhp
9. Joe Torres, lhp
10. Chris Bootcheck, rhp
11. Steven Shell, rhp
12. Rafael Rodriguez, rhp
13. Brendan Donnelly, rhp
14. Derrick Turnbow, rhp
15. Jake Woods, lhp
16. Nathan Haynes, of
17. Robb Quinlan, of
18. Quan Cosby, of
19. Nick Touchstone, lhp
20. Brian Specht, ss

TOP PROSPECTS OF THE DECADE

1994	Brian Anderson, lhp
1995	Andrew Lorraine, lhp
1996	Darin Erstad, of
1997	Jarrod Washburn, lhp
1998	Troy Glaus, 3b
1999	Ramon Ortiz, rhp
2000	Ramon Ortiz, rhp
2001	Joe Torres, lhp
2002	Casey Kotchman, 1b
2003	Francisco Rodriguez, rhp

TOP DRAFT PICKS OF THE DECADE

1994	McKay Christensen, of
1995	Darin Erstad, of
1996	Chuck Abbott, ss (2)
1997	Troy Glaus, 3b
1998	Seth Etherton, rhp
1999	John Lackey, rhp (2)
2000	Joe Torres, lhp
2001	Casey Kotchman, 1b
2002	Joe Saunders, lhp
2003	Brandon Wood, ss

ALL-TIME LARGEST BONUSES

Troy Glaus, 1997	$2,250,000
Joe Torres, 2000	$2,080,000
Casey Kotchman, 2001	$2,075,000
Joe Saunders, 2002	$1,825,000
Chris Bootcheck, 2000	$1,800,000

MINOR LEAGUE
DEPTH CHART

ANAHEIM **ANGELS**

RANK: **3**

Impact potential (A): It would be tough for any organization to match the quality and impact potential of the Angels' top five prospects. Casey Kotchman, Jeff Mathis and Dallas McPherson could hit consecutively in the heart of the order for a first-division club, while Alberto Callaspo might be leading things off at the top.

Depth (B): Injuries to several pitching prospects, including Joe Torres and Joe Saunders, have taken a toll on the system's overall depth. Young pitchers beyond the top 10 have many obstacles to overcome before they can be counted on.

Sleeper: Bobby Wilson, c.   *—Depth charts prepared by **Josh Boyd**. Numbers in parentheses indicate prospect rankings.*

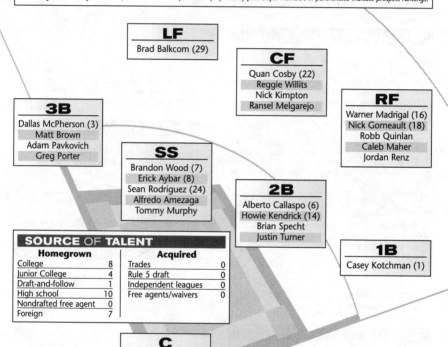

LF
Brad Balkcom (29)

CF
Quan Cosby (22)
Reggie Willits
Nick Kimpton
Ransel Melgarejo

RF
Warner Madrigal (16)
Nick Gorneault (18)
Robb Quinlan
Caleb Maher
Jordan Renz

3B
Dallas McPherson (3)
Matt Brown
Adam Pavkovich
Greg Porter

SS
Brandon Wood (7)
Erick Aybar (8)
Sean Rodriguez (24)
Alfredo Amezaga
Tommy Murphy

2B
Alberto Callaspo (6)
Howie Kendrick (14)
Brian Specht
Justin Turner

1B
Casey Kotchman (1)

SOURCE OF TALENT

Homegrown		Acquired	
College	8	Trades	0
Junior College	4	Rule 5 draft	0
Draft-and-follow	1	Independent leagues	0
High school	10	Free agents/waivers	0
Nondrafted free agent	0		
Foreign	7		

C
Jeff Mathis (2)
Bobby Wilson (17)
Jared Abruzzo (25)
Mike Collins
Ryan Budde

RHP

Starters	Relievers
Ervin Santana (4)	Carlos Morban (23)
Bobby Jenks (5)	Bob Zimmerman (26)
Rafael Rodriguez (9)	Richard Thompson (27)
Steven Shell (10)	Stephen Andrade (30)
Kevin Jepsen (12)	Kevin Gregg
Chris Bootcheck (19)	Greg Jones
Rich Fischer (20)	Scott Dunn
Abel Moreno	Mike Brunet
Jesse Smith	
James Holcomb	
Matt Hensley	
Steve Green	

LHP

Starters	Relievers
Joe Saunders (11)	Matt Lincoln
Jake Woods (13)	Jon Rouwenhorst
Anthony Whittington (15)	
Tim Bittner (21)	
Kyle Pawelczyk (27)	
Nick Touchstone	
Micah Posey	
Scott Hindman	
Joe Torres	
Kelly Shearer	

DRAFT
ANALYSIS

Best Pro Debut: LHP Daniel Davidson (13) went 8-2 and led the Rookie-level Pioneer League with a 1.64 ERA. Though SS Adam Pavkovich's (11) defense was believed to be his strength, he hit .301-2-29 and earned a one-game cameo in Triple-A.

Best Athlete: OF Reggie Willits (7) is a toolsy switch-hitter who runs well and plays a solid center field. He also had a fine debut, batting .300-4-27 in the PL.

Best Pure Hitter: SS Brandon Wood (1) worked out diligently before his high school senior season and turned himself into a threat at the plate, hitting 20 home runs. SS Sean Rodriguez (3) and Pavkovich rank right behind him.

Best Raw Power: Many teams didn't get a good look at OF Blake Balkcom (5), who had minor knee surgery in 2002 and then injured his quadriceps last spring. The Angels think he'll hit for enough power to play in right field.

Fastest Runner: Willits can run the 60-yard dash in 6.6 seconds. He led the Big 12 Conference with 37 steals at Oklahoma.

Best Defensive Player: Wood is a better shortstop than Rodriguez because of his superior hands and instincts. Rodriguez has more arm and flash. His best fit may be behind the plate, though he's reluctant to catch at this point.

Best Fastball: RHP Bob Zimmermann (4)

hit 98 mph as a reliever with Team USA in the summer of 2002. He started much of last spring at Southwest Missouri State and last summer after signing, but fits best in the bullpen. LHP Anthony Whittington (2) and RHP Chris Hunter (41) both get to 94 mph.

Best Breaking Ball: RHP Jesse Smith (6) has a plus curveball and an 88-92 mph fastball.

Most Intriguing Background: Whittington was a volunteer fireman. Smith worked construction and spent two years out of baseball before Illinois Valley CC coach Bob Koopman spotted him at a tryout for the independent Frontier League. Willits' sister Wendi played briefly in the WNBA.

Closest To The Majors: Zimmermann, whose progress will quicken once he moves to the bullpen.

Best Late-Round Pick: The Angels weren't able to land Hunter as a 19th-round draft-and-follow from 2002, but signed him late after drafting him again.

The One Who Got Away: Some clubs considered Jason Donald (20) a possible first-round talent but he was intent on attending Arizona.

Assessment: Scouting director Donny Rowland was fired in August, but his fourth and final draft for the Angels added to the organization's depth of pitchers and up-the-middle position players.

Whittington — JOHN SPEAR

2002 DRAFT — GRADE: C

LHP Joe Saunders (1) and RHP Kevin Jepsen (2) have been derailed by arm problems so far. Later-round picks such as 2B Howie Kendrick (10) and draft-and-follow C Bobby Wilson (48) are picking up some of the slack.

2001 DRAFT — GRADE: A

Perhaps the best draft any team had during the years graded for this book, it started strong with 1B Casey Kotchman (1), C Jeff Mathis (1) and 3B Dallas McPherson (2). RHP Steven Shell (3) and LHP Jake Woods (3) aren't bad, either.

2000 DRAFT — GRADE: C

Mercurial RHP Bobby Jenks (5) will determine how successful this draft is, because first-round pitchers Joe Torres and Chris Bootcheck have hit the wall. Signing a pair of 2003 first-rounders, SS Aaron Hill (7) and OF David Murphy (50), would have helped.

1999 DRAFT — GRADE: C+

The Angels didn't have a first-rounder but still found a World Series with their top pick: RHP John Lackey (2). SS Alfredo Amezaga (13) and OF Robb Quinlan (10) could provide bench depth.

—Draft analysis prepared by Jim Callis. Numbers in parentheses indicate draft rounds.

1b

Casey
Kotchman

Born: Feb. 22, 1983.
Ht.: 6-3. **Wt.:** 210.
Bats: L. **Throws:** L.
School: Seminole (Fla.) HS.
Career Transactions: Selected by Angels in first round (13th overall) of 2001 draft; signed July 28, 2001.

Kotchman has been Anaheim's top position prospect since signing for a $2.075 million bonus in 2001. His father Tom has enjoyed a long career in player development and scouting with the Angels, and he served as Casey's adviser during negotiations. Kotchman was considered one of the most advanced hitters in the draft while leading Seminole High to the 2001 national championship. Various injuries have hampered his progress and limited his playing time in each of his three pro seasons. Last year a torn right hamstring kept him on the shelf for nearly three months in the first half of the season at high Class A Rancho Cucamonga. He was knocked out of the California League playoffs when he was hit by a pitch on the wrist. He was hit in the face during instructional league and then had to be shut down during the Arizona Fall League when he reinjured his hamstring. Wrist and back injuries limited Kotchman during his first two seasons, but nothing seems to keep him from raking when he's in the lineup.

Kotchman has a fluid swing in the classic lefthander's mold of a Todd Helton or Will Clark, and he creates explosive contact with the fat part of the bat on a consistent basis. He displays uncanny strike-zone awareness and early-pitch recognition. He manages to put himself in good hitter's counts by rarely chasing balls out of the zone. He still maintains his aggressiveness, though, and attacks the pitch he's looking for. Kotchman is content to smack hard line drives all over the field and into the alleys. He saves most of his power for batting practice and is still learning when to use it during games. He projects to hit 25-plus homers a year. Defensively, he's as good as any first baseman in the minors, combining good instincts, accurate throws and excellent footwork around the bag. Growing up around pro clubhouses with his father, Kotchman was more prepared for pro ball than most any player coming out of high school. His problem has been staying healthy. Several of Kotchman's injuries have been freak accidents, but some scouts still wonder if he's injury prone and why. Some have noticed his body tighten up since high school. He spent this offseason in Arizona conditioning himself in hopes of preventing another injury. He deserves credit for not allowing the lack of playing time to frustrate him or keep him from hitting, though who knows where he'd be right now had he received consistent playing time. Kotchman doesn't run well, but he isn't a clogger and his instincts give him an advantage on the bases.

The Angels' 2001 draft could go down as one of the strongest in recent history if Kotchman, Jeff Mathis and Dallas McPherson all continue on their current tracks. Anaheim's scouts evaluated all three as first-round talents. Despite his persistent injuries, Kotchman probably would excel in Triple-A now. The Angels are more likely to take a conservative approach and assign him to Double-A Arkansas to begin 2004. He profiles as prototypical No. 3 hitter who will be among the league leaders in average, doubles and on-base percentage on an annual basis.

Year	Club (League)	Class	AVG	G	AB	R	H	2B	3B	HR	RBI	BB	SO	SB	SLG	OBP
2001	Angels (AZL)	R	.600	4	15	5	9	1	0	1	5	3	2	0	.867	.632
	Provo (Pio)	R	.500	7	22	6	11	3	0	7	2	0	0	.636	.542
2002	Cedar Rapids (Mid)	A	.281	81	288	42	81	30	1	5	50	48	37	2	.444	.390
2003	Rancho Cuca. (Cal)	A	.350	57	206	42	72	12	0	8	28	30	16	2	.524	.441
	Angels (AZL)	R	.333	7	27	5	9	1	0	2	6	2	3	0	.593	.379
MINOR LEAGUE TOTALS			.326	156	558	100	182	47	1	16	96	85	58	4	.500	.421

Jeff Mathis, c

Born: March 31, 1983. **Ht.:** 6-2. **Wt.:** 180. **Bats:** R. **Throws:** R. **School:** Marianna (Fla.) HS. **Career Transactions:** Selected by Angels in first round (33rd overall) of 2001 draft; signed June 5, 2001.

Mathis projected as a fifth-round pick heading into the 2001 draft, but the Angels identified him as a potential first-rounder early in the spring and were prepared to take him 13th overall if Casey Kotchman was gone. He turned down a two-sport offer from Florida State, where was recruited as quarterback along with Joe Mauer. Mathis' older brother Jake is an infielder in the Angels system. Mathis has conjured comparisons from Jason Kendall to Mike Lieberthal because of his athleticism, agility and offensive ceiling. His improved pitch recognition has allowed him to make adjustments at the plate and control the barrel of the bat. He has strength and bat speed, and his power numbers have increased each year. He displays all of the attributes of a clubhouse leader and has the makeup to take charge of a pitching staff. While he has above-average arm strength and quick, soft hands, Mathis needs to make subtle adjustments to deter basestealers. He threw out just 25 percent last year. Only Mauer rates ahead of Mathis among the game's catching prospects. Mathis will take over from Bengie Molina in Anaheim no later than 2005.

Year	Club (League)	Class	AVG	G	AB	R	H	2B	3B	HR	RBI	BB	SO	SB	SLG	OBP
2001	Angels (AZL)	R	.304	7	23	1	7	1	0	0	3	2	4	0	.348	.346
	Provo (Pio)	R	.299	22	77	14	23	6	3	0	18	11	13	1	.455	.387
2002	Cedar Rapids (Mid)	A	.287	128	491	75	141	41	3	10	73	40	75	7	.444	.346
2003	Rancho Cuca. (Cal)	A	.323	97	378	73	122	28	3	11	54	35	74	5	.500	.384
	Arkansas (TL)	AA	.284	24	95	19	27	11	0	2	14	12	16	1	.463	.364
MINOR LEAGUE TOTALS			.301	278	1064	182	320	87	9	23	162	100	182	14	.464	.364

Dallas McPherson, 3b

Born: July 23, 1980. **Ht.:** 6-4. **Wt.:** 230. **Bats:** L. **Throws:** R. **School:** The Citadel. **Career Transactions:** Selected by Angels in second round of 2001 draft; signed June 18, 2001.

It would be foolish to doubt the mettle or intensity of McPherson, a former cadet at The Citadel. Last season, he shot himself in a finger with a BB gun and didn't skip a day. After returning from a bulging disc that sidelined him for most of April, he ripped nine home runs in 14 games, highlighted by a double and home run against a rehabbing Randy Johnson. When Johnson beaned him in his third trip to the plate, McPherson stared him down and then stole second. McPherson generates explosive power with good bat speed and natural loft. His ability to make adjustments has helped him become a more complete hitter. While improving his plate discipline, he has worked his way into hitter's counts and he learned to anticipate offspeed stuff better. He has a plus arm. His glove lags behind his bat, though he works on his defense as much as anyone in the system. He cut down on his errors last year thanks to improved footwork and better accuracy on his throws because he didn't rush them. Given the strides McPherson has made to become adequate at third base—not to mention Vladimir Guerrero's arrival—talk of moving him to right field has died down. He could make Troy Glaus expendable with another monster year.

Year	Club (League)	Class	AVG	G	AB	R	H	2B	3B	HR	RBI	BB	SO	SB	SLG	OBP
2001	Provo (Pio)	R	.395	31	124	30	49	11	0	5	29	12	22	1	.605	.449
2002	Cedar Rapids (Mid)	A	.277	132	499	71	138	24	3	15	88	78	128	30	.427	.381
2003	Rancho Cuca. (Cal)	A	.308	77	292	65	90	21	6	18	59	41	79	12	.606	.404
	Arkansas (TL)	AA	.314	28	102	22	32	9	1	5	27	19	25	4	.569	.426
MINOR LEAGUE TOTALS			.304	268	1017	188	309	65	10	43	203	150	254	47	.514	.400

Ervin Santana, rhp

Born: Jan. 10, 1983. **Ht.:** 6-2. **Wt.:** 160. **Bats:** R. **Throws:** R. **Career Transactions:** Signed out of Dominican Republic by Angels, Sept. 2, 2000.

Previously known as Johan and believed to be 10 months younger, Santana was the organization's and California League's 2003 pitcher of the year. He also was selected for the Futures Games. He missed a couple of starts with a tender elbow after a promotion to Double-A but finished the season strong. Santana's electrifying stuff might be as good as any in the minors. His fastball regularly hits the upper 90s, topping out at 98 mph and sitting at 93-97. He throws a nasty 78-87 mph slider for strikes, varying speeds and breaks at will, and has a good feel for his changeup. Santana has a tendency to overthrow and occasionally fly open on the front side of his delivery and collapse in the back, affecting his command. He has displayed the ability to recognize those mistakes and make in-game adjustments on his own. Santana has all the makings of a dominant frontline starter. The additions of Bartolo Colon and Kelvim Escobar in Anaheim buy him an extra year in the upper levels before he's ready to make a push for a job in 2005.

Year	Club (League)	Class	W	L	ERA	G	GS	CG	SV	IP	H	R	ER	HR	BB	SO	AVG
2001	Angels (AZL)	R	3	2	3.22	10	9	1	0	59	40	27	21	0	35	69	.184
	Provo (Pio)	R	2	1	7.71	4	4	0	0	19	19	17	16	1	12	22	.247
2002	Cedar Rapids (Mid)	A	14	8	4.16	27	27	0	0	147	133	75	68	10	48	146	.240
2003	Rancho Cuca. (Cal)	A	10	2	2.53	20	20	1	0	125	98	44	35	9	36	130	.212
	Arkansas (TL)	AA	1	1	3.94	6	6	0	0	30	23	15	13	4	12	23	.211
MINOR LEAGUE TOTALS			30	14	3.64	67	66	2	0	379	313	178	153	24	143	390	.220

5 Bobby Jenks, rhp

Born: March 14, 1981. **Ht.:** 6-3. **Wt.:** 240. **Bats:** R. **Throws:** R. **School:** Inglemoor HS, Bothell, Wash. **Career Transactions:** Selected by Angels in fifth round of 2000 draft; signed June 13, 2000.

Jenks has overcome more obstacles than most 23-year-old prospects. Many of them have been self-inflicted, including a suspension for violating team rules in 2002. Just when he was starting to make the most significant progress of his career last season, he was the subject of a revealing ESPN Magazine article and spent two months on the disabled list with a stress reaction in his elbow. Jenks lights up radar guns, generating easy 93-99 mph readings in every start. He has topped out at 102 but still is learning the importance of command and movement over velocity. His curveball features hard, downward bite and can be an unhittable pitch when he's in rhythm. He rarely uses his change-up, but he'll flash an above-average one on occasion. Jenks is still learning to harness his emotions and his overpowering repertoire. He came into spring last year 30 pounds overweight, which led to complications with his mechanics. His command and breaking ball suffer when he can't repeat his delivery. Angels officials noticed more ambition from Jenks after the magazine article. If he follows up a strong winter in Puerto Rico with a good spring, he likely will head to Triple-A Salt Lake.

Year	Club (League)	Class	W	L	ERA	G	GS	CG	SV	IP	H	R	ER	HR	BB	SO	AVG
2000	Butte (Pio)	R	1	7	7.86	14	12	0	0	53	61	57	46	2	44	42	.290
2001	Cedar Rapids (Mid)	A	3	7	5.27	21	21	0	0	99	90	74	58	10	64	98	.245
	Arkansas (TL)	AA	1	0	3.60	2	2	0	0	10	8	5	4	0	5	10	.200
2002	Arkansas (TL)	AA	3	6	4.66	10	10	1	0	58	49	34	30	2	44	58	.234
	Rancho Cuca. (Cal)	A	3	5	4.82	11	10	1	0	65	50	42	35	4	46	64	.212
2003	Arkansas (TL)	AA	7	2	2.17	16	16	0	0	83	56	23	20	2	51	103	.191
	Angels (AZL)	R	0	0	0.00	1	1	0	0	4	2	0	0	0	0	5	.154
MINOR LEAGUE TOTALS			18	27	4.67	75	72	2	0	372	316	235	193	20	254	380	.231

6 Alberto Callaspo, 2b

Born: April 19, 1983. **Ht.:** 5-10. **Wt.:** 173. **Bats:** B. **Throws:** R. **Career Transactions:** Signed out of Venezuela by Angels, Feb. 16, 2001.

Latin American scouts Carlos Porte and Amador Arias earned kudos for their efforts in discovering Callaspo, a virtual unknown in Venezuela before signing for $8,000. He led the Rookie-level Pioneer League in hits in 2002 before topping the low Class A Midwest League in batting, hits and doubles last year. Callaspo has such uncanny bat control that scouts mention names like Rod Carew and Tony Gwynn when describing his swing. He employs a similar contact-based approach with a short swing. While his raw power is limited, he hits the ball squarely and shows enough sock to drive the ball into the alleys. He has outstanding range with quick, soft hands and is exceptional at turning the double play. He's a solid-average runner who could play shortstop. While Callaspo puts everything he swings at in play, he's not selective and rarely walks. He needs to become more patient as he faces more advanced pitching. Coming off an outstanding winter performance in Venezuela, where he competed for another batting title, Callaspo will head to high Class A. He's probably 2½ years away from Anaheim.

Year	Club (League)	Class	AVG	G	AB	R	H	2B	3B	HR	RBI	BB	SO	SB	SLG	OBP
2001	Angels (DSL)	R	.356	66	275	55	98	11	4	2	39	22	16	14	.447	.403
2002	Provo (Pio)	R	.338	70	299	70	101	16	10	3	60	17	14	13	.488	.374
2003	Cedar Rapids (Mid)	A	.327	133	514	86	168	38	4	2	67	42	28	20	.428	.377
MINOR LEAGUE TOTALS			.337	269	1088	211	367	65	18	7	166	81	58	47	.449	.383

7 Brandon Wood, ss

Born: March 2, 1985. **Ht.:** 6-3. **Wt.:** 185. **Bats:** R. **Throws:** R. **School:** Horizon HS, Scottsdale, Ariz. **Career Transactions:** Selected by Angels in first round (23rd overall) of 2003 draft; signed June 6, 2003.

When Wood was a 5-foot-10, 130-pound freshman, he was so overmatched that his high school team used a DH for his spot in the lineup. It wasn't until he blossomed physically last spring that his draft stock skyrocketed. After hitting 20 homers, two shy of the Arizona prep record, he signed for $1.3 million. Wood fits the profile of modern shortstops such as Cal Ripken and Alan Trammell. He worked hard to develop his swing with former big league manager Jim Lefebvre before his senior season. He stays behind the ball and can drive pitches with plus bat speed. His instincts, hands and plus arm make up for a lack of pure speed. If he plays his way off shortstop, he has the tools to excel at second base, third base or catcher. Wood swung and missed more often than expected after signing. The Angels believe it was just a case of him being overaggressive and trying to hit for too much power. He became too pull-conscious. The Angels compare Wood's makeup to that of Jeff Mathis and Dallas McPherson, so they expect him to adjust and move swiftly. He'll spend 2004 at low Class A Cedar Rapids.

Year	Club (League)	Class	AVG	G	AB	R	H	2B	3B	HR	RBI	BB	SO	SB	SLG	OBP
2003	Angels (AZL)	R	.308	19	78	14	24	8	2	0	13	4	15	3	.462	.349
	Provo (Pio)	R	.278	42	162	25	45	13	2	5	31	16	48	1	.475	.348
MINOR LEAGUE TOTALS			.288	61	240	39	69	21	4	5	44	20	63	4	.471	.348

8 Erick Aybar, ss

Born: Jan. 14, 1984. **Ht.:** 5-11. **Wt.:** 160. **Bats:** B. **Throws:** R. **Career Transactions:** Signed out of Dominican Republic by Angels, Feb. 4, 2002.

Former scouting director Donny Rowland and international supervisor Clay Daniel made several return visits to the Dominican to evaluate Aybar. The younger brother of Dodgers third-base prospect Willy Aybar, Erick lowered his asking price from $250,000 and signed for $100,000. He and Alberto Callaspo have formed all-star double-play combinations in the Pioneer and Midwest leagues the last two years. One scout coined them "Hoover and Oreck" because they vacuum up everything. Aybar is flashier with natural shortstop actions and a strong and accurate arm. He also runs a tick faster, has more thump in his bat and drives the ball more consistently. Aybar doesn't exhibit the same type of bat control as Callaspo and tends to be more of a free swinger. He has the tools for shortstop, though some scouts are concerned about his size and project him as more of a utilityman down the road. Known as *los hermanos* (Siamese twins), Aybar and Callaspo will take their highlight-reel show to high Class A in 2004. Callaspo eventually will face strong competition from within the system in Brandon Wood.

Year	Club (League)	Class	AVG	G	AB	R	H	2B	3B	HR	RBI	BB	SO	SB	SLG	OBP
2002	Provo (Pio)	R	.326	67	273	64	89	15	6	4	29	21	43	15	.469	.395
2003	Cedar Rapids (Mid)	A	.308	125	496	83	153	30	10	6	57	17	54	32	.446	.346
MINOR LEAGUE TOTALS			.315	192	769	147	242	45	16	10	86	38	97	47	.454	.364

9 Rafael Rodriguez, rhp

Born: Sept. 24, 1984. **Ht.:** 6-1. **Wt.:** 170. **Bats:** R. **Throws:** R. **Career Transactions:** Signed out of Dominican Republic by Angels, July 20, 2001.

Rodriguez earned a $780,000 bonus after impressing Angels scouts in a private workout in 2002. He evokes comparisons to Ramon Ortiz and Ervin Santana, though he has been wildly inconsistent and isn't as polished at the same stage. Rodriguez was torched for a 10.17 ERA in five starts last June, then he followed up with a 5-1, 1.86 July. Rodriguez' lightning-quick arm was the first thing that caught scouts' attention. He can dial his fastball up to 97 mph and sits at 90-96. His hard slider has out-pitch potential. Rodriguez has a high-maintenance delivery that instructors have to keep close tabs on. The ball jumps out of his hand, but his command is erratic because he tends to get out of whack with his full-effort mechanics. He shows a feel for a deceptive changeup but needs a more effective weapon against lefties. He has yet to mature physically or emotionally. The Angels believe he'll turn the corner when he masters English. Rodriguez spent his first full season in low Class A at age 18, so he's ahead of schedule. He'll join the high Class A rotation in 2004.

Year	Club (League)	Class	W	L	ERA	G	GS	CG	SV	IP	H	R	ER	HR	BB	SO	AVG
2002	Angels (AZL)	R	2	1	3.99	8	8	0	0	38	37	19	17	4	20	50	.255
	Provo (Pio)	R	1	1	5.96	6	6	0	0	26	26	17	17	3	14	25	.268
2003	Cedar Rapids (Mid)	A	10	11	4.31	26	26	1	0	144	129	85	69	7	59	100	.236
MINOR LEAGUE TOTALS			13	13	4.46	40	40	1	0	208	192	121	103	14	93	175	.243

10 Steven Shell, rhp

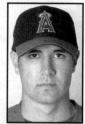

Born: March 10, 1983. **Ht.:** 6-5. **Wt.:** 190. **Bats:** R. **Throws:** R. **School:** El Reno (Okla.) HS. **Career Transactions:** Selected by Angels in third round of 2001 draft; signed June 17, 2001.

Shell has been on the cusp of the top 10 since signing as a projection pick in 2001. He earned the starting assignment for the California League in its 2003 all-star game against the Carolina League, based on the strength of his 6-5, 3.20 record in the first half. A tender elbow robbed him of his effectiveness for much of the second half and cost him most of August. Thanks to his clean delivery, Shell has the best command and control in the organization. He paints both sides of the plate with an 88-92 mph fastball and will max out at 94 when he's healthy. His spike curveball is a reliable weapon and a potential strikeout pitch. His changeup is solid. Shell has to trust his fastball as he did during the first half. He needs to become more consistent with his secondary pitches. He tried to pitch through pain last season and it cost him. The Angels plan on taking a conservative approach with his return, but are optimistic this wasn't a significant setback. If he comes to spring training at 100 percent, Shell could jump to Double-A. Otherwise, he'll repeat high Class A and still be young for that level at 21.

Year	Club (League)	Class	W	L	ERA	G	GS	CG	SV	IP	H	R	ER	HR	BB	SO	AVG
2001	Angels (AZL)	R	1	0	0.00	3	0	0	0	4	1	0	0	0	2	3	.077
	Provo (Pio)	R	0	3	7.17	14	4	0	1	38	52	31	30	3	15	33	.331
2002	Cedar Rapids (Mid)	A	11	4	3.72	22	21	1	0	121	119	59	50	12	26	86	.255
2003	Rancho Cuca. (Cal)	A	6	8	4.24	22	21	1	0	127	123	66	60	13	26	100	.248
MINOR LEAGUE TOTALS			18	15	4.34	61	46	2	1	290	295	156	140	28	69	222	.261

11 Joe Saunders, lhp

Born: June 16, 1981. **Ht.:** 6-2. **Wt.:** 200. **Bats:** L. **Throws:** L. **School:** Virginia Tech. **Career Transactions:** Selected by Angels in first round (12th overall) of 2002 draft; signed June 10, 2002 . . . On disabled list, April 3-Sept. 18, 2003.

Saunders made dramatic progress as a pitcher from the time the Phillies drafted him in the fifth round out of high school until he went 12th overall to the Angels in 2002. After going 9-2, 2.86 with a Big East Conference-leading 102 strikeouts as a junior, he signed a predraft deal with the Angels worth $1.825 million after passing a physical. He was scheduled to join Ervin Santana, Steven Shell and Jake Woods in the Rancho Cucamonga rotation last spring, but he showed up with a torn rotator cuff and partially torn labrum. He managed to avoid surgery, however, when Dr. James Andrews prescribed an aggressive rehabilitation process instead. Saunders is at his best when he works his 89-94 mph fastball to both sides of the plate. Changing speeds is his forte, whether it's off his fastball or with his best pitch, a plus changeup with fade and sink. He fools hitters by maintaining his fastball arm action when he throws his changeup. His curveball never has been a strength, but it's a third pitch he can throw for strikes. Saunders was on the mound in instructional league last fall. His fastball was hitting 87 mph and all reports indicated that he was throwing free and easy, without pain. The Angels say Saunders will be ready by spring training. He'll start the season in high Class A if his arm proves to be sound.

Year	Club (League)	Class	W	L	ERA	G	GS	CG	SV	IP	H	R	ER	HR	BB	SO	AVG
2002	Provo (Pio)	R	2	1	3.62	8	8	0	0	32	40	19	13	1	11	21	.305
	Cedar Rapids (Mid)	A	3	1	1.88	5	5	0	0	29	16	7	6	2	9	27	.168
2003	Did not play—Injured																
MINOR LEAGUE TOTALS			5	2	2.80	13	13	0	0	61	56	26	19	3	20	48	.248

12 Kevin Jepsen, rhp

Born: July 26, 1984. **Ht.:** 6-3. **Wt.:** 200. **Bats:** R. **Throws:** R. **School:** Bishop Manogue HS, Sparks, Nev. **Career Transactions:** Selected by Angels in second round of 2002 draft; signed July 10, 2002.

Jepsen sent a shockwave through the scouting community in the spring of 2002 when he lit up radar guns with 98 mph gas and a 91 mph slider. Angels crosschecker Mark Russo was one of those scouts in attendance for Jepsen's coming-out party, and former national scouting supervisor Hank Sargent clocked Jepsen at 95 in another outing in icy conditions. Jepsen had a shaky introduction to pro ball after signing, which was attributed to a long layoff. He was so impressive in spring training last year, though, that Anaheim started him in low Class A rather than extended spring training. He went 5-0, 1.75 in his first five starts, but five starts later he was shut down with elbow tenderness. Jepsen rehabbed in Arizona before having surgery to remove bone chips. He has drawn physical comparisons to such power pitchers as Curt Schilling and Roger Clemens. His raw stuff is as good as any pitcher in the system outside of Ervin Santana, but Jepsen still is just scratching the surface of his potential. His fastball was regularly clocked in the mid-90s early last season. He throws a heavy ball, though it tends to be straight. His slider is above-average with short, late tilt at 84-87 mph. But he tends to get around it, causing it to lose its sharpness when he's searching for more break. He made strides with his changeup last season, though both it and his command need a lot of work. Jepsen impressed the Angels in some bullpen sessions during the offseason, and they expect him to be ready to return to low Class A this year.

Year	Club (League)	Class	W	L	ERA	G	GS	CG	SV	IP	H	R	ER	HR	BB	SO	AVG
2002	Angels (AZL)	R	1	3	6.84	8	5	0	0	26	29	22	20	3	12	19	.274
2003	Cedar Rapids (Mid)	A	6	3	2.65	10	10	0	0	51	32	24	15	2	28	42	.180
MINOR LEAGUE TOTALS			7	6	4.07	18	15	0	0	77	61	46	35	5	40	61	.215

13 Jake Woods, lhp

Born: Sept. 3, 1981. **Ht.:** 6-1. **Wt.:** 190. **Bats:** L. **Throws:** L. **School:** Bakersfield (Calif.) JC.
Career Transactions: Selected by Angels in third round of 2001 draft; signed June 13, 2001.

Woods followed Bakersfield products Colby Lewis (Rangers, 1999) and Phil Dumatrait (Red Sox, 2000) as picks in the first three rounds, and he broke Dumatrait's school record for strikeouts in 2001. He often is compared to big league relievers such as Mike Stanton, Scott Schoeneweis and Kent Mercker and originally projected as a future situational reliever. Woods, however, has made steady progress as a starter, adding a changeup as a third pitch. Armed with a moving 87-92 mph fastball and a plus curveball, he rarely needed to use a changeup before signing. It since has emerged as more than a show-me pitch. His strikeout rate has dropped each year, but he's learning the importance of pitching with his fastball. Woods has a high-effort delivery that sometimes affects the consistency of his big-breaking curve. He has the arsenal to start and he has been durable, tying Chris Bootcheck for the system lead with 171 innings in 2003. To remain in the rotation, he'll have to get more effective against righthanders. They hit .283 off him last year, compared to a .215 average for lefties. The Angels don't feel rushed to make a decision on Woods' future and will continue to develop him as a starter in Double-A this season.

Year	Club (League)	Class	W	L	ERA	G	GS	CG	SV	IP	H	R	ER	HR	BB	SO	AVG
2001	Provo (Pio)	R	4	3	5.29	15	14	1	0	65	70	41	38	6	29	84	.275
2002	Cedar Rapids (Mid)	A	10	5	3.05	27	27	1	0	153	128	66	52	12	54	121	.228
2003	Rancho Cuca. (Cal)	A	12	7	3.99	28	28	2	0	171	178	90	76	9	54	109	.270
MINOR LEAGUE TOTALS			26	15	3.84	70	69	4	0	389	376	197	166	27	137	314	.255

14 Howie Kendrick, 2b

Born: July 12, 1983. **Ht.:** 5-10. **Wt.:** 180. **Bats:** R. **Throws:** R. **School:** St. John's River (Fla.) CC.
Career Transactions: Selected by Angels in 10th round of 2002 draft; signed June 19, 2002.

Scout/minor league manager Tom Kotchman first identified Kendrick as a potential draft-and-follow selection in 2002. Instead of waiting a year and risking losing him, Kotchman used video of Kendrick to persuade the Angels to sign him immediately for $100,000. Kendrick started 4-for-40 last season in Provo, then hit .423 the rest of the way to finish fourth in the league in hitting. He has a short, direct swing with outstanding hand speed. He stays inside the ball and shows the ability to make adjustments. Kendrick is a contact hitter with the strength to drive the ball into the gaps. He's physical and athletic, comparing to undersized second basemen such as Harold Reynolds and Ray Durham. Kendrick is a steady defender who makes the routine play. His arm strength is solid-average, and he has good hands and is dedicated to improving. Right behind Alberto Callaspo on the system's depth chart at second base, Kendrick is primed for a promotion to low Class A.

Year	Club (League)	Class	AVG	G	AB	R	H	2B	3B	HR	RBI	BB	SO	SB	SLG	OBP
2002	Angels (AZL)	R	.318	42	157	24	50	6	4	0	13	7	11	12	.408	.368
2003	Provo (Pio)	R	.368	63	234	65	86	20	3	3	36	24	28	8	.517	.434
MINOR LEAGUE TOTALS			.348	105	391	89	136	26	7	3	49	31	39	20	.473	.409

15 Anthony Whittington, lhp

Born: Oct. 9, 1984. **Ht.:** 6-5. **Wt.:** 225. **Bats:** R. **Throws:** L. **School:** Buffalo HS, Putnam, W.Va.
Career Transactions: Selected by Angels in second round of 2003 draft; signed July 12, 2003.

Whittington hurled four no-hitters last spring and went 13-2, 0.80 with 187 strikeouts in 82 innings, gaining recognition as West Virginia's best prospect. Expected to go as high as the fifth round early last spring, he kept improving his stock steadily. He threw well for Yankees scouts in a predraft workout in Tampa and could have gone to New York four picks after Anaheim popped him in the second round. A volunteer fireman in high school, Whittington had committed to Oklahoma State because of its fire-management program. It took a month and a $650,000 bonus to lure him to pro ball. While he flashes 94 mph heat, he's a deep projection who has a long way to go with his feel for pitching. He struggled with command and consistency in his debut. His fastball features explosive life and he showed the makings of a tight slider, which too often gets slurvy because he also throws a curveball. At some point the Angels will try to get him to settle on one breaking ball, most likely the slider. Whittington didn't need to mix his changeup in often, but when he did he displayed a nice touch and occasional running action. At 6-foot-5 and 225 pounds, he's physically imposing, and his long, loose and easy arm action make him projectable. He has conjured comparisons to John Rocker for his size and overpowering fastball. Whittington has plenty of room for improvement with his mechanics. He shouldered a heavy workload last year in high school, making four starts over one 10-day stretch. Not surprisingly, his fastball dipped to 84-90 mph before the draft. His velocity was solid again in the Rookie-level Arizona League. He's ticketed for extended spring training and the rotation in Rookie-level Provo. The Angels understood the risk involved in selecting Whittington, but gambled on his upside potential. Other clubs viewed him more as a power reliever down the road.

Year	Club (League)	Class	W	L	ERA	G	GS	CG	SV	IP	H	R	ER	HR	BB	SO	AVG
2003	Angels (AZL)	R	0	3	8.03	9	5	0	0	25	31	24	22	1	17	20	.320
MINOR LEAGUE TOTALS			0	3	8.03	9	5	0	0	25	31	24	22	1	17	20	.320

16 Warner Madrigal, of

Born: March 21, 1984. **Ht.:** 6-0. **Wt.:** 190. **Bats:** R. **Throws:** R. **Career Transactions:** Signed out of Dominican Republic by Angels, July 21, 2001.

Former scouting director Donny Rowland and international scouting supervisor Clay Daniel made three trips to the team's Dominican academy to scout Madrigal, who initially asked for a $1 million bonus. After seeing Madrigal throw and take batting practice, the Angels weren't going to let him get away, eventually landing him for $150,000. He physically resembles Albert Belle, and his swing has similar length and power. Rowland described Madrigal's approach at the plate as "full attack mode with bad intentions." He crushes fastballs and saw a lot of them in Rookie ball. After starting the year with a few minor but nagging injuries in extended spring training, Madrigal proceeded to lead the Pioneer League in runs, hits, doubles and extra-base hits. He'll need to tone down his aggressive, all-out swing and improve his pitch selection and recognition as he progress. Madrigal is a below-average runner who doesn't have great instincts on defense, but he has the best outfield arm in the system and profiles well in right. Anaheim will challenge him with a jump to low Class A, and how he adapts will be a good indication of his future potential.

Year	Club (League)	Class	AVG	G	AB	R	H	2B	3B	HR	RBI	BB	SO	SB	SLG	OBP
2001	Angels (DSL)	R	.181	22	72	5	13	5	0	0	8	0	30	0	.250	.213
2002	Angels (DSL)	R	.229	42	140	22	32	5	3	4	23	10	42	5	.393	.312
2003	Provo (Pio)	R	.369	70	279	75	103	28	2	9	51	12	58	2	.581	.394
MINOR LEAGUE TOTALS			.301	134	491	102	148	38	5	13	82	22	130	7	.479	.344

17 Bobby Wilson, c

Born: April 8, 1983. **Ht.:** 6-0. **Wt.:** 205. **Bats:** R. **Throws:** R. **School:** St. Petersburg (Fla.) JC. **Career Transactions:** Selected by Angels in 48th round of 2002 draft; signed May 17, 2003.

Wilson was Casey Kotchman's teammate and the team MVP on Seminole (Fla.) High's 2001 national championship team. The two close friends played Amateur Athletic Union ball together for 10 years. Wilson committed to Mississippi and was drafted in the 26th round by the Giants out of high school. He spurned both options and attended St. Petersburg Junior College and became the 2003 Florida juco player of the year. Tom Kotchman signed Wilson as a 48th-round draft-and-follow for $150,000 shortly before last year's draft, then managed him at Provo. Wilson topped the Pioneer League in RBIs despite missing a couple of weeks with a wrist injury and garnered comparisons to offensive catchers along the lines of Jim Leyritz, Mike Stanley and Todd Zeile. Wilson's strong, compact body never has thrilled scouts, but he worked hard in college on his conditioning. He generates above-average pop with a short, efficient swing. Behind the plate, he has the tools to evolve into a solid catcher, but he still needs to refine his receiving and catch-and-throw transfer. His pure arm strength is above-average, yet he nabbed just 15 percent of basesteal-ers last year. The Angels are loaded with catching prospects from Jeff Mathis to Wilson to Jared Abruzzo, and there are also high hopes for Australian Mike Collins and defensive-spe-cialist Brett Martinez. With so many backstops around, Wilson has taken grounders at third base, though his value is much higher behind the plate. He's likely to play every day but share time at catcher with Collins in low Class A this year.

Year	Club (League)	Class	AVG	G	AB	R	H	2B	3B	HR	RBI	BB	SO	SB	SLG	OBP
2003	Provo (Pio)	R	.284	57	236	36	67	12	0	6	62	18	31	0	.411	.329
MINOR LEAGUE TOTALS			.284	57	236	36	67	12	0	6	62	18	31	0	.411	.329

18 Nick Gorneault, of

Born: April 19, 1979. **Ht.:** 6-3. **Wt.:** 200. **Bats:** R. **Throws:** R. **School:** University of Massachusetts. **Career Transactions:** Selected by Angels in 19th round of 2001 draft; signed June 7, 2001.

Gorneault made a lasting first impression on former Angels scout Jon Bunnell (now with the Mets) when he homered at Fenway Park in the Beanpot Tournament as a sophomore at UMass. Gorneault continued to rake in front of Bunnell, hitting three bombs and a double against Florida the next time he saw him. Though he batted .369-12-41 as a senior, his unorthodox swing turned off scouts. While his stroke might not be picturesque and he could stand to improve his selectiveness at the plate, Gorneault broke through as an offen-sive force for last season. He batted .328 and led the organization with 91 RBIs. He's more athletic than he gets credit for, though he's a slightly below-average runner. He's cut from the mold of former Dodgers slugger Mike Marshall, a strong and physical outfielder with plus power potential. Gorneault has a knack for making hard contact. He has quick, strong hands, though he hooks around the ball at times and scouts are concerned about his abili-ty to deal with breaking balls at higher levels. His arm is average and he's capable in all three outfield spots. Gorneault will begin 2004 in Double-A, where he finished with a flourish last season.

Year	Club (League)	Class	AVG	G	AB	R	H	2B	3B	HR	RBI	BB	SO	SB	SLG	OBP
2001	Provo (Pio)	R	.315	54	168	38	53	12	4	6	30	11	65	5	.542	.373
2002	Cedar Rapids (Mid)	A	.289	103	346	60	100	17	7	10	53	30	106	12	.465	.346
2003	Rancho Cuca. (Cal)	A	.321	97	374	67	120	36	2	14	72	20	82	11	.540	.363
	Arkansas (TL)	AA	.345	29	110	19	38	6	4	2	19	8	25	2	.527	.395
MINOR LEAGUE TOTALS			.312	283	998	184	311	71	17	32	174	69	278	30	.513	.362

19 Chris Bootcheck, rhp

Born: Oct. 24, 1978. **Ht.:** 6-5. **Wt.:** 200. **Bats:** R. **Throws:** R. **School:** Auburn University. **Career Transactions:** Selected by Angels in first round (20th overall) of 2000 draft; signed Sept. 13, 2000.

Bootcheck reached the big leagues last September, when Ramon Ortiz was on bereave-ment leave because of his father's death. Bootcheck, whose father Dan pitched in the Tigers system in the 1970s but never reached the majors, hasn't lived up to the projections he had coming out of Auburn as a first-rounder in 2000, however. He nearly pitched his way into Anaheim's plans last spring before being optioned to Triple-A, where he again struggled to put hitters away. He was bothered by forearm stiffness before finishing strong. Bootcheck was clocked as high as 97 mph in college, touching 94 on a regular basis, but he has backed off his power and sits at 89-93 with cutting action now. He has been reluctant to adapt to the Angels' organization pitching preference for a full windup. Pitching coordinator Mike Butcher has spent extensive time working with Bootcheck to hone his mechanics. Bootcheck's slider isn't quite the power pitch it was at Auburn, either, though it's still of major league quality with good depth and velocity. His changeup is decent and he incor-porates an average curveball to complete his four-pitch mix. He does a good job of throw-ing strikes. Unless he somehow bumps John Lackey from the rotation in spring training, Bootcheck will head back to Triple-A.

Year	Club (League)	Class	W	L	ERA	G	GS	CG	SV	IP	H	R	ER	HR	BB	SO	AVG
2001	Rancho Cuca. (Cal)	A	8	4	3.93	15	14	1	0	87	84	45	38	11	23	86	.251
	Arkansas (TL)	AA	3	3	5.45	6	6	1	0	36	39	25	22	3	11	22	.265
2002	Arkansas (TL)	AA	8	7	4.81	19	19	3	0	116	130	68	62	11	35	90	.277
	Salt Lake (PCL)	AAA	4	3	3.88	9	9	1	0	58	64	29	25	5	16	38	.283
2003	Salt Lake (PCL)	AAA	8	9	4.25	28	26	3	0	171	194	103	81	19	43	82	.290
	Anaheim (AL)	MAJ	0	1	9.58	4	1	0	0	10	16	13	11	5	6	7	.340
MAJOR LEAGUE TOTALS			0	1	9.58	4	1	0	0	10	16	13	11	5	6	7	.340
MINOR LEAGUE TOTALS			31	26	4.38	77	74	9	0	469	511	270	228	49	128	318	.277

20 Rich Fischer, rhp

Born: Oct. 21, 1980. **Ht.:** 6-3. **Wt.:** 180. **Bats:** R. **Throws:** R. **School:** San Bernardino Valley (Calif.) JC. **Career Transactions:** Selected by Angels in 21st round of 2000 draft; signed June 9, 2000.

Fischer wasn't getting much attention for his bat as a shortstop at San Bernardino Valley Junior College, but his arm strength and fluid, athletic actions prompted Angels area scout Tim Corcoran to work him out as pitcher. Fischer took to the mound immediately, though he tailed off in 2003 after working a system-high 176 innings the year before. His velocity tailed off from the low 90s and was simply average instead of plus. The consistency of his changeup and curveball suffered as well. Pitching coordinator Mike Butcher helped straighten out his mechanics, which were at the root of his problem. Fischer was collapsing his delivery on the backside, causing his stuff to flatten out. Butcher was able to get him to stay behind the ball and drive it downhill. Fischer was on his way to rediscovering his velocity and the sharpness to his slider in the Arizona Fall League before he was shut down with a tender elbow. He must continue to develop his secondary stuff, as he may have become too dependent upon his fastball because he commands it so well. He displays good natural touch with his changeup. Fischer will pitch for a chance to advance to Triple-A this spring.

Year	Club (League)	Class	W	L	ERA	G	GS	CG	SV	IP	H	R	ER	HR	BB	SO	AVG
2000	Butte (Pio)	R	3	5	5.91	18	13	1	1	70	103	63	46	8	26	45	.338
2001	Cedar Rapids (Mid)	A	9	7	4.20	20	20	2	0	131	131	73	61	8	33	97	.261
2002	Rancho Cuca. (Cal)	A	7	8	3.50	19	19	5	0	131	118	61	51	14	29	138	.239
	Arkansas (TL)	AA	1	3	4.23	7	7	0	0	45	40	22	21	8	10	36	.233
2003	Arkansas (TL)	AA	5	11	4.61	26	26	2	0	154	159	91	79	14	43	123	.268
MINOR LEAGUE TOTALS			25	34	4.38	90	85	10	1	531	551	310	258	52	141	439	.267

21 Tim Bittner, lhp

Born: June 9, 1980. **Ht.:** 6-2. **Wt.:** 200. **Bats:** L. **Throws:** L. **School:** Marist University. **Career Transactions:** Selected by White Sox in 10th round of 2001 draft; signed June 8, 2001.

A two-way star at Marist, Bittner became the highest-drafted player in school history when the White Sox selected him in the 10th round in 2001. He nearly won the Rookie-level Appalachian League ERA title in his pro debut, but he fell five innings short of qualifying. The least-known of the five players in the Scott Schoeneweis trade with Chicago last July, Bittner jump-started his career afterward with a scintillating six-start run in high Class A. The White Sox had moved him to the bullpen, but Angels scout Mark Russo recommended that he return to the rotation. Bittner didn't give up an earned run in his first five starts in his new organization and went 5-0, 0.28 in August. He shows a plus fastball at times but typically sits in the 88-90 mph range. He spins a solid slider and mixes in a below-average curveball and average changeup, all from a three-quarters slot with a good arm action and delivery. He already has exceeded expectations and will move to Double-A this year.

Year	Club (League)	Class	W	L	ERA	G	GS	CG	SV	IP	H	R	ER	HR	BB	SO	AVG
2001	Bristol (Appy)	R	6	1	1.10	8	8	1	0	49	34	14	6	0	12	53	.190
	Kannapolis (SAL)	A	0	3	4.43	4	4	0	0	20	21	18	10	1	9	15	.269
2002	Kannapolis (SAL)	A	5	13	4.58	29	29	0	0	157	166	98	80	10	67	123	.274
2003	Kannapolis (SAL)	A	4	4	3.40	10	10	1	0	50	45	24	19	4	26	45	.242
	Winston-Salem (Car)	A	3	3	3.60	17	0	0	1	30	18	13	12	3	12	23	.176
	Rancho Cuca. (Cal)	A	5	0	0.28	6	6	1	0	33	18	5	1	0	14	28	.161
MINOR LEAGUE TOTALS			23	24	3.39	74	57	3	1	340	302	172	128	18	140	287	.239

22 Quan Cosby, of

Born: Dec. 23, 1982. **Ht.:** 5-10. **Wt.:** 190. **Bats:** B. **Throws:** R. **School:** Mart (Texas) HS. **Career Transactions:** Selected by Angels in sixth round of 2001 draft; signed June 6, 2001.

One of the most gifted athletes in the minors, Cosby gave up football and track to sign for $850,000 as a 2001 sixth-round pick. A Texas football recruit, he accounted for 48 touchdowns as a high school senior playing quarterback, cornerback and kick returner. He also won Texas 2-A state championships in the 100 meters (10.46 seconds) and 200 meters (21.31). Though the Angels knew Cosby's development would take time, he made impressive progress during his first two pro seasons. A shoulder injury prevented him from building upon that success last year. He played through the pain but missed most of July. Cosby's best tool is legitimate 80 speed on the 20-80 scouting scale. A switch-hitter, he keeps the ball on the ground to make best use of his wheels. He's fairly patient at the plate, but needs better strike-zone judgment and pitch recognition so he can make better contact and give up fewer at-bats. His approach negates any power potential that he has. Defensively, Cosby covers lots of ground in center field but has a below-average arm. He has worked hard to get better. The Angels expect Cosby to require about 2,500 at-bats in the minors before he's ready. He'll return to low Class A to start 2004.

Year	Club (League)	Class	AVG	G	AB	R	H	2B	3B	HR	RBI	BB	SO	SB	SLG	OBP
2001	Angels (AZL)	R	.243	41	148	21	36	4	1	0	8	9	40	8	.284	.289
2002	Provo (Pio)	R	.302	76	291	66	88	9	4	0	29	45	62	22	.361	.404
2003	Cedar Rapids (Mid)	A	.249	104	370	55	92	4	1	0	21	36	79	17	.265	.316
MINOR LEAGUE TOTALS			.267	221	809	142	216	17	6	0	58	90	181	47	.303	.344

23 Carlos Morban, rhp

Born: Jan. 29, 1983. **Ht.:** 6-6. **Wt.:** 180. **Bats:** R. **Throws:** R. **Career Transactions:** Signed out of Dominican Republic by Angels, Oct. 12, 2000.

Morban and Abel Moreno emerged as the best pitching prospects on a prospect-laden Provo roster last summer. Working out of the bullpen, Morban showcased one of the organization's most powerful arms, while Moreno relied on pitching savvy and the best change-up in the system to keep hitters off balance. Morban began 2003 in low Class A but was demoted to work on his command. He's a prototypical power-armed, one-inning reliever who projects along the lines of Lee Smith or Armando Benitez. He rears back and throws an explosive 92-96 mph fastball with a loose and easy arm action. He pitches on a downhill plane from a three-quarters slot. His power curveball has hard, late bite and the potential to become a second out pitch. Morban needs a better changeup and more maturity. The Angels hope he'll respond as a starter when they send him back to low Class A this year.

Year	Club (League)	Class	W	L	ERA	G	GS	CG	SV	IP	H	R	ER	HR	BB	SO	AVG
2001	Angels (AZL)	R	0	1	13.14	11	1	0	0	12	17	22	18	0	12	10	.315
2002	Angels (AZL)	R	2	0	5.19	17	0	0	1	26	26	19	15	0	15	35	.257
2003	Cedar Rapids (Mid)	A	0	0	5.59	9	0	0	0	10	14	6	6	1	6	13	.341
	Provo (Pio)	R	2	1	3.18	21	0	0	5	23	20	8	8	1	8	26	.238
MINOR LEAGUE TOTALS			4	2	5.99	58	1	0	6	71	77	55	47	2	41	84	.275

24 Sean Rodriguez, ss/2b

Born: April 26, 1985. **Ht.:** 6-0. **Wt.:** 180. **Bats:** R. **Throws:** R. **School:** Braddock HS, Miami. **Career Transactions:** Selected by Angels in third round of 2003 draft; signed June 4, 2003.

Rodriguez transferred from Coral Park (Fla.) High prior to his senior season when he was shifted to center field because of shortstop Robert Valido, who became a fourth-round pick of the White Sox last June. Both shunned commitments to Florida International to sign, with Rodriguez getting $400,000 as a third-round pick. His father John managers in the Marlins system, while his brother Robert is a minor league catcher for the Expos. Rodriguez was regarded as one of the most polished high school players in the draft, but the Angels won't rush him. A polished hitter with four strong tools, he's a versatile infielder in the class of Placido Polanco. Rodriguez has a quick bat and projects to hit for solid power to the gaps. He displays good natural actions at shortstop, but probably will shift to second base because he lacks speed and quickness. Equipped with a plus arm, he also profiles as a catcher. With Howie Kendrick playing second base every day in low Class A, Rodriguez is expected to start 2004 in Provo after time in extended spring training. Of course, his bat could hasten things.

Year	Club (League)	Class	AVG	G	AB	R	H	2B	3B	HR	RBI	BB	SO	SB	SLG	OBP
2003	Angels (AZL)	R	.269	54	216	30	58	8	5	2	25	14	37	11	.380	.332
MINOR LEAGUE TOTALS			.269	54	216	30	58	8	5	2	25	14	37	11	.380	.332

25 Jared Abruzzo, c

Born: Nov. 15, 1981. **Ht.:** 6-3. **Wt.:** 210. **Bats:** B. **Throws:** R. **School:** El Capitan HS, Lakeside, Calif. **Career Transactions:** Selected by Angels in second round of 2000 draft; signed June 20, 2000.

Jeff Mathis was drafted a year after Abruzzo, but blew by him last year and forced Abruzzo to take a step back to low Class A, where he had spent most of 2001. He expected to move up to Double-A to platoon with Ryan Budde, so it took some encouragement from big league manager Mike Scioscia to convince Abruzzo this was a good move for his career. He has been slow to adapt to pro ball and battled throwing problems that stunted his defensive development in 2002. He has a strong arm but erased just 23 percent of runners last year. He also needs work on his receiving and blocking skills after leading the Midwest League with 18 passed balls in 2003. Abruzzo is far more advanced offensively right now. He can drive the ball from both sides of the plate and has a knack for drawing walks. A diligent worker, he impresses the Angels with his conditioning. He's a below-average runner. Abruzzo gets down on himself at times, but the Angels are willing to be patient. He'll go to high Class A this year after playing there in 2002. He ultimately may caddy for Mathis in the majors.

Year	Club (League)	Class	AVG	G	AB	R	H	2B	3B	HR	RBI	BB	SO	SB	SLG	OBP
2000	Butte (Pio)	R	.255	62	208	46	53	11	0	8	45	61	58	1	.423	.423
2001	Cedar Rapids (Mid)	A	.241	87	323	41	78	20	0	10	53	44	104	1	.396	.340
	Rancho Cucamonga (Cal)	A	.208	28	101	13	21	1	0	2	13	9	30	1	.277	.270
2002	Rancho Cucamonga (Cal)	A	.244	101	385	53	94	27	0	16	53	30	124	1	.439	.300
2003	Cedar Rapids (Mid)	A	.271	130	468	64	127	30	1	13	73	59	99	1	.423	.352
MINOR LEAGUE TOTALS			.251	408	1485	217	373	89	1	49	237	203	415	5	.411	.343

26 Bob Zimmermann, rhp

Born: Nov. 17, 1981. **Ht.:** 6-5. **Wt.:** 225. **Bats:** R. **Throws:** R. **School:** Southwest Missouri State University. **Career Transactions:** Selected by Angels in fourth round of 2003 draft; signed June 26, 2003.

Drafted in the 14th round by the Rockies out of high school, Zimmermann set Southwest Missouri State's saves record by the end of his sophomore season. He moved to the rotation last spring and helped the Bears reach their first College World Series. Regarded as first-round material heading into 2003, Zimmermann was inconsistent and lost velocity as a starter. Moved back to relief, he started pumping heavy 94-96 mph fastballs again. After signing for $270,000 as a fourth-rounder, he threw 90-94 in Rookie ball. His repertoire and maximum-effort delivery are best suited for the bullpen. He throws a slider, splitter and changeup but has yet to master any of them consistently. Nevertheless, the Angels feel fortunate to get a quality arm like his where they did. They'll test him by putting Zimmermann in high Class A for his first full pro season.

Year	Club (League)	Class	W	L	ERA	G	GS	CG	SV	IP	H	R	ER	HR	BB	SO	AVG
2003	Provo (Pio)	R	4	2	4.50	11	10	0	0	48	57	29	24	4	8	37	.285
MINOR LEAGUE TOTALS			4	2	4.50	11	10	0	0	48	57	29	24	4	8	37	.285

27 Richard Thompson, rhp

Born: July 1, 1984. **Ht.:** 6-1. **Wt.:** 170. **Bats:** R. **Throws:** R. **Career Transactions:** Signed out of Australia by Angels, Feb. 13, 2002.

The Angels have become more aggressive in scouting Australia and signed promising left-hander Matt Ryan out of the under-18 national tournament in January. Catcher Mike Collins hit .333 while splitting time with Bobby Wilson in Provo in 2003. But the most promising Aussie in the system is Thompson, who gave up one earned run in 29 appearances in low Class A year before a promotion. His dominance was so complete that one scout referred to his curveball as a 14-to-6 breaker because of its height and drop. He throws effortless 88-93 mph fastballs, and his arm speed and ability to spin his curve suggest more velocity to come. Thompson developed a feel for a plus changeup when he raised his arm slot and was tried as a starter in instructional league. Still a teenager, he won't be rushed and will return to high Class A after finishing 2003 there. Thompson has the ingredients to continue to baffle opponents. His stamina could be a question as a starter, but if he takes to the new role he could far exceed the Angels' hopes.

Year	Club (League)	Class	W	L	ERA	G	GS	CG	SV	IP	H	R	ER	HR	BB	SO	AVG
2002	Angels (AZL)	R	2	0	2.70	15	0	0	1	23	14	12	7	0	9	29	.167
2003	Cedar Rapids (Mid)	A	1	2	0.24	31	0	0	9	38	18	5	1	1	13	54	.140
	Rancho Cuca. (Cal)	A	2	2	4.91	24	0	0	8	29	28	19	16	4	18	33	.246
MINOR LEAGUE TOTALS			5	4	2.39	70	0	0	18	90	60	36	24	5	40	116	.183

28 Kyle Pawelczyk, lhp

Born: Nov. 18, 1981. **Ht.:** 6-5. **Wt.:** 180. **Bats:** L. **Throws:** L. **School:** Chipola (Fla.) JC. **Career Transactions:** Selected by Angels in third round of 2002 draft; signed July 10, 2002.

The Angels made a concerted effort to add lefthanded pitching in 2002, drafting Joe Saunders in the first round and signing Scott Hindman, Pawelczyk, Micah Posey and Nick Touchstone. An 11th-round pick of the Expos in 2001, Pawelczyk was one of the more coveted draft-and-follows but declined to sign with Montreal. He had minor labrum surgery in 2002 after he was promoted to low Class A ahead of Saunders. He was healthy last season, throwing 87-90 mph on a tough downhill plane. He touched 92 on occasion. Pawelczyk also has the makings of a plus curveball with good depth, but it needs to become more consistent. His changeup and control are raw. Pawelczyk and Hindman are the most projectable lefties among Anaheim's 2002 crop, and both should open in the low Class A rotation.

Year	Club (League)	Class	W	L	ERA	G	GS	CG	SV	IP	H	R	ER	HR	BB	SO	AVG
2002	Angels (AZL)	R	0	0	0.00	1	1	0	0	3	2	0	0	0	0	2	.200
	Cedar Rapids (Mid)	A	1	2	4.62	7	6	0	0	25	20	13	13	1	27	28	.217
2003	Angels (AZL)	R	0	2	6.49	7	5	0	0	26	32	25	19	1	19	24	.291
	Provo (Pio)	R	3	2	4.03	5	4	0	0	22	19	13	10	1	8	20	.232
MINOR LEAGUE TOTALS			4	6	4.91	20	16	0	0	77	73	51	42	3	54	74	.248

29 Blake Balkcom, of

Born: Aug. 8, 1982. **Ht.:** 6-2. **Wt.:** 225. **Bats:** R. **Throws:** R. **School:** Florida State University.
Career Transactions: Selected by Angels in fifth round of 2003 draft; signed June 20, 2003.

With the system lacking outfield depth, the Angels made outfielders their top priority in the 2003 draft. When all of their targets—Chris Lubanski, Lastings Milledge, Brian Anderson, Brad Snyder—were gone by their 23rd pick, they weren't going to take a lesser outfielder that high just to fill a need. Instead they addressed the position by snagging Balkcom in the fifth round and Reggie Willits in the seventh. After transferring from Chipola (Fla.) Junior College to Florida State in the fall of 2002, Balkcom required minor knee surgery. He tried to come back too early last spring and injured his quadriceps, so many clubs didn't get a good look at him. A big, strong-bodied corner outfielder in the Tom Brunansky mold, Balkcom impressed Angels scouts with his opposite-field juice. His bat stays in the zone for a long time, a promising sign for developing young power hitters. He's trying to shorten and become more consistent with his stroke. He also needs to tighten his strike zone. Balkcom is a below-average runner but runs better once he gets under way. He has average arm strength for a corner outfield position. The Angels are banking on Balkcom's bat to come on in a big way and will send him to high Class A in 2004.

Year	Club (League)	Class	AVG	G	AB	R	H	2B	3B	HR	RBI	BB	SO	SB	SLG	OBP
2003	Provo (Pio)	R	.290	36	131	20	38	12	0	2	28	10	26	0	.427	.345
MINOR LEAGUE TOTALS			.290	36	131	20	38	12	0	2	28	10	26	0	.427	.345

30 Stephen Andrade, rhp

Born: Feb. 6, 1978. **Ht.:** 6-1. **Wt.:** 220. **Bats:** R. **Throws:** R. **School:** Cal State Stanislaus. **Career Transactions:** Selected by Angels in 32nd round of 2001 draft; signed June 7, 2001.

Andrade was 23 and didn't have an overpowering fastball or a projectable body when Angels scout Todd Blyleven tabbed him as a 32nd-rounder in 2001. He's still not a favorite of scouts, who doubt he'll continue to trick more advanced hitters as he rises. But there's no denying that he has a gift for missing bats after he led Double-A Texas League relievers in opponent average (.147) and strikeouts per nine innings (13.1) in 2003. One organization has raised Andrade's OFP (overall future potential) grade nine points since he signed. Andrade throws 87-90 mph and touches 92, but deception achieved through a funky delivery and arm action with a head jerk is the key to his success. He has a deep arm swing in the back and catapults himself towards the plate, a la Robb Nen. Within the organization, Andrade also has been compared to Brendan Donnelly, another minor league reliever who didn't wow scouts. Andrade's command isn't a plus, but he's always around the strike zone. He offers two types of breaking balls, including a wicked biting slurve. He has earned a promotion to Triple-A and is a sleeper candidate to pitch in Anaheim this season.

Year	Club (League)	Class	W	L	ERA	G	GS	CG	SV	IP	H	R	ER	HR	BB	SO	AVG
2001	Provo (Pio)	R	0	0	0.00	1	0	0	0	2	3	0	0	0	0	5	.333
	Cedar Rapids (Mid)	A	2	1	6.52	20	0	0	0	29	33	24	21	3	8	31	.284
2002	Cedar Rapids (Mid)	A	1	1	1.16	46	0	0	11	54	30	7	7	1	16	93	.162
2003	Rancho Cucamonga (Cal)	A	0	0	0.00	3	0	0	1	3	0	0	0	0	3	7	.000
	Arkansas (TL)	AA	5	1	2.65	36	0	0	7	51	26	16	15	2	19	74	.147
MINOR LEAGUE TOTALS			8	3	2.78	106	0	0	19	139	92	47	43	6	46	210	.185

ARIZONA
DIAMONDBACKS

The Diamondbacks and Devil Rays, 1998 expansion brethren, both tried to jumpstart their franchises with free-agent signings while building up their farm systems. It worked in Arizona, as Randy Johnson and Curt Schilling pitched the Diamondbacks past the Yankees in the 2001 World Series.

Because they contended in their second season, the Diamondbacks made trades that sent prospects such as Brad Penny and Vicente Padilla away for veterans. They also spent a lot of money to lure major league free agents as well as amateurs in Travis Lee and John Patterson, two loophole free agents from the 1996 draft. While Arizona has remained in contention, millions of dollars in deferred payments will have to be made soon, forcing the team to trim payroll and go with more youth. The biggest sign of that came when the Diamondbacks traded Schilling to the Red Sox in November. Though Arizona spent some of the savings in the Richie Sexson deal with the Brewers, it reduced the 2004 payroll by roughly $10 million.

At just the right time, the farm system has started to produce. Eight rookie pitchers found their way onto an injury-ravaged staff in 2003, and nine of the team's top 30 prospects entering the season made it to the majors. Righthander Brandon Webb led the surge, going 10-9, 2.84 to win BA's Rookie of

TOP 30 PROSPECTS

1. Scott Hairston, 2b
2. Sergio Santos, ss
3. Dustin Nippert, rhp
4. Chad Tracy, 3b
5. Adriano Rosario, rhp
6. Conor Jackson, of
7. Carlos Quentin, of
8. Brian Bruney, rhp
9. Edgar Gonzalez, rhp
10. Mike Gosling, lhp
11. Luis Terrero, of
12. Josh Kroeger, of
13. Marland Williams, of
14. Jamie D'Antona, 3b
15. Chris Snyder, c
16. Jared Doyle, lhp
17. Brandon Medders, rhp
18. Matt Chico, lhp
19. Jay Garthwaite, of
20. Phil Stockman, rhp
21. Greg Aquino, rhp
22. Shane Nance, lhp
23. Carlos Gonzalez, of
24. Dustin Glant, rhp
25. Sean Luellwitz, 1b
26. Jarred Ball, of
27. Jesus Cota, of
28. Brian Barden, 3b
29. Sergio Lizarraga, rhp
30. Lance Cormier, rhp

By Will Kimmey

the Year award. Oscar Villarreal and Jose Valverde proved to be key arms out of the bullpen, while role players Alex Cintron, Robby Hammock, Matt Kata and Lyle Overbay also contributed.

The future looks even better. The organization's top two prospects, Scott Hairston and Sergio Santos, could form a potent offensive double-play combination. While Hairston and Santos were both early-round draft picks, the Diamondbacks have enjoyed success deeper in the draft, netting college players such as Webb, Overbay, Hammock and more than a half dozen players among their current top 30 after the first five rounds.

Through its affiliates, the Diamondbacks' organizational presence extends all the way across the Mexican border from Texas through Arizona and into Southern California. Arizona's scouts have uncovered several prospects in Mexico, including major leaguers such as Erubiel Durazo and Villarreal.

Arizona hasn't forfeited a pick because of a free-agent signing since the 2000 draft, and parlayed a bonus selection for the loss of Greg Colbrunn into slugger Conor Jackson in 2003. With more high-end selections to come and the hope for continued success in the late rounds and Mexico, the Diamondbacks system is on its way up. It couldn't have happened at a better time for the franchise.

ORGANIZATION
OVERVIEW

General manager: Joe Garagiola Jr. **Farm director:** Tommy Jones. **Scouting director:** Mike Rizzo.

2003 PERFORMANCE

Class	Team	League	W	L	Pct.	Finish*	Manager
Majors	Arizona	National	84	78	.519	9th (16)	Bob Brenly
Triple-A	Tucson Sidewinders	Pacific Coast	73	71	.507	7th (16)	Al Pedrique
Double-A	El Paso Diablos	Texas	67	73	.479	6th (8)	Scott Coolbaugh
High A	Lancaster Jet Hawks	California	73	67	.521	7th (10)	Mike Aldrete
Low A	South Bend Silver Hawks	Midwest	72	64	.529	4th (14)	Von Hayes
Short-season	Yakima Bears	Northwest	45	31	.592	2nd (8)	Bill Plummer
Rookie	Missoula Osprey	Pioneer	36	40	.474	5th (8)	Tony Perezchica
OVERALL 2003 MINOR LEAGUE RECORD			366	346	.514	8th (30)	

*Finish in overall standings (No. of teams in league)

ORGANIZATION LEADERS

BATTING   *Minimum 250 At-Bats
*AVG	Billy Martin, Tucson/El Paso	.348
R	Dan Uggla, Lancaster	104
H	Chad Tracy, Tucson	169
TB	Kyle Nichols, Lancaster	278
2B	Josh Kroeger, El Paso/Lancaster	39
3B	Luis Terrero, Tucson	15
HR	Kyle Nichols, Lancaster	31
RBI	Kyle Nichols, Lancaster	108
BB	Jeff Stanek, Lancaster/South Bend	55
SO	Kyle Nichols, Lancaster	118
SB	Marland Williams, Lancaster	57
*SLG	Billy Martin, Tucson/El Paso	.587
*OBP	Billy Martin, Tucson/El Paso	.424

PITCHING   #Minimum 75 Innings
W	Sam Smith, South Bend	16
L	Matt Henrie, Tucson/El Paso/Lancaster	14
#ERA	Sergio Lizarraga, South Bend	1.78
G	Mark Freed, El Paso	67
CG	Matt Henrie, Tucson/El Paso/Lancaster	4
	Sam Smith, South Bend	4
SV	Matty Wilkinson, South Bend	30
IP	Matt Henrie, Tucson/El Paso/Lancaster	185
BB	Phil Stockman, Tucson/El Paso	68
SO	Phil Stockman, Tucson/El Paso	151

BEST TOOLS

Best Hitter for Average	Scott Hairston
Best Power Hitter	Sergio Santos
Fastest Baserunner	Marland Williams
Best Athlete	Marland Williams
Best Fastball	Brian Bruney
Best Curveball	Dustin Nippert
Best Slider	Brian Bruney
Best Changeup	Mike Gosling
Best Control	Edgar Gonzalez
Best Defensive Catcher	Chris Snyder
Best Defensive Infielder	Jerry Gil
Best Infield Arm	Jerry Gil
Best Defensive Outfielder	Luis Terrero
Best Outfield Arm	Luis Terrero

PROJECTED 2007 LINEUP

Catcher	Chris Snyder
First Base	Richie Sexson
Second Base	Scott Hairston
Third Base	Chad Tracy
Shortstop	Sergio Santos
Left Field	Conor Jackson
Center Field	Luis Terrero
Right Field	Carlos Quentin
No. 1 Starter	Brandon Webb
No. 2 Starter	Dustin Nippert
No. 3 Starter	Adriano Rosario
No. 4 Starter	Edgar Gonzalez
No. 5 Starter	Mike Gosling
Closer	Jose Valverde

LAST YEAR'S TOP 20 PROSPECTS

1. Scott Hairston, 2b	11. Tim Olson, ss/of
2. Mike Gosling, lhp	12. Chris Snyder, c
3. Lyle Overbay, 1b	13. Oscar Villarreal, rhp
4. John Patterson, rhp	14. Adriano Rosario, rhp
5. Brandon Webb, rhp	15. Jesus Cota, of/1b
6. Edgar Gonzalez, rhp	16. Jose Valverde, rhp
7. Sergio Santos, ss	17. Brian Barden, 3b
8. Chad Tracy, 3b	18. Brad Cresse, c
9. Brian Bruney, rhp	19. Dustin Nippert, rhp
10. Luis Terrero, of	20. Bill White, lhp

TOP PROSPECTS OF THE DECADE

1997	Travis Lee, 1b
1998	Travis Lee, 1b
1999	Brad Penny, rhp
2000	John Patterson, rhp
2001	Alex Cintron, ss
2002	Luis Terrero, of
2003	Scott Hairston, 2b

TOP DRAFT PICKS OF THE DECADE

1996	Nick Bierbrodt, lhp
1997	Jack Cust, 1b
1998	Darryl Conyer, of (3)
1999	Corey Myers, ss
2000	Mike Schultz, rhp (2)
2001	Jason Bulger, rhp
2002	Sergio Santos, ss
2003	Conor Jackson, of

ALL-TIME LARGEST BONUSES

Travis Lee, 1996	$10,000,000
John Patterson, 1996	$6,075,000
Byung-Hyun Kim, 1999	$2,000,000
Corey Myers, 1999	$2,000,000
Mike Gosling, 2001	$2,000,000

MINOR LEAGUE
DEPTH CHART

ARIZONA DIAMONDBACKS   RANK: **13**

Impact potential (C): If they can stay at their positions, Scott Hairston and Sergio Santos would form a potent offensive combo up the middle. Dustin Nippert and Adriano Rosario have power arms with potential frontline stuff.

Depth (B): The Diamondbacks have put together a deep system under Mike Rizzo's watch as scouting director, and what's most encouraging about this current crop is the majority of the prospects will be in the upper levels in 2004.

Sleeper: Matt Chico, lhp.   *—Depth charts prepared by Josh Boyd. Numbers in parentheses indicate prospect rankings.*

LF
Conor Jackson (6)
Jarred Ball (26)
Jesus Cota (27)
Doug Devore

CF
Luis Terrero (11)
Marland Williams (13)
Jay Garthwaite (19)
Victor Hall
Mike Goss
Lino Garcia

RF
Carlos Quentin (7)
Josh Kroeger (12)
Carlos Gonzalez (23)
Noochie Varner

3B
Chad Tracy (4)
Jamie D'Antona (14)
Brian Barden (28)
Mayobanex Santana
Dan Uggla

SS
Sergio Santos (2)
Jerry Gil
Tim Olson

2B
Scott Hairston (1)
Andy Green
Danny Richar

1B
Sean Luellwitz (25)
Kyle Nichols
Corey Myers

SOURCE OF TALENT

Homegrown		Acquired	
College	14	Trades	1
Junior College	2	Rule 5 draft	0
Draft-and-follow	2	Independent	0
High school	4	Free agents/waivers	0
Nondrafted free agent	0		
Foreign	7		

C
Chris Snyder (15)
Craig Ansman

LHP

Starters	Relievers
Mike Gosling (10)	Matt Chico (18)
Jared Doyle (16)	Shane Nance (22)
Angel Rocha	Robbie Van
Mark Rosen	Cliff McMachen
Tetsya Yamaguchi	Clint Goocher

RHP

Starters	Relievers
Dustin Nippert (3)	Brian Bruney (8)
Adriano Rosario (5)	Brandon Medders (17)
Edgar Gonzalez (9)	Greg Aquino (21)
Phil Stockman (20)	Dustin Glant (24)
John Allender	Sergio Lizarraga (29)
Casey Daigle	Lance Cormier (30)
William Juarez	Matty Wilkinson
Chris Kinsey	Pete Sikaras
Jason Bulger	Jesus Silva
Beltran Perez	Mike Watson

DRAFT
ANALYSIS

Best Pro Debut: OF Conor Jackson (1) was MVP of the short-season Northwest League, batting .319-6-60, and setting an NWL record with 35 doubles in 68 games. 3B Jamie D'Antona (2) hit .277-15-57 and tied for the NWL homer lead. RHP Dustin Glant (7), a sinker/slider specialist, led the NWL with 18 saves, while 2B Steve Garrabrants (9) topped the league with 30 steals. RHP Adam Bass (10) and LHP Walt Novosel (22) both posted sub-1.00 ERAs.

Best Athlete: OF Jayson Santiago (17), who's raw. OF Jeff Cook (5) is much more refined after four years at Southern Mississippi.

Best Pure Hitter: OF Carlos Quentin (1) or Jackson. Quentin has yet to make his pro debut because he needed Tommy John surgery on his throwing elbow.

Best Raw Power: The Diamondbacks thought D'Antona had more raw power than any player in the draft.

Fastest Runner: Santiago can cover 60 yards in 6.4 seconds. Garrabrants is a step behind him but has better instincts.

Best Defensive Player: Garrabrants and SS Tila Reynolds (11) briefly formed a good double-play combination in the NWL.

Best Fastball: LHP Matt Chico (2) touched 97 mph and sat at 92-93 while working out for the Diamondbacks before the draft. He turned down the Red Sox as a 2001 second-round pick, then flunked out of Southern California and wasn't eligible at Palomar (Calif.) JC last spring.

D'Antona

Best Breaking Ball: RHP Chris Kinsey (4) has two effective breaking pitches, a true curveball and a slurvy slider.

Most Intriguing Background: Jackson's father John is a regular on the CBS series "JAG," and Conor has had bit parts as an actor. RHP Derik Nippert (36) is the twin of Dustin Nippert, one of the top pitching prospects in the system. C Orlando Mercado Jr.'s (6) father caught for eight years in the majors and is the Angels' bullpen coach.

Closest To The Majors: Jackson, because he got a head start on Quentin and is more disciplined than D'Antona.

Best Late-Round Pick: Bass has a big frame (6-foot-6, 210 pounds) and two potential plus pitches in his fastball and slider. He's been clocked as high as 95 mph.

The One Who Got Away: Arizona signed 28 of its first 29 selections. RHP Jeff Manship (50) had one of the best curveballs in the draft and an 88-92 mph fastball, but he fulfilled his commitment to Notre Dame.

Assessment: Arizona may have found the heart of its future batting order with Jackson, Quentin and D'Antona. Chico got back on track and could be a coup if he refines his mechanics and repertoire.

SS Sergio Santos (1) is one of the top infield prospects in the game. RHP Dustin Nippert (15) and C Chris Snyder (2) also could be key parts of Arizona's future.

2B Scott Hairston (3) has more than made up for the disappointment of RHP Jason Bulger (1). 3B Chad Tracy (7) could start for the Diamondbacks sometime soon.

Even without a first-rounder, Arizona still found BA's 2003 Rookie of the Year, RHP Brandon Webb (8). Another late-rounder, RHP Brian Bruney (12), has closer potential.

The Diamondbacks whiffed on both first-rounders, 1B Corey Myers and RHP Casey Daigle. They recovered with 1B Lyle Overbay (18) and LHP Chris Capuano (8), whom they used in the Richie Sexson trade, and INF Matt Kata (9).

*—Draft analysis prepared by **Jim Callis**. Numbers in parentheses indicate draft rounds.*

MEL BAILEY

Scott
Hairston

Born: May 25, 1980.
Ht.: 6-0. **Wt.:** 190.
Bats: R. **Throws:** R.
School: Central Arizona JC.
Career Transactions: Selected by Diamondbacks in third round of 2001 draft; signed June 15, 2001.

Hairston's baseball pedigree is unquestioned. His grandfather Sammy spent most of his career in the Negro Leagues before getting five at-bats in 1951 for the White Sox, the same team for which Hairston's father Jerry played 14 seasons. His uncle John got four at-bats for the 1969 Reds. Brother Jerry Jr. took over as the Orioles' second baseman in 2001. Scott shows the potential to become the best of the lot. He won the Arizona junior college triple crown in 2001 and tied for the minor league lead with 73 extra-base hits in his first full season in 2002. But like his brother, Hairston spent a significant part of 2003 on the disabled list. He pulled a muscle in his back while swinging the bat and tried to play through it. After a month of posting subpar numbers and further aggravating his back, Hairston missed six weeks. MRI exams showed nothing more than muscular damage, so the back problems aren't likely to recur. He took a month off after the regular season ended before reporting to the Arizona Fall League, where he proved there were no lingering effects by hitting .365-3-13.

A majority of scouts would agree Hairston's bat is ready for the majors now and gives him all-star potential as a second baseman. He demonstrates a quiet, balanced approach at the plate and stays on top of and inside the ball well with a short, compact stroke. Hairston's excellent bat speed also allows him to generate plus power. Hairston's total package at the plate could result in Jeff Kent-like production. He runs well enough to reach double-digits in steals, but won't be the threat on the bases that his brother is. The Kent comparisons that follow Hairston are based on his offense and defense. Hairston has trouble making the pivot on double plays and isn't comfortable throwing from different angles. He has worked on his defense in the AFL the last two seasons, and while he has made progress he also boots routine plays. While Hairston's hands, range and arm are average, most scouts project his future at third base or the outfield. Hairston often is one of the first players at the ballpark, but he spends most of that extra time in the batting cage. Some in the organization wonder where he'd be defensively if he spent more time working to improve his weaknesses. Hairston isn't shy about watching home runs or aggressive in charging down the baseline on routine outs. His plate discipline slipped in 2003, but his back problems may have been a contributing factor.

Even after being slowed by injury, Hairston isn't far away from challenging for a major league spot. The Diamondbacks' signing of free agent Roberto Alomar ended any chance he had of grabbing the Arizona second-base job out of spring training. So he'll begin 2004 at Triple-A Tucson and likely spend the whole year there, with a September callup possible.

Year	Club (League)	Class	AVG	G	AB	R	H	2B	3B	HR	RBI	BB	SO	SB	SLG	OBP
2001	Missoula (Pio)	R	.347	74	291	81	101	16	6	14	65	38	50	2	.588	.432
2002	South Bend (Mid)	A	.332	109	394	79	131	35	4	16	72	58	74	9	.563	.426
	Lancaster (Cal)	A	.405	18	79	20	32	11	1	6	26	6	16	1	.797	.442
2003	El Paso (TL)	AA	.276	88	337	53	93	21	7	10	47	30	80	6	.469	.345
	Tucson (PCL)	AAA	.000	1	0	0	0	0	0	0	1	0	0	0	.000	.000
MINOR LEAGUE TOTALS			.324	290	1101	233	357	83	18	46	211	132	220	18	.558	.404

2 Sergio Santos, ss

Born: July 4, 1983. **Ht.:** 6-3. **Wt.:** 190. **Bats:** R. **Throws:** R. **School:** Mater Dei HS, Hacienda Heights, Calif. **Career Transactions:** Selected by Diamondbacks in first round (27th overall) of 2002 draft; signed June 26, 2002.

Scouts viewed Santos as an elite prospect when he was a high school sophomore. His senior year didn't live up to billing, so he slipped to the 27th overall pick, where Arizona was more than happy to pay $1.4 million to keep him from attending Southern California. He earned a promotion to Double-A El Paso less than a month after his 20th birthday. Santos brings a full toolbox to the field, as well as tremendous enthusiasm and confidence. His strength and power stand out. Santos also makes adjustments at the plate. A big-bodied shortstop like Alex Rodriguez, he has a cannon arm to go with solid feet and range. Santos has made 62 errors in 1½ pro seasons. His arm allows him to wait longer on balls, resulting in bad hops or rushed throws, and his hands aren't great for short. Many scouts forecast a move to third base or the outfield. He also could be more patient at the plate, which would help unleash his power potential. Santos and Arizona want him to stay at short, though his bat will play anywhere. He'll return to Double-A to start 2004.

Year	Club (League)	Class	AVG	G	AB	R	H	2B	3B	HR	RBI	BB	SO	SB	SLG	OBP
2002	Missoula (Pio)	R	.272	54	202	38	55	19	2	9	37	29	49	6	.520	.367
2003	Lancaster (Cal)	A	.287	93	341	55	98	13	2	8	49	41	64	5	.408	.368
	El Paso (TL)	AA	.255	37	137	13	35	7	1	2	16	8	25	0	.365	.293
MINOR LEAGUE TOTALS			.276	184	680	106	188	39	5	19	102	78	138	11	.432	.353

3 Dustin Nippert, rhp

Born: May 6, 1981. **Ht.:** 6-7. **Wt.:** 200. **Bats:** R. **Throws:** R. **School:** West Virginia University. **Career Transactions:** Selected by Diamondbacks in 15th round of 2002 draft; signed June 9, 2002.

The Diamondbacks lengthened Nippert's stride after signing him, and it helped him gain command of his power repertoire. He endured a scare during the 2003 season, when doctors found a golf-ball-sized tumor under his left armpit. It was benign and removed arthroscopically, but did cost him two months. Arizona scout Greg Lonigro signed Nippert's identical twin Derik as a 36th-rounder in 2003. Nippert pounds the strike zone with two plus pitches, a 92-96 mph fastball and a power curveball with a 12-to-6 break. He stays tall during his delivery and throws on a downhill plane, getting the most out of his 6-foot-7 frame. Nippert didn't have a third pitch until his changeup gained consistency in the Arizona Fall League. While Nippert throws plenty of strikes, he sometimes delivers too many and can leave his fastball up in the zone at times. He must learn about wasting pitches in pitcher's counts. He also needs to further integrate his changeup into his repertoire. After two strong minor league seasons and a stellar AFL, Nippert will skip a level and jump to Double-A. He has the stuff to develop into a front-of-the-rotation starter.

Year	Club (League)	Class	W	L	ERA	G	GS	CG	SV	IP	H	R	ER	HR	BB	SO	AVG
2002	Missoula (Pio)	R	4	2	1.65	17	11	0	0	55	42	12	10	2	9	77	.208
2003	South Bend (Mid)	A	6	4	2.82	17	17	0	0	96	66	32	30	4	32	96	.191
MINOR LEAGUE TOTALS			10	6	2.39	34	28	0	0	150	108	44	40	6	41	173	.197

4 Chad Tracy, 3b

Born: May 22, 1980. **Ht.:** 6-2. **Wt.:** 200. **Bats:** L. **Throws:** R. **School:** East Carolina University. **Career Transactions:** Selected by Diamondbacks in seventh round of 2001 draft; signed June 9, 2001.

Tracy won the Double-A Texas League batting title with a .344 average in 2002, then led the Triple-A Pacific Coast League in hits and all minor league third basemen in batting as an encore. He's starting to remind scouts of Wade Boggs, whom Tracy had lunch with last summer while at the Futures Game. Tracy rivals Scott Hairston as the organization's best hitter. He should hit .300 in the majors because he's so quick at getting the barrel to the ball and adept at making adjustments. He hits laser-beam doubles to the gaps with regularity. A first baseman for two years in college, Tracy has made tremendous defensive strides over the last year. His footwork has improved and his arm rates average to above. Tracy never has demonstrated enough power for a corner infielder. He worked on lifting the ball better in the Dominican League this winter. He doesn't walk much because he makes contact with such ease. Before the Richie Sexson trade, Tracy had a chance to win the third-base job and keep Shea Hillenbrand at first base. Now Tracy will probably settle for a reserve job behind Hillenbrand in 2004.

Year	Club (League)	Class	AVG	G	AB	R	H	2B	3B	HR	RBI	BB	SO	SB	SLG	OBP
2001	Yakima (NWL)	A	.278	10	36	2	10	1	0	0	5	3	5	1	.306	.350
	South Bend (Mid)	A	.340	54	215	43	73	11	0	4	36	19	19	3	.447	.393
2002	El Paso (TL)	AA	.344	129	514	80	177	39	5	8	74	38	51	2	.486	.389
2003	Tucson (PCL)	AAA	.324	133	522	91	169	31	4	10	80	41	52	0	.456	.372
MINOR LEAGUE TOTALS			.333	326	1287	216	429	82	9	22	195	101	127	6	.462	.382

5 Adriano Rosario, rhp

Born: May 16, 1985. **Ht.:** 6-2. **Wt.:** 190. **Bats:** R. **Throws:** R. **Career Transactions:** Signed out of Dominican Republic by Diamondbacks, June 13, 2002.

Rosario is so mature and confident that some in the low Class A Midwest League questioned his age in 2003. But Arizona hired a private investigator to verify his background before signing him for $400,000. A shortstop growing up, Rosario hit 98 mph at Arizona's Dominican complex that April, prompting scouting director Mike Rizzo to set aside his predraft duties in 2002 to fly down to sign him. Rosario has the makings of three plus pitches. He throws his four-seam fastball up to 97-98 mph, and his two-seamer has more movement at 93-95. His slider and changeup are inconsistent, but could also be out pitches. He has a clean delivery and calm demeanor on the mound. The Diamondbacks don't question his durability, but are curious to see how he'll hold up after going from 77 innings in 2002 to 160 in 2003. He should miss a lot more bats than he did in the MWL. The Diamondbacks don't shy away from saying Rosario has No. 1 starter potential. He could join Dustin Nippert in a powerful Double-A rotation in 2004.

Year	Club (League)	Class	W	L	ERA	G	GS	CG	SV	IP	H	R	ER	HR	BB	SO	AVG
2002	Diamondbacks (DSL)	R	3	1	2.05	10	10	1	0	57	41	16	13	0	7	57	.193
	Missoula (Pio)	R	1	2	6.30	4	4	0	0	20	26	15	14	0	3	14	.321
2003	South Bend (Mid)	A	9	5	2.86	27	27	0	0	160	149	69	51	3	30	119	.247
MINOR LEAGUE TOTALS			13	8	2.96	41	41	1	0	237	216	100	78	3	40	190	.241

6 Conor Jackson, of

Born: May 7, 1982. **Ht.:** 6-3. **Wt.:** 205. **Bats:** R. **Throws:** R. **School:** University of California. **Career Transactions:** Selected by Diamondbacks in first round (19th overall) of 2003 draft; signed June 16, 2003.

After signing for $1.5 million, Jackson set a short-season Northwest League record for doubles and led the circuit in RBIs. Arizona moved him from corner infielder to outfielder because of its infield depth. His father John plays admiral A.J. Chegwidden on TV's "JAG." Jackson is as polished as any hitter from the 2003 draft. He has a quick bat and swings only at pitches he can hit. He was called out on strikes a few times early in his pro career, and Diamondbacks officials said it was because he knew the strike zone better than the umpires. He has an average arm. Shoulder tendinitis forced Jackson to DH for most of the summer, so he's still adjusting to the outfield. He's working on reading balls and taking better routes. The Diamondbacks want Jackson to put more backspin on the ball, which they hope will add carry to take more of his doubles over the fence. He doesn't have great speed but won't clog the bases. Jackson projects as a .300 hitter with 20-30 homers a year. He likely will begin 2004 at high Class A Lancaster.

Year	Club (League)	Class	AVG	G	AB	R	H	2B	3B	HR	RBI	BB	SO	SB	SLG	OBP
2003	Yakima (NWL)	A	.319	68	257	44	82	35	1	6	60	36	41	3	.533	.410
MINOR LEAGUE TOTALS			.319	68	257	44	82	35	1	6	60	36	41	3	.533	.410

7 Carlos Quentin, of

Born: Aug. 28, 1982. **Ht.:** 6-2. **Wt.:** 220. **Bats:** R. **Throws:** R. **School:** Stanford University. **Career Transactions:** Selected by Diamondbacks in first round (29th overall) of 2003 draft; signed July 2, 2003.

A product of San Diego's University High, where he was two years behind Mark Prior, Quentin became one of the best hitters in Stanford history. He played most of the 2003 season with a sore right elbow that required Tommy John surgery, which he had after signing for $1.1 million. He played on Team USA with Conor Jackson in 2002, and they should be reunited in Arizona's outfield of the future. With a powerful bat and arm, Quentin has classic right-field tools. He should regain his plus arm strength.

He drives the ball to all fields and doesn't have to pull pitches to send them out of the park. He's a disciplined hitter who gets on base. While Quentin has a lot of juice in his bat, he needs to do a better job of translating it into homers. He went deep just 35 times in 199 college games. He'll have to rebuild his arm strength, though with his determination that shouldn't be a problem. Quentin started taking batting practice three times a week in November while finishing his political-science degree at Stanford. He'll open 2004 as a DH, probably at high Class A, and should be ready for right field in May.

Year	Club (League)	Class	AVG	G	AB	R	H	2B	3B	HR	RBI	BB	SO	SB	SLG	OBP
2003	Did not play—Injured															

8 Brian Bruney, rhp

Born: Feb. 17, 1982. **Ht.:** 6-3. **Wt.:** 225. **Bats:** R. **Throws:** R. **School:** Warrenton (Ore.) HS. **Career Transactions:** Selected by Diamondbacks in 12th round of 2000 draft; signed June 6, 2000.

Along with Sergio Santos, Bruney is one of the few high school draftees who have panned out for the Diamondbacks, who are increasingly leaning toward college selections. In November, he allowed the ninth-inning homer to Mexico's Luis Garcia that eliminated Team USA from the 2004 Olympics. Bruney's fastball and slider are plus offerings. He can put three digits on radar guns but gets better command when he throws 95-96 mph. His slider took longer to develop, but El Paso pitching coach Claude Osteen helped him turn it into a hard, 85-86 mph breaker last April. Bruney also has the perfect mentality for a closer: a burning desire to take the ball and a short memory. Bruney is a reliever because there's effort in his compact delivery and he has just a passable feel for his changeup. He throws it mainly against lefties, and it moves away from them. Bruney should earn a role in Arizona's bullpen in 2004, possibly in the eighth inning. Among their relief prospects, he's the best suited to be the long-term closer.

Year	Club (League)	Class	W	L	ERA	G	GS	CG	SV	IP	H	R	ER	HR	BB	SO	AVG
2000	Diamondbacks (AZL)	R	4	1	6.48	20	2	0	2	25	21	23	18	2	29	24	.221
2001	South Bend (Mid)	A	1	4	4.13	26	0	0	8	33	24	19	15	1	19	40	.205
	Yakima (NWL)	A	1	2	5.14	15	0	0	2	21	19	14	12	2	11	28	.226
2002	South Bend (Mid)	A	4	3	1.68	37	0	0	10	48	37	15	9	1	17	54	.210
	El Paso (TL)	AA	0	2	2.92	10	0	0	0	12	11	5	4	1	4	14	.268
2003	El Paso (TL)	AA	0	2	2.59	28	0	0	14	31	29	17	9	1	13	28	.234
	Tucson (PCL)	AAA	3	1	2.81	32	0	0	12	32	24	12	10	0	18	32	.207
MINOR LEAGUE TOTALS			13	15	3.42	168	2	0	48	203	165	105	77	8	111	220	.219

9 Edgar Gonzalez, rhp

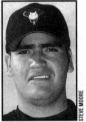

Born: Feb. 23, 1983. **Ht.:** 6-0. **Wt.:** 220. **Bats:** R. **Throws:** R. **Career Transactions:** Signed out of Mexico by Diamondbacks, April 18, 2000 . . . On restricted list, June 12, 2000-April 4, 2002.

Gonzalez signed for $3,500 at age 17, but got homesick and left the Rookie-level Dominican Summer League before throwing an inning. He made his pro debut two years later in 2002, threw a Midwest League no-hitter in his second start, and reached the majors in June 2003. He won his major league debut against the Padres. Gonzalez is crafty, mixing four pitches while moving them all around the strike zone. He throws his fastball at 88-91 mph, keeping 94-95 in his pocket for when he needs it. He also adds and subtracts from his changeup and uses three different curveballs, each with different movement and velocity. Gonzalez doesn't have a true knockout pitch, so he doesn't always miss bats or put hitters away at key moments. While Gonzalez studies hitters, he sometimes toys with lesser threats rather than challenging them and getting rid of them quickly. A future No. 3 starter, Gonzalez spent the winter in Panama to help him prepare for a spring audition for Arizona's rotation.

Year	Club (League)	Class	W	L	ERA	G	GS	CG	SV	IP	H	R	ER	HR	BB	SO	AVG
2000	Did not play																
2001	Did not play																
2002	South Bend (Mid)	A	11	8	2.91	23	23	4	0	151	141	66	49	4	34	110	.246
	Lancaster (Cal)	A	3	0	0.78	4	4	0	0	23	24	7	2	1	3	21	.264
2003	El Paso (TL)	AA	2	2	3.50	6	6	0	0	36	40	18	14	1	11	30	.282
	Tucson (PCL)	AAA	8	7	3.75	20	19	1	0	130	126	65	54	4	28	69	.255
	Arizona (NL)	MAJ	2	1	4.91	9	2	0	0	18	28	10	10	3	7	14	.368
MAJOR LEAGUE TOTALS			2	1	4.91	9	2	0	0	18	28	10	10	3	7	14	.368
MINOR LEAGUE TOTALS			24	17	3.15	53	52	5	0	340	331	156	119	10	76	230	.254

10   Mike Gosling, lhp

Born: Sept. 23, 1980. **Ht.:** 6-2. **Wt.:** 210. **Bats:** L. **Throws:** L. **School:** Stanford University. **Career Transactions:** Selected by Diamondbacks in second round of 2001 draft; signed Aug. 1, 2001.

Gosling fell to the second round of the 2001 draft because of his bonus demands and signed for $2 million—more than 53 of the 66 players taken ahead of him. He ranked as the No. 2 prospect and top pitcher on this list a year ago, then posted the worst ERA among Triple-A qualifiers in 2003. He tried to pitch through a small tear in his shoulder at the end of the season and had arthroscopic surgery afterward. At his best, Gosling flashes four average to above-average pitches and has solid command. He throws an 88-92 mph fastball that reaches 94, a plus curveball, a changeup and a cut fastball that he added as a pro. He showed character by working hard while battling adversity and injury. Mechanics were the biggest culprit in Gosling's struggles. He dropped his elbow and pushed his pitches, which left fastballs up in the strike zone. His durability had been questioned in the past and is an issue again following his shoulder problems. Gosling should be healthy and ready for spring training. He'll begin 2004 at Triple-A and could be one of the first arms summoned to Arizona when a need arises.

Year	Club (League)	Class	W	L	ERA	G	GS	CG	SV	IP	H	R	ER	HR	BB	SO	AVG
2002	El Paso (TL)	AA	14	5	3.13	27	27	2	0	167	149	66	58	7	62	115	.238
2003	Tucson (PCL)	AAA	9	12	5.61	26	26	0	0	136	190	106	85	13	56	89	.330
MINOR LEAGUE TOTALS			23	17	4.25	53	53	2	0	303	339	172	143	20	118	204	.282

11   Luis Terrero, of

Born: May 18, 1980. **Ht.:** 6-2. **Wt.:** 205. **Bats:** R. **Throws:** R. **Career Transactions:** Signed out of Dominican Republic by Diamondbacks, Sept. 27, 1997.

Terrero's been a tease for most of his career. He ranked No. 1 in the organization two years ago and shows flashes of all five tools, but he can't stay healthy. His thin yet sculpted physique is so tight that it constantly breaks down. He has missed time with ribcage, ankle, groin, hamstring and hamate injuries during the last three seasons, then was hospitalized in November when a blood clot led to swelling in his left arm. On the positive side, he hit for the cycle twice in 2002, then cranked a walk-off homer and three-run bomb in back-to-back major league spring training games and tied for the minor league lead in triples in 2003. Long limbs and good wheels allow Terrero to cover ground quickly in the outfield, where he also shows a plus-plus arm, and on the basepaths. He runs into a lot of outs and barely breaks even stealing bases. He's also overaggressive at the plate. He displays power to all fields, but has difficulty laying off bad pitches and racks up too many strikeouts. For all his talent, Terrero never has shown consistent production. Some fear he could turn into another Ruben Rivera. He'll get a crack at sticking with the Diamondbacks this season, and his health and ability to make adjustments will determine if he can be an everyday player or extra outfielder.

Year	Club (League)	Class	AVG	G	AB	R	H	2B	3B	HR	RBI	BB	SO	SB	SLG	OBP
1998	Diamondbacks (DSL)	R	.231	56	169	19	39	7	1	2	15	13	44	9	.320	.301
1999	Missoula (Pio)	R	.287	71	272	74	78	13	7	8	40	32	91	27	.474	.365
2000	High Desert (Cal)	A	.190	19	79	10	15	3	1	0	1	3	16	5	.253	.229
	Missoula (Pio)	R	.261	68	276	48	72	10	0	8	44	10	75	23	.384	.305
2001	South Bend (Mid)	A	.157	24	89	4	14	2	0	1	8	0	29	3	.213	.176
	Yakima (NWL)	A	.317	11	41	7	13	2	1	0	0	2	8	0	.415	.349
	Lancaster (Cal)	A	.451	19	71	16	32	9	1	4	11	1	14	5	.775	.466
	El Paso (TL)	AA	.299	34	147	29	44	13	3	3	8	4	45	9	.490	.331
2002	El Paso (TL)	AA	.286	104	360	49	103	20	6	8	54	23	89	18	.442	.342
2003	Tucson (PCL)	AAA	.287	118	467	83	134	20	15	3	46	31	103	23	.413	.345
	Arizona (NL)	MAJ	.250	5	4	0	1	0	0	0	0	0	1	0	.250	.400
MAJOR LEAGUE TOTALS			.250	5	4	0	1	0	0	0	0	0	1	0	.250	.400
MINOR LEAGUE TOTALS			.276	524	1971	339	544	99	35	37	227	119	514	122	.418	.330

12   Josh Kroeger, of

Born: Aug. 31, 1982. **Ht.:** 6-2. **Wt.:** 200. **Bats:** L. **Throws:** L. **School:** Scripps Ranch HS, San Diego. **Career Transactions:** Selected by Diamondbacks in fourth round of 2000 draft; signed June 6, 2000.

An athletic player with raw power, Kroeger turned down a football scholarship to Division II Truman State (Mo.) as a wide receiver. He advanced to high Class A as a teenager in 2002, and advanced pitchers picked him apart. He returned to Lancaster in 2003 and turned everything around. With a new sense of confidence and an extra year of developing his linebacker-like body, Kroeger started showing his above-average power. He tied for 11th in the minors with 39 doubles after hitting 44 combined in his first three seasons. His strong left-handed swing reminds some of Dave Justice, and Diamondbacks officials believe he can produce similar numbers as a right fielder once he starts making in-game adjustments. Kroeger's above-average speed allows him to play center field if needed, and his strong arm makes him a standout in right. After leveling off after a midseason move to Double-A last year, Kroeger will head back to El Paso in 2004.

Year	Club (League)	Class	AVG	G	AB	R	H	2B	3B	HR	RBI	BB	SO	SB	SLG	OBP
2000	Diamondbacks (AZL)	R	.297	54	222	40	66	9	3	4	28	21	41	5	.419	.359
2001	South Bend (Mid)	A	.274	79	292	36	80	15	1	3	37	18	49	4	.363	.324
2002	Lancaster (Cal)	A	.235	133	497	63	117	20	7	7	58	23	136	2	.346	.274
2003	Lancaster (Cal)	A	.341	78	305	50	104	30	6	5	55	35	58	6	.528	.409
	El Paso (TL)	AA	.274	54	208	26	57	9	2	3	22	10	54	3	.380	.315
MINOR LEAGUE TOTALS			.278	398	1524	215	424	83	19	22	200	107	338	20	.401	.330

13 Marland Williams, of

Born: June 22, 1981. **Ht.:** 5-9. **Wt.:** 175. **Bats:** R. **Throws:** R. **School:** North Florida CC. **Career Transactions:** Selected by Diamondbacks in 36th round of 2001 draft; signed May 10, 2002.

There's not a Diamondbacks prospect quicker or more athletic than Williams. He's a top-of-the-scale runner who gets to maximum speed with an explosive, two-step acceleration. A high school wide receiver recruited by Florida and Florida State, Williams chose baseball and attended North Florida before signing as a draft-and-follow. After he struggled at short-season Yakima in his pro debut, the Diamondbacks aggressively promoted him to high Class A. He met the challenge and showed offensive improvements. Built like Tim Raines, Williams has just enough pop in his bat to get him in trouble. Arizona officials want him to focus on keeping his stroke short and quick and eliminating an uppercut so he can use his feet. He must improve his plate discipline and bunting if he's to be a top-of-the-order hitter. He set a Lancaster franchise record with 57 steals in 2003 and was caught just seven times. His headfirst slides cost him a month of development as he had to sit out after getting his hand spiked during a steal attempt. He's still learning how to get jumps and read pitchers, but he often outruns pickoff attempts, pitchouts and even grounders to the right of shortstop. Williams also outruns balls in center field, showing superior range that makes up for a below-average arm. He'll work on the little ball game in Double-A this year.

Year	Club (League)	Class	AVG	G	AB	R	H	2B	3B	HR	RBI	BB	SO	SB	SLG	OBP
2002	Yakima (NWL)	A	.246	70	280	46	69	4	8	3	17	27	86	51	.350	.311
2003	Lancaster (Cal)	A	.287	102	425	85	122	15	1	4	30	31	99	57	.355	.340
MINOR LEAGUE TOTALS			.271	172	705	131	191	19	9	7	47	58	185	108	.353	.328

14 Jamie D'Antona, 3b

Born: May 12, 1982. **Ht.:** 6-2. **Wt.:** 210. **Bats:** R. **Throws:** R. **School:** Wake Forest University. **Career Transactions:** Selected by Diamondbacks in second round of 2003 draft; signed June 10, 2003.

D'Antona packs the best raw power in the system, and scouts don't have a problem projecting him as a 40-homer guy. He set Wake Forest's career home run mark (58) and was named Atlantic Coast Conference player of the year in 2003. The Diamondbacks thought he had more raw power than any player in the draft, and he tied for the Northwest League homer crown in his pro debut while ranking second to teammate Conor Jackson in RBIs. D'Antona's strength and bat speed are such that he doesn't need to hit the ball squarely to send it over the fence, and he shows that power to all fields. He sometimes gets into trouble by taking monstrous slow-pitch softball cuts. A shorter stroke could help bring up his average a bit, though D'Antona draws a decent number of walks and made adjustments after a slow start at the plate for Yakima. He also throws with great power, having hit 94 mph off the mound at a workout for scouts in college. His other third-base tools aren't as impressive, as he has limited range and his hands are just workable. There aren't any immediate plans to move D'Antona from third base, as he'll be adequate there if he can streamline his body, but first base could be his future destination. He will join 2003 first-rounders Jackson and Carlos Quentin in the heart of the high Class A batting order this year.

Year	Club (League)	Class	AVG	G	AB	R	H	2B	3B	HR	RBI	BB	SO	SB	SLG	OBP
2003	Yakima (NWL)	A	.277	70	271	46	75	18	1	15	57	35	60	0	.517	.356
MINOR LEAGUE TOTALS			.277	70	271	46	75	18	1	15	57	35	60	0	.517	.356

15 Chris Snyder, c

Born: Feb. 12, 1981. **Ht.:** 6-3. **Wt.:** 220. **Bats:** R. **Throws:** R. **School:** University of Houston. **Career Transactions:** Selected by Diamondbacks in second round of 2002 draft; signed June 16, 2002.

Snyder rated as the best defensive catcher in the 2002 draft and has proven why during his two pro seasons. He receives balls well with his soft hands and blocks pitches adroitly with an agile and strong body. He also knows how to handle a staff and call games, which he has done since his days in college. His strong, accurate arm and quick release can quiet the running game. He threw out 29 percent of basestealers in 2003 after catching 39 percent in his debut. Snyder began his second pro season repeating high Class A and put up excellent offensive numbers, but fell flat after a move to Double-A. His struggles were attributed to both the advanced pitching and Snyder's conditioning. He has shown a pattern of wearing down in late July as the rigors of catching more than 100 games take their toll. Snyder must get in better shape and increase his endurance if he's to handle 130 games as an everyday catcher in the majors. His swing can be long at times, but Snyder has the bat speed and loft to hit 20-25 home runs annually. He also makes consistent contact and has enough plate discipline to hit for a solid average as well. Snyder will make a second try at Double-A in 2004.

Year	Club (League)	Class	AVG	G	AB	R	H	2B	3B	HR	RBI	BB	SO	SB	SLG	OBP
2002	Lancaster (Cal)	A	.258	60	217	31	56	16	0	9	44	25	54	0	.456	.337
2003	Lancaster (Cal)	A	.314	69	245	53	77	16	2	10	53	35	43	0	.518	.414
	El Paso (TL)	AA	.202	53	188	21	38	14	0	4	26	19	29	0	.340	.286
MINOR LEAGUE TOTALS			.263	182	650	105	171	46	2	23	123	79	126	0	.446	.352

16 Jared Doyle, lhp

Born: Jan. 30, 1981. **Ht.:** 6-0. **Wt.:** 190. **Bats:** L. **Throws:** L. **School:** James Madison University. **Career Transactions:** Selected by Diamondbacks in third round of 2002 draft; signed June 15, 2002.

Doyle and his twin brother Nathan, a shortstop, helped James Madison to a school-record 177 wins over three years before Jared signed with the Diamondbacks after going 11-3, 2.57 in 2002. Nathan returned for his senior season before joining the Tigers as a 25th-rounder last June. In 2003, Doyle experienced the success expected of a polished college pitcher in low Class A. He tossed a one-hitter and a pair of three-hitters, and he was the leading winner on a South Bend staff that also included Dustin Nippert and Adriano Rosario. Doyle can't match their stuff, but he has a 91-94 mph fastball, a plus curveball and a solid changeup. His deceptive delivery makes it tough for hitters to get a good look at him, and his pitches have above-average movement that compensates for less-than-pinpoint command. Doyle often nibbles early in the count and falls behind, resulting in good hitters' pitches and too many walks. Spring training will determine if he begins 2004 in high Class A or Double-A.

Year	Club (League)	Class	W	L	ERA	G	GS	CG	SV	IP	H	R	ER	HR	BB	SO	AVG
2002	Yakima (NWL)	A	4	4	2.87	16	8	0	1	63	44	24	20	1	29	70	.198
2003	South Bend (Mid)	A	12	8	2.78	27	26	3	0	149	124	64	46	6	65	93	.229
MINOR LEAGUE TOTALS			16	12	2.81	43	34	3	1	211	168	88	66	7	94	163	.220

17 Brandon Medders, rhp

Born: Jan. 26, 1980. **Ht.:** 6-2. **Wt.:** 195. **Bats:** R. **Throws:** R. **School:** Mississippi State University. **Career Transactions:** Selected by Diamondbacks in eighth round of 2001 draft; signed June 11, 2001.

Drafted by the Devil Rays in the 37th round out of high school and by the Royals as an 18th-rounder out of Shelton State (Ala.) Community College, Medders finally signed as an eighth-rounder out of Mississippi State. His ERA has been inflated by launching pads at Lancaster and El Paso the last two years, but he has shown late-inning stuff after moving to the bullpen because of his herky-jerky, max-effort delivery. Medders has a 91-94 mph fastball that sinks and tops out at 96. It has plus life and naturally moves like a cutter. He also shows a good feel for his hard slider, which he can add and subtract from. Medders showed a closer's mentality by assuming that role at El Paso when Brian Bruney was promoted last year. The Diamondbacks added him to the 40-man roster in November and expect him to finish games in Triple-A this year. He could make his major league debut this summer.

Year	Club (League)	Class	W	L	ERA	G	GS	CG	SV	IP	H	R	ER	HR	BB	SO	AVG
2001	Lancaster (Cal)	A	1	2	1.32	31	0	0	3	41	26	8	6	1	15	53	.182
2002	Lancaster (Cal)	A	4	8	5.38	43	12	0	15	99	111	73	59	9	36	104	.282
2003	El Paso (TL)	AA	5	3	4.41	56	0	0	7	69	65	37	34	3	26	72	.244
MINOR LEAGUE TOTALS			10	13	4.26	130	12	0	25	209	202	118	99	13	77	229	.252

18 Matt Chico, lhp

Born: June 10, 1983. **Ht.:** 5-11. **Wt.:** 190. **Bats:** L. **Throws:** L. **School:** Palomar (Calif.) JC. **Career Transactions:** Selected by Diamondbacks in third round of 2003 draft; signed June 12, 2003.

Chico enjoyed plenty of hype coming out of high school, having pitched for two U.S. junior national teams and getting drafted in the second round by the Red Sox. He turned Boston down to attend Southern California and was the Trojans' Opening Day starter in 2002, but left after his freshman year because of academic troubles. He attended Palomar (Calif.) JC last year, but was ineligible to play there because of poor grades. He pitched in a beer league in California and Diamondbacks scouts spotted him there. Chico's body type, mentality and pitching style are similar to Mike Hampton, though he has much more velocity. Chico is a bulldog with a 92-93 mph fastball that tops out at 96-97. He works it to all quadrants of the strike zone. Chico also uses a curveball with a hard downward break and has shown a feel for a changeup. He does struggle with the consistency of his offspeed pitches, and often relies too much on his fastball because he doesn't want to get beat with anything but his best pitch. He'll need to develop his other offerings if he's to reach his ceiling of a middle-of-the-rotation starter. He's also working on adding a cutter. Chico is destined for low Class A in 2004.

Year	Club (League)	Class	W	L	ERA	G	GS	CG	SV	IP	H	R	ER	HR	BB	SO	AVG
2003	Yakima (NWL)	A	7	4	3.53	17	13	0	0	71	75	28	28	4	25	71	.274
MINOR LEAGUE TOTALS			7	4	3.53	17	13	0	0	71	75	28	28	4	25	71	.274

19 Jay Garthwaite, of

Born: Nov. 26, 1980. **Ht.:** 6-2. **Wt.:** 210. **Bats:** R. **Throws:** R. **School:** University of Washington. **Career Transactions:** Selected by Diamondbacks in 14th round of 2002 draft; signed June 11, 2002.

Garthwaite played football in high school and still has the physique to prove it. The Athletics drafted him in the 12th round after his prep career, but Garthwaite instead attended Washington, where he set a freshman record with 12 home runs. His uncle Larry Angel played in the minors and reached Triple-A. Garthwaite has a nice assortment of raw tools, including power to all fields. But he's overaggressive at the plate and gives away too many at-bats with long swings when he fails to recognize breaking balls. A center fielder in college, Garthwaite plays an above-average right field with good speed for his size. His arm is average. He still can play center in a pinch, as he did when Marland Williams missed time at Lancaster with a hand injury last year. Garthwaite is a consummate pro and solid character guy. He'll try to refine his raw tools next year at Double-A, and could show 30-homer power at the major league level.

Year	Club (League)	Class	AVG	G	AB	R	H	2B	3B	HR	RBI	BB	SO	SB	SLG	OBP
2002	Yakima (NWL)	A	.176	14	51	6	9	5	0	1	3	3	12	0	.333	.236
	South Bend (Mid)	A	.247	46	162	21	40	10	2	2	18	11	62	2	.370	.301
	Lancaster (Cal)	A	.364	7	11	2	4	0	0	1	3	2	7	0	.636	.462
2003	Lancaster (Cal)	A	.297	113	437	82	130	33	2	22	87	30	97	3	.533	.351
MINOR LEAGUE TOTALS			.277	180	661	111	183	48	4	26	111	46	178	5	.480	.332

20 Phil Stockman, rhp

Born: Jan. 25, 1980. **Ht.:** 6-6. **Wt.:** 200. **Bats:** R. **Throws:** R. **Career Transactions:** Signed out of Australia by Diamondbacks, Nov. 7, 1997 . . . On disabled list, June 23-Sept. 7, 1999.

Stockman signed out of Australia at age 17 as a tall but rail-thin thrower with limited experience on the mound. Arizona's player-development staff turned Stockman from a project into a prospect by helping him maintain a more consistent and smoother delivery and arm slot. Stockman now throws on a steep downhill plane, using the leverage from his 6-foot-7 frame to bump his velocity into the 89-94 mph range and as high as 96. He most often sinks his fastball at 91-92. Stockman also features a decent breaking ball and changeup. He used that repertoire to rank third in the Texas League in strikeouts last year. He also finished third in walks because he still needs to refine his command and consistency. Blisters also have plagued Stockman for the last three years. Much like Royals lefthander Jeremy Affeldt, he has tried several remedies and may have to move to the bullpen if no solution is found. Stockman will pitch out of the Triple-A rotation in 2004.

Year	Club (League)	Class	W	L	ERA	G	GS	CG	SV	IP	H	R	ER	HR	BB	SO	AVG
1998	Diamondbacks (AZL)	R	0	0	0.00	1	0	0	0	0	0	0	0	0	2	1	.000
1999	Did not play—Injured																
2000	Diamondbacks (AZL)	R	3	2	2.59	14	2	0	1	42	40	22	12	2	23	40	.237
	Missoula (Pio)	R	2	0	2.45	2	2	0	0	11	10	3	3	0	3	4	.233
2001	Lancaster (Cal)	A	0	0	5.09	8	0	0	0	18	11	11	10	2	9	18	.200
	Yakima (NWL)	A	3	4	4.26	15	14	0	0	76	81	39	36	5	22	48	.272
2002	Lancaster (Cal)	A	7	5	4.40	20	20	0	0	108	91	58	53	10	58	108	.232
2003	El Paso (TL)	AA	11	7	3.96	26	26	0	0	148	137	75	65	9	64	146	.244
	Tucson (PCL)	AAA	1	1	1.00	2	1	0	0	9	8	1	1	0	4	5	.258
MINOR LEAGUE TOTALS			27	19	3.94	88	65	0	1	412	378	209	180	28	185	370	.244

21 Greg Aquino, rhp

Born: Jan. 11, 1978. **Ht.:** 6-1. **Wt.:** 150. **Bats:** R. **Throws:** R. **Career Transactions:** Signed out of Dominican Republic by Diamondbacks, Nov. 8, 1995.

If not for his mother, Aquino might not be with the Diamondbacks anymore. He was one of the first players ever signed by the organization, but hit just .229 as a shortstop over his first four seasons. He almost quit after Arizona asked him to see how his arm strength would translate on the mound, but his mother told him not to give up on his dream of playing in the majors. Aquino has shown improvement each year on the mound, topping out at 99-100 mph in a 2003. Though his fastball is straight, its sheer velocity still makes it tough to hit. He also throws a power slider, and is daring enough to throw it in any count despite his inconsistent command. Aquino will show a two-seam fastball and a changeup at times, but he doesn't have a reliable offspeed pitch to complement his hard, hard, harder approach. As a result, the bullpen is the best place for him. Aquino has missed time with elbow and shoulder discomfort and tendinitis over the last year and a half. While he always comes back with his same power stuff, the recurring problems are troubling. The Diamondbacks see him eventually settling into a role like the one Oscar Villarreal had in 2003, getting key outs in middle relief and also serving as a set-up man. Aquino could begin 2004 in Triple-A and move to the majors at midseason.

Year	Club (League)	Class	AVG	G	AB	R	H	2B	3B	HR	RBI	BB	SO	SB	SLG	OBP
1996	Diamondbacks (DSL)	R	.200	58	160	21	32	3	0	0	9	22	11	7	.219	.308
1997	Diamondbacks (DSL)	R	.289	53	180	39	52	9	0	0	14	18	21	3	.339	.355
	South Bend (Mid)	A	.185	8	27	2	5	2	0	0	2	0	7	0	.259	.185
1998	Diamondbacks (AZL)	R	.282	45	163	20	46	11	1	0	11	7	34	2	.362	.310
1999	South Bend (Mid)	A	.156	53	186	18	29	4	2	0	10	9	46	1	.199	.199
2000	South Bend (Mid)	A	.000	29	0	1	0	0	0	0	0	0	0	0	.000	.000
2003	El Paso (TL)	AA	.222	20	9	0	2	0	0	0	0	0	2	0	.222	.222
MINOR LEAGUE TOTALS			.229	266	725	101	166	29	3	0	46	56	121	13	.277	.288

Year	Club (League)	Class	W	L	ERA	G	GS	CG	SV	IP	H	R	ER	HR	BB	SO	AVG
1999	Diamondbacks (AZL)	R	1	2	3.79	13	2	0	0	19	17	11	8	0	13	20	.246
2000	South Bend (Mid)	A	5	7	4.46	29	18	0	0	119	119	67	59	9	56	93	.260
2001	Lancaster (Cal)	A	2	5	8.14	25	4	0	0	42	59	40	38	7	24	39	.331
	Yakima (NWL)	A	4	2	3.30	8	8	0	0	46	39	18	17	2	14	39	.229
2002	Yakima (NWL)	A	1	1	2.06	6	6	0	0	35	26	9	8	0	17	34	.213
	Lancaster (Cal)	A	4	1	3.67	8	8	0	0	49	50	20	20	3	18	50	.267
2003	El Paso (TL)	AA	7	3	3.46	20	20	0	0	107	115	43	41	5	38	91	.278
MINOR LEAGUE TOTALS			24	21	4.12	109	66	0	0	417	425	208	191	26	180	366	.266

22 Shane Nance, lhp

Born: Sept. 7, 1977. **Ht.:** 5-8. **Wt.:** 180. **Bats:** L. **Throws:** L. **School:** University of Houston. **Career Transactions:** Selected by Dodgers in 11th round of 2000 draft; signed June 12, 2000 . . . Traded by Dodgers with RHP Ben Diggins to Brewers for 3B Tyler Houston and a player to be named, July 23, 2002; Dodgers acquired RHP Brian Mallette to complete trade (Oct. 16, 2002) . . . Traded by Brewers with 1B Richie Sexson and a player to be named to Diamondbacks for 2B Junior Spivey, 1B Lyle Overbay, LHP Jorge de la Rosa, C Chad Moeller, INF Craig Counsell and LHP Chris Capuano, Dec. 1, 2003; Diamondbacks acquired OF Noochie Varner to complete trade (Dec. 15, 2003).

Nance was a human yo-yo in 2003, moving between Milwaukee and Triple-A Indianapolis four times. He had trouble sticking with the Brewers because he was hit hard and kept coughing up homers. He tore the biceps muscle in his right arm in 2002, but it didn't hold him back in 2003. Milwaukee sent him to Arizona in the Richie Sexson trade, and Nance will try to fill the lefty specialist role with a new organization. He has pitched well throughout the minors, and to succeed in the majors he's going to have to work down and away more often instead of leaving the ball over the plate. He pitches with a solid fastball, plus changeup and so-so curveball. Generously listed at 5-foot-8, Nance throws on a very flat plane that makes his stuff easier to hit. His command has been fine in the minors, but he has been too tentative in the majors. He'll audition for the Arizona staff in spring training.

Year	Club (League)	Class	W	L	ERA	G	GS	CG	SV	IP	H	R	ER	HR	BB	SO	AVG
2000	Yakima (NWL)	A	2	4	2.48	12	9	0	0	58	41	19	16	1	22	66	.203
2001	Vero Beach (FSL)	A	6	3	2.63	21	0	0	4	48	28	15	14	3	21	63	.164
	Jacksonville (SL)	AA	7	0	1.59	28	0	0	1	45	31	11	8	4	17	44	.195
2002	Las Vegas (PCL)	AAA	11	3	4.17	37	0	0	1	58	58	32	27	6	26	53	.260
	Indianapolis (IL)	AAA	3	0	0.00	9	0	0	0	17	12	0	0	0	6	10	.207
	Milwaukee (NL)	MAJ	0	0	4.26	4	0	0	0	6	4	3	3	1	4	5	.174
2003	Milwaukee (NL)	MAJ	0	2	4.81	26	0	0	0	24	34	16	13	5	10	25	.327
	Indianapolis (IL)	AAA	2	4	1.38	35	1	0	3	52	34	10	8	4	13	53	.185
MAJOR LEAGUE TOTALS			0	2	4.70	30	0	0	0	31	38	19	16	6	14	30	.299
MINOR LEAGUE TOTALS			31	14	2.36	142	10	0	9	279	204	87	73	17	105	289	.205

23 Carlos Gonzalez, of

Born: Oct. 17, 1985. **Ht.:** 6-1. **Wt.:** 170. **Bats:** L. **Throws:** L. **Career Transactions:** Signed out of Venezuela by Diamondbacks, Aug. 3, 2002.

The Diamondbacks can't discuss Gonzalez without mentioning fellow Venezuelan Bobby Abreu. The comparisons are quite strong at the same stage of their careers, though Gonzalez showed more power at 17 while Abreu displayed more of his trademark plate discipline. Like Abreu, Gonzalez is a solid defender with average speed and a strong right-field arm. He actually hit 91 mph off the mound when the Diamondbacks were scouting him. Gonzalez was the Rookie-level Pioneer League's youngest player in 2003, and his advanced bat allowed him to hold his own. The ball jumps off his bat because of the natural loft in his swing. Gonzalez does worry too much about striking out and hates to get into two-strike counts, so he ends up swinging at bad pitches, which leads to poor at-bats. He'll need to show more patience if he's to reach his ceiling as a .290 hitter capable of 20-25 homers annually. Gonzalez will address his biggest need—gaining experience—in low Class A this year.

Year	Club (League)	Class	AVG	G	AB	R	H	2B	3B	HR	RBI	BB	SO	SB	SLG	OBP
2003	Missoula (Pio)	R	.258	72	275	45	71	14	4	6	25	16	61	12	.404	.308
MINOR LEAGUE TOTALS			.258	72	275	45	71	14	4	6	25	16	61	12	.404	.308

24 Dustin Glant, rhp

Born: July 20, 1981. **Ht.:** 6-2. **Wt.:** 200. **Bats:** R. **Throws:** R. **School:** Purdue University. **Career Transactions:** Selected by Diamondbacks in seventh round of 2003 draft; signed June 9, 2003.

Unlike many teams, the Diamondbacks have put late-inning relief prospects into those roles in the minors rather than keeping them in the rotation to get more innings and work on more pitches. The approach has paid off with pitchers such as Byung-Hyun Kim, Mike Koplove, Bret Prinz, Jose Valverde and Oscar Villarreal. Brian Bruney and Brandon Medders are on the verge of the majors. Glant is the best of the closers lower in the system, a group that also includes Pete Sikaras (23 saves at Lancaster) and Matt Wilkinson (30 at South Bend). Glant didn't get much exposure as a closer for a mediocre Purdue team last spring, so Arizona was able to get him in the seventh round. He led the Northwest League with 18 saves, breaking lots of bats with a 90-94 mph fastball with great sinking life similar to Brandon Webb's. Glant also uses an 80-82 mph power slider and a cut changeup. He has a closer's mentality and throws so many strikes that the ninth inning is pretty automatic for him. He'll hop on the fast track to the majors in low Class A this year, with a midseason jump possible.

Year	Club (League)	Class	W	L	ERA	G	GS	CG	SV	IP	H	R	ER	HR	BB	SO	AVG
03	Yakima (NWL)	A	1	2	1.85	34	0	0	18	34	19	9	7	2	9	31	.157
MINOR LEAGUE TOTALS			1	2	1.85	34	0	0	18	34	19	9	7	2	9	31	.157

25 Sean Luellwitz, 1b

Born: Nov. 16, 1979. **Ht.:** 6-5. **Wt.:** 220. **Bats:** R. **Throws:** R. **School:** Vanderbilt University. **Career Transactions:** Selected by Diamondbacks in 28th round of 2002 draft; signed June 6, 2002.

Luellwitz was part of the same Vanderbilt recruiting class as Mark Prior, and he was named Commodores MVP twice during his three years in college. Drafted in 2002 mostly because the Diamondbacks needed an extra first baseman to help fill rosters, Luellwitz tightened up his body after his pro debut by dropping 15 pounds and adding muscle. The results are positive as the Wisconsin native felt right at home in the Midwest League last year, where he ranked second in slugging and fourth in doubles while playing in a tough hitter's park. He shows a short stroke with power to all fields, though he could stand to walk more. Managers rated Luellwitz as the MWL's best defensive first baseman for his range and soft hands, and South Bend pitchers felt more comfortable with him in the lineup. He also emerged as a team leader. Luellwitz was old for low Class A at 22, but he came a long way over the course of the season and was rewarded by staying with the team during its playoff run. He could hit 30 homers in a full year at Lancaster's launching pad in 2004, but he'll probably hop to Double-A as soon as he shows he's ready.

Year	Club (League)	Class	AVG	G	AB	R	H	2B	3B	HR	RBI	BB	SO	SB	SLG	OBP
2002	Yakima (NWL)	A	.317	13	41	6	13	2	0	0	3	5	8	0	.366	.391
	South Bend (Mid)	A	.216	48	162	15	35	9	2	1	21	22	35	0	.315	.323
2003	South Bend (Mid)	A	.291	128	475	59	138	34	1	18	79	49	82	5	.480	.365
MINOR LEAGUE TOTALS			.274	189	678	80	186	45	3	19	103	76	125	5	.434	.356

26 Jarred Ball, of

Born: April 18, 1983. **Ht.:** 6-1. **Wt.:** 170. **Bats:** B. **Throws:** R. **School:** Tomball (Texas) HS.
Career Transactions: Selected by Diamondbacks in ninth round of 2001 draft; signed July 29, 2001.

Ball grew up just outside of Houston, where he learned the game from his father Randy, a former minor league catcher. Ball turned down a college commitment to play for his hometown University of Houston after the Diamondbacks drafted him. He was over-matched as a 19-year-old in low Class A in 2002, not reaching base enough to make use of his plus speed. Ball became an all-star his second time through the Midwest League, show-ing good baserunning instincts and quickness as he swiped 32 bases in 43 attempts. He's a good defender who can play center field, though his arm is below average. A singles and doubles hitter, Ball would fit nicely atop a lineup if he can improve his plate discipline. But his 2-1 strikeout-walk ratio leaves much to be desired from a player who has shown little pop. Ball might have trouble standing out in an organization suddenly rife with outfield tal-ent, especially in center. He'll try to impress again in high Class A in 2004.

Year	Club (League)	Class	AVG	G	AB	R	H	2B	3B	HR	RBI	BB	SO	SB	SLG	OBP
2001	Missoula (Pio)	R	.246	19	57	13	14	2	1	0	3	7	14	1	.316	.348
2002	South Bend (Mid)	A	.240	87	321	48	77	13	4	2	23	42	85	12	.324	.338
2003	South Bend (Mid)	A	.281	125	463	62	130	23	2	4	52	41	84	32	.365	.342
MINOR LEAGUE TOTALS			.263	231	841	123	221	38	7	6	78	90	183	45	.346	.341

27 Jesus Cota, of

Born: Nov. 7, 1981. **Ht.:** 6-3. **Wt.:** 220. **Bats:** L. **Throws:** R. **School:** Pima (Ariz.) CC. **Career Transactions:** Selected by Diamondbacks in 14th round of 2000 draft; signed May 28, 2001.

In many ways, Cota is the second coming of former Diamondbacks first baseman Erubiel Durazo. Both grew up in Hermosillo, Mexico, before polishing their compact but powerful strokes at high schools and junior colleges in Arizona. Cota won the Rookie-level Pioneer League triple crown in 2001. He again posted loud numbers in 2002, though his free-swing-ing ways detracted from his batting average. Like Durazo, Cota suffered from a power out-age in 2003, with his drought the result of a hip flexor that nagged him all year before he was shut down in early August. Playing the outfield regularly for the first time also could have aggravated the condition. Unable to get his hips involved in his swing, Cota often felt for the ball and flailed away. The Diamondbacks will give Cota a pass for 2003, and hope his ability to drive fastballs out of the park to all fields returns this year. He's an average left fielder at best because his speed and arm strength are limited. He's a better fit at first base, where he played most often in his first two pro years. He spent the winter conditioning in Tucson, and a solid spring should send him back there for Triple-A competition.

Year	Club (League)	Class	AVG	G	AB	R	H	2B	3B	HR	RBI	BB	SO	SB	SLG	OBP
2001	Missoula (Pio)	R	.368	75	272	74	100	22	0	16	71	56	52	2	.625	.476
2002	Lancaster (Cal)	A	.280	135	540	73	151	33	3	16	101	38	121	0	.441	.325
2003	El Paso (TL)	AA	.272	98	364	51	99	16	3	1	37	27	57	2	.341	.322
MINOR LEAGUE TOTALS			.298	308	1176	198	350	71	6	33	209	121	230	4	.452	.363

28 Brian Barden, 3b

Born: April 2, 1981. **Ht.:** 5-11. **Wt.:** 195. **Bats:** R. **Throws:** R. **School:** Oregon State University.
Career Transactions: Selected by Diamondbacks in sixth round of 2002 draft; signed June 9, 2002.

Barden is essentially a righthanded-hitting version of Chad Tracy with even less power. It's tough to overcome that rap at an infield corner, and a .399 slugging percentage in the hitter-friendly Texas League last year didn't help his cause. But Barden has overcome plen-ty in his career, becoming a three-time all-Pacific-10 Conference player at Oregon State after taking one of the few scholarship offers he received. He didn't get a lot of draft attention, but still earned a spot on the California League all-star team in his half-season pro debut. Barden's compact stroke and ability to make adjustments should allow him to hit at any level, and in fairness his power was diminished by a thumb injury that cost him a month last summer. Like Jarred Ball, he'll have to draw more walks if he's not going to provide more pop. Barden's quick, athletic play and solid arm give him Gold Glove potential at third base. He reminds some scouts of David Bell or a young Jeff Cirillo. Barden could play second base if needed but isn't nearly the same caliber of defender in the middle of the diamond. If Tracy doesn't make the big league club in his battle with Shea Hillenbrand for Arizona's third-base job, Barden could return to Double-A.

Year	Club (League)	Class	AVG	G	AB	R	H	2B	3B	HR	RBI	BB	SO	SB	SLG	OBP
2002	Yakima (NWL)	A	.333	4	15	5	5	1	0	0	2	1	1	0	.400	.412
	Lancaster (Cal)	A	.335	64	269	58	90	19	1	8	46	16	63	3	.502	.370

2003	El Paso (TL)	AA	.287	109	383	50	110	24	5	3	57	29	78	10	.399 .348
MINOR LEAGUE TOTALS			.307	177	667	113	205	44	6	11	105	46	142	13	.441 .358

29 Sergio Lizarraga, rhp

Born: July 23, 1981. **Ht.:** 6-4. **Wt.:** 190. **Bats:** R. **Throws:** R. **Career Transactions:** Signed out of Mexico by Diamondbacks, Oct. 6, 2000.

After signing Edgar Gonzalez and Oscar Villareal out of Mexico, the Diamondbacks have another find in Lizarraga. He really blossomed in 2003, adding 10 pounds to his skinny 6-foot-4 frame before succeeding in a swing role in low Class A. He moved to the rotation for good in late July and allowed just nine runs over his final seven starts. Lizarraga always had fine command of his three-pitch repertoire and a knack for pitching beyond his years, but the extra strength helped raise his fastball from 87-89 mph to the low 90s. He occasionally hit 94. He also throws a solid slider and a changeup. Lizarraga likes to set hitters up by adding and subtracting velocity from his fastball and slider while moving the pitches around the strike zone. He followed up with a strong winter in the Mexican Pacific League. Lizarraga should move up to the rotation in Lancaster, a hitter's park that will prove a stern test. The Diamondbacks think he ultimately can end up similar to Miguel Batista.

Year	Club (League)	Class	W	L	ERA	G	GS	CG	SV	IP	H	R	ER	HR	BB	SO	AVG
2001	Missoula (Pio)	R	6	2	5.09	15	15	0	0	81	104	57	46	10	23	57	.308
2002	Yakima (NWL)	A	4	8	4.05	16	13	0	0	91	90	48	41	6	19	86	.262
2003	South Bend (Mid)	A	9	2	1.78	42	9	0	1	96	71	22	19	6	29	85	.205
MINOR LEAGUE TOTALS			19	12	3.56	73	37	0	1	268	265	127	106	22	71	228	.258

30 Lance Cormier, rhp

Born: Aug. 19, 1980. **Ht.:** 6-1. **Wt.:** 190. **Bats:** R. **Throws:** R. **School:** University of Alabama. **Career Transactions:** Selected by Diamondbacks in fourth round of 2002 draft; signed June 6, 2002.

Cormier set several school records in a four-year career at Alabama, and his track record, polish and competitive nature attracted the Diamondbacks. In 2003, his first full season, he pitched well after an emergency promotion to Triple-A but had less success in high Class A or Double-A. Cormier throws four solid-average pitches, led by a changeup and curveball. He also has an 88-92 mph fastball and a slider. He delivers all four offerings with pinpoint command but lacks a true out pitch. He could evolve as a back-of-the-rotation starter or return to the bullpen, where he saved 11 games to lead the Southeastern Conference as a freshman. With heated competition set for El Paso's rotation, Cormier could begin 2004 in Triple-A.

Year	Club (League)	Class	W	L	ERA	G	GS	CG	SV	IP	H	R	ER	HR	BB	SO	AVG
2002	Yakima (NWL)	A	0	0	27.00	1	0	0	0	1	4	4	3	0	0	3	.500
	South Bend (Mid)	A	3	0	2.93	11	3	0	1	28	29	9	9	1	2	17	.259
2003	Lancaster (Cal)	A	6	5	3.82	15	15	0	0	94	102	55	40	6	16	59	.280
	Tucson (PCL)	AAA	1	1	2.60	5	4	0	0	28	26	10	8	1	5	11	.260
	El Paso (TL)	AA	2	3	6.10	9	8	0	0	41	59	33	28	3	22	26	.337
MINOR LEAGUE TOTALS			12	9	4.13	41	30	0	1	192	220	111	88	11	45	116	.290

ATLANTA BRAVES

Disappointment has become commonplace for the Braves over the past several Octobers, but their dejection after losing to the Cubs in the 2003 National League Division Series might have topped the charts.

After tying the Yankees for the major league lead with 101 victories only to come up short of the World Series yet again, Atlanta is going through another overhaul at the major league level. The Braves face budget limitations while many of their important contributors from 2003—including Javy Lopez, Greg Maddux and Gary Sheffield, whose salaries totaled $32.75 million, roughly one-third of Atlanta's payroll—departed as free agents. The payroll could be cut to the $80 million range in 2004, which would put the Braves in the middle of the pack.

Despite the potential storm clouds on the horizon, the situation in Atlanta is more sunny than gloomy. The team picked up a $6.2 million option on righthander Russ Ortiz, who led the National League with 21 wins after coming from the Giants. And it traded some of its pitching surplus to bring in J.D. Drew from the Cardinals.

A deep farm system, bolstered by four straight strong drafts under scouting director Roy Clark, also has the Braves in an enviable position. Help is on the way at a variety of key positions, beginning in 2004 at catcher (Johnny Estrada), and followed at third base (Andy Marte) and right field (Jeff Francoeur). If the Braves can combine those prospects with their established standouts, they could field a championship-caliber lineup dominated by homegrown players. Throughout the team's run of success, mixing new players in has been standard procedure.

Clark and the Braves continue to maintain the philosophy of drafting high school players, particularly in the first 10 rounds, with a heavy emphasis on pitching. They also have worked to upgrade the team's catching. In addition to acquiring Estrada from Philadelphia last winter, Atlanta nabbed Brian McCann and Jarrod Saltalamacchia in the first two rounds of the past two drafts.

Atlanta was uncharacteristically successful in the lower minors in 2003, winning its first low Class A South Atlantic League title since 1979 and its first Rookie-level Gulf Coast League championship since 1964. That's another sign the organization's commitment to drafting and developing younger players is working.

One reason the Braves feel confident with that approach is the longevity of their minor league staff. Rick Albert, Randy Ingle and Brian Snitker all have spent at least a quarter-century in the farm system. The Braves also brought back veteran pitching coach Bill Fischer this fall after the surprising firing of roving pitching coordinator Rick Adair.

TOP 30 PROSPECTS

1. Andy Marte, 3b
2. Jeff Francoeur, of
3. Bubba Nelson, rhp
4. Dan Meyer, lhp
5. Adam LaRoche, 1b
6. Macay McBride, lhp
7. Brian McCann, c
8. Kyle Davies, rhp
9. Anthony Lerew, rhp
10. Kelly Johnson, ss
11. Jose Capellan, rhp
12. Wilson Betemit, 3b
13. Gregor Blanco, of
14. Onil Joseph, of
15. Jake Stevens, lhp
16. Blaine Boyer, rhp
17. Matt Merricks, lhp
18. Scott Thorman, 1b
19. Jarrod Saltalamacchia, c
20. Carlos Duran, of
21. Andy Pratt, lhp
22. Jo Jo Reyes, lhp
23. Chuck James, lhp
24. Brayan Pena, c
25. Ryan Langerhans, of
26. Brett Evert, rhp
27. Zach Miner, rhp
28. Charlie Morton, rhp
29. Matt Esquivel, of
30. Paul Bacot, rhp

By Bill Ballew

ORGANIZATION
OVERVIEW

General manager: John Schuerholz. **Farm director:** Dayton Moore. **Scouting director:** Roy Clark.

2003 PERFORMANCE

Class	Team	League	W	L	Pct.	Finish*	Manager
Majors	Atlanta	National	101	61	.623	1st (16)	Bobby Cox
Triple-A	Richmond Braves	International	64	79	.448	13th (14)	Pat Kelly
Double-A	Greenville Braves	Southern	68	70	.493	5th (10)	Brian Snitker
High A	Myrtle Beach Pelicans	Carolina	56	82	.406	8th (8)	Randy Ingle
Low A	Rome Braves	South Atlantic	78	61	.561	+3rd (16)	Rocket Wheeler
Rookie	Danville Braves	Appalachian	36	30	.545	4th (10)	Kevin McMullan
Rookie	GCL Braves	Gulf Coast	38	22	.633	+1st (14)	Ralph Henriquez

OVERALL 2003 MINOR LEAGUE RECORD   340 344 .497 17th (30)

*Finish in overall standings (No. of teams in league). +League champion

ORGANIZATION LEADERS

BATTING
Minimum 250 At-Bats

*AVG	Johnny Estrada, Richmond	.328
R	Jeff Francoeur, Rome	78
H	Jeff Francoeur, Rome	147
TB	Adam LaRoche, Richmond/Greenville	235
2B	Andy Marte, Myrtle Beach	35
	James Jurries, Greenville	35
3B	Wilson Betemit, Richmond	13
HR	Adam LaRoche, Richmond/Greenville	20
RBI	Adam LaRoche, Richmond/Greenville	72
BB	Andy Marte, Myrtle Beach	67
SO	Cory Aldridge, Greenville	134
SB	Gregor Blanco, Myrtle Beach	34
*SLG	Johnny Estrada, Richmond	.494
*OBP	Johnny Estrada, Richmond	.393

PITCHING
#Minimum 75 Innings

W	Matt Wright, Myrtle Beach/Rome	12
	Blaine Boyer, Rome	12
L	Matt Merricks, Myrtle Beach/Rome	15
ERA	Anthony Lerew, Rome	2.38
G	Three tied at	53
CG	Jason Marquis, Richmond	3
	Daniel Curtis, Greenville/Myrtle Beach	3
SV	Joey Dawley, Richmond	23
IP	Macay McBride, Myrtle Beach	165
BB	Andy Pratt, Richmond	77
SO	Andy Pratt, Richmond	161

BEST TOOLS

Best Hitter for Average	Adam LaRoche
Best Power Hitter	Andy Marte
Fastest Baserunner	Gregor Blanco
Best Athlete	Jeff Francoeur
Best Fastball	Jose Capellan
Best Curveball	Charlie Morton
Best Slider	Macay McBride
Best Changeup	Kyle Davies
Best Control	Dan Meyer
Best Defensive Catcher	Brayan Pena
Best Defensive Infielder	Luis Hernandez
Best Infield Arm	Wilson Betemit
Best Defensive Outfielder	Jeff Francoeur
Best Outfield Arm	Adam Stern

PROJECTED 2007 LINEUP

Catcher	Brian McCann
First Base	Chipper Jones
Second Base	Marcus Giles
Third Base	Andy Marte
Shortstop	Rafael Furcal
Left Field	J.D. Drew

Center Field	Andruw Jones
Right Field	Jeff Francoeur
No. 1 Starter	Russ Ortiz
No. 2 Starter	Bubba Nelson
No. 3 Starter	Dan Meyer
No. 4 Starter	Macay McBride
No. 5 Starter	Mike Hampton
Closer	Jose Capellan

LAST YEAR'S TOP 20 PROSPECTS

1. Adam Wainwright, rhp
2. Wilson Betemit, ss
3. Andy Marte, 3b
4. Bubba Nelson, rhp
5. Macay McBride, lhp
6. Jeff Francoeur, of
7. Carlos Duran, of
8. Scott Thorman, 1b
9. Brett Evert, rhp
10. Gonzalo Lopez, rhp
11. Horacio Ramirez, lhp
12. Kelly Johnson, ss
13. Adam LaRoche, 1b
14. Bryan Digby, rhp
15. Zach Miner, rhp
16. Jung Bong, lhp
17. Gregor Blanco, of
18. Dan Meyer, lhp
19. Trey Hodges, rhp
20. Ryan Langerhans, of

TOP PROSPECTS OF THE DECADE

1994	Chipper Jones, ss
1995	Chipper Jones, ss/3b
1996	Andruw Jones, of
1997	Andruw Jones, of
1998	Bruce Chen, lhp
1999	Bruce Chen, lhp
2000	Rafael Furcal, ss
2001	Wilson Betemit, ss
2002	Wilson Betemit, ss
2003	Adam Wainwright, rhp

TOP DRAFT PICKS OF THE DECADE

1994	Jacob Shumate, rhp
1995	*Chad Hutchinson, rhp
1996	A.J. Zapp, 1b
1997	Troy Cameron, ss
1998	Matt Belisle, rhp (2)
1999	Matt Butler, rhp (2)
2000	Adam Wainwright, rhp
2001	Macay McBride, lhp
2002	Jeff Francoeur, of
2003	Luis Atilano, rhp

*Did not sign

ALL-TIME LARGEST BONUSES

Jeff Francoeur, 2002	$2,200,000
Matt Belisle, 1998	$1,750,000
Jung Bong, 1997	$1,700,000
Macay McBride, 2001	$1,340,000
Adam Wainwright, 2000	$1,250,000
Josh Burrus, 2001	$1,250,000

MINOR LEAGUE
DEPTH CHART

ATLANTA BRAVES — RANK: 4

Impact potential (B): Andy Marte is not far off from a Miguel Cabrera-esque breakthrough, Jeff Francoeur adapted quickly to pro pitching and oozes plus tools, while Adam LaRoche is prepared to step in at first base for the Braves this season and could challenge for the Rookie of the Year award.

Depth (A): It's another typical year in the Braves organization. They're stacked with premium talents, balancing athletic outfielders with power arms. Last year's draft haul included six picks in the first three rounds. Don't discount Brian McCann's bat.

Sleeper: Onil Joseph, of.   —Depth charts prepared by **Josh Boyd**. Numbers in parentheses indicate prospect rankings.

LF
Onil Joseph (14)
Adam Stern
Josh Burrus

CF
Jeff Francoeur (2)
Gregor Blanco (13)
Ryan Langerhans (25)
Matt Esquivel (29)
Steven Doetsch
Ardley Jansen

RF
Carlos Duran (20)
Billy McCarthy
Angelo Burrows
Carlos Guzman

3B
Andy Marte (1)
Wilson Betemit (12)
James Jurries
Mike Hessman

SS
Kelly Johnson (10)
T.J. Pena
Luis Hernandez

2B
Richard Lewis
Aaron Herr

1B
Adam LaRoche (5)
Scott Thorman (18)
Carlos Moreta

C
Brian McCann (7)
Jarrod Saltalamacchia (19)
Brayan Pena (24)
Kyle Roat
C.J. Bressoud

SOURCE OF TALENT

Homegrown		Acquired	
College	1	Trades	1
Junior College	2	Rule 5 draft	0
Draft-and-follow	0	Independent	0
High school	19	Free agents/waivers	0
Nondrafted free agent	0		
Foreign	7		

LHP

Starters	Relievers
Dan Meyer (4)	Andy Pratt (21)
Macay McBride (6)	Chuck James (23)
Jake Stevens (15)	Ray Aguilar
Matt Merricks (17)	Devin Anderson
Jo Jo Reyes (22)	
Matt Harrison	
Matt Coenen	

RHP

Starters	Relievers
Bubba Nelson (3)	Jose Capellan (11)
Kyle Davies (8)	Bryan Digby
Anthony Lerew (9)	Luis Atilano
Blaine Boyer (16)	Buddy Hernandez
Brett Evert (26)	Sung Jung
Zach Miner (27)	Roberto Nieves
Charlie Morton (28)	Efigenio Peralta
Paul Bacot (30)	Ralph Roberts
Matt Wright	Kevin Barry
Gonzalo Lopez	
Sean White	

DRAFT
ANALYSIS

Best Pro Debut: OF Steven Doetsch (14) batted .320-8-37, tying for the Rookie-level Gulf Coast League home run title and leading the GCL in hits (73). The Braves had several young pitchers perform well, most notably LHP Jo Jo Reyes (2) and RHP Paul Bacot (2), who helped the GCL club win its first championship in 39 years.

Best Athlete: Doetsch, 6-foot-3 and 205 pounds, has plus speed and arm strength, and plays a fine center field. Bacot, 6-foot-6 and 200 pounds, led his high school team to the 2003 Georgia state 5-A basketball finals as a point guard.

Best Pure Hitter: Though the Braves and other organizations had questions about his swing and approach before the draft, they believe Doetsch is the best hitter they signed. He showed more patience and a greater willingness to use the entire field.

Best Raw Power: 3B Jamie Romak (4), who was limited to 51 at-bats because of a lower-back injury. He's a righthanded version of Scott Thorman, a fellow Canadian they took in 2000's first round.

Fastest Runner: Doetsch covers 60 yards in 6.6-6.7 seconds. He's still learning how to use his speed, as he was caught stealing on nine of his 17 GCL attempts.

Best Defensive Player: C Jarrod Saltalamacchia (1) had the best all-around catching package in the draft. The 6-foot-4

Doetsch

switch-hitter also has offensive upside.

Best Fastball: RHP Ryan Basner (7) has reached 95 mph out of the bullpen. Several high school arms touch 93, including Reyes, Bacot, LHPs Jake Stevens (3) and Matt Harrison (3), and RHPs Chris Vines (5) and Asher Demme (6).

Best Breaking Ball: Stevens' hard curveball ate up GCL hitters.

Most Intriguing Background: Saltalamacchia's older brother Justin, an outfielder/infielder, signed with the Braves as a nondrafted free agent out of UNC Greensboro. C C.J. Bressoud (26), a good defender, is the nephew of Eddie Bressoud, an all-star shortstop with the Red Sox in the 1960s.

Closest To The Majors: RHP Sean White's (8) sinker and command could move him up the ladder quickly.

Best Late-Round Pick: Doetsch. Bressoud and LHP Kyle Bakker (20) were tough signs, but the Braves landed them.

The One Who Got Away: LHP Keith Weiser (18) and RHP/OF Brooks Brown (21) would have added to the haul of high school pitching. Weiser is at Miami (Ohio), while Brown will play both ways for Georgia.

Assessment: The Braves have had success with prep arms in the past, and no club can top their 2003 draft in that regard as they signed seven such pitchers in the first six rounds.

It's impossible to argue with the top three picks: OF Jeff Francoeur (1), LHP Dan Meyer (1) and C Brian McCann (2). But unsigned SS Tyler Greene (2) could be the No. 1 overall pick in 2005.

LHP Macay McBride (1) and RHPs Kyle Davies (4) and Anthony Lerew (11) restocked Atlanta's pitching depth. SS Josh Burrus (1) and 2B Richard Lewis (1) have been disappointing.

RHP Adam Wainwright (1) netted J.D. Drew in an offseason trade, while two late-round sleepers—1B Adam LaRoche (29) and RHP Trey Hodges (17)—could start for the Braves in 2004. RHP Bubba Nelson (2) could help soon, and SS Kelly Johnson (1) and 1B Scott Thorman (1) still have promise. Of four first-rounders, only 2B Aaron Herr has stalled.

Atlanta had no first-rounder and has little to show for huge bonus investments in RHP Matt Butler (2), SS Pat Manning (3) and RHP Matt McClendon (5). The Braves traded the best prospects from this crop, RHP Andrew Brown (6) and LHP Ben Kozlowski (12).

—Draft analysis prepared by Jim Callis. Numbers in parentheses indicate draft rounds.

Andy Marte

Born: Oct. 21, 1983.
Ht.: 6-1. **Wt.:** 180.
Bats: R. **Throws:** R.
Career Transactions: Signed out of Dominican Republic by Braves, Sept. 12, 2000.

After leading the low Class A South Atlantic League with 105 RBIs and finishing the season as the league's all-star third baseman in 2002, Marte jumped to high Class A and continued his emergence as one of the top infield prospects in the game. He overcame a rough start that included a .200 batting average during April to pace the Carolina League in doubles and extra-base hits, and again he finished the season as his league's postseason all-star third baseman. He produced solid power numbers in spite of playing in a difficult hitter's park in Myrtle Beach and seeing a steady diet of offspeed pitches in 2003. That type of turnaround was no surprise because Marte never has had difficulty staying focused. In his first pro season after signing with the Braves for $600,000, he struggled to make contact and batted just .200 at Rookie-level Danville. He learned from that experience and hasn't looked back since, batting better than .280 in both of his full professional seasons.

Marte has a quick, line-drive stroke that continues to become more powerful as his body matures. His pitch recognition is as good as anyone's in the system, and he has the uncanny ability to make adjustments with his swing while the ball is on the way to the plate. For a young player, he already understands the importance of drawing walks and made significant strides in that skill in 2003. He used a new pre-at-bat ritual to help him stay on top of the ball and through it better. While defense was once a struggle for Marte, hard work and experience have paid off for him at third base. He has improved on charging slow rollers and on making accurate throws. He has average speed, and is a smart and effective baserunner. Marte's desire to succeed is strong, yet he never lets his emotions get the best of him. His ability to stay on an even keel and separate the different aspects of the game has put him on the fast track to the major leagues. His defensive footwork could stand some upgrading, especially when he's going back on balls and to his left. But the Braves are confident Marte will develop into no worse than an average defender at the hot corner.

While spending full seasons at both Class A stops, Marte has made rapid progress and shows no sign of slowing down on his way to the big leagues. He's the best third-base prospect in the minors and unquestionably the Braves' long-term answer at the hot corner. The Braves want Marte to spend most of the 2004 season at Double-A Greenville, but his progress and the needs in Atlanta could accelerate his arrival. Regardless of the circumstances, he should make his big league debut no later than a September callup.

Year	Club (League)	Class	AVG	G	AB	R	H	2B	3B	HR	RBI	BB	SO	SB	SLG	OBP
2001	Danville (Appy)	R	.200	37	125	12	25	6	0	1	12	20	45	3	.272	.306
2002	Macon (SAL)	A	.281	126	488	69	137	32	4	21	105	41	114	2	.492	.339
2003	Myrtle Beach (Car)	A	.285	130	463	69	132	35	1	16	63	67	109	5	.469	.372
MINOR LEAGUE TOTALS			.273	293	1076	150	294	73	5	38	180	128	268	10	.456	.350

2 Jeff Francoeur, of

RODGER WOOD

Born: Jan. 8, 1984. **Ht.:** 6-4. **Wt.:** 200. **Bats:** R. **Throws:** R. **School:** Parkview HS, Lilburn, Ga. **Career Transactions:** Selected by Braves in first round (23rd overall) of 2002 draft; signed July 8, 2002.

Many longtime members of the organization consider Francoeur the most complete outfielder the Braves have developed since Dale Murphy. He lived up to the lofty expectations in his first full pro season by ranking as the No. 4 prospect in the South Atlantic League. A high school all-American defensive back who earned a football scholarship to Clemson, Francoeur is the best all-around athlete in the system. He consistently makes solid contact with the barrel of the bat, and his maturing body should produce 30 homers annually down the road. He has the speed and instincts to play center field, and his arm strength is among the best in the organization. Francoeur also has plus makeup and a strong competitive drive. Francoeur's strike-zone judgment could improve. Otherwise, he simply needs experience against better competition to make some minor adjustments. On the verge of becoming one of the premier prospects in the minors, Francoeur is slated to open 2004 with high Class A Myrtle Beach. He could reach Double-A in the second half.

Year	Club (League)	Class	AVG	G	AB	R	H	2B	3B	HR	RBI	BB	SO	SB	SLG	OBP
2002	Danville (Appy)	R	.327	38	147	31	48	12	1	8	31	15	34	8	.585	.395
2003	Rome (SAL)	A	.281	134	524	78	147	26	9	14	68	30	68	14	.445	.325
MINOR LEAGUE TOTALS			.291	172	671	109	195	38	10	22	99	45	102	22	.475	.341

3 Bubba Nelson, rhp

RODGER WOOD

Born: Aug. 26, 1981. **Ht.:** 6-2. **Wt.:** 200. **Bats:** R. **Throws:** R. **School:** Riverdale Baptist HS, Upper Marlboro, Md. **Career Transactions:** Selected by Braves in second round of 2000 draft; signed June 23, 2000.

After leading the minors with a 1.66 ERA in 2002, Nelson ranked sixth in the Southern League in ERA last year before dominating in 11 relief appearances for Triple-A Richmond. He moved to the bullpen in case the Braves needed him for the playoffs. Nelson has impressive life on all his pitches. His heavy heater sits in the 89-93 mph range and shows outstanding movement, not unlike Greg Maddux' slower fastball. He also has a nasty hard slider that looks at times like a slurve. Command, particularly with his fastball, remains Nelson's greatest problem. While he keeps his pitches down, he must improve the location of all his pitches in the strike zone. Though his changeup continues to develop, it's still inconsistent. Nelson is on the verge of reaching the majors. He'll return to the rotation in 2004 in Triple-A, and could see some big league action by the end of the season. Atlanta's bullpen is unsettled, so that could be where he gets his first opportunity.

Year	Club (League)	Class	W	L	ERA	G	GS	CG	SV	IP	H	R	ER	HR	BB	SO	AVG
2000	Braves (GCL)	R	3	2	4.23	12	6	1	0	45	40	24	21	2	13	54	.233
2001	Macon (SAL)	A	12	8	3.93	25	24	2	0	151	144	76	66	16	57	154	.252
2002	Myrtle Beach (Car)	A	11	5	1.72	23	23	0	0	136	98	37	26	4	44	105	.202
	Braves (GCL)	R	0	0	0.00	3	3	0	0	5	1	0	0	0	1	7	.063
2003	Greenville (SL)	AA	8	10	3.18	23	20	0	0	119	106	47	42	7	45	77	.241
	Richmond (IL)	AAA	0	1	1.88	11	0	0	0	14	10	3	3	1	5	7	.222
MINOR LEAGUE TOTALS			34	26	3.03	97	76	3	0	470	399	187	158	30	165	404	.231

4 Dan Meyer, lhp

JOHN SPEAR

Born: July 3, 1981. **Ht.:** 6-3. **Wt.:** 190. **Bats:** R. **Throws:** L. **School:** James Madison University. **Career Transactions:** Selected by Braves in first round (34th overall) of 2002 draft; signed June 7, 2002.

In his first full pro season, Meyer split 2003 between two Class A clubs and pitched as consistently as anyone in the organization. He gave his team a chance to win every time he took the mound, allowing three earned runs or fewer in 24 of his 28 starts. Meyer has above-average stuff and outstanding command. He throws a low-90s fastball with plus movement. His slider is also on the verge of becoming an above-average pitch. His strikeout-walk ratio is a gaudy 4.7-1 in pro ball. Meyer's focus and concentration level are assets, and he wants the ball with the game on the line. Meyer needs to polish his changeup and become more consistent with the pitch. He also needs to do a better job against left-handers, who hit a surprising .306 off him in 2003. Righties batted just .220. With a promotion to Double-A on the immediate horizon, Meyer is moving as quickly as any pitcher in the organization. He could push to join the big league rotation at some point in 2005.

Year	Club (League)	Class	W	L	ERA	G	GS	CG	SV	IP	H	R	ER	HR	BB	SO	AVG
2002	Danville (Appy)	R	3	3	2.74	13	13	1	0	66	47	22	20	4	18	77	.198
2003	Rome (SAL)	A	4	4	2.87	15	15	0	0	82	76	35	26	6	15	95	.248
	Myrtle Beach (Car)	A	3	6	2.87	13	13	0	0	78	69	29	25	7	17	63	.236
MINOR LEAGUE TOTALS			10	13	2.83	41	41	1	0	226	192	86	71	17	50	235	.230

5 Adam LaRoche, 1b

Born: Nov. 6, 1979. **Ht.:** 6-3. **Wt.:** 180. **Bats:** L. **Throws:** L. **School:** Seminole State (Okla.) CC. **Career Transactions:** Selected by Braves in 29th round of 2000 draft; signed June 21, 2000.

A two-way star in junior college, LaRoche signed with the Braves because they liked him better as a hitter. He returned to the Carolina League to open 2002, but he has terrorized pitchers ever since. He led the system with a .317 average in 2002 and in home runs and RBIs in 2003. His father Dave was a two-time all-star reliever, while his brother Andy signed with the Dodgers for $1 million last August. LaRoche has a funky, wide-open stance that produces results with his ability to use his hands and transfer his weight. He hits a lot of line drives into the gaps, yet he proved last summer he can hit for power. He's a smooth defender who could be a perennial Gold Glove candidate. His arm can deliver 90 mph fastballs. Though LaRoche answered questions about his power, he's not the slugger most teams look for at first base. He has below-average speed, which rules out playing the outfield. No Atlanta rookie enters spring training with a better shot of earning a starting job than LaRoche. Manager Bobby Cox loves his all-around game and gritty approach.

Year	Club (League)	Class	AVG	G	AB	R	H	2B	3B	HR	RBI	BB	SO	SB	SLG	OBP
2000	Danville (Appy)	R	.308	56	201	38	62	13	3	7	45	24	46	4	.507	.381
2001	Myrtle Beach (Car)	A	.251	126	471	49	118	31	0	7	47	30	108	10	.361	.305
2002	Myrtle Beach (Car)	A	.336	69	250	30	84	17	0	9	53	27	37	0	.512	.406
	Greenville (SL)	AA	.289	45	173	17	50	9	0	4	19	19	38	1	.410	.363
2003	Greenville (SL)	AA	.283	61	219	42	62	12	1	12	37	34	53	1	.511	.381
	Richmond (IL)	AAA	.295	72	264	33	78	21	0	8	35	27	58	1	.466	.360
MINOR LEAGUE TOTALS			.288	429	1578	209	454	103	4	47	236	161	340	17	.447	.358

6 Macay McBride, lhp

Born: Oct. 24, 1982. **Ht.:** 5-11. **Wt.:** 180. **Bats:** L. **Throws:** L. **School:** Screven County HS, Sylvania, Ga. **Career Transactions:** Selected by Braves in first round (24th overall) of 2001 draft; signed June 6, 2001.

The 2002 South Atlantic League pitcher of the year, McBride continued his steady climb through the organization. He led the Carolina League in innings and strikeouts, ranked sixth in ERA and surrendered three earned runs or fewer in 22 of 27 starts. McBride's best pitch is a sharp slider that reminds some scouts of Steve Carlton's. His fastball has good movement and resides in the low 90s. His changeup has become a plus pitch. McBride knows what he's doing on the mound and mixes his three pitches with precision. He may be the most competitive pitcher in the organization. He gained velocity as the season progressed, though he has raised concerns with his fastball after throwing in the mid-90s in high school. The Braves aren't too worried because he has blossomed into a pitcher instead of the thrower he was as a prepster. McBride has spent a full season at each level. He'll spend 2004 in Greenville and could be pushing for a shot in the big leagues by 2005.

Year	Club (League)	Class	W	L	ERA	G	GS	CG	SV	IP	H	R	ER	HR	BB	SO	AVG
2001	Braves (GCL)	R	4	4	3.76	13	11	0	0	55	51	30	23	0	23	67	.248
2002	Macon (SAL)	A	12	8	2.12	25	25	2	0	157	119	49	37	6	48	138	.209
2003	Myrtle Beach (Car)	A	9	8	2.95	27	27	1	0	165	164	63	54	5	49	139	.262
MINOR LEAGUE TOTALS			25	20	2.72	65	63	3	0	377	334	142	114	11	120	344	.238

7 Brian McCann, c

Born: Feb. 20, 1984. **Ht.:** 6-3. **Wt.:** 190. **Bats:** L. **Throws:** R. **School:** Duluth (Ga.) HS. **Career Transactions:** Selected by Braves in second round of 2002 draft; signed July 11, 2002.

The son of former Marshall head baseball coach Howard McCann and younger brother of Clemson third-base prospect Brad McCann, Brian put together a solid first full season in pro ball. He ranked second in the organization in RBIs and fourth in batting. Drafted for his offensive potential, McCann has a pretty swing and plenty of raw power. But he's far from one-dimensional, as he's just a tick behind Brayan Pena as the top defensive catcher in the system. McCann's arm strength is good and his accuracy is improving. The Braves also love his hard-nosed attitude behind the plate. McCann has made strides with his defense, but he's not a sure thing to remain at catcher. He'll need to continue to improve his footwork and agility. He also must stay in shape in order to remain strong throughout the season. He homered just once during the last two months of the season after going deep 11 times in the first three. He has much more offensive upside than projected 2004 starter Johnny Estrada, and the Braves are thrilled with the progress McCann has shown early in his career. He'll spend 2004 in high Class A.

Year	Club (League)	Class	AVG	G	AB	R	H	2B	3B	HR	RBI	BB	SO	SB	SLG	OBP
2002	Braves (GCL)	R	.220	29	100	9	22	5	0	2	11	10	22	0	.330	.295
2003	Rome (SAL)	A	.290	115	424	40	123	31	3	12	71	24	73	7	.462	.329
MINOR LEAGUE TOTALS			.277	144	524	49	145	36	3	14	82	34	95	7	.437	.322

8 Kyle Davies, rhp

Born: Sept. 9, 1983. **Ht.:** 6-2. **Wt.:** 210. **Bats:** R. **Throws:** R. **School:** Stockbridge (Ga.) HS. **Career Transactions:** Selected by Braves in fourth round of 2001 draft; signed June 15, 2001.

Davies was considered a disappointment prior to the 2003 season, so much in fact that the Braves feared he had peaked in his mid-teens. He dominated youth competition at ages 14 and 15, and was one of the greatest players to ever come from the famed East Cobb program in suburban Atlanta. Davies made a major change in his delivery at the end of 2002. After showing initial reluctance, Davies embraced the adjustments and progressed as much as any pitcher in the organization in 2003. His new delivery helped Davies go from throwing a flat 87-88 mph fastball to a 92-93 mph heater with plus movement that tops out at 95. His changeup is the best in the system, with excellent depth and fade. His command has improved and continues to get better. Davies always has displayed the intangibles necessary to succeed, particularly his intense competitiveness. He must avoid reverting to the tall-and-fall delivery that caused him to push his pitches to the plate. He also needs to improve his slider to give him a solid third pitch as a starter. Davies opened the Braves' eyes with his ability to put away hitters. He'll open 2004 in high Class A, and a jump to Double-A at midseason wouldn't be a surprise.

Year	Club (League)	Class	W	L	ERA	G	GS	CG	SV	IP	H	R	ER	HR	BB	SO	AVG
2001	Braves (GCL)	R	4	2	2.25	12	9	1	0	56	47	17	14	2	8	53	.224
	Macon (SAL)	A	1	0	0.00	1	1	0	0	6	2	0	0	0	1	7	.105
2002	Macon (SAL)	A	0	1	6.00	2	1	0	0	6	6	4	4	1	4	4	.273
	Danville (Appy)	R	5	3	3.50	14	14	0	0	69	73	39	27	2	23	62	.263
2003	Rome (SAL)	A	8	8	2.89	27	27	1	0	146	128	52	47	9	53	148	.238
MINOR LEAGUE TOTALS			18	14	2.92	56	52	2	0	283	256	112	92	14	89	274	.240

9 Anthony Lerew, rhp

Born: Oct. 28, 1982. **Ht.:** 6-3. **Wt.:** 210. **Bats:** L. **Throws:** R. **School:** Northern HS, Wellsville, Pa. **Career Transactions:** Selected by Braves in 11th round of 2001 draft; signed June 6, 2001.

Lerew emerged as a prospect in 2002, when he was co-pitcher of the year in the Rookie-level Appalachian League. He was similarly effective at low Class A Rome, where he was the most consistent starter in a prospect-laden rotation. He also won the opening game of each of two playoff series as the team won the South Atlantic League title in its first season in Rome. Lerew has two plus pitches that have allowed him to dominate the lower minors. His 91-93 mph fastball shows outstanding movement and impressive late sinking action. His changeup is nearly as effective as his heater and acts like a splitter. Lerew also has excellent makeup, size and intimidating mound presence. The development of his slider will determine how successful Lerew will be at higher levels. He used to throw a curveball and needs that third pitch to put better hitters away. Lerew should become even better in the near future if his slider develops as expected. He'll move to high Class A in 2004 and could develop into a middle-of-the-rotation starter in the majors.

Year	Club (League)	Class	W	L	ERA	G	GS	CG	SV	IP	H	R	ER	HR	BB	SO	AVG
2001	Braves (GCL)	R	1	2	2.92	12	7	0	0	49	43	25	16	3	14	40	.228
2002	Danville (Appy)	R	8	3	1.73	14	14	0	0	83	60	23	16	2	25	75	.205
2003	Rome (SAL)	A	7	6	2.38	25	25	0	0	144	112	45	38	7	43	127	.215
MINOR LEAGUE TOTALS			16	11	2.28	51	46	0	0	276	215	93	70	12	82	242	.215

10 Kelly Johnson, ss

Born: Feb. 22, 1982. **Ht.:** 6-1. **Wt.:** 180. **Bats:** L. **Throws:** R. **School:** Westwood HS, Austin. **Career Transactions:** Selected by Braves in first round (38th overall) of 2000 draft; signed June 12, 2000.

The Braves believe Johnson will develop into an everyday player in the big leagues, particularly if the last month of the 2003 season and the Arizona Fall League are any indication. After battling some elbow soreness that limited him to six games in July, Johnson bounced back to post 21 RBIs in August, just three fewer than his total in the first four months. Johnson made some adjustments at the plate, including spreading out his stance and working counts, and once again showed the promise that he could hit for average and decent power at the major league level. With his hitting potential and ability to play a variety of positions, Johnson reminds several longtime members of the organization of a poor man's Chipper Jones. Currently stationed at shortstop, he doesn't have the quickness to remain there. Johnson could wind up at second or third base or one of the outfield corners due to his average-to-plus arm strength and speed. Spring training will determine whether Johnson moves up to Triple-A or remains in Double-A while attempting to become more consistent at the plate and to find a defensive home.

Year	Club (League)	Class	AVG	G	AB	R	H	2B	3B	HR	RBI	BB	SO	SB	SLG	OBP
2000	Braves (GCL)	R	.269	53	193	27	52	12	3	4	29	24	45	6	.425	.349
2001	Macon (SAL)	A	.289	124	415	75	120	22	1	23	66	71	111	25	.513	.404
2002	Myrtle Beach (Car)	A	.255	126	482	62	123	21	5	12	49	51	105	12	.394	.325
2003	Greenville (SL)	AA	.275	98	334	46	92	22	5	6	45	35	81	10	.425	.340
	Braves (GCL)	R	.385	6	26	10	10	1	1	1	3	3	4	1	.615	.467
MINOR LEAGUE TOTALS			.274	407	1450	220	397	78	15	46	192	184	346	54	.443	.358

11 Jose Capellan, rhp

Born: Jan. 13, 1981. **Ht.:** 6-3. **Wt.:** 170. **Bats:** R. **Throws:** R. **Career Transactions:** Signed out of Dominican Republic by Braves, Aug. 6, 1998 . . . On suspended list, June 1-Sept. 9, 2002.

Capellan owns the strongest arm in the Braves system. He blew out his elbow in Rookie ball in 2001 and had Tommy John surgery, but bounced back to reach triple digits on the radar gun on several occasions last year. Prior to the injury, Capellan was a refined pitcher at a young age, showing a 92-94 mph fastball and the ability to spin a breaking ball. His velocity has increased with experience, but the potential of another breakdown remains a concern. Despite possessing an ideal pitcher's frame, Capellan has a shaky delivery. He tends to open his front foot, thereby putting strain on his shoulder and elbow. His secondary pitches need improvement, particularly his changeup. Despite his velocity, he didn't exactly blow hitters away in 2003. His overpowering but limited repertoire suggests that his role down the road could come as a closer. The Braves admitted they were cautious in Capellan's comeback last year. Now a member of the 40-man roster, Capellan needs to prove his durability and start making serious progress, beginning this year in high Class A.

Year	Club (League)	Class	W	L	ERA	G	GS	CG	SV	IP	H	R	ER	HR	BB	SO	AVG
1999	Braves (DSL)	R	3	3	3.58	14	10	0	2	60	54	31	24	1	28	46	.242
2000	Braves (DSL)	R	3	8	3.69	14	14	0	0	68	58	45	28	0	36	68	.221
2001	Danville (Appy)	R	0	0	1.72	3	3	0	0	16	12	7	3	1	4	25	.200
2002	Did not play																
2003	Rome (SAL)	A	1	2	3.80	14	12	1	0	47	43	23	20	2	19	32	.253
	Braves (GCL)	R	0	1	2.65	5	5	0	0	17	18	7	5	0	8	17	.277
MINOR LEAGUE TOTALS			7	14	3.45	50	44	1	2	209	185	113	80	4	95	188	.237

12 Wilson Betemit, 3b

Born: Nov. 2, 1981. **Ht.:** 6-3. **Wt.:** 190. **Bats:** B. **Throws:** R. **Career Transactions:** Signed out of Dominican Republic by Braves, July 28, 1996.

Betemit ranked as the Braves' top prospect entering the 2001 and 2002 seasons, and was expected to move into Atlanta's starting lineup this spring now that third baseman Vinny Castilla's contract has come to a merciful end. Betemit, however, has stagnated during his two full seasons in Triple-A, and he's not ready for the big leagues. The Braves hope he can turn himself around. He showed signs of doing that last July by batting .313, only to continue his roller-coaster ride by hitting .248 in August. Betemit continues to show holes in his swing, which is why he hasn't made consistent contact or developed the power once expected of him. A switch-hitter, he has struggled from the right side, batting just .171 with one homer against lefties in 2003. His speed is average but not enough to keep him at shortstop. He spent most of last season at third base. While his range and consistency are good and his arm is among the strongest of any infielder in the system, Betemit's value is not as high at the hot corner as it was in the past.

Year	Club (League)	Class	AVG	G	AB	R	H	2B	3B	HR	RBI	BB	SO	SB	SLG	OBP
1997	Braves (GCL)	R	.212	32	113	12	24	6	1	0	15	9	32	0	.283	.270
1998	Braves (GCL)	R	.220	51	173	23	38	8	4	5	16	20	49	6	.399	.301
1999	Danville (Appy)	R	.320	67	259	39	83	18	2	5	53	27	63	6	.463	.383
2000	Jamestown (NY-P)	A	.331	69	269	54	89	15	2	5	37	30	37	3	.457	.393
2001	Myrtle Beach (Car)	A	.277	84	318	38	88	20	1	7	43	23	71	8	.412	.324
	Greenville (SL)	AA	.355	47	183	22	65	14	0	5	19	12	36	6	.514	.394
	Atlanta (NL)	MAJ	.000	8	3	1	0	0	0	0	0	2	3	1	.000	.400
2002	Richmond (IL)	AAA	.245	93	343	43	84	17	1	8	34	34	82	8	.370	.312
	Braves (GCL)	R	.263	7	19	2	5	4	0	0	2	5	2	1	.474	.417
2003	Richmond (IL)	AAA	.262	127	478	55	125	23	13	8	65	38	115	8	.414	.315
MAJOR LEAGUE TOTALS			.000	8	3	1	0	0	0	0	0	2	3	1	.000	.400
MINOR LEAGUE TOTALS			.279	577	2155	288	601	125	24	43	284	198	487	46	.419	.338

13 Gregor Blanco, of

Born: Dec. 12, 1983. **Ht.:** 5-11. **Wt.:** 170. **Bats:** L. **Throws:** L. **Career Transactions:** Signed out of Venezuela by Braves, July 4, 2000.

Myrtle Beach manager Randy Ingle was more pleased with Blanco's progress last year than that of anyone else on his team. He made major strides in his maturity, competitiveness and work habits to continue his emergence as one of the top outfielders in the system. For the second straight year, Blanco struggled to open the season, and he was hitting .209 in early May. He shortened his swing and did a better job of employing his plus speed to get on base. Blanco also proved he had gotten stronger by hitting .304 in August after tiring noticeably down the stretch in 2002. With better control of the strike zone, Blanco could become a prototypical leadoff hitter. His center-field defense is above average and his arm is easily strong for the position. The Braves hope he continues his recent advances this season in Double-A.

Year	Club (League)	Class	AVG	G	AB	R	H	2B	3B	HR	RBI	BB	SO	SB	SLG	OBP
2001	Braves 2 (DSL)	R	.330	58	215	45	71	6	10	0	18	31	31	21	.451	.422
2002	Macon (SAL)	A	.271	132	468	87	127	14	9	7	36	85	120	40	.385	.392
2003	Myrtle Beach (Car)	A	.271	126	461	66	125	19	7	5	36	54	114	34	.375	.357
MINOR LEAGUE TOTALS			.282	316	1144	198	323	39	26	12	90	170	265	95	.393	.384

14 Onil Joseph, of

Born: Feb. 12, 1982. **Ht.:** 6-1. **Wt.:** 150. **Bats:** R. **Throws:** R. **Career Transactions:** Signed out of Dominican Republic by Braves, Feb 22, 2000.

Known as Miguel Mota and believed to be a year younger prior to the 2003 season, Joseph continued to make a name for himself in the Atlanta organization. The leadoff hitter set the table for the South Atlantic League champions, combining with Jeff Francoeur and Ardley Jansen to give Rome one of the most promising outfields in the lower minors. With his short, sweet swing and above-average speed, Joseph batted .330 during the final two months to finish 10th in the SAL batting race. His strike-zone judgment is advanced for his age and should improve further. Joseph is a good defender but still is learning how to take the most efficient angles on balls. He has good arm strength, though his accuracy could stand a little improvement. While he has done a good job of adding strength to his wiry frame, Joseph could use a little more muscle. Joseph is headed in the right direction and will move up to high Class A in 2004.

Year	Club (League)	Class	AVG	G	AB	R	H	2B	3B	HR	RBI	BB	SO	SB	SLG	OBP
2000	Braves (DSL)	R	.200	64	190	18	38	5	4	0	9	21	47	7	.268	.285
2001	Braves 1 (DSL)	R	.277	70	249	42	69	7	2	0	21	33	42	23	.321	.366
2002	Braves (GCL)	R	.305	58	213	27	65	8	4	3	28	14	39	12	.423	.353
2003	Rome (SAL)	A	.296	120	483	66	143	16	6	4	47	37	89	32	.379	.349
MINOR LEAGUE TOTALS			.278	312	1135	153	315	36	16	7	105	105	217	74	.356	.343

15 Jake Stevens, lhp

Born: March 15, 1985. **Ht.:** 6-3. **Wt.:** 210. **Bats:** L. **Throws:** L. **School:** Cape Coral (Fla.) HS. **Career Transactions:** Selected by Braves in third round of 2003 draft; signed June 4, 2003.

It didn't take long for Stevens to learn a valuable lesson in pro ball. In his first inning after signing as the 79th overall pick in the 2003 draft, he walked the bases loaded and then surrendered a grand slam. He finished much better than he started, winning the first game of the Rookie-level Gulf Coast League championship series. The Braves believe Stevens discovered in that first inning that he has to be aggressive in the strike zone every time he takes the mound. He does just that with a plus curveball that he throws from a high three-quarters slot, creating a 1-to-7 break. Stevens' fastball also has good movement and sits in the low 90s while topping out at 93. His changeup is also a promising pitch, though it could use a little more fade in order to become a plus offering. Stevens' maximum-effort delivery worried some scouts prior to the draft, but the Braves have made refinements with his mechanics and say he has the makeup to be one of the premier pitchers from the 2003 draft class. He's expected to spend 2004 in the low Class A rotation.

Year	Club (League)	Class	W	L	ERA	G	GS	CG	SV	IP	H	R	ER	HR	BB	SO	AVG
2003	Braves (GCL)	R	3	4	2.87	14	6	0	0	47	49	23	15	2	16	47	.262
MINOR LEAGUE TOTALS			3	4	2.87	14	6	0	0	47	49	23	15	2	16	47	.262

16 Blaine Boyer, rhp

Born: July 11, 1981. **Ht.:** 6-3. **Wt.:** 190. **Bats:** R. **Throws:** R. **School:** Walton HS, Marietta, Ga. **Career Transactions:** Selected by Braves in third round of 2000 draft; signed June 13, 2000.

After spending all of 2002 in the low Class A Macon bullpen, Boyer returned to the same role at the beginning of 2003 in Rome. Shifted to the rotation in mid-April, he won just three of his first 11 decisions. Farm director Dayton Moore had a heart-to-heart talk with him, and from then on he did nothing but dominate, going 9-0, 2.08 over his final 11 starts. His turnaround came because he learned from his mistakes. Previously, Boyer became so emotional on the mound that he struggled to comprehend what was happening and why. With added maturity, he has shown signs of becoming a three-pitch pitcher. His stuff improved during his hot stretch. His heavy fastball ranged from the low to mid-90s with good movement, and his plus curveball maintained its sharp break. He still needs to command his changeup more effectively, but overall he has taken major steps in his development. While he's scheduled to start 2004 in the high Class A rotation, Boyer could develop into a closer in the long term.

Year	Club (League)	Class	W	L	ERA	G	GS	CG	SV	IP	H	R	ER	HR	BB	SO	AVG
2000	Braves (GCL)	R	1	3	2.51	11	5	0	1	32	24	16	9	0	19	27	.200
2001	Danville (Appy)	R	4	5	4.32	13	12	0	0	50	48	35	24	4	19	57	.250
2002	Macon (SAL)	A	5	9	3.07	43	0	0	1	70	52	30	24	0	39	73	.207
2003	Rome (SAL)	A	12	8	3.69	30	26	1	0	137	146	70	56	5	58	115	.271
MINOR LEAGUE TOTALS			22	25	3.51	97	43	1	2	289	270	151	113	9	135	272	.245

17 Matt Merricks, lhp

Born: Aug. 6, 1982. **Ht.:** 5-11. **Wt.:** 180. **Bats:** L. **Throws:** L. **School:** Oxnard (Calif.) HS. **Career Transactions:** Selected by Braves in sixth round of 2000 draft; signed June 26, 2000.

Though Merricks tied for the minor league lead with 15 losses, 2003 was a successful season for him. He solved low Class A in his second attempt at that level, and he pitched well in high Class A despite losing his first seven decisions there. He improved the velocity of his fastball to as high as 95 mph, and his changeup developed into a plus pitch. His stuff is as good as that of any lefty in the organization, and his aggressiveness borders on needing to be channeled. His curveball also could use some refinement, and a bone spur in the back of his elbow is hindering the development of his breaking ball. The biggest thing Merricks needs is more maturity. Spring training will determine whether he reports to high Class A or Double-A to open 2004.

Year	Club (League)	Class	W	L	ERA	G	GS	CG	SV	IP	H	R	ER	HR	BB	SO	AVG
2000	Braves (GCL)	R	1	0	2.53	9	0	0	1	21	21	15	6	0	11	28	.250
2001	Danville (Appy)	R	4	5	2.79	12	11	0	0	58	42	19	18	5	18	78	.209
2002	Macon (SAL)	A	5	5	5.12	19	14	0	0	83	82	54	47	6	51	60	.256
2003	Rome (SAL)	A	5	7	2.82	14	10	0	0	67	58	27	21	1	19	60	.232
	Myrtle Beach (Car)	A	1	8	3.23	11	8	0	0	47	45	29	17	5	23	37	.251
MINOR LEAGUE TOTALS			16	25	3.55	65	43	0	1	276	248	144	109	17	122	263	.240

18 Scott Thorman, 1b

Born: Jan. 6, 1982. **Ht.:** 6-3. **Wt.:** 200. **Bats:** L. **Throws:** R. **School:** Preston HS, Cambridge, Ontario. **Career Transactions:** Selected by Braves in first round (30th overall) of 2000 draft; signed June 19, 2000 . . . On disabled list, June 19-Sept. 18, 2001.

Like Andy Marte, Thorman was another Myrtle Beach Pelican trying to keep his head above water early last year. He didn't climb over the Mendoza Line until mid-May before heating up and earning a trip to the Futures Game, where the native Canadian played for the international team. He became a better hitter and made steady strides in his overall development. No one in the system has more pure power than Thorman, who was hampered by Myrtle Beach's spacious Coastal Federal Field. He batted just .219-8-27 at home and became more conscious of hitting line drives. He still needs to improve his understanding of what pitchers are trying to do, and to stop trying to pull pitches too often. He started going with pitches and hitting to the opposite field at the end of the season. A former third baseman, Thorman has worked hard at becoming a better first baseman and has made major strides with his footwork. He also has a cannon for an arm, which allows him to gun down runners at the plate on relay throws. Thorman is scheduled to move up to Double-A this year, with the hope he'll continue to make the adjustments he showed at the end of 2003.

Year	Club (League)	Class	AVG	G	AB	R	H	2B	3B	HR	RBI	BB	SO	SB	SLG	OBP
2000	Braves (GCL)	R	.227	29	97	15	22	7	1	1	19	12	23	0	.351	.330
2001	Did not play—Injured															
2002	Macon (SAL)	A	.294	127	470	57	138	38	3	16	82	51	83	2	.489	.367
2003	Myrtle Beach (Car)	A	.243	124	445	44	108	26	2	12	56	42	79	0	.391	.311
MINOR LEAGUE TOTALS			.265	280	1012	116	268	71	6	29	157	105	185	2	.433	.339

19 Jarrod Saltalamacchia, c

Born: May 2, 1985. **Ht.:** 6-4. **Wt.:** 195. **Bats:** B. **Throws:** R. **School:** Royal Palm Beach HS, West Palm Beach, Fla. **Career Transactions:** Selected by Braves in first round (36th overall) of 2003 draft; signed June 3, 2003.

For the second straight year, the Braves believe they emerged with the draft's best catcher. After pulling in Brian McCann with a second-round pick in 2002, Atlanta took Saltalamacchia with the 36th overall selection last June. (The Braves also signed his brother Justin, an outfielder/infielder, as a nondrafted free agent out of UNC Greensboro.) Most draft observers rated the catching class last year as weak, but Saltalamacchia's complete package would have had him near the top of the charts in any year. He possesses a strong frame and displays excellent agility and athleticism, especially for his size. His footwork and release were considered to be his primary weaknesses on draft day, though Saltalamacchia made solid progress in those areas after working most of the summer and fall with minor league instruction coordinator Chino Cadahia, one of the best catching teachers in the business. Saltalamacchia is a switch-hitter with good power potential. His swing tends to get long, particularly late in games, but the Braves have been impressed with the adjustments he has made to wood bats. He showed plenty of plate discipline for a teenager. Saltalamacchia will follow McCann's path, jumping to low Class A for his first full season.

Year	Club (League)	Class	AVG	G	AB	R	H	2B	3B	HR	RBI	BB	SO	SB	SLG	OBP
2003	Braves (GCL)	R	.239	46	134	23	32	11	2	2	14	28	33	0	.396	.382
MINOR LEAGUE TOTALS			.239	46	134	23	32	11	2	2	14	28	33	0	.396	.382

20 Carlos Duran, of

Born: Dec. 27, 1982. **Ht.:** 6-1. **Wt.:** 160. **Bats:** L. **Throws:** L. **Career Transactions:** Signed out of Venezuela by Braves, July 29, 1999.

Duran may have had the most disappointing 2003 season of any Braves prospect outside of righthander Gonzalo Lopez, who ranked in the top 10 a year ago. Despite possessing as many tools as anyone in the system, he stumbled throughout the summer in high Class A. Most disappointing was his lack of dedication on a daily basis. He hit just .224, 61 points below his previous career average, constantly giving away at-bats with his lack of patience at the plate. At his best, Duran has a smooth swing with plus speed and the natural instincts to make things happen on the field. Those traits were obvious when he ranked fourth in hits and fifth in runs in the South Atlantic League in 2002. He has shown the legs and ability to man center field, and his arm is strong enough to handle any of the three outfield positions. The Braves hope his maturity and intensity will increase this year, which he may have to start with a return to Myrtle Beach.

Year	Club (League)	Class	AVG	G	AB	R	H	2B	3B	HR	RBI	BB	SO	SB	SLG	OBP
2000	Chico Canonico (VSL)	R	.306	54	196	48	60	12	6	8	41	18	28	13	.551	.378
2001	Braves (GCL)	R	.304	54	204	35	62	10	3	2	17	12	30	16	.412	.349
2002	Macon (SAL)	A	.270	132	534	86	144	22	10	7	50	29	80	23	.388	.312
2003	Myrtle Beach (Car)	A	.224	118	415	45	93	20	6	3	35	17	60	11	.323	.257
MINOR LEAGUE TOTALS			.266	358	1349	214	359	64	25	20	143	76	198	63	.395	.311

21 Andy Pratt, lhp

Born: Aug. 27, 1979. **Ht.:** 6-0. **Wt.:** 180. **Bats:** L. **Throws:** L. **School:** Chino Valley (Ariz.) HS. **Career Transactions:** Selected by Rangers in ninth round of 1998 draft; signed June 8, 1998 . . . Traded by Rangers to Braves for LHP Ben Kozlowski, April 9, 2002.

The Braves' trade of Ben Kozlowski to the Rangers for Pratt looked lopsided in 2002, when Kozlowski shot from high Class A to the majors. Now it looks like it might play out in Atlanta's favor after Kozlowski needed Tommy John surgery and Pratt had a solid 2003 season in Triple-A. On some nights, Pratt can be as dominating as any lefty in the game, only to come back a start or two later and have difficulty finding the strike zone. The son of Cubs minor league pitching coach Tom Pratt, Andy has added velocity to his fastball, which sits in the 92-93 mph range. His slider, which looks like a cut fastball on occasion, is a plus pitch, while his curveball and changeup are at least average offerings. He just needs more consistency. Though somewhat small for a pitcher, Pratt is a good athlete who is getting stronger. He could arrive in the big leagues for an extended ride in the near future.

Year	Club (League)	Class	W	L	ERA	G	GS	CG	SV	IP	H	R	ER	HR	BB	SO	AVG
1998	Rangers (GCL)	R	4	3	3.86	12	8	0	0	56	49	25	24	4	14	49	.238
1999	Savannah (SAL)	A	4	4	2.89	13	13	1	0	72	66	30	23	4	16	100	.242
2000	Charlotte (FSL)	A	7	4	2.72	16	16	2	0	93	68	37	28	8	26	95	.203
	Tulsa (TL)	AA	1	6	7.22	11	11	0	0	52	66	48	42	7	33	42	.303
2001	Tulsa (TL)	AA	8	10	4.61	27	26	3	0	168	175	99	86	18	57	132	.268
2002	Greenville (SL)	AA	4	9	4.26	20	18	1	0	93	92	54	44	5	44	67	.262
	Richmond (IL)	AAA	4	2	3.10	6	6	1	0	41	35	15	14	2	9	36	.232
	Atlanta (NL)	MAJ	0	0	6.75	1	0	0	0	1	1	1	1	0	4	1	.200
2003	Richmond (IL)	AAA	7	10	3.40	28	27	1	0	156	146	77	59	10	77	161	.250
MAJOR LEAGUE TOTALS			0	0	6.75	1	0	0	0	1	1	1	1	0	4	1	.200
MINOR LEAGUE TOTALS			39	48	3.94	133	125	9	0	730	697	385	320	58	276	682	.251

22 Jo Jo Reyes, lhp

Born: Nov. 20, 1984. **Ht.:** 6-2. **Wt.:** 200. **Bats:** L. **Throws:** L. **School:** Riverside Poly HS, Riverside, Calif. **Career Transactions:** Selected by Braves in second round of 2003 draft; signed June 3, 2003.

The Braves gave serious thought to drafting Reyes with their first pick in the supplemental first round and were thrilled when they grabbed him in the second round (43rd overall) last June. He made a seamless move from high school to Rookie ball, which included six scoreless innings in his Gulf Coast League playoff start. He reminded many coaches in the organization of a stockier version of Horacio Ramirez. Reyes has a quick arm action and can throw three pitches for strikes. His delivery creates incredible deception, which makes his 90-93 mph fastball look like 95. He also shows a good feel for pitching and can mix his fastball, changeup and slider well, particularly for a young southpaw. Though some scouts were scared of Reyes' body, which they compared to David Wells', Reyes is a good athlete who dropped 30 pounds before the draft. Nevertheless, he'll have to stay in shape in order to live up to his enormous potential. He's slated to open 2004 in the low Class A rotation.

Year	Club (League)	Class	W	L	ERA	G	GS	CG	SV	IP	H	R	ER	HR	BB	SO	AVG
2003	Braves (GCL)	R	5	3	2.56	11	10	0	0	46	34	16	13	1	14	55	.205
MINOR LEAGUE TOTALS			5	3	2.56	11	10	0	0	46	34	16	13	1	14	55	.205

23 Chuck James, lhp

Born: Nov. 9, 1981. **Ht.:** 6-0. **Wt.:** 170. **Bats:** L. **Throws:** L. **School:** Chattahoochee Valley (Ala.) JC. **Career Transactions:** Selected by Braves in 20th round of 2002 draft; signed July 29, 2002.

James is a stereotypical "little lefty" who knows how to pitch. With his maturity and ability to mix his pitches, change speeds and keep batters off balance, James toyed with the Appalachian League. He limited opponents to a .151 average and never allowed more than two earned runs in any of his outings. His fastball resides in the 89-91 mph range, and his best pitch is his changeup. His third pitch, a slider, is continuing to show improvement. James does an excellent job of hitting his spots, moving all three of his offerings around in the strike zone and employing the same arm action with each of them. He also isn't afraid to throw inside and will saw batters off at the hands. Aside from upgrading his slider, James will need to continue to prove himself against better competition. His next test will come this year in high Class A.

Year	Club (League)	Class	W	L	ERA	G	GS	CG	SV	IP	H	R	ER	HR	BB	SO	AVG
2003	Danville (Appy)	R	2	1	1.25	11	11	0	0	50	26	9	7	1	19	68	.151
MINOR LEAGUE TOTALS			2	1	1.25	11	11	0	0	50	26	9	7	1	19	68	.151

24 Brayan Pena, c

Born: Jan. 7, 1982. **Ht.:** 5-11. **Wt.:** 210. **Bats:** B. **Throws:** R. **Career Transactions:** Signed out of Costa Rica by Braves, Nov. 2, 2000.

Of the Braves' young catching prospects, Pena is the closest to reaching the big leagues. A Cuban defector, he put together a solid 2003 season in high Class A, polishing his defensive skills and rebounding with his bat. Pena's catching ability is more advanced than Brian McCann's. He moves well and does a good job of calling games. One of the more enthusiastic and vocal players in the system, Pena is popular with his teammates, and most pitchers like working with him. Offensively, Pena isn't much of a power threat, but the switch-hitter makes excellent contact and won the Appalachian League batting crown in 2001. The Braves would like to see him exercise a little more patience at the plate. The major concern about Pena has been possible weight problems, which have yet to materialize. As long as he stays in shape, he should be in line to back up Johnny Estrada in Atlanta by late 2005. Pena will begin this year as the starter in Double-A.

Year	Club (League)	Class	AVG	G	AB	R	H	2B	3B	HR	RBI	BB	SO	SB	SLG	OBP
2001	Danville (Appy)	R	.370	64	235	39	87	16	2	1	33	31	30	3	.468	.440
2002	Macon (SAL)	A	.229	81	271	26	62	10	0	3	25	22	37	0	.299	.290
	Myrtle Beach (Car)	A	.211	6	19	3	4	1	0	0	1	3	4	0	.263	.318
2003	Myrtle Beach (Car)	A	.294	82	286	24	84	14	1	2	27	11	28	2	.371	.320
MINOR LEAGUE TOTALS			.292	233	811	92	237	41	3	6	86	67	99	5	.372	.346

25 Ryan Langerhans, of

Born: Feb. 20, 1980. **Ht.:** 6-3. **Wt.:** 190. **Bats:** L. **Throws:** L. **School:** Round Rock (Texas) HS.
Career Transactions: Selected by Braves in third round of 1998 draft; signed June 28, 1998.

A year ago, some members of the Atlanta front office said they thought Langerhans would be their next homegrown player to earn a big league starting job. That still could develop, though it's more likely he'll become a reserve in the majors. He's the son of John Langerhans, who once held the University of Texas home run record and coached Ryan at prep power Round Rock High before retiring after the 2003 season. While making cameo appearances with Atlanta in each of the past two seasons, Langerhans has yet to post break-out numbers in the minors. Despite possessing a quick, fundamentally sound swing, he fights paralysis by analysis, trying to figure out what the pitcher is throwing instead of simply seeing the ball and hitting it. Braves manager Bobby Cox loves Langerhans' hard-nosed approach and his steady defense. He gets good jumps on fly balls and has above-average arm strength. Langerhans also has good baseball speed and excellent instincts on the basepaths. Unless he puts together an impressive spring, he'll return to Triple-A in 2004.

Year	Club (League)	Class	AVG	G	AB	R	H	2B	3B	HR	RBI	BB	SO	SB	SLG	OBP
1998	Braves (GCL)	R	.277	43	148	15	41	10	4	2	19	19	38	2	.439	.357
1999	Macon (SAL)	A	.268	121	448	66	120	30	1	9	49	52	99	19	.400	.352
2000	Myrtle Beach (Car)	A	.212	116	392	55	83	14	7	6	37	32	104	25	.329	.286
2001	Myrtle Beach (Car)	A	.287	125	450	66	129	30	3	7	48	55	104	22	.413	.374
2002	Greenville (SL)	AA	.251	109	391	57	98	23	2	9	62	68	83	10	.389	.366
	Atlanta (NL)	MAJ	.000	1	1	0	0	0	0	0	0	0	0	0	.000	.000
2003	Greenville (SL)	AA	.253	94	336	42	85	23	2	6	38	46	85	10	.387	.348
	Richmond (IL)	AAA	.280	38	132	13	37	10	2	4	11	11	29	2	.477	.338
	Atlanta (NL)	MAJ	.267	16	15	2	4	0	0	0	0	0	6	0	.267	.267
MAJOR LEAGUE TOTALS			.250	17	16	2	4	0	0	0	0	0	6	0	.250	.250
MINOR LEAGUE TOTALS			.258	646	2297	314	593	140	21	43	264	283	542	90	.394	.347

26 Brett Evert, rhp

Born: Oct. 23, 1980. **Ht.:** 6-6. **Wt.:** 200. **Bats:** L. **Throws:** R. **School:** North Salem (Ore.) HS.
Career Transactions: Selected by Braves in seventh round of 1999 draft; signed June 9, 1999.

Considered one of the top righthanders in the system as recently as a year ago, Evert has been mediocre since a hot start in Double-A earned him a trip to the 2002 Futures Game. His mechanics have broken down and he's unable to repeat his delivery, which led to a demotion to the bullpen last year. He showed signs of regaining his consistency and confidence during his stint as a reliever. When in sync, Evert has a low-90s fastball with a good downward angle and decent movement. His hard overhand curveball also can be a devastating pitch with its tight spin and straight drop. Evert's mechanical difficulties have hurt his command, and opponents have teed off when he can keep his pitches down in the strike zone. His changeup also hasn't developed enough depth, which has made him a two-pitch pitcher who may be better suited for the bullpen in the long term. Evert will get a look this spring as a potential reliever with the big league club, and he could move quickly if everything comes together.

Year	Club (League)	Class	W	L	ERA	G	GS	CG	SV	IP	H	R	ER	HR	BB	SO	AVG
1999	Braves (GCL)	R	5	3	2.03	13	10	0	0	49	37	17	11	0	9	39	.208
2000	Macon (SAL)	A	1	4	4.64	7	7	0	0	43	53	27	22	7	9	29	.298
	Jamestown (NY-P)	A	8	3	3.38	15	15	0	0	77	92	52	29	6	19	64	.288
2001	Macon (SAL)	A	1	0	0.74	6	6	0	0	36	25	5	3	0	3	34	.182
	Myrtle Beach (Car)	A	7	2	2.24	13	13	1	0	72	63	25	18	4	15	75	.226
2002	Greenville (SL)	AA	5	8	4.90	16	15	1	0	94	94	59	51	15	35	84	.263
	Myrtle Beach (Car)	A	3	5	3.75	10	10	1	0	58	53	30	24	3	21	51	.241
2003	Greenville (SL)	AA	4	9	4.02	33	15	1	1	116	126	57	52	12	44	103	.283
MINOR LEAGUE TOTALS			34	34	3.47	113	91	4	1	545	543	272	210	47	155	479	.257

27 Zach Miner, rhp

Born: March 12, 1982. **Ht.:** 6-3. **Wt.:** 190. **Bats:** R. **Throws:** R. **School:** Palm Beach Gardens (Fla.) HS. **Career Transactions:** Selected by Braves in fourth round of 2000 draft; signed Sept. 1, 2000.

Miner's stock fell as much as that of any prospect in the organization last year. Despite his obvious abilities, he was reluctant to challenge hitters in high Class A. Some Atlanta coaches say Miner suffers from aluminum-bat syndrome and is nervous about hitters making solid contact, which causes him to live on the outside half of the plate. The Braves would like to see a little more toughness from Miner, especially when it comes to grinding out victories and working through trouble in the middle innings. On the plus side, Miner has a good feel for pitching. He has an easy delivery that produces low-90s fastballs with good sink. His changeup and slider are decent offerings and he has the promise of becoming a solid three-pitch pitcher. While Miner has increased his strength over the past two years, the Braves want him to continue to do so in order to go deeper into games. If he can do that while regaining his aggressiveness, Miner could reclaim his status as one of the system's top pitching prospects.

Year	Club (League)	Class	W	L	ERA	G	GS	CG	SV	IP	H	R	ER	HR	BB	SO	AVG
2001	Jamestown (NY-P)	A	3	4	1.89	15	15	0	0	91	76	26	19	6	16	68	.226
2002	Macon (SAL)	A	8	9	3.28	29	28	1	0	159	143	73	58	10	51	131	.243
2003	Myrtle Beach (Car)	A	6	10	3.69	27	27	2	0	154	150	74	63	10	61	88	.262
MINOR LEAGUE TOTALS			17	23	3.12	71	70	3	0	403	369	173	140	26	128	287	.246

28 Charlie Morton, rhp

Born: Oct. 12, 1983. **Ht.:** 6-4. **Wt.:** 190. **Bats:** R. **Throws:** R. **School:** Joel Barlow HS, Redding, Conn. **Career Transactions:** Selected by Braves in third round of 2002 draft; signed June 19, 2002.

Despite winning just three of his 15 decisions in his first two years in pro ball, Morton is making steady progress and developing into the type of pitcher the Braves thought he could become when they took him in the third round of the 2002 draft. The tall, lanky righthander's best pitch is a power overhand curveball that breaks straight down, making it nearly impossible to hit. His fastball resides in the 91-93 mph range, and his changeup has the makings of becoming a solid-average pitch. The Braves also like Morton's feel for pitching as well as his presence on the mound. Hailing from cold-weather Connecticut, Morton simply needs innings to work on his stuff and command. He'll get them in low Class A in 2004.

Year	Club (League)	Class	W	L	ERA	G	GS	CG	SV	IP	H	R	ER	HR	BB	SO	AVG
2002	Braves (GCL)	R	1	7	4.54	11	5	0	0	40	37	34	20	1	30	32	.243
2003	Danville (Appy)	R	2	5	4.67	14	13	0	0	54	65	32	28	3	25	46	.302
MINOR LEAGUE TOTALS			3	12	4.61	25	18	0	0	94	102	66	48	4	55	78	.278

29 Matt Esquivel, of

Born: Dec. 17, 1982. **Ht.:** 6-2. **Wt.:** 220. **Bats:** R. **Throws:** R. **School:** McArthur HS, San Antonio. **Career Transactions:** Selected by Braves in fifth round of 2001 draft; signed July 10, 2001.

Several Appalachian League managers considered Esquivel to be the circuit's best defensive outfielder in 2003. The 6-foot-2, 220-pounder covered center field from gap to gap and made at least one spectacular play per series. Despite his bulky appearance, Esquivel has above-average speed and excellent acceleration, and makes plays with his ability to get great jumps on balls. His only defensive shortcoming is his arm, which lacks strength and accuracy. Esquivel is expected to hit for enough power to play on an outfield corner should he switch positions at the higher levels. He's an aggressive hitter but needs to make more consistent contact. A fifth-round pick in 2001, he signed late that summer while deciding whether he wanted to try to walk on the University of Nebraska football team as a running back. One of the top high school football players in the San Antonio area, he had surgery as a sophomore to graft bone cells from his hip to fill a gap where bone had died in his knee. After spending the last two years in Rookie ball, he'll get his first taste of full-season ball with a promotion to low Class A in 2004.

Year	Club (League)	Class	AVG	G	AB	R	H	2B	3B	HR	RBI	BB	SO	SB	SLG	OBP
2002	Danville (Appy)	R	.278	61	227	38	63	13	2	5	41	21	67	2	.419	.345
2003	Danville (Appy)	R	.282	61	220	41	62	10	4	11	42	20	72	7	.514	.352
MINOR LEAGUE TOTALS			.280	122	447	79	125	23	6	16	83	41	139	9	.465	.349

30 Paul Bacot, rhp

Born: Aug. 16, 1984. **Ht.:** 6-6. **Wt.:** 205. **Bats:** R. **Throws:** R. **School:** Lakeside HS, Atlanta.
Career Transactions: Selected by Braves in second round of 2003 draft; signed June 3, 2003.

A second-rounder last June, Bacot is a quintessential Braves draft pick. He's a home-state Georgia product, and he's a projectable high school athlete with huge upside. He starred at point guard and helped his Lakeside High team reach the state 5-A basketball finals. He declined scholarships from mid-level NCAA Division I programs to sign for $550,000. Now that he's concentrating solely on baseball, he could really take off. He was untouchable for Atlanta's championship Gulf Coast League team, though he missed the last couple of weeks after being shut down in early August with a tired arm. Bacot has an 88-90 mph fastball that scouts believe will reach the mid-90s once he fills out. He backs it up with an 83-mph slider and an advanced changeup. He also has excellent command to both sides of the plate. If he shows he's sound in spring training, he could open 2004 in low Class A.

Year	Club (League)	Class	W	L	ERA	G	GS	CG	SV	IP	H	R	ER	HR	BB	SO	AVG
2003	Braves (GCL)	R	4	0	0.95	9	6	0	0	38	23	6	4	0	4	26	.168
MINOR LEAGUE TOTALS			4	0	0.95	9	6	0	0	38	23	6	4	0	4	26	.168

BALTIMORE
ORIOLES

The Orioles drew national attention with the signings of shortstop Miguel Tejada and Javy Lopez. Though they couldn't get Vladimir Guerrero to agree to terms, the Orioles are suddenly relevant again after several years in baseball exile. The reconstruction of the franchise actually started more than a year earlier, with the firing of general manager Syd Thrift after the 2002 season ended. Owner Peter Angelos took the unusual step of hiring Jim Beattie and Mike Flanagan to share the GM duties, but their first year yielded promising results.

One of their first moves was hiring Doc Rodgers as farm director to bring stability to a system in disarray. He brought communication and discipline back to player development. Players actually blossomed rather than stagnated in the minors. Rodgers started by putting new managers at five of the organization's seven affiliates. On the first day of minor league spring training last year, he emphasized his old-school principles by telling players to show at least four inches of sock. When several didn't adhere to the rule, Rodgers brought a ruler to a meeting the next day. He also met individually with every player.

The message was consistent, as was the instruction. Instead of hearing different things from different coaches, players worked under a standardized training regimen at every level. The Oriole Way returned.

TOP 30 PROSPECTS

1. Adam Loewen, lhp
2. John Maine, rhp
3. Nick Markakis, of
4. Val Majewski, of
5. Denny Bautista, rhp
6. Matt Riley, lhp
7. Erik Bedard, lhp
8. Rommie Lewis, lhp
9. Mike Fontenot, 2b
10. Dave Crouthers, rhp
11. Ryan Hannaman, lhp
12. Jose Bautista, 3b
13. Chris Ray, rhp
14. Brian Finch, rhp
15. Daniel Cabrera, rhp
16. Don Levinski, rhp
17. Eddy Rodriguez, rhp
18. Brian Forystek, lhp
19. Lorenzo Scott, of
20. Walter Young, 1b/dh
21. Carlos Perez, lhp
22. Tripper Johnson, 3b
23. Mike Huggins, 1b
24. Eli Whiteside, c
25. Darnell McDonald, of
26. Jose Morban, ss/2b
27. Tim Raines Jr., of
28. Richard Stahl, lhp
29. Aaron Rakers, rhp
30. Bryan Bass, ss

By Will Lingo

"It was really just a case of getting back to fundamentals," Rodgers said. "We emphasized work ethic, communication, expectations and accountability, and our players responded."

While making significant changes in the minor leagues, Beattie and Flanagan made few big moves with the big league team before the 2003 season. Knowing a quick fix wouldn't work, they spent time assessing their talent. During the summer, they unloaded Sidney Ponson and Jeff Conine and got five players who should surpass the talent they got in their great purge of 2000. Three years earlier, they dealt six veterans and received only one player of value, Melvin Mora. This time the club got big league righthander Kurt Ainsworth and lefthander Damian Moss (who was nontendered in December) as well as Denny Bautista, Ryan Hannaman and Don Levinski.

The next step was replacing manager Mike Hargrove with the younger, more dynamic Lee Mazzilli. Finally came the free agents, adding premium players to a team devoid of impact talent.

The Orioles have a lot of questions to answer before they print playoff tickets, especially on the pitching staff. And the farm system, while dramatically improved, still isn't among the best in the game. But the organization has made significant steps in the right direction on both fronts.

ORGANIZATION
OVERVIEW

General manager: Jim Beattie/Mike Flanagan. **Farm director:** Doc Rodgers. **Scouting director:** Tony DeMacio.

2003 PERFORMANCE

Class	Team	League	W	L	Pct.	Finish*	Manager
Majors	Baltimore	American	71	91	.438	t-10th (14)	Mike Hargrove
Triple-A	Ottawa Lynx	International	79	65	.549	3rd (14)	Gary Allenson
Double-A	Bowie Baysox	Eastern	69	72	.489	8th (12)	Dave Trembley
High A	Frederick Keys	Carolina	60	75	.444	7th (8)	Tom Lawless
Low A	Delmarva Shorebirds	South Atlantic	67	71	.486	10th (16)	Stan Hough
Short-season	Aberdeen IronBirds	New York-Penn	38	38	.500	t-8th (14)	Joe Almaraz
Rookie	Bluefield Orioles	Appalachian	23	40	.365	9th (10)	Don Buford
Rookie	GCL Orioles	Gulf Coast	32	28	.533	4th (12)	Jesus Alfaro
OVERALL 2003 MINOR LEAGUE RECORD			367	389	.485	20th (30)	

*Finish in overall standings (No. of teams in league)

ORGANIZATION LEADERS

BATTING   *Minimum 250 At-Bats
*AVG	Mike Fontenot, Bowie	.325
R	Tim Raines Jr., Ottawa/Bowie	81
H	Mike Fontenot, Bowie	146
TB	Mike Fontenot, Bowie	216
2B	Val Majewski, Frederick/Delmarva	35
3B	Val Majewski, Frederick/Delmarva	11
HR	Three tied at	14
RBI	Mike Huggins, Frederick	74
BB	Jack Cust, Ottawa	80
SO	Neal Stephenson, Delmarva	137
SB	Tim Raines Jr., Ottawa/Bowie	51
*SLG	Val Majewski, Frederick/Delmarva	.541
*OBP	Jack Cust, Ottawa	.422

PITCHING   #Minimum 75 Innings
W	John Maine, Frederick/Delmarva	13
L	Ryan Keefer, Delmarva	12
#ERA	Scott Rice, Frederick/Delmarva	1.83
G	Darwin Cubillan, Ottawa	65
CG	Four tied at	2
SV	Jeff Montani, Delmarva	23
IP	John Stephens, Ottawa	159
BB	Mike Paradis, Bowie	81
SO	John Maine, Frederick/Delmarva	185

BEST TOOLS

Best Hitter for Average	Nick Markakis
Best Power Hitter	Walter Young
Fastest Baserunner	Tim Raines Jr.
Best Athlete	Lorenzo Scott
Best Fastball	Denny Bautista
Best Curveball	Matt Riley
Best Slider	Dave Crouthers
Best Changeup	Brian Forystek
Best Control	John Maine
Best Defensive Catcher	Eli Whiteside
Best Defensive Infielder	Ed Rogers
Best Infield Arm	Bryan Bass
Best Defensive Outfielder	Darnell McDonald
Best Outfield Arm	Keith Reed

PROJECTED 2007 LINEUP

Catcher	Javy Lopez
First Base	Jay Gibbons
Second Base	Mike Fontenot
Third Base	Jose Bautista
Shortstop	Miguel Tejada
Left Field	Val Majewski
Center Field	Luis Matos

Right Field	Nick Markakis
Designated Hitter	Larry Bigbie
No. 1 Starter	Adam Loewen
No. 2 Starter	John Maine
No. 3 Starter	Sidney Ponson
No. 4 Starter	Matt Riley
No. 5 Starter	Denny Bautista
Closer	Jorge Julio

LAST YEAR'S TOP 20 PROSPECTS

1. Erik Bedard, lhp	11. Corey Shafer, of
2. Darnell McDonald, of	12. Bryan Bass, ss
3. Daniel Cabrera, rhp	13. Val Majewski, of
4. Luis Jimenez, 1b/of	14. Dave Crouthers, rhp
5. Rommie Lewis, lhp	15. Kurt Birkins, lhp
6. Mike Fontenot, 2b	16. Steve Bechler, rhp
7. Richard Stahl, lhp	17. Aaron Rakers, rhp
8. John Maine, rhp	18. Doug Gredvig, 1b
9. Tripper Johnson, 3b	19. Paul Henry, rhp
10. Eli Whiteside, c	20. Eric DuBose, lhp

TOP PROSPECTS OF THE DECADE

1994	Jeffrey Hammonds, of
1995	Armando Benitez, rhp
1996	Rocky Coppinger, rhp
1997	Nerio Rodriguez, rhp
1998	Ryan Minor, 3b
1999	Matt Riley, lhp
2000	Matt Riley, lhp
2001	Keith Reed, of
2002	Richard Stahl, lhp
2003	Erik Bedard, lhp

TOP DRAFT PICKS OF THE DECADE

1994	Tommy Davis, 1b (2)
1995	Alvie Shepherd, rhp
1996	Brian Falkenborg, rhp (2)
1997	Jayson Werth, c
1998	Rick Elder, of
1999	Mike Paradis, rhp
2000	Beau Hale, rhp
2001	Chris Smith, lhp
2002	Adam Loewen, lhp
2003	Nick Markakis, of

ALL-TIME LARGEST BONUSES

Adam Loewen, 2002	$3,200,000
Beau Hale, 2000	$2,250,000
Chris Smith, 2001	$2,175,000
Darnell McDonald, 1997	$1,900,000
Nick Markakis, 2003	$1,850,000

MINOR LEAGUE
DEPTH CHART

BALTIMORE **ORIOLES** RANK: 18

Impact potential (B): The addition of an Adam Loewen and Nick Markakis here and a Denny Bautista and Ryan Hannaman there does wonders for a system that was fighting for breath a year ago. With Matt Riley and Erik Bedard on the comeback trail, things are looking up in Baltimore.

Depth (C): A solid 2003 draft and an influx of prospects through trades provide a big boost for the overall health of a farm system that was ranked last a year ago. There's still a lack of quality bats in the syetem, though.

Sleeper: Daniel Cabrera, rhp. —*Depth charts prepared by* **Josh Boyd**. *Numbers in parentheses indicate prospect rankings.*

LF
Val Majewski (4)
Woody Cliffords
B.J. Littleton

CF
Darnell McDonald (25)
Tim Raines Jr. (27)
Arturo Rivas

RF
Nick Markakis (3)
Lorenzo Scott (19)
Keith Reed
Tim Gilhooly

3B
Jose Bautista (12)
Tripper Johnson (22)
Matt Pulley
Napolean Calzado
Carlos Rijo

SS
Jose Morban (26)
Bryan Bass (30)
Ed Rogers
Brandon Fahey
Nate Spears

2B
Mike Fontenot (9)
Gary Cates
Omar Rogers

1B
Walter Young (20)
Mike Huggins (23)
Corey Shafer
Doug Gredvig
Kris Wilken

SOURCE OF TALENT

Homegrown		Acquired	
College	11	Trade	3
Junior College	2	Rule 5 draft	1
Draft-and-follow	2	Independent	0
High school	6	Free agent/waivers	2
Nondrafted free agent	0		
Foreign	3		

C
Eli Whiteside (24)
Ryan Hubele
Tommy Arko
Juan Gutierrez

RHP

Starters	Relievers
John Maine (2)	Eddy Rodriguez (17)
Denny Bautista (5)	Aaron Rakers (29)
Dave Crouthers (10)	Fredy Deza
Chris Ray (13)	Sendy Rleal
Brian Finch (14)	Jacobo Sequea
Daniel Cabrera (15)	Jayme Sperring
Don Levinski (16)	Paul Henry
Bob McCrory	Ben Knapp
Beau Hale	Cory Morris
Hayden Penn	
Joe Coppinger	
Ryan Keefer	
Mike Paradis	
James Tiller	
Doug Brubaker	

LHP

Starters	Relievers
Adam Loewen (1)	Brian Forystek (18)
Matt Riley (6)	Scott Rice
Erik Bedard (7)	Richard Salazar
Rommie Lewis (8)	
Ryan Hannaman (11)	
Carlos Perez (21)	
Rich Stahl (28)	
Kurt Birkins	
Chris Smith	
Justin Azze	

DRAFT
ANALYSIS

Best Pro Debut: Though most teams had him pegged as a lefthanded pitcher, OF Nick Markakis (1) became a full-time hitter and ranked as the top prospect in the short-season New York-Penn League after batting .283-1-28. And while most clubs didn't have RHP Brian Finch (2) as high on their draft boards as the Orioles did, he had a 1.93 ERA and 29 strikeouts in 28 NY-P innings. RHP Tony Neal (20) put up similar numbers in the NY-P: 1.94 ERA, 43 whiffs in 42 innings.

Best Athlete: Better known as a linebacker for Ball State, OF Lorenzo Scott (17) has power and speed and wasn't as raw as the Orioles thought. He hit .319 with 12 extra-base hits and 11 steals in the Rookie-level Gulf Coast League before returning for his senior football season.

Best Pure Hitter: Markakis, who batted .455-17-74 and .439-21-92 while winning consecutive Baseball America Junior College Player of the Year awards.

Best Raw Power: Scott and 3B Matt Pulley (12).

Fastest Runner: SS Nate Spears (5) used his plus speed to steal 18 bases in 23 tries in the GCL.

Best Defensive Player: Though Markakis was primarily a DH in junior college to protect his prized left arm, he has plus range and arm strength for right field. The Orioles have given him some exposure in center,

Finch

and he may be able to play there.

Best Fastball: Finch and RHPs Chris Ray (3) and Bob McCrory (4) all can pitch in the mid-90s. Finch has more life and sink on his fastball than Ray and McCrory.

Best Breaking Ball: Ray's hard slider, combined with his fastball, allowed him to dominate the Cape Cod League in the summer of 2002. Finch's knuckle-curve and Neal's slider are also plus pitches.

Most Intriguing Background: Unsigned SS David Cash's (21) father Dave was an all-star second baseman in the mid-1970s.

Closest To The Majors: Markakis might have moved faster as a lefthander, but he still should win the race. Ray is the best candidate among the pitchers.

Best Late-Round Pick: Scott, with the credit going to area scout Marc Ziegler. While scouting other Ball State players, Ziegler became enamored with Scott, who started just five games last spring.

The One Who Got Away: LHP Nathan Nery (8) is projectable with a 6-foot-4, 195-pound build and a high-80s fastball. He's attending Stetson.

Assessment: In LHP Adam Loewen and Markakis, the Orioles got the two most coveted draft-and-follows from the 2002 draft. Baltimore also added power arms in Finch, Ray and McCrory.

Draft-and-follow LHP Adam Loewen (1) and RHP John Maine (6) could front Baltimore's rotation in the near future. OF Val Majewski (3) is the system's top position prospect. Unsigned RHP Mark McCormick (11) looks like he'll be a 2005 first-rounder.

Baltimore blew first-rounders on LHP Chris Smith and SS Bryan Bass, though 2B Mike Fontenot (1) started to rebound in 2003. LHP Rommie Lewis (4) and RHP Dave Crouthers (3) also have upside.

RHP Beau Hale (1) has been a disaster, and 3B Tripper Johnson (1) is regressing. Signing RHPs Kyle Sleeth (18) and Tim Stauffer (36), who became the third and fourth overall picks in 2003, would have been huge.

The Orioles had seven first-round picks, but only OF Larry Bigbie (1) and 2B Brian Roberts (1) look like they'll pan out. LHP Erik Bedard (6) could be better than either if he can stay healthy.

—Draft analysis prepared by Jim Callis. Numbers in parentheses indicate draft rounds.

RODGER WOOD

Adam
Loewen

Born: April 9, 1984.
Ht.: 6-6. **Wt.:** 220.
Bats: L. **Throws:** L.
School: Chipola (Fla.) JC.
Career Transactions: Selected by Orioles in first round (fourth overall) of 2002 draft; signed May 26, 2003.

As significant as free agents Miguel Tejada and Javy Lopez were to the major league team, the signing of Loewen was just as important for the farm system. It provided a true impact player to an organization that sorely needed one. It also showed the team's new administration was willing to move boldly to bring in talent. The Orioles took Loewen fourth overall in 2002, making him the highest-drafted Canadian ever, but tried to lowball him in negotiations. With the Orioles' offer at $2.5 million and Loewen standing on a demand of $4 million, he enrolled at Chipola (Fla.) JC, becoming the earliest pick to take the draft-and-follow route in draft history. The Orioles signed him minutes before they would have lost his rights. He received a major league contract with a $3.2 million bonus and a guaranteed value of $4.02 million. It was clear at an early age that Loewen was special. He led a team from British Columbia to the 1996 Little League World Series, handed Korea its only loss at the 2000 World Junior Championship and no-hit the Pirates' Rookie-level Dominican Summer League team during a Team Canada tour in 2001. The Orioles played it safe with Loewen after he signed, giving him just seven starts, none more than five innings, and shutting him down in August.

With two plus pitches and the possibility of two more, Loewen has legitimate No. 1 starter potential. His fastball usually ranges from 90-95 mph, though it was a bit lower at the end of the season as he tired. His curveball, a big 12-to-6 breaker, is his best pitch. He has a good feel for a changeup and has dabbled with a slider as well. He's athletic with smooth mechanics, effortless arm action and good extension. Loewen would have been drafted early as a power-hitting outfielder if he wasn't such a promising pitcher. His low-key demeanor on the mound earns comparisons to Tom Glavine. The Orioles praise his makeup and maturity as much as his physical ability. Because he needed little other than his fastball and curveball as an amateur, Loewen still needs work on his changeup. His fastball command also can improve, and he's still learning to command his offspeed stuff. He'll have to build up his durability and get accustomed to pitching from February through October.

Though they played it safe with Loewen last year, the Orioles expect him to move quickly to the big leagues. He's motivated to get there, calling the team in November to see if he could come to the minor league complex in Sarasota, Fla., to work out. The Orioles told him to wait until January, and after spring training they'll send him to low Class A Delmarva. He'll probably spend half the season there before moving up to high Class A Frederick.

Year	Club (League)	Class	W	L	ERA	G	GS	CG	SV	IP	H	R	ER	HR	BB	SO	AVG
2003	Aberdeen (NY-P)	A	0	2	2.70	7	7	0	0	23	13	7	7	0	9	25	.167
MINOR LEAGUE TOTALS			0	2	2.70	7	7	0	0	23	13	7	7	0	9	25	.167

2 John Maine, rhp

Born: May 8, 1981. **Ht.:** 6-4. **Wt.:** 190. **Bats:** R. **Throws:** R. **School:** UNC Charlotte. **Career Transactions:** Selected by Orioles in sixth round of 2002 draft; signed July 5, 2002.

Maine led the minors in strikeouts and opponent average (.177) in 2003. In his second high Class A start, he threw a seven-inning no-hitter against Winston-Salem and came within a hit batter of a perfect game. Maine's best pitch is a 90-92 mph fastball. He already has major league command of his heater and is able to throw it to both sides of the plate as well as up and down. His fastball also has great life, and the deception in his delivery makes it look even faster. Maine can strike hitters out with his fastball alone, and he threw it 75-90 percent of the time before 2003. He employed his curveball and changeup more last year, though he still needs to use and command them better. Maintaining consistent mechanics is a key. In his first high Class A start, Maine got knocked around a bit and told Frederick's staff that he did not want to be paid for his work that day. The no-hitter against Winston-Salem followed. It's that makeup that makes Maine a special pitcher and could get him to the big leagues as soon as 2004. He'll open at Double-A Bowie.

Year	Club (League)	Class	W	L	ERA	G	GS	CG	SV	IP	H	R	ER	HR	BB	SO	AVG
2002	Aberdeen (NY-P)	A	1	1	1.74	4	2	0	0	10	6	2	2	0	3	21	.154
	Delmarva (SAL)	A	1	1	1.36	6	5	0	0	33	21	8	5	0	4	39	.178
2003	Delmarva (SAL)	A	7	3	1.53	14	14	1	0	76	43	16	13	1	18	108	.165
	Frederick (Car)	A	6	1	3.07	12	12	1	0	70	48	27	24	5	20	77	.190
MINOR LEAGUE TOTALS			15	6	2.08	36	33	2	0	190	118	53	44	6	45	245	.176

3 Nick Markakis, of

Born: Nov. 17, 1983. **Ht.:** 6-1. **Wt.:** 175. **Bats:** L. **Throws:** L. **School:** Young Harris (Ga.) JC. **Career Transactions:** Selected by Orioles in first round (seventh overall) of 2003 draft; signed June 11, 2003.

BA's 2002 and 2003 Junior College Player of the Year, Markakis led the juco ranks in victories (12) and strikeouts (160) as a pitcher as well as RBIs (92) as a DH last spring. He turned down $1.5 million from the Reds as a draft-and-follow, then went seventh overall to Baltimore and signed for $1.85 million. After playing for Greece at the European Championships in July, he earned top prospect honors in the short-season New York-Penn League. Most teams preferred Markakis as a pitcher, but the Orioles think he can be a special hitter. He's quiet at the plate, with a smooth, natural stroke that produces good leverage. He's adept at manipulating the bat head and can drive the ball to all fields. He obviously has a plus arm and is athletic, which should make him a good defender on either corner. Markakis doesn't have much experience against premium competition, particularly as a hitter. He can be overpowered by good fastballs at this point. He needs to add strength to his frame, and he already has added about 10 pounds of muscle since signing. Markakis probably will start 2004 in low Class A. If he performs as expected, he'll move up fast.

Year	Club (League)	Class	AVG	G	AB	R	H	2B	3B	HR	RBI	BB	SO	SB	SLG	OBP
2003	Aberdeen (NY-P)	A	.283	59	205	22	58	14	3	1	28	30	33	13	.395	.372
MINOR LEAGUE TOTALS			.283	59	205	22	58	14	3	1	28	30	33	13	.395	.372

4 Val Majewski, of

Born: June 19, 1981. **Ht.:** 6-2. **Wt.:** 200. **Bats:** L. **Throws:** L. **School:** Rutgers University. **Career Transactions:** Selected by Orioles in third round of 2002 draft; signed July 22, 2002.

Majewski was on his way to putting up monster numbers in his first full pro season when a stress fracture in his femur knocked him out of action for six weeks. The Orioles aren't sure what caused it, but he has fully healed. Despite playing at first base in college and in center field in the minors, Majewski is more of a prototype right fielder. He has a quiet, disciplined approach at the plate and takes a direct path to the ball, centering just about every pitch he hits. He uses the whole ballpark and doesn't have to pull the ball to drive it. The Orioles say his makeup can't be graded high enough. Majewski has a good arm and the potential to be a plus defender in right fielder, but he needs more experience there. He'll have to hit more home runs to fit the right-field profile. Majewski proved enough in 41 games at high Class A to open 2004 in Double-A. He could move quickly through an organization that needs impact bats, especially in the outfield.

Year	Club (League)	Class	AVG	G	AB	R	H	2B	3B	HR	RBI	BB	SO	SB	SLG	OBP
2002	Aberdeen (NY-P)	A	.300	31	110	22	33	7	4	1	15	13	14	8	.464	.376
	Delmarva (SAL)	A	.118	7	17	2	2	0	0	1	3	1	1	0	.294	.158
2003	Delmarva (SAL)	A	.303	56	208	38	63	15	8	7	48	28	20	10	.553	.383
	Orioles (GCL)	R	.333	1	3	0	1	0	0	0	0	1	0	0	.333	.500
	Aberdeen (NY-P)	A	.375	4	16	2	6	2	2	0	3	1	2	1	.750	.412
	Frederick (Car)	A	.289	41	159	15	46	18	1	5	20	7	23	0	.509	.321
MINOR LEAGUE TOTALS			.294	140	513	79	151	42	15	14	89	51	60	19	.517	.358

5 Denny Bautista, rhp

Born: Oct. 23, 1982. **Ht.:** 6-5. **Wt.:** 170. **Bats:** R. **Throws:** R. **Career Transactions:** Signed out of Dominican Republic by Marlins, April 11, 2000 . . . Traded by Marlins with RHP Don Levinski to Orioles for 1B Jeff Conine, Aug. 31, 2003.

Bautista has the highest ceiling of the players Baltimore acquired in midseason trades. Mentored by Pedro and Ramon Martinez in the Dominican Republic, Bautista pitched in the Futures Game and ranked among the top prospects in the high Class A Florida State and Double-A Southern leagues. Bautista has an electric arm, with an explosive fastball that sits in the mid-90s and can touch 98 mph. In one Double-A start, he was clocked at 96 mph 18 times. His curveball also could be a plus pitch, and he has a projectable body. While Bautista's arm ranks with the best in the minors, his command doesn't. His mechanics can get out of sync and he throws across his body. His changeup is a potential plus pitch, but he needs to use it more to develop it. Bautista has the ability to pitch at the top of a rotation, but he'll need to hone his command and delivery to make that happen. He's a potential closer if starting doesn't work out. He could move up to Triple-A Ottawa to start the season and should be ready to contribute in the big leagues by 2005.

Year	Club (League)	Class	W	L	ERA	G	GS	CG	SV	IP	H	R	ER	HR	BB	SO	AVG
2000	Marlins (GCL)	R	6	2	2.43	11	11	2	0	63	49	24	17	1	17	58	.209
	Marlins (DSL)	R	0	1	2.57	3	3	0	0	14	11	6	4	2	9	17	.216
	Utica (NY-P)	A	0	0	3.60	1	1	0	0	5	4	3	2	0	2	5	.222
2001	Kane County (Mid)	A	3	1	4.35	8	7	0	0	39	43	21	19	2	14	20	.281
	Utica (NY-P)	A	3	1	2.08	7	7	0	0	39	25	16	9	0	6	31	.174
2002	Jupiter (FSL)	A	4	6	4.99	19	15	0	0	88	80	52	49	6	40	79	.242
2003	Jupiter (FSL)	A	8	4	3.21	14	14	0	0	84	68	32	30	2	35	77	.219
	Carolina (SL)	AA	4	5	3.71	11	11	0	0	53	45	33	22	5	35	61	.226
MINOR LEAGUE TOTALS			28	20	3.54	74	69	2	0	386	325	187	152	18	158	348	.226

6 Matt Riley, lhp

Born: Aug. 2, 1979. **Ht.:** 6-1. **Wt.:** 207. **Bats:** L. **Throws:** L. **School:** Sacramento CC. **Career Transactions:** Selected by Orioles in third round of 1997 draft; signed May 28, 1998 . . . On disabled list, April 1-Nov. 19, 2001.

After the obligatory year of mediocre performance following Tommy John surgery, Riley showed the form that made him the organization's top prospect entering 1999 and 2000. He finished the season with two strong starts against the Blue Jays in September and has regained his old stuff. His fastball sits in the low 90s and touches 94, and his big curveball is an out pitch. His changeup has improved significantly, as he has command of all three pitches. Immaturity held him back before his injury, but Riley showed more focus and determination after the heat-related death of close friend Steve Bechler in spring training. Riley had trouble repeating his delivery in the past but seems to have straightened his mechanics out. All that's left is to polish his command and feel for pitching. The organization's higher expectations on and off the field have helped Riley get ready for the big leagues. He'll go to spring training with a chance to win a job in Baltimore's rotation.

Year	Club (League)	Class	W	L	ERA	G	GS	CG	SV	IP	H	R	ER	HR	BB	SO	AVG
1998	Delmarva (SAL)	A	5	4	1.19	16	14	0	0	83	42	19	11	0	44	136	.152
1999	Frederick (Car)	A	3	2	2.61	8	8	0	0	52	34	19	15	5	14	58	.188
	Bowie (EL)	AA	10	6	3.22	20	20	3	0	126	113	53	45	13	42	131	.241
	Baltimore (AL)	MAJ	0	0	7.36	3	3	0	0	11	17	9	9	4	13	6	.378
2000	Rochester (IL)	AAA	0	2	14.14	2	2	0	0	7	15	12	11	3	4	8	.417
	Bowie (EL)	AA	5	7	6.08	19	14	2	1	74	74	56	50	9	49	66	.262
2001	Did not play—Injured																
2002	Bowie (EL)	AA	4	10	6.34	22	22	0	0	109	136	84	77	12	48	105	.306
2003	Bowie (EL)	AA	5	2	3.11	14	14	1	0	72	56	27	25	4	23	73	.210
	Ottawa (IL)	AAA	4	2	3.58	13	13	0	0	70	70	30	28	4	28	77	.261
	Baltimore (AL)	MAJ	1	0	1.80	2	2	0	0	10	7	2	2	1	5	8	.194
MAJOR LEAGUE TOTALS			1	0	4.71	5	5	0	0	21	24	11	11	5	18	14	.296
MINOR LEAGUE TOTALS			36	35	3.97	114	107	6	1	593	540	300	262	50	252	654	.243

7 Erik Bedard, lhp

Born: March 6, 1979. **Ht.:** 6-1. **Wt.:** 191. **Bats:** L. **Throws:** L. **School:** Norwalk (Conn.) CC. **Career Transactions:** Selected by Orioles in sixth round of 1999 draft; signed June 8, 1999.

Bedard was the organization's best prospect and was tearing up Double-A when the Bowie staff let him exceed his pitch count in a July 2002 game. He promptly blew out his elbow and had Tommy John surgery two months later. He returned to the mound last August and the Orioles say he could have pitched in the majors in September, but they didn't want to rush his comeback. Surprisingly, Bedard's fastball velocity was almost all the way back to his customary 92 mph when he first came back. His plus curveball also showed its old snap. The hard work Bedard put into rehab paid off and showed his determination. While his stuff looked promising in August, Bedard still has to prove himself over the long haul. The year off cost Bedard time he needed to develop his changeup and his approach. The Orioles expect Bedard to be healthy and ready to go in spring training. Still, they may play it cautiously and have him open the season in Double-A.

Year	Club (League)	Class	W	L	ERA	G	GS	CG	SV	IP	H	R	ER	HR	BB	SO	AVG
1999	Orioles (GCL)	R	2	1	1.86	8	6	0	0	29	20	7	6	1	13	41	.192
2000	Delmarva (SAL)	A	9	4	3.57	29	22	1	2	111	98	48	44	2	35	131	.233
2001	Frederick (Car)	A	9	2	2.15	17	17	0	0	96	68	27	23	4	26	130	.198
	Orioles (GCL)	R	0	1	3.00	2	2	0	0	6	4	2	2	0	3	7	.200
2002	Bowie (EL)	AA	6	3	1.97	13	12	0	0	69	43	18	15	0	30	66	.176
	Baltimore (AL)	MAJ	0	0	13.50	2	0	0	0	1	2	1	1	0	0	1	.500
2003	Orioles (GCL)	R	0	0	1.13	3	3	0	0	8	4	1	1	0	2	11	.154
	Aberdeen (NY-P)	A	0	0	2.35	2	2	0	0	8	7	2	2	0	1	13	.233
	Frederick (Car)	A	0	1	7.36	1	1	0	0	4	5	3	3	1	1	2	.357
MAJOR LEAGUE TOTALS			0	0	13.50	2	0	0	0	1	2	1	1	0	0	1	.500
MINOR LEAGUE TOTALS			26	12	2.62	75	65	1	2	330	249	108	96	8	111	401	.207

8 Rommie Lewis, lhp

Born: Sept. 2, 1982. **Ht.:** 6-6. **Wt.:** 203. **Bats:** L. **Throws:** L. **School:** Newport HS, Bellevue, Wash. **Career Transactions:** Selected by Orioles in fourth round of 2001 draft; signed June 9, 2001.

Among the many changes made by the Orioles' new player-development staff was moving Lewis from reliever to starter. Though his numbers weren't outstanding, they were pleased with the results. He went to the bullpen in August to save wear and tear on his arm. Lewis' feel for pitching stands out more than his stuff, making it that much stranger that he was pitching in relief. His fastball went from 93 mph out of the bullpen to 90-91 in the rotation last year, but that's still good velocity for a lefty. He spots his fastball well, and he can add and subtract velocity from it. His curveball and changeup were much improved. Lewis' savvy actually gets him in trouble sometimes, as he racks up high pitch counts playing cat-and-mouse games with batters. The Orioles want him to be more aggressive early in the count. He also needs to get in better shape to handle the workload of starting. With a season of starting under his belt and another year of physical maturity, Lewis should be able to handle more innings and produce better results in 2004. Even if he returns to high Class A to open the season, he'll spend most of it in Double-A.

Year	Club (League)	Class	W	L	ERA	G	GS	CG	SV	IP	H	R	ER	HR	BB	SO	AVG
2001	Orioles (GCL)	R	1	1	2.14	10	7	0	0	34	37	16	8	3	6	27	.276
	Frederick (Car)	A	0	1	9.00	1	0	0	0	4	8	7	4	1	1	2	.400
2002	Delmarva (SAL)	A	1	2	2.15	53	0	0	25	71	50	19	17	1	20	77	.198
2003	Frederick (Car)	A	4	9	3.34	26	20	1	0	113	108	54	42	9	60	69	.251
MINOR LEAGUE TOTALS			6	13	2.88	90	27	1	25	222	203	96	71	14	87	175	.242

9 Mike Fontenot, 2b

Born: June 9, 1980. **Ht.:** 5-8. **Wt.:** 160. **Bats:** L. **Throws:** R. **School:** Louisiana State University. **Career Transactions:** Selected by Orioles in first round (19th overall) of 2001 draft; signed Sept. 5, 2001.

After batting .219 in April, Fontenot looked like he might be headed down the same path to oblivion as fellow Orioles 2001 first-rounders Chris Smith and Bryan Bass. Then he got contact lenses in May and got locked in at the plate, batting .360 over the last three months to earn Double-A Eastern League all-star honors. Fontenot is an offensive second baseman. He works counts, gets on base and laces line drives from gap to gap. He has good power for his size and should hit 10-15 homers annually. He also runs well and could steal 20 bases a year. Fontenot's glove lags behind his bat, but he showed enough improvement in 2003 that he can become an average defender. He cleaned up his footwork and throws, his two biggest problems in the past. The Orioles give a lot of credit to Bowie manager Dave Trembley for getting the best out of Fontenot, challenging him every day while helping him improve. Fontenot could be trade bait because of the organization's depth at second base, but for now he'll try to continue his success in Triple-A.

Year	Club (League)	Class	AVG	G	AB	R	H	2B	3B	HR	RBI	BB	SO	SB	SLG	OBP
2002	Frederick (Car)	A	.264	122	481	61	127	16	4	8	53	42	117	13	.364	.333
2003	Bowie (EL)	AA	.325	126	449	63	146	24	5	12	66	50	89	16	.481	.399
MINOR LEAGUE TOTALS			.294	248	930	124	273	40	9	20	119	92	206	29	.420	.365

10 Dave Crouthers, rhp

Born: Dec. 18, 1979. **Ht.:** 6-3. **Wt.:** 203. **Bats:** R. **Throws:** R. **School:** Southern Illinois University-Edwardsville. **Career Transactions:** Selected by Orioles in third round of 2001 draft; signed June 7, 2001.

Crouthers was an all-conference outfielder for three years running at NCAA Division II Southern Illinois-Edwardsville. He doubled as a starting pitcher in 2001, when he set Cougars season records for RBIs and pitching strikeouts (breaking Orioles farmhand Aaron Rakers' mark). Baltimore saw his frame and pictured him as a workhorse starter. Crouthers' strong build earns comparisons to that of Dave Stieb and Matt Clement, and he has an easy arm action. His fastball sits at 93-94 mph and touches 96. His slider also can be an above-average pitch at times. When everything is working Crouthers can be dominant, but that doesn't happen often enough. His slider and command need more consistency, and he needs to use his changeup more. The Orioles used a pitching script that compelled him to throw the changeup in certain counts, and it has the potential to be a plus pitch. Crouthers remains a work in progress, but on the right day he looks ready for the majors. The Orioles will send him back to Double-A to start 2004.

Year	Club (League)	Class	W	L	ERA	G	GS	CG	SV	IP	H	R	ER	HR	BB	SO	AVG
2001	Bluefield (Appy)	R	2	3	4.43	10	10	1	0	45	41	28	22	7	18	45	.243
2002	Delmarva (SAL)	A	8	6	3.34	25	25	1	0	129	117	66	48	4	58	108	.243
2003	Frederick (Car)	A	7	5	3.59	18	18	0	0	93	83	47	37	1	43	82	.243
	Bowie (EL)	AA	4	2	3.80	9	9	0	0	45	37	20	19	4	18	29	.220
MINOR LEAGUE TOTALS			21	16	3.64	62	62	2	0	312	278	161	126	16	137	264	.240

11 Ryan Hannaman, lhp

Born: Aug. 28, 1981. **Ht.:** 6-3. **Wt.:** 200. **Bats:** L. **Throws:** L. **School:** Murphy HS, Mobile, Ala. **Career Transactions:** Selected by Giants in fourth round of 2000 draft; signed June 11, 2000 . . . Traded by Giants with RHP Kurt Ainsworth and LHP Damian Moss to Orioles for RHP Sidney Ponson, July 31, 2003.

The Sidney Ponson trade couldn't have worked out any better for the Orioles. For two months of Ponson, the Giants sent righthander Kurt Ainsworth and lefties Hannaman and Damian Moss to Baltimore last July. Baltimore nontendered Moss, but Ainsworth, Hannaman and Ponson (who returned as a free agent in January) all could play major roles on the big league staff. San Francisco first scouted Hannaman as a position player but moved him to the mound after he signed. His lack of pitching experience and nagging injuries have held him back a bit—he hasn't made it past high Class A—and he struggled with biceps tendinitis last year. But he has a potentially special arm, throwing his fastball in the mid-90s with a lot of life. His slider is a little slurvy at times and needs tightening, and his changeup also needs work. But command is his biggest issue. Indicative of the extremes Hannaman offers, in one of his final starts of the season he walked the bases loaded and then struck out the side. Some of his problems are mechanical, as he has a bit of a long arm action and needs to find a consistent delivery. If the Orioles can polish his power arm, he could be dominant. If not, he likely would head to the bullpen. He'll open 2004 in Double-A with a good spring.

Year	Club (League)	Class	W	L	ERA	G	GS	CG	SV	IP	H	R	ER	HR	BB	SO	AVG
2000	Giants (AZL)	R	0	1	21.60	5	0	0	0	3	4	8	8	0	11	6	.333
	Salem-Keizer (NWL)	A	0	0	0.00	1	0	0	0	1	1	0	0	0	1	1	.250
2001	Giants (AZL)	R	4	1	2.00	11	11	0	0	54	34	14	12	1	31	67	.182
	Salem-Keizer (NWL)	A	1	1	2.08	3	3	0	0	13	8	5	3	1	8	19	.170
2002	Hagerstown (SAL)	A	7	6	2.80	24	24	1	0	132	129	54	41	9	46	145	.256
	San Jose (Cal)	A	0	0	3.00	1	1	0	0	6	3	2	2	1	3	7	.158
2003	San Jose (Cal)	A	4	4	4.71	13	13	1	0	63	66	41	33	7	32	77	.260
	Giants (AZL)	R	1	1	4.38	4	4	0	0	12	8	6	6	0	7	14	.190
	Frederick (Car)	A	1	3	3.79	5	5	0	0	19	14	9	8	2	17	22	.206
MINOR LEAGUE TOTALS			18	17	3.35	67	61	2	0	303	267	139	113	21	156	358	.235

12 Jose Bautista, 3b

Born: Oct. 19, 1980. **Ht.:** 6-0. **Wt.:** 190. **Bats:** R. **Throws:** R. **School:** Chipola (Fla.) JC. **Career Transactions:** Selected by Pirates in 20th round of 2000 draft; signed May 19, 2001 . . . Selected by Orioles from Pirates in Rule 5 major league draft, Dec.15, 2003.

Bautista has as high a ceiling as any 2003 major league Rule 5 pick. Pittsburgh drafted him in 2000 and signed him as a draft-and-follow the following spring after he was the Florida junior college player of the year as a center fielder. The Pirates moved him to third base after signing him. Bautista has a quick bat and can catch up with the best fastballs. His power potential is his best tool. He shows good actions around third base and also has a strong arm. He's a streaky hitter who usually gets off to torrid starts before hitting a lull. While in a slump last May, he punched a garbage can after a strikeout, breaking his right hand and costing him 2½ months. Bautista is a good athlete, but that hasn't always translated to the basepaths, where he tends to tread with caution. Though he hasn't played above high Class A, the Orioles say his versatility gives him a chance to stick on their 25-man roster. If he doesn't, they have to put him through waivers and offer him back to Pittsburgh for half the $50,000 draft price before sending him to the minors. Baltimore retained Rule 5 pick Jose Morban a year ago and will try to find a way to keep the much more talented Bautista.

Year	Club (League)	Class	AVG	G	AB	R	H	2B	3B	HR	RBI	BB	SO	SB	SLG	OBP
2001	Williamsport (NY-P)	A	.286	62	220	43	63	10	3	5	30	21	41	8	.427	.364
2002	Hickory (SAL)	A	.301	129	438	72	132	26	3	14	57	67	104	3	.470	.402
2003	Lynchburg (Car)	A	.242	51	165	28	40	14	2	4	20	27	48	1	.424	.359
	Pirates (GCL)	R	.348	7	23	5	8	1	0	1	3	4	7	0	.522	.429
MINOR LEAGUE TOTALS			.287	249	846	148	243	51	8	24	110	119	200	12	.452	.385

13 Chris Ray, lhp

Born: Jan. 12, 1982. **Ht.:** 6-3. **Wt.:** 200. **Bats:** R. **Throws:** R. **School:** College of William & Mary. **Career Transactions:** Selected by Orioles in third round of 2003 draft; signed July 10, 2003.

Ray was a potential first-round pick for the 2003 draft after putting up a 1.93 ERA with 10 saves in the Cape Cod League the previous summer. He moved into the William & Mary rotation last spring to more fully develop his assortment of pitches, but he struggled with the adjustment and fell to the third round. That still made him the highest draftee in school history. He pitched in the short-season Aberdeen rotation and showed the great fastball that is his calling card. He throws it at 93-95 mph, and it was clocked as high as 98 in college. He also has a hard slider with late bite. His splitter is effective, but Baltimore isn't sure he should use it extensively, and his changeup needs work. Ray has a loose arm but is inconsistent with his mechanics, sometimes rushing his lower half or showing effort in his delivery. Ray was able to dominate in the New York-Penn League by blowing people away, and he'll move up to one of the Orioles' Class A stops to see if he can do the same to more advanced hitters. He'll remain a starter for now but could become a power reliever.

Year	Club (League)	Class	W	L	ERA	G	GS	CG	SV	IP	H	R	ER	HR	BB	SO	AVG
2003	Aberdeen (NY-P)	A	2	0	2.82	9	8	0	0	38	32	15	12	0	10	44	.225
MINOR LEAGUE TOTALS			2	0	2.82	9	8	0	0	38	32	15	12	0	10	44	.225

14 Brian Finch, rhp

Born: Sept. 27, 1981. **Ht.:** 6-4. **Wt.:** 195. **Bats:** R. **Throws:** R. **School:** Texas A&M University. **Career Transactions:** Selected by Orioles in second round of 2003 draft; signed June 13, 2003.

Finch was a 23rd-round draft pick of the Angels in 2000 but went to Texas A&M, where he never settled into a role. That made him a surprise as a second-round pick, but his early results make him look like a potential steal. Finch has a powerful build and a power arm. His fastball sits comfortably at 94-95 mph and ranges from 91-96. The sink on his heater is nearly as good as its velocity. His breaking pitch is a big knuckle-curve that's a potential plus pitch. He hasn't thrown his changeup a lot, but he does get good sinking action on it. Finch also has a good feel for pitching. The lone negative in his pro debut came when he was shut down with a strained elbow after pitching a combined 93 innings between college and Aberdeen. He's fine now and his health isn't a concern. Despite his initial success, he still has a lot of refinements to make, particularly with his changeup and command. Finch has a ceiling as a middle-of-the-rotation starter, and like Chris Ray he could fall back on a role as a late-inning reliever. He'll probably open his first full season in low Class A.

Year	Club (League)	Class	W	L	ERA	G	GS	CG	SV	IP	H	R	ER	HR	BB	SO	AVG
2003	Aberdeen (NY-P)	A	1	3	1.93	8	5	0	0	28	19	9	6	0	5	29	.183
MINOR LEAGUE TOTALS			1	3	1.93	8	5	0	0	28	19	9	6	0	5	29	.183

15 Daniel Cabrera, rhp

Born: May 28, 1981. **Ht.:** 6-7. **Wt.:** 220. **Bats:** R. **Throws:** R. **Career Transactions:** Signed out of Dominican Republic by Orioles, March 11, 1999.

After ranking third on this list a year ago, Cabrera was maddeningly inconsistent in his first full season. He reported to spring training late because he spent a few extra days with his ill mother back in the Dominican Republic. He still made the low Class A rotation and stayed in it throughout the season, mixing brilliant starts with brutal ones. In August, for example, he followed a stretch when he allowed one earned run in 17 innings by giving up seven runs (six earned) in 1⅓ innings. Cabrera has as high a ceiling as anyone in the organization because of his power arm, which generates mid-90s fastballs. He has a hard slider that also could be a plus pitch, and a developing changeup. His big problem is his command, which regressed in 2003. His inability to throw strikes consistently makes him run up high pitch counts, which gets him run out of games early. Most of his problems are mechanical, as he's still learning to handle his huge frame. He did pitch well enough to stay on the 40-man roster and move up to high Class A this year.

Year	Club (League)	Class	W	L	ERA	G	GS	CG	SV	IP	H	R	ER	HR	BB	SO	AVG
1999	Orioles (DSL)	R	2	4	4.71	14	10	1	0	57	60	42	30	3	42	74	.260
2000	Orioles (DSL)	R	8	1	2.52	12	10	2	0	71	45	26	20	3	38	44	.167
2001	Orioles (GCL)	R	2	3	5.53	12	7	0	0	41	31	29	25	1	39	36	.215
2002	Bluefield (Appy)	R	5	2	3.28	12	12	0	0	60	52	25	22	0	25	69	.234
2003	Delmarva (SAL)	A	5	9	4.24	26	26	1	0	125	105	74	59	6	78	120	.225
MINOR LEAGUE TOTALS			22	19	3.95	76	65	4	0	355	293	196	156	13	222	343	.220

16 Don Levinski, rhp

Born: Oct. 20, 1982. **Ht.:** 6-4. **Wt.:** 200. **Bats:** R. **Throws:** R. **School:** Weimar (Texas) HS. **Career Transactions:** Selected by Expos in second round of 2001 draft; signed Aug. 4, 2001 . . . Traded by Expos to Marlins, Aug. 5, 2002, completing trade in which Marlins sent OF Cliff Floyd, 2B Wilton Guerrero, RHP Claudio Vargas and cash to Expos for RHP Carl Pavano, LHP Graeme Lloyd, RHP Justin Wayne, 2B Mike Mordecai and a player to be named (July 11, 2002) . . . Traded by Marlins with RHP Denny Bautista to Orioles for 1B Jeff Conine, Aug. 31, 2003.

In little more than two years after being drafted, Levinski was traded twice. After each trade, he was shut down for the season. Levinski came down with a slight rotator-cuff tear just before he became the player to be named in a Cliff Floyd trade in 2002, but the Marlins elected to keep him in the deal. That problem cleared up, but when Levinski had shoulder discomfort after joining the Orioles in a deal for Jeff Conine, they played it safe. He didn't pitch until instructional league, and even there he only worked out in the bullpen. When healthy, Levinski throws a heavy 88-93 mph sinker and power curveball. His changeup still is developing. The Orioles also like his size and makeup. They've made adjustments to his arm action to try to relieve the stress on his shoulder. They also hope that will improve his command, which completely fell apart last year. Levinski should be 100 percent in spring training, and he'll likely return to high Class A as Baltimore tries to get him back on track.

Year	Club (League)	Class	W	L	ERA	G	GS	CG	SV	IP	H	R	ER	HR	BB	SO	AVG
2001	Expos (GCL)	R	0	0	3.46	3	3	0	0	13	15	5	5	1	7	15	.300
2002	Clinton (Mid)	A	12	6	3.02	21	21	1	0	119	92	48	40	6	55	125	.212
2003	Jupiter (FSL)	A	4	11	4.03	21	21	0	0	87	75	48	39	1	70	77	.235
MINOR LEAGUE TOTALS			16	17	3.45	45	45	1	0	219	182	101	84	8	132	217	.227

17 Eddy Rodriguez, rhp

Born: Aug. 8, 1981. **Ht.:** 6-1. **Wt.:** 194. **Bats:** R. **Throws:** R. **Career Transactions:** Signed out of Dominican Republic by Orioles, March 11, 1999.

Rodriguez steadily has pitched his way into the Orioles' plans, emerging as a legitimate prospect last season in Double-A. When Melvin Mora had a rehabilitation stint with the Baysox, he tabbed Rodriguez as the Bowie player who could contribute in the major leagues. Manager Dave Trembley called him the team's MVP, and he was promoted to Triple-A for the International League playoffs. Rodriguez throws 91-93 mph, but his fastball seems harder because of the funkiness in his delivery. He has a sharp slider, but not much of a change-up because he has been a reliever throughout his career. More important, he has ice water in his veins, shows poise on the mound and wants the ball every night. He still needs to improve his command and is learning to pitch. At his size, Rodriguez profiles more as set-up guy than a closer, but his future is definitely in the bullpen. He's slated for Triple-A to open 2004 and could reach Baltimore later in the year.

Year	Club (League)	Class	W	L	ERA	G	GS	CG	SV	IP	H	R	ER	HR	BB	SO	AVG
1999	Orioles (DSL)	R	2	2	4.78	25	0	0	8	49	51	35	26	5	21	47	.266

Year	Club (League)	Class	W	L	ERA	G	GS	CG	SV	IP	H	R	ER	HR	BB	SO	AVG
2000	Orioles (GCL)	R	2	1	2.00	18	0	0	6	27	17	8	6	0	19	31	.185
	Delmarva (SAL)	A	0	0	1.80	4	0	0	0	5	5	1	1	1	2	3	.263
2001	Delmarva (SAL)	A	5	3	3.39	41	0	0	1	61	58	27	23	4	23	64	.247
	Bowie (EL)	AA	1	1	2.08	5	0	0	2	9	7	2	2	0	6	10	.241
2002	Frederick (Car)	A	0	3	2.23	38	0	0	11	48	28	14	12	3	20	58	.169
	Bowie (EL)	AA	0	0	5.63	6	0	0	1	8	6	6	5	1	7	7	.200
2003	Bowie (EL)	AA	3	4	2.34	56	0	0	13	73	49	26	19	3	35	66	.188
MINOR LEAGUE TOTALS			13	14	3.02	193	0	0	42	280	221	119	94	17	133	286	.216

18 Brian Forystek, lhp

Born: Oct. 30, 1978. **Ht.:** 6-1. **Wt.:** 177. **Bats:** L. **Throws:** L. **School:** Illinois State University. **Career Transactions:** Selected by Orioles in 14th round of 2000 draft; signed June 26, 2000.

Signed out of Illinois State for $5,000, Forystek looked like an organizational player until last year. After he made eight scoreless relief appearances in Double-A, he got a chance to pitch in the rotation in May and ran with it. He made the Eastern League's midseason all-star team and finished ninth in the league in ERA. His turnaround was a combination of gaining confidence and command of his secondary pitches. His fastball is 88-89 mph, occasionally touching 90, with good sink and life. He got a handle on his changeup in 2002 and excelled with it in 2003. It gives him another weapon against righthanders, while his slider is more useful against lefties. Forystek commands those pitches better than his fastball, a point of emphasis for him going into 2004. He must be more effective against lefthanders, who batted .322 against him (compared to .228 for righties). He also has to get his lower half in better shape after tiring down the stretch. Forystek could become an end-of-the-rotation starter or middle reliever. He'll try to prove himself in Triple-A this year.

Year	Club (League)	Class	W	L	ERA	G	GS	CG	SV	IP	H	R	ER	HR	BB	SO	AVG
2000	Orioles (GCL)	R	4	0	3.72	11	0	0	1	19	18	10	8	1	8	28	.240
	Frederick (Car)	A	1	0	1.35	3	0	0	0	7	5	1	1	0	1	7	.185
2001	Frederick (Car)	A	1	3	2.88	41	1	0	0	59	61	27	19	3	30	68	.269
2002	Frederick (Car)	A	1	4	4.50	43	1	0	3	70	71	47	35	4	36	79	.258
2003	Bowie (EL)	AA	9	9	3.39	29	21	1	0	125	116	57	47	8	42	103	.251
MINOR LEAGUE TOTALS			16	16	3.54	127	23	1	4	280	271	142	110	16	117	285	.254

19 Lorenzo Scott, of

Born: March 1, 1982. **Ht.:** 6-3. **Wt.:** 210. **Bats:** L. **Throws:** L. **School:** Ball State University. **Career Transactions:** Selected by Orioles in 17th round of 2003 draft; signed June 9, 2003.

Scott was a two-sport performer at Ball State, earning much more acclaim for his football accomplishments as a linebacker. He led the Cardinals in tackles for three straight years and played baseball only sparingly, but area scout Marc Ziegler spotted him and persuaded the Orioles to take a 17th-round flier on him last June. Scott signed with the stipulation that he could return for his senior season of football. He once again topped Ball State in tackles, earning team MVP honors and all-Mid-American Conference recognition. While he played just 33 games in the Rookie-level Gulf Coast League, he made quite an impression with his athleticism. He has a body suited for the NFL, much less baseball. Though he's inexperienced, he had more polish than Baltimore thought he would. He showed off a tantalizing power-speed combination and plus range in the outfield. Pitchers were reluctant to challenge him, so he drew a lot of walks. What the Orioles liked most of all was his makeup and instincts. Scott will have to make more contact to succeed against better pitching, and he still needs to make up for his lack of experience. His potential is exciting and the Orioles will be patient, sending him to Aberdeen in 2004.

Year	Club (League)	Class	AVG	G	AB	R	H	2B	3B	HR	RBI	BB	SO	SB	SLG	OBP
2003	Orioles (GCL)	R	.319	33	116	30	37	8	4	0	24	25	28	11	.457	.441
MINOR LEAGUE TOTALS			.319	33	116	30	37	8	4	0	24	25	28	11	.457	.441

20 Walter Young, 1b/dh

Born: Feb. 18, 1980. **Ht.:** 6-5. **Wt.:** 290. **Bats:** L. **Throws:** R. **School:** Purvis (Miss.) HS. **Career Transactions:** Selected by Pirates in 31st round of 1999 draft; signed June 3, 1999 . . . Claimed on waivers by Orioles from Pirates, Nov. 20, 2003.

Before taking Jose Bautista from the Pirates in the major league Rule 5 draft, the Orioles snatched Young from Pittsburgh off waivers. He immediately became Baltimore's best first-base prospect and top power hitter in the minors. Young committed to play defensive end at Louisiana State until the Pirates swayed him with a $500,000 signing bonus in 1999. He broke through with an MVP performance in the low Class A South Atlantic League in 2002. He encored by leading the high Class A Carolina League in RBIs despite being slowed by a groin injury early last year. Young is a huge man with intriguing light-tower power. He's fairly mobile for a big man and has decent actions around first base, making plays on the balls he can reach. But his size is a major concern. It hampers his ability to get around on inside pitches or cover much ground defensively. He may profile best as a DH. Young also needs to improve his plate discipline. The Orioles will unleash him on Double-A to open 2004.

Year	Club (League)	Class	AVG	G	AB	R	H	2B	3B	HR	RBI	BB	SO	SB	SLG	OBP
1999	Pirates (GCL)	R	.231	37	130	9	30	6	2	0	15	4	34	2	.308	.270
2000	Pirates (GCL)	R	.296	45	162	32	48	11	1	10	34	8	29	3	.562	.357
	Williamsport (NY-P)	A	.185	24	92	5	17	4	0	2	12	1	26	0	.293	.200
2001	Williamsport (NY-P)	A	.289	66	232	40	67	10	1	13	47	19	43	1	.509	.353
2002	Hickory (SAL)	A	.333	132	492	84	164	34	2	25	103	36	102	2	.563	.390
2003	Lynchburg (Car)	A	.278	117	431	76	120	15	2	20	87	35	88	2	.462	.348
MINOR LEAGUE TOTALS			.290	421	1539	246	446	80	8	70	298	103	322	10	.489	.349

21 Carlos Perez, lhp

Born: May 20, 1982. **Ht.:** 6-1. **Wt.:** 185. **Bats:** L. **Throws:** L. **Career Transactions:** Signed out of Dominican Republic by Orioles, Sept. 9, 1999.

Perez has made steady progress as the Orioles have taken an exceptionally patient approach since signing him out of the Dominican in 1999. He still hasn't advanced past Rookie ball, but he made the step up from the Gulf Coast League to the Appalachian League in 2003 and finished fourth in the league in ERA. Toward the end of the season, he allowed two earned runs or fewer in six consecutive starts. Perez' biggest strength is his advanced command of three pitches, led by a low-90s fastball that touches 95 mph. He also has a sharp slider and a work-in-progress changeup. He's competitive and intelligent, and he already speaks English fluently. The Orioles will push him to low Class A in 2004.

Year	Club (League)	Class	W	L	ERA	G	GS	CG	SV	IP	H	R	ER	HR	BB	SO	AVG
2000	Orioles (DSL)	R	3	6	3.39	12	11	0	0	64	56	35	24	1	42	51	.242
2001	Orioles (GCL)	R	1	1	5.46	14	0	0	0	30	29	22	18	1	17	29	.246
2002	Orioles (GCL)	R	2	2	2.63	12	5	0	0	38	35	18	11	2	17	32	.257
2003	Bluefield (Appy)	R	5	5	2.01	12	11	0	0	58	52	23	13	4	11	58	.232
MINOR LEAGUE TOTALS			11	14	3.14	50	27	0	0	189	172	98	66	8	87	170	.243

22 Tripper Johnson, 3b

Born: April 28, 1982. **Ht.:** 6-1. **Wt.:** 200. **Bats:** R. **Throws:** R. **School:** Newport HS, Bellevue, Wash. **Career Transactions:** Selected by Orioles in first round (32nd overall) of 2000 draft; signed June 26, 2000.

Johnson had a storybook high school career in suburban Seattle. In addition to being a teammate of Rommie Lewis, he starred in basketball and football, winning The Seattle Times' male athlete of the year award in 2000. His pro career has proceeded more slowly, as he has moved a level at a time and hasn't had a breakout season yet. Johnson battled nagging back problems in 2003, which may have sapped his power. He has a potentially special bat and has improved his approach in the last couple of years, but he needs to hit the ball with authority more consistently. He has too many at-bats where he just puts the ball in play rather than driving it. Johnson also hasn't improved as much defensively as the Orioles had hoped. He'll have to work on his reactions as well as improving his quickness. Johnson could return to high Class A to open 2004 in hopes of getting him off to a hot start.

Year	Club (League)	Class	AVG	G	AB	R	H	2B	3B	HR	RBI	BB	SO	SB	SLG	OBP
2000	Orioles (GCL)	R	.306	48	180	22	55	5	3	2	33	13	38	7	.400	.355
2001	Bluefield (Appy)	R	.261	43	157	24	41	6	1	2	26	11	37	4	.350	.312
2002	Delmarva (SAL)	A	.260	136	493	73	128	32	6	11	71	62	88	19	.416	.349
2003	Frederick (Car)	A	.273	123	417	43	114	25	3	5	50	46	92	7	.384	.359
MINOR LEAGUE TOTALS			.271	350	1247	162	338	68	13	20	180	132	255	37	.395	.349

23 Mike Huggins, 1b

Born: Aug. 29, 1980. **Ht.:** 6-3. **Wt.:** 212. **Bats:** R. **Throws:** R. **School:** Baylor University. **Career Transactions:** Selected by Orioles in 13th round of 2002 draft; signed June 7, 2002.

Huggins is one of the organization's biggest overachievers. He was a football and baseball standout in high school in San Antonio, and was recruited by Big 12 Conference football programs before deciding to play baseball at Baylor. After redshirting in 1999, he was a three-year starter who turned down the Rockies in the 25th round as a draft-eligible sophomore. In his first full year as a pro, he led the organization in RBIs. Huggins has average tools across the board and plays above his ability. He has a good approach at the plate and should be a run producer. Baltimore hopes he'll continue the power growth he showed in 2003. Huggins is a good athlete for his size, making him an adequate first baseman and more than a clogger on the bases. He also has strong makeup, winning community-service awards from both his minor league team in Frederick and from the Orioles last year. Huggins is in line for a promotion to Double-A, but he'll have to compete with Walter Young and Doug Gredvig for at-bats. One of those players likely will be assigned elsewhere.

Year	Club (League)	Class	AVG	G	AB	R	H	2B	3B	HR	RBI	BB	SO	SB	SLG	OBP
2002	Aberdeen (NY-P)	A	.262	76	271	32	71	15	2	1	27	31	55	9	.343	.340
2003	Frederick (Car)	A	.293	126	454	66	133	32	0	13	74	55	93	3	.449	.367
MINOR LEAGUE TOTALS			.281	202	725	98	204	47	2	14	101	86	148	12	.410	.357

24 Eli Whiteside, c

Born: Oct. 22, 1979. **Ht.:** 6-2. **Wt.:** 213. **Bats:** R. **Throws:** R. **School:** Delta State (Miss.) University. **Career Transactions:** Selected by Orioles in sixth round of 2001 draft; signed June 7, 2001.

The Orioles drafted Whiteside because of his defensive skills, and he has lived up to his reputation. He has a strong body and an above-average arm, throwing out 37 percent of basestealers in Double-A last year. He still needs to work on his receiving skills and footwork. Most important, Whiteside has to improve offensively. He battled injuries throughout 2003, most notably a high ankle sprain, and hit a career-low .204. He went to the Arizona Fall League but played just one game before being shut down with elbow tendinitis. Whiteside needs at-bats, because if he can hit at all he'll be a big league backup on the strength of his defense. But while he has a little pop, he has a poor approach at the plate. He chases everything and might struggle to bat .230 in the majors. Despite his struggles, Whiteside remains the organization's top catching prospect. He'll return to Double-A in an effort to get his bat going.

Year	Club (League)	Class	AVG	G	AB	R	H	2B	3B	HR	RBI	BB	SO	SB	SLG	OBP
2001	Delmarva (SAL)	A	.250	61	212	30	53	11	0	7	28	9	45	1	.401	.300
2002	Frederick (Car)	A	.259	80	313	34	81	19	0	8	42	14	57	0	.396	.296
	Bowie (EL)	AA	.263	27	99	11	26	5	0	2	11	4	18	0	.374	.311
2003	Bowie (EL)	AA	.204	81	265	21	54	13	1	1	23	5	44	0	.272	.230
	Orioles (GCL)	R	.333	1	3	0	1	1	0	0	1	1	0	0	.667	.500
	Aberdeen (NY-P)	A	.700	2	10	0	7	3	0	0	4	0	1	1	1.000	.700
MINOR LEAGUE TOTALS			.246	252	902	96	222	52	1	18	108	33	166	2	.366	.285

25 Darnell McDonald, of

Born: Nov. 17, 1978. **Ht.:** 5-11. **Wt.:** 208. **Bats:** R. **Throws:** R. **School:** Cherry Creek HS, Englewood, Colo. **Career Transactions:** Selected by Orioles in first round (26th overall) of 1997 draft; signed Aug. 8, 1997.

What was supposed to be McDonald's long-awaited breakout year didn't happen. Ranked No. 2 on this list a year ago, he looked like he was about to fulfill his first-round promise after his 2002 performance, and he said he had rediscovered his passion for the game. After his mother died of a heart attack in 1999, McDonald said it took him several years to get over it. He was a two-sport star in high school in Colorado, and the Orioles gave him a $1.9 million bonus to keep him from going to Texas as a running back. He opened 2003 in Triple-A and got off to a solid start, but he tore the labrum in his right shoulder and had surgery in May, ending his year. Like his brother Donzell, McDonald is a standout athlete with a dazzling package of tools. His bat has started to come around as he has shown more patience and a much better approach. Yet he never has been able to translate his strength into power, and he has good speed but not enough to steal many bases or quite handle center field. Better suited for an outfield corner defensively, he'll need to show more pop to fit the offensive profile there. He's expected to be healthy for spring training and will return to Triple-A. The Orioles kept him on their 40-man roster, so they expect him to bounce back.

Year	Club (League)	Class	AVG	G	AB	R	H	2B	3B	HR	RBI	BB	SO	SB	SLG	OBP
1998	Delmarva (SAL)	A	.261	134	528	87	138	24	5	6	44	33	117	35	.360	.308
	Frederick (Car)	A	.222	4	18	3	4	2	0	1	2	3	6	2	.500	.333
1999	Frederick (Car)	A	.266	130	507	81	135	23	5	6	73	61	92	26	.367	.347
2000	Bowie (EL)	AA	.242	116	459	59	111	13	5	6	43	29	87	11	.331	.290
2001	Bowie (EL)	AA	.282	30	117	16	33	7	1	3	21	9	28	3	.436	.336
	Rochester (IL)	AAA	.238	104	391	37	93	19	2	2	35	29	75	13	.312	.291
2002	Bowie (EL)	AA	.292	37	144	21	42	9	1	4	15	22	27	9	.451	.393
	Rochester (IL)	AAA	.289	91	332	43	96	21	6	6	35	32	78	11	.443	.353
2003	Ottawa (IL)	AAA	.296	40	152	19	45	7	1	0	20	18	27	5	.355	.374
MINOR LEAGUE TOTALS			.263	686	2648	366	697	125	26	34	288	236	537	115	.369	.326

26 Jose Morban, ss/2b

Born: Dec. 2, 1979. **Ht.:** 6-1. **Wt.:** 170. **Bats:** R. **Throws:** R. **Career Transactions:** Signed out of Dominican Republic by Rangers, Dec. 15, 1996 . . . Selected by Twins from Rangers in Rule 5 major league draft, Dec. 16, 2002 . . . Claimed on waivers by Orioles from Twins, March 28, 2003.

Morban came up in the Rangers organization but was taken by the Twins in the major league Rule 5 draft in December 2002. Minnesota couldn't keep him on its big league roster and had to place him on waivers, where the Orioles grabbed him. Baltimore kept him in the majors all season while getting him limited work. Morban is an athletic, toolsy middle infielder. He has the defensive skills and arm to play anywhere in the infield. Baltimore has talked about moving him to third base because of Miguel Tejada's presence at shortstop and a glut of talent at second. The problem is that his bat won't play at the hot corner unless Morban makes major strides. He hadn't played above high Class A when he became a Rule 5 pick, and he showed poor pitch recognition and plate discipline in the minors. Morban does have some pop but needs to shorten his swing to make better contact. He also has plus speed. In spite of his flaws, he's the organization's best shortstop prospect, though he might eventually fit best as a utility player. The Orioles will give him a full season in the minors, starting in Double-A, to see exactly what they have.

Year	Club (League)	Class	AVG	G	AB	R	H	2B	3B	HR	RBI	BB	SO	SB	SLG	OBP
1997	Rangers (DSL)	R	.313	13	16	5	5	0	0	0	2	4	7	3	.313	.450
1998	Rangers (DSL)	R	.232	54	168	31	39	10	5	4	25	24	35	13	.423	.338
1999	Rangers (GCL)	R	.283	54	205	45	58	10	5	4	18	31	70	19	.439	.378
2000	Savannah (SAL)	A	.220	80	273	44	60	8	4	4	28	41	79	27	.322	.330
	Pulaski (Appy)	R	.225	30	120	21	27	3	2	3	17	12	35	6	.358	.293
2001	Savannah (SAL)	A	.251	122	474	71	119	20	11	8	47	42	119	46	.390	.313
2002	Charlotte (FSL)	A	.260	126	485	75	126	27	12	8	66	46	111	21	.414	.326
2003	Baltimore (AL)	MAJ	.141	61	71	14	10	0	0	2	5	3	21	8	.225	.187
MAJOR LEAGUE TOTALS			.141	61	71	14	10	0	0	2	5	3	21	8	.225	.187
MINOR LEAGUE TOTALS			.249	479	1741	292	434	78	39	31	203	200	456	135	.392	.330

27 Tim Raines Jr., of

Born: Aug. 31, 1979. **Ht.:** 5-10. **Wt.:** 189. **Bats:** R. **Throws:** R. **School:** Seminole HS, Sanford, Fla. **Career Transactions:** Selected by Orioles in sixth round of 1998 draft; signed June 15, 1998.

Raines completed a remarkable turnaround in 2003, going off the Orioles' 40-man roster and getting back on within a year. Raines, who debuted in the big leagues in 2001 and got the opportunity to play with his father Tim Sr., was sent back to Double-A in 2002 and performed poorly. His attitude also didn't endear him to the organization, and he was designated for assignment in January 2003. He returned to Bowie and got back on track, earning promotions to Triple-A and then to the majors. Baltimore kept him on the 40-man roster after the season. As it was for his father, speed is Raines' best tool. He's a basestealing threat and an outstanding defender in center field. He has improved his approach at the plate and made better contact last year, though he has to prove he can do the same in the big leagues. He looked overmatched by major league pitching at times. Raines still doesn't hustle all the time, failing to run after a ball that went over his head in a game against the Blue Jays, for instance. Still, his speed and defense give him a chance to make the Baltimore roster as a backup outfielder. If his offense continues to progress, he eventually could be a starter.

Year	Club (League)	Class	AVG	G	AB	R	H	2B	3B	HR	RBI	BB	SO	SB	SLG	OBP
1998	Orioles (GCL)	R	.244	56	197	40	48	7	4	1	13	30	53	37	.335	.377
1999	Delmarva (SAL)	A	.248	117	415	80	103	24	8	2	49	71	130	49	.359	.359
2000	Frederick (Car)	A	.236	127	457	89	108	21	3	2	36	67	106	81	.309	.348
2001	Frederick (Car)	A	.250	23	84	15	21	3	1	3	13	13	23	14	.417	.351
	Bowie (EL)	AA	.291	65	254	46	74	14	1	4	30	34	60	29	.402	.380
	Rochester (IL)	AAA	.256	40	133	19	34	5	1	2	12	11	30	11	.353	.313
	Baltimore (AL)	MAJ	.174	7	23	6	4	2	0	0	0	3	8	3	.261	.269
2002	Bowie (EL)	AA	.261	123	491	66	128	17	4	5	25	34	101	33	.342	.310
2003	Bowie (EL)	AA	.308	66	247	44	76	15	4	4	26	21	40	28	.449	.371
	Ottawa (IL)	AAA	.299	52	214	37	64	11	5	3	23	19	37	23	.439	.357
	Baltimore (AL)	MAJ	.140	20	43	4	6	1	1	0	2	2	12	0	.209	.196
MAJOR LEAGUE TOTALS			.152	27	66	10	10	3	1	0	2	5	20	3	.227	.222
MINOR LEAGUE TOTALS			.263	669	2492	436	656	117	31	26	227	300	580	305	.366	.350

28 Richard Stahl, lhp

Born: April 11, 1981. **Ht.:** 6-7. **Wt.:** 222. **Bats:** R. **Throws:** L. **School:** Newton HS, Covington, Ga. **Career Transactions:** Selected by Orioles in first round (18th overall) of 1999 draft; signed Aug. 31, 1999.

No. 1 on this list just two years ago, Stahl serves as the representative for the Orioles' flock of talented but oft-injured pitching prospects. Along with first-round picks Beau Hale and Chris Smith, Stahl is expected to be healthy for spring training and anxious to put his arm troubles behind them. Baltimore didn't protect any of them on its 40-man roster, but no team took them in the major league Rule 5 draft. Though Stahl has pitched sparingly the last three years because of back and shoulder injuries, he still has the biggest upside of the group. He stayed in extended spring training last year with a strained lower back, but stayed healthy once he reported to low Class A. The Orioles used him cautiously out of the bullpen, seeking only to keep him in one piece and to get his confidence back. His results weren't good, but that was a minor consideration. When healthy, Stahl has a mid-90s fastball and a curveball that's a potential second plus pitch. Because he has been missed so much time, his changeup is unrefined and his mechanics are out of whack. He doesn't throw as free and easy as he once did, leading to command problems. He has worked with roving pitching instructor Moe Drabowsky to get a consistent, smooth delivery. Stahl likely will head back to low Class A, where he'll get a chance to pitch in the rotation.

Year	Club (League)	Class	W	L	ERA	G	GS	CG	SV	IP	H	R	ER	HR	BB	SO	AVG
2000	Delmarva (SAL)	A	5	6	3.34	20	20	0	0	89	97	47	33	3	51	83	.280
2001	Delmarva (SAL)	A	2	3	2.67	6	6	0	0	34	24	15	10	3	15	31	.205
	Frederick (Car)	A	1	1	1.95	6	6	1	0	32	26	13	7	1	15	24	.232
	Orioles (GCL)	R	0	0	0.00	1	1	0	0	2	1	0	0	0	1	1	.167
2002	Delmarva (SAL)	A	1	1	5.59	2	2	0	0	10	10	8	6	3	5	9	.278
2003	Delmarva (SAL)	A	1	3	5.48	28	1	0	1	48	47	41	29	4	50	46	.261
MINOR LEAGUE TOTALS			10	14	3.57	63	36	1	1	214	205	124	85	14	137	194	.257

29 Aaron Rakers, rhp

Born: Jan. 22, 1977. **Ht.:** 6-3. **Wt.:** 205. **Bats:** R. **Throws:** R. **School:** Southern Illinois University-Edwardsville. **Career Transactions:** Selected by Orioles in 23rd round of 1999 draft; signed June 7, 1999.

A teammate of Dave Crouthers at Southern Illinois-Edwardsville, Rakers continues to inch toward a possible big league bullpen job. After spending parts of four seasons in Double-A, he finally moved up to Triple-A and has put elbow problems behind him. Though he sometimes struggled with Ottawa because of command problems, he made up for that performance with a strong Arizona Fall League, going 5-0, 1.96 with a 24-4 strikeout-walk ratio in 18 innings. Rakers' out pitch is his splitter, but there's concern that big league hitters will lay off it and sit on his fastball, which is 90 mph and tends to straighten out. Rakers has become more effective against lefthanders, so now he just needs to show the same command that he did in the AFL. He'll be a darkhorse candidate for the big league bullpen in spring training but more likely will return to Triple-A to start the season.

Year	Club (League)	Class	W	L	ERA	G	GS	CG	SV	IP	H	R	ER	HR	BB	SO	AVG
1999	Bluefield (Appy)	R	0	0	2.57	3	0	0	0	7	5	2	2	1	3	12	.200
	Delmarva (SAL)	A	4	1	1.42	18	0	0	8	25	9	6	4	0	13	38	.108
2000	Frederick (Car)	A	1	1	1.55	26	0	0	8	41	23	8	7	2	12	57	.163
	Bowie (EL)	AA	3	2	2.79	24	0	0	8	29	20	11	9	5	10	21	.194
2001	Bowie (EL)	AA	4	4	2.39	51	0	0	14	60	53	21	16	8	20	74	.227
2002	Bowie (EL)	AA	5	1	2.06	36	0	0	10	48	39	12	11	3	12	45	.232
2003	Bowie (EL)	AA	5	0	2.75	31	0	0	8	39	27	12	12	7	19	42	.196
	Ottawa (IL)	AAA	2	4	5.13	21	0	0	1	26	19	18	15	1	11	26	.202
MINOR LEAGUE TOTALS			24	13	2.48	210	0	0	57	276	195	90	76	27	100	315	.198

30 Bryan Bass, ss

Born: April 12, 1982. **Ht.:** 6-1. **Wt.:** 180. **Bats:** B. **Throws:** R. **School:** Seminole (Fla.) HS. **Career Transactions:** Selected by Orioles in first round (31st overall) of 2001 draft; signed July 13, 2001.

Bass' tools alone would put him among the elite prospects in the organization, but the way he uses them threatens his future. He grew up in Alabama and moved to Florida in his draft year to get more exposure, but an eligibility snafu kept him off the field. The Orioles still gave him a $1.15 million bonus to lure him away from a football scholarship to play wide receiver at Alabama. Bass looked like he would be worth the investment in his pro debut, but he has regressed since. Last year was a disaster, as he played poorly while repeating low Class A and was worse after a demotion to Aberdeen. Bass could be a standout offensive player if he made consistent contact, as he has shown the ability to drive the ball from both sides of the plate. His defense similarly has deteriorated each year in spite of his physical ability. He committed 52 errors between his two stops last year. It's probably time to move him over to third base. More than anything else, Bass needs to mature and come to the field ready to play every day. Like many young players, he has excelled with pure ability for so long that it's taking time for him to figure out how to work. Bass is still young, so the Orioles haven't given up on him, but he needs to show something this season.

Year	Club (League)	Class	AVG	G	AB	R	H	2B	3B	HR	RBI	BB	SO	SB	SLG	OBP
2001	Orioles (GCL)	R	.297	21	74	12	22	3	6	0	7	5	25	4	.500	.333
	Bluefield (Appy)	R	.324	19	71	17	23	6	1	5	20	10	17	0	.648	.407
2002	Delmarva (SAL)	A	.221	130	457	60	101	20	7	6	59	40	146	15	.335	.299
2003	Delmarva (SAL)	A	.205	60	205	23	42	8	7	0	21	21	58	7	.312	.284
	Aberdeen (NY-P)	A	.193	70	254	26	49	11	1	2	14	24	75	11	.268	.273
MINOR LEAGUE TOTALS			.223	300	1061	138	237	48	22	13	121	100	321	37	.347	.300

BOSTON
RED SOX

After their first full year with John Henry as owner and Theo Epstein as general manager, it's abundantly clear that these are not the Red Sox of old. Or even of the turn of the millennium. They may have finished second in the American League East for the sixth straight season and had their hearts broken by the Yankees yet again in 2003. But the Sox also implemented several changes designed to overtake New York as the long-term team to beat in baseball's most competitive division.

When the Red Sox named Epstein GM in November 2003, there was much ado about how he became the youngest GM in big league history at 28. Youth aside, Epstein has established himself as an intelligent and relentless executive. He helped steer Boston to its first postseason berth since 1999 with a series of successful signings (Mike Timlin, Bill Mueller, David Ortiz) and trades (Todd Walker, Byung-Hyun Kim, Scott Williamson), plus one creative purchase (getting Kevin Millar out of a deal to play in Japan). Epstein made only two regrettable moves, signing free agent Ramiro Mendoza and trading Freddy Sanchez, who could fill the club's second-base hole, for Scott Sauerbeck and Jeff Suppan.

Henry made a fortune in the investment business by analyzing market trends and relying on data and formulas. He wants his team run in the same fashion. That's why Boston hired adviser Bill James, who popularized the statistical analysis of baseball with his Baseball Abstracts in the 1980s. That's also why former manager Grady Little's tenure was doomed before he left Pedro Martinez in to pitch the eighth inning of the AL Championship Series. The Red Sox also have applied a statistical approach in areas beyond the big league team. They've shifted their focus in the draft to college players, taking just one high schooler with their first 18 choices in 2003. When looking for minor league coaches and instructors, they've checked how teams performed under those men.

Thanks to the offseason additions of Curt Schilling and Keith Foulke, Boston may have supplanted New York as the AL East favorite in 2004. Restocking the farm system is going to take significantly longer. Epstein's resourcefulness and the team's willingness to take on payroll have helped make up for a lack of minor league talent, but that can't last indefinitely.

It's too early to know for sure, but the Red Sox appear to have taken a positive first step forward with the 2003 draft. Cuban righty Gary Galvez and Dominican shortstop Luis Soto highlighted Boston's international efforts. Shortly after signing Soto, however, director of international scouting Louie Eljaua took a job with the Pirates.

TOP 30 PROSPECTS

1. Hanley Ramirez, ss
2. Kelly Shoppach, c
3. David Murphy, of
4. Kevin Youkilis, 3b
5. Matt Murton, of
6. Chad Spann, 3b
7. Abe Alvarez, lhp
8. Jon Lester, lhp
9. Juan Cedeno, lhp
10. Manny Delcarmen, rhp
11. Luis Mendoza, rhp
12. Anastacio Martinez, rhp
13. Mickey Hall, of
14. Jon Papelbon, rhp
15. Beau Vaughan, rhp
16. Jerome Gamble, rhp
17. Charlie Zink, rhp
18. Dustin Brown, c
19. Aneudis Mateo, rhp
20. Tim Hamulack, lhp
21. Gary Galvez, rhp
22. Luis Soto, ss
23. Billy Simon, rhp
24. Jessie Corn, rhp
25. Mark Malaska, lhp
26. Jamie Brown, rhp
27. Kyle Jackson, rhp
28. Jose Vaquedano, rhp
29. Carlos Morla, rhp
30. Harvey García, rhp

By Jim Callis

ORGANIZATION
OVERVIEW

General manager: Theo Epstein. **Farm director:** Ben Cherington. **Scouting director:** David Chadd.

2003 PERFORMANCE

Class	Team	League	W	L	Pct.	Finish*	Manager
Majors	Boston	American	95	67	.586	3rd (30)	Grady Little
Triple-A	Pawtucket Red Sox	International	83	61	.576	1st (14)	Buddy Bailey
Double-A	Portland Sea Dogs	Eastern	72	70	.507	t-5th (12)	Ron Johnson
High A	Sarasota Red Sox	Florida State	63	67	.485	8th (12)	Tim Leiper
Low A	Augusta GreenJackets	South Atlantic	49	87	.360	16th (16)	Russ Morman
Short-season	Lowell Spinners	New York-Penn	39	35	.527	6th (14)	Jon Deeble
Rookie	GCL Red Sox	Gulf Coast	33	26	.559	3rd (14)	Ralph Treuel
OVERALL 2003 MINOR LEAGUE RECORD			339	345	.496	18th (30)	

*Finish in overall standings (No. of teams in league)

ORGANIZATION LEADERS

BATTING
*Minimum 250 At-Bats
*AVG	Sean McGowan, Portland/Sarasota	.320
R	Kevin Youkilis, Pawtucket/Portland	83
H	Andy Abad, Pawtucket	153
TB	Andy Abad, Pawtucket	233
2B	Andy Abad, Pawtucket	35
3B	Anton French, Pawtucket	10
HR	Earl Snyder, Pawtucket	22
RBI	Andy Abad, Pawtucket	93
BB	Kevin Youkilis, Pawtucket/Portland	104
SO	Jeremy Owens, Portland	161
SB	Anton French, Pawtucket	40
*SLG	Andy Dominique, Pawtucket/Portland	.508
*OBP	Kevin Youkilis, Pawtucket/Portland	.441

PITCHING
#Minimum 75 Innings
W	Bronson Arroyo, Pawtucket	12
L	Luis Villarreal, Augusta	11
#ERA	Jamie Brown, Pawtucket	2.95
G	Three tied at	51
CG	Tim Kester, Portland	3
SV	Juan Perez, Portland/Sarasota	18
IP	Charlie Zink, Portland/Sarasota	175
BB	Charlie Zink, Portland/Sarasota	78
SO	Bronson Arroyo, Pawtucket	155

BEST TOOLS

Best Hitter for Average	Kevin Youkilis
Best Power Hitter	Matt Murton
Fastest Baserunner	Jeremy Owens
Best Athlete	Hanley Ramirez
Best Fastball	Juan Cedeno
Best Curveball	Anastacio Martinez
Best Slider	Jessie Corn
Best Changeup	Abe Alvarez
Best Control	Abe Alvarez
Best Defensive Catcher	Edgar Martinez
Best Defensive Infielder	Ignacio Suarez
Best Infield Arm	Hanley Ramirez
Best Defensive Outfielder	Jeremy Owens
Best Outfield Arm	Willy Mota

PROJECTED 2007 LINEUP

Catcher	Jason Varitek
First Base	David Ortiz
Second Base	Hanley Ramirez
Third Base	Kevin Youkilis
Shortstop	Nomar Garciaparra
Left Field	David Murphy
Center Field	Johnny Damon
Right Field	Trot Nixon
Designated Hitter	Manny Ramirez
No. 1 Starter	Pedro Martinez
No. 2 Starter	Derek Lowe
No. 3 Starter	Abe Alvarez
No. 4 Starter	Byung-Hyun Kim
No. 5 Starter	Jon Lester
Closer	Keith Foulke

LAST YEAR'S TOP 20 PROSPECTS

1. Hanley Ramirez, ss	11. Michael Goss, of
2. Kelly Shoppach, c	12. Dustin Brown, c/of
3. Kevin Youkilis, 3b	13. Scott White, 3b
4. Freddy Sanchez, ss/2b	14. Andy Shibilo, rhp
5. Phil Dumatrait, lhp	15. Kason Gabbard, lhp
6. Manny Delcarmen, rhp	16. Rene Miniel, rhp
7. Billy Simon, rhp	17. Chris Smith, rhp
8. Jon Lester, lhp	18. Anastacio Martinez, rhp
9. Jorge de la Rosa, lhp	19. Chad Spann, 3b
10. Aneudis Mateo, rhp	20. Matt White, lhp

TOP PROSPECTS OF THE DECADE

1994	Trot Nixon, of
1995	Nomar Garciaparra, ss
1996	Donnie Sadler, ss
1997	Nomar Garciaparra, ss
1998	Brian Rose, rhp
1999	Dernell Stenson, of
2000	Steve Lomasney, c
2001	Dernell Stenson, of/1b
2002	Seung Song, rhp
2003	Hanley Ramirez, ss

TOP DRAFT PICKS OF THE DECADE

1994	Nomar Garciaparra, ss
1995	Andy Yount, rhp
1996	John Garrett, rhp
1997	John Curtice, rhp
1998	Adam Everett, ss
1999	Rick Asadoorian, of
2000	Phil Dumatrait, lhp
2001	Kelly Shoppach, c (2)
2002	Jon Lester, lhp (2)
2003	David Murphy, of

ALL-TIME LARGEST BONUSES

Adam Everett, 1998	$1,725,000
Rick Asadoorian, 1998	$1,725,000
David Murphy, 2003	$1,525,000
Phil Dumatrait, 2000	$1,250,000
Robinson Checo, 1996	$1,150,000

MINOR LEAGUE
DEPTH CHART

BOSTON RED SOX   RANK: 24

Impact potential (C): Hanley Ramirez could still turn out to be a frontline star, but he'll have to improve upon last season's performance, on and off the field.

Depth (D): The 2003 draft helped stock a barren system. Their focus on college players will help address their needs in the upper levels. Boston's top five prospects are position players, though the club has tried to address its need for pitching through the draft and Latin America.

Sleeper: Charlie Zink, rhp.   —Depth charts prepared by **Josh Boyd**. Numbers in parentheses indicate prospect rankings.

LF
Matt Murton (5)

CF
David Murphy (3)
Chris Turner
Robert Evans
Chris Durbin

RF
Mickey Hall (13)
Brandon Moss
Claudio Arias

3B
Kevin Youkilis (4)
Chad Spann (6)
Heriberto Guzman
Scott White

SS
Hanley Ramirez (1)
Luis Soto (22)
Alex Penalo
Christian Lara

2B
Kenny Perez

1B
Jeremy West
John Hattig
Carlos Torres

SOURCE OF TALENT

Homegrown		Acquired	
College	8	Trade	2
Junior College	1	Rule 5 draft	0
Draft-and-follow	2	Independent	1
High school	6	Free agent/waivers	3
Nondrafted free agent	0		
Foreign	7		

C
Kelly Shoppach (2)
Dustin Brown (18)
Michel Hernandez
Salvador Paniagua
Andy Dominique

RHP

Starters	Relievers
Manny Delcarmen (10)	Luis Mendoza (11)
Jon Papelbon (14)	Anastacio Martinez (12)
Beau Vaughan (15)	Jerome Gamble (16)
Charlie Zink (17)	Jessie Corn (24)
Aneudis Mateo (19)	Jamie Brown (26)
Gary Galvez (21)	Carlos Morla (29)
Billy Simon (23)	Jason Shiell
Kyle Jackson (27)	Edwin Almonte
Jose Vaquedano (28)	Bryan Hebson
Harvey Garcia (30)	Colter Bean
Jesus Delgado	Kevin Huang
Chris Smith	

LHP

Starters	Relievers
Abe Alvarez (7)	Tim Hamulack (20)
Jon Lester (8)	Mark Malaska (25)
Juan Cedeno (9)	Lenny DiNardo
Kason Gabbard	Phil Seibel
David Sanders	Brian Marshall
Adam Blackley	
Mario Pena	

DRAFT
ANALYSIS

Best Pro Debut: LHPs Abe Alvarez (2) and Justin Sturge (12) backed up their reputations as control specialists. Alvarez didn't allow an earned run in nine short-season starts. Sturge went 4-0, 1.08 with a 36-6 K-BB ratio in 42 innings overall.

Best Athlete: The Red Sox added several quality athletes to a system sorely in need of them. OFs David Murphy (1), Mickey Hall (2), Chris Durbin (10) and Chris Turner (15) are multi-tooled players, and Boston believes they all have good chances to play center field.

Best Pure Hitter: OF Matt Murton (1) over Murphy and Hall. Murton flourished with wood bats in the Cape Cod League the last two summers.

Best Raw Power: Murton. His bat and power are plus tools, and his speed and range are average. The only tool he's lacking is arm strength, relegating him to left field.

Fastest Runner: Turner has plus speed. Most of the Red Sox' position-player picks are average runners.

Best Defensive Player: SS Ignacio Suarez (24) can field with any shortstop in the system, but hit .222 with short-season Lowell.

Best Fastball: RHP Jon Papelbon (4) pitches at 89-94 mph and reaches 96 mph out of the bullpen. RHP Jason Smith (49) hit 95-96 mph last summer but pitched at 88-92 as a high school senior.

Papelbon

Best Breaking Ball: RHP Beau Vaughan (3) has three average or better pitches, starting with his slider. Vaughan adds a 90-94 mph fastball and a changeup.

Most Intriguing Background: The Red Sox drafted four relatives of their employees. Only C Erich Cloninger (35), the grandson of Boston pitching coach Tony Cloninger, turned pro. LHP Brian Marshall's (5) twin brother Sean signed with the Cubs as a sixth-round pick.

Closest To The Majors: As an advanced lefthander in a thin system, Alvarez will get to the big leagues faster than most 2003 draftees. The Red Sox signed only two high school players.

Best Late-Round Pick: LHP David Sanders (30), Smith and Turner all have much more upside than their draft position would indicate. Turner and Smith were considered tough signs. Sanders showed three fringe-average pitches on the Cape in 2002.

The One Who Got Away: Six-foot-5, 230-pound OF Josh Morris (20) would have given the Red Sox another athletic outfielder if he hadn't decided to go to Georgia.

Assessment: Boston shifted its focus heavily to college players, with Hall and Smith its only high school signees. The Red Sox added athletes and players who could advance quickly to restock the upper levels of their system.

2002 DRAFT   GRADE: C

The Red Sox had no first-rounder and may rue not signing RHP Jason Neighborgall (7). But they did grab LHP Jon Lester (2) and 3B Chad Spann (6), plus trade bait with LHP Tyler Pelland (9) and OF Mike Goss (11).

2001 DRAFT   GRADE: C+

Boston again didn't pick until the second round, but found two potential big league regulars in C Kelly Shoppach (2) and 3B Kevin Youkilis (8).

2000 DRAFT   GRADE: C+

The Red Sox traded their best picks in this draft, SS Freddy Sanchez (11) and LHP Phil Dumatrait (1). RHP Manny Delcarmen (2) has a higher ceiling than either but must come back from Tommy John surgery.

1999 DRAFT   GRADE: C

All three first-rounders—LHP Casey Fossum, RHP Brad Baker and OF Rick Asadoorian— have been dealt, and only Fossum looks like he'll be productive. Boston also traded OF Lew Ford (12) and won't reap any direct benefits from this draft.

—Draft analysis prepared by Jim Callis. Numbers in parentheses indicate draft rounds.

STEVE MOORE

Hanley
Ramirez

Born: Dec. 23, 1983.
Ht.: 6-1. **Wt.:** 170.
Bats: B. **Throws:** R.
Career Transactions: Signed out of Dominican Republic by Red Sox, July 2, 2000.

While the Red Sox have Nomar Garciaparra and pursued a trade for Alex Rodriguez, they have another potential five-tool shortstop coming up in Ramirez. His first two pro seasons were nothing short of sensational, as he batted a combined .349/.400/.541. He was Boston's Rookie-level Dominican Summer Player of the Year in 2001, and the No. 1 prospect in both the Rookie-level Gulf Coast and short-season New York-Penn leagues as an encore. Ramirez' ascent slowed in 2003, his first exposure to full-season ball. He started slowly at low Class A Augusta, then was banished to extended spring training for 10 days in early May after he made an obscene gesture to fans in a game at South Georgia. He settled down after he returned and finished with steady if not spectacular numbers for a teenaged infielder in the South Atlantic League. Though he didn't tear up low Class A or force a midseason promotion, the Red Sox are pleased with what they call a solid developmental year.

Tampa Bay's B.J. Upton is the only minor league shortstop whose raw tools compare to Ramirez'. He's the best athlete and has the strongest infield arm in the Red Sox system—and he's most dangerous at the plate. Ramirez has quick hands, a smooth stroke and lots of bat speed. He has pitch recognition beyond his years, so he's not vulnerable to breaking balls and is able to hit deep in counts. If he puts it all together, he could be a .300/.370/.500 shortstop in the majors. He improved his baserunning skills in 2003, and his combination of speed and aggressiveness makes him a stolen base threat. His arm also got better last year, as he maintained plus arm strength throughout the season for the first time. He has classic shortstop actions and reliable hands. The Red Sox have tried to temper the hype swirling around Ramirez because it has come so quickly that he hasn't handled it well. His May suspension wasn't an isolated incident. He was sent home from instructional league in 2002 after he cursed at a trainer. Ramirez did a better job of keeping his composure and acting more professionally when he came back from extended spring training. He needs to let the game come to him instead of trying to do too much. Ramirez is too worried about hitting the ball out of the park, so he lengthens his swing and gets overaggressive. He should be able to work counts and draw walks, but his impatience often gets the best of him. He made 36 errors at Augusta, mostly on throws where he had little chance to get the runner or where he just got careless.

Once Ramirez becomes a true professional, he should take off. The Red Sox hope that will happen in 2004 at high Class A Sarasota. If Boston re-signs Garciaparra, Ramirez could become a valuable trading chip.

Year	Club (League)	Class	AVG	G	AB	R	H	2B	3B	HR	RBI	BB	SO	SB	SLG	OBP
2001	Red Sox (DSL)	R	.345	54	197	32	68	18	2	5	34	15	22	13	.533	.397
2002	Red Sox (GCL)	R	.341	45	164	29	56	11	3	6	26	16	15	8	.555	.402
	Lowell (NY-P)	A	.371	22	97	17	36	9	2	1	19	4	14	4	.536	.400
2003	Augusta (SAL)	A	.275	111	422	69	116	24	3	8	50	32	73	36	.403	.327
MINOR LEAGUE TOTALS			.314	232	880	147	276	62	10	20	129	67	124	61	.475	.365

2 Kelly Shoppach, c

Born: April 29, 1980. **Ht.:** 5-11. **Wt.:** 210. **Bats:** R. **Throws:** R. **School:** Baylor University. **Career Transactions:** Selected by Red Sox in second round of 2001 draft; signed Aug. 17, 2001.

Shoppach was the first college catcher drafted in 2001, and Boston's top pick (second round) after it forfeited its first-round selection for signing Manny Ramiez. After rotator-cuff surgery last offseason, he was back catching by late April and hit throughout the regular season and the Arizona Fall League. Managers rated Shoppach the best defensive backstop in the Double-A Eastern League, and his arm bounced back fine as he threw out 31 percent of basestealers. While his catch-and-throw skills and take-charge leadership stand out the most, he's also a capable hitter. He has a line-drive approach that generates gap power, and he also has the patience that the Red Sox value. In the AFL, Shoppach's receiving was sloppy. The Red Sox believe he got tired and needs to improve his conditioning. With 195 strikeouts in 208 pro games, he'll have to close some holes in his swing before he gets to the majors. He's a below-average runner. Shoppach's game is similar to all-star Jason Varitek's. If the Red Sox let Varitek walk as a free agent after 2004, Shoppach could be ready to step in following a season at Triple-A Pawtucket.

Year	Club (League)	Class	AVG	G	AB	R	H	2B	3B	HR	RBI	BB	SO	SB	SLG	OBP
2002	Sarasota (FSL)	A	.271	116	414	54	112	35	1	10	66	59	112	2	.432	.369
2003	Portland (EL)	AA	.282	92	340	45	96	30	2	12	60	35	83	0	.488	.353
MINOR LEAGUE TOTALS			.276	208	754	99	208	65	3	22	126	94	195	2	.458	.362

3 David Murphy, of

Born: Oct. 18, 1981. **Ht.:** 6-4. **Wt.:** 192. **Bats:** L. **Throws:** L. **School:** Baylor University. **Career Transactions:** Selected by Red Sox in first round (17th overall) of 2003 draft; signed June 12, 2003.

For the second time in three years, Baylor produced Boston's top draft pick. Murphy's stock began to rise in the Cape Cod League during the summer of 2002 and didn't stop until he went 17th overall last June. The Red Sox adore Murphy's approach at the plate, exemplified by his first two pro at-bats. He took the first eight pitches he saw, drawing a walk and working a 3-0 count before lacing an opposite-field double on his first swing. He may be able to stick in center field after Chris Durbin (Boston's 10th-round pick) kept him in right at Baylor. Murphy's arm and speed are solid average. While Murphy has raw power, he'll need to add strength and more loft to his swing in order to tap into it. He's still learning to play center field and lacks the speed usually associated with the position, though his instincts and athleticism work in his favor. Murphy will return to high Class A after scuffling there in 2003. Ideally, he'd be ready for Boston when Johnny Damon's contract ends after the 2005 season.

Year	Club (League)	Class	AVG	G	AB	R	H	2B	3B	HR	RBI	BB	SO	SB	SLG	OBP
2003	Lowell (NY-P)	A	.346	21	78	13	27	4	0	0	13	16	9	4	.397	.453
	Sarasota (FSL)	A	.242	45	153	18	37	5	1	1	18	20	33	6	.307	.329
MINOR LEAGUE TOTALS			.277	66	231	31	64	9	1	1	31	36	42	10	.338	.373

4 Kevin Youkilis, 3b

Born: March 15, 1979. **Ht.:** 6-1. **Wt.:** 220. **Bats:** R. **Throws:** R. **School:** University of Cincinnati. **Career Transactions:** Selected by Red Sox in eighth round of 2001 draft; signed June 11, 2001.

Youkilis already has exceeded expectations for an eighth-round senior sign. In 2003 alone, he played in the Futures Game, led the Eastern League in on-base percentage, finished third in the minors with an overall .441 OBP and reached base in 71 consecutive games. Youkilis is an on-base machine. His controlled, line-drive approach frustrates pitchers. An intensive workout regimen last offseason has helped make him into an average defender and a decent athlete. Despite Youkilis' plate discipline, he has yet to show much power. He drove the ball more often after adjusting his hands toward the end of his tenure at Double-A Portland, but reverted to his previous form once he slumped at Pawtucket. Pitchers exploited Youkilis' patience there, so he'll have to get more aggressive earlier in the count. He's a below-average runner. Often compared to Bill Mueller, Youkilis eventually will have to unseat the defending AL batting champion to win Boston's third-base job. He's ticketed for a return to Triple-A in 2004.

Year	Club (League)	Class	AVG	G	AB	R	H	2B	3B	HR	RBI	BB	SO	SB	SLG	OBP
2001	Lowell (NY-P)	A	.317	59	183	52	58	14	2	3	28	70	28	4	.464	.512
	Augusta (SAL)	A	.167	5	12	0	2	0	0	0	0	3	3	0	.167	.375
2002	Augusta (SAL)	A	.283	15	53	5	15	5	0	0	6	13	8	0	.377	.433
	Sarasota (FSL)	A	.295	76	268	45	79	16	0	3	48	49	37	0	.388	.422
	Trenton (EL)	AA	.344	44	160	34	55	10	0	5	26	31	18	5	.500	.462
2003	Portland (EL)	AA	.327	94	312	74	102	23	1	6	37	86	40	7	.465	.487
	Pawtucket (IL)	AAA	.165	32	109	9	18	3	0	2	15	18	21	0	.248	.295
MINOR LEAGUE TOTALS			.300	325	1097	219	329	71	3	19	160	270	155	16	.422	.451

5 Matt Murton, of

RODGER WOOD

Born: Oct. 3, 1981. **Ht.:** 6-1. **Wt.:** 215. **Bats:** R. **Throws:** R. **School:** Georgia Tech. **Career Transactions:** Selected by Red Sox in first round (32nd overall) of 2003 draft; signed July 8, 2003.

Murton and fellow 2003 first-rounder David Murphy teamed to win back-to-back Cape Cod League championships in 2001-02. Chris Durbin, Boston's 10th-round pick in 2003, completed the 2002 Wareham outfield. Initially projected as a first-rounder, Murton lasted 32 picks in June because he slumped as a junior. He got pull conscious and lengthened his swing last spring, but he hits better with wood bats because he shortens his stroke and lets his power come naturally. The Cape's 2002 home run derby winner, he has more pop than any hitter in the system. Boston makes all of its players in Class A or below keep notebooks on hitting, something Murton already did on his own. He runs well for his size and is a four-tool player. His weak arm relegates him to left field. His swing has more effort than Murphy's does. If he gets much bigger or stronger, his speed and range likely will dip below average. Murton will reunite with Murphy again in 2004, this time in high Class A. If all goes as expected, they'll play together again, this time in Boston, by mid-2006.

Year	Club (League)	Class	AVG	G	AB	R	H	2B	3B	HR	RBI	BB	SO	SB	SLG	OBP
2003	Lowell (NY-P)	A	.286	53	189	30	54	11	2	2	29	27	39	9	.397	.374
MINOR LEAGUE TOTALS			.286	53	189	30	54	11	2	2	29	27	39	9	.397	.374

6 Chad Spann, 3b

DAVID SCHOFIELD

Born: Oct. 25, 1983. **Ht.:** 6-1. **Wt.:** 190. **Bats:** R. **Throws:** R. **School:** Southland Academy, Americus, Ga. **Career Transactions:** Selected by Red Sox in fifth round of 2002 draft; signed June 10, 2002.

Drafted from a private high school in rural Georgia, Spann faced a huge jump in competition when he turned pro. His work ethic and maturity convinced the Red Sox he could handle low Class A in 2003, and he became Augusta's player of the year and a South Atlantic League all-star. Spann has an advanced hitting gameplan, especially considering his age and background. For now he's content to make contact and use the middle of the field, but he should develop average to plus power once he gets stronger and more pull conscious. A football and basketball star in high school, he's more athletic than most third basemen. Though managers named Spann the SAL's best defender at third base, he's still a work in progress. His arm and range are fine but can improve, and his hands aren't especially soft. He doesn't draw as many walks as the Red Sox would like. The organization's most improved player in 2003, Spann will join a prospect-laden Sarasota club this year. Bill Mueller and Kevin Youkilis are formidable obstacles ahead of him at third base.

Year	Club (League)	Class	AVG	G	AB	R	H	2B	3B	HR	RBI	BB	SO	SB	SLG	OBP
2002	Red Sox (GCL)	R	.222	57	203	20	45	8	3	6	28	12	37	1	.379	.271
2003	Augusta (SAL)	A	.312	116	414	55	129	21	3	5	63	40	64	9	.413	.379
MINOR LEAGUE TOTALS			.282	173	617	75	174	29	6	11	91	52	101	10	.402	.345

7 Abe Alvarez, lhp

RICH ABEL

Born: Oct. 17, 1982. **Ht.:** 6-2. **Wt.:** 190. **Bats:** L. **Throws:** L. **School:** Long Beach State University. **Career Transactions:** Selected by Red Sox in second round (49th overall) of 2003 draft; signed June 27, 2003.

Alvarez pitched just three innings as a Long Beach State freshman in 2001, then was Big West Conference pitcher of the year in each of the next two seasons. Eased into pro ball with tight pitch counts, he didn't allow an earned run in 19 innings at short-season Lowell. The Red Sox put a premium on pitching savvy, and Alvarez is loaded with it. He has the best command and changeup in the system, and his 85-88 mph fastball is arguably the best as well because he effortlessly pains the black with it. Alvarez also has a big league average curveball and an uncanny knack for varying speeds, looks and locations. He has a gift for discerning a hitter's weakness and exploiting it to get outs, and shuts down the running game with his pickoff move. Alvarez' below-average velocity will draw its share of skeptics. A childhood accident left him legally blind in one eye, but it doesn't hamper him on the mound. Alvarez will open 2004 in high Class A and should reach Boston quickly because he's a lefty who knows how to pitch. He has a ceiling as a No. 3 starter.

Year	Club (League)	Class	W	L	ERA	G	GS	CG	SV	IP	H	R	ER	HR	BB	SO	AVG
2003	Lowell (NY-P)	A	0	0	0.00	9	9	0	0	19	9	2	0	0	2	19	.138
MINOR LEAGUE TOTALS			0	0	0.00	9	9	0	0	19	9	2	0	0	2	19	.138

8 Jon Lester, lhp

RODGER WOOD

Born: Jan. 7, 1984. **Ht.:** 6-3. **Wt.:** 200. **Bats:** L. **Throws:** L. **School:** Bellarmine Prep, Puyallup, Wash. **Career Transactions:** Selected by Red Sox in second round of 2002 draft; signed Aug. 13, 2002.

If the Red Sox had pulled off the Alex Rodriguez trade, Lester would have been headed to Texas. And if they adopted their college emphasis a year earlier, it's unlikely they would have spent their first pick (second round) in 2002 on him. Signability concerns knocked him out of the first round, but he turned pro for $1 million. A former basketball standout and a legitimate prospect as a first baseman, Lester has good athletic ability. That allows him to repeat his delivery, locate pitches on both sides of the plate and keep the ball down in the zone. He has an 88-92 mph fastball and the makings of an average curveball, average-to-plus changeup and plus command. His feel, presence and cerebral approach are impressive for his age. Lester needs time to develop his stuff and strength. He missed a start in May with shoulder tightness and was kept on a 70-80 pitch count down the stretch. Ready for high Class A, Lester is at least 2½ years away from the majors.

Year	Club (League)	Class	W	L	ERA	G	GS	CG	SV	IP	H	R	ER	HR	BB	SO	AVG
2002	Red Sox (GCL)	R	0	1	13.50	1	1	0	0	1	5	6	1	0	1	1	.714
2003	Augusta (SAL)	A	6	9	3.65	24	21	0	0	106	102	54	43	7	44	71	.262
MINOR LEAGUE TOTALS			6	10	3.71	25	22	0	0	107	107	60	44	7	45	72	.270

9 Juan Cedeno, lhp

RODGER WOOD

Born: Aug. 19, 1983. **Ht.:** 6-1. **Wt.:** 175. **Bats:** L. **Throws:** L. **Career Transactions:** Signed out of Dominican Republic by Red Sox, Jan. 5, 2001.

Cedeno came to the United States in 2002 and made an impression in instructional league, where he blew away Minnesota's Joe Mauer in two at-bats. In his first full season last year, he had a 10.29 ERA in April and a 2.48 mark afterward. He allowed three or fewer earned runs in 18 of his last 19 outings. Cedeno has the best fastball in the system. He sat at 92-93 mph and touched 95 last summer, and reportedly hit 97 this winter in the Dominican League. He resembles countryman Pedro Martinez with a small, thin body, big hands and quick arm. He spins his curveball well and it could give him a second plus pitch. He's competitive and confident. He needs to understand that less can be more. Cedeno is enthralled with his fastball and overthrows it. He tries to hit 100 mph while the Red Sox want him to be content at 92-93 with more strikes and life. His changeup lags behind his heater and curve. Cedeno's velocity, approach and stuff may fit better in the bullpen in the long term. He'll remain in the rotation this year in high Class A.

Year	Club (League)	Class	W	L	ERA	G	GS	CG	SV	IP	H	R	ER	HR	BB	SO	AVG
2001	Red Sox (DSL)	R	3	3	3.38	14	14	0	0	64	45	30	24	0	37	77	.198
2002	Red Sox (GCL)	R	2	5	4.19	11	7	0	0	43	55	31	20	1	12	32	.297
2003	Augusta (SAL)	A	7	9	3.02	23	21	0	0	101	87	38	34	8	44	87	.235
MINOR LEAGUE TOTALS			12	17	3.37	48	42	0	0	208	187	99	78	9	93	196	.239

10 Manny Delcarmen, rhp

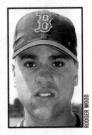

RODGER WOOD

Born: Feb. 16, 1982. **Ht.:** 6-2. **Wt.:** 190. **Bats:** R. **Throws:** R. **School:** West Roxbury (Mass.) HS. **Career Transactions:** Selected by Red Sox in second round of 2000 draft; signed Aug. 22, 2000.

Delcarmen entered 2003 with the highest ceiling of any Red Sox pitching prospect. He tied a career high with 11 strikeouts in his second start and was improving rapidly, pushing for a promotion to Double-A by the end of April. Then he blew out his elbow throwing a changeup in his fourth outing and had Tommy John surgery in May. Delcarmen always showed arm strength as a pro, regularly hitting 92-94 mph. He excited the Red Sox by making the transition from thrower to pitcher in high Class A. He improved his fastball command, delivery and mental approach. He made the most strides with his changeup, showing a willingness to throw it after finding a new grip. His curveball already was a plus pitch at times. He has worked diligently in rehabilitation, turning himself into a better athlete. Reconstructive elbow surgery will cost Delcarmen critical development time. Boston won't know if his stuff will bounce back until 2005, though he will return to the mound in June. If he can regain his form, he can be a front-of-the-rotation starter.

Year	Club (League)	Class	W	L	ERA	G	GS	CG	SV	IP	H	R	ER	HR	BB	SO	AVG
2001	Red Sox (GCL)	R	4	2	2.54	11	8	0	1	46	35	16	13	0	19	62	.211
2002	Augusta (SAL)	A	7	8	4.10	26	24	0	0	136	124	77	62	15	56	136	.242
2003	Sarasota (FSL)	A	1	1	3.13	4	3	0	0	23	16	9	8	1	7	16	.200
MINOR LEAGUE TOTALS			12	11	3.64	41	35	0	1	205	175	102	83	16	82	214	.231

11 Luis Mendoza, rhp

Born: Oct. 31, 1983. **Ht.:** 6-3. **Wt.:** 180. **Bats:** L. **Throws:** R. **Career Transactions:** Signed out of Mexico by Red Sox, July 12, 2000.

Mendoza's fastball has steadily improved since he signed in 2000. His velocity was 83-85 mph at that point, improved to 87-91 in 2002 and was 91-94 in 2003. He's one of the most coveted Red Sox pitchers in trade talks. Now Mendoza must achieve similar improvement with his curveball and changeup. They're the culprits responsible for him striking out less than one batter every two innings last year despite his plus fastball. His curve is a lazy, off-speed breaking ball that's effective about one of every three times he throws it. He does show feel for the changeup and for pitching overall. And while Mendoza hasn't blown hitters away yet, they haven't made good contact against him either. He throws strikes and has an easy, consistent delivery that allows him to pitch to the bottom of the strike zone. It's hard to drive his fastball because it sinks and bores in on righthanders. Mendoza is intelligent and learned English quickly. He lost two months of development time when a line drive broke his right foot, though he did return with a strong performance in August. He'll continue to work on his secondary pitches in high Class A this year.

Year	Club (League)	Class	W	L	ERA	G	GS	CG	SV	IP	H	R	ER	HR	BB	SO	AVG
2001	San Joaquin (VSL)	R	6	0	2.27	13	9	0	1	67	46	20	17	0	10	61	—
2002	Ciudad Alianza (VSL)	R	0	3	3.03	15	4	0	2	36	44	29	12	2	15	32	.293
	Red Sox (GCL)	R	3	4	4.21	13	10	0	1	58	76	36	27	3	8	21	.329
2003	Augusta (SAL)	A	3	3	2.26	13	11	0	0	60	46	19	15	1	14	29	.210
	Red Sox (GCL)	R	0	0	0.00	2	2	0	0	5	4	0	0	0	0	3	.222
MINOR LEAGUE TOTALS			12	10	2.84	56	36	0	4	225	216	104	71	6	47	146	.275

12 Anastacio Martinez, rhp

Born: Nov. 3, 1978. **Ht.:** 6-2. **Wt.:** 180. **Bats:** R. **Throws:** R. **Career Transactions:** Signed out of Dominican Republic Red Sox, Jan. 6, 1998 . . . Traded by Red Sox with RHP Brandon Lyon to Pirates for LHP Scott Sauerbeck and LHP Mike Gonzalez, July 22, 2003 . . . Traded by Pirates with RHP Jeff Suppan and RHP Brandon Lyon to Red Sox for SS Freddy Sanchez, LHP Mike Gonzalez and cash, July 31, 2003.

If the condition of Brandon Lyon's elbow hadn't been disputed, Martinez would be a Pirate. They went to Pittsburgh last July for Scott Sauerbeck and minor league lefty Mike Gonzalez, but when the Pirates insisted Lyon wasn't healthy, the Red Sox gave up top second-base prospect Freddy Sanchez and returned Gonzalez for Jeff Suppan, Lyon and Martinez. After struggling as a starter in Double-A in 2002, Martinez returned to the bullpen last year and had much more success. His fastball sat at 92-95 mph in his new role, and it's an explosive pitch that can sink or bore in the last few feet before it gets to the plate. He has the best curveball in the system, a power breaker that isn't consistent. He had an average changeup early in his career as a starter but got away from throwing it and it isn't what it used to be. Though Martinez is hard to hit, he doesn't throw enough strikes to be trusted as a closer. He's more suited as a sixth- or seventh-inning set-up man. He also has to watch his weight. Martinez pitched well in Triple-A during August and the playoffs, and after returning there to start 2004 he could help Boston in the second half.

Year	Club (League)	Class	W	L	ERA	G	GS	CG	SV	IP	H	R	ER	HR	BB	SO	AVG
1998	Red Sox (DSL)	R	0	1	13.50	2	2	0	0	7	13	11	10	0	7	8	.433
	Red Sox (GCL)	R	2	3	3.18	12	10	0	0	51	45	28	18	2	12	50	.232
1999	Augusta (SAL)	A	2	4	6.30	10	10	0	0	40	44	37	28	7	18	36	.262
	Lowell (NY-P)	A	0	3	3.68	11	11	0	0	51	61	36	21	4	18	43	.289
2000	Augusta (SAL)	A	9	6	4.64	23	23	0	0	120	130	69	62	8	50	107	.279
	Red Sox (GCL)	R	0	1	9.45	2	1	0	0	7	15	9	7	0	3	1	.441
2001	Sarasota (FSL)	A	9	12	3.35	25	24	1	0	145	130	69	54	12	39	123	.236
2002	Trenton (EL)	AA	5	12	5.31	27	27	0	0	139	152	98	82	12	75	127	.276

Year	Club (League)	Class	W	L	ERA	G	GS	CG	SV	IP	H	R	ER	HR	BB	SO	AVG
2003	Portland (EL)	AA	3	1	2.25	34	0	0	14	40	31	13	10	3	24	37	.212
	Altoona (EL)	AA	0	0	2.25	3	0	0	0	4	6	1	1	1	1	1	.400
	Pawtucket (IL)	AAA	2	1	1.93	8	0	0	0	14	12	3	3	2	3	15	.226
MINOR LEAGUE TOTALS			32	44	4.31	157	108	1	14	618	639	374	296	51	250	548	.264

13 Mickey Hall, of

Born: May 20, 1985. **Ht.:** 6-1. **Wt.:** 195. **Bats:** L. **Throws:** L. **School:** Walton HS, Marietta, Ga. **Career Transactions:** Selected by Red Sox in second round of 2003 draft; signed July 11, 2003.

Outfield was the weakest position in the Red Sox system entering 2003 and they addressed it in the draft, loading up with David Murphy (first round), Matt Murton (supplemental first), Hall (second), Chris Durbin (10th) and Chris Turner (15th). Had he not signed for $800,000, Hall would have replaced Murton in the lineup at Georgia Tech, where his brother Jake is an infielder. One of only two high school signees by Boston, Hall has good baseball skills but lacks the strength needed for pro ball, Hall is physically mature and was able to make the jump successfully. Boston looked past its college focus and took Hall in part because he has a mature approach for a teenaged hitter. He has a pretty lefthanded swing and plus-plus bat speed, and the Red Sox like his strike-zone knowledge. He will have to make adjustments, such as adding loft to his swing to hit for power and getting a little more aggressive so he won't fall behind in the count against better pitching. Hall is one of the better athletes in the system, running a 6.65-second 60-yard dash and throwing 88 mph off the mound in high school. Boston has entertained the possibility that he could play center field but he fits better in right, where he played in the Gulf Coast League. His arm is accurate as well as strong. Because Hall is advanced for his age and has a strong instructional league, he likely will open 2004 in low Class A at age 18.

Year	Club (League)	Class	AVG	G	AB	R	H	2B	3B	HR	RBI	BB	SO	SB	SLG	OBP
2003	Red Sox (GCL)	R	.227	21	66	7	15	6	0	0	9	19	24	1	.318	.400
MINOR LEAGUE TOTALS			.227	21	66	7	15	6	0	0	9	19	24	1	.318	.400

14 Jon Papelbon, rhp

Born: Nov. 23, 1980. **Ht.:** 6-4. **Wt.:** 230. **Bats:** R. **Throws:** R. **School:** Mississippi State University. **Career Transactions:** Selected by Red Sox in fourth round of 2003 draft; signed June 12, 2003.

Though Papelbon never started a game in three years at Mississippi State, the Red Sox believe he can pitch in the rotation. He split time between starting and relieving in his pro debut, being kept on tight pitch counts and having more success than his numbers would indicate. Papelbon has the strong, durable frame and stuff to make the conversion work. His fastball usually sits at 92-93 mph and ranges from 89-96. His slider fluctuates from 45-60 on the 20-80 scouting scale. The changeup is a relatively new pitch for him, but his feel for it is promising. Papelbon was more of a thrower in 2002, when the Athletics drafted him in the 40th round as a sophomore-eligible, but is becoming a more savvy pitcher. With his size and quick arm, he pitches on a nice downward angle and gets good life on his pitches. He has good control but must improve his pitch selection with runners on base. He'll work out of the rotation in low Class A this year.

Year	Club (League)	Class	W	L	ERA	G	GS	CG	SV	IP	H	R	ER	HR	BB	SO	AVG
2003	Lowell (NY-P)	A	1	2	6.34	13	6	0	0	33	43	23	23	2	9	36	.312
MINOR LEAGUE TOTALS			1	2	6.34	13	6	0	0	33	43	23	23	2	9	36	.312

15 Beau Vaughan, rhp

Born: June 4, 1981. **Ht.:** 6-4. **Wt.:** 230. **Bats:** B. **Throws:** R. **School:** Arizona State University. **Career Transactions:** Selected by Red Sox in third round of 2003 draft; signed June 23, 2003.

Vaughan wasn't drafted out of Phoenix Junio College (2000), South Mountain (Ariz.) Community College (2001) or New Orleans (2002), so he transferred to Arizona State and blossomed into a third-round pick. He's similar to Jon Papelbon, who went one round later last June. They're the same size and have similar stuff, though Papelbon's is slightly better. They're two of the more physical pitchers in the system. Vaughan's best pitch is his 90-94 mph fastball, though he doesn't throw it enough. He has an 82-84 mph slider that he used to trick college hitters using aluminum bats, and the Red Sox are trying to get him to understand that his fastball will work better against wood. His changeup is better than Papelbon's, but his command, delivery and conditioning aren't quite as good. Vaughan and Papelbon should move through the minors together, beginning 2004 in the low Class A rotation.

Year	Club (League)	Class	W	L	ERA	G	GS	CG	SV	IP	H	R	ER	HR	BB	SO	AVG
2003	Lowell (NY-P)	A	1	0	2.32	11	6	0	0	31	27	8	8	1	15	30	.235
MINOR LEAGUE TOTALS			1	0	2.32	11	6	0	0	31	27	8	8	1	15	30	.235

16 Jerome Gamble, rhp

Born: April 5, 1980. **Ht.:** 6-2. **Wt.:** 200. **Bats:** R. **Throws:** R. **School:** Benjamin Russell HS, Alexander City, Ala. **Career Transactions:** Selected by Red Sox in fourth round of 1998 draft; signed June 9, 1998 . . . Selected by Reds from Red Sox in Rule 5 major league draft, Dec. 16, 2002 . . . Returned to Red Sox, March 7, 2003.

The Red Sox left Gamble and Wil Ledezma their 40-man roster after the 2002 season because both had a long history of injuries and had worked a combined eight innings above low Class A. The Reds took Gamble and the Tigers selected Ledezma in the major league Rule 5 draft, but Gamble returned to Boston after failing to retire a batter in his lone big league spring-training appearance for Cincinnati. Gamble has one of the best arms in the Red Sox system. Strong and athletic, he throws a 92-94 mph fastball. At times he'll get good spin on a 12-6 breaking ball that some consider the best curve in the system. But it's inconsistent, and both his curveball and changeup need refinement. More than anything, Gamble must stay healthy. They 87 innings he logged in 2003 represented a career high, and he missed seven weeks with a sore elbow. Gamble also had elbow soreness in 2000, a precursor to Tommy John surgery the following year. His arm action has changed since the operation, making it more difficult for him to stay on top of his curveball. He'll pitch in Double-A in 2004.

Year	Club (League)	Class	W	L	ERA	G	GS	CG	SV	IP	H	R	ER	HR	BB	SO	AVG
1998	Red Sox (GCL)	R	2	3	4.43	11	6	0	1	43	33	24	21	4	19	49	.204
1999	Lowell (NY-P)	A	1	0	1.75	5	5	0	0	26	18	7	5	1	9	37	.196
2000	Augusta (SAL)	A	5	3	2.52	15	15	0	0	79	69	26	22	1	32	71	.235
2001	Sarasota (FSL)	A	0	0	7.88	3	2	0	1	8	11	8	7	0	4	7	.333
2002	Augusta (SAL)	A	1	2	1.82	14	14	0	0	49	34	12	10	2	22	42	.192
2003	Sarasota (FSL)	A	6	4	3.66	17	14	0	0	76	68	36	31	2	21	51	.239
	Portland (EL)	AA	2	0	4.91	2	2	0	0	11	10	6	6	0	1	11	.238
MINOR LEAGUE TOTALS			17	12	3.15	67	58	0	2	292	243	119	102	10	108	268	.224

17 Charlie Zink, rhp

Born: Aug. 26, 1979. **Ht.:** 6-1. **Wt.:** 190. **Bats:** R. **Throws:** R. **School:** Savannah (Ga.) School of Art and Design. **Career Transactions:** Signed by independent Yuma (Western), Aug. 2001 . . . Signed by Red Sox, April 1, 2002.

The premier knuckleballer in the minor leagues, Zink's entered pro ball as a conventional pitcher. He was undrafted out of the Savannah College of Art and Design, where his college coach was former Red Sox great Luis Tiant. Zink hooked up with an independent Western League team and was toying with trying to make the PGA golf tour before Boston signed him on Tiant's recommendation. In 2002, he excelled as a low Class A reliever by keeping hitters off balance with a hard, overhand curveball he could throw for strikes at any time in the count. Zink also dabbled with a knuckleball that caught the eye of minor league pitching coordinator Goose Gregson. The Red Sox gave Zink two options for 2003: He could stay with his normal stuff and pitch in the high Class A bullpen, or become a full-time knuckleballer and move to the rotation. Zink chose the latter and did more than Boston expected. He met with big league knuckleballer Tim Wakefield in spring training and joined Sarasota after two weeks of preparing for the transition in extended spring. Gregson says Charlie Hough told him years ago to stick with any fledgling knuckleballer who could throw one good floater out of 10. Gregson estimates that Zink threw 30 percent quality knucklers in 2003. It's a legitimate swing-and-miss pitch and he commands it as well as can be expected. He has the fearless mentality required to live and die with the knuckler. He finished the season strong in Double-A in August, coming within one out of a no-hitter in his final start, and did OK in the Arizona Fall League. The Red Sox say Zink's knuckleball will continue to improve and are certain that he'll pitch in the majors. He's still learning to adapt his other pitches to the knuckleball delivery. He must use the same motion so hitters won't know what's coming. Zink had an 86-87 mph fastball in 2002 and he's aiming for the low 80s as a knuckleballer. His curveball isn't as sharp because he can't stay on top of it, though he still throws it for strikes. He throws the knuckler roughly 90 percent of the time. Zink will begin 2004 in Double-A, and if he can continue to progress at the same rate he did last year, he could help the Red Sox by the end of the season.

Year	Club (League)	Class	W	L	ERA	G	GS	CG	SV	IP	H	R	ER	HR	BB	SO	AVG
2001	Yuma (West)	IND	0	0	5.40	4	0	0	0	5	4	3	3	1	4	6	.235
2002	Augusta (SAL)	A	1	2	1.68	26	0	0	0	48	42	17	9	1	16	48	.240
	Sarasota (FSL)	A	0	0	0.00	4	0	0	0	9	2	1	0	0	3	11	.071
2003	Sarasota (FSL)	A	7	9	3.90	24	19	2	0	136	123	69	59	10	64	94	.245
	Portland (EL)	AA	3	2	3.43	6	6	0	0	39	21	16	15	1	14	18	.154
MINOR LEAGUE TOTALS			11	13	3.21	60	25	2	0	233	188	103	83	12	97	171	.224

18 Dustin Brown, c

Born: June 19, 1982. **Ht.:** 6-0. **Wt.:** 180. **Bats:** R. **Throws:** R. **School:** Yavapai (Ariz.) JC. **Career Transactions:** Selected by Red Sox in 35th round of 2000 draft; signed May 25, 2001.

Jason Varitek and Kelly Shoppach loom large at the top of the organization ladder, but the Red Sox also like Brown's potential behind the plate. He does too, after showing reluctance to catch and seeing time in right field in 2002. Brown's first season as a full-time catcher went well, with the exception of a nagging hamstring injury that bothered him through June. He didn't cross the Mendoza Line for good until May 31, but once he was healthy he hit .297/.363/.442 over the last two months. Brown has promising raw power that he hasn't tapped into and the ability to draw walks. He's a good athlete for a catcher and was a sound defensive right fielder. He has a strong arm and should improve his receiving and success rate nabbing basestealers (28 percent in 2003) once he gets more experience. His game-calling skills already have improved noticeably. Brown will catch in high Class A this year.

Year	Club (League)	Class	AVG	G	AB	R	H	2B	3B	HR	RBI	BB	SO	SB	SLG	OBP
2001	Red Sox (GCL)	R	.254	36	126	15	32	5	4	0	14	7	24	1	.357	.289
2002	Red Sox (GCL)	R	.321	45	159	28	51	12	2	1	20	23	24	11	.440	.404
	Lowell (NY-P)	A	.282	21	78	12	22	3	1	0	12	8	20	1	.346	.371
2003	Augusta (SAL)	A	.263	87	285	27	75	17	6	2	41	37	69	7	.386	.358
MINOR LEAGUE TOTALS			.278	189	648	82	180	37	13	3	87	75	137	20	.389	.359

19 Aneudis Mateo, rhp

Born: Oct. 3, 1982. **Ht.:** 6-4. **Wt.:** 180. **Bats:** R. **Throws:** R. **Career Transactions:** Signed out of Dominican Republic by Red Sox, March 17, 2000.

For the most part, the Red Sox spend conservatively in Latin America. Top prospect Hanley Ramirez cost them just a $22,000 bonus, while intriguing lefthander Juan Cedeno signed for $30,000. Mateo is an exception, as Boston paid $400,000 to win a bidding war for him in 2000. After winning Boston's Gulf Coast League pitcher of the year award in 2002, he regressed last season. Mateo was waylaid by blister problems and elbow tendinitis. Physical condition is a key for him, as his stuff is good when he's in shape and pedestrian when he's not. At his best, Mateo has an 89-93 mph fastball with heavy sink that one club official likened to a bowling ball. He slings the ball from a low three-quarters angle that's tough on hitters. His late-breaking curveball is an effective pitch when he stays on top of it. Mateo needs to work on his changeup, his command within the strike zone and his delivery. He lands heavily on his front heel, creating recoil and stress on his shoulder that worries some scouts. The Red Sox also would like him to firm up midsection and strengthen his lower body before he arrives in spring training. Reports from the Dominican Republic were that he was working harder than ever. Mateo faces a critical year in 2004, as he'll try to re-establish himself as one of Boston's top mound prospects while pitching in Class A.

Year	Club (League)	Class	W	L	ERA	G	GS	CG	SV	IP	H	R	ER	HR	BB	SO	AVG
2000	Red Sox (DSL)	R	2	4	3.27	9	7	0	0	33	38	16	12	2	5	34	.275
2001	Red Sox (GCL)	R	0	1	0.00	3	2	0	0	8	6	4	0	0	6	6	.200
2002	Red Sox (GCL)	R	4	3	1.76	11	11	2	0	51	45	14	10	1	11	45	.232
	Lowell (NY-P)	A	2	0	1.45	3	3	0	0	19	8	3	3	1	2	13	.133
2003	Augusta (SAL)	A	0	5	4.89	13	11	0	0	53	62	33	29	2	16	34	.292
	Red Sox (GCL)	R	0	0	1.80	2	2	0	0	5	4	1	1	0	0	6	.222
MINOR LEAGUE TOTALS			8	13	2.93	41	36	2	0	169	163	71	55	6	34	138	.250

20 Tim Hamulack, lhp

Born: Nov. 14, 1976. **Ht.:** 6-4. **Wt.:** 210. **Bats:** L. **Throws:** L. **School:** Montgomery (Md.) CC. **Career Transactions:** Selected by Astros in 32nd round of 1995 draft; signed May 12, 1996 . . . Selected by Royals from Astros in Rule 5 minor league draft, Dec. 11, 2000 . . . Contract purchased by Marlins from Royals, Dec. 12, 2000 . . . Granted free agency, Oct. 15, 2002 . . . Signed by Mariners, Nov. 4, 2002 . . . Granted free agency, Oct. 15, 2003 . . . Signed by Red Sox, Nov. 19, 2003.

Hamulack was one of the top prizes on the minor league free-agent market this offseason, and he was No. 1 on Boston's priority list. The Mariners hoped to re-sign him but the Red Sox won out by offering him a spot on their 40-man roster. That was a far cry from the 2000-01 offseason, when the Astros didn't protect Hamulack with one of their 78 big league or Triple-A roster spots and lost him in the minor league Rule 5 draft. He has made significant strides since then. He has a solid-average fastball that sits at 89-91 mph and was up to 94 this winter in Puerto Rico. He uses his hard three-quarters slurve more than he used to and has better command of his changeup. Hamulack has a funky delivery with a long arm action, a shoulder turn and some gyration, and the combination hides the ball from hitters. One National League scout whose team had interest in him said Hamulack could be more than a situational southpaw and called him a blue-collar lefty in the mold of Scott Stewart. The Red Sox spent all of 2003 looking for a second lefthander to team with Alan Embree in their bullpen, and they're still looking. After a strong winter league performance, Hamulack could win that job in spring training.

Year	Club (League)	Class	W	L	ERA	G	GS	CG	SV	IP	H	R	ER	HR	BB	SO	AVG
1996	Astros (GCL)	R	4	1	2.33	22	0	0	2	27	23	9	7	1	13	24	.230
1997	Astros (GCL)	R	1	1	4.20	23	0	0	9	45	56	31	21	3	18	38	.311
1998	Quad City (Mid)	A	0	2	3.24	52	0	0	0	58	58	23	21	3	26	52	.265
1999	Michigan (Mid)	A	3	0	3.04	25	0	0	0	27	23	9	9	0	11	32	.235
2000	Kissimmee (FSL)	A	3	1	4.98	41	0	0	1	56	67	37	31	3	21	54	.296
2001	Brevard County (FSL)	A	2	4	3.15	40	0	0	1	71	83	42	25	3	21	39	.287
2002	Portland (EL)	AA	8	4	2.88	38	1	0	6	78	73	32	25	6	29	53	.252
2003	Tacoma (PCL)	AAA	1	0	3.86	10	0	0	0	14	16	6	6	1	8	12	.302
	San Antonio (TL)	AA	0	1	2.09	40	0	0	1	47	32	13	11	0	15	54	.192
MINOR LEAGUE TOTALS			22	14	3.31	291	1	0	20	424	431	202	156	20	162	358	.266

21 Gary Galvez, rhp

Born: March 24, 1984. **Ht.:** 6-3. **Wt.:** 210. **Bats:** R. **Throws:** R. **Career Transactions:** Signed out of Dominican Republic by Red Sox, Feb. 15, 2003.

Scouts first noticed Galvez when he played first base and pitched in relief for Cuba's 16-and-under team at the 2000 Pan American Championship in Monterrey, Mexico. He was projected as Cuba's ace at the 2002 World Junior Championship before being pulled from the roster the day before the team left for Quebec. The government considered him a threat to defect, and when Galvez realized he'd probably never be allowed to travel outside of Cuba with future national teams, he resolved to leave. After three aborted attempts, he was smuggled off the island with 22 other Cubans on August 22. Galvez spent a month in a U.S. detention center before getting processed and establishing residency in the Dominican Republic. The Red Sox beat out the Dodgers, Mariners, Phillies and Yankees to sign Galvez for $450,000 plus college scholarship money, though their offer was $50,000 less than the highest bid. Galvez didn't get his visa paperwork straightened out until last September, so he spent the summer in the Dominican Summer League and didn't come to the United States until instructional league. Boston is enthused by his advanced approach for his age, and his birthdate hasn't been questioned. Galvez already shows the aptitude to sink his fastball, hit either corner with it and change speeds with his heater and curveball. His fastball usually sits around 90 mph and should pick up velocity. His curveball, slider and changeup are all average pitches, and his command makes them play better than that. Galvez has a smooth delivery that allows him to throw strikes with ease. It also features a high leg kick that gives him deception. While in the DSL, he pitched backward for much of the season, using too many breaking balls before starting to pitch off his fastball in August. Though it's uncertain where Galvez will make his U.S. debut, he could advance to low Class A by the end of the season.

Year	Club (League)	Class	W	L	ERA	G	GS	CG	SV	IP	H	R	ER	HR	BB	SO	AVG
2003	Red Sox East (DSL)	R	6	3	1.64	14	11	0	2	71	66	26	13	0	10	65	.234
MINOR LEAGUE TOTALS			6	3	1.64	14	11	0	2	71	66	26	13	0	10	65	.234

22 Luis Soto, ss

Born: Dec. 7, 1985. **Ht.:** 6-1. **Wt.:** 180. **Bats:** B. **Throws:** R. **Career Transactions:** Signed out of Dominican Republic by Red Sox, Nov. 25, 2003.

The Red Sox have beefed up their shortstop depth in the lower minors with Latin American signings over the last three year. In 2001 they signed Dominican Alex Penalo, who has topped .300 in both his pro seasons while showing above-average defensive tools. They went to Venezuela the following year for Christian Lara, who was their 2003 Dominican Summer League player of the year. Last December they landed Soto for $500,000. Soto stood out at October's World Wood Bat Championship showcase in Jupiter, Fla., where he was one of three Latin players to participate. He's the type of player the new Boston regime has put an emphasis on finding: one with strong physical tools and a mature approach beyond his years. At 18, Soto already knows how to recognize and deal with breaking pitches, and he also shows some aptitude for pulling the ball. He has a fluid stroke and quick hands at the plate. Soto also has plus speed and shortstop skills, with range, arm strength and actions. Because he's so advanced, it's likely that he'll come straight to the United States for his pro debut. He could share time with Lara in the Gulf Coast League.

Year	Club (League)	Class	AVG	G	AB	R	H	2B	3B	HR	RBI	BB	SO	SB	SLG	OBP
2003	Did not play—Signed 2004 contract															

23 Billy Simon, rhp

Born: Nov. 11, 1982. **Ht.:** 6-6. **Wt.:** 220. **Bats:** R. **Throws:** R. **School:** Wellington (Fla.) Community HS. **Career Transactions:** Selected by Red Sox in ninth round of 2001 draft; signed July 27, 2001 . . . On disabled list, April 3-Sept. 16, 2003.

Simon had the most frustrating 2003 of any Red Sox prospect. He entered the year ranked right behind Manny Delcarmen among the system's righthanders but never pitched in a game. Simon was bothered by a sore neck in spring training, tried to pitch through it and went on the disabled list in April. Doctors later diagnosed a hereditary verterbra condition, and Boston spent the offseason searching for a rehabilitation program that could get Simon back on the mound. On the positive side, the problem isn't believed to be career threatening and doesn't involve his arm. Before he was sidelined, Simon looked like a ninth-round steal out of Wellington Community High, which also produced first-rounders Bobby Bradley (1999), Sean Burnett (2000) and Justin Pope (2001 after attending Central Florida) and Brian Snyder (2003 after attending Stetson). Simon fell in the 2001 draft because of his commitment to Louisiana State yet signed for $325,000, fourth-round money. In 2002, he showed a 90-92 mph fastball with late sink, a hard overhand curveball and a developing changeup. He was the most impressive pitcher in Boston's instructional league camp after that season. With just 42 innings to show for three pro innings, Simon desperately needs innings and experience. It's uncertain when and where he'll return to the mound, but once healthy he could start to move quickly through the minors.

Year	Club (League)	Class	W	L	ERA	G	GS	CG	SV	IP	H	R	ER	HR	BB	SO	AVG
2001	Red Sox (GCL)	R	0	0	1.00	3	3	0	0	9	6	2	1	0	1	7	.207
2002	Red Sox (GCL)	R	1	1	1.64	6	5	0	0	22	12	6	4	0	5	24	.156
	Lowell (NY-P)	A	0	1	1.64	3	3	0	0	11	10	6	2	0	6	12	.238
2003	Did not play—Injured																
MINOR LEAGUE TOTALS			1	2	1.50	12	11	0	0	42	28	14	7	0	12	43	.189

24 Jessie Corn, rhp

Born: July 16, 1982. **Ht.:** 6-0. **Wt.:** 190. **Bats:** R. **Throws:** R. **School:** Jacksonville State University. **Career Transactions:** Selected by Red Sox in sixth round of 2003 draft; signed June 9, 2003.

Corn reflects the shift in Boston's draft philosophy. His size (6-foot-1) and velocity (87-90 mph) didn't wow scouts, but the Red Sox coveted his pitching acumen and performance record, which included a 37-inning scoreless streak and Atlantic Sun Conference bests in ERA (2.27) and strikeouts (119 in 115 innings) as a junior last spring. Corn had a combined 4-10, 5.16 in his first two years at Jacksonville State, mainly because Gamecocks coaches wouldn't let him throw his slider. That's easily his best pitch, rating as the best in the organization and grading as a 65 on the 20-80 scouting scale. He reached 92 mph with his fastball in instructional league but won't overpower hitters. Instead, Corn will get ahead in the count with precise command of his full repertoire, which also includes a curveball and changeup, then put them away with the slider. He had a tired arm after the college season and pitched just four innings during the summer, though he looked refreshed by instructional league. Boston will use Corn as a starter in one of its Class A rotations this year to give him innings to refine his changeup. Long term he might fit better as a reliever and could reach the majors fairly quickly in that role.

Year	Club (League)	Class	W	L	ERA	G	GS	CG	SV	IP	H	R	ER	HR	BB	SO	AVG
2003	Lowell (NY-P)	A	0	0	0.00	4	0	0	0	4	2	5	0	0	3	4	.118
MINOR LEAGUE TOTALS			0	0	0.00	4	0	0	0	4	2	5	0	0	3	4	.118

25 Mark Malaska, lhp

Born: Jan. 17, 1978. **Ht.:** 6-3. **Wt.:** 190. **Bats:** L. **Throws:** L. **School:** University of Akron. **Career Transactions:** Selected by Devil Rays in eighth round of 2000 draft; signed June 19, 2000 . . . Claimed on waivers by Red Sox from Devil Rays, Dec. 8, 2003.

The Red Sox spent the offseason collecting lefthanded relievers to back up Alan Embree in the big league bullpen. They signed Tim Hamulack as a minor league free agent and claimed Phil Seibel off waivers from the Mets in November, took Malaska off waivers from the Devil Rays and Lenny DiNardo in the Rule 5 draft from the Mets in December, then signed Bobby M. Jones and Nick Bierbrodt as free agents in January. Malaska is the only member of the group to pitch in the big leagues last year and has perhaps the best chance of breaking camp with Boston. He was strictly an outfielder in his first two college seasons at Akron and pitched just 24 innings as a two-way player as a junior, but that was enough to get him drafted in the eighth round in 2000. He moved from the rotation to the bullpen in 2003 and reached the majors in mid-July. Malaska's doesn't have a standout pitch but he pitches craftily around a marginal 86-90 mph fastball. His changeup is his best offering, and he commands his curveball well and mixes in a slider. He does an excellent job of keeping the ball in strike zone, allowing just one homer every 17 innings as a pro. Though Malaska permitted runs in just five of his 22 major league outings, Tampa Bay manager Lou Piniella got down on him because he didn't challenge hitters enough. After watching Scott Sauerbeck battle the strike zone last year, the Red Sox won't tolerate a lefty reliever who can't find the plate.

Year	Club (League)	Class	W	L	ERA	G	GS	CG	SV	IP	H	R	ER	HR	BB	SO	AVG
2000	Charleston, SC (SAL)	A	0	0	9.00	2	0	0	0	2	3	2	2	1	0	3	.375
	Hudson Valley (NY-P)	A	0	2	4.91	10	5	0	0	40	44	27	22	1	14	36	.273
2001	Charleston, SC (SAL)	A	7	12	2.92	25	25	1	0	157	153	71	51	11	35	152	.249
	Bakersfield (Cal)	A	2	1	4.08	3	3	0	0	18	14	8	8	1	5	13	.219
2002	Bakersfield (Cal)	A	7	4	2.96	15	15	2	0	91	98	48	30	5	12	94	.263
	Orlando (SL)	AA	4	5	3.69	12	11	1	1	71	82	37	29	4	28	49	.292
2003	Orlando (SL)	AA	1	1	2.16	19	0	0	1	25	21	6	6	2	4	22	.236
	Durham (IL)	AAA	1	1	4.30	15	0	0	0	23	24	12	11	1	8	22	.270
	Tampa Bay (AL)	MAJ	2	1	2.81	22	0	0	0	16	13	7	5	0	12	17	.232
MAJOR LEAGUE TOTALS			2	1	2.81	22	0	0	0	16	13	7	5	0	12	17	.232
MINOR LEAGUE TOTALS			22	26	3.35	101	59	4	2	427	439	211	159	26	106	391	.261

26 Jamie Brown, rhp

Born: March 31, 1977. **Ht.:** 6-2. **Wt.:** 200. **Bats:** R. **Throws:** R. **School:** Meridian (Miss.) JC. **Career Transactions:** Selected by Indians in 21st round of 1996 draft; signed May 15, 1997 . . . Released by Indians, Sept. 1, 2001; re-signed by Indians, Oct. 9, 2001 . . . Traded by Indians to Red Sox for 2B Angel Santos, June 22, 2003.

Acquired for second baseman Angel Santos in midseason trade of Triple-A players, Brown earned a 40-man roster spot with the Red Sox, who believe he's on the verge of pitching in the majors. Brown was on the fast track in the Indians system, reaching Double-A in his first full pro season, before injuries intervened. He had shoulder tendinitis in 1999, lower back problems in 2000 and Tommy John surgery in 2001. Fully healthy again, Brown commands four pitches: a low-90s fastball, a good changeup, a slider and a curveball. His breaking stuff is fringy, and he can use it to throw strikes but not to get outs. When he keeps his fastball down, it sinks and bores in on righthanders. Brown projects as a big league swingman. Used primarily in relief after switching organizations, he'll pitch out of the Triple-A rotation at the outset of this season.

Year	Club (League)	Class	W	L	ERA	G	GS	CG	SV	IP	H	R	ER	HR	BB	SO	AVG
1997	Watertown (NY-P)	A	10	2	3.08	13	13	1	0	73	66	35	25	6	15	57	.235
1998	Kinston (Car)	A	11	9	3.81	27	27	2	0	173	162	91	73	12	44	148	.250
	Akron (EL)	AA	1	0	2.57	1	1	0	0	7	5	2	2	1	1	5	.192
1999	Akron (EL)	AA	5	9	4.57	23	23	1	0	138	140	72	70	11	39	98	.271
	Buffalo (IL)	AAA	1	0	5.40	1	0	0	0	5	8	4	3	0	1	2	.400
2000	Akron (EL)	AA	7	6	4.38	17	17	1	0	97	95	49	47	12	26	57	.251
2001	Akron (EL)	AA	1	1	5.03	4	4	0	0	20	22	11	11	2	7	12	.278
2002	Akron (EL)	AA	9	5	2.78	18	17	0	0	104	98	41	32	5	17	72	.249
2003	Buffalo (IL)	AAA	4	4	3.52	13	10	0	0	61	45	26	24	4	17	26	.206
	Pawtucket (IL)	AAA	4	1	2.26	18	3	0	1	52	40	17	13	1	5	39	.209
MINOR LEAGUE TOTALS			53	37	3.71	135	115	5	1	729	681	348	300	54	172	516	.247

27 Kyle Jackson, rhp

Born: April 9, 1983. **Ht.:** 6-3. **Wt.:** 180. **Bats:** R. **Throws:** R. **School:** St. Petersburg (Fla.) JC. **Career Transactions:** Selected by Red Sox in 32nd round of 2001 draft; signed May 22, 2002.

Jackson was New Hampshire's top prospect when he came out of high school in 2001, though he fell to the 32nd round in part because he was committed to St. John's. After the Red Sox drafted him in the 32nd round he opted to go to St. Petersburg, where he won a junior college state title before signing as a draft-and-follow. He pitched just two innings after signing in 2002 because of a tired arm, but he rebounded to win Boston's Gulf Coast League pitcher of the year award last summer. Jackson could have three average or better pitches. His curveball ranks as one of the best in the system, and he also has an 88-93 mph fastball. His changeup is further behind but shows promise. His biggest needs are to get more consistent with his delivery and to develop a pitch to put hitters away with. Jackson earned a late-season promotion to Lowell, so he could begin 2004 in low Class A.

Year	Club (League)	Class	W	L	ERA	G	GS	CG	SV	IP	H	R	ER	HR	BB	SO	AVG
2002	Red Sox (GCL)	R	0	0	0.00	1	1	0	0	2	0	0	0	0	0	1	.000
2003	Red Sox (GCL)	R	5	2	1.85	12	12	0	0	58	40	14	12	3	11	37	.195
	Lowell (NY-P)	A	1	1	0.93	2	2	0	0	10	7	6	1	0	2	2	.200
MINOR LEAGUE TOTALS			6	3	1.67	15	15	0	0	70	47	20	13	3	13	40	.191

28 Jose Vaquedano, rhp

Born: July 9, 1981. **Ht.:** 6-4. **Wt.:** 170. **Bats:** R. **Throws:** R. **School:** Vernon Regional (Texas) JC. **Career Transactions:** Selected by Red Sox in 35th round of 2002 draft; signed June 8, 2002.

Vaquedano is bidding to become the first player born in Honduras to reach the majors, though he'll have competition from Indians prospect Mariano Gomez. Drafted in the 35th round in 2002 after two seasons at Vernon Regional Junior College, he took a step forward last year when he moved from the bullpen to the rotation. He returned to Lowell and was named the team's pitcher of the year. Tall and lean, Vaquedano pitches down in the strike zone and gets natural sink on his 90-92 mph fastball and his changeup. He has a fluid arm action and an easy, repeatable delivery, which allow him to throw strikes. Vaquedano still needs to add strength and improve his secondary pitches. He can throw his slurvy breaking ball for strikes but it's not especially sharp. He's ready for his first taste of full-season ball and will start in low Class A this year.

Year	Club (League)	Class	W	L	ERA	G	GS	CG	SV	IP	H	R	ER	HR	BB	SO	AVG
2002	Lowell (NY-P)	A	1	3	4.35	22	0	0	0	39	46	33	19	4	18	35	.293
2003	Lowell (NY-P)	A	7	4	3.30	14	10	0	0	74	67	30	27	4	15	70	.241
MINOR LEAGUE TOTALS			8	7	3.66	36	10	0	0	113	113	63	46	8	33	105	.260

29 Carlos Morla, rhp

Born: April 15, 1982. **Ht.:** 6-0. **Wt.:** 140. **Bats:** R. **Throws:** R. **Career Transactions:** Signed out of Dominican Republic by Red Sox, Oct. 9, 1999 . . . On disabled list, June 2-Aug. 31, 2001.

Morla didn't make it to Augusta until mid-May last year because his entry into the United States was delayed after it was learned that he had been playing under a false identity. Previously known as Denny Tussen, he also turned out to be a year older than previously believed. Because he has the best sheer velocity in the system, his prospect status was unaffected. There's some Pedro Martinez in Morla, who's a 6-foot Dominican with long fingers, a quick arm, a low three-quarters arm slot and lively 93-97 mph heat. But the similarities end there, as Morla is a one-pitch guy with shaky command. The Red Sox think he'd be more effective at a higher arm angle, and it varies so much that it's hard for him to be consistent with his pitches. He's in love with his fastball and hasn't developed his other pitches. At times he'll get bite on his curveball, but when he doesn't stay on top of the pitch it becomes a less effective slurve. He rarely throws his changeup. Morla missed all of 2001 with elbow problems but has been healthy since. He projects as a reliever but still needs at least one more pitch for that role. He'll move up to high Class A in 2004.

Year	Club (League)	Class	W	L	ERA	G	GS	CG	SV	IP	H	R	ER	HR	BB	SO	AVG
2000	Red Sox (DSL)	R	3	2	2.32	12	8	0	0	54	57	29	14	0	10	38	.251
2001	Did not play—Injured																
2002	Red Sox (GCL)	R	2	2	2.60	12	3	0	0	52	48	28	15	1	15	37	.246
2003	Augusta (SAL)	A	2	2	5.40	28	0	0	7	40	33	25	24	3	22	37	.224
MINOR LEAGUE TOTALS			7	6	3.26	52	11	0	7	146	138	82	53	4	47	112	.243

30 Harvey Garcia, rhp

Born: March 16, 1984. **Ht.:** 6-2. **Wt.:** 170. **Bats:** R. **Throws:** R. **Career Transactions:** Signed out of Venezuela by Marlins, July 2, 2000 . . . Released by Marlins, June 7, 2002 . . . Signed by Red Sox, June 14, 2002.

Louie Elajua was Marlins director of Latin American scouting when the club signed Garcia in 2000. He had moved on to Boston as international scouting director with owner John Henry and Co. when Florida released Garcia in June 2002, and the Red Sox quickly signed him a week later. That moves looks wise, as Garcia was one of the better pitching prospects in the Gulf Coast League last year. He can reach 95 mph with his fastball and should add velocity as he fills out. His heater has explosive late life, and because he throws with little effort he commands it well. Garcia still has a long way to go with the rest of his repertoire. He no-hit the GCL Reds for six innings by throwing almost exclusively fastballs and doesn't trust his curveball or changeup. One observer said he needs to finish his delivery better to reduce the risk of injury. Because Garcia is so raw, he'll probably open 2004 in extended spring training and advance to Lowell in June.

Year	Club (League)	Class	W	L	ERA	G	GS	CG	SV	IP	H	R	ER	HR	BB	SO	AVG
2001	Ciudad Alianza (VSL)	R	2	2	3.58	12	4	0	0	33	36	20	13	0	18	23	—
2002	San Joaquin (VSL)	R	0	2	6.08	4	3	0	0	13	16	11	9	3	8	12	.320
	Ciudad Alianza (VSL)	R	2	3	2.68	9	7	0	0	40	32	15	12	0	14	31	.221
2003	Red Sox North (DSL)	R	0	2	1.20	3	3	0	0	15	10	4	2	0	3	10	.172
	Red Sox (GCL)	R	3	0	1.89	9	8	0	0	33	21	11	7	2	12	32	.179
MINOR LEAGUE TOTALS			7	9	2.87	37	25	0	0	135	115	61	43	5	55	108	.214

CHICAGO
CUBS

The Cubs were five outs away from making their first trip to the World Series in 58 years. They couldn't close the deal, but that shouldn't tarnish the club's unexpected National League Central title or bright future.

Chicago hasn't had consecutive winning seasons since a six-year run from 1967-72 under Hall of Fame manager Leo Durocher. Under Dusty Baker, their best skipper since Durocher, the Cubs improved by 21 games in 2003. They should eclipse the one-hit wonders of 1984, '89 and '98. A big reason is that no team can match Chicago's collection of young pitching, which is primarily homegrown. Coaces Mark Prior and Kerry Wood were first-round picks, while Carlos Zambrano is the biggest jewel the Cubs have mined out of their Latin American program.

There's more pitching on the way. Venezuelan right-hander Angel Guzman was on the verge of a big league callup before tearing his labrum in July. The Cubs stocked up on arms in the 2001 draft, getting Prior second overall and lefthander Andy Sisco one round later, and again in 2002, when they grabbed lefties Justin Jones and Luke Hagerty and righties Bobby Brownlie, Chadd Blasko and Billy Petrick in the first three rounds.

Chicago has so many pitching prospects that it doesn't have enough minor league rotation spots to accommodate them all.

TOP 30 PROSPECTS

1. Angel Guzman, rhp
2. Justin Jones, lhp
3. Ryan Harvey, of
4. Andy Sisco, lhp
5. Felix Pie, of
6. Bobby Brownlie, rhp
7. Chadd Blasko, rhp
8. Brendan Harris, 3b/2b
9. David Kelton, of
10. Jae-Kuk Ryu, rhp
11. Luke Hagerty, lhp
12. Jason Dubois, of/1b
13. Todd Wellemeyer, rhp
14. Nic Jackson, of
15. Sergio Mitre, rhp
16. Francis Beltran, rhp
17. Brian Dopirak, 1b
18. Billy Petrick, rhp
19. Jason Wylie, rhp
20. Ricky Nolasco, rhp
21. Felix Sanchez, lhp
22. Jon Leicester, rhp
23. Sean Marshall, lhp
24. Renyel Pinto, lhp
25. John Webb, rhp
26. Carmen Pignatiello, lhp
27. Rich Hill, rhp
28. Darin Downs, lhp
29. Bear Bay, rhp
30. Matt Craig, 3b

By Jim Callis

Many of the up-and-coming pitchers could become trade bait to address the system's main shortcoming as of late: producing big league hitters.

The Cubs didn't develop any of the 10 position players who started a postseason game for them. Center fielder Corey Patterson showed improvement in 2003, but tore up his knee in July. First baseman Hee Seop Choi showed off slugging prowess before sustaining a concussion in June, but didn't hit afterward and was traded for Derrek Lee in the offseason. The Cubs envision Ryan Harvey and Felix Pie eventually joining Patterson in their outfield, but both are teenagers and a few years away from Wrigley Field. Infielder Brendan Harris and outfielders David Kelton and Jason Dubois are the hitters closest to the majors, but they're not ready for starting jobs.

Chicago is in a position to emerge as a perennial contender. Every other club in its division is either aging and pushing the envelope on its budget (Houston, St. Louis) or in a long-term rebuilding project (Cincinnati, Milwaukee, Pittsburgh). The Cubs also are in the good hands of general manager Jim Hendry, who demonstrated a keen eye for talent when he was the team's farm and scouting director. In his first full season as GM, he hired the right manager and made the right trades to bring his team to the postseason. Now the challenge is to return, and Hendry and his team appear up to it.

ORGANIZATION
OVERVIEW

General manager: Jim Hendry. **Farm director:** Oneri Fleita. **Scouting director:** John Stockstill.

2003 PERFORMANCE

Class	Team	League	W	L	Pct.	Finish*	Manager
Majors	Chicago	National	88	74	.543	4th (16)	Dusty Baker
Triple-A	Iowa Cubs	Pacific Coast	70	72	.493	t-9th (16)	Mike Quade
Double-A	West Tenn Diamond Jaxx	Southern	65	73	.471	9th (10)	Bobby Dickerson
High A	Daytona Cubs	Florida State	66	71	.482	9th (12)	Rick Kranitz
Low A	Lansing Lugnuts	Midwest	69	66	.511	+t-6th (14)	Julio Garcia
Short-season	Boise Hawks	Northwest	27	49	.355	8th (8)	Steve McFarland
Rookie	AZL Cubs	Arizona	25	24	.510	t-5th (9)	Carmelo Martinez
OVERALL 2003 MINOR LEAGUE RECORD			322	355	.476	25th (30)	

*Finish in overall standings (No. of teams in league) +League champion

ORGANIZATIONAL LEADERS

BATTING *Minimum 250 At-Bats
*AVG	Trenidad Hubbard, Iowa	.319
R	Three tied at	72
H	Felix Pie, Lansing	144
TB	Phil Hiatt, Iowa	242
2B	Phil Hiatt, Iowa	35
3B	Alberto Garcia, AZL Cubs	10
HR	Phil Hiatt, Iowa	25
RBI	Phil Hiatt, Iowa	89
BB	Dwaine Bacon, West Tenn/Daytona	66
SO	Mike Mallory, Daytona	136
SB	Dwaine Bacon, West Tenn/Daytona	74
*SLG	Phil Hiatt, Iowa	.506
*OBP	Trenidad Hubbard, Iowa	.405

PITCHING #Minimum 75 Innings
W	Anderson Tavarez, Lansing	12
L	Carlos Vasquez, Lansing	13
#ERA	Chadd Blasko, Daytona/Lansing	1.95
G	Mark Carter, Daytona/Lansing	61
CG	Andy Sisco, Lansing	3
SV	Jason Wylie, Lansing	29
IP	Carmen Pignatiello, West Tenn/Daytona	162
BB	Steve Smyth, Iowa	72
SO	Mike Nannini, West Tenn	158

BEST TOOLS

Best Hitter for Average	Brendan Harris
Best Power Hitter	Ryan Harvey
Fastest Baserunner	Dwaine Bacon
Best Athlete	Ryan Harvey
Best Fastball	Angel Guzman
Best Curveball	Bobby Brownlie
Best Slider	Jared Blasdell
Best Changeup	Angel Guzman
Best Control	Chadd Blasko
Best Defensive Catcher	Tony Richie
Best Defensive Infielder	Ronny Cedeno
Best Infield Arm	Ronny Cedeno
Best Defensive Outfielder	Felix Pie
Best Outfield Arm	Ryan Harvey

PROJECTED 2007 LINEUP

Catcher	Michael Barrett
First Base	Derrek Lee
Second Base	Brendan Harris
Third Base	Aramis Ramirez
Shortstop	Alex Gonzalez
Left Field	Sammy Sosa
Center Field	Corey Patterson

Right Field	Ryan Harvey
No. 1 Starter	Mark Prior
No. 2 Starter	Kerry Wood
No. 3 Starter	Angel Guzman
No. 4 Starter	Carlos Zambrano
No. 5 Starter	Justin Jones
Closer	Kyle Farnsworth

LAST YEAR'S TOP 20 PROSPECTS

1. Hee Seop Choi, 1b
2. Angel Guzman, rhp
3. Andy Sisco, lhp
4. Felix Pie, of
5. Nic Jackson, of
6. Francis Beltran, rhp
7. Luke Hagerty, lhp
8. Brendan Harris, 3b/2b
9. David Kelton, 3b/1b
10. Todd Wellemeyer, rhp
11. Jae-Kuk Ryu, rhp
12. Justin Jones, lhp
13. Felix Sanchez, lhp
14. Luis Montanez, ss/2b
15. Alfredo Francisco, 3b
16. Steve Smyth, lhp
17. Billy Petrick, rhp
18. Matt Bruback, rhp
19. Ricky Nolasco, rhp
20. John Webb, rhp

TOP PROSPECTS OF THE DECADE

1994	Brooks Kieschnick, of
1995	Brooks Kieschnick, of
1996	Brooks Kieschnick, of
1997	Kerry Wood, rhp
1998	Kerry Wood, rhp
1999	Corey Patterson, of
2000	Corey Patterson, of
2001	Corey Patterson, of
2002	Mark Prior, rhp
2003	Hee Seop Choi, 1b

TOP DRAFT PICKS OF THE DECADE

1994	Jayson Peterson, rhp
1995	Kerry Wood, rhp
1996	Todd Noel, rhp
1997	Jon Garland, rhp
1998	Corey Patterson, of
1999	Ben Christensen, rhp
2000	Luis Montanez, ss
2001	Mark Prior, rhp
2002	Bobby Brownlie, rhp
2003	Ryan Harvey, of

ALL-TIME LARGEST BONUSES

Mark Prior, 2001	$4,000,000
Corey Patterson, 1998	$3,700,000
Luis Montanez, 2000	$2,750,000
Bobby Brownlie, 2002	$2,500,000
Ryan Harvey, 2003	$2,400,000

MINOR LEAGUE
DEPTH CHART

CHICAGO CUBS RANK: 7

Impact potential (B): The Cubs might have graded higher, except their premium prospects have questions (Angel Guzman's shoulder) or have yet to reach high Class A, making the them riskier bets.

Depth (B): It's always impressive when prospects such as Luke Hagerty—who could be an impact player after coming back from Tommy John surgery—Jason Dubois and Todd Wellemeyer can't crack the top 10. The Cubs are loaded with pitching depth, but not as many sure things offensively.

Sleeper: Billy Petrick, rhp. —*Depth charts prepared by Josh Boyd. Numbers in parentheses indicate prospect rankings.*

LF
David Kelton (9)
Jason Dubois (12)
J.J. Johnson

CF
Felix Pie (5)
Nic Jackson (14)
Dwaine Bacon

RF
Ryan Harvey (3)
Kyle Boyer
Carlos Mejia

3B
Matt Craig (30)
Francisco Salas
Alfredo Francisco

SS
Buck Coats
Ronnie Cedeno
Ryan Theriot

2B
Brendan Harris (8)
Luis Montanez
Robinson Chirinos

1B
Brian Dopirak (17)
Micah Hoffpauir
Brandon Sing

SOURCE OF TALENT

Homegrown		Acquired	
College	12	Trades	0
Junior College	2	Rule 5 draft	0
Draft-and-follow	1	Independent leagues	0
High school	9	Free agents/waivers	0
Nondrafted free agents	0		
Foreign	6		

C
Tony Richie
Jake Fox

RHP

Starters	Relievers
Angel Guzman (1)	Francis Beltran (16)
Bobby Brownlie (6)	Jason Wylie (19)
Chadd Blasko (7)	Jon Leicester (22)
Jae-Kuk Ryu (10)	Jared Blasdell
Todd Wellemeyer (13)	Wes O'Brien
Sergio Mitre (15)	David Cash
Billy Petrick (18)	Scott Chiasson
Ricky Nolasco (20)	
John Webb (25)	
Bear Bay (29)	
Carlos Marmol	
Rocky Cherry	
Robert Ransom	
Matt Clanton	
Anderson Tavares	

LHP

Starters	Relievers
Justin Jones (2)	Felix Sanchez (21)
Andy Sisco (4)	Renyel Pinto (24)
Luke Hagerty (11)	Carmen Pignatiello (26)
Sean Marshall (23)	Rich Hill (27)
Darin Downs (28)	Russ Rohlicek
Carlos Vasquez	Yorkin Ferreras
Andy Santana	Steve Smyth
	Jordan Gerk

DRAFT
ANALYSIS

Best Pro Debut: LHP Sean Marshall (6) went 6-6, 2.34 with 99 strikeouts in 91 innings between the short-season Northwest League and low Class A Midwest League. In the MWL playoffs, he pitched scoreless ball for 6⅔ innings to win his lone start. Marshall's body (6-foot-6, 195 pounds), high-80s fastball and curveball all have a lot of projection.

Best Athlete: OF Ryan Harvey (1) has been compared to two-time National League MVP Dale Murphy because of his size (6-foot-5, 215 pounds), power and all-around tools. He's a potential Gold Glove right fielder who had above-average speed and a 90-93 mph fastball before blowing out his right knee in an outfield collision at a November 2002 showcase. He should be fully recovered by spring training.

Best Pure Hitter: Harvey's .235 average and 21 strikeouts in 51 Rookie-level at-bats are attributable to the rust from a mostly inactive spring and summer.

Best Raw Power: Harvey wrests the honor of most powerful Cubs minor leaguer from Brian Dopirak, his former teammate at Dunedin (Fla.) High.

Fastest Runner: Nondrafted free agent OF Ryan Fitzgerald has 70 speed on the 20-80 scouting scale, but the Cubs didn't sign any draftees with those kind of wheels.

Best Defensive Player: The best receiver in the 2003 draft, C Tony Richie (4) frames

Downs

pitches like a big leaguer. He also has an average, accurate arm. After surgery on his throwing shoulder, he had to be shut down when it bothered him again last summer.

Best Fastball: The Cubs signed RHP Robert Ransom (23) after he touched 94 mph last summer in the Cape Cod League. His fastball could use more movement.

Best Breaking Ball: LHP Darin Downs (5) had a plus-plus curveball before coming down with shoulder tendinitis last spring.

Most Intriguing Background: Marshall's twin Brian was Boston's fifth-round pick. RHP Ryan Kalita (17) followed brother Tim, a lefty in the Tigers system, to Notre Dame and into pro ball.

Closest To The Majors: Marshall, especially if he shifts to the bullpen as he gets closer to Wrigley Field.

Best Late-Round Pick: Ransom.

The One Who Got Away: OF Sam Fuld (24) fell after a disappointing junior season at Stanford, then rebounded with a banner summer in the Cape Cod League. C Landon Powell (25) will try to become the first college senior drafted in 2004 after using the summer to get himself in better shape.

Assessment: Harvey was a consensus top-five choice and just the type of slugger the Cubs needed in their system, and they got him when the Royals decided to save money by taking Chris Lubanski at No. 5.

As if the Cubs didn't already have enough pitching, they loaded up with LHPs Justin Jones (2) and Luke Hagerty (1), and RHPs Bobby Brownlie (1), Chadd Blasko (1), Billy Petrick (3) and Jason Wylie (12).

RHP Mark Prior (1) would win this class an "A" by himself. But Chicago also signed LHP Andy Sisco (2), 3B/2B Brendan Harris (5) and RHP Sergio Mitre (7).

The Cubs have traded LHP Dontrelle Willis (8) and 2B Bobby Hill (2), but they have held onto OF/1B Jason Dubois (14), RHP Todd Wellemeyer (4) and OF Nic Jackson (3).

The only blemish on Chicago's report card. Injuries have hampered the progress of RHPs Ben Christensen (1) and John Webb (19) and LHP Steve Smyth (4).

—Draft analysis prepared by Jim Callis. Numbers in parentheses indicate draft rounds.

rhp

Angel Guzman

Born: Dec. 14, 1981.
Ht.: 6-3. **Wt.:** 180.
Bats: R. **Throws:** R.
Career Transactions: Signed out of Venezuela by Royals, March 4, 1999 . . . Contract voided, June 24, 1999 . . . Signed by Cubs, Nov. 12, 1999.

The Cubs thought Guzman was ready to make a Mark Prior-like ascent in 2003, beginning the season in Double-A West Tenn and getting to the majors by midseason. If Chicago didn't have so much pitching, he could have pressed for a big league job. Guzman led the Cubs with a 1.13 ERA in the Cactus League, and his teammates voted him the most impressive rookie in big league camp. He caught fire in late May, going 3-1, 1.01 over his next five starts. After shutting out eventual Southern League champion Carolina for seven innings on June 20, Guzman was picked to pitch in the Futures Game and would have been the logical callup when Prior hurt his shoulder in mid-July. But Guzman never threw another pitch in 2003, as his shoulder was bothering him. Doctors diagnosed a slight tear in his labrum, and he had it corrected with arthroscopic surgery. The Cubs added him to the 40-man roster for the first time in October. His brother Daniel pitches in the Indians system.

Guzman has enjoyed nothing but success since the Cubs gave him a second chance. The Royals originally signed him for $5,500 but voided his contact after he failed his physical. After landing with Chicago for $30,000, he has gone 24-9, 2.33. Guzman's fastball and changeup are the best in the Cubs system, and his curveball ranks near the top. When they're on, they're each 70 pitches on the 20-80 scouting scale. Notable for both its velocity (91-96 mph) and explosive sink, his fastball may be the best of his offerings. His development accelerated in 2002 when he regained the curve he flashed when he signed. Managers rated Guzman's command the best in the Southern League, and he not only throws strikes but also keeps the ball down in the zone. He has permitted just one homer per 23.7 innings as a pro. He shows a lot of athleticism and poise on the mound. Guzman's mechanics and easy delivery augured well for his health—before his shoulder injury. Now the Cubs are holding their breath and hoping he comes back with the stuff he had before he was sidelined. His rehabilitation was going well at the Cubs' spring-training base in Mesa, Ariz., but they won't know for sure until he takes the mound in a game situation. He also had a stress fracture in his elbow during his first pro season in 2000.

Guzman's physical condition is the only concern at this point. He was ready for the major leagues when he got hurt. The Cubs are going to take things slowly with Guzman's valuable right arm. He'll be back in big league camp this spring, but he may not make his 2004 debut until May. He likely will return to Double-A to begin his comeback. Guzman has the stuff of a No. 1 starter, though he may never rise above No. 3 if Prior and Kerry Wood stay in Chicago.

Year	Club (League)	Class	W	L	ERA	G	GS	CG	SV	IP	H	R	ER	HR	BB	SO	AVG
2000	La Pradera (VSL)	R	1	1	1.93	7	6	0	0	33	24	13	7	0	5	25	.197
2001	Boise (NWL)	A	9	1	2.23	14	14	0	0	77	68	27	19	2	19	63	.233
2002	Lansing (Mid)	A	5	2	1.89	9	9	1	0	62	42	18	13	3	16	49	.186
	Daytona (FSL)	A	6	2	2.39	16	15	1	0	94	99	34	25	2	33	74	.268
2003	West Tenn (SL)	AA	3	3	2.81	15	15	0	0	90	83	30	28	8	26	87	.249
MINOR LEAGUE TOTALS			24	9	2.33	61	59	2	0	355	316	122	92	15	99	298	.235

2 Justin Jones, lhp

Born: Sept. 25, 1984. **Ht.:** 6-4. **Wt.:** 190. **Bats:** L. **Throws:** L. **School:** Kellam HS, Virginia Beach. **Career Transactions:** Selected by Cubs in second round of 2002 draft; signed June 25, 2002.

Jones looked like a possible first-round pick early in 2002 but didn't pitch well in front of crosscheckers, so the Cubs were able to grab him in the second. They planned on pitching him at short-season Boise in 2003 before injuries created an opening at low Class A Lansing. Jones excelled as one of the youngest pitchers in the Midwest League. His 89-94 mph fastball and his curveball are both plus pitches. With his age and frame, he projects to add velocity. His changeup is advanced for his age, as is most of his package. He also throws an occasional splitter. Lefties went 5-for-58 (.086) with no extra-base hits against him in 2003. Like several of Chicago's top pitching prospects, Jones didn't make it through the full season. He was shut down twice with a tired arm and didn't pitch after Aug. 5. He didn't need surgery but needs to get stronger. His command can get better. The Cubs have sought a good lefty starter for years, and Jones will race Andy Sisco and Luke Hagerty to Wrigley Field. Jones should be 100 percent for spring training and will spend 2004 at high Class A Daytona.

Year	Club (League)	Class	W	L	ERA	G	GS	CG	SV	IP	H	R	ER	HR	BB	SO	AVG
2002	Cubs (AZL)	R	3	1	1.80	11	11	0	0	50	31	12	10	0	18	63	.181
	Boise (NWL)	A	1	0	1.80	1	1	0	0	5	4	1	1	0	3	4	.211
2003	Lansing (Mid)	A	3	5	2.28	16	16	0	0	71	56	29	18	1	32	87	.215
MINOR LEAGUE TOTALS			7	6	2.07	28	28	0	0	126	91	42	29	1	53	154	.202

3 Ryan Harvey, of

Born: Aug. 30, 1984. **Ht.:** 6-5. **Wt.:** 220. **Bats:** R. **Throws:** R. **School:** Dunedin (Fla.) HS. **Career Transactions:** Selected by Cubs in first round (sixth overall) of 2003 draft; signed June 21, 2003.

Seven months after blowing out his right knee in an outfield collision at a high school showcase, Harvey was a candidate to go No. 1 overall in the 2003 draft. The Cubs ranked him third on their draft board and were elated to get him with the sixth pick. Though he signed quickly for $2.4 million, the team had him focus on rehabbing his knee until the final two weeks of the season. Scouts compare Harvey to Dale Murphy. Harvey has huge power, as well as the strongest outfield arm and the best power/speed combination in the system. He threw 90-93 mph off the mound before giving up pitching in the wake of his injury. Harvey hasn't quite regained his 6.7-second speed in the 60-yard dash. His rust also showed at the plate in the Rookie-level Arizona League. His swing can get long at times and he'll have to keep it shorter with wood bats. The last Cubs outfield prospect with this much promise was Corey Patterson. They rushed Patterson and vow not to do the same with Harvey. Sammy Sosa's eventual successor may begin 2004 in extended spring training before heading to Boise.

Year	Club (League)	Class	AVG	G	AB	R	H	2B	3B	HR	RBI	BB	SO	SB	SLG	OBP
2003	Cubs (AZL)	R	.235	14	51	9	12	3	2	1	7	6	21	0	.431	.339
MINOR LEAGUE TOTALS			.235	14	51	9	12	3	2	1	7	6	21	0	.431	.339

4 Andy Sisco, lhp

Born: Jan. 13, 1983. **Ht.:** 6-9. **Wt.:** 260. **Bats:** L. **Throws:** L. **School:** Eastlake HS, Sammamish, Wash. **Career Transactions:** Selected by Cubs in second round of 2001 draft; signed June 26, 2001.

After snaring Mark Prior with the No. 2 overall pick in 2001, the Cubs followed up with another potential ace in Sisco in the second round. As a senior he pitched in the same rotation as Cardinals No. 1 prospect Blake Hawksworth. Recruited as a defensive end by Pacific-10 Conference football programs, he signed for $1 million. He missed two months with a broken pitching hand in 2003, but finished strong by not allowing an earned run in two starts as Lansing won the Midwest League playoffs. Sisco is a huge left-hander who already throws 92-94 mph and projects to add more heat, so he draws obvious comparisons to Randy Johnson. And while he has to polish the rest of his game, he has better mechanics and command than the Big Unit had at the same age. Sisco already has an effective changeup and at times shows a plus curveball. Sisco's curve is far from a finished product, as one in four he throws is above-average. He'd be better off throwing fewer split-

ters and focusing on his other pitches. The Cubs like his competitive makeup, but he also can be immature. Once he masters his curveball, Sisco will take off. The Cubs will keep him and Jones together again in 2004 in high Class A.

Year	Club (League)	Class	W	L	ERA	G	GS	CG	SV	IP	H	R	ER	HR	BB	SO	AVG
2001	Cubs (AZL)	R	1	0	5.24	10	7	0	0	34	36	28	20	1	10	31	.267
2002	Boise (NWL)	A	7	2	2.43	14	14	0	0	78	51	23	21	3	39	101	.188
2003	Lansing (Mid)	A	6	8	3.54	19	19	3	0	94	76	44	37	3	31	99	.220
MINOR LEAGUE TOTALS			14	10	3.41	43	40	3	0	206	163	95	78	7	80	231	.217

5 Felix Pie, of

Born: Feb. 8, 1985. **Ht.:** 6-2. **Wt.:** 170. **Bats:** L. **Throws:** L. **Career Transactions:** Signed out of Dominican Republic by Cubs, July 3, 2001.

Pie appeared in the 2003 Futures Game at 18 years and five months, just two months older than Florida's Miguel Cabrera was in 2001 when he became the youngest ever to appear in the prospect showcase. Pie, who hit .429 and drove in the winning run in the Midwest League playoffs, also won championships in the Arizona and Northwest leagues in 2002. Pie shows four intriguing tools, most noticeably 70 speed on the 20-80 scouting scale. He had no trouble hitting for average as a teenager in the MWL, where managers rated him the league's best defensive outfielder. He plays a shallow center field and has a solid arm. Though Pie will add strength, he won't hit for much power because his swing and approach are designed more to make contact. Though he runs well, he lacks basestealing instincts and was nabbed 13 times in 32 tries in 2003. He has a good concept of the strike zone for such a young player, but he still needs more discipline. The Cubs envision Pie as their leadoff hitter of the future, and he could push Corey Patterson to an outfield corner. He'll spend 2004 in high Class A.

Year	Club (League)	Class	AVG	G	AB	R	H	2B	3B	HR	RBI	BB	SO	SB	SLG	OBP
2002	Cubs (AZL)	R	.321	55	218	42	70	16	13	4	37	21	47	17	.569	.385
	Boise (NWL)	A	.125	2	8	1	1	1	0	0	1	1	1	0	.250	.222
2003	Lansing (Mid)	A	.285	124	505	72	144	22	9	4	47	41	98	19	.388	.346
MINOR LEAGUE TOTALS			.294	181	731	115	215	39	22	8	85	63	146	36	.440	.356

6 Bobby Brownlie, rhp

Born: Oct. 5, 1980. **Ht.:** 6-0. **Wt.:** 210. **Bats:** R. **Throws:** R. **School:** Rutgers University. **Career Transactions:** Selected by Cubs in first round (21st overall) of 2003 draft; signed March 5, 2003.

Once considered the top prospect in the 2002 draft, Brownlie came down with biceps tendinitis in his junior season and fell to the 21st pick. He didn't sign until March 2003, receiving $2.5 million. Because he worked hard to get into pitching shape during the offseason so he could pitch for the Cubs in January, he ran out of gas in early July, when he was shut down with a sore shoulder and tired arm. Brownlie has always dazzled scouts with his 12-to-6 curveball, and it's the best breaking pitch in the system. He also has a low-90s fastball that touched 97 mph when he was in college. He augments his stuff with good command and feel for pitching. Brownlie's changeup lags behind his fastball and curve but should be an effective pitch in time. The Cubs aren't too concerned about his health. An MRI showed no structural damage in his shoulder and he was back to 100 percent in instructional league. Chicago officials say he'll be fine now that he's on a baseball schedule. Brownlie was pushing for a promotion to Double-A when he wore down, and he'll get one to start 2004. If all goes well, he could reach Wrigley Field in September.

Year	Club (League)	Class	W	L	ERA	G	GS	CG	SV	IP	H	R	ER	HR	BB	SO	AVG
2003	Daytona (FSL)	A	5	4	3.00	13	13	1	0	66	48	26	22	2	24	59	.201
MINOR LEAGUE TOTALS			5	4	3.00	13	13	1	0	66	48	26	22	2	24	59	.201

7 Chadd Blasko, rhp

Born: March 9, 1981. **Ht.:** 6-7. **Wt.:** 220. **Bats:** R. **Throws:** R. **School:** Purdue University. **Career Transactions:** Selected by Cubs in first round (36th overall) of 2002 draft; signed Aug. 31, 2002.

One of three college pitchers taken by the Cubs in 2002's supplemental first round, Blasko broke out in his 2003 pro debut while Luke Hagerty and Matt Clanton were hurt. Many scouts had projected him as a reliever because of his long arm action, but Blasko was unhittable as a starter. He needed just two outings before earning a promotion to high Class A, where he led the Florida State League in ERA. The Cubs drafted Blasko for his size and his fastball. He throws in the low to mid-90s and commands his fastball with precision. The key for him in 2003 was coming up with a consistent breaking ball, a big curveball that looks like a hanger before suddenly dropping through the strike zone. While Blasko also improved his changeup and slider, those pitches still need further refinement. He may not have a picture-perfect delivery, but it's deceptive and he throws strikes, so the Cubs aren't going to touch it. Blasko will head to Double-A, and he and Brownlie could compete for a big league rotation spot in 2005.

Year	Club (League)	Class	W	L	ERA	G	GS	CG	SV	IP	H	R	ER	HR	BB	SO	AVG
2003	Lansing (Mid)	A	0	1	1.64	2	2	0	0	11	10	3	2	0	5	6	.256
	Daytona (FSL)	A	10	5	1.98	24	24	1	0	136	100	33	30	3	43	131	.205
MINOR LEAGUE TOTALS			10	6	1.95	26	26	1	0	147	110	36	32	3	48	137	.209

8 Brendan Harris, 3b/2b

Born: Aug. 26, 1980. **Ht.:** 6-1. **Wt.:** 190. **Bats:** R. **Throws:** R. **School:** College of William & Mary. **Career Transactions:** Selected by Cubs in fifth round of 2001 draft; signed July 21, 2001.

Harris couldn't match the .328 average and 15 homers he put up in his first full pro season in 2002, but the Cubs were still pleased with his development. They gave him a look at catcher during spring training, but ended that experiment when the physical toll proved to be too much. Harris missed the final two weeks of the season with broken ribs, then returned to hit .302 in the Arizona Fall League. Harris is a consistent line-drive hitter with gap power. He hasn't shown typical home run pop for a third baseman, but the Cubs believe it will come. He has one of the strongest infield arms in the system, and he displays good athleticism at both second and third base. Harris has played more at the hot corner than at second base, and it shows. He's not as smooth at second and needs to improve his double-play pivots. His intense makeup is an overall plus, yet it sometimes works against him. Harris will continue to see playing time at both second and third base in 2004 at Triple-A Iowa. He'll challenge for a big league job at one of those spots in 2005.

Year	Club (League)	Class	AVG	G	AB	R	H	2B	3B	HR	RBI	BB	SO	SB	SLG	OBP
2001	Lansing (Mid)	A	.274	32	113	25	31	5	1	4	22	17	26	5	.442	.370
2002	Daytona (FSL)	A	.329	110	425	82	140	35	6	13	54	43	57	16	.532	.395
	West Tenn (SL)	AA	.321	13	53	8	17	4	1	2	11	2	5	1	.547	.345
2003	West Tenn (SL)	AA	.280	120	435	56	122	34	7	5	52	51	72	6	.425	.364
MINOR LEAGUE TOTALS			.302	275	1026	171	310	78	15	24	139	113	160	28	.478	.376

9 David Kelton, of

Born: Dec. 17, 1979. **Ht.:** 6-3. **Wt.:** 200. **Bats:** R. **Throws:** R. **School:** Troup County HS, La Grange, Ga. **Career Transactions:** Selected by Cubs in second round of 1998 draft; signed June 3, 1998.

The Cubs finally gave up on Kelton filling their perennial void at third base. Since having shoulder surgery in high school, he repeatedly had mental and physical struggles making throws from the hot corner. After committing 11 errors in 33 games there to start 2003, he asked to move to the outfield and got his wish. Kelton has the tools to handle his new position. His bat speed and plate coverage should make him a .275 hitter with 20-25 homers annually. He has the athleticism and arm strength to play on either corner and could fill in as a center fielder in a pinch. Kelton has been steady but rarely spectacular in the minors, and he'll have to step up his production to gain playing time in the outfield or at first base, where he played extensively in 2002. Doing a better job of controlling the strike zone would help. He would have been a natural fit as a platoon partner had the Cubs chosen to stick with Hee Seop Choi or Randall Simon at first base, but the Derrek

Lee trade leaves Kelton vying for a backup role at best this year. To do that he'll have to prove himself to manager Dusty Baker in spring training.

Year	Club (League)	Class	AVG	G	AB	R	H	2B	3B	HR	RBI	BB	SO	SB	SLG	OBP
1998	Cubs (AZL)	R	.265	50	181	39	48	7	5	6	29	23	58	16	.459	.353
1999	Lansing (Mid)	A	.269	124	509	75	137	17	4	13	68	39	121	22	.395	.322
2000	Daytona (FSL)	A	.268	132	523	75	140	30	7	18	84	38	120	7	.455	.317
2001	West Tenn (SL)	AA	.313	58	224	33	70	9	4	12	45	24	55	1	.549	.378
2002	West Tenn (SL)	AA	.261	129	498	68	130	28	6	20	79	52	129	12	.462	.332
2003	Iowa (PCL)	AAA	.269	121	442	62	119	24	3	16	67	46	115	8	.446	.338
	Chicago (NL)	MAJ	.167	10	12	1	2	1	0	0	1	0	5	0	.250	.167
MAJOR LEAGUE TOTALS			.167	10	12	1	2	1	0	0	1	0	5	0	.250	.167
MINOR LEAGUE TOTALS			.271	614	2377	352	644	115	29	85	372	222	598	66	.451	.334

10 Jae-Kuk Ryu, rhp

Born: May 30, 1983. **Ht.:** 6-3. **Wt.:** 210. **Bats:** R. **Throws:** R. **Career Transactions:** Signed out of Korea by Cubs, June 1, 2001.

Ryu has pitched well since the Cubs signed him out of Korea for $1.6 million, but his performance and potential were overshadowed by an incident in April 2003. Ryu killed an osprey by throwing a baseball and knocking it from its perch atop a light pole at Daytona's Jackie Robinson Ballpark. He dominated low Class A after a punitive demotion, then was inconsistent in his first try at Double-A. Ryu can toy with hitters when he's on. His 92-93 mph fastball and his curveball are his primary pitches, and he commands them well. He gets good run on his changeup. Ryu could use better control of his changeup, and his overall command deteriorated in Double-A. Some Cubs officials aren't enamored with his splitter. But his biggest need is to mature and acclimate himself to the United States. In addition to the osprey attack, Ryu also has had multiple run-ins with teammates. Ryu wasn't ready for Double-A last year, but the Cubs couldn't send him back to Daytona. He'll get another look in 2004.

Year	Club (League)	Class	W	L	ERA	G	GS	CG	SV	IP	H	R	ER	HR	BB	SO	AVG
2001	Cubs (AZL)	R	1	0	0.61	4	3	0	0	15	11	2	1	0	5	20	.196
2002	Boise (NWL)	A	6	1	3.57	10	10	0	0	53	45	28	21	1	25	56	.223
	Lansing (Mid)	A	1	2	7.11	5	4	0	0	19	26	16	15	1	8	21	.333
2003	Daytona (FSL)	A	0	1	3.05	4	4	0	0	21	14	14	7	1	11	22	.187
	Lansing (Mid)	A	6	1	1.75	11	11	0	0	72	59	19	14	2	19	57	.225
	West Tenn (SL)	AA	2	5	5.43	11	11	1	0	58	63	37	35	3	25	45	.280
MINOR LEAGUE TOTALS			16	10	3.53	45	43	1	0	237	218	116	93	8	93	221	.243

11 Luke Hagerty, lhp

Born: April 1, 1981. **Ht.:** 6-7. **Wt.:** 230. **Bats:** R. **Throws:** L. **School:** Ball State University. **Career Transactions:** Selected by Cubs in first round (32nd overall) of 2002 draft; signed June 27, 2002 . . . On disabled list, June 11-Sept. 1, 2003.

Hagerty looked so good in spring training last year that scouts wondered how he could have lasted 32 picks in the 2003 draft, or gone 31 picks after his former Ball State teammate, Bryan Bullington. Hagerty's lively fastball was crackling in the mid-90s, and his slider was much improved, giving him a second nasty pitch. But while warming up for his final spring training start, Hagerty felt a pop in his elbow. Then he received an unwanted 22nd birthday present: An MRI that revealed he needed Tommy John surgery. The operation and rehabilitation have gone well, and Hagerty should return to the mound in mid-2004. The track record of Tommy John patients is good, and Kerry Wood on the parent Cubs provides a local source of inspiration. Hagerty will have to regain his plus stuff, which he should be able to do given his work ethic, and develop a reliable changeup. The elbow injury was a total shock because he hadn't experienced any physical problems and he has stress-free mechanics, especially for a pitcher as large as he is. Like most Tommy John survivors, it probably will take him two years to get back to 100 percent, which would be 2005 in his case. Loaded with quality pitchers, the Cubs are more than willing to wait for another.

Year	Club (League)	Class	W	L	ERA	G	GS	CG	SV	IP	H	R	ER	HR	BB	SO	AVG
2002	Boise (NWL)	A	5	3	1.13	10	10	0	0	48	32	15	6	2	15	50	.189
2003	Did not play—Injured																
MINOR LEAGUE TOTALS			5	3	1.13	10	10	0	0	48	32	15	6	2	15	50	.189

12 Jason Dubois, of/1b

Born: March 26, 1979. **Ht.:** 6-5. **Wt.:** 220. **Bats:** R. **Throws:** R. **School:** Virginia Commonwealth University. **Career Transactions:** Selected by Cubs in 14th round of 2000 draft; signed June

11, 2000 . . . On disabled list, June 26-Sept. 15, 2000 . . . Selected by Blue Jays from Cubs in Rule 5 major league draft, Dec. 16, 2002 . . . Returned to Cubs, March 15, 2003.

The Cubs nearly lost Dubois a year ago. He had a solid track record of hitting, setting the career home run record and winning the 2000 Colonial Athletic Association triple crown at Virginia Commonwealth, then leading the Florida State League in slugging and ranking second in on-base percentage in 2002. Nevertheless, Chicago didn't protect him on its 40-man roster and watched Toronto select him in the major league Rule 5 draft. When Dubois went 3-for-18 in big league camp, the Jays decided they couldn't keep him on their big league roster and the Cubs gladly took him back. Dubois responded with another solid season and was named Arizona Fall League MVP after hitting .358 with a league-best nine homers. Chicago likely will buy out Moises Alou's $11.5 million option for 2005, and David Kelton and Dubois are the best in-house candidates to take over in left field. Dubois has more raw power than Kelton, which could be his ticket to winning the job. His size and his opposite-field pop are signs that he annually can double the 15 homers he hit last season. Kelton is more of a pure hitter, but Dubois has better patience and on-base skills. He's somewhat of a dead high ball hitter, but he's doing a good job of closing some of his holes. He has below-average speed and isn't the athlete Kelton is, but Dubois can play either outfield corner or first base adequately. He won 19 games as a pitcher at VCU and his arm strength helps him in the outfield. He'll spend most of this season in Triple-A, preparing for the challenge of 2005.

Year	Club (League)	Class	AVG	G	AB	R	H	2B	3B	HR	RBI	BB	SO	SB	SLG	OBP
2000	Did not play—Injured															
2001	Lansing (Mid)	A	.296	118	443	76	131	28	9	24	92	46	120	1	.562	.377
2002	Daytona (FSL)	A	.321	99	361	64	116	25	1	20	85	57	95	6	.562	.422
2003	West Tenn (SL)	AA	.269	130	443	57	119	31	4	15	73	57	118	2	.458	.367
MINOR LEAGUE TOTALS			.294	347	1247	197	366	84	14	59	250	160	333	9	.525	.387

13 Todd Wellemeyer, rhp

Born: Aug. 30, 1978. **Ht.:** 6-3. **Wt.:** 200. **Bats:** R. **Throws:** R. **School:** Bellarmine (Ky.) University. **Career Transactions:** Selected by Cubs in fourth round of 2000 draft; signed June 10, 2000.

On most teams, Wellemeyer would be going to big league camp as a frontrunner to win a rotation spot. On the pitching-rich Cubs, he's not even guaranteed of finding a role as the last man in the bullpen. Wellemeyer has legitimate starter stuff. He can hit 96 mph with his four-seam fastball and achieve plenty of sink with his two-seamer. Iowa pitching coach Jerry Reuss helped him add more tilt to his slider and he gets good movement on his changeup. Wellemeyer needs to remember that location matters as much as power. He sometimes overthrows, leaving his fastball up in the strike zone and losing command. His slider and changeup also need more consistency, as big league hitters learned to sit on his fastball. If Chicago decides to keep him in relief, he could become a set-up man in time. Wellemeyer will try to crack the Cubs staff in spring training, and he'll return to Triple-A if he can't.

Year	Club (League)	Class	W	L	ERA	G	GS	CG	SV	IP	H	R	ER	HR	BB	SO	AVG
2000	Eugene (NWL)	A	4	4	3.67	15	15	0	0	76	62	35	31	3	33	85	.225
2001	Lansing (Mid)	A	13	9	4.16	27	27	1	0	147	165	85	68	14	74	167	.288
2002	Daytona (FSL)	A	2	4	3.79	14	14	0	0	74	63	33	31	7	19	87	.230
	West Tenn (SL)	AA	3	3	4.70	8	8	1	0	46	33	25	24	2	18	37	.204
2003	West Tenn (SL)	AA	1	1	5.48	4	4	0	0	21	19	13	13	1	10	34	.238
	Iowa (PCL)	AAA	5	5	5.18	13	12	0	0	66	68	39	38	7	33	56	.272
	Chicago (NL)	MAJ	1	1	6.51	15	0	0	1	28	25	22	20	5	19	30	.245
MAJOR LEAGUE TOTALS			1	1	6.51	15	0	0	1	28	25	22	20	5	19	30	.245
MINOR LEAGUE TOTALS			28	26	4.29	81	80	2	0	430	410	230	205	34	187	466	.254

14 Nic Jackson, of

Born: Sept. 25, 1979. **Ht.:** 6-3. **Wt.:** 200. **Bats:** L. **Throws:** R. **School:** University of Richmond. **Career Transactions:** Selected by Cubs in third round of 2000 draft; signed June 20, 2000.

Jackson could push himself into the mix to replace Moises Alou in 2005 if he can remain healthy—something he has done in just one of his four pro seasons. He had a ligament injury in his right middle finger in 2000 and a fractured right shin in 2002. Jackson stayed in one piece until mid-August last year, when he hurt his shoulder diving for a fly ball. He has one of the best packages of tools in the system but his development has been stalled since managers named him the Florida State League's most exciting player in 2001. He has a quick bat, strength and speed, and he often gets compared to fellow University of Richmond product Brian Jordan. While Jackson started poorly in Triple-A, his production increased each month until he got injured. He needs more at-bats to make further adjustments. He still has problems with pitches on the outer half of the plate and with breaking balls, and he doesn't use the opposite field as much as he should. Jackson has enough range for center field but his arm is his weakest tool and may not be strong enough for right. He'll head back to Triple-A in 2005, where he could be flanked by David Kelton and Jason Dubois in the Iowa outfield.

Year	Club (League)	Class	AVG	G	AB	R	H	2B	3B	HR	RBI	BB	SO	SB	SLG	OBP
2000	Eugene (NWL)	A	.255	74	294	39	75	12	7	6	47	22	64	25	.405	.308
2001	Daytona (FSL)	A	.296	131	503	87	149	30	6	19	85	39	96	24	.493	.355
2002	West Tenn (SL)	AA	.290	32	131	18	38	9	1	3	20	6	23	8	.443	.329
2003	Iowa (PCL)	AAA	.253	125	458	56	116	19	4	11	44	35	102	17	.384	.315
MINOR LEAGUE TOTALS			.273	362	1386	200	378	70	18	39	196	102	285	74	.434	.330

15 Sergio Mitre, rhp

Born: Feb. 16, 1981. **Ht.:** 6-4. **Wt.:** 210. **Bats:** R. **Throws:** R. **School:** San Diego CC. **Career Transactions:** Selected by Cubs in seventh round of 2001 draft; signed June 7, 2001.

Mitre doesn't have the front-of-the-rotation profile of the pitchers ahead of him on this list, but he has enjoyed consistent success throughout the minors and reached Chicago for a pair of emergency starts barely two years after he signed out of San Diego City College. His stuff has gotten a little better each year to the point where it's average across the board. His velocity fluctuates from 86-94 mph, and his fastball is more notable for its sink. He's a strikethrowing, ground-ball machine who also works with a curveball or changeup. Mitre isn't overpowering and doesn't have much margin for error, which big league hitters showed by letting him fall behind in the count before pounding him. He has a ceiling as a No. 4 or 5 starter, and he'd also be effective as a middle reliever with a knack for getting double plays. There's no opening for him on the current big league staff, so he'll spend this year in Triple-A. The Cubs fielded several trade inquiries about Mitre last summer and could be tempted to deal him in 2004.

Year	Club (League)	Class	W	L	ERA	G	GS	CG	SV	IP	H	R	ER	HR	BB	SO	AVG
2001	Boise (NWL)	A	8	4	3.07	15	15	1	0	91	85	37	31	2	18	71	.243
2002	Lansing (Mid)	A	8	10	2.83	27	27	2	0	169	166	72	53	7	22	96	.261
2003	West Tenn (SL)	AA	7	9	3.34	25	24	0	0	146	162	75	54	6	41	128	.282
	Chicago (NL)	MAJ	0	1	8.31	3	2	0	0	9	15	8	8	1	4	3	.395
MAJOR LEAGUE TOTALS			0	1	8.31	3	2	0	0	9	15	8	8	1	4	3	.395
MINOR LEAGUE TOTALS			23	23	3.06	67	66	3	0	405	413	184	138	15	86	295	.265

16 Francis Beltran, rhp

Born: Nov. 29, 1979. **Ht.:** 6-6. **Wt.:** 230. **Bats:** R. **Throws:** R. **Career Transactions:** Signed out of Dominican Republic by Cubs, Nov. 15, 1996.

After pitching in the Futures Game, showing the best fastball in the Southern League and making his big league debut in 2002, Beltran had a forgettable 2003. His numbers were good but he wasn't his usual dominant self in Triple-A, and he pitched just twice after June 22 because of triceps tendinitis. He reportedly was on the list of prospects the Pirates could choose from in the Aramis Ramirez/Kenny Lofton trade, and Beltran's physical condition probably contributed to Pittsburgh's decision to take Bobby Hill. When he's right, Beltran can chew hitters up with a 95-98 mph fastball and a mid-80s slider. He'll throw a splitter to keep hitters off balance. It's the closest thing he has to a changeup, the pitch that prevented him from progressing as a starter. Beltran pitched well in his native Dominican Republic this winter, so his health is no longer a concern. Command remains his weakness, and once he improves in that regard he'll be ready to help the Cubs. He'll get a look in spring training but almost certainly will begin 2004 in Triple-A.

Year	Club (League)	Class	W	L	ERA	G	GS	CG	SV	IP	H	R	ER	HR	BB	SO	AVG
1997	Cubs (AZL)	R	0	1	3.42	16	0	0	1	24	27	18	9	1	8	17	.276
1998	Cubs (AZL)	R	1	1	5.55	12	5	0	0	36	49	23	22	1	14	26	.343
1999	Cubs (AZL)	R	0	1	0.00	7	0	0	2	11	5	3	0	0	1	8	.139
	Eugene (NWL)	A	0	2	8.36	16	0	0	0	28	41	32	26	2	14	28	.331
2000	Lansing (Mid)	A	1	1	9.68	16	0	0	0	18	24	22	19	0	19	16	.338
	Eugene (NWL)	A	2	2	2.68	25	0	0	8	44	28	16	13	1	20	52	.178
2001	Daytona (FSL)	A	6	9	5.00	21	18	0	0	95	93	62	53	10	40	72	.251
2002	West Tenn (SL)	AA	2	2	2.59	39	0	0	23	42	28	14	12	2	19	43	.192
	Chicago (NL)	MAJ	0	0	7.50	11	0	0	0	12	14	11	10	2	16	11	.311
2003	Iowa (PCL)	AAA	6	2	2.96	31	2	0	4	49	46	17	16	2	19	33	.247
MAJOR LEAGUE TOTALS			0	0	7.50	11	0	0	0	12	14	11	10	2	16	11	.311
MINOR LEAGUE TOTALS			18	21	4.43	183	25	0	38	345	341	207	170	19	154	295	.256

17 Brian Dopirak, 1b

Born: Dec. 20, 1983. **Ht.:** 6-4. **Wt.:** 230. **Bats:** R. **Throws:** R. **School:** Dunedin (Fla.) HS. **Career Transactions:** Selected by Cubs in second round of 2002 draft; signed Aug. 4, 2002.

There must be something about Dunedin (Fla.) High and power hitters. Some scouts considered Dopirak to have the most raw power in the 2002 draft, even more than Brewers first-rounder Prince Fielder. Now Dopirak has been surpassed in his own organization by 2003 first-rounder Ryan Harvey, his former Dunedin teammate. Harvey is more of a well-rounded athlete while Dopirak is more of a grip-it-and-rip-it slugger, but when Dopirak makes contact he can drive a ball out of sight. He earned Northwest League all-star honors last year and after starting 2-for-22 following a promotion to low Class A, he hit .337 the rest of the way (including the playoffs). His plate discipline still leaves a lot to be desired and Midwest League pitchers got him to chase most anything. He'll have to make more adjustments to climb through the minors. Dopirak's power will have to carry him, because he won't hit for a high average, he doesn't run well and he's just adequate at first base. That said, few players in the minors have his Dopirak's 40- or 50-homer ceiling. The Cubs do like his attitude and he has put in time trying to get better defensively. He'll advance one step at the time, meaning he should spend 2004 back in the MWL.

Year	Club (League)	Class	AVG	G	AB	R	H	2B	3B	HR	RBI	BB	SO	SB	SLG	OBP
2002	Cubs (AZL)	R	.253	21	79	10	20	4	0	0	6	6	23	0	.304	.306
2003	Boise (NWL)	A	.240	52	192	25	46	4	0	13	37	24	58	0	.464	.330
	Lansing (Mid)	A	.269	19	78	8	21	3	0	2	10	2	22	0	.385	.305
MINOR LEAGUE TOTALS			.249	92	349	43	87	11	0	15	53	32	103	0	.410	.319

18 Billy Petrick, rhp

Born: April 29, 1984. **Ht.:** 6-6. **Wt.:** 240. **Bats:** B. **Throws:** R. **School:** Morris (Ill.) HS. **Career Transactions:** Selected by Cubs in third round of 2002 draft; signed July 19, 2002.

The Cubs weren't able to keep former draft picks Quincy Carter and Antwaan Randle El away from college football, and ultimately the NFL. But they lured Petrick, one of the nation's top long snapper recruits, from a Washington State football scholarship by giving him $459,500 as a 2002 third-round pick. He's strong and athletic for a pitcher, and his lower half reminds the Cubs of Mark Prior's. Petrick is still raw and has much to learn, but he also has the makings of a power pitcher. He throws a low-90s fastball that can reach 96 mph, and he's tough to homer against because he throws on a steep downward plane and has good sink. He's still putting together the rest of his repertoire. His curveball was too big and loopy, so he replaced it with a slider that's in its formative stages. His changeup can become a solid-average pitch in time. His command also needs improvement. Chicago can afford to show lots of patience with Petrick, who will move up to low Class A this year.

Year	Club (League)	Class	W	L	ERA	G	GS	CG	SV	IP	H	R	ER	HR	BB	SO	AVG
2002	Cubs (AZL)	R	2	1	1.71	6	6	0	0	32	21	8	6	0	6	35	.189
2003	Boise (NWL)	A	2	5	4.76	14	14	0	0	64	60	49	34	4	27	64	.241
MINOR LEAGUE TOTALS			4	6	3.75	20	20	0	0	96	81	57	40	4	33	99	.225

19 Jason Wylie, rhp

Born: May 27, 1981. **Ht.:** 6-5. **Wt.:** 230. **Bats:** R. **Throws:** R. **School:** University of Utah. **Career Transactions:** Selected by Cubs in 12th round of 2002 draft; signed June 6, 2002.

Wylie is another victim of Chicago's tremendous pitching depth. His scintillating 2002 pro debut showed that he was a steal as a 12th-rounder, and the Cubs realized that he had the stuff to do more than close games. But they didn't have a rotation opening in Class A last year, so he stayed in relief and continued to excel. He led the Midwest League in appearances and for the second time in as many years, he made a major postseason contribution to a championship club. Lansing ran the table with seven straight playoff wins, with Wylie saving four of them. Hitters just don't make good contact against Wylie, who has permitted a .178 opponent average and one homer as a pro. He gets great sink and bore on a low- to mid-90s fastball, and hitters can't think about sitting on it because he can beat them with his curveball and slider. He also throws a changeup. Wylie needs more consistency with his command, but he's on the verge of moving quickly. He'll probably start 2004 in high Class A with a chance for a midseason promotion.

Year	Club (League)	Class	W	L	ERA	G	GS	CG	SV	IP	H	R	ER	HR	BB	SO	AVG
2002	Boise (NWL)	A	1	1	1.99	24	0	0	11	41	26	9	9	1	7	44	.187
2003	Lansing (Mid)	A	1	2	1.38	57	0	0	29	59	36	13	9	0	22	54	.171
MINOR LEAGUE TOTALS			2	3	1.63	81	0	0	40	99	62	22	18	1	29	98	.178

20 Ricky Nolasco, rhp

Born: Dec. 13, 1982. **Ht.:** 6-2. **Wt.:** 220. **Bats:** R. **Throws:** R. **School:** Rialto (Calif.) HS. **Career Transactions:** Selected by Cubs in fourth round of 2001 draft; signed July 31, 2001.

Nolasco is the stealth pitching prospect in the Cubs system. Drafted in the fourth round in 2001, when Chicago started its draft by taking Mark Prior and Andy Sisco, Nolasco never has received much attention. Yet he has a 19-7, 2.69 career record and skipped a level en route to a successful year in high Class A at age 20. He and Felix Sanchez were headed to Texas last summer in a trade for Rafael Palmeiro before Palmeiro nixed returning to the Cubs. The younger brother of Brewers minor league righthander Dave Nolasco, Ricky has a feel for pitching and a competitive makeup. When he got shelled for a 11.57 ERA through his first three Florida State League starts, he didn't panic and went 11-3, 2.23 the rest of the way. Nolasco's stuff is pretty nice, too. He throws a fastball in the low 90s, and it sinks and bores in on righthanders. His curveball is a solid second pitch, and he can change speeds on it. His changeup is on the road to becoming an average pitch. Nolasco puts his pitches where he wants to and gets lots of groundouts. He's ready for Double-A and could be pitching in Chicago by the end of 2005.

Year	Club (League)	Class	W	L	ERA	G	GS	CG	SV	IP	H	R	ER	HR	BB	SO	AVG
2001	Cubs (AZL)	R	1	0	1.50	5	4	0	0	18	11	3	3	0	5	23	.175
2002	Boise (NWL)	A	7	2	2.48	15	15	0	0	91	72	32	25	1	25	92	.214
2003	Daytona (FSL)	A	11	5	2.96	26	26	1	0	149	129	58	49	7	48	136	.232
MINOR LEAGUE TOTALS			19	7	2.69	46	45	1	0	258	212	93	77	8	78	251	.222

21 Felix Sanchez, lhp

Born: Aug. 3, 1981. **Ht.:** 6-3. **Wt.:** 180. **Bats:** R. **Throws:** L. **Career Transactions:** Signed out of Dominican Republic by Cubs, Sept. 15, 1998.

In Dusty Baker's first big league camp as Chicago's manager, few players opened his eyes as much as Sanchez, who posted a 1.29 ERA in 14 innings. Not many lefties can light up a radar gun like Sanchez, who can pitch in the mid-90s and touch 97 when working out of the bullpen. The Cubs hoped to make him a starter, but his inability to develop his secondary pitches will have them settle for a power lefty reliever instead. He went to the bullpen full-time in 2003, though he pitched out of the rotation at the end of the year to make up for innings lost when a torn pectoral muscle sidelined him for five weeks. Sanchez' slider is an average pitch at times but not frequently enough. He also has a decent changeup he doesn't throw as much out of the bullpen. He needs to do a better job of repeating his delivery, which would help his slider and his command. Chicago signed Kent Mercker as a free agent, buying a year of development time for Sanchez in Triple-A.

Year	Club (League)	Class	W	L	ERA	G	GS	CG	SV	IP	H	R	ER	HR	BB	SO	AVG
1999	Cubs (DSL)	R	1	3	3.28	7	7	0	0	25	27	18	9	1	9	27	.273
2000	Cubs (DSL)	R	4	2	3.15	13	13	0	0	54	45	26	19	2	15	61	.223
2001	Cubs (AZL)	R	2	5	4.01	12	9	0	0	61	57	38	27	2	22	55	.250
	Boise (NWL)	A	2	0	1.56	3	3	0	0	17	11	4	3	0	10	16	.180
2002	Lansing (Mid)	A	6	6	4.15	26	21	0	2	119	130	67	55	7	44	101	.286
2003	West Tenn (SL)	AA	2	2	3.23	30	8	0	0	64	57	30	23	3	31	55	.235
	Cubs (AZL)	R	0	0	0.00	1	1	0	0	2	2	0	0	0	0	3	.250
	Chicago (NL)	MAJ	0	0	10.80	3	0	0	0	2	2	2	2	1	3	2	.333
MAJOR LEAGUE TOTALS			0	0	10.80	3	0	0	0	2	2	2	2	1	3	2	.333
MINOR LEAGUE TOTALS			17	18	3.58	92	62	0	2	342	329	183	136	15	131	318	.254

22 Jon Leicester, rhp

Born: Feb. 7, 1979. **Ht.:** 6-2. **Wt.:** 220. **Bats:** R. **Throws:** R. **School:** University of Memphis. **Career Transactions:** Selected by Cubs in 11th round of 2000 draft; signed June 19, 2000.

The Cubs did a masterful job of finding pitching in the late rounds of the 2000 draft. They signed 2003 National League rookie of the year Dontrelle Willis in the eighth round, Leicester in the 11th, Carmen Pignatiello in the 20th and Jason Szuminski (lost to the Padres in December's major league Rule 5 draft) in the 27th. Area scout Mark Adair had to do a lot of projection on Leicester, who went 0-11, 6.72 and performed better as a shortstop that year at the University of Memphis. While he never has had a winning record or posted an ERA lower than 3.89 as pro, Leicester has made good progress and has been protected on the 40-man roster for the last two years. The Cubs still aren't sure if he'll wind up being a starter, set-up man or closer. Though he had a lower ERA in relief (3.35) than in the rotation (4.44) in Double-A, he actually pitched better as a starter. Leicester has one of the best pure arms in the system, throwing 95-96 mph and topping out at 98 last year. Leicester also can over-match hitters with his slider and splitter at times. The key for him is command, in terms of both throwing all his pitches for strikes and locating them in the zone. He pitches high in the strike zone too often, which won't be as easy to get away with in the majors. He'll spend 2004 in Triple-A.

Year	Club (League)	Class	W	L	ERA	G	GS	CG	SV	IP	H	R	ER	HR	BB	SO	AVG
2000	Eugene (NWL)	A	1	5	5.44	17	7	0	0	50	47	36	30	4	22	31	.247
2001	Lansing (Mid)	A	9	10	5.29	28	27	1	0	153	182	117	90	16	58	109	.297
2002	Daytona (FSL)	A	2	3	3.97	20	14	0	0	82	77	43	36	2	48	57	.248
	West Tenn (SL)	AA	2	2	4.61	5	4	0	0	27	24	16	14	1	13	18	.231
2003	West Tenn (SL)	AA	6	7	3.89	45	9	1	6	106	89	54	46	7	53	106	.227
	Iowa (PCL)	AAA	0	0	7.20	1	1	0	0	5	6	4	4	0	2	4	.316
MINOR LEAGUE TOTALS			20	27	4.68	116	62	2	6	423	425	270	220	30	196	325	.261

23 Sean Marshall, lhp

Born: Aug. 30, 1982. **Ht.:** 6-5. **Wt.:** 185. **Bats:** L. **Throws:** L. **School:** Virginia Commonwealth University. **Career Transactions:** Selected by Cubs in sixth round of 2003 draft; signed June 7, 2003.

Marshall and his twin brother Brian helped Virginia Commonwealth lead NCAA Division I with a 2.54 team ERA in 2003. Afterward, Brian signed with the Red Sox as a fifth-rounder and Sean went to the Cubs in the sixth round. Though he has a ways to go to reach his ceiling, Marshall has similar upside to Andy Sisco. He has a projectable body at 6-foot-6 and 195 pounds. While he currently pitches in the high 80s, he has touched 93 mph and could get there regularly. And while it's not overpowering at this point, his heater is tough to hit because of its movement and his command of it. He varies the speeds on a curveball that can be a plus pitch, and he's not afraid to throw his changeup in any count. Marshall throws strikes and keeps the ball down in the zone. He just needs to work on adding strength and establishing his fastball more often. He has an advanced feel for pitching and could move quickly. Marshall could handle a promotion to high Class A but the Cubs' logjam of pitching may send him to low Class A to begin 2004.

Year	Club (League)	Class	W	L	ERA	G	GS	CG	SV	IP	H	R	ER	HR	BB	SO	AVG
2003	Boise (NWL)	A	5	6	2.57	14	14	0	0	74	66	31	21	1	23	88	.237
	Lansing (Mid)	A	1	0	0.00	1	1	0	0	7	5	1	0	0	0	11	.192
MINOR LEAGUE TOTALS			6	6	2.34	15	15	0	0	81	71	32	21	1	23	99	.233

24 Renyel Pinto, lhp

Born: July 8, 1982. **Ht.:** 6-4. **Wt.:** 190. **Bats:** L. **Throws:** L. **Career Transactions:** Signed out of Venezuela by Cubs, Jan. 31, 1999.

Pinto's 2003 season started on the wrong foot. He missed the first four weeks with a sprained ankle, then gave up a total of three earned runs in his first four starts—and had a 0-2 record to show with it. Though his run support never came around, he finished the year on a positive note when the Cubs added him to the 40-man roster for the first time. Pinto throws his fastball in the low 90s and misses bats because hitters have a hard time picking up his pitches from his low three-quarters arm angle. He's still turning his curveball and changeup into consistently effective pitches, but he shows pretty good command. If his secondary pitches don't come around, he'd make a good lefty reliever. Pinto will pitch in the Double-A rotation this year.

Year	Club (League)	Class	W	L	ERA	G	GS	CG	SV	IP	H	R	ER	HR	BB	SO	AVG
1999	Cubs (DSL)	R	4	5	4.38	13	13	1	0	64	70	35	31	5	22	62	.289
2000	Cubs (AZL)	R	0	2	6.30	9	4	0	0	30	42	29	21	3	16	23	.326
2001	Lansing (Mid)	A	4	8	5.22	20	20	1	0	88	94	64	51	9	44	69	.278
2002	Daytona (FSL)	A	3	3	5.51	7	7	0	0	33	45	23	20	5	11	24	.338
	Lansing (Mid)	A	7	5	3.31	17	16	0	0	98	79	39	36	9	28	92	.221
2003	Daytona (FSL)	A	3	8	3.22	20	19	0	0	115	91	47	41	4	45	104	.221
MINOR LEAGUE TOTALS			21	31	4.22	86	79	2	0	427	421	237	200	35	166	374	.261

25 John Webb, rhp

Born: May 23, 1979. **Ht.:** 6-3. **Wt.:** 220. **Bats:** R. **Throws:** R. **School:** Manatee (Fla.) CC. **Career Transactions:** Selected by Cubs in 19th round of 1999 draft; signed June 16, 1999.

Webb had Tommy John surgery in 2001, and he started to regain his previous stuff in the Arizona Fall League after the 2003 season. After throwing 88-91 mph during the summer, he bumped his fastball up to 91-94 mph in the AFL. Webb's heater has late sinking life, but he needs to work it inside more often. A full-time shortstop and part-time reliever at Manatee (Fla.) Community College, he brings good athleticism to the mound. That should help him repeat his delivery better, the key to improved command and secondary pitches.

Webb will show a slider with some power and depth, but not on a consistent basis. His curveball and changeup are just ordinary at best. If he can continue to pitch like he did in the AFL, he could help the Cubs after a season in Triple-A.

Year	Club (League)	Class	W	L	ERA	G	GS	CG	SV	IP	H	R	ER	HR	BB	SO	AVG
1999	Cubs (AZL)	R	0	0	3.58	18	0	0	3	33	33	20	13	0	8	39	.246
	Eugene (NWL)	A	1	0	0.00	2	0	0	1	4	1	0	0	0	1	3	.077
2000	Lansing (Mid)	A	7	6	2.47	21	21	1	0	135	125	53	37	4	40	108	.250
	Daytona (FSL)	A	1	1	4.76	4	2	0	1	17	17	11	9	1	3	18	.250
2001	Daytona (FSL)	A	1	1	5.40	5	4	0	0	20	23	13	12	0	7	20	.280
2002	Daytona (FSL)	A	5	3	3.43	10	10	1	0	58	43	23	22	3	23	65	.207
	West Tenn (SL)	AA	4	5	4.52	11	11	0	0	62	52	33	31	5	22	45	.231
2003	West Tenn (SL)	AA	5	8	4.50	30	22	0	1	132	135	74	66	11	52	85	.270
MINOR LEAGUE TOTALS			24	24	3.72	101	70	2	6	460	429	227	190	24	156	383	.248

26 Carmen Pignatiello, lhp

Born: Sept. 12, 1982. **Ht.:** 6-0. **Wt.:** 180. **Bats:** R. **Throws:** L. **School:** Providence Catholic HS, New Lenox, Ill. **Career Transactions:** Selected by Cubs in 20th round of 2000 draft; signed June 28, 2000.

Though his fastball resides in the 83-85 mph range, Pignatiello led the Florida State League in strikeouts last year. With that lack of velocity, he'll have to keep proving himself, but he also has an impressive résumé dating back to when he won a gold medal with Team USA at the 1999 World Junior Championship. He was a high school teammate of righthander Kris Honel, who was drafted in the first round in 2001 by Chicago's other big league team. Pignatiello survives with below-average velocity because he has a plus curveball and command, along with a good changeup. He draws the standard comparisons to Jamie Moyer and Kirk Rueter, though he'll probably have to develop more fastball to move all the way up the ladder. Pignatiello is vulnerable when he doesn't locate his pitches, as evidenced by him topping the FSL in runs, earned runs and homers allowed. He has earned a promotion to Double-A in 2004.

Year	Club (League)	Class	W	L	ERA	G	GS	CG	SV	IP	H	R	ER	HR	BB	SO	AVG
2000	Cubs (AZL)	R	4	1	4.46	9	3	0	0	36	48	26	18	1	13	32	.314
2001	Boise (NWL)	A	7	3	3.00	16	12	0	1	78	70	37	26	2	22	83	.230
2002	Lansing (Mid)	A	9	11	3.17	27	27	1	0	167	152	76	59	10	51	139	.240
2003	Daytona (FSL)	A	8	11	4.38	26	26	1	0	156	144	87	76	13	55	140	.241
	West Tenn (SL)	AA	1	0	1.50	1	1	0	0	6	3	1	1	1	2	11	.150
MINOR LEAGUE TOTALS			29	26	3.65	79	69	2	1	444	417	227	180	27	143	405	.244

27 Rich Hill, lhp

Born: March 11, 1980. **Ht.:** 6-5. **Wt.:** 190. **Bats:** L. **Throws:** L. **School:** University of Michigan. **Career Transactions:** Selected by Cubs in fourth round of 2002 draft; signed July 10, 2002.

Drafted in the seventh round by the Angels in 2001 when he was sophomore-eligible, Hill turned them down to return to Michigan. Had Hill pitched enough innings to qualify, his 13.7 strikeouts per nine innings easily would have topped the minors in 2003. While he has no trouble missing bats, he has problems missing the strike zone. He has given up nearly as many walks as hits since turning pro, and his control was off so much last year that he had to be demoted from low Class A at age 23. Hill led the short-season Northwest League in strikeouts, thanks to his lively 91-93 mph fastball and knee-buckling curveball. But he's going to have to throw a lot more strikes to have a chance at being even a big league reliever. The Cubs think his control is more a mental than physical issue. Hill's pitches move so much that he gets himself in trouble by trying to paint the corners rather than challenging hitters. His changeup also needs improvement, but his command obviously is the key. He'll try to figure it out in low Class A this year.

Year	Club (League)	Class	W	L	ERA	G	GS	CG	SV	IP	H	R	ER	HR	BB	SO	AVG
2002	Boise (NWL)	A	0	2	8.36	6	5	0	0	14	15	19	13	0	14	12	.268
2003	Lansing (Mid)	A	0	1	2.76	15	4	0	0	29	14	12	9	0	36	50	.141
	Boise (NWL)	A	1	6	4.35	14	14	0	0	68	57	40	33	5	32	99	.233
MINOR LEAGUE TOTALS			1	9	4.43	35	23	0	0	112	86	71	55	5	82	161	.215

28 Darin Downs, lhp

Born: Dec. 26, 1984. **Ht.:** 6-3. **Wt.:** 176. **Bats:** R. **Throws:** L. **School:** Santaluces HS, Boynton Beach, Fla. **Career Transactions:** Selected by Cubs in fifth round of 2003 draft; signed June 7, 2003.

Downs got rocked in the Rookie-level Arizona League in his professional debut, but that wasn't a true indication of his potential. He missed a month of his high school senior season with shoulder tendinitis and was never 100 percent after signing for $225,000 as a fifth-round pick. When Downs was sound last spring, one scout said he had the best command he had seen in 20 years and could handle Double-A. His curveball rated a 70 on the 20-80 scouting scale, and some observers thought his changeup was just as good. With those two offerings and an advanced feel for pitching, he compensates for an 85-89 mph fastball that lacks plus velocity or life. Downs' shoulder is fine now and shouldn't be a long-term problem. The Cubs took things slowly with him last summer and probably will do so again in 2004, which could mean some time in extended spring and a June assignment to short-season Boise.

Year	Club (League)	Class	W	L	ERA	G	GS	CG	SV	IP	H	R	ER	HR	BB	SO	AVG
2003	Cubs (AZL)	R	0	2	6.57	13	11	0	0	38	48	30	28	2	17	32	.318
MINOR LEAGUE TOTALS			0	2	6.57	13	11	0	0	38	48	30	28	2	17	32	.318

29 Bear Bay, rhp

Born: Aug. 7, 1983. **Ht.:** 6-2. **Wt.:** 160. **Bats:** R. **Throws:** R. **School:** Angelina (Texas) JC.
Career Transactions: Selected by Cubs in 25th round of 2002 draft; signed May 22, 2003.

The Cubs unveiled another wave of pitching in the Arizona League last year. Besides Darin Downs, they also featured the league's wins leader in Bay and strikeout king in hard-throwing Carlos Marmol. Bay signed as a draft-and-follow out of Angelina (Texas) Junior College in May, then drew the support of managers as the AZL's top pitching prospect. He throws four pitches for strikes and delivers them all from the same arm slot. He can get up to 94 mph with his four-seam fastball, and he also uses a two-seamer, curveball and changeup. The Cubs made minor mechanical adjustments, getting Bay to stay back longer and shorten his stride, and he had no problem filling the strike zone afterward. He tired late in the summer, so he'll need to get stronger, which could add more juice to his fastball. He could open 2004 in the low Class A rotation.

Year	Club (League)	Class	W	L	ERA	G	GS	CG	SV	IP	H	R	ER	HR	BB	SO	AVG
2003	Cubs (AZL)	R	7	1	2.50	10	6	0	0	58	51	18	16	2	9	69	.237
	Boise (NWL)	A	1	2	3.74	4	4	0	0	22	17	9	9	1	7	24	.213
MINOR LEAGUE TOTALS			8	3	2.84	14	10	0	0	79	68	27	25	3	16	93	.231

30 Matt Craig, 3b

Born: April 16, 1981. **Ht.:** 6-3. **Wt.:** 200. **Bats:** B. **Throws:** R. **School:** University of Richmond.
Career Transactions: Selected by Cubs in third round of 2002 draft; signed June 17, 2002.

Virginia isn't considered the most fertile breeding ground for prospects, but area scout Billy Swoope found six of the Cubs' top 30 prospects there: Justin Jones (No. 2), Brendan Harris (No. 8), Jason Dubois (No. 12), Nic Jackson (No. 14), Sean Marshall (No. 23) and Craig. Though Craig struggled mightily in his 2002 pro debut, the Cubs jumped him to high Class A last year and he passed the test. He's an offense-first player with a nice swing from both sides of the plate. He's similar offensively to Harris, hitting for average with gap power and a decent amount of walks. Craig should hit more homers as he fills out. The biggest difference between the two is that Harris is more athletic and capable of playing second or third base. Craig's speed, hands and arm are below average, and he may not be able to stick at the hot corner. Left field is his fallback position, and moving there would require him to provide more offense. He'll play regularly at third in Double-A this year.

Year	Club (League)	Class	AVG	G	AB	R	H	2B	3B	HR	RBI	BB	SO	SB	SLG	OBP
2002	Boise (NWL)	A	.193	37	140	19	27	2	0	5	20	12	28	0	.314	.252
2003	Daytona (FSL)	A	.285	119	442	56	126	25	2	11	66	46	87	4	.425	.357
MINOR LEAGUE TOTALS			.263	156	582	75	153	27	2	16	86	58	115	4	.399	.332

CHICAGO
WHITE SOX

By Phil Rogers

Some years the White Sox are sellers, and some years they are buyers. The latter was the case in 2003. Having added one 20-game winner in Bartolo Colon and discovered another in Eseban Loiaza, general manager Ken Williams figured he had a team with staying power. So he made a flurry of trades that cost Chicago six of its top 30 prospects entering the season. The moves helped the White Sox recover from a 45-49 first half and take a two-game lead in the American League Central on Sept. 9. But Chicago lost the last five games of its season series with Minnesota and ultimately finished four games behind the Twins.

The White Sox were left with nothing to show for thinning out their prospect depth. Add in the stunted development of outfielder Joe Borchard, lefty Corwin Malone and righty Jon Rauch—all considered among the game's top young talents at one point—and the departure of 1999 first-round pick Brian West to play football at Louisiana State, and it was a negative year for Chicago's system.

There were some bright spots. Miguel Olivo jumped from Double-A to the majors, establishing himself as the regular catcher despite hitting just .237. Outfielder Jeremy Reed and lefty Neal Cotts also emerged as likely contributors in the not-too-distant future. Reed won the minor league batting title at .373, while Cotts salvaged something from the Keith Foulke-Billy Koch deal with the Athletics.

While the system saw upheaval, so too did the front office. Scouting director Doug Laumann was demoted to special-assignment scout in July. In three years on the job, Laumann drafted the system's top two prospects in Reed and righty Kris Honel. He had a strong draft in 2003, which included outfielders Ryan Sweeney and Brian Anderson, plus shortstop Robert Valido.

Farm director Bob Fontaine Jr. was interested in replacing Laumann, returning to the scouting director's role after previously serving in that capacity for the Angels. That didn't happen, so Fontaine became scouting director for the Mariners.

Duane Shaffer, Sox senior director of player personnel, reassumed scouting director duties after holding that post from 1991-2000. His draft picks include Mark Buehrle, a 38th-rounder in 1998, and Borchard. The new farm director is Dave Wilder, who held that job for the Cubs before becoming an assistant GM with them and the Brewers.

Shaffer and Wilder have their work cut out for them. The White Sox aren't bereft of talent, but they're weaker than they have been in years. They can begin restocking with the 2004 draft, as they own six picks in the first two rounds after losing Colon and Tom Gordon to free agency.

ORGANIZATION
OVERVIEW

General manager: Ken Williams. **Farm director:** Dave Wilder. **Scouting director:** Duane Shaffer.

2003 PERFORMANCE

Class	Team	League	W	L	Pct.	Finish*	Manager
Majors	Chicago	American	86	76	.531	t-6th (14)	Jerry Manuel
Triple-A	Charlotte Knights	International	74	70	.514	6th (14)	Nick Capra
Double-A	Birmingham Barons	Southern	73	64	.533	3rd (10)	Wally Backman
High A	Winston-Salem Warthogs	Carolina	71	67	.514	+5th (8)	Razor Shines
Low A	Kannapolis Intimidators	South Atlantic	55	82	.401	15th (16)	John Orton
Rookie	Great Falls White Sox	Pioneer	38	38	.500	4th (7)	Chris Cron
Rookie	Bristol White Sox	Appalachian	33	33	.500	6th (10)	Jerry Hairston
OVERALL 2003 MINOR LEAGUE RECORD			344	354	.493	19th (30)	

*Finish in overall standings (No. of teams in league). +League champion.

ORGANIZATION LEADERS

BATTING   *Minimum 250 At-Bats
*AVG Jeremy Reed, Birmingham/Winston-Salem .. .373
R Jeremy Reed, Birmingham/Winston-Salem 88
H Jeremy Reed, Birmingham/Winston-Salem .. 173
TB Ross Gload, Charlotte 266
2B Ross Gload, Charlotte 40
3B Ross Gload, Charlotte 6
HR Brian Becker, Winston-Salem 19
RBI Jeremy Reed, Birmingham/Winston-Salem 95
BB Jeremy Reed, Birmingham/Winston-Salem 70
SO Charlie Lisk, Kannapolis/Great Falls 104
SB Ruddy Yan, Winston-Salem 76
*SLG Jeremy Reed, Birmingham/Winston-Salem .. .537
*OBP Jeremy Reed, Birmingham/Winston-Salem .. .453

PITCHING   #Minimum 75 Innings
W Brian Cooper, Charlotte 15
L Three tied at 12
#ERA Ryan Meaux, Birmingham/Winston-Salem .. 1.55
G Josh Fields, Winston-Salem 58
CG Kris Honel, Birmingham/Winston-Salem 3
SV Josh Fields, Winston-Salem 20
IP Brian Cooper, Charlotte 174
BB Wyatt Allen, Winston-Salem 89
SO Kris Honel, Birmingham/Winston-Salem....... 135

BEST TOOLS

Best Hitter for Average .... Jeremy Reed
Best Power Hitter.. Joe Borchard
Fastest Baserunner .... Ruddy Yan
Best Athlete .... Chris Young
Best Fastball .... Enemencio Pacheco
Best Curveball .... Kris Honel
Best Slider .... Ryan Wing
Best Changeup .... Neal Cotts
Best Control.. Ryan Meaux
Best Defensive Catcher .... Chris Stewart
Best Defensive Infielder............................. Robert Valido
Best Infield Arm .... Andy Gonzalez
Best Defensive Outfielder....................... Brian Anderson
Best Outfield Arm .... Brian Anderson

PROJECTED 2007 LINEUP

Catcher.. Miguel Olivo
First Base.. Paul Konerko
Second Base .... Willie Harris
Third Base .... Joe Crede
Shortstop .... Robert Valido
Left Field.. Ryan Sweeney
Center Field .... Jeremy Reed
Right Field .... Magglio Ordonez

Designated Hitter .... Carlos Lee
No. 1 Starter .... Mark Buehrle
No. 2 Starter .... Esteban Loaiza
No. 3 Starter .... Kris Honel
No. 4 Starter.. Jon Garland
No. 5 Starter... Neal Cotts
Closer.. Damaso Marte

LAST YEAR'S TOP 20 PROSPECTS

1. Joe Borchard, of	11. Neal Cotts, lhp
2. Miguel Olivo, c	12. Micah Schnurstein, 3b
3. Anthony Webster, of	13. Dave Sanders, lhp
4. Kris Honel, rhp	14. Ryan Wing, lhp
5. Jon Rauch, rhp	15. Brian West, rhp
6. Corwin Malone, lhp	16. Brian Miller, rhp
7. Andy Gonzalez, ss	17. Tim Hummel, ss/2b
8. Felix Diaz, rhp	18. Daniel Haigwood, lhp
9. Arnie Munoz, lhp	19. Pedro Lopez, 2b
10. Royce Ring, lhp	20. Jason Stumm, rhp

TOP PROSPECTS OF THE DECADE

1994 .... James Baldwin, rhp
1995 .... Scott Ruffcorn, rhp
1996.. Chris Snopek, ss/3b
1997 .... Mike Cameron, of
1998 .... Mike Caruso, ss
1999 .... Carlos Lee, 3b
2000 .... Kip Wells, rhp
2001 .... Jon Rauch, rhp
2002 .... Joe Borchard, of
2003 .... Joe Borchard, of

TOP DRAFT PICKS OF THE DECADE

1994 .... Mark Johnson, c
1995.. Jeff Liefer, 3b
1996.. *Bobby Seay, lhp
1997 .... Jason Dellaero, ss
1998 .... Kip Wells, rhp
1999 .... Jason Stumm, rhp
2000 .... Joe Borchard, of
2001 .... Kris Honel, rhp
2002 .... Royce Ring, lhp
2003 .... Brian Anderson, of
*Did not sign.

ALL-TIME LARGEST BONUSES

Joe Borchard, 2000 .... $5,300,000
Jason Stumm, 1999..................................... $1,750,000
Royce Ring, 2002 .... $1,600,000
Brian Anderson, 2003 .... $1,600,000
Kris Honel, 2001 .... $1,500,000

MINOR LEAGUE
DEPTH CHART

CHICAGO **WHITE SOX**   RANK: **21**

Impact potential (D): When Joe Borchard faltered in Triple-A, Jeremy Reed exploded onto the scene. While Reed has a knack for hitting that has already exceeded expectations, his power will have to develop for him to become an impact player in the majors. Ryan Sweeney has a high ceiling, but is several years away.

Depth (D): Just a few years ago, this organization seemed to be bursting at the seams with up-and-coming talent. Last summer's deadline deals, however, took much of the remaining depth in the team's failed effort to reach the postseason, leaving few surefire prospects.

Sleeper: Robert Valido, ss.   *—Depth charts prepared by Josh Boyd. Numbers in parentheses indicate prospect rankings.*

LF
Scott Bikowski
Clinton King

CF
Jeremy Reed (1)
Brian Anderson (7)
Chris Young (9)
Michael Spidale

RF
Ryan Sweeney (4)
Joe Borchard (5)
Ricardo Nanita (24)
Thomas Brice

3B
Micah Schnurstein (21)

SS
Robert Valido (13)
Michael Morse (17)
Andy Gonzalez (25)
Guillermo Reyes

2B
Pedro Lopez (20)
Antoin Gray (23)
Ruddy Yan (27)

1B
Ross Gload
Brian Becker
Casey Rogowski
Brandon Bounds

C
Chris Stewart
Charlie Lisk

SOURCE OF TALENT			
Homegrown		**Acquired**	
College	7	Trade	5
Junior College	2	Rule 5 draft	0
Draft-and-follow	1	Independent	0
High school	11	Free agent/waivers	0
Nondrafted free agent	0		
Foreign	4		

RHP

Starters	**Relievers**
Kris Honel (2)	Shingo Takatsu (8)
Brandon McCarthy (11)	Felix Diaz (18)
Brian Miller (12)	Gary Majewski
Jon Rauch (14)	Jon Adkins
Enemencio Pacheco (15)	Josh Fields
Orionny Lopez (29)	Jeff Bajenaru
Jason Stumm (30)	
Todd Deininger	
Jason Grilli	
Mitch Wylie	
Wyatt Allen	
Matt Nachreiner	

LHP

Starters	**Relievers**
Neal Cotts (3)	Arnie Munoz (10)
Ryan Wing (6)	Fabio Castro (16)
Corwin Malone (22)	Ryan Meaux (19)
Tim Tisch (26)	Dave Sanders
Josh Stewart (28)	Tetsu Yofu
Byeong Hak An	Jim Bullard
Daniel Haigwood	
Heath Phillips	
Paulino Reynoso	
Ryan Rodriguez	

DRAFT
ANALYSIS

Best Pro Debut: OF Ricardo Nanita (14) finished second in the Rookie-level Pioneer League batting race, hitting .384-5-37 with 11 steals. The White Sox' first four picks all topped .300, with the biggest surprise being SS Robert Valido (4), who hit .307-6-31 in the Rookie-level Appalachian League.

Best Athlete: Brian Anderson (1) and Ryan Sweeney (2) are five-tool outfielders who have shown potential on the mound. Anderson threw 92-93 mph as a freshman at Arizona, while Sweeney pitched at 88-92 last spring and drew legitimate interest as a lefthander.

Casey

Best Pure Hitter: Sweeney's bat speed, swing plane and approach should allow him to produce for both power and average.

Best Raw Power: Anderson can launch 400-foot line drives. OF Clint King (3) gets nice loft with his swing.

Fastest Runner: The White Sox went for power more than speed. Valido is the best runner, rating a 55 on the 20-80 scale.

Best Defensive Player: Valido could be an outstanding shortstop. His instincts and range allow him to cover ground, and he has soft hands and a strong arm.

Best Fastball: Chicago signed three strong arms out of the state of Texas. RHP John Russ (8) pitches at 90-92 mph and topped out at 96 during the spring. RHPs Matt Nachreiner (5) and James Casey (7) both throw 91-93, and Nachreiner achieves Derek Lowe-like sink on his fastball.

Best Breaking Ball: Russ' curveball has been compared to Mike Mussina's. But for all his stuff, he doesn't miss many bats. He allowed a .301 opponent average in the Pioneer League.

Most Intriguing Background: LHP Greg Moviel (15) and RHP Paul Moviel (36) are brothers. Greg, who already has a 90-92 mph fastball and is projectable at 6-foot-7 and 225 pounds, turned down the White Sox for Vanderbilt.

Closest To The Majors: Anderson, though he was set back by his second wrist surgery in the last year.

Best Late-Round Pick: Nanita. LHP Fraser Dizard (10) would have gone much higher had he not hurt his elbow in 2002 and pitched poorly last spring. When he's right, Dizard commands an 88-92 mph fastball, a plus changeup and an average curveball.

The One Who Got Away: LHP Donald Veal (12), SS Wes Hodges (13) and Greg Moviel. Veal, who went to Arizona, reminded some scouts of Dontrelle Willis. Hodges, now at Georgia Tech, slid when his power was muted by a broken hamate bone.

Assessment: The White Sox were short on position-player prospects before this hitter-heavy draft. Scouting director Doug Laumann's reward? Getting reassigned for political reasons.

OF Jeremy Reed (2) led the minors in hitting in 2003. LHP Royce Ring (1) and RHP Josh Rupe (3) were used in deals for Roberto Alomar and Carl Everett last year.

RHP Kris Honel (1) and LHP Ryan Wing (2) are two of the system's top pitching prospects. OF Chris Young (16) and RHP Brian Miller (20) could be late-round steals.

$5.3 million OF Joe Borchard (1) isn't earning Mark McGwire comparisons any longer. If he ever decided to pursue the NFL, he might wind up throwing passes to OF Freddie Mitchell (50).

Once heralded as a classic pitching draft, this crop might not produce much for the White Sox in the long run. RHPs Matt Ginter (1), Danny Wright (2), Jon Rauch (3) and Joe Valentine (26) and LHPs Josh Stewart (5) and David Sanders (6) have all pitched in the majors but haven't succeeded. 2B Scott Hairston (18) would be starting in Chicago had he signed.

—Draft analysis prepared by Jim Callis. Numbers in parentheses indicate draft rounds.

Jeremy
Reed

Born: June 15, 1981.
Ht.: 6-0. **Wt.:** 180.
Bats: L. **Throws:** L.
School: Long Beach State University.
Career Transactions: Selected by White Sox in second round of 2002 draft; signed June 25, 2002.

Doug Laumann, who lasted three years as the White Sox' scouting director, may have hit a home run with Reed. Reed played mostly first base during his first two seasons at Long Beach State before moving to the outfield as a junior. Laumann and scouts Joe Butler and Matt Hattabaugh saw enough to project him as a big league center fielder. They may turn out to be exactly right. It required less faith to envision Reed producing with a wood bat. He used wood when he won the Alaska League MVP award in 2000, and again when he led Team USA in hitting with a .366 average in 2001. But even Chicago has been surprised at how quickly Reed has adapted to pro ball. After hitting .319 at low Class A Kannapolis in his pro debut, Reed led the minors with a .373 average and .453 on-base percentage last year. He was at his best after a promotion to Double-A Birmingham, hitting .409-7-43 with 18 steals in 66 games. After the season, Reed started in the outfield for the Team USA squad that was upset by Mexico in the Olympic qualifying tournament.

Reed can really hit. He not only has a simple stroke that allows him to make contact almost at will but he also has a terrific eye for the strike zone. He walked nearly twice as much as he struck out in 2003. Wally Backman, his manager at Birmingham last year, says Reed has such an advanced ability to anticipate pitches that he sometimes helps teammates prepare for at-bats. Like a young Rafael Palmeiro, Reed uses the whole park with his line-drive stroke and should develop more power in time, though he'll generate a lot more doubles than homers. He'll probably max out at 15-20 homers annually. He doesn't have any problems with lefthanders, hitting them at a .352 clip last year. Reed runs well and has a natural aggressiveness that allows him to stretch hits into an extra base. He has become an average center fielder and should get better with more experience there. His arm is average, and he could possibly play right field if he can't stick in center. Reed's aggressiveness occasionally turns into recklessness. He needs to pick his spots better as a basestealer after getting caught in 13 of 31 attempts in Double-A. If he proves unable to handle center field, he won't have the home run power typical of a corner outfielder. Nevertheless, he should provide enough offense to hold down a job in left or right. Reed sprained his right wrist while with the U.S. qualifying team, but he's expected to be fine by spring training.

After finishing third behind Twins catcher Joe Mauer and Royals righthander Zack Greinke in BA's 2003 Minor League Player of the Year race, Reed is on the fast track to Chicago. He'll go to big league camp as a nonroster invitee, and the White Sox don't have a clear-cut center fielder. Several club officials would like to see Reed get a full season at Triple-A Charlotte, however, and he'll likely open the season playing alongside Joe Borchard there. With Magglio Ordonez one year away from free agency, it's conceivable both Reed and Borchard will be regulars in 2005.

Year	Club (League)	Class	AVG	G	AB	R	H	2B	3B	HR	RBI	BB	SO	SB	SLG	OBP
2002	Kannapolis (SAL)	A	.319	57	210	37	67	15	0	4	32	11	24	17	.448	.377
2003	Winston-Salem (Car)	A	.333	65	222	37	74	18	1	4	52	41	17	27	.477	.431
	Birmingham (SL)	AA	.409	66	242	51	99	17	3	7	43	29	19	18	.591	.474
MINOR LEAGUE TOTALS			.356	188	674	125	240	50	4	15	127	81	60	62	.509	.430

2 Kris Honel, rhp

RODGER WOOD

Born: Nov. 7, 1982. **Ht.:** 6-5. **Wt.:** 190. **Bats:** R. **Throws:** R. **School:** Providence Catholic HS, New Lenox, Ill. **Career Transactions:** Selected by White Sox in first round (16th overall) of 2001 draft; signed June 14, 2001.

A local product, Honel went 16th overall in the 2001 draft, making him the earliest Illinois prep pitcher picked since Bob Kipper was chosen eighth in 1982. Honel continues to justify his selection, earning all-star recognition in both of his full seasons. He helped Winston-Salem capture the high Class A Carolina League championship in 2003 with two wins in the playoffs, including the clincher. Since his mid-teens, Honel has thrown a knee-buckling knuckle-curve, and he'll use it in any count. His fastball climbed back to 91-93 mph last year after dipping a little in 2002. He has a lot of natural movement on his heater, with late break down and away from righthanders. He gets deception from a natural snap at the end of his delivery. He repeats his delivery well, giving him good command. Honel has enough fastball now, but his frame is so projectable that the White Sox continue to watch for him to develop more velocity. That's all he needs to have front-of-the-rotation stuff. The Sox rushed Jon Garland and Dan Wright to the majors but are more cautious these days. They want Honel to be ready when he gets there, with the second half of 2005 a reasonable goal. He'll pitch in Double-A this year.

Year	Club (League)	Class	W	L	ERA	G	GS	CG	SV	IP	H	R	ER	HR	BB	SO	AVG
2001	White Sox (AZL)	R	2	0	1.80	3	1	0	0	10	9	3	2	0	3	8	.257
	Bristol (Appy)	R	2	3	3.13	8	8	0	0	46	41	19	16	4	9	45	.240
2002	Kannapolis (SAL)	A	9	8	2.82	26	26	0	0	153	128	57	48	12	52	152	.228
	Winston-Salem (Car)	A	0	0	1.69	1	1	0	0	5	3	2	1	0	3	8	.150
2003	Winston-Salem (Car)	A	9	7	3.11	24	24	3	0	133	122	51	46	7	42	122	.248
	Birmingham (SL)	AA	1	0	3.75	2	2	0	0	12	9	6	5	2	6	13	.205
MINOR LEAGUE TOTALS			23	18	2.95	64	62	3	0	360	312	138	118	25	115	348	.236

3 Neal Cotts, lhp

Born: March 25, 1980. **Ht.:** 6-2. **Wt.:** 200. **Bats:** L. **Throws:** L. **School:** Illinois State University. **Career Transactions:** Selected by Athletics in second round of 2001 draft; signed June 13, 2001 . . . Traded by Athletics with OF Daylan Holt to White Sox, Dec. 16, 2002, completing trade in which White Sox sent RHP Keith Foulke, C Mark Johnson, RHP Joe Valentine and cash to Athletics for RHP Billy Koch and two players to be named (Dec. 3, 2002).

Unsung when he was traded, Cotts has become the best part of the Billy Koch-Keith Foulke deal for the White Sox. He started the 2003 Futures Game at U.S. Cellular Field and would have won the Double-A Southern League ERA title had he not fallen 3 1/2 innings shy of qualifying. His first big league promotion lasted four starts, as he left a poor impression because of wildness. Cotts has averaged 11.2 strikeouts per nine innings in the minors despite a fastball that tops out at 91 mph. His motion deceives hitters and makes his fastball look harder. His changeup is his best pitch, and his curveball improved last year. He does a good job changing speeds and using his secondary pitches to set up his fastball. He keeps the ball down in the strike zone and rarely gives up homers. Cotts will have to iimprove his control before he gets another shot with the White Sox. Big league hitters didn't chase his pitches out of the strike zone, and they didn't swing and miss too often when his stuff came over the plate. He doesn't have an obvious out pitch for the majors. A strong spring training could put Cotts into immediate consideration for a spot in the Chicago rotation. More likely, he'll go to Triple-A and be in line for a big league job in 2005.

Year	Club (League)	Class	W	L	ERA	G	GS	CG	SV	IP	H	R	ER	HR	BB	SO	AVG
2001	Vancouver (NWL)	A	1	0	3.09	9	7	0	0	35	28	14	12	2	13	44	.215
	Visalia (Cal)	A	3	2	2.32	7	7	0	0	31	27	14	8	0	15	34	.225
2002	Modesto (Cal)	A	12	6	4.12	28	28	0	0	138	123	72	63	5	87	178	.239
2003	Birmingham (SL)	AA	9	7	2.16	21	21	0	0	108	67	32	26	2	56	133	.178
	Chicago (AL)	MAJ	1	1	8.10	4	4	0	0	13	15	12	12	1	17	10	.294
MAJOR LEAGUE TOTALS			1	1	8.10	4	4	0	0	13	15	12	12	1	17	10	.294
MINOR LEAGUE TOTALS			25	15	3.14	65	63	0	0	312	245	132	109	9	171	389	.215

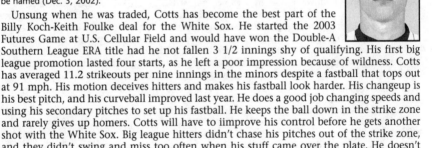

4 Ryan Sweeney, of

Born: Feb. 20, 1985. **Ht.:** 6-4. **Wt.:** 200. **Bats:** L. **Throws:** L. **School:** Xavier HS, Cedar Rapids, Iowa. **Career Transactions:** Selected by White Sox in second round of 2003 draft; signed July 12, 2003.

Sweeney had a chance to become Iowa's first high school first-rounder, but a lackluster performance at a predraft showcase dropped him to the second round. Scouted as both a pitcher and hitter, he signed for $785,000. Because he had college basketball potential, the White Sox were able to spread his bonus over five years. Sweeney drew rave reviews in instructional league. He is a competitor in an ultra-athletic package. He's considered a pure hitter with gap power, in the mold of John Olerud. He has great plate coverage and surprisingly good plate discipline for such a raw talent. He has a plus arm, showing an 88-92 mph fastball and promising curveball last spring, and is suited for right field. Having put on 15 pounds of muscle, Sweeney looks like a power hitter but has yet to become one with a wood bat. He sometimes appears too pull-conscious. His fielding skills are raw. The consensus is that he has more offensive upside than 2003 first-rounder Brian Anderson. With his strong debut, Sweeney showed that he's ready for low Class A this year.

Year	Club (League)	Class	AVG	G	AB	R	H	2B	3B	HR	RBI	BB	SO	SB	SLG	OBP
2003	Bristol (Appy)	R	.313	19	67	11	21	3	0	2	5	7	10	3	.448	.387
	Great Falls (Pio)	R	.353	10	34	0	12	2	0	0	4	2	3	0	.412	.389
MINOR LEAGUE TOTALS			.327	29	101	11	33	5	0	2	9	9	13	3	.436	.387

5 Joe Borchard, of

Born: Nov. 25, 1978. **Ht.:** 6-5. **Wt.:** 220. **Bats:** B. **Throws:** R. **School:** Stanford University. **Career Transactions:** Selected by White Sox in first round (12th overall) of 2000 draft; signed Aug. 8, 2000.

Borchard is under increasing pressure to justify the record $5.3 million bonus he was given to forsake a career as an NFL quarterback. He has gone backward the last two years, largely because he chases too many bad pitches. Somewhat limited by a broken foot in 2002, he had no excuses last season. Borchard's athleticism and leadership skills give him an edge over most ballplayers. He generates easy power and can hit monster home runs, especially from the left side. He has a strong arm, which he once showed by throwing five touchdown passes in a game against UCLA. Strikeouts are a concern, especially because his walk totals have diminished the last two years. Borchard's plate discipline has worsened even as the organization has emphasized its importance. He has become a particularly suspect hitter from the right side. He can play three outfield positions but is below-average in center, Chicago's original goal for him. After he played nonstop for 2½ years, the White Sox gave Borchard the winter off. He used the time to get married. It's unlikely he'll hit his way to Chicago in spring training and is destined for a third season in Triple-A.

Year	Club (League)	Class	AVG	G	AB	R	H	2B	3B	HR	RBI	BB	SO	SB	SLG	OBP
2000	White Sox (AZL)	R	.414	7	29	3	12	4	0	0	8	4	4	0	.552	.485
	Winston-Salem (Car)	A	.288	14	52	7	15	3	0	2	7	6	9	0	.462	.377
	Birmingham (SL)	AA	.227	6	22	3	5	0	1	0	3	3	8	0	.318	.308
2001	Birmingham (SL)	AA	.295	133	515	95	152	27	1	27	98	67	158	5	.509	.384
2002	Winston-Salem (Car)	A	.000	2	3	1	0	0	0	0	0	6	0	0	.000	.667
	Charlotte (IL)	AAA	.272	117	438	62	119	35	2	20	59	49	139	2	.498	.349
	Chicago (AL)	MAJ	.222	16	36	5	8	0	0	2	5	1	14	0	.389	.243
2003	Charlotte (IL)	AAA	.253	114	435	62	110	20	2	13	53	27	103	2	.398	.307
	Chicago (AL)	MAJ	.184	16	49	5	9	1	0	1	5	5	18	0	.265	.246
MAJOR LEAGUE TOTALS			.200	32	85	10	17	1	0	3	10	6	32	0	.318	.245
MINOR LEAGUE TOTALS			.276	393	1494	233	413	89	6	62	228	162	421	9	.469	.354

6 Ryan Wing, lhp

Born: Feb. 1, 1982. **Ht.:** 6-2. **Wt.:** 170. **Bats:** L. **Throws:** L. **School:** Riverside (Calif.) CC. **Career Transactions:** Selected by White Sox in second round of 2001 draft; signed July 23, 2001.

Selected one round after Kris Honel in the 2001 draft, Wing has been in lockstep with him ever since. He started and won the California-Carolina League all-star game last year and teamed with Honel to pitch Winston-Salem to a championship. Wing is a nightmare for lefthanders because of his arm angle and stuff. He has a low-90s fastball with hard, sinking action. He uses his sinker to set up an excellent slider. He doesn't hesitate to knock hitters off the plate. He's difficult to run on, leading Carolina League pitchers last year with 67 percent of basestealers getting caught against him. Wing sometimes struggles with his mechanics, which in turn leads to spotty control. That's the biggest difference between him and Honel. Wing should improve his command with more experience. Wing and Honel will team up again in Double-A this year. The White Sox have promoted plenty of pitchers from Birmingham to the majors, including Neil Cotts in 2003, and could get interested in Wing quickly if he has a good first half. More realistically, he needs another 300 minor league innings before getting the call.

Year	Club (League)	Class	W	L	ERA	G	GS	CG	SV	IP	H	R	ER	HR	BB	SO	AVG
2001	Bristol (Appy)	R	1	0	9.00	1	0	0	0	1	1	1	1	0	0	2	.200
2002	Kannapolis (SAL)	A	12	7	3.78	25	21	0	0	124	111	64	52	6	60	109	.240
2003	Winston-Salem (Car)	A	9	7	2.98	26	26	0	0	145	116	62	48	9	67	107	.227
MINOR LEAGUE TOTALS			22	14	3.37	52	47	0	0	270	228	127	101	15	127	218	.233

7 Brian Anderson, of

RODGER WOOD

Born: March 11, 1982. **Ht.:** 6-2. **Wt.:** 205. **Bats:** R. **Throws:** R. **School:** University of Arizona. **Career Transactions:** Selected by White Sox in first round (15th overall) of 2003 draft; signed June 19, 2003.

After a Freshman All-America season in 2001, Anderson slumped mightily as a sophomore at Arizona. He reworked his swing and his approach last spring, and it paid off as he went 15th overall in the draft and signed for $1.6 million. He made the most of the chance to audition for the White Sox, who train in Tucson and sent 16 scouts and coaches to watch him. Anderson got off to a fast start at Rookie-level Great Falls before being sidelined by minor wrist surgery. Anderson has all five tools and is a slightly better athlete than Ryan Sweeney. He's a polished hitter who can work counts and wait for a pitch to drive. He runs well and is a plus defender in center field. He has an outstanding arm and was clocked up to 93 mph as a reliever in his first two years with the Wildcats. Health is an issue. Anderson battled knee and wrist injuries in 2002, and his wrist began bothering him after he turned pro. Doctors shaved down a bone that was causing him irritation, and he's expected to be ready to go in spring training. With Chris Young slated to play center field in low Class A, Anderson likely will go to high Class A for his first full pro season. His big league ETA is mid-2006.

Year	Club (League)	Class	AVG	G	AB	R	H	2B	3B	HR	RBI	BB	SO	SB	SLG	OBP
2003	Great Falls (Pio)	R	.388	13	49	6	19	2	1	2	13	9	10	3	.592	.492
MINOR LEAGUE TOTALS			.388	13	49	6	19	2	1	2	13	9	10	3	.592	.492

8 Shingo Takatsu, rhp

RON VESELY

Born: Nov. 25, 1968. **Ht.:** 5-11. **Wt.:** 160. **Bats:** R. **Throws:** R. **Career Transactions:** Signed out of Japan by White Sox, Jan. 21, 2004.

Drawn to the city and the opportunity, Takatsu became the first Japanese veteran to sign with a Chicago team when he agreed to a one-year deal worth a guaranteed $1 million. He spent 13 years with the Yakult Swallows, surpassing Kazuhiro Sasaki in 2003 to take over Japan's all-time saves lead with 260. Takatsu was at his best in the Japan Series, going 2-0 with nine saves and a 0.00 ERA—this his nickname, "Mr. Zero"—helping the Swallows to four titles. Using a sidearm delivery, Takatsu is extremely deceptive and durable. He has plus command with three different pitches, changing speeds on his sinker, slider and changeup so well that he essentially has six different offerings. He can throw his changeup like a screwball and make his sinking fastball move toward either side of the plate. There's nothing overpowering about Takatsu. His fastball rarely climbs above 88 mph and often parks at 85-86. His control slipped a notch last year and he has averaged just 5.8 strikeouts per nine innings over the last two seasons. For a sinkerball pitcher, he gives up a surprising number of homers.Takatsu will work either as a set-up man or closer for the White Sox, depending on the performance of Billy Koch. The Sox hold a $2.5 million option on his contract for 2005.

Year	Club (League)	Class	W	L	ERA	G	GS	CG	SV	IP	H	R	ER	HR	BB	SO	AVG
1991	Yakult (CL)	JPN	1	1	4.23	13	1	1	0	28	34	15	13	4	6	25	—
1992	Yakult (CL)	JPN	5	3	4.68	23	8	3	0	83	84	48	43	10	36	63	—
1993	Yakult (CL)	JPN	6	4	2.30	56	1	0	20	78	69	28	20	3	24	72	—
1994	Yakult (CL)	JPN	8	4	2.86	47	0	0	19	72	63	25	23	7	30	54	—
1995	Yakult (CL)	JPN	1	3	2.61	39	0	0	28	48	42	14	14	2	14	36	—
1996	Yakult (CL)	JPN	2	6	3.24	39	0	0	21	50	56	18	18	7	16	35	—
1997	Yakult (CL)	JPN	7	4	2.04	51	3	0	7	79	55	20	18	9	20	68	—

1998	Yakult (CL)	JPN	2	3	5.56	42	0	0	3	45	54	29	28	6	26	32	—
1999	Yakult (CL)	JPN	1	1	2.18	40	0	0	30	41	32	11	10	6	8	38	—
2000	Yakult (CL)	JPN	0	1	2.08	35	0	0	29	35	32	8	8	4	8	29	—
2001	Yakult (CL)	JPN	0	4	2.61	52	0	0	27	52	49	17	15	3	13	39	—
2002	Yakult (CL)	JPN	0	2	3.89	44	0	0	32	42	37	19	18	6	11	28	—
2003	Yakult (CL)	JPN	2	3	3.00	44	0	0	34	42	42	18	14	7	21	26	—
JAPANESE LEAGUE TOTALS			35	39	3.13	525	13	4	260	695	649	270	242	74	233	545	—

9 Chris Young, of

Born: Sept. 5, 1983. **Ht.:** 6-2. **Wt.:** 170. **Bats:** R. **Throws:** R. **School:** Bellaire (Texas) HS. **Career Transactions:** Selected by White Sox in 16th round of 2001 draft; signed Aug. 19, 2001.

Young led Texas prepsters in steals in 2001 at perennial power Bellaire High, which went 34-2 and was ranked sixth nationally. He lasted 16 rounds in the draft, mostly because he was scrawny. He has filled out as a pro and made great strides in 2003, when he ranked as the No. 2 prospect in the Rookie-level Appalachian League. Speed remains Young's best tool. He has been clocked at 4.0 seconds to first base from the right side of the plate. He's always a threat to steal bases, including third. Young has learned to use the whole field while developing surprising power and improved strike-zone judgment. He's an above-average center fielder who played 50 consecutive errorless games last year. Young sometimes looks bad against breaking pitches. He needs to do a better job making contact to take full advantage of his speed. He has a below-average arm and didn't register an assist in 2003. The White Sox hope Young can continue to establish himself as he moves to low Class A. They have little need to rush him with Jeremy Reed, Joe Borchard and Brian Anderson ahead of him on the center-field depth chart.

Year	Club (League)	Class	AVG	G	AB	R	H	2B	3B	HR	RBI	BB	SO	SB	SLG	OBP
02	White Sox (AZL)	R	.217	55	184	26	40	13	1	5	17	19	54	7	.380	.308
03	Bristol (Appy)	R	.290	64	238	47	69	18	3	7	28	23	40	21	.479	.357
	Great Falls (Pio)	R	.176	10	34	5	6	3	0	0	1	1	10	0	.265	.200
MINOR LEAGUE TOTALS			.252	129	456	78	115	34	4	12	45	43	104	28	.423	.326

10 Arnie Munoz, lhp

Born: June 21, 1982. **Ht.:** 5-9. **Wt.:** 170. **Bats:** L. **Throws:** L. **Career Transactions:** Signed out of Dominican Republic by White Sox, Dec. 20, 1998.

Munoz was named pitcher of the year in the Dominican League after the 2002 season, and he paid for it. He barely had any time off before spring training and the workload showed. His snapdragon curveball didn't have its usual bite as he failed to impress in big league camp and started slowly in Triple-A. When it's on, Munoz' curveball is one of the best in the minors. He uses tremendous arm speed to get the same violent break as Barry Zito. Munoz' fastball can touch 90 mph. Those two pitches account for his ratio of 10.9 strikeouts per nine innings as a pro and make him a scourge on lefthanders, who hit just .128 against him last year. He's poised and controls the running game exceptionally well. Munoz continues working on his changeup and slider. He needs something more to get righties out after they torched him for a .339 average in 2003. The White Sox haven't given him a chance to start because he's a maximum-effort pitcher who wears down after one trip through the lineup. The Sox appear set with lefties Damaso Marte and Kelly Wunsch in their bullpen, but Munoz has intriguing talent. He figures to arrive in Chicago at some point in 2004 and has Eddie Guarado potential.

Year	Club (League)	Class	W	L	ERA	G	GS	CG	SV	IP	H	R	ER	HR	BB	SO	AVG
99	White Sox (AZL)	R	0	2	5.25	14	0	0	1	12	13	10	7	1	8	12	.255
00	Burlington (Mid)	A	2	3	6.81	22	0	0	0	38	45	34	29	2	25	44	.294
01	Kannapolis (SAL)	A	6	3	2.49	60	0	0	12	80	41	24	22	2	42	115	.161
02	Birmingham (SL)	AA	6	0	2.61	51	0	0	6	72	62	29	21	6	29	78	.231
03	Charlotte (IL)	AAA	4	3	4.75	49	0	0	6	55	52	35	29	7	27	63	.254
MINOR LEAGUE TOTALS			18	11	3.78	196	0	0	25	257	213	132	108	18	131	312	.229

11 Brandon McCarthy, rhp

Born: July 7, 1983. **Ht.:** 6-7. **Wt.:** 180. **Bats:** R. **Throws:** R. **School:** Lamar (Colo.) CC. **Career Transactions:** Selected by White Sox in 17th round of 2002 draft; signed June 7, 2002.

McCarthy has gone 25-8 over the last two seasons, including a 12-0 run at Lamar (Colo.) CC that drew the attention of Sox scouts Joe Butler and John Kazanas. He led national juco pitchers by averaging 14.0 strikeouts per nine innings in 2002, and he has topped the

Rookie-level Arizona and Pioneer leagues in innings and whiffs in his two pro seasons. McCarthy is a blue-collar version of former White Sox star Jack McDowell. He stands tall, challenges hitters and wins games. He doesn't blow the ball past hitters, getting his fastball up to just 91 mph, but he has a hard curveball with diving action plus an improving changeup. The best thing he does is throw strikes. McCarthy doesn't get a lot of movement on his fastball and is relatively hittable. He needs to work on commanding the inner half of the plate because hitters sometimes get too comfortable against him. McCarthy should gain velocity as he continues to fill out his frame. He'll probably advance a step to low Class A but is polished enough to be considered for a jump to high Class A.

Year	Club (League)	Class	W	L	ERA	G	GS	CG	SV	IP	H	R	ER	HR	BB	SO	AVG
02	White Sox (AZL)	R	4	4	2.76	14	14	0	0	78	78	40	24	6	15	79	.255
03	Great Falls (Pio)	R	9	4	3.65	16	15	1	0	101	105	49	41	7	15	125	.263
MINOR LEAGUE TOTALS			13	8	3.26	30	29	1	0	179	183	89	65	13	30	204	.259

12 Brian Miller, rhp

Born: Oct. 18, 1982. **Ht.:** 6-3. **Wt.:** 200. **Bats:** R. **Throws:** R. **School:** Charlotte (Mich.) HS.
Career Transactions: Selected by White Sox in 20th round of 2001 draft; signed Aug. 15, 2001.

Miller had been rated as the top prep pitcher in Michigan in 2001, but most organizations believed it would be impossible to get him to break his commitment to Michigan State. The White Sox waited until the 20th round to select him, negotiated hard and got him signed. They have taken it slowly with him as he seeks consistency. He has the best arm among the system's righthanders, and when it's on he can be spectacular, as he was in a seven-inning no hitter last year. At times he fights his mechanics, which causes him to have nights where finding the strike zone is a major task. His fastball qualifies as easy heat, climbing into the mid-90s without any effort to his delivery. He has a classic pitcher's body and should only get stronger. He came into the organization with a good changeup and has improved it. His breaking ball is another matter. Some scouts say Miller's arm action isn't conducive to throwing a good breaker, and he has yet to prove them wrong. Miller is on target to advance to high Class A in 2004. He has a ceiling of a middle-of-the-rotation starter.

Year	Club (League)	Class	W	L	ERA	G	GS	CG	SV	IP	H	R	ER	HR	BB	SO	AVG
02	Bristol (Appy)	R	7	3	4.30	13	13	0	0	61	57	32	29	3	30	63	.251
03	Kannapolis (SAL)	A	8	12	5.30	25	25	1	0	126	124	85	74	7	61	93	.258
MINOR LEAGUE TOTALS			15	15	4.97	38	38	1	0	186	181	117	103	10	91	156	.256

13 Robert Valido, ss

Born: May 16, 1985. **Ht.:** 6-2. **Wt.:** 180. **Bats:** R. **Throws:** R. **School:** Coral Park HS, Miami.
Career Transactions: Selected by White Sox in fourth round of 2003 draft; signed June 4, 2003.

Competition will be nothing new for Valido. He had to beat out two other highly regarded prospects, Sean Rodriguez (Anaheim's third-round pick in 2003) and Guillermo Martinez (the White Sox' 17th-rounder, who opted to attend South Alabama) to win the shortstop's job at Coral Park High. The Miami school also produced shortstop Luis Montanez, the No. 3 overall pick in 2000 by the Cubs. Valido is a gifted fielder who has a strong arm, range and soft hands. Scouts and coaches gush about his instincts and his willingness to take coaching, with Jerry Hairston, his manager at Rookie-level Bristol, saying Valido will do anything it takes to play in the big leagues. Valido lasted until the fourth round of the draft because teams were concerned about his hitting. But he went straight to the Appalachian League and held his own against older players, finishing ninth in the batting race and showing surprising power. He makes good contact but could draw a few more walks. Though his speed is only slightly above average, he was a force on the bases in his pro debut. Valido will compete against older shortstops in spring training to try to win a starting job in low Class A.

Year	Club (League)	Class	AVG	G	AB	R	H	2B	3B	HR	RBI	BB	SO	SB	SLG	OBP
03	Bristol (Appy)	R	.307	58	215	39	66	15	2	6	31	17	28	17	.479	.364
MINOR LEAGUE TOTALS			.307	58	215	39	66	15	2	6	31	17	28	17	.479	.364

14 Jon Rauch, rhp

Born: Sept. 27, 1978. **Ht.:** 6-11. **Wt.:** 260. **Bats:** R. **Throws:** R. **School:** Morehead State University. **Career Transactions:** Selected by White Sox in third round of 1999 draft; signed June 9, 1999.

Yes, it has been three seasons since Rauch was BA's 2000 Minor League Player of the Year and a key part of the gold medal-winning U.S. Olympic starting rotation. But the tallest pitcher in major league history still remains on the radar screen despite seemingly going into the witness-protection program. He was a forgotten man after spring training last season. He went to camp as a favorite to pitch in the White Sox rotation but lost out to Esteban

Loaiza and wasn't heard from again. Rauch turned in a solid Triple-A, recovering from a midseason sore shoulder—the same one he had operated on in 2001—to finish strong. He's not overpowering but gets seldom-seen arm angles from his height and has become a polished pitcher. His height causes his 91-92 fastball to appear harder than it is. He seems on top of hitters when he releases it. Rauch also has two above-average breaking balls and a decent changeup, but he must command of all his pitches to succeed. He's in the picture for a 2004 spot with the Sox, who praise his positive attitude. This will be a make-it-or-break-it year for Rauch, who's likely to be traded elsewhere if he doesn't secure a job in Chicago.

Year	Club (League)	Class	W	L	ERA	G	GS	CG	SV	IP	H	R	ER	HR	BB	SO	AVG
99	Bristol (Appy)	R	4	4	4.45	14	9	0	2	57	65	44	28	4	16	66	.269
	Winston-Salem (Car)	A	0	0	3.00	1	1	0	0	6	4	3	2	1	3	7	.174
00	Winston-Salem (Car)	A	11	3	2.86	18	18	1	0	110	102	49	35	10	33	124	.249
	Birmingham (SL)	AA	5	1	2.25	8	8	2	0	56	36	18	14	4	16	63	.179
01	Charlotte (IL)	AAA	1	3	5.79	6	6	0	0	28	28	20	18	8	7	27	.248
02	Chicago (AL)	MAJ	2	1	6.59	8	6	0	0	29	28	26	21	7	14	19	.248
	Charlotte (IL)	AAA	7	8	4.28	19	19	1	0	109	91	60	52	14	42	97	.226
03	Charlotte (IL)	AAA	7	1	4.11	24	23	1	0	125	121	60	57	16	35	94	.258
MAJOR LEAGUE TOTALS			2	1	6.59	8	6	0	0	29	28	26	21	7	14	19	.248
MINOR LEAGUE TOTALS			35	20	3.78	90	84	5	2	491	447	254	206	57	152	478	.240

15 Enemencio Pacheco, rhp

Born: Aug. 31, 1978. **Ht.:** 6-1. **Wt.:** 170. **Bats:** R. **Throws:** R. **Career Transactions:** Signed out of Dominican Republic by Rockies, Jan. 15, 1997 . . . Traded by Rockies to White Sox for C Sandy Alomar, July 29, 2002.

It's hard to understand why a general manager on a non-contender would give up a pitcher who throws 95 mph to give Sandy Alomar Jr. an extended tryout, but that's what Colorado's Dan O'Dowd did two years ago. The White Sox not only got a surprisingly good prospect in Pacheco, but also re-signed Alomar after he spent two months with the Rockies. Pacheco was considered a hard thrower without a clue during five seasons in the Colorado organization but showed enough last year in Double-A to be added to the 40-man roster. He barely earned his spot on the Birmingham roster out of spring training and opened the season as a long reliever, but he emerged as the top starter on a playoff team. Pacheco ended the season on a seven-game winning streak and then threw 13 shutout innings in the Southern League playoffs. The Barons went 20-4 in his regular-season starts, compared to 53-60 behind everyone else. The Sox are excited about the thunder in Pacheco's arm. In addition to his fastball, he also has a hard slider. He doesn't have much in the way of an off-speed, but got by with his power stuff and improved command as a starter. Chicago views him as a versatile pitcher who could either round out a starting rotation or serve as an Octavio Dotel-style set-up man. He would benefit from a full season at Triple-A but could push for a big league job with an impressive spring training.

Year	Club (League)	Class	W	L	ERA	G	GS	CG	SV	IP	H	R	ER	HR	BB	SO	AVG
97	Rockies (DSL)	R	1	6	5.26	11	10	1	0	51	70	49	30	3	22	39	.320
98	Rockies (AZL)	R	5	0	3.99	12	11	0	0	59	51	31	26	1	17	59	.234
	Asheville (SAL)	A	0	0	6.75	2	0	0	0	4	5	5	3	1	1	2	.278
99	Asheville (SAL)	A	3	9	5.29	15	15	1	0	85	98	60	50	4	29	59	.287
	Portland (NWL)	A	4	3	3.95	12	12	1	0	73	73	43	32	7	21	44	.248
00	Asheville (SAL)	A	8	10	3.69	21	21	0	0	117	129	67	48	9	35	79	.283
01	Salem (Car)	A	4	2	4.68	27	3	0	1	42	55	27	22	4	18	29	.313
	Asheville (SAL)	A	1	2	4.21	7	7	0	0	36	38	23	17	0	9	34	.264
02	Salem (Car)	A	2	2	3.16	41	0	0	6	51	52	22	18	1	26	31	.263
	Winston-Salem (Car)	A	1	1	4.74	8	4	0	0	25	31	17	13	1	8	24	.298
03	Birmingham (SL)	AA	12	2	2.56	30	24	0	0	151	131	51	43	5	51	116	.234
MINOR LEAGUE TOTALS			41	37	3.91	186	107	3	7	695	733	395	302	36	237	516	.269

16 Fabio Castro, lhp

Born: Jan. 20, 1985. **Ht.:** 5-8. **Wt.:** 157. **Bats:** L. **Throws:** L. **Career Transactions:** Signed out of Dominican Republic by White Sox, Dec. 26, 2001.

If his talent came in a bigger package, Castro already would have become a highly touted prospect. Don't be surprised if he emerges as one in the next couple of years. All the under-sized lefthander has done for the last two years is get outs, first in the Rookie-level Dominican Summer League and then as an 18-year-old in the Appalachian League, where he faced mostly hitters coming from college. Castro has very good command of an 89-91 mph fastball, a breaking ball and a changeup. His secondary pitches need more consistency, as is typical with young pitchers. He made two late-season starts in low Class A, impressing with his poise as much as his stuff. Should he catch a growth spurt, he could turn into a monster. He'll return to Kannapolis in 2004 and could get a full-time look as a starter.

Year	Club (League)	Class	W	L	ERA	G	GS	CG	SV	IP	H	R	ER	HR	BB	SO	AVG
02	White Sox (DSL)	R	10	2	1.95	25	2	0	8	65	37	17	14	3	23	89	.159
03	Bristol (Appy)	R	6	2	1.72	19	0	0	2	47	29	14	9	1	19	59	.173
	Kannapolis (SAL)	A	0	2	3.27	2	2	0	0	11	8	5	4	0	5	16	.200
MINOR LEAGUE TOTALS			16	6	1.98	46	4	0	10	123	74	36	27	4	47	164	.168

17 Mike Morse, ss

Born: March 22, 1982. **Ht.:** 6-4. **Wt.:** 180. **Bats:** R. **Throws:** R. **School:** Nova HS, Davie, Fla.
Career Transactions: Selected by White Sox in third round of 2000 draft; signed June 19, 2000.

Morse teamed with Ruddy Yan to give Carolina League champion Winston-Salem a dynamic double-play combination. Morse provided uncommon power for a middle infielder, while Yan led the league in steals. Morse has made a station-to-station climb through the system since being drafted in the third round in 2000. His pop is his strong suit, but he needs to make more contact and take more walks. At 6-foot-4, Morse is taller than most shortstops and there's some worry that he might outgrow the position. But he has a solid arm and still covers enough ground. He was steadier defensively last year after spending some time at third base in 2002. A return trip to high Class A might make some sense, giving Morse a chance to build on success.

Year	Club (League)	Class	AVG	G	AB	R	H	2B	3B	HR	RBI	BB	SO	SB	SLG	OBP
00	White Sox (AZL)	R	.256	45	180	32	46	6	1	2	24	15	29	5	.333	.308
01	Bristol (Appy)	R	.227	57	181	23	41	7	3	4	27	17	57	6	.365	.324
02	Kannapolis (SAL)	A	.257	113	417	43	107	30	4	2	56	25	73	7	.362	.310
03	Winston-Salem (Car)	A	.245	122	432	45	106	30	2	10	55	25	91	4	.394	.296
MINOR LEAGUE TOTALS			.248	337	1210	143	300	73	10	18	162	82	250	22	.369	.307

18 Felix Diaz, rhp

Born: July 27, 1980. **Ht.:** 6-1. **Wt.:** 180. **Bats:** R. **Throws:** R. **Career Transactions:** Signed out of Dominican Republic by Giants, March 20, 1998 . . . Traded by Giants with LHP Ryan Meaux to White Sox for OF Kenny Lofton, July 28, 2002.

Diaz once was one of the Giants' top pitching prospects, but they gave him up to rent Kenny Lofton for the stretch run in 2002. Now the White Sox have their own mixed feelings about Diaz. They've seen enough to put him on their 40-man roster but have yet to give him serious consideration for a big league role. He spent 2003 in Triple-A, where the good news was that he stayed healthy and set a career high for innings. The bad news was that he didn't distinguish himself. Diaz throws 92-94 mph but doesn't get a lot of movement on his fastball. His mid-80s slider and changeup are solid pitches. He throws strikes, too. Yet the total package is somehow less than the sum of its individual parts. Diaz will have to turn it on in Triple-A this year to have a chance at starting for the Sox. He's a wild card for an organization that no longer has many guys with plus arms knocking on the door.

Year	Club (League)	Class	W	L	ERA	G	GS	CG	SV	IP	H	R	ER	HR	BB	SO	AVG
98	Giants (DSL)	R	0	4	7.55	14	5	0	0	39	52	44	33	4	26	34	.306
99	Giants (DSL)	R	0	0	0.75	3	3	0	0	12	6	2	1	0	7	19	.150
00	Giants (AZL)	R	3	4	4.16	11	11	0	0	63	56	35	29	0	16	58	.232
	Salem-Keizer (NWL)	A	0	1	8.10	3	0	0	0	3	6	6	3	2	1	2	.400
01	Hagerstown (SAL)	A	1	4	3.66	15	12	0	0	52	49	27	21	4	16	56	.245
02	Shreveport (TL)	AA	3	5	2.70	12	12	1	0	60	54	22	18	1	23	48	.240
	Birmingham (SL)	AA	4	0	3.48	7	6	0	0	31	25	14	12	4	8	30	.207
03	Charlotte (IL)	AAA	5	7	3.97	27	18	1	0	116	122	59	51	12	33	83	.270
MINOR LEAGUE TOTALS			16	25	4.02	92	67	2	0	376	370	209	168	27	130	330	.253

19 Ryan Meaux, lhp

Born: Oct. 5, 1978. **Ht.:** 5-11. **Wt.:** 170. **Bats:** R. **Throws:** L. **School:** Lamar (Colo.) CC. **Career Transactions:** Selected by Giants in 25th round of 2001 draft; signed June 10, 2001 . . . Traded by Giants with RHP Felix Diaz to White Sox for OF Kenny Lofton, July 28, 2002.

Meaux was far less regarded than Felix Diaz when they arrived in the Kenny Lofton trade, but he appears a good bet to reach the majors as a situational lefthander or, possibly, a setup man. He's part of the same Lamar (Colo.) CC pipeline that produced Brandon McCarthy. Meaux doesn't have a plus pitch and has to be seen with the game on the line to be appreciated. His makeup is outstanding. He knows how to pitch and has developed tremendous command of all his pitches: a mid-80s fastball, a good curveball and a changeup he throws infrequently. He doesn't beat himself, permitting just four unintentional walks and two homers in 93 innings last year. He could earn a spot in Triple-A in spring training and be in Chicago before the year is over.

Year	Club (League)	Class	W	L	ERA	G	GS	CG	SV	IP	H	R	ER	HR	BB	SO	AVG
01	Salem-Keizer (NWL)	A	2	2	5.59	17	3	0	0	29	39	20	18	4	11	27	.325
02	Hagerstown (SAL)	A	4	3	2.63	44	0	0	17	55	41	22	16	1	12	44	.203
	Kannapolis (SAL)	A	0	2	1.35	10	0	0	6	13	19	10	2	1	0	13	.322
03	Winston-Salem (Car)	A	1	3	1.15	32	0	0	10	55	49	14	7	2	3	43	.239
	Birmingham (SL)	AA	1	2	2.13	26	0	0	2	38	39	11	9	0	3	29	.277
MINOR LEAGUE TOTALS			8	12	2.46	129	3	0	35	190	187	77	52	8	29	156	.257

20 Pedro Lopez, 2b/ss

Born: April 28, 1984. **Ht.:** 6-1. **Wt.:** 160. **Bats:** R. **Throws:** R. **Career Transactions:** Signed out of Dominican Republic by White Sox, Sept. 14, 2000.

Lopez excelled in two years of Rookie ball but found the going rougher in low Class A last year. He continued to show outstanding bat control but didn't approach his previous .316 career average. Lopez doesn't have much power but has bought into playing the little game. He makes contact, sprays the ball around the entire field and bunts for base hits. He needs to draw more walks, though he hurts his own cause by putting the ball in play most of the time when he swings. He has plus speed but is just a moderate threat as a basestealer. He could develop into a classic No. 2 hitter. Lopez stands out more on defense. Signed as a shortstop, he mostly has played second base with Andy Gonzalez playing alongside him. He has range, soft hands and above-average instincts. He'll probably team with Gonzalez again in high Class A this year.

Year	Club (League)	Class	AVG	G	AB	R	H	2B	3B	HR	RBI	BB	SO	SB	SLG	OBP
01	White Sox (AZL)	R	.312	50	199	26	62	11	3	1	19	16	24	12	.412	.359
02	Bristol (Appy)	R	.319	63	260	42	83	11	0	0	35	20	27	22	.362	.370
03	Kannapolis (SAL)	A	.264	109	390	40	103	23	0	0	33	26	43	24	.323	.314
	Winston-Salem (Car)	A	.231	4	13	1	3	0	0	0	0	1	0	0	.231	.286
MINOR LEAGUE TOTALS			.291	226	862	109	251	45	3	1	87	63	94	58	.354	.341

21 Micah Schnurstein, 3b

Born: July 18, 1984. **Ht.:** 6-1. **Wt.:** 200. **Bats:** R. **Throws:** R. **School:** Basic HS, Henderson, Nev. **Career Transactions:** Selected by White Sox in seventh round of 2002 draft; signed June 7, 2002.

A surprise seventh-round pick in 2002, Schnurstein introduced himself by terrorizing pitchers in the Arizona League, where he set a record with 26 doubles in 50 games. He encountered much more adversity in his first full pro season. He hoped to begin the season in low Class A but was assigned to extended spring training. After reporting to Great Falls in June, he missed time with a wrist injury. He didn't look like the Schnurstein of 2002 at the plate, failing to drive the ball. The White Sox were impressed by how he took his lumps in stride and didn't get overly frustrated. Power should be his best tool. He's an aggressive hitter who doesn't walk much. Stockily built, he's a below-average runner. Schnurstein converted to third base midway through his high school senior season and has played well there. He has good reactions, soft hands and a solid arm. Schnurstein will go to low Class A this year and try to put 2003 behind him.

Year	Club (League)	Class	AVG	G	AB	R	H	2B	3B	HR	RBI	BB	SO	SB	SLG	OBP
02	White Sox (AZL)	R	.332	50	205	28	68	26	1	3	48	12	34	1	.512	.373
03	Great Falls (Pio)	R	.264	50	193	35	51	9	1	1	16	11	39	0	.337	.313
MINOR LEAGUE TOTALS			.299	100	398	63	119	35	2	4	64	23	73	1	.427	.344

22 Corwin Malone, lhp

Born: July 3, 1980. **Ht.:** 6-3. **Wt.:** 200. **Bats:** R. **Throws:** L. **School:** Thomasville (Ala.) HS. **Career Transactions:** Selected by White Sox in ninth round of 1999 draft; signed June 7, 1999.

Two years after he ranked as the organization's top lefty prospect and one of the best in the entire game, Malone has slid back. He has spent back-to-back seasons mired in Double-A, plagued by wildness and elbow problems. He missed the final month of 2002 and two months in the middle of 2003. Recruited as a linebacker by Alabama-Birmingham, Malone can overpower hitters with his 92-93 mph as long as he gets his sharp-breaking curveball over the plate. That hasn't happened often enough in Double-A, where he has issued as many walks as strikeouts. There isn't much finesse to Malone, who needs a lot of improvement with his changeup and control. If that doesn't happen, he may face a future as a reliever. The White Sox were encouraged by Malone's showing in instructional league, but they can't be expected to keep him on the 40-man roster forever. He enters 2004 with his career at a crossroads.

Year	Club (League)	Class	W	L	ERA	G	GS	CG	SV	IP	H	R	ER	HR	BB	SO	AVG
99	White Sox (AZL)	R	0	2	8.00	10	0	0	0	18	16	19	16	1	16	24	.219
00	Burlington (Mid)	A	2	3	4.90	38	1	0	0	72	67	52	39	4	60	82	.244

	Class	W	L	ERA	G	GS	CG	SV	IP	H	R	ER	HR	BB	SO	AVG
01 Kannapolis (SAL)	A	11	4	2.00	18	18	2	0	112	83	30	25	2	44	119	.208
Winston-Salem (Car)	A	0	1	1.72	5	5	0	0	37	25	10	7	1	10	38	.192
Birmingham (SL)	AA	2	0	2.33	4	4	0	0	19	8	5	5	2	12	20	.127
02 Birmingham (SL)	AA	10	7	4.71	22	22	0	0	124	116	77	65	6	89	89	.248
03 Birmingham (SL)	AA	4	2	5.40	8	8	0	0	40	50	26	24	2	28	28	.305
Bristol (Appy)	R	0	0	5.14	4	4	0	0	14	17	8	8	2	3	15	.298
Kannapolis (SAL)	A	0	3	5.11	5	5	1	0	25	27	19	14	2	10	29	.273
MINOR LEAGUE TOTALS		29	22	3.96	114	67	3	0	461	409	246	203	22	272	444	.237

23 Antoin Gray, 2b/3b

Born: May 19, 1981. **Ht.:** 5-9. **Wt.:** 195. **Bats:** R. **Throws:** R. **School:** Southern University. **Career Transactions:** Selected by White Sox in 25th round of 2003 draft; signed June 6, 2003.

Gray finished fourth in the NCAA Division I batting race with a .449 average in 2002, finishing behind future first-round picks Rickie Weeks and Khalil Greene, as well as Curtis Granderson, who has hit .304 since signing with the Tigers. One of six players drafted off Southern's 44-7 team last year, Gray hit .407-26-133 in 108 games in his two years in the same lineup as Weeks. Though he faced a huge jump in competition when he turned pro, there was a minimal learning curve for Gray. He continued to hit, finishing third in the Pioneer League in runs and doubles. He has promising power and a keen eye for walks, though he must improve his bunting and cut down on his strikeouts. Beyond his bat, Gray doesn't have a plus tool. He played third base at Southern while Weeks played second, the position Gray is better suited for. His arm fits better at second base, though he'll need a lot of work defensively, especially on the double-play pivot. If Gray can become adequate defensively, he could have a big league career as an offensive second baseman. Unless the White Sox decide to hold Pedro Lopez back, Gray will report to low Class A to start 2004.

Year	Club (League)	Class	AVG	G	AB	R	H	2B	3B	HR	RBI	BB	SO	SB	SLG	OBP
03	Great Falls (Pio)	R	.292	69	277	63	81	20	0	8	43	49	62	4	.451	.406
MINOR LEAGUE TOTALS			.292	69	277	63	81	20	0	8	43	49	62	4	.451	.406

24 Ricardo Nanita, of

Born: June 12, 1981. **Ht.:** 6-1. **Wt.:** 180. **Bats:** L. **Throws:** L. **School:** Florida International University. **Career Transactions:** Selected by White Sox in 14th round of 2003 draft; signed June 7, 2003.

Born in the Dominican Republic, Nanita came to the United States to combine baseball with college. He spent two years at Chipola (Fla.) JC before moving to Florida International for his junior season. He used wood bats during fall practice with the Panthers, and his experience showed as he put together a 30-game hitting streak in his pro debut. Nanita can do a lot of things at the plate, bunting for hits, shooting the ball through holes in the infield or driving it into the gaps. He doesn't project as a home run threat but will surprise pitchers who get careless. He has a good idea of the strike zone and runs well enough to steal 25-plus bases annually. Nanita has outstanding instincts on the bases and in center field. He has a plus arm but will be run on until he increases his accuracy. His outstanding debut may allow Nanita to skip a level and go to high Class A in 2004.

Year	Club (League)	Class	AVG	G	AB	R	H	2B	3B	HR	RBI	BB	SO	SB	SLG	OBP
03	Great Falls (Pio)	R	.384	47	185	38	71	7	4	5	37	17	28	11	.546	.445
MINOR LEAGUE TOTALS			.384	47	185	38	71	7	4	5	37	17	28	11	.546	.445

25 Andy Gonzalez, ss

Born: Dec. 15, 1981. **Ht.:** 6-2. **Wt.:** 180. **Bats:** R. **Throws:** R. **School:** Florida Air Academy, Melbourne, Fla. **Career Transactions:** Selected by White Sox in fifth round of 2001 draft; signed June 16, 2001.

Just a year ago, the White Sox saw Gonzalez as their shortstop of the future. No longer. His 2003 season raised major questions about his approach as a hitter, and his problems at the plate seemed to carry over to the field. Outside of drawing walks, Gonzalez couldn't do anything against low Class A pitching. He didn't hit the ball with any authority and didn't deal with adversity well. Projections for his power aren't nearly as kind as they were before, and the Sox would like him to just focus on raising his average. He runs well but gets caught stealing more than he should. Gonzalez has the tools to be a good defensive shortstop, starting with a strong arm that had some clubs considering drafting him as a pitcher out of high school. His range is adequate but he must cut down on his errors. With the addition of Robert Valido and the emergence of Mike Morse, Gonzalez suddenly faces a lot of competition to see who becomes the organization's first homegrown regular at shortstop since Bucky Dent. He has a lot to prove in 2004, when he'll probably start in high Class A.

Year	Club (League)	Class	AVG	G	AB	R	H	2B	3B	HR	RBI	BB	SO	SB	SLG	OBP
01	White Sox (AZL)	R	.323	48	189	33	61	18	1	5	30	15	36	13	.508	.382
02	Bristol (Appy)	R	.280	66	254	48	71	17	0	1	45	32	43	5	.358	.358
03	Kannapolis (SAL)	A	.231	123	429	58	99	17	1	1	39	69	82	22	.282	.347
MINOR LEAGUE TOTALS			.265	237	872	139	231	52	2	7	114	116	161	40	.353	.357

26 Tim Tisch, lhp

Born: April 11, 1980. **Ht.:** 6-5. **Wt.:** 190. **Bats:** L. **Throws:** L. **School:** Mesa (Ariz.) JC. **Career Transactions:** Selected by White Sox in 34th round of 2001 draft; signed May 22, 2002.

A 34th-round draft-and-follow from 2001, Tisch showed enough to merit being signed a year later but wasn't considered a top prospect. He was a tall, projectable lefty with a mid-80s fastball. Winless in his pro debut, he snuck onto the prospect radar last year, when he threw a seven-inning no-hitter in July. More important, he gained strength and improved his mechanics. That allowed him to boost his fastball into the low 90s and to throw strikes more easily. He comes straight over the top at hitters, and the ball seems to explode out of his hand. Tisch also has a decent slider and changeup. He doesn't miss a lot of bats, but hitters also don't get good swings against him. He figures to spend this year in the low Class A rotation.

Year	Club (League)	Class	W	L	ERA	G	GS	CG	SV	IP	H	R	ER	HR	BB	SO	AVG
02	White Sox (AZL)	R	0	3	4.50	17	0	0	0	22	30	13	11	0	14	14	.316
03	Bristol (Appy)	R	3	5	3.13	11	11	1	0	60	52	21	21	4	21	44	.235
	Kannapolis (SAL)	A	1	0	1.93	3	2	0	0	14	11	5	3	0	8	11	.212
MINOR LEAGUE TOTALS			4	8	3.27	31	13	1	0	96	93	39	35	4	43	69	.253

27 Ruddy Yan, 2b

Born: Jan. 13, 1981. **Ht.:** 6-0. **Wt.:** 160. **Bats:** B. **Throws:** R. **Career Transactions:** Signed out of Dominican Republic by Pirates, Jan. 4, 1999 . . . Traded by Pirates with LHP Damaso Marte to White Sox for RHP Matt Guerrier, March 27, 2002.

Tremendous speed hasn't translated to a quick climb up the ladder for the slightly built Yan. He has run into a roadblock despite 164 stolen bases the last two years, tops in the minor leagues. He was a Carolina League all-star last year after posting league bests in runs, steals and hitting streak (26 games). But Yan didn't make the progress at the plate that the White Sox hoped for when they had him repeat high Class A. He's a blazer who forces the infield in and still gets hits on squibbers and choppers. But he hasn't developed the authority, especially from the left side, to drive the ball past infielders or over outfielders, who also play him shallow. Yan needs more strength and more discipline, as he doesn't reach base enough to inspire the belief he could bat leadoff at the upper levels. He did improve his defense significantly last season, covering lots of ground and making fewer mistakes. Chicago also discovered that Yan was a year older than originally believed, which didn't help his case. He'll have to hit better to survive Double-A in 2004.

Year	Club (League)	Class	AVG	G	AB	R	H	2B	3B	HR	RBI	BB	SO	SB	SLG	OBP
99	Pirates (DSL)	R	.300	69	250	61	75	6	1	3	21	49	49	48	.368	.424
00	Pirates (GCL)	R	.357	12	42	10	15	0	1	0	1	12	8	5	.405	.500
01	Hickory (SAL)	A	.283	128	446	58	126	8	4	2	24	42	62	56	.332	.347
02	Winston-Salem (Car)	A	.253	132	490	78	124	6	7	4	35	42	57	88	.318	.312
03	Winston-Salem (Car)	A	.264	130	485	85	128	11	3	2	24	47	73	76	.311	.328
MINOR LEAGUE TOTALS			.273	471	1713	292	468	31	16	11	105	192	249	273	.329	.348

28 Josh Stewart, lhp

Born: Dec. 5, 1978. **Ht.:** 6-3. **Wt.:** 200. **Bats:** L. **Throws:** L. **School:** University of Memphis. **Career Transactions:** Selected by White Sox in fifth round of 1999 draft; signed June 7, 1999.

Stewart probably doesn't know whether to laugh or cry when he thinks back to 2003. He followed up a breakout season in 2002 with a typically unflappable performance in his first big league spring training. He challenged hitters the same way he had in the Arizona Fall League and got results. In fact, he took advantage of an injury to Danny Wright to leave Tucson as the Chicago's fifth starter. He beat Cleveland to pick up his first major league win before taking a line drive from Jeff Conine in the chest in his next start. Stewart missed a turn and then got pounded by Seattle and was sent to Triple-A, where he bothered by a circulatory problem in his left hand and worked just 26 more innings. Stewart lost his grip on both the ball and his spot on the 40-man roster. When he's right, he throws in the high 80s and has a plus curveball. He changes speeds and locations to keep hitters off balance. If Stewart is healthy and can recapture his 2002 magic, he can pitch himself back into the Sox' good graces this year.

Year	Club (League)	Class	W	L	ERA	G	GS	CG	SV	IP	H	R	ER	HR	BB	SO	AVG
99	Bristol (Appy)	R	1	0	1.50	5	0	0	1	18	13	5	3	0	5	25	.206
	Burlington (Mid)	A	2	0	7.28	16	0	0	1	30	32	25	24	6	21	35	.283
00	Burlington (Mid)	A	9	9	4.57	25	25	1	0	138	157	84	70	14	58	82	.290
01	Winston-Salem (Car)	A	4	6	3.82	12	12	1	0	64	64	41	27	6	28	38	.258
	Birmingham (SL)	AA	3	4	6.67	16	16	0	0	82	110	68	61	7	42	47	.330
02	Birmingham (SL)	AA	11	7	3.53	26	26	1	0	150	145	65	59	11	56	92	.255
03	Chicago (AL)	MAJ	1	2	5.96	5	5	0	0	26	28	18	17	4	16	13	.272
	Charlotte (IL)	AAA	0	3	6.15	5	5	0	0	26	38	18	18	4	6	10	.345
	Bristol (Appy)	R	0	0	0.00	2	2	0	0	6	5	0	0	0	2	5	.227
MAJOR LEAGUE TOTALS			1	2	5.96	5	5	0	0	26	28	18	17	4	16	13	.272
MINOR LEAGUE TOTALS			30	29	4.58	107	86	3	2	514	564	306	262	48	218	334	.282

29 Orionny Lopez, rhp

Born: April 1, 1984. **Ht.:** 6-2. **Wt.:** 170. **Bats:** R. **Throws:** R. **School:** Forest Hill HS, West Palm Beach, Fla. **Career Transactions:** Selected by White Sox in 10th round of 2002 draft; signed June 8, 2002.

Lopez doesn't have stuff that leaves scouts drooling, but he knows how to pitch and make the most of an average arm. Though his fastball hangs out in the 87-89 mph range, he keeps hitters from sitting on it by mixing in a plus curveball and changeup. He throws hitters off balance by using a deceptive delivery and maintaining the same arm action with all his pitches. He also has good command and tremendous mound presence. Lopez had a 0.50 ERA in early August last year before tiring markedly down the stretch. The White Sox want him to gain some strength, figuring that will increase his stamina and perhaps his velocity as well. He faces a longer season in low Class A this year.

Year	Club (League)	Class	W	L	ERA	G	GS	CG	SV	IP	H	R	ER	HR	BB	SO	AVG
02	White Sox (AZL)	R	1	4	3.97	17	3	0	3	34	31	15	15	3	11	38	.244
03	Bristol (Appy)	R	5	3	2.37	17	0	0	2	49	38	18	13	2	18	53	.213
MINOR LEAGUE TOTALS			6	7	3.02	34	3	0	5	83	69	33	28	5	29	91	.226

30 Jason Stumm, rhp

Born: April 13, 1981. **Ht.:** 6-2. **Wt.:** 210. **Bats:** R. **Throws:** R. **School:** Centralia (Wash.) HS. **Career Transactions:** Selected by White Sox in first round (15th overall) of 1999 draft; signed June 21, 1999.

This is the year the White Sox hope to be rewarded for their patience with Stumm, who was compared to Roger Clemens when they made him a first-round pick in 1999. He had Tommy John surgery the next season, a shoulder operation in 2002 and has pitched just 206 innings in five pro seasons. Stumm has regained the mid-90s velocity on his fastball and Chicago believes he has a high upside, probably as a reliever. But the odds are against him reaching his ceiling unless he can stay healthy. His slider, changeup and command all need a lot of work. The Sox liked how he finished 2003 and expect him to come into spring training ready to compete. If he doesn't perform well in the Cactus League, he could lose his spot on the 40-man roster. He'll probably open the year in Double-A.

Year	Club (League)	Class	W	L	ERA	G	GS	CG	SV	IP	H	R	ER	HR	BB	SO	AVG
99	White Sox (AZL)	R	0	0	3.27	3	2	0	0	11	13	8	4	2	3	9	.310
	Burlington (Mid)	A	3	3	5.32	10	10	0	0	44	47	31	26	4	27	33	.276
00	Burlington (Mid)	A	2	7	4.61	13	13	2	0	66	66	44	34	6	30	62	.262
01	White Sox (AZL)	R	0	2	2.25	4	4	0	0	12	6	4	3	0	5	12	.154
02	Kannapolis (SAL)	A	0	1	2.25	22	0	0	5	40	37	10	10	1	12	45	.245
03	Winston-Salem (Car)	A	1	0	3.60	20	0	0	0	25	28	10	10	1	11	23	.295
	Birmingham (SL)	AA	0	0	4.50	7	0	0	0	8	8	4	4	1	6	8	.267
MINOR LEAGUE TOTALS			6	13	3.97	79	29	2	5	206	205	113	91	15	94	192	.263

CINCINNATI
REDS

The opening of the Great American Ball Park in 2003 created high expectations for the Reds, but they weren't able to rejuvenate their fan base. Cincinnati finished 24 games below .500, 19 games behind the Cubs in the National League Central.

Though the Reds were just 2½ games out at the beginning of July, they fired general manager Jim Bowden three days before the July 31 trade deadline. To replace Bowden, who had been calling the shots since October 1992, chief operating officer John Allen took over baseball operations with the assistance of interim GMs Brad Kullman (who had been assistant GM) and Leland Maddox (scouting director). Over the next 72 hours, that team executed four cost-cutting deals that sent Aaron Boone, Jose Guillen, Gabe White and Scott Williamson to contenders. The big league roster was decimated, while Bowden analyzed the moves as a commentator on ESPN. The Reds went 20-34 over the final two months.

Cincinnati tabbed Rangers assistant GM Dan O'Brien as GM after the season to turn things around. A 26-year front office veteran who spent 15 years in the Astros' scouting and player-development departments, O'Brien helped spearhead Houston's Latin American revival. He announced his intention to follow the Astros' blueprint, focusing on homegrown talent, specifically pitching.

TOP 30 PROSPECTS

1. Ryan Wagner, rhp
2. Edwin Encarnacion, 3b
3. Brandon Claussen, lhp
4. Dustin Moseley, rhp
5. Joey Votto, 1b
6. Phil Dumatrait, lhp
7. Stephen Smitherman, of
8. Tyler Pelland, lhp
9. Chris Gruler, rhp
10. Ty Howington, lhp
11. Miguel Perez, c
12. William Bergolla, 2b
13. Josh Hall, rhp
14. Richie Gardner, rhp
15. Rainer Feliz, rhp
16. Joe Valentine, rhp
17. Bobby Basham, rhp
18. Thomas Pauly, rhp
19. David Mattox, rhp
20. Habelito Hernandez, 3b/2b
21. Matt Belisle, rhp
22. Tony Blanco, 3b
23. Alex Farfan, rhp
24. Ricardo Aramboles, rhp
25. Jim Paduch, rhp
26. Brian Shackelford, lhp
27. Charlie Manning, lhp
28. Dane Sardinha, c
29. Willy Jo Ronda, ss/2b
30. Kenny Lewis, of

By Josh Boyd

"It starts and ends with starting pitching," O'Brien said at his first press conference. He said developing quality pitching is "the quickest way to being competitive."

In recent years, too many of the organization's promising young arms have lost time to injuries. Chris Gruler, No. 1 on this list a year ago, was limited to six innings by shoulder surgery. Ricardo Aramboles and Luke Hudson went down with torn labrums in spring training. Josh Hall tore his after reaching the majors in September. Bobby Basham, Ty Howington and Josh Thigpen all saw their velocity plummet, though doctors found no structural damage and Howington finished on a positive note.

The additions of lefthanders Brandon Claussen, Phil Dumatrait, Tyler Pelland and Charlie Manning and righties Joe Valentine and Matt Belisle through trades added depth. Cincinnati also picked up pitching in the draft, with first-rounder Ryan Wagner going almost straight to the majors.

Promoting harmony between scouting and player development will be one of O'Brien's first chores, as the rift between the two departments is well known in the industry. He reassigned Maddox to major league scout and replaced him with former Dodgers scouting director Terry Reynolds.

"We have a lot of work to do," O'Brien said, acknowledging the system's weaknesses. "The challenges are significant."

ORGANIZATION
OVERVIEW

General manager: Dan O'Brien. **Farm director:** Tim Naehring. **Scouting director:** Terry Reynolds.

2003 PERFORMANCE

Class	Team	League	W	L	Pct.	Finish*	Manager(s)
Majors	Cincinnati	National	69	93	.426	13th (16)	Bob Boone/Dave Miley
Triple-A	Louisville RiverBats	International	79	64	.552	2nd (14)	Dave Miley/Rick Burleson
Double-A	Chattanooga Lookouts	Southern	66	74	.471	8th (10)	Phillip Wellman
High A	Potomac Cannons	Carolina	62	77	.446	6th (8)	Jayhawk Owens
Low A	Dayton Dragons	Midwest	61	78	.439	13th (14)	Donnie Scott
Rookie	Billings Mustangs	Pioneer	41	35	.539	+3rd (8)	Rick Burleson/Jay Sorg
Rookie	GCL Reds	Gulf Coast	26	34	.433	10th (12)	Edgar Caceres
OVERALL 2003 MINOR LEAGUE RECORD			335	362	.481	23rd (30)	

*Finish in overall standings (No. of teams in league). + League champion

ORGANIZATION LEADERS

BATTING   *Minimum 250 At-Bats
*AVG	Brandon Larson, Louisville	.323
R	Luis Bolivar, Dayton/Billings	83
H	Kevin Howard, Dayton	145
TB	Jesse Gutierrez, Chattanooga/Potomac	230
2B	Jesse Gutierrez, Chattanooga/Potomac	34
3B	Three tied at	5
HR	Brandon Larson, Louisville	20
	Jesse Gutierrez, Chattanooga/Potomac	20
RBI	Jesse Gutierrez, Chattanooga/Potomac	96
BB	Joey Votto, Dayton/Billings	90
SO	Mark Schramek, Chatt./Potomac/Dayton	155
SB	William Bergolla, Potomac	52
*SLG	Brandon Larson, Louisville	.617
*OBP	Joey Votto, Dayton/Billings	.406

PITCHING   #Minimum 75 Innings
W	Eddy Valdez, Potomac/Dayton	16
L	Daylan Childress, Chattanooga/Potomac	13
#ERA	Todd Coffey, Potomac/Dayton	2.16
G	Todd Coffey, Potomac/Dayton	50
CG	Three tied at	2
SV	Nathan Cotton, Chattanooga/Potomac	28
IP	Eddy Valdez, Potomac/Dayton	169
BB	Daylan Childress, Chattanooga/Potomac	71
SO	Daylan Childress, Chattanooga/Potomac	124

BEST TOOLS

Best Hitter for Average	Joey Votto
Best Power Hitter	Joey Votto
Fastest Baserunner	Kenny Lewis
Best Athlete	Kenny Lewis
Best Fastball	Alex Farfan
Best Curveball	Phil Dumatrait
Best Slider	Ryan Wagner
Best Changeup	David Mattox
Best Control	Dustin Moseley
Best Defensive Catcher	Dane Sardinha
Best Defensive Infielder	Hector Tiburcio
Best Infield Arm	Edwin Encarnacion
Best Defensive Outfielder	Chris Dickerson
Best Outfield Arm	Ben Himes

PROJECTED 2007 LINEUP

Catcher	Jason LaRue
First Base	Joey Votto
Second Base	D'Angelo Jimenez
Third Base	Edwin Encarnacion
Shortstop	Rainer Olmedo
Left Field	Adam Dunn
Center Field	Ken Griffey Jr.

Right Field	Austin Kearns
No. 1 Starter	Brandon Claussen
No. 2 Starter	Dustin Moseley
No. 3 Starter	Phil Dumatrait
No. 4 Starter	Tyler Pelland
No. 5 Starter	Chris Gruler
Closer	Ryan Wagner

LAST YEAR'S TOP 20 PROSPECTS

1. Chris Gruler, rhp
2. Bobby Basham, rhp
3. Wily Mo Pena, of
4. Edwin Encarnacion, 3b
5. Dustin Moseley, rhp
6. Ty Howington, lhp
7. Ricardo Aramboles, rhp
8. Brandon Larson, 3b
9. Josh Hall, rhp
10. Mark Schramek, 3b
11. Luke Hudson, rhp
12. Josh Thigpen, rhp
13. Stephen Smitherman, of
14. Joey Votto, 3b/c
15. Dane Sardinha, c
16. Justin Gillman, rhp
17. Jerome Gamble, rhp
18. Daylan Childress, rhp
19. Rainer Olmedo, ss/2b
20. Gookie Dawkins, ss/2b

TOP PROSPECTS OF THE DECADE

1994	Pokey Reese, ss
1995	Pokey Reese, ss
1996	Pokey Reese, ss
1997	Aaron Boone, 3b
1998	Damian Jackson, ss/2b
1999	Rob Bell, rhp
2000	Gookie Dawkins, ss
2001	Austin Kearns, of
2002	Austin Kearns, of
2003	Chris Gruler, rhp

TOP DRAFT PICKS OF THE DECADE

1994	C.J. Nitkowski, lhp
1995	Brett Tomko, rhp (2)
1996	John Oliver, of
1997	Brandon Larson, ss/3b
1998	Austin Kearns, of
1999	Ty Howington, lhp
2000	David Espinosa, ss
2001	*Jeremy Sowers, lhp
2002	Chris Gruler, rhp
2003	Ryan Wagner, rhp

*Did not sign

ALL-TIME LARGEST BONUSES

Chris Gruler, 2002	$2,500,000
Austin Kearns, 1998	$1,950,000
Ty Howington, 1999	$1,750,000
Ryan Wagner, 2003	$1,400,000
Brandon Larson, 1997	$1,330,000

MINOR LEAGUE
DEPTH CHART

CINCINNATI REDS   RANK: 26

Impact potential (D): Ryan Wagner went from the draft to the Reds bullpen in less than two months. He could establish himself as a dominant closer within two years. Edwin Encarnacion, Joey Votto and Miguel Perez show intriguing potential at the plate, but need to make adjustments to fulfill that potential.

Depth (C): The system is not in great shape, but was bolstered by last summer's deadline deals, especially the one that produced lefties Phil Dumatrait and Tyler Pelland from the Red Sox. The Reds' new front office needs to find an immediate remedy for the recurring injuries that have plagued the organization's most promising young arms.

Sleeper: Rainer Feliz, rhp.   —*Depth charts prepared by **Josh Boyd**. Numbers in parentheses indicate prospect rankings.*

LF
Stephen Smitherman (7)
Jordan Belcher

CF
Kenny Lewis (30)
Chris Dickerson

RF
Ben Himes

3B
Edwin Encarnacion (2)
Tony Blanco (22)
Mark Schramek

SS
Hector Tiburcio
Luis Bolivar
Jeff Bannon

2B
William Bergolla (12)
Habelito Hernandez (20)
Willy Jo Ronda (29)
Tim Hummel
Kevin Howard

1B
Joey Votto (5)

SOURCE OF TALENT

Homegrown		Acquired	
College	7	Trades	10
Junior College	0	Rule 5 draft	1
Draft-and-follow	0	Independent leagues	0
High school	7	Free agents/Waivers	0
Nondrafted free agents	0		
Foreign	5		

C
Miguel Perez (11)
Dane Sardinha (28)
Jesse Gutierrez
Jeff Urgelles
Jarrod Schmidt

RHP

Starters	Relievers
Dustin Moseley (4)	Ryan Wagner (1)
Chris Gruler (9)	Joe Valentine (16)
Josh Hall (13)	Alex Farfan (23)
Richie Gardner (14)	Luke Hudson
Rainer Feliz (15)	Joel Barreto
Bobby Basham (17)	Josh Thigpen
Thomas Pauly (18)	Juan Cerros
David Mattox (19)	Chris Booker
Matt Belisle (21)	Todd Coffey
Ricardo Aramboles (24)	Nathan Cotton
Jim Paduch (25)	Carlos Guevara
Justin Gillman	
David Gil	
Daylan Childress	
Jeff Bruksch	
Ryan Mottl	
Eddy Valdez	

LHP

Starters	Relievers
Brandon Claussen (3)	Brian Shackelford (26)
Phil Dumatrait (6)	Phil Norton
Tyler Pelland (8)	Casey Dehart
Ty Howington (10)	Jan Granado
Charlie Manning (27)	
Juan Frias	
Camilo Vazquez	

DRAFT
ANALYSIS

Best Pro Debut: RHP Ryan Wagner (1) reached Cincinnati 46 days after going 14th overall and went 2-0, 1.66 with 25 strikeouts in 22 innings.

Best Athlete: OF Kenny Lewis (4), a Virginia Tech football recruit, was the fastest player in the draft and can put on a show in BP.

Best Pure Hitter: SS Willy Jo Ronda (3) is an offensive infielder who may outgrow his current position and warrant a move to second or third base. He has enough bat to make either move.

Best Raw Power: When the Reds worked out OF Ben Himes (9) in 2002, special assistant Bob Zuk loved him. Himes missed the year with a knee injury and turned down Cincinnati as a 50th-round pick. He stayed healthy and batted .317-7-42 in the Pioneer League after signing.

Fastest Runner: The Reds have clocked Lewis at an amazing 6.2 seconds in the 60-yard dash, and at 3.5 seconds from the left side of the plate to first base on a drag bunt.

Best Defensive Player: OF Chris Dickerson (16) made an impression in center field during instructional league.

Best Fastball: RHP Brock Till's (17) max-imum-effort delivery generates 93-96 mph heat. Like Till, RHP Damian Ursin (8) is 6 feet tall, and he has a 92-95 mph fastball. Wagner and RHPs Thomas Pauly (2) and Richie Gardner (6) all pitch up to 94 mph.

Lewis

Best Breaking Ball: Wagner's slider is so devastating that it may have to be outlawed.

Most Intriguing Background: The Reds drafted Notre Dame QB Carlyle Holliday (44) as an outfielder though he hasn't played baseball for the Irish. They weren't able to sign him or OF Dennis Dixon (20), whose power/speed/arm combination could have made him a second-round pick if not for his football prowess; he was the top gridiron recruit in Oregon's 2003 class. Because the Ducks don't have a baseball program, the Reds can sign him as a draft-and-follow.

Closest To The Majors: Wagner's trip to the majors was the swiftest since Ariel Prieto went from No. 5 overall to the Athletics in 28 days in 1995.

Best Late-Round Pick: The Reds say Dickerson could handle the majors defensively right now. He still has to prove he can hit after batting .243 at Nevada last spring and .244 in the Pioneer League last summer.

The One Who Got Away: RHP Marc Cornell (5) was in the running to be the No. 1 pick by the Devil Rays until he hurt his shoulder. He spent the summer rehabbing before returning to Ohio University, where he hopes to regain his 94-98 mph fastball.

Assessment: Wagner provided an instant payoff, and Cincinnati also expects big things from Pauly, Ronda and Lewis.

2002 DRAFT — GRADE: D

RHP Chris Gruler (1) pitched just 50 innings before needing shoulder surgery, and the commissioner's office didn't let the Reds spend enough to sign LHP/OF Nick Markakis (23), who went seventh overall in 2003. 1B Joey Votto (2) is this group's best hope.

2001 DRAFT — GRADE: F

Cincinnati drafted LHP Jeremy Sowers (1) with little intention of signing him, and now he'll be a first-rounder in 2004. RHP Bobby Basham's (7) stock took a severe downturn last year.

2000 DRAFT — GRADE: C

OF David Espinosa (1) was a disappointment before he was traded, but the Reds found two keepers in RHP Dustin Moseley (1) and OF Stephen Smitherman (23). LHP Ryan Snare (2) could pitch in the Texas rotation this year.

1999 DRAFT — GRADE: C

LHP Ty Howington (1) has a high ceiling but wasn't protected on the 40-man roster this offseason. 1B Ben Broussard (2) and RHP Michael Neu (29) reached the majors with other clubs after trades.

—Draft analysis prepared by Jim Callis. Numbers in parentheses indicate draft rounds.

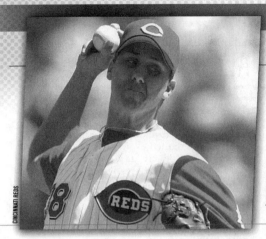

CINCINNATI REDS

Ryan Wagner

Born: July 15, 1982.
Ht.: 6-4. **Wt.:** 210.
Bats: R. **Throws:** R.
School: University of Houston.
Career Transactions: Selected by Reds in first round (14th overall) of 2003 draft; signed June 13, 2003.

Because he turned 21 within 45 days of the draft, Wagner was eligible following his sophomore season at Houston. Undrafted out of high school partly because he asked for $500,000 to sign, he became last spring's most pleasant draft surprise. He went from being an unheralded freshman to an All-American to a first-rounder to a major leaguer by the middle of July. He needed just 46 days and all of nine innings between Double-A Chattanooga and Triple-A Louisville to earn a promotion to Cincinnati after signing for $1.4 million. His rapid trek to the big leagues was the fastest since Athletics 1995 first-rounder Ariel Prieto needed just 28 days in the minors. Wagner broke a 39-year-old NCAA Division I record by fanning 16.8 hitters per nine innings, while limiting college opponents to a .147 average. He held big leaguers to a meager .173 clip, but was shut down as a precaution after shouldering a heavy workload: 79 innings for Houston and 31 more after signing. It was nothing more than a precaution, as Wagner was exhausted and the Reds didn't want to risk taxing his arm.

Wagner's 84-87 mph slider is downright unhittable and grades as a top-of-the-scouting-scale 80 pitch at times. It features sharp, late tilt in the zone and darts away from the barrel of the bat. Hitters have a difficult time identifying his slider, and often think it's a splitter or true curveball because of its depth. Wagner isn't a one-trick pony, however. His fastball sits at 91-94 mph and features hard sink and boring action to induce ground balls. His fastball movement is so good that hitters will have a tough time laying off his slider and sitting on his fastball. He showed enough resiliency and durability to work multiple-inning stints for Houston. Though he rarely needs it, Wagner shows a feel for an average changeup, leading some scouts to think he could hold down a rotation spot. Not many scouts project Wagner as a starter, however, because his delivery and arm action might not be conducive to a rotation workload. While he'll drop his arm slot at times to create more movement on his fastball, that also causes additional stress on his shoulder—even more than when he relies heavily on his slider. The Reds would like him to become more consistent with his slot and repeating his delivery.

Following Wagner's promotion to the majors, the Reds discussed moving him to the rotation in 2004, but they now seem content to groom him as their future closer. College closers don't often duplicate their success in the majors, but there's little doubt Wagner can over-match hitters at any level. If he's not Cincinnati's closer coming out of spring training, he'll be one of the better set-up men in the National League.

Year	Club (League)	Class	W	L	ERA	G	GS	CG	SV	IP	H	R	ER	HR	BB	SO	AVG
2003	Chattanooga (SL)	AA	1	0	0.00	5	0	0	0	5	2	1	0	0	2	6	.125
	Louisville (IL)	AAA	0	1	4.50	4	0	0	0	4	5	2	2	0	0	4	.313
	Cincinnati (NL)	MAJ	2	0	1.66	17	0	0	0	22	13	4	4	2	12	25	.173
MAJOR LEAGUE TOTALS			2	0	1.66	17	0	0	0	22	13	4	4	2	12	25	.173
MINOR LEAGUE TOTALS			1	1	2.00	9	0	0	0	9	7	3	2	0	2	10	.219

2 Edwin Encarnacion, 3b

RODGER WOOD

Born: Jan. 7, 1983. **Ht.:** 6-1. **Wt.:** 195. **Bats:** R. **Throws:** R. **School:** Manuela Toro HS, Caguas, P.R. **Career Transactions:** Selected by Rangers in ninth round of 2000 draft; signed June 12, 2000 . . . Traded by Rangers with OF Ruben Mateo to Reds for RHP Rob Bell, June 15, 2001.

Former Reds special assistant Al Goldis was scouting Hank Blalock in the Rookie-level Gulf Coast League in 2000 when he came across Encarnacion, who was playing shortstop. Cincinnati acquired him the following year in the Ruben Mateo-Rob Bell trade with Texas. A two-level jump to Double-A last spring proved to be a tad overzealous, and he was forced to step back and make adjustments. Encarnacion has special bat speed and plus-plus power potential. He's advanced at recognizing pitches early. He still shows middle-of-the-diamond actions, along with above-average strength. During his struggles in Double-A, Encarnacion's attitude and work ethic were concerns. He needs to use the opposite field more effectively by allowing outside pitches to get deeper. He has the bat quickness to do so. Like many developing hitters, he needs to lay off breaking balls down and away. Encarnacion made encouraging strides with both his hitting approach and his demeanor after being sent to high Class A Potomac. He's better prepared for a second tour of Double-A in 2004.

Year	Club (League)	Class	AVG	G	AB	R	H	2B	3B	HR	RBI	BB	SO	SB	SLG	OBP
2000	Rangers (GCL)	R	.311	51	177	31	55	6	3	0	36	21	27	3	.379	.381
2001	Savannah (SAL)	A	.306	45	170	23	52	9	2	4	25	12	34	3	.453	.355
	Dayton (Mid)	A	.162	9	37	2	6	2	0	1	6	1	5	0	.297	.184
	Billings (Pio)	R	.261	52	211	27	55	8	2	5	26	15	29	8	.389	.307
2002	Dayton (Mid)	A	.282	136	518	80	146	32	4	17	73	40	108	25	.458	.338
2003	Chattanooga (SL)	AA	.272	67	254	40	69	13	1	5	36	22	44	8	.390	.331
	Potomac (Car)	A	.321	58	215	40	69	15	1	6	29	24	32	7	.484	.387
MINOR LEAGUE TOTALS			.286	418	1582	243	452	85	13	38	231	135	279	54	.428	.343

3 Brandon Claussen, lhp

Born: May 1, 1979. **Ht.:** 6-2. **Wt.:** 200. **Bats:** R. **Throws:** L. **School:** Howard (Texas) JC. **Career Transactions:** Selected by Yankees in 34th round of 1998 draft; signed May 20, 1999 . . . Traded by Yankees with LHP Charlie Manning and cash to Reds for 3B Aaron Boone, July 31, 2003.

The top pitcher in the Yankees system, Claussen went to the Reds at last year's trade deadline in a deal for Aaron Boone. Though he returned ahead of schedule from Tommy John surgery in June 2002, Claussen was shut down with a tired arm for precautionary reasons after three starts in August. Claussen topped out at 94 mph before the operation, and pitched from 87-92 in 2003. He fires slightly across his body, creating good arm-side tail on his fastball and adding tilt and depth to his plus 78 mph slider. His changeup is an average big league pitch. He has good command and can work both sides of the plate. The good news is the Reds sidelined Claussen before he reinjured his arm. The red flag is that healthy pitchers usually don't need to be shut down and his velocity isn't all the way back. Provided there aren't further setbacks, Claussen will get every opportunity to win a job in the Reds' revamped rotation in spring training. He profiles as a solid middle-of-the-rotation starter.

Year	Club (League)	Class	W	L	ERA	G	GS	CG	SV	IP	H	R	ER	HR	BB	SO	AVG
1999	Yankees (GCL)	R	0	1	3.18	2	2	0	0	11	7	4	4	2	2	16	.175
	Staten Island (NY-P)	A	6	4	3.38	12	12	1	0	72	70	30	27	4	12	89	.253
	Greensboro (SAL)	A	0	1	10.50	1	1	1	0	6	8	7	7	1	2	5	.296
2000	Greensboro (SAL)	A	8	5	4.05	17	17	1	0	98	91	49	44	9	44	98	.251
	Tampa (FSL)	A	2	5	3.10	9	9	1	0	52	49	24	18	1	17	44	.245
2001	Tampa (FSL)	A	5	2	2.73	8	8	0	0	56	47	21	17	2	13	69	.224
	Norwich (EL)	AA	9	2	2.13	21	21	1	0	131	101	42	31	6	55	151	.210
2002	Columbus (IL)	AAA	2	8	3.28	15	15	0	0	93	85	47	34	4	46	73	.242
2003	Tampa (FSL)	A	2	0	1.64	4	4	0	0	22	16	5	4	0	3	26	.198
	Columbus (IL)	AAA	2	1	2.75	11	11	1	0	69	53	28	21	4	18	39	.213
	New York (AL)	MAJ	1	0	1.42	1	1	0	0	6	8	2	1	1	1	5	.296
	Louisville (IL)	AAA	0	1	7.47	3	3	0	0	16	17	13	13	3	6	16	.293
MAJOR LEAGUE TOTALS			1	0	1.42	1	1	0	0	6	8	2	1	1	1	5	.296
MINOR LEAGUE TOTALS			36	30	3.16	103	103	6	0	626	544	270	220	36	218	626	.233

4 Dustin Moseley, rhp

Born: Dec. 26, 1981. **Ht.:** 6-4. **Wt.:** 200. **Bats:** R. **Throws:** R. **School:** Arkansas HS, Texarkana, Ark. **Career Transactions:** Selected by Reds in first round (34th overall) of 2000 draft; signed Nov. 22, 2000.

Moseley signed late in 2000 for $930,000 and has advanced rapidly, earning midseason promotions during each of the last two seasons and reaching Triple-A at age 21. Moseley's mature knack for pitching has enabled him to move swiftly up the ladder. While he's not overpowering with his 88-92 mph fastball, he has plus movement and manipulates the ball to both sides of the plate with a cutter and two-seamer. His 77-81 mph curveball with 12-to-6 break and his deceptive sinking changeup are among the best in the organization. His delivery is clean and effortless, potentially allowing him to add to his fastball. Because he doesn't have plus velocity, Moseley has to rely on location and setting up hitters. Scouts say he doesn't have a true out pitch, so he won't be able to carry a pitching staff. Though his ceiling is limited, Moseley is a good bet to enjoy a long and productive career in the majors. He reminds scouts of control artists like Rick Reed and Bob Tewksbury. He'll start 2004 in Triple-A and could help the Reds rotation before the all-star break.

Year	Club (League)	Class	W	L	ERA	G	GS	CG	SV	IP	H	R	ER	HR	BB	SO	AVG
2001	Dayton (Mid)	A	10	8	4.20	25	25	0	0	148	158	83	69	10	42	108	.271
2002	Stockton (Cal)	A	6	3	2.74	14	14	2	0	89	60	28	27	3	21	80	.188
	Chattanooga (SL)	AA	5	6	4.13	13	13	0	0	81	91	47	37	5	37	52	.293
2003	Chattanooga (SL)	AA	5	6	3.83	18	18	0	0	113	116	55	48	10	28	73	.264
	Louisville (IL)	AAA	2	3	2.70	8	8	0	0	50	46	19	15	5	14	27	.245
MINOR LEAGUE TOTALS			28	26	3.68	78	78	2	0	480	471	232	196	33	142	340	.256

5 Joey Votto, 1b

Born: Sept. 10, 1983. **Ht.:** 6-3. **Wt.:** 200. **Bats:** L. **Throws:** R. **School:** Richview Collegiate Institute, Toronto. **Career Transactions:** Selected by Reds in second round of 2002 draft; signed June 5, 2002.

Votto was a surprise second-rounder in 2002, in part because he signed for a below-market $600,000, but Cincinnati brass also fell in love with him after he put on an impressive power display at Cinergy Field. Drafted as a catcher, he primarily played third base in high school and now has moved to first base to expedite his development. He was one of several Reds prospects who had to be demoted after initially struggling in 2003. Reds scouts envision Votto as a middle-of-the-lineup force. He's short and direct to the ball with natural loft in his swing, which will lend itself to big-time power potential as he matures. A dead-pull hitter in 2002, he moved closer to the plate and started driving the ball to left field last season. Votto draws lots of walks but is often too patient at the plate, putting himself into poor hitting counts by taking a lot of borderline pitches. Defense will never be his strong suit. A coach's dream, Votto is a baseball rat who studies the art of hitting. He'll return to low Class A Dayton, but could emerge quickly without the rigors of catching holding him back.

Year	Club (League)	Class	AVG	G	AB	R	H	2B	3B	HR	RBI	BB	SO	SB	SLG	OBP
2002	Reds (GCL)	R	.269	50	175	29	47	13	3	9	33	21	45	7	.531	.342
2003	Dayton (Mid)	A	.231	60	195	19	45	8	0	1	20	34	64	2	.287	.348
	Billings (Pio)	R	.317	70	240	47	76	17	3	6	38	56	80	4	.488	.452
MINOR LEAGUE TOTALS			.275	180	610	95	168	38	6	16	91	111	189	13	.436	.389

6. Phil Dumatrait, lhp

Born: July 12, 1981. **Ht.:** 6-2. **Wt.:** 185. **Bats:** R. **Throws:** L. **School:** Bakersfield (Calif.) JC. **Career Transactions:** Selected by Red Sox in first round (22nd overall) of 2000 draft; signed July 10, 2000 . . . Traded by Red Sox with a player to be named to Reds for RHP Scott Williamson, July 30, 2003.

Undrafted out of high school, Dumatrait blossomed into a first-rounder at Bakersfield JC thanks to a spike in velocity. Regarded as the Red Sox' best pitching prospect heading into last spring, Dumatrait was dealt with Tyler Pelland for closer Scott Williamson in July. Dumatrait's curveball is the best in the organization. He adds and subtracts from the pitch, using a slower curve to get ahead in the count and a sharper hammer to finish hitters. His fastball sits at 88-90 and features outstanding late life that makes it difficult to command, but he has learned to harness it. He's athletic and operates with a free and easy delivery. Dumatrait needs to incorporate his changeup into his mix more often. His command isn't always sharp and is the key to him achieving his ceiling as a major league starter. The Reds say Dumatrait has good enough stuff to succeed as a situational reliever in the majors right now. While that could ultimately be his role, his stuff is good enough to start and he'll continue to do so in Double-A.

Year	Club (League)	Class	W	L	ERA	G	GS	CG	SV	IP	H	R	ER	HR	BB	SO	AVG
2000	Red Sox (GCL)	R	0	1	1.65	6	6	0	0	16	10	6	3	0	12	12	.172
2001	Red Sox (GCL)	R	3	0	2.76	8	8	0	0	33	27	10	10	0	9	33	.229
	Lowell (NY-P)	A	1	1	3.48	2	2	0	0	10	9	4	4	0	4	15	.225
2002	Augusta (SAL)	A	8	5	2.77	22	22	1	0	120	109	44	37	5	47	108	.249
	Sarasota (FSL)	A	0	2	3.86	4	4	0	0	14	10	9	6	0	15	16	.192
2003	Sarasota (FSL)	A	7	5	3.02	21	20	0	1	104	74	41	35	4	59	74	.204
	Potomac (Car)	A	4	1	3.35	7	7	1	0	38	36	17	14	2	14	32	.248
MINOR LEAGUE TOTALS			23	15	2.92	70	69	2	1	336	275	131	109	11	160	290	.227

7 Stephen Smitherman, of

Born: Sept. 1, 1978. **Ht.:** 6-4. **Wt.:** 235. **Bats:** R. **Throws:** R. **School:** University of Arkansas-Little Rock. **Career Transactions:** Selected by Reds in 23rd round of 2000 draft; signed June 7, 2000.

Smitherman followed up a breakthrough 2002 campaign by leading the Double-A Southern League in on-base percentage and finishing second in slugging. He also hit the game-winning homer for the U.S. in the Futures Game. Unlike most aggressive power hitters, Smitherman has become more selective at the plate while maintaining his ability to drive the ball. His natural prowess to put the barrel on the ball has been consistently underrated. He runs well for a big man. Though he learned to lay off some balls out of the strike zone, Smitherman still has holes and can get tied up with hard stuff inside. He's also susceptible to breaking balls down and away, but he can punish fastballs. A diabetic, he suffered a scary episode in June when he had to be helped off the field. But he didn't miss any time. Smitherman struggled during a brief trip to the majors and never got back into a groove afterward. He'll have to prove himself in Triple-A in 2004, but already has exceeded expectations.

Year	Club (League)	Class	AVG	G	AB	R	H	2B	3B	HR	RBI	BB	SO	SB	SLG	OBP
2000	Billings (Pio)	R	.316	70	301	61	95	16	5	15	65	23	67	14	.551	.373
2001	Dayton (Mid)	A	.280	134	497	89	139	45	2	20	73	43	113	16	.499	.348
2002	Stockton (Cal)	A	.313	128	482	78	151	36	1	19	99	39	126	17	.510	.362
2003	Chattanooga (SL)	AA	.310	105	365	60	113	21	2	19	73	54	95	11	.534	.402
	Cincinnati (NL)	MAJ	.159	21	44	3	7	2	0	1	6	3	9	1	.273	.213
	Louisville (IL)	AAA	.127	17	63	1	8	0	0	0	5	4	19	0	.127	.188
MAJOR LEAGUE TOTALS			.159	21	44	3	7	2	0	1	6	3	9	1	.273	.213
MINOR LEAGUE TOTALS			.296	454	1708	289	506	118	10	73	315	163	420	58	.505	.363

8 Tyler Pelland, lhp

Born: Oct. 9, 1983. **Ht.:** 6-0. **Wt.:** 190. **Bats:** R. **Throws:** L. **School:** Mount Abraham HS, Bristol, Vt. **Career Transactions:** Selected by Red Sox in ninth round of 2002 draft; signed Aug. 17, 2002 . . . Traded with LHP Phil Dumatrait by Red Sox to Reds for RHP Scott Williamson, July 29, 2003.

Former Reds special assistant Al Goldis' work in the Gulf Coast League also paid off with Pelland. Goldis recommended that the Reds acquire him from the Red Sox last July, and they did later than month in the Scott Williamson deal. Pelland would have gone in the first five rounds in 2002 if not for his commitment to Clemson, and he got fourth-round money ($240,000) as a ninth-rounder. Pelland has a 90-95 mph fastball with good late life in the strike zone. He's mechanically sound, drawing comparisons to Mike Hampton. His changeup has good action and deception. He shows a good feel for setting up hitters. He has made significant strides with his stuff in just one season as a pro. Because of his stocky build, Pelland isn't projectable, though he already flashes plus velocity. He has a feel for a power breaking ball, but it's inconsistent at this point. Reds officials say Pelland will be able to handle a jump to low Class A, coming off an impressive showing in instructional league. He probably won't surface in Cincinnati until 2007.

Year	Club (League)	Class	W	L	ERA	G	GS	CG	SV	IP	H	R	ER	HR	BB	SO	AVG
2003	Red Sox (GCL)	R	3	4	1.62	11	8	0	0	39	26	12	7	0	18	34	.186
	Reds (GCL)	R	0	0	0.00	1	1	0	0	3	3	0	0	0	0	1	.273
MINOR LEAGUE TOTALS			3	4	1.51	12	9	0	0	42	29	12	7	0	18	35	.192

9 Chris Gruler, rhp

Born: Sept. 11, 1983. **Ht.:** 6-3. **Wt.:** 200. **Bats:** R. **Throws:** R. **School:** Liberty Union HS, Brentwood, Calif. **Career Transactions:** Selected by Reds in first round (third overall) of 2002 draft; signed June 5, 2002.

Rated as the Reds' top prospect entering 2003, Gruler never got the chance to build on that status. He was shut down with a sore shoulder during instructional league in 2002, but after an offseason of rest and rehab was pronounced ready for Dayton's rotation. After three disastrous starts, he had season-ending shoulder surgery. Reds special adviser Johnny Bench compared Gruler's stuff to Tom Seaver's after a predraft workout in 2002. He worked with a free and easy arm action and polished delivery, making his shoulder injury all the more surprising and frustrating. He generates 89-95 mph heat when healthy, and his hard curveball ranked among the best in the system. He's a hard worker, which will help in his comeback. Gruler has been healthy enough to tally just 50 pro innings. He's had little time to work on his changeup. When he returns, it may take time before he's as sharp as he was during his debut. Gruler has to prove his arm is sound. He has had only one minor setback with tendinitis, though his rehab will continue into the 2004 season. He should take the mound in low Class A by May.

Year	Club (League)	Class	W	L	ERA	G	GS	CG	SV	IP	H	R	ER	HR	BB	SO	AVG
2002	Billings (Pio)	R	0	0	1.08	4	4	0	0	17	11	3	2	1	6	11	.183
	Dayton (Mid)	A	0	1	5.60	7	7	0	0	27	23	19	17	2	16	31	.228
2003	Dayton (Mid)	A	0	2	27.00	3	3	0	0	6	10	19	17	0	12	6	.370
MINOR LEAGUE TOTALS			0	3	6.52	14	14	0	0	50	44	41	36	3	34	48	.234

10 Ty Howington, lhp

Born: Nov. 4, 1980. **Ht.:** 6-5. **Wt.:** 220. **Bats:** B. **Throws:** L. **School:** Hudson's Bay HS, Vancouver, Wash. **Career Transactions:** Selected by Reds in first round (14th overall) of 1999 draft; signed Nov. 1, 1999.

Howington appeared on the cusp of the big leagues after reaching Double-A before his 21st birthday. But he has battled elbow and shoulder problems for much of the last two seasons and posted a 5.45 ERA in Double-A in that span. At his best—and he was close to it in the second half of 2003—Howington can pour 89-93 mph heat with above-average life in the strike zone. He has developed a good cutter to complement one of the most effective changeups in the system, and his curveball will be at least average. Howington hasn't gotten back to 94 mph, which he hit regularly in 2001, and his arm troubles are a concern. His velocity was in the mid-80s in early 2003. The injuries limited his range of motion, which affected his mechanics and arm action and ultimately his command. Coming off another encouraging showing in instructional league, Howington is ready for a fourth shot at Double-A at age 23. The Reds surprised many people by leaving him off their 40-man roster, but he was not taken in the Rule 5 draft. He has the potential to be a workhorse in the Andy Pettitte mold if he can stay healthy.

Year	Club (League)	Class	W	L	ERA	G	GS	CG	SV	IP	H	R	ER	HR	BB	SO	AVG
2000	Dayton (Mid)	A	5	15	5.27	27	26	0	0	142	150	91	83	7	86	119	.275
2001	Dayton (Mid)	A	4	0	1.15	6	6	1	0	39	15	7	5	0	9	47	.116
	Mudville (Cal)	A	3	2	2.43	7	7	0	0	37	33	18	10	2	20	44	.234
	Chattanooga (SL)	AA	1	3	3.27	7	7	0	0	41	36	18	15	3	24	38	.240
2002	Chattanooga (SL)	AA	1	5	5.12	15	15	1	0	65	65	39	37	5	33	51	.261
	Stockton (Cal)	A	1	1	3.09	2	2	0	0	12	7	6	4	1	4	9	.171
2003	Potomac (Car)	A	7	7	3.53	19	19	0	0	99	103	44	39	4	34	86	.271
	Chattanooga (SL)	AA	0	2	6.91	4	4	0	0	14	15	12	11	1	20	16	.273
MINOR LEAGUE TOTALS			22	35	4.09	87	86	2	0	449	424	235	204	23	230	410	.251

11 Miguel Perez, c

Born: Sept. 25, 1983. **Ht.:** 6-3. **Wt.:** 190. **Bats:** R. **Throws:** R. **Career Transactions:** Signed out of Venezuela by Reds, Nov. 15, 2000.

Perez passed Dane Sardinha on the organization's catching depth chart despite a midseason demotion to Rookie-level Billings. One Reds official said Perez could be the best catching prospect to come through the organization in recent years. His defense is ahead of his offense at this point, and he has room for improvement in both areas. While he's not as refined defensively as Sardinha, Perez projects to be a frontline defender in time. He has a plus arm and is working on speeding up his release. He committed 17 errors and permitted 16 passed balls, while throwing out 34 percent of basestealers in Billings. He was overmatched at low Class A, where he fell into the habit of cheating with his hands and continually got off balance at the plate. Nevertheless, Reds minor league hitting instructor Leon Roberts was impressed with Perez' ability to use his hands in spite of his mechanical flaws. He has the potential to drive the ball for power when he stays loaded and keeps both halves of his body in sync. He's a bit of a project and will get another shot at low Class A in 2004.

Year	Club (League)	Class	AVG	G	AB	R	H	2B	3B	HR	RBI	BB	SO	SB	SLG	OBP
2001	Cagua (VSL)	R	.331	48	163	20	54	3	1	0	19	12	33	6	.362	.377
2002	Cagua (VSL)	R	.213	34	108	14	23	4	0	2	18	9	23	1	.306	.320
	Reds (GCL)	R	.360	26	86	12	31	1	0	0	11	2	9	3	.372	.396
2003	Dayton (Mid)	A	.172	20	58	3	10	0	0	0	3	4	19	1	.172	.273
	Billings (Pio)	R	.339	60	227	46	77	11	2	1	25	18	27	1	.419	.410
MINOR LEAGUE TOTALS			.304	188	642	95	195	19	3	3	76	45	111	12	.357	.372

12 William Bergolla, 2b

Born: Feb. 4, 1983. **Ht.:** 6-0. **Wt.:** 175. **Bats:** R. **Throws:** R. **Career Transactions:** Signed out of Venezuela by Reds, Nov. 15, 1999.

Bergolla first caught the attention of special assistant to the GM Johnny Almaraz with his quick hands and natural righthanded stroke during a tryout camp in Venezuela in 1999. Last year, Bergolla was hitting .209 and bothered by an injured thumb in early May, but bounced back to lead the high Class A Carolina League in hits. He has a simple approach with a sound, mechanical stroke. He exhibits excellent bat control, putting the ball in play with regularity, and stays inside the ball well. His ability to make contact works against him in that he rarely draws walks. Bergolla's strength is hitting line drives, and he shows occasional pop to the alleys. He stole a system-best 52 bases in 2003, more a testament to his instincts and quickness than his pure speed. Bergolla moved across the bag to second base full-time after spending portions of the previous two seasons at shortstop. The Reds want him to improve his strength and conditioning to hold up better over the course of a season. He broke his left hamate bone during a practice after the season in Venezuela, but the injury won't require surgery and he'll open the year in Double-A.

Year	Club (League)	Class	AVG	G	AB	R	H	2B	3B	HR	RBI	BB	SO	SB	SLG	OBP
2000	Cagua (VSL)	R	.372	13	43	6	16	3	2	0	5	8	3	1	.535	.481
	Reds (GCL)	R	.182	8	22	2	4	0	0	0	0	4	2	3	.182	.308
2001	Billings (Pio)	R	.323	57	232	47	75	5	3	4	24	24	21	22	.422	.387
2002	Dayton (Mid)	A	.248	68	274	38	68	13	1	3	23	16	36	13	.336	.291
	Billings (Pio)	R	.352	53	210	35	74	9	1	3	29	24	26	16	.448	.408
2003	Potomac (Car)	A	.272	128	523	77	142	25	3	2	31	29	59	52	.342	.309
MINOR LEAGUE TOTALS			.291	327	1304	205	379	55	10	12	112	105	147	107	.376	.342

13 Josh Hall, rhp

Born: Dec. 16, 1980. **Ht.:** 6-2. **Wt.:** 190. **Bats:** R. **Throws:** R. **School:** E.C. Glass HS, Lynchburg, Va. **Career Transactions:** Selected by Reds in seventh round of 1998 draft; signed June 11, 1998 . . . On disabled list, June 16-Sept. 13, 1999.

Hall's approach on the mound mirrors Dustin Moseley's. He uses his headiness to set up hitters more than trying to blow them away. After emerging as one of the Reds' best prospects in 2002, he made his major league debut last August following another solid season in Double-A. Though he shut out the Cubs for seven innings in one start, Hall mostly struggled in Cincinnati before his season ended with a torn labrum. His second reconstructive shoulder surgery—the first cost him all of 1999 and much of 2000—is expected to keep him out for six to nine months. Hall's fastball is average, sitting around 89-91 mph, but like Moseley he moves it around, keeps the ball down and changes speeds efficiently. Hall's plus curveball, a 12-to-6 downer, might be a touch better than Moseley's, and he also offers a plus changeup. When Hall rebounded from his first shoulder surgery, he impressed Reds brass so much they wanted to use his rehab as a blueprint for injured pitchers. His work ethic is beyond reproach, which will benefit him, but this setback is potentially devastating.

Year	Club (League)	Class	W	L	ERA	G	GS	CG	SV	IP	H	R	ER	HR	BB	SO	AVG
1998	Billings (Pio)	R	5	4	5.00	14	14	1	0	81	89	53	45	6	33	50	.276
1999	Did not play—Injured																
2000	Reds (GCL)	R	0	5	10.57	6	6	0	0	15	26	25	18	2	13	20	.371
2001	Dayton (Mid)	A	11	5	2.65	22	22	2	0	132	117	52	39	4	39	122	.232
2002	Stockton (Cal)	A	4	0	2.27	7	7	1	0	44	31	13	11	1	13	51	.194
	Chattanooga (SL)	AA	7	8	3.75	22	22	1	0	132	140	75	55	7	50	116	.276
2003	Chattanooga (SL)	AA	8	10	3.47	26	25	2	0	153	152	73	59	9	53	114	.260
	Cincinnati (NL)	MAJ	0	2	6.57	6	5	0	0	25	33	22	18	4	15	18	.314
MAJOR LEAGUE TOTALS			0	2	6.57	6	5	0	0	25	33	22	18	4	15	18	.314
MINOR LEAGUE TOTALS			35	32	3.67	97	96	7	0	557	555	291	227	29	201	473	.258

14 Richie Gardner, rhp

Born: Feb. 1, 1982. **Ht.:** 6-3. **Wt.:** 185. **Bats:** R. **Throws:** R. **School:** University of Arizona.
Career Transactions: Selected by Reds in sixth round of 2003 draft; signed Aug. 23, 2003.

Drafted in the 24th round by the Rangers out of high school, Gardner went to Santa Rosa (Calif.) JC. After missing most of his sophomore season with mononucleosis and a concussion (he got hit in the head during batting practice), he transferred to Arizona. He emerged as the Wildcats' ace in his lone season in Tucson, then was the talk of the Reds' instructional league camp after signing late for $160,000. Gardner dialed his fastball up to 94 mph, sitting comfortably between 90-93 with sink and tail. His changeup, which features splitter tumble, already rates as one of the best offspeed pitches in the system, and he flashed an above-average breaking ball during the fall. He has an ideal pitcher's frame and sound mechanics. His pro debut may come in high Class A and he could move quickly.

Year	Club (League)	Class	W	L	ERA	G	GS	CG	SV	IP	H	R	ER	HR	BB	SO	AVG
					Has not played—Signed 2004 Contract												

15 Rainer Feliz, rhp

Born: March 22, 1983. **Ht.:** 6-5. **Wt.:** 170. **Bats:** R. **Throws:** R. **Career Transactions:** Signed out of Dominican Republic by Reds, Nov. 20, 2000.

Thanks to injuries, the system lacks projectable power arms. While righthander Alex Farfan has the best velocity now, Feliz has the potential for more. The velocity on his 90-92 mph fastball is likely to increase, considering his loose arm and immature, wiry build. Feliz already demonstrates an advanced feel for pitching for his age. He was throwing 84-87 when the Reds signed him out of a tryout camp at their academy in the Dominican Republic. Feliz throws a quality slider with tight rotation and good velocity, and he has the makings of a good changeup. While he has good control, he'll face the challenge to maintain sound mechanics as his body changes. Feliz and Richie Gardner were the most impressive Reds prospects in instructional league, and one scout said Feliz could be the best pitching prospect in the system in a year. He's slated to make his full-season debut in low Class A.

Year	Club (League)	Class	W	L	ERA	G	GS	CG	SV	IP	H	R	ER	HR	BB	SO	AVG
2001	Reds (DSL)	R	2	2	6.46	12	5	0	0	24	36	22	17	2	6	12	.346
2002	Reds (DSL)	R	3	3	3.70	12	11	1	0	66	65	33	27	3	18	44	.258
2003	Reds (GCL)	R	2	2	3.20	10	10	0	0	45	39	17	16	0	13	36	.239
MINOR LEAGUE TOTALS			7	7	4.02	34	26	1	0	134	140	72	60	5	37	92	.270

16 Joe Valentine, rhp

Born: Dec. 24, 1979. **Ht.:** 6-2. **Wt.:** 195. **Bats:** R. **Throws:** R. **School:** Jefferson Davis (Ala.) JC.
Career Transactions: Selected by White Sox in 26th round of 1999 draft; signed June 26, 1999 . . . Selected by Expos from White Sox in Rule 5 major league draft, Dec. 13, 2001 . . . Contract purchased by Tigers from Expos, Dec. 13, 2001 . . . Returned to White Sox, April 5, 2002 . . . Traded by White Sox with RHP Keith Foulke, C Mark Johnson and cash to Athletics for RHP Billy Koch and two players to be named, Dec. 3, 2002; White Sox acquired LHP Neal Cotts and OF Daylan Holt to complete trade (Dec. 16, 2002) . . . Traded by Athletics with RHP Aaron Harang and RHP Jeff Bruksch to Reds for OF Jose Guillen, July 30, 2003.

Valentine has seen his name on the transaction wire more than most minor leaguers, but he soon may find a home in the Cincinnati bullpen. After nearly making the Tigers bullpen in 2002 as a major league Rule 5 selection, he's been involved in deadline deals in each of the last two seasons. He made his major league debut for the Reds in August. Valentine's fastball tops out at 96 mph with good life, and his slider features hard, late biting action. Command always has been an issue, as he works with a long arm action and full-effort delivery. He needs to work on his path to the plate because he tends to over-rotate and fall off toward first base. Some scouts would like to see more separation in velocity between his two pitches. Valentine profiles as a closer but could be relegated to a lesser role if his control doesn't improve. He'll have a shot to make the big league bullpen in spring training.

Year	Club (League)	Class	W	L	ERA	G	GS	CG	SV	IP	H	R	ER	HR	BB	SO	AVG
1999	White Sox (AZL)	R	0	0	0.00	3	0	0	0	4	2	0	0	0	1	2	.154
	Bristol (Appy)	R	0	0	7.02	11	0	0	0	17	27	17	13	2	9	14	.360
2000	Bristol (Appy)	R	2	1	2.88	19	0	0	7	25	14	10	8	1	12	30	.163
2001	Kannapolis (SAL)	A	2	2	2.93	30	0	0	14	31	21	10	10	0	10	33	.194
	Winston-Salem (Car)	A	5	1	1.01	27	0	0	8	45	18	7	5	0	27	50	.122
2002	Birmingham (SL)	AA	4	1	1.97	55	0	0	36	59	36	16	13	1	30	63	.173
2003	Sacramento (PCL)	AAA	1	3	4.82	40	0	0	4	52	44	33	28	5	37	53	.222
	Louisville (IL)	AAA	1	0	0.79	9	0	0	1	11	5	1	1	0	3	8	.132
	Cincinnati (NL)	MAJ	0	0	18.00	2	0	0	0	2	5	4	4	1	1	1	.455
MAJOR LEAGUE TOTALS			0	0	18.00	2	0	0	0	2	5	4	4	1	1	1	.455
MINOR LEAGUE TOTALS			15	8	2.87	194	0	0	70	244	167	94	78	9	129	253	.191

17 Bobby Basham, rhp

Born: March 7, 1980. **Ht.:** 6-3. **Wt.:** 205. **Bats:** R. **Throws:** R. **School:** University of Richmond.
Career Transactions: Selected by Reds in seventh round of 2001 draft; signed July 18, 2001.

After Basham capped a 2002 breakout campaign with a shutout in the California League playoffs and a solid performance in the Arizona Fall League, many Reds officials said he was the system's top prospect. The former Richmond backup quarterback did nothing to dissuade them by tossing 4⅓ scoreless innings in big league camp last spring. But by May, Basham's velocity was down and he was getting hit hard. His fastball dipped from 90-93 mph to as low as 83, and his slider—his out pitch—lost its sharpness. Basham was shut down with a tired arm in July. Doctors didn't discover any structural damage but also couldn't find an answer for the lack of life in his arm. Scouts saw a change in his mechanics, especially his arm action, which wasn't working as fluidly. When he's right, Basham shows a lively fastball with sink and tail, plus a hard slider with depth. He did manage to develop a decent changeup. Cincinnati expects him to return to the mound in spring training, and he'll likely repeat Double-A before advancing cautiously.

Year	Club (League)	Class	W	L	ERA	G	GS	CG	SV	IP	H	R	ER	HR	BB	SO	AVG
2001	Billings (Pio)	R	1	2	4.85	6	6	0	0	30	36	23	16	2	17	37	.300
2002	Dayton (Mid)	A	6	4	1.64	13	13	4	0	88	64	25	16	4	9	97	.195
2003	Chattanooga (SL)	AA	5	10	5.17	17	17	0	0	94	133	72	54	16	24	56	.331
	Potomac (Car)	A	0	1	2.70	1	1	0	0	7	5	3	2	0	1	1	.200
MINOR LEAGUE TOTALS			12	17	3.63	37	37	4	0	218	238	123	88	22	51	191	.272

18 Thomas Pauly, rhp

Born: July 28, 1981. **Ht.:** 6-1. **Wt.:** 195. **Bats:** R. **Throws:** R. **School:** Princeton University.
Career Transactions: Selected by Reds in second round of 2003 draft; signed June 13, 2003.

In high school, Pauly hardly seemed destined for professional baseball. He was a better swimmer than pitcher, and his 82 mph fastball didn't get scouts' attention. Things started to come together for him at Princeton, though he was so frustrated after his collegiate debut he popped a blood vessel in his right hand when he punched a bathroom door. As his velocity soared into the 90s, Pauly developed into a closer and set Princeton's career record for saves. He maintained his 92-94 mph fastball with late sinking action even after moving into the rotation in low Class A, and the Reds plan on developing him as a starter. Pauly's slider can be nasty. He has tinkered with different grips on his changeup, a pitch he'll need to make a successful transition to the rotation. He shows the potential to have three above-average major league offerings, which has Reds officials projecting Pauly as a No. 2 starter. He spent one week in instructional league before returning to Princeton to complete his sociology degree. High Class A is the logical next step in 2004.

Year	Club (League)	Class	W	L	ERA	G	GS	CG	SV	IP	H	R	ER	HR	BB	SO	AVG
2003	Dayton (Mid)	A	2	5	4.02	12	12	0	0	47	45	26	21	5	10	36	.247
MINOR LEAGUE TOTALS			2	5	4.02	12	12	0	0	47	45	26	21	5	10	36	.247

19 David Mattox, rhp

Born: May 24, 1980. **Ht.:** 6-2. **Wt.:** 195. **Bats:** R. **Throws:** R. **School:** Anderson (S.C.) College.
Career Transactions: Selected by Mets in 11th round of 2001 draft; signed June 8, 2001 . . . Selected by Reds from Mets in Rule 5 major league draft, Dec. 15, 2003.

Of all the pitchers taken in the 2003 major league Rule 5 draft, Mattox has the best chance of becoming a major league starter, and the Reds will give him every chance to make their rotation. A college shortstop who converted to the mound as a senior, Mattox has shown flashes of being a solid No. 3 starter in the majors but still has plenty of kinks to get out of his mechanics before he puts it all together. He struggles at times with his command, largely because he never has settled on a consistent arm slot. He also has had problems with rotating his shoulder too early. However, Mattox does throw with a free and easy motion. His changeup is a potentially dominant pitch, as he throws it with excellent arm speed and it has good sink. He also has a 90-91 mph fastball with above-average life. Mattox throws a curveball and slider, but both breaking pitches are inconsistent. He's working on developing his slider to bust batters inside, but he hasn't gained a consistent feel for it yet.

Year	Club (League)	Class	W	L	ERA	G	GS	CG	SV	IP	H	R	ER	HR	BB	SO	AVG
2001	Kingsport (Appy)	R	5	1	2.40	14	8	1	0	56	48	22	15	3	19	58	.225
	Brooklyn (NY-P)	A	1	0	0.90	2	2	0	0	10	5	2	1	0	3	12	.147
2002	Capital City (SAL)	A	8	2	3.55	17	17	0	0	91	78	42	36	3	42	92	.234
	St. Lucie (FSL)	A	4	4	2.82	9	9	2	0	51	46	21	16	2	24	34	.245
2003	Binghamton (EL)	AA	8	7	3.49	21	20	0	0	113	103	50	44	7	40	86	.246
MINOR LEAGUE TOTALS			26	14	3.13	63	56	3	0	322	280	137	112	15	128	282	.236

20 Habelito Hernandez, 3b/2b

Born: Jan. 11, 1981. **Ht.:** 6-0. **Wt.:** 180. **Bats:** R. **Throws:** R. **Career Transactions:** Signed out of Dominican Republic by Reds, June 3, 2000.

Unlike many of the infielders the Reds have signed out of Latin America, Hernandez has serious sock in his bat, though he doesn't possess the defensive gifts of some others. At the plate, Hernandez employs an overly aggressive approach but has tremendous bat speed and hand-eye coordination. The Reds tried to tone him down by telling him he couldn't swing until he got ahead in the count, and he still finished with two walks last year. Hernandez is a dead-red fastball hitter with plus power to all fields. He was sidelined for three weeks after he dislocated his right shoulder on a collision at third base, and his arm hadn't bounced back by instructional league. While he didn't show the quickness needed at second base, he demonstrated better reactions and average arm strength at the hot corner. Hernandez finished the season at high Class A, but he'll likely start 2004 in low Class A. If he learns to work counts better, he could return to high Class A by the end of the year.

Year	Club (League)	Class	AVG	G	AB	R	H	2B	3B	HR	RBI	BB	SO	SB	SLG	OBP
2000	Reds (DSL)	R	.222	49	162	32	36	4	1	3	21	11	32	9	.315	.284
2001	Reds (DSL)	R	.293	66	242	40	71	13	5	9	40	6	37	8	.500	.314
2002	Reds (GCL)	R	.235	27	98	11	23	5	1	1	11	1	19	2	.337	.257
2003	Billings (Pio)	R	.377	36	162	42	61	14	5	8	32	1	22	5	.673	.392
	Reds (GCL)	R	.200	3	10	1	2	0	0	0	0	0	2	0	.200	.200
	Potomac (Car)	A	.250	8	28	2	7	0	0	0	1	1	7	0	.250	.267
MINOR LEAGUE TOTALS			.285	189	702	128	200	36	12	21	105	20	119	24	.460	.313

21 Matt Belisle, rhp

Born: June 6, 1980. **Ht.:** 6-3. **Wt.:** 190. **Bats:** B. **Throws:** R. **School:** McCallum HS, Austin. **Career Transactions:** Selected by Braves in second round of 1998 draft; signed Aug. 23, 1998 . . . On disabled list, April 6-Sept. 18, 2001 . . . Traded by Braves to Reds, Aug. 14, 2003, completing trade in which Reds sent LHP Kent Mercker to Braves for a player to be named (Aug. 12, 2003).

Three years removed from back surgery that cost him the entire 2001 season, Belisle was acquired from the Braves in August. Once considered one of the brightest pitching prospects in the Atlanta system, Belisle hasn't been quite the same since the ruptured disc. Still, one scout calls him a lock to pitch in the majors as a No. 4 or 5 starter. Belisle is a hard worker with competitive makeup and three solid-average pitches and good command. No longer capable of cranking his fastball up to 94 mph, he fills the strike zone with an average 88-91 mph heater. His curveball is average and has depth, though he needs to develop more deception with the pitch. That would help him fare better against lefthanders, who batted .303 against him in the minors last year. Belisle's arm action is somewhat stiff, and Braves pitching coaches were working with him to shorten his arm swing in the back. Cincinnati's rotation is unsettled, so Belisle will get a long look in spring training.

Year	Club (League)	Class	W	L	ERA	G	GS	CG	SV	IP	H	R	ER	HR	BB	SO	AVG
1999	Danville (Appy)	R	2	5	4.67	14	14	0	0	71	86	50	37	3	23	60	.291
2000	Macon (SAL)	A	9	5	2.37	15	15	1	0	102	79	37	27	7	18	97	.216
	Myrtle Beach (Car)	A	3	4	3.43	12	12	0	0	79	72	32	30	5	11	71	.246
2001	Did not play—Injured																
2002	Greenville (SL)	AA	5	9	4.35	26	26	1	0	159	162	91	77	18	39	123	.261
2003	Greenville (SL)	AA	6	8	3.52	21	21	1	0	125	128	59	49	5	42	94	.272
	Richmond (IL)	AAA	1	1	2.25	3	3	0	0	20	17	6	5	1	0	10	.230
	Louisville (IL)	AAA	1	3	3.81	4	4	0	0	26	31	15	11	2	5	15	.304
	Cincinnati (NL)	MAJ	1	1	5.19	6	0	0	0	9	10	5	5	1	2	6	.303
MAJOR LEAGUE TOTALS			1	1	5.19	6	0	0	0	9	10	5	5	1	2	6	.303
MINOR LEAGUE TOTALS			27	35	3.64	95	95	3	0	583	575	290	236	41	138	470	.259

22 Tony Blanco, 3b

Born: Nov. 10, 1981. **Ht.:** 6-1. **Wt.:** 175. **Bats:** R. **Throws:** R. **Career Transactions:** Signed out of Dominican Republic by Red Sox, July 2, 1998 . . . Traded by Red Sox with RHP Josh Thigpen to Reds, Dec. 16, 2002, completing trade in which Reds sent 2B Todd Walker to Red Sox for two players to be named (Dec. 12, 2002).

Blanco was Boston's top position-player prospect for two years running, but fell out of favor when he failed to show the ability to adjust. Upon joining Cincinnati, he was hampered by the after-effects of elbow surgery, which forced him to play first base and DH in 2003. He's shaking several bad habits, including changing his style and approach from at-bat to at-bat. Blanco also gets beat with fastballs when he's worrying about breaking balls. He has the best raw power and bat speed in the system. When healthy, he also has a cannon for an arm. The Reds saw him make progress during the final week of instructional league. His opportunity to finally make his Double-A debut is complicated by Edwin Encarnacion's presence at third base, though Blanco could get a look at first base or left field.

Year	Club (League)	Class	AVG	G	AB	R	H	2B	3B	HR	RBI	BB	SO	SB	SLG	OBP
1999	Red Sox (DSL)	R	.277	67	249	36	69	12	5	8	41	29	65	12	.462	.366
2000	Red Sox (GCL)	R	.384	52	190	32	73	13	1	13	50	18	38	6	.668	.442
	Lowell (NY-P)	A	.143	9	28	1	4	1	0	0	0	2	12	1	.179	.226
2001	Augusta (SAL)	A	.265	96	370	44	98	23	2	17	69	17	78	1	.476	.308
2002	Sarasota (FSL)	A	.221	65	244	22	54	13	2	6	32	6	70	2	.365	.250
2003	Potomac (Car)	A	.266	69	241	33	64	17	2	10	49	26	62	0	.477	.338
MINOR LEAGUE TOTALS			.274	358	1322	168	362	79	12	54	241	98	325	22	.474	.333

23 Alex Farfan, rhp

Born: Jan. 6, 1983. **Ht.:** 6-3. **Wt.:** 200. **Bats:** R. **Throws:** R. **Career Transactions:** Signed out Venezuela by Reds, June 15, 2000.

Farfan has bulked up his frame since signing as a wiry 6-foot-3, 175-pounder. With more muscle, better conditioning and a permanent move to the bullpen, he added velocity to his fastball. Farfan now touches 97 mph and is regularly timed at 93-96 mph. He also features a hard slider, which is occasionally a plus pitch. But for all his stuff, he hasn't missed many bats because his command and control need to improve. The Reds are fine-tuning his delivery to address those weaknesses. Farfan, who has a full arm swing in the back, tends to throw across his body. He also must learn to use his front side better in his delivery to create leverage and improve his downhill plane. Farfan has the best arm in the system and the stuff to close games but is learning how to harness it. He'll pitch at high Class A this year.

Year	Club (League)	Class	W	L	ERA	G	GS	CG	SV	IP	H	R	ER	HR	BB	SO	AVG
2000	Cagua (VSL)	R	0	4	12.15	8	3	0	0	13	17	24	18	0	16	11	.327
2001	Cagua (VSL)	R	0	2	3.74	16	5	0	2	34	22	19	14	0	37	26	—
2002	Reds (GCL)	R	3	4	5.18	20	5	0	4	40	28	28	23	3	20	31	.194
2003	Dayton (Mid)	A	5	3	3.73	40	0	0	4	80	73	35	33	2	30	43	.246
MINOR LEAGUE TOTALS			8	13	4.75	84	13	0	10	167	140	106	88	5	103	111	.239

24 Ricardo Aramboles, rhp

Born: Dec. 4, 1981. **Ht.:** 6-4. **Wt.:** 220. **Bats:** R. **Throws:** R. **Career Transactions:** Signed out of Dominican Republic by Marlins, July 2, 1996 . . . Contract voided, Dec. 3, 1997 . . . Signed by Yankees Feb. 26, 1998 . . . Traded by Yankees to Reds for RHP Mark Wohlers, June 30, 2001 . . . On disabled list, April 3-Sept. 9, 2003.

After being limited to just 23 innings with a tender elbow in 2002, Aramboles was throwing the ball as well as anyone in Reds camp last spring when he had another setback. Already a survivor of Tommy John surgery in 1999, he had a season-ending operation to repair a torn labrum in April. He attended instructional league for one week following the season, throwing on flat ground. The Reds expect him to be ready to throw off a mound by spring training. The question is whether Aramboles will regain his clean arm action, 92-94 mph fastball, power curveball and devastating changeup. If all goes well, he could get a taste of the big leagues in September and hope for a 2005 arrival in their bullpen. He'd still be just 23. But the list of recoveries from labrum surgeries is much shorter than those from Tommy John surgery, so the odds are stacked against Aramboles.

Year	Club (League)	Class	W	L	ERA	G	GS	CG	SV	IP	H	R	ER	HR	BB	SO	AVG
1997	Marlins (DSL)	R	1	1	1.71	8	2	0	0	21	15	7	4	0	7	14	.200
1998	Yankees (GCL)	R	2	1	2.93	10	9	0	0	40	33	14	13	0	13	44	.231
	Oneonta (NY-P)	A	1	0	1.50	1	1	0	0	6	4	2	1	1	1	8	.190
1999	Yankees (GCL)	R	2	3	3.89	9	7	0	0	35	35	18	15	1	14	42	.276
	Greensboro (SAL)	A	1	2	2.34	6	6	1	0	35	25	9	9	1	12	34	.205
2000	Greensboro (SAL)	A	5	13	4.31	25	25	2	0	138	150	81	66	12	47	150	.274
2001	Tampa (FSL)	A	7	2	4.06	12	11	0	0	69	72	37	31	5	19	59	.271
	Columbus (IL)	AAA	1	3	3.04	4	4	0	0	24	26	11	8	2	4	14	.283
	Chattanooga (SL)	AA	0	2	8.00	2	1	0	0	9	12	8	8	1	0	5	.324
	Dayton (Mid)	A	1	2	3.66	4	4	0	0	20	23	8	8	2	4	9	.299
2002	Chattanooga (SL)	AA	1	0	3.13	4	4	0	0	23	22	8	8	0	8	22	.268
2003	Did not play—Injured																
MINOR LEAGUE TOTALS			22	29	3.68	85	74	3	0	418	417	203	171	25	129	401	.262

25 Jim Paduch, rhp

Born: Nov. 2, 1982. **Ht.:** 6-3. **Wt.:** 185. **Bats:** R. **Throws:** R. **School:** Concordia (Ill.) University. **Career Transactions:** Selected by Reds in 12th round of 2003 draft; signed June 9, 2003.

The 2003 Northern Illinois-Iowa Conference player of the year, Paduch was primarily a shortstop in his first two years of college, pitching only in relief. The Reds credit area scout Mike Keenan for identifying Paduch as a sleeper. While not overpowering, he has the ability to locate his 87-91 mph fastball. He also varies speeds with a changeup and two types of breaking balls. He was invited to throw out the first pitch before a game at Great American

Ball Park after clinching the Pioneer League championship with a no-hitter. Paduch's poise and advanced feel for pitching might earn him a quick promotion to high Class A to start 2004.

Year	Club (League)	Class	W	L	ERA	G	GS	CG	SV	IP	H	R	ER	HR	BB	SO	AVG
2003	Billings (Pio)	R	7	1	1.94	15	15	0	0	79	72	28	17	1	20	65	.242
MINOR LEAGUE TOTALS			7	1	1.94	15	15	0	0	79	72	28	17	1	20	65	.242

26 Brian Shackelford, lhp

Born: Aug. 30, 1976. **Ht.:** 6-1. **Wt.:** 190. **Bats:** L. **Throws:** L. **School:** University of Oklahoma.
Career Transactions: Selected by Royals in 13th round of 1998 draft; signed June 4, 1998 . . . Traded by Royals with RHP Jeff Austin to Reds for 3B Damaso Espino and OF Alan Moye, March 6, 2003.

A two-way player in college, Shackelford saw more time in the outfield than on the mound and the Royals drafted him as a position player. He hit .241 as an outfielder before shifting to the mound midway through 2002. His stock soared in the Arizona Fall League in 2002, prompting the Reds to seek him in a minor league trade. He has made tremendous progress on the mound, reaching Triple-A within a year of switching positions. Shackelford has the makings of four major league pitches, including an 88-92 mph tailing fastball, a cutter, a slider and a changeup. After a demotion to high Class A last year, he settled on a comfortable arm slot. His new high three-quarters release helped him find the strike zone more frequently. Shackelford just needs innings to hone his repertoire. His future role will depend upon his ability to get lefthanders out. He'll probably start the year in Triple-A.

Year	Club (League)	Class	AVG	G	AB	R	H	2B	3B	HR	RBI	BB	SO	SB	SLG	OBP
1998	Spokane (NWL)	A	.293	70	266	35	78	21	1	10	55	35	52	3	.492	.378
1999	Charleston, WV (SAL)	A	.200	73	260	25	52	14	2	10	30	26	80	1	.385	.274
2000	Wilmington (Car)	A	.234	113	423	44	99	23	1	11	63	30	83	4	.371	.290
2001	Wichita (TL)	AA	.260	110	366	62	95	18	3	20	72	33	79	4	.489	.326
2002	Wichita (TL)	AA	.217	86	244	29	53	10	0	6	31	23	42	3	.332	.288
2003	Chattanooga (SL)	AA	.000	13	2	1	0	0	0	0	0	1	1	0	.000	.333
	Louisville (IL)	AAA	.000	13	1	0	0	0	0	0	0	0	0	0	.000	.000
MINOR LEAGUE TOTALS			.241	478	1562	196	377	86	7	57	251	148	337	15	.415	.311

Year	Club (League)	Class	W	L	ERA	G	GS	CG	SV	IP	H	R	ER	HR	BB	SO	AVG
2001	Wichita (TL)	AA	0	0	18.00	1	0	0	0	1	3	2	2	0	1	0	.500
2002	Wichita (TL)	AA	3	1	3.51	22	0	0	0	26	23	12	10	1	26	15	.258
2003	Chattanooga (SL)	AA	3	2	6.30	13	1	0	1	20	26	18	14	3	14	19	.313
	Potomac (Car)	A	0	1	1.98	18	0	0	1	27	17	6	6	1	8	20	.181
	Louisville (IL)	AAA	1	0	2.30	12	0	0	0	16	15	4	4	0	7	10	.259
MINOR LEAGUE TOTALS			7	4	3.61	66	1	0	2	90	84	42	36	5	56	64	.255

27 Charlie Manning, lhp

Born: March 31, 1979. **Ht.:** 6-2. **Wt.:** 180. **Bats:** L. **Throws:** L. **School:** University of Tampa.
Career Transactions: Selected by Yankees in ninth round of 2001 draft; signed June 11, 2001 . . . Traded by Yankees with LHP Brandon Claussen to Reds for 3B Aaron Boone, July 31, 2003.

Manning put his name on the prospect radar after striking out 146 in 163 innings between high Class A and Double-A in 2002. He struggled to duplicate that success when a triceps strain robbed him of his effectiveness early in 2003 at Double-A. He was shipped to the bullpen and demoted to high Class A before he was traded for Gabe White. Manning's velocity dropped from its usual 87-89 mph range and bottomed out at 83. By season's end, however, he was back to normal and peaking at 93 mph. He developed a cut fastball that helped him against righthanders. Manning worked with Reds pitching instructor Sammy Ellis on commanding his two-seamer to improve his effectiveness against lefties. He does a good job of keeping the ball down in the zone. He also has a sharp slider and good change-up. Drafted as a college senior, he has to prove himself in Double-A before moving on.

Year	Club (League)	Class	W	L	ERA	G	GS	CG	SV	IP	H	R	ER	HR	BB	SO	AVG
2001	Staten Island (NY-P)	A	8	4	3.49	14	14	0	0	80	73	33	31	4	21	87	.245
2002	Tampa (FSL)	A	6	4	3.24	17	16	0	0	100	82	48	36	4	31	85	.221
	Norwich (EL)	AA	4	2	3.57	11	11	1	0	63	55	27	25	1	26	61	.235
2003	Trenton (EL)	AA	0	2	6.26	23	6	0	0	46	53	34	32	1	35	34	.303
	Tampa (FSL)	A	2	4	3.45	6	6	0	0	31	27	14	12	2	15	25	.233
	Potomac (Car)	A	5	0	1.19	6	6	0	0	38	24	7	5	1	11	31	.182
MINOR LEAGUE TOTALS			25	16	3.54	77	59	1	0	358	314	163	141	13	139	323	.237

28 Dane Sardinha, c

Born: April 8, 1979. **Ht.:** 6-0. **Wt.:** 215. **Bats:** R. **Throws:** R. **School:** Pepperdine University.
Career Transactions: Selected by Reds in second round of 2000 draft; signed Sept. 1, 2000.

Sardinha hit .256 in Double-A last year, raising his minor league average to .229—not what the Reds envisioned when they gave him a $1.75 million major league contract three years earlier. He began last year on the disabled list after tearing a ligament in his left knee during spring training, and he ended it by being removed from Cincinnati's 40-man roster for the second time. His development was accelerated by his big league deal, which meant he would have been out of options in 2004, and the Reds say he'll make more progress without that pressure. Sardinha made his second consecutive trip to the Arizona Fall League, where he worked on his hitting mechanics. He hasn't shown the ability to make adjustments at the plate and too often chases bad pitches. He hasn't been able to shake his bad habit of pulling off the ball because his hips and legs don't work in sync with his hands and upper body. He's a potential defensive stalwart with advanced receiving and throwing skills. The Reds have asked him to be more assertive in handling pitchers, a key ingredient to his future as a backup catcher. Sardinha likely will be the everyday catcher in Triple-A this year.

Year	Club (League)	Class	AVG	G	AB	R	H	2B	3B	HR	RBI	BB	SO	SB	SLG	OBP
2001	Mudville (Cal)	A	.235	109	422	45	99	24	2	9	55	12	97	0	.365	.259
2002	Chattanooga (SL)	AA	.206	106	394	34	81	20	0	4	40	14	114	0	.287	.234
2003	Chattanooga (SL)	AA	.256	72	246	21	63	15	0	3	32	22	61	5	.354	.313
	Cincinnati (NL)	MAJ	.000	1	2	0	0	0	0	0	0	0	1	0	.000	.000
MAJOR LEAGUE TOTALS			.000	1	2	0	0	0	0	0	0	0	1	0	.000	.000
MINOR LEAGUE TOTALS			.229	287	1062	100	243	59	2	16	127	48	272	5	.333	.263

29 Willy Jo Ronda, ss

Born: June 8, 1985. **Ht.:** 6-2. **Wt.:** 175. **Bats:** B. **Throws:** R. **School:** Gabriela Mistral HS, San Juan, P.R. **Career Transactions:** Selected by Reds in third round of 2003 draft; signed June 20, 2003.

The Reds were high on several of Puerto Rico's top prospects after seeing them in a pre-draft showcase on the island, and Ronda's offensive upside in the middle of the diamond helped him emerge as their favorite. Then-scouting director Leland Maddox fell in love with Ronda's makeup after visiting with him and watching his brother throw batting practice to him every night at a field across the street from his house. A switch-hitter, Ronda is more comfortable from the left side and often neglects his righthanded stroke. He uses his hands well at the plate, which enables him to center the ball consistently and make solid contact. He has a natural uppercut which should lead to more home run power as he develops. He also starts his hip before his hands, causing his front side to fly off the ball. Defensively, he might not have the speed to stay at shortstop. Depending on how he develops at the plate, he could move to second or third base. Catching is also a long-term possibility because of his plus arm strength and strong lower half. If he doesn't start 2004 at low Class A, he could get there by the end of the season.

Year	Club (League)	Class	AVG	G	AB	R	H	2B	3B	HR	RBI	BB	SO	SB	SLG	OBP
2003	Reds (GCL)	R	.301	47	173	25	52	16	2	2	26	13	40	5	.451	.353
	Billings (Pio)	R	.667	1	3	2	2	0	0	0	0	1	1	1	.667	.750
MINOR LEAGUE TOTALS			.307	48	176	27	54	16	2	2	26	14	41	6	.455	.361

30 Kenny Lewis, of

Born: Oct. 13, 1984. **Ht.:** 5-9. **Wt.:** 195. **Bats:** L. **Throws:** L. **School:** George Washington HS, Danville, Va. **Career Transactions:** Selected by Reds in fourth round of 2003 draft; signed June 17, 2003.

Lewis didn't play baseball in high school until his junior year, and even then football commanded much of his attention. It's a testament to his natural athleticism that he was attracting crosscheckers and scouting directors by the dozens last spring. His father Kenny Sr. spent four years in the NFL as a running back for the Jets. He was going to follow in his father's footsteps at Virginia Tech before deciding to sign for $300,000. The fastest player in the 2003 draft, Lewis was clocked at 6.2 seconds in the 60-yard dash in a May workout. He led the Gulf Coast League in steals with his speed and tools recalling those of Deion Sanders. But Lewis is very raw. The Reds will have to mold Lewis into a slap-and-run contact hitter who can shoot grounders through the left side of the infield. He tends to drop his hands and swings uphill, resulting in too many fly balls and strikeouts. His stroke is also geared to pull everything. Lewis worked on bunting for hits during instructional league. In center field, he needs to improving his reads and routes on fly balls. After playing Rookie ball, Lewis was thrust into the Southern League playoff race to provide speed off the bench, but he was overmatched at the plate. It should give him an idea of what he needs to do to get back to that level. He'll start working on those things in low Class A this year.

Year	Club (League)	Class	AVG	G	AB	R	H	2B	3B	HR	RBI	BB	SO	SB	SLG	OBP
2003	Reds (GCL)	R	.242	55	194	40	47	8	4	0	14	29	66	37	.325	.345
	Chattanooga (SL)	AA	.118	6	17	4	2	1	0	0	0	4	9	3	.176	.318
MINOR LEAGUE TOTALS			.232	61	211	44	49	9	4	0	14	33	75	40	.313	.343

CLEVELAND
INDIANS

The Indians did a lot of winning during the 2003 season. Everywhere, that is, but at the major league level.

Indeed, the most dramatic evidence of the organization's rebuilding process can be found in the winning percentages. At the major league level, Cleveland's .420 winning percentage was its 10th-worst since it began play in 1901. The Tribe's six minor league clubs, however, combined for a .575 mark, the second-best in baseball. At 97-43, low Class A Lake County had the best record of any team in the majors or minors. Double-A Akron went 88-53, the fourth-best mark in the minors, and won the Eastern League championship.

In the majors, winning took a back seat to development. While the loss total soared, so too did the stock of many of the 25 rookies who appeared with the Indians. Outfielder Jody Gerut finished fourth in the American League rookie of the year balloting. The Indians also pushed many young players through the system, trying to accelerate the rebuilding process.

Cleveland also continued to bring in more talent, taking advantage of multiple first-round picks for the fourth straight draft. The Indians made the most of their highest draft slot in 10 years by taking Tulane first baseman Michael Aubrey, who hit .348 at Lake County. They used their other first-rounders on Ball State outfielder

TOP 30 PROSPECTS

1. Grady Sizemore, of
2. Jeremy Guthrie, rhp
3. Fausto Carmona, rhp
4. Jake Dittler, rhp
5. Fernando Cabrera, rhp
6. Michael Aubrey, 1b
7. Jason Cooper, of
8. Brad Snyder, of
9. Adam Miller, rhp
10. Matt Whitney, 3b
11. Nick Pesco, rhp
12. Kazuhito Tadano, rhp
13. Corey Smith, 3b
14. Francisco Cruceta, rhp
15. Rafael Perez, lhp
16. Jason Stanford, lhp
17. Mariano Gomez, lhp
18. Brian Tallet, lhp
19. Nathan Panther, of
20. Travis Foley, rhp
21. Dan Denham, rhp
22. J.D. Martin, rhp
23. Aaron Laffey, lhp
24. Ivan Ochoa, ss
25. Javi Herrera, c
26. Brian Slocum, rhp
27. Nelson Hiraldo, rhp
28. David Wallace, c
29. Ben Francisco, of
30. Sean Smith, rhp

By Jim Ingraham

Brad Snyder and Texas high school righthander Adam Miller, who also looked good in their pro debuts. The Tribe added another first-round talent in righty Nick Pesco, a 25th-round draft-and-follow from 2002 who signed for $1.1 million.

Many longtime Indians employees say it has been decades since the organization had this much depth in its farm system. Cleveland has so much talent, in fact, that several legitimate prospects with eye-catching numbers couldn't crack the organization's top 30. That group includes pitchers Dan Eisentrager (12-3, 1.72); Keith Ramsey (13-6, 2.99); Todd Pennington (0.72 ERA, minor league bests with 14.1 strikeouts per nine innings and .138 opponent average); third baseman Shaun Larkin (.266-20-80); and Scott (.276-20-81).

There were a few negatives on the development side last year, however. The last two No. 1 prospects in the organization, infielder Brandon Phillips and Smith, didn't progress as hoped. Phillips had a disastrous year, hitting .208 in Cleveland and .175 in Triple-A. Smith still hasn't had a breakout season after batting .271-9-64 at Akron.

But they were the exception and not the rule. The Indians aren't ready to contend in the AL Central this year, but they should be able to challenge no later than 2006. Their only division rival whose future looks as bright is the Twins.

ORGANIZATION
OVERVIEW

General manager: Mark Shapiro. **Farm director:** John Farrell. **Scouting director:** John Mirabelli.

2003 PERFORMANCE

Class	Team	League	W	L	Pct.	Finish*	Manager
Majors	Cleveland	American	68	94	.420	12th (14)	Eric Wedge
Triple-A	Buffalo Bisons	International	73	70	.510	t-7th (14)	Marty Brown
Double-A	Akron Aeros	Eastern	88	53	.624	+1st (12)	Brad Komminsk
High A	Kinston Indians	Carolina	73	66	.525	4th (8)	Torey Lovullo
Low A	Lake County Captains	South Atlantic	97	43	.693	1st (16)	Luis Rivera
Short-season	Mahoning Valley Indians	New York-Penn	38	36	.514	7th (14)	Ted Kubiak
Rookie	Burlington Indians	Appalachian	37	31	.544	5th (10)	Rouglas Odor
OVERALL 2003 MINOR LEAGUE RECORD			406	299	.576	2nd (30)	

*Finish in overall standings (No. of teams in league). +League champion.

ORGANIZATION LEADERS

BATTING
*Minimum 250 At-Bats
*AVG	Victor Martinez, Buffalo/Akron	.329
R	Grady Sizemore, Akron	96
H	Grady Sizemore, Akron	151
TB	Jason Cooper, Kinston/Lake County	260
2B	Jason Cooper, Kinston/Lake County	34
3B	Grady Sizemore, Akron	11
HR	Alex Escobar, Buffalo	24
RBI	Luke Scott, Akron/ Kinston	81
BB	Shaun Larkin, Lake County	73
SO	Alex Escobar, Buffalo	133
SB	Willy Taveras, Kinston	57
*SLG	Jason Cooper, Kinston/Lake County	.542
*OBP	Joe Inglett, Kinston/Akron	.396

PITCHING
#Minimum 75 Innings
W	Fausto Carmona, Akron/Lake County	17
L	Jeremy Guthrie, Buffalo/Akron	11
#ERA	Shea Douglas, Akron/Lake County	1.42
G	Lee Gronkiewicz, Kinston	51
CG	Francisco Cruceta, Akron	6
SV	Lee Gronkiewicz, Kinston	37
IP	Francisco Cruceta, Akron	163
BB	Jim Ed Warden, Akron/Kinston/Lake County	74
SO	Francisco Cruceta, Akron	134

BEST TOOLS

Best Hitter for Average	Michael Aubrey
Best Power Hitter	Jason Cooper
Fastest Baserunner	Ricardo Rojas
Best Athlete	Grady Sizemore
Best Fastball	Fernando Cabrera
Best Curveball	Dan Eisentrager
Best Slider	Rafael Perez
Best Changeup	Jake Dittler
Best Control	Fausto Carmona
Best Defensive Catcher	Dave Wallace
Best Defensive Infielder	Ivan Ochoa
Best Infield Arm	Corey Smith
Best Defensive Outfielder	Ricardo Rojas
Best Outfield Arm	Ricardo Rojas

PROJECTED 2007 LINEUP

Catcher	Victor Martinez
First Base	Michael Aubrey
Second Base	Brandon Phillips
Third Base	Matt Whitney
Shortstop	John Peralta
Left Field	Grady Sizemore
Center Field	Milton Bradley

Right Field	Jody Gerut
Designated Hitter	Travis Hafner
No. 1 Starter	C.C. Sabathia
No. 2 Starter	Cliff Lee
No. 3 Starter	Jason Davis
No. 4 Starter	Jeremy Guthrie
No. 5 Starter	Fausto Carmona
Closer	Fernando Cabrera

LAST YEAR'S TOP 20 PROSPECTS

1. Brandon Phillips, ss/2b
2. Victor Martinez, c
3. Cliff Lee, lhp
4. Jeremy Guthrie, rhp
5. Travis Hafner, 1b
6. Ricardo Rodriguez, rhp
7. Grady Sizemore, of
8. Billy Traber, lhp
9. Brian Tallet, lhp
10. Jason Davis, rhp
11. Corey Smith, 3b
12. Francisco Cruceta, rhp
13. Alex Escobar, of
14. J.D. Martin, rhp
15. Josh Bard, c
16. Dan Denham, rhp
17. Johnny Peralta, ss
18. Travis Foley, rhp
19. Matt Whitney, 3b
20. Luis Garcia, of/1b

TOP PROSPECTS OF THE DECADE

1994	Manny Ramirez, of
1995	Jaret Wright, rhp
1996	Bartolo Colon, rhp
1997	Bartolo Colon, rhp
1998	Sean Casey, 1b
1999	Russell Branyan, 3b
2000	C.C. Sabathia, lhp
2001	C.C. Sabathia, lhp
2002	Corey Smith, 3b
2003	Brandon Phillips, ss/2b

TOP DRAFT PICKS OF THE DECADE

1994	Jaret Wright, rhp
1995	David Miller, 1b/of
1996	Danny Peoples, 1b/of
1997	Tim Drew, rhp
1998	C.C. Sabathia, lhp
1999	Will Hartley, c (2)
2000	Corey Smith, 3b
2001	Dan Denham, rhp
2002	Jeremy Guthrie, rhp
2003	Michael Aubrey, 1b

ALL-TIME LARGEST BONUSES

Danys Baez, 1999	$4,500,000
Jeremy Guthrie, 2002	$3,000,000
Michael Aubrey, 2003	$2,010,000
Dan Denham, 2001	$1,860,000
Tim Drew, 1997	$1,600,000

MINOR LEAGUE
DEPTH CHART

CLEVELAND **INDIANS**

RANK: 6

Impact potential (B): Grady Sizemore can do it all. Only his below-average arm keeps him from achieving five-tool status. He also has the intangibles to become a standout in the majors. Michael Aubrey and Brad Snyder, products of the 2003 draft, also have high-end potential, and Matt Whitney, coming off knee surgery, shouldn't be forgotten.

Depth (A): Eight of the Indians top 10 prospects from a year ago graduated to the big leagues, and that didn't even include Jody Gerut, Alex Escobar or Ben Broussard. Not many systems are strong enough to sustain that type of exodus and still be among the deepest in the game. Another strong draft by Indians scouting director John Mirabelli and another wave of promising Latin prospects are sure to keep the Indians on top for years.

Sleeper: Mariano Gomez, lhp. *—Depth charts prepared by Josh Boyd. Numbers in parentheses indicate prospect rankings.*

LF
Jason Cooper (7)
Luke Scott
Ryan Goleski
Mike Conroy

CF
Grady Sizemore (1)
Brad Snyder (8)
Ben Francisco (29)
Ricardo Rojas

RF
Nathan Panther (19)

3B
Matt Whitney (10)
Corey Smith (13)
Shaun Larkin
Rodney Choy Foo
Kevin Kouzmanoff
Pat Osborn

SS
Ivan Ochoa (24)
Chris De La Cruz

2B
Micah Schilling
Eider Torres
Joe Inglett

1B
Michael Aubrey (6)
Eric Crozier

SOURCE OF TALENT

Homegrown		Acquired	
College	8	Trades	2
Junior College	3	Rule 5 draft	0
Draft-and-follow	0	Independent	0
High school	9	Free agents/waivers	0
Nondrafted free agent	2		
Foreign	6		

C
Javier Herrera (25)
David Wallace (28)
Ryan Garko

RHP

Starters	Relievers
Jeremy Guthrie (2)	Fernando Cabrera (5)
Fausto Carmona (3)	Kazuhito Tadano (12)
Jake Dittler (4)	Todd Pennington
Adam Miller (9)	Carlos De la Cruz
Nick Pesco (11)	Rafael Betancourt
Francisco Cruceta (14)	Matt Davis
Travis Foley (20)	
Dan Denham (21)	
J.D. Martin (22)	
Brian Slocum (26)	
Nelson Hiraldo (27)	
Sean Smith (30)	
Kyle Denney	
Kyle Evans	
Dan Eisentrager	
Matthew Haynes	

LHP

Starters	Relievers
Rafael Perez (15)	Michael Hernandez
Jason Stanford (16)	Cliff Bartosh
Mariano Gomez (17)	Shea Douglas
Brian Tallet (18)	Blake Allen
Aaron Laffey (23)	Juan Lara
Keith Ramsey	
Derrick Van Dusen	
Dan Cevette	

DRAFT ANALYSIS

Best Pro Debut: 1B Michael Aubrey (1) went straight to low Class A and hit .348-5-19. RHP Adam Miller (1) was the Rookie-level Appalachian League's No. 1 prospect, though his record was 0-4, 4.96. LHP Aaron Laffey (16) was untouchable in the Appy League, going 3-1, 2.91 with 46 strikeouts and just 22 hits in 34 innings.

Best Athlete: OF Brad Snyder (1) showed his tools by hitting .284-6-31 with 14 steals in the short-season New York-Penn League.

Best Pure Hitter: Scouts considered Aubrey the second-best hitter in the college draft pool, behind No. 2 overall pick Rickie Weeks.

Best Raw Power: 1B Ryan Goleski (24) earned NY-P all-star honors by batting .296-8-37. He set Eastern Michigan and Mid-American Conference career home run records with 51 in three seasons.

Fastest Runner: OF Juan Valdes (5) ran a 6.6-second 60 during instructional league.

Best Defensive Player: C Javi Herrera (2) is an advanced receiver with a good arm, though he was ineffective combating the running game in 2003. SS Brandon Pinckney (12) has good hands and made the Appy all-star team by hitting .272-1-27.

Best Fastball: Miller has a 90-95 fastball with 55 sink and 60 command on the 20-80 scouting scale. RHP Scott Roehl (10) has similar arm strength but doesn't have the same

Herrera

life or control. Draft-and-follow RHP Nick Pesco (25 in 2002) reached 94 mph in instructional league and has a power curveball, yet his best pitch may be his changeup.

Best Breaking Ball: RHP Matt Davis (7) tightened up his slurvy breaking ball after signing, turning it into an 82-84 mph strikeout slider. He went 4-4, 1.54 and limited NY-P hitters to a .199 average.

Most Intriguing Background: Snyder recovered from a horrific car accident in the summer of 2001 that nearly forced him to have his right big toe amputated.

Closest To The Majors: Aubrey should reach Double-A in 2004. His main need is at-bats against quality lefthanders.

Best Late-Round Pick: Laffey, who has a good feel for pitching. He has an 86-89 mph fastball and gets strikeouts with two average breaking balls, a curveball and slider.

The One Who Got Away: Toolsy OF Ben Harrison (4) wanted second-round money, even after breaking his hamate bone in the Cape Cod League. He returned to Florida.

Assessment: The Indians took steps to rectify the American League's second-worst offense by starting their draft with Aubrey and Snyder. Miller had one of the best high school arms in the draft, and Pesco is a draft-and-follow signing in the tradition of Jason Davis (2000) and Sean Smith (2002).

If RHP Jeremy Guthrie (1), OF Jason Cooper (3), 3B Matt Whitney (3) and draft-and-follow RHP Nick Pesco (25) keep progressing, this grade will rise.

Of Cleveland's four first-rounders, RHP Dan Denham has been slow to develop, RHP Alan Horne didn't sign, RHP J.D. Martin got hurt and OF Michael Conroy hasn't hit. RHPs Jake Dittler (2) and Travis Foley (4) have passed them.

3B Corey Smith (1) is starting to plateau and likely won't produce as much as OF Conor Jackson (31), who became a 2003 first-rounder after rebuffing the Indians. LHP Brian Tallet (2) reached the majors quickly but blew out his elbow and needed Tommy John surgery.

This draft was a disaster in the early rounds but rebounded with RHPs Jason Davis (21) and Fernando Cabrera (10).

—Draft analysis prepared by Jim Callis. Numbers in parentheses indicate draft rounds.

Grady
Sizemore

Born: Aug. 2, 1982.
Ht.: 6-2. **Wt.:** 200.
Bats: L. **Throws:** L.
School: Cascade HS, Everett, Wash.
Career Transactions: Selected by Expos in third round of 2000 draft; signed June 16, 2000 . . . Traded by Expos with 1B Lee Stevens, SS Brandon Phillips and LHP Cliff Lee to Indians for RHP Bartolo Colon and a player to be named, June 27, 2002; Expos acquired RHP Tim Drew to complete trade (June 28, 2002).

Sizemore was considered the third-best prospect in the trade that brought him from Montreal to Cleveland for Bartolo Colon in mid-2002. Since switching organizations, Sizemore has eclipsed infielder Brandon Phillips and lefty Cliff Lee, who came with him from the Expos, and established that he has a higher ceiling than anyone in the system. A high school quarterback who signed a letter of intent with Washington after being recruited by several other Pacific-10 Conference schools, Sizemore gave up football to sign for $2 million. He's a high-energy, intense competitor who draws comparisons to other football-to-baseball converts such as Kirk Gibson. Sizemore looks like he made the right decision. In 2003, he led Indians minor leaguers in runs and hits, topped the Double-A Eastern League in triples and was named MVP of the Futures Game. He hit .412 as Akron won the EL playoffs, then batted third for Team USA at the Olympic qualifying tournament in November.

It has been a long time since a player with this many tools has emerged from the Indians system. Sizemore has the full package, the potential to be a marquee player, and is as close to being an untouchable as the Indians have in their minor league system. He uses the entire field and controls the strike zone well, projecting as a .300 hitter in the majors. His power is coming quicker than expected, as he stroked 13 homers last year after totaling six in his first three seasons. There's a lot more to come, as he was an EL all-star at the tender age of 20. Sizemore's speed and center-field range are well-above-average. He's quick out of the batter's box and has tremendous baserunning instincts. He's still learning the art of basestealing but should become at least a 20-20 player as he matures. Along with all his physical skills, Sizemore also has off-the-charts makeup. He's an aggressive, blue-collar player with a tremendous desire to succeed. There are few flaws in Sizemore's overall game. His arm grades as a 35 on the 20-80 scouting scale, though it's playable in center field. He compensates by getting to balls and unloading them quickly. Sizemore's walk rate declined in 2003, though it was still respectable. That seems to be the tradeoff, at least at first, for the increase in power. After succeeding on just 57 percent of his steal attempts the last two years, he must improve his reads and jumps.

Sizemore isn't far from being major league-ready at age 21. With a surplus of young outfielders on the major league roster, the Indians have no need to push him and he'll start 2004 as the center fielder in Triple-A Buffalo. He should make his big league debut at some point during the season.

Year	Club (League)	Class	AVG	G	AB	R	H	2B	3B	HR	RBI	BB	SO	SB	SLG	OBP
2000	Expos (GCL)	R	.293	55	205	31	60	8	3	1	14	23	24	16	.376	.380
2001	Clinton (Mid)	A	.268	123	451	64	121	16	4	2	61	81	92	32	.335	.381
2002	Brevard County (FSL)	A	.258	75	256	37	66	15	4	0	26	36	41	9	.348	.351
	Kinston (Car)	A	.343	47	172	31	59	9	3	3	20	33	30	14	.483	.451
2003	Akron (EL)	AA	.304	128	496	96	151	26	11	13	78	46	73	10	.480	.373
MINOR LEAGUE TOTALS			.289	428	1580	259	457	74	25	19	199	219	260	81	.404	.381

2 Jeremy Guthrie, rhp

Born: April 8, 1979. **Ht.:** 6-1. **Wt.:** 200. **Bats:** B. **Throws:** R. **School:** Stanford University. **Career Transactions:** Selected by Indians in first round (22nd overall) of 2002 draft; signed Oct. 3, 2002.

After signing a major league contract worth a guaranteed $4 million (including a $3 million bonus) in October 2002, Guthrie reached Triple-A in his first season as a professional. The last Indians pitcher to advance that high in his introduction to pro ball was another Stanford product, Steve Dunning, who went straight to the majors in 1970. Guthrie easily dominated the Eastern League but got hit hard in the Triple-A International League, though he impressed observers at both stops. He has command of four pitches, starting with a 90-93 mph fastball that touches 95. His slider and changeup have the potential to be plus pitches, and he also throws a curveball. He also fields his position well. Intelligent and coachable, he's a great competitor with a strong work ethic. Like many inexperienced pitchers, Guthrie tends to rely too much on his fastball when he gets into trouble. He didn't locate his pitches as well in Triple-A as he had in Double-A. IL hitters got ahead in the count and pounced on his mistakes. The Indians hoped Guthrie would compete for a spot in the major league rotation in spring training. The choppy waters he experienced at Buffalo last year mean he'll start the season back there this year instead, though he still could reach Cleveland during the 2004 season.

Year	Club (League)	Class	W	L	ERA	G	GS	CG	SV	IP	H	R	ER	HR	BB	SO	AVG
2003	Akron (EL)	AA	6	2	1.44	10	9	2	0	63	44	11	10	0	14	35	.196
	Buffalo (IL)	AAA	4	9	6.52	18	18	1	0	97	129	75	70	15	30	62	.321
MINOR LEAGUE TOTALS			10	11	4.52	28	27	3	0	159	173	86	80	15	44	97	.276

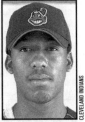

3 Fausto Carmona, rhp

Born: Dec. 7, 1983. **Ht.:** 6-4. **Wt.:** 180. **Bats:** R. **Throws:** R. **Career Transactions:** Signed out of Dominican Republic by Indians, Dec. 28, 2000.

Nobody in the organization made more dramatic progress in 2003 than Carmona, who emerged as a breakout candidate last spring. He tied for the minor league high in wins and led the low Class A South Atlantic League in ERA. The Indians could have promoted him but wanted to ease his transition to the United States as a teenager. Carmona threw a higher percentage of strikes than any pitcher in the organization last year. He has uncanny control of his 92-95 mph fastball, which he drives downhill in the zone, making it difficult for hitters to lift the ball. His athleticism allows him to repeat his delivery efficiently. His changeup is an advanced pitch. Carmona needs to further develop his slider, which will dictate how quickly he moves. He pitches to contact by design, but has good enough control to pitch out of the zone more often and draw more swings and misses. Carmona profiles as at least a quality No. 3 starter. He'll start the year at high Class A Kinston and could reach Double-A by midseason.

Year	Club (League)	Class	W	L	ERA	G	GS	CG	SV	IP	H	R	ER	HR	BB	SO	AVG
2001	Indians (DSL)	R	4	2	3.11	14	13	0	0	75	69	36	26	0	12	47	.234
2002	Burlington (Appy)	R	2	4	3.30	13	11	0	1	76	89	36	28	4	10	42	.295
	Mahoning Valley (NY-P)	A	0	0	0.00	3	0	0	0	4	2	0	0	0	1	0	.182
2003	Lake County (SAL)	A	17	4	2.06	24	24	1	0	148	117	48	34	10	14	83	.214
	Akron (EL)	AA	0	0	4.50	1	1	0	0	6	8	3	3	1	0	3	.308
MINOR LEAGUE TOTALS			23	10	2.64	55	49	1	1	310	285	123	91	15	37	175	.241

4 Jake Dittler, rhp

Born: Nov. 24, 1982. **Ht.:** 6-4. **Wt.:** 220. **Bats:** R. **Throws:** R. **School:** Green Valley HS, Henderson, Nev. **Career Transactions:** Selected by Indians in second round of 2001 draft; signed July 21, 2001.

Dittler is a product of national prep power Green Valley High, which also produced first-round picks Chad Hermansen (1995) and Mike Nannini (1998). The Indians took three pitchers ahead of Dittler in the first round of the 2001 draft, but he has surpassed Dan Denham, Alan Horne (who didn't sign) and J.D. Martin as a prospect. Dittler went just 6-13, 4.19 over his first two seasons before breaking out last year. Dittler relies on a sinking, boring fastball that sits at 90-94 mph. Physical maturity has allows him to sustain his arm slot, giving his fastball consistent velocity and action in the zone. He also throws a hard curveball. Dittler's control improved noticeably in 2003. His strong build and confidence are reminiscent of Curt Schilling. Dittler needs to improve the consistency and rotation of his curve, and also must refine his changeup. He must be able to throw his secondary pitches for strikes so hitters don't sit on his fastball. Dittler will start the 2004 season in Double-A. He needs at least a year and a half in the upper minors before he's ready for Cleveland.

Year	Club (League)	Class	W	L	ERA	G	GS	CG	SV	IP	H	R	ER	HR	BB	SO	AVG
2001	Burlington (Appy)	R	1	2	3.68	6	5	0	0	22	25	14	9	0	12	20	.287
2002	Columbus (SAL)	A	5	11	4.28	25	25	0	0	128	127	77	61	4	51	108	.257
2003	Lake County (SAL)	A	6	4	2.63	17	17	1	0	89	86	39	26	4	20	82	.244
	Kinston (Car)	A	5	1	2.40	8	8	1	0	49	47	17	13	2	11	32	.257
MINOR LEAGUE TOTALS			17	18	3.41	56	55	2	0	288	285	147	109	10	94	242	.255

5 Fernando Cabrera, rhp

RICH ABEL

Born: Nov. 16, 1981. **Ht.:** 6-4. **Wt.:** 170. **Bats:** R. **Throws:** R. **School:** Disciples of Christ Academy, Bayamon, P.R. **Career Transactions:** Selected by Indians in 10th round of 1999 draft; signed Aug. 23, 1999.

After being used almost exclusively as a starter in his first 3½ years in the organization, Cabrera moved to the bullpen in late June last year. He finished the season as Akron's closer, converting his last five regular-season save opportunities and turning in three scoreless outings in the playoffs. Cabrera throws an overpowering 92-96 mph fastball and a splitter that's an effective No. 2 pitch. His stuff and his temperament are well suited for a late-inning role, and he also had success as a starter. His fastball command improved in 2003. Cabrera needs to make hitters more aware of his splitter, which would make his fastball more effective. His slider and changeup lag behind his main two pitches, though he won't need them as much in relief. He must improve his fielding and ability to control the running game after giving up 27 steals in 31 attempts (87 percent) last year. Cabrera will begin 2004 in Triple-A. He'll reach Cleveland after he shows command of more than his fastball. The Indians don't have an obvious closer on their current roster, and Cabrera could fill that role in time.

Year	Club (League)	Class	W	L	ERA	G	GS	CG	SV	IP	H	R	ER	HR	BB	SO	AVG
2000	Burlington (Appy)	R	3	7	4.61	13	13	0	0	68	64	42	35	4	20	50	.252
2001	Columbus (SAL)	A	5	6	3.61	20	20	0	0	95	89	49	38	7	37	96	.242
2002	Kinston (Car)	A	6	8	3.52	21	21	0	0	110	83	48	43	7	40	107	.206
	Akron (EL)	AA	1	2	5.33	7	4	0	1	27	26	16	16	1	12	29	.252
2003	Akron (EL)	AA	9	4	2.97	36	15	0	5	109	96	41	36	8	40	115	.237
MINOR LEAGUE TOTALS			24	27	3.70	97	73	0	6	409	358	196	168	27	149	397	.234

6 Michael Aubrey, 1b

RICH ABEL

Born: April 15, 1982. **Ht.:** 6-0. **Wt.:** 195. **Bats:** L. **Throws:** L. **School:** Tulane University. **Career Transactions:** Selected by Indians in first round (11th overall) of 2003 draft; signed June 14, 2003.

Aubrey was a two-way star when BA named him Freshman of the Year in 2001, but he eventually settled in as strictly a first baseman. Among college players in the 2003 draft, scouts considered only No. 2 overall pick Rickie Weeks a better pure hitter than Aubrey. He projected to go as high as No. 6, but Aubrey went 11th and signed for $2.01 million. An advanced hitter, Aubrey was as good as advertised in his pro debut. He makes outstanding contact, has good plate discipline and projects as a .300 hitter with 35 doubles and 15-20 homers in the majors. He has solid-average speed and Gold Glove potential at first base. He threw 90-92 mph off the mound as a Tulane freshman and has a good arm for his position. Though he sometimes gets tied up on inside fastballs, Aubrey should be able to adjust. He gets pull-conscious at times, leading to an uppercut swing, and needs to a better job of identifying pitches he can drive. He doesn't have much experience facing quality lefthanders and hit .250 against southpaws in his debut. Aubrey won't need much time in the minors. He'll begin 2004 in high Class A and should reach Double-A in the second half.

Year	Club (League)	Class	AVG	G	AB	R	H	2B	3B	HR	RBI	BB	SO	SB	SLG	OBP
2003	Lake County (SAL)	A	.348	38	138	22	48	13	0	5	19	14	22	0	.551	.409
MINOR LEAGUE TOTALS			.348	38	138	22	48	13	0	5	19	14	22	0	.551	.409

7 Jason Cooper, of

Born: Dec. 6, 1980. **Ht.:** 6-2. **Wt.:** 220. **Bats:** L. **Throws:** L. **School:** Stanford University. **Career Transactions:** Selected by Indians in third round of 2002 draft; signed July 23, 2002.

Cooper was part of a vaunted 1999 senior class at Moses Lake (Wash.) High, along with outfielder B.J. Garbe (first round, Twins) and catcher Ryan Doumit (second, Pirates). Cooper turned down the Phillies as a second-rounder to attend Stanford, where he was also a backup punter. He led Tribe farmhands with a .542 slugging percentage in his first full season. Cooper could move fast. He has big league power and is a more complete hitter than he was at Stanford, where injuries and an uppercut swing held him back. He's gaining a better understanding of the strike zone and using the whole field, and now projects as a .280 hitter with 30 homers annually. He has average speed and plays with tremendous intensity. At times, Cooper can get pull-conscious and his stroke can get long. He hurt his shoulder in college and his arm strength hasn't come back, limiting him to left field. He has improved as an outfielder but can get better. The Indians have several left-handed-hitting outfielders in the majors, so they won't rush Cooper. He'll head to Double-A in 2004.

Year	Club (League)	Class	AVG	G	AB	R	H	2B	3B	HR	RBI	BB	SO	SB	SLG	OBP
2002	Columbus (SAL)	A	.255	17	55	9	14	5	0	4	17	6	17	0	.564	.339
2003	Lake County (SAL)	A	.297	69	263	50	78	17	7	12	36	32	52	3	.551	.385
	Kinston (Car)	A	.307	61	218	36	67	17	2	9	36	25	46	3	.528	.380
MINOR LEAGUE TOTALS			.297	147	536	95	159	39	9	25	89	63	115	6	.543	.378

8 Brad Snyder, of

Born: May 25, 1982. **Ht.:** 6-3. **Wt.:** 200. **Bats:** L. **Throws:** L. **School:** Ball State University. **Career Transactions:** Selected by Indians in first round (18th overall) of 2003 draft; signed June 15, 2003.

After growing up as an Indians fan in Bellevue, Ohio, Snyder was thrilled when his local team drafted him. His career was threatened by an auto accident after his freshman year at Ball State, but he made a full recovery. He was the 2003 Mid-American Conference player of the year and the fourth first-round pick in Ball State history. Snyder has all-around tools. He's a patient hitter with a quick bat and the ability to turn on pitches. When he extends his arms, he can drive the ball out of any part of the park. He's an average runner but covers enough ground to play center field. His arm is average as well. Snyder struck out 82 times in 62 games and will have to make better contact. He has a slight loop in his swing that he'll have to iron out, and he'll have to adapt to quality breaking stuff. His reads on the basepaths and in center field also need work. A right fielder at Ball State, Snyder will enhance his value as a pro if he can stay in center. The Indians plan on keeping him there, and he'll spend 2004 in Class A.

Year	Club (League)	Class	AVG	G	AB	R	H	2B	3B	HR	RBI	BB	SO	SB	SLG	OBP
2003	Mahoning Valley (NY-P)	A	.284	62	225	52	64	11	6	6	31	41	82	14	.467	.393
MINOR LEAGUE TOTALS			.284	62	225	52	64	11	6	6	31	41	82	14	.467	.393

9 Adam Miller, rhp

Born: Nov. 26, 1984. **Ht.:** 6-4. **Wt.:** 175. **Bats:** R. **Throws:** R. **School:** McKinney (Texas) HS. **Career Transactions:** Selected by Indians in first round (31st overall) of 2003 draft; signed June 10, 2003.

The Indians used eight first-round picks on pitchers in the previous six years. Seven of those arms came from the high school ranks, including Miller, who surged into the first round with a strong finish last spring. Though a sore shoulder and strict pitch counts limited him in his pro debut, he still ranked as the No. 1 prospect in the Rookie-level Appalachian League. Miller is mature for a high schooler and has a projectable power pitcher's frame. Some scouts have compared him to two-time Cy Young Award winner Bret Saberhagen. Miller throws strikes with a heavy, boring 90-95 mph fastball. He also has a plus slider that has touched 87 mph. Miller didn't need his changeup in high school, so the development of that pitch has lagged. At 6-foot-5 he needs to work on keeping his mechanics together and consistently repeating his delivery. His shoulder isn't a long-term concern but still raised a red flag. Miller was at his best by instructional league last fall, showing no signs of shoulder trouble. He'll move into the rotation at low Class A Lake County this year.

Year	Club (League)	Class	W	L	ERA	G	GS	CG	SV	IP	H	R	ER	HR	BB	SO	AVG
2003	Burlington (Appy)	R	0	4	4.96	10	10	0	0	33	30	20	18	2	9	23	.250
MINOR LEAGUE TOTALS			0	4	4.96	10	10	0	0	33	30	20	18	2	9	23	.250

10 Matt Whitney, 3b

Born: Feb. 13, 1984. **Ht.:** 6-4. **Wt.:** 190. **Bats:** R. **Throws:** R. **School:** Palm Beach Gardens (Fla.) HS. **Career Transactions:** Selected by Indians in first round (33rd overall) of 2002 draft; signed June 14, 2002 . . . On disabled list, April 3-Sept. 15, 2003.

A supplemental first-round pick in 2002, Whitney was so impressive in his pro debut that the Indians invoked Manny Ramirez' name when discussing his offensive potential. But last February, Whitney broke his left leg in a freak accident playing basketball while in minor league camp. He required two separate surgeries and missed the entire season. Whitney has middle-of-the-lineup talent. He has a sweet swing that generates power to all fields. The ball jumps off his bat and has tremendous carry. He quickly made adjustments to pro pitching and wood bats. He's athletic for his size and has made a nice transition to third base after playing mostly first base and the outfield in high school. First and foremost, Whitney needs to get 100 percent healthy. His arm is solid for the hot corner, though he tended to push his throws in 2002. He's a below-average runner but not a baseclogger. Whitney's rehab program continued through the offseason, and the Indians hope he'll be ready to resume full activity by the start of spring training. He may start the year in extended spring training with a target of getting to low Class A in May.

Year	Club (League)	Class	AVG	G	AB	R	H	2B	3B	HR	RBI	BB	SO	SB	SLG	OBP
2002	Burlington (Appy)	R	.286	45	175	33	50	12	1	10	33	18	49	5	.537	.359
	Columbus (SAL)	A	.111	6	18	0	2	0	0	0	0	3	4	0	.111	.238
2003	Did not play—Injured															
MINOR LEAGUE TOTALS			.269	51	193	33	52	12	1	10	33	21	53	5	.497	.347

11 Nick Pesco, rhp

Born: Sept. 17, 1983. **Ht.:** 6-6. **Wt.:** 200. **Bats:** R. **Throws:** R. **School:** Cosumnes River (Calif.) CC. **Career Transactions:** Selected by Indians in 25th round of 2002 draft; signed May 19, 2003.

After taking Pesco as a 25th-round draft-and-follow in 2002, the Indians watched him blossom into a potential first-rounder as a Cosumnes River sophomore last spring. They signed him in May for $1.1 million, and he finished second to teammate Rafael Perez in the Appalachian League ERA race in his pro debut. A big, strong righthander who has been compared to Jason Davis, Pesco throws a 91-94 mph fastball on a good downward plane. He also has a 12-to-6 power curveball and slider, yet his best pitch may be his changeup. He's durable and has good command within the strike zone. Cleveland has made minor adjustments to Pesco's mechanics, and he needs to maintain his lengthened stride. He also must learn how to attack hitters, and the weapons to do so are there. Pesco should be a draft-and-follow signing in the tradition of Jason Davis in 2000 and Sean Smith in 2002. He will join Adam Miller in anchoring what should be another powerhouse rotation at Lake County in 2004.

Year	Club (League)	Class	W	L	ERA	G	GS	CG	SV	IP	H	R	ER	HR	BB	SO	AVG
2003	Burlington (Appy)	R	3	1	1.82	13	13	0	0	54	36	16	11	0	22	55	.188
MINOR LEAGUE TOTALS			3	1	1.82	13	13	0	0	54	36	16	11	0	22	55	.188

12 Kazuhito Tadano, rhp

Born: April 25, 1980. **Ht.:** 6-0. **Wt.:** 180. **Bats:** R. **Throws:** R. **Career Transactions:** Signed out of Japan by Indians, March 8, 2003.

The first Japanese-born player signed by the Indians, Tadano's past created a stir in the midst of his professional debut last year. While at Rikkyo University in 2000, he and several of his teammates participated in a pornographic video that contained homosexual acts. Japanese teams ignored him in their 2002 draft after he was projected as an early first-round pick, and a couple of U.S. clubs interested in signing him backed off after learning of the video. The Indians excused the incident as a youthful mistake and took a chance on Tadano for the bargain price of $67,000. He certainly looks like a bargain so far. By all accounts, he fit in well with teammates at all three of his minor league stops in 2003. Tadano has numerous strengths, beginning with two plus secondary pitches, a slider and splitter. His fastball sits at 88-91 mph. He has been compared to countryman Shigetoshi Hasegawa, but with better command of his secondary pitches. Very durable, Tadano wants the ball every day and has a work ethic that's off the charts. His quick times to the plate make it difficult for baserunners to get good jumps against him, and just two tried to steal on him last summer. Tadano needs to improve his approach to lefthanders. He's also getting acclimated to the U.S. culture and spent part of the offseason in an English class in Tokyo. He'll compete for a big league bullpen job in spring training, and the Indians tried to defuse controversy about his past by making him available to the press in the offseason. The story will probably never go away, but it should become a footnote as Tadano makes a name with his ability.

Year	Club (League)	Class	W	L	ERA	G	GS	CG	SV	IP	H	R	ER	HR	BB	SO	AVG
2003	Kinston (Car)	A	2	1	1.89	7	1	0	0	19	13	5	4	0	3	28	.191
	Akron (EL)	AA	4	1	1.24	31	0	0	3	73	62	15	10	4	15	78	.226
	Buffalo (IL)	AAA	0	0	3.86	2	0	0	0	7	6	3	3	0	4	6	.231
MINOR LEAGUE TOTALS			6	2	1.55	40	1	0	3	99	81	23	17	4	22	112	.220

13 Corey Smith, 3b

Born: April 15, 1982. **Ht.:** 6-1. **Wt.:** 200. **Bats:** R. **Throws:** R. **School:** Piscataway (N.J.) HS. **Career Transactions:** Selected by Indians in first round (26th overall) of 2000 draft; signed June 15, 2000.

Even as a premium high school prospect, Smith's talent was universally acknowledged but no one spoke about him in glowing terms. The trend has continued in his professional career. While Smith clearly has good tools, the Indians are still waiting for him to have a breakthrough season. A first-round pick in 2000 who was considered the organization's top prospect two years later, Smith has seen his stock drop since. He has above-average bat speed and strength, but hasn't translated his raw power into homers. He did cut down on his strikeouts in 2003, but he's still a guess hitter who can be fooled easily. Smith also has a plus arm but is a defensive liability at the hot corner. Poor footwork and uncertain hands have led to him leading his league's third baseman in errors in each of his four pro seasons. He made 44 miscues last year to lead Eastern League third basemen, a year after leading Carolina League third basemen with 34 errors. Smith is an average runner with good instincts on the bases. He worked hard in the Arizona Fall League after the season but still showed the same weaknesses. Smith will return to Double-A in 2004, repeating a level for the first time in his career.

Year	Club (League)	Class	AVG	G	AB	R	H	2B	3B	HR	RBI	BB	SO	SB	SLG	OBP
2000	Burlington (Appy)	R	.256	57	207	21	53	8	2	4	39	27	50	8	.372	.339
2001	Columbus (SAL)	A	.260	130	500	59	130	26	5	18	85	37	149	10	.440	.312
2002	Kinston (Car)	A	.255	134	505	71	129	29	2	13	67	59	141	7	.398	.341
2003	Akron (EL)	AA	.271	127	473	51	128	27	3	9	64	50	99	7	.397	.340
MINOR LEAGUE TOTALS			.261	448	1685	202	440	90	12	44	255	173	439	32	.407	.332

14 Francisco Cruceta, rhp

Born: July 4, 1981. **Ht.:** 6-2. **Wt.:** 180. **Bats:** R. **Throws:** R. **Career Transactions:** Signed out of Dominican Republic by Dodgers, May 20, 1999 . . . Traded by Dodgers with LHP Terry Mulholland and RHP Ricardo Rodriguez to Indians for RHP Paul Shuey, July 28, 2002.

Cruceta was more of an unknown than Ricardo Rodriguez when they were acquired from the Dodgers for Paul Shuey in July 2002, though he had started to emerge in the spring of 2002 with a strong spring training performance and a no-hitter in April for low Class A South Georgia. Rodriguez since has been traded for Ryan Ludwick, while Cruceta has a bright future with the Indians. He led Eastern League pitchers in strikeouts and complete games last year, while finishing second in wins, third in innings and fourth in ERA. Cruceta relies on a 92-93 mph sinker, a solid-average to plus slider and a changeup. He struggles at times with the command of his fastball, particularly early in games. He needs to trust his stuff more and throw strikes more frequently. His ability to do so will determine whether his future role will be as a starter or reliever. He'll begin 2004 in the Triple-A rotation.

Year	Club (League)	Class	W	L	ERA	G	GS	CG	SV	IP	H	R	ER	HR	BB	SO	AVG
1999	Dodgers (DSL)	R	3	2	7.56	14	1	0	0	25	33	34	21	4	15	21	.308
2000	Dodgers (DSL)	R	4	2	3.31	21	6	0	3	49	33	29	18	1	36	49	.180
2001	Dodgers (DSL)	R	0	4	1.50	11	9	0	0	48	35	24	8	1	24	47	.200
2002	South Georgia (SAL)	A	8	5	2.80	20	20	3	0	113	98	42	35	7	34	111	.231
	Kinston (Car)	A	2	0	2.50	7	7	0	0	40	31	13	11	2	25	37	.217
2003	Akron (EL)	AA	13	9	3.09	27	25	6	0	163	141	70	56	7	66	134	.232
MINOR LEAGUE TOTALS			30	22	3.06	100	68	9	3	438	371	212	149	22	200	399	.226

15 Rafael Perez, lhp

Born: May 15, 1982. **Ht.:** 6-3. **Wt.:** 170. **Bats:** L. **Throws:** L. **Career Transactions:** Signed out of Dominican Republic by Indians, Jan. 25, 2002.

A long, lanky lefty, Perez has produced eye-popping numbers in his two seasons with the Indians. He was known as Hanlet Ramirez when he helped his Indians squad to the 2002 championship in the Rookie-level Dominican Summer League. He was named Appalachian League pitcher of the year in his U.S. debut last year, leading the league in wins and ERA while ranking second in innings and fifth in strikeouts. He already throws an 89-91 mph, and has a projectable frame that should be able to add velocity. His fastball is effective because it tails away late from righthanders. His slider is tough on lefthanders, and he also throws a complementary changeup. His tremendous control of his pitches and emotions could allow him to move quickly through the minors, and because he usually pitches ahead in the count it makes his otherwise average offerings more effective. He mixes his pitches well and keeps hitters off balance. Perez needs to get stronger and prove he can handle the rigors of starting over a full season. Cleveland will give him the chance to do that this year in high Class A, skipping him a level because they have to determine whether he merits a 40-man roster spot after the season.

Year	Club (League)	Class	W	L	ERA	G	GS	CG	SV	IP	H	R	ER	HR	BB	SO	AVG
2002	Cleveland W (DSL)	R	7	1	0.96	13	13	1	0	75	58	14	8	3	16	81	.208
2003	Burlington (Appy)	R	9	3	1.70	13	12	0	0	69	56	23	13	1	16	63	.220
MINOR LEAGUE TOTALS			16	4	1.31	26	25	1	0	144	114	37	21	4	32	144	.214

16 Jason Stanford, lhp

Born: Jan. 23, 1977. **Ht.:** 6-2. **Wt.:** 200. **Bats:** L. **Throws:** L. **School:** UNC Charlotte. **Career Transactions:** Signed as nondrafted free agent by Indians, Nov. 16, 1999.

An overachiever signed as a nondrafted free agent, Stanford has been a consistent winner wherever he's pitched. He has gone 3-0, 0.75 for Team USA in international competitions after the 2001 and 2003 seasons, pitching 12 innings in the unsuccessful effort at the Olympic qualifying tournament in November, and would have been a prime candidate for the 2004 Olympics had the United States qualified. Stanford has a great feel for pitching and has met the challenge every time he has moved up a level. His fastball ranges between 87-90 mph, but that's enough velocity for him because he has a good changeup that he'll throw in any count. He's working on tightening his slider to give it late action and keep righthanders honest. Stanford won't overpower hitters yet he believes in his stuff. He pitched effectively in a swing role for Cleveland in the second half of 2003, shutting out the Blue Jays for six innings to earn his first big league win. He'll go to spring training with a chance to win the No. 5 starter's job.

Year	Club (League)	Class	W	L	ERA	G	GS	CG	SV	IP	H	R	ER	HR	BB	SO	AVG
2000	Columbus (SAL)	A	7	4	2.73	14	14	0	0	79	82	32	24	3	20	72	.265
	Kinston (Car)	A	4	3	2.57	11	11	1	0	70	68	22	20	2	17	58	.250
	Akron (EL)	AA	1	0	1.59	1	1	0	0	6	5	1	1	0	1	5	.238
2001	Akron (EL)	AA	6	11	4.07	24	24	1	0	142	152	71	64	11	32	108	.276
	Buffalo (IL)	AAA	1	0	0.00	1	1	1	0	9	3	0	0	0	0	10	.103
2002	Akron (EL)	AA	7	6	3.43	18	18	1	0	102	108	44	39	3	33	86	.276
	Buffalo (IL)	AAA	3	1	2.78	6	5	0	0	36	33	12	11	5	11	23	.244
2003	Buffalo (IL)	AAA	10	4	3.43	20	20	1	0	126	124	57	48	13	25	108	.261
	Cleveland (AL)	MAJ	1	3	3.60	13	8	0	0	50	48	20	20	5	16	30	.246
MAJOR LEAGUE TOTALS			1	3	3.60	13	8	0	0	50	48	20	20	5	16	30	.246
MINOR LEAGUE TOTALS			39	29	3.27	95	94	5	0	569	575	239	207	37	139	470	.263

17 Mariano Gomez, lhp

Born: Sept. 12, 1982. **Ht.:** 6-5. **Wt.:** 170. **Bats:** L. **Throws:** L. **Career Transactions:** Signed out Honduras by Indians, July 1, 1999.

Signed at age 16 out of Honduras, Gomez has made impressive strides in full-season ball over the last two years. His size, strength and mix of pitches are all positive attributes. Gomez whips his fastball at 89-90 mph with a quick arm. He also has a plus breaking ball with slurvy action, as well as a changeup. He tends to get too emotional at times, which prevents him from maintaining his delivery. Gomez is very intelligent—fluent in three languages—but a worrier, dwelling on things he can't control rather than concentrating on that which he can. He's inconsistent with his breaking ball at this point. Gomez has added 30 pounds since he signed, and at 6-foot-5 he has the frame to handle more, which could mean additional velocity. He's poised for a breakout campaign but needs to prove he can handle the rigors of a complete season. Last year, he didn't pitch after July 14 because of a strained ligament in his left middle finger. He'll move a step up to Double-A in 2004.

Year	Club (League)	Class	W	L	ERA	G	GS	CG	SV	IP	H	R	ER	HR	BB	SO	AVG
2000	Burlington (Appy)	R	0	5	4.31	13	11	0	0	54	77	44	26	7	16	30	.341
2001	Burlington (Appy)	R	2	8	6.07	13	12	0	0	59	69	47	40	4	21	57	.289
	Mahoning Valley (NY-P)	A	1	0	5.40	1	1	0	0	5	5	3	3	1	2	6	.263
2002	Columbus (SAL)	A	8	2	2.75	34	13	0	1	111	106	44	34	3	40	98	.247
2003	Kinston (Car)	A	6	4	3.67	18	18	1	0	101	91	49	41	11	38	69	.243
MINOR LEAGUE TOTALS			17	19	3.92	79	55	1	1	331	348	187	144	26	117	260	.270

18 Brian Tallet, lhp

Born: Sept. 21, 1977. **Ht.:** 6-7. **Wt.:** 200. **Bats:** L. **Throws:** L. **School:** Louisiana State University.
Career Transactions: Selected by Indians in second round of 2000 draft; signed Aug. 1, 2000.

The ace of Louisiana State's 2000 College World Series championship team, Tallet won 15 games and started the CWS title game against Stanford. The Tigers won with a late rally, so Tallet didn't figure into the decision. He rushed through the minors and reached Cleveland in little more than two years after signing. However, he blew out his elbow shortly after being demoted to Triple-A for the third time last year. He had Tommy John surgery that is expected to knock him out for all of 2004. When healthy, Tallet goes after hitters with a solid-average repertoire. He throws an 89-92 mph fastball with good sinking action, a slider and changeup. When he returns to the mound, his next challenge will be to improve the command of his fastball and add strength. The 6-foot-7 Tallet has such a long, levered body that his delivery tends to get out of whack, and he has trouble maintaining his arm slot. He faces a full year of rehabilitation.

Year	Club (League)	Class	W	L	ERA	G	GS	CG	SV	IP	H	R	ER	HR	BB	SO	AVG
2000	Mahoning Valley (NY-P)	A	0	0	1.15	6	6	0	0	16	10	2	2	0	3	20	.172
2001	Kinston (Car)	A	9	7	3.04	27	27	2	0	160	134	62	54	12	38	164	.224
2002	Akron (EL)	AA	10	1	3.08	18	16	1	0	102	93	41	35	9	32	73	.243
	Buffalo (IL)	AAA	2	3	3.07	8	7	0	0	44	47	17	15	1	16	25	.281
	Cleveland (AL)	MAJ	1	0	1.50	2	2	0	0	12	9	3	2	0	4	5	.214
2003	Buffalo (IL)	AAA	4	4	5.14	15	15	0	0	84	89	50	48	10	34	67	.270
	Cleveland (AL)	MAJ	0	2	4.74	5	3	0	0	19	23	14	10	2	8	9	.303
MAJOR LEAGUE TOTALS			1	2	3.48	7	5	0	0	31	32	17	12	2	12	14	.271
MINOR LEAGUE TOTALS			25	15	3.41	74	71	3	0	406	373	172	154	32	123	349	.243

19 Nathan Panther, of

Born: July 12, 1981. **Ht.:** 6-2. **Wt.:** 180. **Bats:** L. **Throws:** L. **School:** Muscatine (Iowa) CC.
Career Transactions: Selected by Indians in 15th round of 2002 draft; signed June 7, 2002.

Panther ranked third among national junior college hitters with a .479 average as a two-way star at Muscatine Community College in 2002. Yet he was a relative unknown until he stood out at a predraft showcase. Based on his first full season, he looks like a 15th-round steal. Panther is an all-around outfielder who resembles a young Steve Finley. He's a line-drive hitter with gap power and plus speed. He needs to get stronger, which would help boost his home run totals. If he reaches his ceiling, he could be a 20-20 player. Panther's arm is another asset. He played mainly right field last year but may also have the range for center, where he saw some brief action. He'll get more time in center field this year in high Class A.

Year	Club (League)	Class	AVG	G	AB	R	H	2B	3B	HR	RBI	BB	SO	SB	SLG	OBP
2002	Burlington (Appy)	R	.240	34	125	17	30	7	4	2	21	16	22	3	.408	.324
2003	Lake County (SAL)	A	.285	108	428	88	122	22	6	13	52	45	75	38	.456	.356
	Akron (EL)	AA	.000	3	9	0	0	0	0	0	1	0	3	0	.000	.000
MINOR LEAGUE TOTALS			.270	145	562	105	152	29	10	15	74	61	100	41	.438	.344

20 Travis Foley, rhp

Born: March 11, 1983. **Ht.:** 6-1. **Wt.:** 180. **Bats:** R. **Throws:** R. **School:** Butler HS, Louisville.
Career Transactions: Selected by Indians in fourth round of 2001 draft; signed June 13, 2001.

Of all the pitching prospects the Indians signed out of the 2001 draft, none can match Foley's 25 victories in pro ball (J.D. Martin has 24.). He has a solid-average fastball that sits at 90 mph and tops out at 93. He has made major improvements to his changeup, which is now a plus pitch. His third offering is a tight, late-breaking slider that has replaced a slow curveball. Foley's build isn't very projectable, so it would help if he could regain the 1-2 mph of velocity that he lost in 2003. He's also working on refining his changeup and developing more command of his slider. He needs a better breaking ball to remain a starter, and otherwise faces a future as a middle reliever. Foley will pitch in the Double-A rotation this year.

Year	Club (League)	Class	W	L	ERA	G	GS	CG	SV	IP	H	R	ER	HR	BB	SO	AVG
2001	Burlington (Appy)	R	2	3	2.80	10	10	0	0	45	26	16	14	4	15	59	.171
2002	Columbus (SAL)	A	13	4	2.82	26	26	1	0	137	108	47	43	9	44	138	.215
2003	Kinston (Car)	A	10	10	3.69	24	24	1	0	127	115	54	52	7	54	96	.254
MINOR LEAGUE TOTALS			25	17	3.17	60	60	2	0	309	249	117	109	20	113	293	.225

21 Dan Denham, rhp

Born: Dec. 24, 1982. **Ht.:** 6-2. **Wt.:** 190. **Bats:** R. **Throws:** R. **School:** Deer Valley HS, Antioch, Calif. **Career Transactions:** Selected by Indians in first round (17th overall) of 2001 draft; signed July 7, 2001.

Denham was the top pick in Cleveland's pitching-rich 2001 draft class, signing for what was then a club-record $1.86 million bonus. His brother Jason, who also attends Deer Valley High, is an outfielder who attended the Area Code Games last summer and will be eligible for the 2004 draft. While Dan's development has been slow, the Indians remain high on him. His only extended success came when he repeated low Class A last year, and he tailed off following a promotion. He went 3-0, 1.49 in his final six starts for Kinston. When he first signed, Denham tended to overthrow, but he has settled down and learned to pitch at 90-93 mph with his fastball. He's durable and competitive. His reworked delivery is strong and compact, though it can get mechanical and lacks deception. Denham did a better job of throwing strikes last year, but still needs to refine his curveball, slider and changeup. He also can improve at locating his fastball on both sides of the plate. Denham will return to high Class A to start 2004.

Year	Club (League)	Class	W	L	ERA	G	GS	CG	SV	IP	H	R	ER	HR	BB	SO	AVG
2001	Burlington (Appy)	R	0	4	4.40	8	8	0	0	31	30	21	15	5	26	31	.256
2002	Columbus (SAL)	A	9	8	4.76	28	28	0	0	125	123	76	66	7	65	109	.265
2003	Lake County (SAL)	A	5	2	3.08	14	14	0	0	73	75	28	25	4	22	63	.263
	Kinston (Car)	A	5	5	4.50	14	14	1	0	72	82	42	36	2	27	39	.298
MINOR LEAGUE TOTALS			19	19	4.26	64	64	1	0	300	310	167	142	18	140	242	.272

22 J.D. Martin, rhp

Born: Jan. 2, 1983. **Ht.:** 6-4. **Wt.:** 170. **Bats:** R. **Throws:** R. **School:** Burroughs HS, Ridgecrest, Calif. **Career Transactions:** Selected by Indians in first round (35th overall) of 2001 draft; signed June 20, 2001.

Martin got off to a faster start than any of the pitchers in the Tribe's 2001 draft, including Dan Denham and Travis Foley, by posting a 1.38 ERA in his pro debut and winning 14 games in his first full season. But he also had the most disappointing 2003 season of that group because he was shut down in late July with a strained elbow ligament. The good news was that Martin avoided surgery and should be fine after an offseason of rest and rehabilitation. His strong suits are his command and feel for changing speeds. His 87-89 mph fastball isn't overpowering, but he locates it well and does the same with his overhand curveball, slider and changeup. Lean and wiry, he has room on his frame to add velocity, but that hasn't happened for him. Durability and stamina always have been issues for Martin, who has worked hard to add eight pounds to his frame since signing. Expected to be 100 percent by the start of spring training, Martin will rejoin fellow 2001 first-rounder Dan Denham in the high Class A rotation.

Year	Club (League)	Class	W	L	ERA	G	GS	CG	SV	IP	H	R	ER	HR	BB	SO	AVG
2001	Burlington (Appy)	R	5	1	1.38	10	10	0	0	46	26	9	7	3	11	72	.164
2002	Columbus (SAL)	A	14	5	3.90	27	26	0	0	138	141	76	60	12	46	131	.266
2003	Kinston (Car)	A	5	3	4.27	16	16	0	0	86	95	50	41	7	30	57	.281
MINOR LEAGUE TOTALS			24	9	3.60	53	52	0	0	270	262	135	108	22	87	260	.255

23 Aaron Laffey, lhp

Born: April 15, 1985. **Ht.:** 6-0. **Wt.:** 170. **Bats:** L. **Throws:** L. **School:** Allegany HS, Foxburg, Md. **Career Transactions:** Selected by Indians in 16th round of 2003 draft; signed July 1, 2003.

Laffey's father is a former teammate of Braves pitching coach Leo Mazzone. He didn't give up an earned run in 44 innings as a high school senior, but he plummeted in the draft when his agent told area scouts that he'd have to go in the top 75 picks to sign. He had a commitment to Virginia Tech, and some scouts said his style was reminiscent of former Tech lefty Joe Saunders, a first-round pick of the Angels in 2002. The Indians took a flier on Laffey in the 16th round, and when fourth-round choice Ben Harrison insisted on first-round money, they used the money earmarked for Harrison to sign Laffey for $363,000. He responded with a dominating debut at Rookie-level Burlington, where he averaged 12.2 strikeouts per nine innings and held opponents to a .183 average—both better numbers than more celebrated teammates Adam Miller, Rafael Perez and Nick Pesco. Laffey has a well-above-average slider. Though he's just 6 feet tall, he's able to pitch down in the zone with his 86-88 mph fastball because it has good sink. He throws strikes and has good command within the zone. He's a good athlete who played shortstop when he wasn't pitching for his high school team, and he was a standout for his high school basketball team. He controls the running game by keeping basestealers off balance with varied looks. Laffey's build doesn't leave room for much projection. He relied too heavily on baffling Appalachian League hitters with his slider. He'll have to use his fastball more and develop his changeup at higher levels. He'll pitch in low Class A this year.

Year	Club (League)	Class	W	L	ERA	G	GS	CG	SV	IP	H	R	ER	HR	BB	SO	AVG
2003	Burlington (Appy)	R	3	1	2.91	9	4	0	0	34	22	13	11	0	15	46	.183
MINOR LEAGUE TOTALS			3	1	2.91	9	4	0	0	34	22	13	11	0	15	46	.183

24 Ivan Ochoa, ss

Born: Dec. 16, 1982. **Ht.:** 5-10. **Wt.:** 140. **Bats:** R. **Throws:** R. **Career Transactions:** Signed out of Venezuela by Indians, May 3, 2000.

Omar Vizquel isn't the only slick-fielding Venzuelan shortstop in the organization. Ochoa, who broke into pro ball as a third baseman, is the best defensive infielder in the system. Like many young shortstops, his glove is way ahead of his bat. His range, hands and arm are all major league-quality right now, but he needs to avoid mental lapses. Sound fundamentally, he can make acrobatic plays as well as routine ones. Ochoa has 55 speed on the 20-80 scouting scale and has been a basestealing threat in the lower minors. The huge question surrounding him is how much offense he'll be able to provide. Ochoa is slim and lacks strength. He offers next to no power—he's still looking for his first homer as a pro—so he's going to have to learn how to get on base. He shows some aptitude for working counts and handling the bat, but pitchers have been able to overpower him. While his defense is so exceptional that he won't have to be a force offensively, he's going to have to hit more to have a career like Indians reserve John McDonald's. Hampered by hamstring problems in 2003, Ochoa should spend the full year in high Class A.

Year	Club (League)	Class	AVG	G	AB	R	H	2B	3B	HR	RBI	BB	SO	SB	SLG	OBP
2000	San Felipe (VSL)	R	.344	38	122	36	42	5	3	0	14	29	22	14	.434	.506
2001	Burlington (Appy)	R	.216	51	176	30	38	2	0	0	14	24	57	14	.227	.346
2002	Columbus (SAL)	A	.217	125	391	54	85	9	3	0	28	54	87	47	.256	.324
2003	Kinston (Car)	A	.253	82	296	42	75	12	3	0	23	31	67	28	.314	.336
MINOR LEAGUE TOTALS			.244	296	985	162	240	28	9	0	79	138	233	103	.290	.357

25 Javi Herrera, c

Born: Jan. 8, 1981. **Ht.:** 6-1. **Wt.:** 195. **Bats:** R. **Throws:** R. **School:** University of Tennessee. **Career Transactions:** Selected by Indians in second round of 2003 draft; signed June 8, 2003.

The Indians took catchers with consecutive early-round picks in the 2003 draft, and they're opposite players. Third-rounder Ryan Garko is an offensive player who has to improve behind the plate, while Herrera is a classic catch-and-throw guy who'll have to prove he can hit. Herrera's unquestioned strength is his ability to handle pitchers and call a game. He had to adjust to wood bats, learning to call more fastballs and trying to induce contract rather than trying to fool hitters with breaking pitches. Herrera has polished receiving skills and his arm has bounced back after he had arthroscopic shoulder surgery in 2002. He erased just 20 percent of basestealers in college and 17 percent in pro ball last year, but should improve on those marks in the future. As a hitter, Herrera needs to focus on staying patient and making consistent contact. He projects as a .250-.260 hitter with gap power and few homers. He's a below-average runner but quicker than most catchers. Cleveland promoted Herrera ahead of Garko last summer, but they may have to split the catching duties in low Class A this year.

Year	Club (League)	Class	AVG	G	AB	R	H	2B	3B	HR	RBI	BB	SO	SB	SLG	OBP
2003	Mahoning Valley (NY-P)	A	.289	12	45	9	13	3	0	0	8	5	11	0	.356	.353
	Lake County (SAL)	A	.240	46	154	15	37	14	0	1	22	17	32	0	.351	.324
MINOR LEAGUE TOTALS			.251	58	199	24	50	17	0	1	30	22	43	0	.352	.330

26 Brian Slocum, rhp

Born: March 27, 1981. **Ht.:** 6-4. **Wt.:** 190. **Bats:** R. **Throws:** R. **School:** Villanova. **Career Transactions:** Selected by Indians in second round of 2002 draft; signed June 21, 2002.

Slocum took his offseason conditioning program into his own hands following the 2002 season, and the results were not what he or the Indians wanted. He added 12 pounds of muscle but also restricted his range of motion. That caused a loss of velocity and eventually shoulder inflammation that got him shut down in mid-August. Slocum didn't need surgery, but it was the third straight year he was hampered by physical ailments. He had a sore shoulder in 2001 and biceps tendinitis in 2002. When healthy, Slocum features a low-90s fastball, a solid changeup and an improving slider. He throws strikes and keeps the ball down in the zone. During instructional league, he was put on a program designed to trim some of his bulk. He regained flexibility, arm speed and velocity. A slimmer Slocum will return to high Class A this year.

Year	Club (League)	Class	W	L	ERA	G	GS	CG	SV	IP	H	R	ER	HR	BB	SO	AVG
2002	Mahoning Valley (NY-P)	A	5	2	2.60	11	11	0	0	55	47	19	16	1	14	48	.230
2003	Kinston (Car)	A	6	7	4.46	22	21	0	1	107	112	61	53	7	41	66	.266
MINOR LEAGUE TOTALS			11	9	3.83	33	32	0	1	162	159	80	69	8	55	114	.254

27 Nelson Hiraldo, rhp

Born: Sept. 17, 1983. **Ht.:** 6-0. **Wt.:** 160. **Bats:** R. **Throws:** R. **Career Transactions:** Signed out of Dominican Republic by Indians, May 9, 2001.

Following a pair of nice seasons in the short-season Dominican Summer League, Hiraldo made a successful U.S. debut in 2003, finishing it off with four scoreless innings in the South Atlantic League playoffs. Though he isn't tall, Hiraldo has a quick arm, which allows him to generate a 90-93 mph fastball, and is athletic, which allows him to repeat his delivery well and have good command. He also has a solid changeup and flashes a good slider at times. When he doesn't stay on top of his slider, it flattens out on him. Hiraldo has a fearlessness about him that was evident even while he was acclimating himself to a new culture. He'll probably spend the entire 2004 season in low Class A.

Year	Club (League)	Class	W	L	ERA	G	GS	CG	SV	IP	H	R	ER	HR	BB	SO	AVG
2001	Indians (DSL)	R	6	3	2.54	15	14	0	0	74	72	32	21	4	21	61	.247
2002	Indians (DSL)	R	6	3	2.22	15	15	0	0	81	63	29	20	2	10	55	.204
2003	Burlington (Appy)	R	6	1	3.81	12	6	0	0	52	48	23	22	3	11	52	.241
	Lake County (SAL)	A	1	1	3.14	3	2	0	0	14	11	5	5	3	2	14	.212
MINOR LEAGUE TOTALS			19	8	2.76	45	37	0	0	222	194	89	68	12	44	182	.228

28 David Wallace, c

Born: Oct. 17, 1979. **Ht.:** 6-4. **Wt.:** 220. **Bats:** R. **Throws:** R. **School:** Vanderbilt University. **Career Transactions:** Signed as nondrafted free agent by Indians, Aug. 9, 2001.

Wallace played little baseball in three years at Vanderbilt, collecting just 125 at-bats in three years. His most notable baseball memory may have been striking out to end Mark Prior's first college game, a 2-1 loss to Belmont (Tenn.). Wallace accomplished more on the gridiron, where he started six games at quarterback as a freshman. The Indians spotted Wallace playing summer ball in Alaska and signed him as a nondrafted free agent. He has emerged as a sturdy, dependable catcher with significant upside. Wallace's leadership skills, which helped him as a quarterback, have translated on the diamond. He excels at calling games and handling pitchers. His receiving and throwing are solid-average and can get better. He threw out 30 percent of basestealers in 2003. Wallace is progressing as a hitter. He can drive balls into the gaps and draws a fair share of walks. He needs to do a better job of plate coverage, particularly on the outer half of the plate, in order to cut down on his strikeouts. Because Wallace is 24, Cleveland would like to start moving him more quickly. He'll begin this year in high Class A but is a candidate for promotion to Double-A as soon as he starts to hit more consistently.

Year	Club (League)	Class	AVG	G	AB	R	H	2B	3B	HR	RBI	BB	SO	SB	SLG	OBP
2002	Mahoning Valley (NY-P)	A	.255	45	145	22	37	5	0	3	17	11	48	3	.352	.345
2003	Lake County (SAL)	A	.291	64	223	39	65	14	2	6	36	37	52	5	.453	.413
	Kinston (Car)	A	.224	44	147	20	33	13	0	2	14	16	43	1	.354	.321
MINOR LEAGUE TOTALS			.262	153	515	81	135	32	2	11	67	64	143	9	.396	.369

29 Ben Francisco, of

Born: Oct. 23, 1981. **Ht.:** 6-1. **Wt.:** 180. **Bats:** R. **Throws:** R. **School:** UCLA. **Career Transactions:** Selected by Indians in fifth round of 2002 draft; signed June 19, 2002.

After winning the short-season New York-Penn League batting title with a .349 average in 2002, Francisco missed the first two months of last season. He broke the hamate bone in his left wrist during spring training and required surgery. Once he returned, he continued to show all the tools he flashed in his pro debut. Francisco is a natural hitter with doubles power. He employs a pure swing with a direct path to the ball. He uses the entire field and shows potential as a leadoff hitter. Francisco is aggressive at the plate, but he's not a free swinger. He's an above-average runner who possesses good instincts and reads pitchers well. Defensively, Francisco is still a little unrefined and has fringy arm strength. He doesn't profile well in any of the three outfield slots because he lacks the arm for right, the range for center and the power for left. He'll split time in left and center this year, when he could skip a level and go to Double-A.

Year	Club (League)	Class	AVG	G	AB	R	H	2B	3B	HR	RBI	BB	SO	SB	SLG	OBP
2002	Mahoning Valley (NY-P)	A	.349	58	235	55	82	23	2	3	23	22	28	22	.502	.416
2003	Lake County (SAL)	A	.287	80	289	57	83	21	1	11	48	31	50	15	.481	.359
MINOR LEAGUE TOTALS			.315	138	524	112	165	44	3	14	71	53	78	37	.490	.384

30 Sean Smith, rhp

Born: Oct. 13, 1983. **Ht.:** 6-4. **Wt.:** 180. **Bats:** R. **Throws:** R. **School:** Sacramento CC. **Career Transactions:** Selected by Indians in 16th round of 2001 draft; signed May 29, 2002.

Just like Nick Pesco a year after him, Smith received $1.1 million from the Indians as a draft-and-follow. His fastball hit 94 mph at Sac City before he signed, but he hasn't shown as much velocity while working regularly in a pro rotation. Smith's heater now sits at 88-91 mph, but its effective because he mixes it with a 12-6 curveball and a fading changeup. He also throws a slider. Smith is at his best when he keeps his fastball down in the zone. That's tough to do when he lapses into overthrowing. His delivery is solid, but he needs better command. Though Smith isn't as far along as Cleveland expected he would be, he'll still compete for a spot in the high Class A rotation.

Year	Club (League)	Class	W	L	ERA	G	GS	CG	SV	IP	H	R	ER	HR	BB	SO	AVG
2002	Burlington (Appy)	R	1	1	3.24	10	9	0	0	33	29	14	12	1	12	29	.236
2003	Lake County (SAL)	A	11	4	3.71	26	26	0	0	121	100	62	50	17	67	101	.229
MINOR LEAGUE TOTALS			12	5	3.61	36	35	0	0	155	129	76	62	18	79	130	.230

COLORADO ROCKIES

The Rockies have suffered through five losing seasons in the last six years and fell below three million in attendance for the first time in franchise history the last two seasons. Yet they gave general manager Dan O'Dowd a two-year contract extension and picked up the 2005 and '06 options in manager Clint Hurdle's pact. Ownership made a major statement. Stability is crucial, and they believe the Rockies will succeed long-term because of a farm system that has made major strides. Just eight current GM/manager tandems have been in place longer than O'Dowd (who replaced original GM Bob Gebhard in September 1999) and Hurdle (who became manager in April 2002). O'Dowd is 12th in seniority among GM's, while Hurdle ranks 13th in terms of continuous service among managers.

One reason for the confidence in O'Dowd is the work done by the men he hired to be scouting director (Bill Schmidt) and farm director (Bill Geivett). Their efforts are critical now that the Rockies have decided they can't do business as originally thought. They're not a big-market franchise. They have to be careful in the long-term commitments they make after blowing millions on players such as Mike Hampton and Denny Neagle. They have to depend on their system to produce players.

Indications are that it will do just that.

TOP 30 PROSPECTS

1. Chin-Hui Tsao, rhp
2. Ian Stewart, 3b
3. Jeff Francis, lhp
4. Ubaldo Jimenez, rhp
5. Jayson Nix, 2b
6. Rene Reyes, of
7. Jason Young, rhp
8. Zach Parker, lhp
9. Matt Holliday, of
10. Ching-Lung Lo, rhp
11. Brad Hawpe, of/1b
12. Jeff Baker, 3b
13. Garrett Atkins, 3b
14. Scott Dohmann, rhp
15. Oscar Materano, ss
16. Neil Wilson, c
17. Choo Freeman, of
18. Juan Morillo, rhp
19. J.D. Closser, c
20. Jeff Salazar, of
21. Clint Barmes, ss
22. Cory Sullivan, of
23. Mike Esposito, rhp
24. Tony Miller, of
25. Aaron Miles, 2b
26. Sandy Nin, rhp
27. Justin Hampson, lhp
28. Ben Crockett, rhp
29. Justin Huisman, rhp
30. Aaron Marsden, lhp

By Tracy Ringolsby

Colorado's six minor league affiliates posted a .508 winning percentage in 2003, the 10th-best in baseball and second-best in Rockies history.

At the major league level, 11 homegrown players saw time with the Rockies. All-star first baseman Todd Helton and starters Jason Jennings and Shawn Chacon had established themselves previously. Youngsters such as right-handers Chin-Hui Tsao, Aaron Cook and Jason Young, outfielder Rene Reyes and third baseman Garrett Atkins gave Colorado fans a glimpse at the team's future.

The Rockies have been aggressive signing players in the draft and on the international market. Schmidt has one of the highest college/high school ratios among scouting directors, but he has spent three first-round picks and two second-round selections on prepsters. Two of them, 2003 first-rounder Ian Stewart and 2001 second-rounder Jayson Nix, are the best position-player prospects in the organization.

Four of their top 10 prospects were signed on the international market, including their best in Tsao. The others are Dominican righthander Ubaldo Jimenez, Reyes (Venezuela) and Taiwanese righty Ching-Lung Lo. They also have hopes for Venezuelan shortstop Oscar Materano and Dominican righty Juan Morillo, as well as a pair of 2003 signees, Australian lefty Shane Lindsay and Japanese righty Yusuke Arakawa.

ORGANIZATION
OVERVIEW

General manager: Dan O'Dowd. **Farm director:** Bill Geivett. **Scouting director:** Bill Schmidt.

2003 PERFORMANCE

Class	Team	League	W	L	Pct.	Finish*	Manager
Majors	Colorado	National	74	88	.457	12th (16)	Clint Hurdle
Triple-A	Colo. Springs Sky Sox	Pacific Coast	73	70	.510	6th (16)	Rick Sofield
Double-A	Tulsa Drillers	Texas	74	64	.536	2nd (8)	Marv Foley
High A	Visalia Oaks	California	79	61	.564	1st (10)	Stu Cole
Low A	Asheville Tourists	South Atlantic	74	65	.532	6th (16)	Joe Mikulik
Short-season	Tri-City Dust Devils	Northwest	33	43	.434	6th (8)	Ron Gideon
Rookie	Casper Rockies	Pioneer	28	48	.368	7th (8)	P.J. Carey
OVERALL 2003 MINOR LEAGUE RECORD			361	350	.508	10th (30)	

*Finish in overall standings (No. of teams in league)

ORGANIZATION LEADERS

BATTING
*Minimum 250 At-Bats
*AVG	Rene Reyes, Colorado Springs	.343
R	Jeff Salazar, Visalia/Asheville	110
H	Cory Sullivan, Tulsa	167
TB	Jayson Nix, Visalia	267
2B	Jayson Nix, Visalia	46
3B	Sandy Almonte, Tri-City	9
HR	Jeff Salazar, Visalia/Asheville	29
RBI	Jeff Salazar, Visalia/Asheville	98
BB	Jeff Salazar, Visalia/Asheville	77
SO	Justin Lincoln, Visalia	151
SB	K.J. Hendricks, Asheville	50
*SLG	Andy Tracy, Tulsa	.563
*OBP	Ryan Shealy, Visalia	.391

PITCHING
#Minimum 75 Innings
W	Justin Hampson, Tulsa/Visalia	14
L	Ben Crockett, Visalia/Asheville	12
#ERA	Steve Reba, Asheville	2.66
G	Jentry Beckstead, Asheville	63
CG	Cory Vance, Colorado Springs	3
SV	Brad Clontz, Colorado Springs	30
IP	Ben Crockett, Visalia/Asheville	184
BB	Ubaldo Jimenez, Visalia/Asheville	68
SO	Jeff Francis, Visalia	153

BEST TOOLS

Best Hitter for Average	Brad Hawpe
Best Power Hitter	Ian Stewart
Fastest Baserunner	K.J. Hendricks
Best Athlete	Choo Freeman
Best Fastball	Juan Morillo
Best Curveball	Ubaldo Jimenez
Best Slider	Chin-Hui Tsao
Best Changeup	Jeff Francis
Best Control	Jeff Francis
Best Defensive Catcher	Neil Wilson
Best Defensive Infielder	Oscar Materano
Best Infield Arm	Oscar Materano
Best Defensive Outfielder	Cory Sullivan
Best Outfield Arm	Rene Reyes

PROJECTED 2007 LINEUP

Catcher	Neil Wilson
First Base	Todd Helton
Second Base	Jayson Nix
Third Base	Ian Stewart
Shortstop	Oscar Materano
Left Field	Matt Holliday
Center Field	Preston Wilson

Right Field	Rene Reyes
No. 1 Starter	Chin-Hui Tsao
No. 2 Starter	Jeff Francis
No. 3 Starter	Ubaldo Jimenez
No. 4 Starter	Jason Jennings
No. 5 Starter	Shawn Chacon
Closer	Aaron Cook

LAST YEAR'S TOP 20 PROSPECTS

1. Aaron Cook, rhp
2. Chin-Hui Tsao, rhp
3. Rene Reyes, of/1b
4. Jason Young, rhp
5. Choo Freeman, of
6. Jayson Nix, 2b
7. Jeff Baker, 3b
8. Zach Parker, lhp
9. Jeff Francis, lhp
10. Brad Hawpe, 1b
11. Ubaldo Jimenez, rhp
12. Oscar Matareno, ss
13. Garrett Atkins, 3b
14. Ching-Lung Lo, rhp
15. Tony Miller, of
16. Matt Holliday, of
17. J.D. Closser, c
18. Chris Buglovsky, rhp
19. Mike Esposito, rhp
20. Brian Fuentes, lhp

TOP PROSPECTS OF THE DECADE

1994	John Burke, rhp
1995	Doug Million, lhp
1996	Derrick Gibson, of
1997	Todd Helton, 1b
1998	Todd Helton, 1b
1999	Choo Freeman, of
2000	Choo Freeman, of
2001	Chin-Hui Tsao, rhp
2002	Chin-Hui Tsao, rhp
2003	Aaron Cook, rhp

TOP DRAFT PICKS OF THE DECADE

1994	Doug Million, lhp
1995	Todd Helton, 1b
1996	Jake Westbrook, rhp
1997	Mark Mangum, rhp
1998	Choo Freeman, of
1999	Jason Jennings, rhp
2000	*Matt Harrington, rhp
2001	Jayson Nix, ss
2002	Jeff Francis, lhp
2003	Ian Stewart, 3b

*Did not sign.

ALL-TIME LARGEST BONUSES

Jason Young, 2000	$2,750,000
Chin-Hui Tsao, 1999	$2,200,000
Ian Stewart, 2003	$1,950,000
Jeff Francis, 2002	$1,850,000
Jason Jennings, 1999	$1,675,000

MINOR LEAGUE
DEPTH CHART

COLORADO ROCKIES
RANK: 15

Impact potential (B-): The Rockies have never developed a pitcher with the electric stuff of Chin-Hui Tsao, and he's just about ready to step into the big league rotation. Ian Stewart might have the most upside of any position player they've developed since Todd Helton. One of the youngest players in the minors, Ching-Lung Lo is raw but he could step forward in the next two years.

Depth (C+): For all of their efforts to find pitching, the Rockies system is well stocked with position players. Outfielders Choo Freeman, Jeff Salazar, Cory Sullivan and Tony Miller have impressive tools packages, but didn't crack an improved top 10.

Sleeper: Tony Miller, of.   *—Depth charts prepared by Josh Boyd. Numbers in parentheses indicate prospect rankings.*

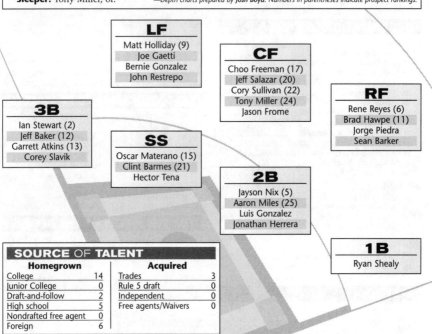

LF
Matt Holliday (9)
Joe Gaetti
Bernie Gonzalez
John Restrepo

CF
Choo Freeman (17)
Jeff Salazar (20)
Cory Sullivan (22)
Tony Miller (24)
Jason Frome

RF
Rene Reyes (6)
Brad Hawpe (11)
Jorge Piedra
Sean Barker

3B
Ian Stewart (2)
Jeff Baker (12)
Garrett Atkins (13)
Corey Slavik

SS
Oscar Materano (15)
Clint Barmes (21)
Hector Tena

2B
Jayson Nix (5)
Aaron Miles (25)
Luis Gonzalez
Jonathan Herrera

1B
Ryan Shealy

SOURCE OF TALENT

Homegrown		Acquired	
College	14	Trades	3
Junior College	0	Rule 5 draft	0
Draft-and-follow	2	Independent	0
High school	5	Free agents/Waivers	0
Nondrafted free agent	0		
Foreign	6		

C
Neil Wilson (16)
J.D. Closser (19)
Alvin Colina
Garret Gentry
Rick Guarno

RHP

Starters	Relievers
Chin-Hui Tsao (1)	Scott Dohmann (14)
Ubaldo Jimenez (4)	Juan Morillo (18)
Jason Young (7)	Sandy Nin (26)
Ching-Lung Lo (10)	Justin Huisman (29)
Mike Esposito (23)	Allan Simpson
Ben Crockett (28)	Scott Beerer
Alberto Arias	Gerrit Simpson
Ryan Kibler	Yusuke Arakawa
Marc Kaiser	Manuel Corpas
Shane Lindsay	Jentry Beckstead
	Emmanuel Ramirez

LHP

Starters	Relievers
Jeff Francis (3)	Matt White
Zach Parker (8)	Jonathan Valcarcel
Justin Hampson (27)	
Aaron Marsden (30)	
Cory Vance	

DRAFT
ANALYSIS

Best Pro Debut: 3B Ian Stewart (1) had no trouble jumping from high school to the Rookie-level Pioneer League, batting .317-10-43.

Best Athlete: RHP Scott Beerer (2) was as versatile as any college player last spring. He batted .335-11-57 while starting at left field, first base and third for Texas A&M, and set a school record with 13 saves. C Rick Guarno (4) is athletic for his position.

Best Pure Hitter: The organization has depth at third base with Garrett Atkins and Jeff Baker, and Stewart may be a better all-around hitter than either of them.

Best Raw Power: Stewart.

Fastest Runner: Guarno and OF John Restrepo (11) both have above-average speed.

Best Defensive Player: Guarno shows good catch-and-throw skills and quick feet behind the plate.

Best Fastball: Beerer throws 91-95 mph with plus life. RHP Darric Merrell (10) hit 94 mph in 2002 but didn't show the same velocity last year while battling elbow problems. OF Ryan Fox (21) wanted to start his pro career as a position player, but the Rockies plan to move him to the mound, where he has shown a 92-93 mph fastball.

Best Breaking Ball: LHP Aaron Marsden's (3) best weapon is a plus-plus slider.

Most Intriguing Background: Unsigned

Guarno

2B Eric Young Jr.'s (30) dad was an all-star second baseman for the Rockies and spent 2003 with the Brewers and Giants. OF Joe Gaetti's (12) father Gary made two All-Star Games and won four Gold Gloves with the Twins.

Closest To The Majors: Besides his slider, Marsden also has an 87-91 mph fastball with good movement and plus command.

Best Late-Round Pick: RHP Marc Kaiser (10) was a 2000 fourth-round pick out of high school by the Reds. He began his college career as a two-way player at Arizona before transferring to Lewis-Clark (Idaho) State. He's a more well-rounded pitcher after refining his two-seam fastball and slider.

The One Who Got Away: RHP Jim Brauer (17) pitched just five innings at Michigan last spring before being sidelined by scar tissue in his elbow. He was healthy in the Cape Cod League last summer, though his four-pitch mix wasn't as sharp. The Rockies pursued him, but not strongly enough to keep him from returning to the Wolverines.

Assessment: The Rockies concentrated on college players as usual, taking 24 in the first 25 rounds, but couldn't pass on Stewart's bat with the No. 10 overall choice. He's on his way to becoming their best homegrown hitter since 1995 first-rounder Todd Helton.

LHP Jeff Francis (1), 3B Jeff Baker (4) and C Neil Wilson (5) all could be a big part of Colorado's future, and OF Jeremy Salazar (8) just missed a 30-30 season in Class A last year. Unsigned RHPs Micah Owings (2) and Justin Hoyman (43) could go very early in the 2004 draft.

2B Jayson Nix (1) is by far the best middle infielder in the system. OFs Cory Sullivan (7) and Tony Miller (10) are decent prospects.

The Rockies failed to sign RHP Matt Harrington (1)—or OF Michael Vick (30). RHP Jason Young (2), draft-and-follow LHP Zach Parker (21), OF/1B Brad Hawpe (11), 3B Garrett Atkins (5) and RHP Scott Dohmann (6) all rank among the organization's best prospects.

RHP Jason Jennings (1) was the 2002 National League rookie of the year, while C Josh Bard (3) was given to Cleveland in an ill-advised trade. Unsigned RHP Bobby Brownlie (26), a 2002 first-rounder, likely will be better than either.

—Draft analysis prepared by Jim Callis. Numbers in parentheses indicate draft rounds.

Chin-Hui
Tsao

Born: June 2, 1981.
Ht.: 6-2. **Wt.:** 175.
Bats: R. **Throws:** R.
Career Transactions: Signed out of Taiwan by Rockies, Oct. 7, 1999.

Tsao became the first Taiwanese pitcher and just the second Taiwanese player to appear in the majors when he pitched 6⅓ innings to beat the Brewers on July 25. Overall, he survived his first taste of the big leagues despite allowing first-inning homers in four of his eight starts. He missed nearly a month when he went on the disabled list with a strained hamstring, which kept his innings down enough so that he retained his rookie eligibility. Because Tsao was on the DL at the end of August, however, he couldn't be sent to the minors and thus be allowed to pitch for Taiwan in the Asian Games, the qualifying event for the Olympics. The Rockies had agreed to make Tsao available in order to have the government waive his mandatory 18 months of military service, but there was no way around Major League Baseball's rules. Taiwan went on to earn a berth in the Olympics, along with Japan. Colorado's first major international signing, Tsao received a $2.2 million bonus in 1999. He has mastered English and has shown he has fully recovered from Tommy John surgery in 2001. Before joining the Rockies, he made a strong impression in his half-season at Double-A Tulsa, ranking as the top prospect in the Texas League.

Tsao has a devastating slider, though he has been limited in how he can use it since his elbow surgery. The Rockies don't want him to overextend himself with the slider, which has given him more opportunity to refine his changeup. He has an exploding fastball that can run up to 96 mph and usually sits in the low 90s. He can add and subtract from his heater, depending on what the situation calls for. Just as important as his stuff, Tsao has command of the strike zone. He has averaged 10.5 strikeouts and just 2.3 walks per nine innings during his minor league career. He is athletic and moves off the mound quickly. He also is a good baserunner, able to challenge an outfielder's arm. Pressure isn't an issue for Tsao. He's carrying the hopes of an entire nation, so what's a baseball game? Tsao's focus came under question in Colorado. Until arriving at Coors Field he always had been so much more talented than his competition that he was able to excel with ease. In the big leagues, he's going to have to develop game plans. He must adjust to what the advance scouts, pitching coach and catcher believe he should do instead of continually shaking off his catcher. He needs to get stronger and develop more stamina so he can carry his stuff later into games.

Projected as Colorado's future ace, Tsao will go to spring training with a solid chance to be part of the Rockies rotation. However, he'll have to earn the job. If not, the Rockies won't hesitate sending him to Colorado Springs for Triple-A seasoning. He skipped that step on his way up and could benefit from time with pitching guru Bob McClure.

Year	Club (League)	Class	W	L	ERA	G	GS	CG	SV	IP	H	R	ER	HR	BB	SO	AVG
2000	Asheville (SAL)	A	11	8	2.73	24	24	0	0	145	119	54	44	8	40	187	.220
2001	Salem (Car)	A	0	4	4.67	4	4	0	0	17	23	11	9	1	5	18	.333
2002	Tri-City (NWL)	A	0	0	0.00	3	3	0	0	11	6	2	0	0	2	16	.150
	Salem (Car)	A	4	2	2.09	9	9	0	0	47	34	13	11	3	12	45	.204
2003	Tulsa (TL)	AA	11	4	2.46	18	18	0	0	113	88	34	31	7	26	125	.214
	Colorado (NL)	MAJ	3	3	6.02	9	8	0	0	43	48	30	29	11	20	29	.284
MAJOR LEAGUE TOTALS			3	3	6.02	9	8	0	0	43	48	30	29	11	20	29	.284
MINOR LEAGUE TOTALS			26	18	2.56	58	58	0	0	334	270	114	95	19	85	391	.220

Ian Stewart, 3b

Born: April 5, 1985. **Ht.:** 6-3. **Wt.:** 205. **Bats:** L. **Throws:** R. **School:** La Quinta HS, Garden Grove, Calif. **Career Transactions:** Selected by Rockies in first round (10th overall) of 2003 draft; signed June 11, 2003.

Stewart set local records with 16 homers and 61 RBIs last spring, helping La Quinta High win 30 games and an 11th consecutive league championship. After signing for $1.95 million, Stewart earned top prospect honors in the Rookie-level Pioneer League. A legitimate run producer, Stewart had no problems adjusting to wood bats. He started hitting the day he got to Casper, driving the ball out of the ballpark in all directions. He has quality plate coverage and is strong on the inner half of the plate. He has below-average speed but excellent instincts on the bases. Stewart may have to move to first base. While he's not a slick fielder, the Rockies say he can become a solid third baseman. As a defender, Rockies adviser Walt Weiss compares him to Chipper Jones with the potential to be Scott Rolen. The key is that Stewart accepts instruction and is driven to succeed. Most important, he wants to play third. Within three years, Stewart could be in the middle of the Colorado lineup. He figures to start 2004 at low Class A Asheville, but he'll move as quickly as he handles the challenge of each level.

Year	Club (League)	Class	AVG	G	AB	R	H	2B	3B	HR	RBI	BB	SO	SB	SLG	OBP
2003	Casper (Pio)	R	.317	57	224	40	71	14	5	10	43	29	54	4	.558	.401
MINOR LEAGUE TOTALS			.317	57	224	40	71	14	5	10	43	29	54	4	.558	.401

Jeff Francis, lhp

Born: Jan. 8, 1981. **Ht.:** 6-5. **Wt.:** 200. **Bats:** L. **Throws:** L. **School:** University of British Columbia. **Career Transactions:** Selected by Rockies in first round (ninth overall) of 2002 draft; signed June 19, 2002.

Francis was the ninth player selected in the 2002 draft, making him the second-highest Canadian selection ever. His pro debut was cut short when he sustained a concussion after being hit in the head with a liner while sitting in the Asheville dugout. He struggled to start the 2003 season, but went 10-1, 1.06 in his final 13 starts, including 15 shutout innings in two playoff wins. Francis has excellent command of a solid fastball. He pitches at 90 mph and figures to add velocity as he builds upper-body strength. His curveball is a plus pitch at times. He has fluid mechanics that will allow him to advance quickly. His strong finish highlighted his ability to deal with adversity and move forward. Francis needs more consistency with his curveball. He also is working on his changeup, which will be a critical pitch as he reaches higher levels. Francis will open the 2004 season at Double-A Tulsa. He could follow the paths of righthanders Jason Jennings, Aaron Cook and Chin-Hui Tsao, finishing his first full season above Class A in the majors.

Year	Club (League)	Class	W	L	ERA	G	GS	CG	SV	IP	H	R	ER	HR	BB	SO	AVG
2002	Tri-City (NWL)	A	0	0	0.00	4	3	0	0	11	5	0	0	0	4	16	.143
	Asheville (SAL)	A	0	0	1.80	4	4	0	0	20	16	6	4	2	4	23	.232
2003	Visalia (Cal)	A	12	9	3.47	27	27	2	0	161	135	66	62	8	45	153	.229
MINOR LEAGUE TOTALS			12	9	3.10	35	34	2	0	191	156	72	66	10	53	192	.225

Ubaldo Jimenez, rhp

Born: Jan. 22, 1984. **Ht.:** 6-2. **Wt.:** 165. **Bats:** R. **Throws:** R. **Career Transactions:** Signed out of Dominican Republic by Rockies, April 25, 2001.

In his first year in the United States, Jimenez posted a 6.53 ERA in the Pioneer League. In his second, he put together such a strong second half at Asheville that he was promoted to high Class A Visalia at age 19 for the California League playoffs. Jimenez has legitimate power-pitcher potential. He has a four-seam fastball that reaches 96-97 mph, and a two-seamer with excellent running action. He also throws a big, sharp-breaking curveball that buckles righthanders, and he uses it against lefties as well. Jimenez needs to develop a third pitch. He shows a big league changeup in side sessions but hasn't taken it to the mound yet. Like most young pitchers, he'll have to improve his command. He should be able to make these adjustments with experience. Jimenez figures to start the 2004 season at Visalia but could reach Double-A by the middle of the year. Once he develops his changeup he'll have the stuff to pitch at the top of a big league rotation.

Year	Club (League)	Class	W	L	ERA	G	GS	CG	SV	IP	H	R	ER	HR	BB	SO	AVG
2001	Rockies (DSL)	R	2	5	4.88	13	13	0	0	48	41	36	26	1	44	36	.225
2002	Rockies (DSL)	R	2	0	0.00	3	3	0	0	18	10	1	0	0	6	25	.152
	Casper (Pio)	R	3	5	6.53	14	14	0	0	62	72	46	45	6	29	65	.288
2003	Asheville (SAL)	A	10	6	3.46	27	27	0	0	154	129	67	59	11	67	138	.230
	Visalia (Cal)	A	1	0	0.00	1	0	0	0	5	3	0	0	0	1	7	.176
MINOR LEAGUE TOTALS			18	16	4.08	58	57	0	0	287	255	150	130	18	147	271	.237

5 Jayson Nix, 2b

Born: Aug. 26, 1982. **Ht.:** 5-11. **Wt.:** 180. **Bats:** R. **Throws:** R. **School:** Midland (Texas) HS. **Career Transactions:** Selected by Rockies in first round (44th overall) of 2001 draft; signed July 14, 2001.

STEVE MOORE

The brother of Rangers outfielder Laynce Nix, Jayson was a star short-stop/righthander in high school in Texas. He was moved to second base in instructional league following his 2001 pro debut, and adapted well enough that talk about a possible conversion to catcher was tabled. He tied for the minor league lead with 46 doubles in 2003. Able to drive pitches into either gap, Nix has plus power potential for a middle infielder. He has an excellent sense of how to play the game and is able to make adjustments. He shows leadership and is never intimidated. He'll be known as an offensive player, but his range and speed at second base are solid-average and he has a strong arm. Nix swings and misses more than he should when he gets too pull-conscious. He's still learning the nuances of positioning himself at second base. Nix hit in the first three spots in the Visalia lineup and will be best suited for hitting second or third in the majors. He'll move up to Double-A in 2004 and should be in the big leagues to stay the following year.

Year	Club (League)	Class	AVG	G	AB	R	H	2B	3B	HR	RBI	BB	SO	SB	SLG	OBP
2001	Casper (Pio)	R	.294	42	153	28	45	10	1	5	24	21	43	1	.471	.385
2002	Asheville (SAL)	A	.246	132	487	73	120	29	2	14	79	62	105	14	.400	.340
2003	Visalia (Cal)	A	.281	137	562	107	158	46	0	21	86	54	131	24	.475	.351
MINOR LEAGUE TOTALS			.269	311	1202	208	323	85	3	40	189	137	279	39	.444	.351

6 Rene Reyes, of

Born: Feb. 21, 1978. **Ht.:** 5-11. **Wt.:** 215. **Bats:** B. **Throws:** R. **Career Transactions:** Signed out of Venezuela by Rockies, Aug. 29, 1996 . . . On disabled list, April 6-Sept. 29, 2000.

Originally signed as a catcher, Reyes moved to the outfield after shoulder and knee surgeries. A former MVP in the Rookie-level Arizona and low Class A South Atlantic leagues, he played in the Futures Games in July 2003 and received his first big league callup shortly afterward. He topped all minor league switch-hitters in batting in 2003. He doesn't have a picturesque swing, but Reyes can hit. He gets the bat head through the zone and makes solid contact, with a career .329 average in the minors. He has gap power now and should pull more pitches as he matures. He runs well enough to steal some bases and shows fringe-average ability in center field, though he's better suited for an outfield corner. Reyes can get lackadaisical until he's challenged. He needs to show a desire to get better rather than be satisfied with getting by. He puts the bat on the ball so easily that he rarely walks. Reyes figures to be a fourth outfielder in Colorado to open the 2004 season. With his bat, he should be ready to claim a starting job on one of the corners the following year.

Year	Club (League)	Class	AVG	G	AB	R	H	2B	3B	HR	RBI	BB	SO	SB	SLG	OBP
1997	Guacara 1 (VSL)	R	.220	38	82	8	18	2	2	1	9	7	14	1	.329	.281
1998	Rockies (AZL)	R	.429	49	177	40	76	9	4	5	39	8	15	16	.610	.493
1999	Rockies (AZL)	R	.361	22	97	21	35	4	4	1	20	4	14	6	.515	.398
	Asheville (SAL)	A	.350	40	160	26	56	6	1	3	19	6	22	1	.456	.377
2000	Did not play—Injured															
2001	Asheville (SAL)	A	.322	128	484	71	156	27	2	11	61	28	80	53	.455	.371
2002	Carolina (SL)	AA	.292	123	455	64	133	33	4	14	54	29	69	10	.475	.339
2003	Colo. Spr. (PCL)	AAA	.343	98	370	60	127	23	3	6	50	22	56	12	.470	.380
	Colorado (NL)	MAJ	.259	53	116	13	30	7	1	2	7	5	19	2	.388	.287
MAJOR LEAGUE TOTALS			.259	53	116	13	30	7	1	2	7	5	19	2	.388	.287
MINOR LEAGUE TOTALS			.329	498	1825	290	601	104	20	41	252	104	270	99	.476	.375

7 Jason Young, rhp

Born: Sept. 28, 1979. **Ht.:** 6-5. **Wt.:** 215. **Bats:** R. **Throws:** R. **School:** Stanford University. **Career Transactions:** Selected by Rockies in second round of 2000 draft; signed Sept. 26, 2000.

The Rockies were set to take Young in 2000's first round, but went for Matt Harrington when he slid to the No. 7 overall pick. While Colorado couldn't sign Harrington, it landed Young in the second round and signed him for a franchise-record $2.75 million. He pitched in the Futures Game in 2001 and 2002, and had eight brief big league stints in 2003. Young uses the entire strike zone with four pitches. His top pitch is a 92-93 mph four-seam fastball, and he has refined a Vulcan changeup that he'll throw in any count. He's intelligent and mature, and he's an excellent competitor. Young still is trying to decide on his breaking ball. The slider is easier to learn, but because its velocity is too similar to that of his two-seam fastball, his curveball is more useful as an offspeed pitch. Young also needs more upper-body strength and added deception with his delivery. Projected as an eventual starter, Young will get a look as a reliever in big league camp. More likely, though, he'll begin 2004 in Triple-A.

Year	Club (League)	Class	W	L	ERA	G	GS	CG	SV	IP	H	R	ER	HR	BB	SO	AVG
2001	Salem (Car)	A	6	7	3.44	17	17	2	0	105	104	47	40	8	28	91	.259
2002	Carolina (SL)	AA	7	4	2.64	14	14	1	0	89	71	30	26	1	30	76	.219
	Colo. Spr. (PCL)	AAA	6	5	4.97	13	13	0	0	80	87	52	44	10	38	74	.272
2003	Colo. Spr. (PCL)	AAA	6	7	3.95	23	21	2	0	116	128	63	51	10	37	99	.271
	Colorado (NL)	MAJ	0	2	8.44	8	3	0	0	21	34	22	20	8	9	18	.354
MAJOR LEAGUE TOTALS			0	2	8.44	8	3	0	0	21	34	22	20	8	9	18	.354
MINOR LEAGUE TOTALS			25	23	3.72	67	65	5	0	389	390	192	161	29	133	340	.257

8 Zach Parker, lhp

Born: Aug. 19, 1981. **Ht.:** 6-2. **Wt.:** 205. **Bats:** R. **Throws:** L. **School:** San Jacinto (Texas) JC. **Career Transactions:** Selected by Rockies in 21st round of 2000 draft; signed May 27, 2001.

Parker could be the best San Jacinto lefthander since Andy Pettitte, but he needs to stay on the mound to realize his potential. He has pitched just 285 innings as pro. He was shut down early in 2001 because of his juco workload and again in 2003 with bone spurs in his elbow. In between, he won 16 games in low Class A in his one healthy season. Parker commands a 90 mph fastball that should bump up a notch or two as he gets stronger. He backs it up with a solid changeup and an intense competitive drive. He has totally shackled lefties in two years in Class A, holding them to a .180 average and two homers in 233 at-bats. Because he has spent so much time on the sidelines, Parker's breaking ball is still a project. He has toyed with both a curveball and slider, and lately he has focused on the curveball. He'll have to prove he can stay healthy over the long haul. After full seasons in Double-A and Triple-A, Parker should get to Colorado in 2006. For now, the Rockies hope he can hold up for the entire year at Tulsa.

Year	Club (League)	Class	W	L	ERA	G	GS	CG	SV	IP	H	R	ER	HR	BB	SO	AVG
2001	Casper (Pio)	R	1	2	7.52	8	8	0	0	26	42	26	22	2	12	19	.389
2002	Asheville (SAL)	A	16	7	4.01	28	28	1	0	168	174	89	75	11	64	119	.274
2003	Visalia (Cal)	A	5	5	3.69	16	16	1	0	90	85	38	37	10	27	52	.250
MINOR LEAGUE TOTALS			22	14	4.23	52	52	2	0	285	301	153	134	23	103	190	.278

9 Matt Holliday, of

Born: Jan. 10, 1980. **Ht.:** 6-4. **Wt.:** 230. **Bats:** R. **Throws:** R. **School:** Stillwater (Okla.) HS. **Career Transactions:** Selected by Rockies in seventh round of 1998 draft; signed July 24, 1998.

The Rockies signed Holliday for $840,000 out of high school, when he was a premium quarterback prospect. When the Miami and Tennessee football programs tried to lure him in 2001, Colorado gave him a six-year big league contract with a $700,000 guarantee. He finally began to live up to expectations in the second half of 2003, and he played so well in the Arizona Fall League that he was added to the U.S. Olympic qualifying team. Though the numbers don't add up, the Rockies see considerable physical potential. Holliday has legitimate big league power despite never hitting more than 12 homers in a season. A former third baseman, he has worked hard to become a solid left fielder. To unlock his power in games, Holliday needs to get his hands in a cocked position so he's ready to hit more quickly. He's still rebuilding his arm strength after having Tommy John surgery in July 2001. After two years in Double-A, Holliday will move to Triple-A in 2004. If he shows consistent power, he'll be called up.

Year	Club (League)	Class	AVG	G	AB	R	H	2B	3B	HR	RBI	BB	SO	SB	SLG	OBP
1998	Rockies (AZL)	R	.342	32	117	20	40	4	1	5	23	15	21	2	.521	.413
1999	Asheville (SAL)	A	.264	121	444	76	117	28	0	16	64	53	116	10	.435	.350
2000	Salem (Car)	A	.274	123	460	64	126	28	2	7	72	43	74	11	.389	.335
2001	Salem (Car)	A	.275	72	255	36	70	16	1	11	52	33	42	11	.475	.358
2002	Carolina (SL)	AA	.276	130	463	79	128	19	2	10	64	67	102	16	.391	.375
2003	Tulsa (TL)	AA	.253	135	522	65	132	28	5	12	72	43	74	15	.395	.313
MINOR LEAGUE TOTALS			.271	613	2261	340	613	123	11	61	347	254	429	65	.416	.349

10 Ching-Lung Lo, rhp

Born: Aug. 20, 1985. **Ht.:** 6-6. **Wt.:** 190. **Bats:** R. **Throws:** R. **Career Transactions:** Signed out of Taiwan by Rockies, Oct. 20, 2001.

Lo signed for $1.4 million out of Taiwan's Koio Yuan High, the same school that produced Chin-Hui Tsao. Lo tied for the short-season Northwest League in losses in 2003, but his 10th-place finish in ERA is more telling of how well he pitched. The Taiwanese national team hoped to use Lo in the Asian Games, but the Rockies denied permission so they could limit his workload. Lo enters his third pro season at 18 and he already throws an 89-90 mph sinker. He can turn his velocity up in key situations and should add more as he fills out his upper body. He has improved his change-up in his two seasons in the United States. He also has the mental toughness to battle through mistakes and adversity. Lo's slider is inconsistent, though it shows flashes of being a plus pitch. He needs to throw it more often in order to improve it. As with many tall, thin athletes, he can look awkward and have difficulty repeating his delivery at times. The Rockies won't rush Lo as they let him build up strength. Headed to Asheville for his first year of full-season ball, he may not get to Colorado until late 2007.

Year	Club (League)	Class	W	L	ERA	G	GS	CG	SV	IP	H	R	ER	HR	BB	SO	AVG
2002	Casper (Pio)	R	2	4	3.20	14	9	0	0	45	44	22	16	3	22	21	.246
2003	Tri-City (NWL)	A	3	7	2.85	14	14	0	0	76	66	27	24	1	27	48	.237
MINOR LEAGUE TOTALS			5	11	2.98	28	23	0	0	121	110	49	40	4	49	69	.241

11 Brad Hawpe, of/1b

Born: June 22, 1979. **Ht.:** 6-3. **Wt.:** 200. **Bats:** L. **Throws:** L. **School:** Louisiana State University. **Career Transactions:** Selected by Rockies in 11th round of 2000 draft; signed June 21, 2000.

The question about Hawpe isn't whether he can hit, because it's obvious that he can. Whether he can play the outfield is the key for him, because he's not going to move Todd Helton off first base in Colorado. Hawpe tied the NCAA Division I record with 36 doubles in 2000, when he won a College World Series with Louisiana State, and he was the high Class A Carolina League MVP in 2002. Hawpe's bat is going to carry him. He generates legitimate power with bat speed, and he understands the value of using all fields. He does need to be more selective, particularly against lefthanders, if he expects to play every day. A below-average runner with good instincts, he can take the extra base but isn't a threat to steal. Hawpe is better suited for right field than left, where he still has some problems with the angle of the ball off the bat. Having played first base, he's more accustomed to seeing balls hit to the right side. At best, he'll be an adequate defender wherever he plays. Hawpe missed six weeks late in the 2003 season with a separated shoulder but made a solid return in the Arizona Fall League, where he hit .359 after a 4-for-34 (.118) start. He'll move to Triple-A this year with expectation of being ready for the big leagues within a year.

Year	Club (League)	Class	AVG	G	AB	R	H	2B	3B	HR	RBI	BB	SO	SB	SLG	OBP
2000	Portland (NWL)	A	.288	62	205	38	59	19	2	7	29	40	51	2	.502	.398
2001	Asheville (SAL)	A	.267	111	393	78	105	22	3	22	72	59	113	7	.506	.363
2002	Salem (Car)	A	.347	122	450	87	156	38	2	22	97	81	84	1	.587	.447
2003	Tulsa (TL)	AA	.277	93	346	52	96	27	0	17	68	31	84	1	.503	.338
MINOR LEAGUE TOTALS			.298	388	1394	255	416	106	7	68	266	211	332	11	.531	.390

12 Jeff Baker, 3b

Born: June 21, 1981. **Ht.:** 6-2. **Wt.:** 210. **Bats:** R. **Throws:** R. **School:** Clemson University. **Career Transactions:** Selected by Rockies in fourth round of 2002 draft; Sept. 27, 2002.

The start of Baker's pro career has been a struggle. After falling to the fourth round of the

2002 draft because of a lackluster junior season, a checkered history with wood bats and signability concerns, he signed that October. After landing a $2 million big league contract with a $50,000 bonus, Baker was set to make his debut last year. But ongoing problems with his left wrist have resulted in two surgeries since he signed (he had a third while at Clemson) and limited him to 70 games in 2003. Baker hits the ball hard and has big-time power, but he needs to do a better job of making contact. He has good hand-eye coordination and balance at the plate, but pitch selection is a challenge for him. His strength is in the middle of the field and he has the ability to turn on hanging breaking balls. Baker has legitimate third-base tools. He has nice hands, quick reflexes and a strong arm. He moves around well enough that he could wind up at second base, which could be needed with Ian Stewart coming behind him. Baker most likely will open 2004 in high Class A, but if he's healthy and plays as expected, he'll move quickly to Double-A.

Year	Club (League)	Class	AVG	G	AB	R	H	2B	3B	HR	RBI	BB	SO	SB	SLG	OBP
2003	Asheville (SAL)	A	.289	70	263	44	76	17	0	11	44	30	79	4	.479	.377
MINOR LEAGUE TOTALS			.289	70	263	44	76	17	0	11	44	30	79	4	.479	.377

13 Garrett Atkins, 3b

Born: Dec. 12, 1979. **Ht.:** 6-3. **Wt.:** 210. **Bats:** R. **Throws:** R. **School:** UCLA. **Career Transactions:** Selected by Rockies in fifth round of 2000 draft; signed June 22, 2000.

Atkins was converted from first to third base in 2002 because of the presence of Todd Helton at Coors Field. He had played third in high school and early in his career at UCLA, where he set a school record with a 33-game hitting streak. Atkins is a career .303 hitter in the minors. His brief big league audition last year didn't go as well, however, and exposed some holes in his game. Some question how driven he is to address his deficiencies, particularly on defense. Those who believe in Atkins are convinced he has a desire to succeed but just doesn't let it show. His footwork is a major problem at the hot corner, affecting his ability to field grounders and make throws. He does have offensive ability. Atkins is very good at recognizing problems in his swing. He has some raw power, but he prefers to use a line-drive approach and doesn't project to hit enough homers to carry him at third base unless he becomes at least avearge in the field. He'll get a look in spring training but figures to open the season back in Triple-A.

Year	Club (League)	Class	AVG	G	AB	R	H	2B	3B	HR	RBI	BB	SO	SB	SLG	OBP
2000	Portland (NWL)	A	.303	69	251	34	76	12	0	7	47	45	48	2	.434	.411
2001	Salem (Car)	A	.325	135	465	70	151	43	5	5	67	74	98	6	.471	.421
2002	Carolina (SL)	AA	.271	128	510	71	138	27	3	12	61	59	77	6	.406	.345
2003	Colo. Spr. (PCL)	AAA	.319	118	439	80	140	30	1	13	67	45	52	2	.481	.382
	Colorado (NL)	MAJ	.159	25	69	6	11	2	0	0	4	3	14	0	.188	.205
MAJOR LEAGUE TOTALS			.159	25	69	6	11	2	0	0	4	3	14	0	.188	.205
MINOR LEAGUE TOTALS			.303	450	1665	255	505	112	9	37	242	223	275	16	.448	.387

14 Scott Dohmann, rhp

Born: Feb. 13, 1978. **Ht.:** 6-1. **Wt.:** 180. **Bats:** R. **Throws:** R. **School:** University of Louisiana-Lafayette. **Career Transactions:** Selected by Rockies in sixth round of 2000 draft; signed June 23, 2000.

The top winner on Louisiana-Lafayette's College World Series team and the Sun Belt Conference pitcher of the year in 2000, Dohmann won in double figures and led his league in starts in each of his first two full pro seasons. After four starts in 2003, however, Dohmann was moved to the bullpen. He welcomed the change, feeling it would speed his path to the big leagues. He didn't have much of a ceiling as a starter but opened eyes out of the bullpen. His fastball, which had sat at 89 mph, suddenly moved to 93-95. He has a slider and used the Arizona Fall League to work on his changeup, a pitch he'll need against left-handers. Dohmann can get out of whack with his delivery and suffer through spurts where he battles his command. He has toned his motion down and generally has good control. Dohmann will get a chance to make the Rockies out of spring training, but likely will open the year in Triple-A.

Year	Club (League)	Class	W	L	ERA	G	GS	CG	SV	IP	H	R	ER	HR	BB	SO	AVG
2000	Portland (NWL)	A	2	1	0.78	5	4	0	0	23	14	3	2	0	5	23	.177
	Asheville (SAL)	A	1	5	6.06	7	7	0	0	33	43	24	22	3	8	36	.319
2001	Asheville (SAL)	A	11	13	4.32	28	28	0	0	165	88	83	27	33	154	.251
2002	Salem (Car)	A	13	5	4.23	28	28	0	0	170	149	85	80	22	53	131	.233
2003	Tulsa (TL)	AA	9	4	4.13	50	4	0	4	94	94	47	43	11	29	102	.259
MINOR LEAGUE TOTALS			36	28	4.20	118	71	3	4	493	465	247	230	63	128	446	.248

15 Oscar Materano, ss

Born: Nov. 18, 1981. **Ht.:** 6-1. **Wt.:** 170. **Bats:** R. **Throws:** R. **Career Transactions:** Signed out of Venezuela by Rockies, July 18, 1998.

Materano is the next in the line of Caribbean shortstops produced by Colorado, and he has better tools than predecessors Neifi Perez and Juan Uribe. Materano has plus arm strength and the ability to go into the hole and make outstanding plays. The Rockies also like his offensive potential, though he has yet to hit much. He has a live bat that will produce some extra-base pop once he develops a better knowledge of the strike zone. He's over-aggressive at the plate and out of control in the field. Style, not substance, is his priority, and he hasn't shown the maturity to make adjustments. Though he has big hands, they are a bit stiff. He's an average runner. Materano will repeat low Class A in 2004, a move designed to make him realize that he has to develop better focus.

Year	Club (League)	Class	AVG	G	AB	R	H	2B	3B	HR	RBI	BB	SO	SB	SLG	OBP
1999	Universidad (VSL)	R	.220	44	159	8	35	11	2	0	26	11	44	2	.314	.280
2000	Rockies (AZL)	R	.243	31	115	19	28	3	3	0	13	10	25	5	.322	.331
2001	Casper (Pio)	R	.251	69	271	34	68	11	0	6	38	9	59	5	.358	.291
2002	Tri-City (NWL)	A	.259	68	270	38	70	14	0	9	40	11	61	7	.411	.293
2003	Asheville (SAL)	A	.251	82	339	48	85	14	1	4	30	17	78	8	.333	.292
MINOR LEAGUE TOTALS			.248	294	1154	147	286	53	6	19	147	58	267	27	.354	.294

16 Neil Wilson, c

Born: Dec. 7, 1983. **Ht.:** 6-1. **Wt.:** 190. **Bats:** R. **Throws:** R. **School:** Vero Beach (Fla.) HS. **Career Transactions:** Selected by Rockies in fifth round of 2002 draft; signed June 21, 2002.

Wilson is a sleeper who has been a catcher for just two years. He played shortstop in high school in 2001 because he was a year behind Pirates draftee Chris Torres. Wilson, whose older brother Andy is an outfielder in the Mets system, has been limited to 60 games in his two pro seasons. He shared the catching job at Casper in 2002, then had his 2003 season truncated by a right wrist injury. Wilson has the offensive potential to be a run-producing catcher. He can drive the ball and showed improved plate discipline last year. The key will be how well Wilson develops behind the plate. He does move well and has excellent arm strength. He's still learning the mechanics behind the plate and trying to smooth out his footwork, the biggest reason why he has thrown out just 18 percent of basestealers as a pro. He has benefited from spending the last two years with Casper manager P.J. Carey, one of the best catching instructors in the game. Wilson should move to low Class A in 2004.

Year	Club (League)	Class	AVG	G	AB	R	H	2B	3B	HR	RBI	BB	SO	SB	SLG	OBP
2002	Casper (Pio)	R	.239	37	134	18	32	2	3	2	17	10	30	0	.343	.296
2003	Casper (Pio)	R	.295	23	78	13	23	6	1	2	12	19	15	3	.474	.439
MINOR LEAGUE TOTALS			.259	60	212	31	55	8	4	4	29	29	45	3	.392	.352

17 Choo Freeman, of

Born: Oct. 20, 1979. **Ht.:** 6-2. **Wt.:** 200. **Bats:** R. **Throws:** R. **School:** Dallas Christian HS, Mesquite, Texas. **Career Transactions:** Selected by Rockies in first round (36th overall) of 1998 draft; signed July 13, 1998.

Freeman set a Texas high school record with 50 touchdown receptions and was Texas A&M's top wide receiver recruit in 1998. He turned down the Aggies to sign for a then-Rockies record $1.4 million. His baseball skills were unrefined, so he has made a slow climb through the system, similar to his cousin Torii Hunter's rise with Minnesota. Freeman had a breakout season in 2002 but had trouble repeating it last year. He missed three weeks after his mother-in-law died, and another three weeks with an ankle injury. Freeman has a tremendous work ethic and doesn't cheat himself. He's very athletic and continues to translate that ability to the baseball field. His best tool is his speed, which helps him take extra bases and cover ground in center field. He's still honing his basestealing instincts, however. Similarly, he has raw power but has yet to unleash it much in games. His arm is below average but is getting stronger. Freeman will return to Triple-A this year, with the Rockies hoping he can recapture his 2002 form.

Year	Club (League)	Class	AVG	G	AB	R	H	2B	3B	HR	RBI	BB	SO	SB	SLG	OBP
1998	Rockies (AZL)	R	.320	40	147	35	47	3	6	1	24	15	25	14	.442	.391
1999	Asheville (SAL)	A	.274	131	485	82	133	22	4	14	66	39	132	16	.423	.336
2000	Salem (Car)	A	.266	127	429	73	114	18	7	5	54	37	104	16	.375	.326
2001	Salem (Car)	A	.240	132	517	63	124	16	5	8	42	31	108	19	.337	.292
2002	Carolina (SL)	AA	.291	124	430	81	125	18	6	12	64	64	101	15	.444	.400
2003	Colo. Spr. (PCL)	AAA	.254	103	327	44	83	9	4	7	36	23	71	2	.370	.315
MINOR LEAGUE TOTALS			.268	657	2335	378	626	86	32	47	286	209	541	82	.393	.338

18 Juan Morillo, rhp

Born: Nov. 5, 1983. **Ht.:** 6-1. **Wt.:** 160. **Bats:** R. **Throws:** R. **Career Transactions:** Signed out of Dominican Republic by Rockies, April 26, 2001.

After two seasons in the Rookie-level Dominican Summer League, Morillo came to the United States last summer and created much more excitement than his statistics would indicate. He struggled early with the cultural differences, but began to turn things around at the end of the season and then in instructional league. Morillo has a big-time fastball. He usually pitches in the mid-90s and will hit 98-99 mph a few times each game. He has a free arm action and, when he follows through, great extension. He already has drawn comparisons to Bartolo Colon at the same stages of their careers. Morillo's hard slider is inconsistent but shows upside. He's learning a changeup and needs to throw a lot more strikes. He's a long-range projection who has the fastball to close games and the potential to develop into a frontline starter. The Rockies may play it conservatively and send him to short-season Tri-City in 2004.

Year	Club (League)	Class	W	L	ERA	G	GS	CG	SV	IP	H	R	ER	HR	BB	SO	AVG
2001	Rockies (DSL)	R	2	4	6.81	14	7	0	0	36	35	31	27	1	38	20	.248
2002	Rockies (DSL)	R	1	5	4.75	14	11	0	0	55	49	44	29	1	33	43	.230
2003	Casper (Pio)	R	1	6	5.91	15	15	0	0	64	85	73	42	6	40	44	.318
MINOR LEAGUE TOTALS			4	15	5.70	43	33	0	0	155	169	148	98	8	111	107	.272

19 J.D. Closser, c

Born: Jan. 15, 1980. **Ht.:** 5-10. **Wt.:** 175. **Bats:** B. **Throws:** R. **School:** Monroe HS, Alexandria, Ind. **Career Transactions:** Selected by Diamondbacks in fifth round of 1998 draft; signed June 28, 1998 . . . Traded by Diamondbacks with OF Jack Cust to Rockies for LHP Mike Myers, Jan. 7, 2002.

Considered the lesser prospect in the January 2002 trade that sent Mike Myers to Arizona, Closser will do more for the Rockies than Jack Cust, who was considered the key to the deal. Cust since has been passed on to the Orioles, while Closser projects as Colorado's starting catcher in 2005. He has benefited from playing for catchers-turned-managers P.J. Carey and Marv Foley the last two seasons, earning Texas League all-star honors in 2003. Closser is a switch-hitter with power from both sides. He overswings at times, which is unnecessary because he has the bat speed to hit good fastballs, though he has shown the patience to draw walks. Closser plays full speed ahead. He's good at blocking the plate as well as balls in the dirt, and he has improved his game-calling. He has ample arm strength but is erratic with his throws because he needs better footwork and mechanics. Nevertheless, he ranked fifth in the Texas League by erasing 33 percent of basestealers. He has below-average speed but runs better than many catchers. Closser is ready for Triple-A after two years at Double-A and a winter assignment in the Dominican Republic.

Year	Club (League)	Class	AVG	G	AB	R	H	2B	3B	HR	RBI	BB	SO	SB	SLG	OBP
1998	Diamondbacks (AZL)	R	.313	45	150	26	47	13	2	4	21	37	36	3	.507	.453
	South Bend (Mid)	A	.214	4	14	3	3	1	0	0	2	2	7	0	.286	.313
1999	South Bend (Mid)	A	.241	52	174	29	42	8	0	3	27	34	37	0	.339	.363
	Missoula (Pio)	R	.324	76	275	73	89	22	0	10	54	71	57	9	.513	.458
2000	South Bend (Mid)	A	.224	101	331	54	74	19	1	8	37	60	61	6	.360	.347
2001	Lancaster (Cal)	A	.291	128	468	85	136	26	6	21	87	65	106	6	.506	.377
2002	Carolina (SL)	AA	.283	95	315	43	89	27	1	13	62	44	69	9	.498	.369
2003	Tulsa (TL)	AA	.283	118	410	62	116	28	5	13	54	47	79	3	.471	.359
MINOR LEAGUE TOTALS			.279	619	2137	375	596	144	15	72	344	360	452	36	.461	.383

20 Jeff Salazar, of

Born: Nov. 24, 1980. **Ht.:** 6-0. **Wt.:** 180. **Bats:** L. **Throws:** L. **School:** Oklahoma State University. **Career Transactions:** Selected by Rockies in eighth round of 2002 draft; signed June 11, 2002.

Signed as a college senior out of Oklahoma State, where Matt Holliday's father Tom was the coach, Salazar led the South Atlantic League in homers and RBIs in his first full pro season. He nearly put together a 30-30 year. While his power numbers were embellished by the short right-field fence at Asheville's McCormick Field, Salazar has legitimate life in his bat. He'll hit for average with at least gap power in the majors. He uses all fields and controls the strike zone. A plus runner, he's learning how to bunt. He gets himself in trouble when he gets too pull-happy. Salazar is a good center fielder who's technically proficient at the position. His arm is below average. The Rockies love his attitude, as he shows up at the ballpark ready to work every day. Based on his success and his age, he could jump to Double-A this year.

Year	Club (League)	Class	AVG	G	AB	R	H	2B	3B	HR	RBI	BB	SO	SB	SLG	OBP
2002	Tri-City (NWL)	A	.235	72	268	38	63	5	4	4	21	47	43	10	.328	.351
2003	Asheville (SAL)	A	.284	129	486	109	138	23	4	29	98	77	74	28	.527	.387
	Visalia (Cal)	A	.000	1	5	1	0	0	0	0	0	0	0	0	.000	.000
MINOR LEAGUE TOTALS			.265	202	759	148	201	28	8	33	119	124	117	38	.453	.372

21 Clint Barmes, ss

Born: March 6, 1979. **Ht.:** 6-0. **Wt.:** 175. **Bats:** R. **Throws:** R. **School:** Indiana State University.
Career Transactions: Selected by Rockies in 10th round of 2000 draft; signed June 9, 2000.

Two years ago, the thought was that Barmes, a center fielder at Indiana State, could be a quality utility infielder. A year ago, there was talk he could become an everyday second baseman. Now, the Rockies are convinced he could be a solid shortstop, along the lines of Walt Weiss, a special adviser for the team. Barmes is an acquired taste. He's best appreciated when you watch how hard he works and how consistent he plays. Barmes can hit for a decent average with gap power. He has to stay on the ball and drive it into right-center to be successful at the plate. He does have a lot of movement in his batting stance, and would benefit if he simplified it and got into hitting position quicker. When his timing is good he can handle breaking balls, but he gets in trouble when he rushes himself. More selectivity also would help. Barmes has good speed and great instincts on the bases. At shortstop, he has enough arm and positions himself well enough to offset his limited range. Barmes will get a chance to compete for Colorado's shortstop job in the spring and could make the team as a utilityman. If he isn't assured ample playing time, he'll head back to Triple-A to get experience.

Year	Club (League)	Class	AVG	G	AB	R	H	2B	3B	HR	RBI	BB	SO	SB	SLG	OBP
2000	Portland (NWL)	A	.282	45	181	37	51	6	4	2	16	18	28	12	.392	.361
	Asheville (SAL)	A	.173	19	81	11	14	4	0	0	4	10	13	4	.222	.269
2001	Asheville (SAL)	A	.260	74	285	40	74	14	1	5	24	17	37	21	.368	.314
	Salem (Car)	A	.248	38	121	17	30	3	3	0	9	15	20	4	.322	.350
2002	Carolina (SL)	AA	.272	103	438	62	119	23	2	15	60	31	72	15	.436	.329
2003	Colo. Spr. (PCL)	AAA	.276	136	493	63	136	35	1	7	54	22	63	12	.394	.316
	Colorado (NL)	MAJ	.320	12	25	2	8	2	0	0	2	0	10	0	.400	.357
MAJOR LEAGUE TOTALS			.320	12	25	2	8	2	0	0	2	0	10	0	.400	.357
MINOR LEAGUE TOTALS			.265	415	1599	230	424	85	11	29	167	113	233	68	.386	.325

22 Cory Sullivan, of

Born: Aug. 20, 1979. **Ht.:** 6-0. **Wt.:** 180. **Bats:** L. **Throws:** L. **School:** Wake Forest University.
Career Transactions: Selected by Rockies in seventh round of 2001 draft; signed June 7, 2001.

Sullivan has handled the challenges of going directly from Wake Forest, where he was a two-way star and earned a degree in psychology, to full-season baseball. He led the Texas League in hits in 2003. He doesn't have a particularly eye-opening skill, but is a very capable center fielder with leadoff skills. He handles the bat and runs well, and he has a good understanding of situational baseball. He uses a line-drive approach and has good speed. Offensively, he needs to draw more walks and refine his basestealing ability. He gets excellent breaks on balls in the outfield and has an above-average arm for center. Sullivan has an innate feel for the game and doesn't make mental mistakes. He'll go to Triple-A in 2004 with the expectation he'll be at least a fourth outfielder in the big leagues by the following year.

Year	Club (League)	Class	AVG	G	AB	R	H	2B	3B	HR	RBI	BB	SO	SB	SLG	OBP
2001	Asheville (SAL)	A	.275	67	258	36	71	12	1	5	22	25	56	13	.388	.344
2002	Salem (Car)	A	.288	138	560	90	161	42	6	12	67	36	70	26	.448	.340
2003	Tulsa (TL)	AA	.300	135	557	81	167	34	8	5	61	39	83	17	.417	.347
MINOR LEAGUE TOTALS			.290	340	1375	207	399	88	15	22	150	100	209	56	.424	.344

23 Mike Esposito, rhp

Born: Sept. 27, 1981. **Ht.:** 6-0. **Wt.:** 190. **Bats:** R. **Throws:** R. **School:** Arizona State University.
Career Transactions: Selected by Rockies in 12th round of 2002 draft; signed Aug. 29, 2002.

One of the top college pitching prospects entering 2002, Esposito scared off teams when he developed forearm stiffness late that spring. He already had Tommy John surgery two years earlier, and he dropped to the 12th round. When the Rockies were unable to sign second-rounder Micah Owings away from Georgia Tech, they used the money earmarked for him to give Esposito a $750,000 bonus. He signed too late to pitch that season, but after a tuneup in instructional league, he went directly to high Class A for his pro debut. Esposito has solid command of four average pitches. His two-seam and four-seam fastballs range from 88-93 mph, and he also throws a curveball and changeup. He still needs to learn to trust himself. Esposito pitches away from contact early in the count, rather than aggressively challenging hitters. At 6 feet tall, he doesn't generate much downhill plane on his pitches, though he does generate good sink on his two-seamer. He'll make the move to Double-A to open 2004.

Year	Club (League)	Class	W	L	ERA	G	GS	CG	SV	IP	H	R	ER	HR	BB	SO	AVG
2003	Visalia (Cal)	A	12	6	3.75	27	27	1	0	161	173	83	67	14	55	116	.277
MINOR LEAGUE TOTALS			12	6	3.75	27	27	1	0	161	173	83	67	14	55	116	.277

24 Tony Miller, of

Born: Aug. 18, 1980. **Ht.:** 5-9. **Wt.:** 180. **Bats:** R. **Throws:** R. **School:** University of Toledo. **Career Transactions:** Selected by Rockies in 10th round of 2001 draft; signed June 7, 2001.

Miller is younger than his 23 in baseball terms. A defensive back at Toledo, he hasn't put in as much time on the diamond as most players his age. Miller has the tools to be a center fielder who bats at the top of the lineup, but his game still needs refinement and a hyper-extended left knee in 2003 cost him half the year. If he perfects his bunting, he has a chance to be a .300 hitter. Compared to Cory Sullivan, he has more pop, more speed and more patience for drawing walks. Sullivan has an advantage in plate discipline and defensive ability. Miller gets good breaks on balls and has a slightly below-average arm. Coming off an impressive showing in instructional leauge last fall, he'll return to Double-A and try to make up for lost time.

Year	Club (League)	Class	AVG	G	AB	R	H	2B	3B	HR	RBI	BB	SO	SB	SLG	OBP
2001	Casper (Pio)	R	.306	70	268	68	82	17	3	10	34	41	63	28	.504	.399
2002	Asheville (SAL)	A	.283	129	501	109	142	23	4	17	48	88	129	50	.447	.396
2003	Visalia (Cal)	A	.248	67	266	47	66	14	5	4	31	40	58	11	.383	.349
MINOR LEAGUE TOTALS			.280	266	1035	224	290	54	12	31	113	169	250	89	.445	.385

25 Aaron Miles, 2b

Born: Dec. 15, 1976. **Ht.:** 5-8. **Wt.:** 170. **Bats:** B. **Throws:** R. **School:** Antioch (Calif.) HS. **Career Transactions:** Selected by Astros in 19th round of 1995 draft; signed June 17, 1995 . . . Selected by White Sox from Astros in Rule 5 minor league draft, Dec. 11, 2000 . . . Granted free agency, Oct. 15, 2001; re-signed by White Sox, Nov. 16, 2001 . . . Granted free agency, Oct. 15, 2002; re-signed by White Sox, Oct. 25, 2002 . . . Traded by White Sox to Rockies for SS Juan Uribe, Dec. 2, 2003.

Miles needed two years to get out of Rookie ball and three more to escape low Class A. His perseverance finally paid off in 2003, when he made his major league debut with the White Sox. Following a December trade for disappointing Juan Uribe, Miles could be the Rockies' Opening Day starter at second base. Though his big league résumé consists of a 4-for-12 performance with three doubles last September, Miles is a better hitter than his competition, which consists of Benji Gil, Denny Hocking and Damian Jackson. He broke through with an MVP season in the Double-A Southern League in 2002, and he encored with a rookie-of-the-year performance in the Triple-A International League last year. He's not big and looks like a David Eckstein-style pest at the plate, but he has legitimate gap power. He's a tremendous contact hitter from both sides of the plate, though he doesn't draw many walks. IL managers rated him the league's best defender at his position, but he's really an offensive second baseman. His speed, range and arm are ordinary, though he does have soft hands. He has superb instincts and does the little things well, which is how he survived in the minors as long as he did. If Miles can't make Colorado's starting lineup, the Greek Olympic team wants him for theirs. His great-grandfather was born in Greece, which could be Miles' ticket to the Athens Games if he's not in the majors in August.

Year	Club (League)	Class	AVG	G	AB	R	H	2B	3B	HR	RBI	BB	SO	SB	SLG	OBP
1995	Astros (GCL)	R	.257	47	171	32	44	9	3	0	18	14	14	9	.345	.312
1996	Astros (GCL)	R	.294	55	214	48	63	3	2	0	15	20	18	14	.327	.357
1997	Quad City (Mid)	A	.262	97	370	55	97	13	2	1	35	30	45	18	.316	.318
1998	Quad City (Mid)	A	.244	108	369	42	90	22	6	2	37	25	52	28	.352	.293
1999	Michigan (Mid)	A	.317	112	470	72	149	28	8	10	71	28	33	17	.474	.353
2000	Kissimmee (FSL)	A	.292	75	295	40	86	20	1	2	36	28	29	11	.386	.352
2001	Birmingham (SL)	AA	.259	84	343	53	89	16	3	8	42	26	35	3	.394	.313
2002	Birmingham (SL)	AA	.322	138	531	67	171	39	1	9	68	40	45	25	.450	.369
2003	Charlotte (IL)	AAA	.304	133	546	80	166	34	5	11	50	40	52	8	.445	.351
	Chicago (AL)	MAJ	.333	8	12	3	4	3	0	0	2	0	0	0	.583	.333
MAJOR LEAGUE TOTALS			.333	8	12	3	4	3	0	0	2	0	0	0	.583	.333
MINOR LEAGUE TOTALS			.289	849	3309	489	955	184	31	43	372	251	323	133	.402	.338

26 Sandy Nin, rhp

Born: Aug. 13, 1980. **Ht.:** 6-0. **Wt.:** 170. **Bats:** R. **Throws:** R. **Career Transactions:** Signed out of Dominican Republic by Blue Jays, July 11, 2000 . . . Traded by Blue Jays to Rockies, Dec. 15, 2003, completing three-way trade in which Blue Jays received RHP Justin Speier from Rockies, Rockies received LHP Joe Kennedy from Devil Rays and a player to named from Blue Jays, and Devil Rays received LHP Mark Hendrickson from Blue Jays (Dec. 14, 2003).

Rather than face arbitration with Justin Speier, the Rockies gave him up in a three-team trade that landed Joe Kennedy from the Devil Rays and Nin from the Blue Jays. Nin led the Dominican Summer League in wins and strikeouts in his 2001 pro debut and hasn't slowed down since arriving in the United States. He pitched in tough luck last year in low Class A, and finished up with a quality start in Double-A—at age 19. Nin has a strong arm, with a 90-93 mph fastball and a power slider. His changeup has potential but still needs improvement. He doesn't get as many strikeouts as his stuff would indicate he should because he's just 6 feet tall and his pitches arrive at the plate on a flat plane. He should make his Rockies debut in high Class A.

Year	Club (League)	Class	W	L	ERA	G	GS	CG	SV	IP	H	R	ER	HR	BB	SO	AVG
2001	Blue Jays (DSL)	R	11	1	1.12	14	14	3	0	97	70	23	12	1	19	105	—
2002	Blue Jays (DSL)	R	2	0	1.25	3	2	1	0	22	10	4	3	2	1	25	.132
	Auburn (NY-P)	A	4	4	2.92	17	11	0	2	74	61	29	24	3	11	61	.225
2003	Charleston, WV (SAL)	A	7	8	2.89	23	23	1	0	131	124	50	42	4	19	87	.250
	New Haven (EL)	AA	0	1	2.57	1	1	0	0	7	5	2	2	1	0	9	.200
MINOR LEAGUE TOTALS			24	14	2.26	58	51	5	2	330	270	108	83	11	50	287	.230

27 Justin Hampson, lhp

Born: May 24, 1980. **Ht.:** 6-1. **Wt.:** 180. **Bats:** L. **Throws:** L. **School:** Belleville Area (Ill.) CC. **Career Transactions:** Selected by Rockies in 28th round of 1999 draft; signed May 22, 2000.

Hampson took a little while to get going as a prospect. Selected in the 28th round in 1999, he didn't sign as a draft-and-follow until the following year. He went 1-8 in his pro debut and spent his first two seasons in short-season ball. He has continued to improve over the last two years, leading the system with 14 victories and making the California League all-star team in 2003. Hampson ranges from 87-91 mph on his fastball, sitting primarily at 88-89, and he pitches inside to both lefthanders and righthanders. His best pitch is his changeup, though he needs to be more aggressive and not nibble at the strike zone with it. He also must refine his fastball command and his curveball. He sometimes dips his front shoulder in his delivery, which puts his curve on the same plane as his fastball. He's ready for Double-A.

Year	Club (League)	Class	W	L	ERA	G	GS	CG	SV	IP	H	R	ER	HR	BB	SO	AVG
2000	Portland (NWL)	A	1	8	3.54	14	13	0	0	69	74	43	27	5	27	44	.271
2001	Tri-City (NWL)	A	4	6	4.52	15	15	0	0	82	84	55	41	5	23	63	.266
2002	Asheville (SAL)	A	9	8	3.83	27	27	1	0	164	162	87	70	12	58	123	.261
2003	Visalia (Cal)	A	14	7	3.68	26	26	1	0	159	153	73	65	12	51	150	.252
	Tulsa (TL)	AA	0	1	13.50	1	1	0	0	4	8	6	6	0	3	0	.421
MINOR LEAGUE TOTALS			28	30	3.94	83	82	2	0	478	481	264	209	34	162	380	.262

28 Ben Crockett, rhp

Born: Dec. 19, 1979. **Ht.:** 6-3. **Wt.:** 200. **Bats:** R. **Throws:** R. **School:** Harvard University. **Career Transactions:** Selected by Rockies in third round of 2002 draft; signed June 17, 2002.

Crockett set every conceivable strikeout record at Harvard, and his ability to throw strikes has carried over from college to the pros. He has averaged 1.8 walks per nine innings as a pro. Crockett's biggest assets are his command and his intelligence. He adjusts from at-bat to at-bat with a hitter, never making the same pitch twice. He's very efficient with his pitches, which include a four-seam fastball that hits 91-92 mph, a two-seamer that sits around 86 mph and a cut fastball with similar velocity. He throw his changeup in any count. Crockett is inconsistent with his curveball, which is more a slurve than a true breaking hammer. He doesn't project to get much better and has a ceiling as a fourth or fifth starter. He tore an elbow ligament in 2001 but didn't require surgery and hasn't had any problems since. Crockett will open 2004 in high Class A with a chance to move to Double-A in the second half.

Year	Club (League)	Class	W	L	ERA	G	GS	CG	SV	IP	H	R	ER	HR	BB	SO	AVG
2002	Tri-City (NWL)	A	0	1	2.88	7	6	0	0	25	26	8	8	2	3	21	.263
	Asheville (SAL)	A	2	3	7.36	6	6	0	0	29	51	25	24	4	6	18	.372
2003	Asheville (SAL)	A	10	9	2.49	23	23	2	0	152	152	60	42	11	32	117	.259
	Visalia (Cal)	A	2	3	4.50	5	5	0	0	32	35	18	16	5	7	26	.278
MINOR LEAGUE TOTALS			14	16	3.40	41	40	2	0	238	264	111	90	22	48	182	.278

29 Justin Huisman, rhp

Born: April 16, 1979. **Ht.:** 6-1. **Wt.:** 195. **Bats:** R. **Throws:** R. **School:** University of Mississippi.
Career Transactions: Selected by Rockies in 15th round of 2000 draft; signed June 14, 2000.

Huisman played with his brothers Jason (a former outfielder in the Angels system) and Josh at Mississippi, where he was a shortstop/closer. He has made a smooth transition to full-time pitcher, posting a 1.85 ERA in his pro debut and a 2.22 mark in his four-year career. Huisman's high-80s two-seam fastball isn't overpowering, but it fools hitters because it doesn't look like a sinker until it drops straight down when it gets to the plate. He also has an average slider and pinpoint command. There's a little violence to Huisman's delivery, but it's deceptive. He needs to improve his changeup, which also sinks, to help him against more advanced lefthanded hitters. Huisman will be in big league camp this spring, but he most likely will open the season at Triple-A.

Year	Club (League)	Class	W	L	ERA	G	GS	CG	SV	IP	H	R	ER	HR	BB	SO	AVG
2000	Portland (NWL)	A	3	6	1.85	16	3	0	1	44	31	16	9	1	17	32	.196
2001	Asheville (SAL)	A	0	3	1.70	55	0	0	30	58	35	20	11	1	14	53	.167
2002	Salem (Car)	A	3	4	1.57	41	0	0	20	52	47	11	9	0	14	24	.250
	Carolina (SL)	AA	0	3	6.66	18	0	0	2	24	30	22	18	4	12	10	.291
2003	Tulsa (TL)	AA	7	2	1.75	57	0	0	26	62	55	22	12	1	7	46	.234
MINOR LEAGUE TOTALS			13	18	2.22	187	3	0	79	240	198	91	59	7	64	165	.221

30 Aaron Marsden, lhp

Born: Nov. 18, 1981. **Ht.:** 6-5. **Wt.:** 225. **Bats:** L. **Throws:** L. **School:** University of Nebraska.
Career Transactions: Selected by Rockies in third round of 2003 draft; signed June 21, 2003.

Like fellow North Dakotan Darin Erstad, Marsden starred at Nebraska. He was the Big 12 Conference pitcher of the year in 2003, when he also earned academic All-America honors with a 3.95 grade-point average in finance. Marsden's strong suits are his command and plus-plus slider. He has average velocity on his two-seam and four-seam fastballs, which run away from lefthanders. He also throws a changeup with sinking action and a curveball. He's tough on hitters because he's a big lefthander with a deceptive delivery, though there's a bit of effort to it. The Rockies were impressed with how he took a leadership role in the short-season Tri-City clubhouse. He should jump to low Class A in 2004 and could move quickly.

Year	Club (League)	Class	W	L	ERA	G	GS	CG	SV	IP	H	R	ER	HR	BB	SO	AVG
2003	Tri-City (NWL)	A	4	3	2.79	13	10	0	1	61	49	21	19	2	18	46	.217
MINOR LEAGUE TOTALS			4	3	2.79	13	10	0	1	61	49	21	19	2	18	46	.217

DETROIT
TIGERS

As horrible as 2003 got in the major leagues for the Tigers, who barely avoided matching the 1962 Mets' total of 120 defeats, it was nearly as disappointing at the minor league level. For years, Detroit has banked on its emphasis on player development paying off. But it hasn't. And based on the performance of players who were considered the organization's top prospects last season, the future doesn't appear much brighter than the present.

Baseball America initially rated the Tigers' 2001 draft as the best in baseball, but most of the players who showed so much promise then have struggled since. Righthander Kenny Baugh (first round) has had shoulder problems. Second baseman Michael Woods (supplemental first) has had two knee surgeries and hit .205 in high Class in 2003. Righty Preston Larrison (second) couldn't handle the jump to Double-A last year. Neither could Jack Hannahan (third), who no longer looks like the third baseman of the future.

Those are far from the only disappointments. Detroit once had high hopes for lefties Tim Kalita and Andy Van Hekken, righthander Matt Wheatland, shortstop Anderson Hernandez and outfielders Neil Jenkins and Nook Logan. All labored through last season, except for Wheatland, who didn't pitch at all because of a shoulder ailment. He has pitched just 69 innings

TOP 30 PROSPECTS

1. Kyle Sleeth, rhp
2. Brent Clevlen, of
3. Joel Zumaya, rhp
4. Rob Henkel, lhp
5. Tony Giarratano, ss
6. Kody Kirkland, 3b
7. Scott Moore, 3b
8. Curtis Granderson, of
9. Jay Sborz, rhp
10. Kenny Baugh, rhp
11. Ryan Raburn, 3b/2b
12. Wilkin Ramirez, 3b
13. Chris Shelton, 1b/c
14. Cody Ross, of
15. Humberto Sanchez, rhp
16. Fernando Rodney, rhp
17. Preston Larrison, rhp
18. Jon Connolly, lhp
19. Donald Kelly, ss/3b
20. Nook Logan, of
21. Roberto Novoa, rhp
22. Eulogio de la Cruz, rhp
23. Josh Rainwater, rhp
24. Gilberto Mejia, ss
25. Anderson Hernandez, ss
26. Eric Eckenstahler, lhp
27. Lino Urdaneta, rhp
28. Mike Bumatay, lhp
29. Juan Tejeda, 1b
30. Michael Woods, 2b

By Pat Caputo

since the Tigers picked him eighth overall in 2000.

Where other organizations invariably find lightning in a bottle, the Tigers have been struck by it. Typical was the unveiling of Detroit's double-play combination of Omar Infante and Ramon Santiago in 2003. Both fell so short of expectations, as have former top prospects Brandon Inge and Nate Cornejo, that the Tigers decided to move on this offseason. They signed free agent Fernando Vina and traded Santiago to Seattle for Carlos Guillen.

Detroit clearly lacks impact players. Jeremy Bonderman, acquired from the Athletics in a three-way deal that sent Jeff Weaver to the Yankees, appears to be the only big leaguer with star potential. Carlos Pena and Franklyn German, acquired in the same trade, haven't shown nearly as much promise. General manager Dave Dombrowski has tried to compensate by trading veterans and getting prospects in return. The Tigers also carried three major league Rule 5 pitchers in the majors last season and went back for three more in December, giving the organization improved depth.

Dombrowski's approach is to move young players with promise to the majors quickly. In Florida, his previous post, the carry-over from that philosophy paid off in a 2003 World Series championship. Given the Tigers' dismal track record, Dombrowski's current task is much more daunting.

ORGANIZATION
OVERVIEW

General manager: Dave Dombrowski. **Farm director:** Rick Bennett. **Scouting director:** Greg Smith.

2003 PERFORMANCE

Class	Team	League	W	L	Pct.	Finish*	Manager
Majors	Detroit	American	43	119	.265	14th (14)	Alan Trammell
Triple-A	Toledo Mud Hens	International	65	78	.455	11th (14)	Larry Parrish
Double-A	Erie Sea Wolves	Eastern	72	70	.507	t-5th (12)	Kevin Bradshaw
High A	Lakeland Tigers	Florida State	55	78	.414	11th (12)	Gary Green
Low A	West Michigan Whitecaps	Midwest	67	73	.479	9th (14)	Phil Regan
Shot-season	Oneonta Tigers	New York-Penn	45	30	.600	4th (14)	Randy Ready
Rookie	GCL Tigers	Gulf Coast	28	29	.491	5th (12)	Howard Bushong

OVERALL 2003 MINOR LEAGUE RECORD 332 358 .481 22nd (30)
*Finish in overall standings (No. of teams in league)

ORGANIZATION LEADERS

BATTING
*Minimum 250 At-Bats

*AVG	Donald Kelly, Erie/Lakeland	.306
R	Cody Ross, Toledo	74
H	Curtis Granderson, Lakeland	136
TB	Cody Ross, Toledo	242
2B	Brant Ust, Toledo/Erie	36
3B	Three tied at	11
HR	Ernie Young, Toledo	21
RBI	Ernie Young, Toledo	84
BB	Brent Clevlen, West Michigan	72
SO	Neil Jenkins, Lakeland	150
SB	Nook Logan, Erie	37
*SLG	Cody Ross, Toledo	.515
*OBP	Donald Kelly, Erie/Lakeland	.396

PITCHING
#Minimum 75 Innings

W	Jon Connolly, West Michigan	16
L	Preston Larrison, Toledo/Erie	13
#ERA	Jon Connolly, West Michigan	1.41
G	Ian Ostlund, Lakeland/West Michigan	61
CG	Jon Connolly, West Michigan	5
SV	Brian Schmack, Erie	29
IP	Pat Ahearne, Toledo/Erie	184
BB	Humberto Sanchez, West Michigan	78
SO	Joel Zumaya, West Michigan	126

BEST TOOLS

Best Hitter for Average	Chris Shelton
Best Power Hitter	Brent Clevlen
Fastest Baserunner	Nook Logan
Best Athlete	Bo Flowers
Best Fastball	Joel Zumaya
Best Curveball	Rob Henkel
Best Slider	Kyle Sleeth
Best Changeup	Rob Henkel
Best Control	Kenny Baugh
Best Defensive Catcher	Maxim St. Pierre
Best Defensive Infielder	Anderson Hernandez
Best Infield Arm	Anderson Hernandez
Best Defensive Outfielder	Nook Logan
Best Outfield Arm	Cody Ross

2007 LINEUP

Catcher	Ivan Rodriguez
First Base	Carlos Pena
Second Base	Ryan Raburn
Third Base	Kody Kirkland
Shortstop	Carlos Guillen
Left Field	Dmitri Young
Center Field	Curtis Granderson
Right Field	Brent Clevlen
Designated Hitter	Eric Munson
No. 1 Starter	Jeremy Bonderman
No. 2 Starter	Kyle Sleeth
No. 3 Starter	Joel Zumaya
No. 4 Starter	Rob Henkel
No. 5 Starter	Wil Ledezma
Closer	Franklyn German

LAST YEAR'S TOP 20 PROSPECTS

1. Jeremy Bonderman, rhp	11. Chad Petty, lhp
2. Preston Larrison, rhp	12. Cody Ross, of
3. Franklyn German, rhp	13. Matt Coenen, lhp
4. Omar Infante, ss/2b	14. Andy Van Hekken, lhp
5. Eric Munson, 1b/3b	15. Jack Hannahan, 3b
6. Scott Moore, ss	16. Andres Torres, of
7. Nook Logan, of	17. Kenny Baugh, rhp
8. Rob Henkel, lhp	18. Curtis Granderson, of
9. Brent Clevlen, of	19. Humberto Sanchez, rhp
10. Anderson Hernandez, ss	20. Michael Woods, 2b

TOP PROSPECTS OF THE DECADE

1994	Justin Thompson, lhp
1995	Tony Clark, 1b
1996	Mike Drumright, rhp
1997	Mike Drumright, rhp
1998	Juan Encarnacion, of
1999	Gabe Kapler, of
2000	Eric Munson, 1b/c
2001	Brandon Inge, c
2002	Nate Cornejo, rhp
2003	Jeremy Bonderman, rhp

TOP DRAFT PICKS OF THE DECADE

1994	Cade Gaspar, rhp
1995	Mike Drumright, rhp
1996	Seth Greisinger, rhp
1997	Matt Anderson, rhp
1998	Jeff Weaver, rhp
1999	Eric Munson, c/1b
2000	Matt Wheatland, rhp
2001	Kenny Baugh, rhp
2002	Scott Moore, ss
2003	Kyle Sleeth, rhp

ALL-TIME LARGEST BONUSES

Eric Munson, 1999	$3,500,000
Kyle Sleeth, 2003	$3,350,000
Matt Anderson, 1997	$2,505,000
Scott Moore, 2002	$2,300,000
Matt Wheatland, 2000	$2,150,000

MINOR LEAGUE
DEPTH CHART

DETROIT TIGERS
RANK: 22

Impact potential (C): Kyle Sleeth, the third pick in the 2003 draft, should advance rapidly through the system after making his debut this spring. He may be the only pitcher in the organization with frontline stuff, and the Tigers are banking on him to anchor their staff in the near future.

Depth (D): This is an organization that needs to be aggressive in the amateur market, given the state of its major league roster. Detroit stole Kody Kirkland from the Pirates last year, and he projects as a solid everyday big leaguer, as do Brent Clevlen and Tony Giarratano.

Sleeper: Wilkin Ramirez, 3b. —*Depth charts prepared by Josh Boyd. Numbers in parentheses indicate prospect rankings.*

LF
Curtis Granderson (8)
Wilton Reynlds
David Espinosa

CF
Nook Logan (20)
Victor Mendez
Vincent Blue
Corey Richardson

RF
Brent Clevlen (2)
Cody Ross (14)
Marcus Thames
Michael Brown

3B
Kody Kirkland (6)
Scott Moore (7)
Wilkin Ramirez (12)
Donald Kelly (19)
Jack Hannahan

SS
Tony Giarratano (5)
Anderson Hernandez (25)

2B
Ryan Raburn (11)
Gilberto Mejia (24)
Michael Woods (30)
Pablo Ozuna
Eric Rodland
Scott Tousa

1B
Chris Shelton (13)
Juan Tejeda (29)

SOURCE OF TALENT

Homegrown		Acquired	
College	7	Trade	3
Junior College	2	Rule 5 draft	3
Draft-and-follow	2	Independent	0
High school	7	Free agent/waivers	0
Nondrafted free agent	0		
Foreign	6		

C
Cody Collet
Maxim St. Pierre
Mike Rabelo
Alex Trezza

RHP

Starters	Relievers
Kyle Sleeth (1)	Humberto Sanchez (15)
Joel Zumaya (3)	Fernando Rodney (16)
Jay Sborz (9)	Roberto Novoa (21)
Kenny Baugh (10)	Eulogio de la Cruz (22)
Preston Larrison (17)	Lino Urdaneta (27)
Josh Rainwater (23)	Chris Mears
Shane Loux	Jair Jurrjens
John Ennis	Jorge Cordova
Troy Pickford	Jordan Tata
Matt Pender	Chris Homer
Jeremy Johnson	Michael Howell

LHP

Starters	Relievers
Rob Henkel (4)	Eric Eckenstahler (26)
Jon Connolly (18)	Mike Bumatay (28)
Danny Zell	Corey Hamman
Andy Van Hekken	
Adrian Burnside	

DRAFT
ANALYSIS

Best Pro Debut: Arguably the best all-around pure college shortstop in the draft, SS Tony Giarratano (3) surprised the Tigers with his quick adjustment to wood bats. After hitting .187 in the Cape Cod League in 2002, he batted .328-3-27 in the short-season New York-Penn League. His double-play partner, 2B Eric Rodland (9), hit .328-0-27 with 13 steals. RHP Chris Homer (24) tied for the NY-P lead with 15 saves.

Best Athlete: OF Jeremy Laster's (12) power and speed give him a huge ceiling, though he's raw.

Rodland

Best Pure Hitter: Rodland is an offensive second baseman who holds Gonzaga's career hits record with 269.

Best Raw Power: C Cody Collet (6) edges OF Michael Brown (13). Collet signed late and didn't play a pro game, while back problems limited Brown to one home run.

Fastest Runner: After loading up on athletes in 2002, the Tigers concentrated on bats. Laster has plus speed but isn't as fast as 2002 draftees Robbie Sovie and Bo Flowers.

Best Defensive Player: Giarratano's arm and hands are both well above-average tools.

Best Fastball: The first pitcher taken in the 2003 draft, RHP Kyle Sleeth (1) sat at 93-94 mph and touched 96 consistently all spring. RHP Jay Sborz (2) has similar velocity but can't match Sleeth's command and consistency. RHP Josh Rainwater (4) hit 95 mph in high school before the draft.

Best Breaking Ball: Sleeth has two good breaking pitches. The Tigers think his power curveball is better than his low-80s slider.

Most Intriguing Background: Sleeth tied an NCAA record by winning 26 consecutive games from 2001-03. SS Nathan Doyle's (25) twin brother Jared, a lefty, is one of the Diamondbacks' best pitching prospects.

Closest To The Majors: Sleeth signed too late to make his pro debut, but he's so advanced that he could push Detroit to start him in Double-A this year.

Best Late-Round Pick: RHP Jordan Tata (16) showed average stuff during the spring but consistently popped 93 mph after signing. He also has a solid curveball and keeps his pitches down in the strike zone.

The One Who Got Away: The Tigers either signed or still control the rights to all but three of their 50 draftees. Their biggest regret is losing RHP Ryan Muller (35) to the University of San Francisco. He has a promising fastball and curveball.

Assessment: One benefit of losing big is premium draft position, which allowed the Tigers to spend the No. 3 overall pick on Sleeth, arguably the most promising pitcher they've ever drafted. He and Giarratano could provide quick help in Detroit.

2002 DRAFT   GRADE: C+

OF Brent Clevlen (2) is the organization's top position prospect. RHP Joel Zumaya (11), 3B Scott Moore (1) and OF Curtis Granderson (3) also are among the best the system has to offer.

2001 DRAFT   GRADE: C

Both first-rounders, RHP Kenny Baugh and 2B Michael Woods, have been held back by injuries. A once-promising draft no longer looks as bright, though there's still hope for Baugh, 3B/2B Ryan Raburn (5) and draft-and-follow RHP Humberto Sanchez (31). Sleeper LHP Jon Connolly (28) led the minors in ERA last year.

2000 DRAFT   GRADE: F

RHP Matt Wheatland (1) hasn't pitched since 2001 because of shoulder woes. OF Nook Logan (3) is the highlight of this draft, and that's not saying much.

1999 DRAFT   GRADE: C

3B Eric Munson (1) has developed much more slowly than expected but showed signs of life in 2003. OF Cody Ross (4) continues to overachieve.

—Draft analysis prepared by Jim Callis. Numbers in parentheses indicate draft rounds.

rhp

Kyle
Sleeth

Born: Dec. 20, 1981.
Ht.: 6-5. **Wt.:** 205.
Bats: R. **Throws:** R.
School: Wake Forest University.
Career Transactions: Selected by Tigers in first round (third overall) of 2003 draft; signed Aug. 8, 2003.

An 18th-round pick out of a Colorado high school in 2000, Sleeth opted to attend Wake Forest instead. He went 31-6 in three seasons, tying an NCAA record by winning 26 consecutive decisions. Sleeth entered 2003 as the top amateur pitching prospect and exited the draft as the first pitcher selected and third overall pick. Scouts considered him better than Bryan Bullington, who went No. 1 overall to the Pirates the year before. Sleeth didn't sign until August, receiving a $3.35 million bonus. By that time, the Tigers decided that he shouldn't make his pro debut until 2004. They didn't want him to work many innings last summer in any case, after watching 2001 first-rounder Kenny Baugh develop shoulder problems shortly after signing. Like Baugh, Sleeth pitched a lot of innings in college. After signing, he worked out with the major league club and then with Triple-A Toledo. Sleeth did pitch during instructional league and was impressive.

Sleeth has far and away the highest ceiling among Tigers farmhands. He had one of the best fastballs available in the 2003 draft, both in terms of velocity and life. He usually pitches between 92-94 mph and touches 96. His fastball seems even firmer, however, because of its movement. It bores down and in on righthanders. It's a heavy ball. Sleeth throws both a power curveball and a low-80s slider. The curveball is the better breaking pitch, as he throws it in the high 70s and it features a lot of depth and bite. His slider improved last spring, though some scouts say it's a bit slurvy. His changeup has the potential to be an average major league pitch. Sleeth has a strong, projectable frame and was durable at Wake Forest. He's quiet and confident. When the Demon Deacons struggled behind him last spring, he remained poised. Though not demonstrative, Sleeth exudes competitiveness. To move quickly through the minors and to be effective in the majors, Sleeth will have to be more consistent with each of his pitches. His ability to repeat pitches is still questionable. He sometimes loses his delivery, causing him to throw across his body or leave pitches up in the strike zone. Sleeth also has to decide whether he wants to use three or four pitches. His slider is too similar to his curveball.

If Sleeth had signed shortly after the draft and pitched last summer, he likely would start 2004 at Double-A Erie and be in line to reach Detroit by September. Now the Tigers won't push him quite that hard, so he'll probably make his pro debut at high Class A Lakeland. If he enjoys immediate success, the club won't hesitate to promote him to Double-A, and he still could make it to the majors this year. He has that type of ability and makeup, and Tigers general manager Dave Dombrowski won't hesitate to bring deserving prospects to the majors.

Year	Club (League)	Class	W	L	ERA	G	GS	CG	SV	IP	H	R	ER	HR	BB	SO	AVG
2003	Did not play—Signed 2004 contract																

2 Brent Clevlen, of

Born: Oct. 27, 1983. **Ht.:** 6-2. **Wt.:** 190. **Bats:** R. **Throws:** R. **School:** Westwood HS, Cedar Park, Texas. **Career Transactions:** Selected by Tigers in second round of 2002 draft; signed July 23, 2002.

Clevlen was a versatile high school athlete who could have played college football as a quarterback if not for his prowess on the diamond, where he starred as an outfielder and pitcher. He outdueled Expos 2002 first-rounder Clint Everts in the Texas 5-A playoffs shortly before signing for $805,000. A second-round pick, he has outperformed No. 8 overall selection Scott Moore, his teammate in each of his first two pro seasons. Clevlen is a fluid, natural athlete with a terrific swing. He's a selective hitter who uses the entire field. Low Class A West Michigan's notoriously pitcher-friendly Fifth Third Ballpark hurt his numbers last year, but he revealed his power potential on the road, hitting .290 with 10 homers in 70 games. He has good instincts, solid speed and a strong right-field arm. Clevlen's biggest fault as a hitter is that he can be too passive and fall behind in the count. He sometimes takes questionable routes on fly balls and has trouble with balls hit directly over his head. He'll begin this year in high Class A, where he'll again team up with Moore. Clevlen is on course to reach Detroit in mid-2006.

Year	Club (League)	Class	AVG	G	AB	R	H	2B	3B	HR	RBI	BB	SO	SB	SLG	OBP
2002	Tigers (GCL)	R	.330	28	103	14	34	2	3	3	21	8	24	2	.495	.372
2003	West Michigan (Mid)	A	.260	138	481	67	125	22	7	12	63	72	111	6	.410	.359
MINOR LEAGUE TOTALS			.272	166	584	81	159	24	10	15	84	80	135	8	.425	.361

3 Joel Zumaya, rhp

Born: Nov. 9, 1984. **Ht.:** 6-3. **Wt.:** 210. **Bats:** R. **Throws:** R. **School:** Bonita Vista HS, Chula Vista, Calif. **Career Transactions:** Selected by Tigers in 11th round of 2002 draft; signed June 20, 2002.

When the Tigers selected Zumaya in the 11th round of the 2002 draft, they figured he was just another high school righty with raw arm strength who would need time to develop. But his fastball suddenly gained velocity and he has progressed much faster than expected. He would have led minor league starters in strikeouts per nine innings last year (12.6) had he pitched enough innings to qualify. Zumaya's fastball consistently reaches the mid-90s, and he has hit 97-98 mph on several occasions, but that's not the only reason he gets so many strikeouts. He also has uncanny velocity on a nasty curveball, throwing it in the low 80s. He has a bulldog approach and takes to coaching well. Improved mechanics are the key to his improved stuff. Zumaya has a maximum-effort delivery, which led to back problems that knocked him out for six weeks last year. He sometimes drops his arm angle, causing his pitches to flatten out. He needs more consistency with his curve and a great deal of refinement with his changeup, which he doesn't throw often enough. If Zumaya stays healthy and keeps winning in high Class A this year, he could reach Double-A by midseason. His approach, power stuff and lack of a changeup could make him a closer in the long run.

Year	Club (League)	Class	W	L	ERA	G	GS	CG	SV	IP	H	R	ER	HR	BB	SO	AVG
2002	Tigers (GCL)	R	2	1	1.93	9	8	0	0	37	21	9	8	2	11	46	.163
2003	West Michigan (Mid)	A	7	5	2.79	19	19	0	0	90	69	35	28	3	38	126	.209
MINOR LEAGUE TOTALS			9	6	2.54	28	27	0	0	128	90	44	36	5	49	172	.196

4 Rob Henkel, lhp

Born: Aug. 3, 1978. **Ht.:** 6-2. **Wt.:** 210. **Bats:** R. **Throws:** L. **School:** UCLA. **Career Transactions:** Selected by Marlins in third round of 2000 draft; signed Sept. 19, 2000 . . . Traded by Marlins with RHP Gary Knotts and LHP Nate Robertson to Tigers for LHP Mark Redman and RHP Jerrod Fuell, Jan. 11, 2003.

Henkel was the key pitcher for Detroit in the January 2003 trade that sent Mark Redman to Florida and also netted Gary Knotts and Nate Robertson. Henkel pitched up to expectations in Double-A, but his season was marred by back spasms that forced him to miss numerous starts, including his scheduled Arizona Fall League stint. Henkel is a legitimate three-pitch lefthander. His fastball consistently touches 90 mph and while it doesn't have a lot of movement, he locates it well. His out pitch is a tight curveball—the best in the system—that he commands well. His changeup is also effective and he throws it for strikes. He has a high three-quarters delivery that seems difficult for hitters to pick up. Henkel's health is a major question mark. He had Tommy John surgery at UCLA and came down with shoulder problems shortly after he signed in 2000, costing him velocity on what had been a 93-95 mph heater. Even when he's going good, his teams hold their breath wondering if he's about to break down. Added to the 40-man roster this offseason, Henkel is good enough to pitch in the majors in 2004 if he can stay healthy. He'll start the year in Triple-A.

Year	Club (League)	Class	W	L	ERA	G	GS	CG	SV	IP	H	R	ER	HR	BB	SO	AVG
2001	Marlins (GCL)	R	1	3	1.52	9	8	0	0	30	17	9	5	0	11	38	.156
	Utica (NY-P)	A	0	0	4.32	3	3	0	0	8	7	4	4	0	6	11	.212
	Kane County (Mid)	A	0	0	4.50	1	1	0	0	4	6	3	2	0	1	2	.316
2002	Jupiter (FSL)	A	8	3	2.51	14	12	0	0	75	55	22	21	4	22	82	.206
	Portland (EL)	AA	5	4	3.86	13	13	0	0	70	54	31	30	6	27	68	.212
2003	Erie (EL)	AA	9	3	3.38	16	16	0	0	83	67	33	31	7	27	70	.220
MINOR LEAGUE TOTALS			23	13	3.10	56	53	0	0	270	206	102	93	17	94	271	.209

5 Tony Giarratano, ss

Born: Nov. 29, 1982. **Ht.:** 6-0. **Wt.:** 180. **Bats:** B. **Throws:** R. **School:** Tulane University. **Career Transactions:** Selected by Tigers in third round of 2003 draft; signed June 30, 2003.

Giarratano had arguably the best all-around tools among college short-stops in the 2003 draft, and his all-star debut in the short-season New York-Penn League did nothing to detract from his claim. After hitting .238 for Tulane and .187 in the Cape Cod League in 2002, he improved dramatically at the plate last year. He stands out defensively and ranks just behind Anderson Hernandez among the system's infielders. Giarratano has plus speed for a shortstop and a strong, accurate arm. His hands and actions are also better than average. A natural righthanded hitter, he's more effective from the left side. He made a surprisingly easy transition from aluminum bats and should be able to hit for a solid average with gap power and a few steals. Giarratano handles the bat well but must improve his patience. He won't have much power, so he'll need good on-base skills. Giarratano entered the organization at a perfect time. The Tigers were disappointed by upper-level shortstops Omar Infante, Ramon Santiago and Anderson Hernandez in 2003. Even after trading Santiago for Carlos Guillen, Detroit will give Giarratano the chance to move quickly. He'll skip a level and play in high Class A this year.

Year	Club (League)	Class	AVG	G	AB	R	H	2B	3B	HR	RBI	BB	SO	SB	SLG	OBP
2003	Oneonta (NY-P)	A	.328	47	189	31	62	11	4	3	27	12	22	9	.476	.369
MINOR LEAGUE TOTALS			.328	47	189	31	62	11	4	3	27	12	22	9	.476	.369

6 Kody Kirkland, 3b

Born: June 9, 1983. **Ht.:** 6-4. **Wt.:** 200. **Bats:** R. **Throws:** R. **School:** JC of Southern Idaho. **Career Transactions:** Selected by Pirates in 30th round of 2001 draft; signed May 24, 2002 . . . Traded by Pirates to Tigers, May 24, 2003, completing trade in which Tigers sent 1B Randall Simon to Pirates for LHP Adrian Burnside and two players to be named (Nov. 25, 2002); Tigers also acquired RHP Roberto Novoa (Dec. 16, 2002).

The Tigers had no intention of going to arbitration with Randall Simon after the 2002 season, so they traded him to the Pirates for three players, most notably Kirkland. Because Kirkland signed in late May 2002, he couldn't switch organizations until a year later, so he began last season in extended spring training. Kirkland is an impressive hitter with a compact stroke and projectable power. He drives balls to all fields and has a decent idea of the strike zone. Defensively, he has average range and arm strength to go with good hands. He's a smart player who likes to compete. While Kirkland has topped .300 in each of his two pro seasons, he'll have to make more consistent contact to do well against more advanced pitchers. The accuracy of his throws varies, the main reason behind his 15 errors in 65 games last summer. Kirkland would have started 2003 in low Class A if not for the trade. He'll probably head there rather than high Class A this year because 2002 first-rounder Scott Moore is one level ahead of him.

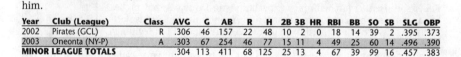

Year	Club (League)	Class	AVG	G	AB	R	H	2B	3B	HR	RBI	BB	SO	SB	SLG	OBP
2002	Pirates (GCL)	R	.306	46	157	22	48	10	2	0	18	14	39	2	.395	.373
2003	Oneonta (NY-P)	A	.303	67	254	46	77	15	11	4	49	25	60	14	.496	.390
MINOR LEAGUE TOTALS			.304	113	411	68	125	25	13	4	67	39	99	16	.457	.383

7 Scott Moore, 3b

Born: Nov. 17, 1983. **Ht.:** 6-2. **Wt.:** 180. **Bats:** L. **Throws:** R. **School:** Cypress HS, Long Beach, Calif. **Career Transactions:** Selected by Tigers in first round (eighth overall) of 2002 draft; signed June 4, 2002.

Moore was drafted eighth overall in 2002 as a shortstop and spent his first pro season there in the Rookie-level Gulf Coast League. Scouts and Tigers officials projected him as a third baseman, and he moved there last spring. He spent three weeks in extended spring training learning the position before going to low Class A. Moore's calling card is his classic lefthanded stroke. When he makes contact, he hits the ball hard and shows considerable power potential. He has soft hands and good arm strength. Moore has struck out 141 times in 147 games as a pro, more the result of his inconsistent approach than his swing. He's overaggressive at times and not aggressive enough at others. He has trouble with the footwork at third base, which leads to bad throws and errors. He doesn't run well, especially for someone drafted as a shortstop. Moore looks like a one-dimensional player who will go as far as his bat will carry him, and he's going to have to make adjustments if it's going to carry him to the majors. The Tigers would like to move Moore to high Class A to begin 2004, but they question whether he's ready for the leap.

Year	Club (League)	Class	AVG	G	AB	R	H	2B	3B	HR	RBI	BB	SO	SB	SLG	OBP
02	Tigers (GCL)	R	.293	40	133	18	39	6	2	4	25	10	31	1	.459	.349
03	West Michigan (Mid)	A	.239	107	372	40	89	16	6	6	45	41	110	2	.363	.325
MINOR LEAGUE TOTALS			.253	147	505	58	128	22	8	10	70	51	141	3	.388	.332

8 Curtis Granderson, of

Born: March 16, 1981. **Ht.:** 6-1. **Wt.:** 180. **Bats:** L. **Throws:** R. **School:** University of Illinois-Chicago. **Career Transactions:** Selected by Tigers in third round of 2002 draft; signed June 28, 2002.

Granderson finished runner-up in the NCAA Division I (.483) and New York-Penn League (.344) batting races in 2002. After continuing to impress during spring training last year, he skipped a level and jumped to high Class A. Though his numbers weren't as good, he maintained his consistency against significantly better competition. Granderson has no trouble hitting for average with his short stroke, ability to make contact and willingness to use all fields. He has no glaring weakness in his game. He has gap power, runs OK and can play all three outfield positions. Though Granderson doesn't have any big holes, his only standout tool is his hitting. He's not a big home run or stolen base threat, and he fits best in left field, where he'll have to do more than hit for average. Because he puts the bat on the ball with ease, he doesn't draw a lot of walks and doesn't always wait for the best pitch to hit. Granderson will advance to Double-A in 2004 and could reach Detroit sometime next year. It remains to be seen whether he'll be a solid big league regular or just a good fourth outfielder.

Year	Club (League)	Class	AVG	G	AB	R	H	2B	3B	HR	RBI	BB	SO	SB	SLG	OBP
02	Oneonta (NY-P)	A	.344	52	212	45	73	15	4	3	34	20	35	9	.495	.417
03	Lakeland (FSL)	A	.286	127	476	71	136	29	10	11	51	49	91	10	.458	.365
MINOR LEAGUE TOTALS			.304	179	688	116	209	44	14	14	85	69	126	19	.469	.381

9 Jay Sborz, rhp

Born: Jan. 24, 1985. **Ht.:** 6-4. **Wt.:** 210. **Bats:** R. **Throws:** R. **School:** Langley HS, Great Falls, Va. **Career Transactions:** Selected by Tigers in second round of 2003 draft; signed June 30, 2003.

The Tigers believe they landed a first-round talent when they got Sborz with the 40th overall pick last June. He had one of the best pure arms in the draft, and it cost $865,000 to sign him away from a commitment to Arizona State. He looked raw in the Gulf Coast League but pitched better during instructional league. Sborz is a true power pitcher. He has a 93-95 mph fastball and a hard, sharp-breaking slider that often touches 80. He has a strong frame with room to grow, so there's more velocity in there. Some scouts project that he could put up triple digits on the radar gun. Sborz is a thrower, not a pitcher. He has a violent delivery and doesn't repeat his arm slot or pitches well. He struggles to throw strikes and has no semblance of a changeup. Some teams were concerned about his immaturity, but the Tigers say his behavior has been good. Sborz showed enough during instructional league to possibly earn a spot in low Class A this year. Detroit will use him as a starter to give him innings, but his explosive fastball and lack of offspeed stuff could lead to a future as a closer.

Year	Club (League)	Class	W	L	ERA	G	GS	CG	SV	IP	H	R	ER	HR	BB	SO	AVG
2003	Tigers (GCL)	R	0	2	4.85	8	7	0	0	26	20	18	14	2	14	35	.206
MINOR LEAGUE TOTALS			0	2	4.85	8	7	0	0	26	20	18	14	2	14	35	.206

10 Kenny Baugh, rhp

RICH ABEL

Born: Feb. 5, 1979. **Ht.:** 6-4. **Wt.:** 190. **Bats:** R. **Throws:** R. **School:** Rice University. **Career Transactions:** Selected by Tigers in first round (11th overall) of 2001 draft; signed June 5, 2001 . . . On disabled list, April 4-Oct. 10, 2002.

The 11th overall pick in 2001, Baugh pitched well in Double-A that summer and seemed on the verge of joining Detroit's rotation. But shoulder problems surfaced that August, requiring arthroscopic surgery to repair a labrum tear. He missed all of 2002 and didn't look the same when he returned last year. Baugh knows how to pitch. He has excellent command of his fastball and can work it to any quadrant of the strike zone. His curveball might be his best pitch and was more consistent than ever in 2003. He also has a good changeup, giving him the chance to have three average pitches. His makeup and work ethic are excellent. Baugh didn't light up the radar gun before he got hurt, usually pitching at 90 mph, and his velocity was down to 85-88 in 2003. The movement on his fastball is also ordinary, so it can get hammered if he doesn't locate with precision. There also are obvious concerns about his shoulder. Baugh will begin 2004 in Triple-A. How far he goes depends on his ability to stay healthy and regain arm strength.

Year	Club (League)	Class	W	L	ERA	G	GS	CG	SV	IP	H	R	ER	HR	BB	SO	AVG
2001	West Michigan (Mid)	A	2	1	1.59	6	6	0	0	34	31	14	6	0	10	39	.238
	Erie (EL)	AA	1	3	2.97	5	5	1	0	30	23	16	10	5	6	30	.207
2002	Did not play—Injured																
2003	Lakeland (FSL)	A	3	0	3.86	4	4	0	0	21	21	14	9	2	11	12	.263
	Erie (EL)	AA	7	9	4.60	19	19	1	0	110	111	71	56	16	32	58	.262
MINOR LEAGUE TOTALS			13	13	3.74	34	34	2	0	195	186	115	81	23	59	139	.250

11 Ryan Raburn, 3b/2b

Born: April 17, 1981. **Ht.:** 6-0. **Wt.:** 180. **Bats:** R. **Throws:** R. **School:** South Florida CC. **Career Transactions:** Selected by Tigers in fifth round of 2001 draft; signed June 20, 2001.

After two years regaining his health and hitting stroke, Raburn's stature rose during instructional league when he moved from third base to second. He dominated in his pro debut in the New York-Penn League in 2001, but dislocated his hip that offseason in an all-terrain vehicle accident. Raburn, whose brother Johnny is an outfielder in the Brewers system, has struggled in game action since returning late in the 2002 season. But at the end of 2003 and during instructional league, he found his quick, compact swing, which offers lots of power potential. He stings the ball to all fields and has a good idea when it comes to the strike zone. Though he's fairly athletic, moves well and has decent hands, he was a poor defensive third baseman. He struggled with his footwork on throws and made too many errors. A center fielder at University of Florida before transferring to junior college, Raburn seems to have found a home at second base. He was remarkably solid there during the fall, and some scouts say he has the ceiling of a Jeff Kent. Raburn likely will advance to Double-A because Michael Woods will have to repeat high Class A.

Year	Club (League)	Class	AVG	G	AB	R	H	2B	3B	HR	RBI	BB	SO	SB	SLG	OBP
2001	Tigers (GCL)	R	.155	19	58	4	9	2	0	1	5	9	19	2	.241	.300
	Oneonta (NY-P)	A	.363	44	171	25	62	17	8	8	42	17	42	1	.696	.418
2002	Tigers (GCL)	R	.300	8	30	4	9	3	1	1	5	3	7	0	.567	.364
	West Michigan (Mid)	A	.220	40	150	27	33	10	1	6	28	16	46	0	.420	.306
2003	West Michigan (Mid)	A	.351	16	57	14	20	7	0	3	12	6	14	1	.632	.431
	Lakeland (FSL)	A	.222	95	325	52	72	14	3	12	56	45	89	2	.394	.332
MINOR LEAGUE TOTALS			.259	222	791	126	205	53	13	31	148	96	217	6	.477	.351

12 Wilkin Ramirez, 3b

Born: Oct. 25, 1985. **Ht.:** 6-2. **Wt.:** 190. **Bats:** R. **Throws:** R. **Career Transactions:** Signed out of Dominican Republic by Tigers, Feb. 5, 2003.

The Tigers beat out several teams and spent $300,000 to sign Ramirez out of the Dominican Republic last February, and it appears at this point to be a good investment. He's a big, strong, righthanded hitter who idolizes Manny Ramirez (no relation), and he has copied many of his mannerisms. Ramirez struck out frequently during his pro debut in the

Gulf Coast League but when he did connect, he showed power to all fields. He's advanced for a teenager, as he hits offspeed stuff surprisingly well and doesn't chase many pitches out of the strike zone. He has average speed and arm strength, but he's raw defensively. He led GCL third basemen with 21 errors in 48 games. Detroit likes Ramirez' makeup and may jump him to low Class A to begin 2004.

Year	Club (League)	Class	AVG	G	AB	R	H	2B	3B	HR	RBI	BB	SO	SB	SLG	OBP
2003	Tigers (GCL)	R	.275	54	200	34	55	6	7	5	35	13	51	6	.450	.321
MINOR LEAGUE TOTALS			.275	54	200	34	55	6	7	5	35	13	51	6	.450	.321

13 Chris Shelton, 1b/c

Born: June 26, 1980. **Ht.:** 6-0. **Wt.:** 220. **Bats:** R. **Throws:** R. **School:** University of Utah. **Career Transactions:** Selected by Pirates in 33rd round of 2001 draft; signed June 10, 2001 . . . Selected by Tigers from Pirates in Rule 5 major league draft, Dec. 15, 2003.

The Tigers popped Shelton out of the Pirates system with the first pick in December's major league Rule 5 draft. Given Shelton's track record for hitting, many teams were surprised that Pittsburgh left their minor league player of the year unprotected. After leading the low Class A South Atlantic League in on-base and slugging percentage in 2002, he did the same in the high Class A Carolina League last year. He also added batting and home run titles en route to winning the CL MVP award. A 33rd-round pick in 2001, Shelton was ticketed for a backup role in short-season ball that summer before an injury to another player gave him an opening as a starter. He may not excite scouts with his stocky build, but he can hit all pitches to all fields, both for power and average. He also works the count well and draws lots of walks. Shelton's biggest need is to find a position. He's subpar defensively and can't run. He doesn't move well behind the plate or at first base, and he threw out just 25 percent of basestealers last year. In many ways, he's similar to the Pirates' Craig Wilson, who came up through the minors as a catcher. Shelton also tried third base and left field in instructional league with the Pirates. If he keeps hitting, his lack of athleticism will be overlooked. The Tigers have been disappointed with Carlos Pena so far and don't have much in the way of first-base prospects, so they'll make every effort to keep Shelton. If he doesn't stay on their 25-man roster all year, they have to slide him through waivers and then offer him back to Pittsburgh for half the $50,000 draft price. Detroit retained all three of its major league Rule 5 picks a year ago and should be able to do the same with Shelton.

Year	Club (League)	Class	AVG	G	AB	R	H	2B	3B	HR	RBI	BB	SO	SB	SLG	OBP
2001	Williamsport (NY-P)	A	.305	50	174	22	53	11	0	2	33	33	31	4	.402	.415
2002	Hickory (SAL)	A	.340	93	332	72	113	27	2	17	65	47	74	0	.587	.425
2003	Lynchburg (Car)	A	.359	95	315	71	113	24	1	21	69	68	67	1	.641	.478
	Altoona (EL)	AA	.279	35	122	17	34	10	1	0	14	8	23	0	.377	.331
MINOR LEAGUE TOTALS			.332	273	943	182	313	72	4	40	181	156	195	5	.544	.430

14 Cody Ross, of

Born: Dec. 23, 1980. **Ht.:** 5-11. **Wt.:** 180. **Bats:** R. **Throws:** L. **School:** Carlsbad (N.M.) HS. **Career Transactions:** Selected by Tigers in fourth round of 1999 draft; signed June 12, 1999.

There's a lot of debate among scouts and baseball officials when it comes to Ross' tools. Yet there's no denying his solid, consistent production throughout the minor leagues. He made his major league debut last July, and after a September callup he hit a grand slam off Cleveland's Cliff Lee. Later in that game he tore the anterior cruciate ligament in his left knee while legging out a bunt. Scouts who like Ross see him as a poor man's Craig Biggio or Bobby Higginson. He's tough and has surprising power for someone his size. Scouts who aren't high on him see a smallish player with more heart than tools. He doesn't run like Biggio did in his prime or have Higginson's pull power. He has good outfield instincts and can play in center, but he fits better in right with his strong, accurate arm. Ross isn't selective and will have to tighten his strike zone against big league pitchers. His grit has helped him during his rehabilitation, which has gone well. Ross will get a shot to make the Tigers during spring training but likely will begin the season in Triple-A.

Year	Club (League)	Class	AVG	G	AB	R	H	2B	3B	HR	RBI	BB	SO	SB	SLG	OBP
1999	Tigers (GCL)	R	.218	42	142	19	31	8	3	4	18	16	28	3	.401	.304
2000	West Michigan (Mid)	A	.267	122	434	71	116	17	9	7	68	55	83	11	.396	.356
2001	Lakeland (FSL)	A	.276	127	482	84	133	34	5	15	80	44	96	28	.461	.337
2002	Erie (EL)	AA	.280	105	400	73	112	28	3	19	72	44	86	16	.508	.352
2003	Toledo (IL)	AAA	.287	124	470	74	135	35	6	20	61	32	86	15	.515	.333
	Detroit (AL)	MAJ	.211	6	19	1	4	1	0	1	5	1	3	0	.421	.286
MAJOR LEAGUE TOTALS			.211	6	19	1	4	1	0	1	5	1	3	0	.421	.286
MINOR LEAGUE TOTALS			.273	520	1928	321	527	122	26	65	299	191	379	73	.465	.341

15 Humberto Sanchez, rhp

Born: May 28, 1983. **Ht.:** 6-6. **Wt.:** 230. **Bats:** R. **Throws:** R. **School:** Connors State (Okla.) JC.
Career Transactions: Selected by Tigers in 31st round of 2001 draft; signed May 27, 2002.

Sanchez had surgery to remove scar tissue from his arm as a freshman at Rockland (N.Y.) Community College in April 2001, but the Tigers took him anyway that year as a draft-and-follow in the 31st round. When he flashed first-round talent at Connors State the following spring, they signed him for $1 million. Sanchez reminds scouts of Roberto Hernandez because he has the same build and arm action. He can intimidate hitters with his fastball, which sits at 92-93 mph and has plus-plus heavy sink. His curveball is improving and is an above-average pitch at times. Sanchez didn't dominate as expected last season because his mechanics kept going awry. When that happens, he can't command his pitches. Because he's not athletic, he has trouble repeating his delivery. Sanchez has yet to develop an effective changeup, so his future may be in relief. He remains a long-term project and will begin 2004 in high Class A.

Year	Club (League)	Class	W	L	ERA	G	GS	CG	SV	IP	H	R	ER	HR	BB	SO	AVG
2002	Oneonta (NY-P)	A	2	2	3.62	9	9	0	0	32	29	18	13	1	21	26	.244
2003	West Michigan (Mid)	A	7	7	4.42	23	23	0	0	116	107	71	57	3	78	96	.249
MINOR LEAGUE TOTALS			9	9	4.25	32	32	0	0	148	136	89	70	4	99	122	.248

16 Fernando Rodney, rhp

Born: March 18, 1977. **Ht.:** 5-11. **Wt.:** 200. **Bats:** R. **Throws:** R. **Career Transactions:** Signed out of Dominican Republic by Tigers, Nov. 1, 1997.

A couple of years ago, the Tigers considered Rodney one of the best young prospects in the organization. Then they discovered that he was born in 1977 rather than 1981, so "young" no longer applied. Rodney remains a prospect, however, because he throws 98 mph consistently and has had success as a closer at the higher levels of the minors. He also throws an above-average changeup and a serviceable slider. In two extensive stints in the major leagues, Rodney has been hit hard because of poor pitch selection and location. Time after time he has gone to his changeup as an out pitch and left it up and over the plate. Though his fastball has plenty of heat, it's straight and arrives on a flat plane. In order to stick as a big leaguer, Rodney must learn to work his fastball around the edges of the strike zone to set up hitters for his changeup. Detroit, which didn't have a pitcher with more than five saves last year, will include Rodney in its closer competition this spring.

Year	Club (League)	Class	W	L	ERA	G	GS	CG	SV	IP	H	R	ER	HR	BB	SO	AVG
1998	Tigers (DSL)	R	1	3	3.38	11	5	0	1	32	25	16	12	4	19	37	.214
1999	Tigers (GCL)	R	3	3	2.40	22	0	0	9	30	20	8	8	1	21	39	.200
	Lakeland (FSL)	A	1	0	1.42	4	0	0	2	6	7	1	1	0	1	5	.304
2000	West Michigan (Mid)	A	6	4	2.94	22	10	0	2	83	74	34	27	2	35	56	.238
2001	Lakeland (FSL)	A	4	2	3.42	16	9	0	0	55	53	26	21	2	19	44	.249
	Tigers (GCL)	R	0	0	0.00	1	1	0	0	1	0	0	0	0	1	1	.000
	Erie (EL)	AA	0	0	4.26	4	0	0	1	6	7	3	3	1	3	8	.292
2002	Erie (EL)	AA	1	0	1.33	21	0	0	11	20	14	4	3	0	5	18	.194
	Detroit (AL)	MAJ	1	3	6.00	20	0	0	0	18	25	15	12	2	10	10	.329
	Toledo (IL)	AAA	1	1	0.81	20	0	0	4	22	13	4	2	1	9	25	.171
2003	Toledo (IL)	AAA	1	1	1.33	38	0	0	23	41	22	6	6	0	13	58	.163
	Detroit (AL)	MAJ	1	3	6.07	27	0	0	3	30	35	20	20	2	17	33	.294
MAJOR LEAGUE TOTALS			2	6	6.04	47	0	0	3	48	60	35	32	4	27	43	.308
MINOR LEAGUE TOTALS			18	14	2.52	159	25	0	51	297	235	102	83	11	126	291	.219

17 Preston Larrison, rhp

Born: Nov. 19, 1980. **Ht.:** 6-4. **Wt.:** 230. **Bats:** R. **Throws:** R. **School:** University of Evansville.
Career Transactions: Selected by Tigers in second round of 2001 draft; signed July 13, 2001.

Larrison picked up the victory at the 2003 Futures Game, but he arrived at the minor league all-star contest with a 5.32 ERA and in the midst of a three-month winless drought. It was a rare highlight for Larrison, who plummeted from his No. 2 ranking on this list a year ago. Going back to his college days, he has struggled to maintain success from season to season. Projected as a first-round pick entering his junior season in 2001, he didn't perform well under the pressure of his draft. He pitched well in high Class A in 2002 before laboring last year in Double-A. It's not a matter of stuff. Larrison has good command of a heavy 92 mph sinker and a plus changeup. But he can't put away hitters because he doesn't have an effective breaking ball. His fastball and changeup arrive on the same plane, another reason he's easy to hit. He was out of shape and needs to concentrate on physical conditioning. After nearly making Detroit's staff out of spring training in 2003, he pressed too much and tried to be too fine with his pitches, falling behind in the count too often. Though he was added to the 40-man roster in November, he'll have to pitch well this spring to avoid returning to Double-A.

Year	Club (League)	Class	W	L	ERA	G	GS	CG	SV	IP	H	R	ER	HR	BB	SO	AVG
2001	Oneonta (NY-P)	A	1	3	2.47	10	8	0	0	47	37	22	13	1	21	50	.208
2002	Lakeland (FSL)	A	10	5	2.39	21	19	3	0	120	86	39	32	6	45	92	.200
2003	Erie (EL)	AA	4	12	5.61	24	24	0	0	127	161	89	79	10	59	53	.322
	Toledo (IL)	AAA	0	1	3.38	1	1	0	0	5	3	3	2	1	2	3	.158
MINOR LEAGUE TOTALS			15	21	3.78	56	52	3	0	300	287	153	126	18	127	198	.254

18 Jon Connolly, lhp

Born: Aug. 24, 1983. **Ht.:** 6-0. **Wt.:** 200. **Bats:** R. **Throws:** L. **School:** Oneonta (N.Y.) HS.
Career Transactions: Selected by Tigers in 28th round of 2001 draft; signed June 26, 2001.

Let the debate over his ultimate value rage. Connolly topped the minors in ERA and fell one victory short of tying for the minor league lead last year, but he did it with a plus-plus changeup and excellent command. Skeptics point to his 83-88 mph fastball and below-average curveball and wonder how he'll be able to succeed at higher levels. Those who believe in him say he can locate any of his pitches wherever he wants and has such superb feel that he could become a No. 5 starter. Connolly, whose brother Mike pitches in the Pirates system, spent 2002 pitching in his hometown (short-season Oneonta) with no hint of this success. He doesn't project to throw any harder, so a key for him will be improving his curve. In addition to his lack of velocity, there are concerns about Connolly's athleticism and whether he'll be able to control his weight. He'll have to prove himself all over again this year in high Class A.

Year	Club (League)	Class	W	L	ERA	G	GS	CG	SV	IP	H	R	ER	HR	BB	SO	AVG
2001	Tigers (GCL)	R	1	1	3.82	8	6	0	0	35	30	16	15	0	10	23	.227
	Oneonta (NY-P)	A	0	1	18.00	1	1	0	0	3	8	6	6	1	1	1	.533
2002	Oneonta (NY-P)	A	5	3	4.01	14	14	0	0	85	102	46	38	7	10	50	.294
2003	West Michigan (Mid)	A	16	3	1.41	25	25	5	0	166	128	37	26	4	38	104	.212
MINOR LEAGUE TOTALS			22	8	2.64	48	46	5	0	290	268	105	85	12	59	178	.244

19 Donald Kelly, ss/3b

Born: Feb. 15, 1980. **Ht.:** 6-4. **Wt.:** 190. **Bats:** L. **Throws:** R. **School:** Point Park (Pa.) College.
Career Transactions: Selected by Tigers in eighth round of 2001 draft; signed June 12, 2001.

Unlike Omar Infante, Ramon Santiago and Anderson Hernandez, Kelly was a young shortstop who didn't disappoint the Tigers in 2003. Kelly was the high Class A Florida State League's all-star shortstop—though he played just 20 games there and served a utility role at Lakeland in deference to Hernandez—and held his own following a promotion to Double-A. His biggest assets are his knowledge of the strike zone and his ability to put the ball in play. In an organization where hitters tend to strike out too much and don't draw enough walks, his approach is refreshing. Tall and rangy, he has sure hands but lacks the range to be an everyday shortstop in the big leagues. He has solid-average speed and covers ground better at third base. However, Kelly doesn't have anywhere near the pop necessary to play regularly at the hot corner in the majors. Unless he develops a power stroke, which appears unlikely at this point, his future lies as a utilityman. Added to the 40-man roster this offseason, he could make his big league debut late in 2004.

Year	Club (League)	Class	AVG	G	AB	R	H	2B	3B	HR	RBI	BB	SO	SB	SLG	OBP
2001	Oneonta (NY-P)	A	.286	67	262	41	75	8	3	0	25	25	16	8	.340	.345
2002	West Michigan (Mid)	A	.286	128	455	72	130	21	5	1	59	59	40	9	.360	.368
2003	Lakeland (FSL)	A	.317	87	303	48	96	17	4	1	38	45	25	15	.409	.401
	Erie (EL)	AA	.265	22	83	14	22	5	1	1	13	15	9	0	.386	.378
MINOR LEAGUE TOTALS			.293	304	1103	175	323	51	13	3	135	144	90	32	.371	.373

20 Nook Logan, of

Born: Nov. 28, 1979. **Ht.:** 6-2. **Wt.:** 180. **Bats:** B. **Throws:** R. **School:** Copiah-Lincoln (Miss.) CC. **Career Transactions:** Selected by Tigers in third round of 2000 draft; signed July 8, 2000.

Converted from a center fielder into a shortstop and turned into a switch-hitter after his first pro season, Logan continues to intrigue the Tigers. His speed grades as a 70 on the 20-80 scouting scale, and he's a surehanded, instinctive center fielder with an average arm. But it's still not clear whether he'll ever hit enough to become a factor in the major leagues. His numbers have been remarkably consistent during his three years in full-season ball, and that's not a good thing. His lack of strength is the main problem, as he can't pull the ball or hit it the opposite way with authority from either side of the plate. His plate discipline also is weak, and the bottom line is that he can't get on base enough to take advantage of his speed. At 24, Logan no longer is young in baseball terms. He spent the offseason at Detroit's spring-training base in Lakeland, Fla., trying to build up his strength. The Tigers will find out if his hard work pays off this year in Triple-A.

Year	Club (League)	Class	AVG	G	AB	R	H	2B	3B	HR	RBI	BB	SO	SB	SLG	OBP
2000	Tigers (GCL)	R	.279	43	136	29	38	2	2	0	14	31	36	20	.324	.412
	Lakeland (FSL)	A	.333	11	42	4	14	1	0	0	3	2	13	2	.357	.364
2001	West Michigan (Mid)	A	.262	128	522	82	137	19	8	1	27	53	129	67	.335	.330
2002	Lakeland (FSL)	A	.269	124	506	75	136	14	7	2	26	40	111	55	.336	.321
2003	Erie (EL)	AA	.251	136	514	71	129	16	7	4	38	51	103	37	.333	.316
MINOR LEAGUE TOTALS			.264	442	1720	261	454	52	24	7	108	177	392	181	.334	.332

21 Roberto Novoa, rhp

Born: Aug. 15, 1979. **Ht.:** 6-5. **Wt.:** 200. **Bats:** R. **Throws:** R. **Career Transactions:** Signed out of Dominican Republic by Pirates, July 3, 1999 . . . Traded by Pirates to Tigers, Dec. 17, 2002, as part of trade in which Tigers sent 1B Randall Simon to Pirates for two players to be named (Nov. 25, 2002).

Along with Kody Kirkland, Novoa and lefthander Adrian Burnside were the players acquired from the Pirates for Randall Simon. The reason the Tigers wanted Novoa remains the reason why they're confident he'll be part of the big league staff in the near future. He's a tall righthander who consistently throws between 93-95 mph with nice sink on his fastball. He also has a quick-breaking curveball that some scouts refer to as a slurve. Novoa commands both pitches well. He's also developing a splitter that hasn't become a factor yet. Novoa was used as a starter last season, but doesn't have a useable changeup and is essentially a two-pitch pitcher. In all likelihood he'll be a set-up man in the majors, but he'll probably pitch out of the Double-A rotation in 2004 to give him more innings to work on a third pitch.

Year	Club (League)	Class	W	L	ERA	G	GS	CG	SV	IP	H	R	ER	HR	BB	SO	AVG
2000	Pirates (DSL)	R	4	6	4.15	13	13	1	0	82	99	65	38	5	29	44	.289
2001	Williamsport (NY-P)	A	5	5	3.39	14	13	1	0	80	76	40	30	4	20	55	.255
2002	Hickory (SAL)	A	1	5	5.48	10	10	0	0	43	61	30	26	2	15	29	.335
	Williamsport (NY-P)	A	8	3	3.65	12	12	0	0	67	62	32	27	4	8	56	.240
2003	Lakeland (FSL)	A	4	5	3.73	19	15	2	0	99	93	45	41	8	25	71	.243
MINOR LEAGUE TOTALS			22	24	3.94	68	63	4	0	370	391	212	162	23	97	255	.267

22 Eulogio de la Cruz, rhp

Born: March 12, 1984. **Ht.:** 5-11. **Wt.:** 170. **Bats:** R. **Throws:** R. **Career Transactions:** Signed out of Dominican Republic by Tigers, Sept. 6, 2001.

De la Cruz has pitched well the last two years in the Gulf Coast League but has been hammered in brief stints in the New York-Penn League. He enjoyed being thrust into the closer's role in 2003, excelling thanks to his fastball. He hits 96 mph consistently and made strides last season in terms of getting ahead in the count with his heater. He also has a good feel for pitching and the competitive nature needed to finish games. De la Cruz has the makings of a good breaking ball, though it has only intermittent success at this early stage of his development. He needs to refine his secondary pitches and his command. Because he's short, he's at a disadvantage because his fastball comes at hitters on a flat plane. He showed enough last year that he may begin 2004 in low Class A.

Year	Club (League)	Class	W	L	ERA	G	GS	CG	SV	IP	H	R	ER	HR	BB	SO	AVG
2002	Tigers (GCL)	R	1	1	2.63	20	0	0	1	38	40	24	11	0	21	46	.260
	Oneonta (NY-P)	A	0	0	23.14	2	0	0	0	2	7	8	6	0	4	4	.500
2003	Tigers (GCL)	R	2	2	2.59	22	0	0	7	24	18	10	7	0	15	30	.205
	Oneonta (NY-P)	A	0	0	10.80	2	0	0	0	3	6	4	4	0	1	4	.400
MINOR LEAGUE TOTALS			3	3	3.72	46	0	0	8	68	71	46	28	0	41	84	.262

23 Josh Rainwater, rhp

Born: April 9, 1985. **Ht.:** 6-1. **Wt.:** 220. **Bats:** R. **Throws:** R. **School:** DeRidder (La.) HS. **Career Transactions:** Selected by Tigers in fourth round of 2003 draft; signed June 7, 2003.

The Tigers look at getting a high school prospect with Rainwater's arm strength in the fourth round of the 2003 draft as a pleasant fallout of the "Moneyball" craze for college players. Detroit officials said in past years, Rainwater could have gone as high as the second round. Rainwater capped his high school career by tossing a no-hitter in the Louisiana 4-A semifinals and then coming back the next day to strike out six of the seven batters he faced to save the finale. Because he worked so hard, the Tigers kept him on tight pitch counts in the Gulf Coast League. He reached 95 mph during the spring but sat at 89-92 mph in his pro debut. He's relatively refined for a high school pitcher, but his fastball command and his offspeed pitches are inconsistent. There's some concern within the organization about his lack of athleticism, and Detroit would like him to shed weight and get in better condition. He could start this year in low Class A.

Year	Club (League)	Class	W	L	ERA	G	GS	CG	SV	IP	H	R	ER	HR	BB	SO	AVG
2003	Tigers (GCL)	R	1	2	4.78	10	9	0	0	38	41	23	20	4	20	40	.273
MINOR LEAGUE TOTALS			1	2	4.78	10	9	0	0	38	41	23	20	4	20	40	.273

24 Gilberto Mejia, ss

Born: Sept. 1, 1982. **Ht.:** 5-9. **Wt.:** 160. **Bats:** B. **Throws:** R. **Career Transactions:** Signed out of Dominican Republic by Tigers, April 26, 2000.

Mejia failed to establish himself in low Class A in both 2002 and 2003, but he took off after a demotion to the Gulf Coast League last June. He led the GCL in hitting and slugging while finishing second in stolen bases. The downside is that he was old for a complex league at 20. Mejia has good physical tools. He has above-average speed and can drive the ball with authority to all fields. Primarily a second baseman in the past, he moved to shortstop in the GCL. His hands are suspect and his arm isn't strong or accurate, so the Tigers may try him in the outfield in 2004. His future probably lies as a utilityman. Mejia still has to prove he can hit and control the strike zone above the lowest levels of the minors. Detroit hopes his third try at West Michigan will be the charm.

Year	Club (League)	Class	AVG	G	AB	R	H	2B	3B	HR	RBI	BB	SO	SB	SLG	OBP
2000	Tigers (DSL)	R	.248	39	129	28	32	6	3	1	16	20	28	5	.364	.353
2001	Tigers (DSL)	R	.270	65	241	53	65	12	4	0	22	38	40	16	.353	.374
2002	West Michigan (Mid)	A	.246	19	69	17	17	4	2	2	15	11	23	4	.449	.341
2003	West Michigan (Mid)	A	.200	34	115	14	23	2	1	1	9	8	31	0	.261	.252
	Oneonta (NY-P)	A	.238	6	21	4	5	1	1	0	5	3	3	1	.381	.333
	Tigers (GCL)	R	.360	44	175	36	63	11	9	5	29	13	29	23	.611	.400
MINOR LEAGUE TOTALS			.273	207	750	152	205	36	20	9	96	93	154	49	.411	.354

25 Anderson Hernandez, ss

Born: Oct. 30, 1982. **Ht.:** 5-9. **Wt.:** 160. **Bats:** B. **Throws:** R. **Career Transactions:** Signed out of Dominican Republic by Tigers, April 23, 2001.

Shaken by the death of his father and struggling with other off-field issues, Hernandez had a disappointing season in 2003. He remains the best defensive infielder in the system, with exceptional range, extraordinarily fluid movements, a cannon arm and soft hands. But just when it was expected he would step up his offensive production, it declined while he repeated high Class A. Hernandez lacks strength and plate discipline. He seldom pulls the ball and he swings at way too many bad pitches. He has plus speed but doesn't reach base enough to use it. There also are concerns surrounding his makeup. Hernandez' career is at a crossroads and he'll have to rebound in 2004, probably in Double-A. Last year's third-round pick, Tony Giarratano, has already moved way past him as the system's top shortstop.

Year	Club (League)	Class	AVG	G	AB	R	H	2B	3B	HR	RBI	BB	SO	SB	SLG	OBP
2001	Tigers (GCL)	R	.264	55	216	37	57	5	11	0	18	13	38	34	.389	.303
	Lakeland (FSL)	A	.190	7	21	2	4	0	1	0	1	0	8	0	.286	.190
2002	Lakeland (FSL)	A	.259	123	410	52	106	13	7	2	42	33	102	16	.339	.310
2003	Lakeland (FSL)	A	.229	106	380	47	87	11	4	2	28	27	69	15	.295	.278
MINOR LEAGUE TOTALS			.247	291	1027	138	254	29	23	4	89	73	217	65	.332	.295

26 Eric Eckenstahler, lhp

Born: Dec. 17, 1976. **Ht.:** 6-7. **Wt.:** 220. **Bats:** L. **Throws:** L. **School:** Illinois State University. **Career Transactions:** Selected by Tigers in 32nd round of 1999 draft; signed May 25, 2000.

Eckenstahler is 27, an elderly age for a prospect, and he has pitched just 23 innings in the majors. Signed as a fifth-year senior draft-and-follow out of Illinois State, he doesn't project as either a starter or a late-inning reliever. But he could have a big league career in middle relief because he's a 6-foot-7 lefthander with a 90 mph fastball. He has a somewhat deceptive motion that hitters have difficulty picking up, and he has enough slider and command to go once through an order. When Eckenstahler struggles, it's because he tends to nibble too much. He's effective against righthanders, so he's not limited to a situational role. Sometimes compared to Graeme Lloyd, he should break camp with the Tigers. Though he worked just 16 innings for Detroit in 2003, his 2.87 ERA was the lowest on the big league staff.

Year	Club (League)	Class	W	L	ERA	G	GS	CG	SV	IP	H	R	ER	HR	BB	SO	AVG
2000	West Michigan (Mid)	A	0	2	5.79	10	3	0	1	19	21	15	12	4	11	22	.280
	Oneonta (NY-P)	A	0	0	1.64	8	0	0	0	11	7	3	2	0	3	13	.175
2001	Lakeland (FSL)	A	1	0	1.50	4	0	0	1	6	3	1	1	0	2	7	.158
	Erie (EL)	AA	4	2	3.90	46	0	0	4	65	65	32	28	7	31	73	.257
2002	Toledo (IL)	AAA	2	4	4.43	52	0	0	0	67	57	37	33	8	35	69	.234
	Detroit (AL)	MAJ	1	0	5.63	7	0	0	0	8	14	5	5	1	2	13	.378
2003	Toledo (IL)	AAA	3	6	3.16	39	0	0	0	43	32	21	15	2	25	40	.213
	Detroit (AL)	MAJ	0	0	2.87	20	0	0	0	16	9	6	5	0	15	12	.167
MAJOR LEAGUE TOTALS			1	0	3.80	27	0	0	0	24	23	11	10	1	17	25	.253
MINOR LEAGUE TOTALS			10	14	3.90	159	3	0	6	210	185	109	91	21	107	224	.237

27 Lino Urdaneta, rhp

Born: Nov. 20, 1979. **Ht.:** 6-1. **Wt.:** 168. **Bats:** R. **Throws:** R. **Career Transactions:** Signed out of Venezuela by Dodgers, Aug. 31, 1996 . . . Granted free agency, Oct. 15, 2003 . . . Signed by Indians, Nov. 10, 2003 . . . Selected by Tigers from Indians in Rule 5 major league draft, Dec. 15, 2003.

After seven seasons in the Dodgers system, Urdaneta signed with the Indians as a minor league free agent in November. A month later, the Tigers took him in the third round of the major league Rule 5 draft because they clocked him at 98 mph in the Venezuelan League. They carried three Rule 5 picks though the entire 2003 season, but after actively signing free agents this offseason, it will be harder to keep all three of their Rule 5 choices in 2004: first baseman/catcher Chris Shelton, situational lefty Mike Bumatay and Urdaneta. After saving 32 games in 2002, Urdaneta couldn't repeat that success in Double-A last year. While he complements his fastball with a hard slider, he has trouble repeating his pitches, doesn't throw enough strikes and doesn't miss enough bats. Urdaneta's velocity alone makes him a worthwhile gamble, but he has to be put on waivers and offered back to Cleveland for half the $50,000 draft price if Detroit can't give him a roster spot all season.

Year	Club (League)	Class	W	L	ERA	G	GS	CG	SV	IP	H	R	ER	HR	BB	SO	AVG
1997	San Joaquin 2 (VSL)	R	6	3	2.04	13	0	0	0	62	46	23	14	3	21	37	—
1998	Dodgers (DSL)	R	6	1	2.26	12	12	1	0	56	43	18	14	1	26	44	.214
1999	Vero Beach (FSL)	A	5	4	4.84	27	5	0	0	67	74	42	36	10	20	43	.286
2000	Vero Beach (FSL)	A	5	4	5.42	27	5	0	1	78	103	60	47	7	24	40	.325
2001	Wilmington (SAL)	A	1	2	7.61	10	4	0	0	24	31	23	20	7	11	16	.330
2002	Vero Beach (FSL)	A	2	2	2.41	52	0	0	32	52	39	15	14	3	17	30	.207
	Jacksonville (SL)	AA	0	0	0.00	1	0	0	0	1	3	0	0	0	1	1	.600
2003	Jacksonville (SL)	AA	0	8	4.29	44	0	0	6	65	68	37	31	4	24	42	.280
MINOR LEAGUE TOTALS			25	24	3.92	186	26	1	39	404	407	218	176	35	144	253	.276

28 Mike Bumatay, lhp

Born: Oct. 9, 1979. **Ht.:** 6-0. **Wt.:** 170. **Bats:** L. **Throws:** L. **School:** Clovis (Calif.) HS. **Career Transactions:** Selected by Pirates in 21st round of 1998 draft; signed June 20, 1998 . . . Selected by Rockies from Pirates in Rule 5 minor league draft, Dec. 16, 2002 . . . Selected by Tigers from Rockies in Rule 5 major league draft, Dec.15, 2003.

Another major league Rule 5 pick, Bumatay was targeted by the Tigers as a situational lefthander and has a better chance of sticking with the big league club than Luis Urdaneta. Bumatay was selected from the Rockies, who had taken him from the Pirates in the 2002 minor league Rule 5 draft. He got hit hard in Double-A at the beginning of last season, but righted himself after a demotion and was untouchable over the last three months. His deceptive delivery is tough on lefties. Bumatay's best pitch is a 72-75 mph curveball, and he backs it up with an 87-89 mph fastball and an average changeup. His fastball runs in on lefties, while his changeup sinks. Bumatay isn't afraid to throw inside to righties, and his fastball picked up 1-2 mph last year. His biggest need is to improve his command. His stuff won't overmatch big league hitters by any means, so he'll have to locate his pitches to succeed. Colorado nearly protected Bumatay on its 40-man roster and probably would take him back if Detroit can't keep him on the big league roster.

Year	Club (League)	Class	W	L	ERA	G	GS	CG	SV	IP	H	R	ER	HR	BB	SO	AVG
1998	Pirates (GCL)	R	2	3	3.18	13	5	0	1	40	46	29	14	1	16	37	.282
1999	Pirates (GCL)	R	2	1	2.90	11	3	0	2	40	35	16	13	4	8	39	.241
2000	Williamsport (NY-P)	A	1	0	2.84	7	0	0	2	13	10	4	4	1	7	17	.217
	Hickory (SAL)	A	3	0	1.78	16	0	0	8	25	20	7	5	1	12	32	.217
2001	Lynchburg (Car)	A	1	7	7.27	23	1	0	2	43	55	39	35	4	26	40	.302
	Hickory (SAL)	A	1	0	2.73	15	1	0	0	26	20	10	8	0	8	31	.208
2002	Lynchburg (Car)	A	5	2	3.24	52	0	0	2	67	50	27	24	2	31	79	.208
2003	Tulsa (TL)	AA	4	1	2.60	40	0	0	1	55	42	20	16	4	29	69	.210
	Visalia (Cal)	A	0	0	0.00	8	0	0	2	9	1	0	0	0	5	16	.037
MINOR LEAGUE TOTALS			19	14	3.36	185	10	0	20	319	279	152	119	17	142	360	.234

29 Juan Tejeda, 1b

Born: Jan. 26, 1982. **Ht.:** 6-2. **Wt.:** 190. **Bats:** R. **Throws:** R. **Career Transactions:** Signed out of Dominican Republic by Tigers, July 7, 1999.

Tejeda has hit for average and produced runs since arriving in the United States in 2001, leading the Midwest League with 106 RBIs in 2002. He has good knowledge of the strike zone and puts the ball in play consistently. Yet most scouts say Tejeda lacks the pop to be an impact player in the majors and may not reach that level. He has a long, slow stroke and has yet to show any pull power. He also lacks speed and is a liability on defense, especially with his poor footwork and range. Unless he starts yanking pitches out of the park, Tejeda will have to hit for an even higher average and produce even more runs to make it to Comerica Park. He'll start 2004 in Double-A.

Year	Club (League)	Class	AVG	G	AB	R	H	2B	3B	HR	RBI	BB	SO	SB	SLG	OBP
1999	Tigers (DSL)	R	.276	42	152	26	42	9	2	5	26	14	33	1	.461	.360
2000	Tigers (DSL)	R	.312	66	260	52	81	20	3	10	46	16	45	2	.527	.374
2001	Tigers (GCL)	R	.295	50	173	17	51	8	1	4	37	8	32	0	.422	.344
2002	West Michigan (Mid)	A	.300	137	524	68	157	34	6	11	106	60	89	5	.450	.372
2003	Lakeland (FSL)	A	.280	125	461	63	129	28	4	10	76	56	68	6	.423	.360
MINOR LEAGUE TOTALS			.293	420	1570	226	460	99	16	40	291	154	267	14	.453	.365

30 Michael Woods, 2b

Born: Sept. 11, 1980. **Ht.:** 6-1. **Wt.:** 200. **Bats:** R. **Throws:** R. **School:** Southern University. **Career Transactions:** Selected by Tigers in second round of 2001 draft; signed June 29, 2001.

The Tigers were thrilled when Woods was available to them with the 32nd overall pick in 2001, when he beat out Southern teammate Rickie Weeks (who would become the No. 2 overall pick in 2003 for the Brewers) for the Southwestern Athletic Conference batting title. After a solid pro debut, Woods injured his knee in his first game in 2002 and required arthroscopic surgery. He came back later that season, only to hurt his other knee, and his career has been a struggle ever since. Woods still has the quick hands that attracted scouts to him in the first place, but he hits the ball with a lot of topspin and his drives tend to die in the gaps. If he's going to be a big league hitter, he'll have to get more lift on the ball. While he draws a lot of walks, he'll also have to make more consistent contact. Woods has average speed and the hands and arm to play second base, though he's not always fluid defensively. Converted third baseman Ryan Raburn has moved past Woods, who'll head back to high Class A.

Year	Club (League)	Class	AVG	G	AB	R	H	2B	3B	HR	RBI	BB	SO	SB	SLG	OBP
2001	Oneonta (NY-P)	A	.270	9	37	6	10	2	0	0	3	4	5	5	.324	.357
	West Michigan (Mid)	A	.270	44	163	30	44	8	4	0	17	32	44	13	.368	.401
2002	Lakeland (FSL)	A	.225	33	111	20	25	6	4	2	11	28	25	7	.405	.385
	Tigers (GCL)	R	.286	7	21	2	6	1	1	0	2	3	6	3	.429	.375
2003	Lakeland (FSL)	A	.205	116	361	38	74	12	4	0	27	52	92	10	.260	.304
MINOR LEAGUE TOTALS			.229	209	693	96	159	29	13	2	60	119	172	38	.317	.346

FLORIDA
MARLINS

Marlins owner Jeffrey Loria, team president David Samson and general manager Larry Beinfest considered 2002 a practice run of sorts after taking over franchise operations just days before the start of spring training. They promised 2003 would be different in every way. On the field. At the gate. In the community.

Then they went out and won the World Series, much to the shock and dismay of their former constituency in Montreal. Consider Marlins management officially rehabilitated after a season when plenty of things went wrong but all the big things went right.

With their front-office team in place for the start of 2002-03 offseason planning, the Marlins worked out a three-way deal with the Rockies and Braves that ranked among the most creative ever assembled. Mike Hampton wound up in Atlanta, Charles Johnson and Preston Wilson wound up in Colorado and Florida was left with Juan Pierre, Tim Spooneybarger and $23.5 million worth of Hampton's remaining obligation.

With their savings, the Marlins were able to add 10-time all-star Pudge Rodriguez as a free agent and deal for underachieving lefty Mark Redman. After the season started, Florida added Ugeuth Urbina and Chad Fox to its bullpen and Jeff Conine to its lineup. The Redman, Urbina and Conine deals cost the Marlins system eight quality prospects,

TOP 30 PROSPECTS

1. Jeremy Hermida, of
2. Jason Stokes, 1b
3. Jeff Allison, rhp
4. Scott Olsen, lhp
5. Yorman Bazardo, rhp
6. Josh Willingham, c
7. Bill Murphy, lhp
8. Eric Reed, of
9. Jai Miller, of
10. Trevor Hutchinson, rhp
11. Lincoln Holdzkom, rhp
12. Cole Seifrig, 2b
13. Lee Mitchell, 3b/ss
14. Ronald Belizario, rhp
15. Robert Andino, ss
16. Kevin Cave, rhp
17. Wilson Valdez, ss/2b
18. Chris Aguila, of
19. Franklyn Gracesqui, lhp
20. Jon-Michael Nickerson, lhp
21. Josh Wilson, ss
22. Victor Prieto, rhp
23. Logan Kensing, rhp
24. Josh Johnson, rhp
25. Mike Flannery, rhp
26. Pablo Sosa, 3b
27. David Marchbanks, lhp
28. Jonathan Fulton, ss
29. Chris Resop, rhp
30. Chip Ambres, of

By Mike Berardino

including Adrian Gonzalez, the No. 1 overall pick in 2000, and six other players who once had ranked among their Top 10 Prospects.

The two biggest additions, however, came from Double-A Carolina, where lefthander Dontrelle Willis (14 wins) and third baseman/outfielder Miguel Cabrera (62 RBIs in 87 games) began the year. A day after Willis arrived in the majors, manager Jeff Torborg and pitching coach Brad Arnsberg were fired after a 16-22 start. Under 72-year-old replacement Jack McKeon, the Marlins posted the majors' best record from May 23 on and became the second team in history to win the World Series after firing their manager during the season.

In the end, the Marlins' $54 million payroll ranked 21st in the majors. They were able to win 91 games, posting just the second winning mark in club history. They also made up a $110 million payroll difference to defeat the Yankees in six stirring games for the championship, their second in seven seasons. Florida still ranked 28th in home attendance, but its average of 16,290 was a 62 percent improvement over 2002.

Despite the loss of Willis, Cabrera and all three players in the Urbina deal, Double-A Carolina rolled to the Southern League title. Triple-A Albuquerque and high Class A Jupiter also reached the playoffs as the Marlins system went a combined 345-342, the second winning record in six seasons.

ORGANIZATION
OVERVIEW

General manager: Larry Beinfest. **Farm director:** Marc DelPiano. **Scouting director:** Stan Meek.

2003 PERFORMANCE

Class	Team	League	W	L	Pct.	Finish*	Manager(s)
Majors	Florida	National	91	71	.562	3rd (16)	J. Torborg/J. McKeon
Triple-A	Albuquerque Isotopes	Pacific Coast	74	70	.514	5th (16)	Dean Treanor
Double-A	Carolina Mudcats	Southern	80	58	.580	+1st (10)	Tracy Woodson
High A	Jupiter Hammerheads	Florida State	76	62	.551	3rd (12)	Luis Dorante
Low A	Greensboro Hornets	South Atlantic	67	69	.493	9th (16)	Steve Phillips
Short-season	Jamestown Jammers	New York-Penn	22	51	.301	13th (14)	Benny Castillo
Rookie	GCL Marlins	Gulf Coast	26	32	.448	11th (12)	Tim Cossins

OVERALL 2003 MINOR LEAGUE RECORD   345 342 .502 13th (30)

*Finish in overall standings (No. of teams in league). +League champion.

ORGANIZATION LEADERS

BATTING   *Minimum 250 At-Bats
*AVG	Miguel Cabrera, Carolina	.365
R	Eric Reed, Jupiter	86
H	Eric Reed, Jupiter	154
TB	Jason Wood, Albuquerque	222
2B	Jason Stokes, Jupiter	31
3B	Chip Ambres, Carolina	8
	Eric Reed, Jupiter	8
HR	Rob Stratton, Albuquerque	32
RBI	Jason Stokes, Jupiter	89
BB	Jeremy Hermida, Albuquerque/Greensboro	80
SO	Rob Stratton, Albuquerque	175
SB	Eric Reed, Jupiter	53
*SLG	Miguel Cabrera, Carolina	.609
*OBP	Matt Erickson, Albuquerque	.442

PITCHING   #Minimum 75 Innings
W	Phil Akens, Jupiter/Greensboro	13
L	Justin Wayne, Albuquerque/Jupiter	12
#ERA	Chris Key, Carolina/Jupiter	1.66
G	Ozwaldo Mairena, Albuquerque	61
CG	Yorman Bazardo, Greensboro	4
SV	Mike Flannery, Carolina	23
	Kevin Cave, Jupiter	23
IP	Nick Ungs, Carolina/Jupiter	170
BB	Three tied at	70
SO	Denny Bautista, Carolina/Jupiter	138

BEST TOOLS

Best Hitter for Average	Jeremy Hermida
Best Power Hitter	Jason Stokes
Fastest Baserunner	Eric Reed
Best Athlete	Jai Miller
Best Fastball	Jeff Allison
Best Curveball	Jeff Allison
Best Slider	Scott Olsen
Best Changeup	Mike Neu
Best Control	Nick Ungs
Best Defensive Catcher	Ryan Jorgensen
Best Defensive Infielder	Robert Andino
Best Infield Arm	Robert Andino
Best Defensive Outfielder	Eric Reed
Best Outfield Arm	Juan Lindesey

PROJECTED 2007 LINEUP

Catcher	Ramon Castro
First Base	Jason Stokes
Second Base	Luis Castillo
Third Base	Mike Lowell
Shortstop	Alex Gonzalez
Left Field	Miguel Cabrera
Center Field	Juan Pierre
Right Field	Jeremy Hermida
No. 1 Starter	Josh Beckett
No. 2 Starter	Dontrelle Willis
No. 3 Starter	Jeff Allison
No. 4 Starter	A.J. Burnett
No. 5 Starter	Scott Olsen
Closer	Yorman Bazardo

LAST YEAR'S TOP 20 PROSPECTS

1. Miguel Cabrera, 3b
2. Jason Stokes, 1b
3. Adrian Gonzalez, 1b
4. Dontrelle Willis, lhp
5. Jeremy Hermida, of
6. Don Levinski, rhp
7. Justin Wayne, rhp
8. Blaine Neal, rhp
9. Will Smith, of
10. Josh Wilson, ss
11. Ryan Snare, lhp
12. Ronald Belizario, rhp
13. Denny Bautista, rhp
14. Chip Ambres, of
15. Kevin Hooper, ss/2b
16. Abraham Nunez, of
17. Eric Reed, of
18. Victor Prieto, rhp
19. Robert Andino, ss
20. Scott Olsen, rhp

TOP PROSPECTS OF THE DECADE

1994	Charles Johnson, c
1995	Charles Johnson, c
1996	Edgar Renteria, ss
1997	Felix Heredia, lhp
1998	Mark Kotsay, of
1999	A.J. Burnett, rhp
2000	A.J. Burnett, rhp
2001	Josh Beckett, rhp
2002	Josh Beckett, rhp
2003	Miguel Cabrera, 3b

TOP DRAFT PICKS OF THE DECADE

1994	Josh Booty, 3b
1995	Jaime Jones, of
1996	Mark Kotsay, of
1997	Aaron Akin, rhp
1998	Chip Ambres, of
1999	Josh Beckett, rhp
2000	Adrian Gonzalez, 1b
2001	Garrett Berger, rhp (2)
2002	Jeremy Hermida, of
2003	Jeff Allison, rhp

ALL-TIME LARGEST BONUSES

Josh Beckett, 1999	$3,625,000
Adrian Gonzalez, 2000	$3,000,000
Livan Hernandez, 1996	$2,500,000
Jason Stokes, 2000	$2,027,000
Jeremy Hermida, 2002	$2,012,500

MINOR LEAGUE
DEPTH CHART

FLORIDA MARLINS
RANK: 14

Impact potential (B): Even after promoting Miguel Cabrera and Dontrelle Willis, and trading prospects Adrian Gonzalez and Denny Bautista, the Marlins system still boasts high-ceiling potential with Jeremy Hermida, Jason Stokes, Jeff Allison and Scott Olsen. Stokes' power is among the best in the minors, but he'll need to bounce back from an injury-riddled 2003 season.

Depth (C): The Marlins depth was so good that they were able to acquire the necessary pieces (Ugueth Urbina, Jeff Conine, Mark Redman) to push them over the top last October. Trades left them particularly thin in the upper levels, though there are encouraging signs coming from their drafts and strong Latin American presence.

Sleeper: Cole Seifrig, 2b.

—Depth charts prepared by Josh Boyd. Numbers in parentheses indicate prospect rankings.

LF
Chris Aguila (18)

CF
Eric Reed (8)
Jai Miller (9)
Chip Ambres (30)
Jose Aponte
Travis Ezi
Xavier Arroyo

RF
Jeremy Hermida (1)
Abraham Nunez
Kenny Berkenbosch

3B
Lee Mitchell (13)
Pablo Sosa (26)

SS
Robert Andino (15)
Wilson Valdez (17)
Josh Wilson (21)
Jonathan Fulton (28)

2B
Cole Seifrig (12)
Kevin Hooper

1B
Jason Stokes (2)
J.T. Restko
Ryan Bear
Pat Magness

SOURCE OF TALENT

Homegrown		Acquired	
College	7	Trades	1
Junior College	1	Rule 5 draft	1
Draft-and-follow	1	Independent	0
High school	14	Free agents/waivers	1
Nondrafted free agent	0		
Foreign	4		

C
Josh Willingham (6)
Ryan Jorgensen
Patrick Arlis

LHP

Starters	Relievers
Scott Olsen (4)	Franklyn Gracesqui (19)
Bill Murphy (7)	Zach McCormack
Jon-Michael Nickerson (20)	
David Marchbanks (27)	
Todd Moser	

RHP

Starters	Relievers
Jeff Allison (3)	Lincoln Holdzkom (11)
Yorman Bazardo (5)	Ronald Belizario (14)
Trevor Hutchinson (10)	Kevin Cave (16)
Victor Prieto (22)	Mike Flannery (25)
Logan Kensing (23)	Chris Resop (29)
Josh Johnson (24)	Nate Bump
Justin Wayne	Michael Neu
Nic Ungs	Mike Nannini
Jason Iehl	Jon Asahina
Phil Akens	Dustin Kupper
Randall Messenger	Jerrod Fuell
Allen Baxter	Casey Blalock
Henricus Vanden Hurk	Ross Wolf

DRAFT
ANALYSIS

2003 DRAFT

Best Pro Debut: LHP Jon Nickerson (16) went 5-1, 1.86 and threw a no-hitter in the Rookie-level Gulf Coast League. Finesse LHP David Marchbanks (7) posted a 1.91 ERA between three stops, including a quality start in Double-A.

Best Athlete: OF Jai Miller (4) and 2B Cole Seifrig (5) were both surprise early-round picks because most clubs figured they'd follow through on football scholarships. With Preston Wilson tools, Miller is the best athlete in the Marlins system. Seifrig isn't far behind.

Best Pure Hitter: Seifrig's sweet stroke gives him the most upside at the plate. He hit .280 between the GCL and the short-season New York-Penn League.

Best Raw Power: Miller batted just .206 with one homer in the GCL and NY-P, but the ball jumps off his bat. As he focuses on baseball, makes adjustments at the plate and fills out his 6-foot-3, 190-pound frame, he'll show more game power.

Fastest Runner: Miller's speed rates a 75 on the 20-80 scouting scale. He can go from the right side to first in 4.05 seconds.

Best Defensive Player: Miller is a natural center fielder. Lee Mitchell (6) is a good third baseman with a strong arm.

Best Fastball: RHP Jeff Allison (1) had the most electric arm in the 2003 draft. He gets a lot of movement on a 92-97 mph fastball. RHP Logan Kensing (2) can't match Allison's velocity, but he throws 90-94 mph and has even more impressive life with his fastball's heavy sink.

Best Breaking Ball: Allison's breaking pitch is as good as his fastball. When he gets on top of it, it's an untouchable 80-83 mph.

Most Intriguing Background: Unsigned RHPs Chilion (47) and Ashkelon Stapleton (48) are identical twins whom the Marlins will pursue as draft-and-follows in 2004.

Closest To The Majors: Kensing or Marchbanks. The Marlins may find it hard to hold back a pitcher with Allison's stuff.

Best Late-Round Pick: The Marlins spotted Nickerson while evaluating Miller in an Alabama high school all-star game. Nickerson, who had been more of a basketball player, has a very good changeup and life on a fastball that reaches 90-91 mph.

The One Who Got Away: LHP Tony Watson (23), who opted to attend Nebraska, is more advanced than Nickerson. Watson's projectable at 6-foot-4 and 185 pounds. He touches 90 mph and shows a feel for a curveball. The Marlins inked their top 16 picks.

Assessment: Allison slid out of the top 10 based on signability, but Florida was able to sign him for $1.85 million. After grabbing Kensing, projected as a first-rounder during the spring, the Marlins concentrated on athletes who offer high risks and high rewards.

Marchbanks — RICH ABEL

2002 DRAFT — GRADE: B+

OF Jeremy Hermida (1) has one of the sweetest swings in the game. The Marlins also have high hopes for LHP Scott Olsen (6), OF Eric Reed (9) and RHP Trevor Hutchinson (3).

2001 DRAFT — GRADE: F

Florida didn't have a first-rounder and its top two picks, RHPs Garrett Berger (2) and Allen Baxter (3), have barely pitched because of injuries. Unless RHP Lincoln Holdzkom (7) puts it all together, this draft looks bleak.

2000 DRAFT — GRADE: B+

1B Jason Stokes (2) possesses light-tower power. 1B Adrian Gonzalez (1), LHP Rob Henkel (3) and OF Will Smith (6) were used in deals for Ugueth Urbina and Mark Redman, who were crucial to the Marlins' 2003 championship run. Also keep an eye on C/1B Josh Willingham (17).

1999 DRAFT — GRADE: A

Florida doesn't make it to the World Series, let alone win it, without RHP Josh Beckett (1). How many Cy Young Awards are in his future? LHP Nate Robertson (5) was part of the Redman trade.

—Draft analysis prepared by Jim Callis. Numbers in parentheses indicate draft rounds.

Jeremy
Hermida

Born: Jan. 30, 1984.
Ht.: 6-4. **Wt.:** 200.
Bats: L. **Throws:** R.
School: Wheeler HS, Marietta, Ga.
Career Transactions: Selected by Marlins in first round (11th overall) of 2002 draft; signed July 5, 2002.

F ormer Marlins scouting director Jim Fleming (now the team's assistant general manager) could hardly believe his good fortune when Hermida was still available with the 11th pick in the 2002 draft. Rated the best pure high school hitter and the fourth-best position player overall, Hermida was projected as high as the second pick. The Marlins chose him over prep lefty Scott Kazmir (who ranks as the Mets' top prospect), then gave Hermida a $2,012,500 bonus. A natural righthanded hitter, Hermida was converted to the left side at age 4 by his father. He began practicing with a wood bat at 13 and received tutelage from former Braves outfielder Terry Harper. He later starred in Georgia's famed East Cobb youth program. A slow start at low Class A Greensboro in 2003 was attributed in part to poor weather that limited his extra work. Still, he finished the season as the No. 5 prospect in the South Atlantic League and led the league in walks.

Some scouts called Hermida the best high school hitter since Eric Chavez. Others saw a young Andy Van Slyke or Paul O'Neill. Hermida himself identified more with Shawn Green. Whichever comparison you prefer, there's no denying his polished hitting approach and advanced maturity. He has a smooth, quick stroke, top-notch plate discipline, a strong work ethic and first-rate makeup. He's comfortable working deep in counts and has no trouble taking pitches on the outer half to the gap in left-center. Hermida is durable, as he played through a minor ankle problem in 2002 and a minor heel injury in 2003. Though just an average runner, he has excellent instincts on the bases. He was thrown out just twice in 30 steal attempts last season, both on the back end of double steals. His arm is much improved to where it's now average. Though he has come a long way defensively, Hermida is far better coming in on balls than going back at this point. He needs to improve his upper-body strength to keep from wearing down over the course of the season. He hasn't shown much power so far but the Marlins believe that will increase as he adds lift to his swing and bulk to his tall, lean, broad-shouldered frame. Some see him as a 25-plus homer man in the majors because of his above-average bat speed. He still has trouble at times with pitches on his hands.

Hermida should start 2004 at high Class A Jupiter, but a midyear promotion to Double-A Carolina isn't out of the question. He could arrive in the majors by the end of 2005 if he continues on this career path.

Year	Club (League)	Class	AVG	G	AB	R	H	2B	3B	HR	RBI	BB	SO	SB	SLG	OBP
2002	Marlins (GCL)	R	.224	38	134	15	30	7	3	0	14	15	25	5	.321	.316
	Jamestown (NY-P)	A	.319	13	47	8	15	2	1	0	7	7	10	1	.404	.407
2003	Greensboro (SAL)	A	.284	133	468	73	133	23	5	6	49	80	100	28	.393	.387
	Albuquerque (PCL)	AAA	.000	1	3	0	0	0	0	0	0	0	3	0	.000	.000
MINOR LEAGUE TOTALS			.273	185	652	96	178	32	9	6	70	102	138	34	.377	.373

2 Jason Stokes, 1b

Born: Jan. 23, 1982. **Ht.:** 6-4. **Wt.:** 225. **Bats:** R. **Throws:** R. **School:** Coppell (Texas) HS. **Career Transactions:** Selected by Marlins in second round of 2000 draft; signed Aug. 29, 2000.

Considered the top high school power hitter in the 2000 draft, Stokes dropped because of signability concerns and yet signed for $2.027 million. He challenged for the low Class A Midwest League triple crown in 2002 despite a painful cyst on his left wrist. He had surgery, including a bone graft, near the end of 2002, and the complicated procedure kept him from letting go at the plate until two months into the 2003 season. Light-tower power remains Stokes' greatest tool. He has cranked some mammoth shots and has shown good plate judgment in the past, though he regressed in that area last year. He has decent hands at first base. Wrist surgery and the huge parks of the high Class A Florida State League may have caused Stokes to alter his approach and chase pitches. He doesn't run well and remains an average defender, though he has picked up a half step through strict conditioning. Stokes had passed Adrian Gonzalez in the Marlins' plans at first base before they sent Gonzalez to the Rangers, though now he has to contend with Hee Seop Choi's presence . He should begin 2004 at Double-A Carolina, where the ball travels better and his natural power should be rewarded, and could challenge for a big league job in 2005.

Year	Club (League)	Class	AVG	G	AB	R	H	2B	3B	HR	RBI	BB	SO	SB	SLG	OBP
2001	Utica (NY-P)	A	.231	35	130	12	30	2	1	6	19	11	48	0	.400	.299
2002	Kane County (Mid)	A	.341	97	349	73	119	25	0	27	75	47	96	1	.645	.421
2003	Jupiter (FSL)	A	.258	121	462	67	119	31	3	17	89	36	135	6	.448	.312
MINOR LEAGUE TOTALS			.285	253	941	152	268	58	4	50	183	94	279	7	.514	.352

3 Jeff Allison, rhp

Born: Nov. 7, 1984. **Ht.:** 6-2. **Wt.:** 195. **Bats:** R. **Throws:** R. **School:** Veterans Memorial HS, Peabody, Mass. **Career Transactions:** Selected by Marlins in first round (16th overall) of 2003 draft; signed July 22, 2003.

BA's 2003 High School Player of the Year, Allison went 9-0, 0.00 with 142 strikeouts in 64 innings, allowing just 13 hits, nine walks and one unearned run. He was a top 10 prospect for the draft but fell because of perceived bonus demands. The Marlins took him 16th and signed him for $1.85 million. Often compared to World Series MVP Josh Beckett for his stuff, mound demeanor and cocky attitude, Allison could enjoy a similarly rapid pass through the minors. Allison had the best fastball (92-97 mph with life) and curveball (80-86 with sharp downward break) in the 2003 draft. He also has a tight slider. He throws from a high three-quarters arm slot, which aids his plus natural movement. Allison has broad shoulders, but his upper body needs work. A minor bout with shoulder tendinitis limited his pro debut to three starts. He rarely threw his changeup in high school because no one could hit his first two pitches. Allison should start 2004 in low Class A, with a taste of high Class A likely. If he proves as special as everybody thinks, he might not need more than the 200 minor league innings Beckett got.

Year	Club (League)	Class	W	L	ERA	G	GS	CG	SV	IP	H	R	ER	HR	BB	SO	AVG
2003	Marlins (GCL)	R	0	2	1.00	3	3	0	0	9	7	2	1	0	4	11	.206
MINOR LEAGUE TOTALS			0	2	1.00	3	3	0	0	9	7	2	1	0	4	11	.206

4 Scott Olsen, lhp

Born: Jan. 12, 1984. **Ht.:** 6-4. **Wt.:** 170. **Bats:** L. **Throws:** L. **School:** Crystal Lake (Ill.) South HS. **Career Transactions:** Selected by Marlins in sixth round of 2002 draft; signed June 9, 2002.

Scot Engler was the Marlins' 2002 scout of the year, and Olsen had a little something to do with that. Relatively unknown in high school, Olsen signed for $160,000 as a tall, projectable lefty with a loose arm and an easy delivery. He threw across his body and fell off toward third base, but Rookie-level Gulf Coast League pitching coach Jeff Schwarz got him pointed in the right direction. Olsen pitched at 90-92 mph and topped out at 94, about 3 mph higher than he did in his first pro season. He's aggressive, competitive and receptive to teaching. He has a bit of a mean streak, too, glaring at opposing hitters from the mound. He admires Randy Johnson and wears the same No. 51. His slider went from average early in the year to a plus pitch by the second half after he shelved his curveball. His command also took over after the break. Olsen has a slight frame that could stand another 15-20 pounds of muscle. He needs to add maturity and improve his changeup. After turning it up in the second half, Olsen should start the year in high Class A. A midyear promotion to Double-A would surprise no one.

Year	Club (League)	Class	W	L	ERA	G	GS	CG	SV	IP	H	R	ER	HR	BB	SO	AVG
2002	Marlins (GCL)	R	2	3	2.96	13	11	0	0	52	39	18	17	0	17	50	.204
2003	Greensboro (SAL)	A	7	9	2.81	25	24	0	0	128	101	51	40	4	59	129	.220
MINOR LEAGUE TOTALS			9	12	2.85	38	35	0	0	180	140	69	57	4	76	179	.215

5 Yorman Bazardo, rhp

Born: July 11, 1984. **Ht.:** 6-2. **Wt.:** 170. **Bats:** R. **Throws:** R. **Career Transactions:** Signed out of Venezuela by Marlins, July 19, 2000.

Signed for $85,000, Bazardo has shown an exciting arm. The new Marlins regime stuck him in the bullpen for his first season in the United States, then moved him to the rotation in 2003 when he came out of extended spring training. He opened the season with 17 scoreless innings and finished it with 17 more. Tall and long-limbed, Bazardo pitches at 92-94 mph and has touched 97. His stuff holds up, as he threw 95-97-94 to finish his second straight shutout in his final start of the year. He has a plus changeup, and he's athletic and projectable. He has a sunny disposition and solid makeup. Bazardo's power curveball needs work. He's prone to overthrowing. He needs to be more aggressive rather than sitting back and waiting until he's in trouble to get locked in. His mechanics can betray him at times, as he has a tendency to drift toward first base. Bazardo will open 2004 in the Florida State League, where the pitcher-friendly atmosphere should help his growing confidence. The Marlins will be careful not to rush him.

Year	Club (League)	Class	W	L	ERA	G	GS	CG	SV	IP	H	R	ER	HR	BB	SO	AVG
2001	Ciudad Alianza (VSL)	R	7	2	2.43	12	12	1	0	70	59	26	19	0	18	62	—
2002	Jamestown (NY-P)	A	5	0	2.72	25	0	0	6	36	39	11	11	0	6	26	.275
2003	Greensboro (SAL)	A	9	8	3.12	21	21	4	0	130	132	56	45	8	26	70	.261
MINOR LEAGUE TOTALS			21	10	2.85	58	33	5	6	237	230	93	75	8	50	158	.264

6 Josh Willingham, c

Born: Feb. 17, 1979. **Ht.:** 6-1. **Wt.:** 200. **Bats:** R. **Throws:** R. **School:** University of North Alabama. **Career Transactions:** Selected by Marlins in 17th round of 2000 draft; signed June 8, 2000.

Blocked at both corner infield spots, Willingham agreed to try catching during instructional league after the 2002 season. He showed enough potential to rocket up the organizational charts. He tore up high Class A to earn a June promotion to Double-A, but a knee injury interrupted his surge. Arthroscopic surgery caused him to miss seven weeks. Willingham has a short swing, power to all fields and a willingness to work counts and take walks. He has good arm strength and has shown an aptitude for game-calling. Makeup is a definite plus as he's a genuine throwback. With just 40 regular season games behind the plate, Willingham still has much to learn. He threw out just 20 percent of basestealers. He should start 2004 back in Double-A. Depending on who the Marlins settle on as their everyday catcher in the wake of Ivan Rodriguez' departure to free agency, Willingham could be a season from getting a major league shot or looking for another position.

Year	Club (League)	Class	AVG	G	AB	R	H	2B	3B	HR	RBI	BB	SO	SB	SLG	OBP
2000	Utica (NY-P)	A	.263	65	205	37	54	16	0	6	29	39	55	9	.429	.400
2001	Kane County (Mid)	A	.259	97	320	57	83	20	2	7	36	53	85	24	.400	.382
2002	Jupiter (FSL)	A	.274	107	376	72	103	21	4	17	69	63	88	18	.487	.394
2003	Jupiter (FSL)	A	.264	59	193	46	51	17	1	12	34	46	42	9	.549	.422
	Carolina (SL)	AA	.299	22	67	15	20	2	1	5	14	13	20	0	.582	.434
	Marlins (GCL)	R	.429	2	7	3	3	1	0	1	3	1	2	0	1.000	.500
MINOR LEAGUE TOTALS			.269	352	1168	230	314	77	8	48	185	215	292	60	.472	.400

7 Bill Murphy, lhp

Born: May 9, 1981. **Ht.:** 6-0. **Wt.:** 190. **Bats:** L. **Throws:** L. **School:** Cal State Northridge. **Career Transactions:** Selected by Athletics in third round of 2002 draft; signed June 26, 2002 . . . Traded by Athletics to Marlins, Dec. 23, 2003, completing an earlier trade in which Marlins sent LHP Mark Redman to Athletics for RHP Mike Neu and a player to be named.

When the Marlins decided they couldn't afford going to arbitration with 14-game winner Mark Redman, they traded him to the Athletics for Murphy and righthander Mike Neu. While Neu has the best changeup in the system and could help Florida sooner, it's Murphy who's the prize of the deal. He went to Cal State Northridge as an outfielder/pitcher before moving to the mound full-time as a sophomore. He quickly established himself as one of Oakland's top pitching prospects, tossing a no-hitter in low Class A and reaching Double-A in 2003, his first full pro season. He generates a lot of swing-and-misses with the life on his 89-91 mph fastball and his deceptive delivery. He also throws a curveball, which can be a plus pitch at times, and a changeup. Murphy came down with a dead arm in 2002 and wore down again at the end of last season. In addition to building up his strength, he also must improve his command and pitch sequencing. If he can do that, he projects as a No. 3 starter in the majors. Murphy needs another half-season in Double-A and could be ready for the big leagues in 2005.

Year	Club (League)	Class	W	L	ERA	G	GS	CG	SV	IP	H	R	ER	HR	BB	SO	AVG
2002	Vancouver (NWL)	A	1	4	4.57	13	9	0	0	41	28	23	21	2	35	46	.192
2003	Midland (TL)	AA	3	3	4.09	11	11	0	0	55	44	25	25	4	26	34	.220
	Kane County (Mid)	A	7	4	2.25	14	14	1	0	92	61	27	23	5	32	87	.188
MINOR LEAGUE TOTALS			11	11	3.30	38	34	1	0	188	133	75	69	11	93	167	.199

8 Eric Reed, of

Born: Dec. 2, 1980. **Ht.:** 5-11. **Wt.:** 170. **Bats:** L. **Throws:** L. **School:** Texas A&M University. **Career Transactions:** Selected by Marlins in ninth round of 2002 draft; signed June 6, 2002.

Reed led the Cape Cod League in hitting in 2001 but fell in the 2002 draft after a poor junior season at Texas A&M. Despite a wiry frame, he's a former high school powerlifting champion who squatted 450 pounds in college. He signed for $85,000 and has wasted little time showing the Marlins they got a steal. Reed is close to an 80 runner on the 20-80 scouting scale. He's an excellent bunter, even with two strikes. An Ichiro Suzuki admirer, he understands his limitations and doesn't bother trying to lift balls. Widely considered the best defender in the system, he shows remarkable range and jumps in center field. He also has an average to slightly better arm. Naturally aggressive, Reed is working on taking more pitches and getting comfortable in deep counts. His pitch recognition needs work, and he's still learning how to turn on inside pitches rather than trying to slap everything the other way. He also needs to get better leads and hone his basestealing skills. The organization's 2003 player of the year, Reed figures to move up to Double-A in 2004. His arrival could synchronize nicely with the end of Juan Pierre's contract after 2005.

Year	Club (League)	Class	AVG	G	AB	R	H	2B	3B	HR	RBI	BB	SO	SB	SLG	OBP
2002	Jamestown (NY-P)	A	.308	60	250	35	77	5	1	0	17	17	30	19	.336	.348
	Kane County (Mid)	A	.360	12	50	11	18	1	0	0	2	3	11	7	.380	.396
2003	Jupiter (FSL)	A	.300	134	514	86	154	15	8	0	25	52	83	53	.360	.367
MINOR LEAGUE TOTALS			.306	206	814	132	249	21	9	0	44	72	124	79	.354	.363

9 Jai Miller, of

Born: Jan. 17, 1985. **Ht.:** 6-4. **Wt.:** 195. **Bats:** R. **Throws:** R. **School:** Selma (Ala.) HS. **Career Transactions:** Selected by Marlins in fourth round of 2003 draft; signed June 3, 2003.

The first three-sport all-state athlete in Alabama prep history, Miller was headed to Stanford as a wide receiver and point guard. The Marlins signed him for $250,000, in large part because area scout Dave Dangler had established a strong relationship with Miller's father. Miller's mother and grandmother were killed in a car crash, but he overcame that tragedy and impressed Marlins officials with his intelligence and positive outlook. Miller may already have the quickest bat in the organization. He projects as a five-tool talent who reminds some of Preston Wilson. His makeup and work ethic are both pluses. A 70 runner on the 20-80 scouting scale, Miller has been timed at 4.05 seconds to first base from the right side. Miller is raw in every way. He must refine his approach at the plate and use his legs more. Defensively, he is fine going back on balls and chasing them to either side but needs to get better at coming in. He has a strong arm but has to improve his technique. He'll open his first full season in low Class A. Once his experience starts to catch up with his raw talent, he could take off.

Year	Club (League)	Class	AVG	G	AB	R	H	2B	3B	HR	RBI	BB	SO	SB	SLG	OBP
2003	Marlins (GCL)	R	.199	46	146	17	29	4	1	1	15	15	45	9	.260	.279
	Jamestown (NY-P)	A	.233	11	43	5	10	3	0	0	6	3	15	1	.302	.292
MINOR LEAGUE TOTALS			.206	57	189	22	39	7	1	1	21	18	60	10	.270	.282

10 Trevor Hutchinson, rhp

STEVE MOORE

Born: Oct. 8, 1979. **Ht.:** 6-5. **Wt.:** 220. **Bats:** R. **Throws:** R. **School:** University of California. **Career Transactions:** Selected by Marlins in third round of 2002 draft; signed Feb. 24, 2003.

Hutchinson is the younger brother of Chad Hutchinson, the former Cardinals pitching prospect and current Dallas Cowboys quarterback. Drafted as a college senior, Trevor held out before signing for $375,000 just before the start of 2003 spring training. An allergic reaction to a bee sting landed him in the hospital in July, but he came back to earn MVP honors in the Double-A Southern League playoffs, winning the clinching game. Advanced physically and mentally, Hutchinson throws a heavy sinker at 88-92 mph. He complements that with a slider and changeup, both solid-average pitches. He has a good feel for pitching, changing speeds and quadrants and outthinking young hitters. Hutchinson's stuff isn't overwhelming, and his age means there isn't much room for improvement. He projects as a fifth starter on a quality staff and could wind up as a workhorse set-up man. Hutchinson figures to return to Double-A in 2004. He could get a look in the big leagues depending on need and his progress, but more likely will challenge for a full-time spot in 2005.

Year	Club (League)	Class	W	L	ERA	G	GS	CG	SV	IP	H	R	ER	HR	BB	SO	AVG
2003	Jupiter (FSL)	A	9	2	2.77	14	13	2	0	84	77	30	26	3	16	58	.243
	Carolina (SL)	AA	3	3	3.86	8	6	0	0	35	32	21	15	1	13	18	.244
MINOR LEAGUE TOTALS			12	5	3.09	22	19	2	0	119	109	51	41	4	29	76	.243

11 Lincoln Holdzkom, rhp

Born: March 23, 1982. **Ht.:** 6-4. **Wt.:** 240. **Bats:** R. **Throws:** R. **School:** Arizona Western CC. **Career Transactions:** Selected by Marlins in seventh round of 2001 draft; signed June 5, 2001.

Kicked off his junior college team for insubordination, Holdzkom spent his first 2½ pro seasons showing flashes of obstinacy. The turning point came in June, when he and Greensboro manager Steve Phillips had a heated shouting match. Phillips challenged Holdzkom to live up to his vast talent, which he soon began doing. A body builder in high school, Holdzkom is physically imposing and can intimidate batters with his hulking appearance. He pitches in the mid-90s and touchs 97 with his fastball, which he complements with a hard-breaking curve. While Holdzkom appears to have closer stuff, some wonder whether he has the makeup to be anything more than a set-up man. Command has been a problem when he's been asked to close out wins as opposed to pitching the seventh or eighth innings. He can be slow to the plate and needs to improve his pickoff move. A late sub for fellow hardhead Randall Messenger in the Arizona Fall League, Holdzkom was added to the 40-man roster in November and could begin 2004 in Double-A with a good spring.

Year	Club (League)	Class	W	L	ERA	G	GS	CG	SV	IP	H	R	ER	HR	BB	SO	AVG
2001	Marlins (GCL)	R	1	3	2.49	12	7	0	2	43	26	18	12	0	27	43	.176
2002	Kane County (Mid)	A	1	5	2.53	30	0	0	11	32	21	11	9	0	29	42	.181
2003	Greensboro (SAL)	A	1	4	2.84	43	0	0	4	57	36	24	18	0	27	74	.182
	Jupiter (FSL)	A	0	2	3.07	13	0	0	2	15	9	6	5	0	7	20	.167
MINOR LEAGUE TOTALS			3	14	2.69	98	7	0	19	147	92	59	44	0	90	179	.178

12 Cole Seifrig, 2b

Born: Sept. 10, 1984. **Ht.:** 6-3. **Wt.:** 190. **Bats:** R. **Throws:** R. **School:** Heritage Hills HS, Lincoln City, Ind. **Career Transactions:** Selected by Marlins in fifth round in 2003 draft; signed June 11, 2003.

No less an authority than fellow southern Indiana product Don Mattingly congratulated Marlins officials at the World Series for drafting Seifrig. A Purdue football recruit as a wide receiver, he accepted a $200,000 bonus to play baseball instead. The son of a military officer who has been serving in the Middle East, he's serious, disciplined and a hard worker. He has a short, quick swing and quiet hands, a hitting package that evokes both Paul Molitor and Ryne Sandberg. Seifrig could move to third base eventually or stay at second, where his throwing mechanics have vastly improved since he signed. His actions around the bag are sound if not flashy. Center field might be another option as he runs well. Seifrig needs to improve his plate judgment and draw more walks, but for now gets by with an aggressive approach and excellent hand-eye coordination. Area scout Scot Engler and part-time scout Darren Blair did tons of legwork before assistant GM Jim Fleming and national crosschecker Joe Jordan came to see Seifrig, lest they alert their competitors. When they finally saw him, it was for a makeup night game that became a virtual command performance. When Seifrig stayed until 10 p.m. for extra batting practice against Jordan, the Marlins knew they had their man. He'll play in low Class A this year.

Year	Club (League)	Class	AVG	G	AB	R	H	2B	3B	HR	RBI	BB	SO	SB	SLG	OBP
2003	Marlins (GCL)	R	.285	50	186	27	53	7	2	2	7	10	44	11	.376	.335
	Jamestown (NY-P)	A	.261	11	46	3	12	3	0	0	8	2	12	2	.326	.286
MINOR LEAGUE TOTALS			.280	61	232	30	65	10	2	2	15	12	56	13	.366	.325

13 Lee Mitchell, 3b/ss

Born: April 21, 1982. **Ht.:** 6-1. **Wt.:** 198. **Bats:** R. **Throws:** R. **School:** University of Georgia. **Career Transactions:** Selected by Marlins in sixth round of 2003 draft; signed June 16, 2003.

The Marlins camp was split on Mitchell, who had a strong Cape Cod League performance in 2002 but followed up with a so-so junior year at Georgia. Eastern scouting supervisor Mike Cadahia was so adamant about Mitchell's ability that the Marlins took him in the sixth round and immediately were rewarded for their faith. Tall and slender, he drew comparisons to a young Aaron Boone. While none of Mitchell's tools are a plus, everything is solid average, with the possible exception of his legs. At the plate, he's aggressive with deceptively good power, considering his frame. He could stand to add another 15-20 pounds of muscle. Defensively, Mitchell has a reliable arm and complements it with good footwork and solid range. He can handle slow rollers but needs work on balls to his backhand side. He played 19 games at shortstop at short-season Jamestown, mainly to give more playing time at third base to Pablo Sosa. Mitchell spent his time in low Class A exclusively at the hot corner. He loves to compete and has high standards for himself and his teammates. With his advanced understanding of the game, he could start 2004 in high Class A.

Year	Club (League)	Class	AVG	G	AB	R	H	2B	3B	HR	RBI	BB	SO	SB	SLG	OBP
2003	Jamestown (NY-P)	A	.308	46	169	21	52	5	2	2	19	16	39	3	.396	.365
	Greensboro (SAL)	A	.228	23	79	7	18	4	0	2	7	6	17	1	.354	.282
MINOR LEAGUE TOTALS			.282	69	248	28	70	9	2	4	26	22	56	4	.383	.339

14 Ronald Belizario, rhp

Born: Dec. 31, 1982. **Ht.:** 6-2. **Wt.:** 150. **Bats:** R. **Throws:** R. **Career Transactions:** Signed out of Venezuela by Marlins, Aug. 2, 1999.

Few members of this list have proven as maddening to Marlins brass as Belizario. Last year alone he missed curfew the night before a scheduled start, skipped conditioning sessions and showed up his pitching coach during mound visits. His immaturity and hard-headed nature got him shipped back to extended spring training in May, where for three weeks he was forced to report at 7 a.m. for early cardiovascular work. Once he got the message, farm director Marc DelPiano sent him back out to Greensboro, where Belizario pitched at 94-95 mph and touched 98. He has a decent change, a sweeping slider and a cutter some in the organization would rather see him shelve. In terms of pure stuff, some believe he outranks even Yorman Bazardo and Scott Olsen. A minor shoulder problem led the Marlins to shut Belizario down near the end of the regular season and caused him to miss the Florida State League playoffs. He projects as a premium set-up man or perhaps a closer, but first he'll have to get his emotions under control and bring his work ethic up to a consistently acceptable level. He'll also have to show more consistent command. He should start 2004 back in high Class A.

Year	Club (League)	Class	W	L	ERA	G	GS	CG	SV	IP	H	R	ER	HR	BB	SO	AVG
2000	Universidad (VSL)	R	2	3	7.39	17	5	0	6	35	37	34	29	1	18	27	.253
2001	Marlins (GCL)	R	4	6	2.34	13	10	1	0	73	62	29	19	4	20	54	.229
2002	Kane County (Mid)	A	6	5	3.46	23	22	1	0	140	131	67	54	4	56	98	.247
2003	Greensboro (SAL)	A	5	1	3.00	10	8	1	0	48	41	23	16	3	18	45	.229
	Jupiter (FSL)	A	1	2	4.91	6	4	0	0	18	20	10	10	0	8	13	.278
MINOR LEAGUE TOTALS			18	17	3.66	69	49	3	6	315	291	163	128	12	120	237	.243

15 Robert Andino, ss

Born: April 25, 1984. **Ht.:** 6-0. **Wt.:** 170. **Bats:** R. **Throws:** R. **School:** Southridge HS, Miami. **Career Transactions:** Selected by Marlins in second round of 2002 draft; signed Aug. 4, 2002.

On paper, Andino had a miserable year with the bat in his first full pro season. He struck out once every 3.3 at-bats and appeared overmatched at times, but the Marlins remain high on the slick-fielding shortstop from Miami. Andino, who signed for $750,000 after a two-month holdout in 2002, showed excellent bat speed but consistently jumped at pitches. The more he struggled, the harder it was for him to stay under control. Strength isn't a problem as he has a solid frame and a thick lower half. Defensively, Andino has tremendous range, a plus arm and a flair for the dramatic. His 28 errors were due mainly to carelessness, especially on throws, but still represent a low total for a teenage shortstop in his first full year. The Marlins also were impressed that he didn't let his offensive struggles affect his defense or his attitude. The son of a former professional player in Puerto Rico, Andino has just average speed and isn't much of a basestealer. Rated behind only B.J. Upton among shortstops on the Marlins draft board a year ago, Andino again took a back seat to Upton and a class of promising young shortstops in the low Class A South Atlantic League. It might be good for Andino to get a refresher course in the SAL so he can get his bat going.

Year	Club (League)	Class	AVG	G	AB	R	H	2B	3B	HR	RBI	BB	SO	SB	SLG	OBP
2002	Marlins (GCL)	R	.259	9	27	2	7	0	0	0	2	5	6	3	.259	.364
	Jamestown (NY-P)	A	.167	9	36	2	6	1	1	0	3	1	9	1	.250	.189
2003	Greensboro (SAL)	A	.188	119	416	45	78	17	2	2	27	46	128	6	.252	.266
MINOR LEAGUE TOTALS			.190	137	479	49	91	18	3	2	32	52	143	10	.253	.266

16 Kevin Cave, rhp

Born: May 25, 1980. **Ht.:** 6-2. **Wt.:** 220. **Bats:** R. **Throws:** R. **School:** Xavier University. **Career Transactions:** Selected by Marlins in 17th round of 2001 draft; signed June 5, 2001.

After blowing a number of saves at low Class A Kane County in 2002, Cave was nearly lights-out at high Class A last season, converting 23 of 25 chances. A minor bout of elbow tendinitis caused him to be shut down in August, but his year was an unqualified success. A classic late bloomer, Cave was an outfielder for most of his college career at Xavier and was hampered by a broken foot as a draft-eligible sophomore. Strong work by former Marlins scouts Brad Del Barba and Tom Keefe led to Cave's selection as a 17th-rounder when most teams thought he was ineligible as a college sophomore. He features a 94-95 mph fastball with late, hard sink and a plus changeup he uses to neutralize lefthanders. His hard curveball still needs work but could end up being a plus pitch as well. Projected as a set-up man in the majors, he could work his way into a more prominent role, a la Tim Worrell. Cave's primary weakness is mound inexperience. He also must control his emotions better, but so far has shown the short memory any reliever must have. He should start the year in Double-A.

Year	Club (League)	Class	W	L	ERA	G	GS	CG	SV	IP	H	R	ER	HR	BB	SO	AVG
2001	Utica (NY-P)	A	1	2	3.26	14	5	0	1	39	38	16	14	4	14	23	.260
2002	Kane County (Mid)	A	3	7	4.58	41	0	0	10	55	53	32	28	3	21	60	.259
2003	Jupiter (FSL)	A	2	2	1.60	39	0	0	23	45	36	11	8	0	14	43	.217
MINOR LEAGUE TOTALS			6	11	3.25	94	5	0	34	139	127	59	50	7	49	126	.246

17 Wilson Valdez, ss/2b

Born: May 20, 1978. **Ht.:** 5-11. **Wt.:** 160. **Bats:** R. **Throws:** R. **Career Transactions:** Signed out of Dominican Republic by Expos, Feb. 4, 1997 . . . Claimed on waivers by Marlins from Expos, March 29, 2002.

Stuck playing second base in Double-A at the start of 2003, Valdez made huge strides in terms of his offense and his attitude. A long talk with Ozzie Guillen, then the Marlins' third-base coach and now the White Sox' manager, got him headed in the right direction at spring training. Valdez went from a moody, occasionally surly sort to a consistently hard worker who played with tremendous energy. Valdez earned an early-season callup to Triple-A Albuquerque, swapping places with the disappointing Jesus Medrano and pushing Kevin Hooper off shortstop and over to second base. Plucked off waivers from the Expos in the spring of 2002, Valdez has good bat speed with minimal gap power and an understanding of his limitations. Wiry strong, he slaps the ball around, bunts often, moves runners, keeps his strikeouts low and projects as a solid No. 2 or No. 8 hitter. His instincts on the bases are strong and he has shown the ability to convert his above-average speed into a high stolen-base percentage. He's a plus defender at shortstop with a solid-average arm and plus range. A late-season thumb injury on his glove hand required surgery but Valdez should challenge for a big league utility job in the spring.

Year	Club (League)	Class	AVG	G	AB	R	H	2B	3B	HR	RBI	BB	SO	SB	SLG	OBP
1997	Expos (DSL)	R	.303	62	244	39	74	13	1	2	29	25	19	19	.389	.370
1998	Expos (DSL)	R	.300	64	247	42	74	9	0	3	30	19	12	15	.372	.352
1999	Expos (GCL)	R	.293	22	82	12	24	2	0	0	7	5	7	10	.317	.330
	Vermont (NY-P)	A	.246	36	130	19	32	7	0	1	10	7	21	4	.323	.283
2000	Cape Fear (SAL)	A	.245	15	49	6	12	2	0	0	3	2	9	3	.286	.275
	Vermont (NY-P)	A	.266	65	248	32	66	8	1	1	30	17	32	16	.319	.312
2001	Clinton (Mid)	A	.252	59	214	31	54	8	1	0	11	9	22	6	.299	.286
	Jupiter (FSL)	A	.249	64	233	34	58	13	2	2	19	10	33	7	.348	.286
2002	Portland (EL)	AA	.261	114	375	51	98	19	5	1	30	15	47	18	.347	.294
2003	Carolina (SL)	AA	.313	37	144	28	45	6	2	0	14	15	17	16	.382	.373
	Albuquerque (PCL)	AAA	.287	90	338	45	97	12	4	0	18	19	37	33	.346	.326
MINOR LEAGUE TOTALS			.275	628	2304	339	634	99	16	10	201	143	256	147	.345	.319

18 Chris Aguila, of

Born: Feb. 23, 1979. **Ht.:** 5-11. **Wt.:** 180. **Bats:** R. **Throws:** R. **School:** McQueen HS, Reno, Nev. **Career Transactions:** Selected by Marlins in third round of 1997 draft; signed June 18, 1997.

Aguila also ranked 18th on this list after the 2000 season, then dropped completely off the next two years before re-establishing himself with the Southern League batting title in 2003. Aguila won the crown despite missing 41 games after an errant pitch by Joe Winkelsas left him with a hairline fracture in his right wrist on June 3. Aguila, whose 29 home runs as a senior at McQueen High in Reno remain tied for the national high school single-season record, changed from an extreme inside-out stroke to a more power-laden swing that showcased his ability to pull inside mistakes with authority. He pounds fastballs, even plus fastballs, from the middle in. He's not as successful with pitches on the outer half, sometimes rolling over good breaking balls. A modest-sized late bloomer, Aguila has plus bat speed, a strong situational approach and average power that projects to 15-20 homers in a full big-league season. He's an average runner but an excellent defender who can handle all three outfield spots. He takes good routes, has an above-average arm and shows a strong desire to keep improving. Aguila also has a reputation for being upbeat, unselfish and a good teammate. When the organization asked Miguel Cabrera to learn left field last season, Aguila took it upon himself to talk at length with his young Carolina teammate about outfield play, even working with him during batting practice. He's ready for Triple-A.

Year	Club (League)	Class	AVG	G	AB	R	H	2B	3B	HR	RBI	BB	SO	SB	SLG	OBP
1997	Marlins (GCL)	R	.217	46	157	12	34	7	0	1	17	21	49	2	.280	.309
1998	Marlins (GCL)	R	.269	51	171	29	46	12	3	4	29	19	49	6	.444	.349
1999	Kane County (Mid)	A	.244	122	430	74	105	21	7	15	78	40	127	14	.430	.320
2000	Brevard County (FSL)	A	.241	136	518	68	125	27	3	9	56	37	105	8	.357	.292
2001	Brevard County (FSL)	A	.276	73	272	44	75	15	3	10	34	21	54	8	.463	.328
	Portland (EL)	AA	.257	64	241	25	62	16	1	4	29	18	50	5	.382	.312
2002	Portland (EL)	AA	.294	130	429	62	126	28	4	6	46	48	101	14	.420	.369
2003	Carolina (SL)	AA	.320	93	337	58	108	21	3	11	55	36	67	6	.499	.384
	Marlins (GCL)	R	.750	1	4	1	3	0	0	1	2	0	1	0	1.500	.750
MINOR LEAGUE TOTALS			.267	716	2559	373	684	147	24	61	346	240	603	63	.415	.333

19 Franklyn Gracesqui, lhp

Born: Aug. 20, 1979. **Ht.:** 6-5. **Wt.:** 210. **Bats:** B. **Throws:** L. **School:** George Washington HS, New York. **Career Transactions:** Selected by Blue Jays in 21st round of 1998 draft; signed June 7, 1998 . . . Selected by Marlins from Blue Jays in minor league Rule 5 draft, Dec. 16, 2002.

After the 2001 season, Gracesqui merited a spot on Toronto's 40-man roster, but the Blue Jays left him unprotected after 2002 and the Marlins grabbed him in the minor league Rule 5 draft. A tall, physical lefty, he has a plus fastball that gets on hitters late. He pitches at 93-94 mph and touches 96. Thanks to some deception in his funky three-quarters delivery, hitters don't get many good looks against him. He lacks a second plus pitch, however. At times he commands his slider in the zone, but it acts more like a cutter. Despite being essentially a 1½-pitch pitcher with shaky command, he has averaged better than a strikeout per inning in his career. Like Manny Ramirez, he's a Dominican who came through the strong baseball program at New York's George Washington High. Gracesqui is durable, capable of working three straight days, and projects as a valuable situational reliever in the majors. He must improve his work ethic, and he rubs some of his teammates the wrong way with his nonchalant attitude. He should start the year in Triple-A.

Year	Club (League)	Class	W	L	ERA	G	GS	CG	SV	IP	H	R	ER	HR	BB	SO	AVG
1998	St. Catharines (NY-P)	A	1	0	6.61	11	0	0	0	16	16	12	12	2	12	19	.242
1999	St. Catharines (NY-P)	A	2	3	5.05	15	10	0	1	46	44	30	26	4	41	45	.253
2000	Medicine Hat (Pio)	R	0	1	2.63	8	4	0	0	24	15	11	7	1	21	20	.185
	Hagerstown (SAL)	A	0	1	4.91	3	1	0	0	7	4	4	4	1	9	6	.174

2001	Charleston, WV (SAL)	A	2	8	3.17	35	2	0	1	65	60	40	23	1	34	66	.245
	Dunedin (FSL)	A	1	0	0.00	4	0	0	0	6	2	0	0	0	8	6	.125
2002	Tennessee (SL)	AA	4	2	4.64	41	0	0	1	43	40	26	22	3	34	48	.258
	Dunedin (FSL)	A	2	1	2.49	10	0	0	1	22	15	8	6	1	11	25	.192
2003	Carolina (SL)	AA	3	3	2.48	44	0	0	5	58	44	19	16	0	43	75	.211
MINOR LEAGUE TOTALS			15	19	3.63	171	17	0	9	287	240	150	116	13	213	310	.229

20 Jon-Michael Nickerson, lhp

Born: Dec. 4, 1984. **Ht.:** 6-5. **Wt.:** 180. **Bats:** L. **Throws:** L. **School:** Stanhope Elmore HS, Millbrook, Ala. **Career Transactions:** Selected by Marlins in 16th round of 2003 draft; signed June 4, 2003.

Tall and rail-thin, Nickerson concentrated more on basketball than baseball in high school. He largely flew under the radar until Marlins national crosschecker Joe Jordan and area scout Dave Dangler happened across him at an all-star game in rural Alabama. There to see Florida's eventual 2003 fourth-round pick Jai Miller, they immediately noticed Nickerson's broad shoulders, easy arm action and projectable frame. Nickerson threw just 23 innings as a high school senior but signed for $40,000 as a 16th-rounder. The Jacksonville State basketball signee pitched a no-hitter in the Gulf Coast League. Despite his inexperience, he already has shown the ability to throw his breaking ball for strikes. He never really learned a changeup until the Marlins got hold of him, but it quickly became his most effective pitch as he dominated the GCL. His fastball sits at 87-89 mph and he touched 91 after a late-season promotion to Greensboro. Nickerson throws downhill, has sound mechanics and projects to add velocity and strength. His makeup is another plus as he is receptive to coaching and looks his elders in the eye. As with Scott Olsen a year before, the Marlins believe they got another steal in Nickerson. He'll return to low Class A in 2004.

Year	Club (League)	Class	W	L	ERA	G	GS	CG	SV	IP	H	R	ER	HR	BB	SO	AVG
2003	Marlins (GCL)	R	5	1	1.87	12	12	1	0	53	36	15	11	1	23	50	.191
	Greensboro (SAL)	A	0	0	1.80	1	1	0	0	5	3	1	1	1	1	2	.188
MINOR LEAGUE TOTALS			5	1	1.86	13	13	1	0	58	39	16	12	2	24	52	.191

21 Josh Wilson, ss

Born: March 26, 1981. **Ht.:** 6-1. **Wt.:** 160. **Bats:** R. **Throws:** R. **School:** Mount Lebanon (Pa.) HS. **Career Transactions:** Selected by Marlins in third round of 1999 draft; signed June 5, 1999.

After breaking into the top 10 on this list a year ago, Wilson took a decided step backward in 2003. He missed the last month with a broken left hand after being hit by a pitch, but the frustration already had taken hold. Wilson showed a nagging inability to identify strikes, refused to take his walks and fell into a disturbing pattern of lofting easy fly balls to the opposite field. Wilson's father Mike is the baseball coach at Duquesne University and remains a strong influence on his son's career. Some wonder if that connection hasn't slowed Josh's progress. He's resistant to suggested changes to his inside-out swing, which can get long and loopy, and he refuses to lift weights seriously. Tall and thin, he still needs to add upper-body strength. He's an average runner and poor basestealer. Though he has shown he can play second base, he is expected to remain at shortstop, where he reminds some of the Pirates' Jack Wilson (no relation). Previous comparisons to Jay Bell are no longer offered. Wilson has soft hands, quick feet, plus range and an above-average arm but his bat remains in question. He may need to repeat Double-A, especially if Wilson Valdez starts 2004 in Triple-A.

Year	Club (League)	Class	AVG	G	AB	R	H	2B	3B	HR	RBI	BB	SO	SB	SLG	OBP
1999	Marlins (GCL)	R	.266	53	203	29	54	9	4	0	27	24	36	14	.350	.352
2000	Kane County (Mid)	A	.269	13	52	2	14	3	1	1	6	3	14	0	.423	.316
	Utica (NY-P)	A	.344	66	259	43	89	13	6	3	43	29	47	9	.475	.418
2001	Kane County (Mid)	A	.285	123	506	65	144	28	5	4	61	28	60	17	.383	.325
2002	Jupiter (FSL)	A	.256	111	398	51	102	17	1	11	50	28	67	7	.387	.318
	Portland (EL)	AA	.341	12	41	5	14	3	0	2	5	2	6	0	.561	.372
2003	Carolina (SL)	AA	.253	118	434	53	110	30	6	3	58	27	70	6	.371	.294
MINOR LEAGUE TOTALS			.278	496	1893	248	527	103	23	24	250	141	300	53	.395	.333

22 Victor Prieto, rhp

Born: April 24, 1983. **Ht.:** 6-2. **Wt.:** 175. **Bats:** R. **Throws:** R. **Career Transactions:** Signed out of Venezuela by Marlins, July 2, 1999.

Prieto took a huge leap forward in his first U.S. season, then fell back in 2003. One of many intriguing prospects signed out of Venezuela by former Marlins scout Miguel Garcia, Prieto struggled with his command and went winless at Jamestown. He still has a big arm and quick arm action. He fires his heavy fastball at 94-97 mph with an outstanding 12-to-6 curveball and the makings of a plus changeup, though he doesn't use it as much as Florida officials would like. He's quiet and hard to read, even for fellow Spanish speakers. Prieto has a tendency to overthrow and tries to do too much on the mound. He can be too aggressive at times. With his thin frame that borders on being frail, Prieto's health must be monitored closely. He has been shut down several times in the past with a tired arm and a sore shoulder, and he needs to add more strength. Though extremely raw, Prieto's high ceiling should buy him plenty of developmental time. He's not ready for full-season ball yet.

Year	Club (League)	Class	W	L	ERA	G	GS	CG	SV	IP	H	R	ER	HR	BB	SO	AVG
2000	Universidad (VSL)	R	5	3	3.36	14	10	0	0	59	67	30	22	1	32	65	.293
2001	Ciudad Alianza (VSL)	R	2	2	3.19	13	5	0	0	31	19	14	11	0	21	34	—
2002	Marlins (GCL)	R	4	2	3.16	8	7	1	0	31	14	17	11	0	19	21	.135
2003	Jamestown (NY-P)	A	0	6	5.52	13	11	0	0	46	40	29	28	0	40	45	.242
MINOR LEAGUE TOTALS			11	13	3.88	48	33	1	0	167	140	90	72	1	112	165	.243

23 Logan Kensing, rhp

Born: July 3, 1982. **Ht.:** 6-1. **Wt.:** 185. **Bats:** R. **Throws:** R. **School:** Texas A&M University. **Career Transactions:** Selected by Marlins in second round of 2003 draft; signed June 21, 2003.

If the 2003 draft had been held in April rather than June, Kensing would have been a first-round pick. Primarily a shortstop in high school and a part-time reliever as a Texas A&M freshman in 2002, he was one of the most impressive pitchers in the college ranks at the outset of last year. But while his lack of pitching experience means he has a fresh arm, he also wasn't conditioned to hold up over the entire college season. He didn't have any arm problems but his stuff wasn't as crisp in the second half, which is why the Marlins were able to snag him in the second round and sign him for $675,000. When he's on, Kensing throws a heavy 90-94 mph sinker with tremendous boring action out of a three-quarters slot. His slider can be a plus pitch as well but it also can flatten out. Too often he has trouble repeating his delivery, which detracts from his stuff. He drops his front shoulder, costing him valuable leverage. At times, the Matt Clement-like movement Kensing achieves with his pitches makes them difficult to command. He's competitive and athletic and has shown leadership qualities. He could start back at low A Greensboro with the potential to move fast once he gets his mechanics sorted out.

Year	Club (League)	Class	W	L	ERA	G	GS	CG	SV	IP	H	R	ER	HR	BB	SO	AVG
2003	Jamestown (NY-P)	A	2	4	5.73	8	6	0	0	33	48	23	21	1	6	20	.333
	Greensboro (SAL)	A	0	2	4.50	4	4	0	0	20	18	10	10	2	5	11	.243
MINOR LEAGUE TOTALS			2	6	5.26	12	10	0	0	53	66	33	31	3	11	31	.303

24 Josh Johnson, rhp

Born: Jan. 31, 1984. **Ht.:** 6-7. **Wt.:** 220. **Bats:** L. **Throws:** R. **School:** Jenks HS, Tulsa. **Career Transactions:** Selected by Marlins in fourth round of 2002 draft; signed June 8, 2002.

Once considered a late first- or second-round selection in 2002, Johnson had a disappointing senior season in high school and slid to the fourth round of the draft. Troubled first by shoulder tendinitis and later a pulled hip flexor after signing for $300,000, he was shut down for a time but bounced back with a solid first full season in 2003. Despite his size and bulk, he's not a power pitcher. He commands his fastball at 88-92 mph, mixing in a developing changeup and an average slider that showed signs of improvement late in the year. In his final two starts, after making some adjustments with Greensboro pitching coach Scott Mitchell, Johnson's slider showed more bite and tilt than before. He also threw a little harder as the year wore on due to other mechanical changes. Some see him as a Carl Pavano type, a workhorse who throws downhill and can eat innings. Johnson is strong mentally, works hard and has honed a solid frame. His makeup and intelligence make him a strong candidate to keep improving as he climbs the ladder. He'll move up to high Class A in 2004.

Year	Club (League)	Class	W	L	ERA	G	GS	CG	SV	IP	H	R	ER	HR	BB	SO	AVG
2002	Marlins (GCL)	R	2	0	0.60	4	3	0	0	15	8	3	1	0	3	11	.154
	Jamestown (NY-P)	A	0	2	12.38	2	2	0	0	8	15	15	11	0	7	5	.385
2003	Greensboro (SAL)	A	4	7	3.61	17	17	0	0	82	69	44	33	5	29	59	.223
MINOR LEAGUE TOTALS			6	9	3.84	23	22	0	0	105	92	62	45	5	39	75	.230

25 Mike Flannery, rhp

Born: Sept. 20, 1979. **Ht.:** 6-1. **Wt.:** 195. **Bats:** R. **Throws:** R. **School:** Gloucester County (N.J.) JC. **Career Transactions:** Selected by Marlins in 33rd round of 1999 draft; signed May 30, 2000.

A draft-and-follow out of Gloucester County (N.J.) Junior College, Flannery has developed steadily as he has grown stronger. His fastball now touches 96 mph, and he complements it with a slider that has shown flashes of being a plus pitch. More often, though, the slider is just average, causing Flannery to rely even more on his fastball command and a bulldog mentality. Like Kevin Cave a level below, Flannery has worked his way up from a modest draft position to prospect status. Flannery showed the ability to close for a Carolina team that won the Southern League crown, but he probably projects as more of a set-up man. He was slated to represent the Marlins in the Arizona Fall League before a tired arm caused the organization to rethink the decision. Added to the 40-man roster for the first time, Flannery figures to start the year in Triple-A. He could see his first big league action at some point in 2004.

Year	Club (League)	Class	W	L	ERA	G	GS	CG	SV	IP	H	R	ER	HR	BB	SO	AVG
2000	Utica (NY-P)	A	2	7	4.89	13	13	0	0	70	71	51	38	8	20	44	.256
2001	Kane County (Mid)	A	3	4	4.79	53	0	0	16	56	58	35	30	5	31	47	.262
2002	Jupiter (FSL)	A	2	5	2.21	58	0	0	26	61	58	20	15	4	10	44	.250
2003	Carolina (SL)	AA	7	3	2.31	56	0	0	23	58	42	20	15	1	26	50	.199
MINOR LEAGUE TOTALS			14	19	3.59	180	13	0	65	246	229	126	98	18	87	185	.243

26 Pablo Sosa, 3b

Born: Aug. 11, 1982. **Ht.:** 6-1. **Wt.:** 180. **Bats:** R. **Throws:** R. **Career Transactions:** Signed out of the Dominican Republic by Marlins, Aug. 15, 2001.

Built more like a strong safety than a prototypical ballplayer, Sosa is tooled up but exceedingly raw. While he has great potential and a very high ceiling, he could take several years to smooth over some very rough edges. His arm, range and power are plus tools, and he has 75 bat speed on the 20-80 scale thanks to his strong hands and forearms. His strength is natural as he rarely lifts weights. In batting practice, he hits balls harder and farther than almost anyone in the system. Trouble is, he has no idea about pitch recognition once he gets into games. Extremely aggressive at the plate, Sosa drew just six walks in his first season in the United States. His speed is average and he projects as a prototype third baseman. His arrival at Jamestown pushed sixth-rounder Lee Mitchell over to shortstop. Sosa plays hard but still has a tendency to get out of control at times. He figures to start in low Class A this year.

Year	Club (League)	Class	AVG	G	AB	R	H	2B	3B	HR	RBI	BB	SO	SB	SLG	OBP
2002	Marlins (DSL)	R	.375	65	251	33	94	16	2	6	42	8	28	4	.526	.398
2003	Marlins (GCL)	R	.296	21	71	10	21	2	1	0	5	4	9	2	.352	.333
	Jamestown (NY-P)	A	.243	35	136	10	33	7	2	0	8	2	27	1	.324	.262
MINOR LEAGUE TOTALS			.323	121	458	53	148	25	5	6	55	14	64	7	.439	.348

27 David Marchbanks, lhp

Born: Feb. 3, 1982. **Ht.:** 6-3. **Wt.:** 205. **Bats:** L. **Throws:** L. **School:** University of South Carolina. **Career Transactions:** Selected by Marlins in seventh round of 2003 draft; signed July 6, 2003.

Nothing about Marchbanks jumps out. Repeated viewings, however, seem to inspire support. The Southeastern Conference's 2003 pitcher of the year, he has much more savvy than raw stuff. Pegged by Eastern scouting supervisor Mike Cadahia, Marchbanks signed for $144,000 and immediately made that seem like a bargain. Marchbanks pitches at 87-89 mph and occasionally will touch 90. His slider is average and his changeup projects as a plus pitch. A strike-thrower, Marchbanks has some deception in his delivery because of a high leg kick. Lean and deceptively strong, he projects to add a little more velocity as he fills out. He works fast, keeps the defense on its toes and shows good durability. He has a good makeup and shows a professional demeanor on and off the mound. Some have compared his approach to ex-Marlins 14-game winner Mark Redman. Both are crafty lefties with college experience and the intelligence to compensate for below-average velocity. Marchbanks could be the first player from Florida's 2003 draft to reach the majors. He finished his first pro summer with a quality start in Double-A and likely will begin this year in high Class A.

Year	Club (League)	Class	W	L	ERA	G	GS	CG	SV	IP	H	R	ER	HR	BB	SO	AVG
2003	Jamestown (NY-P)	A	0	0	1.23	5	3	0	0	15	11	2	2	1	3	12	.204
	Greensboro (SAL)	A	0	1	2.12	3	3	0	0	17	16	5	4	0	1	15	.250
	Carolina (SL)	AA	0	1	3.00	1	1	1	0	6	4	2	2	0	5	3	.222
MINOR LEAGUE TOTALS			0	2	1.91	9	7	1	0	38	31	9	8	1	9	30	.228

28 Jonathan Fulton, ss

Born: Dec. 1, 1983. **Ht.:** 6-4. **Wt.:** 200. **Bats:** R. **Throws:** R. **School:** George Washington HS, Danville, Va. **Career Transactions:** Selected by Marlins in third round of 2003 draft; signed June 5, 2003.

For the first six or so weeks of his pro career, Fulton was dreadfully overmatched at the plate. He hit .150 in his first 133 pro at-bats. Once Marlins officials noticed he was squinting an awful lot, he was sent out for eye tests and fitted with contact lenses and prescription sunglasses. Upon his return, Fulton went 13-for-35 (.371) the rest of the way and showed plus power. He has a good frame but lacks strength, in part because of a poor diet in high school. He does, however, have strong hands. He needs to add at least 20 pounds but showed smooth actions and a plus arm at shortstop. He projects to make the move to third, where some in the system see a young Scott Rolen. A former high school quarterback, he has more athleticism than a typical third baseman. Fulton is quiet and raw but receptive to teaching. Area scout Joel Matthews was one of his biggest backers. Extra work with roving hitting instructor John Mallee at a year-end minicamp helped Fulton show marked improvement. He's older than most high school draftees, turning 20 in the December after his pro debut. He figures to start 2004 in extended spring training.

Year	Club (League)	Class	AVG	G	AB	R	H	2B	3B	HR	RBI	BB	SO	SB	SLG	OBP
2003	Marlins (GCL)	R	.196	47	168	9	33	9	0	1	13	9	51	0	.268	.247
MINOR LEAGUE TOTALS			.196	47	168	9	33	9	0	1	13	9	51	0	.268	.247

29 Chris Resop, rhp

Born: Nov. 4, 1982. **Ht.:** 6-3. **Wt.:** 200. **Bats:** R. **Throws:** R. **School:** Barron Collier HS, Naples, Fla. **Career Transactions:** Selected by Marlins in fourth round of 2001 draft; signed July 12, 2001.

A strong two-way talent in high school, Resop entered pro ball as an outfielder and was an abject failure at the plate. Despite putting on regular shows in batting practice, he hit .193 in three years with just one home run in 269 at-bats. His status changed overnight, however, when he consented to the Marlins' mid-July suggestion that he give pitching another try. He showed precious little mound rust upon his return. After a few weeks of work with Greensboro pitching coach Scott Mitchell, Resop soon started pumping 95-mph fastballs and flashing a sharp curveball out of a three-quarters arm slot. His changeup remains rudimentary. Pitching exclusively in relief, he showed a competitive streak and a good feel for pitching. A good athlete, Resop can field his position and shows the ability to hold runners. He's a strike thrower who threw just two balls in one 23-pitch outing. Resop could move quickly through the system now that he apparently has found his true calling. He'll probably begin the year back in low Class A.

Year	Club (League)	Class	AVG	G	AB	R	H	2B	3B	HR	RBI	BB	SO	SB	SLG	OBP
2001	Marlins (GCL)	R	.116	26	86	5	10	2	0	0	5	7	34	0	.140	.189
	Utica (NY-P)	A	.333	2	3	0	1	0	0	0	0	0	2	0	.333	.333
2002	Marlins (GCL)	R	.264	28	91	7	24	5	2	0	11	5	21	1	.363	.323
2003	Greensboro (SAL)	A	.191	37	89	6	17	4	1	1	8	1	29	0	.292	.209
MINOR LEAGUE TOTALS			.193	93	269	18	52	11	3	1	24	13	86	1	.268	.243

Year	Club (League)	Class	W	L	ERA	G	GS	CG	SV	IP	H	R	ER	HR	BB	SO	AVG
2003	Greensboro (SAL)	A	0	1	4.97	11	0	0	0	13	11	7	7	1	5	15	.224
MINOR LEAGUE TOTALS			0	1	4.97	11	0	0	0	13	11	7	7	1	5	15	.224

30 Chip Ambres, of

Born: Dec. 19, 1979. **Ht.:** 6-1. **Wt.:** 190. **Bats:** R. **Throws:** R. **School:** West Brook HS, Beaumont, Texas. **Career Transactions:** Selected by Marlins in first round (27th overall) of 1998 draft; signed Aug. 3, 1998.

Ambres hasn't really been around since the Marlins' inaugural season in 1993. It only seems that way. Slowed by leg injuries, including hamstring problems and a broken right fibula in 2001 that required surgery, the 1998 first-rounder continues to tantalize. He plays an acceptable center field but projects as a left fielder down the road. No longer more than an average runner, thanks in part to a metal plate in his right leg, Ambres had his worst year as a basestealer in 2003. He has struggled at times to keep his weight down. His best attributes at this point are strong plate discipline and solid gap power. Extra work with roving hitting coordinator John Mallee seemingly had returned Ambres to the fast track in the fall of 2002, but he followed up with a so-so Double-A debut. Ambres has a solid makeup and work ethic and could wind up a late bloomer who reaches the majors as an extra outfielder. A Texas A&M football signee out of high school, the former quarterback has resisted annual overtures to give the gridiron another try.

Year	Club (League)	Class	AVG	G	AB	R	H	2B	3B	HR	RBI	BB	SO	SB	SLG	OBP
1999	Marlins (GCL)	R	.353	37	139	29	49	13	3	1	15	25	19	22	.511	.452
	Utica (NY-P)	A	.267	28	105	24	28	3	6	5	15	21	25	11	.552	.388
2000	Kane County (Mid)	A	.231	84	320	46	74	16	3	7	28	52	72	26	.366	.342
2001	Kane County (Mid)	A	.265	96	377	79	100	26	8	5	41	53	81	19	.416	.369
2002	Jupiter (FSL)	A	.236	123	509	88	120	25	7	9	37	57	98	23	.365	.323
2003	Carolina (SL)	AA	.258	127	380	75	98	23	8	10	55	72	81	9	.439	.376
MINOR LEAGUE TOTALS			.256	495	1830	341	469	106	35	37	191	280	376	110	.413	.361

The Astros were Baseball America's Organization of the Year in 2001, when they posted the top record in the National League as well as the best combined winning percentage in the minor leagues. The only negatives were the lack of a high Class A team and a failure to get past the first round of the playoffs.

Houston rectified the first problem with the addition of a Carolina League affiliate in 2003, but still has nary a postseason series victory to show for its 43 seasons. Even worse, the Astros let opportunities to end that streak pass by underachieving in each of the last two seasons. Most galling was their 2003 performance, when 88 victories would have won the NL Central. The Astros outhit and outpitched the Cubs, yet finished one game behind them.

While that's the smallest of gaps, it could widen. While cleaning out his locker at the end of the season, closer Billy Wagner questioned owner Drayton McLane's willingness to make the financial commitment to build a championship club. Houston entered the offseason seeking what general manager Gerry Hunsicker called payroll flexibility. Though the Astros signed free agent Andy Pettitte to a three-year, $31.5 million contract, they won't spend more than the $72.5 million they committed to player salaries in 2003, and they may spend less. Roger Clemens' one-year deal was so backloaded

TOP 30 PROSPECTS

1. Taylor Buchholz, rhp
2. Jason Lane, of
3. John Buck, c
4. Chris Burke, 2b/ss
5. Fernando Nieve, rhp
6. Hector Gimenez, c
7. Chad Qualls, rhp
8. Jason Hirsh, rhp
9. Matt Albers, rhp
10. Jimmy Barthmaier, rhp
11. Willy Taveras, of
12. Mitch Talbot, rhp
13. Mike Gallo, lhp
14. Tommy Whiteman, ss/3b
15. Ezequiel Astacio, rhp
16. Jared Gothreaux, rhp
17. Cliff Davis, rhp
18. Josh Anderson, of
19. Raymar Diaz, rhp
20. Scott Robinson, 1b
21. Jesse Carlson, lhp
22. Rodrigo Rosario, rhp
23. Charlton Jimerson, of
24. Todd Self, 1b/of
25. Ryan McKeller, rhp
26. D.J. Houlton, rhp
27. Jimmy Barrett, rhp
28. Tony Pluta, rhp
29. Derick Grigsby, rhp
30. Felipe Paulino, rhp

By Jim Callis

that he will receive just $1 million in 2004.

Their first move—not surprisingly considering his comments and their bullpen depth—was to send Wagner to the Phillies for Brandon Duckworth and minor league righthanders Taylor Buchholz and Ezequiel Astacio. The Astros also were looking to rid themselves of Richard Hidalgo's $12 million salary for 2004. Even team icon Jeff Bagwell has become a financial albatross. Coming off his worst back-to-back seasons in a decade, Bagwell will make $45 million over the next three seasons.

Duckworth will step right into the rotation and Buchholz immediately became the best prospect in the system. But the system isn't as strong as it appeared two years ago, when BA rated it the third-best in baseball. The majority of the Astros' Top 10 Prospects from then have either gotten hurt (lefthander Carlos Hernandez, righties Anthony Pluta and Rodrigo Rosario) or leveled off (catcher John Buck, infielders Chris Burke and Tommy Whiteman, righty Chad Qualls). Only Brad Lidge and Morgan Ensberg have met expectations, though Jason Lane could do the same if Houston finds him an outfield spot.

In order to compete with the Cubs, who have more money and a better stock of prospects, as well as the rest of the NL Central, the Astros will need the farm system to be as productive as it was in the 1990s.

ORGANIZATION
OVERVIEW

General manager: Gerry Hunsicker. **Farm director:** Tim Purpura. **Scouting director:** David Lakey.

2003 PERFORMANCE

Class	Team	League	W	L	Pct.	Finish*	Manager
Majors	Houston	National	87	75	.537	5th (16)	Jimy Williams
Triple-A	New Orleans Zephyrs	Pacific Coast	71	73	.493	8th(16)	Chris Maloney
Double-A	Round Rock Express	Texas	46	94	.329	8th (8)	Jackie Moore
High A	Salem Avalanche	Carolina	73	65	.529	3rd (8)	John Massarelli
Low A	Lexington Legends	South Atlantic	75	63	.543	5th (16)	Russ Nixon
Short-season	Tri-City Valley Cats	New York-Penn	44	32	.579	5th (14)	Ivan DeJesus
Rookie	†Martinsville Astros	Appalachian	42	23	.646	1st (10)	Jorge Orta
OVERALL 2003 MINOR LEAGUE RECORD			351	350	.501	15th (30)	

*Finish in overall standings (No. of teams in league). †Franchise will move to Greeneville, Tenn., in 2004.

ORGANIZATION LEADERS

BATTING
*Minimum 250 At-Bats
*AVG	Colin Porter, New Orleans	.320
R	Chris Burke, Round Rock	88
H	Chris Burke, Round Rock	165
TB	Henri Stanley, New Orleans	225
2B	T.J. Soto, Salem/Lexington	29
	Brooks Conrad, Salem/Lexington	29
3B	Three tied at	8
HR	John Fagan, Lexington	18
RBI	T.J. Soto, Salem/Lexington	82
BB	Todd Self, Salem	87
SO	Freddy Acevedo, Lexington	132
SB	Chris Burke, Round Rock	34
*SLG	Colin Porter, New Orleans	.511
*OBP	Todd Self, Salem	.433

PITCHING
#Minimum 75 Innings
W	Fernando Nieve, Lexington	14
L	Ruddy Lugo, Round Rock	15
#ERA	Chris Sampson, Salem/Lexington	1.90
G	Kirk Bullinger, New Orleans	55
	Miguel Saladin, New Orleans	55
CG	Tim McClaskey, Round Rock	7
SV	Juan Campos, Round Rock/Salem	24
IP	Chad Qualls, Round Rock	175
BB	Jailen Peguero, Lexington	69
SO	D.J. Houlton, New Orleans/Round Rock	149

BEST TOOLS

Best Hitter for Average	Jason Lane
Best Power Hitter	Jason Lane
Fastest Baserunner	Jeff Jorgensen
Best Athlete	Charlton Jimerson
Best Fastball	Fernando Nieve
Best Curveball	Taylor Buchholz
Best Slider	Jared Gothreaux
Best Changeup	Max Tremblay
Best Control	Taylor Buchholz
Best Defensive Catcher	Hector Gimenez
Best Defensive Infielder	Eric Bruntlett
Best Infield Arm	Jason Alfaro
Best Defensive Outfielder	Willy Taveras
Best Outfield Arm	Charlton Jimerson

PROJECTED 2007 LINEUP

Catcher	John Buck
First Base	Jeff Bagwell
Second Base	Chris Burke
Third Base	Morgan Ensberg
Shortstop	Adam Everett
Left Field	Lance Berkman
Center Field	Jason Lane
Right Field	Richard Hidalgo
No. 1 Starter	Roy Oswalt
No. 2 Starter	Wade Miller
No. 3 Starter	Andy Pettitte
No. 4 Starter	Taylor Buchholz
No. 5 Starter	Tim Redding
Closer	Octavio Dotel

LAST YEAR'S TOP 20 PROSPECTS

1. John Buck, c
2. Jason Lane, of
3. Brad Lidge, rhp
4. Jimmy Barrett, rhp
5. Chris Burke, 2b/ss
6. Tommy Whiteman, ss
7. Rodrigo Rosario, rhp
8. Hector Gimenez, c
9. Chad Qualls, rhp
10. Santiago Ramirez, rhp
11. Derick Grigsby, rhp
12. Henri Stanley, of
13. Anthony Pluta, rhp
14. Gavin Wright, of
15. Jeriome Robertson, lhp
16. Manny Santillan, rhp
17. Miguel Saladin, rhp
18. Victor Hall, of
19. Greg Miller, lhp
20. Fernando Nieve, rhp

TOP PROSPECTS OF THE DECADE

1994	Phil Nevin, 3b
1995	Brian Hunter, of
1996	Billy Wagner, lhp
1997	Richard Hidalgo, of
1998	Richard Hidalgo, of
1999	Lance Berkman, of
2000	Wilfredo Rodriguez, lhp
2001	Roy Oswalt, rhp
2002	Carlos Hernandez, lhp
2003	John Buck, c

TOP DRAFT PICKS OF THE DECADE

1994	Ramon Castro, c
1995	Tony McKnight, rhp
1996	Mark Johnson, rhp
1997	Lance Berkman, 1b
1998	Brad Lidge, rhp
1999	Mike Rosamond, of
2000	Robert Stiehl, rhp
2001	Chris Burke, ss
2002	Derick Grigsby, rhp
2003	Jason Hirsh, rhp (2)

ALL-TIME LARGEST BONUSES

Chris Burke, 2001	$2,125,000
Robert Stiehl, 2000	$1,250,000
Derick Grigsby, 2002	$1,125,000
Brad Lidge, 1998	$1,070,000
Lance Berkman, 1997	$1,000,000

HOUSTON ASTROS

RANK: **29**

Impact potential (D): A 27-year-old Jason Lane would have held the top spot on the Astros' prospect list had they not picked up Taylor Buchholz from the Phillies after the 2003 season for Billy Wagner. Some scouts still project Lane as an impact bat. Buchholz has two power pitches, but needs to refine his command and consistency to pitch at the front of a rotation.

Depth (F): Lane, John Buck and Chris Burke look like average big leaguers, but beyond that the Astros aren't developing the type of talent to compare with such players as Lance Berkman, Richard Hidalgo and Bobby Abreu in the past. Their strength lies in a raw crop of intriguing, but unrefined young arms led by Fernando Nieve.

Sleeper: Raymar Diaz, rhp.   —*Depth charts prepared by Josh Boyd. Numbers in parentheses indicate prospect rankings.*

LF
Mike Rodriguez
Anthony Acevedo
Gavin Wright

CF
Willy Taveras (11)
Josh Anderson (18)
Charlton Jimerson (23)
Jeff Jorgensen

RF
Jason Lane (2)
Freddy Acevedo
Ervin Alcantara

3B
Jason Alfaro
Saul Torres

SS
Tommy Whiteman (14)
Wade Robinson
Eric Bruntlett
Osvaldo Fernando

2B
Chris Burke (4)
Brooks Conrad
Dave Matranga

1B
Scott Robinson (20)
Todd Self (24)
Royce Huffman

SOURCE OF TALENT

Homegrown		Acquired	
College	11	Trades	2
Junior College	1	Rule 5 draft	1
Draft-and-follow	4	Independent	0
High school	6	Free agents/waivers	1
Nondrafted free agent	0		
Foreign	4		

C
John Buck (3)
Hector Gimenez (6)

RHP

Starters	Relievers
Taylor Buchholz (1)	Chad Qualls (7)
Fernando Nieve (5)	Ezequiel Astacio (15)
Jason Hirsh (8)	Jared Gothreaux (16)
Matt Albers (9)	Ryan McKeller (25)
Jimmy Barthmaier (10)	D.J. Houlton (26)
Mitch Talbot (12)	Tony Pluta (28)
Cliff Davis (17)	Felipe Paulino (30)
Raymar Diaz (19)	Miguel Saladin
Rodrigo Rosario (22)	Brandon Backe
Jimmy Barrett (27)	Santiago Ramirez
Derick Grigsby (29)	Daniel Freeman
Joey DeLeon	Doug Sessions
Chance Douglass	Jamie Merchant
Rory Shortell	Ruddy Lugo
	Robert Stiehl

LHP

Starters	Relievers
Josh Muecke	Mike Gallo (13)
Wandy Rodriguez	Jesse Carlson (21)
	Phil Barzilla
	Mark McLemore

DRAFT
ANALYSIS

Best Pro Debut: OF Josh Anderson (4) batted .286-3-30 with 26 steals to make the short-season New York-Penn League all-star team. 3B Brock Koman (9) tied for the NY-P lead with 25 doubles and batted .267-3-29.

Best Athlete: Anderson, who led NCAA Division I in stolen bases, has five tools, including 70 speed on the 20-80 scouting scale. He also starred at guard for his high school basketball team. OF Jeff Jorgensen (7) is faster than Anderson, though not as strong. RHPs Cliff Davis (6) and Jimmy Barthmaier (13) were sought-after as quarterbacks.

Best Pure Hitter: Anderson has the speed and batting ability to hit for average, though he'll need to show more discipline to bat at the top of the order.

Best Raw Power: 1Bs Beau Hearod (10) and Kevin Vital (18). Hearod led the Southeastern Conference with 20 homers and 82 RBIs for Alabama last spring. The 6-foot, 245-pound Vital batted cleanup behind No. 2 overall pick Rickie Weeks at Southern.

Fastest Runner: Jorgensen gets from home to first in 3.9 seconds from the right side. He was a nationally rated 60-meter sprinter in high school and originally attended Rice on a track scholarship. He missed the summer recovering from a broken foot.

Best Defensive Player: SS Wade Robinson (12) has the range, hands, arm

Anderson

and actions to make all the plays at his position. He batted .306-3-29 in the NY-P.

Best Fastball: RHP Jason Hirsh (2), at 6-foot-8 and 250 pounds, can reach 96 mph with his fastball and 86 with his slider. LHP Josh Muecke (5), Davis and Barthmaier all push 94 mph.

Best Breaking Ball: Area scout Mike Maggart, who signed Wade Miller and Tim Redding, found RHP Jamie Merchant (16) at the University of Vermont. Merchant's 77-78 mph curve was better than expected.

Most Intriguing Background: Jorgensen tried out for baseball only at the behest of high school teammate Austin Davis, a Rice outfielder. He graduated with a triple-major in May.

Closest To The Majors: Hirsh will have two plus-plus pitches once he becomes more consistent with his fastball and slider.

Best Late-Round Pick: Barthmaier might have been a first-round pick had football not clouded his signability.

The One Who Got Away: OF Drew Stubbs (3) was a quarterback, basketball player and state-champion relay runner in high school who went to Texas.

Assessment: The Astros lost their first-round pick for signing Jeff Kent and didn't help their cause by losing Stubbs to the Longhorns. They did compensate by going well over slot money to get Barthmaier.

RHP Derick Grigsby's (1) pro debut in 2003 was terribly disappointing, though RHP Mitch Talbot's (2) was encouraging. RHPs Jared Gothreaux (16) and Raymar Diaz (47, draft-and-follow) are intriguing sleepers.

2B Chris Burke (1) is Jeff Kent's heir apparent, and draft-and-follow RHP Matt Albers (23) has one of the best arms in the system. RHP Kirk Saarloos (3) shot to the majors quickly. Interestingly, the Astros drafted but failed to sign Gothreaux (37) and Diaz (29).

Power RHPs Robert Stiehl (1) and Tony Pluta (3) have been derailed by major surgery. RHP Chad Qualls (2) turned the corner in 2003 and could be the next Brad Lidge. SS Tommy Whiteman (6) may push Adam Everett.

OF Mike Rosamond (1) has washed out, but OF Jason Lane (6) would be Houston's best center-field option and just needs a chance to play. Mike Gallo (5) is the lefty set-up man the club has sought for years.

—Draft analysis prepared by Jim Callis. Numbers in parentheses indicate draft rounds.

DAVID SCHOFIELD

Taylor Buchholz

Born: Oct. 13, 1981.
Ht.: 6-4. **Wt.:** 220.
Bats: R. **Throws:** R.
School: Springfield (Pa.) HS.
Career Transactions: Selected by Phillies in sixth round of 2000 draft; signed June 19, 2000 . . . Traded by Phillies with RHP Brandon Duckworth and RHP Ezequiel Astacio to Astros for LHP Billy Wagner, Nov. 3, 2003.

The Phillies first approached the Astros about a trade in September, searching for a reasonably priced alternative to David Bell and inquiring about Geoff Blum. After Philadelphia held its offseason organizational meetings, it shifted its top priority to closer and came looking for Billy Wagner, Houston's career leader in saves. The Astros were rebuffed when they asked to build a trade around one of two pitching prospects, Cole Hamels and Gavin Floyd. The Phillies initially turned them down on Buchholz as well but relented when they realized it would be a deal-breaker. His commitment to North Carolina caused him to slide in the 2000 draft. His hometown Phillies may have been the only team that could have signed him, and they gave him fourth-round money ($365,000) as a sixth-round pick. Buchholz went 3-13 in his first calendar year after signing before everything started to click. He was the FSL pitcher of the year in 2002 and the youngest player selected for the Double-A Eastern League all-star game in 2003.

Buchholz' signature pitch is a hard curveball he picked up in low Class A in 2001. One scout compared its quality and his feel for it to Josh Beckett's and Kerry Wood's, while Phillies assistant general manager Mike Arbuckle said Buchholz' curve could be one of the five best in the National League within a few years. He throws the bender at 76-79 mph, and can change speeds off it to further befuddle hitters. Buchholz also has a quality fastball that sits in the low 90s, touches 95 mph and has heavy life. He'll flash an average changeup at times. He has a strong, durable frame that has held up well through 78 starts over the last three seasons. He shows good poise on the mound and never let a lack of run support fluster him at Double-A Reading. Buchholz succeeds so easily with his fastball and curve that he hasn't thrown his changeup much. He needs to use it more often to improve its quality and command. He pitched with bone chips in his elbow in 2003, but the problem resolved itself without surgery. Buchholz doesn't always trust his natural stuff and will try to overthrow. Then his front shoulder flies open in his delivery and he leaves pitches up in the strike zone. He needs to do a better job of holding baserunners.

The Wagner trade made sense on several levels for Houston. Wagner was unhappy with the direction of the club, he made more money than the Astros wanted to pay when they had a lower-cost alternative in Octavio Dotel, and they got three potential starting pitchers. Buchholz will open 2004 at Triple-A New Orleans. Given how Houston went through 12 starters in 2003, he could get promoted quickly if injuries strike. Buchholz projects as a No. 2 or 3 starter.

Year	Club (League)	Class	W	L	ERA	G	GS	CG	SV	IP	H	R	ER	HR	BB	SO	AVG
2000	Phillies (GCL)	R	2	3	2.25	12	7	0	0	44	46	22	11	2	14	41	.269
2001	Lakewood (SAL)	A	9	14	3.36	28	26	5	0	177	165	83	66	8	57	136	.250
2002	Clearwater (FSL)	A	10	6	3.29	23	23	4	0	159	140	66	58	11	51	129	.233
	Reading (EL)	AA	0	2	7.43	4	4	0	0	23	29	19	19	5	6	17	.315
2003	Reading (EL)	AA	9	11	3.55	25	24	1	0	145	136	62	57	14	33	114	.249
MINOR LEAGUE TOTALS			30	36	3.47	92	84	10	0	547	516	252	211	40	161	437	.249

Jason Lane, of

JOHN SPEAR

Born: Dec. 22, 1976. **Ht.:** 6-2. **Wt.:** 210. **Bats:** R. **Throws:** L. **School:** University of Southern California. **Career Transactions:** Selected by Astros in sixth round of 1999 draft; signed June 7, 1999.

Lane started getting taken seriously as a prospect after winning two league MVP awards and three RBI titles in his first three pro seasons. But when the Astros moved Craig Biggio to center field, it left Lane without a spot to crack the big league lineup. Lane is the lone impact hitter in the system. He has consistently hit for power and average as a pro. He's not a burner and fits best on an outfield corner, but he's a better center fielder than any of Houston's regulars. The Astros wanted him to become less pull-conscious and more disciplined in 2003, and he accomplished both missions. Lane has worked hard to eliminate glaring flaws from his game. The only negative in 2003 was a sports hernia that led to two lengthy stints on the disabled list and postseason surgery. He has nothing left to prove in the minors and will break camp with the Astros. But unless the Astros can move Richard Hidalgo's $12 million salary, Lane will serve as a fourth outfielder.

Year	Club (League)	Class	AVG	G	AB	R	H	2B	3B	HR	RBI	BB	SO	SB	SLG	OBP
1999	Auburn (NY-P)	A	.279	74	283	46	79	18	5	13	59	38	46	6	.516	.366
2000	Michigan (Mid)	A	.299	133	511	98	153	38	0	23	104	62	91	20	.509	.375
2001	Round Rock (TL)	AA	.316	137	526	103	166	36	2	38	124	61	98	14	.608	.407
2002	New Orleans (PCL)	AAA	.272	111	426	65	116	36	2	15	83	31	90	13	.472	.328
	Houston (NL)	MAJ	.290	44	69	12	20	3	1	4	10	10	12	1	.536	.375
2003	New Orleans (PCL)	AAA	.298	71	248	37	74	17	0	7	39	30	26	2	.452	.374
	Houston (NL)	MAJ	.296	18	27	5	8	2	0	4	10	0	2	0	.815	.296
MAJOR LEAGUE TOTALS			.292	62	96	17	28	5	1	8	20	10	14	1	.615	.355
MINOR LEAGUE TOTALS			.295	526	1994	349	588	145	9	96	409	222	351	55	.521	.373

John Buck, c

MORRIS FOSTOFF

Born: July 7, 1980. **Ht.:** 6-3. **Wt.:** 210. **Bats:** R. **Throws:** R. **School:** Taylorsville (Utah) HS. **Career Transactions:** Selected by Astros in seventh round of 1998 draft; signed June 11, 1998.

Buck emerged as one of the game's top catching prospects in 2001. While he still maintains that status, he faded down the stretch in 2002 and started to slump again in June 2003 before breaking his right hand in a baserunning accident. With power to all fields and the ability to crush mistakes, Buck has 20-25 home run potential. Managers rated him the best defensive catcher in the Pacific Coast League because of his arm strength and soft hands. He exudes leadership and relishes taking charge of a pitching staff. Buck probably won't hit for much of an average, though he can improve if he improves his recognition of breaking pitches and the strike zone. He has a long release that limited him to erasing just 26 percent of basestealers. He doesn't run well and has bulked up too much in the last two years, though he got into better shape while out with the broken hand. Buck may have been pushed too quickly and definitely needs more time in Triple-A. The Astros re-signed Brad Ausmus as a stopgap and will have him mentor Buck when he's ready.

Year	Club (League)	Class	AVG	G	AB	R	H	2B	3B	HR	RBI	BB	SO	SB	SLG	OBP
1998	Astros (GCL)	R	.286	36	126	24	36	9	0	3	15	13	22	2	.429	.362
1999	Auburn (NY-P)	A	.245	63	233	36	57	17	0	3	29	25	48	7	.356	.328
	Michigan (Mid)	A	.100	4	10	1	1	1	0	0	0	2	3	0	.200	.250
2000	Michigan (Mid)	A	.282	109	390	57	110	33	0	10	71	55	81	2	.444	.374
2001	Lexington (SAL)	A	.275	122	443	72	122	24	1	22	73	37	84	4	.483	.345
2002	Round Rock (TL)	AA	.263	120	448	48	118	29	3	12	89	31	93	2	.422	.314
2003	New Orleans (PCL)	AAA	.255	78	274	32	70	18	2	2	39	14	53	1	.358	.301
MINOR LEAGUE TOTALS			.267	532	1924	270	514	131	6	52	316	177	384	18	.423	.336

Chris Burke, 2b/ss

Born: March 11, 1980. **Ht.:** 5-11. **Wt.:** 180. **Bats:** R. **Throws:** R. **School:** University of Tennessee. **Career Transactions:** Selected by Astros in first round (10th overall) of 2001 draft; signed June 22, 2001.

Forced to Double-A before he was ready because the Astros didn't have a high Class A affiliate in 2002, Burke floundered. His struggles convinced him that what worked in college wasn't going to cut it in the pros, and he made a successful return to Round Rock in 2003, earning Texas League all-star honors. He started for Team USA at the Olympic qualifying tournament in Panama. Burke is ideally suited for the No. 2 spot in a lineup.

He gets on base, handles the bat well, has gap power and the speed and instincts to steal bases. He has the quickness and athleticism to be a good second baseman. Burke sometimes has too much power for his own good and must realize hitting homers isn't his game. He needs to take more grounders at second base, so he can improve his ability to read and charge balls. He has played a fair amount of shortstop as a pro but lacks the arm for the position. Unless Burke flops in Triple-A, he'll be Houston's starting second baseman in 2005. Buying Jeff Kent out for $700,000 will be more palatable to the Astros than paying him a $9 million salary.

Year	Club (League)	Class	AVG	G	AB	R	H	2B	3B	HR	RBI	BB	SO	SB	SLG	OBP
2001	Michigan (Mid)	A	.300	56	233	47	70	11	6	3	17	26	31	21	.438	.376
2002	Round Rock (TL)	AA	.264	136	481	66	127	19	8	3	37	39	61	16	.356	.330
2003	Round Rock (TL)	AA	.301	137	549	88	165	23	8	3	41	57	57	34	.388	.379
MINOR LEAGUE TOTALS			.287	329	1263	201	362	53	22	9	95	122	149	71	.385	.360

5 Fernando Nieve, rhp

Born: July 15, 1982. **Ht.:** 6-0. **Wt.:** 195. **Bats:** R. **Throws:** R. **Career Transactions:** Signed out of Venezuela by Astros, May 11, 1999.

Though Nieve had pitched just three innings above Rookie ball, the Astros fretted about possibly losing him in the 2002 Rule 5 draft. They're glad they didn't after watching him mature as a pitcher and a person and lead Houston farmhands with 14 victories. He has continued to build on that success by dominating in the Venezuelan League (4-1, 1.88). He doesn't have the highest radar-gun readings, but Nieve's fastball is the best in the system because it combines velocity (91-95 mph) with heavy sink and boring action that rides in on righthanders. His curveball improved dramatically in 2003, as did his approach. He's now a pitcher rather than a thrower who believes he can survive on fastballs alone. Nieve still is learning to throw a changeup and doesn't throw it often. He'll need that pitch and possibly a four-seamer to combat lefthanders at higher levels. He has trouble pitching lefties inside because his two-seamer tends to run back over the plate. Nieve's progress was the farm system's most pleasant development in 2003. Ticketed for high Class A Salem, he's at least two years away from Minute Maid Park.

Year	Club (League)	Class	W	L	ERA	G	GS	CG	SV	IP	H	R	ER	HR	BB	SO	AVG
1999	La Pradera (VSL)	R	0	6	4.55	11	7	0	0	32	31	22	16	0	16	41	—
2000	Venoco (VSL)	R	3	4	2.71	14	13	0	0	80	56	29	24	5	28	64	.199
2001	Martinsville (Appy)	R	4	2	3.79	12	8	1	0	38	27	20	16	2	21	49	.197
2002	Martinsville (Appy)	R	4	1	2.39	13	13	0	0	68	46	23	18	5	27	60	.185
	Lexington (SAL)	A	0	1	6.00	1	1	0	0	3	6	5	2	0	0	2	.353
2003	Lexington (SAL)	A	14	9	3.65	28	28	1	0	150	133	69	61	10	65	144	.238
MINOR LEAGUE TOTALS			25	23	3.33	79	70	2	0	371	299	168	137	22	157	360	.216

6 Hector Gimenez, c

Born: Sept. 28, 1982. **Ht.:** 5-10. **Wt.:** 180. **Bats:** B. **Throws:** R. **Career Transactions:** Signed out of Venezuela by Astros, July 2, 1999.

While the Astros system has slipped, not many organizations have a pair of potential starting catchers like John Buck and Gimenez. Managers have ranked Gimenez the best defensive catcher in the low Class A South Atlantic and high Class A Carolina leagues in his two domestic seasons. One CL manager said he tried to run on Salem just because he liked watching Gimenez' arm in action. Gimenez has a plus arm and ranked second in the CL by throwing out 39 percent of basestealers. He throws better and has more agility than Buck. He's similar offensively, producing more for power than for average. As a bonus, he's a switch-hitter. Still adapting to the United States, Gimenez doesn't have Buck's leadership skills. Gimenez needs to improve his English so he can better handle a pitching staff. He sometimes lets bad at-bats affect his defense. As a hitter, he has only a raw grasp of the strike zone. Like most catchers, he has below-average speed. Gimenez is two years behind Buck. The Astros will return him to high Class A in 2004 and promote him once he gets going offensively.

Year	Club (League)	Class	AVG	G	AB	R	H	2B	3B	HR	RBI	BB	SO	SB	SLG	OBP
2000	Venoco (VSL)	R	.297	34	91	9	27	8	0	1	13	12	21	0	.418	.396
2001	Venoco (VSL)	R	.278	42	144	27	40	12	3	5	34	26	30	4	.507	.388
2002	Lexington (SAL)	A	.263	85	297	41	78	16	1	11	42	25	78	2	.434	.320
2003	Salem (Car)	A	.247	109	381	41	94	17	1	7	54	29	75	2	.352	.304
MINOR LEAGUE TOTALS			.262	270	913	118	239	53	5	24	143	92	204	8	.410	.333

7 Chad Qualls, rhp

STEVE MOORE

Born: Aug. 17, 1978. **Ht.:** 6-5. **Wt.:** 220. **Bats:** R. **Throws:** R. **School:** University of Nevada. **Career Transactions:** Selected by Astros in second round of 2000 draft; signed Aug. 16, 2000.

Like Chris Burke, Qualls was promoted to Double-A before his time in 2002. While he led the Texas League with 142 strikeouts, he went 6-13, 4.36. His Round Rock encore started no better, as he went 3-8, 5.42 in the first three months. Then he finished with a 5-3, 1.93 flourish, establishing himself as the Astros' most advanced starting pitching prospect until they traded for Taylor Buchholz. Qualls' resurgence started when he realized that he's not a power pitcher. His out pitch is a slider, and he wins when he gets his 87-94 mph fastball to sink. He improved his changeup and started throwing a splitter. He's durable and mentally tough. Qualls has difficulty maintaining his mechanics. When he drops down too low, he loses his heavy sink and hitters sit on flat fastballs. His inconsistent delivery also hampers his control. He still has work to do with his changeup, the pitch that ultimately will determine whether he's a big league starter or reliever. Houston's plan is for Qualls to begin 2004 as a Triple-A starter. But he could be an attractive relief option for the Astros by midseason.

Year	Club (League)	Class	W	L	ERA	G	GS	CG	SV	IP	H	R	ER	HR	BB	SO	AVG
2001	Michigan (Mid)	A	15	6	3.72	26	26	3	0	162	149	77	67	8	31	125	.239
2002	Round Rock (TL)	AA	6	13	4.36	29	29	0	0	163	174	92	79	9	67	142	.273
2003	Round Rock (TL)	AA	8	11	3.85	28	28	3	0	175	174	85	75	12	61	132	.264
MINOR LEAGUE TOTALS			29	30	3.98	83	83	6	0	500	497	254	221	29	159	399	.259

8 Jason Hirsh, rhp

RICH ABEL

Born: Feb. 20, 1982. **Ht.:** 6-8. **Wt.:** 250. **Bats:** R. **Throws:** R. **School:** California Lutheran University. **Career Transactions:** Selected by Astros in second round of 2003 draft; signed July 3, 2003.

Hirsh threw just 86-88 mph in high school, attracting no interest from NCAA Division I programs. Thanks to weight work and mechanical adjustments at Division III Cal Lutheran, he boosted his fastball up to 96 mph and his slider up to 86 last spring, when he recorded 17- and 18-strikeout games. The Astros took him with their top pick after forfeiting their first-rounder to sign free agent Jeff Kent. By the time he reaches the majors, Hirsh could have two 70 pitches on the 20-80 scouting scale. His fastball sits at 92-93 mph and shows nice arm-side run at times. He has intimidating presence on the mound and is athletic for his size. He was more polished than the Astros expected. Hirsh needs more consistency with all of his pitches. At times his fastball is straight, and his slider is far less reliable. His changeup has its moments but his inexperience throwing offspeed stuff shows. Hirsh could be a formidable starter or reliever. Some have projected him as a set-up man, but that might be underestimating him. He'll pitch in the low Class A Lexington rotation in 2004.

Year	Club (League)	Class	W	L	ERA	G	GS	CG	SV	IP	H	R	ER	HR	BB	SO	AVG
2003	Tri-City (NY-P)	A	3	1	1.95	10	8	0	0	32	22	10	7	0	7	33	.190
MINOR LEAGUE TOTALS			3	1	1.95	10	8	0	0	32	22	10	7	0	7	33	.190

9 Matt Albers, rhp

RICH ABEL

Born: Jan. 20, 1983. **Ht.:** 6-0. **Wt.:** 205. **Bats:** L. **Throws:** R. **School:** San Jacinto (Texas) JC. **Career Transactions:** Selected by Astros in 23rd round of 2001 draft; signed May 31, 2002.

Albers is a local product, drafted out of a suburban Houston high school and signed after a year in junior college. He made tremendous strides from his first pro summer to his second, topping the New York-Penn League in strikeouts and turning in quality starts in each of his last six outings. Despite a short, stocky frame, Albers generates 91-95 mph fastballs with little effort. He also has a quick, sharp breaking ball and is picking up a changeup. His fearless makeup might be as good as his stuff. He did a better job controlling his mechanics and his pitches in 2003. His feel for his craft also improved. Houston has had success with short pitchers, but Albers not only was short but also had a soft, pudgy body when he signed. The Astros challenged him to improve his conditioning and he responded, though he'll have to continually watch himself. His secondary pitches require more work. Albers will team up with Jason Hirsh again in low Class A. Hirsh has a higher ceiling, but Albers is more polished and consistent at this point.

Year	Club (League)	Class	W	L	ERA	G	GS	CG	SV	IP	H	R	ER	HR	BB	SO	AVG
2002	Martinsville (Appy)	R	2	3	5.13	13	13	0	0	60	61	38	34	2	38	72	.274
2003	Tri-City (NY-P)	A	5	4	2.92	15	14	0	0	86	69	37	28	1	25	94	.214
MINOR LEAGUE TOTALS			7	7	3.82	28	27	0	0	146	130	75	62	3	63	166	.239

10 Jimmy Barthmaier, rhp

Born: Jan. 6, 1984. **Ht.:** 6-4. **Wt.:** 210. **Bats:** R. **Throws:** R. **School:** Roswell (Ga.) HS. **Career Transactions:** Selected by Astros in 13th round of 2003 draft; signed July 3, 2003.

Barthmaier could have gone in 2003's supplemental first round, but several Southeastern Conference football programs recruited him as a quarterback, clouding his signability. When the Braves passed on him, other teams followed suit, but Barthmaier had told Astros area scout Ellis Dungan that he was open to turning pro. He signed for $750,000 as a 13th-rounder—$125,000 more than Houston gave Jason Hirsh as a second-rounder. Barthmaier is loaded with physical tools. He has size, athleticism and arm strength. He throws a heavy fastball at 91-94 mph and should add velocity. His slider is a second power pitch, registering as high as 85 mph. He soaks up instruction quickly. Because he divided his time between two sports, Barthmaier is raw. He used to throw his slider with a football motion, and he barely has used a changeup. He throws across his body and varies his arm slots, so he'll have to clean up his mechanics. Barthmaier will need plenty of time to develop. He'll begin the 2004 season in extended spring training and report to short-season Tri-City. He probably won't see full-season ball until 2005.

Year	Club (League)	Class	W	L	ERA	G	GS	CG	SV	IP	H	R	ER	HR	BB	SO	AVG
2003	Martinsville (Appy)	R	1	1	2.49	8	3	0	0	22	19	9	6	0	7	18	.226
MINOR LEAGUE TOTALS			1	1	2.49	8	3	0	0	22	19	9	6	0	7	18	.226

11 Willy Taveras, of

Born: Dec. 25, 1981. **Ht.:** 6-0. **Wt.:** 160. **Bats:** R. **Throws:** R. **Career Transactions:** Signed out of Dominican Republic by Indians, May 27, 1999 . . . Selected by Astros from Indians in Rule 5 major league draft, Dec. 15, 2003.

The Astros lack center-field prospects and have been stretching it defensively at that position in the majors with Richard Hidalgo, Lance Berkman and Craig Biggio. With that in mind, they spent a major league Rule 5 pick on a center fielder for the second straight year. The Astros had to return Victor Hall to the Diamondbacks in 2003 but may be able to retain Taveras. If they can't keep him on their 25-man roster all year, they'll have to put him through waivers and offer him back to Indians for half the $50,000 draft price. Cleveland liked Taveras but had too many prospects to protect on its 40-man roster. Taveras is a potential leadoff hitter whose line-drive approach and control of the strike zone suit him well for the role. He has to get stronger to keep pitchers honest, but power never will be a big part of his game. Taveras' best tool is his speed, which made a huge impression on Carolina League managers in 2003. They rated him the fastest baserunner, best baserunner and best defensive outfielder in the league. Not only can he fly, but he also has basestealing aptitude, succeeding on 57 of his 69 attempts last year. Taveras can cover more ground than any outfielder in the organization, including the majors, and he has a solid arm. He really needs to be playing every day in Double-A at this stage of his career, so if Houston holds on to Taveras, it will come at the expense of stunting his development.

Year	Club (League)	Class	AVG	G	AB	R	H	2B	3B	HR	RBI	BB	SO	SB	SLG	OBP
1999	Indians (DSL)	R	.354	68	277	57	98	19	6	3	44	32	32	26	.498	.435
2000	Burlington (Appy)	R	.263	50	190	46	50	4	3	1	16	23	44	36	.332	.356
2001	Columbus (SAL)	A	.271	97	395	55	107	15	7	3	32	22	73	29	.367	.317
2002	Columbus (SAL)	A	.265	85	313	68	83	14	1	4	27	45	68	54	.355	.385
2003	Kinston (Car)	A	.282	113	397	64	112	9	6	2	35	52	68	57	.350	.381
MINOR LEAGUE TOTALS			.286	413	1572	290	450	61	23	13	154	174	285	202	.379	.373

12 Mitch Talbot, rhp

Born: Oct. 17, 1983. **Ht.:** 6-2. **Wt.:** 175. **Bats:** R. **Throws:** R. **School:** Canyon View, HS, Cedar City, Utah. **Career Transactions:** Selected by Astros in second round of 2002 draft; signed Aug. 20, 2002.

Since they signed him as a second-rounder in 2002, the Astros have compared Talbot's repertoire to that of former all-star Ron Darling. Because the Astros temporarily embargoed signing draft picks that summer, he didn't make his pro debut until 2003 at Rookie-level Martinsville. The layoff didn't hurt him, as Talbot showed a lot of polish for a teenager.

Hitters have trouble making solid contact because he has a quick, deceptive arm action and gets a lot of boring and sinking action on his fastballs. He sits at 89-92 mph with his two-seam fastball and can get up to 95 with a four-seamer. His curveball, changeup and ability to pitch are all advanced for his age. He should have three average or better pitches when he reaches the majors. Talbot still needs to tighten his curveball and refine his mechanics a little bit. He'll work on that in low Class A this year.

Year	Club (League)	Class	W	L	ERA	G	GS	CG	SV	IP	H	R	ER	HR	BB	SO	AVG
2003	Martinsville (Appy)	R	4	4	2.83	12	12	0	0	54	45	26	17	1	11	46	.224
MINOR LEAGUE TOTALS			4	4	2.83	12	12	0	0	54	45	26	17	1	11	46	.224

13 Mike Gallo, lhp

Born: April 2, 1977. **Ht.:** 6-0. **Wt.:** 175. **Bats:** L. **Throws:** L. **School:** Long Beach State University. **Career Transactions:** Selected by Astros in fifth round of 1999 draft; signed June 3, 1999.

The presence of lefty closer Billy Wagner obscured the fact that the Astros lacked a reliable southpaw set-up man from 1999-2002. Gallo filled the void when he was promoted last June, and Houston says he can become more than a lefty specialist. The 1999 Big West Conference pitcher of the year (beating out Chad Qualls and Kirk Saarloos, among others), Gallo moved to the bullpen as a pro in mid-2000. He spent three full years in Class A before rocketing from Double-A to Triple-A to the majors in less than three months last year. Gallo goes right after hitters with an 88-91 mph fastball, a big-breaking curveball he'll throw to lefthanders and righthanders, a compact slider and a changeup. His fastball jumps in on lefties and he uses the changeup to combat righties. Gallo has improved his ability to locate his pitches in the strike zone. He incorporates a leg kick and a lot of motion into his delivery, making him deceptive. He does the little things such as fielding his position well and holding runners, allowing just four steals in eight tries last year. Gallo isn't big and can hang his slider when he doesn't stay on top of it. He needs to do a better job against big league righties, who hit .295 against him, and some Houston officials would like to see him drop down occasionally versus lefties. Gallo was sharp in the Arizona Fall League, recording a 0.89 ERA and 11-0 strikeout-walk ratio in 11 innings, reinforcing the Astros' faith in him.

Year	Club (League)	Class	W	L	ERA	G	GS	CG	SV	IP	H	R	ER	HR	BB	SO	AVG
1999	Auburn (NY-P)	A	1	0	1.23	3	3	0	0	15	13	4	2	0	7	11	.232
	Michigan (Mid)	A	2	3	5.85	12	12	0	0	60	76	47	39	6	23	32	.315
2000	Michigan (Mid)	A	8	3	4.86	24	13	0	0	91	104	58	49	6	27	56	.285
2001	Michigan (Mid)	A	9	2	3.84	44	0	0	4	84	83	38	36	4	19	67	.252
2002	Lexington (SAL)	A	4	4	1.83	42	2	0	8	88	69	29	18	6	26	93	.211
	Round Rock (TL)	AA	0	0	6.75	1	0	0	0	1	1	1	1	1	0	0	.200
2003	Round Rock (TL)	AA	1	1	1.37	17	0	0	2	20	17	3	3	1	6	22	.246
	New Orleans (PCL)	AAA	3	0	2.08	16	0	0	0	17	13	4	4	0	3	11	.217
	Houston (NL)	MAJ	1	0	3.00	32	0	0	0	30	28	10	10	3	10	16	.267
MAJOR LEAGUE TOTALS			1	0	3.00	32	0	0	0	30	28	10	10	3	10	16	.267
MINOR LEAGUE TOTALS			28	13	3.64	159	30	0	14	376	376	184	152	24	111	292	.259

14 Tommy Whiteman, ss/3b

Born: July 14, 1979. **Ht.:** 6-3. **Wt.:** 180. **Bats:** R. **Throws:** R. **School:** University of Oklahoma. **Career Transactions:** Selected by Astros in sixth round of 2000 draft; signed June 16, 2000.

Whiteman, whose Native American name is Owner of Outstanding Horses, is believed to be the first pro athlete from the Crow Nation. Along with Jimmy Barrett, he was one of the system's biggest disappointments in 2003. He tailed off badly after a hot start in Double-A, with his performance declining each month. Even worse, he refused to take responsibility or acknowledge the slippage. The Astros finally got his attention by moving him to third base and playing Chris Burke at shortstop, not that the move jump-started Whiteman's bat. His trip to the Arizona Fall League was a waste of time, as he went 0-for-9 before leaving with soreness in his right scapula. What has been especially frustrating for the Astros is that Whiteman has shown five tools at shortstop. He has the bat speed to hit for average and gap power, and he's a solid-average runner once he gets going. Defensively, he has plus instincts and hands, and his quick first step gives him good range. But Whiteman has to show more energy and dedication to become a big league regular. He needs more strength and plate discipline, as he can be beaten with good fastballs inside and he chases breaking balls. He hasn't corrected a tendency to flip his throws on routine plays, which hurts his accuracy, though that may have been related to his scapula problem. The injury only required rest and rehabilitation, not surgery, so he'll be good to go for spring training. Because they've put him on the 40-man roster for two straight years, the Astros will push Whiteman to

Triple-A in 2004. If he doesn't make adjustments and improve, he won't be protected a third time.

Year	Club (League)	Class	AVG	G	AB	R	H	2B	3B	HR	RBI	BB	SO	SB	SLG	OBP
2000	Auburn (NY-P)	A	.250	70	232	33	58	10	3	1	22	22	52	7	.332	.318
2001	Lexington (SAL)	A	.319	114	389	58	124	26	8	18	57	34	106	17	.566	.380
	Round Rock (TL)	AA	.250	4	16	1	4	0	0	1	1	0	5	0	.438	.294
2002	Round Rock (TL)	AA	.179	15	56	3	10	2	1	0	5	4	17	1	.250	.246
	Lexington (SAL)	A	.303	90	350	50	106	29	2	10	49	36	66	6	.483	.374
2003	Round Rock (TL)	AA	.261	133	532	65	139	18	2	13	70	35	102	3	.376	.310
MINOR LEAGUE TOTALS			.280	426	1575	210	441	85	16	43	204	131	348	34	.436	.341

15 Ezequiel Astacio, rhp

Born: Nov. 4, 1979. **Ht.:** 6-3. **Wt.:** 180. **Bats:** R. **Throws:** R. **Career Transactions:** Signed out of Dominican Republic by Phillies, Feb. 22, 1998 . . . Traded by Phillies with RHP Brandon Duckworth and RHP Taylor Buchholz to Astros for LHP Billy Wagner, Nov. 3, 2003.

Taylor Buchholz and Brandon Duckworth were the centerpieces of the Billy Wagner trade with Philadelphia, but the Astros got a third potential starter in the deal with Astacio. After filling out in the offseason and adding 3 mph to his fastball, he led the Florida State League and the Phillies system with 15 wins in 2003. Astacio throws strikes with all three of his pitches: an 88-93 mph fastball, a curveball that's average now and has plus potential, and a changeup. He needs to become more consistent with his curve and learn to use his change-up better. He'll abandon it for stretches, then rely on it too much. While Astacio is stingy with walks, he's hittable because he catches too much of the strike zone and doesn't pitch inside enough. He's intelligent and should be able to make those adjustments. There's also room for more projection with his long, loose arm. Headed for Double-A, he projects as a No. 5 starter or middle reliever.

Year	Club (League)	Class	W	L	ERA	G	GS	CG	SV	IP	H	R	ER	HR	BB	SO	AVG
1998	Phillies (DSL)	R	0	3	7.71	15	4	0	0	21	26	29	18	3	22	16	.283
1999	Phillies (DSL)	R	5	2	2.67	12	12	0	0	64	50	24	19	4	27	42	.221
2000	Phillies (DSL)	R	7	5	2.20	15	15	0	0	90	70	40	22	1	20	97	.207
2001	Phillies (GCL)	R	4	2	2.30	9	9	0	0	47	48	16	12	2	10	42	.268
2002	Lakewood (SAL)	A	10	7	3.31	25	25	1	0	152	159	61	56	9	46	100	.275
2003	Clearwater (FSL)	A	15	5	3.29	25	22	2	0	148	140	60	54	9	29	83	.247
MINOR LEAGUE TOTALS			41	24	3.12	101	87	3	0	522	493	230	181	28	154	380	.249

16 Jared Gothreaux, rhp

Born: Jan. 27, 1980. **Ht.:** 6-0. **Wt.:** 200. **Bats:** R. **Throws:** R. **School:** McNeese State University. **Career Transactions:** Selected by Astros in 16th round of 2002 draft; signed June 6, 2002.

Gothreaux is similar to Ezequiel Astacio. They posted virtually identical statistics in 2003, led high Class A leagues in victories and have comparable stuff. Gothreaux began the season in the Salem bullpen and didn't crack the rotation until late April, yet topped the Carolina League in wins and finished third in ERA. His best pitch is his breaking ball, which has slider velocity (81-82 mph) and drops like a power curveball. He also has an 88-93 mph fastball and can vary speeds with both pitches. Gothreaux also shows good touch with his changeup and used it more as a starter last season. He keeps the ball down in the zone, pitching to contact and inducing grounders. Like Astacio, Gothreaux doesn't beat himself with walks but doesn't miss many bats. He's fully developed and doesn't figure to get better than he is now. He has the same projection (fifth starter or middle reliever) and destination (Double-A) as Astacio.

Year	Club (League)	Class	W	L	ERA	G	GS	CG	SV	IP	H	R	ER	HR	BB	SO	AVG
2002	Tri-City (NY-P)	A	2	3	2.72	28	0	0	4	46	55	23	14	3	12	53	.288
2003	Salem (Car)	A	13	4	2.82	29	22	1	1	147	144	54	46	4	26	85	.259
MINOR LEAGUE TOTALS			15	7	2.80	57	22	1	5	193	199	77	60	7	38	138	.266

17 Cliff Davis, rhp

Born: Dec. 31, 1984. **Ht.:** 6-5. **Wt.:** 215. **Bats:** R. **Throws:** R. **School:** Eupora (Miss.) HS. **Career Transactions:** Selected by Astros in sixth round of 2003 draft; signed June 16, 2003.

Jimmy Barthmaier wasn't the only top quarterback recruit that Houston signed away from college football in 2003. After leading Eupora High to the Mississippi 2-A finals in baseball and football, Davis was ticketed for the University of Alabama—where former baseball prospects Brody Croyle and Spencer Pennington are one-two on the quarterback depth chart. The Astros changed Davis' mind with a $200,000 bonus. Because he hadn't received much instruction or focused on baseball in the past, he's raw. He'll take considerable time to refine, but he is a strong athlete with a classic pitcher's body (6-foot-6, 215 pounds) and the opportunity for two plus pitches. Davis won two games in five days to give Eupora the state baseball title, leaving him worn out by the time he signed. His velocity dipped from 92-94 mph in the spring to 86-89 mph, but Houston expects the velocity and rising life on his fastball to return. He also shows a hard, knee-buckling curveball at times and has a decent feel for a changeup. Davis' command was off during his pro debut at Rookie-level Martinsville, and the Astros will try to improve his mechanics. He has a funky delivery, throwing from a three-quarters arm slot and holding the ball close to his head. While he needs a lot of innings and a lot more consistency, his ceiling is high. He'll report to extended spring in April, and to either Tri-City or the organization's relocated Rookie-level Appalachian League team in Greeneville, Tenn., in June.

Year	Club (League)	Class	W	L	ERA	G	GS	CG	SV	IP	H	R	ER	HR	BB	SO	AVG
2003	Martinsville (Appy)	R	1	0	7.50	12	1	0	0	18	13	15	15	1	17	13	.213
MINOR LEAGUE TOTALS			1	0	7.50	12	1	0	0	18	13	15	15	1	17	13	.213

18 Josh Anderson, of

Born: Aug. 10, 1982. **Ht.:** 6-2. **Wt.:** 195. **Bats:** L. **Throws:** R. **School:** Eastern Kentucky University. **Career Transactions:** Selected by Astros in fourth round of 2003 draft; signed June 13, 2003.

Speed was the system's biggest deficiency entering 2003, and the Astros addressed that in June by drafting Anderson in the fourth round and Jeff Jorgensen in the seventh. Jorgensen, who missed the summer with a broken foot that kept him out of the College World Series with Rice, is faster. But Anderson is nearly as quick—he can go from the left side of the plate to first base in 3.95-4.0 seconds—plus he's stronger and more polished. He led NCAA Division I with 57 steals in 65 attempts at Eastern Kentucky last spring, and he finished third in hitting behind first-round picks Rickie Weeks (Brewers) and Mitch Maier (Royals) at .447. While some scouts viewed Anderson as having questionable power and no more than fourth-outfielder potential, Houston loves his tools across the board. He made a surprisingly quick adjustment to wood bats. The Astros say he'll be a dangerous stolen base threat while hitting for respectable power. Anderson covers a lot of ground and gets good jumps in center field. He also has a strong arm and can throw nearly as well lefthanded as righthanded. Houston officials describe him as an untamed stallion who can get too reckless in the field and on the bases. A more patient approach at the plate also would benefit him, as would shortening his swing and improving his bunting. After earning New York-Penn League all-star recognition in his pro debut, Anderson likely will begin 2004 in low Class A.

Year	Club (League)	Class	AVG	G	AB	R	H	2B	3B	HR	RBI	BB	SO	SB	SLG	OBP
2003	Tri-City (NY-P)	A	.286	74	297	44	85	11	4	3	30	16	53	26	.380	.339
MINOR LEAGUE TOTALS			.286	74	297	44	85	11	4	3	30	16	53	26	.380	.339

19 Raymar Diaz, rhp

Born: Nov. 13, 1983. **Ht.:** 6-7. **Wt.:** 190. **Bats:** R. **Throws:** R. **School:** Laredo (Texas) JC. **Career Transactions:** Selected by Astros in 47th round of 2002 draft; signed May 6, 2003.

The Astros signed three draft-and-follows from the 2002 draft, and all of them made the top 30. While Scott Robinson (seventh round) and Ryan McKeller (45th) were drafted higher and received more exposure, initial returns indicate that Diaz (47th) is the best of the group. Houston originally drafted Diaz in the 29th round in 2001, as an outfielder out of a Puerto Rican high school. He went to Laredo (Texas) JC, where the Astros again drafted him as an outfielder in 2002. The Astros liked his speed and arm strength, and his 6-foot-7 frame projected power though there were questions about his bat. Laredo started using Diaz as a reliever last spring, and he immediately hit 91-92 mph with his fastball. Houston made him a full-time pitcher after signing him in May, and he surpassed their expectations with a 0.90 ERA and .162 opponent average in Rookie ball. He then surprised the Astros by joining Santurce in the Puerto Rican League and pitching well in middle relief. Diaz touches the mid-90s at times and has good spin on his inconsistent curveball. He still needs to hone his curve and command and develop a changeup, but he's coordinated and has a good delivery for someone of his size and inexperience. His winter showing makes it that much easier to send him to low Class A in 2004.

Year	Club (League)	Class	W	L	ERA	G	GS	CG	SV	IP	H	R	ER	HR	BB	SO	AVG
2003	Martinsville (Appy)	R	4	0	0.90	19	0	0	5	30	17	4	3	1	13	29	.162
MINOR LEAGUE TOTALS			4	0	0.90	19	0	0	5	30	17	4	3	1	13	29	.162

20 Scott Robinson, 1b

Born: Oct. 14, 1983. **Ht.:** 6-1. **Wt.:** 185. **Bats:** L. **Throws:** S. **School:** Palomar (Calif.) JC. **Career Transactions:** Selected by Astros in 7th round of 2002 draft; signed May 23, 2003.

The Astros really wanted to sign Robinson, the best pure hitter they drafted in 2002, out of high school but had to settle for catching a break. Though he couldn't come to terms, he changed his college plans from San Diego State to Palomar (Calif.) JC, meaning Houston retained his rights as an unexpected draft-and-follow. The move paid off for Robinson, who ultimately signed for $225,000. Robinson's father Bruce was the 21st overall pick in the June 1975 draft and played briefly in the majors, as did his uncle Dave. The only high school player ever to play in the Alaska League, Robinson went 4-for-18 as a rising senior with the Alaska Goldpanners in 2001. He returned after graduating in 2002 and was team MVP as the Goldpanners won the National Baseball Congress World Series. Robinson is often compared to Mark Grace. He has a good feel at the plate, controls the bat well and should be able to hit for average with line-drive power. He can handle good fastballs already. He also has athleticism and moves well around the first-base bag. He throws equally well with both hands. Also like Grace, he doesn't have typical first-base power. Robinson could top out at 10-15 homers annually, and he must add upper-body strength to help him drive more balls. He makes consistent contact yet must draw more walks. Following his so-so pro debut in the New York-Penn League, the Astros expect he'll hit more this year in low Class A.

Year	Club (League)	Class	AVG	G	AB	R	H	2B	3B	HR	RBI	BB	SO	SB	SLG	OBP
2003	Tri-City (NY-P)	A	.253	73	277	36	70	23	0	4	36	17	32	4	.379	.297
MINOR LEAGUE TOTALS			.253	73	277	36	70	23	0	4	36	17	32	4	.379	.297

21 Jesse Carlson, lhp

Born: Dec. 31, 1980. **Ht.:** 6-1. **Wt.:** 160. **Bats:** L. **Throws:** L. **School:** University of Connecticut. **Career Transactions:** Selected by Tigers in 15th round of 2002 draft; signed June 6, 2002 . . . Released by Tigers, March 28, 2003 . . . Signed by Astros, March 31, 2003.

Carlson wound up with the Astros because he was in the wrong place at the wrong time. While in minor league camp with the Tigers, he was an innocent participant in an off-color skit that insulted Oneonta manager Randy Ready's wife. Though Carlson had a strong pro debut in 2002, Detroit released him and two other players because of the incident. After signing with Houston, Carlson was unhittable at Lexington, where he was named team MVP. His best pitch is a sharp, late-breaking slider, and he's especially tough on lefthanders because he throws from a low three-quarters slot. His fastball arrives at 88-91 mph and he mixes in an occasional changeup. Carlson's stuff is nastier than Mike Gallo's, though Gallo has proved himself four levels higher than Carlson has at this point. Houston will give him the chance to catch up in 2004, when their rights to Carlson end if he's not kept on the 40-man roster after the season. He'll start the year in Double-A and move to Triple-A as soon as he shows he's ready.

Year	Club (League)	Class	W	L	ERA	G	GS	CG	SV	IP	H	R	ER	HR	BB	SO	AVG
2002	Oneonta (NY-P)	A	2	2	1.66	19	0	0	0	38	19	8	7	1	10	47	.146
2003	Lexington (SAL)	A	3	0	1.56	53	0	0	13	63	37	11	11	2	16	84	.168
MINOR LEAGUE TOTALS			5	2	1.60	72	0	0	13	101	56	19	18	3	26	131	.160

22 Rodrigo Rosario, rhp

Born: March 14, 1978. **Ht.:** 6-2. **Wt.:** 165. **Bats:** R. **Throws:** R. **Career Transactions:** Signed out of Dominican Republic by Astros, July 6, 1996 . . . Released by Astros, Nov. 19, 2003 . . . Signed by Astros, Jan. 9, 2004.

Rosario's first two big league starts couldn't have been any different. He beat the Rangers in his big league debut, allowing just four hits and two runs (one earned) in six innings. Six days later he faced Texas again, but this time a sore shoulder forced him to leave after two scoreless innings and signaled the end of his season. When Rosario had surgery in August, the damage was worse than initially believed. He had labrum and rotator-cuff tears plus instability in the shoulder, not to mention a torn biceps tendon. A healthy Rosario would have ranked third on this list, but he probably won't pitch at all in 2004. The Astros released him in November and brought him back on a minor league contract in January. Hitters have difficulty making solid contact against Rosario. Though he threw 93-95 mph in his brief major league stint, he usually sits at 91-92 mph and gets a lot more movement when he does. He doesn't have a classic slider, but when he stays on top of the pitch it works for him. He had shown an improved slider and changeup before he got hurt. Because Rosario has a slight build, his durability may always be questioned. So will his future until he returns to the mound and shows if he can recapture his ability to miss bats.

Year	Club (League)	Class	W	L	ERA	G	GS	CG	SV	IP	H	R	ER	HR	BB	SO	AVG
1997	Astros (DSL)	R	6	4	2.46	15	14	0	0	91	63	30	25	2	24	81	.195
1998	Astros (GCL)	R	2	2	4.12	13	12	0	0	68	61	36	31	6	30	65	.245
	Auburn (NY-P)	A	0	0	0.00	2	0	0	0	2	0	0	0	0	3	2	.000
1999	Martinsville (Appy)	R	5	5	4.69	14	14	0	0	79	78	46	41	9	32	86	.267
2000	Auburn (NY-P)	A	5	6	3.45	14	14	0	0	76	67	36	29	3	32	67	.232
2001	Lexington (SAL)	A	13	4	2.14	30	21	1	2	147	105	46	35	8	36	131	.198
2002	Round Rock (TL)	AA	11	6	3.11	26	23	0	0	130	106	56	45	5	59	94	.222
2003	New Orleans (PCL)	AAA	5	7	4.03	15	15	1	0	87	71	40	39	7	32	68	.222
	Houston (NL)	MAJ	1	0	1.13	2	2	0	0	8	5	2	1	0	3	6	.172
MAJOR LEAGUE TOTALS			1	0	1.13	2	2	0	0	8	5	2	1	0	3	6	.172
MINOR LEAGUE TOTALS			47	34	3.24	129	113	2	2	680	551	290	245	40	248	594	.222

23 Charlton Jimerson, of

Born: Sept. 22, 1979. **Ht.:** 6-3. **Wt.:** 210. **Bats:** R. **Throws:** R. **School:** University of Miami. **Career Transactions:** Selected by Astros in fifth round of 2001 draft; signed June 23, 2001.

Jimerson dominated the 2001 College World Series. His power, speed and defense carried Miami to the national championship, and his backstory was even better. His mother was a crack addict who abandoned Jimerson and his younger brother, while his father was abusive toward his mom and became homeless. Raised by an older sister, Jimerson attended Miami on an academic scholarship and played sparingly until midway through his senior year. He left the Hurricanes with one CWS Most Outstanding Player award, two national titles and a computer-science degree. The question now is how happy the baseball ending will be. Jimerson is the best athlete in the system and could become another Eric Davis if everything clicks. But thus far it hasn't and he hasn't progressed past high Class A. Physically, he has it all. Few players in the organization can match his raw power and plus speed, and none of them runs out grounders harder than Jimerson does. He has outstanding range in center field and a strong arm as well. But he's still unrefined and lacks instincts. He has a long stroke, swings through too many pitches and doesn't read breaking balls, often leaving him defenseless at the plate. He's intelligent and works hard but hasn't been able to make adjustments. Missing six weeks early last season after a pitch broke his right hand was a huge setback because he needs at-bats. Jimerson reminds one scout of Jesse Barfield, who was almost released in Double-A before blossoming into an American League home run champion. Houston hopes Jimerson can take a similar path and showed faith in him by adding him to the 40-man roster this offseason. That decision makes it likely that he'll spend 2004 in Double-A.

Year	Club (League)	Class	AVG	G	AB	R	H	2B	3B	HR	RBI	BB	SO	SB	SLG	OBP
2001	Pittsfield (NY-P)	A	.234	51	197	35	46	12	1	9	31	18	79	15	.442	.304
2002	Lexington (SAL)	A	.228	125	439	65	100	22	4	14	57	36	168	34	.392	.295
2003	Salem (Car)	A	.265	97	336	53	89	19	3	12	55	25	109	27	.446	.317
MINOR LEAGUE TOTALS			.242	273	972	153	235	53	8	35	143	79	356	76	.421	.305

24 Todd Self, 1b/of

Born: Nov. 9, 1978. **Ht.:** 6-5. **Wt.:** 215. **Bats:** L. **Throws:** R. **School:** University of Louisiana-Monroe. **Career Transactions:** Selected by Astros in 15th round of 2000 draft; signed June 8, 2000.

Self made news last August when he got trapped in a dugout bathroom during a game at Kinston. He slammed the door in anger after a bad at-bat in the top of the ninth, then missed the bottom of the inning and was stuck for 20 minutes after the game ended. Now if he can just unlock his power. Self was a defensive hitter when he entered pro ball, letting himself fall into bad counts. Now he works pitchers masterfully, and managers rated his strike-zone judgment the best in the Carolina League last year. Self is getting stronger and makes consistent, solid contact, but at 25 he has just 22 homers in 387 pro games. He's still learning to recognize which pitches he can drive, and he must start punishing fastballs rather than serving them to the opposite field for singles. He made great strides against left-handers in 2003. While Self's strong arm is suitable for right field, his below-average speed and poor routes make him better suited for first base. If he doesn't start producing more homers, his ceiling will be as a bench player in the majors. Self will move to Double-A this year.

Year	Club (League)	Class	AVG	G	AB	R	H	2B	3B	HR	RBI	BB	SO	SB	SLG	OBP
2000	Auburn (NY-P)	A	.194	52	160	13	31	3	1	1	19	28	42	10	.244	.326
2001	Pittsfield (NY-P)	A	.303	73	261	52	79	13	4	3	49	46	61	10	.418	.403
2002	Michigan (Mid)	A	.310	136	491	81	152	36	5	12	94	65	104	10	.477	.394
2003	Salem (Car)	A	.318	126	431	84	137	27	2	6	57	87	93	2	.432	.433
MINOR LEAGUE TOTALS			.297	387	1343	230	399	79	12	22	219	226	300	32	.423	.401

25 Ryan McKeller, rhp

Born: July 8, 1983. **Ht.:** 6-5. **Wt.:** 210. **Bats:** R. **Throws:** R. **School:** New Mexico JC. **Career Transactions:** Selected by Astros in 45th round of 2002 draft; signed May 12, 2003.

McKeller has some of the best pure stuff in the system, and the Astros are trying to help him figure out how to make the most of it. As with Raymar Diaz, Houston had to draft McKeller twice and then wait another year to land him as a draft-and-follow. The Astros took him in the 38th round out of high school in 2001, but he chose to attend McLennan (Texas) Community College. He was too wild to earn many innings there as a freshman, so he transferred to New Mexico JC in 2002. McKeller had limited success with the Thunderbirds, going 6-3, 9.77 last spring, but the Astros made sure to lock him up before he could re-enter the draft again. Minor league pitching coordinator Dewey Robinson and Martinsville pitching coach Jack Billingham have made good initial adjustments to McKeller's mechanics, getting him to slow down his delivery and throw more strikes. He has a 91-95 mph fastball with good late life. His curveball had its moments in instructional league but still needs a lot of work, and his changeup is further away. While he's currently a one-pitch guy who can locate that pitch only adequately, McKeller is lean and lanky and should get stronger or better. He can be intimidating with his velocity, size, wildness and a funky twist in his delivery that makes his pitches hard to pick up. He might be best served with an assignment to extended spring training and then Tri-City this year.

Year	Club (League)	Class	W	L	ERA	G	GS	CG	SV	IP	H	R	ER	HR	BB	SO	AVG
2003	Martinsville (Appy)	R	3	0	3.58	15	4	0	3	38	33	16	15	4	19	46	.241
MINOR LEAGUE TOTALS			3	0	3.58	15	4	0	3	38	33	16	15	4	19	46	.241

26 D.J. Houlton, rhp

Born: Aug. 12, 1979. **Ht.:** 6-4. **Wt.:** 220. **Bats:** R. **Throws:** R. **School:** University of the Pacific. **Career Transactions:** Selected by Astros in 11th round of 2001 draft; signed June 9, 2001.

Selecting college seniors is one way to save money in the draft, and the Astros are nothing if not thrifty. They're also efficient at spotting talent that has been overlooked. Big leaguers Morgan Ensberg and Kirk Saarloos were senior signs, as were eight members of this top 30. Houlton handled the jump from low A to Double-A last year with aplomb, though he hit the wall in Triple-A. He doesn't have a standout pitch but he has succeeded with a deep repertoire, good command and a feel for mixing locations and speeds. The Astros give him credit for getting further with his stuff than most pitchers would. The consensus is that Houlton's best pitch is his big 12-to-6 curveball, with his changeup right behind. His fastball runs from 86-92 mph, and he gets nice bore on his two-seamer. He doesn't hesitate to challenge batters inside. He also throws a cutter, slider and a splitter. Houlton got into trouble in Triple-A when he changed his style and tried to become more of a power pitcher. He tried to impress the radar guns and went to too many four-seam fastballs, which lacked movement and got pounded when he didn't spot them on the corners. He also went with his slider more than his curveball. If Houlton gets back to his basics in Triple-A this year, he could reach Houston by September.

Year	Club (League)	Class	W	L	ERA	G	GS	CG	SV	IP	H	R	ER	HR	BB	SO	AVG
2001	Martinsville (Appy)	R	5	4	2.50	13	13	1	0	72	67	24	20	7	7	71	.240
	Michigan (Mid)	A	0	1	5.40	1	1	0	0	5	7	5	3	0	1	4	.304
2002	Michigan (Mid)	A	14	5	3.14	35	16	0	2	141	120	57	49	12	30	138	.223
2003	Round Rock (TL)	AA	5	4	3.47	18	18	1	0	109	93	45	42	11	28	101	.226
	New Orleans (PCL)	AAA	3	4	5.40	11	11	0	0	62	70	39	37	12	19	48	.288
MINOR LEAGUE TOTALS			27	18	3.50	78	59	2	2	388	357	170	151	42	85	362	.239

27 Jimmy Barrett, rhp

Born: June 7, 1981. **Ht.:** 6-2. **Wt.:** 190. **Bats:** R. **Throws:** R. **School:** Fort Hill HS, Cumberland, Md. **Career Transactions:** Selected by Astros in third round of 1999 draft; signed June 25, 1999.

Barrett emerged as the system's best starting pitching prospect in 2002. He came into 2003 trying to cruise on his ability and justify his spot on the 40-man roster, and he didn't do either. Barrett completely lost his feel for pitching and his curveball, and he got pounded for three months. He did recover to go 5-3, 3.45 in his last 10 starts, and he took steps forward in instructional league. The natural cutting life on his fastball returned as it sat at 89-91 mph and topped out at 94. He's replacing his curveball, which was too loopy, with a slider that's slurvy at this point. Barrett's changeup, command and delivery also need improvement. If there was any good to come out of 2003, Barrett was humbled and learned he must be a pitcher rather than a thrower. Houston kept Barrett on the 40-man roster and will send him back to high Class A in 2004.

Year	Club (League)	Class	W	L	ERA	G	GS	CG	SV	IP	H	R	ER	HR	BB	SO	AVG
1999	Martinsville (Appy)	R	0	1	4.42	6	3	0	0	18	15	9	9	0	10	12	.227
2000	Martinsville (Appy)	R	6	2	4.73	13	13	0	0	67	60	37	35	4	32	72	.239
2001	Michigan (Mid)	A	10	5	4.48	27	25	1	0	131	122	76	65	12	62	98	.242
2002	Lexington (SAL)	A	9	5	2.81	27	22	0	1	134	112	53	42	13	40	131	.230
2003	Salem (Car)	A	7	10	5.33	26	26	0	0	138	160	87	82	13	56	75	.292
MINOR LEAGUE TOTALS			32	23	4.29	99	89	1	1	488	469	262	233	42	200	388	.253

28 Tony Pluta, rhp

Born: Oct. 28, 1982. **Ht.:** 6-2. **Wt.:** 210. **Bats:** R. **Throws:** R. **School:** Las Vegas HS. **Career Transactions:** Selected by Astros in third round of 2000 draft; signed Aug. 22, 2000.

After getting shelled in low Class A in 2002 and knocked around in his first two starts last year, Pluta was cruising with a shutout for four-plus innings in his next outing. Then he felt a pop in his elbow while throwing a changeup, and his season was over. Pluta had Tommy John surgery in June and was doing well in his rehabilitation. Many pitchers come back stronger after the operation, and Pluta may benefit from adopting more of a finesse approach. He had explosive life on a 94-96 mph fastball but not much to go with it. He showed a good overhand curveball during his pro debut, but his breaking ball devolved into a three-quarters slurve. He also had only sporadic feel for his changeup, and exerted so much effort in his delivery that it cost him command. Pluta's best fit may be as a late-inning reliever, though he'd still need to come up with at least one more pitch. He'll start throwing again this June and may get back on the mound by the end of the season.

Year	Club (League)	Class	W	L	ERA	G	GS	CG	SV	IP	H	R	ER	HR	BB	SO	AVG
2001	Lexington (SAL)	A	12	4	3.20	26	26	0	0	132	107	52	47	7	86	138	.231
2002	Michigan (Mid)	A	11	13	5.92	28	28	1	0	143	155	100	94	18	83	120	.277
2003	Salem (Car)	A	0	1	5.84	3	3	0	0	12	13	8	8	1	8	14	.271
MINOR LEAGUE TOTALS			23	18	4.66	57	57	1	0	288	275	160	149	26	177	272	.257

29 Derick Grigsby, rhp

Born: June 30, 1982. **Ht.:** 6-0. **Wt.:** 190. **Bats:** R. **Throws:** R. **School:** Northeast Texas CC. **Career Transactions:** Selected by Astros in first round (29th overall) of 2002 draft; signed Aug. 11, 2002.

Grigsby didn't look like the same pitcher Houston drafted when he made his pro debut last year. In junior college he threw a 95-96 mph fastball and power slider from a high three-quarters slot. In 2003, his arm angle dropped slightly and his stuff dropped a lot. Grigsby showed only an average fastball, though it did have good life when he kept it down in the strike zone, and his slider morphed into a slurve. His changeup remains raw, and his command was only slightly better. Grigsby showed signs of getting more aggressive in instructional league, where his stuff began to rebound. The Astros will handle him carefully because he's reserved and has had to deal with tough family circumstances. Grigsby's mother died unexpectedly during routine surgery in 2001. He used part of his $1.125 million bonus to buy his father a motorcycle, and his dad was seriously injured (including losing toes on his left foot) in a motorcycle accident when Grigsby reported to instructional league last year. Grigsby will try to recover his previous form in high Class A in 2004.

Year	Club (League)	Class	W	L	ERA	G	GS	CG	SV	IP	H	R	ER	HR	BB	SO	AVG
2003	Lexington (SAL)	A	2	2	4.79	12	9	0	0	36	40	19	19	2	14	21	.294
	Tri-City (NY-P)	A	5	5	4.86	15	15	0	0	76	73	44	41	7	32	62	.252
MINOR LEAGUE TOTALS			7	7	4.84	27	24	0	0	112	113	63	60	9	46	83	.265

30 Felipe Paulino, rhp

Born: Oct. 5, 1983. **Ht.:** 6-2. **Wt.:** 180. **Bats:** R. **Throws:** R. **Career Transactions:** Signed out of Venezuela by Astros, July 2, 2001.

Paulino has the best raw arm strength in the system. He announced his presence with his first pitch in the United States, a 96 mph heater last June in Martinsville. His fastball sat at 94-98 mph in the Appalachian League, and he topped out in triple digits. Velocity and a strong frame are the only things Paulino has going for him right now, but they're hard to ignore. He doesn't command his fastball well, and doesn't have much consistency with his hard slider. His mechanics are rough and he's still learning how to pitch, both from a mental and physical standpoint. If the Astros can refine Paulino they might have a future closer. He'll begin the year in extended spring training and head to Tri-City or Greeneville in June.

Year	Club (League)	Class	W	L	ERA	G	GS	CG	SV	IP	H	R	ER	HR	BB	SO	AVG
2002	Venoco (VSL)	R	0	0	1.29	4	0	0	0	7	4	1	1	1	6	4	.182
2003	Venoco (VSL)	R	1	0	5.59	5	0	0	0	10	6	6	6	0	12	13	.194
	Martinsville (Appy)	R	2	2	5.61	16	0	0	1	26	23	20	16	0	19	27	.235
MINOR LEAGUE TOTALS			3	2	4.89	25	0	0	1	42	33	27	23	1	37	44	.219

KANSAS CITY
ROYALS

Royals manager Tony Pena coined the phrase in spring training, passing out "We Believe" t-shirts to his players. That must have been a hard sell after general manager Allard Baird had been forced to trim $10 million from the payroll of a 2002 team that registered a franchise-record 100 losses and boasted a farm system with few impact prospects. Kansas City looked sure to extend its string of losing seasons to nine. But the upbeat clubhouse environment Pena fostered allowed the Royals to streak to a 9-0 start and collect 16 wins in their first 19 games. It jump-started a fan base that was further stoked as the "Believe" mantra emerged as a marketing campaign.

The Royals were the feel-good story of the first half as they sat in first place in the American League Central, buoyed by a young and largely homegrown pitching staff and eventual AL rookie of the year Angel Berroa. Pitching injuries and inexperience caught up with Kansas City after the all-star break, though Baird did his best to plug major league holes in a cost-effective manner. In the end it wasn't enough to hold off the hard-charging Twins, who posted the best record in the majors over the second half, or the White Sox. Still, the Royals led the division for more days than any other team and showed a 21-game improvement that ranked as the sixth-best turnaround in

TOP 30 PROSPECTS

1. Zack Greinke, rhp
2. Chris Lubanski, of
3. Mitch Maier, of/3b
4. David DeJesus, of
5. Colt Griffin, rhp
6. Donald Murphy, 2b
7. Shane Costa, of
8. Brian Bass, rhp
9. Andres Blanco, ss
10. Byron Gettis, of
11. Ruben Gotay, 2b
12. Jonah Bayliss, rhp
13. Adam Donachie, c
14. Kyle Middleton, rhp
15. Carlos Rosa, rhp
16. Jorge Vasquez, rhp
17. Rich Thompson, of
18. Travis Chapman, 3b/1b
19. Alexis Gomez, of
20. Ryan Bukvich, rhp
21. Mike Tonis, c
22. Mike Aviles, ss
23. Kenard Springer, of
24. Chad Santos, 1b
25. Kila Kaaihue, 1b
26. Brian McFall, 1b
27. Devon Lowery, rhp
28. Dustin Hughes, lhp
29. Danny Christensen, lhp
30. Ambiorix Burgos, rhp

By Will Kimmey

the majors since 1900.

The success spread to the farm system as well. Right-hander Zack Greinke, the club's top pick in 2002, earned a Futures Game berth by going 11-1, 1.14 at high Class A Wilmington. The Royals went after more polished players like Greinke in the 2003 draft, going away from high-risk, high-reward high schoolers like 2001 choices Colt Griffin and Roscoe Crosby. Scouting director Deric Ladnier made savvy use of the college ranks to manage one of the game's lowest signing-bonus budgets.

The bottom line also received a boost as the extra wins brought out extra fans and attendance increased by more than 400,000 fans to 1.7 million. That allowed Baird to hold on to the team's best player, Carlos Beltran, though he likely will be too costly to re-sign when he becomes a free agent after the 2004 season. The team's performance also satisfied a clause in Mike Sweeney's contract that would have allowed him to become a free agent if the team didn't post a winning season by 2004.

Baird made more smart and thrifty moves over the offseason, eschewing big-ticket free agents to add solid performers at reasonable prices. If the young arms bounce back this year and the farm system can produce two or three contributors, the Royals are in a good position to chase the pennant in a weak AL Central.

ORGANIZATION
OVERVIEW

General manager: Allard Baird. **Farm director:** Shaun McGinn. **Scouting director:** Deric Ladnier.

2003 PERFORMANCE

Class	Team	League	W	L	Pct.	Finish*	Manager
Majors	Kansas City	American	83	79	.512	8th (14)	Tony Pena
Triple-A	Omaha Royals	Pacific Coast	70	73	.490	11th (16)	Mike Jirschele
Double-A	Wichita Wranglers	Texas	71	69	.507	4th (8)	Keith Bodie
High A	Wilmington Blue Rocks	Carolina	80	60	.571	1st (8)	Billy Gardner
Low A	Burlington Bees	Midwest	64	74	.464	14th (16)	Joe Szekely
Rookie	†AZL Royals I	Arizona	31	18	.633	+2nd (9)	Lloyd Simmons
Rookie	AZL Royals II	Arizona	32	22	.593	4th (9)	Kevin Boles
OVERALL 2003 MINOR LEAGUE RECORD			348	316	.524	7th (30)	

*Finish in overall standings (No. of teams in league). +League champion. †Affiliate will be in Idahol Falls (Pioneer) in 2004.

ORGANIZATION LEADERS

BATTING   *Minimum 250 At-Bats
*AVG	Donald Murphy, Burlington	.313
R	Mel Stocker, Wilmington/Burlington	91
H	Donald Murphy, Burlington	158
TB	Byron Gettis, Wichita	241
2B	Jarrod Patterson, Omaha	33
3B	Brandon Powell, Royals I	15
HR	Jarrod Patterson, Omaha	18
RBI	Byron Gettis, Wichita	103
BB	Chris Fallon, Wilmington	84
SO	Chad Santos, Wichita	116
SB	Mel Stocker, Wilmington/Burlington	41
*SLG	Mike Kelly, Omaha	.495
*OBP	David DeJesus, Omaha/Wichita	.414

PITCHING   #Minimum 75 Innings
W	Zack Greinke, Wichita/Wilmington	15
L	Danny Tamayo, Wichita	14
#ERA	Zack Greinke, Wichita/Wilmington	1.93
G	Jorge Vasquez, Wichita/Wilmington	53
CG	Jamey Wright, Omaha	3
	Zack Greinke, Wichita/Wilmington	3
SV	Jorge Vasquez, Wichita/Wilmington	29
IP	Kyle Middleton, Wilmington	160
BB	Colt Griffin, Wilmington/Burlington	97
SO	Jonah Bayliss, Burlington	133

BEST TOOLS

Best Hitter for Average	Mitch Maier
Best Power Hitter	Brian McFall
Fastest Baserunner	Chris Lubanski
Best Athlete	Chris Lubanski
Best Fastball	Colt Griffin
Best Curveball	Brian Bass
Best Slider	Colt Griffin
Best Changeup	Zack Greinke
Best Control	Zack Greinke
Best Defensive Catcher	Mike Tonis
Best Defensive Infielder	Andres Blanco
Best Infield Arm	Donald Murphy
Best Defensive Outfielder	David DeJesus
Best Outfield Arm	Byron Gettis

PROJECTED 2007 LINEUP

Catcher	Adam Donachie
First Base	Mike Sweeney
Second Base	Angel Berroa
Third Base	Donald Murphy
Shortstop	Andres Blanco
Left Field	Chris Lubanski
Center Field	Carlos Beltran

Right Field	Mitch Maier
Designated Hitter	Juan Gonzalez
No. 1 Starter	Zack Greinke
No. 2 Starter	Jeremy Affeldt
No. 3 Starter	Jimmy Gobble
No. 4 Starter	Runelvys Hernandez
No. 5 Starter	Colt Griffin
Closer	Mike MacDougal

LAST YEAR'S TOP 20 PROSPECTS

1. Zack Greinke, rhp
2. Angel Berroa, ss
3. Jimmy Gobble, lhp
4. Ken Harvey, 1b
5. Mike MacDougal, rhp
6. Alexis Gomez, of
7. Colt Griffin, rhp
8. Kyle Snyder, rhp
9. Andres Blanco, ss
10. Jeremy Hill, rhp
11. Ryan Bukvich, rhp
12. Danny Christensen, lhp
13. Ruben Gotay, 2b
14. Alejandro Machado, ss
15. Mike Tonis, c
16. Brad Voyles, rhp
17. Ian Ferguson, rhp
18. Wes Obermuller, rhp
19. David DeJesus, of
20. Roscoe Crosby, of

TOP PROSPECTS OF THE DECADE

1994	Jeff Granger, lhp
1995	Johnny Damon, of
1996	Jim Pittsley, rhp
1997	Glendon Rusch, lhp
1998	Dee Brown, of
1999	Carlos Beltran, of
2000	Dee Brown, of
2001	Chris George, rhp
2002	Angel Berroa, ss
2003	Zack Greinke, rhp

TOP DRAFT PICKS OF THE DECADE

1994	Matt Smith, lhp/1b
1995	Juan LeBron, of
1996	Dee Brown, of
1997	Dan Reichert, rhp
1998	Jeff Austin, rhp
1999	Kyle Snyder, rhp
2000	Mike Stodolka, lhp
2001	Colt Griffin, rhp
2002	Zack Greinke, rhp
2003	Chris Lubanski, of

ALL-TIME LARGEST BONUSES

Jeff Austin, 1998	$2,700,000
Mike Stodolka, 2000	$2,500,000
Zack Greinke, 2002	$2,475,000
Colt Griffin, 2001	$2,400,000
Kyle Snyder, 1999	$2,100,000
Chris Lubanski, 2003	$2,100,000

MINOR LEAGUE
DEPTH CHART

KANSAS CITY **ROYALS**

RANK: 19

Impact potential (B): Zack Greinke had his way with minor leaguers last year and is one of the top pitching prospects in baseball. He profiles along the lines of Orel Hershiser and Bret Saberhagen. Chris Lubanski is a premium athlete who projects as outfielder in the mold of Rocco Baldelli.

Depth (D): The Royals' depth took a hit, mostly because they graduated seven players from last year's list to the majors, including American League rookie of the year Angel Berroa. They dealt three others. Their 2003 draft class was a plus and David DeJesus, Donald Murphy and Brian Bass took significant steps forward.

Sleeper: Adam Donachie, c. *—Depth charts prepared by **Josh Boyd**. Numbers in parentheses indicate prospect rankings.*

LF
Mitch Maier (3)
Shane Costa (7)
Kenard Springer (23)
Tim Frend

CF
Chris Lubanski (2)
David DeJesus (4)
Rich Thompson (17)
Alexis Gomez (19)
James Shanks

RF
Byron Gettis (10)
Derik Lytle

3B
Travis Chapman (18)
Miguel Vega
Damaso Espino
Jarrod Patterson
Justin Gemoll

SS
Andres Blanco (9)
Mike Aviles (22)
Angel Sanchez
Irving Falu

2B
Donald Murphy (6)
Ruben Gotay (11)
Brandon Powell

1B
Chad Santos (24)
Kila Kaaihue (25)
Brian McFall (26)
Chamar McDonald
Dave Jensen

SOURCE OF TALENT

Homegrown		Acquired	
College	8	Trade	1
Junior College	2	Rule 5 draft	0
Draft-and-follow	2	Independent	0
High school	11	Free agent/waivers	0
Nondrafted free agent	1		
Foreign	5		

C
Adam Donachie (13)
Mike Tonis (21)
Matt Tupman
Scott Walter

LHP

Starters	Relievers
Danny Christensen (29)	Dustin Hughes (28)
John Gragg	
Shaun Shiery	
Mike Stodolka	

RHP

Starters	Relievers
Zack Greinke (1)	Jorge Vasquez (16)
Colt Griffin (5)	Ryan Bukvich (20)
Brian Bass (8)	Ryan Braun
Jonah Bayliss (12)	Ira Brown
Kyle Middleton (14)	Mike Natale
Carlos Rosa (15)	
Devon Lowery (27)	
Ambiorix Burgos (30)	
Greg Atencio	
Zach McClellan	
Chris Goodman	
Ian Ferguson	
Danny Tamayo	

DRAFT
ANALYSIS

Best Pro Debut: The Royals drafted mainly college players, and several of them tore up the Rookie-level Arizona League, led by SS Mike Aviles (7). Aviles won the MVP award after hitting .363-6-39 with 11 steals and league highs in doubles (19) and runs (51). Managers rated OF Chris Lubanski (1) the league's top prospect after he batted .326-4-27. OF/3B Mitch Maier (1) hit .350-2-45 and OF Shane Costa (2) batted .368-1-24, including a stint in high Class A.

Best Athlete: Lubanski is a 6-foot-3 athlete with strong tools across the board except for arm strength.

Best Pure Hitter: Costa or Maier. Maier finished second in the Division I batting race at .448 and has more power than Costa.

Best Raw Power: 1B Brian McFall (3), a surprise early-round pick, has the most present power. 3B Miguel Vega (4) may develop more loft power in time.

Fastest Runner: Lubanski gets from the left side to first base in 3.9-4.0 seconds. He was just 9-for-19 on steals in the AZL.

Best Defensive Player: Lubanski has the tools to be a Gold Glove center fielder but needs work on his reads and jumps. For now, Aviles is better.

Best Fastball: RHP Ryan Braun (7) hit 97 mph during the spring and 94-95 during the summer. RHP Chris Goodman (5) pitches at 90-92 mph and gets to 94.

McFall

JOHN SPEAR

Best Breaking Ball: If he improves his command, Braun has closer stuff with his fastball and his 85-86 mph slider. His hard curveball also is effective at times.

Most Intriguing Background: Aviles' uncle Ramon was a big league infielder and is a minor league coach for the Phillies. Michael was named NCAA Division II player of the year after leading that level in hitting (.500), slugging (1.016), runs (83) and homers (22).

Closest To The Majors: Costa may beat Maier because he won't have to learn a new position. Maier was a college catcher but couldn't stay there.

Best Late-Round Pick: LHP Dustin Hughes (11) was an AZL all-star after going 5-2, 2.84 with 54 strikeouts in 51 innings. He commands a slightly above-average fastball to both sides of the plate and backs it up with a slider.

The One Who Got Away: The Royals couldn't lure RHP Pat Bresnehan (23) away from attending Arizona State. Based on sheer ability, he would have gone in the first three rounds.

Assessment: The Royals signed just three high schoolers after landing in the first four rounds a year ago. They drafted well despite facing budget constraints that led to below-slot deals with both first-rounders and $1,000 bonuses for the fifth-through ninth-round choices.

2002 DRAFT   GRADE: B+

RHP Zack Greinke (1) could be the first high school draftee from 2002 to reach the majors. 2B Donald Murphy (5) and C Adam Donachie (2) are also part of Kansas City's future.

2001 DRAFT   GRADE: D

The Royals took a huge risk with RHP Colt Griffin (1) and OF Roscoe Crosby (2), and their $4.15 million investment doesn't look like it will pay off with a huge reward. Besides Griffin, no one else shows much promise.

2000 DRAFT   GRADE: C

OF David DeJesus (4) is angling for a big league job, somewhat offsetting LHP Mike Stodolka (1) going bust. RHP Brian Bass' (6) stuff keeps improving. RHP Ryan Bukvich (11) has had his moments.

1999 DRAFT   GRADE: B+

RHP Mike MacDougal (1) was an all-star closer in his first full season in the majors. Fellow first-round pitchers Jimmy Gobble and Kyle Snyder joined him in Kansas City last year, though RHP Jay Gehrke's (1) career stopped in 2001. Since-traded 2B Mark Ellis (9) and 1B Ken Harvey (5) were big league regulars in 2003.

—Draft analysis prepared by Jim Callis. Numbers in parentheses indicate draft rounds.

Zack Greinke

Born: Oct. 21, 1983.
Ht.: 6-2. **Wt.:** 190.
Bats: R. **Throws:** R.
School: Apopka HS, Orlando.
Career Transactions: Selected by Royals in first round (sixth overall) of 2002 draft; signed July 13, 2002.

The Royals wanted to draft an advanced college pitcher in the first round in 2002 because they used their first two picks the previous year on a pair of risky raw talents, Colt Griffin and Roscoe Crosby. But Kansas City's scouts said Greinke was the most polished and poised pitcher available, even though he spent most of his time as a shortstop before his senior year of high school. He got in just 12 innings in his pro debut after signing for $2.475 million, but the Royals were convinced he was mature enough to handle a trip to the Puerto Rican League. He more than held his own there, working with Braves pitching guru Guy Hansen. Another bold move by the Royals put Greinke in high Class A Wilmington to begin the 2003 season. He dominated the competition, winning his first nine decisions. He ranked as the Carolina League's best prospect, earning a berth in the Futures Game and a promotion to Double-A Wichita. He allowed three earned runs or more just three times all year en route to a 1.93 composite ERA, the third-best in the minors. He missed one start with a strained back, but it was more to give him a mental and physical break because the competitive Greinke told coaches he could pitch if needed.

Greinke loves the game and has great makeup. He spent time during spring training evaluating players with scouting director Deric Ladnier, offering his insights on their strengths and weaknesses. He also took to watching batting practice, learning where hitters liked the ball and what they had trouble with. Greinke is a constant tinkerer and thinker with impeccable control of an array of pitches. He likes developing new pitches and variations by adding and subtracting velocity and changing grips. He throws his fastball in the high 80s most of the time, but can rev it up to the mid-90s when he wants. A new grip on his two-seamer makes it dive toward the ground. His slider ranks as a put-away pitch with depth and a hard, late bite. His changeup is his third-best pitch, but still grades as above-average and ranks as the organization's best. Greinke now throws his curveball with a spike grip for more action. His ability to improvise sometimes gets him in trouble. He might get beat trying a new pitch in a situation when an outside fastball or biting slider would work fine. He doesn't strike out as many hitters as he could because he revels in breaking bats and inducing weak contact to create better pitch economy. He could rack up more whiffs if he just threw his slider more in two-strike counts. Consistency on his secondary pitches is about the only area Greinke needs to improve. He'd be even more lethal if he located all the different variations in his repertoire on one occasion. He normally just goes with what feels best that day.

Greinke secured an invite to major league spring training, but the Royals might send him out of big league camp earlier than he deserves because they don't want to raise any hope that he might make the rotation. He'll probably begin the year back in Double-A to build confidence, receiving a quick bump to Triple-A Omaha as soon as he dominates. He still has a chance to make his major league debut late in the year.

Year	Club (League)	Class	W	L	ERA	G	GS	CG	SV	IP	H	R	ER	HR	BB	SO	AVG
2002	Royals (GCL)	R	0	0	1.93	3	3	0	0	5	3	1	1	0	3	4	.200
	Spokane (NWL)	A	0	0	7.71	2	2	0	0	5	9	4	4	0	0	5	.391
	Wilmington (Car)	A	0	0	0.00	1	0	0	0	2	1	0	0	0	0	0	.167
2003	Wilmington (Car)	A	11	1	1.14	14	14	3	0	87	56	16	11	5	13	78	.178
	Wichita (TL)	AA	4	3	3.23	9	9	0	0	53	58	20	19	5	5	34	.286
MINOR LEAGUE TOTALS			15	4	2.08	29	28	3	0	151	127	41	35	10	21	121	.226

2 Chris Lubanski, of

Born: March 24, 1985. **Ht.:** 6-3. **Wt.:** 185. **Bats:** L. **Throws:** L. **School:** Kennedy-Kenrick HS, Schwenksville, Pa. **Career Transactions:** Selected by Royals in first round (fifth overall) of 2003 draft; signed June 6, 2003.

Lubanski enjoyed a standout amateur career, hitting for the cycle twice in a doubleheader as a senior and playing on Team USA's youth and junior squads. He projected to go no higher than the seventh pick in the draft, but the Royals liked him enough to draft him at No. 5 on merit. After signing for $2.1 million, he ranked as the top prospect in the Rookie-level Arizona League. Lubanski's speed rates the best of his four above-average tools. He's a 70 runner on the 20-80 scouting scale. He has an athletic body with broad shoulders, and is capable of developing 25-homer power while also producing a strong average. He shows good pop now, especially when he centers the ball. He has great makeup and took a leadership role on his college-heavy AZL squad. Lubanski improved his throwing, but it will never rate much better than average. He's still learning what to do with certain pitches and gets anxious and a little out of control at the plate, on the bases and in the field. Lubanski draws comparisons to a young Kirk Gibson, and he also reminds Royals officials of Johnny Damon and Carlos Beltran. He's ticketed for low Class A Burlington, but a strong spring could lead Kansas City to challenge him with a jump to high Class A.

Year	Club (League)	Class	AVG	G	AB	R	H	2B	3B	HR	RBI	BB	SO	SB	SLG	OBP
2003	Royals 1 (AZL)	R	.326	53	221	41	72	4	6	4	27	18	50	9	.452	.382
MINOR LEAGUE TOTALS			.326	53	221	41	72	4	6	4	27	18	50	9	.452	.382

3 Mitch Maier, of/3b

Born: June 30, 1982. **Ht.:** 6-2. **Wt.:** 200. **Bats:** L. **Throws:** R. **School:** University of Toledo. **Career Transactions:** Selected by Royals in first round (30th overall) of 2003 draft; signed June 4, 2003.

Maier was an all-state quarterback growing up near Michigan and had an offer to walk on to the Wolverines football team as a safety, but he turned it down to play baseball at Toledo. He led the Mid-American Conference in batting as a freshman and junior, also topping the league in steals as a junior. He signed for $900,000 as the 30th overall pick. The Royals drafted Maier for his bat. His build and offensive approach recall Twins prospect Joe Mauer's. Maier understands the strike zone, makes consistently hard contact and has natural loft power that could lead to 25 homers a year. He hits lefthanders as well as righthanders. Maier's speed, acceleration and smarts could allow him to reach double figures in steals. Maier needs a defensive home. A quirk in his throwing motion limited his effectiveness at catcher, so the Royals addressed an organization weakness by moving him to third base in instructional league. He'll probably play the outfield in 2004, as they just want him to get comfortable at the plate and not worry about defense for the time being. Maier was hurt more than any Royals player by the organization's two Arizona League teams last year. He'll make a small jump this year to low Class A, where he'll flank Chris Lubanski as a corner outfielder.

Year	Club (League)	Class	AVG	G	AB	R	H	2B	3B	HR	RBI	BB	SO	SB	SLG	OBP
2003	Royals 1 (AZL)	R	.350	51	203	41	71	14	6	2	45	18	25	7	.507	.403
MINOR LEAGUE TOTALS			.350	51	203	41	71	14	6	2	45	18	25	7	.507	.403

4 David DeJesus, of

Born: Dec. 20, 1979. **Ht.:** 6-0. **Wt.:** 170. **Bats:** L. **Throws:** L. **School:** Rutgers University. **Career Transactions:** Selected by Royals in fourth round of 2000 draft; signed Aug. 22, 2000 . . . On disabled list, June 19-Sept. 17, 2001.

DeJesus plays with an almost reckless aggression, which has resulted in several trips to the disabled list and postponed his pro debut for two years. Last year, he injured his right shoulder twice diving for balls in the outfield but recovered to make his big league debut in September. DeJesus is instinctive and plays above the sum of his tools. He shows gap-to-gap power, good control of the strike zone and above-average speed, which should make him an effective leadoff or No. 2 hitter. He's a solid center fielder, with decent range and an arm that rates a tick above-average. DeJesus doesn't have a lot of power but did show more juice in the Arizona Fall League, especially when driving inside pitches. Despite his high on-base percentages, he has a knack for making weak contact against poor pitches. The Royals will give DeJesus a shot at winning their left-field job this spring, but he won't make the team unless management projects at least 300 at-bats for him. He could take over center field when Carlos Beltran leaves.

Year	Club (League)	Class	AVG	G	AB	R	H	2B	3B	HR	RBI	BB	SO	SB	SLG	OBP
2001	Did not play—Injured															
2002	Wilmington (Car)	A	.296	87	334	69	99	22	6	4	41	48	42	15	.434	.400
	Wichita (TL)	AA	.253	25	79	7	20	5	2	2	15	8	10	3	.443	.347
2003	Wichita (TL)	AA	.338	17	71	14	24	4	0	2	10	9	8	1	.479	.422
	Omaha (PCL)	AAA	.298	59	215	49	64	16	3	5	23	34	30	8	.470	.412
	Kansas City (AL)	MAJ	.286	12	7	0	2	0	1	0	0	1	2	0	.571	.444
MAJOR LEAGUE TOTALS			.286	12	7	0	2	0	1	0	0	1	2	0	.571	.444
MINOR LEAGUE TOTALS			.296	188	699	139	207	47	11	13	89	99	90	27	.451	.400

5 Colt Griffin, rhp

Born: Sept. 29, 1982. **Ht.:** 6-4. **Wt.:** 200. **Bats:** R. **Throws:** R. **School:** Marshall (Texas) HS. **Career Transactions:** Selected by Royals in first round (ninth overall) of 2001 draft; signed Aug. 8, 2001.

Griffin was set to play first base at Louisiana Tech before becoming the first documented high school pitcher to hit 100 mph. He rocketed into the first round and received a $2.4 million bonus. While he has struggled with mechanics and control, one scout who saw him in 2003 said he had never seen a power pitcher improve so much in one season. Griffin dialed down his velocity for more control and now pitches at 94 mph and tops out at 97. A hard-biting 87-89 mph slider that can tie up lefthanders inside gives him two plus-plus pitches. Burlington pitching coach Tom Burgmeier got Griffin to use a more consistent arm slot and shorter arm stroke on his delivery, which greatly improved his command. He must make more progress with his control after leading the minors in walks and finishing second in wild pitches (23). Kansas City isn't worried that his strikeout rates aren't as high as expected, as he has been told to concentrate on inducing weak contract. His changeup may never be an average pitch, but the Royals say he can succeed with just his fastball and slider. The Royals drafted Griffin knowing he was raw and a great deal of patience would be required. They feel good about his future after the strides he made. He'll pitch in high Class A this year and could shoot through the system if everything clicks.

Year	Club (League)	Class	W	L	ERA	G	GS	CG	SV	IP	H	R	ER	HR	BB	SO	AVG
2001	Spokane (NWL)	A	0	1	27.00	3	2	0	0	2	4	7	7	0	7	0	.364
2002	Burlington (Mid)	A	6	6	5.36	19	19	0	0	91	75	60	54	1	82	66	.233
	Wilmington (Car)	A	0	1	3.86	3	0	0	0	5	3	2	2	0	5	3	.214
2003	Burlington (Mid)	A	9	11	3.91	27	27	0	0	150	127	80	65	7	97	107	.233
	Wilmington (Car)	A	1	0	0.00	1	1	0	0	6	3	1	0	0	0	5	.143
MINOR LEAGUE TOTALS			16	19	4.55	53	49	0	0	253	212	150	128	8	191	181	.232

6 Donald Murphy, 2b

Born: March 10, 1983. **Ht.:** 5-10. **Wt.:** 180. **Bats:** R. **Throws:** R. **School:** Orange Coast (Calif.) JC. **Career Transactions:** Selected by Royals in fifth round of 2002 draft; signed June 23, 2002.

Murphy didn't qualify academically to play at Long Beach State in 2002, so he attended Orange Coast Junior College. He received plenty of exposure from scouts who flocked there to watch supplemental first-round pick Matt Clanton. Murphy's makeup, bat and stocky, short-legged build remind Royals officials of Marcus Giles, though he should have a better glove. Murphy has the bat to become a regular as an offense-first second baseman. He's a well-rounded hitter with a great approach and knowledge of the strike zone. He makes consistent contact and often waits longer on inside pitches before rapping them the opposite way. The ball jumps off his bat, leading scouts to project more power. Murphy's solid hands and plus arm strength allow him to make all the routine plays at second, and he isn't afraid of contact when turning the double play. Murphy is a below-average runner, so he must use his instincts and positioning to supplement his range. He must improve his footwork at second base. He should have enough bat if he has to move to third base. The Royals think Murphy is the safest bet of any of their middle-infield prospects to make the majors. He'll move up to high Class A in 2004.

Year	Club (League)	Class	AVG	G	AB	R	H	2B	3B	HR	RBI	BB	SO	SB	SLG	OBP
2002	Spokane (NWL)	A	.303	28	109	20	33	10	2	0	15	6	17	0	.431	.356
	Burlington (Mid)	A	.225	33	120	12	27	6	3	0	15	11	31	0	.325	.300
2003	Burlington (Mid)	A	.313	132	504	77	158	29	6	5	98	65	78	15	.425	.397
MINOR LEAGUE TOTALS			.297	193	733	109	218	45	11	5	128	82	126	15	.409	.375

7 Shane Costa, of

Born: Dec. 12, 1981. **Ht.:** 6-0. **Wt.:** 200. **Bats:** L. **Throws:** R. **School:** Cal State Fullerton. **Career Transactions:** Selected by Royals in second round of 2003 draft; signed July 17, 2003.

After grabbing Mitch Maier at the end of the first round, the Royals opted for another polished college hitter in Costa. The 2003 Big West Conference player of the year, he signed for $750,000 after playing in the College World Series. His father Leo is a former college football player and national bodybuilding champion who works as a personal trainer. Costa's hands are quick and nimble, allowing him to react to all types of pitches. He shows good bat control and plate discipline, and he uses the whole field. He's fast and aggressive on the bases and in the outfield. Costa's upright stance with his feet close together was more tailored for aluminum bats, so the Royals spread him out in hopes of generating more power. He also must focus on going with pitches, not trying to pull balls on the outer third or inside-out offerings on the inner half. His arm is limited but shouldn't prevent him from playing center field. He likes working out, but Kansas City has cautioned him about getting too muscle-bound and losing flexibility. Costa received a late promotion to high Class A, where he doubled in his lone playoff start. He'll begin there in 2004 as he pushes his way to the majors as a player in the mold of Rusty Greer.

Year	Club (League)	Class	AVG	G	AB	R	H	2B	3B	HR	RBI	BB	SO	SB	SLG	OBP
2003	Royals 2 (AZL)	R	.386	23	88	22	34	6	4	1	24	6	7	4	.580	.444
	Wilmington (Car)	A	.143	3	7	1	1	1	0	0	0	2	1	0	.286	.400
MINOR LEAGUE TOTALS			.368	26	95	23	35	7	4	1	24	8	8	4	.558	.440

8 Brian Bass, rhp

Born: Jan. 6, 1982. **Ht.:** 6-0. **Wt.:** 190. **Bats:** R. **Throws:** R. **School:** Robert E. Lee HS, Montgomery, Ala. **Career Transactions:** Selected by Royals in sixth round of 2000 draft; signed June 9, 2000.

Bass treaded water in low Class A for a year and a half before mental and physical maturation allowed him to go 4-3, 3.64 over the second half in 2002. He continued his success last year, ranking fourth in the Carolina League in ERA, strikeouts and innings pitched. He took a no-hitter into the ninth inning against Winston-Salem before surrendering a two-out home run. Bass' stuff has improved dramatically since 2002. His fastball went from 87-89 mph to topping out at 93-94, while his curveball moved from below-average to plus and became the system's best. He shows great command to both sides of the plate and keeps the ball down in the zone, eliciting plenty of groundouts. He's a good athlete with sound mechanics and fields his position well. Bass doesn't have a great changeup, but it's improving and eventually should be an average weapon against lefties. He's also working to refine his slider. Bass announced himself as a prospect in 2003 and was added to the 40-man roster in the offseason. This year will offer more evidence as to whether he can be a middle-of-the-rotation starter as he moves from a pitcher's paradise in Wilmington to a hitter's haven in Wichita.

Year	Club (League)	Class	W	L	ERA	G	GS	CG	SV	IP	H	R	ER	HR	BB	SO	AVG
2000	Royals (GCL)	R	3	5	3.89	12	9	0	0	44	36	27	19	0	18	44	.211
	Charleston, WV (SAL)	A	0	0	6.75	1	1	0	0	4	6	3	3	0	0	1	.333
2001	Burlington (Mid)	A	3	10	4.65	26	26	1	0	139	138	82	72	16	53	75	.257
2002	Burlington (Mid)	A	5	7	3.83	20	20	1	0	110	103	57	47	8	31	60	.246
2003	Wilmington (Car)	A	9	8	2.84	26	26	2	0	152	129	59	48	7	43	119	.229
MINOR LEAGUE TOTALS			20	30	3.78	85	82	4	0	450	412	228	189	31	145	299	.241

9 Andres Blanco, ss

Born: April 11, 1984. **Ht.:** 5-10. **Wt.:** 150. **Bats:** B. **Throws:** R. **Career Transactions:** Signed out of Venezuela by Royals, Aug. 2, 2000.

American League rookie of the year Angel Berroa is an exceptional defender, but the Royals say Blanco possesses a better arm and range. He earned all-star honors in high Class A as an 18-year-old last season after spending most of 2002 in Rookie ball. Blanco plays shortstop like Omar Vizquel with his tremendous hands, arm strength and range. He makes errors, but many happen because he gets to more balls than his peers. Bat control isn't a problem for Blanco, who can bunt and make contact with ease. His quick hands and wrists allow him to shoot balls through the infield for hits. Blanco must get stronger in order to hit enough to play regularly in the majors. He's a career .259 hitter with no homers and a .299 slugging percentage. He needs to become less flashy and erratic, remembering to set his feet properly to reduce throwing errors and raising his bases-stealing percentage by running in better counts. Blanco's bat will determine when he reaches the big league. He'll need to hone his offensive survival kit—walking, bunting and hit-and-run skills—this year in Double-A.

Year	Club (League)	Class	AVG	G	AB	R	H	2B	3B	HR	RBI	BB	SO	SB	SLG	OBP
2001	Royals (DSL)	R	.298	54	188	39	56	0	3	0	16	28	23	9	.330	.411
2002	Royals (GCL)	R	.249	52	193	27	48	8	0	0	14	15	29	16	.290	.315
	Wilmington (Car)	A	.308	5	13	2	4	1	0	0	0	1	4	0	.385	.357
2003	Wilmington (Car)	A	.244	113	394	61	96	11	3	0	25	44	50	13	.287	.330
MINOR LEAGUE TOTALS			.259	224	788	129	204	20	6	0	55	88	106	38	.299	.347

10 Byron Gettis, of

Born: March 13, 1980. **Ht.:** 6-0. **Wt.:** 240. **Bats:** R. **Throws:** R. **School:** Cahokia (Ill.) HS. **Career Transactions:** Signed as nondrafted free agent by Royals, June 29, 1998.

Gettis had a scholarship to play quarterback at Minnesota, then signed with the Royals after finalizing negotiations in a bowling alley. He's the cousin of former NFL linebacker Dana Howard. Gettis and didn't play a lot of baseball as a youth, so it took a while for his athleticism to translate into baseball success. He needed two years at each level before exploding at Double-A, winning the organization's minor league player of the year award in 2003. Most of Gettis' success can be attributed to a better grasp of the strike zone. He had always been a dead-red fastball hitter, but learned to lay off breaking balls and got himself in more hitter's counts by focusing on driving the ball up the middle. He's one of the stronger hitters in the system. His arm and athleticism make him an average right fielder. Gettis carries a lot of weight on his 6-foot frame, leading to concerns his body could get soft. He still has holes in his swing, but his newfound plate discipline makes them harder to exploit. Gettis could become a regular with 30-homer power, or he could wind up as a fourth outfielder. The Royals will have a better idea after he spends 2004 in Triple-A.

Year	Club (League)	Class	AVG	G	AB	R	H	2B	3B	HR	RBI	BB	SO	SB	SLG	OBP
1998	Royals (GCL)	R	.216	27	88	11	19	2	0	0	4	4	20	0	.239	.247
1999	Royals (GCL)	R	.316	28	95	20	30	6	2	5	21	17	21	3	.579	.424
	Charleston, WV (SAL)	A	.295	43	149	19	44	7	2	2	13	10	36	10	.409	.361
2000	Wilmington (Car)	A	.155	30	97	13	15	2	0	0	10	13	33	2	.175	.265
	Charleston, WV (SAL)	A	.215	94	344	43	74	18	3	5	50	31	95	11	.328	.297
2001	Burlington (Mid)	A	.314	37	140	26	44	9	2	5	26	14	25	4	.514	.385
	Wilmington (Car)	A	.251	82	303	34	76	21	2	6	51	20	70	4	.393	.321
2002	Wilmington (Car)	A	.283	120	449	76	127	33	2	8	70	48	103	10	.419	.364
2003	Wichita (TL)	AA	.302	140	510	80	154	31	4	16	103	55	110	15	.473	.377
MINOR LEAGUE TOTALS			.268	601	2175	322	583	129	17	47	348	212	513	59	.408	.346

11 Ruben Gotay, 2b

Born: Dec. 25, 1982. **Ht.:** 5-11. **Wt.:** 160. **Bats:** B. **Throws:** R. **School:** Indian Hills (Iowa) CC. **Career Transactions:** Selected by Royals in 31st round of 2000 draft; signed May 28, 2001.

Gotay led the low Class A Midwest League in doubles and extra-base hits in 2002, but regressed offensively last season. He ranked fifth in the Carolina League in doubles, but his average dipped. The Royals attribute that to opponents focusing on Gotay, who hit third in the Wilmington lineup, and avoiding throwing him fastballs. He did rebound in Puerto Rico over the winter. Gotay has gap power and the ability to use the entire field. He must improve his strength and conditioning. He has tired out down the stretch the last two seasons, and the extra strength would add more carry to his drives. Gotay has struggled against lefthanders throughout his career. He's limited defensively, with fringe arm strength and footwork that need improvement. He compensates for his arm with a quick release. He and shortstop Andres Blanco developed a strong defensive rapport working together for the first time in high Class A, and he also served as Blanco's translator. Gotay played third base in Puerto Rico but doesn't project to have the power for the position. A purely offensive second baseman, Gotay will benefit by moving from Wilmington to Wichita in 2004.

Year	Club (League)	Class	AVG	G	AB	R	H	2B	3B	HR	RBI	BB	SO	SB	SLG	OBP
2001	Royals (GCL)	R	.315	52	184	29	58	15	1	3	19	26	22	5	.457	.398
2002	Burlington (Mid)	A	.285	133	509	87	145	42	9	9	83	73	110	5	.456	.377
2003	Wilmington (Car)	A	.261	134	502	68	131	31	2	9	72	60	97	8	.384	.343
MINOR LEAGUE TOTALS			.279	319	1195	184	334	88	12	21	174	159	229	18	.426	.366

12 Jonah Bayliss, rhp

Born: Aug. 13, 1980. **Ht.:** 6-2. **Wt.:** 200. **Bats:** R. **Throws:** R. **School:** Trinity (Conn.) College.
Career Transactions: Selected by Royals in seventh round of 2002 draft; signed June 11, 2002.

Bayliss was the New England Small College Athletic Conference pitcher of the year as a junior at Trinity in 2002, going 8-1, 2.43. He threw a seven-inning no-hitter with 14 strikeouts for Trinity, then topped the feat with a nine-inning, nine-strikeout no-no for Burlington last year. It was his best performance of an otherwise ugly second half, as he wore down. Bayliss has a 91-94 mph fastball that tops out at 96 and has good life. His slider, a second above-average pitch, reaches the low 80s. His curveball is a 12-to-6 hammer but is inconsistent. His changeup has a chance to be average but is mostly a show-me pitch. Bayliss works a lot of deep counts and must gain better command so he can throw quality strikes rather than laying pitches cross the heart of the plate. He can be guilty of trying to throw everything hard in a quest for strikeouts and could benefit from pitching to contact more often. Bayliss has a workhorse build but sometimes throws across his body and fails to finish pitches. The Royals adjusted his delivery slightly in instructional league, and it made his stuff more consistent. He and Colt Griffin will anchor the high Class A rotation this year.

Year	Club (League)	Class	W	L	ERA	G	GS	CG	SV	IP	H	R	ER	HR	BB	SO	AVG
2002	Spokane (NWL)	A	4	8	5.35	15	15	0	0	71	70	46	42	9	29	38	.264
2003	Burlington (Mid)	A	7	12	3.86	26	26	2	0	140	129	78	60	11	69	133	.242
MINOR LEAGUE TOTALS			11	20	4.36	41	41	2	0	211	199	124	102	20	98	171	.249

13 Adam Donachie, c

Born: March 3, 1984. **Ht.:** 6-2. **Wt.:** 180. **Bats:** R. **Throws:** R. **School:** Timber Creek HS, Orlando. **Career Transactions:** Selected by Royals in second round of 2002 draft; signed June 20, 2002.

Donachie enjoyed a strong instructional league to wrest the catcher-of-the-future mantle from Mike Tonis. Donachie is quiet behind the plate with sure hands, great arm strength, and game-calling and blocking skills. His quick exchange and release don't show in his statistics, as he nabbed just 24 percent of basestealers in 2003. Similarly, his power potential doesn't show up in his numbers. He led all Florida high schoolers with 15 home runs as a senior in 2002, including one off first-round pick Zack Greinke. Donachie began switch-hitting in high school, but his coach didn't let him swing from the left side in conference games. He didn't resume work on that side of the plate until instructional league after the 2003 season. The Royals expect him to eventually hit about .260 with 15 homers annually. He reminds them of A.J. Pierzynski because he seems to do everything with ease. He also impressed with a decided improvement in his focus, as he had been immature in his first pro season. Donachie's playing time has been limited as a pro because of an ankle injury and a glut of catchers in the system. He'll try to turn his promise into production this year, either at Kansas City's new Rookie-level Idaho Falls affiliate or in low Class A.

Year	Club (League)	Class	AVG	G	AB	R	H	2B	3B	HR	RBI	BB	SO	SB	SLG	OBP
2002	Royals (GCL)	R	.206	21	68	7	14	3	0	0	3	9	12	0	.250	.304
2003	Royals 2 (AZL)	R	.444	2	9	3	4	1	0	0	0	1	4	0	.556	.500
	Royals 1 (AZL)	R	.222	20	63	8	14	3	1	0	7	9	12	0	.302	.338
MINOR LEAGUE TOTALS			.229	43	140	18	32	7	1	0	10	19	28	0	.293	.331

14 Kyle Middleton, rhp

Born: June 13, 1980. **Ht.:** 6-6. **Wt.:** 230. **Bats:** R. **Throws:** R. **School:** Jefferson Davis (Ala.) JC.
Career Transactions: Selected by Royals in 49th round of 1999 draft; signed May 31, 2000.

Despite standing 6-foot-6, Middleton isn't a power pitcher. He's not athletic and throws his fastball in the 88-90 mph range with good sinking action, occasionally touching 92. But he's a tremendous competitor with great makeup and a big-breaking curveball that he improved in instructional league. Once he gains more consistency with it, it should become more of a strikeout pitch. His changeup is borderline average. He doesn't issue many walks, but still needs to improve the quality of his strikes and keep the ball down more. Even without a put-away pitch, Middleton led the Carolina League in ERA, ranked second in innings and tied Zack Greinke for second in wins. Middleton is probably a safer bet than Brian Bass, whom he'll join in the Double-A rotation in 2004, but doesn't have as high a ceiling.

Year	Club (League)	Class	W	L	ERA	G	GS	CG	SV	IP	H	R	ER	HR	BB	SO	AVG
2000	Royals (GCL)	R	0	2	14.85	15	1	0	0	20	32	34	33	2	17	14	.352
2001	Spokane (NWL)	A	3	6	4.65	16	14	0	0	79	92	48	41	5	23	68	.300
2002	Burlington (Mid)	A	14	5	3.74	29	17	0	1	125	124	67	52	6	31	64	.254
2003	Wilmington (Car)	A	11	8	2.41	27	27	1	0	160	155	59	43	6	35	75	.256
MINOR LEAGUE TOTALS			28	21	3.95	87	59	1	1	385	403	208	169	19	106	221	.270

15 Carlos Rosa, rhp

Born: Sept. 21, 1984. **Ht.:** 6-2. **Wt.:** 170. **Bats:** R. **Throws:** R. **Career Transactions:** Signed out of Dominican Republic by Royals, Nov. 29, 2001.

Next to Chris Lubanski, Rosa is the Royals' best prospect under 20. His live arm pumps 90-94 mph fastballs. The Royals project Rosa to add velocity as he matures, and he already can work his fastball to both sides of the plate. A plus slider and solid changeup, for which he shows a good feel, give him the chance to reach the majors with three above-average pitches. He's very athletic, smart and driven. He picked up English quickly and has shown the ability to retain instruction and make his own adjustments on the mound. Rosa has a good arm action but there's some effort to his delivery. Though he has added three inches and 35 pounds since signing as a 5-foot-10 135-pounder in 2001, he still must add strength to his thin frame. He also must work on controlling his emotions. His burning desire to win often leads to him getting down on himself when he struggles, but also delivers the work ethic that will help him reach the majors. He'll get his first chance at full-season ball in low Class A this year.

Year	Club (League)	Class	W	L	ERA	G	GS	CG	SV	IP	H	R	ER	HR	BB	SO	AVG
2002	Royals (DSL)	R	1	0	1.80	1	1	0	0	5	3	1	1	0	0	2	.167
	Royals (GCL)	R	0	4	6.19	10	9	0	0	32	52	32	22	3	12	11	.361
2003	Royals (AZL)	R	5	3	3.63	15	11	0	0	69	79	36	28	4	18	54	.288
MINOR LEAGUE TOTALS			6	7	4.32	26	21	0	0	106	134	69	51	7	30	67	.307

16 Jorge Vasquez, rhp

Born: July 16, 1978. **Ht.:** 6-1. **Wt.:** 160. **Bats:** R. **Throws:** R. **Career Transactions:** Signed out of Dominican Republic by Royals, Sept. 1, 1998.

Vasquez entered 2003 with a 7-22 career record and eight saves to his credit. He always had a penchant not only for racking up strikeouts, but also for allowing runs. After a strong start in high Class A, he was even better in Double-A. Vasquez ranked fourth in the Texas League with 22 saves and 10th in the minors with 29 overall. That success and a nasty slider earned Vasquez a spot on the 40-man roster this offseason. He loves his plus slider and its late, hard break so much that at times he'll use it exclusively and still dominate hitters because he commands it so well. The Royals would like him to get more use out of his 90-92 mph fastball, which he can spot to both sides of the plate. They would also like him to look at possibly adding a splitter or improving his changeup so he has a better weapon to use against lefthanders. He also could stand to refine his command. Vasquez reminds some in the organization of 2002 major league Rule 5 pick D.J. Carrasco. He'll have a shot to make the Kansas City bullpen in spring training, just as Carrasco did last year.

Year	Club (League)	Class	W	L	ERA	G	GS	CG	SV	IP	H	R	ER	HR	BB	SO	AVG
1999	Royals (DSL)	R	2	6	3.09	21	10	1	2	76	105	42	26	6	24	78	—
2000	Royals (DSL)	R	2	8	4.54	23	7	0	0	73	76	48	37	5	19	70	.260
2001	Royals (GCL)	R	0	1	1.13	4	2	0	0	16	10	2	2	0	1	19	.167
	Spokane (NWL)	A	1	6	5.01	10	8	0	0	50	50	33	28	3	13	67	.259
2002	Burlington (Mid)	A	2	1	1.57	22	0	0	6	46	22	8	8	3	15	55	.141
	Wilmington (Car)	A	0	0	4.91	10	0	0	0	11	12	6	6	1	3	17	.255
2003	Wilmington (Car)	A	1	2	1.96	17	0	0	7	23	19	7	5	1	14	31	.224
	Wichita (TL)	AA	3	1	1.92	36	0	0	22	52	39	12	11	3	18	52	.212
MINOR LEAGUE TOTALS			11	25	3.19	143	27	1	37	347	333	158	123	22	107	389	.224

17 Rich Thompson, of

Born: April 23, 1979. **Ht.:** 6-3. **Wt.:** 180. **Bats:** L. **Throws:** R. **School:** James Madison University. **Career Transactions:** Selected by Blue Jays in sixth round of 2000 draft; signed June 19, 2000 . . . Traded by Blue Jays to Pirates for RHP John Wasdin, July 8, 2003 . . . Selected by Padres from Pirates in Rule 5 major league draft, Dec. 15, 2003 . . . Traded by Padres to Royals for RHP Jason Szuminski and cash, Dec. 15, 2003.

The Royals became Thompson's fourth organization in five months shortly after December's major league Rule 5 draft ended. He began 2003 in the Blue Jays system and was traded to the Pirates for John Wasdin in July. When Pittsburgh didn't protect Thompson on its 40-man roster, the Padres drafted him and sent him to Kansas City in a prearranged deal for Rule 5 righthander Jason Szuminski and cash. Thompson's excellent speed affords him the range to be an above-average defender and the ability to steal bases. It also factors into his offensive approach, as he'll bunt and slap singles while also legging out doubles and triples. He has just four career home runs and has never walked a lot, but flashed more power and plate discipline in the Arizona Fall League last offseason to raise his profile heading into the Rule 5 draft. He led the AFL with 28 runs, four triples and 13 steals in 25 games, and scouts ranked him as the league's fastest baserunner. Thompson's ability to play all three outfield positions and pinch-run should help him stick with the Royals as a fifth outfielder, but he'll also have to improve his offensive production. If he doesn't, he has to clear waivers and be offered back to the Pirates for half the $50,000 draft price before he can be sent to the minors.

Year	Club (League)	Class	AVG	G	AB	R	H	2B	3B	HR	RBI	BB	SO	SB	SLG	OBP
2000	Queens (NY-P)	A	.262	68	252	42	66	9	5	1	27	45	57	28	.349	.386
2001	Dunedin (FSL)	A	.311	112	454	90	141	14	6	1	60	44	72	39	.374	.380
	Syracuse (IL)	AAA	.245	17	53	5	13	0	1	0	3	4	12	5	.283	.293
2002	Tennessee (SL)	AA	.280	135	554	109	155	13	4	2	44	50	86	45	.329	.361
2003	New Haven (EL)	AA	.313	49	182	39	57	5	1	0	9	10	24	15	.352	.373
	Syracuse (IL)	AAA	.295	28	112	13	33	2	1	0	7	9	10	11	.330	.373
	Nashville (PCL)	AAA	.257	35	109	17	28	3	2	0	11	9	21	22	.321	.333
MINOR LEAGUE TOTALS			.287	444	1716	315	493	46	20	4	161	171	282	165	.344	.368

18 Travis Chapman, 3b/1b

Born: June 5, 1978. **Ht.:** 6-2. **Wt.:** 180. **Bats:** R. **Throws:** R. **School:** Mississippi State University. **Career Transactions:** Selected by Phillies in 17th round of 2000 draft; signed June 18, 2000 . . . Selected by Indians from Phillies in Rule 5 major league draft, Dec. 16, 2002 . . . Contract purchased by Tigers from Indians, Dec. 16, 2002 . . . Returned to Phillies, March 26, 2003 . . . Granted free agency, Dec. 20, 2003 . . . Signed with Royals, Jan. 25, 2004.

Chapman spent the first part of his offseason in the Arizona Fall League playing first base to prepare to win a role as a utility corner infielder and pinch-hitter with the Phillies. But he tore the labrum in his throwing shoulder while working out during the winter, and Philadelphia chose not to offer him a contract for 2004, making him a free agent. The Royals signed him in late January to help address their lack of organizational depth at the hot corner. Chapman isn't blessed with plus tools, but he has worked relentlessly to improve himself every year. He was solid in his first two seasons as a pro, then answered concerns about a lack of power by spending his entire offseason following the 2001 campaign working out. He added 10 pounds of muscle and transformed himself from an organizational player to a prospect. He's an average hitter who sometimes gets pull-conscious and can be worked hard inside and then away with offspeed pitches. Chapman finished fourth in the Triple-A International League in RBIs last year, when he also played in the Triple-A all-star game and led the Phillies system in doubles. He could develop into a Joe Randa type who hits .270 with a handful of home runs. Chapman has mediocre range but is a steady defender at either infield corner. He may not be ready to take the field until June, when he's expected to return to Triple-A.

Year	Club (League)	Class	AVG	G	AB	R	H	2B	3B	HR	RBI	BB	SO	SB	SLG	OBP
2000	Phillies (GCL)	R	.188	9	32	3	6	3	1	0	5	4	4	0	.344	.308
	Batavia (NY-P)	A	.316	49	174	23	55	10	2	1	28	12	24	0	.414	.379
2001	Clearwater (FSL)	A	.307	96	329	39	101	22	0	4	50	44	39	3	.410	.400
	Reading (EL)	AA	.182	7	22	3	4	0	0	1	3	0	5	0	.318	.250
2002	Reading (EL)	AA	.301	136	478	64	144	35	1	15	76	54	77	3	.473	.388
2003	Scranton/W-B (IL)	AAA	.272	134	478	62	130	36	0	12	82	44	97	2	.423	.348
	Philadelphia (NL)	MAJ	.000	1	1	0	0	0	0	0	0	0	0	0	.000	.000
MAJOR LEAGUE TOTALS			.000	1	1	0	0	0	0	0	0	0	0	0	.000	.000
MINOR LEAGUE TOTALS			.291	431	1513	194	440	106	4	33	244	158	246	8	.432	.374

19 Alexis Gomez, of

Born: Aug. 6, 1978. **Ht.:** 6-2. **Wt.:** 180. **Bats:** L. **Throws:** L. **Career Transactions:** Signed out of Dominican Republic by Royals, Feb. 21, 1997.

Gomez is an excellent athlete who played on the Dominican Republic's junior national volleyball team, but he has yet to translate his plus tools into baseball success and doesn't show great instincts in any phase of the game. He looks great in a uniform, but the Royals are still waiting for the light to come on for him. His status wasn't helped when it was revealed last spring that Gomez was two years older than previously thought. He has above-average range in center or right field, plus one of the better outfield arms in the system. Plate discipline and pitch recognition are his biggest downfalls. He strikes out too much, struggles against fastballs on the inner half and doesn't make in-game adjustments. His walk rate plummeted in his first exposure to Triple-A and he stopped using his plus speed to steal bases. Gomez has solid power, but often gets homer-happy and lets his swing get too long. He'd be better off shortening his stroke down and becoming a gap-to-gap hitter who makes use of his wheels. Gomez has one option left, and looks to be headed back to Triple-A for what might be his last chance. He profiles as a fourth outfielder at best.

Year	Club (League)	Class	AVG	G	AB	R	H	2B	3B	HR	RBI	BB	SO	SB	SLG	OBP
1997	Royals (DSL)	R	.351	64	248	51	87	12	9	0	42	33	52	9	.472	.430
1998	Royals (DSL)	R	.283	67	233	51	66	11	3	1	34	50	46	17	.369	.421
1999	Royals (GCL)	R	.276	56	214	44	59	12	1	5	31	32	48	13	.411	.371
2000	Wilmington (Car)	A	.254	121	461	63	117	13	4	1	33	45	121	21	.306	.322
2001	Wilmington (Car)	A	.302	48	169	29	51	8	2	1	9	11	43	7	.391	.348
	Wichita (TL)	AA	.281	83	342	55	96	15	6	4	34	27	70	16	.395	.337
2002	Wichita (TL)	AA	.295	114	461	72	136	21	8	14	75	45	84	36	.466	.359
	Kansas City (AL)	MAJ	.200	5	10	0	2	0	0	0	0	0	2	0	.200	.200
2003	Omaha (PCL)	AAA	.269	121	457	49	123	23	8	8	58	26	92	4	.407	.307
MAJOR LEAGUE TOTALS			.200	5	10	0	2	0	0	0	0	0	2	0	.200	.200
MINOR LEAGUE TOTALS			.284	674	2585	414	735	115	41	34	316	269	556	123	.400	.354

20 Ryan Bukvich, rhp

Born: May 13, 1978. **Ht.:** 6-2. **Wt.:** 250. **Bats:** R. **Throws:** R. **School:** University of Mississippi.
Career Transactions: Selected by Royals in 11th round of 2000 draft; signed June 9, 2000.

Bukvich experienced two poor seasons at Mississippi and was academically ineligible as a senior, but area scout Mark Willoughby remembered Bukvich's arm strength from his freshman year at NCAA Division II Delta State (Miss.). Bukvich raced through the minors but has struggled somewhat since first reaching the majors in July 2002. He opened last year as a set-up man in Kansas City, but his control soon deserted him and led to a demotion to Triple-A in May. He earned a second brief promotion at the end of June, but spent most of the year in Omaha struggling to refine his command. While his 92-96 mph fastball can be dominant, Bukvich often fails to finish pitches and leaves the ball up in the zone, resulting in home runs of falling behind in the count. First-pitch strikes are key because he can't use his fringe-average splitter or slurvy slider unless he's ahead in the count. None of his struggles are new, as they've been constant shortcomings throughout his career. How Bukvich addresses those concerns will determine whether he spends 2004 in Kansas City or Triple-A.

Year	Club (League)	Class	W	L	ERA	G	GS	CG	SV	IP	H	R	ER	HR	BB	SO	AVG
2000	Spokane (NWL)	A	2	0	0.64	10	0	0	2	14	5	1	1	0	9	15	.111
	Charleston, WV (SAL)	A	0	0	1.88	11	0	0	4	14	6	3	3	0	7	17	.128
	Wilmington (Car)	A	0	1	18.00	2	0	0	0	2	3	4	4	0	5	3	.375
2001	Wilmington (Car)	A	0	1	1.72	37	0	0	13	58	41	16	11	1	31	80	.194
	Wichita (TL)	AA	0	0	3.75	7	0	0	0	12	9	6	5	2	2	14	.200
2002	Wichita (TL)	AA	1	1	1.31	23	0	0	8	34	17	8	5	0	15	47	.145
	Omaha (PCL)	AAA	1	0	0.00	12	0	0	8	14	4	0	0	0	7	17	.093
	Kansas City (AL)	MAJ	1	0	6.12	26	0	0	0	25	26	19	17	2	19	20	.277
2003	Kansas City (AL)	MAJ	1	0	9.58	9	0	0	0	10	12	11	11	2	9	8	.293
	Omaha (PCL)	AAA	1	2	4.91	34	0	0	5	37	39	21	20	2	25	44	.273
MAJOR LEAGUE TOTALS			2	0	7.13	35	0	0	0	35	38	30	28	4	28	28	.281
MINOR LEAGUE TOTALS			5	5	2.39	136	0	0	40	185	124	59	49	5	101	237	.188

21 Mike Tonis, c

Born: Feb. 9, 1979. **Ht.:** 6-3. **Wt.:** 220. **Bats:** R. **Throws:** R. **School:** University of California.
Career Transactions: Selected by Royals in second round of 2000 draft; signed July 12, 2000.

The Royals angled for their catcher of the future when they selected Tonis and Scott Walter out of college in the second and third rounds in 2000. They expected one of them to make it to Kansas City by 2003, but Tonis hasn't stayed healthy and Walter hasn't shown the defensive skills. Tonis had knee surgery after the 2001 season, a shoulder operation during spring training in 2002, then broke his jaw five games into an August rehab assignment that year. He missed about a month in 2003 with a strained left hand. Despite the injuries, Tonis still ranks as the system's best defensive catcher. He works well with pitchers, calls a solid game and owns good catch-and-throw skills. He threw out 34 percent of basestealers last year. Tonis' offense has suffered with all the down time. He has a slow bat and hasn't developed the 15-20 home run power the Royals expected. He doesn't recognize breaking balls well and hit just .219 against righthanders last year. He's even-tempered and works hard, but now looks more likely to be a backup rather than a regular in the majors. How Tonis fares this season in Triple-A will be pivotal in determining his future with the club.

Year	Club (League)	Class	AVG	G	AB	R	H	2B	3B	HR	RBI	BB	SO	SB	SLG	OBP
2000	Charleston, WV (SAL)	A	.200	28	100	10	20	8	0	0	17	9	22	1	.280	.268
	Omaha (PCL)	AAA	.500	2	8	1	4	0	0	0	3	0	3	0	.500	.500
2001	Wilmington (Car)	A	.252	33	123	15	31	8	0	3	18	15	34	0	.390	.343
	Wichita (TL)	AA	.270	63	226	36	61	11	1	9	43	22	41	1	.447	.344
2002	Royals (GCL)	R	.176	6	17	2	3	0	0	1	3	2	3	0	.353	.300
2003	Wichita (TL)	AA	.238	87	307	34	73	18	0	2	24	23	52	3	.316	.296
MINOR LEAGUE TOTALS			.246	219	781	98	192	45	1	15	108	71	155	5	.364	.316

22 Mike Aviles, ss

Born: March 13, 1981. **Ht.:** 5-11. **Wt.:** 193. **Bats:** R. **Throws:** R. **School:** Concordia (N.Y.) College. **Career Transactions:** Selected by Royals in seventh round of 2003 draft; signed June 12, 2003.

Area scout Steve Connelly pushed to select Aviles as a college junior in 2002, then watched him explode to become the NCAA Division II player of the year as a senior. Aviles shortened his stroke and led Division II players in batting (.500), slugging (1.016), homers (22) and runs (83). The Royals had to draft him earlier than expected in the 2003 draft, but still signed him for $1,000 as a seventh-rounder. He delivered an MVP year in the Arizona League, leading the circuit in runs and doubles. Aviles is a contact hitter with a knack for making adjustments. He should have average power. He's a natural fielder with good hands, an above-average arm and average speed, but he sometimes tries to be too flashy. He ultimately may not have the range for shortstop and might have to move to second base. He spent the offseason in Puerto Rico, playing for Carolina, where his uncle Ramon (a former big leaguer) is a bench coach. The Royals will push Aviles through the system quickly, and he'll begin 2004 in high Class A.

Year	Club (League)	Class	AVG	G	AB	R	H	2B	3B	HR	RBI	BB	SO	SB	SLG	OBP
2003	Royals 1 (AZL)	R	.363	52	212	51	77	19	5	6	39	13	28	11	.585	.404
MINOR LEAGUE TOTALS			.363	52	212	51	77	19	5	6	39	13	28	11	.585	.404

23 Kenard Springer, of

Born: Sept. 18, 1983. **Ht.:** 6-0. **Wt.:** 210. **Bats:** R. **Throws:** R. **School:** Nettleton (Miss.) HS. **Career Transactions:** Selected by Royals in eighth round of 2002 draft; signed June 7, 2002.

Springer tells anyone who asks that he's from Tupelo, Miss., the birthplace of Elvis Presley. He's athletic and was an all-state running back in high school. A cousin of Brewers shortstop Bill Hall, Springer needed two seasons of Rookie ball to complete his transition from a high school third baseman wielding an aluminum bat to a professional outfielder using wood. Royals hitting instructor Andre David had Springer wear ankle weights in the batting cage to quiet his approach at the plate, and helped him eliminate a bad case of bat wrap. The result was a 27-game hitting streak and the sixth-best average in the Arizona League in 2003, when Springer was the organization's most improved player. He's strong, shows good power and has the ability to recognize and adjust to breaking balls. He needs to shorten his swing despite excellent bat speed and must tighten his strike zone. Springer has a long way to go defensively, especially reading balls and getting jumps. He'll always have limitations as a fielder, most notably a below-average left-field arm, but he's faster than his build would indicate. He could return to the infield down the road if he gets crowded out of the outfield by 2003 draftees Chris Lubanski, Mitch Maier and Shane Costa. Low Class A should provide a proving ground for Springer's bat in 2004.

Year	Club (League)	Class	AVG	G	AB	R	H	2B	3B	HR	RBI	BB	SO	SB	SLG	OBP
2002	Royals (GCL)	R	.189	38	95	11	18	2	0	0	2	9	13	5	.211	.280
2003	Royals 1 (AZL)	R	.346	49	182	35	63	15	1	3	39	10	20	7	.489	.388
MINOR LEAGUE TOTALS			.292	87	277	46	81	17	1	3	41	19	33	12	.394	.351

24 Chad Santos, 1b

Born: April 28, 1981. **Ht.:** 5-11. **Wt.:** 220. **Bats:** L. **Throws:** L. **School:** St. Louis School, Honolulu. **Career Transactions:** Selected by Royals in 22nd round of 1999 draft; signed June 8, 1999.

Santos is one of two Hawaiian first-base prospects for the Royals, joining Kila Kaaihue, and he's the best defender at the position in the system. He has soft hands and solid range. He also rivals another first baseman, 2003 third-rounder Brian McFall, for the most pure power in the organization. Santos can drive the ball out of any park, but he struggles desperately against lefthanders. He has yet to hit better than .165 against southpaws in his career, posting a .116 mark with 44 strikeouts in 86 at-bats against them last year. He sometimes gets caught trying to hit everything out of the park and could help himself by going the other way more and gaining a better grasp on the strike zone. Santos will return to Double-A to continue working on his approach against lefthanders.

Year	Club (League)	Class	AVG	G	AB	R	H	2B	3B	HR	RBI	BB	SO	SB	SLG	OBP
1999	Royals (GCL)	R	.271	48	177	20	48	9	0	4	35	12	54	1	.390	.319
2000	Charleston, WV (SAL)	A	.209	59	187	16	39	9	2	4	18	27	62	0	.342	.307
	Spokane (NWL)	A	.251	73	267	40	67	18	0	14	47	36	103	1	.476	.344
2001	Burlington (Mid)	A	.252	121	444	58	112	32	0	16	83	52	101	0	.432	.337
2002	Wilmington (Car)	A	.240	110	379	46	91	21	0	9	54	46	122	0	.367	.330
2003	Wichita (TL)	AA	.270	111	396	48	107	21	3	11	49	35	116	3	.422	.332
MINOR LEAGUE TOTALS			.251	522	1850	228	464	110	5	58	286	208	558	5	.410	.331

25 Kila Kaaihue, 1b

Born: March 29, 1984. **Ht.:** 6-3. **Wt.:** 210. **Bats:** L. **Throws:** R. **School:** Iolani HS, Honolulu. **Career Transactions:** Selected by Royals in 15th round of 2002 draft; signed June 24, 2002.

Scouting director Deric Ladnier first saw Kaaihue when he went to Hawaii to check out Bronson Sardinha and Brandon League in 2001. A year later, he remembered Kaaihue's power potential and bloodlines—his father Kala caught in the minors for the Cardinals and Pirates—and drafted him in spite of a poor senior season. Kaaihue was overmatched in low Class A at the beginning of 2003, hitting .194 with three home runs and 31 strikeouts in 154 at-bats through May. He caught up during the second half, hitting .266 with eight homers and 46 strikeouts in 241 at-bats. He has a sweet swing with long extension and loft power, and his excellent bat speed gets the barrel through the zone quickly. He sometimes has trouble wrapping his bat, but he stayed inside the ball better late in the year after making an adjustment. Kaaihue doesn't chase pitches out of the strike zone and does draw walks, though he sometimes gets on a power jag and values muscle over contact. Elbow and biceps injuries limited Kaaihue to DH in 2002. He showed good hands with below-average range and speed in 2003. He will remain in low Class A to start 2004, allowing him to build on the confidence he gained in the second half of last year.

Year	Club (League)	Class	AVG	G	AB	R	H	2B	3B	HR	RBI	BB	SO	SB	SLG	OBP
2002	Royals (GCL)	R	.259	43	139	15	36	8	0	3	21	26	35	0	.381	.381
2003	Burlington (Mid)	A	.238	114	395	53	94	21	1	11	63	67	87	1	.380	.355
MINOR LEAGUE TOTALS			.243	157	534	68	130	29	1	14	84	93	122	1	.380	.362

26 Brian McFall, 1b

Born: June 17, 1984. **Ht.:** 6-3. **Wt.:** 205. **Bats:** R. **Throws:** R. **School:** Chandler-Gilbert (Ariz.) JC. **Career Transactions:** Selected by Royals in third round of 2003 draft; signed June 3, 2003.

McFall wasn't on the radar for many teams early in the 2003 draft, but the Royals rated his power potential among the best in the class. They signed him for $385,000. He was one of five players drafted last year out of Chandler-Gilbert, where he also showed promise on the mound. McFall's future won't be on the mound, however, because the ball really jumps off his bat. He has as much raw power as anyone in the system, but he has a ways to go in understanding breaking balls and working himself into hitter's counts. He didn't see too many fastballs in the Arizona League, where he often batted cleanup. McFall is an intense player who works hard and runs out every ball, but he sometimes plays out of control. He's an above-average runner for his body type and can play third base a little bit, though he's better at first base. He's still a below-average defender, though he has made strides. McFall hit 92 mph off the mound in college, so he has the arm to go with the athleticism to move to the outfield if needed. He'll stay in Rookie ball this year.

Year	Club (League)	Class	AVG	G	AB	R	H	2B	3B	HR	RBI	BB	SO	SB	SLG	OBP
2003	Royals 1 (AZL)	R	.220	51	191	34	42	9	4	6	36	17	50	1	.403	.296
MINOR LEAGUE TOTALS			.220	51	191	34	42	9	4	6	36	17	50	1	.403	.296

27 Devon Lowery, rhp

Born: March 24, 1983. **Ht.:** 6-1. **Wt.:** 190. **Bats:** L. **Throws:** R. **School:** South Point HS, Belmont, N.C. **Career Transactions:** Selected by Royals in 14th round of 2001 draft; signed June 9, 2001.

One of North Carolina's top high school quarterbacks in 2001, Lowery was recruited by Wake Forest and other NCAA Division I football programs. He settled on playing baseball, however, and is one of the best athletes in the system. Lowery spent most of his career in the bullpen before moving to the rotation last July. He added strength after the 2002 season, boosting his fastball 3-4 mph to 94. It has good life, especially when he keeps it down in the zone. Lowery throws his late-breaking slider for strikes against righthanders and uses a fading changeup against lefties. He's a smart pitcher who retains coaching well, and he shows a good feel for working hitters. He wore down last year after setting a career high in innings but should have enough stamina once he gets used to being a starter. Lowery impressed the Royals so much that he almost received a late promotion to high Class A when Wilmington needed an extra pitcher. Lowery will start 2004 there to continue developing his repertoire. He might return to the bullpen because he has a knack for getting groundballs and his secondary pitches might come up a little short at the major league level.

Year	Club (League)	Class	W	L	ERA	G	GS	CG	SV	IP	H	R	ER	HR	BB	SO	AVG
2001	Royals (GCL)	R	2	3	4.17	11	6	0	1	41	38	25	19	2	12	19	.238
2002	Royals (GCL)	R	0	3	3.86	15	0	0	4	26	25	13	11	1	11	26	.255
2003	Burlington (Mid)	A	6	4	3.36	26	10	0	5	96	78	39	36	9	34	74	.222
MINOR LEAGUE TOTALS			8	10	3.64	52	16	0	10	163	141	77	66	12	57	119	.232

28 Dustin Hughes, lhp

Born: June 29, 1982. **Ht.:** 5-9. **Wt.:** 195. **Bats:** L. **Throws:** L. **School:** Delta State (Miss.) University. **Career Transactions:** Selected by Royals in 11th round of 2003 draft; signed June 20, 2003.

Area scout Mark Willoughby first spotted Ryan Bukvich at NCAA Division II Delta State, where he also found Hughes. Hughes ranked third in Division II with 12.4 strikeouts per nine innings last spring, then made the Arizona League all-star team in his pro debut. He succeeds with above-average command of two plus pitches: a 90-94 mph fastball and a low-80s slider with a hard, late break. Hughes also works with an average changeup and over-matched the AZL's young hitters with his ability to throw offspeed pitches behind in the count. He was much better out of the bullpen, posting an 0.45 ERA in relief versus a 4.40 mark in the rotation. His strong lower half and compact, stocky build are reminiscent of Mike Stanton. Hughes should move quickly through the organization, ultimately ending up as a set-up man. He'll begin 2004 in the high Class A rotation if he has a good spring.

Year	Club (League)	Class	W	L	ERA	G	GS	CG	SV	IP	H	R	ER	HR	BB	SO	AVG
2003	Royals 1 (AZL)	R	5	2	2.84	11	6	0	0	51	38	21	16	4	18	54	.207
MINOR LEAGUE TOTALS			5	2	2.84	11	6	0	0	51	38	21	16	4	18	54	.207

29 Danny Christensen, lhp

Born: Aug. 10, 1983. **Ht.:** 6-2. **Wt.:** 200. **Bats:** L. **Throws:** L. **School:** Xaverian HS, Brooklyn. **Career Transactions:** Selected by Royals in fourth round of 2002 draft; signed June 8, 2002.

A strong pro debut earned Christensen comparisons to fellow 2002 high school draftee Zack Greinke. They have a similar competitive nature, polish and feel for pitching. Christensen was expected to leap to high Class A in 2003, but he reported to spring training pudgy and out of shape after developing poor eating habits. As a result, he tired quickly, struggled to finish his pitches and left the ball up in the zone to get blasted—especially by lefties, who hit .355 against him. He ended up tied for second in the Midwest League with 12 losses before getting sent down to the Arizona League, where he made adjustments and regrouped. Christensen also spent time on the disabled list with a blister on his middle finger, which came from throwing his big-breaking curveball, a plus pitch when he throws it for strikes. His fastball has plenty of life at 87-90 mph, topping out at 92. He also throws a circle changeup. The Royals challenged Christensen to get in better shape, and he hired a personal trainer for the offseason. He also needs to improve his command. He likely will head back to low Class A to start 2004.

Year	Club (League)	Class	W	L	ERA	G	GS	CG	SV	IP	H	R	ER	HR	BB	SO	AVG
2002	Royals (GCL)	R	1	3	3.10	7	6	0	0	29	20	13	10	2	14	28	.196
	Spokane (NWL)	A	2	0	1.10	6	6	0	0	33	24	6	4	3	14	23	.198
2003	Burlington (Mid)	A	1	12	5.92	17	16	0	0	79	83	62	52	11	31	46	.269
	Royals 1 (AZL)	R	0	0	2.25	4	2	0	0	12	8	4	3	0	5	12	.178
MINOR LEAGUE TOTALS			4	15	4.07	34	30	0	0	153	135	85	69	16	64	109	.234

30 Ambiorix Burgos, rhp

Born: April 19, 1984. **Ht.:** 6-0. **Wt.:** 180. **Bats:** R. **Throws:** R. **Career Transactions:** Signed out of Dominican Republic by Royals, Nov. 14, 2000.

Burgos is the only other player in the system with a pure power arm that can rival Colt Griffin's. Burgos made his U.S. debut last year after two seasons in the Rookie-level Dominican Summer League. He threw 87-88 mph when he signed in 2002, climbed to 94-95 a year later and now unleashed 96-97 mph heat. Burgos already shows an advanced feel for his changeup and is working on a slider and curveball. He has solid mechanics but still is adjusting to having grown four inches since signing. His high waist and long arms lead to effortless velocity. He just needs to maintain a more consistent release point and overall focus. Burgos can dominate on the mound with his physical stature and raw stuff, but he has really struggled with cultural adjustments, including learning English. He grew up in a rough area of the Dominican and can be tough to coach at times. Burgos shows the baseball skills to move to low Class A, but his maturity will dictate whether he goes to Burlington or Rookie-level Idaho Falls. Though he has a front-of-the-rotation ceiling, he's a long way from reaching it.

Year	Club (League)	Class	W	L	ERA	G	GS	CG	SV	IP	H	R	ER	HR	BB	SO	AVG
2001	Royals (DSL)	R	2	5	4.97	13	11	0	0	51	51	36	28	1	35	38	.262
2002	Royals (DSL)	R	0	9	5.47	13	12	0	0	51	47	42	31	1	28	33	.241
2003	Royals 1 (AZL)	R	3	2	4.00	9	7	0	0	36	37	22	16	1	16	43	.261
	Burlington (Mid)	A	0	1	5.40	2	2	0	0	5	3	3	3	1	6	4	.200
MINOR LEAGUE TOTALS			5	17	4.92	37	32	0	0	143	138	103	78	4	85	118	.252

LOS ANGELES
DODGERS

I n his second attempt to purchase a major league franchise, Boston-based real-estate developer Frank McCourt paid $430 million to buy the Dodgers from Fox in October. McCourt, who outbid but lost out to John Henry for the Red Sox in 2002, won't officially take over the team until major league owners ratify the sale, a vote that has been pushed back several times because McCourt's financing plan is highly leveraged.

The uncertainly put the Dodgers organization in limbo after a tumultuous season. McCourt reportedly has plans for Corey Busch, a former Giants executive vice president who currently serves as an adviser to commissioner Bud Selig, to take over as club president. Rumors that Athletics general manager Billy Beane already was lobbying McCourt to head the baseball operation couldn't make Dan Evans comfortable as he prepared for his third season as GM.

Evans' first year on the job was solid but unspectacular, as he was strapped by some immovable contracts left behind by Kevin Malone's regime. But his second year was met with harsh criticism, as a team with a $109 million payroll didn't make the playoffs and Evans couldn't pull the big deal to push them over the top. The local media piled on, and though the Dodgers contended all season, they extended a playoff drought that dates back to 1996.

TOP 30 PROSPECTS

1. Edwin Jackson, rhp
2. Greg Miller, lhp
3. Franklin Gutierrez, of
4. James Loney, 1b
5. Joel Hanrahan, rhp
6. Chad Billingsley, rhp
7. Xavier Paul, of
8. Andy LaRoche, 2b/ss
9. Koyie Hill, c
10. Reggie Abercrombie, of
11. Joel Guzman, ss
12. Steve Colyer, lhp
13. Willy Aybar, 3b
14. Jonathan Broxton, rhp
15. Chuck Tiffany, lhp
16. Chin-Feng Chen, of/1b
17. Jonathan Figueroa, lhp
18. Russell Martin, c
19. Mike Megrew, lhp
20. Andrew Brown, rhp
21. Delwyn Young, 2b
22. Ching-Lung Hu, ss
23. Yhency Brazoban, rhp
24. Joe Thurston, 2b
25. Orlando Rodriguez, lhp
26. Mike Nixon, c
27. James McDonald, rhp
28. Juan Rivera, ss
29. Brian Pilkington, rhp
30. Zach Hammes, rhp

By Josh Boyd

Evans and his front office proceeded with business as usual, trying to improve the Dodgers' inept offense. Los Angeles finished dead last in the majors in runs scored last year. In-season attempts to punch up the offense by trading for Jeromy Burnitz and Robin Ventura didn't cost them much but did little to help, either. Acquiring a difference-maker has proven to be a challenge for the Dodgers, who seem tentative at times in the market.

Their scouting and player development staff is hitting on all cylinders, however. The farm system, which ranked in the bottom five in talent when Evans took over, has been bolstered by two productive drafts by scouting director Logan White. BA rated his 2003 draft the best in the game. Considered unsignable because of a scholarship from Rice, LaRoche changed his mind for a $1 million bonus. Righthander Edwin Jackson emerged as one of the most promising pitching prospects in baseball and won a surprise spot start in September. And some scouts say lefthander Greg Miller is even better than Jackson.

Former farm director Bill Bavasi deserves credit for straightening out the organization's player-development plan, and the Mariners hired him as GM in November. His position wasn't likely to be filled until the ownership change. Assistant GM Kim Ng led the department in the meantime.

ORGANIZATION
OVERVIEW

General manager: Dan Evans. **Acting farm director:** Kim Ng. **Scouting director:** Logan White.

2003 PERFORMANCE

Class	Team	League	W	L	Pct.	Finish*	Manager
Majors	Los Angeles	National	85	77	.525	t-7th (16)	Jim Tracy
Triple-A	Las Vegas 51s	Pacific Coast	76	66	.535	3rd (16)	John Shoemaker
Double-A	Jacksonville Suns	Southern	66	73	.475	6th (10)	Dino Ebel
High A	Vero Beach Dodgers	Florida State	62	69	.473	10th (12)	Scott Little
Low A	South Georgia Waves	South Atlantic	64	72	.471	11th (16)	Dann Bilardello
Rookie	Ogden Raptors	Pioneer	35	41	.461	6th (8)	Travis Barbary
Rookie	GCL Dodgers	Gulf Coast	29	31	.483	6th (12)	Luis Salazar
OVERALL 2003 MINOR LEAGUE RECORD			332	352	.486	21st (30)	

*Finish in overall standings (No. of teams in league)

ORGANIZATIONAL LEADERS

BATTING
Minimum 250 At-Bats

*AVG	Bubba Crosby, Las Vegas	.361
R	Chin-Feng Chen, Las Vegas	84
H	Joe Thurston, Las Vegas	156
TB	Franklin Gutierrez, Jacksonville/Vero Beach	258
2B	Delwyn Young, South Georgia	38
3B	Bubba Crosby, Las Vegas	8
HR	Chin-Feng Chen, Las Vegas	26
RBI	Chin-Feng Chen, Las Vegas	86
BB	Tarrik Brock, Las Vegas/Jacksonville	62
SO	Reggie Abercrombie, Jacksonville	164
SB	Wilkin Ruan, Las Vegas	41
*SLG	Bubba Crosby, Las Vegas	.635
*OBP	Bubba Crosby, Las Vegas	.410

PITCHING
#Minimum 75 Innings

W	Brian Pilkington, Jacksonville/Vero Beach	13
L	Heath Totten, Jacksonville	12
#ERA	Greg Miller, Jacksonville/Vero Beach	2.21
G	Bryan Corey, Las Vegas	60
CG	Heath Totten, Jacksonville	2
	T.J. Nall, Vero Beach	2
SV	Steve Colyer, Las Vegas	23
	Jason Frasor, Jacksonville/Vero Beach	23
IP	Heath Totten, Jacksonville	181
BB	Joel Hanrahan, Las Vegas/Jacksonville	73
SO	Edwin Jackson, Jacksonville	157

BEST TOOLS

Best Hitter for Average	James Loney
Best Power Hitter	Franklin Gutierrez
Fastest Baserunner	Jerome Milons
Best Athlete	Reggie Abercrombie
Best Fastball	Edwin Jackson
Best Curveball	Greg Miller
Best Slider	Greg Miller
Best Changeup	Alfredo Gonzalez
Best Control	Brian Pilkington
Best Defensive Catcher	Edwin Bellorin
Best Defensive Infielder	Ching-Lung Hu
Best Infield Arm	Andy LaRoche
Best Defensive Outfielder	Wilkin Ruan
Best Outfield Arm	Xavier Paul

PROJECTED 2007 LINEUP

Catcher	Koyie Hill
First Base	James Loney
Second Base	Andy LaRoche
Third Base	Adrian Beltre
Shortstop	Cesar Izturis
Left Field	Franklin Gutierrez
Center Field	Xavier Paul
Right Field	Shawn Green
No. 1 Starter	Edwin Jackson
No. 2 Starter	Greg Miller
No. 3 Starter	Odalis Perez
No. 4 Starter	Joel Hanrahan
No. 5 Starter	Kazuhisha Ishii
Closer	Eric Gagne

LAST YEAR'S TOP 20 PROSPECTS

1. James Loney, 1b
2. Jonathan Figueroa, lhp
3. Edwin Jackson, rhp
4. Reggie Abercrombie, of
5. Joey Thurston, 2b/ss
6. Koyie Hill, c
7. Alfredo Gonzalez, rhp
8. Joel Hanrahan, rhp
9. Joel Guzman, ss
10. Chin-Feng Chen, of/1b
11. Hong-Chih Kuo, lhp
12. Victor Diaz, 3b/2b
13. Greg Miller, lhp
14. Andrew Brown, rhp
15. Derek Thompson, lhp
16. Franklin Gutierrez, of
17. Willy Aybar, 3b
18. Jonathan Broxton, rhp
19. Wilkin Ruan, of
20. Mike Nixon, c

TOP PROSPECTS OF THE DECADE

1994	Darren Dreifort, rhp
1995	Todd Hollandsworth, of
1996	Karim Garcia, of
1997	Paul Konerko, 3b
1998	Paul Konerko, 1b
1999	Angel Pena, c
2000	Chin-Feng Chen, of
2001	Ben Diggins, rhp
2002	Ricardo Rodriguez, rhp
2003	James Loney, 1b

TOP DRAFT PICKS OF THE DECADE

1994	Paul Konerko, c
1995	David Yocum, lhp
1996	Damian Rolls, 3b
1997	Glenn Davis, 1b
1998	Bubba Crosby, of
1999	Jason Repko, ss/of
2000	Ben Diggins, rhp
2001	Brian Pilkington, rhp (2)
2002	James Loney, 1b
2003	Chad Billingsley, rhp

ALL-TIME LARGEST BONUSES

Joel Guzman, 2001	$2,250,000
Ben Diggins, 2000	$2,200,000
Hideo Nomo, 1995	$2,000,000
Kazuhisha Ishii, 2002	$1,500,000
James Loney, 2002	$1,500,000

MINOR LEAGUE
DEPTH CHART

LOS ANGELES **DODGERS**   RANK: 2

Impact potential (A): Edwin Jackson and Greg Miller are arguably the top two pitching prospects in the game. Franklin Gutierrez is rising fast after tapping into his raw power last season, and James Loney continues to play at a high level despite being the youngest player in his league.

Depth (A): The Dodgers turned things around in a hurry after talent on the farm all but dried up in the late 1990s. Scouting director Logan White has turned in back-to-back strong drafts, and management has shown a renewed willingness to spend on the amateur market. Los Angeles should once again emerge as a scouting force in Latin America under Rene Francisco's watch.

Sleeper: James McDonald, rhp.   *—Depth charts prepared by Josh Boyd. Numbers in parentheses indicate prospect rankings.*

LF
Xavier Paul (7)
Chin-Feng Chen (16)
Matt Kemp

CF
Reggie Abercrombie (10)
Jerome Milons
Jason Romano
Jason Repko
Wilkin Ruan
Shane Victorino

RF
Franklin Gutierrez (3)

3B
Joel Guzman (11)
Wiliy Aybar (13)
Brennan King
Luis Castillo

SS
Ching-Lung Hu (22)
Juan Rivera (28)
Travis Denker
Russ Mitchell
Etanislao Abreu

2B
Andy LaRoche (8)
Delwyn Young (21)
Joe Thurston (24)
Lucas May

1B
James Loney (4)

SOURCE OF TALENT

Homegrown		Acquired	
College	1	Trades	3
Junior College	4	Rule 5 draft	0
Draft-and-follow	2	Independent leagues	0
High school	13	Free agents/waivers	0
Nondrafted free agent	0		
Foreign	7		

C
Koyie Hill (9)
Russell Martin (18)
Mike Nixon (26)
Edwin Bellorin

LHP

Starters	Relievers
Greg Miller (2)	Steve Colyer (12)
Chuck Tiffany (15)	Orlando Rodriguez (25)
Jonathan Figueroa (17)	Luis Gonzalez
Mike Megrew (19)	Eric Stults
Hong-Chih Kuo	Chad Bailey

RHP

Starters	Relievers
Edwin Jackson (1)	Yhency Brazoban (23)
Joel Hanrahan (5)	Marcos Carvajal
Chad Billingsley (6)	Duaner Sanchez
Jonathan Broxton (14)	Alfredo Gonzalez
Andrew Brown (20)	Brian Falkenborg
James McDonald (27)	Steve Schmoll
Brian Pilkington (29)	Jason Frasor
Zach Hammes (30)	Franquelis Osoria
Jordan Pratt	Agustin Montero
Brandon Weeden	Jose Diaz
Heath Totten	
Jose Obispo	
Jose Rojas	

DRAFT
ANALYSIS

Best Pro Debut: The first pitcher and hitter drafted by the Dodgers both had immediate success. RHP Chad Billingsley (1) looked polished while going 5-4, 2.83 in the Rookie-level Pioneer League. OF Xavier Paul (4) batted .307-7-47 with a PL-best six triples.

Best Athlete: Paul's bat, power, speed and arm are all plus tools. He started throwing in the low 90s as a high school freshman. More accomplished in basketball, OF Matt Kemp (6) is a raw, 6-foot-5 package of power and speed.

May

Best Pure Hitter: SS Andy LaRoche (39) was the best position player in the Cape Cod League last summer, but the Dodgers say Paul is slightly better at the plate. 3B Lucas May (8) and SS Russ Mitchell (15) also have potential.

Best Raw Power: LaRoche has more strength than Paul, though Paul bombed a ball off a warehouse roof in Ogden.

Fastest Runner: Paul runs the 60-yard dash in 6.45-6.6 seconds. His speed and instincts make him an asset on the bases and in the outfield.

Best Defensive Player: LaRoche isn't speedy or flashy, but he's surehanded and has a strong arm. The Dodgers project him as a second baseman.

Best Fastball: Billingsley's fastball ranges from 90-97 mph and sits at 93. LHP Chuck Tiffany (2) has a heater that can reach 94.

RHPs Jordan Pratt (5) and Phil Sobkow (10) are in the same neighborhood.

Best Breaking Ball: Billingsley's curveball and slider are both plus pitches at times; his curve is slightly better. Tiffany has a good hook as well as the best changeup among Dodgers draftees.

Most Intriguing Background: C Thomas Piazza (26) is the younger brother of Mike, who began what will be a Hall of Fame career in Los Angeles. LaRoche's father Dave was a two-time all-star reliever, while his brother Adam is a top first-base prospect in the Braves system. 1B James Peterson (16) is the second-leading home run hitter in national high school history with 73.

Closest To The Majors: High schoolers such as Edwin Jackson, James Loney and Greg Miller are speeding through the Dodgers system, and the club thinks Billingsley, Paul and Tiffany can too.

Best Late-Round Pick: LaRoche. He would have been a mid-first-round pick in 2004, which is why he cost $1 million.

The One Who Got Away: LHP Cory Van Allen (3) has a more polished repertoire than Tiffany. He's now at Baylor.

Assessment: While more teams covet college players now, the Dodgers have had success with high schoolers. Their first eight selections were high school players, a mix of strong arms and productive bats.

LHP Greg Miller (1) and 1B James Loney (1) look like future stars. The next five picks—RHPs Zach Hammes (2) and Jonathan Broxton (2), C Mike Nixon (3), 2B Delwyn Young (4) and LHP Mike Megrew (5)—are legitimate prospects as well.

The Dodgers had no first-rounder and their top pick, RHP Brian Pilkington (2), has battled shoulder trouble. But they stole RHP Edwin Jackson (6) and used RHP Kole Strayhorn (4) in a deal for Jeromy Burnitz. Pilkington is starting to rebound, too.

RHP Ben Diggins (1) blew out his elbow after getting dealt to the Brewers. RHP Joel Hanrahan (2), C Koyie Hill (4) and 2B Victor Diaz have brighter futures.

Draft-and-follow OF Reggie Abercrombie (23) has a huge ceiling and huge problems making contact. 2B Joey Thurston (4) failed to seize a big league opportunity in 2003.

—Draft analysis prepared by Jim Callis. Numbers in parentheses indicate draft rounds.

LARRY GOREN

rhp

Edwin
Jackson

Born: Sept. 9, 1983.
Ht.: 6-3. **Wt.:** 190.
Bats: R. **Throws:** R.
School: Shaw HS, Columbus, Ga.
Career Transactions: Selected by Dodgers in sixth round of 2001 draft; signed June 18, 2001.

First spotted by Dodgers scouts Jim Lester (now with the Pirates) and Lon Joyce when he was a center fielder at Shaw High in Columbus, Ga., Jackson also was the No. 3 starter behind Nick Long, now an Expos prospect, and Steven Register, now Auburn's closer. Jackson reached 91 mph at the time, but Joyce's first instinct was to make the most of his athleticism and bat potential in the outfield. The Dodgers weren't sure which direction his career would head, so they allowed him to DH when he wasn't pitching during in the Rookie-level Gulf Coast League in 2001. They abandoned any thoughts of developing him as an outfielder the following spring, and his career took off. After beginning 2002 in extended spring training, Jackson jumped to low Class A South Georgia. He carried a no-hitter into the seventh inning of his first start and fell seven innings short of qualifying for the South Atlantic League ERA title, which he would have won. Jackson skipped another level to start the 2003 season as one of the youngest pitchers in Double-A. He became the youngest pitcher since Dwight Gooden to win his major league debut when he beat Randy Johnson in September.

Jackson's picturesque delivery, clean arm action and premium athleticism aid him in making 98 mph fastballs look effortless. He sits between 91-97 and can maintain his velocity deep into games. His slider and changeup both have come a long way since he made the full-time conversion to pitching, and while he's not consistent with his secondary pitches he flashes above-average potential with both offerings. Each of his three pitches features plus life, with his fastball boring up into the zone, his slider showing hard bite and depth at times, and his circle changeup fading and sinking. Jackson demonstrates an advanced feel for pitching too, not afraid to pitch inside or double up on sliders and changeups. The Dodgers have done a fine job limiting Jackson's workload. He was limited to around 100 pitches a start, and he was scratched from the Arizona Fall League to avoid putting more innings on his arm. Jackson has been unfazed by his rapid ascent. He still needs to gain consistency and confidence with his slider and changeup. Like many strikeout pitchers, he can amass lofty pitch counts.

With three potential out pitches and plus command, that shouldn't be an issue for long. Jackson is the complete package, and fits the profile of a top-of-the-line starting pitcher to a tee. He established himself as one of the elite prospects in baseball even before his September callup, and his performance all but guaranteed him a spot in the Los Angeles rotation for 2004. He's the best homegrown pitching prospect the Dodgers have developed since Pedro Martinez, and they don't plan on letting this one get away.

Year	Club (League)	Class	W	L	ERA	G	GS	CG	SV	IP	H	R	ER	HR	BB	SO	AVG
2001	Dodgers (GCL)	R	2	1	2.45	12	2	0	0	22	14	12	6	1	19	23	.173
2002	South Georgia (SAL)	A	5	2	1.98	19	19	0	0	105	79	34	23	2	33	85	.206
2003	Jacksonville (SL)	AA	7	7	3.70	27	27	0	0	148	121	68	61	9	53	157	.220
	Los Angeles (NL)	MAJ	2	1	2.45	4	3	0	0	22	17	6	6	2	11	19	.221
MAJOR LEAGUE TOTALS			2	1	2.45	4	3	0	0	22	17	6	6	2	11	19	.221
MINOR LEAGUE TOTALS			14	10	2.95	58	48	0	0	275	214	114	90	12	105	265	.211

2 Greg Miller, lhp

Born: Nov. 3, 1984. **Ht.:** 6-5. **Wt.:** 190. **Bats:** L. **Throws:** L. **School:** Esperanza HS, Yorba Linda, Calif. **Career Transactions:** Selected by Dodgers in first round (31st overall) of 2002 draft; signed June 14, 2002.

Several Dodgers scouts say Miller is even better than Edwin Jackson. After going 2-2, 5.03 in his first six starts, Miller dominated the high Class A Florida State League and earned a promotion to Double-A Jacksonville as an 18-year-old. Miller's velocity has increased from the mid-80s in high school to the low 90s, and he regularly hit 95 mph in 2003. His power curveball is among the best in the organization, and he added a cutter that has morphed into a nasty slider. His average changeup gives a fourth pitch with which to attack hitters. He completes the package with command, intelligence and uncanny poise. Miller's season ended with shoulder bursitis, and some wonder if the stress of throwing a slider contributed to his problems. Other than staying healthy, he has little to work on. Though the Dodgers opted for Jackson when Hideo Nomo got hurt, Miller got serious consideration for a September spot start. He'll be given an outside chance to make the big league rotation in the spring, but most likely will return to Double-A.

Year	Club (League)	Class	W	L	ERA	G	GS	CG	SV	IP	H	R	ER	HR	BB	SO	AVG
2002	Great Falls (Pio)	R	3	2	2.37	11	7	0	0	38	27	14	10	1	13	37	.199
2003	Vero Beach (FSL)	A	11	4	2.49	21	21	1	0	116	103	40	32	5	41	111	.240
	Jacksonville (SL)	AA	1	1	1.01	4	4	0	0	27	15	5	3	1	7	40	.156
MINOR LEAGUE TOTALS			15	7	2.25	36	32	1	0	180	145	59	45	7	61	188	.219

3 Franklin Gutierrez, of

Born: Feb. 21, 1983. **Ht.:** 6-2. **Wt.:** 175. **Bats:** R. **Throws:** R. **Career Transactions:** Signed out of Venezuela by Dodgers, Nov. 18, 2000.

Gutierrez didn't emerge as a full-fledged prospect until 2003, when he homered six times in as many games to start the season at high Class A Vero Beach. He ranked among the Florida State League leaders in home runs and slugging before a promotion to Double-A. Gutierrez' raw power became above-average game power last year. He has a balanced approach with outstanding bat speed and natural lift to his swing. He's wiry strong and athletic, with the speed to run down balls in center field. He has plus arm strength and enough bat to handle a move to right if needed. His swing gets long, creating holes, especially up and in. Improving his pitch recognition would help Gutierrez make better contact. Like many young hitters, he's vulnerable to good breaking stuff and needs to learn to take pitches the other way. Gutierrez has developed into a dynamic five-tool prospect and there's still room for projection. A future heart-of-the-order masher, he was the talk of the Venezuelan League, which should further accelerate his timetable. He'll open 2004 in Double-A.

Year	Club (League)	Class	AVG	G	AB	R	H	2B	3B	HR	RBI	BB	SO	SB	SLG	OBP
2001	Dodgers (GCL)	R	.269	56	234	38	63	16	0	4	30	16	39	9	.389	.324
2002	South Georgia (SAL)	A	.283	92	361	61	102	18	4	12	45	31	88	13	.454	.344
	Las Vegas (PCL)	AAA	.300	2	10	2	3	2	0	0	2	1	4	0	.500	.364
2003	Vero Beach (FSL)	A	.282	110	425	65	120	28	5	20	68	39	111	17	.513	.345
	Jacksonville (SL)	AA	.313	18	67	12	21	3	2	4	12	7	20	3	.597	.387
MINOR LEAGUE TOTALS			.282	278	1097	178	309	67	11	40	157	94	262	42	.472	.343

4 James Loney, 1b

Born: May 7, 1984. **Ht.:** 6-3. **Wt.:** 200. **Bats:** L. **Throws:** L. **School:** Elkins HS, Missouri City, Texas. **Career Transactions:** Selected by Dodgers in first round (19th overall) of 2002 draft; signed June 11, 2002.

Loney led Elkins High to a national championship in 2002 as a two-way star. The Dodgers went against the consensus in drafting him as a first baseman, not a lefthander. He reached high Class A in his debut season before a pitch broke his left wrist. He struggled early in 2003 before regaining strength in his wrist. A disciplined hitter with good pitch recognition and a classic lefthanded stroke that recalls Mark Grace, Loney sprays line drives to all fields and has power to the alleys. He's still growing and projects to hit 30 homers annually. Defensively, he works well around the bag and his arm is as good as it gets at first base. His instincts and makeup are off the charts. Since his hand injury, Loney tends to pull off pitches and collapse his back side on occasion. This also might be a result of trying to hit for more power, instead of letting it come naturally. He has below-average speed but is a smart baserunner. The Dodgers have been aggressive with Loney. He might be best off with a season each in Double-A and Triple-A before he breaks into the majors.

Year	Club (League)	Class	AVG	G	AB	R	H	2B	3B	HR	RBI	BB	SO	SB	SLG	OBP
2002	Great Falls (Pio)	R	.371	47	170	33	63	22	3	5	30	25	18	5	.624	.457
	Vero Beach (FSL)	A	.299	17	67	6	20	6	0	0	5	6	10	0	.388	.356
2003	Vero Beach (FSL)	A	.276	125	468	64	129	31	3	7	46	43	80	9	.400	.337
MINOR LEAGUE TOTALS			.301	189	705	103	212	59	6	12	81	74	108	14	.452	.369

5 Joel Hanrahan, rhp

Born: Oct. 6, 1981. **Ht.:** 6-3. **Wt.:** 215. **Bats:** R. **Throws:** R. **School:** Norwalk (Iowa) Community HS. **Career Transactions:** Selected by Dodgers in second round of 2000 draft; signed June 22, 2000.

Hanrahan threw a pair of no-hitters in high Class A in 2002, then won the Double-A Southern League ERA title last year. Strong and physical, Hanrahan has established himself as a workhorse with the power repertoire to match. He throws a heavy 90-94 mph sinker and touches 95 at times. He tries to get ahead in the count with his fastball and put away hitters with a plus mid-80s slider. He works down in the zone and keeps the ball in the park. Hanrahan has an average changeup but must use it more often. He doesn't consistently repeat his release point, and he needs to stay on top of his slider. His walk rate soared at Triple-A Las Vegas when he tired and his mechanics got sloppy. He can lean on his slider too much at times. Ticketed for a return to Triple-A, Hanrahan is on the cusp of a major league promotion. It may not happen in Los Angeles, but he should be a solid middle-of-the-rotation starter for many years.

Year	Club (League)	Class	W	L	ERA	G	GS	CG	SV	IP	H	R	ER	HR	BB	SO	AVG
2000	Great Falls (Pio)	R	3	1	4.75	12	11	0	0	55	49	32	29	4	23	40	.231
2001	Wilmington (SAL)	A	9	11	3.38	27	26	0	0	144	136	71	54	13	55	116	.250
2002	Vero Beach (FSL)	A	10	6	4.20	25	25	2	0	144	129	74	67	11	51	139	.242
	Jacksonville (SL)	AA	1	1	10.64	3	3	0	0	11	15	14	13	2	7	10	.326
2003	Jacksonville (SL)	AA	10	4	2.43	23	23	1	0	133	117	44	36	5	53	130	.239
	Las Vegas (PCL)	AAA	1	2	10.08	5	5	0	0	25	36	28	28	2	20	13	.343
MINOR LEAGUE TOTALS			34	25	3.99	95	93	3	0	512	482	263	227	37	209	448	.250

6 Chad Billingsley, rhp

Born: July 29, 1984. **Ht.:** 6-2. **Wt.:** 215. **Bats:** R. **Throws:** R. **School:** Defiance (Ohio) HS. **Career Transactions:** Selected by Dodgers in first round (24th overall) of 2003 draft; signed June 9, 2003.

A preseason All-American, Billingsley entered last spring as one of the hottest high school prospects in the 2003 draft class. Clubs' wariness of drafting prep righthanders, combined with his slow start in the cold Midwest, contributed to his stock sliding. But the Dodgers watched all of his outings and didn't hesitate signing him for $1.375 million. A power pitcher built along the lines of Jaret Wright or Jeremy Bonderman, Billingsley runs his fastball up to 97 mph, sitting at 90-94 with average riding action. He throws both a late-breaking 86-87 mph slider and a hammer curveball, and he also shows a good feel for a changeup. He commands all four pitches well. Billingsley has advanced mechanics and pounds the strike zone, but he needs to become more consistent in repeating his arm slot. He tends to get under his slider, causing it to flatten out. He also can improve his pitch selection. One of just two high school righties drafted in the first round, Billingsley will move fast for the Dodgers. He'll spend 2004 in Class A.

Year	Club (League)	Class	W	L	ERA	G	GS	CG	SV	IP	H	R	ER	HR	BB	SO	AVG
2003	Ogden (Pio)	R	5	4	2.83	11	11	0	0	54	49	24	17	0	15	62	.243
MINOR LEAGUE TOTALS			5	4	2.83	11	11	0	0	54	49	24	17	0	15	62	.243

7 Xavier Paul, of

Born: Feb. 25, 1985. **Ht.:** 6-0. **Wt.:** 200. **Bats:** L. **Throws:** R. **School:** Slidell (La.) HS. **Career Transactions:** Selected by Dodgers in fourth round of 2003 draft; signed June 11, 2003.

Paul first attracted the attention of scouts as a high school sophomore. Most teams overlooked him in the 2003 draft because of his size and commitment to Tulane, but he shined for the Dodgers in a predraft workout in New Orleans. Area scout Clarence Johns did his homework on Paul's signability and Los Angeles got him for $270,000. Paul has a strong, compact body with a short swing and surprising raw power. He shows the discipline and plate awareness to hit at the top of the lineup. He already puts together the best combination of power and natural hitting ability in the organization. He hits the ball where it's pitched and uses the whole field. Paul is a plus runner once he gets going and has a plus-plus arm in the outfield. He touched 94 mph as a prep pitcher. Paul needs to stay focused and improve his routes in the outfield. He'll increase his value if he can handle a move to center field in 2004. Never afraid to challenge their prospects, the Dodgers could jump Paul to high Class A this year. He's not a premium basestealing threat, but he profiles as a potent top-of-the-order hitter.

Year	Club (League)	Class	AVG	G	AB	R	H	2B	3B	HR	RBI	BB	SO	SB	SLG	OBP
2003	Ogden (Pio)	R	.307	69	264	60	81	15	6	7	47	34	58	11	.489	.384
MINOR LEAGUE TOTALS			.307	69	264	60	81	15	6	7	47	34	58	11	.489	.384

8 Andy LaRoche, 2b/ss

Born: Sept. 13, 1983. **Ht.:** 5-11. **Wt.:** 185. **Bats:** R. **Throws:** R. **School:** Grayson County (Texas) CC. **Career Transactions:** Selected by Dodgers in 39th round of 2003 draft; signed Aug. 14, 2003.

The son of former all-star Dave LaRoche and brother of Braves prospect Adam, Andy was considered unsignable and headed for Rice when the Dodgers took a flier on him last June. When he tore up the Cape Cod League and projected as a 2004 first-rounder, the Dodgers went against MLB's recommendations and signed him for $1 million. An aggressive hitter, LaRoche caught scouts off guard by displaying well-above-average raw power in the Cape. It was evident again in instructional league, where he launched several tape-measure shots. His arm strength is the best in the organization, and he has a natural feel for the game. The question about LaRoche is where he will play. He may lack the quickness to stay at shortstop, but he isn't a defensive liability and his versatility gives the Dodgers options, including catcher. He can get pull-happy, making him susceptible to off-speed pitches. LaRoche broke his leg early in the Cape season and wasn't cleared to play shortstop until the fall. The Dodgers expect him to be fully recovered this spring, when they'll move him to second base and promote him to high Class A.

Year	Club (League)	Class	AVG	G	AB	R	H	2B	3B	HR	RBI	BB	SO	SB	SLG	OBP
2003	Ogden (Pio)	R	.211	6	19	1	4	1	0	0	5	1	4	0	.263	.238
MINOR LEAGUE TOTALS			.211	6	19	1	4	1	0	0	5	1	4	0	.263	.238

9 Koyie Hill, c

Born: March 9, 1979. **Ht.:** 6-0. **Wt.:** 190. **Bats:** B. **Throws:** R. **School:** Wichita State University. **Career Transactions:** Selected by Dodgers in fourth round of 2000 draft; signed June 22, 2000.

Hill was disappointed to start 2003 back in Double-A for a second straight season, but David Ross blocked him in Triple-A. Hill turned his year around after a promotion to Las Vegas in May. A line-drive hitter with a level swing from both sides of the plate, Hill makes consistent contact and sprays the ball to all fields, showing enough power to carry the alleys. A patient hitter, Hill rarely chases bad pitches. A third baseman in college, Hill converted to catcher after signing. He has good hands, athleticism and arm strength but must improve his receiving mechanics, release and throwing accuracy. He nabbed just 27 percent of basestealers in 2003. His walk rate plummeted last year, though his strikeout rate did as well. He's a well below-average runner. If the Dodgers can trade Paul Lo Duca, Hill will share the big league catching job with Ross. Though he has work to do behind the plate, Hill already is better defensively than Lo Duca and won't be a significant dropoff offensively.

Year	Club (League)	Class	AVG	G	AB	R	H	2B	3B	HR	RBI	BB	SO	SB	SLG	OBP
2000	Yakima (NWL)	A	.259	64	251	26	65	13	1	2	29	25	47	0	.343	.324
2001	Wilmington (SAL)	A	.301	134	498	65	150	20	2	8	79	49	82	21	.398	.368
2002	Jacksonville (SL)	AA	.271	130	468	67	127	25	1	11	64	76	88	5	.400	.368
2003	Jacksonville (SL)	AA	.228	25	101	9	23	7	0	0	7	6	19	2	.297	.271
	Las Vegas (PCL)	AAA	.314	85	312	48	98	18	0	3	36	15	39	5	.401	.345
	Los Angeles (NL)	MAJ	.333	3	3	0	1	0	0	0	0	0	2	0	.667	.333
MAJOR LEAGUE TOTALS			.333	3	3	0	1	1	0	0	0	0	2	0	.667	.333
MINOR LEAGUE TOTALS			.284	438	1630	215	463	83	4	24	215	171	275	33	.384	.352

10 Reggie Abercrombie, of

Born: July 15, 1980. **Ht.:** 6-3. **Wt.:** 210. **Bats:** R. **Throws:** R. **School:** Lake City (Fla.) CC. **Career Transactions:** Selected by Dodgers in 23rd round of 1999 draft; signed May 24, 2000.

Abercrombie entertained college football scholarships before his parents persuaded him to focus on baseball. He has added more than 40 pounds of muscle since signing and draws comparisons to premium athletes such as Eric Davis, Torii Hunter and Preston Wilson. Many scouts say Abercrombie is the best physical specimen in baseball. His speed, center-field range and arm strength all earn 70 on the 20-80 scouting scale. He has tremendous bat speed and the strength to drive pitches out of any park to all fields. Abercrombie's plate discipline has been downright awful. He appeared to make progress after getting contact lenses in May 2002, but his strikeout-walk ratio worsened in 2003. Though he works hard on pitch-recognition drills, he continues to struggle in that area. He's overaggressive, gets off balance and chases too many pitches in the dirt and out of the zone. Abercrombie tore the ACL in his right knee chasing a fly ball in the Arizona Fall League and could be out until May. The Dodgers still protected him on their 40-man roster. Once he returns to Double-A, it will be time for him to start making adjustments.

Year	Club (League)	Class	AVG	G	AB	R	H	2B	3B	HR	RBI	BB	SO	SB	SLG	OBP
2000	Great Falls (Pio)	R	.273	54	220	40	60	7	1	2	29	22	66	32	.341	.360
2001	Wilmington (SAL)	A	.226	125	486	63	110	17	3	10	41	19	154	44	.335	.272
2002	Vero Beach (FSL)	A	.276	132	526	80	145	23	13	10	56	27	158	41	.426	.321
	Jacksonville (SL)	AA	.250	1	4	1	1	0	0	0	0	0	1	1	.250	.250
2003	Jacksonville (SL)	AA	.261	116	448	59	117	25	7	15	54	16	164	28	.449	.298
MINOR LEAGUE TOTALS			.257	428	1684	243	433	72	24	37	180	84	543	146	.394	.306

11 Joel Guzman, ss

Born: Nov. 24, 1984. **Ht.:** 6-4. **Wt.:** 198. **Bats:** R. **Throws:** R. **Career Transactions:** Signed out of Dominican Republic by Dodgers, July 2, 2001.

When Guzman signed for a Dominican-record $2.25 million bonus in 2001, he was showered with hyperbole, and not just from the Dodgers. But he hasn't made the immediate impact a typical can't-miss prospect would in the lower levels of the minors. Guzman received a promotion to high Class A last year not on merit but solely because of a conflict between him and South Georgia manager Dann Billardello. Los Angeles hoped the change of environment would help motivate him. It's easy to forget he won't turn 20 until after the 2004 season, but he needs to mature. Guzman offers an intriguing package of plus raw tools, including well above-average raw power and plus arm strength. After working with Dominican instructor Antonio Bautista and roving hitting instructor Bob Mariano, he has shown significant progress staying back against breaking balls, though they still give him trouble. He's a free swinger who swings and misses too frequently to take advantage of his immense power potential. Guzman is quickly outgrowing shortstop, and it's only a matter of time before he shifts to third base or even first base. The Dodgers should slow his development down and let him experience an extended period of success this year in Class A.

Year	Club (League)	Class	AVG	G	AB	R	H	2B	3B	HR	RBI	BB	SO	SB	SLG	OBP
2002	Dodgers (GCL)	R	.212	10	33	4	7	2	0	0	2	5	8	1	.273	.316
	Great Falls (Pio)	R	.252	43	151	19	38	8	2	3	27	18	54	5	.391	.331
2003	South Georgia (SAL)	A	.235	58	217	33	51	13	0	8	29	9	62	4	.406	.263
	Vero Beach (FSL)	A	.246	62	240	30	59	13	1	5	24	11	60	0	.371	.279
MINOR LEAGUE TOTALS			.242	173	641	86	155	36	3	16	82	43	184	10	.382	.289

12 Steve Colyer, lhp

Born: Feb. 22, 1979. **Ht.:** 6-4. **Wt.:** 205. **Bats:** L. **Throws:** L. **School:** Meramec (Mo.) JC. **Career Transactions:** Selected by Dodgers in second round of 1997 draft; signed May 23, 1998.

The Dodgers had two of the worst consecutive drafts ever in 1997-98, and Colyer is all they have to show for a '97 effort that started with first-rounder Glenn Davis and unsigned second-rounder Chase Utley. Colyer spent four years in Class A as a starter, showing little hope of harnessing his overpowering arsenal until he moved to the bullpen in 2002. His aggressive delivery and linebacker-like approach are best suited for a late-inning role. He generates explosive life on his fastball, which is one of the best in the organization at 93-98 mph. His hard slider gives him a second weapon with which to attack hitters, but command is still an issue. Colyer was impressive in big league camp last year, fanning 13 in 10 innings before Tom Martin beat him out for the lefty set-up job. Colyer rode the Las Vegas-Los Angeles shuttle five times last year, and was inexplicably left to sit in the Dodgers bullpen for two weeks in July without making an appearance before he was sent back to Triple-A. Colyer should join Martin in the big league bullpen this year, and he could close out games in the future if he figures out the importance of throwing strikes.

Year	Club (League)	Class	W	L	ERA	G	GS	CG	SV	IP	H	R	ER	HR	BB	SO	AVG
1998	Yakima (NWL)	A	2	2	4.96	15	12	0	0	65	72	46	36	2	36	75	.277
1999	San Bernardino (Cal)	A	7	9	4.70	27	25	1	0	146	145	82	76	12	86	131	.269
2000	Vero Beach (FSL)	A	5	7	5.76	26	18	1	0	95	97	74	61	9	68	80	.272
2001	Vero Beach (FSL)	A	4	8	3.96	24	24	0	0	120	101	62	53	16	77	118	.234
2002	Jacksonville (SL)	AA	5	4	3.45	59	0	0	21	63	50	29	24	6	40	68	.214
2003	Los Angeles (NL)	MAJ	0	0	2.75	13	0	0	0	20	22	6	6	0	9	16	.297
	Las Vegas (PCL)	AAA	2	3	3.21	44	0	0	23	48	44	18	17	1	22	50	.243
MAJOR LEAGUE TOTALS			0	0	2.75	13	0	0	0	20	22	6	6	0	9	16	.297
MINOR LEAGUE TOTALS			25	33	4.47	195	79	2	44	537	509	311	267	46	329	522	.254

13 Willy Aybar, 3b

Born: March 9, 1983. **Ht.:** 6-0. **Wt.:** 175. **Bats:** B. **Throws:** R. **Career Transactions:** Signed out of Dominican Republic by Dodgers, Jan. 31, 2000.

Aybar, who signed for a then-Dominican-record $1.4 million in January 2000 (since eclipsed by Joel Guzman's $2.25 million deal), bounced back from a disappointing 2002 season. He never got untracked that year after visa problems caused him to miss spring training and arrive at high Class A a month into the season. His younger brother Erick is a hot shortstop prospect on the way up in the Angels organization. At the plate, Aybar hits line drives from both sides of the plate, showing more bat speed from the right side and a smooth, easy stroke from the left. He hit .298 batting lefthanded versus .224 righthanded in 2003. He keeps his hands back and hitting offspeed stuff well. He's patient but scouts don't believe that necessarily equates into good plate discipline or pitch recognition. Defensively, Aybar is one of the best defensive infielders in the system, capable of making plays on the run and throwing strikes to first with his plus arm strength. He still needs to mature and improve his overall approach. If his power doesn't come, some in the organization think Aybar could slide over to second base. Aybar is one prospect the Dodgers need to promote cautiously. After two years in high Class A, he's ready for Double-A.

Year	Club (League)	Class	AVG	G	AB	R	H	2B	3B	HR	RBI	BB	SO	SB	SLG	OBP
2000	Great Falls (Pio)	R	.263	70	266	39	70	15	1	4	49	36	45	5	.372	.349
2001	Wilmington (SAL)	A	.237	120	431	45	102	25	2	4	48	43	64	7	.332	.307
	Vero Beach (FSL)	A	.286	2	7	0	2	0	0	0	1	2	0	.286	.375
2002	Vero Beach (FSL)	A	.215	108	372	56	80	18	2	11	65	69	54	15	.363	.339
2003	Vero Beach (FSL)	A	.274	119	445	47	122	29	3	11	74	41	70	9	.427	.336
MINOR LEAGUE TOTALS			.247	419	1521	187	376	87	8	30	236	190	235	36	.374	.331

14 Jonathan Broxton, rhp

Born: June 16, 1984. **Ht.:** 6-4. **Wt.:** 240. **Bats:** R. **Throws:** R. **School:** Burke County HS, Waynesboro, Ga. **Career Transactions:** Selected by Dodgers in second round of 2002 draft; signed June 30, 2002.

After an impressive spring, Broxton was hampered by wrist tendinitis and later a biceps strain throughout most of the regular season. None of that prevented him from blowing 97-mph heat in instructional league, as he had done in spring training. Known as "The Bull," Broxton creates outstanding leverage to the plate with his 6-foot-4 frame and high three-quarters arm slot. His fastball dipped to 86-87 when he was nagged by the biceps injury, but it rarely dips below 90 and sits around 94 with heavy sink when he's healthy. He demonstrates excellent command of his 85-86 mph slider, which breaks sharply off the table. After learning a changeup from minor league pitching instructor Mark Brewer in 2002, Broxton continued to show a feel for the pitch after working on it with South Georgia pitching coach Roger McDowell last year. Broxton has a high-maintenance body that requires extra attention. His weight soared as high as 277 during the season. The Dodgers envision him as a workhorse and don't expect the injuries he battled last season to linger and affect his development. He'll continue to build innings as a starter in high Class A, though some scouts project him eventually moving to the bullpen. Broxton does have three potential plus pitches, which is more than enough to keep him in the rotation.

Year	Club (League)	Class	W	L	ERA	G	GS	CG	SV	IP	H	R	ER	HR	BB	SO	AVG
2002	Great Falls (Pio)	R	2	0	2.76	11	6	0	2	29	22	9	9	0	16	33	.212
2003	South Georgia (SAL)	A	4	2	3.13	9	8	0	0	37	27	15	13	1	22	30	.208
MINOR LEAGUE TOTALS			6	2	2.97	20	14	0	2	67	49	24	22	1	38	63	.209

15 Chuck Tiffany, lhp

Born: Jan. 25, 1985. **Ht.:** 6-1. **Wt.:** 195. **Bats:** L. **Throws:** L. **School:** Charter Oak HS, Covina, Calif. **Career Transactions:** Selected by Dodgers in second round of 2003 draft; signed Aug. 6, 2003.

Tiffany tied Dodgers 2003 first-rounder Chad Billingsley and Twins 16th-rounder Michael Rogers for the U.S. junior national team lead with four wins in the summer of 2002. That wasn't his biggest amateur achievement. He was MVP of the PONY League World Series as a 14-year-old. Los Angeles exceeded the commissioner's office's bonus recommendation by buying Tiffany out of his Cal State Fullerton commitment with a $1.2 million bonus. His pro debut was delayed until late August because of the negotiations, and then he was limited by a hamstring injury, which also hampered him during high school. Often compared to Mike Stanton because of his strong, stocky build, Tiffany can run his fastball up to 94 mph. He regularly sits in the 90-92 mph range with his two- and four-seamers. His circle change-up is major league-quality already, featuring late sink and fade away from righthanders. His arm works free and easy, helping his fastball ride up in the zone. His curveball projects as average, but he's still inconsistent because he doesn't always stay on top of his pitches. Tiffany needs to work on his flexibility to avoid further hamstring issues, and he'll have to keep close tabs on his weight because of his stocky frame. The Dodgers would like to get Tiffany acclimated with full-season ball by starting him in low Class A.

Year	Club (League)	Class	W	L	ERA	G	GS	CG	SV	IP	H	R	ER	HR	BB	SO	AVG
2003	Ogden (Pio)	R	0	0	10.13	3	0	0	0	3	4	4	3	0	2	4	.364
MINOR LEAGUE TOTALS			0	0	10.13	3	0	0	0	3	4	4	3	0	2	4	.364

16 Chin-Feng Chen, of/1b

Born: Oct. 28, 1977. **Ht.:** 6-1. **Wt.:** 189. **Bats:** R. **Throws:** R. **Career Transactions:** Signed out of Taiwan by Dodgers, Jan. 4, 1999.

Chen became the first Taiwanese player to reach the majors in 2002, and he hit .579 with three homers in 19 at-bats in big league camp. That still wasn't enough to crack the Dodgers outfield, so he spent his second consecutive season in Triple-A. After becoming the first player in high Class A California League history to join the 30-30 club in his 1999 pro debut, Chen looked like a multitooled phenom on the fast track to Chavez Ravine. Four years later, his below-average tools are preventing him from advancing and the Dodgers are counting on his lone plus attribute (power) to carry him to the majors. A dead-red fastball hitter, Chen is capable of producing 30 homers annually in the majors. He generates power to all fields with quick, strong wrists and above-average bat speed. He swings and misses too often, though. In the outfield, his arm is a liability and he doesn't read balls off the bat well enough to compensate for his lack of range. The Dodgers tried to make him a full-time first baseman in 2002, but his footwork was terrible. A key cog in Taiwan's lineup, Chen led the World Cup in home runs in 2001 and his 6-for-12 performance in the Asian Games last fall helped his country earn a berth in the 2004 Olympics. They'll have to play without him if he's in the big leagues in August.

Year	Club (League)	Class	AVG	G	AB	R	H	2B	3B	HR	RBI	BB	SO	SB	SLG	OBP
1999	San Bernardino (Cal)	A	.316	131	510	98	161	22	10	31	123	75	129	31	.580	.404
2000	San Antonio (TL)	AA	.277	133	516	66	143	27	3	6	67	61	131	23	.376	.355
2001	Vero Beach (FSL)	A	.268	62	235	38	63	15	3	5	41	28	56	2	.421	.359
	Jacksonville (SL)	AA	.313	66	224	47	70	16	2	17	50	41	65	5	.629	.422
2002	Las Vegas (PCL)	AAA	.284	137	511	90	145	26	4	26	84	58	160	1	.503	.352
	Los Angeles (NL)	MAJ	.000	3	5	1	0	0	0	0	0	1	3	0	.000	.167
2003	Las Vegas (PCL)	AAA	.281	133	474	84	133	30	5	26	86	59	106	6	.530	.360
	Los Angeles (NL)	MAJ	.000	1	1	0	0	0	0	0	0	0	0	0	.000	.000
MAJOR LEAGUE TOTALS			.000	4	6	1	0	0	0	0	0	1	3	0	.000	.143
MINOR LEAGUE TOTALS			.289	662	2470	423	715	136	27	111	451	322	647	68	.501	.372

17 Jonathan Figueroa, lhp

Born: Sept. 15, 1983. **Ht.:** 6-5. **Wt.:** 205. **Bats:** L. **Throws:** L. **Career Transactions:** Signed out of Venezuela by Dodgers, Jan. 22, 2002.

The Dodgers signed Figueroa for $500,000 following an outstanding performance on the Perfect Game showcase circuit in the spring of 2002. He was so dominant in his pro debut that some Los Angeles officials believed he could have handled a jump to the major league bullpen. But Figueroa came down with shoulder tendinitis in instructional league following the 2002 season. As a result, his mechanics got out of whack and his velocity and command suffered. It didn't help when Figueroa showed up out of shape last spring. He lost his fluid arm action trying to compensate for his shoulder soreness, and only after extensive work with South Georgia pitching coach Roger McDowell did Figueroa begin to show flashes of past form. His fastball didn't approach the 93-94 mph range he's capable of, but rather sat at 86-88 and topped out at 91. His breaking ball is a plus pitch and a devastating sight for lefthanders, coming out of Figueroa's low three-quarters slot. He's still developing a change-up. Rated the No. 2 prospect in the system a year ago, Figueroa has seen his stock drop. While he has a chance to bounce back, most scouts are projecting him as a reliever now. If he looks like his old self in spring training, Figueroa could open 2004 in high Class A.

Year	Club (League)	Class	W	L	ERA	G	GS	CG	SV	IP	H	R	ER	HR	BB	SO	AVG
2002	Great Falls (Pio)	R	2	1	1.42	7	7	0	0	32	16	7	5	0	19	48	.147
	South Georgia (SAL)	A	5	2	1.42	8	8	0	0	44	22	10	7	1	20	57	.148
2003	South Georgia (SAL)	A	1	8	4.94	17	17	0	0	78	79	60	43	4	42	74	.264
MINOR LEAGUE TOTALS			8	11	3.21	32	32	0	0	154	117	77	55	5	81	179	.210

18 Russell Martin, c

Born: Feb. 15, 1983. **Ht.:** 5-11. **Wt.:** 202. **Bats:** R. **Throws:** R. **School:** Chipola (Fla.) JC. **Career Transactions:** Selected by Dodgers in 17th round of 2002 draft; signed June 13, 2002.

Martin led the Canadian junior national team with a .414 average and two home runs in 29 at-bats at the 2000 World Junior Championship. Drafted as a third baseman, that's where he spent his first summer in pro ball, but the Dodgers shifted him behind the plate in instructional league 2002 at the suggestion of area scout Clarence Johns. Martin's athleticism, soft hands and well above-average arm strength originally prompted his conversion. Under the tutelage of minor league catching instructor Jon Debus, Martin has made tremendous strides receiving and blocking balls. He still lacks polish, as indicated by his 27 passed balls and 23 percent success rate throwing out basestealers in the Rookie-level Pioneer League. The Dodgers love the Canadian's hockey mentality and believe it has helped him with the transition. At the plate, Martin has a fluid line-drive stroke with raw power potential. He needs to stay behind the ball more consistently, though, as he tends to get overly pull-conscious. He has done an excellent job thus far of controlling the strike zone. The Dodgers plan on keeping Martin and fellow catching conversion prospect Mike Nixon at separate levels. They'll compete for a chance to move up to high Class A in 2004.

Year	Club (League)	Class	AVG	G	AB	R	H	2B	3B	HR	RBI	BB	SO	SB	SLG	OBP
2002	Dodgers (GCL)	R	.286	41	126	22	36	3	3	0	10	23	18	7	.357	.412
2003	South Georgia (SAL)	A	.286	25	98	15	28	4	1	3	14	9	11	5	.439	.343
	Ogden (Pio)	R	.271	52	188	25	51	13	0	6	36	26	26	3	.436	.368
MINOR LEAGUE TOTALS			.279	118	412	62	115	20	4	9	60	58	55	15	.413	.376

19 Mike Megrew, lhp

Born: Jan. 29, 1984. **Ht.:** 6-6. **Wt.:** 210. **Bats:** L. **Throws:** L. **School:** Chariho Regional HS, Hope Valley, R.I. **Career Transactions:** Selected by Dodgers in fifth round of 2002 draft; signed June 5, 2002.

Dodgers scouting director Logan White calls Megrew a poster boy for projectable lefties. As with Greg Miller, Megrew's velocity steadily has increased since high school. Area scout Jon Kosciak did a tremendous job evaluating Megrew when he clocked him in the mid-80s as a senior. While Megrew hasn't reached Miller's mid-90s levels yet, he's topping out at 92 mph. At a lanky 6-foot-6 and 210 pounds, Megrew isn't done growing and the Dodgers project him to sit at 90-93 before long. He'll flash a plus curveball at times and changes speeds masterfully. He demonstrates excellent feel for throwing a power changeup, which is occasionally a plus-plus pitch and helps play his fastball up. The Dodgers were conservative with Megrew last year, but after finishing second in the Pioneer League in strikeouts, he won't be held back this season. He'll start 2004 in South Georgia.

Year	Club (League)	Class	W	L	ERA	G	GS	CG	SV	IP	H	R	ER	HR	BB	SO	AVG
2002	Dodgers (GCL)	R	1	1	2.03	5	4	0	0	13	8	4	3	0	3	12	.178
2003	Ogden (Pio)	R	5	3	3.40	14	14	0	0	77	64	40	29	6	24	99	.222
MINOR LEAGUE TOTALS			6	4	3.20	19	18	0	0	90	72	44	32	6	27	111	.216

20 Andrew Brown, rhp

Born: Feb. 17, 1981. **Ht.:** 6-6. **Wt.:** 230. **Bats:** R. **Throws:** R. **School:** Trinity Christian Academy, Jacksonville. **Career Transactions:** Selected by Braves in sixth round of 1999 draft; signed June 3, 1999 . . . On disabled list, June 19-Sept. 6, 2000 . . . Traded by Braves with OF Brian Jordan and LHP Odalis Perez to Dodgers for OF Gary Sheffield, Jan. 15, 2002.

Injuries to top pitching prospects Jonathan Figueroa (shoulder), Brown and Alfredo Gonzalez (shoulder) were among the few Dodgers disappointments in the minor leagues in 2003. Brown, an afterthought in the Gary Sheffield trade with the Braves before the 2002 season, looked ready to assert himself as one of the brightest pitching prospects in the minors. Three years removed from Tommy John surgery in 2000, he opened eyes in big league camp last spring. He was throwing an effortless 93-96 mph fastball, along with a pair of plus breaking balls and an average changeup. Then Brown was pulled from his only regular-season start after one inning because of a twinge in his elbow. He had surgery to remove bone chips in June and didn't resurface until instructional league. Even then, he threw only 45-50 pitch bullpen sessions. His delivery is clean and his arm works well, though his command has been inconsistent in the past. First and foremost, Brown must prove his durability. He could put himself in the Dodgers' big league plans after starting back in Double-A.

Year	Club (League)	Class	W	L	ERA	G	GS	CG	SV	IP	H	R	ER	HR	BB	SO	AVG
1999	Braves (GCL)	R	1	1	2.34	11	11	0	0	42	40	15	11	4	16	57	.247
2000	Did not play–Injured																
2001	Jamestown (NY-P)	A	3	4	3.92	14	12	0	0	64	50	29	28	5	31	59	.215
2002	Vero Beach (FSL)	A	10	10	4.11	25	24	1	0	127	97	63	58	13	62	129	.215
2003	Jacksonville (SL)	AA	0	0	0.00	1	1	0	0	1	0	0	0	0	0	1	.000
MINOR LEAGUE TOTALS			14	15	3.72	51	48	1	0	235	187	107	97	22	109	246	.220

21 Delwyn Young, 2b

Born: June 30, 1982. **Ht.:** 5-10. **Wt.:** 180. **Bats:** B. **Throws:** R. **School:** Santa Barbara (Calif.) CC. **Career Transactions:** Selected by Dodgers in fourth round of 2002 draft; signed June 12, 2002.

The Braves failed to sign Young as a 29th-round draft-and-follow before the 2002 draft, and his stock soared after an impressive predraft workout at Dodger Stadium with GM Dan Evans looking on. He has had no problem making the transition to wood bats, leading the South Atlantic League in extra-base hits (60) and slugging percentage last season. He worked hard to shorten his swing and became more compact and direct to the ball in 2003. Young might have the best bat speed in the organization. He's an aggressive hitter who shows the ability to crush the ball to all fields from both sides of the plate. Strong and stocky at 5-foot-10, Young lacks quickness at second base and might eventually have to move to third base or left field. He has an above-average arm, but the Dodgers would like to see him take his defense more seriously. Young's advanced hitting approach could help him skip high Class A and start 2004 in Double-A. His presence enabled the Dodgers to include second-base prospect Victor Diaz in a midseason trade for Jeromy Burnitz.

Year	Club (League)	Class	AVG	G	AB	R	H	2B	3B	HR	RBI	BB	SO	SB	SLG	OBP
2002	Great Falls (Pio)	R	.300	59	240	42	72	18	1	10	41	27	60	4	.508	.380
2003	South Georgia (SAL)	A	.323	119	443	67	143	38	7	15	73	36	87	5	.542	.381
MINOR LEAGUE TOTALS			.315	178	683	109	215	56	8	25	114	63	147	9	.530	.381

22 Ching-Lung Hu, ss

Born: Feb. 2, 1984. **Ht.:** 5-9. **Wt.:** 150. **Bats:** R. **Throws:** R. **Career Transactions:** Signed out of Taiwan by Dodgers, Jan. 31, 2003.

The Dodgers have a long history of success in the Far East and continue to be one of the more active major league clubs in that region. They're still waiting on returns from their Taiwanese investments in Chin-Feng Chen and oft-injured Hong-Chih Kuo, and Hu is their latest signee. He signed after special assistant to the GM Jeff Schugel scouted the 2002 World Junior Championship, where Hu hit .474 with four home runs in 38 at-bats as Taiwan's leadoff man. The Dodgers' 2003 draft brought an influx of potential middle infielders, but none of them can match Hu's athleticism and natural shortstop actions. He already has garnered comparisons to Rey Ordonez for his acrobatic defensive plays and strong arm. Despite his small stature, Hu doesn't get the bat knocked out of his hands. He's deceptively strong, capable of driving the ball with his line-drive swing and plus bat speed. He's also an above-average runner. Hu is fairly selective at the plate but needs to learn how to better cover the plate, use the whole field and draw more walks. He'll hit near the top of the lineup in low Class A this year.

Year	Club (League)	Class	AVG	G	AB	R	H	2B	3B	HR	RBI	BB	SO	SB	SLG	OBP
2003	Ogden (Pio)	R	.305	53	220	34	67	9	5	3	23	14	33	5	.432	.343
MINOR LEAGUE TOTALS			.305	53	220	34	67	9	5	3	23	14	33	5	.432	.343

23 Yhency Brazoban, rhp

Born: June 11, 1980. **Ht.:** 6-1. **Wt.:** 170. **Bats:** R. **Throws:** R. **Career Transactions:** Signed out of Dominican Republic by Yankees, July 10, 1997 . . . Traded by Yankees with RHP Jeff Weaver and RHP Brandon Weeden to Dodgers for RHP Kevin Brown, Dec. 13, 2003.

The Yankees were down on Brazoban when they sent him along with righthanders Jeff Weaver, Brandon Weeden and $2.6 million to the Dodgers for Kevin Brown. But some clubs viewed the fireballing Brazoban as one of New York's brightest prospects. His off-the-field behavior and lazy work ethic have been issues since before he converted from outfielder to reliever in mid-2002. A toolsy outfielder, he never showed the ability to make adjustments at the plate and was easy prey for pitchers in the lower levels. But his arm graded out as an 80 on the 20-80 scouting scale, prompting former Yankees farm director Rob Thomson to suggest a position change. After moving to the mound, Brazoban consistently has dialed up 92-97 mph heat, topping out at 99 on occasion. He also throws a good power slider for strikes. He's still raw and more of a thrower than pitcher at this point, but the Dodgers hope he can emerge along the lines of another former position player, Guillermo Mota. Brazoban needs to mature and improve his mound demeanor before achieving those type of expectations. He's easily rattled when things don't go his way on the mound. He's likely to kick his Dodgers career off in Double-A.

Year	Club (League)	Class	AVG	G	AB	R	H	2B	3B	HR	RBI	BB	SO	SB	SLG	OBP
1998	Yankees (DSL)	R	.319	68	251	51	80	19	2	9	46	31	75	10	.518	.399
1999	Yankees (GCL)	R	.320	56	200	33	64	14	5	1	26	12	47	7	.455	.367
2000	Greensboro (SAL)	A	.188	12	48	6	9	3	0	0	8	3	15	1	.250	.231
	Yankees (GCL)	R	.303	54	201	36	61	14	4	5	28	11	28	2	.488	.349
2001	Greensboro (SAL)	A	.273	124	469	51	128	23	3	6	52	19	98	6	.373	.311
	Columbus (IL)	AAA	.200	1	5	2	1	1	0	0	0	0	2	0	.400	.200
2002	Greensboro (SAL)	A	.242	69	252	33	61	11	2	3	28	15	74	0	.337	.290
MINOR LEAGUE TOTALS			.283	384	1426	212	404	85	16	24	188	91	339	26	.416	.334

Year	Club (League)	Class	W	L	ERA	G	GS	CG	SV	IP	H	R	ER	HR	BB	SO	AVG
2002	Yankees (GCL)	R	0	0	4.50	6	0	0	0	6	3	3	3	0	4	11	.136
2003	Tampa (FSL)	A	0	2	2.83	24	0	0	15	29	27	13	9	0	12	34	.245
	Trenton (EL)	AA	2	2	7.81	20	0	0	3	28	33	25	24	5	14	19	.314
	Yankees (GCL)	R	0	0	6.00	3	0	0	0	3	5	3	2	0	1	5	.385
MINOR LEAGUE TOTALS			2	4	5.23	53	0	0	18	65	68	44	38	5	31	69	.272

24 Joe Thurston, 2b

Born: Sept. 29, 1979. **Ht.:** 5-11. **Wt.:** 190. **Bats:** L. **Throws:** R. **School:** Sacramento CC. **Career Transactions:** Selected by Dodgers in fourth round of 1999 draft; signed June 6, 1999.

Thurston headed into last spring with little competition for the Dodgers' second-base job opened by the trade of Mark Grudzielanek. But after leading the minors in hits and total bases in 2002, Thurston hit a soft .241 and played lackluster defense in big league camp. The rookie-of-the-year candidate got just 10 big league at-bats all season and wasn't nearly as productive in his second tour of the Pacific Coast League. While there are still some scouts who view him as an everyday second baseman, he might be better suited for a utility role in the Mark McLemore mold. Thurston's makeup is off the charts and his overachieving ways made him an organization favorite long ago. He was Los Angeles' minor league player of the year in 2001 and 2002. The question is whether his tools will measure up in the big leagues. Thurston dives into the plate and didn't drive the ball well last season. He might encounter the same problem against power stuff in the majors. He's aggressive and draws few walks, but he has a knack for putting the bat on the ball. Thurston added some weight before 2003 and it seemed to affect his agility in the field and on the bases. He's an average runner yet was thrown out 12 times in 13 attempts after averaging 21 steals the previous two years. He lacks soft hands but gets the job done defensively. Even after Alex Cora's injury, the Dodgers are more likely to look outside the organization than to hand the position to Thurston.

Year	Club (League)	Class	AVG	G	AB	R	H	2B	3B	HR	RBI	BB	SO	SB	SLG	OBP
1999	Yakima (NWL)	A	.285	71	277	48	79	10	3	0	32	27	34	27	.343	.387
	San Bernardino (Cal)	A	.000	2	3	0	0	0	0	0	0	0	1	0	.000	.250
2000	San Bernardino (Cal)	A	.303	138	551	97	167	31	8	4	70	56	61	43	.410	.380
2001	Jacksonville (SL)	AA	.267	134	544	80	145	25	7	7	46	48	65	20	.377	.338
2002	Las Vegas (PCL)	AAA	.334	136	587	106	196	39	13	12	55	25	60	22	.506	.372
	Los Angeles (NL)	MAJ	.462	8	13	1	6	1	0	0	1	0	1	0	.538	.429
2003	Las Vegas (PCL)	AAA	.290	132	538	77	156	27	6	7	68	31	48	1	.401	.345
	Los Angeles (NL)	MAJ	.200	12	10	2	2	0	0	0	0	1	1	0	.200	.273
MAJOR LEAGUE TOTALS			.348	20	23	3	8	1	0	0	1	1	2	0	.391	.360
MINOR LEAGUE TOTALS			.297	613	2500	408	743	132	37	30	271	187	269	113	.416	.362

25 Orlando Rodriguez, lhp

Born: Nov. 28, 1980. **Ht.:** 5-10. **Wt.:** 155. **Bats:** L. **Throws:** L. **Career Transactions:** Signed out of Dominican Republic by White Sox, Jan. 12, 2000 . . . Traded by White Sox with RHP Gary Majewski and RHP Andre Simpson to Dodgers for RHP Antonio Osuna and LHP Carlos Ortega, March 22, 2001.

The Dodgers boast a deep crop of power lefthanders lefthanders, including Greg Miller, Steve Colyer, Chuck Tiffany, Jonathan Figueroa, Mike Megrew, Rodriguez and Chad Bailey. Though he has battled injuries in each of the last two seasons, Rodriguez was a steal as a throw-in to the Antonio Osuna deal with the White Sox in 2001. Elbow tendinitis sidelined him for half of the 2002 season, but he didn't allow a run in 27 outings in Class A. Another bout with tendinitis in 2003 prevented him from pitching until August. He was impressive enough to earn a spot on the Dodgers' 40-man roster after the season, as his lively 91-93 mph fastball and downer curveball surely would have attracted interest in the major league Rule 5 draft. Rodriguez shows a changeup but mainly leans on his two plus pitches. His arm works well out of his compact delivery, and he generates good sink on his fastball. He must improve his control and, more important, he desperately needs to stay healthy for a full season. If he does, he could jump to the majors in 2004 if Tom Martin or Steve Colyer needs backup.

Year	Club (League)	Class	W	L	ERA	G	GS	CG	SV	IP	H	R	ER	HR	BB	SO	AVG
2000	White Sox (AZL)	R	2	5	4.20	16	5	0	0	41	36	30	19	3	32	53	.234
	White Sox (DSL)	R	1	1	4.20	3	3	0	0	15	11	8	7	3	4	25	.177
2001	Great Falls (Pio)	R	3	3	4.15	15	10	0	1	61	58	41	28	11	26	79	.240
2002	South Georgia (SAL)	A	3	0	0.00	20	0	0	5	28	12	0	0	0	10	42	.135
	Vero Beach (FSL)	A	0	0	0.00	7	0	0	1	7	6	0	0	0	3	10	.240
2003	Jacksonville (SL)	AA	1	2	3.75	11	0	0	0	12	10	5	5	1	7	14	.233
MINOR LEAGUE TOTALS			10	11	3.24	72	18	0	7	164	133	84	59	18	82	223	.216

26 Mike Nixon, c

Born: Aug. 17, 1983. **Ht.:** 6-3. **Wt.:** 210. **Bats:** R. **Throws:** R. **School:** Sunnyslope HS, Phoenix. **Career Transactions:** Selected by Dodgers in third round of 2002 draft; signed June 8, 2002.

It took a $950,000 bonus to sign Nixon away from a football commitment at UCLA, where he was slated to play safety. Notre Dame and Arizona State also recruited him as a quarterback. Named Arizona's 2001 prep football player of the year, he still holds the state 4-A passing record with 8,091 career yards. Nixon also was a menace on defense, recording over 100 tackles as a senior, and he led Sunnyslope High to a state title in basketball. Considering he used to play baseball just three months out of the year, Nixon has made a relatively smooth transition to wood bats and pro pitching. He has established himself as a line-drive hitter with a good idea at the plate. His short, quick stroke and bat control aid him with two strikes. He'll need to make more quality contact to generate more power, and he occasionally cuts himself off at the plate. He also could stand to draw more walks. Nixon has plenty of work to do behind the plate, too. While he shows solid fundamentals in receiving and pitchers like the way he calls a game, Nixon proved to be easy prey for South Atlantic League basestealers in 2003. He threw out just 12 percent and allowed a league-high 163 thefts. His raw arm strength is solid average, but because of inconsistent throwing mechanics his release point varies and his pop times are slow. Not everyone in the organization is convinced he'll make enough improvement defensively, but his bat should be able to carry him as a third baseman or left fielder. The Dodgers love his makeup and work ethic. With Russell Martin's emergence, a promotion to high Class A isn't a lock for Nixon. Given his inexperience, a return to low Class A shouldn't be viewed as a setback.

Year	Club (League)	Class	AVG	G	AB	R	H	2B	3B	HR	RBI	BB	SO	SB	SLG	OBP
2002	Great Falls (Pio)	R	.311	55	219	33	68	10	0	1	31	11	36	7	.370	.355
2003	South Georgia (SAL)	A	.274	102	390	58	107	20	1	1	38	33	76	13	.338	.334
MINOR LEAGUE TOTALS			.287	157	609	91	175	30	1	2	69	44	112	20	.350	.341

27 James McDonald, rhp

Born: Oct. 19, 1984. **Ht.:** 6-5. **Wt.:** 195. **Bats:** L. **Throws:** R. **School:** Golden West (Calif.) JC. **Career Transactions:** Selected by Dodgers in 11th round of 2002 draft; signed May 26, 2003.

McDonald's father James spent four years in the NFL as a tight end for the Rams and Lions, and his cousins Donzell and Darnell McDonald are minor league outfielders. McDonald's Long Beach Poly High lost to Delmon Young and Camarillo High in the California state semifinals in 2002. He caught the attention of Dodgers scouts by ripping a ball of the wall against Young (the No. 1 overall pick in 2003), who was throwing 93-94 mph. After Los Angeles took him in the 11th round, McDonald elected to attend Golden West (Calif.) JC in hopes of improving his draft status. He did just that, signing for $300,000 as a draft-and-follow. The Dodgers initially were split on whether to develop McDonald as a pitcher or outfielder, but the extra year helped convince them his future is on the mound. Compared to Edwin Jackson for his two-way athleticism, McDonald needs polish but already flashes plus velocity on his fastball. It normally sits in the 87-92 mph range, while his curveball has tight bite and depth. His changeup is a work in progress. The Dodgers think he could follow a similar path to Jackson's and will start him on the fast track at one of their Class A affiliates in 2004.

Year	Club (League)	Class	W	L	ERA	G	GS	CG	SV	IP	H	R	ER	HR	BB	SO	AVG
2003	Dodgers (GCL)	R	2	4	3.33	12	9	0	0	49	39	20	18	3	15	47	.220
MINOR LEAGUE TOTALS			2	4	3.33	12	9	0	0	49	39	20	18	3	15	47	.220

28 Juan Rivera, ss

Born: March 17, 1987. **Ht.:** 6-0. **Wt.:** 150. **Bats:** B. **Throws:** R. **Career Transactions:** Signed out of Dominican Republic by Dodgers, July 21, 2003.

Rivera could be the first significant contribution to the system made by Dominican scout Rene Francisco. Francisco, who signed Rafael Furcal, came over from the Braves in 2002. Under Francisco's watch, the Dodgers aren't as likely to spend wildly as they have done in the past on Joel Guzman and Willy Aybar. First identified by Dominican scout Angel Santana, Rivera signed for $100,000. A switch-hitter with a more advanced approach from the left side, Rivera reminds some scouts of former all-star Tony Fernandez. Though Rivera ran a 7.25 60-yard dash when he signed, he has improved and projects as an above-average runner. He has natural shortstop actions, with good footwork and a strong arm. He worked out at the Dodgers' complex in Vero Beach, Fla., after signing and was treated to a tour of Dodger Stadium before returning to the Dominican for the winter. Rivera should make his pro debut in the Gulf Coast League this year.

Year	Club (League)	Class	AVG	G	AB	R	H	2B	3B	HR	RBI	BB	SO	SB	SLG	OBP
2003	Did not play—Signed 2004 contract															

29 Brian Pilkington, rhp

Born: Sept. 17, 1982. **Ht.:** 6-5. **Wt.:** 210. **Bats:** R. **Throws:** R. **School:** Santiago HS, Garden Grove, Calif. **Career Transactions:** Selected by Dodgers in second round of 2001 draft; signed June 14, 2001.

A nephew of 287-game winner Bert Blyleven, Pilkington isn't overpowering but has moved swiftly up the ladder by filling up the strike zone. Pilkington, who had arthroscopic shoulder surgery after the Dodgers took him with their first pick (second round) in 2001, reached Double-A before turning 21. Though his stuff is just average across the board—88-91 mph sinker, solid three-quarters-breaking curveball, fading changeup—he has pinpoint command that can make his offerings a grade better. Pilkington is around the strike zone too frequently, however. The Dodgers are trying to encourage him to try to make hitters chase more pitches out of the zone because his control is good enough that he can work behind in the count. He profiles as a back-of-the-rotation starter with John Burkett upside. Pilkington attracts a lot of attention in trade talks and is slated for a return to Double-A in 2004.

Year	Club (League)	Class	W	L	ERA	G	GS	CG	SV	IP	H	R	ER	HR	BB	SO	AVG
2001	Great Falls (Pio)	R	0	1	5.63	5	2	0	0	16	19	11	10	2	2	17	.297
2002	South Georgia (SAL)	A	8	4	3.45	20	18	1	0	112	129	61	43	8	13	78	.283
	Vero Beach (FSL)	A	2	1	2.37	3	3	0	0	19	16	7	5	2	3	10	.235
2003	Vero Beach (FSL)	A	10	6	3.88	21	21	1	0	125	136	55	54	9	16	74	.276
	Jacksonville (SL)	AA	3	0	3.34	5	5	0	0	32	31	13	12	3	2	24	.250
MINOR LEAGUE TOTALS			23	12	3.66	54	49	2	0	305	331	147	124	24	36	203	.275

30 Zach Hammes, rhp

Born: May 15, 1984. **Ht.:** 6-6. **Wt.:** 225. **Bats:** R. **Throws:** R. **School:** Iowa City (Iowa) HS. **Career Transactions:** Selected by Dodgers in second round of 2002 draft; signed June 21, 2002.

When it comes to drafting pitchers, the Dodgers like tall, projectable lefties a la Greg Miller and big, strong righthanders along the lines of Jonathan Broxton. At 6-foot-6 and 220 pounds, Hammes falls into the latter category. Scouting director Logan White blew out his elbow as a minor league pitchers, and two of his main points of emphasis for pitchers are good mechanics and clean arm action. Hammes has the arm action part down but has spent most of his first two seasons trying to get his delivery ironed out. He has made strides yet still needs to continue improving his flexibility. Hammes has trouble finishing his delivery because he has a short stride and often cuts his pitches off, thus taking some of the natural power away from his stuff. He tops out at 92-93 mph and sits at 88-91 with his fastball. He has a power curveball but is inconsistent, occasionally hanging it. He has a feel for a straight changeup. Once Hammes learns to repeat his delivery, he'll benefit from additional velocity and command and start to move fast. He could return to low Class A to begin 2004.

Year	Club (League)	Class	W	L	ERA	G	GS	CG	SV	IP	H	R	ER	HR	BB	SO	AVG
2002	Dodgers (GCL)	R	2	2	3.27	10	8	0	0	33	26	14	12	0	15	27	.217
2003	South Georgia (SAL)	A	7	11	5.54	25	24	0	0	117	138	91	72	11	65	75	.295
MINOR LEAGUE TOTALS			9	13	5.04	35	32	0	0	150	164	105	84	11	80	102	.279

MILWAUKEE
BREWERS

TOP 30 PROSPECTS

1. Rickie Weeks, 2b
2. Prince Fielder, 1b
3. J.J. Hardy, ss
4. Manny Parra, lhp
5. Brad Nelson, of/1b
6. Mike Jones, rhp
7. Corey Hart, 3b/of
8. Ben Hendrickson, rhp
9. David Krynzel, of
10. Jorge de la Rosa, lhp
11. Lou Palmisano, c
12. Dennis Sarfate, rhp
13. Luis Martinez, lhp
14. Tom Wilhelmsen, rhp
15. Chris Capuano, lhp
16. Dana Eveland, lhp
17. Anthony Gwynn, of
18. Pedro Lirano, rhp
19. Tim Bausher, rhp
20. Jeff Housman, lhp
21. Ben Diggins, rhp
22. Charlie Fermaint, of
23. Gilberto Acosta, ss
24. Jeff Bennett, rhp
25. Steve Moss, of
26. Greg Kloosterman, lhp
27. Mike Adams, rhp
28. Tommy Hawk, rhp
29. Greg Bruso, rhp
30. Jason Belcher, of

By Tom Haudricourt

After taking over a team beaten down by years of losing, general manager Doug Melvin and manager Ned Yost had two simple goals for 2003: Create an atmosphere conducive to winning, and show improvement in terms of wins and losses.

It was mission accomplished on both fronts. The Brewers had their 11th consecutive losing season, but the franchise's leadership said the organization was headed in the right direction after bottoming out in 2002. "We've heard from a lot of scouts, people that have been through here, coaches from other teams," Yost said. "People would warn them that this is not the old Brewers. 'Don't take them lightly.' That was good to hear."

After generating enough enthusiasm for a perennial last-place club to draw 1.7 million people to Miller Park, however, much of that goodwill was lost. The team's board of directors, claiming the franchise was still losing money, called for slashing the payroll to a major league-low $30 million for 2004, which caused a huge public-relations fallout. Team president Ulice Payne, who came in as part of the team's overhaul after the 2002 season, spoke out against the move and then decided to have the remaining four years of his contract bought out. Fans spoke out, and legislators called for an audit of the Brewers' books. After promises that a publicly funded new stadium would allow the Brewers to generate enough money to put together a competitive team, they instead have cut payroll. The trade of Richie Sexson to the Diamondbacks provided a lightning rod for the criticism. Topping off the winter of discontent was the announcement in January that the Selig family plans to sell the franchise.

Brewers fans have reason to be impatient, but in improving from 56 victories in 2002 to 68 in 2003, the Brewers showed a spirit that wasn't evident in previous years. Outfielder Scott Podsednik, a waiver claim, finished second in the National League rookie of the year voting.

While trying to stabilize the big league team, Melvin and his staff decided to keep groups of prospects intact at Double-A Huntsville and low Class A Beloit to foster a winning attitude, and both clubs made their league finals. Scouts in other organizations said the Brewers, thanks in large part to scouting director Jack Zduriencik's 2000-03 drafts, have the most improved system in the game, and Baseball America rates their minor league talent as the best in the game.

The Brewers know player development is their only hope for winning again. Some prospects could trickle into the major leagues in 2004, and Melvin and his staff expect a noticeable impact the following year. As far as long-suffering Brewers fans are concerned, it can't happen soon enough.

ORGANIZATION
OVERVIEW

General manager: Doug Melvin. **Farm director:** Reid Nichols. **Scouting director:** Jack Zduriencik.

2003 PERFORMANCE

Class	Team	League	W	L	Pct.	Finish*	Manager
Majors	Milwaukee	National	68	94	.420	14th (16)	Ned Yost
Triple-A	Indianapolis Indians	International	64	78	.451	12th (14)	Cecil Cooper
Double-A	Huntsville Stars	Southern	75	63	.543	2nd (10)	Frank Kremblas
High A	High Desert Mavericks	California	42	98	.300	10th (10)	Tim Blackwell
Low A	Beloit Snappers	Midwest	75	61	.551	2nd (14)	Don Money
Rookie	Helena Brewers	Pioneer	48	28	.632	2nd (8)	Ed Sedar
Rookie	AZL Brewers	Arizona	15	34	.306	9th (9)	Hector Torres
OVERALLL 2003 MINOR LEAGUE RECORD			319	362	.469	26th (30)	

*Finish in overall standings (No. of teams in league).

ORGANIZATION LEADERS

BATTING
*Minimum 250 At-Bats

*AVG	Terry Trofholz, Helena	.349
R	Kennard Bibbs, Beloit	85
H	Prince Fielder, Beloit	157
TB	Prince Fielder, Beloit	264
2B	Corey Hart, Huntsville	40
3B	Dave Krynzel, Huntsville	11
HR	Prince Fielder, Beloit	27
RBI	Prince Fielder, Beloit	112
BB	Rich Paz, Indianapolis/Huntsville	74
SO	Jeff Eure, Beloit	128
SB	Chris Morris, High Desert	67
*SLG	Prince Fielder, Beloit	.526
*OBP	Rich Paz, Indianapolis/Huntsville	.422

PITCHING
#Minimum 75 Innings

W	Derek Lee, Indianapolis /Huntsville	13
L	Dan Hall, High Desert	14
#ERA	Luis Martinez, Indianapolis/Huntsville	2.13
G	Rob Giron, Indianapolis	52
	Josh Alliston, Beloit	52
CG	Several tied at	1
SV	Rob Giron, Indianapolis	15
IP	Luis Martinez, Indianapolis/Huntsville	161
BB	Luis Martinez, Indianapolis/Huntsville	73
SO	Luis Martinez, Indianapolis/Huntsville	162

BEST TOOLS

Best Hitter for Average	Prince Fielder
Best Power Hitter	Prince Fielder
Fastest Baserunner	David Krynzel
Best Athlete	David Krynzel
Best Fastball	Tom Wilhelmsen
Best Curveball	Ben Hendrickson
Best Slider	Tim Bausher
Best Changeup	Jeff Housman
Best Control	Manny Parra
Best Defensive Catcher	Lou Palmisano
Best Defensive Infielder	J.J. Hardy
Best Infield Arm	J.J. Hardy
Best Defensive Outfielder	David Krynzel
Best Outfield Arm	Steve Moss

PROJECTED 2007 LINEUP

Catcher	Lou Palmisano
First Base	Prince Fielder
Second Base	Rickie Weeks
Third Base	Corey Hart
Shortstop	J.J. Hardy
Left Field	Geoff Jenkins

Center Field	David Krynzel
Right Field	Brad Nelson
No. 1 Starter	Ben Sheets
No. 2 Starter	Manny Parra
No. 3 Starter	Mike Jones
No. 4 Starter	Ben Hendrickson
No. 5 Starter	Jorge de la Rosa
Closer	Dennis Sarfate

LAST YEAR'S TOP 20 PROSPECTS

1. Brad Nelson, 1b/of
2. Mike Jones, rhp
3. Prince Fielder, 1b
4. Ben Hendrickson, rhp
5. Corey Hart, 3b/1b
6. J.J. Hardy, ss
7. David Krynzel, of
8. Manny Parra, lhp
9. Ben Diggins, rhp
10. Matt Ford, lhp
11. Enrique Cruz, 3b/ss
12. Pedro Liriano, rhp
13. Keith Ginter, 3b
14. Ozzie Chavez, ss
15. Shane Nance, lhp
16. Steve Moss, of
17. Jayson Durocher, rhp
18. Bill Hall, ss
19. Eric M. Thomas, rhp
20. Mike Adams, rhp

TOP PROSPECTS OF THE DECADE

1994	Jeff D'Amico, rhp
1995	Antone Williamson, 3b
1996	Jeff D'Amico, rhp
1997	Todd Dunn, of
1998	Valerio de los Santos, lhp
1999	Ron Belliard, 2b
2000	Nick Neugebauer, rhp
2001	Ben Sheets, rhp
2002	Nick Neugebauer, rhp
2003	Brad Nelson, 1b

TOP DRAFT PICKS OF THE DECADE

1994	Antone Williamson, 3b
1995	Geoff Jenkins, of
1996	Chad Green, of
1997	Kyle Peterson, rhp
1998	J.M. Gold, rhp
1999	Ben Sheets, rhp
2000	David Krynzel, of
2001	Mike Jones, rhp
2002	Prince Fielder, 1b
2003	Rickie Weeks, 2b

ALL-TIME LARGEST BONUSES

Rickie Weeks, 2003	$3,600,000
Ben Sheets, 1999	$2,450,000
Prince Fielder, 2002	$2,400,000
Mike Jones, 2001	$2,075,000
David Krynzel, 2000	$1,950,000

MINOR LEAGUE
DEPTH CHART

MILWAUKEE BREWERS   RANK: 1

Impact potential (A+): While Milwaukee's big league situation continues to be bleak, there is hope on the way. Phenoms Rickie Weeks, Prince Fielder and J.J. Hardy lead the charge and are on pace for a complete infield overhaul by 2005. Brad Nelson should bounce back after a broken hand stymied his progress last year.

Depth (B+): The Brewers' resurgence is a tribute to the job Jack Zduriencik and his scouting staff have done in the last four years. Five years ago, prospects with the profiles of Lou Palmisano, Dennis Sarfate, Tom Wilhelmsen and Anthony Gwynn would've been locks for the top 10, but now they take a back seat to a more advanced group of up-and-comers.

Sleeper: Charlie Fermaint, of.   *—Depth charts prepared by Josh Boyd. Numbers in parentheses indicate prospect rankings.*

LF
Brad Nelson (5)
Steve Moss (25)
Jason Belcher (30)
Drew Anderson
Adam Mannon

CF
Dave Krynzel (9)
Anthony Gwynn (17)
Charlie Fermaint (22)
Manuel Melo

RF
Corey Hart (7)
Francisco Plasencia
Daryl Clark
Terry Trofholz

3B
Enrique Cruz
Froilan Villanueva

SS
J.J. Hardy (3)
Gilberto Acosta (23)
Josh Murray
Ozzie Chavez

2B
Rickie Weeks (1)
Alejandro Machado
Callix Crabbe
Ralph Santana

1B
Prince Fielder (2)
Manuel Ramirez
Barrett Whitney

SOURCE OF TALENT

Homegrown		Acquired	
College	5	Trades	5
Junior College	2	Rule 5 draft	1
Draft-and-follow	2	Independent leagues	1
High school	12	Free agents/waivers	0
Nondrafted free agent	0		
Foreign	2		

C
Lou Palmisano (11)
Brian Opdyke
Kade Johnson
John Vanden Berg

RHP

Starters	Relievers
Mike Jones (6)	Tim Bausher (19)
Ben Hendrickson (8)	Jeff Bennett (24)
Dennis Sarfate (12)	Mike Adams (27)
Tom Wilhelmsen (14)	Matt Childers
Pedro Liriano (18)	Adrian Hernandez
Ben Diggins (21)	Josh Alliston
Tommy Hawk (28)	Robbie Wooley
Greg Bruso (29)	
Jason Shelley	
Chris Saenz	
Khalid Ballouli	
Alvaro Martinez	
Eric Thomas	

LHP

Starters	Relievers
Manny Parra (4)	Dana Eveland (16)
Jorge de la Rosa (10)	Matt Ford
Luis Martinez (13)	Brian Adams
Chris Capuano (15)	
Jeff Housman (20)	
Greg Kloosterman (26)	
Chad Petty	

DRAFT
ANALYSIS

Best Pro Debut: C Lou Palmisano (3) was MVP of the Rookie-level Pioneer League and won the batting (.391), on-base (.458) and slugging (.592) titles. He broke his left ankle busting up a double play in August. 2B Rickie Weeks (1) hit .349 with more extra-base hits (10) and walks (15) than strikeouts (nine) in low Class A. RHP Tommy Hawk (17) went 2-1, 2.31 and led the Rookie-level Arizona League in ERA.

Best Athlete: The Brewers like the athleticism of their top four picks—Weeks, OF Anthony Gwynn (2), Palmisano and OF Charlie Fermaint (4)—but it's hard to beat Weeks' package. His offensive ceiling is as high as any player's in the 2003 draft.

Best Pure Hitter: Weeks won back-to-back Division I batting titles in 2002-03 and holds the NCAA career record with a .473 average. He might have the quickest hands of any draftee since Gary Sheffield, the No. 6 overall pick by Milwaukee in June 1986.

Best Raw Power: Weeks. Palmisano and C Brian Opdyke (5) have intriguing potential.

Fastest Runner: Fermaint was clocked at 6.5 seconds in the 60-yard dash before he pulled a hamstring during the spring, which caused him to slide in the draft.

Best Defensive Player: Though Gwynn has his famous father's hitting approach, he distinguishes himself with his play in center field. Palmisano is agile behind the plate

Gwynn

and has solid arm strength.

Best Fastball: RHPs Robbie Wooley (6) and Ryan Marion (8) both touch 94 mph, with RHP Brian Montalbo (7) right behind them at 93.

Best Breaking Ball: LHP Greg Kloosterman (9), a two-way star at Bethel (Ind.) College, has the most refined curveball. He went 6-1, 3.28 with 78 strikeouts in 69 innings in the Rookie-level Pioneer League.

Most Intriguing Background: Gwynn's father Tony coached him at San Diego State. Montalbo's dad Mel played two games in the NFL as a defensive back. Palmisano's brother Nicholas, a first baseman, was a 33rd-round pick by the Pirates. 1B Carlos Corporan's (12) brother Elvis is a third baseman in the Yankees system.

Closest To The Majors: Weeks got there in September, going 2-for-12, and likely will begin 2004 in Double-A.

Best Late-Round Pick: Hawk, who was ticketed for Cal State Fullerton.

The One Who Got Away: The Brewers signed their first 12 picks. They liked the bat of C Garrett Bussiere (14), who escaped to the University of California.

Assessment: Scouting director Jack Zduriencik continues to add talent to an improving system. The Brewers got arguably the best hitter (Weeks) and catcher (Palmisano) in the draft.

1B Prince Fielder (1) was considered a risky No. 7 overall pick, but no longer. RHP Tom Wilhelmsen (7) has an electric arm and just needs to figure out how to use it.

The best of scouting director Jack Zduriencik's four revitalizing drafts for the Brewers. This one landed four of the system's top six prospects—SS J.J. Hardy (2), draft-and-follow LHP Manny Parra (26), OF/1B Brad Nelson (4), RHP Mike Jones (1)—plus RHP Dennis Sarfate (9).

3B Corey Hart (11), the 2003 Southern League MVP, and OF David Krynzel (1) are two more building blocks in Milwaukee's reconstruction.

RHP Ben Sheets (1) is the Brewers' best homegrown pitcher since Dan Plesac. RHP Ben Hendrickson (10) should join him in the big league rotation at some point in 2004.

—Draft analysis prepared by Jim Callis. Numbers in parentheses indicate draft rounds.

BILL MITCHELL

Rickie
Weeks

Born: Sept. 13, 1982.
Ht.: 6-0. **Wt.:** 195.
Bats: R. **Throws:** R.
School: Southern University.
Career Transactions: Selected by Brewers in first round (second overall) of 2003 draft; signed Aug. 7, 2003.

Holding the second pick in the 2003 draft, the Brewers knew they were going to get an offensive prodigy, either prep star Delmon Young or Weeks. When Tampa Bay selected Young No. 1 overall, the Brewers happily took Weeks, Baseball America's College Player of the Year and two-time NCAA batting champion. After two months of negotiations, the Brewers finally signed Weeks to a five-year major league contract—a first in franchise history—that included a $3.6 million bonus and guaranteed at least $4.8 million. The Brewers sent Weeks to low Class A Beloit for the final weeks of the Midwest League season, then summoned him to Milwaukee in mid-September to get a taste of big league life. Keeping Weeks in the fast lane, the Brewers assigned him to the Arizona Fall League. He wowed scouts with his progress at Southern, where he finished with an NCAA-record .473 career batting average. He was a two-time All-American and considered by far the closest to the major leagues among position players available in the draft. Not bad for a guy who went undrafted and barely recruited out of a Florida high school.

Weeks has a lightning-quick bat and was the purest hitter in the 2003 draft. His bat is so quick through the zone that he can make good contact even when he's fooled on a pitch. Weeks has surprising pop for his size, as well as tremendous speed and quickness on the basepaths, a combination that has many scouts comparing him to a young Joe Morgan. He also has a good eye at the plate and gets hit by a lot of pitches, which will allow him to post high on-base percentages. Weeks has worked hard to improve his defensive play. He's a superior athlete who takes instruction well and always looks for ways to get better. "He has a special focus," Brewers scouting director Jack Zduriencik said. There's not much to quibble with about Weeks' package. He does some fundamental things wrong defensively, such as throwing from odd angles at times, but there's nothing that good coaching and experience can't correct. He'll also have to improve his double-play pivot. He makes up for his minor flaws with good hands, quickness and determination. Some have suggested he's better suited for center field, though the Brewers have no plans to move him from second base. Whether he'll hit for as much power as he did in college remains to be seen.

For a first-year pro, Weeks got a lot of experience, appearing in the big leagues and then heading to the AFL, where he hit .319-1-15 with nine stolen bases. The Brewers will continue to expedite his development, starting him at Double-A Huntsville in 2004 and getting him to the majors to stay no later than 2005.

Year	Club (League)	Class	AVG	G	AB	R	H	2B	3B	HR	RBI	BB	SO	SB	SLG	OBP
2003	Brewers (AZL)	R	.500	1	4	0	2	0	0	0	4	0	2	1	.500	.600
	Beloit (Mid)	A	.349	20	63	13	22	8	1	1	16	15	9	2	.556	.494
	Milwaukee (NL)	MAJ	.167	7	12	1	2	1	0	0	0	1	6	0	.250	.286
MAJOR LEAGUE TOTALS			.167	7	12	1	2	1	0	0	0	1	6	0	.250	.286
MINOR LEAGUE TOTALS			.358	21	67	13	24	8	1	1	20	15	11	3	.552	.500

2 Prince Fielder, 1b

Born: May 9, 1984. **Ht.:** 6-0. **Wt.:** 260. **Bats:** L. **Throws:** R. **School:** Eau Gallie HS, Melbourne, Fla. **Career Transactions:** Selected by Brewers in first round (seventh overall) of 2002 draft; signed June 17, 2002.

The son of former big league slugger Cecil Fielder is a completely different hitter than his dad. He bats lefthanded, hits for average, covers the plate well and goes the other way with pitches. His signature tool, however, is the same as his father's: power. One of the Midwest League's youngest players, he won the league MVP award at age 19. All of the aforementioned offensive skills make Fielder a prodigy at the plate. Few hitters with his youth or power are as accomplished and as knowledgeable. He takes walks when pitchers decide to work around him. His pitch recognition and quick bat make him a tough out at the plate. Fielder admittedly worked little on his fielding in high school, and it shows. He made strides last year under Beloit manager Don Money, who made him work long hours on his moves around the bag. Through discipline and use of a personal trainer, he has his weight under control but must continue to be diligent. Fielder's bat should get him to the big leagues in relatively short order, though the Brewers don't want to rush him. He should be ready for Double-A in 2004, when he'll again be young for his league.

Year	Club (League)	Class	AVG	G	AB	R	H	2B	3B	HR	RBI	BB	SO	SB	SLG	OBP
2002	Ogden (Pio)	R	.390	41	146	35	57	12	0	10	40	37	27	3	.678	.531
	Beloit (Mid)	A	.241	32	112	15	27	7	0	3	11	10	27	0	.384	.320
2003	Beloit (Mid)	A	.313	137	502	81	157	22	2	27	112	71	80	2	.526	.409
MINOR LEAGUE TOTALS			.317	210	760	131	241	41	2	40	163	118	134	5	.534	.423

3 J.J. Hardy, ss

Born: Aug. 19, 1982. **Ht.:** 6-2. **Wt.:** 180. **Bats:** R. **Throws:** R. **School:** Sabino HS, Tucson. **Career Transactions:** Selected by Brewers in second round of 2001 draft; signed July 16, 2001.

The Brewers haven't been afraid to push Hardy, whom they consider a special player. He spent 2003 in Double-A at age 20, making the Futures Game and Southern League all-star team. He also served as the backup shortstop on the U.S. Olympic qualifying team. Not a bad resume at this point of his career. Hardy has a strong arm and good range at shortstop. Scouts were uncertain about his hitting ability when he was an amateur, but he has surprising pop and rarely strikes out because of his plate discipline. What the Brewers really like about Hardy, however, is his competitive nature. His makeup is off the charts. Hardy sometimes gets long with his swing and goes into funks at the plate. He doesn't run particularly well and isn't exceptionally quick, but he makes up for those shortcomings with keen baseball instincts. His intense nature causes him to wear down at times. It wouldn't be a shock to see Hardy in the Brewers' Opening Day lineup. If not, many in the organization believe he'll arrive in the majors later in 2004. He's expected to be Milwaukee's starting shortstop for a long time.

Year	Club (League)	Class	AVG	G	AB	R	H	2B	3B	HR	RBI	BB	SO	SB	SLG	OBP
2001	Brewers (AZL)	R	.250	5	20	6	5	2	1	0	1	1	2	0	.450	.286
	Ogden (Pio)	R	.248	35	125	20	31	5	0	2	15	15	12	1	.336	.326
2002	High Desert (Cal)	A	.293	84	335	53	98	19	1	6	48	19	38	9	.409	.327
	Huntsville (SL)	AA	.228	38	145	14	33	7	0	1	13	9	19	1	.297	.269
2003	Huntsville (SL)	AA	.279	114	416	67	116	26	0	12	62	58	54	6	.428	.368
MINOR LEAGUE TOTALS			.272	276	1041	160	283	59	2	21	139	102	125	17	.393	.335

4 Manny Parra, lhp

Born: Oct. 30, 1982. **Ht.:** 6-3. **Wt.:** 200. **Bats:** L. **Throws:** L. **School:** American River (Calif.) JC. **Career Transactions:** Selected by Brewers in 26th round of 2001 draft; signed May 27, 2002.

Parra is a poster boy for the draft-and-follow system. After he went back to junior college for the 2002 season, he improved so much that the Brewers gave him first-round money ($1.55 million). He blossomed in 2003, when he was considered one of the top pitchers in the Midwest League. Parra features a rare combination of stuff and control, especially for a lefthander. He throws his fastball consistently in the 90-93 mph range, and he has a good curveball and an improving changeup. Parra keeps hitters off balance with two-seamers, four-seamers and cutters. He attacks the strike zone, usually working in good pitcher's counts. He's also a competitor who drives himself to be better. Parra needs to improve command of his curve and changeup. He strained a pectoral muscle near the end of the season and must stay on top of his mechanics to avoid future breakdowns. Parra has all the ingredients to move steadily through the system, perhaps skipping a step or two along the way. He likely will open 2004 at high Class A High Desert and could reach Double-A by the end of the year.

Year	Club (League)	Class	W	L	ERA	G	GS	CG	SV	IP	H	R	ER	HR	BB	SO	AVG
2002	Brewers (AZL)	R	0	0	4.50	1	1	0	0	2	1	1	1	1	0	4	.143
	Ogden (Pio)	R	3	1	3.21	11	10	0	0	48	59	30	17	3	10	51	.298
2003	Beloit (Mid)	A	11	2	2.73	23	23	1	0	139	127	50	42	9	24	117	.243
MINOR LEAGUE TOTALS			14	3	2.87	35	34	1	0	188	187	81	60	13	34	172	.257

5 Brad Nelson, of/1b

Born: Dec. 23, 1982. **Ht.:** 6-2. **Wt.:** 220. **Bats:** L. **Throws:** R. **School:** Bishop Garrigan HS, Algona, Iowa. **Career Transactions:** Selected by Brewers in fourth round of 2001 draft; signed July 25, 2001.

Nelson was the Brewers' 2002 minor league player of the year after leading the minors with 49 doubles and 116 RBIs at age 19. He broke the hamate bone in his right wrist early in 2003, however, and never recovered. He went to the Arizona Fall League to try to make up for lost time, but struggled there as well. When healthy, Nelson has a solid approach at the plate. He uses the entire field and can hit with power the other way. Switched to left field in an effort to clear the way at first base for Prince Fielder, Nelson made the adjustment. His arm remains strong, thanks to his amateur days as a pitcher. He has good makeup and work ethic. The broken hamate bone robbed Nelson of his power, and he'll have to work to get his quick power stroke back. Like most young hitters, Nelson needs better plate discipline. Though a better athlete than he's given credit for, he has limited speed and range. The Brewers say Nelson will get back on track in 2004. They moved him to Double-A in the second half despite his injury, and he'll probably return there to open the season.

Year	Club (League)	Class	AVG	G	AB	R	H	2B	3B	HR	RBI	BB	SO	SB	SLG	OBP
2001	Brewers (AZL)	R	.302	17	63	10	19	6	1	0	13	8	18	0	.429	.392
	Ogden (Pio)	R	.262	13	42	5	11	4	0	0	10	3	9	0	.357	.298
2002	Beloit (Mid)	A	.297	106	417	70	124	38	2	17	99	34	86	4	.520	.353
	High Desert (Cal)	A	.255	26	102	24	26	11	0	3	17	12	28	0	.451	.333
2003	High Desert (Cal)	A	.311	41	167	23	52	9	1	1	18	12	22	2	.395	.363
	Huntsville (SL)	AA	.210	39	143	15	30	12	0	1	14	11	34	2	.315	.274
MINOR LEAGUE TOTALS			.281	242	934	147	262	80	4	22	171	80	197	8	.445	.341

6 Mike Jones, rhp

Born: April 23, 1983. **Ht.:** 6-4. **Wt.:** 200. **Bats:** R. **Throws:** R. **School:** Thunderbird HS, Phoenix. **Career Transactions:** Selected by Brewers in first round (12th overall) of 2001 draft; signed June 27, 2001.

Jones was pushed to Double-A despite not turning 20 until a month into the season. He was performing up to expectations, making the mid-season Southern League all-star team, until a lingering elbow problem prompted the Brewers to shut him down and monitor his health closely. When healthy, Jones throws a fastball in the low to mid-90s. He also has a tough curveball that he delivers from a three-quarters angle. Beyond his fluid delivery and athletic ability, Jones has impressed Brewers officials with his work ethic and poise. Scouts loved the ease with which Jones threw the ball in high school, but he fought his mechanics at times in 2003 as his strikeout-walk ratio declined. His changeup is decent but not completely deceptive. He sometimes gets too cute and gives hitters too much credit instead of just trusting his stuff, which is plenty good. There has been disagreement regarding the severity of Jones' elbow injury, and some feared he was headed for Tommy John surgery. But the Brewers said he would be OK with rest and rehabilitation, and late in the winter doctors diagnosed only a strained elbow ligament. A second opinion by Angels orthopedic specialist Lewis Yocum confirmed the diagnosis. Jones still will be closely watched when he reports to spring training, but the Brewers were hopeful he could open the season at Triple-A Indianapolis.

Year	Club (League)	Class	W	L	ERA	G	GS	CG	SV	IP	H	R	ER	HR	BB	SO	AVG
2001	Ogden (Pio)	R	4	1	3.74	9	7	0	0	34	29	17	14	1	10	32	.236
2002	Beloit (Mid)	A	7	7	3.12	27	27	0	0	139	135	63	48	3	62	132	.256
2003	Huntsville (SL)	AA	7	2	2.40	17	17	0	0	98	87	35	26	4	47	63	.238
MINOR LEAGUE TOTALS			18	10	2.93	53	51	0	0	270	251	115	88	8	119	227	.247

7 Corey Hart, 3b/of

RODGER WOOD

Born: March 24, 1982. **Ht.:** 6-6. **Wt.:** 200. **Bats:** R. **Throws:** R. **School:** Greenwood HS, Bowling Green, Ky. **Career Transactions:** Selected by Brewers in 11th round of 2000 draft; signed June 12, 2000.

Just as they did with Brad Nelson, the Brewers moved Hart to a new position in an effort to break up their logjam of first basemen. He had a difficult adjustment to third base, though the switch didn't harm his offensive production. He was named the Southern League MVP at age 21. With a body that draws comparisons to Richie Sexson, Hart would make a nice big league first baseman. Like Sexson, he makes up for his lanky build with a short, compact stroke that generates good power, particularly in the gaps. Hart has a good arm and runs well for a big guy. Scouts say Hart is no third baseman. Though he continues to work hard on his footwork and overall defense, he committed 32 errors in 119 starts, most on throws because of poor fundamentals. The Brewers decided to shift him to the outfield before spring training. Hart also is a free swinger who doesn't take many walks. Once the Brewers get Hart settled into the proper position, probably right field, his future will become better known. The plan is to move him up to Indianapolis in 2004.

Year	Club (League)	Class	AVG	G	AB	R	H	2B	3B	HR	RBI	BB	SO	SB	SLG	OBP
2000	Ogden (Pio)	R	.287	57	216	32	62	9	1	2	30	13	27	6	.366	.332
2001	Ogden (Pio)	R	.340	69	262	53	89	18	1	11	62	26	47	14	.542	.395
2002	High Desert (Cal)	A	.288	100	393	76	113	26	10	22	84	37	101	24	.573	.356
	Huntsville (SL)	AA	.266	28	94	16	25	3	0	2	15	7	16	3	.362	.340
2003	Huntsville (SL)	AA	.302	130	493	70	149	40	1	13	94	28	101	25	.467	.340
MINOR LEAGUE TOTALS			.300	384	1458	247	438	96	13	50	285	111	292	72	.487	.353

8 Ben Hendrickson, rhp

STEVE MOORE

Born: Feb. 4, 1981. **Ht.:** 6-4. **Wt.:** 190. **Bats:** R. **Throws:** R. **School:** Jefferson HS, Bloomington, Minn. **Career Transactions:** Selected by Brewers in 10th round of 1999 draft; signed Sept. 1, 1999.

Hendrickson has some of the best stuff in the organization and has methodically moved up the ladder. He had elbow problems in 2003, however, and was shut down for a couple of months. Hendrickson pitched well after returning, including a standout stint in the Arizona Fall League, so club officials believe the tender elbow isn't a long-term problem. Hendrickson has a solid 89-93 mph fastball and a cutter, but what sets him apart is his outstanding curveball. He throws it over the top and it has a sharp 12-to-6 break, freezing hitters even when they're expecting it. Hendrickson has nice arm action, good command, poise and knowledge of how to set up hitters. Hendrickson relies on his curveball too much, which may have contributed to his elbow soreness. He took a regular turn throughout 2002 but must prove his durability again after making just 16 starts at Huntsville. He continues to work on his changeup. Because Hendrickson looked so sharp in the AFL, the Brewers won't hesitate to promote him to Triple-A in 2004. With his curveball and history of success, he could join Milwaukee's rotation in the near future.

Year	Club (League)	Class	W	L	ERA	G	GS	CG	SV	IP	H	R	ER	HR	BB	SO	AVG
2000	Ogden (Pio)	R	4	3	5.68	13	7	0	1	51	50	37	32	7	29	48	.245
2001	Beloit (Mid)	A	8	9	2.84	25	25	1	0	133	122	58	42	3	72	133	.246
2002	High Desert (Cal)	A	5	5	2.55	14	14	0	0	81	61	31	23	3	41	70	.209
	Huntsville (SL)	AA	4	2	2.97	13	13	0	0	70	57	31	23	2	35	50	.231
2003	Huntsville (SL)	AA	7	6	3.45	17	16	0	0	78	82	35	30	6	28	56	.278
MINOR LEAGUE TOTALS			28	25	3.27	82	75	1	1	413	372	192	150	21	205	357	.243

9 David Krynzel, of

RODGER WOOD

Born: Nov. 7, 1981. **Ht.:** 6-1. **Wt.:** 180. **Bats:** L. **Throws:** L. **School:** Green Valley HS, Henderson, Nev. **Career Transactions:** Selected by Brewers in first round (11th overall) of 2000 draft; signed June 12, 2000.

Much to the Brewers' delight, Krynzel got off to a fast start in Double-A, earning selections to the Southern League midseason all-star team and the Futures Game. He went into a swoon in the second half, batting .137 in August and losing nearly 50 points off his average by season's end. His bat continued to run hot and cold in the AFL. Speed is Krynzel's calling card, and he uses it to create havoc on the bases as well as to chase down balls from gap to gap in center field. Augmenting his range in the outfield, Krynzel has good arm strength. He has prototypical leadoff tools. Despite his slump, he's mentally tough. The

Brewers would like to see Krynzel bunt more, take more pitches and continue to slap the ball around. He needs to stop striking out more than 100 times a year, which is unacceptable in the leadoff role. He doesn't possess great instincts on the bases and must improve his ability to read pitchers. Despite the emergence of Scott Podsednik, Krynzel still is seen as Milwaukee's center fielder of the future. He'll start the 2004 season in Triple-A.

Year	Club (League)	Class	AVG	G	AB	R	H	2B	3B	HR	RBI	BB	SO	SB	SLG	OBP
2000	Ogden (Pio)	R	.359	34	131	25	47	8	3	1	29	16	23	8	.489	.442
2001	Beloit (Mid)	A	.305	35	141	22	43	1	1	1	19	9	28	11	.348	.364
	High Desert (Cal)	A	.277	89	383	65	106	19	5	5	33	27	122	34	.392	.329
2002	High Desert (Cal)	A	.268	97	365	76	98	13	12	11	45	64	100	29	.460	.391
	Huntsville (SL)	AA	.240	31	129	13	31	2	3	2	13	4	30	13	.349	.269
2003	Huntsville (SL)	AA	.267	124	457	72	122	13	11	2	34	60	119	43	.357	.357
MINOR LEAGUE TOTALS			.278	410	1606	273	447	56	35	22	173	180	422	138	.398	.360

10 Jorge de la Rosa, lhp

Born: April 5, 1981. **Ht.:** 6-1. **Wt.:** 190. **Bats:** L. **Throws:** L. **Career Transactions:** Signed out of Mexico by Diamondbacks, March 20, 1998 . . . Contract purchased by Monterrey (Mexican) from Diamondbacks, April 2, 2000 . . . Contract purchased by Red Sox from Monterrey, Feb. 22, 2001 . . . Traded by Red Sox with LHP Casey Fossum, RHP Brandon Lyon and OF Mike Goss to Diamondbacks for RHP Curt Schilling, Nov. 28, 2003 . . . Traded by Diamondbacks with 2B Junior Spivey, 1B Lyle Overbay, C Chad Moeller, INF Craig Counsell and LHP Chris Capuano to Brewers for 1B Richie Sexson, LHP Shane Nance and a player to be named, Dec. 1, 2003.

This offseason, de la Rosa was the key prospect in separate transactions involving two of the game's elite players. Three days after the Red Sox sent him to the Diamondbacks in a deal for Curt Schilling, Arizona turned around and shipped him to the Brewers in a nine-player trade for Richie Sexson. De la Rosa was Boston's best pitching prospect, and he has accomplished more at a higher level than any of the top arms in the Milwaukee system. When the Red Sox bought him from Mexico's Monterrey Sultans in 2001, then-general manager Dan Duquette dubbed de la Rosa "the Mexican John Rocker" because he projected as a hard-throwing lefty closer. While he still lights up radar guns from 90-95, he has shown potential as a big league starter. Besides his heater, he has a curveball that's a plus pitch at times, as well as a changeup that has made significant improvement. He still needs to refine his command and become more consistent with his secondary pitches, but he's not too far away from the majors. The back of Milwaukee's rotation is unsettled, so he should make his big league debut at some point in 2004.

Year	Club (League)	Class	W	L	ERA	G	GS	CG	SV	IP	H	R	ER	HR	BB	SO	AVG
1998	Diamondbacks (DSL)	R	1	0	4.50	13	0	0	1	14	8	7	7	3	8	21	.160
1999	Diamondbacks (AZL)	R	0	0	3.21	8	0	0	2	14	12	5	5	1	3	17	.226
	High Desert (Cal)	A	0	0	0.00	2	0	0	0	3	1	0	0	0	2	5	.100
	Missoula (Pio)	R	0	1	7.98	13	0	0	2	15	22	17	13	2	9	14	.333
2000	Monterrey (Mex)	AAA	3	2	6.28	37	0	0	1	39	38	27	27	2	32	50	.257
2001	Sarasota (FSL)	A	0	1	1.21	12	0	0	2	30	13	7	4	0	12	27	.127
	Trenton (EL)	AA	1	3	5.84	29	0	0	0	37	56	35	24	4	20	27	.348
2002	Sarasota (FSL)	A	7	7	3.65	23	23	1	0	121	105	53	49	10	52	95	.231
	Trenton (EL)	AA	1	2	5.50	4	4	0	0	18	17	12	11	0	9	15	.239
2003	Portland (EL)	AA	6	3	2.80	22	20	0	1	100	87	39	31	6	36	102	.236
	Pawtucket (IL)	AAA	1	2	3.75	5	5	0	0	24	27	14	10	0	12	17	.278
MINOR LEAGUE TOTALS			20	21	3.94	168	52	1	9	413	386	216	181	28	195	388	.244

11 Lou Palmisano, c

Born: Sept. 16, 1982. **Ht.:** 6-1. **Wt.:** 185. **Bats:** R. **Throws:** R. **School:** Broward (Fla.) CC. **Career Transactions:** Selected by Brewers in third round of 2003 draft; signed June 3, 2003.

Palmisano hurt his shoulder in 2002 and required surgery, but bounced back with a solid year in junior college that had some scouts calling him the best catcher in the draft. In desperate need of help behind the plate, the Brewers happily snapped him up in the third round. He earned MVP honors in the Rookie-level Pioneer League, leading the circuit in batting, on-base percentage and slugging. The only negative was that he broke his left ankle trying to bust up a double play. Palmisano is athletic behind the plate, with good quickness, soft hands and a strong arm. He also calls a good game and is a take-charge guy. At the plate, he has a quick bat and power to all fields. He runs well for a catcher. Palmisano arrived at the Brewers' rookie camp with a definite hitch in his swing, and pitchers were able to exploit it. He made adjustments and the glitch wasn't as noticeable. Sometimes he's too aggressive for his own good, chasing high fastballs. Palmisano will be put on a fast track. His aggressive nature and leadership skills should serve him well as he moves toward the big leagues. He should see high Class A at some point in 2004.

Year	Club (League)	Class	AVG	G	AB	R	H	2B	3B	HR	RBI	BB	SO	SB	SLG	OBP
2003	Helena (Pio)	R	.391	47	174	32	68	13	2	6	43	18	29	13	.592	.458
MINOR LEAGUE TOTALS			.391	47	174	32	68	13	2	6	43	18	29	13	.592	.458

12 Dennis Sarfate, rhp

Born: April 9, 1981. **Ht.:** 6-4. **Wt.:** 210. **Bats:** R. **Throws:** R. **School:** Chandler-Gilbert (Ariz.) CC. **Career Transactions:** Selected by Brewers in ninth round of 2001 draft; signed June 18, 2001.

No pitcher in the organization boosted his stock more in 2003 than Sarfate, who had a breakthrough season in low Class A. He won his final 11 decisions, including both of his starts in the Midwest League playoffs. "He always had a good arm," scouting director Jack Zduriencik said, "but he really grew up as a pitcher." He responded well to coaching, started to mix his pitches and set hitters up, and developed into a strikeout pitcher. Sarfate has a heavy fastball in the 91-96 mph range, a sharp slider and a deceptive changeup. His confidence soared when he started clicking off victories. He does overthrow at times, and he must develop more consistency with his breaking ball and more belief in his changeup. He also needs to cut down on his walks and keeping his pitches off the fat part of the plate. Sarfate has an aggressive nature that would suit him well as a closer if he can't put together the whole package of three pitches. He probably will begin 2004 in Double-A.

Year	Club (League)	Class	W	L	ERA	G	GS	CG	SV	IP	H	R	ER	HR	BB	SO	AVG
2001	Ogden (Pio)	R	1	2	4.63	9	4	0	1	23	20	13	12	4	10	32	.230
2002	Brewers (AZL)	R	0	0	2.57	5	5	0	0	14	6	4	4	0	7	22	.125
	Ogden (Pio)	R	0	0	9.00	1	0	0	0	1	2	1	1	0	1	2	.400
2003	Beloit (Mid)	A	12	2	2.84	26	26	0	0	140	114	50	44	11	66	140	.227
MINOR LEAGUE TOTALS			13	4	3.08	41	35	0	1	178	142	68	61	15	84	196	.221

13 Luis Martinez, lhp

Born: Jan. 20, 1980. **Ht.:** 6-6. **Wt.:** 200. **Bats:** L. **Throws:** L. **Career Transactions:** Signed out of Dominican Republic by Brewers, Oct. 12, 1996.

The Brewers didn't know what to expect from Martinez, who spun his wheels and showed a distinct lack of maturity while in Double-A in 2002. Last year, the light bulb suddenly turned on as he made a triumphant return to Huntsville, then pitched even better in Triple-A. His stuff is not particularly awe-inspiring: 90-92 mph fastball, plus changeup, so-so curveball. But the big lefty has a funky delivery with a slight hesitation that adds to his deception. His unusual mechanics also can work against him, leading to command problems at times because he struggles to repeat his arm action. When he stays ahead in the count, he racks up strikeouts, and when he keeps the ball down, he's effective. Martinez didn't do that during a September callup and got hammered by big league hitters. In the Brewers' eyes, that shellacking didn't detract from the progress he made in 2003. They'll give him a shot to make their rotation in spring training.

Year	Club (League)	Class	W	L	ERA	G	GS	CG	SV	IP	H	R	ER	HR	BB	SO	AVG
1997	Brewers (DSL)	R	0	2	12.96	11	2	0	0	17	21	27	24	3	24	17	.288
1998	Helena (Pio)	R	0	9	10.13	17	10	0	0	48	64	73	54	5	66	47	.318
1999	Ogden (Pio)	R	0	7	6.97	15	7	0	1	50	66	65	39	3	34	43	.304
2000	Beloit (Mid)	A	5	7	3.79	28	13	0	0	93	71	49	39	8	61	77	.209
2001	High Desert (Cal)	A	8	9	5.19	22	22	0	0	113	112	67	65	9	64	121	.263
	Huntsville (SL)	AA	0	0	6.75	7	0	0	0	9	13	7	7	0	9	13	.333
2002	Huntsville (SL)	AA	8	8	5.20	29	18	0	1	109	114	70	63	6	65	106	.277
2003	Huntsville (SL)	AA	8	5	2.58	20	20	1	0	115	93	46	33	4	54	116	.224
	Indianapolis (IL)	AAA	4	0	0.99	7	7	0	0	46	37	5	5	0	19	46	.237
	Milwaukee (NL)	MAJ	0	3	9.92	4	4	0	0	16	25	18	18	3	15	10	.373
MAJOR LEAGUE TOTALS			0	3	9.92	4	4	0	0	16	25	18	18	3	15	10	.373
MINOR LEAGUE TOTALS			33	47	4.94	156	99	1	2	599	591	409	329	38	396	586	.259

14 Tom Wilhelmsen, rhp

Born: Dec. 16, 1983. **Ht.:** 6-6. **Wt.:** 190. **Bats:** R. **Throws:** R. **School:** Tucson Magnet HS, Tucson. **Career Transactions:** Selected by Brewers in seventh round of 2002 draft; signed Aug. 19, 2002.

Wilhelmsen didn't pitch in 2002 after signing late, so the Brewers didn't know what to expect when they sent him to low Class A last year at age 19. To say the least, they were pleasantly surprised. "He might have the best arm in the organization," scouting director Jack Zduriencik said. One National League scout went a step further, saying Wilhelmsen was the best righthander he had ever seen in the Midwest League. He gets his fastball to the plate regularly in the mid-90s, and his lanky body should fill out with time and make him even stronger. His heater does lack movement, however, because he throws straight over the top. He also has a good curveball and a decent changeup, and the NL scout graded both as plus-plus pitches in one outing. Wilhelmsen did experience elbow problems that caused him to be shut down for most of the second half. He also has maturity issues. Some call him a flake, others merely a free spirit. In other words, he's a lefthander trapped in a righthander's body. Once Wilhelmsen grows up, there should be no stopping him because he has the raw stuff to win big. Despite his youth, he could start 2004 in Double-A.

Year	Club (League)	Class	W	L	ERA	G	GS	CG	SV	IP	H	R	ER	HR	BB	SO	AVG
2003	Beloit (Mid)	A	5	5	2.76	15	15	1	0	88	78	35	27	6	27	63	.241
	Brewers (AZL)	R	0	1	4.50	2	2	0	0	4	5	2	2	0	4	4	.313
MINOR LEAGUE TOTALS			5	6	2.84	17	17	1	0	92	83	37	29	6	31	67	.244

15 Chris Capuano, lhp

Born: Aug. 19, 1978. **Ht.:** 6-2. **Wt.:** 220. **Bats:** L. **Throws:** L. **School:** Duke University. **Career Transactions:** Selected by Diamondbacks in eighth round of 1999 draft; signed Aug. 24, 1999 . . . Traded by Diamondbacks with 2B Junior Spivey, 1B Lyle Overbay, LHP Jorge de la Rosa, C Chad Moeller and INF Craig Counsell to Brewers for 1B Richie Sexson, LHP Shane Nance and a player to be named, Dec. 1, 2003.

Trading Richie Sexson was an unpopular move, but the Brewers did deepen their stock of lefthanders by picking up Jorge de la Rosa and Capuano in the nine-player deal. Capuano missed most of the 2002 season following Tommy John surgery, but he returned to spring training just nine months later, befitting his tough-as-nails mentality. He made his major league debut with a scoreless 10th inning against the Braves in early May before returning to Triple-A, where he posted the best ERA of any Pacific Coast League lefthander. He topped out at 94 mph before surgery and pitched more in the 87-89 range in 2003, peaking at 91. Power pitching was never his forte, anyway. He succeeds by commanding the strike zone vertically and horizontally with his entire repertoire, led by a slurvy, looping breaking ball. Capuano showed an improved feel for his changeup last year, and uses a cutter the second or third time through an order. His must gain better control of his mechanics, as he tends to drop his arm and sling the ball toward the plate. Capuano profiles as a back-of-the-rotation starter and could win that job out of spring training.

Year	Club (League)	Class	W	L	ERA	G	GS	CG	SV	IP	H	R	ER	HR	BB	SO	AVG
2000	South Bend (Mid)	A	10	4	2.21	18	18	0	0	102	68	35	25	2	45	105	.193
2001	El Paso (TL)	AA	10	11	5.31	28	28	2	0	159	184	109	94	13	75	167	.290
2002	Tucson (PCL)	AAA	4	1	2.72	6	6	0	0	36	30	12	11	1	11	29	.227
2003	Tucson (PCL)	AAA	9	5	3.34	23	23	0	0	143	133	66	53	9	43	108	.250
	Arizona (NL)	MAJ	2	4	4.64	9	5	0	0	33	27	19	17	3	11	23	.231
MAJOR LEAGUE TOTALS			2	4	4.64	9	5	0	0	33	27	19	17	3	11	23	.231
MINOR LEAGUE TOTALS			33	21	3.74	75	75	2	0	440	415	222	183	25	174	409	.251

16 Dana Eveland, lhp

Born: Oct. 29, 1983. **Ht.:** 6-1. **Wt.:** 220. **Bats:** L. **Throws:** L. **School:** JC of Canyons (Calif.). **Career Transactions:** Selected by Brewers in 16th round of 2002 draft; signed May 26, 2003.

A draft-and-follow signed before the 2003 draft, Eveland was made the closer at Rookie-level Helena because the Brewers were worried about how many innings he had logged in junior college. He responded to the new role with 14 saves in 19 appearances and an average of 14.2 strikeouts per nine innings, earning Pioneer League all-star honors. Coming out of the bullpen, he saw his fastball jump to 94-95 mph, and he also has a good curveball. His slider and changeup need work Scouts worry about his maximum-effort delivery and his David Wells build (though he's in better shape than Wells). Because Eveland has a deep repertoire, the Brewers may return him to a starting role, but club officials certainly liked the way he handled the pressure of finishing games. He showed good mound presence and went right after hitters. Eveland will spend 2004 in Class A.

Year	Club (League)	Class	W	L	ERA	G	GS	CG	SV	IP	H	R	ER	HR	BB	SO	AVG
2003	Helena (Pio)	R	2	1	2.08	19	0	0	14	26	30	9	6	1	8	41	.286
MINOR LEAGUE TOTALS			2	1	2.08	19	0	0	14	26	30	9	6	1	8	41	.286

17 Anthony Gwynn, of

Born: Oct. 4, 1982. **Ht.:** 6-0. **Wt.:** 185. **Bats:** L. **Throws:** R. **School:** San Diego State University. **Career Transactions:** Selected by Brewers in second round of 2003 draft; signed June 19, 2003.

The Brewers did Gwynn a favor by picking him with the second pick of 2003's second round. The Padres were set to grab him with the next choice, which would have created added pressure of following in the footsteps of his father, former San Diego great and future

Hall of Famer Tony Gwynn. Unlike his dad, who coached him at San Diego State, Anthony was known best for his defense in college. He has great instincts in center field and the wheels to chase down drives in either gap. He reads the ball well off the bat and gets good jumps. Gwynn uses his father's approach at the plate, spraying the ball all over the field. He makes good contact and controls the strike zone, and he uses his above-average speed to leg out hits and steal bases. Also like his dad, he has all of the intangibles and knows the game. The more the Brewers watched him, the more they liked him. But Gwynn has little or no power, so scouts wonder how much he'll hit and how effective he'll be at the higher levels. Not only would he benefit from more pop at the plate, but he also needs more strength to make it through the long pro season. He went straight to low Class A and hit .322 in his first month as a pro, but he wore down and batted just .240 the rest of the way. He'll advance to high Class A this year.

Year	Club (League)	Class	AVG	G	AB	R	H	2B	3B	HR	RBI	BB	SO	SB	SLG	OBP
2003	Beloit (Mid)	A	.280	61	236	35	66	8	0	1	33	32	31	14	.326	.364
MINOR LEAGUE TOTALS			.280	61	236	35	66	8	0	1	33	32	31	14	.326	.364

18 Pedro Liriano, rhp

Born: Oct. 23, 1980. **Ht.:** 6-2. **Wt.:** 170. **Bats:** R. **Throws:** R. **Career Transactions:** Signed out of Dominican Republic by Angels, Nov. 10, 1998 . . . Traded by Angels to Brewers, Sept. 20, 2002, completing trade in which Brewers sent OF Alex Ochoa and C Sal Fasano to Angels for C Jorge Fabregas and two players to be named (July 31, 2002); Brewers also acquired 2B Johnny Raburn (Aug. 14, 2002).

The Brewers often compare Liriano to Pedro Martinez, but they're talking about his wiry physique and not his stuff. Liriano throws a sinker in the high 80s to low 90s, and his best pitch is a slider that hitters can't help but chase. He has a deceptive delivery with a quick arm from a low three-quarters slingy slot. The Angels gave him up to get Alex Ochoa from Milwaukee for their stretch run in 2002. Liriano ran hot and cold in his Brewers system debut at Double-A in 2003, though he pitched well in the Southern League playoffs. When he commands his pitches and has an effective changeup, he wins. When he doesn't, he struggles because he can't just overpower hitters. If he doesn't improve at Triple-A this year, he may be destined to become a middle reliever.

Year	Club (League)	Class	W	L	ERA	G	GS	CG	SV	IP	H	R	ER	HR	BB	SO	AVG
1999	Angels (DSL)	R	7	2	1.83	17	9	3	0	79	46	23	16	3	23	61	.172
2000	Angels (DSL)	R	5	1	1.25	12	11	1	0	79	36	19	11	3	29	78	.132
2001	Provo (Pio)	R	11	2	2.78	15	14	0	0	78	80	39	24	3	31	76	.265
2002	Rancho Cucamonga (Cal)	A	10	14	3.60	28	28	1	0	167	129	86	67	14	74	176	.212
2003	Huntsville (SL)	AA	9	13	3.79	27	26	0	0	143	138	77	60	12	62	116	.256
MINOR LEAGUE TOTALS			42	32	2.94	99	88	5	0	545	429	244	178	35	219	507	.216

19 Tim Bausher, rhp

Born: April 23, 1979. **Ht.:** 6-4. **Wt.:** 200. **Bats:** R. **Throws:** R. **School:** Kutztown (Pa.) University. **Career Transactions:** Selected by Mariners in 27th round of 2001 draft; signed June 7, 2001 . . . Released by Mariners, April 24, 2002 . . . Signed by independent Berkshire (Northeast), May 2003 . . . Contract purchased by Brewers from Berkshire, June 2, 2003.

It was understandable if Bausher's head was spinning a bit at the end of 2003. The Mariners drafted him in the 27th round in 2001, but he quickly injured his shoulder and had surgery, earning his release the following year. Deciding to give baseball a final shot in 2003, he signed with Pittsfield in the independent Northeast League last May. He pitched in one game and got spotted by the Brewers, who purchased him and sent him to low Class A. He was closing games by the end of the season and earned a trip to the Arizona Fall League, where he continued to open eyes. Bausher, whose older brother Andy pitched at Triple-A in the Padres system last year, has two closer-caliber pitches. His fastball registers in the mid-90s and he complements it with a hard, sharp slider. When he needs a strikeout, he has the stuff to get one. Because he missed nearly two years after his shoulder injury, the Brewers were careful with his workload. He just needs to stay healthy, keep throwing his two power pitches and find the strike zone more consistently. Because Bausher will be 25 in 2004, Milwaukee hopes he can at least reach Double-A by the end of the year.

Year	Club (League)	Class	W	L	ERA	G	GS	CG	SV	IP	H	R	ER	HR	BB	SO	AVG
2001	Everett (NWL)	A	0	3	8.62	11	1	0	1	16	25	15	15	2	8	18	.352
2002	Did not play																
2003	Berkshire (NE)	IND	0	0	2.25	1	1	0	0	4	3	1	1	0	3	8	.200
	Beloit (Mid)	A	1	2	3.33	19	0	0	3	27	19	12	10	3	12	39	.194
MINOR LEAGUE TOTALS			1	5	5.27	30	1	0	4	43	44	27	25	5	20	57	.260

20 Jeff Housman, lhp

Born: Aug. 4, 1981. **Ht.:** 6-3. **Wt.:** 180. **Bats:** L. **Throws:** L. **School:** Cal State Fullerton. **Career Transactions:** Selected by Brewers in 33rd round of 2002 draft; signed June 10, 2002.

If it seems like Housman came out of nowhere, it's because he did. A high school team-mate of Shane Costa, Housman transferred to Fullerton from College of the Sequoias JC for his junior season. He went 0-4, 4.89. He got roughed up on a regular basis in Rookie ball during his pro debut in 2002, yet he ended his first full season by holding his own in Double-A. Farm director Reid Nichols compares Housman to Doug Davis, who pitched well for the Brewers in the second half last year, using deception and location instead of power. Housman's fastball tops out in the high 80s and his slider is inconsistent, but he fools hitters with his changeup and works both sides of the plate. He shows good poise on the mound, an ability to set up hitters and plenty of savvy. The Brewers will see if he can pass muster in Triple-A this year.

Year	Club (League)	Class	W	L	ERA	G	GS	CG	SV	IP	H	R	ER	HR	BB	SO	AVG
2002	Ogden (Pio)	R	1	3	8.07	16	5	0	0	32	55	38	29	5	12	23	.372
2003	Beloit (Mid)	A	2	7	1.81	20	15	0	0	89	79	40	18	5	26	50	.231
	Huntsville (SL)	AA	3	2	3.30	8	8	1	0	46	49	21	17	4	17	26	.274
MINOR LEAGUE TOTALS			6	12	3.43	44	28	1	0	168	183	99	64	14	55	99	.274

21 Ben Diggins, rhp

Born: June 13, 1979. **Ht.:** 6-7. **Wt.:** 230. **Bats:** R. **Throws:** R. **School:** University of Arizona. **Career Transactions:** Selected by Dodgers in first round (17th overall) of 2000 draft; signed Aug. 23, 2000 . . . Traded by Dodgers with LHP Shane Nance to Brewers for 3B Tyler Houston and a player to be named, July 23, 2002; Dodgers acquired RHP Brian Mallete to complete trade (Oct. 16, 2002).

Acquired from the Dodgers in a July 2002 deal for Tyler Houston, Diggins immediately became one of the top pitching prospects in the Brewers system. He was off to a nice start in Double-A last year when his elbow began bothering him. Two months of rehab did nothing to solve the problem, so he had Tommy John surgery. Now if he takes the mound at any point in 2004, it will be a significant accomplishment. A big guy with a power arm, he consistently threw in the low 90s before getting hurt, but hasn't consistently hit the mid 90s since college. Not only will he have to regain his velocity when he returns, but he also has plenty of unfinished business. His command and average curveball were inconsistent, and his changeup was below-average. Diggins may benefit from relearning his mechanics on the comeback trail from elbow surgery. At some point, the Brewers must decide if Diggins has the repertoire to be a starter, or whether he'd be better off in a late-inning role that would allow him to use his fastball more.

Year	Club (League)	Class	W	L	ERA	G	GS	CG	SV	IP	H	R	ER	HR	BB	SO	AVG
2001	Wilmington (SAL)	A	7	6	3.58	21	21	0	0	106	88	49	42	5	48	79	.224
2002	Vero Beach (FSL)	A	6	10	3.63	20	19	0	0	114	103	54	46	8	41	101	.238
	Huntsville (SL)	AA	2	1	1.91	7	7	0	0	38	26	13	8	0	15	34	.208
	Milwaukee (NL)	MAJ	0	4	8.63	5	5	0	0	24	28	24	23	4	18	15	.298
2003	Huntsville (SL)	AA	3	2	2.36	8	8	0	0	46	41	18	12	2	16	32	.236
MAJOR LEAGUE TOTALS			0	4	8.63	5	5	0	0	24	28	24	23	4	18	15	.298
MINOR LEAGUE TOTALS			18	19	3.21	56	55	0	0	303	258	134	108	15	120	246	.230

22 Charlie Fermaint, of

Born: Oct. 11, 1985. **Ht.:** 5-10. **Wt.:** 170. **Bats:** R. **Throws:** R. **School:** Jose S. Alegria HS, Dorado, P.R. **Career Transactions:** Selected by Brewers in fourth round of 2003 draft; signed June 5, 2003.

One of the youngest players selected in the 2003 draft, Fermaint didn't turn 18 until after the season. His primary asset is his blazing speed. Clocked at 6.5 seconds in the 60-yard dash early last spring, he pulled a hamstring and slid until the fourth round of the draft. Injuries got him again in the Rookie-level Arizona League, where he hurt his shoulder diving for a ball in the outfield. He's raw, but his speed gives him the chance to be a top-notch base-stealer and center fielder. He must learn plate discipline to take full advantage of his quickness. Fermaint has a short stroke and could develop power as he matures. In the meantime, he's being encouraged to bunt and hit the ball on the ground more often. The Brewers like his athletic skills and believe he'll only improve with experience. Because he's so young and not advanced, he probably won't see full-season ball until 2005.

Year	Club (League)	Class	AVG	G	AB	R	H	2B	3B	HR	RBI	BB	SO	SB	SLG	OBP
2003	Brewers (AZL)	R	.300	25	100	16	30	3	3	1	9	3	19	6	.420	.327
MINOR LEAGUE TOTALS			.300	25	100	16	30	3	3	1	9	3	19	6	.420	.327

23 Gilberto Acosta, ss

Born: Oct. 5, 1982. **Ht.:** 6-1. **Wt.:** 150. **Bats:** B. **Throws:** R. **Career Transactions:** Signed out of Venezuela by Brewers, Aug. 7, 1999.

Acosta has moved slowly, spending two years each in the Rookie-level Dominican Summer and Arizona leagues, but scouts who saw him in 2003 liked his tools. He has good hands and a strong arm at short, though only average range at this point of his young career. Acosta has plus speed—he led the AZL with 30 steals while being caught just three times—and he puts the ball in play. He recognizes the importance of drawing walks and getting on base. The switch-hitting Acosta has little or no power, but that's not his game. His slight frame could use some filling out to get him through the daily grind of a full season. He'll move up to low Class A this year.

Year	Club (League)	Class	AVG	G	AB	R	H	2B	3B	HR	RBI	BB	SO	SB	SLG	OBP
2000	Brewers (DSL)	R	.279	26	86	16	24	2	0	2	13	10	11	5	.372	.361
2001	Brewers (DSL)	R	.230	70	248	38	57	9	2	0	35	34	31	16	.282	.332
2002	Brewers (AZL)	R	.315	50	184	38	58	9	2	0	25	26	29	4	.386	.415
2003	Brewers (AZL)	R	.349	50	189	43	66	8	4	1	26	20	30	30	.450	.413
MINOR LEAGUE TOTALS			.290	196	707	135	205	28	8	3	99	90	101	55	.365	.379

24 Jeff Bennett, rhp

Born: June 10, 1980. **Ht.:** 6-3. **Wt.:** 200. **Bats:** R. **Throws:** R. **School:** Gordonsville (Tenn.) HS. **Career Transactions:** Selected by Pirates in 19th round of 1998 draft; signed June 4, 1998 . . . Selected by Brewers from Pirates in Rule 5 major league draft, Dec. 15, 2003.

Bennett gained little recognition as a prospect in his first five seasons in the Pirates system, repeating both the Rookie and high Class A levels. His career took off last season when Pittsburgh switched him from starter to reliever. He pitched well in Double-A, and though he struggled in Triple-A the Brewers still saw enough to take him in the major league Rule 5 draft in December. He has to stick on Milwaukee's 25-man roster all season, or else clear waivers and be offered back to the Pirates for half the $50,000 draft price. Relieving agrees with Bennett because he can throw harder in short bursts instead of worrying about pacing himself. Bennett's fastball jumped from 90 to 95 mph in the bullpen, giving him the out pitch he lacked as starter. He also throws a good slider that prevents hitters from sitting on his fastball, though he didn't use it enough after making the jump to the Pacific Coast League. It wasn't a surprise that Pittsburgh lost him in the Rule 5 draft, though there's some concern that he had a sore shoulder in the Arizona Fall League. Considering how hard he now throws, it's not out of the question that Bennett eventually could emerge as a closer.

Year	Club (League)	Class	W	L	ERA	G	GS	CG	SV	IP	H	R	ER	HR	BB	SO	AVG
1998	Pirates (GCL)	R	2	4	4.63	13	11	0	0	47	50	29	24	4	13	18	.265
1999	Pirates (GCL)	R	3	4	4.23	8	8	0	0	45	53	27	21	1	9	28	.296
	Hickory (SAL)	A	2	2	5.91	8	6	0	0	35	48	25	23	5	9	16	.322
2000	Hickory (SAL)	A	10	13	4.40	27	27	1	0	172	189	116	84	14	47	126	.276
2001	Lynchburg (Car)	A	11	10	3.42	25	25	2	0	166	171	78	63	14	30	98	.268
	Altoona (EL)	AA	0	1	3.86	1	1	0	0	7	9	3	3	0	2	6	.300
2002	Lynchburg (Car)	A	10	6	3.62	24	20	0	0	124	137	64	50	7	30	90	.280
2003	Altoona (EL)	AA	4	4	2.72	33	2	0	1	60	45	22	18	2	23	62	.201
	Nashville (PCL)	AAA	1	3	6.56	9	5	0	0	23	26	21	17	4	12	16	.277
MINOR LEAGUE TOTALS			43	47	4.02	148	105	3	1	678	728	385	303	51	175	460	.272

25 Steve Moss, of

Born: Jan. 12, 1984. **Ht.:** 6-2. **Wt.:** 180. **Bats:** R. **Throws:** R. **School:** Notre Dame HS, Sherman Oaks, Calif. **Career Transactions:** Selected by Brewers in 29th round of 2002 draft; signed July 13, 2002.

Moss plummeted in the 2002 draft because he had an ankle injury and a strong commitment to UCLA, so the Brewers think they may have gotten a steal when they landed him in the 29th round. Milwaukee didn't get to see much of Moss last year because he dislocated his left shoulder diving for a ball in the outfield. Though his aggressive nature led to the injury, it's also one of the attributes that makes him a potentially special player. Moss has a nice, short stroke and good patience at the plate. He needs to make better contact and develop more power. Though he has plus speed, he's still learning to read pitchers' moves and get good jumps on the bases. That's not a problem defensively, where he tracks the ball well and also shows a strong arm in center field. It would have been interesting to see how the Brewers would have aligned the Beloit outfield if Moss had been healthy when Anthony Gwynn arrived there. Moss could return to low Class A to begin 2004.

Year	Club (League)	Class	AVG	G	AB	R	H	2B	3B	HR	RBI	BB	SO	SB	SLG	OBP
2002	Brewers (AZL)	R	.292	30	106	20	31	8	2	1	20	22	32	3	.434	.414
	Ogden (Pio)	R	.500	5	8	3	4	2	1	0	3	1	1	0	1.000	.538
2003	Beloit (Mid)	A	.290	57	186	25	54	8	3	1	22	32	44	7	.382	.398
MINOR LEAGUE TOTALS			.297	92	300	48	89	18	6	2	45	55	77	10	.417	.409

26 Greg Kloosterman, lhp

Born: June 21, 1982. **Ht.:** 6-3. **Wt.:** 205. **Bats:** L. **Throws:** L. **School:** Bethel (Ind.) College.
Career Transactions: Selected by Brewers in ninth round of 2003 draft; signed June 4, 2003.

Kloosterman was the 2003 National Christian College Athletic Association player of the year after a strong two-way performance at tiny Bethel (Ind.). He did more damage at the plate, batting .413 with 20 homers to set school records for single-season and career (40) homers, but the Brewers drafted him as a pitcher. Though he's strong and athletic, Milwaukee and other teams believed his future was on the mound after seeing his sharp curveball. It totally overmatched Rookie-level hitters. Kloosterman also throws an 85-90 mph fastball and a decent changeup. He has good command and consistent mechanics, especially for someone who divided his attention between hitting and pitching in college. The Brewers think Kloosterman will continue to get better as he focuses on pitching. As long as he has his killer curve, hitters can't sit on his fastball. He probably will start 2004 in low Class A.

Year	Club (League)	Class	W	L	ERA	G	GS	CG	SV	IP	H	R	ER	HR	BB	SO	AVG
2003	Helena (Pio)	R	6	1	3.28	14	14	0	0	69	68	28	25	4	23	76	.258
MINOR LEAGUE TOTALS			6	1	3.28	14	14	0	0	69	68	28	25	4	23	76	.258

27 Mike Adams, rhp

Born: July 29, 1978. **Ht.:** 6-5. **Wt.:** 190. **Bats:** R. **Throws:** R. **School:** Texas A&M University.
Career Transactions: Signed as nondrafted free agent by Brewers, May 15, 2001.

Adams looks more like a basketball player than a baseball player. Accordingly, he first went to Texas A&M-Kingsville as a two-sport athlete on a hoops scholarship. His basketball career was derailed by a broken ankle, and he signed as a fifth-year senior before the 2001 draft. Adams uses his tall, lanky frame and the torque from his long arms to generate a low-to mid-90s fastball and a tough slider. He has reached Double-A without minor league hitters able to catch up to him. They've batted .209 against him while he has averaged 11.0 strikeouts per nine innings. Adams closed out games in Double-A last year and has the durability to work multiple-inning stints and make an occasional start. At times his mechanics get out of whack and he suffers command problems, but for the most part Adams has thrown strikes with his two primary pitches. He'll get a chance to prove himself in Triple-A this year.

Year	Club (League)	Class	W	L	ERA	G	GS	CG	SV	IP	H	R	ER	HR	BB	SO	AVG
2001	Ogden (Pio)	R	2	2	2.81	23	0	0	12	32	26	10	10	4	6	44	.220
2002	Beloit (Mid)	A	0	0	2.93	11	0	0	5	15	13	6	5	1	2	21	.228
	High Desert (Cal)	A	2	1	2.57	10	0	0	5	14	9	6	4	2	7	23	.173
	Huntsville (SL)	AA	1	0	3.38	13	0	0	1	19	14	11	7	3	12	17	.209
2003	Huntsville (SL)	AA	3	7	3.15	45	2	0	14	74	58	30	26	6	33	83	.208
MINOR LEAGUE TOTALS			8	10	3.03	102	2	0	37	154	120	63	52	16	60	188	.209

28 Tommy Hawk, rhp

Born: Feb. 7, 1985. **Ht.:** 6-3. **Wt.:** 210. **Bats:** R. **Throws:** R. **School:** Cabrillo HS, Lompoc, Calif.
Career Transactions: Selected by Brewers in 17th round of 2003 draft; signed June 6, 2003.

Hawk could have gone as high as the sixth round in the 2003 draft if clubs thought they could sign him away from Cal State Fullerton. Milwaukee landed him as a 17th-rounder and he won the Arizona League ERA title in his pro debut. His fastball tops out at 93 mph but is more notable for its life than its velocity. He has a curveball that varies between good and too loopy, and he uses a splitter as a changeup. The Brewers liked his work ethic and competitiveness on the mound. Hawk is raw and has a somewhat violent delivery that could cause problems down the road. At this point, he simply needs innings and instruction. He'll likely open this year in low Class A.

Year	Club (League)	Class	W	L	ERA	G	GS	CG	SV	IP	H	R	ER	HR	BB	SO	AVG
2003	Brewers (AZL)	R	2	1	2.31	12	6	0	0	47	47	17	12	3	17	30	.261
MINOR LEAGUE TOTALS			2	1	2.31	12	6	0	0	47	47	17	12	3	17	30	.261

29 Greg Bruso, rhp

Born: May 5, 1980. **Ht.:** 6-3. **Wt.:** 190. **Bats:** R. **Throws:** R. **School:** UC Davis. **Career Transactions:** Selected by Giants in 16th round of 2002 draft; signed June 10, 2002 . . . Traded by Giants to Brewers for 2B Eric Young, Aug. 19, 2003.

Like Tommy Hawk, Bruso was a late-round pick who won an ERA title (in the short-season Northwest League) in his pro debut. When the Brewers traded Eric Young to the Giants last August, they were pleased to get Bruso in return. He already had reached Double-A by that point, and he performed well in the Southern League playoffs. His changeup is his out pitch, and he also throws a high-80s fastball and an adequate slider. He relies on hitting his spots and keeping batters off balance. While he pitched well in Double-A, he didn't miss many bats. Bruso projects more as a middle reliever than as a starter, but his acquisition helped Milwaukee accomplish one of its primary goals last year: to create more pitching depth. He could earn a spot in Triple-A with a strong spring training.

Year	Club (League)	Class	W	L	ERA	G	GS	CG	SV	IP	H	R	ER	HR	BB	SO	AVG
2002	Salem-Keizer (NWL)	A	4	3	1.99	14	13	0	0	81	58	23	18	5	17	78	.201
2003	San Jose (Cal)	A	7	5	3.11	14	13	1	0	84	69	34	29	5	11	77	.218
	Norwich (EL)	AA	5	4	3.42	11	11	2	0	76	72	32	29	6	11	45	.254
	Huntsville (SL)	AA	1	1	3.60	2	2	0	0	10	13	5	4	1	6	5	.351
MINOR LEAGUE TOTALS			17	13	2.86	41	39	3	0	252	212	94	80	17	45	205	.229

30 Jason Belcher, of

Born: Jan. 13, 1982. **Ht.:** 6-1. **Wt.:** 190. **Bats:** L. **Throws:** R. **School:** Walnut Ridge (Ark.) HS. **Career Transactions:** Selected by Brewers in fifth round of 2000 draft; signed June 30, 2000.

When the Brewers took Belcher in the 2000 draft, they had high hopes that he'd become the first quality catcher they had developed since B.J. Surhoff and David Nilsson. But he was so poor defensively—he threw out just four of 53 basestealers (8 percent) in low Class A in 2002—that they made him a full-time outfielder last year. The good news is that he continued to show promise with the bat. He has hit for average and shown a knack for getting on base throughout his pro career. He'll need to generate more power as a corner outfielder, however. Belcher also is a liability as an outfielder and might be best suited for DH. He broke his left wrist in an outfield misadventure, costing him the last six weeks of the season. The Brewers may push him to Double-A in 2004 to see how his bat responds.

Year	Club (League)	Class	AVG	G	AB	R	H	2B	3B	HR	RBI	BB	SO	SB	SLG	OBP
2000	Helena (Pio)	R	.333	46	162	30	54	18	2	4	36	20	25	3	.543	.403
2001	Beloit (Mid)	A	.326	38	144	23	47	6	0	2	23	15	16	0	.410	.394
2002	Beloit (Mid)	A	.261	98	348	44	91	19	0	6	38	45	42	3	.368	.348
2003	High Desert (Cal)	A	.320	91	350	43	112	23	3	5	54	26	35	4	.446	.370
MINOR LEAGUE TOTALS			.303	273	1004	140	304	66	5	17	151	106	118	10	.429	.371

MINNESOTA
TWINS

By Josh Boyd

After facing the possibility of contraction following the 2001 season, the Twins posted their first consecutive 90-win seasons in a decade. Contrary to commissioner Bud Selig's assertion that they were an aberration, they've become the model for small-market success. General manager Terry Ryan holds the blueprint. It starts and ends with scouting and player development, the lifeblood of the organization. Despite their recent turnaround, which has included consecutive American League Central titles, the Twins still deal with strict financial constraints. That puts more pressure on the farm system to have major league-ready talent on call. Minnesota doesn't have the payroll to keep its predominantly homegrown roster at home for long.

In one of the rare instances when the Twins were a factor in the trade market, Ryan sent Bobby Kielty to the Blue Jays for Shannon Stewart last July, sparking a second-half turnaround. But in order to retain Stewart as a free agent following the season, Minnesota couldn't re-sign Eddie Guardado and LaTroy Hawkins. They freed up more payroll by trading Eric Milton and A.J. Pierzynski.

Scouting director Mike Radcliff—one of the game's most respected evaluators—farm director Jim Rantz and their staffs have been up to the task, churning out enough big leaguers to keep pace with departing free agents. An impressive core of power pitching prospects waits in the wings to help replace Guardado and Hawkins in the bullpen. Joe Nathan, part of the Pierzynski trade with the Giants, could open the season as the closer. Their most anxiously awaited arrival, however, is 2003 Minor League Player of the Year Joe Mauer. He's the best prospect in the game and the best all-around catcher to come along since Pudge Rodriguez. His rapid development allowed the Twins to part with Pierzynski.

Minnesota will be able to add another haul of prospects in June, when they'll have four extra first-round picks as compensation for the loss of Guardado and Hawkins. Whether the Twins will be able to sign all those premium picks remains to be seen.

Beyond the draft, the Twins have been one of the most progressive organizations in scouting Australia, and have branched out into Europe and Africa. Australians Grant Balfour and Brad Thomas will be counted on to contribute to the pitching staff this season. Venezuela has also proven to be a fruitful scouting ground. Righthander Juan Rincon turned in a solid rookie campaign last year, while countryman Luis Rivas hasn't lived up to lofty expectations yet. The Twins have lacked a presence in the Dominican Republic, and are moving into the academy formerly operated by the Blue Jays and Diamondbacks.

TOP 30 PROSPECTS

1. Joe Mauer, c
2. Justin Morneau, 1b
3. Matt Moses, 3b
4. J.D. Durbin, rhp
5. Jesse Crain, rhp
6. Jason Bartlett, ss
7. Denard Span, of
8. Jason Kubel, of
9. Grant Balfour, rhp
10. Michael Restovich, of
11. Adam Harben, rhp
12. Alexander Smit, lhp
13. Alex Romero, of
14. Evan Meek, rhp
15. Errol Simonitsch, lhp
16. Lew Ford, of
17. Boof Bonser, rhp
18. Francisco Liriano, lhp
19. Scott Baker, rhp
20. Dave Shinskie, rhp
21. Scott Tyler, rhp
22. Colby Miller, rhp
23. Terry Tiffee, 3b
24. Rob Bowen, c
25. Michael Ryan, of
26. Luke Hughes, ss
27. Michael Rogers, lhp
28. Jose Morales, c
29. Trent Oeltjen, of
30. Johnny Woodard, 1b

ORGANIZATION
OVERVIEW

General manager: Terry Ryan. **Farm director:** Jim Rantz. **Scouting director:** Mike Radcliff.

2003 PERFORMANCE

Class	Team	League	W	L	Pct.	Finish*	Manager
Majors	Minnesota	American	90	72	.556	5th (14)	Ron Gardenhire
Triple-A	Rochester Red Wings	International	68	75	.476	9th (14)	Phil Roof
Double-A	New Britain Rock Cats	Eastern	73	68	.518	4th (12)	Stan Cliburn
High A	Fort Myers Miracle	Florida State	73	63	.537	5th (12)	Jose Marzan
Low A	Quad City River Bandits	Midwest	59	78	.431	14th (14)	Jeff Carter
Rookie	Elizabethton Twins	Appalachian	42	24	.636	+2nd (10)	Ray Smith
Rookie	GCL Twins	Gulf Coast	28	31	.475	7th (14)	Rudy Hernandez
OVERALL 2003 MINOR LEAGUE RECORD			343	339	.503	11th (30)	

*Finish in overall standings (No. of teams in league) +League champion

ORGANIZATION LEADERS

BATTING   *Minimum 250 At-Bats
*AVG	Joe Mauer, New Britain/Fort Myers	.338
R	Jason Bartlett, New Britain	96
H	Joe Mauer, New Britain/Fort Myers	172
TB	Jeff Deardorff, Rochester/New Britain	249
2B	Kevin West, New Britain	41
3B	Jason Bartlett, New Britain	8
	Trent Oeltjen, Quad City	8
HR	Justin Morneau, Rochester/New Britain	22
RBI	Terry Tiffee, New Britain	93
BB	Jason Bartlett, New Britain	58
SO	Jeff Deardorff, Rochester/New Britain	130
	Dusty Gomon, Quad City/Elizabethton	130
SB	Jason Bartlett, New Britain	41
*SLG	Justin Morneau, Rochester/New Britain	.526
*OBP	Joe Mauer, New Britain/Fort Myers	.398

PITCHING   #Minimum 75 Innings
W	J.D. Durbin, New Britain/Fort Myers	15
L	Scott Tyler, Quad City	12
#ERA	Jesse Crain, Roch./New Britain/Fort Myers	1.93
G	Beau Kemp, New Britain/Fort Myers	58
CG	Four tied at	2
SV	Beau Kemp, New Britain/Fort Myers	22
IP	J.D. Durbin, New Britain/Fort Myers	182
BB	Scott Tyler, Quad City	82
SO	J.D. Durbin, New Britain/Fort Myers	139

BEST TOOLS

Best Hitter for Average	Joe Mauer
Best Power Hitter	Justin Morneau
Fastest Baserunner	Denard Span
Best Athlete	Denard Span
Best Fastball	J.D. Durbin
Best Curveball	J.D. Durbin
Best Slider	Jesse Crain
Best Changeup	Julio DePaula
Best Control	Colby Miller
Best Defensive Catcher	Joe Mauer
Best Defensive Infielder	Jason Bartlett
Best Infield Arm	Omar Burgos
Best Defensive Outfielder	B.J. Garbe
Best Outfield Arm	Jason Kubel

PROJECTED 2007 LINEUP

Catcher	Joe Mauer
First Base	Doug Mientkiewicz
Second Base	Matt Moses
Third Base	Corey Koskie
Shortstop	Jason Bartlett
Left Field	Shannon Stewart
Center Field	Torii Hunter

Right Field	Michael Cuddyer
Designated Hitter	Justin Morneau
No. 1 Starter	Johan Santana
No. 2 Starter	Kyle Lohse
No. 3 Starter	J.D. Durbin
No. 4 Starter	Brad Radke
No. 5 Starter	Grant Balfour
Closer	Jesse Crain

LAST YEAR'S TOP 20 PROSPECTS

1. Joe Mauer, c
2. Justin Morneau, 1b
3. Michael Cuddyer, of
4. Michael Restovich, of
5. Denard Span, of
6. Scott Tyler, rhp
7. J.D. Durbin, rhp
8. Jason Kubel, of
9. Lew Ford, of
10. Adam Johnson, rhp
11. Dusty Gomon, 1b
12. Jesse Crain, rhp
13. Alex Romero, of
14. Matt Yeatman, rhp
15. Brad Thomas, lhp
16. Sandy Tejada, rhp
17. Beau Kemp, rhp
18. Trent Oeltjen, of
19. Grant Balfour, rhp
20. Matt Vorwald, rhp

TOP PROSPECTS OF THE DECADE

1994	Rich Becker, of
1995	LaTroy Hawkins, rhp
1996	Todd Walker, 2b
1997	Todd Walker, 2b
1998	Luis Rivas, ss
1999	Michael Cuddyer, 3b
2000	Michael Cuddyer, 3b
2001	Adam Johnson, rhp
2002	Joe Mauer, c
2003	Joe Mauer, c

TOP DRAFT PICKS OF THE DECADE

1994	Todd Walker, 2b
1995	Mark Redman, lhp
1996	*Travis Lee, 1b
1997	Michael Cuddyer, ss
1998	Ryan Mills, lhp
1999	B.J. Garbe, of
2000	Adam Johnson, rhp
2001	Joe Mauer, c
2002	Denard Span, of
2003	Matt Moses, 3b

*Did not sign.

ALL-TIME LARGEST BONUSES

Joe Mauer, 2001	$5,150,000
B.J. Garbe, 1999	$2,750,000
Adam Johnson, 2000	$2,500,000
Ryan Mills, 1998	$2,000,000
Michael Cuddyer, 1997	$1,850,000

MINOR LEAGUE
DEPTH CHART

MINNESOTA **TWINS**

RANK: **5**

Impact potential (A): Joe Mauer has been all the Twins hoped for when they decided to draft him with Mark Prior on the board in 2001. He and Justin Morneau will likely hit in the 3-4 holes for the Twins for the next decade. Matt Moses is a few years behind, but has a special bat that reminds some scouts of Hank Blalock.

Depth (A): Their last two draft hauls are loaded with potential. What has made Mike Radcliff and his scouting department so successful over the long haul is their ability to uncover mid-round gems, while establishing niches in Australia and Europe.

Sleeper: Adam Harben, rhp. *—Depth charts prepared by **Josh Boyd**. Numbers in parentheses indicate prospect rankings.*

LF
Michael Restovich (10)
Michael Ryan (25)
Trent Oeltjen (29)
Josh Rabe

CF
Denard Span (7)
Lew Ford (16)
James Tomlin
Javier Lopez

RF
Jason Kubel (8)
Alex Romero (13)
Kevin West
B.J. Garbe

3B
Matt Moses (3)
Terry Tiffee (23)

SS
Jason Bartlett (6)
Luke Hughes (26)

2B
Luis Rodriguez
Paul Rutgers
Luis Mata

1B
Justin Morneau (2)
Johnny Woodard (30)
Dusty Gomon
David Winfree

SOURCE OF TALENT

Homegrown		Acquired	
College	3	Trade	4
Junior College	3	Rule 5 draft	0
Draft-and-follow	1	Independent	0
High school	14	Free agent/waivers	0
Nondrafted free agent	0		
Foreign	5		

C
Joe Mauer (1)
Rob Bowen (24)
Jose Morales (28)
Kyle Phillips

RHP

Starters	Relievers
J.D. Durbin (4)	Jesse Crain (5)
Grant Balfour (9)	Pat Neshek
Adam Harben (11)	Brian Wolfe
Evan Meek (14)	Julio DePaula
Boof Bonser (17)	Travis Bowyer
Scott Baker (19)	Justin Olson
Dave Shinskie (20)	Mike Nakamura
Scott Tyler (21)	Jon Pridie
Colby Miller (22)	Adam Johnson
Angel Garcia	Kevin Cameron
Chris Schutt	
Josh Hill	
Matt Yeatman	
Sandy Tejada	
Henry Bonilla	

LHP

Starters	Relievers
Alexander Smit (12)	Brad Thomas
Errol Simonitsch (15)	Javier Martinez
Francisco Liriano (18)	Brent Hoard
Michael Rogers (27)	
Jason Miller	

DRAFT
ANALYSIS

Best Pro Debut: RHP Scott Baker (2) has command of four pitches. He debuted at low Class A and put up a 3-1, 2.49 record. RHP Chris Schutt (7) led the Rookie-level Appalachian League with 82 strikeouts in 55 innings and went 5-1, 1.98. LHP Errol Simonitsch (6) was just as effective at the same level, going 5-1, 1.76.

Best Athlete: LHP Michael Rogers (16) and Schutt pulled double duty as pitcher/center fielders before turning pro. Rogers would have been one of college baseball's top two-way players had the Twins not signed him away from Texas.

Best Pure Hitter: 3B Matt Moses (1) had one of the best bats in the high school ranks and hit .385 in a short stint in the Rookie-level Gulf Coast League. 1B Johnny Woodard (3) should hit for power and average.

Best Raw Power: 1B David Winfree (13) has a strong body and power swing, but went just 9-for-70 (.129) in the GCL.

Fastest Runner: OF John Rumsey (41) is a 60 runner on the 20-80 scouting scale.

Best Defensive Player: SS Patrick Ortiz (24) makes all the plays, though he hit just .208 in the GCL.

Best Fastball: Baker's fastball runs from 88-93 mph and sits at 90, but is an above-average pitch because it features so much life. Draft-and-follow RHP Evan Meek (11 in 2002) can reach 96 mph.

Baker — JOHN SPEAR

Best Breaking Ball: Schutt's slider and Rogers' curveball have the most potential.

Most Intriguing Background: A routine physical revealed that Moses had a tiny hole in his heart, but he's fine and feeling better than ever after a 20-minute operation. C Gregory Najac (20) may be the first player ever selected out of Belgium. His father is in the U.S. Air Force; Najac was draft-eligible because he began his high school career in New York. RHP David Shinskie (4) and C Eli Tintor (18) would have been college quarterbacks at Delaware and Minnesota-Duluth had they not turned pro. Tintor's father Rick works for the Twins as an associate scout and was GM Terry Ryan's catcher in Class A.

Closest To The Majors: Baker, Simonitsch and Schutt, in that order.

Best Late-Round Pick: If Rogers were taller (he's 6 feet), he could have been a first-rounder. Both he and Winfree exceeded recommended bonuses for their rounds.

The One Who Got Away: SS Brandon McArthur (5) has a chance to have average tools across the board with plus offensive potential. He's at the University of Florida.

Assessment: Moses evokes 1997 Minnesota first-rounder Michael Cuddyer. He and Baker were a nice start to the Twins' draft, which received a significant boost when they decided to pay extra for Rogers.

RHP Jesse Crain (2) could be closing games for the Twins this year. OF Denard Span (1) and RHPs Adam Harben (15) and Evan Meek (11, draft-and-follow) also rank among the organization's best prospects. So would C Jeff Clement (12), LHP Ryan Schreppel (20), RHPs Garrett Mock (14) and Mark Sauls (3), OF Clete Thomas (5) and 1B Adam Lind (8)—had they signed.

Sure, Minnesota passed on Mark Prior with the No. 1 overall pick and did little after making that choice. But C Joe Mauer (1) rates a top grade all by himself.

RHP J.D. Durbin (2) is nearly ready for the majors, while OF Jason Kubel (12) is one of the game's unsung prospects. They've surpassed RHP Adam Johnson (1), and the Twins failed to sign their other first-rounder, RHP Aaron Heilman.

OF B.J. Garbe (1) hit .178 in Double-A last year, but Minnesota did find an offensive force in 1B Justin Morneau (3). OF Ricky Manning (22) signed and became a star—though as a cornerback for the Carolina Panthers.

—Draft analysis prepared by Jim Callis. Numbers in parentheses indicate draft rounds.

Joe Mauer

Born: April 19, 1983.
Ht.: 6-4. **Wt.:** 220.
Bats: L. **Throws:** R.
School: Cretin-Derham Hall, St. Paul, Minn.

Career Transactions: Selected by Twins in first round (first overall) of 2001 draft; signed July 17, 2001.

G rowing up in St. Paul as a Twins fan just 10 minutes from the Metrodome, Mauer seemed destined to play for the hometown team. He had options coming out of high school in 2001, however. Mauer was regarded as one of the top quarterback recruits in the nation and nearly followed fellow Cretin-Derham Hall grad Chris Weinke to Florida State. Twins scouts saw Mauer play more than 100 times as an amateur, and ultimately chose him over Mark Prior with the No. 1 overall pick in the draft. While Prior already has become a star in the majors, Mauer isn't too far behind. He won BA's Minor League Player of the Year award in 2003 and is set to make his big league debut at 20 when he opens this season as Minnesota's regular catcher. His .338 average led all minor league catchers last season. Mauer was a member of the U.S. team that fell short of the Olympic qualifying tournament, though he was inexplicably left out of the starting lineup in the deciding game against Mexico. His older brothers Jake, a second baseman, and Bill, a righthander, also are Minnesota farmhands.

Mauer combines a picture-perfect lefthanded stroke with impeccable strike-zone judgment to generate high batting averages and on-base percentages. His natural approach and swing path lend themselves more to a batting title than a home run crown. He's geared to hit line drives back up the middle and toward left-center. Defensively, Mauer had no equals at the minor league level. Some scouts say he'll be the best receiver in the American League when he debuts in April. Despite his size—only Sandy Alomar Jr. is bigger among major league catchers—Mauer is an expert at blocking pitches with his soft hands and moves quickly on balls in front of the plate. Outstanding arm strength gives him a third present 80 tool on the 20-80 scouting scale to go with his bat and his defensive ability. Mauer has a quick release and consistently puts his throws on the bag with uncanny accuracy, which led to him nabbing 52 percent of basestealers last year. He's a quiet leader who exudes confidence but maintains a low profile. The Twins wanted Mauer to become more comfortable at running a pitching staff, and he did just that. He runs better and has more athleticism than most catchers. Mauer really doesn't have any weaknesses. He has just nine homers in 277 pro games, though Twins scouts insist he has the power to one day hit 35-40 in a season if he wants to. He may add more loft to his swing as he develops, and showed signs of doing that in Double-A.

Most scouts give Mauer the nod over Devil Rays shortstop B.J. Upton as the best prospect in the game. The Twins cleared Mauer's path to the majors by dealing all-star A.J. Pierzynski to the Giants in November. Mauer, who will bat seventh or eighth to start 2004, is an early favorite for American League rookie of the year. There's no reason he shouldn't develop into a perennial all-star.

Year	Club (League)	Class	AVG	G	AB	R	H	2B	3B	HR	RBI	BB	SO	SB	SLG	OBP
2001	Elizabethton (Appy)	R	.400	32	110	14	44	6	2	0	14	19	10	4	.491	.492
2002	Quad City (Mid)	A	.302	110	411	58	124	23	1	4	62	61	42	0	.392	.393
2003	Fort Myers (FSL)	A	.335	62	233	25	78	13	1	1	44	24	24	3	.412	.395
	New Britain (EL)	AA	.341	73	276	48	94	17	1	4	41	25	25	0	.453	.400
MINOR LEAGUE TOTALS			.330	277	1030	145	340	59	5	9	161	129	101	7	.423	.406

2 Justin Morneau, 1b

Born: May 15, 1981. **Ht.:** 6-4. **Wt.:** 220. **Bats:** L. **Throws:** R. **School:** New Westminster (B.C.) SS. **Career Transactions:** Selected by Twins in third round of 1999 draft; signed June 17, 1999.

Morneau has been hobbled by various injuries in each of his five seasons since originally signing as a catcher in 1999. The most serious was an intestinal virus that caused him to drop 20 pounds before the 2002 season, but last year's broken toe couldn't stop him from hitting a team-high .429 in spring training. He batted .400 with five homers in six games to lead Canada to second place at the Olympic qualifying tournament in November, earning a spot in the 2004 Athens Games. Morneau has legitimate power with a classic finish and natural loft to his swing. He generates easy pop and has the plus bat speed to drive good fastballs. Morneau struggled with offspeed stuff in the big leagues and will have to adjust. Strong defense has been a signature of the Twins over the last two seasons, but Morneau will be just adequate at first base despite working hard to improve. Morneau is likely to start the year at Triple-A Rochester, but should get at least 200-250 at-bats for the Twins between first base and DH. He should wrest the first-base job from Doug Mientkiewicz and bat cleanup for Minnesota in 2005.

Year	Club (League)	Class	AVG	G	AB	R	H	2B	3B	HR	RBI	BB	SO	SB	SLG	OBP
1999	Twins (GCL)	R	.302	17	53	3	16	5	0	0	9	2	6	0	.396	.333
2000	Twins (GCL)	R	.402	52	194	47	78	21	0	10	58	30	18	3	.665	.478
	Elizabethton (Appy)	R	.217	6	23	4	5	0	0	1	3	1	6	0	.348	.250
2001	Quad City (Mid)	A	.356	64	236	50	84	17	2	12	53	26	38	0	.597	.420
	Fort Myers (FSL)	A	.294	53	197	25	58	10	3	4	40	24	41	0	.437	.385
	New Britain (EL)	AA	.158	10	38	3	6	1	0	0	4	3	8	0	.184	.214
2002	New Britain (EL)	AA	.298	126	494	72	147	31	4	16	80	42	88	7	.474	.356
2003	New Britain (EL)	AA	.329	20	79	14	26	3	1	6	13	7	14	0	.620	.384
	Rochester (IL)	AAA	.268	71	265	39	71	11	1	16	42	28	56	0	.498	.344
	Minnesota (AL)	MAJ	.226	40	106	14	24	4	0	4	16	9	30	0	.377	.287
MAJOR LEAGUE TOTALS			.226	40	106	14	24	4	0	4	16	9	30	0	.377	.287
MINOR LEAGUE TOTALS			.311	419	1579	257	491	99	11	65	302	163	275	10	.511	.379

3 Matt Moses, 3b

Born: Feb. 20, 1985. **Ht.:** 6-0. **Wt.:** 210. **Bats:** L. **Throws:** R. **School:** Mills Godwin HS, Richmond, Va. **Career Transactions:** Selected by Twins in first round (21st overall) of 2003 draft; signed July 9, 2003.

Moses rated as one of the best pure hitters among 2003 high school draftees. A routine physical after he agreed to a $1.45 million bonus revealed an irregularity in his heart. A 20-minute procedure patched a tiny hole and has permitted him to proceed with his career without concern. Moses consistently hits the ball squarely thanks to a sound, compact swing. Scouts liken him to Hank Blalock, and the Twins say Moses has all the components at the plate to develop power and move on the fast track in a similar fashion. Because he's a baseball rat who loves to hit, he has advanced pitch recognition and solid plate discipline. A shortstop in high school, Moses was announced as a third baseman on draft day. He has impressed Minnesota by putting in extra work to improve defensively, but he's still fringe-average in the field. His arm is average at best, and his throwing mechanics are inconsistent, leading to erratic throws. He has below-average speed. Moses will move to low Class A Quad City this season. His bat is going to be special, and he should have little difficulty adjusting to pitchers at each level.

Year	Club (League)	Class	AVG	G	AB	R	H	2B	3B	HR	RBI	BB	SO	SB	SLG	OBP
2003	Twins (GCL)	R	.385	18	65	6	25	5	1	0	11	5	9	0	.492	.417
MINOR LEAGUE TOTALS			.385	18	65	6	25	5	1	0	11	5	9	0	.492	.417

4 J.D. Durbin, rhp

Born: Feb. 24, 1982. **Ht.:** 6-0. **Wt.:** 190. **Bats:** R. **Throws:** R. **School:** Coronado HS, Scottsdale, Ariz. **Career Transactions:** Selected by Twins in second round of 2000 draft; signed July 18, 2000.

Nicknamed "Real Deal," Durbin oozes confidence and personality. He was a two-way star in high school and also was recruited as a wide receiver. He made two scoreless appearances in relief for Team USA at the Olympic qualifying tournament. Durbin attacks hitters with a 94-95 mph fastball, which he can maintain deep into games, and a pair of deadly breaking balls. He uses a slurvy-breaking curveball, keeping his 87 mph slider in reserve. With a compact yet full-effort delivery, he's able to repeat his mechanics and fill the strike zone with quality offerings. Some scouts doubt Durbin's size and delivery will hold up in a starting role. He must continue to establish his changeup and build confidence in the pitch. More often than not, it comes in as a batting-practice fastball and gets crushed. He has to stay on top of his pitches to avoid flattening them out. Durbin likely will be the Opening Day starter in Triple-A. He should make his big league debut in 2004, and the lack of a clear-cut closer in Minnesota could present an opportunity for him.

Year	Club (League)	Class	W	L	ERA	G	GS	CG	SV	IP	H	R	ER	HR	BB	SO	AVG
2000	Twins (GCL)	R	0	0	0.00	2	0	0	0	2	2	0	0	0	0	4	.222
2001	Elizabethton (Appy)	R	3	2	1.87	8	7	0	0	34	23	13	7	2	17	39	.190
2002	Quad City (Mid)	A	13	4	3.19	27	27	0	0	161	144	66	57	14	51	163	.239
2003	Fort Myers (FSL)	A	9	2	3.09	14	14	0	0	87	73	35	30	3	22	69	.224
	New Britain (EL)	AA	6	3	3.14	14	14	2	0	95	102	39	33	10	29	70	.278
MINOR LEAGUE TOTALS			31	11	3.02	65	62	2	0	379	344	153	127	29	119	345	.241

5 Jesse Crain, rhp

Born: July 5, 1981. **Ht.:** 6-1. **Wt.:** 200. **Bats:** R. **Throws:** R. **School:** University of Houston. **Career Transactions:** Selected by Twins in second round of 2002 draft; signed July 13, 2002.

Crain preceded Reds top prospect Ryan Wagner as the closer at Houston, where he was an All-America shortstop/reliever in 2002. He didn't allow an earned run until his final appearance of his junior season, and has been nearly as stingy as a pro. He also participated in the Olympic qualifying tournament, working three scoreless innings for Team USA. Like Wagner, Crain dominates hitters with two plus-plus pitches, and his fastball is a couple of ticks better than Wagner's. Crain tops out at 96 mph and usually deals at 92-94. His slider is a true strikeout pitch with vicious, late break. He repeats his delivery, throws strikes and manages to get good leverage despite his stature. Crain needs to be more consistent at driving the ball down in the zone. His changeup is just usable, but he doesn't need it. There's no question Crain is going to get the ball with the game on the line. The only question is whether he'll be a premium set-up man or a quality closer. The Twins believe he's capable of either and could give him save opportunities this season.

Year	Club (League)	Class	W	L	ERA	G	GS	CG	SV	IP	H	R	ER	HR	BB	SO	AVG
2002	Elizabethton (Appy)	R	2	1	0.57	9	0	0	2	16	4	2	1	0	7	18	.082
	Quad City (Mid)	A	1	1	1.50	9	0	0	1	12	6	3	2	0	4	11	.154
2003	Fort Myers (FSL)	A	2	1	2.84	10	0	0	0	19	10	6	6	0	5	25	.154
	New Britain (EL)	AA	1	1	0.69	22	0	0	9	39	13	4	3	0	10	56	.099
	Rochester (IL)	AAA	3	1	3.12	23	0	0	10	26	24	10	9	0	10	33	.245
MINOR LEAGUE TOTALS			9	5	1.69	73	0	0	22	112	57	25	21	0	36	143	.149

6 Jason Bartlett, ss

Born: Oct. 30, 1979. **Ht.:** 6-0. **Wt.:** 170. **Bats:** R. **Throws:** R. **School:** University of Oklahoma. **Career Transactions:** Selected by Padres in 13th round of 2001 draft; signed June 14, 2001 . . . Traded by Padres to Twins for OF Brian Buchanan, July 12, 2002.

Since the Twins traded for Cristian Guzman and developed Luis Rivas, their system has had a gaping hole in the middle infield. They addressed it in July 2002 by trading Brian Buchanan to the Padres for Bartlett, who has exceeded their expectations. While Twins scout John Leavitt projected Bartlett as an everyday big league shortstop, Minnesota would have been content with a utility infielder in the mold of Denny Hocking. Bartlett turns in quality at-bat after quality at-bat. He protects the plate well with quick hands and good bat control. While his tools aren't overwhelming in the middle of the diamond, he has the arm to make strong, accurate throws from the hole and enough range to both sides. Though Bartlett has proven to be a table-setter, he doesn't project to make much of an impact with his bat. A tick above-average as a runner, he led the system in steals but needs to improve his jumps and technique. He topped the minors by getting caught 24 times last year. Guzman's tenure as Minnesota's shortstop likely will run out when his contract ends after 2004. After a full season in Triple-A, Bartlett is his heir apparent.

Year	Club (League)	Class	AVG	G	AB	R	H	2B	3B	HR	RBI	BB	SO	SB	SLG	OBP
2001	Eugene (NWL)	A	.300	68	267	49	80	12	4	3	37	28	47	12	.408	.371
2002	Lake Elsinore (Cal)	A	.250	75	308	57	77	14	4	1	33	32	53	24	.331	.329
	Fort Myers (FSL)	A	.262	39	145	24	38	7	0	2	9	17	24	11	.352	.341
2003	New Britain (EL)	AA	.296	139	548	96	162	31	8	8	48	58	67	41	.425	.380
MINOR LEAGUE TOTALS			.282	321	1268	226	357	64	16	14	127	135	191	88	.390	.361

7 Denard Span, of

STEVE MOORE

Born: Feb. 27, 1984. **Ht.:** 6-1. **Wt.:** 180. **Bats:** L. **Throws:** L. **School:** Tampa Catholic HS. **Career Transactions:** Selected by Twins in first round (20th overall) of 2002 draft; signed Aug. 15, 2002.

Span helped Tampa Catholic win the Florida 3-A title as a junior after transferring from Hillsborough High (home of Carl Everett, Dwight Gooden and Gary Sheffield). Also a star wide receiver, he almost went ninth overall in 2002 until predraft negotiations broke down with the Rockies. The Twins took him 20th and signed him for $1.7 million until late in the summer, delaying his pro debut until last June. Span is the fastest player in the system and has impact basestealing potential, though nagging ankle and leg injuries hampered him in 2003. He made encouraging strides in honing his leadoff skills. He shortened his stroke and cut down some of his natural uppercut, which improved his ability to hit grounders to the left side and let his speed turn them into singles. Span is still unrefined in most aspects of the game. His speed disguises many of his mistakes in the outfield, and his arm is below-average. His new approach at the plate isn't conducive to power, though the Twins say he'll learn to drive the ball to the gaps as he matures. The Twins understand Span will need time to develop into a premium leadoff man. He'll play in low Class A this season and likely will need a full year at each level.

Year	Club (League)	Class	AVG	G	AB	R	H	2B	3B	HR	RBI	BB	SO	SB	SLG	OBP
2003	Elizabethton (Appy)	R	.271	50	207	34	56	5	1	1	18	23	34	14	.319	.355
MINOR LEAGUE TOTALS			.271	50	207	34	56	5	1	1	18	23	34	14	.319	.355

8 Jason Kubel, of

RODGER WOOD

Born: May 25, 1982. **Ht.:** 5-11. **Wt.:** 190. **Bats:** L. **Throws:** R. **School:** Highland HS, Palmdale, Calif. **Career Transactions:** Selected by Twins in 12th round of 2000 draft; signed June 13, 2000.

Like many things the Twins do, Kubel has remained under the radar despite a productive start to his young career. He tied for second in RBIs and finished fourth in hitting in the high Class A Florida State League last year. He has been an all-star in each of his two full seasons. Kubel has a professional approach at the plate. He understands the strike zone and doesn't chase bad pitches. He displays pop to the opposite field with good leverage and finish to his quick, compact stroke. He hits lefties (.306) and righties (.294) alike. He has prototypical right-field arm strength and is a solid-average outfielder. Kubel's slugging percentage dropped from .521 in low Class A to .400 last year in the pitcher-friendly FSL. Selectively aggressive, he needs to make more quality contact to tap into his raw power. A below-average runner, he won't be a threat on the bases. Equipped with a strong, compact body, Kubel profiles as a poor man's Brian Giles. He's on the verge of a breakout season and will be Double-A New Britain's everyday right fielder in 2004.

Year	Club (League)	Class	AVG	G	AB	R	H	2B	3B	HR	RBI	BB	SO	SB	SLG	OBP
2000	Twins (GCL)	R	.282	23	78	17	22	3	2	0	13	10	9	0	.372	.367
2001	Twins (GCL)	R	.331	37	124	14	41	10	4	1	30	19	14	3	.500	.422
2002	Quad City (Mid)	A	.321	115	424	60	136	26	4	17	69	41	48	3	.521	.380
2003	Fort Myers (FSL)	A	.298	116	420	56	125	20	4	5	82	48	54	4	.400	.361
MINOR LEAGUE TOTALS			.310	291	1046	147	324	59	14	23	194	118	125	10	.459	.376

9 Grant Balfour, rhp

Born: Dec. 30, 1977. **Ht.:** 6-2. **Wt.:** 190. **Bats:** R. **Throws:** R. **Career Transactions:** Signed out of Australia by Twins, Jan. 19, 1997.

The Twins have been one of the pioneers in scouting Australia, and Balfour and lefty Brad Thomas will pay the first dividends. After moving to the bullpen in mid-2000, the same year he pitched in the Olympics, Balfour filled a hole in the Rochester rotation last June. It was scheduled to be a brief stay, but he flourished and found a new role. Balfour operates with a lightning-quick arm and fills the strike zone with four pitches. He relied on his 91-94 mph fastball and his slider out of the bullpen. As a starter, he dusted off his curveball, which emerged as his best pitch, and a dependable changeup. He also has enough stamina to maintain his peak velocity deep into starts. There were doubts about how Balfour would hold up, even as a reliever, because of his slender build. The same concerns still apply because he never has worked more than 97 innings in a season. His control was a little shaky in the majors last year. The Twins hope Balfour can handle the No. 4 slot in their rotation. If he can't, he can fall back on a career in relief.

Year	Club (League)	Class	W	L	ERA	G	GS	CG	SV	IP	H	R	ER	HR	BB	SO	AVG
1997	Twins (GCL)	R	2	4	3.76	13	12	0	0	67	73	31	28	1	20	43	.292
1998	Elizabethton (Appy)	R	7	2	3.36	13	13	0	0	78	70	36	29	7	27	75	.240
1999	Quad City (Mid)	A	8	5	3.53	19	14	0	1	92	66	39	36	7	37	95	.204
2000	Fort Myers (FSL)	A	8	5	4.25	35	10	0	6	89	91	46	42	8	34	90	.263
2001	New Britain (EL)	AA	2	1	1.08	35	0	0	13	50	26	6	6	1	22	72	.149
	Minnesota (AL)	MAJ	0	0	13.50	2	0	0	0	3	3	4	4	2	3	2	.333
	Edmonton (PCL)	AAA	2	2	5.51	11	0	0	0	16	18	11	10	2	10	17	.305
2002	Edmonton (PCL)	AAA	2	4	4.16	58	0	0	8	71	60	34	33	3	30	88	.231
2003	Rochester (IL)	AAA	5	2	2.41	21	11	0	5	71	48	21	19	6	16	87	.188
	Minnesota (AL)	MAJ	1	0	4.15	17	1	0	0	26	23	12	12	4	14	30	.235
MAJOR LEAGUE TOTALS			1	0	5.02	19	1	0	0	29	26	16	16	6	17	32	.243
MINOR LEAGUE TOTALS			36	25	3.42	205	60	0	33	534	452	224	203	35	196	567	.231

10 Michael Restovich, of

Born: Jan. 3, 1979. **Ht.:** 6-4. **Wt.:** 240. **Bats:** R. **Throws:** R. **School:** Mayo HS, Rochester, Minn. **Career Transactions:** Selected by Twins in second round of 1997 draft; signed Aug. 15, 1997.

Restovich ranked in the top five on this list from 1999-2003, but he took a step in the wrong direction when he repeated Triple-A last year. Though he hit .283 in a brief stay in Minnesota, the Twins were disappointed with his lack of power and sent him to winter ball in Puerto Rico, where his manager was Twins bench coach Steve Liddle. Restovich's raw power is his calling card. He can hit fastballs a mile with his fluid, direct swing. He concentrated on making consistent contact and hitting the ball to right field last year. While he showed versatility with his new approach, Restovich needs to hit the ball out of the park and be a run producer. That won't happen by inside-outing balls to the opposite field. His strikeout rates have risen as he has advanced. He's just adequate as a baserunner and corner outfielder. This is a pivotal year in Restovich's career. With a crowded outfield in Minnesota, he appears headed for a third straight year in Triple-A. The Twins have turned down several trade inquiries for him, but a change of scenery might be best at this point.

Year	Club (League)	Class	AVG	G	AB	R	H	2B	3B	HR	RBI	BB	SO	SB	SLG	OBP
1998	Elizabethton (Appy)	R	.355	65	242	68	86	20	1	13	64	54	58	5	.607	.489
	Fort Wayne (Mid)	A	.444	11	45	9	20	5	2	0	6	4	12	0	.644	.490
1999	Quad City (Mid)	A	.312	131	493	91	154	30	6	19	107	74	100	7	.513	.412
2000	Fort Myers (FSL)	A	.263	135	475	73	125	27	9	8	64	61	100	19	.408	.350
2001	New Britain (EL)	AA	.269	140	501	69	135	33	4	23	84	54	125	15	.489	.345
2002	Edmonton (PCL)	AAA	.286	138	518	95	148	32	7	29	98	53	151	11	.542	.353
	Minnesota (AL)	MAJ	.308	8	13	3	4	0	0	1	1	1	4	1	.538	.357
2003	Rochester (IL)	AAA	.275	119	454	75	125	34	2	16	72	47	117	10	.465	.346
	Minnesota (AL)	MAJ	.283	24	53	10	15	3	2	0	4	10	12	0	.415	.406
MAJOR LEAGUE TOTALS			.288	32	66	13	19	3	2	1	5	11	16	1	.439	.397
MINOR LEAGUE TOTALS			.291	739	2728	480	793	181	31	108	495	347	663	67	.499	.376

11 Adam Harben, rhp

Born: Aug. 19, 1983. **Ht.:** 6-5. **Wt.:** 210. **Bats:** R. **Throws:** R. **School:** Westark (Ark.) CC. **Career Transactions:** Selected by Twins in 15th round of 2002 draft; signed July 10, 2002.

Harben was drafted in the 38th round by the Tigers in 2001 out of Central Arkansas Christian High, the same school that produced A.J. Burnett six years earlier. Instead of signing, Harben went to Westark, where he roomed with Minnesota manager Ron Gardenhire's son Toby. Area scout Gregg Miller did a good job following Harben and tabbing him in the 15th round, while Toby Gardenhire served as something of a bird-dog scout. When questions about Harben's makeup came up, Gardenhire was able to provide the Twins with inside info to confirm Miller's reports. Harben has shown nothing but solid work ethic since signing and has exceeded expectations as a mid-round pick. His arm works free and easy, pumping 91-95 mph fastballs on a downhill plane. Gangly but athletic, he throws a good slider and is developing a solid changeup with late fade. The Twins projected him as more of a reliever, but Harben refined his mechanics and improved his conditioning. He benefited from more drive from his lower half. His mechanics and command need to become more consistent. He didn't miss as many bats as he should with his stuff because he doesn't locate his pitches well. Harben will pitch in the rotation at high Class A Fort Myers this year.

Year	Club (League)	Class	W	L	ERA	G	GS	CG	SV	IP	H	R	ER	HR	BB	SO	AVG
2002	Twins (GCL)	R	4	1	3.20	12	3	0	0	25	27	11	9	0	8	27	.270
2003	Quad City (Mid)	A	5	6	4.33	16	15	0	0	87	91	54	42	5	35	77	.259
MINOR LEAGUE TOTALS			9	7	4.07	28	18	0	0	113	118	65	51	5	43	104	.261

12 Alexander Smit, lhp

Born: Oct. 2, 1985. **Ht.:** 6-3. **Wt.:** 190. **Bats:** L. **Throws:** L. **Career Transactions:** Signed out of Netherlands by Twins, July 14, 2002.

The Twins don't usually get involved in high-stakes bidding on the international market, but they didn't want to let Smit get away and signed him for $800,000. The first time Twins scout Howard Norsetter saw him, he was a 13-year-old first baseman. He has come a long way since then and was named the top junior (16-18 years old) pitcher in the Netherlands in 2001 and 2002. He made a promising pro debut in the Rookie-level Gulf Coast League last summer, taking a break in July to pitch Holland to an Olympic berth. Though at 18 he's the equivalent of a high school senior, Smit could be the ace of the Dutch national team at the Athens Games. Smit topped out at 92 mph last year and there's more velocity in his slender frame. His fastball regularly sits at 86-90 mph, and he already can repeat his clean delivery on a consistent basis. Smit dominated the GCL, primarily with two pitches. His changeup is advanced, but the Twins would like to seem him incorporate his knuckle-curve into his mix more often. His breaking ball is inconsistent, but they were encouraged by the progress he made with it. He also will need to throw more strikes against more advanced hitters. Smit has a ceiling of a No. 2 or 3 starter, and Minnesota believes he can handle a jump to low Class A to start the season.

Year	Club (League)	Class	W	L	ERA	G	GS	CG	SV	IP	H	R	ER	HR	BB	SO	AVG
2003	Twins (GCL)	R	3	0	1.18	8	7	0	0	38	19	8	5	0	20	40	.156
MINOR LEAGUE TOTALS			3	0	1.18	8	7	0	0	38	19	8	5	0	20	40	.156

13 Alex Romero, of

Born: Sept. 9, 1983. **Ht.:** 6-0. **Wt.:** 170. **Bats:** B. **Throws:** R. **Career Transactions:** Signed out of Venezuela by Twins, July 2, 2000.

Romero finished fifth in the Rookie-level Venezuelan Summer League batting race in his pro debut, hitting .347 as a third baseman. He moved to the outfield when he came to the United States and has continued to impress over the last two years. It took Romero a while in 2003 to get acclimated to the low Class A Midwest League, his first experience playing in cold weather, but he rebounded after hitting .149 in April. When he signed he was more of a slashing-style hitter, but he since has added strength and thickness to his frame, helping him to drive the ball with more regularity. Because he has such a good idea of the strike zone, he has an advantage over many of his peers. There's still a wide range of opinion within the organization on Romero's potential, however. The question is where he profiles, as he isn't a pure center fielder and doesn't have the juice to start on a corner. He does display good instincts in the outfield and his routes are already more direct to the ball than Denard Span's. Romero has a solid-average arm and plus speed. Romero was one of the top rookies in the Venezuelan winter league, and he should step forward as he moves up to high Class A in 2004.

Year	Club (League)	Class	AVG	G	AB	R	H	2B	3B	HR	RBI	BB	SO	SB	SLG	OBP
2001	San Joaquin (VSL)	R	.347	49	167	22	58	9	0	2	30	11	9	10	.437	.388
2002	Twins (GCL)	R	.333	56	186	31	62	13	2	2	42	29	14	16	.457	.423
2003	Quad City (Mid)	A	.296	120	423	50	125	16	3	4	40	43	43	11	.376	.359
MINOR LEAGUE TOTALS			.316	225	776	103	245	38	5	8	112	83	66	37	.409	.381

14 Evan Meek, rhp

Born: May 12, 1983. **Ht.:** 6-1. **Wt.:** 190. **Bats:** R. **Throws:** R. **School:** Inglemoor (Wash.) HS. **Career Transactions:** Selected by Twins in 11th round of 2002 draft; signed May 27, 2003.

Meek was one of 10 Twins draft picks left unsigned from the first 20 rounds of the 2002 draft. Of that group, catcher Jeff Clement (now at Southern California), lefthander Ryan Schreppel (Cal State Fullerton) and righthander Mark Sauls (Florida State) all project as potential first-rounders in the class of 2005. Meek, however, signed as a draft-and-follow for $180,000 after going 5-4, 1.67 with 95 strikeouts in 65 innings for Bellevue (Wash.) CC. He has added 25 pounds to his strong, durable frame since his senior year of high school. He draws comparisons to J.D. Durbin for his frame and his aggressive mound presence, and Meek's two-pitch power arsenal reminds Twins scouts of Jesse Crain. Meek consistently throws his fastball between 90-96 mph with running movement and features a put-away curveball with good late snap. His changeup flashes the makings of a solid third pitch. Meek has to improve his overall feel for pitching, including his command and control. As soon as he can address those weaknesses, he can move into the upper echelon in the Twins organization. For now, he'll jump into the low Class A rotation.

Year	Club (League)	Class	W	L	ERA	G	GS	CG	SV	IP	H	R	ER	HR	BB	SO	AVG
2003	Elizabethton (Appy)	R	7	1	2.47	14	8	0	1	51	33	15	14	2	24	47	.178
MINOR LEAGUE TOTALS			7	1	2.47	14	8	0	1	51	33	15	14	2	24	47	.178

15 Errol Simonitsch, lhp

Born: Aug. 24, 1982. **Ht.:** 6-4. **Wt.:** 225. **Bats:** L. **Throws:** L. **School:** Gonzaga University.
Career Transactions: Selected by Twins in sixth round of 2003 draft; signed June 28, 2003.

Simonitsch was sidelined with shoulder tendinitis last spring, which limited him to just eight starts at Gonzaga and prevented Twins scouting director Mike Radcliff from seeing Simonitsch in person. Area scout Bill Lohr and scouting supervisor Deron Johnson had seen all they needed, however, and convinced Radcliff to grab him in the sixth round, about three rounds lower than where he would have gone sans tendinitis. Simonitsch was cleared to pitch upon signing and helped led Elizabethton to the Rookie-level Appalachian League championship. He works effectively down in the zone with an 88-90 mph fastball and a plus curveball. His changeup really came on over the course of the season. Simonitsch works with a good delivery and loose arm action. He is polished and still projectable, conjuring comparisons to Mark Redman, another big, strong-bodied southpaw originally signed by Minnesota. Armed with three quality offerings and command, Simonitsch has the stuff to move quickly. He'll skip a level and pitch in high Class A this year.

Year	Club (League)	Class	W	L	ERA	G	GS	CG	SV	IP	H	R	ER	HR	BB	SO	AVG
2003	Elizabethton (Appy)	R	5	1	1.76	10	8	0	0	46	39	13	9	1	6	57	.220
MINOR LEAGUE TOTALS			5	1	1.76	10	8	0	0	46	39	13	9	1	6	57	.220

16 Lew Ford, of

Born: Aug. 12, 1976. **Ht.:** 6-0. **Wt.:** 190. **Bats:** R. **Throws:** R. **School:** Dallas Baptist University.
Career Transactions: Selected by Red Sox in 12th round of 1999 draft; signed June 7, 1999 . . . Traded by Red Sox to Twins for RHP Hector Carrasco, Sept. 10, 2000.

An unheralded prospect for much of his career, Ford busted into the Twins' big league plans last year after a hot start in Rochester. He has the tools to be a starting center fielder elsewhere, but isn't likely to crack the Minnesota. The Twins do value his versatility, though, and he gave them the confidence to trade Bobby Kielty and Dustan Mohr last year. Ford just needs to stay healthy now. He hit .357 in his first 16 major league games before breaking his right forearm and missing seven weeks. When he tried to make up for lost time in the Venezuelan winter league, he dislocated a thumb after just four games. Ford has a quick bat and can drive the ball into the alleys or out of the yard with surprising juice. He homered four times in one game in 2001 and won the home run derby at the Double-A all-star game in 2002. Ford has an ideal leadoff man's mentality and is geared to get on base and score runs. Ford is an above-average runner with good basestealing instincts. His plus range and average arm enable him to play all three outfield sports. He should be fully recovered by spring training, where he's supposed to nail down a big league job as a fourth outfielder. Ford would be a capable fill-in if any of the regulars were to get injured.

Year	Club (League)	Class	AVG	G	AB	R	H	2B	3B	HR	RBI	BB	SO	SB	SLG	OBP
1999	Lowell (NY-P)	A	.280	62	250	48	70	17	4	7	34	19	35	15	.464	.339
2000	Augusta (SAL)	A	.315	126	514	122	162	35	11	9	74	52	83	52	.479	.390
2001	Fort Myers (FSL)	A	.298	67	265	42	79	15	2	2	24	21	30	19	.392	.373
	New Britain (EL)	AA	.218	62	252	30	55	9	3	7	25	20	35	5	.361	.289
2002	New Britain (EL)	AA	.311	93	373	81	116	27	2	15	51	49	47	17	.515	.401
	Edmonton (PCL)	AAA	.332	47	193	40	64	11	2	5	24	13	21	11	.487	.390
2003	Rochester (IL)	AAA	.303	53	211	33	64	18	2	3	31	10	28	4	.450	.357
	Minnesota (AL)	MAJ	.329	34	73	16	24	7	1	3	15	8	9	2	.575	.402
MAJOR LEAGUE TOTALS			.329	34	73	16	24	7	1	3	15	8	9	2	.575	.402
MINOR LEAGUE TOTALS			.296	510	2058	396	610	132	26	48	263	184	279	123	.456	.368

17 Boof Bonser, rhp

Born: Oct. 14, 1981. **Ht.:** 6-4. **Wt.:** 230. **Bats:** R. **Throws:** R. **School:** Gibbs HS, St. Petersburg, Fla. **Career Transactions:** Selected by Giants in first round (21st overall) of 2000 draft; signed July 3, 2000 . . . Traded by Giants with RHP Joe Nathan and LHP Francisco Liriano to Twins for C A.J. Pierzynski and a player to be named, Nov. 14, 2003.

Bonser easily would have made our Giants Top 10 Prospects list before he was dealt along with Joe Nathan and live-armed Francisco Liriano for all-star catcher A.J. Pierzynski in November. His status on this list speaks more to the depth of the Twins system than the way they feel about him. Bonser, who legally changed his name from John to Boof in high school, made encouraging progress in 2003. After earning a promotion to Triple-A Fresno, he continued to impress with his repertoire in the Arizona Fall League despite a 6.07 ERA there. Bonser's fastball isn't overpowering at 89-92 mph, though he has shown mid-90s heat in the past. His breaking ball has been vital to his development, and he has started to flash plus curveballs with tight, biting rotation on a more consistent basis. Now he needs to hone his changeup to remain a starter. Bonser will get an opportunity to make the Rochester rotation. With the back of Minnesota's rotation open for competition, he should garner some major league time in 2004.

Year	Club (League)	Class	W	L	ERA	G	GS	CG	SV	IP	H	R	ER	HR	BB	SO	AVG
2000	Salem-Keizer (NWL)	A	1	4	6.00	10	9	0	0	33	21	23	22	2	29	41	.188
2001	Hagerstown (SAL)	A	16	4	2.49	27	27	0	0	134	91	40	37	7	61	178	.192
2002	Shreveport (TL)	AA	1	2	5.55	5	5	0	0	24	30	15	15	3	14	23	.316
	San Jose (Cal)	A	8	6	2.88	23	23	0	0	128	89	44	41	9	70	139	.195
2003	Norwich (EL)	AA	7	10	4.00	24	24	1	0	135	122	80	60	11	67	103	.245
	Fresno (PCL)	AAA	1	2	3.13	4	4	0	0	23	17	13	8	4	8	28	.195
MINOR LEAGUE TOTALS			34	28	3.45	93	92	1	0	478	370	215	183	36	249	512	.215

18 Francisco Liriano, lhp

Born: Oct. 26, 1983. **Ht.:** 6-2. **Wt.:** 185. **Bats:** L. **Throws:** L. **Career Transactions:** Signed out of Dominican Republic by Giants, Sept. 9, 2000 . . . Traded by Giants with RHP Boof Bonser and RHP Joe Nathan to Twins for C A.J. Pierzynski and a player to be named, Nov. 14, 2003.

Liriano headed into last season regarded as one of the best lefthanders in the minors. But after leaving his first outing of the year, he didn't return to the mound except for making four rehab stars in the Rookie-level Arizona League in August. It was the second straight season he broke down with shoulder trouble. Liriano registered 93-97 mph gun readings in instructional league last fall, enough to convince Twins scout Sean Johnson that his arm was sound and worth pursuing in the A.J. Pierzynski trade. Liriano arrived at a Dominican tryout camp in 2000 as an outfielder, but the Giants immediately moved him to the mound. His hammer curveball is a second potential out pitch, but his changeup and control aren't very advanced. While he has tremendous upside, his durability presents a serious red flag at this point. The Twins probably will send him to high Class A, and he could advance quickly if he stays healthy.

Year	Club (League)	Class	W	L	ERA	G	GS	CG	SV	IP	H	R	ER	HR	BB	SO	AVG
2001	Giants (AZL)	R	5	4	3.63	13	12	0	0	62	51	26	25	3	24	67	.232
	Salem-Keizer (NWL)	A	0	0	5.00	2	2	0	0	9	7	5	5	2	1	12	.206
2002	Hagerstown (SAL)	A	3	6	3.49	16	16	0	0	80	61	45	31	6	31	85	.210
2003	San Jose (Cal)	A	0	1	54.00	1	1	0	0	1	5	4	4	0	2	0	.714
	Giants (AZL)	R	0	1	4.32	4	4	0	0	8	5	4	4	1	6	9	.192
MINOR LEAGUE TOTALS			8	12	3.88	36	35	0	0	160	129	84	69	12	64	173	.223

19 Scott Baker, rhp

Born: Sept. 19, 1981. **Ht.:** 6-4. **Wt.:** 190. **Bats:** R. **Throws:** R. **School:** Oklahoma State University. **Career Transactions:** Selected by Twins in second round of 2003 draft; signed June 20, 2003.

Drafted in the 36th round by the Pirates out of high school in 2000, Baker opted to attend Oklahoma State and emerged as a possible first-round pick with a breakthrough summer in the Cape Cod League in 2002. He tied for the Big 12 Conference lead with 12 victories last spring before the Twins grabbed him with a late second-round pick. Baker operates with command of four pitches and a polished delivery. He throws 88-93 mph with sink when he keeps his fastball down. He has plus fastball command, as well as an advanced changeup, a short, quick slider and a knuckle-curve. Baker's health history raises a minor red flag. He sat out most of his freshman season with a strained elbow ligament, which required a visit to Dr. James Andrews but not surgery. Baker admits he may not have been 100 percent as a sophomore either, though he's in tremendous physical condition now. Minnesota is excited about the pitching depth it acquired in 2003. While Errol Simonitsch and Dave Shinskie have higher ceilings despite being drafted behind him, Baker will move on the fast track. He'll join Simonitsch in the high Class A rotation and could finish his first full season in Double-A.

Year	Club (League)	Class	W	L	ERA	G	GS	CG	SV	IP	H	R	ER	HR	BB	SO	AVG
2003	Quad City (Mid)	A	3	1	2.49	11	11	0	0	51	45	16	14	4	8	47	.234
MINOR LEAGUE TOTALS			3	1	2.49	11	11	0	0	51	45	16	14	4	8	47	.234

20 Dave Shinskie, rhp

Born: May 4, 1984. **Ht.:** 6-4. **Wt.:** 205. **Bats:** R. **Throws:** R. **School:** Mt. Carmel Area HS, Kulpmont, Pa. **Career Transactions:** Selected by Twins in fourth round of 2003 draft; signed July 11, 2003.

Shinskie was recruited by several Big Ten Conference football programs as a quarterback before deciding to play two sports at Delaware. He passed for 6,334 yards and 57 touchdowns as a prepster, winning two Pennsylvania 2-A titles at Mount Carmel High. But he put all thoughts of the gridiron behind him after signing for $280,000 as a fourth-round pick. Shinskie fastball reached 93 mph with boring action during the spring, when he went just 1-5 at Mount Carmel, and sat at 89-91 mph in his pro debut. The Twins project him to consistently reach the low 90s as he becomes more accustomed to pitching every fifth day. His 81-mph slider is just OK right now, though he locates it well and it has good downward movement. Shinskie needs to refine his 75-76 mph circle changeup and improve his feel for pitching. He tends to overthrow when he falls behind in the count. He has the strong body, athleticism and competitive makeup to develop into a workhorse. He'll move slow like most of Twins high school draftees, starting 2004 in extended spring training.

Year	Club (League)	Class	W	L	ERA	G	GS	CG	SV	IP	H	R	ER	HR	BB	SO	AVG
2003	Twins (GCL)	R	1	4	7.41	5	5	0	0	17	20	18	14	0	10	13	.294
MINOR LEAGUE TOTALS			1	4	7.41	5	5	0	0	17	20	18	14	0	10	13	.294

21 Scott Tyler, rhp

Born: Aug. 20, 1982. **Ht.:** 6-5. **Wt.:** 230. **Bats:** R. **Throws:** R. **School:** Downingtown (Pa.) HS. **Career Transactions:** Selected by Twins in second round of 2001 draft; signed July 8, 2001.

After ranking sixth on this list a year ago, Tyler struggled to make adjustments in low Class A. The Twins always have known he would be a long-term project, but he excited them by making encouraging strides and leading the Appalachian League in strikeouts in 2002. He's still capable of blowing hitters away with his mid-90s fastball. He just needs to learn how to locate it and keep it down in the zone. Physically imposing at 6-foot-6 and 220 pounds, Tyler is a bit of a stiff-bodied pitcher, which makes it more difficult for him to drive the ball down. While his command might always be an issue, he's not all over the place throwing balls to the backstop. His problem is throwing fastballs at the chest instead of the knees. Tyler's slider is a solid-average offering and his changeup is a reliable third pitch. He worked behind in the count so often last year that he piled up high pitch counts and lasted through six innings just twice. Minnesota refers to 2003 as a speed bump for Tyler, and still projects him as a quality power pitcher as either a starter or reliever. He'll return to Quad City as the Opening Day starter.

Year	Club (League)	Class	W	L	ERA	G	GS	CG	SV	IP	H	R	ER	HR	BB	SO	AVG
2001	Twins (GCL)	R	0	1	6.75	5	3	0	0	11	11	8	8	0	2	14	.256
2002	Elizabethton (Appy)	R	8	1	2.93	14	13	0	0	68	37	23	22	5	46	92	.161
2003	Quad City (Mid)	A	6	12	5.50	30	20	0	0	106	93	70	65	7	82	110	.234
MINOR LEAGUE TOTALS			14	14	4.63	49	36	0	0	185	141	101	95	12	130	216	.210

22 Colby Miller, rhp

Born: March 19, 1982. **Ht.:** 6-2. **Wt.:** 190. **Bats:** R. **Throws:** R. **School:** Weatherford (Okla.) HS. **Career Transactions:** Selected by Twins in third round of 2000 draft; signed June 19, 2000.

The Twins and share the Metrodome with the Vikings, and after looking at their record of drafting quarterbacks it seems they share scouting reports as well. Righthanders Andy Persby (Minnesota) and T.J. Prunty (Miami) were backup quarterbacks in college. Catchers Joe Mauer (Florida State) and Eli Tintor (Minnesota-Duluth) and righty David Shinskie (Delaware) would have played college football if they hadn't signed baseball contract. Outfielder B.J. Garbe, the fifth overall pick in 1999, drew interest from Stanford as a QB. Miller passed Weatherford High to the Oklahoma state 4-A football title in the fall of 1999, then followed up by leading the baseball team to a 41-0 record and another championship the next spring. His fastball sat at 90-94 mph at that point, prompting the Twins to draft him in the second round. Since then, however, Miller's plus velocity has inexplicably been absent for the most part. He pitched at 86-88 mph before sneaking up to 89-91 with good movement last year. Unable to simply overpower hitters, Miller has made significant progress with his slider and changeup. He doesn't have to throw hard to continue moving toward the majors, because his secondary pitches are advanced and he has the best command in the system. Miller profiles as a quality starter in the back half of a rotation. He's ready for Double-A.

Year	Club (League)	Class	W	L	ERA	G	GS	CG	SV	IP	H	R	ER	HR	BB	SO	AVG
2000	Twins (GCL)	R	3	2	3.09	14	10	0	0	55	44	26	19	2	21	55	.218
	Quad City (Mid)	A	0	1	6.75	2	2	0	0	7	10	6	5	0	7	6	.345
2001	Elizabethton (Appy)	R	5	1	2.44	15	6	0	0	48	39	15	13	4	12	61	.217
2002	Quad City (Mid)	A	10	11	3.78	27	27	1	0	155	143	71	65	11	67	139	.249
2003	Fort Myers (FSL)	A	9	6	2.71	26	26	1	0	156	139	58	47	10	43	114	.241
MINOR LEAGUE TOTALS			27	21	3.19	84	71	2	0	421	375	176	149	27	150	375	.240

23 Terry Tiffee, 3b

Born: April 21, 1979. **Ht.:** 6-3. **Wt.:** 210. **Bats:** B. **Throws:** R. **School:** Pratt (Kan.) CC. **Career Transactions:** Selected by Twins in 26th round of 1999 draft; signed Aug. 17, 1999.

Tiffee has come a long way since being drafted out of Pratt CC, where he was the MVP of the Kansas Jayhawk Community College Conference in 1999. Out of shape at 260 pounds in high school, he was down to 230 by the time he was drafted and has trimmed his body to 215 these days. No matter how he looked, Tiffee always has been able to hit. He has a contact-oriented approach from both sides of the plate and produces consistent line drives. He displays more loft power batting righthanded, as opposed to a smooth, level cut form the left side. He's an aggressive hitter early in the count and had one of the lowest pitch/at-bat ratios in the system last year. Tiffee has worked hard to improve at third base, where he has an average arm and hands. He makes routine plays but lacks lateral mobility. The Twins have challenged Tiffee, who led the system in RBIs in 2003, to see more pitches and drive the ball for more power. After hitting .305 in the Arizona Fall League, he'll address those concerns in Triple-A.

Year	Club (League)	Class	AVG	G	AB	R	H	2B	3B	HR	RBI	BB	SO	SB	SLG	OBP
2000	Quad City (Mid)	A	.254	129	493	59	125	25	0	7	60	29	73	2	.347	.292
2001	Quad City (Mid)	A	.309	128	495	65	153	32	1	11	86	32	48	3	.444	.347
2002	Fort Myers (FSL)	A	.281	126	473	47	133	31	0	8	64	25	49	0	.397	.316
2003	New Britain (EL)	AA	.315	139	530	77	167	31	3	14	93	31	49	4	.464	.351
MINOR LEAGUE TOTALS			.290	522	1991	248	578	119	4	40	303	117	219	9	.414	.327

24 Rob Bowen, c

Born: Feb. 24, 1981. **Ht.:** 6-3. **Wt.:** 220. **Bats:** B. **Throws:** R. **School:** Homestead HS, Fort Wayne, Ind. **Career Transactions:** Selected by Twins in second round of 1999 draft; signed July 10, 1999.

It would have been easy to write Bowen off after a dismal 2002 campaign that saw his average plummet to .185 in Class A. He never has demonstrated good strike-zone judgment, and it cost him. But the Twins remained confident in his ability because there were no major mechanical flaws in his swing. Bowen may have felt the pressure of Joe Mauer's presence, though he seemed more comfortable in 2003. He improved his pitch selection last year and made his major league debut in September. He shows solid power potential with natural loft in his lefthanded swing. Scouts have some questions about his bat speed from the right side. He's not Mauer's equal defensively, but Bowen's work behind the plate is his strength. He has a plus arm and quick release, allowing him to throw out 39 percent of basestealers in the minors last year. Extremely agile out of the crouch, Bowen could be even better than Mauer at blocking pitches. He has the tools and intangibles to profile as a big league regular. Of course, if he stays with the Twins, he'll be caddying for Mauer for years. The Twins want Bowen playing on a daily basis, so they might send him back to Double-A to start 2004 with defensive specialist Brandon Marsters ticketed for Triple-A.

Year	Club (League)	Class	AVG	G	AB	R	H	2B	3B	HR	RBI	BB	SO	SB	SLG	OBP
1999	Twins (GCL)	R	.260	29	77	10	20	4	0	0	11	20	15	2	.312	.400
2000	Elizabethton (Appy)	R	.288	21	73	17	21	3	0	4	19	11	18	0	.493	.381
2001	Quad City (Mid)	A	.255	106	385	47	98	18	2	18	70	37	112	4	.452	.321
2002	Fort Myers (FSL)	A	.184	100	342	52	63	12	1	10	49	38	69	1	.313	.272
	Quad City (Mid)	A	.190	5	21	1	4	1	0	0	0	2	4	0	.238	.261
2003	New Britain (EL)	AA	.306	42	134	17	41	13	0	1	16	13	24	0	.425	.376
	Rochester (IL)	AAA	.257	30	105	14	27	7	0	6	17	11	25	0	.495	.333
	Minnesota (AL)	MAJ	.100	7	10	0	1	0	0	0	1	0	4	0	.100	.091
MAJOR LEAGUE TOTALS			.100	7	10	0	1	0	0	0	1	0	4	0	.100	.091
MINOR LEAGUE TOTALS			.241	333	1137	158	274	58	3	39	182	132	267	7	.400	.322

25 Michael Ryan, of

Born: July 6, 1977. **Ht.:** 6-0. **Wt.:** 180. **Bats:** L. **Throws:** R. **School:** Indiana (Pa.) HS. **Career Transactions:** Selected by Twins in fifth round of 1996 draft; signed June 7, 1996.

Ryan is a good example of a natural line-drive hitter developing power as he matures. Along with Lew Ford, Ryan was so impressive last September that the Twins felt comfortable dealing Dustan Mohr in December to clear the way for them as reserve outfielders in 2004. Originally signed as a third baseman, Ryan shifted to second base in 1999 because he lacked pop. When his defense didn't come around, he moved to the outfield full-time in 2002, when he exploded for a career-best 31 home runs and tied Diamondbacks top prospect Scott Hairston for the minor league lead in extra-base hits. Outside of Joe Mauer, Ryan might have the best pure swing in the system. His stroke is so fluid and he makes solid, square contact. Most of his power is to right field and he's a bit of a guess hitter. Ryan is in attack mode early in the count, looking to crush the first pitch he sees in his zone, which isn't conducive to drawing walks. Though he's been tabbed as a platoon player, he hangs in against lefties. He's adequate defensively with fringe-average range and arm strength. He doesn't have a high ceiling, but is an ideal extra outfielder with lefthanded juice off the bench. After hitting .404 in September, Ryan hit .303 with six homers in 89 at-bats in Venezuela over the winter.

Year	Club (League)	Class	AVG	G	AB	R	H	2B	3B	HR	RBI	BB	SO	SB	SLG	OBP
1996	Twins (GCL)	R	.197	43	157	12	31	8	2	0	13	13	20	3	.274	.260
1997	Elizabethton (Appy)	R	.300	62	220	44	66	10	0	3	29	38	39	2	.386	.404
1998	Fort Wayne (Mid)	A	.318	113	412	68	131	24	6	9	72	44	92	7	.471	.381
1999	Fort Myers (FSL)	A	.274	131	507	85	139	26	5	8	71	63	60	3	.393	.356
2000	New Britain (EL)	AA	.277	122	481	64	133	23	8	11	69	34	79	4	.426	.323
	Salt Lake (PCL)	AAA	.222	3	9	1	2	0	0	0	2	3	2	0	.222	.417
2001	Edmonton (PCL)	AAA	.288	135	527	89	152	36	7	18	73	52	121	1	.486	.353
2002	Edmonton (PCL)	AAA	.261	131	540	92	141	36	6	31	101	55	124	4	.522	.330
	Minnesota (AL)	MAJ	.091	7	11	3	1	0	0	0	0	0	2	0	.091	.091
2003	Rochester (IL)	AAA	.225	115	408	56	92	20	4	15	60	38	89	6	.404	.289
	Minnesota (AL)	MAJ	.393	27	61	13	24	7	0	5	13	6	12	2	.754	.441
MAJOR LEAGUE TOTALS			.347	34	72	16	25	7	0	5	13	6	14	2	.653	.392
MINOR LEAGUE TOTALS			.272	855	3261	511	887	183	38	95	490	340	626	30	.439	.341

26 Luke Hughes, ss

Born: Aug. 2, 1984. **Ht.:** 5-11. **Wt.:** 160. **Bats:** R. **Throws:** R. **Career Transactions:** Signed out of Australia by Twins, July 19, 2002.

The Twins are excited about the hitting potential of two young Australian infielders signed by Howard Norsetter. Paul Rutgers, who batted .353 in the Gulf Coast League last year, profiles as an offensive second baseman. Hughes has the athleticism to play shortstop but may end up as a third baseman in the Joe Randa mold. Minnesota signed him out of Major League Baseball's academy in Australia. He was one of his nation's top hitters but injuries kept him out of major international competition in 2001 and 2002. A GCL all-star along with Rutgers, Hughes impresses the Twins with his instincts and makeup. He doesn't currently possess a lot of power, but he shows enough strength to drive the ball with a good swing. Hughes has played against older competition for years in Australia's Claxton Shield tournament, providing scouts the opportunity to see him handle plus fastballs. He uses the whole field and makes good contact. A 4.5-second runner down the first-base line when he signed, Hughes cut his time to 4.3 seconds, which is average speed. He makes the plays and has a plus arm at shortstop, but his range is better suited for the hot corner. He'll probably head to Elizabethton after opening 2004 in extended spring training.

Year	Club (League)	Class	AVG	G	AB	R	H	2B	3B	HR	RBI	BB	SO	SB	SLG	OBP
2003	Twins (GCL)	R	.305	54	190	22	58	9	4	2	25	15	22	5	.426	.361
MINOR LEAGUE TOTALS			.305	54	190	22	58	9	4	2	25	15	22	5	.426	.361

27 Michael Rogers, lhp

Born: June 11, 1985. **Ht.:** 5-10. **Wt.:** 175. **Bats:** L. **Throws:** L. **School:** Del City (Okla.) HS. **Career Transactions:** Selected by Twins in 16th round of 2003 draft; signed July 30, 2003.

Rogers had borderline first-round talent but fell to the 16th round in June because he stands 5-foot-10 and was strongly committed to the University of Texas, where he would have pitched and played the outfield. After failing to sign fifth-rounder Brandon McArthur, the Twins had extra money in their draft budget and lured Rogers with a $300,000 bonus. He was a surprise coup for an organization notorious for leaving premium talent unsigned. His stature and full-effort delivery scared off some teams, but he's athletic and throws his fastball at 88-92 mph with a quick arm. His tight curveball is an equalizer with the potential to be the best in the system. Rogers often relies too much on his breaking ball, and the Twins want him to establish his fastball more. He needs to become more consistent with his arm speed on his changeup so he won't tip hitters off. Rogers overthrows at times, affecting his command. He wasn't in great shape during instructional league, but topped out at 90 mph and impressed scouts with his plus curve. He signed a 2004 contract and probably will make his pro debut in Elizabethton.

Year	Club (League)	Class	W	L	ERA	G	GS	CG	SV	IP	H	R	ER	HR	BB	SO	AVG
2003	Did not play—Signed 2004 contract																

28 Jose Morales, c

Born: Feb. 20, 1983. **Ht.:** 5-11. **Wt.:** 180. **Bats:** B. **Throws:** R. **School:** Academie la Providencia HS, Rio Piedras, P.R. **Career Transactions:** Selected by Twins in third round of 2001 draft; signed June 30, 2001.

Once the Twins convinced Morales he wasn't going to fulfill his aspirations of becoming the next Roberto Alomar, he began to thrive as a catcher. He moved from second base in instructional league following the 2002 season. Despite Minnesota's lack of middle-infield depth, he was getting heavy in his lower half and losing the quickness needed at second. His above-average raw arm strength and good hands are well-suited for catching. He still has to get used to the rigors of catching after missing most of May and August with nagging back injuries last season. He threw out 29 percent of basestealers in the Midwest League, an admirable rate for a first-time catcher in a full-season circuit. At the plate, he shows line-drive, gap-hitting ability and enough bat for a catcher. His biggest need offensively is to show more patience. Morales' name comes up a lot in trade talks but Minnesota wants to hold onto him. He'll return to high Class A, where he was raking in 2003 before straining his back.

Year	Club (League)	Class	AVG	G	AB	R	H	2B	3B	HR	RBI	BB	SO	SB	SLG	OBP
2001	Twins (GCL)	R	.248	35	117	13	29	6	2	0	18	6	26	4	.333	.296
2002	Twins (GCL)	R	.309	53	175	25	54	7	2	0	28	7	28	3	.371	.347
2003	Fort Myers (FSL)	A	.357	12	42	6	15	3	1	0	2	1	5	0	.476	.372
	Quad City (Mid)	A	.271	48	170	14	46	10	1	2	25	5	32	0	.376	.302
MINOR LEAGUE TOTALS			.286	148	504	58	144	26	6	2	73	19	91	7	.373	.322

29 Trent Oeltjen, of

Born: Feb. 28, 1983. **Ht.:** 6-1. **Wt.:** 180. **Bats:** L. **Throws:** L. **Career Transactions:** Signed out of Australia by Twins, Feb. 7, 2001.

Some Twins scouts rate Oeltjen ahead of Alex Romero. Minnesota started following him in Australia when he was 15. He had Tommy John surgery a year later and is now fully recovered. Romero has more power potential, while Oeltjen is a classic line-drive hitter. His swing is loose and fluid, and he puts the ball in play. The Twins think he'll show more gap power as he fills out his athletic frame, and they've likened him to Michael Ryan, a pure hitter who developed plus power well into his career. Oeltjen has quick hands and generates good bat speed, keeping the bat head in the zone for a long time helping him handle lefties and righties alike. He needs to draw more walks so he can take fuller advantage of his plus speed. He has solid instincts on the bases and in the outfield. Oeltjen's arm is below average, the same as it was before his elbow was reconstructed. He needs a full season at each level and will spend 2004 in high Class A.

Year	Club (League)	Class	AVG	G	AB	R	H	2B	3B	HR	RBI	BB	SO	SB	SLG	OBP
2001	Twins (GCL)	R	.321	45	134	21	43	7	3	0	18	14	16	10	.418	.387
	Elizabethton (Appy)	R	.233	9	30	4	7	1	0	0	4	0	6	2	.267	.226
2002	Elizabethton (Appy)	R	.298	54	215	36	64	7	2	3	18	16	34	7	.391	.363
	Quad City (Mid)	A	.240	10	25	4	6	1	0	0	1	3	2	1	.280	.321
2003	Quad City (Mid)	A	.298	123	466	73	139	12	8	4	44	37	57	29	.384	.371
MINOR LEAGUE TOTALS			.298	241	870	138	259	28	13	7	85	70	115	49	.384	.366

30 Johnny Woodard, 1b

Born: Sept. 15, 1984. **Ht.:** 6-4. **Wt.:** 208. **Bats:** L. **Throws:** R. **School:** Cosumnes River (Calif.) JC. **Career Transactions:** Selected by Twins in third round of 2003 draft; signed June 4, 2003.

Another product of the 2003 draft, Woodard was a surprise third-round pick. The Twins admittedly grabbed him earlier than he was expected to go off the board, but they didn't want to miss the opportunity to add another potential impact bat. Woodard played more basketball than baseball in high school, taking his junior year off from the diamond. Minnesota first noticed him as a senior and was able to keep close tabs on him last spring in junior college, when he was the Bay Valley Conference player of the year. Tony Bloomfield, his coach at Cosumnes River (Calif.) JC, works for the Twins as an associate scout. Because of his inexperience, Woodard was overmatched in his pro debut. But he has a good fluid swing with power potential, and he should be able to adapt. The system is loaded at first base, with Justin Morneau on the brink of the majors, and Woodard, Dusty Gomon and David Winfree in the lower minors. Woodard could get a look in the outfield after showing an above-average arm and good hands at first base. He did make too many careless errors, leading Gulf Coast League first basemen with 13 miscues. Woodard is a long-term project who will begin 2004 in extended spring training.

Year	Club (League)	Class	AVG	G	AB	R	H	2B	3B	HR	RBI	BB	SO	SB	SLG	OBP
2003	Twins (GCL)	R	.238	52	172	19	41	6	1	1	15	22	42	1	.302	.330
MINOR LEAGUE TOTALS			.238	52	172	19	41	6	1	1	15	22	42	1	.302	.330

MONTREAL
EXPOS

For the past five years, the conclusion of baseball's regular season raised the question of whether the Expos would be back in Montreal the following spring. They will be again in 2004, but the long-term future of the franchise remains muddled as ever. Owned and operated by Major League Baseball, the Expos played three homestands in Puerto Rico during the 2003 season in an effort to generate more revenue. Unhappy with the extra travel, the players voted against a similar arrangement for 2004. A compromise was struck that will again have the Expos playing 22 games in San Juan, but all games are scheduled before the all-star break, rather than spread throughout the season.

The travel took its toll on a team that stayed on the fringes of the playoff race all season in 2003. That isn't likely to be a problem in 2004, after the Expos lost their cornerstone pitcher, Javier Vazquez, and hitter, Vladimir Guerrero, with the departure of Orlando Cabrera and Jose Vidro likely to follow if the club isn't sold soon. The Expos did get Nick Johnson and Juan Rivera from the Yankees in the Vazquez trade, but they will not make up for all the talent that has been lost.

On the field, the news was surprisingly positive for Montreal in 2003. Though MLB's payroll constraints forced an offseason trade of Bartolo Colon, the Expos actu-

TOP 30 PROSPECTS

1. Clint Everts, rhp
2. Mike Hinckley, lhp
3. Larry Broadway, 1b
4. Josh Karp, rhp
5. Chad Cordero, rhp
6. Shawn Hill, rhp
7. Darrell Rasner, rhp
8. Seung Song, rhp
9. Terrmel Sledge, of
10. Ryan Church, of
11. Rogearvin Bernadina, of
12. Jason Bergmann, rhp
13. Scott Hodges, 3b
14. Brandon Watson, of
15. Rich Rundles, lhp
16. Val Pascucci, of/1b
17. Jerry Owens, of
18. Daryl Thompson, rhp
19. Chris Young, rhp
20. Antonio Sucre, of
21. Luke Lockwood, lhp
22. Vince Rooi, 3b
23. Edgardo Baez, of
24. Frank Diaz, of
25. Chad Bentz, lhp
26. Danny Rueckel, rhp
27. Roy Corcoran, rhp
28. Alexis Morales, rhp
29. Wilton Chavez, rhp
30. Josh Labandeira, ss

By Michael Levesque

ally led the wild-card race in late August and had consecutive winning seasons for the first time since 1993-94. They wilted in September as a grueling schedule (which included 103 games away from Montreal) and injuries exacted their toll. MLB didn't permit the club to expand its roster in September, when it needed reinforcements.

In the minors, the Expos are still feeling the effects of the great purge of 2002. In a vain attempt to contend, general manager Omar Minaya traded away most of the system's best prospects, including Jason Bay, Cliff Lee, Donald Levinski, Brandon Phillips, Grady Sizemore, Matt Watson and Justin Wayne. Montreal's affiliates combined for the worst record in the minors in 2003, going 300-386 (.437).

Scouting director Dana Brown has tried to restock the system. After landing top prospect Clint Everts with his first selection in the 2002 draft, he added righthanders Darrell Rasner (second round) and Jason Bergmann (11th), and brought in the power bat of Larry Broadway in the third round. In 2003, he surprised everyone by nabbing Chad Cordero with the 20th overall pick, but Cordero reached the majors in late August and dominated out of the bullpen. Outfielders Jerry Owens (second) and Edgardo Baez (fourth) also show promise, as do righthanders Daryl Thompson (eighth) and Alex Morales (46th).

ORGANIZATION
OVERVIEW

General manager: Omar Minaya. **Farm director:** Adam Wogan. **Scouting director:** Dana Brown.

2003 PERFORMANCE

Class	Team	League	W	L	Pct.	Finish*	Manager
Majors	Montreal	National	83	79	.512	10th (16)	Frank Robinson
Triple-A	Edmonton Trappers	Pacific Coast	73	69	.514	4th (16)	Dave Huppert
Double-A	Harrisburg Senators	Eastern	60	82	.423	12th (12)	Dave Machemer
High A	Brevard County Manatees	Florida State	65	66	.496	7th (12)	Doug Sisson
Low A	Savannah Sand Gnats	South Atlantic	58	80	.420	13th (16)	Joey Cora
Short-season	Vermont Expos	New York-Penn	19	56	.253	14th (14)	Dave Barnett
Rookie	GCL Expos	Gulf Coast	25	33	.431	10th (12)	Bobby Henley

OVERALL 2003 MINOR LEAGUE RECORD 300 386 .437 30th (30)
*Finish in overall standings (No. of teams in league).

ORGANIZATION LEADERS

BATTING *Minimum 250 At-Bats
*AVG	Terrmel Sledge, Edmonton	.324
R	Terrmel Sledge, Edmonton	95
H	Brandon Watson, Harrisburg	180
TB	Terrmel Sledge, Edmonton	271
2B	Larry Broadway, Harrisburg/Savannah/Brevard	35
3B	Terrmel Sledge, Edmonton	9
HR	Terrmel Sledge, Edmonton	22
RBI	Terrmel Sledge, Edmonton	92
BB	Val Pascucci, Edmonton	101
SO	Val Pascucci, Edmonton	132
SB	Reggie Fitzpatrick, Savannah	36
*SLG	Terrmel Sledge, Edmonton	.545
*OBP	Noah Hall, Harrisburg	.434

PITCHING #Minimum 75 Innings
W	Mike Hinckley, Brevard County/Savannah	13
L	Nick Long, Savannah/Vermont	16
#ERA	Nehomar Ochoa, Vermont/GCL Expos	2.04
G	Chad Bentz, Harrisburg	52
CG	Scott Downs, Edmonton	3
	Mike Hinckley, Brevard/Savannah	3
SV	Chad Bentz, Harrisburg	16
IP	Shawn Hill, Harrisburg/Brevard County	147
BB	Nick Long, Savannah/Vermont	67
SO	Mike Hinckley, Brevard County/Savannah	134

BEST TOOLS

Best Hitter for Average	Brandon Watson
Best Power Hitter	Larry Broadway
Fastest Baserunner	Jerry Owens
Best Athlete	Jerry Owens
Best Fastball	Robert Martinez
Best Curveball	Danny Rueckel
Best Slider	Alex Morales
Best Changeup	Clint Everts
Best Control	Chad Cordero
Best Defensive Catcher	Drew McMillan
Best Defensive Infielder	Shawn Norris
Best Infield Arm	Kory Casto
Best Defensive Outfielder	Danny Rombley
Best Outfield Arm	Lorvin Louisa

PROJECTED 2007 LINEUP

Catcher	Brian Schneider
First Base	Nick Johnson
Second Base	Jose Vidro
Third Base	Tony Batista
Shortstop	Orlando Cabrera
Left Field	Carl Everett
Center Field	Brad Wilkerson

Right Field	Juan Rivera
No. 1 Starter	Clint Everts
No. 2 Starter	Mike Hinckley
No. 3 Starter	Tony Armas
No. 4 Starter	Zach Day
No. 5 Starter	Livan Hernandez
Closer	Chad Cordero

LAST YEAR'S TOP 20 PROSPECTS

1. Clint Everts, rhp
2. Mike Hinckley, lhp
3. Josh Karp, rhp
4. Zach Day, rhp
5. Seung Song, rhp
6. Darrell Rasner, rhp
7. Claudio Vargas, rhp
8. Chris Young, rhp
9. Scott Hodges, 3b
10. Larry Broadway, 1b
11. Eric Good, lhp
12. Brandon Watson, of
13. Luke Lockwood, lhp
14. Rich Rundles, lhp
15. Cristobal Rodriguez, rhp
16. Ron Calloway, of
17. Terrmel Sledge, of
18. Val Pascucci, of
19. Rob Caputo, rhp
20. Matt Cepicky, of

TOP PROSPECTS OF THE DECADE

1994	Cliff Floyd, 1b/of
1995	Ugueth Urbina, rhp
1996	Vladimir Guerrero, of
1997	Vladimir Guerrero, of
1998	Brad Fullmer, 1b
1999	Michael Barrett, 3b/c
2000	Tony Armas, rhp
2001	Donnie Bridges, rhp
2002	Brandon Phillips, ss
2003	Clint Everts, rhp

TOP DRAFT PICKS OF THE DECADE

1994	Hiram Bocachica, ss
1995	Michael Barrett, ss
1996	*John Patterson, rhp
1997	Donnie Bridges, rhp
1998	Josh McKinley, ss
1999	Josh Girdley, lhp
2000	Justin Wayne, rhp
2001	Josh Karp, rhp
2002	Clint Everts, rhp
2003	Chad Cordero, rhp

*Did not sign

ALL-TIME LARGEST BONUSES

Justin Wayne, 2000	$2,950,000
Josh Karp, 2001	$2,650,000
Clint Everts, 2002	$2,500,000
Grady Sizemore, 2000	$2,000,000
Josh Girdley, 1999	$1,700,000

MINOR LEAGUE
DEPTH CHART

MONTREAL EXPOS

RANK: 30

Impact potential (D): The Expos have to bank on their top two pitching prospects to make an impact in the majors, and Clint Everts is still a long-term project. Larry Broadway hits enough to be a productive first baseman, but most of the Expos' other top prospects are just middle-of-the-road players.

Depth (F): Scouting director Dana Brown has done an admirable job considering the circumstances he works in, but the majority of the Expos' talent has been undervalued and dealt. By the time this franchise is sold by Major League Baseball, the cupboard will be almost bare.

Sleeper: Alexis Morales, rhp. — *Depth charts prepared by Josh Boyd. Numbers in parentheses indicate prospect rankings.*

LF
Terrmel Sledge (9)
Chad Chop
Matt Cepicky

CF
Rogearvin Bernadina (11)
Brandon Watson (14)
Jerry Owens (17)
Danny Rombley
Reg Fitzpatrick

RF
Ryan Church (10)
Val Pascucci (16)
Antonio Sucre (20)
Edgardo Baez (23)
Frank Diaz (24)

3B
Scott Hodges (13)
Vince Rooi (22)
Shawn Norris
Kory Casto

SS
Josh Labandiera (30)
Maicer Izturis
Jose Contreras
Trey Webb

2B
Eduardo Nunez

1B
Larry Broadway (3)
Josh Whitesell

SOURCE OF TALENT

Homegrown		Acquired	
College	10	Trades	6
Junior College	1	Rule 5 draft	0
Draft-and-follow	0	Independent	0
High school	8	Free agents/waivers	0
Nondrafted free agent	1		
Foreign	4		

C
Brad Cresse
Josh McKinley

RHP

Starters	Relievers
Clint Everts (1)	Chad Cordero (5)
Josh Karp (4)	Danny Rueckel (26)
Shawn Hill (6)	Roy Corcoran (27)
Darrell Rasner (7)	Alexis Morales (28)
Seung Song (8)	Chris Schroder
Jason Bergmann (12)	Ignacio Puello
Darryl Thompson (18)	Rob Caputo
Chris Young (19)	Gustavo Mata
Wilton Chavez (29)	Manny Santillan
Armando Galarraga	Ed Diaz
Nehomar Ochoa	
Anthony Pearson	

LHP

Starters	Relievers
Mike Hinckley (2)	Chad Bentz (25)
Rich Rundles (15)	Ben Dequin
Luke Lockwood (21)	Jason Stevenson
A.J. Wideman	David Maust
Brett Nyquist	Mike O'Connor
Jason Norderum	
Brett Price	

DRAFT
ANALYSIS

Best Pro Debut: RHP Chad Cordero (1) didn't receive as much publicity as the Reds' Ryan Wagner, but he too shot to the majors and pitched well. Cordero went 1-0, 1.64 with one save in Montreal. A surprise first-rounder, he made sense for the Expos because he was affordable and could pay off quickly.

Best Athlete: A wide receiver for current Baltimore Ravens quarterback Kyle Boller in high school, OF Jerry Owens (2) entered UCLA on a football scholarship. After transferring to The Master's (Calif.) College to play baseball, he wanted to pitch before he was persuaded to take advantage of his speed.

Whitesell

Best Pure Hitter: OF Edgardo Baez (4) has a quick bat and led all Expos draftees with a .274 average in his debut. He played in the Rookie-level Gulf Coast League.

Best Raw Power: 1B Josh Whitesell (6) sold the Expos on his power with his batting-practice displays using wood bats at Loyola Marymount.

Fastest Runner: Few 2003 draftees can outrun Owens. The lefthanded hitter gets to first base in 3.85-3.95 seconds, and cuts that time to 3.5 seconds on a drag bunt.

Best Defensive Player: SS Trey Webb (5) was one of the best pure shortstops in the draft. His arm and range are strengths, though he's error-prone and committed 17 miscues in 54 games in low Class A.

Best Fastball: Cordero and RHPs Daryl Thompson (8) and Alexis Morales (46) all can touch 94 mph. Thompson's fastball has the most upside because he's just 17.

Best Breaking Ball: Cordero's slider is a big reason he was able to succeed in the majors. It peaks at 85 mph and he commands it well.

Most Intriguing Background: Owens. 2B Oscar Bernazard's (28) uncle Tony played 10 seasons in the big leagues and is now a special assistant with the Major League Baseball Players Association.

Closest To The Majors: Cordero. The Expos think RHP Devin Perrin (7), a sleeper who relies on command, could move fast.

Best Late-Round Pick: Area scout Zack Hoyrst looked past Morales' 5-foot-11 build and his arm soreness last spring. After returning to full strength, Morales showed a plus fastball and an 82 mph slider.

The One Who Got Away: The Expos signed their first 19 picks—the best rate of any organization—but couldn't find the money to sign Iowa Western CC RHP Joe Bisenius (21), now at Oklahoma State.

Assessment: Handicapped by a small draft budget and a tiny scouting staff, the Expos have to work that much harder. While no hitters had strong debuts, Cordero, Perrin, Thompson and Morales offer promise on the mound.

2002 DRAFT — GRADE: C

The Expos had to hastily assemble a scouting staff three months before the draft, yet still came away with RHP Clint Everts (1), 1B Larry Broadway (3) and RHP Darrell Rasner (2).

2001 DRAFT — GRADE: C

LHP Mike Hinckley (3) ranks right behind Everts at the top of the Montreal prospect list. RHP Josh Karp (1) still has a high ceiling, as does RHP Donald Levinski (2), part of a shortsighted deal for Cliff Floyd in 2002.

2000 DRAFT — GRADE: A

The good news: The Expos scored big with OFs Grady Sizemore (3) and Jason Bay (22), plus LHP Cliff Lee (4). The bad news: They traded them away for Bartolo Colon and Lou Collier, and have little to show for either at this point. RHP Justin Wayne (1) has fizzled after being dealt. The best member of this class still with Montreal is RHP Shawn Hill (6).

1999 DRAFT — GRADE: C+

As in 2000, the top pick (LHP Josh Girdley, 1) hasn't panned out and the best choice (SS Brandon Phillips, 2) was part of the package for Colon. OF Brandon Watson (9) is the cream of the crop still with the Expos.

—Draft analysis prepared by Jim Callis. Numbers in parentheses indicate draft rounds.

rhp

Clint Everts

Born: Aug. 10, 1984.
Ht.: 6-2. **Wt.:** 170.
Bats: R. **Throws:** R.
School: Cypress Falls HS, Houston.
Career Transactions: Selected by Expos in first round (fifth overall) of 2002 draft; signed Aug. 24, 2002.

The fifth overall selection in 2002, Everts was an outstanding two-way player at Cypress Falls High in Houston. He and Scott Kazmir (Mets) became the first pair of pitchers from the same high school to go in the same first round, and Everts could have gone in the top three rounds purely as a shortstop. But teams focused on him as a pitcher because he had the best curveball in the draft, not to mention age, command and a feel for pitching that all worked in his favor. He signed too late to play in 2002 and spent the fall at Baylor, where he took accounting classes and worked out with the baseball team. Everts had a brief stint in big league camp last spring before heading to extended spring training, then made his pro debut with short-season Vermont in mid-June. The victim of tight pitch counts and poor run support, he went just 2-7 in 2003 but pitched better than his record would indicate. Promoted to low Class A Savannah on his 19th birthday, he allowed two runs or fewer in four of his five starts, but went 0-3.

Everts is an outstanding athlete with a projectable body and the makings of three plus major league pitches. He has a solid, balanced delivery and a clean, easy arm action, which enables him to generate lightning-quick arm speed. His fastball sat at 88-92 mph with good movement in 2003, and he should increase his velocity as he adds strength to his slender frame. The development of his changeup and curveball are further along at this point. His curveball, an 80-84 mph bender with great depth and tight spin, grades as a 70 on the 20-80 scouting scale. It projects as a strikeout pitch in the majors. Everts' 78-81 mph changeup is almost as good as his curve. It's a plus pitch that he has an exceptional feel for. He didn't turn 19 until late in the 2003 season, so he's well ahead of most pitchers his age. Everts had become so reliant on his curveball at one point that the Expos limited his use of his out pitch. He threw it just 15 percent of the time so he could work on his fastball command, which still needs further improvement. He struggled with walks at times, in part because his curve breaks so much that it would leave the strike zone and/or fool umpires. Because of his limited pitching experience, he needs to improve his mound presence and get more aggressive.

With Everts' stuff and the weakened state of the Expos farm system, he can fly through the organization. He's expected to start 2004 at Savannah and could be at high Class A Brevard County by midseason. He has the potential to be a top-of-the-rotation starter in the majors.

Year	Club (League)	Class	W	L	ERA	G	GS	CG	SV	IP	H	R	ER	HR	BB	SO	AVG
2003	Vermont (NY-P)	A	2	4	4.17	10	10	0	0	54	49	26	25	4	35	50	.247
	Savannah (SAL)	A	0	3	3.46	5	5	0	0	26	23	13	10	1	10	21	.230
MINOR LEAGUE TOTALS			2	7	3.94	15	15	0	0	80	72	39	35	5	45	71	.242

STEVE MOORE

2 Mike Hinckley, lhp

Born: Oct. 5, 1982. **Ht.:** 6-3. **Wt.:** 170. **Bats:** R. **Throws:** L. **School:** Moore (Okla.) HS. **Career Transactions:** Selected by Expos in third round of 2001 draft; signed July 5, 2001.

Hinckley ranked second behind Everts on this list entering the 2003 season. He went 4-3, 5.64 in his first 12 starts before finishing the year on a 9-2, 1.37 run. He's rapidly developing into one of the top lefthanded pitching prospects in the game. Hinckley is a projectable lefty with three average to above-average pitches. His arm action and delivery allow him to run his fastball to 91-94 mph with little effort. He learned to manipulate his fastball in the second half of the season, cutting it in on righties and fading it away from lefties. His curveball is a swing-and-miss pitch with good depth and two-plane break. He throws strikes and doesn't allow many home runs. Hinckley's changeup is the weakest of his three offerings but should become an average big league pitch. He must continue to improve his fastball command. Hinckley projects as a No. 2 or 3 starter in the majors. He should start 2004 with Brevard County, but with a good spring he could surprise and open the season with Double-A Harrisburg.

Year	Club (League)	Class	W	L	ERA	G	GS	CG	SV	IP	H	R	ER	HR	BB	SO	AVG
2001	Expos (GCL)	R	2	2	5.24	8	5	0	0	34	46	23	20	1	12	28	.329
2002	Vermont (NY-P)	A	6	2	1.37	16	16	0	0	92	60	19	14	4	30	66	.188
2003	Savannah (SAL)	A	9	5	3.64	23	23	2	0	121	124	54	49	4	41	111	.271
	Brevard County (FSL)	A	4	0	0.72	4	4	1	0	25	14	2	2	1	1	23	.159
MINOR LEAGUE TOTALS			21	9	2.81	51	48	3	0	272	244	98	85	10	84	228	.243

3 Larry Broadway, 1b

RICH ABEL

Born: Dec. 17, 1980. **Ht.:** 6-4. **Wt.:** 230. **Bats:** L. **Throws:** L. **School:** Duke University. **Career Transactions:** Selected by Expos in third round of 2002 draft; signed June 13, 2002.

The only hitter among the first eight prospects on this list, Broadway tore up the South Atlantic League to open his first full season. Managers rated him the league's best batting prospect, power prospect and defensive first baseman at midseason. He also won the home run derby at the all-star game. After reaching Double-A in mid-August, Broadway homered three times in his first six games. Broadway has a balanced, slightly open stance with good leverage and loft in his swing. He generates top-of-the-scale raw power. He executed a better game plan at the plate in 2003, enabling him to get better pitches to hit. He also showed the ability to make adjustments. He hit .300 or better against lefthanders at all three levels. Broadway's biggest weakness is his speed. He has a strong arm for a first baseman, but his defense is merely adequate. After playing in the Arizona Fall League, Broadway likely will return to Double-A to start 2004. With the acquisition of Nick Johnson, the Expos can afford to be more patient with his development.

Year	Club (League)	Class	AVG	G	AB	R	H	2B	3B	HR	RBI	BB	SO	SB	SLG	OBP
2002	Vermont (NY-P)	A	.315	35	127	13	40	3	0	4	23	13	33	0	.433	.379
	Expos (GCL)	R	.250	4	8	1	2	0	0	0	0	4	4	0	.250	.500
2003	Savannah (SAL)	A	.307	83	290	56	89	25	4	14	51	44	70	3	.566	.400
	Brevard County (FSL)	A	.224	25	76	8	17	7	1	1	7	18	20	0	.382	.367
	Harrisburg (EL)	AA	.321	21	78	13	25	3	0	5	18	7	15	0	.551	.371
MINOR LEAGUE TOTALS			.299	168	579	91	173	38	5	24	99	86	142	3	.506	.389

4 Josh Karp, rhp

RODGER WOOD

Born: Sept. 21, 1979. **Ht.:** 6-5. **Wt.:** 210. **Bats:** R. **Throws:** R. **School:** UCLA. **Career Transactions:** Selected by Expos in first round (sixth overall) of 2001 draft; signed Sept. 27, 2001.

The sixth overall choice in the 2001 draft, Karp hasn't had nearly the success of Joe Mauer, Mark Prior, Gavin Floyd and Mark Teixeira, who were picked right before him. He was winless from May 30 until his last start of the 2003 season. Poor run support was a factor, but his ERA also was 5.65 during that stretch. Despite his record, Karp's stuff showed a huge improvement from 2002. He has a short arm action from a three-quarters slot that enables him to command all his pitches. He topped out at 95 mph with his fastball, pitching consistently at 93-94 with good tailing action to both sides of the plate. When he keeps his fastball down, he also achieves good sink. His curveball bites though the strike zone and is a potential out pitch. His changeup is a third plus pitch at times. Karp has never won as much as his stuff would indicate he should. His pitches are inconsistent, as is his pitch selection. He needs to be more assertive on the mound. When the timing is off in his delivery, he drops his elbow and gets under the ball. Karp has all the ingredients. He should start 2004 with Triple-A Edmonton and could be in Montreal by the end of the year.

Year	Club (League)	Class	W	L	ERA	G	GS	CG	SV	IP	H	R	ER	HR	BB	SO	AVG
2002	Brevard County (FSL)	A	4	1	1.59	7	7	0	0	45	31	9	8	1	11	43	.190
	Harrisburg (EL)	AA	7	5	3.84	16	16	0	0	87	83	43	37	6	34	69	.256
2003	Harrisburg (EL)	AA	4	10	4.99	23	23	1	0	123	126	76	68	12	49	77	.266
MINOR LEAGUE TOTALS			15	16	3.99	46	46	1	0	255	240	128	113	19	94	189	.250

5 Chad Cordero, rhp

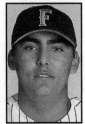

Born: March 18, 1982. **Ht.:** 6-0. **Wt.:** 195. **Bats:** R. **Throws:** R. **School:** Cal State Fullerton. **Career Transactions:** Selected by Expos in first round (20th overall) of 2003 draft; signed June 27, 2003.

Cordero became the second member of the 2003 draft class to make his major league debut last summer, following in the footsteps of the Reds' Ryan Wagner. Cordero was a surprise pick at No. 20 overall, but he was a good fit for the Expos because he signed for $1.35 million, below market value, and didn't need much seasoning. Cordero projects as a closer in the majors, possibly as early as 2004. He's aggressive with his heavy 90-94 mph fastball and sharp slider. He's not big, but he generates power with good lower-half drive and extension in his delivery. Cordero has a mature body with strong legs and rounded shoulders, so his stuff won't get much better. He's thick through his hips and will need to watch his weight. He occasionally leaves his circle changeup high in the strike zone and needs to scrap a slower version of his slider. Based on his September showing in Montreal, Cordero should make the Opening Day roster with a good spring. Rocky Biddle isn't the most reliable closer, so Cordero could take his job quickly.

Year	Club (League)	Class	W	L	ERA	G	GS	CG	SV	IP	H	R	ER	HR	BB	SO	AVG
2003	Brevard County (FSL)	A	1	1	2.05	19	0	0	6	26	17	8	6	1	10	17	.198
	Montreal (NL)	MAJ	1	0	1.64	12	0	0	1	11	4	2	2	1	3	12	.111
MAJOR LEAGUE TOTALS			1	0	1.64	12	0	0	1	11	4	2	2	1	3	12	.111
MINOR LEAGUE TOTALS			1	1	2.05	19	0	0	6	26	17	8	6	1	10	17	.198

6 Shawn Hill, rhp

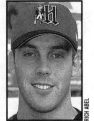

Born: April 28, 1981. **Ht.:** 6-2. **Wt.:** 180. **Bats:** R. **Throws:** R. **School:** Bishop Reding HS, Georgetown, Ontario. **Career Transactions:** Selected by Expos in sixth round of 2000 draft; signed June 16, 2000.

After a lethargic April, Hill found his groove in 2003. He won 12 games for the second straight year and represented Canada in the Futures Game at midseason. He finished the season in Double-A and joined Team Canada for the Olympic qualifying tournament in Panama. Hill threw his sinker at 90-91 mph consistently all year. He also showed an effective curveball and changeup, along with excellent control. With the help of Brevard County pitching coach Mark Grater, he cleaned up his mechanics and improved his arm speed. For someone who was more of a shortstop as a Canadian amateur, Hill is polished. Because he doesn't have an overpowering pitch, Hill doesn't miss a lot of bats. That leaves him little margin for error, though his command has allowed him to succeed. He needs to maintain his delivery because when he rushes his sinker rises. Hill boosted his stock more than any pitcher in the system. He should begin 2004 in Double-A and projects as a mid-rotation workhorse in the majors.

Year	Club (League)	Class	W	L	ERA	G	GS	CG	SV	IP	H	R	ER	HR	BB	SO	AVG
2000	Expos (GCL)	R	1	3	4.81	7	7	0	0	24	25	17	13	0	10	20	.250
2001	Vermont (NY-P)	A	2	2	2.27	7	7	0	0	36	22	12	9	0	8	23	.172
2002	Clinton (Mid)	A	12	7	3.44	25	25	0	0	147	149	75	56	7	35	99	.261
2003	Brevard County (FSL)	A	9	4	2.56	22	21	2	0	127	118	47	36	3	26	66	.248
	Harrisburg (EL)	AA	3	1	3.54	4	4	0	0	20	23	12	8	0	11	12	.280
MINOR LEAGUE TOTALS			27	17	3.10	65	64	2	0	354	337	163	122	10	90	220	.248

7 Darrell Rasner, rhp

Born: Jan. 13, 1981. **Ht.:** 6-3. **Wt.:** 210. **Bats:** R. **Throws:** R. **School:** University of Nevada. **Career Transactions:** Selected by Expos in second round of 2002 draft; signed July 2, 2002.

Drafted behind Everts in 2002, Rasner was off to a good start in his first full pro season before a minor case of shoulder tendinitis sidelined him for a month. He pitched well when he first came off the disabled list before wilting in August. He established several school records during his three-year career at Nevada. Rasner has a prototype pitcher's body with a broad upper torso and strong legs. He has a quick arm action from a three-quarters slot and gets good extension in his delivery. His 88-94 mph fastball features heavy sink and run. He complements it with an average to plus 75-76 mph curveball and an 82 mph circle changeup. When Rasner pumps his fastball up to 94 mph, it lacks the running action he gets when he throws in the high 80s. At times he'll get inside the ball, which also costs him movement. He needs to continue to improve his command of his curveball. Rasner will move up another step to high Class A in 2004. He could reach Double-A by mid-season and the majors by the end of 2005.

Year	Club (League)	Class	W	L	ERA	G	GS	CG	SV	IP	H	R	ER	HR	BB	SO	AVG
2002	Vermont (NY-P)	A	2	5	4.33	10	10	0	0	44	44	27	21	1	18	49	.262
2003	Savannah (SAL)	A	7	7	4.19	22	22	2	0	105	106	53	49	8	36	90	.268
MINOR LEAGUE TOTALS			9	12	4.23	32	32	2	0	149	150	80	70	9	54	139	.266

8 Seung Song, rhp

Born: June 29, 1980. **Ht.:** 6-1. **Wt.:** 190. **Bats:** R. **Throws:** R. **Career Transactions:** Signed out of Korea by Red Sox, Feb. 2, 1999 . . . Traded by Red Sox with RHP Sun-Woo Kim to Expos for OF Cliff Floyd, July 30, 2002.

Song was the key player for the Expos in the Cliff Floyd trade with Boston in July 2002. He became the first Harrisburg pitcher since Lew Krausse Sr. in 1933 to throw a no-hitter in the Eastern League when he beat Erie 2-1 on April 28, 2003. In July, he became the first player to appear in three Futures Games. Song throws strikes. The Expos adjusted his delivery, shortening his arm action. His fastball was a constant 88-90 mph in 2003, and his 72-74 mph curveball is a plus pitch when he commands it. He also throws a changeup and has played around with a splitter. Despite his no-hitter, Song hasn't been as dominant as he was in the Red Sox system. He lost about four miles an hour off both his fastball and curve. His strikeout rate declined even more dramatically, from 10.1 per nine innings over his first four pro seasons to 5.2 in 2003. Though Song rated as Boston's top prospect entering 2002, now he looks like a back-of-the-rotation starter. He should get a shot at cracking the Expos staff in 2004.

Year	Club (League)	Class	W	L	ERA	G	GS	CG	SV	IP	H	R	ER	HR	BB	SO	AVG
1999	Red Sox (GCL)	R	5	5	2.30	13	9	0	0	55	47	29	14	2	20	61	.227
2000	Lowell (NY-P)	A	5	2	2.60	13	13	0	0	73	63	26	21	1	20	93	.233
2001	Augusta (SAL)	A	3	2	2.04	14	14	0	0	75	56	24	17	3	18	79	.208
	Sarasota (FSL)	A	5	2	1.68	8	8	0	0	48	28	11	9	1	18	56	.164
2002	Trenton (EL)	AA	7	7	4.39	21	21	0	0	109	106	61	53	11	37	116	.256
	Harrisburg (EL)	AA	0	0	0.00	1	1	0	0	5	5	2	0	0	0	5	.250
2003	Harrisburg (EL)	AA	5	2	2.35	13	13	1	0	73	55	26	19	5	24	44	.208
	Edmonton (PCL)	AAA	7	2	3.79	13	13	1	0	74	69	34	31	6	33	40	.254
MINOR LEAGUE TOTALS			37	22	2.89	96	92	2	0	511	429	213	164	29	170	494	.227

9 Terrmel Sledge, of

Born: March 18, 1977. **Ht.:** 6-0. **Wt.:** 180. **Bats:** L. **Throws:** L. **School:** Long Beach State U. **Career Transactions:** Selected by Mariners in eighth round of 1999 draft; signed June 18, 1999 . . . Traded by Mariners to Expos, Sept. 27, 2000, completing trade in which Expos sent C Chris Widger to Mariners for two players to be named (Aug. 8, 2000); Expos also acquired LHP Sean Spencer (Aug. 10, 2000).

Sledge pounded Pacific Coast League pitching in 2003, leading the league in runs while finishing second in slugging and third in batting. Because Major League Baseball wouldn't permit the Expos to expand their roster in September, Sledge never got a look in the majors. After the season, Sledge made headlines by becoming the second player on a major league roster to test positive for steroids. He tested positive during Team USA tryouts in October, though the U.S. Anti-Doping Agency did not announce the results until January. Because the test was

not conducted by Major League Baseball and took place in 2003, Sledge will not face any sanctions under MLB's new steroid policy. Sledge has a compact stroke that allows him to spray line drives to the gaps. He has a game plan and always has quality at-bats. He waits for his pitch and is aggressive when he gets it. He did a better job of using the whole field and hitting pitches up in the strike zone in 2003. His 22 homers doubled his previous career high. He's athletic and has above-average speed. Because he doesn't project as a big league center fielder, Sledge needs to add more power in order to start on a corner. He needs to work on his routes on fly balls and his throwing. He has average arm strength, but his throws are low and lack carry. After the Expos brought in Carl Everett and Juan Rivera in the offseason to fill their outfield holes, Sledge has little opportunity for a regular big league job in 2004. He could win a spot on the bench, and might be a better long-term fit as a fourth outfielder anyway.

Year	Club (League)	Class	AVG	G	AB	R	H	2B	3B	HR	RBI	BB	SO	SB	SLG	OBP
1999	Everett (NWL)	A	.318	62	233	43	74	8	3	5	32	27	35	9	.442	.406
2000	Wisconsin (Mid)	A	.217	7	23	5	5	2	2	0	3	3	3	1	.478	.333
	Lancaster (Cal)	A	.339	103	384	90	130	22	7	11	75	72	49	35	.518	.458
2001	Harrisburg (EL)	AA	.277	129	448	66	124	22	6	9	48	51	72	30	.413	.359
2002	Harrisburg (EL)	AA	.301	102	396	74	119	18	6	8	43	55	70	11	.437	.401
	Ottawa (IL)	AAA	.263	24	80	12	21	5	2	1	11	11	15	1	.413	.359
2003	Edmonton (PCL)	AAA	.324	131	497	95	161	26	9	22	92	61	93	13	.545	.397
MINOR LEAGUE TOTALS			.308	558	2061	385	634	103	35	56	304	280	337	100	.473	.400

10 Ryan Church, of

STEVE MOORE

Born: Oct. 14, 1978. **Ht.:** 6-1. **Wt.:** 190. **Bats:** L. **Throws:** L. **Career Transactions:** Selected by Indians in 14th round of 2000 draft; signed June 7, 2000 . . . Traded by Indians with SS Maicer Izturis to Expos for LHP Scott Stewart, Jan. 5, 2004..

Church has a solid all-around package of tools, but he was stuck behind a group of talented young outfielders in the Indians system. Thus his career received a huge boost when he joined the Expos in the Scott Stewart trade in January. Church began his college career as a pitcher before hurting his arm, and he has persevered and overachieved since entering pro ball as a 14th-round pick. His strong build, quick bat, slight uppercut and ability to make hard contact give him above-average raw power. He projects as a .275 hitter with 25 homers annually in the majors, though he needs more consistency and better plate discipline. He's predominantly a pull hitter and must use the opposite field more often. Though Church is a slighty below-average runner, he's capable of playing all three outfield positions. He's best suited for right field because of his strong arm. He'll probably start 2004 in Triple-A but could push for a promotion in the second half, especially if Juan Rivera should struggle in right field.

Year	Club (League)	Class	AVG	G	AB	R	H	2B	3B	HR	RBI	BB	SO	SB	SLG	OBP
2000	Mahoning Valley (NY-P)	A	.298	73	272	51	81	16	5	10	65	38	49	11	.504	.396
2001	Columbus (SAL)	A	.287	101	363	64	104	23	3	17	76	54	79	4	.507	.385
	Kinston (Car)	A	.241	24	83	16	20	7	0	5	15	18	23	1	.506	.379
2002	Kinston (Car)	A	.326	53	181	30	59	12	1	10	30	31	51	4	.569	.433
	Akron (EL)	AA	.296	71	291	39	86	17	4	12	51	12	58	1	.505	.325
2003	Akron (EL)	AA	.261	99	371	47	97	17	3	13	52	32	64	4	.429	.325
MINOR LEAGUE TOTALS			.286	421	1561	247	447	92	16	67	289	185	324	25	.495	.368

11 Rogearvin Bernadina, of

Born: June 12, 1984. **Ht.:** 6-0. **Wt.:** 170. **Bats:** L. **Throws:** L. **Career Transactions:** Signed out of the Netherlands by Expos, Nov. 3, 2001.

Bernadina is the last player former Expos director of international operations Fred Ferreira signed before moving to the Marlins. Ferreira signed him out of Montreal's academy in the Netherlands. Bernadina made his full-season debut in 2003 as one of the youngest regulars in the South Atlantic League. Bernadina is a raw, toolsy outfielder with perhaps the highest upside of any position player in the organization. He's a pure hitter with a smooth stroke and quick hands. He shows gap power now and projects to hit with average power. He's a spectacular center fielder with excellent instincts and an average arm. He has above-average speed and should be a factor on the basepaths with more experience. Bernadina comes from a limited baseball background and still has a ways to go in learning the intricacies of the game. He needs to improve his plate discipline but has a solid approach at the plate, considering his age and limited baseball experience. Bernadina profiles as a five-tool center fielder in the majors, and Expos officials often compare his bat to Garret Anderson's. He'll start 2004 as a teenager in high Class A.

Year	Club (League)	Class	AVG	G	AB	R	H	2B	3B	HR	RBI	BB	SO	SB	SLG	OBP
2002	Expos (GCL)	R	.276	57	196	22	54	7	0	3	18	19	25	1	.357	.348
2003	Savannah (SAL)	A	.237	77	278	36	66	12	3	4	39	19	53	11	.345	.292
MINOR LEAGUE TOTALS			.253	134	474	58	120	19	3	7	57	38	78	12	.350	.316

12 Jason Bergmann, rhp

Born: Sept. 25, 1981. **Ht.:** 6-4. **Wt.:** 190. **Bats:** R. **Throws:** R. **School:** Rutgers University. **Career Transactions:** Selected by Expos in 11th round of 2002 draft; signed June 12, 2002.

Bergmann sprained his right ankle when he slipped on ice at home in New Jersey in January 2003. He couldn't walk for two weeks and was behind the other pitchers when he reported to spring training. Despite the setback, he had a good first half and was selected to the South Atlantic League's all-star game, before slumping down the stretch. Bergmann has a long, lean body and a live arm. From a low three-quarters angle, he can run his fastball into the 91-94 mph range. His heater has boring action up in the zone and will sink and tail when he keeps it down. He has a 72-76 mph downer curveball with good depth and a 78-82 mph changeup with tumbling action. He has a sound delivery but will rush sometimes, causing his front side to fly open. That leads to problems with his control. Bergmann likely will move to high Class A in 2004.

Year	Club (League)	Class	W	L	ERA	G	GS	CG	SV	IP	H	R	ER	HR	BB	SO	AVG
2002	Vermont (NY-P)	A	7	4	2.89	14	14	0	0	72	48	27	23	4	33	57	.194
2003	Savannah (SAL)	A	6	11	4.29	23	22	1	0	109	108	57	52	8	53	82	.264
MINOR LEAGUE TOTALS			13	15	3.74	37	36	1	0	181	156	84	75	12	86	139	.237

13 Scott Hodges, 3b

Born: Dec. 26, 1978. **Ht.:** 6-0. **Wt.:** 190. **Bats:** L. **Throws:** R. **School:** Henry Clay HS, Lexington, Ky. **Career Transactions:** Selected by Expos in first round (38th overall) of 1997 draft; signed June 5, 1997.

Hodges has been battling colitis for a couple of years, which has made it difficult for him to maintain his strength. He managed a full season in 2003 and showed improvement later in the year. His hitting actions are good but he needs more patience at the plate if he's going to provide enough offense for a third baseman. He should develop more over-the-fence power once he learns to turn on balls and drive them. Drafted as a shortstop, Hodges moved to the hot corner after signing and now displays Gold Glove-caliber skills. He has fluid fielding actions with quick hands, good range and lateral movement with a quick first step, and a lot of body control. Hodges has above-average arm strength, plus the ability to get rid of the ball quickly and make accurate throws. Though third base opened up when the Expos let Fernando Tatis go, they opted to sign Tony Batista rather than turn the position over to Hodges.

Year	Club (League)	Class	AVG	G	AB	R	H	2B	3B	HR	RBI	BB	SO	SB	SLG	OBP
1997	Expos (GCL)	R	.235	57	196	26	46	13	2	2	23	23	47	2	.352	.317
1998	Vermont (NY-P)	A	.278	67	266	35	74	13	3	3	35	11	59	8	.383	.305
1999	Cape Fear (SAL)	A	.258	127	449	62	116	31	2	8	59	45	105	8	.390	.324
2000	Jupiter (FSL)	A	.306	111	422	75	129	32	1	14	83	49	66	8	.486	.373
	Harrisburg (EL)	AA	.176	6	17	2	3	0	0	1	5	2	4	1	.353	.238
2001	Harrisburg (EL)	AA	.275	85	305	30	84	11	2	5	32	25	56	3	.374	.328
2002	Harrisburg (EL)	AA	.272	135	526	79	143	35	2	9	68	63	102	2	.397	.351
2003	Edmonton (PCL)	AAA	.288	126	482	67	139	21	3	12	66	29	93	5	.419	.327
MINOR LEAGUE TOTALS			.276	714	2663	376	734	156	15	54	371	247	532	37	.406	.336

14 Brandon Watson, of

Born: Sept. 30, 1981. **Ht.:** 6-1. **Wt.:** 170. **Bats:** L. **Throws:** R. **School:** Westchester HS, Los Angeles. **Career Transactions:** Selected by Expos in ninth round of 1999 draft; signed June 7, 1999.

After batting .236 through mid-May, Watson was one of the minors' hottest leadoff hitters over the remainder of the 2003 season. He hit .349 with 64 runs over his final 101 games, finishing fifth in the Eastern League in hitting. Watson began to improve as he developed more patience at the plate, though he still needs to draw more walks if he's going to be a tablesetter. He has a quick bat, makes good contact and shows the ability to hit to all fields. He lacks power, partly because he collapses his back shoulder, making his swing path longer and creating a loss of leverage. Watson is also an efficient bunter who can get down the line in 3.7 seconds when he drags the ball. He has plus speed, but needs to improve his jumps and baserunning skills. He has Gold Glove potential in center field, with superb flychasing skills and an average arm. Endy Chavez didn't seize Montreal's center-field job in 2003, and Watson could make a push to take it in the near future.

Year	Club (League)	Class	AVG	G	AB	R	H	2B	3B	HR	RBI	BB	SO	SB	SLG	OBP
1999	Expos (GCL)	R	.303	33	119	15	36	2	0	0	12	11	11	4	.319	.361
2000	Vermont (NY-P)	A	.291	69	278	53	81	9	1	0	30	25	38	26	.331	.354
2001	Clinton (Mid)	A	.327	117	489	74	160	16	9	2	38	29	65	33	.409	.364
2002	Brevard County (FSL)	A	.267	111	424	57	113	16	2	0	24	27	53	22	.314	.314
	Harrisburg (EL)	AA	.333	2	6	2	2	0	0	0	0	1	0	0	.333	.429
2003	Harrisburg (EL)	AA	.319	139	565	86	180	17	6	1	39	38	60	18	.375	.362
MINOR LEAGUE TOTALS			.304	471	1881	287	572	60	18	3	143	131	227	103	.360	.351

15 Rich Rundles, lhp

Born: June 3, 1981. **Ht.:** 6-5. **Wt.:** 180. **Bats:** L. **Throws:** L. **School:** Jefferson County HS, Dandridge, Tenn. **Career Transactions:** Selected by Red Sox in third round of 1999 draft; signed July 9, 1999 . . . Traded by Red Sox with RHP Tomo Ohka to Expos for RHP Ugueth Urbina, July 31, 2001.

Rundles joined the Expos along with Tomo Ohka in the Ugueth Urbina trade in July 2001. In his first full season in the organization, Rundles made just 11 starts because of elbow tendinitis. He was relatively healthy in his return to high Class A, experiencing only minor elbow soreness that cost him a few starts, and would have ranked seventh in the Florida State League in ERA if he hadn't fallen three innings short of qualifying. Rundles is a tall, lanky lefthander with good command of his 87-91 mph fastball. His 77-81 mph changeup is a plus pitch with late fade and tumble, but he needs to tighten up his slow 69-73 mph curveball. Rundles has an easy arm action and balanced delivery, but his arm path is long in back and fails to generate arm speed. Added strength is a must to improve his durability. He'll advance to Double-A in 2004.

Year	Club (League)	Class	W	L	ERA	G	GS	CG	SV	IP	H	R	ER	HR	BB	SO	AVG
1999	Red Sox (GCL)	R	1	0	2.13	5	1	0	0	13	13	3	3	1	1	11	.255
2000	Red Sox (GCL)	R	3	1	2.45	9	6	0	0	40	31	15	11	3	10	32	.218
2001	Augusta (SAL)	A	7	6	2.43	19	19	0	0	115	109	46	31	5	10	94	.247
	Clinton (Mid)	A	1	1	2.33	4	4	0	0	27	26	10	7	0	3	20	.248
2002	Brevard County (FSL)	A	2	7	4.08	12	11	0	0	57	66	34	26	5	16	31	.296
2003	Brevard County (FSL)	A	5	6	2.95	19	19	2	0	107	111	44	35	2	24	76	.268
MINOR LEAGUE TOTALS			19	21	2.83	68	60	2	0	359	356	152	113	16	64	264	.259

16 Val Pascucci, of/1b

Born: Nov. 17, 1978. **Ht.:** 6-6. **Wt.:** 230. **Bats:** R. **Throws:** R. **School:** U. of Oklahoma. **Career Transactions:** Selected by Expos in 15th round of 1999 draft; signed June 2, 1999.

After leading the Eastern League with 27 homers in 2002, Pascucci graduated to the Pacific Coast League, where he placed second with a .419 on-base percentage. Pascucci has a large frame and generates excellent leverage with power to all fields, but his ability to draw walks has also made him somewhat passive at the plate. Instead of feasting on pitches he could drive, Pascucci watched too many go by for strikes as he piled up a career-high 132 whiffs. Despite playing in more favorable parks, he dipped to 15 homers. His speed and arm are average, and he's adequate at right field and first base. Like Sledge, he might have been recalled in September had the Expos been permitted to expand their roster. With the Expos' offseason acquisitions at first base and in the outfield, Pascucci likely won't win a big league job in 2004 and could return to Triple-A.

Year	Club (League)	Class	AVG	G	AB	R	H	2B	3B	HR	RBI	BB	SO	SB	SLG	OBP
1999	Vermont (NY-P)	A	.351	72	259	62	91	26	1	7	48	53	46	17	.541	.482
2000	Cape Fear (SAL)	A	.319	20	69	17	22	4	0	3	10	16	15	5	.507	.442
	Jupiter (FSL)	A	.284	113	405	70	115	30	2	14	66	66	98	14	.472	.394
2001	Harrisburg (EL)	AA	.244	138	476	79	116	17	1	21	67	65	114	8	.416	.344
2002	Harrisburg (EL)	AA	.235	137	459	73	108	14	1	27	82	93	115	2	.447	.374
2003	Edmonton (PCL)	AAA	.281	138	459	80	129	29	1	15	85	101	132	3	.447	.419
MINOR LEAGUE TOTALS			.273	618	2127	381	581	120	6	87	358	394	520	49	.458	.397

17 Jerry Owens, of

Born: Feb. 16, 1981. **Ht.:** 6-3. **Wt.:** 195. **Bats:** L. **Throws:** L. **School:** The Masters (Calif.) College. **Career Transactions:** Selected by Expos in second round of 2003 draft; signed June 11, 2003.

Owens gave up baseball after his sophomore season at Hart High in Newhall, Calif., where he starred as a wide receiver catching passes from childhood friend Kyle Boller, who now starts for the NFL's Baltimore Ravens after going 19th overall in the 2003 NFL draft. Owens spent two injury-plagued years on UCLA's football team before enrolling at The Master's (Calif.) College and returning to the diamond. He initially wanted to pitch, but coaches convinced him that he needed to take advantage of his speed by playing a position. Owens did just that, hitting .451 with 30 stolen bases to win the Golden State Athletic Conference's 2003 player of the year award. He was one of the premier athletes in the 2003 draft, and the

Expos considered taking him 20th overall before opting for Chad Cordero. Owens has a lean, wiry physique with sinewy muscles. He can get down the line from the left side of the plate in 3.85-3.95 seconds, and has been clocked as quick as 3.5 seconds on a drag bunt. He projects as an electrifying basestealer in the majors, though he's raw and will need time to develop as a hitter. He lost valuable time last summer when he ran into an outfield wall during his second pro game, missing the rest of the season after minor operations on his throwing shoulder and a pre-existing hernia. Owens has a compact swing, good bat control and a line-drive approach. His bat occasionally drags through the zone and he needs to get his hands more extended. Owens has a below-average arm, but with his range probably will stay in center field. He'll play in low Class A in 2004.

Year	Club (League)	Class	AVG	G	AB	R	H	2B	3B	HR	RBI	BB	SO	SB	SLG	OBP
2003	Vermont (NY-P)	A	.125	2	8	0	1	0	0	0	0	0	2	1	.125	.125
MINOR LEAGUE TOTALS			.125	2	8	0	1	0	0	0	0	0	2	1	.125	.125

18 Daryl Thompson, rhp

Born: Nov. 2, 1985. **Ht.:** 6-1. **Wt.:** 170. **Bats:** R. **Throws:** R. **School:** La Plata HS, Mechanicsville, Md. **Career Transactions:** Selected by Expos in eighth round of 2003 draft; signed June 8, 2003.

Thompson was relatively unknown entering the 2003 season, but soon created a stir among scouts and drew comparisons to Oil Can Boyd for his pitching style and appearance. The Expos selected him in the eighth round and were more than pleased with his debut. Lean and wiry with long arms and legs, plus large hands and fingers, Thompson has good growth and strength potential. He has a loose arm action and somewhat funky mechanics. He drops and drives through his delivery, reaching down and back to fling his fastball consistently 90-91 mph and up to 94. Thompson works from an overhand three-quarters slot, getting good boring action up and down to righthanders with his fastball. His curve is a potential average big league pitch with quick downer rotation, while his changeup is effective. Thompson is athletic, showing plus running speed and solid defensive skills. The Expos have moved their young pitchers slowly in recent years, so Vermont could be his next step in 2004.

Year	Club (League)	Class	W	L	ERA	G	GS	CG	SV	IP	H	R	ER	HR	BB	SO	AVG
2003	Expos (GCL)	R	1	2	2.15	12	10	0	0	46	49	16	11	1	11	18	.288
MINOR LEAGUE TOTALS			1	2	2.15	12	10	0	0	46	49	16	11	1	11	18	.288

19 Chris Young, rhp

Born: May 25, 1979. **Ht.:** 6-10. **Wt.:** 250. **Bats:** R. **Throws:** R. **School:** Princeton University. **Career Transactions:** Selected by Pirates in third round of 2000 draft; signed Sept. 6, 2000 . . . Traded by Pirates with RHP Jon Searles to Expos for RHP Matt Herges, Dec. 20, 2002.

When Expos scouting director Dana Brown was an area scout with the Pirates, he engineered the $1.65 million signing of Young as a third-round pick in 2000. Young was an all-Ivy League center at Princeton with NBA potential, and his deal was heralded as a coup for Pittsburgh. But he developed slowly with the Pirates and fell out of favor with the new regime after general manager Dave Littlefield took over. Pittsburgh traded Young and righthander Jon Searles for Matt Herges in December 2002, then released Herges at the end of spring training. After switching organizations, Young was unhittable in high Class A and so-so in Double-A. At 6-foot-10 and 250 pounds, he has a commanding presence on the mound. He has smooth mechanics and a clean arm action for a pitcher so tall, but doesn't throw harder than 87-93 mph. The Expos sent Young to the Arizona Fall League to work on increasing his arm speed and adding some explosiveness to his delivery. After throwing a slider, he scrapped it in favor of an improving 76-80 mph curveball. It's a 12-to-6 downer that should be at least an average big league pitch. His changeup is also developing. Young should get his first taste of Triple-A at some point in 2004.

Year	Club (League)	Class	W	L	ERA	G	GS	CG	SV	IP	H	R	ER	HR	BB	SO	AVG
2001	Hickory (SAL)	A	5	3	4.12	12	12	2	0	74	79	39	34	6	20	72	.269
2002	Hickory (SAL)	A	11	9	3.11	26	26	1	0	145	127	57	50	11	34	136	.234
2003	Brevard County (FSL)	A	5	2	1.62	8	8	0	0	50	26	9	9	3	5	39	.150
	Harrisburg (EL)	AA	4	4	4.01	15	15	0	0	83	83	39	37	9	22	64	.259
MINOR LEAGUE TOTALS			25	18	3.32	61	61	3	0	352	315	144	130	29	81	311	.237

20 Antonio Sucre, of

Born: Aug. 13, 1983. **Ht.:** 6-2. **Wt.:** 180. **Bats:** R. **Throws:** R. **Career Transactions:** Signed out of Venezuela by Expos, July 20, 2000.

After signing as a 16-year-old in July 2000, Sucre appears ready for his first extended taste of full-season ball in low Class A this year. He has five-tool potential and has been brought along slowly because of his age and lack of refinement. He spent all of 2002-03 in the Rookie-level Gulf Coast League, except for one game in high Class A, where he fanned in both his at-bats. Sucre has a lanky, athletic body with plenty of room to add weight. He has a smooth righthanded stroke with good bat speed and leverage, and he projects to have above-average power as his body matures. But his ability to hit for average will be tested unless he makes some adjustments at the plate. He doesn't show much patience and currently struggles against breaking pitches because his swing can get long. Sucre is sound defensively with good range and an average arm. He's a plus runner who has yet to learn how to translate his speed into stolen bases.

Year	Club (League)	Class	AVG	G	AB	R	H	2B	3B	HR	RBI	BB	SO	SB	SLG	OBP
2001	Cagua (VSL)	R	.286	9	14	4	4	0	0	1	3	6	6	1	.500	.500
	Expos (DSL)	R	.235	28	98	13	23	2	2	4	15	7	30	2	.418	.324
2002	Expos (GCL)	R	.272	37	114	12	31	6	1	2	17	12	28	3	.395	.349
2003	Expos (GCL)	R	.229	48	166	28	38	10	2	4	28	13	45	1	.386	.309
	Brevard County (FSL)	A	.000	1	2	0	0	0	0	0	0	0	2	0	.000	.000
MINOR LEAGUE TOTALS			.244	123	394	57	96	18	5	11	63	38	111	7	.398	.331

21 Luke Lockwood, lhp

Born: July 21, 1981. **Ht.:** 6-3. **Wt.:** 170. **Bats:** L. **Throws:** L. **School:** Silverado HS, Victorville, Calif. **Career Transactions:** Selected by Expos in eighth round of 1999 draft; signed June 3, 1999.

Lockwood had been on the prospect radar screen for a couple of years, primarily because he was a lefthander who knew how to pitch and projected to add velocity. But in his first taste of Double-A, he struggled for most of the 2003 season before going 5-0, 1.47 in August. Lockwood started pitching better after the Expos remade his arm action. Earlier in the season, he had a long arm arc and batters got a good look at the ball. After he quickened his arm action in back and improved his tempo, he gained better deception. Lockwood pitches with an 85-88 mph fastball, an average changeup and an improving curveball. Unless he comes up with an out pitch, he may be relegated to middle relief. He's dependent on his defense to make plays for him, and he has to figure out a way to combat righthanders, who hit .330 and slugged .507 against him last year.

Year	Club (League)	Class	W	L	ERA	G	GS	CG	SV	IP	H	R	ER	HR	BB	SO	AVG
1999	Expos (GCL)	R	1	2	4.57	11	7	0	0	41	46	21	21	3	13	32	.275
2000	Jupiter (FSL)	A	0	1	10.93	3	3	0	0	14	24	17	17	3	5	2	.407
	Vermont (NY-P)	A	1	0	2.25	2	2	0	0	12	12	3	3	1	1	8	.279
	Cape Fear (SAL)	A	2	4	4.50	9	9	0	0	48	49	32	24	3	20	33	.271
2001	Clinton (Mid)	A	5	10	2.70	26	26	3	0	163	152	78	49	8	49	114	.248
2002	Brevard County (FSL)	A	10	7	3.37	26	26	0	0	147	155	69	55	13	38	86	.274
2003	Harrisburg (EL)	AA	8	11	5.16	26	26	2	0	145	175	89	83	16	41	64	.303
MINOR LEAGUE TOTALS			27	35	3.98	103	99	5	0	570	613	309	252	47	167	339	.278

22 Vince Rooi, 3b

Born: Dec. 13, 1981. **Ht.:** 6-1. **Wt.:** 190. **Bats:** R. **Throws:** R. **Career Transactions:** Signed out of the Netherlands by Expos, Aug. 4, 1998.

Rooi missed part of the 2003 season when he suited up for the Dutch national team. He led the European championship with two homers and was named the tournament's best defensive player as he helped the Netherlands to a first-place finish. Then he played a part-time role as the Dutch finished second at Europe's Olympic qualifying tournament to earn a berth in the 2004 Athens Olympics. Rooi has made slow but steady progress in the Expos system. He returned for his second stint at high Class A last season and showed marked improvement at the plate. He has a medium-sized frame with a muscular upper body and strong wrists. He has good power potential and a fairly compact stroke, but his body is wound so tightly that there's stiffness in his swing. Rooi has a solid approach at the plate but must improve his flexibility and bat speed to have success as he moves up the ladder. His .254 average and .379 slugging percentages were career highs, yet far short of the production he's going to need to make it to the majors. Defensively, he has quick actions at third base. His hands, range and arm are all assets. Rooi will begin 2004 in Double-A.

Year	Club (League)	Class	AVG	G	AB	R	H	2B	3B	HR	RBI	BB	SO	SB	SLG	OBP
1999	Expos (GCL)	R	.189	36	111	17	21	4	0	0	10	22	24	3	.225	.328
2000	Vermont (NY-P)	A	.231	65	234	36	54	9	1	6	43	40	60	9	.355	.348
2001	Clinton (Mid)	A	.254	120	422	53	107	22	0	9	60	61	94	5	.370	.349
2002	Brevard County (FSL)	A	.193	118	367	38	71	11	1	4	38	52	86	7	.242	.295
2003	Brevard County (FSL)	A	.254	97	319	34	81	19	0	7	52	36	70	3	.379	.334
MINOR LEAGUE TOTALS			.230	436	1453	178	334	65	2	26	203	211	334	27	.331	.330

23 Edgardo Baez, of

Born: July 12, 1985. **Ht.:** 6-2. **Wt.:** 190. **Bats:** R. **Throws:** R. **School:** Jose S. Alegria HS, Dorado, P.R. **Career Transactions:** Selected by Expos in fourth round of 2003 draft; signed July 1, 2003.

Baez was the consensus top prospect in Puerto Rico before the Excellence Games, a pre-draft showcase held on the island in May. He didn't perform well there, which caused him to slide to the Expos in the fourth round. After arriving in the Gulf Coast League, he again showed his middle-of-the-order potential. He has a well-proportioned, athletic frame with room for added strength. He has a fluid stroke at the plate, featuring quickness and a slight uppercut. Baez is aggressive and projects to have average power. He does have a hitch in his swing, which causes him difficulty with inside pitches. He's a slow runner out of the box and is decent once he gets under way. He doesn't cover a lot of ground in the outfield, but he does own an average arm and can handle right field. Baez' most likely destination in 2004 is Vermont.

Year	Club (League)	Class	AVG	G	AB	R	H	2B	3B	HR	RBI	BB	SO	SB	SLG	OBP
2003	Expos (GCL)	R	.274	34	117	12	32	7	1	3	15	9	31	1	.427	.323
MINOR LEAGUE TOTALS			.274	34	117	12	32	7	1	3	15	9	31	1	.427	.323

24 Frank Diaz, of

Born: Oct. 6, 1983. **Ht.:** 6-2. **Wt.:** 180. **Bats:** R. **Throws:** R. **Career Transactions:** Signed out of Venezuela by Expos, July 4, 2000.

After two seasons in the Gulf Coast League, Diaz made the jump to low Class A in 2003 and held his own as a 19-year old. Signed as a righthanded pitcher, he never made it to the mound because the Expos converted him to the outfield after they saw him swing the bat. Diaz has a solid, athletic body and projects as a power-hitting right fielder in the majors. He has good bat speed and a smooth line-drive stroke, but his swing can get long at times and he needs to incorporate a better trigger mechanism. Starting from a slightly open stance, Diaz generates above-average power potential but will have to concentrate on hitting the ball to all fields. He tends to get pull-conscious. He also needs to show more patience at the plate or run the risk of being exploited by pitchers at higher levels. Diaz has average speed and keen baserunning instincts. A good defender with a plus arm, he can play all three outfield positions. He's destined for high Class A this year.

Year	Club (League)	Class	AVG	G	AB	R	H	2B	3B	HR	RBI	BB	SO	SB	SLG	OBP
2001	Expos (GCL)	R	.219	38	128	10	28	5	1	0	8	12	27	10	.273	.297
2002	Expos (GCL)	R	.277	51	173	33	48	8	2	5	24	19	28	8	.434	.370
	Brevard County (FSL)	A	.226	10	31	3	7	2	0	0	1	6	4	3	.290	.351
2003	Savannah (SAL)	A	.270	122	440	63	119	28	4	7	49	15	73	19	.400	.298
MINOR LEAGUE TOTALS			.262	221	772	109	202	43	7	12	82	52	132	40	.382	.317

25 Chad Bentz, lhp

Born: May 5, 1980. **Ht.:** 6-2. **Wt.:** 210. **Bats:** R. **Throws:** L. **School:** Long Beach State University. **Career Transactions:** Selected by Expos in seventh round of 2001 draft; signed June 10, 2001.

Similar to Jim Abbott, Bentz was born without a complete right hand. That handicap hasn't impeded his baseball progress, as he pitched in Double-A in his second full season. An Alaska high school product who pitched with limited success at Long Beach State, Bentz broke into pro ball as a starter in 2001, moved to the bullpen in his first full season and became a closer midway through 2003. He's the best lefthanded reliever in the system. With a solid delivery and durable frame, Bentz throws a 91-93 mph fastball with late life and a plus slider. He also throws a cutter to get in on righthanders and has the confidence to throw any pitch at any time. His changeup is effective but still needs improvement. His command slipped against more experienced hitters last season. After pitching with nerve damage in his left foot in 2002, Bentz was relatively healthy. He had a case of pink eye early in the season and a pulled upper stomach muscle in August. He was supposed to head to the Arizona Fall League in October, but the Expos changed their minds and decided not to send him because he had thrown too many innings. He should start the 2004 season in Triple-A.

Year	Club (League)	Class	W	L	ERA	G	GS	CG	SV	IP	H	R	ER	HR	BB	SO	AVG
2001	Vermont (NY-P)	A	1	3	4.91	8	8	0	0	37	39	23	20	2	11	38	.264
2002	Brevard County (FSL)	A	0	1	3.64	23	0	0	5	30	30	14	12	1	14	34	.259
2003	Harrisburg (EL)	AA	1	4	2.55	52	0	0	16	85	72	31	24	4	39	56	.241
MINOR LEAGUE TOTALS			2	8	3.34	83	8	0	21	151	141	68	56	7	64	128	.250

26 Danny Rueckel, rhp

Born: Sept. 25, 1979. **Ht.:** 6-0. **Wt.:** 170. **Bats:** R. **Throws:** R. **School:** Furman University. **Career Transactions:** Selected by Expos in 12th round of 2002 draft; signed June 14, 2002.

Though Clint Everts' noted curveball has received much more attention, the Expos insist that Rueckel's is better. It's a devastating 78-82 mph curve with hard bite, and it grades as a 75 on the 20-80 scouting scale. He gained command of it down the stretch and was unhittable in August, not allowing a run and fanning 19 in 13 innings while opponents batted .075 against him. It was a stunning conclusion to his first full season as a pitcher, as he had been a four-year starter at shortstop at Furman. Rueckel is an athletic righthander with a medium frame. He can run his fastball into the 89-92 mph range with late movement. If he can continue to progress like he did at the end of 2003, he'll advance rapidly. For now, he's ticketed for high Class A.

Year	Club (League)	Class	W	L	ERA	G	GS	CG	SV	IP	H	R	ER	HR	BB	SO	AVG
2002	Vermont (NY-P)	A	1	1	1.53	10	0	0	3	18	12	8	3	0	3	23	.188
	Clinton (Mid)	A	3	1	4.15	14	0	0	0	26	23	12	12	1	10	25	.232
2003	Savannah (SAL)	A	1	3	4.06	40	1	0	14	69	68	38	31	4	16	64	.260
MINOR LEAGUE TOTALS			5	5	3.69	64	1	0	17	112	103	58	46	5	29	112	.242

27 Roy Corcoran, rhp

Born: May 11, 1980. **Ht.:** 5-10. **Wt.:** 170. **Bats:** R. **Throws:** R. **School:** Louisiana State University. **Career Transactions:** Signed as nondrafted free agent by Expos, June 15, 2001.

Signed as a nondrafted free agent out of Louisiana State in 2001, Corcoran rocketed through the system. He started 2003 in high Class A and was called up to Montreal in late July, giving up one run in five big league appearances. While he lacks the size scouts desire in a pitcher, his arm action is so quick it looks like he is throwing harder than he actually is. Corcoran has a heavy 91-92 mph fastball, good command and a knack for keeping the ball down in the strike zone. His tight 78-80 mph curveball is a second plus pitch that rates as a 65 on the 20-80 scouting scale. His changeup lags behind his other two pitches, but isn't as crucial in a relief role. Corcoran is a candidate to return to the big league bullpen in 2004.

Year	Club (League)	Class	W	L	ERA	G	GS	CG	SV	IP	H	R	ER	HR	BB	SO	AVG
2001	Expos (GCL)	R	2	0	1.56	13	0	0	2	17	12	4	3	2	2	21	.185
	Jupiter (FSL)	A	0	0	0.00	1	0	0	0	2	0	0	0	0	2	0	.000
2002	Clinton (Mid)	A	3	4	4.16	48	1	0	11	80	82	51	37	5	24	106	.253
2003	Brevard County (FSL)	A	5	3	1.91	28	0	0	12	33	19	8	7	1	11	35	.171
	Harrisburg (EL)	AA	1	1	0.38	14	0	0	3	24	14	4	1	0	7	26	.167
	Montreal (NL)	MAJ	0	0	1.23	5	0	0	0	7	7	2	1	0	3	2	.250
	Edmonton (PCL)	AAA	0	0	0.00	2	0	0	0	2	0	0	0	0	0	1	.000
MAJOR LEAGUE TOTALS			0	0	1.23	5	0	0	0	7	7	2	1	0	3	2	.250
MINOR LEAGUE TOTALS			11	8	2.73	106	1	0	28	158	127	67	48	8	46	189	.213

28 Alexis Morales, rhp

Born: Dec. 8, 1982. **Ht.:** 5-11. **Wt.:** 170. **Bats:** R. **Throws:** R. **School:** Oakton (Ill.) CC. **Career Transactions:** Signed by independent Joliet (Northern), June 2003 . . . Selected by Expos in 46th round of 2003 draft; signed July 8, 2003.

The Expos regarded Morales as a sixth- to ninth-round talent in the 2003 draft, but he had some arm soreness in junior college and they thought he was unsignable. Then area scout Zack Hoyrst learned that Morales was academically ineligible to return to school, so Montreal grabbed him in the 46th round and signed him for 10th-round money. After the draft Morales went to play for the Joliet JackHammers in the independent Northern League, where his junior college head coach Mike Pinto was the JackHammers' pitching coach. The Expos saw he was healthy and signed him, and he threw so well that they advanced him to high Class A. Morales is a smallish righthander with a power arm. He has a short, quick arm action that generates fastballs up to 94 mph and sliders up to 82. His slider is the better of the two pitches, a sharp breaker with good tilt that grades as a 70 on the 20-80 scouting scale. He also has a decent changeup with late tumble. The Expos aren't sure yet what they have in Morales. He could be a late-inning reliever or end up in the rotation. He'll probably return to the Florida State League this year.

Year	Club (League)	Class	W	L	ERA	G	GS	CG	SV	IP	H	R	ER	HR	BB	SO	AVG
2003	Joliet (NorC)	IND	0	2	5.14	5	2	0	0	14	10	10	8	1	12	12	.200
	Expos (GCL)	R	1	1	0.90	6	0	0	1	10	10	4	1	0	1	10	.256
	Brevard County (FSL)	A	0	0	0.00	2	0	0	1	5	3	0	0	0	3	8	.158
MINOR LEAGUE TOTALS			1	1	0.59	8	0	0	2	15	13	4	1	0	4	18	.224

29 Wilton Chavez, rhp

Born: June 13, 1978. **Ht.:** 6-2. **Wt.:** 160. **Bats:** R. **Throws:** R. **Career Transactions:** Signed out of Dominican Republic by Cubs, Feb. 3, 1998 . . . Traded by Cubs to Expos for OF/3B Jose Macias, Dec. 19, 2003.

In one of his best trades as Montreal's GM, Omar Minaya somehow turned soft-hitting Jose Macias into Chavez, who was buried behind a slew of more talented arms in the Cubs system. Macias was eligible for arbitration and about to be nontendered, while Chavez could crack the Expos rotation in the near future. Chavez led the short-season Northwest League in strikeouts in 2000, but his stock has dropped since. He was discovered to be nearly three years older than he was believed to be when he signed. He lacks a true plus pitch, though he has gotten by with an 87-91 mph fastball, a slurvy slider and a changeup. When it's on, his slider is his best offering. Chavez throws strikes and has been able to miss enough bats to be effective. He didn't fool many Triple-A lefthanders—they batted .286 and slugged .466 against him—so he probably needs to return to that level before he's ready for Montreal.

Year	Club (League)	Class	W	L	ERA	G	GS	CG	SV	IP	H	R	ER	HR	BB	SO	AVG
1998	Cubs (DSL)	R	7	5	2.48	20	5	2	1	83	58	33	23	5	20	84	.196
1999	Cubs (AZL)	R	5	5	5.88	14	13	1	0	67	89	57	44	5	31	68	.309
2000	Eugene (NWL)	A	7	1	1.69	15	15	0	0	90	69	28	17	0	25	103	.208
2001	Lansing (Mid)	A	2	6	4.02	8	8	2	0	47	38	24	21	4	27	60	.220
	Daytona (FSL)	A	3	4	4.12	17	16	0	0	90	96	46	41	8	30	59	.269
2002	Daytona (FSL)	A	0	3	4.74	8	6	0	0	25	30	18	13	2	12	25	.300
	West Tenn (SL)	AA	8	5	3.76	18	18	0	0	103	97	48	43	7	39	86	.256
2003	Iowa (PCL)	AAA	11	7	4.24	26	22	1	0	140	144	69	66	17	51	113	.269
	West Tenn (SL)	AA	0	0	2.25	2	1	0	0	8	5	2	2	0	2	15	.172
MINOR LEAGUE TOTALS			43	36	3.72	128	104	6	1	653	626	325	270	48	237	613	.252

30 Josh Labandeira, ss

Born: Feb. 25, 1979. **Ht.:** 5-7. **Wt.:** 180. **Bats:** R. **Throws:** R. **School:** Fresno State University. **Career Transactions:** Selected by Expos in sixth round of 2001 draft; signed June 13, 2001.

The 2001 Western Athletic Conference player of the year, Labandeira broke his leg in his first pro game that summer. He made up for lost time by reaching Double-A midway through 2003, but hit the wall and struggled offensively. Labandeira is a sparkplug who plays hard at all times. He has a tightly wound body that has reached full maturity. He has a short, compact swing with gap power, but also shows some stiffness and a tendency to chase pitches up in the strike zone. He's flashy on defense with soft hands and a plus arm, but has trouble coming across the bag at second, which could be due to the lingering effects from his leg injury. Labandeira is an intelligent baserunner with average speed. He'll need to prove he can handle Double-A pitching before advancing further, but for now he's the top shortstop prospect in the organization.

Year	Club (League)	Class	AVG	G	AB	R	H	2B	3B	HR	RBI	BB	SO	SB	SLG	OBP
2001	Vermont (NY-P)	A	.333	1	3	2	1	0	0	0	0	0	0	0	.333	.333
2002	Clinton (Mid)	A	.286	129	493	60	141	27	3	8	67	45	73	15	.402	.350
2003	Brevard County (FSL)	A	.324	62	238	41	77	13	4	0	25	24	35	6	.412	.386
	Harrisburg (EL)	AA	.239	60	238	25	57	18	2	2	26	20	38	0	.357	.298
MINOR LEAGUE TOTALS			.284	252	972	128	276	58	9	10	118	89	146	21	.393	.346

NEW YORK
METS

TOP 30 PROSPECTS

1. Kazuo Matsui, ss
2. Scott Kazmir, lhp
3. David Wright, 3b
4. Matt Peterson, rhp
5. Lastings Milledge, of
6. Justin Huber, c
7. Bob Keppel, rhp
8. Jeremy Griffiths, rhp
9. Victor Diaz, 2b
10. Craig Brazell, 1b
11. Aaron Baldiris, 3b
12. Tyler Yates, rhp
13. Royce Ring, lhp
14. Kole Strayhorn, rhp
15. Mike Jacobs, c
16. Danny Garcia, 2b
17. Joselo Diaz, rhp
18. Matt Lindstrom, rhp
19. Prentice Redman, of
20. Orber Moreno, rhp
21. Bob Malek, of
22. Shawn Bowman, 3b
23. Jason Anderson, rhp
24. Pat Strange, rhp
25. Blake McGinley, lhp
26. P.J. Bevis, rhp
27. Tyler Davidson, of/1b
28. Yusmeiro Petit, rhp
29. Wayne Lydon, of
30. Anderson Garcia, rhp

By J.J. Cooper

When the most successful team in baseball sits a subway ride away, it's never easy to accept that it's time to rebuild. So before the 2003 season began, the Mets tried to erase the nightmare of 2002 with another plunge into free agency.

But neither the signings of Cliff Floyd, Tom Glavine, Rey Sanchez and Mike Stanton, nor the addition of new manager Art Howe did much to turn around the club. The Mets once again were an ill-conceived, underachieving club, and injury problems only made matters worse. New York finished 66-95, its worst record in a decade. General manager Steve Phillips finally lost his job on June 12, and was replaced by senior assistant GM/farm director Jim Duquette. Duquette, who didn't have the "interim" tag removed from his GM title until Oct. 28, immediately realized the Mets weren't going to challenge for a playoff spot. So for the first time in recent history, the franchise focused on building through its farm system.

Righthander Jae Weong Seo and third baseman Ty Wigginton made the Opening Day roster, and catcher/first baseman Jason Phillips came up in May when Mike Piazza got hurt. Shortstop Jose Reyes, the team's top prospect, had been promoted two days before Phillips was dismissed. The Mets gave auditions to righthanders Jeremy Griffiths and Aaron Heilman, second baseman Danny Garcia, and outfielders Jeff Duncan and Prentice Redman.

Duquette also tried to bolster the farm system by dumping veterans for youngsters. Roberto Alomar, Armando Benitez, Jeromy Burnitz, Graeme Lloyd and Sanchez were dispatched for a total of 11 prospects, most notably second baseman Victor Diaz and righthander relievers Kole Strayhorn and Joselo Diaz and lefty reliever Royce Ring.

After the season, Duquette and the Mets went back to the free-agent market to fill gaps. Mike Cameron will take over in center field, and much will be expected of touted Japanese shortstop Kazuo Matsui. Matsui's signing was a bit puzzling because it forced Reyes to move from shortstop to second base, but the Mets expect the combination to be a dynamic one.

The Mets don't have as many farmhands who will be ready to contribute in 2004, but their system has more depth than it has had recently. New York has done a nice job with its first-round picks, including righthander Bob Keppel and third baseman David Wright (both 2000), Heilman (2001), lefthander Scott Kazmir (2002) and outfielder Lastings Milledge (2003).

Mets fans will have to be patient as their club goes through an overhaul. But they do have some young talent to bank on, and just as important, the team has a long-term plan in place rather than playing for only the immediate future.

ORGANIZATION
OVERVIEW

General manager: Jim Duquette. **Farm director:** Kevin Morgan. **Scouting director:** Jack Bowen.

2003 PERFORMANCE

Class	Team	League	W	L	Pct.	Finish*	Manager
Majors	New York	National	66	95	.410	15th (16)	Art Howe
Triple-A	Norfolk Tides	International	67	76	.469	10th (14)	Bobby Floyd
Double-A	Binghamton Mets	Eastern	63	78	.447	9th (12)	John Stearns
High A	St. Lucie Mets	Florida State	77	62	.554	+2nd (12)	Ken Oberkfell
Low A	Capital City Bombers	South Atlantic	73	65	.529	7th (16)	Tony Tijerina
Short-season	Brooklyn Cyclones	New York-Penn	47	28	.627	2nd (14)	Tim Teufel
Rookie	Kingsport Mets	Appalachian	25	39	.391	8th (10)	Mookie Wilson
OVERALL 2003 MINOR LEAGUE RECORD			352	348	.503	12th (30)	

*Finish in overall standings (No. of teams in league). +League champion.

ORGANIZATION LEADERS

BATTING
Minimum 250 At-Bats

*AVG	Mike Jacobs, Binghamton	.329
R	Wayne Lydon, St. Lucie	83
H	Aaron Baldiris, Capital City/Brooklyn	155
TB	Rodney Nye, Norfolk/Binghamton	229
2B	Rodney Nye, Norfolk/Binghamton	41
3B	Tyler Davidson, Brooklyn/Kingsport	8
HR	Mike Jacobs, Binghamton	17
	Craig Brazell, Norfolk/Binghamton	17
RBI	Aaron Baldiris, Capital City/Brooklyn	86
BB	Jon Slack, Capital City/Brooklyn	77
SO	Blake Whealy, Capital City/Brooklyn	148
SB	Wayne Lydon, St. Lucie	75
*SLG	Mike Jacobs, Binghamton	.548
*OBP	Aaron Baldiris, Capital City/ Brooklyn	.406

PITCHING
#Minimum 75 Innings

W	Miguel Pinango, Capital City	13
L	Jason Roach, Norfolk	11
	Lenny Dinardo, Binghamton/St. Lucie	11
#ERA	Blake McGinley, St. Lucie	1.02
G	Pete Zamora, Norfolk	55
CG	Miguel Pinango, Capital City	3
SV	Robert Paulk, St.Lucie/Capital City/Brooklyn	22
IP	Kevin Deaton, Capital City	135
BB	Mike Cox, Binghamton/St.Lucie	63
SO	Scott Kazmir, St Lucie/Capital City	145

BEST TOOLS

Best Hitter for Average	Kazuo Matsui
Best Power Hitter	Craig Brazell
Fastest Baserunner	Wayne Lydon
Best Athlete	Lastings Milledge
Best Fastball	Scott Kazmir
Best Curveball	Matt Peterson
Best Slider	Tyler Yates
Best Changeup	Bob Keppel
Best Control	Blake McGinley
Best Defensive Catcher	Joe Hietpas
Best Defensive Infielder	Kazuo Matsui
Best Infield Arm	Corey Ragsdale
Best Defensive Outfielder	Prentice Redman
Best Outfield Arm	Bob Malek

PROJECTED 2007 LINEUP

Catcher	Justin Huber
First Base	Mike Piazza
Second Base	Jose Reyes
Third Base	David Wright
Shortstop	Kazuo Matsui
Left Field	Lastings Milledge

Center Field	Mike Cameron
Right Field	Cliff Floyd
No. 1 Starter	Scott Kazmir
No. 2 Starter	Matt Peterson
No. 3 Starter	Bob Keppel
No. 4 Starter	Jae Weong Seo
No. 5 Starter	Aaron Heilman
Closer	Braden Looper

LAST YEAR'S TOP 20 PROSPECTS

1. Jose Reyes, ss
2. Scott Kazmir, lhp
3. Aaron Heilman, rhp
4. David Wright, 3b
5. Justin Huber, c
6. Matt Peterson, rhp
7. Pat Strange, rhp
8. Jaime Cerda, lhp
9. Bob Keppel, rhp
10. Craig Brazell, 1b
11. Phil Seibel, lhp
12. Neal Musser, lhp
13. Jason Phillips, c
14. Jeremy Griffiths, rhp
15. David Mattox, rhp
16. Prentice Redman, of
17. Jeff Duncan, of
18. Heath Bell, rhp
19. Angel Pagan, of
20. Tyler Walker, rhp

TOP PROSPECTS OF THE DECADE

1994	Bill Pulsipher, lhp
1995	Bill Pulsipher, lhp
1996	Paul Wilson, rhp
1997	Jay Payton, of
1998	Grant Roberts, rhp
1999	Alex Escobar, of
2000	Alex Escobar, of
2001	Alex Escobar, of
2002	Aaron Heilman, rhp
2003	Jose Reyes, ss

TOP DRAFT PICKS OF THE DECADE

1994	Paul Wilson, rhp
1995	Ryan Jaroncyk, ss
1996	Robert Stratton, of
1997	Geoff Goetz, lhp
1998	Jason Tyner, of
1999	Neal Musser, lhp (2)
2000	Billy Traber, lhp
2001	Aaron Heilman, rhp
2002	Scott Kazmir, lhp
2003	Lastings Milledge, of

ALL-TIME LARGEST BONUSES

Scott Kazmir, 2002	$2,150,000
Lastings Milledge, 2003	$2,075,000
Geoff Goetz, 1997	$1,700,000
Paul Wilson, 1994	$1,550,000
Aaron Heilman, 2001	$1,508,750

MINOR LEAGUE
DEPTH CHART

NEW YORK METS

RANK: 10

Impact potential (A): The Mets system had made steady progress in recent years—even before signing Japanese free agent Kazuo Matsui, who will step in and contribute immediately. Scott Kazmir and David Wright look like an imposing pair of elite prospects. Lastings Milledge has the raw tools to make an impact down the road, but will face significant challenges adapting to pro ball.

Depth (C): The Mets are loaded with hard throwers. The only problem is most of them are limited to relief roles. They should continue to improve their depth and quality as new GM Jim Duquette, who had overseen the farm system, allocates more resources to scouting and development.

Sleeper: Yusmeiro Petit, rhp.   —*Depth charts prepared by Josh Boyd. Numbers in parentheses indicate prospect rankings.*

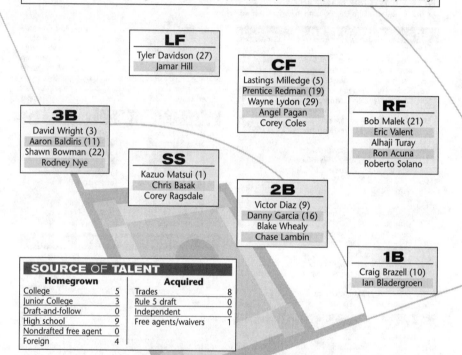

LF
Tyler Davidson (27)
Jamar Hill

CF
Lastings Milledge (5)
Prentice Redman (19)
Wayne Lydon (29)
Angel Pagan
Corey Coles

RF
Bob Malek (21)
Eric Valent
Alhaji Turay
Ron Acuna
Roberto Solano

3B
David Wright (3)
Aaron Baldiris (11)
Shawn Bowman (22)
Rodney Nye

SS
Kazuo Matsui (1)
Chris Basak
Corey Ragsdale

2B
Victor Diaz (9)
Danny Garcia (16)
Blake Whealy
Chase Lambin

1B
Craig Brazell (10)
Ian Bladergroen

SOURCE OF TALENT

Homegrown		Acquired	
College	5	Trades	8
Junior College	3	Rule 5 draft	0
Draft-and-follow	0	Independent	0
High school	9	Free agents/waivers	1
Nondrafted free agent	0		
Foreign	4		

C
Justin Huber (6)
Mike Jacobs (15)
Jim Anderson
Joe Hietpas

RHP

Starters	Relievers
Matt Peterson (4)	Kole Strayhorn (14)
Bob Keppel (7)	Joselo Diaz (17)
Jeremy Griffiths (8)	Orber Moreno (20)
Tyler Yates (12)	Jason Anderson (23)
Matt Lindstrom (18)	P.J. Bevis (26)
Pat Strange (24)	Anderson Garcia (30)
Yusmeiro Petit (28)	Carlos Muniz
Kevin Deaton	Celso Rondon
Miguel Pinango	Jeremy Hill
Ken Chenard	Robert Paulk
Brian Bannister	Jake Joseph
Mateo Miramontes	
Andrew Sides	
Ryan Bicondoa	
Vince Cordova	

LHP

Starters	Relievers
Scott Kazmir (2)	Royce Ring (13)
Neal Musser	Blake McGinley (25)
	Shane Hawk

DRAFT
ANALYSIS

Best Pro Debut: RHP Brian Bannister (7) made the short-season New York-Penn League all-star team after going 4-1, 2.15 with 42 strikeouts in 46 innings. RHP Carlos Muniz (13) picked up 13 saves and had a 0.45 ERA in the NY-P before he broke his thumb.

Best Athlete: OF Lastings Milledge (1) had the best five-tool package in the draft, though he'll need refinement. OF Cory Wells (28) is another gifted athlete, but he's raw. Six-foot-7 RHP Andy Sides (11) was an all-state basketball player at his Missouri high school.

Hawk

Best Pure Hitter: Milledge struggled at times at wood-bat showcases and against quality breaking pitches, but the Mets aren't worried about his ability to hit. They love his bat speed and approach.

Best Raw Power: Milledge or OF Seth Pietsch (8). Pietsch, who's built like Brian Giles at 5-foot-9 and 195 pounds, homered on the first pro pitch he saw.

Fastest Runner: Milledge has 6.4-6.5 second speed in the 60-yard dash.

Best Defensive Player: Milledge covers a lot of ground and has a strong arm for a center fielder. The same is true of OF Corey Coles (5), who pitched at Louisiana-Lafayette.

Best Fastball: The Mets mostly went for guys who knew how to pitch with average stuff. Their strongest arm belongs to RHP Mateo Miramontes (6), who works at 90-91 mph and maxes out at 92.

Best Breaking Ball: Bannister's curveball is a cut above Miramontes' and RHP Vince Cordova's (9). Before the draft, the Mets targeted all three of them and would have considered themselves fortunate to get two.

Most Intriguing Background: Bannister's father Floyd was the No. 1 overall pick in the June 1976 draft and was an all-star in 1982.

Closest To The Majors: LHP Shane Hawk (4) was an obvious candidate, with his solid fastball and slider, but he came down with a sore shoulder. Bannister and Cordova are two other possibilities.

Best Late-Round Pick: Sides could be a steal with his projectable body and feel for his offspeed pitches. The Mets also like Muniz' sinker/slider combination.

The One Who Got Away: RHP Kyle McCulloch (18), who decided to attend Texas, has a solid-average fastball and an advanced changeup. He reminded the Mets of two of their better pitching prospects, Bob Keppel and Matt Peterson.

Assessment: This Mets draft was similar to their last one. In both cases, they had a premier player slide to their first-round pick (Scott Kazmir in 2002) and forfeited their second- and third-round choices to sign free agents. After that, their drafts were ordinary.

2002 DRAFT   GRADE: B

The Mets felt fortunate when LHP Scott Kazmir (1) fell to the 15th pick, especially because they didn't have second- or third-rounders. They didn't get much else, but Kazmir alone is a pretty solid draft.

2001 DRAFT   GRADE: B

3B David Wright (1) is one of the best hitting prospects in the minors. The other first-rounder, RHP Aaron Heilman, will try again to crack New York's rotation. 2B Danny Garcia (5) also will press for playing time.

2000 DRAFT   GRADE: C+

The Mets did well with their first three choices: LHP Billy Traber (1) and RHPs Bob Keppel (1) and Matt Peterson (2). Traber, sent to Cleveland in the Roberto Alomar trade, had Tommy John surgery last year.

1999 DRAFT   GRADE: D

This draft is looking bleak beyond RHP Jeremy Griffiths (3) and C Mike Jacobs (38). New York didn't have a first-rounder and spent its top pick on LHP Neal Musser (2).

—Draft analysis prepared by Jim Callis. Numbers in parentheses indicate draft rounds.

Kazuo
Matsui

Born: Oct. 23, 1975.
Ht.: 5-10. **Wt.:** 185.
Bats: B. **Throws:** R.
Career Transactions: Signed out of Japan by Mets, Dec. 10, 2003.

He doesn't have the teen-idol quality of Ichiro Suzuki or the admiration of his entire country nation like Hideki Matsui, but Kazuo Matsui has always had flair. Between his often-changing hair color, his blazing speed and his flashy glovework, the latest high-profile Japanese import arrives in the United States with nearly as much fanfare as Hideki Matsui (no relation) brought to New York a year ago. Coveted by several big league teams, he became a free agent and signed a three-year, $20.1 million contract with the Mets that included a $100,000 signing bonus and annual salaries of $5 million, $7 million and $8 million. Selected third overall in 1993 in the Japan draft as a pitcher by the Seibu Lions, he quickly converted to shortstop and made his Japanese big league debut at age 20, two years later. The following year, he learned how to switch-hit as on-the-job training in the majors. Matsui broke in as a speedy slap hitter and blossomed into a power threat after maturing physically and training with weights. His list of awards is lengthy: seven all-star selections, four Gold Gloves, three stolen-base crowns, one Pacific League MVP award (1998). He set a PL record by playing in 1,143 consecutive games, and fans voted him Japan's best shortstop of the 20th century. Matsui raised his profile with U.S. scouts when he hit .423 against a team of U.S. major leaguers during a 2002 exhibition series. He homered from both sides of the plate in one game, going deep against Miguel Batista and Scott Schoeneweis.

Matsui has been compared with all of the best shortstops in the majors, and the most apt may be Rafael Furcal. Though Matsui was a 30-30 player in Japan, the Mets would view any homers as a bonus. He's more likely to show off his Ichiro-esque speed and is expected to bat in one of the first two spots in New York's lineup. That said, he is stronger than Ichiro and doesn't use Ichiro's slap-hitting approach. Matsui's solid on-base percentages in Japan were based more on his high batting averages than on his ability to draw walks. As his power numbers grew, so did his strikeouts, and there's concern that he might struggle making contact in his first year in the States. There are fewer worries about his glove.

One Pacific Rim scout predicted that Matsui immediately will become the best defensive shortstop in the game, while a second compared him to Omar Vizquel. The consensus is that Matsui has good range, smooth hands and a plus arm. Another scout said he worries a little about Matsui's arm strength and range, because he played shallow and was more rigid than a classic shortstop in Japan. But he's in the minority. Matsui should be one of the better shortstops in the National League, and the Mets believe he's good enough to force Jose Reyes, baseball's best young shortstop, to second base.

Year	Club (League)	Class	AVG	G	AB	R	H	2B	3B	HR	RBI	BB	SO	SB	SLG	OBP
1995	Seibu (PL)	JPN	.221	69	204	25	45	9	1	2	62	7	26	21	.304	.245
1996	Seibu (PL)	JPN	.283	130	473	51	134	22	5	1	29	14	93	50	.357	.307
1997	Seibu (PL)	JPN	.309	135	576	91	178	23	13	7	63	44	89	62	.431	.362
1998	Seibu (PL)	JPN	.311	135	575	92	179	38	5	9	58	55	89	43	.442	.370
1999	Seibu (PL)	JPN	.330	135	539	87	178	29	4	15	67	56	75	32	.482	.389
2000	Seibu (PL)	JPN	.322	135	550	99	177	40	11	23	90	46	60	26	.560	.372
2001	Seibu (PL)	JPN	.308	140	552	94	170	28	2	24	76	46	83	26	.496	.365
2002	Seibu (PL)	JPN	.332	140	582	119	193	46	6	36	87	53	112	33	.617	.389
2003	Seibu (PL)	JPN	.305	140	587	104	179	36	4	33	84	55	124	13	.549	.365
JAPANESE LEAGUE TOTALS			.309	1159	4638	762	1433	271	51	150	569	376	751	306	.486	.361

Scott Kazmir, lhp

Born: Jan. 24, 1984. **Ht.:** 6-0. **Wt.:** 170. **Bats:** L. **Throws:** L. **School:** Cypress Falls HS, Houston. **Career Transactions:** Selected by Mets in first round (15th overall) of 2002 draft; signed Aug. 2, 2002.

The Mets have been careful with their prized arm, as Kazmir has yet to throw more than seven innings in any game and the Mets held him to a 75-pitch limit for much of the 2003 season. He finished it in style, winning the clinching game in the high Class A Florida State League playoffs. Kazmir's 94-96 mph fastball ranks as one of the best in baseball and he throws it with a relatively easy motion. His 81-84 mph slider is also a well-above-average pitch, and it has good tilt and a sharp break. It projects to get nastier in the future, because he should throw harder as he fills out. His fastball/slider combination can be unhittable, as Kazmir proved by easily leading minor league starters with 11.9 strikeouts per nine innings. Kazmir also shows a major league changeup at times. Kazmir wasn't economical with his pitches to start the season, wasting pitches looking for a strikeout. Some scouts wonder if Kazmir's build will lend itself to the durability needed for a starter, and he had a tender elbow at the start of the season. He must make his changeup more consistent, and his curveball needs a lot of refinement to become a big league pitch. It wouldn't be a surprise if the Mets started Kazmir back in high Class A in 2004 to avoid the April chills in the Double-A Eastern League. Wherever he starts the season, expect him to spend most of the year in Binghamton. He could see Shea Stadium at some point in 2005.

Year	Club (League)	Class	W	L	ERA	G	GS	CG	SV	IP	H	R	ER	HR	BB	SO	AVG
2002	Brooklyn (NY-P)	A	0	1	0.50	5	5	0	0	18	5	2	1	0	7	34	.089
2003	Capital City (SAL)	A	4	4	2.36	18	18	0	0	76	50	26	20	6	28	105	.185
	St. Lucie (FSL)	A	1	2	3.27	7	7	0	0	33	29	15	12	0	16	40	.240
MINOR LEAGUE TOTALS			5	7	2.33	30	30	0	0	127	84	43	33	6	51	179	.188

David Wright, 3b

Born: Dec. 20, 1982. **Ht.:** 6-0. **Wt.:** 200. **Bats:** R. **Throws:** R. **School:** Hickory HS, Chesapeake, Va. **Career Transactions:** Selected by Mets in first round (38th overall) of 2001 draft; signed July 12, 2001.

Considered one of the best pure hitters in the 2001 draft, Wright quickly showed he also has an advanced knowledge of the strike zone to go with his power potential. Wright led the Florida State League with 56 extra-base hits in 2003, ranking third in slugging percentage and fourth in on-base percentage. At his best, Wright is a scout's dream. He flashes the potential to be a .300 hitter with 25-30 homers and 80-plus walks. He makes all the plays at third base. He's one of the best in the minors at charging bunts and choppers, and he also shows a major league arm with good accuracy. Wright has average speed and runs the bases well. He responds to instruction well. In each of his two full pro seasons, Wright has been a streaky hitter. In 2003, he hit .200 through May and June. He works so hard before home games that he wears himself out, and the Mets think he'll be more consistent now that they've gotten him to pace himself. Wright has steadily moved one level at a time, which should continue in 2004 as he heads to Double-A. He could push for the Mets' third-base job at the end of 2005.

Year	Club (League)	Class	AVG	G	AB	R	H	2B	3B	HR	RBI	BB	SO	SB	SLG	OBP
2001	Kingsport (Appy)	R	.300	36	120	27	36	7	0	4	17	16	30	9	.458	.391
2002	Capital City (SAL)	A	.266	135	496	85	132	30	2	11	93	76	114	21	.401	.367
2003	St. Lucie (FSL)	A	.270	133	466	69	126	39	2	15	75	72	98	19	.459	.369
MINOR LEAGUE TOTALS			.272	304	1082	181	294	76	4	30	185	164	242	49	.433	.370

Matt Peterson, rhp

Born: Feb. 11, 1982. **Ht.:** 6-5. **Wt.:** 210. **Bats:** R. **Throws:** R. **School:** Rapides HS, Alexandria, La. **Career Transactions:** Selected by Mets in second round of 2000 draft; signed Aug. 9, 2000.

After spending the last month of the 2003 season in Double-A, the Mets sent Peterson down for the Florida State League postseason. He thrived in the playoff atmosphere, going 2-0, 0.64 in two starts, including a seven-inning one-hitter in his last outing of the year. Peterson has a solid 90-92 mph fastball that he throws to both sides of the plate, but his out pitch is a 12-to-6 curveball that will be a plus pitch with more consistency. His changeup should be a solid offering. Peterson has an advanced feel for pitching and did a better job with his preparation in 2003. Peterson's command isn't bad,

but it needs to get better before he's ready for the majors. He junked his curve at one point for a slurve and now throws a slider as a secondary breaking pitch, but it's a ways from being usable. Peterson has a chance to be a No. 2 starter if he puts everything together. He got a taste of Double-A in 2003 and probably will return there to start 2004. A midseason promotion to Triple-A Norfolk is a possibility.

Year	Club (League)	Class	W	L	ERA	G	GS	CG	SV	IP	H	R	ER	HR	BB	SO	AVG
2001	Capital City (SAL)	A	2	6	4.99	18	14	0	0	79	87	46	44	9	29	72	.275
	Brooklyn (NY-P)	A	2	2	1.62	6	6	0	0	33	26	7	6	0	14	19	.217
2002	Capital City (SAL)	A	8	10	3.86	26	26	1	0	138	109	67	59	13	61	153	.221
	St. Lucie (FSL)	A	1	0	1.50	1	1	0	0	6	5	2	1	0	2	5	.217
2003	St. Lucie (FSL)	A	9	2	1.71	15	15	1	0	84	65	24	16	2	24	73	.212
	Binghamton (EL)	AA	1	2	3.45	6	6	0	0	31	29	18	12	2	20	23	.248
MINOR LEAGUE TOTALS			23	22	3.34	72	68	2	0	372	321	164	138	26	150	345	.233

5 Lastings Milledge, of

Born: April 5, 1985. **Ht.:** 6-1. **Wt.:** 185. **Bats:** R. **Throws:** R. **School:** Lakewood Ranch HS, Palmetto, Fla. **Career Transactions:** Selected by Mets in first round (12th overall) of 2003 draft; signed Aug. 19, 2003.

One of the most well-known and well-scouted players in the 2003 draft, Milledge starred for Team USA at the 2001 World Youth Championship and the 2002 World Junior Championship. He dropped to the No. 12 pick for a variety of reasons: an inconsistent history with wood bats, signability questions, and allegations of improper sexual conduct. Milledge never was charged, and after the Mets conducted their own investigation they signed him for $2.075 million. Milledge's five-tool potential reminds the Mets of former outfield prospect Brian Cole, who was killed in a car accident in 2001. The best athlete in the 2003 high school crop, Milledge wows scouts with his bat speed, foot speed and arm strength. Offensively and defensively, Milledge has to get used to wood bats. He struggled at times reading balls off the bat in instructional league, though he should become an above-average center fielder. He needs to lay off breaking pitches and work counts better. After signing late, Milledge has to make up for lost time. He could start 2004 at low Class A Capital City with a strong spring.

Year	Club (League)	Class	AVG	G	AB	R	H	2B	3B	HR	RBI	BB	SO	SB	SLG	OBP
2003	Kingsport (Appy)	R	.231	7	26	4	6	2	0	0	2	3	4	5	.308	.323
MINOR LEAGUE TOTALS			.231	7	26	4	6	2	0	0	2	3	4	5	.308	.323

6 Justin Huber, c

Born: July 1, 1982. **Ht.:** 6-5. **Wt.:** 190. **Bats:** R. **Throws:** R. **Career Transactions:** Signed out of Australia by Mets, July 26, 2000.

While he's somewhat raw because he's from Australia, Huber has played baseball and been a fixture on Australian national teams for years. He signed with the Mets right before earning all-tournament honors at the 2000 World Junior Championship. Since arriving in the United States, the only thing that has slowed him down has been a strained pectoral muscle that cost him the first four weeks of the 2003 season. Huber is an offensive catcher. He has the ability to hit for average with 20 homers annually, and the Mets rave about his raw power. He also has shown the ability to get on-base with a career .382 OBP. He has solid catch-and-throw potential, and he handles pitchers well. Huber is still raw defensively. At times he looks mechanical with poor footwork. When his mechanics are out of whack, his average-at-best arm becomes a liability. He threw out just 24 percent of basestealers in 2003. With Jason Phillips' and Mike Jacobs' strong showings in 2003, there's no need to rush Huber. He'll return to Double-A to start 2004.

Year	Club (League)	Class	AVG	G	AB	R	H	2B	3B	HR	RBI	BB	SO	SB	SLG	OBP
2001	St. Lucie (FSL)	A	.000	2	6	0	0	0	0	0	0	0	2	0	.000	.000
	Kingsport (Appy)	R	.314	47	159	24	50	11	1	7	31	17	42	4	.528	.415
	Brooklyn (NY-P)	A	.000	3	9	0	0	0	0	0	0	0	4	0	.000	.000
2002	Capital City (SAL)	A	.291	95	330	49	96	22	2	11	78	45	81	1	.470	.408
	St. Lucie (FSL)	A	.270	28	100	15	27	2	1	3	15	11	18	0	.400	.370
2003	St. Lucie (FSL)	A	.284	50	183	26	52	15	0	9	36	17	30	1	.514	.370
	Binghamton (EL)	AA	.264	55	193	16	51	13	0	6	36	19	54	0	.425	.350
MINOR LEAGUE TOTALS			.282	280	980	130	276	63	4	36	196	109	231	6	.464	.382

7 Bob Keppel, rhp

Born: June 11, 1982. **Ht.:** 6-5. **Wt.:** 205. **Bats:** R. **Throws:** R. **School:** DeSmet HS, St. Louis. **Career Transactions:** Selected by Mets in first round (36th overall) of 2000 draft; signed July 7, 2000.

As a junior point guard, Keppel led DeSmet High to its first Missouri state title, and he almost ended up playing basketball at Notre Dame. He threw the first regular-season no-hitter in Binghamton franchise history in August. Despite lacking a true plus pitch, Keppel held his own as a 21-year-old in Double-A. One scout compared him with John VanBenschoten of the Pirates, largely because of Keppel's uncanny ability to make the right pitch at the right time. His 90-91 mph fastball touches 94, though it's more effective and has better movement when he throws it free and easy. His changeup is a major league pitch. Keppel's slider is solid but inconsistent. His curveball isn't as advanced as his other three pitches. He throws strikes, but the Mets want to see better command. After missing a month in 2003 with a strained forearm, he was supposed to get work in the Arizona Fall League but had to be shut down with shoulder stiffness. Keppel should be fine by spring training. He's ticketed for Triple-A and could make his major league debut later in 2004.

Year	Club (League)	Class	W	L	ERA	G	GS	CG	SV	IP	H	R	ER	HR	BB	SO	AVG
2000	Kingsport (Appy)	R	1	2	6.83	8	6	0	0	29	31	22	22	1	13	29	.261
2001	Capital City (SAL)	A	6	7	3.11	26	20	1	0	124	118	58	43	6	25	87	.249
2002	St. Lucie (FSL)	A	9	7	4.32	27	26	0	0	152	162	83	73	13	43	109	.277
2003	Binghamton (EL)	AA	7	4	3.04	18	17	2	0	95	92	36	32	6	27	46	.264
	Brooklyn (NY-P)	A	2	0	2.51	3	3	0	0	14	10	5	4	0	2	13	.189
MINOR LEAGUE TOTALS			25	20	3.78	82	72	3	0	414	413	204	174	26	110	284	.262

8 Jeremy Griffiths, rhp

Born: March 22, 1978. **Ht.:** 6-6. **Wt.:** 240. **Bats:** R. **Throws:** R. **School:** University of Toledo. **Career Transactions:** Selected by Mets in third round of 1999 draft; signed June 9, 1999.

One of a number of quality arms to come out of the Mid-American Conference in recent years, Griffiths was the league's 1999 pitcher of the year. He improved his command in 2002 and accelerated his development, culminating with his promotion to the majors in '03. The rangy Griffiths has gotten his delivery under control, which allows him to command four solid pitches. He works with a 90-91 mph fastball that touches 94, an 81-84 mph slider, a changeup and a curveball. The Mets liked that he became more aggressive in the minors and started busting hitters inside. Griffiths wasn't ready for the majors in 2003 and it showed. He was too tentative and hitters took advantage of him. He needs to regain his feel for his curveball, which he couldn't throw consistently for strikes. Some in the organization say Griffiths is more capable of handling the big leagues now than 2001 first-rounder Aaron Heilman. He'd be best served by another half-season in Triple-A, but he'll be a candidate for New York's rotation in spring training.

Year	Club (League)	Class	W	L	ERA	G	GS	CG	SV	IP	H	R	ER	HR	BB	SO	AVG
1999	Kingsport (Appy)	R	3	5	3.30	14	14	1	0	76	68	40	28	6	36	74	.243
2000	Capital City (SAL)	A	7	12	4.34	26	26	0	0	129	120	78	62	12	39	138	.242
2001	St. Lucie (FSL)	A	7	8	3.75	23	20	2	0	132	126	63	55	9	35	95	.253
	Binghamton (EL)	AA	2	0	0.69	2	2	1	0	13	8	3	1	0	4	12	.174
2002	Binghamton (EL)	AA	8	6	3.89	27	26	2	0	153	157	75	66	12	54	126	.272
2003	Norfolk (IL)	AAA	7	6	2.74	21	19	1	1	115	94	43	35	6	26	78	.224
	New York (NL)	MAJ	1	4	7.02	9	6	0	0	41	57	34	32	5	19	25	.328
MAJOR LEAGUE TOTALS			1	4	7.02	9	6	0	0	41	57	34	32	5	19	25	.328
MINOR LEAGUE TOTALS			34	37	3.60	113	107	7	1	618	573	302	247	45	194	523	.247

9 Victor Diaz, 2b

Born: Dec. 10, 1981. **Ht.:** 6-0. **Wt.:** 200. **Bats:** R. **Throws:** R. **School:** Grayson County (Texas) JC. **Career Transactions:** Selected by Dodgers in 37th round of 2000 draft; signed May 19, 2001 . . . Traded by Dodgers with RHP Kole Strayhorn and RHP Joselo Diaz to Mets for OF Jeromy Burnitz, July 14, 2003.

Diaz won two batting titles in his first two pro seasons before the Dodgers packaged him with righthanders Joselo Diaz and Kole Strayhorn in the Jeromy Burnitz trade in July. Born in the Dominican Republic, Diaz played high school baseball in Chicago before becoming a junior college all-American. Scouts and managers have compared Diaz to Carlos Baerga, another stocky second baseman with a live bat. Line drives fly off of Diaz' bat despite his unorthodox hitting approach. He's strong and has good opposite-field power. Diaz doesn't control his weight well, which has hurt his range and speed. The Dodgers tried him at first, second and third base without finding a good fit. If he stays in shape, he might have enough range to go with his good hands at second. He needs to show more patience at the plate. Diaz hit .320-3-17 in the Dominican League over the winter to win the league's rookie of the year award, and he worked on his defense and getting in better shape. He should move up to Triple-A, but with the signing of Kazuo Matsui and the move of Jose Reyes to second, his long-term role with the Mets is in question.

Year	Club (League)	Class	AVG	G	AB	R	H	2B	3B	HR	RBI	BB	SO	SB	SLG	OBP
2001	Dodgers (GCL)	R	.354	53	195	36	69	22	2	3	31	16	23	6	.533	.414
2002	South Georgia (SAL)	A	.350	91	349	64	122	26	2	10	58	27	69	20	.521	.407
	Jacksonville (SL)	AA	.211	42	152	22	32	7	0	4	24	7	42	7	.336	.258
2003	Jacksonville (SL)	AA	.291	85	316	42	92	20	2	10	55	27	60	8	.462	.353
	Binghamton (EL)	AA	.354	45	175	29	62	11	0	6	23	8	32	7	.520	.382
MINOR LEAGUE TOTALS			.318	316	1187	193	377	86	6	33	191	85	226	48	.484	.371

10 Craig Brazell, 1b

Born: May 10, 1980. **Ht.:** 6-3. **Wt.:** 210. **Bats:** L. **Throws:** R. **School:** Jeff Davis HS, Montgomery, Ala. **Career Transactions:** Selected by Mets in fifth round of 1998 draft; signed June 4, 1998.

RICH ABEL

The son of Ted Brazell, a former Tigers minor league catcher and manager, Craig caught in high school but moved to first base after signing. He has tied for the system's home run lead in each of the last two seasons. Brazell can put on a show in batting practice and does a good job of converting his raw power into game production. Despite an aggressive approach, he has shown he can also hit for average. He has soft hands at first base. Brazell takes big swings looking for fastballs early in the count, which allows pitchers to get ahead of him. He rarely walks and strikes out in bunches. His speed and defensive range are below-average. Brazell's path to the majors appears blocked by Mike Piazza's move to first base. Brazell tried the outfield during instructional league to increase his versatility, but first base still appears to be his best position. He'll start 2004 in Triple-A.

Year	Club (League)	Class	AVG	G	AB	R	H	2B	3B	HR	RBI	BB	SO	SB	SLG	OBP
1998	Mets (GCL)	R	.298	13	47	6	14	3	1	1	6	2	13	0	.468	.340
1999	Kingsport (Appy)	R	.385	59	221	27	85	16	1	6	39	7	34	6	.548	.422
2000	Capital City (SAL)	A	.241	112	406	35	98	28	0	8	57	15	82	3	.369	.279
2001	Capital City (SAL)	A	.308	83	331	51	102	25	5	19	72	15	74	0	.586	.343
2002	St. Lucie (FSL)	A	.266	100	402	38	107	25	3	16	82	13	78	2	.463	.292
	Binghamton (EL)	AA	.308	35	130	14	40	8	0	6	19	1	28	0	.508	.343
2003	Binghamton (EL)	AA	.292	111	432	58	126	23	2	17	76	23	97	2	.472	.331
	Norfolk (IL)	AAA	.261	12	46	4	12	3	0	0	1	1	8	1	.326	.292
MINOR LEAGUE TOTALS			.290	525	2015	233	584	131	12	73	352	77	414	14	.475	.325

11 Aaron Baldiris, 3b

Born: Jan. 5, 1983. **Ht.:** 6-2. **Wt.:** 195. **Bats:** R. **Throws:** R. **Career Transactions:** Signed out of Venezuela by Mets, July 2, 1999 . . . On disabled list, June 19-Sept. 20, 2001.

Baldiris has topped .300 in all but one of his six minor league stops. The only thing that has slowed his ascent was a shoulder injury that sidelined him for the entire 2001 season. Baldiris wears No. 13, just like his boyhood hero Edgardo Alfonzo, and they have similar games. Both hit for average with line-drive power and slick gloves. Baldiris shows an advanced approach and the ability to stay inside the ball. If pitchers try to bust him inside, he can turn on pitches and flash power. He exudes patience and makes good contact. At third base, he has outstanding range to his left, good hands and an average arm. Big league teams want more power at third base than Baldiris has shown to this point. If he doesn't add more pop as he fills out, he could move to second base. Baldiris' August demotion was a clear attempt to stack Brooklyn for the New York-Penn League playoffs and no reflection on his play. He'll move to high Class A in 2004, one step behind David Wright.

Year	Club (League)	Class	AVG	G	AB	R	H	2B	3B	HR	RBI	BB	SO	SB	SLG	OBP
2000	Universidad (VSL)	R	.353	44	139	24	49	9	1	7	35	37	23	4	.583	.489
	Kingsport (Appy)	R	.219	32	105	14	23	3	1	2	20	7	20	2	.324	.265
2001	Did not play—Injured															
2002	Kingsport (Appy)	R	.327	58	217	31	71	9	1	3	24	14	24	9	.419	.390
	Brooklyn (NY-P)	A	.303	9	33	5	10	1	0	0	2	1	2	2	.333	.343
2003	Capital City (SAL)	A	.313	107	393	55	123	19	4	6	68	51	55	13	.427	.396
	Brooklyn (NY-P)	A	.364	26	88	20	32	5	2	0	18	14	13	2	.466	.451
MINOR LEAGUE TOTALS			.316	276	975	149	308	46	9	18	167	124	137	32	.437	.399

12 Tyler Yates, rhp

Born: Aug. 7, 1977. **Ht.:** 6-4. **Wt.:** 220. **Bats:** R. **Throws:** R. **School:** University of Hawaii-Hilo. **Career Transactions:** Selected by Athletics in 23rd round of 1998 draft; signed June 10, 1998 . . . Traded by Athletics with LHP Mark Guthrie to Mets for OF David Justice and cash, Dec. 14, 2001.

Yates was dominating Triple-A in 2002 before he blew out his elbow. After having Tommy John surgery, he returned to the mound last April. To get him consistent innings, the Mets made the former closer a starter. If he hadn't broken the pinky on his pitching hand when he slammed a wall in frustration after his last minor league start, he would have made his major league debut in September. Yates also missed the Arizona Fall league when he developed shoulder stiffness that shut him down for the winter. His fastball touched 100 mph before he got hurt and has dipped since, but he still has plenty of velocity and could regain more. His four-seam fastball sits at 94 mph, while his two-seamer arrives in the low 90s with good movement. Forced to use his secondary pitches more as a starter, he developed a solid changeup to go with his hard, 88-89 mph slider. If Yates is going to start in the majors, he'll need more confidence in his curveball. He'll show a big league curve in side sessions but doesn't trust it enough to throw it in games. His command still needs work, and as the broken finger attests, he needs to control his emotions. While Yates' first year as a starter was an eye-opener, the Mets have a more pressing need for relievers and will give him a chance to win a bullpen job this spring.

Year	Club (League)	Class	W	L	ERA	G	GS	CG	SV	IP	H	R	ER	HR	BB	SO	AVG
1998	Athletics (AZL)	R	0	0	3.91	15	0	0	2	23	28	12	10	0	14	20	.304
	S. Oregon (NWL)	A	0	0	0.00	2	0	0	1	2	2	0	0	0	0	1	.222
1999	Visalia (Cal)	A	2	5	5.47	47	1	0	4	82	98	64	50	12	35	74	.290
2000	Modesto (Cal)	A	4	2	2.86	30	0	0	1	57	50	23	18	2	23	61	.237
	Midland (TL)	AA	1	1	6.15	22	0	0	0	26	28	20	18	2	15	24	.275
2001	Midland (TL)	AA	4	6	4.31	56	0	0	17	63	66	39	30	4	27	61	.261
	Sacramento (PCL)	AAA	1	0	0.00	4	0	0	1	5	3	0	0	0	1	3	.167
2002	Norfolk (IL)	AAA	2	2	1.32	24	0	0	6	34	29	10	5	1	13	34	.227
2003	St. Lucie (FSL)	A	1	2	4.31	14	11	0	0	48	41	28	23	5	24	49	.232
	Binghamton (EL)	AA	1	2	4.35	8	8	0	0	39	33	21	19	4	17	36	.223
	Norfolk (IL)	AAA	1	2	4.05	4	4	0	0	20	22	9	9	1	9	15	.289
MINOR LEAGUE TOTALS			17	22	4.10	226	24	0	32	400	400	226	182	31	178	378	.258

13 Royce Ring, lhp

Born: Dec. 21, 1980. **Ht.:** 6-0. **Wt.:** 220. **Bats:** L. **Throws:** L. **School:** San Diego State University. **Career Transactions:** Selected by White Sox in first round (18th overall) of 2002 draft; signed June 10, 2002 . . . Traded by White Sox with RHP Edwin Almonte and 2B Andrew Salvo to Mets for 2B Roberto Alomar, July 1, 2003.

The key player for the Mets in the Roberto Alomar trade with the White Sox, Ring has spent nearly his entire career as a reliever. As an amateur, he set San Diego State records for single-season and career saves, and he was dominant in relief for Team USA. He also pitched a scoreless inning for the national team at the Olympic qualifying tournament in Panama in November. Ring used to touch 94 mph with his fastball, but as a pro he more often sits in the high 80s and occasionally touches 90. His fastball remains effective, however, because it has plenty of movement. He also has a sweeping, 73-75 mph slider that's tough on lefties. Ring needs to improve his command and conditioning. When he came to the Mets, they tried to use him in multiple-inning stints, but he didn't respond well. He has a chunky physique, and it's possible that he would gain stamina and maybe a couple of miles on his fastball if he lost weight. Though he has served as a closer in college and in the minors, he projects as a lefty set-up man unless he regains velocity. With the Mets needing bullpen help, Ring will have a shot to make the big league club in spring training.

Year	Club (League)	Class	W	L	ERA	G	GS	CG	SV	IP	H	R	ER	HR	BB	SO	AVG
2002	White Sox (AZL)	R	0	0	0.00	3	0	0	0	5	2	0	0	0	0	9	.118
	Winston-Salem (Car)	A	2	0	3.91	21	0	0	5	23	20	11	10	2	11	22	.247
2003	Birmingham (SL)	AA	1	4	2.52	36	0	0	19	36	33	11	10	1	14	44	.237
	Binghamton (EL)	AA	3	0	1.66	18	0	0	7	22	13	4	4	2	11	18	.176
MINOR LEAGUE TOTALS			6	4	2.53	78	0	0	31	85	68	26	24	5	36	93	.219

14 Kole Strayhorn, rhp

Born: Oct. 1, 1982. **Ht.:** 6-0. **Wt.:** 185. **Bats:** R. **Throws:** R. **School:** Shawnee (Okla.) HS. **Career Transactions:** Selected by Dodgers in fourth round of 2001 draft; signed June 9, 2001 . . . Traded with 3B Victor Diaz and RHP Joselo Diaz to Mets for OF Jeromy Burnitz, July 14, 2003.

Strayhorn caught scouts' eyes when he touched 96 mph at the Area Code Games as a rising high school senior. Despite his top-notch fastball, he dropped to the fourth round of the

2001 draft because of concerns with his maximum-effort delivery. As a minor leaguer, Strayhorn has retained the big fastball, a thick body that seems to signal he can be a horse, and the delivery that makes him more of a thrower than a polished pitcher. Strayhorn's fastball sits at 95 mph and touches 97, but it lacks the movement to make it a true strikeout pitch. As a closer, he has backed up his fastball with a get-over curveball. At times, he'll show a lively two-seam fastball and a decent splitter that serves as a changeup. Strayhorn and Joselo Diaz project to fill similar roles as late-inning relievers, with Strayhorn the more polished of the two. He likely will start 2004 in Binghamton.

Year	Club (League)	Class	W	L	ERA	G	GS	CG	SV	IP	H	R	ER	HR	BB	SO	AVG
2001	Great Falls (Pio)	R	0	0	15.43	2	0	0	0	2	4	4	4	1	1	1	.364
	Dodgers (GCL)	R	5	3	2.19	12	6	0	0	53	41	15	13	1	17	47	.216
2002	South Georgia (SAL)	A	1	7	4.24	31	13	0	4	93	99	61	44	4	38	50	.273
2003	Vero Beach (FSL)	A	5	2	2.93	30	0	0	7	46	42	17	15	2	13	44	.236
	St. Lucie (FSL)	A	1	1	1.17	16	0	0	10	15	7	2	2	0	9	16	.140
MINOR LEAGUE TOTALS			12	13	3.34	91	19	0	21	210	193	99	78	8	78	158	.244

15 Mike Jacobs, c

Born: Oct. 30, 1980. **Ht.:** 6-2. **Wt.:** 200. **Bats:** L. **Throws:** R. **School:** Grossmont (Calif.) JC. **Career Transactions:** Selected by Mets in 38th round of 1999 draft; signed June 25, 1999.

While many players hit the wall in Double-A, Jacobs emerged as a prospect and had the best season of his five-year pro career there in 2003. He finished second among minor league catchers in batting and slugging. He earned the Mets' minor league player of the year award and a spot on their 40-man roster. Jacobs has outstanding opposite-field power, similar to Mike Piazza. But he still has plenty of work to do to make the majors. He's overly aggressive at the plate, which pitchers exploited in the past and may do so again. Defensively, he's a below-average receiver with below-average arm strength. He threw out just 20 percent of basestealers last year and stopped catching regularly once Justin Huber was promoted to Binghamton in June. Jacobs spent the rest of the season at DH and started six games at first base at the end of August. Some scouts consider Jacobs a lefthanded-hitting version of Pittsburgh's Craig Wilson, a slugger best suited for first base but capable of being a reserve catcher. The Mets will move him to Triple-A in 2004, leaving Huber at Double-A with the hope that Jacobs will improve his catching skills with regular duty behind the plate.

Year	Club (League)	Class	AVG	G	AB	R	H	2B	3B	HR	RBI	BB	SO	SB	SLG	OBP
1999	Mets (GCL)	R	.333	44	147	18	49	12	0	4	30	14	30	2	.497	.383
2000	Capital City (SAL)	A	.214	18	56	1	12	5	0	0	6	6	19	1	.304	.290
	Kingsport (Appy)	R	.270	59	204	28	55	15	4	7	40	33	62	6	.485	.371
2001	Brooklyn (NY-P)	A	.288	19	66	12	19	5	0	1	15	6	11	1	.409	.364
	Capital City (SAL)	A	.278	46	180	18	50	13	0	2	16	13	46	0	.383	.328
2002	St. Lucie (FSL)	A	.251	118	467	62	117	26	1	11	64	25	95	2	.381	.291
2003	Binghamton (EL)	AA	.329	119	407	56	134	36	1	17	81	28	87	0	.548	.376
MINOR LEAGUE TOTALS			.286	423	1527	195	436	112	6	42	264	125	350	12	.449	.342

16 Danny Garcia, 2b

Born: April 12, 1980. **Ht.:** 6-1. **Wt.:** 175. **Bats:** R. **Throws:** R. **School:** Pepperdine University. **Career Transactions:** Selected by Mets in fifth round of 2001 draft; signed June 22, 2001.

Garcia was a center fielder for two seasons at Pepperdine before moving to second base in 2001, where he profiled better as a pro. Just two years later he was starting for the Mets, as injuries and trades created an opening. He'll be a reserve at best now after New York signed Kazuo Matsui and shifted Jose Reyes from shortstop to second. There's nothing spectacular about Garcia. He has shown a solid batting eye but has no plus tool. Compared to Victor Diaz, he has much less star potential but is much more likely to reach his ceiling. Garcia is an adequate second baseman with decent speed on the basepaths and the ability to hit for average with doubles power. His best long-term fit may be as a utility infielder. He played 18 games at shortstop in high Class A and has seen time in the outfield. If he doesn't make the Mets out of spring training, he'll probably share second base with Diaz and gain experience at other positions in Triple-A.

Year	Club (League)	Class	AVG	G	AB	R	H	2B	3B	HR	RBI	BB	SO	SB	SLG	OBP
2001	Brooklyn (NY-P)	A	.321	15	56	10	18	2	0	1	6	4	10	3	.411	.387
	Capital City (SAL)	A	.301	30	103	25	31	12	1	2	16	15	18	7	.495	.409
2002	St. Lucie (FSL)	A	.273	122	432	69	118	34	5	4	52	53	77	13	.403	.369
2003	Binghamton (EL)	AA	.333	32	117	22	39	12	1	3	22	10	20	2	.530	.391
	Norfolk (IL)	AAA	.263	101	388	45	102	23	3	4	54	22	60	11	.369	.313
	New York (NL)	MAJ	.214	19	56	5	12	2	0	2	6	2	11	0	.357	.274
MAJOR LEAGUE TOTALS			.214	19	56	5	12	2	0	2	6	2	11	0	.357	.274
MINOR LEAGUE TOTALS			.281	300	1096	171	308	83	10	14	150	104	185	36	.413	.357

17 Joselo Diaz, rhp

Born: April 13, 1980. **Wt.:** 6-0. **Wt.:** 225. **Bats:** R. **Throws:** R. **Career Transactions:** Signed out of Dominican Republic by Dodgers, Aug. 24, 1996 . . . Traded by Dodgers with 2B Victor Diaz and RHP Kole Strayhorn to Mets for OF Jeromy Burnitz and cash, July 14, 2003.

Diaz has a lot to learn about pitching, not surprising considering he was a catcher in 2002. He peaked in high Class A as a position player, and it became clear that his strong arm wouldn't make up for a .195 career average. He quickly has developed two potential plus pitches, though he's still more of a thrower than a pitcher. Diaz has a 95-96 mph fastball. He tired after getting traded from the Dodgers and popped the mitt at just 91-92 in the Arizona Fall League. He has flashed a changeup that some scouts think can be a plus pitch, but he doesn't feature it enough during games. He throws his curveball too hard, almost giving it a slider action and making it nearly impossible for him to locate it consistently. He also needs to work on keeping his head still during his delivery, which has contributed to his wildness. Though Diaz has a long way to go, there's a high ceiling to go with the high risk. He'll head to Double-A this year.

Year	Club (League)	Class	AVG	G	AB	R	H	2B	3B	HR	RBI	BB	SO	SB	SLG	OBP
1997	Dodgers (DSL)	R	.147	30	95	12	14	1	0	1	5	6	30	3	.189	.212
1998	Dodgers (DSL)	R	.209	51	163	24	34	6	0	1	27	15	34	4	.264	.299
1999	Did not play—Injured															
2000	Great Falls (Pio)	R	.219	57	210	29	46	9	1	7	31	18	52	2	.371	.292
2001	Wilmington (SAL)	A	.175	23	80	7	14	4	0	2	5	4	31	1	.300	.214
	Great Falls (Pio)	R	.189	48	159	18	30	8	0	3	17	15	38	2	.296	.284
2002	Vero Beach (FSL)	A	.200	3	10	3	2	0	0	1	3	1	3	0	.500	.333
MINOR LEAGUE TOTALS			.195	212	717	93	140	28	1	15	88	59	188	12	.300	.274

Year	Club (League)	Class	W	L	ERA	G	GS	CG	SV	IP	H	R	ER	HR	BB	SO	AVG
2001	Great Falls (Pio)	R	0	0	0.00	1	0	0	0	1	0	0	0	0	0	2	.000
2002	South Georgia (SAL)	A	3	1	4.21	19	0	0	1	26	14	12	12	1	25	33	.163
2003	Vero Beach (FSL)	A	5	2	3.50	15	11	0	1	62	39	25	24	2	48	69	.181
	Jacksonville (SL)	AA	1	0	0.00	5	0	0	0	8	5	1	0	0	3	7	.185
	St. Lucie (FSL)	A	2	2	2.97	11	2	0	1	30	16	12	10	0	25	41	.162
MINOR LEAGUE TOTALS			11	5	3.28	51	13	0	3	126	74	50	46	3	101	152	.172

18 Matt Lindstrom, rhp

Born: Feb. 11, 1980. **Ht.:** 6-4. **Wt.:** 205. **Bats:** R. **Throws:** R. **School:** Ricks (Idaho) JC. **Career Transactions:** Selected by Mets in 10th round of 2002 draft; signed June 14, 2002.

Lindstrom made the 2003 New York-Penn League all-star team, but he was a 23-year-old in short-season ball. Yet he has the chance to be a third or fourth starter in the majors if he can catch up after putting his career on hold for a two-year Mormon mission. He's extremely raw and has trouble repeating his delivery, but he made strides last year. Lindstrom had a very herky-jerky motion when he signed, but he has managed to tame it somewhat. He has a 92-94 mph fastball that touches 96. His slider, which reaches the high 80s and has good bite, shows flashes of becoming a plus pitch. His curveball needs more differentiation from his slider, and he needs to learn to trust his changeup more. He also must continue to improve his mechanics and command. Considering his advanced age, the Mets would like him to have a strong spring training so he could jump to high Class A.

Year	Club (League)	Class	W	L	ERA	G	GS	CG	SV	IP	H	R	ER	HR	BB	SO	AVG
2002	Kingsport (Appy)	R	0	6	4.84	12	11	0	0	48	56	45	26	6	21	39	.280
2003	Capital City (SAL)	A	2	3	2.86	12	11	0	0	57	46	21	18	2	33	50	.228
	Brooklyn (NY-P)	A	7	3	3.44	14	14	0	0	65	61	28	25	2	27	52	.250
MINOR LEAGUE TOTALS			9	12	3.65	38	36	0	0	170	163	94	69	10	81	141	.252

19 Prentice Redman, of

Born: Aug. 23, 1979. **Ht.:** 6-3. **Wt.:** 185. **Bats:** R. **Throws:** R. **School:** Bevill State (Ala.) CC. **Career Transactions:** Selected by Mets in 10th round of 1999 draft; signed June 4, 1999.

One of the best athletes in the system, Redman is hanging on the precipice between being an extra outfielder or a regular center fielder. Interestingly, his older brother Tike faces the same dilemma in the Pirates organization. Redman has wowed the Mets with his raw power since signing, but he has yet to translate it into production because he struggles to make contact. Named Binghamton's MVP in 2002, he regressed in 2003 as he once again struggled with pitch recognition. Redman's speed makes him a stolen-base threat, and he has the range and arm to play anywhere in the outfield. But he's running out of time to prove he can be an everyday player. He faces a crucial season in 2004 in Triple-A.

Year	Club (League)	Class	AVG	G	AB	R	H	2B	3B	HR	RBI	BB	SO	SB	SLG	OBP
1999	Kingsport (Appy)	R	.295	58	200	40	59	14	1	6	29	24	42	16	.465	.373
2000	Capital City (SAL)	A	.260	131	497	60	129	19	1	3	46	52	90	26	.320	.332
2001	St. Lucie (FSL)	A	.261	132	495	70	129	18	1	9	65	42	91	29	.356	.322
2002	Binghamton (EL)	AA	.283	135	491	79	139	35	2	11	63	59	112	43	.430	.367
2003	Norfolk (IL)	AAA	.254	128	433	60	110	29	2	11	48	40	96	24	.406	.326
	New York (NL)	MAJ	.125	15	24	3	3	1	0	1	2	1	9	2	.292	.192
MAJOR LEAGUE TOTALS			.125	15	24	3	3	1	0	1	2	1	9	2	.292	.192
MINOR LEAGUE TOTALS			.267	584	2116	309	566	115	7	40	251	217	431	138	.385	.341

20 Orber Moreno, rhp

Born: April 27, 1977. **Ht.:** 6-3. **Wt.:** 200. **Bats:** R. **Throws:** R. **Career Transactions:** Signed out of Venezuela by Royals, Nov. 10, 1993 . . . On disabled list, March 24-Oct. 12, 2000 . . . Released by Royals, Oct. 3, 2002 . . . Signed by Mets, March 6, 2003.

Projected as the Royals' closer of the future when he was promoted to the majors in May 1999, he overthrew and blew out his elbow. He finally started to bounce back last season. He showed his old 92-95 mph fastball early in 2003, along with a slightly above-average changeup and a useable curveball. He dominated Triple-A hitters but wore down as the season went along. By the time he joined the Mets, Moreno's fastball was down to 91-92 and he struggled to show his best stuff on back-to-back nights. He can be a solid major league reliever thanks to his fastball life and his ability to throw his change in any count. Concerns remain about his durability. If he shows he's fully healthy, he could be a nice sleeper in the New York bullpen.

Year	Club (League)	Class	W	L	ERA	G	GS	CG	SV	IP	H	R	ER	HR	BB	SO	AVG
1994	Royals/Rockies (DSL)	R	3	3	3.19	16	11	0	1	68	51	33	24	3	27	44	.203
1995	Royals (GCL)	R	1	1	2.45	8	3	0	0	22	15	9	6	0	7	21	.188
1996	Royals (GCL)	R	5	1	1.36	12	7	0	1	46	37	15	7	2	10	50	.214
1997	Lansing (Mid)	A	4	8	4.81	27	25	0	0	138	150	83	74	15	45	128	.278
1998	Wilmington (Car)	A	3	2	0.82	23	0	0	7	33	8	3	3	1	10	50	.077
	Wichita (TL)	AA	0	1	2.88	24	0	0	7	34	28	13	11	1	12	40	.215
1999	Omaha (PCL)	AAA	3	1	2.10	16	0	0	4	26	17	6	6	2	4	30	.183
	Kansas City (AL)	MAJ	0	0	5.63	7	0	0	0	8	4	5	5	1	6	7	.143
	Royals (GCL)	R	0	0	0.00	1	1	0	0	1	0	0	0	0	0	1	.000
2000	Did not play—Injured																
2001	Wilmington (Car)	A	1	1	2.53	8	1	0	0	11	12	5	3	1	1	16	.261
	Wichita (TL)	AA	0	0	0.00	5	0	0	1	9	3	0	0	0	2	10	.107
	Omaha (PCL)	AAA	1	1	4.71	17	0	0	3	21	19	11	11	4	8	25	.232
2002	Royals (GCL)	R	0	0	0.00	2	2	0	0	2	1	0	0	0	0	3	.143
2003	Binghamton (EL)	AA	2	0	1.69	4	0	0	1	5	4	1	1	1	1	7	.200
	Norfolk (IL)	AAA	5	1	1.90	38	0	0	12	52	36	11	11	1	17	58	.191
	New York (NL)	MAJ	0	0	7.88	7	0	0	0	8	10	7	7	1	3	5	.313
MAJOR LEAGUE TOTALS			0	0	6.75	14	0	0	0	16	14	12	12	2	9	12	.233
MINOR LEAGUE TOTALS			28	20	3.02	201	50	0	37	468	381	190	157	31	144	483	.218

21 Bob Malek, of

Born: July 6, 1981. **Ht.:** 6-3. **Wt.:** 205. **Bats:** L. **Throws:** R. **School:** Michigan State University. **Career Transactions:** Selected by Mets in fourth round of 2002 draft; signed June 6, 2002.

A 2002 first-team All-American after hitting .402-16-66 with 16 steals for Michigan State, Malek lasted until the fourth round because he faced Tommy John surgery. The Mets regarded him as a second- or third-round talent in a year when they gave up those two picks to sign free agents David Weathers and Roger Cedeno. Malek has fully recovered from the elbow surgery to show the system's best outfield arm. He also has good instincts and takes good routes in the outfield, but his range is borderline in right field. At the plate, Malek has a nice, easy swing. He projects as a John Vander Wal type who hits for average with a good on-base percentage, but he'll have to show a lot more power. He has shown more speed (it's just average) than pop since adjusting to wood bats. He'll move to Double-A in 2004.

Year	Club (League)	Class	AVG	G	AB	R	H	2B	3B	HR	RBI	BB	SO	SB	SLG	OBP
2002	Brooklyn (NY-P)	A	.207	28	111	7	23	3	1	0	10	3	20	4	.252	.235
2003	Capital City (SAL)	A	.262	43	149	20	39	11	0	1	26	26	22	11	.356	.369
	St. Lucie (FSL)	A	.280	79	286	45	80	20	1	2	36	30	50	17	.378	.354
MINOR LEAGUE TOTALS			.260	150	546	72	142	34	2	3	72	59	92	32	.346	.336

22 Shawn Bowman, 3b

Born: Dec. 9, 1984. **Ht.:** 6-2. **Wt.:** 190. **Bats:** R. **Throws:** R. **School:** Dr. Charles Best SS, Coquitlam, B.C. **Career Transactions:** Selected by Mets in 12th round of 2002 draft; signed Aug. 18, 2002.

That .187 batting average isn't a misprint. But despite his tough pro debut, the Mets still say Bowman has a chance to be a major league third baseman. He had mechanical problems in 2003, getting off balance because he was leaning too far toward the plate. After a couple of tweaks to his stance, Bowman was hitting the ball well again in instructional league. He batted .395 with a team-high four homers for Canada at the 2002 World Junior Championship, and there was debate as to whether he or Adam Loewen (now Baltimore's top prospect as a lefthander) was the club's top hitter. New York expects Bowman to develop into a solid power hitter despite his complete lack of power production in 2003. He has soft hands, an above-average arm and good body control at third base. Bowman obviously has a long way to go, but the Mets wouldn't be surprised if he has a breakout season at Brooklyn in 2004.

Year	Club (League)	Class	AVG	G	AB	R	H	2B	3B	HR	RBI	BB	SO	SB	SLG	OBP
2003	Brooklyn (NY-P)	A	.203	42	138	10	28	7	1	0	5	10	49	2	.268	.260
	Kingsport (Appy)	R	.121	10	33	2	4	1	0	0	3	1	13	0	.152	.216
MINOR LEAGUE TOTALS			.187	52	171	12	32	8	1	0	8	11	62	2	.246	.251

23 Jason Anderson, rhp

Born: June 9, 1979. **Ht.:** 6-0. **Wt.:** 190. **Bats:** L. **Throws:** R. **School:** University of Illinois. **Career Transactions:** Selected by Yankees in 10th round of 2000 draft; signed June 13, 2000 . . . Traded by Yankees with RHP Anderson Garcia and RHP Ryan Bicondoa to Mets for RHP Armando Benitez, July 16, 2003.

One of the top pitchers in University of Illinois history, Anderson won a school-record 14 games and was Big 10 Conference pitcher of the year in 2000. He was only a so-so prospect because he had average velocity, but when the Yankees moved him to the bullpen in the New York-Penn League playoffs that summer, his 88-91 mph fastball jumped to 93-95. His newfound velocity, which peaks at 97 mph, rocketed him through the Yankees system. The key player for the Mets in the Armando Benitez trade, he came up last August and could be part of their bullpen in 2004. Some Mets officials considered trying Anderson as a starter, but he seems much more comfortable coming out of the bullpen and pitched better in that role in Triple-A. He doesn't have much feel or confidence in his secondary pitches, which was his undoing at the major league level. His slider could be a solid-average pitch, but it needs plenty of polish. His changeup and cutter are further away.

Year	Club (League)	Class	W	L	ERA	G	GS	CG	SV	IP	H	R	ER	HR	BB	SO	AVG
2000	Staten Island (NY-P)	A	6	5	4.03	15	15	0	0	80	84	41	36	1	25	73	.273
2001	Greensboro (SAL)	A	7	9	3.76	23	19	1	1	124	127	68	52	9	40	101	.267
	Staten Island (NY-P)	A	5	1	1.70	7	7	0	0	48	32	9	9	2	12	56	.190
2002	Tampa (FSL)	A	4	2	4.07	12	3	0	1	24	27	13	11	2	3	22	.281
	Norwich (EL)	AA	1	1	0.93	16	0	0	2	19	14	2	2	1	5	21	.212
	Columbus (IL)	AAA	5	1	3.15	26	0	0	7	34	26	13	12	3	11	28	.211
2003	New York (AL)	MAJ	1	0	4.79	22	0	0	0	21	23	13	11	3	14	9	.280
	Columbus (IL)	AAA	0	0	0.00	6	0	0	3	8	3	0	0	0	2	13	.115
	Norfolk (IL)	AAA	1	3	2.70	10	5	0	4	23	18	8	7	3	7	9	.214
	New York (NL)	MAJ	0	0	5.06	6	0	0	0	11	10	6	6	2	5	7	.256
MAJOR LEAGUE TOTALS			1	0	4.88	28	0	0	0	31	33	19	17	5	19	16	.273
MINOR LEAGUE TOTALS			29	22	3.21	115	49	1	18	361	331	154	129	21	105	323	.246

24 Pat Strange, rhp

Born: Aug. 23, 1980. **Ht.:** 6-5. **Wt.:** 245. **Bats:** R. **Throws:** R. **School:** Central HS, Springfield, Mass. **Career Transactions:** Selected by Mets in second round of 1998 draft; signed July 29, 1998.

A year ago, Strange was thought to be ready for the majors. Instead he struggled through his worst season. Strange's stuff didn't really go away, as he still has a 91-94 mph fastball, an average slider and a good changeup. But his command deserted him. He doesn't maintain his arm slot and worked way too many deep counts last year. His maximum-effort delivery might mean he fits better as a reliever than as a starter, and he was demoted to the Triple-A bullpen last July. Strange has refined his changeup, as what once was almost a curveball has become a more conventional change with good sink. Despite his struggles, he should get a shot to win a spot in the Mets' bullpen this spring.

Year	Club (League)	Class	W	L	ERA	G	GS	CG	SV	IP	H	R	ER	HR	BB	SO	AVG
1998	Mets (GCL)	R	1	1	1.42	4	4	0	0	19	18	3	3	0	7	19	.254
1999	Capital City (SAL)	A	12	5	2.63	28	21	2	1	154	138	57	45	4	29	113	.238
2000	St. Lucie (FSL)	A	10	1	3.58	19	13	2	0	88	78	48	35	4	32	77	.240
	Binghamton (EL)	AA	4	3	4.55	10	10	0	0	55	62	30	28	2	30	36	.287
2001	Binghamton (EL)	AA	11	6	4.87	26	24	1	0	153	171	94	83	18	52	106	.288
	Norfolk (IL)	AAA	1	0	0.00	1	1	0	0	6	4	0	0	0	1	6	.182
2002	Norfolk (IL)	AAA	10	10	3.82	29	25	2	0	165	165	77	70	12	59	109	.265
	New York (NL)	MAJ	0	0	1.13	5	0	0	0	8	6	1	1	0	4	4	.207
2003	Norfolk (IL)	AAA	5	4	5.74	31	10	0	1	89	111	61	57	8	44	64	.313
	New York (NL)	MAJ	0	0	11.00	6	0	0	0	9	13	11	11	4	11	5	.351
MAJOR LEAGUE TOTALS			0	0	6.35	11	0	0	0	17	19	12	12	4	12	9	.288
MINOR LEAGUE TOTALS			54	30	3.96	148	108	7	2	730	747	370	321	48	254	530	.268

25 Blake McGinley, lhp

Born: Aug. 2, 1978. **Ht.:** 6-1. **Wt.:** 175. **Bats:** R. **Throws:** L. **School:** Texas Tech. **Career Transactions:** Selected by Mets in 21st round of 2001 draft; signed June 10, 2001.

While Shawn Bowman makes this list despite his 2003 stats, McGinley cracks the top 30 because of his. Though his repertoire doesn't exactly scream "prospect," he dominated the Florida State League with an 85-89 mph fastball, average curveball and changeup, and the ability to change speeds. It wasn't the first time that McGinley has exceeded expectations. He's had a sub-2.00 ERA with more than a strikeout an inning at three of his four minor league stops. Scouts are baffled about how exactly he continues to thrive. His motion isn't particularly deceptive, but his fastball has good life and he moves the ball inside and out while changing speeds. McGinley will face a big test in 2004, as the Mets will give him the chance to prove he can get Double-A hitters out.

Year	Club (League)	Class	W	L	ERA	G	GS	CG	SV	IP	H	R	ER	HR	BB	SO	AVG
2001	Brooklyn (NY-P)	A	5	0	1.94	18	0	0	4	46	30	12	10	3	11	59	.182
2002	Capital City (SAL)	A	1	1	1.80	26	0	0	10	35	19	9	7	3	6	53	.154
	St. Lucie (FSL)	A	1	1	5.97	18	0	0	4	32	40	22	21	2	13	22	.299
2003	St. Lucie (FSL)	A	9	1	1.02	37	0	0	7	79	51	11	9	0	20	86	.183
MINOR LEAGUE TOTALS			16	3	2.20	99	0	0	25	192	140	54	47	8	50	220	.200

26 P.J. Bevis, rhp

Born: July 28, 1980. **Ht.:** 6-3. **Wt.:** 175. **Bats:** R. **Throws:** R. **Career Transactions:** Signed out of Australia by Diamondbacks, May 17, 1998 . . . Traded by Diamondbacks to Mets for OF Mark Little, Aug. 20, 2002.

The Australian native spent three years in Rookie ball and emerged as a prospect once he went to a low three-quarters delivery. Unlike most sidearmers, he's not a soft tosser. He features a nasty 93-94 mph fastball complemented by a big-breaking 66-67 mph curve. Bevis has had success getting strikeouts with his curve in the minors, but some scouts say it won't be as effective in the majors, as it's more of a surprise pitch than an effective breaking ball. Scouts also worry about his delivery, which combines a long arm action, a stiff shoulder and plenty of effort. Still, Bevis has struck out more than a batter an inning at every stop since he went sidearm, including an impressive 12.7 strikeouts per nine innings in Double-A. He's unlikely to make the Mets bullpen out of spring training, but could make his big league debut later in 2004.

Year	Club (League)	Class	W	L	ERA	G	GS	CG	SV	IP	H	R	ER	HR	BB	SO	AVG
1998	Diamondbacks (AZL)	R	3	3	5.96	14	9	0	0	45	55	39	30	6	10	48	.289
1999	Missoula (Pio)	R	6	2	4.62	15	15	0	0	86	83	51	44	11	30	69	.261
2000	Missoula (Pio)	R	3	6	3.33	14	14	0	0	84	92	50	31	4	22	63	.281
2001	Yakima (NWL)	A	1	1	0.64	12	0	0	8	14	9	1	1	0	7	22	.180
	El Paso (TL)	AA	0	0	2.16	14	0	0	6	17	11	4	4	2	6	19	.183
2002	El Paso (TL)	AA	4	5	2.83	49	0	0	11	64	50	22	20	3	29	62	.220
	Binghamton (EL)	AA	1	0	1.29	4	0	0	0	7	5	1	1	0	3	14	.208
2003	Binghamton (EL)	AA	4	7	4.18	46	0	0	6	71	55	37	33	4	30	100	.210
	Norfolk (IL)	AAA	1	0	0.00	4	0	0	0	8	2	0	0	2	8	.074
MINOR LEAGUE TOTALS			23	24	3.73	172	38	0	31	395	362	205	164	30	139	405	.244

27 Tyler Davidson, of/1b

Born: Sept. 23, 1980. **Ht.:** 6-5. **Wt.:** 240. **Bats:** R. **Throws:** R. **School:** University of Washington. **Career Transactions:** Selected by Mets in eighth round of 2002 draft; signed June 8, 2002 . . . On disabled list, July 1-Sept. 11, 2002.

Davidson's pro debut was delayed when he tore a tendon in his wrist while taking batting practice before his first game at Brooklyn in 2002. He wasn't fully healed by spring training 2003, so he was held back in extended spring. Sent to Rookie-level Kingsport, he dominated, as would be expected for a 22-year-old with college experience. Promoted to Brooklyn for the final two weeks, he continued to show the raw power that excited the Mets when they drafted him. Though he batted a combined .330, he projects more as a slugger than a high-average hitter. He's a below-average runner and his lack of speed carries over to the outfield. He's an adequate defender with a left-field arm. Davidson also got work last season at first base, a position he hadn't played since high school. While he's raw, he did show aptitude there. Because of his age, Davidson could skip a level and start 2004 in high Class A.

Year	Club (League)	Class	AVG	G	AB	R	H	2B	3B	HR	RBI	BB	SO	SB	SLG	OBP
2002	Did not play—Injured															
2003	Kingsport (Appy)	R	.337	50	172	29	58	11	8	10	35	15	36	3	.669	.394
	Brooklyn (NY-P)	A	.304	15	46	7	14	2	0	1	5	2	14	4	.413	.347
MINOR LEAGUE TOTALS			.330	65	218	36	72	13	8	11	40	17	50	7	.615	.384

28 Yusmeiro Petit, rhp

Born: Nov. 22, 1984. **Ht.:** 6-0. **Wt.:** 180. **Bats:** R. **Throws:** R. **Career Transactions:** Signed out of Venezuela by Mets, Nov. 15, 2001.

Despite his lack of a dominant pitch, Petit quickly has established himself as one of the best strikeout pitchers in the system. After blowing away Rookie-level Venezuelan Summer League hitters in 2002, he continued to leave hitters shaking their heads in his first season in the United States. Petit throws an 88-90 mph fastball that touches 92, a changeup that could end up being a plus pitch and an average curveball. What makes him effective is his ability to throw all three pitches for strikes, and to throw his changeup and curve in fastball counts. Though Petit's build isn't projectable, the Mets hope he can add a little more velocity to his fastball. He'll get his first exposure to full-season ball at Capital City in 2004.

Year	Club (League)	Class	W	L	ERA	G	GS	CG	SV	IP	H	R	ER	HR	BB	SO	AVG
2002	Universidad (VSL)	R	3	5	2.43	12	11	0	0	56	53	25	15	1	16	62	.252
2003	Kingsport (Appy)	R	3	3	2.32	12	12	0	0	62	47	19	16	2	8	65	.219
	Brooklyn (NY-P)	A	1	0	2.19	2	2	0	0	12	5	3	3	0	2	20	.119
MINOR LEAGUE TOTALS			7	8	2.35	26	25	0	0	130	105	47	34	3	26	147	.225

29 Wayne Lydon, of

Born: April 17, 1981. **Ht.:** 6-2. **Wt.:** 190. **Bats:** B. **Throws:** R. **School:** Valley View HS, Archbald, Pa. **Career Transactions:** Selected by Mets in ninth round of 1999 draft; signed June 4, 1999.

In an organization filled with speedy outfielders, Lydon is the fastest baserunner of them all. An all-state defensive back for his Pennsylvania high school, Lydon turned down a Penn State football scholarship to turn pro. The Mets converted him to switch-hitting to take advantage of his speed. He looked like a lost cause in 2000 and 2001, but he has developed the ability to slap the ball as a lefty. Because he can go from the left side of the plate to first base in 3.9 seconds, he's tough to throw out when he puts the ball on the ground. Despite good size, he shows little power from either side of the plate, but he has started to work counts and draw walks, vital skills if he's going to become a leadoff hitter. Once he reaches base, Lydon takes one of the biggest leads in baseball—big enough that the Mets tell their other prospects to watch and learn from him—and he can outrun pitchouts and pickoff moves. He finished second in the minors in steals in 2002, and third last year. He's a solid center fielder who covers plenty of ground, but his arm is below-average. Lydon has been on a steady step-a-season progression, which he'll continue in Double-A this year.

Year	Club (League)	Class	AVG	G	AB	R	H	2B	3B	HR	RBI	BB	SO	SB	SLG	OBP
1999	Mets (GCL)	R	.183	37	60	13	11	3	0	0	5	7	13	0	.233	.279
2000	Kingsport (Appy)	R	.203	55	172	34	35	4	1	3	20	24	47	35	.291	.300
2001	Kingsport (Appy)	R	.184	26	98	14	18	7	0	0	8	11	35	15	.255	.266
	Brooklyn (NY-P)	A	.246	21	57	12	14	1	1	0	1	7	18	10	.298	.348
2002	Capital City (SAL)	A	.294	127	473	93	139	9	5	0	46	54	104	87	.334	.368
2003	St. Lucie (FSL)	A	.264	133	488	83	129	14	7	4	44	52	96	75	.346	.342
MINOR LEAGUE TOTALS			.257	399	1348	249	346	38	14	7	124	155	313	222	.321	.337

30 Anderson Garcia, rhp

Born: March 23, 1981. **Ht.:** 6-2. **Wt.:** 170. **Bats:** R. **Throws:** R. **Career Transactions:** Signed out of Dominican Republic by Yankees, April 25, 2001 . . . Traded by Yankees with RHP Jason Anderson and RHP Ryan Bicondoa to Mets for RHP Armando Benitez, July 17, 2003.

While the Mets had to go outside the organization in their search for a major league closer for 2004, they have plenty of future possibilities stacked throughout the minors. Count Garcia, part of the Armando Benitez trade with the Yankees, among the group. He has a 91-94 mph fastball that touches 97 mph and has good arm-side run. It's a potentially dominant pitch. He also shows a good, if inconsistent, slider with a tight, late break and an average straight changeup. Though he has split time between the rotation and bullpen for both the Mets and Yankees, Garcia projects as a reliever. He has trouble keeping his delivery under control, and it's closer to maximum effort than free and easy. He has plenty of work to do on maintaining his mechanics, but with his fastball he'll get plenty of chances to get it put together. He should start this season in high Class A.

Year	Club (League)	Class	W	L	ERA	G	GS	CG	SV	IP	H	R	ER	HR	BB	SO	AVG
2001	Yankees (DSL)	R	2	3	3.15	14	8	0	1	66	52	29	23	3	25	49	.217
	Staten Island (NY-P)	A	0	0	5.79	1	0	0	0	5	7	3	3	0	1	1	.368
2002	Yankees (GCL)	R	4	1	2.30	11	9	1	0	59	43	22	15	1	22	41	.204
2003	Battle Creek (Mid)	A	3	6	3.32	16	11	1	0	76	57	35	28	2	36	62	.208
	Capital City (SAL)	A	0	1	4.26	5	2	0	0	13	10	6	6	1	2	12	.217
MINOR LEAGUE TOTALS			9	12	3.10	47	31	2	1	218	169	95	75	7	86	165	.214

NEW YORK
YANKEES

For Yankees owner George Steinbrenner, just reaching the World Series is unacceptable. In the midst of a three-year championship drought, Steinbrenner has taken full control of the team's day-to-day operations—as if he wasn't already calling the shots. Following New York's World Series loss to the Marlins, who had a payroll less than one-third of the Yankees' $180 million, Steinbrenner targeted nearly every major free agent in sight, spending wildly as the 2004 payroll approached $200 million. As second-time offenders of major league baseball's luxury tax, the Yankees will have to pay a 30 percent penalty on every dollar they spend over $120.5 million.

With the team already aging rapidly, Steinbrenner brought 35-year-olds Gary Sheffield and Paul Quantrill, 36-year-olds Tom Gordon and Kenny Lofton and 39-year-old Kevin Brown on board with multiyear contracts. New York fans were outraged to see Andy Pettitte accept less money to go to Houston, ending his 13-year tenure in the organization, and even more upset when Roger Clemens joined him. The way the Yankees handled Pettitte exemplified Steinbrenner's impersonal corporate mentality.

Compared to Steinbrenner's antics in the late 1970s and '80s, however, highlighted by a managerial carousel, the stability has been shocking since Joe Torre took over in 1996.

TOP 30 PROSPECTS

1. Dioner Navarro, c
2. Eric Duncan, 3b
3. Rudy Guillen, of
4. Joaquin Arias, ss
5. Ramon Ramirez, rhp
6. Robinson Cano, 2b
7. Ferdin Tejeda, ss
8. Jorge DePaula, rhp
9. Estee Harris, of
10. Bronson Sardinha, 3b
11. Edwardo Sierra, rhp
12. Chien-Ming Wang, rhp
13. Scott Proctor, rhp
14. Danny Borrell, lhp
15. Matt DeSalvo, rhp
16. Hector Made, ss
17. Sean Henn, lhp
18. Mark Phillips, lhp
19. Melky Cabrera, of
20. Jose Garcia, rhp
21. Jose Valdez, rhp
22. Michael Vento, of
23. J.T. Stotts, ss/2b
24. Brad Halsey, lhp
25. Jason Stephens, rhp
26. Jon-Mark Sprowl, c
27. Erick Almonte, ss
28. Tyler Clippard, rhp
29. Ben Julianel, lhp
30. Mike Knox, rhp

By Josh Boyd

General manager Brian Cashman has held his title since 1998. But even the Yankees brass was in an uproar this offseason. Chief major league scout Gene Michael, who deserves a lot of credit for constructing the dynasty, voiced his displeasure about not being consulted before the Brown deal was made with the Dodgers. Days after Cashman announced plans to leave after his contract ended in 2004, Steinbrenner invoked a club option for 2005, clearly out of spite.

A year after Mark Newman was pushed out of the Tampa offices in favor of Gordon Blakeley, Newman returned to head up the baseball-operations department, overseeing scouting and player development. Blakeley, who was denied permission to interview for the Mariners' GM vacancy, reportedly upset The Boss by standing up to him on various matters, including the way employees are treated. Farm director Rob Thomson was reassigned to special-assignment scout.

While Steinbrenner's empire has more than enough capital to absorb mistakes, especially with amateur talent, the farm system has suffered in recent years. Drew Henson's flight to football is underscored by the $9 million the Yankees spent on him. What's more troubling is that Yankees officials say they could have eased his development had they not been forced to rush him to the upper minors.

ORGANIZATION
OVERVIEW

General manager: Brian Cashman. **Farm director:** Damon Oppenheimer. **Scouting director:** Lin Garrett.

2003 PERFORMANCE

Class	Team	League	W	L	Pct.	Finish*	Manager
Majors	New York	American	101	61	.623	1st (14)	Joe Torre
Triple-A	Columbus Clippers	International	76	68	.528	4th (14)	Bucky Dent
Double-A	Trenton Thunder	Eastern	70	71	.496	7th (12)	Stump Merrill
High A	Tampa Yankees	Florida State	68	64	.515	6th (12)	Bill Masse
Low A	Battle Creek Yankees	Midwest	73	64	.533	3rd (14)	Mitch Seoane
Short-season	Staten Island Yankees	New York-Penn	29	43	.403	11th (14)	Andy Stankiewicz
Rookie	GCL Yankees	Gulf Coast	26	31	.456	8th (12)	Dan Radison
OVERALL 2003 MINOR LEAGUE RECORD			342	341	.501	14th (30)	

*Finish in overall standings (No. of teams in league)

ORGANIZATIONAL LEADERS

BATTING
*Minimum 250 At-Bats
*AVG	Fernando Seguignol, Columbus/Trenton	.342
R	Brian Myrow, Trenton	99
H	Mike Vento, Columbus/Trenton	151
TB	Jayson Drobiak, Battle Creek	279
2B	Drew Henson, Columbus	40
3B	Three tied at	8
HR	Jayson Drobiak, Battle Creek	30
RBI	Mitch Jones, Trenton	91
BB	Brian Myrow, Trenton	107
SO	Mitch Jones, Trenton	131
SB	Kevin Thompson, Trenton/Tampa	63
*SLG	Fernando Seguignol, Columbus/Tampa	.617
*OBP	Brian Myrow, Trenton	.447

PITCHING
#Minimum 75 Innings
W	Brad Halsey, Trenton/Tampa	17
L	Jeremy King, Tampa/Battle Creek	13
#ERA	Rik Currier, Trenton/Tampa	2.16
G	David Shepard, Columbus/Trenton	61
CG	Jose Garcia, Tampa/Battle Creek	4
SV	Matt Brumit, Tampa/Battle Creek	24
IP	Brad Halsey, Trenton/Tampa	175
BB	Javier Ortiz, Trenton	71
SO	Brad Halsey, Trenton/Tampa	134

BEST TOOLS

Best Hitter for Average	Dioner Navarro
Best Power Hitter	Eric Duncan
Fastest Baserunner	Joaquin Arias
Best Athlete	Rudy Guillen
Best Fastball	Scott Proctor
Best Curveball	Mark Phillips
Best Slider	Ramon Ramirez
Best Changeup	Jorge DePaula
Best Control	Danny Borrell
Best Defensive Catcher	Dioner Navarro
Best Defensive Infielder	Ferdin Tejeda
Best Infield Arm	Joaquin Arias
Best Defensive Outfielder	Melky Cabrera
Best Outfield Arm	Rudy Guillen

PROJECTED 2007 LINEUP

Catcher	Dioner Navarro
First Base	Jorge Posada
Second Base	Joaquin Arias
Third Base	Eric Duncan
Shortstop	Derek Jeter
Left Field	Hideki Matsui
Center Field	Alfonso Soriano
Right Field	Gary Sheffield

Designated Hitter	Jason Giambi
No. 1 Starter	Javier Vazquez
No. 2 Starter	Jose Contreras
No. 3 Starter	Mike Mussina
No. 4 Starter	Ramon Ramirez
No. 5 Starter	Jon Lieber
Closer	Mariano Rivera

LAST YEAR'S TOP 20 PROSPECTS

1. Jose Contreras, rhp
2. Hideki Matsui, of
3. Juan Rivera, of
4. Bronson Sardinha, of
5. Brandon Claussen, lhp
6. Drew Henson, 3b
7. Chien-Ming Wang, rhp
8. Robinson Cano, 2b/ss
9. Danny Borrell, lhp
10. Julio DePaula, rhp
11. Rudy Guillen, of
12. Sean Henn, lhp
13. Ferdin Tejada, ss
14. Charlie Manning, lhp
15. Andy Phillips, 2b
16. Joaquin Arias, 2b/ss
17. Jason Anderson, rhp
18. Javier Ortiz, rhp
19. Brandon Weeden, rhp
20. Jose Valdez, rhp

TOP PROSPECTS OF THE DECADE

1994	Derek Jeter, ss
1995	Ruben Rivera, of
1996	Ruben Rivera, of
1997	Ruben Rivera, of
1998	Eric Milton, lhp
1999	Nick Johnson, 1b
2000	Nick Johnson, 1b
2001	Nick Johnson, 1b
2002	Drew Henson, 3b
2003	Jose Contreras, rhp

TOP DRAFT PICKS OF THE DECADE

1994	Brian Buchanan, of
1995	Shea Morenz, of
1996	Eric Milton, lhp
1997	*Tyrell Godwin, of
1998	Andy Brown, of
1999	David Walling, rhp
2000	David Parrish, c
2001	John-Ford Griffin, of
2002	Brandon Weeden, rhp (2)
2003	Eric Duncan, 3b

*Did not sign.

ALL-TIME LARGEST BONUSES

Hideki Irabu, 1997	$8,500,000
Jose Contreras, 2002	$6,000,000
Wily Mo Pena, 1999	$2,440,000
Drew Henson, 1998	$2,000,000
Chien-Ming Wang, 2000	$1,900,000

MINOR LEAGUE
DEPTH CHART

NEW YORK **YANKEES**   RANK: **27**

Impact potential (D): When scouts talk about the likes of Rudy Guillen and Joaquin Arias, they can't help but mention their high upside. They also point out how raw and unrefined they are, which could mean they don't amount to much. Coming off a breakthrough season, Dioner Navarro is much more of a safe bet. He could become Jorge Posada lite.

Depth (C): While the Yankees' international scouting is flourishing, their recent drafts have been coming up short. Last year they took bigger risks by taking high school players in the early rounds, adding upside in Eric Duncan and Estee Harris and rolling the dice on prep pitchers like Jason Stephens and Tyler Clippard.

Sleeper: Hector Made, ss.   *—Depth charts prepared by **Josh Boyd**. Numbers in parentheses indicate prospect rankings.*

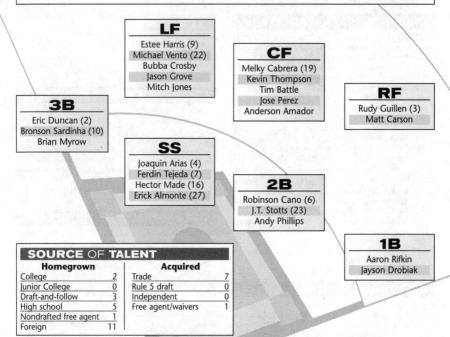

LF
Estee Harris (9)
Michael Vento (22)
Bubba Crosby
Jason Grove
Mitch Jones

CF
Melky Cabrera (19)
Kevin Thompson
Tim Battle
Jose Perez
Anderson Amador

RF
Rudy Guillen (3)
Matt Carson

3B
Eric Duncan (2)
Bronson Sardinha (10)
Brian Myrow

SS
Joaquin Arias (4)
Ferdin Tejeda (7)
Hector Made (16)
Erick Almonte (27)

2B
Robinson Cano (6)
J.T. Stotts (23)
Andy Phillips

1B
Aaron Rifkin
Jayson Drobiak

SOURCE OF TALENT			
Homegrown		**Acquired**	
College	2	Trade	7
Junior College	0	Rule 5 draft	0
Draft-and-follow	3	Independent	0
High school	5	Free agent/waivers	1
Nondrafted free agent	1		
Foreign	11		

C
Dioner Navarro (1)
Jon-Mark Sprowl (27)

RHP
Starters	**Relievers**
Ramon Ramirez (5)	Jorge De Paula (8)
Chien-Ming Wang (12)	Edwardo Sierra (11)
Matt Desalvo (15)	Scott Proctor (13)
Jose Garcia (20)	Jose Valdez (21)
Jason Stephens (25)	Sam Marsonek
Tyler Clippard (28)	Rik Currier
Mike Knox (30)	Eric Schmitt
Elvys Quezada	Edison Reynoso
Justin Pope	
Jeff Karstens	
T.J. Beam	

LHP
Starters	**Relievers**
Danny Borrell (14)	Sean Henn (17)
Mark Phillips (18)	Ben Julianel (29)
Brad Halsey (26)	
Alex Graman	
Andy Beal	
Matt Smith	
Abel Gomez	
Edgar Soto	
Chase Wright	

DRAFT
ANALYSIS

Best Pro Debut: Managers rated 3B Eric Duncan (1) the top prospect in the Rookie-level Gulf Coast League, and he hit .373 after a late promotion to the short-season New York-Penn League. Between the two stops, he batted .301-4-41. RHP Tyler Clippard (9) went 3-3, 2.89 in 44 GCL innings. RHP Elvys Quezada (15) went 5-0, 1.72 between the NY-P and low Class A.

Best Athlete: OFs Estee Harris (2), Tim Battle (3) and Jose Perez (7) all can fly, have center-field skills and have power potential.

Best Pure Hitter: Duncan, whose bat is more advanced than his glove. The Yankees believe he can stay at the hot corner, but he'll need time to work on his defense.

Best Raw Power: Duncan or Harris. Harris is reminiscent of a young Chili Davis. He's just 6 feet and 170 pounds, but the ball jumps off his bat.

Fastest Runner: Battle can run the 60-yard dash in 6.4 seconds.

Best Defensive Player: Battle gets the nod over Harris because he's a little quicker and has a stronger arm. He was clocked at 90-92 mph on the mound in high school.

Best Fastball: The Yankees weren't able to sign him as a draft-and-follow after taking him in the 18th round in 2001, but they finally got RHP Josh Smith (8). His fastball usually runs from 92-95 mph. RHP T.J. Beam

Beam

(10) sits at 90-91 mph, but generates a tough downward plane with his 6-foot-7 frame.

Best Breaking Ball: RHP Jason Stephens' (6) curveball is better than Clippard's. The Yankees spent $500,000 to sign Stephens because he's projectable.

Most Intriguing Background: 1B Taylor Mattingly's (42) father Don and 2B Andre Randolph's (45) dad Willie were all-stars for the Yankees and are employed by the club. 2B Enrique Cruz' (14) brother Jose Jr. plays for the Devil Rays, and his father Jose and uncles Hector and Tommy were former big leaguers.

Closest To The Majors: Beam or Quezada, whose fastball and slider are above-average pitches at times.

Best Late-Round Pick: Quezada or Cruz. Cruz is an offensive second baseman who'll have to work defensively.

The One Who Got Away: RHP Daniel Bard (20) had a borderline first-round arm but fulfilled his commitment to North Carolina. LHP David Purcey (17) can be inconsistent, but he could go high in the 2004 draft after a strong Cape Cod League.

Assessment: In a departure from recent years, the Yankees gambled on younger, less polished players with higher ceilings. They're starting from the bottom as they begin replenishing a system depleted by trades and disappointments.

2002 DRAFT   GRADE: F

New York had one pick in the first three rounds: RHP Brandon Weeden (2), whom they dispatched in the Kevin Brown trade. The best prospect from this crop is middling LHP Brad Halsey (8).

2001 DRAFT   GRADE: C

In a rarity for the Yankees, they had three first-round choices: OFs John-Ford Griffin and Bronson Sardinha and oft-injured RHP Jon Skaggs. Griffin and RHP Jason Arnold (2) were dealt for Jeff Weaver. The best player selected looks like RHP Philip Humber (29), who didn't sign and should be a first-rounder in 2004.

2000 DRAFT   GRADE: D

C David Parrish was a shocking first-round choice that hasn't paid off. LHP Danny Borrell (2) and draft-and-follow RHP Sean Henn (26) have upside—and health questions. RHP Jason Anderson (10) was traded for Armando Benitez shortly after reaching the majors.

1999 DRAFT   GRADE: F

RHP Dave Walling (1) developed a mental block and didn't pitch at all in 2003. LHP Alex Graman (3) is this group's best hope.

—Draft analysis prepared by Jim Callis. Numbers in parentheses indicate draft rounds.

Dioner
Navarro

Born: Feb. 9, 1984.
Ht.: 5-10. **Wt.:** 190.
Bats: B. **Throws:** R.
Career Transactions: Signed out of Venezuela by Yankees, Aug. 21, 2000.

U sually it's the Yankees' money that wins out in the free-agent market, but their tradition and worldwide appeal often provides an extra boost, especially on the international front. Venezuelan scouts Carlos Rios, Ricardo Finol and Hector Rincones established a relationship with Navarro before he signed. When the Braves topped New York's $260,000 bid, Navarro still went with the Yankees because he had spent time around their staff and players in Tampa. Navarro quickly earned the nickname "Pudgito" for his defensive skills and physical resemblance to Pudge Rodriguez. Though he entered last season with a .252 career average, he has been an organization favorite since hitting .280 in his 2001 Rookie-level Gulf Coast League debut. The Yankees planned to keep him in high Class A Tampa all season in 2003, but he handled the bat so well they promoted him to Double-A Trenton by June. Nagging injuries—including an inner-thigh infection that led to a sty in his eye, and a hand injury from a home-plate collision—weren't enough to stop him from raking. His combined .321 average ranked fourth among minor league catchers.

Navarro was a second and third baseman as an amateur, and his successful move behind the plate has conjured comparisons to another infielder turned catcher, Jorge Posada. While Navarro doesn't project to hit for the same power, he has separated himself from the pack by working counts and making hard contact to all fields. His set-up and smooth, natural stroke from both sides of the plate bring to mind Roberto Alomar. Navarro has a short, compact swing but manages to cover the plate, and he's tough to strike out. He stays back on breaking balls and has the bat speed to catch up to plus fastballs. He shows more power potential from the right side, though he can get a little pull-happy and could top out at 20 home runs. Navarro's cat-like quickness around the plate impresses scouts and he has above-average arm strength. Aside from not displaying big-time power, there aren't many flaws with Navarro's bat. There are mixed opinions on his defense. He needs to improve his game-calling skills, though that isn't uncommon for a young catcher. He threw out 33 percent of basestealers last year, and that number should improve with slight refinements to his mechanics.

Navarro has gone from advancing a level a season to the fast track. He's slated to return to Double-A in 2004 but could find himself at Triple-A Columbus before the end of the season. A September callup isn't out of the question. Navarro should be ready to serve as Posada's backup at some point in 2005. He's in line to take the job in 2007, when Posada is due either a $12 million salary or $4 million buyout.

Year	Club (League)	Class	AVG	G	AB	R	H	2B	3B	HR	RBI	BB	SO	SB	SLG	OBP
2001	Yankees (GCL)	R	.280	43	143	27	40	10	1	2	22	17	23	6	.406	.345
2002	Greensboro (SAL)	A	.238	92	328	41	78	12	2	8	36	39	61	1	.360	.326
	Tampa (FSL)	A	.500	1	2	1	1	0	0	0	0	0	0	0	.500	.500
2003	Tampa (FSL)	A	.299	52	197	28	59	16	4	3	28	17	27	1	.467	.364
	Trenton (EL)	AA	.341	58	208	28	71	15	0	4	37	18	26	2	.471	.388
MINOR LEAGUE TOTALS			.284	246	878	125	249	53	7	17	123	91	137	10	.418	.352

2 Eric Duncan, 3b

Born: Dec. 7, 1984. **Ht.:** 6-3. **Wt.:** 195. **Bats:** L. **Throws:** R. **School:** Seton Hall Prep, Florham Park, N.J. **Career Transactions:** Selected by Yankees in first round (27th overall) of 2003 draft; signed June 11, 2003.

Duncan emerged as an early-round target for the Yankees at the 2002 Area Code Games, and he followed up with a strong spring. He collected three hits to earn the MVP award in a high school all-America game played near his New Jersey home before signing for $1.25 million. Managers rated him the No. 1 prospect in the Gulf Coast League. Duncan's approach reminds the Yankees of Nick Johnson, though Duncan can drive the ball to left field with more power. He has similarly solid plate discipline and a short, simple stroke. His even-keeled nature is ideal for New York and he embodies the Derek Jeter blueprint of ability, durability and character. Some teams compared Duncan's lefthanded power potential to Jim Thome's. As with Thome, Duncan's defense at third base may force him to move across the diamond to first. He can get pull-conscious, which should be corrected as he adjusts to wood bats. Duncan could move to high Class A with a good spring. He profiles as a middle-of-the-order run producer. His arrival in the Bronx could coincide with the end of Jason Giambi's contract.

Year	Club (League)	Class	AVG	G	AB	R	H	2B	3B	HR	RBI	BB	SO	SB	SLG	OBP
2003	Yankees (GCL)	R	.278	47	180	24	50	12	2	2	28	18	33	0	.400	.348
	Staten Island (NY-P)	A	.373	14	59	11	22	5	4	2	13	2	11	1	.695	.413
MINOR LEAGUE TOTALS			.301	61	239	35	72	17	6	4	41	20	44	1	.473	.364

3 Rudy Guillen, of

Born: Nov. 23, 1983. **Ht.:** 6-3. **Wt.:** 185. **Bats:** R. **Throws:** R. **Career Transactions:** Signed out of Dominican Republic by Yankees, July 2, 2000.

After signing for $100,000, Guillen showed his power potential by leading the Rookie-level Dominican Summer League with 11 home runs in 2001. In 2003, he moved to center field, the position at which scout Victor Mata first spotted him, and made the jump to full-season ball. An exciting athlete, Guillen makes the game look easy with his graceful actions and projectable tools. He's an above-average runner with a strong arm and solid instincts for center field. He still shows more raw power than game power, but the ball jumps off his bat. Guillen is a bit of a wild swinger. An aggressive hitter early in the count, he too often falls behind and is susceptible to breaking balls. He worked on becoming more selective this offseason at the Yankees' complex in the Dominican. Last summer he drew 13 of his 32 walks in August, more than enough to win a dinner bet with Dodgers prospect Joel Guzman over who would draw more free passes. Guillen has as much upside as any player in the system. He'll spend 2004 in high Class A.

Year	Club (League)	Class	AVG	G	AB	R	H	2B	3B	HR	RBI	BB	SO	SB	SLG	OBP
2001	Yankees (DSL)	R	.281	62	231	38	65	13	2	11	41	15	50	11	.498	.337
2002	Yankees (GCL)	R	.306	59	219	38	67	7	2	3	35	14	39	7	.397	.351
2003	Battle Creek (Mid)	A	.260	133	493	64	128	29	4	13	79	32	87	13	.414	.311
MINOR LEAGUE TOTALS			.276	254	943	140	260	49	8	27	155	61	176	31	.431	.327

4 Joaquin Arias, ss

Born: Sept. 21, 1984. **Ht.:** 6-2. **Wt.:** 160. **Bats:** R. **Throws:** R. **Career Transactions:** Signed out of Dominican Republic by Yankees, July 12, 2001.

When Victor Mata first saw Arias as a wiry, 140-pound 16-year-old, he almost didn't give him a chance to swing the bat at a workout. Once Mata heard the thump of the ball coming off his bat, he kept Arias at the Yankees' academy for nearly a year. Arias signed for $300,000 after growing up in a house with a dirt floor and no furniture. His brother Alberto pitches in the Rockies system. Nicknamed "Spiderman" because his arms and legs appear to be going in every direction at once, Arias displays good body control in the field. He's flashier than New York's other shortstop prospects, showing plus-plus range and speed to go with a plus arm. He has outstanding bat speed and raw power. Arias hits out of a slight crouch and tends to swing uphill, and the Yankees would like to see him level his stroke out. He's too aggressive at the plate, though he demonstrates a good feel for the bat head and makes consistent contact. Like Guillen, Arias has five-tool potential and will continue to move at an aggressive pace. He'll start in high Class A this season as a 19-year-old.

Year	Club (League)	Class	AVG	G	AB	R	H	2B	3B	HR	RBI	BB	SO	SB	SLG	OBP
2002	Yankees (GCL)	R	.300	57	203	29	61	7	6	0	21	12	16	2	.394	.338
2003	Battle Creek (Mid)	A	.266	130	481	60	128	12	8	3	48	26	44	12	.343	.306
MINOR LEAGUE TOTALS			.276	187	684	89	189	19	14	3	69	38	60	14	.358	.316

5 Ramon Ramirez, rhp

STEVE MOORE

Born: Aug. 31, 1981. **Ht.:** 5-11. **Wt.:** 170. **Bats:** R. **Throws:** R. **Career Transactions:** Signed out of Dominican Republic by Rangers, Dec. 27, 1996 . . . Released by Rangers, June 4, 1998 . . . Signed by Hiroshima (Japan), 2002 . . . Signed by Yankees, March 5, 2003.

Released by the Rangers after one season as an outfielder in the Dominican Summer League, Ramirez signed with the Hiroshima Carp as a pitcher in 2002 but pitched just three innings in the Japanese majors. After he impressed Yankees scouts in winter ball, they outbid the Phillies by purchasing his rights from the Carp for $350,000. Ramirez signed for $175,000. He got better as the 2003 season went on, learning to mix his pitches and to work effectively behind in the count. His fastball maxes out at 95 mph and sits at 92-94, while his power curveball features hard downward bite and is his best pitch. Ramirez had Japanese-style mechanics with a hip-turn and hesitations, but pitching instructors Billy Connors and Greg Pavlick converted him to a more conventional over-the-top delivery. Ramirez led the Arizona Fall League with a 1.44 ERA, likely earning him a job in the Triple-A rotation. His stature and two power pitches might make him a candidate for short relief in the future.

Year	Club (League)	Class	AVG	G	AB	R	H	2B	3B	HR	RBI	BB	SO	SB	SLG	OBP
1997	Rangers (DSL)	R	.245	39	94	12	23	4	0	2	9	16	21	2	.351	.355
MINOR LEAGUE TOTALS			.245	39	94	12	23	4	0	2	9	16	21	2	.351	.355

Year	Club (League)	Class	W	L	ERA	G	GS	CG	SV	IP	H	R	ER	HR	BB	SO	AVG
2002	Hiroshima (CL)	JPN	0	0	3.00	2	0	0	0	3	3	1	1	0	2	3	—
2003	Tampa (FSL)	A	2	8	5.21	14	14	0	0	74	88	47	43	7	20	70	.291
	Trenton (EL)	AA	1	1	1.69	4	3	0	0	21	18	8	4	3	8	21	.231
	Columbus (IL)	AAA	0	1	4.50	2	1	0	0	6	5	5	3	1	1	5	.208
MINOR LEAGUE TOTALS			3	10	4.43	20	18	0	0	102	111	60	50	11	29	96	.275

6 Robinson Cano, 2b

RICK BATTLE

Born: Oct. 22, 1982. **Ht.:** 6-0. **Wt.:** 170. **Bats:** L. **Throws:** R. **Career Transactions:** Signed out of Dominican Republic by Yankees, Jan. 5, 2001.

The Yankees' willingness to move prospects quickly under former player-personnel chief Gordon Blakeley is illustrated by Cano's progress in 2003. His father Jose reached the majors briefly in 1989. One of the most confident hitters in the system, Cano can sting hard line drives to right field with an easy, level swing. He's capable of producing more power than he did last year because he has plus bat speed and natural strength, but he needs to learn to lift the ball. As Cano has filled out, especially in his lower half, he has lost his quickness. He doesn't get down the line well and on defense, his range is lacking at second base, which could prompt a move to third. Cano has the arm strength and projects to hit for enough power to justify a move to the hot corner. For now he'll remain at second base and return to Double-A.

Year	Club (League)	Class	AVG	G	AB	R	H	2B	3B	HR	RBI	BB	SO	SB	SLG	OBP
2001	Yankees (GCL)	R	.230	57	200	37	46	14	2	3	34	28	27	11	.365	.330
	Staten Island (NY-P)	A	.250	2	8	0	2	0	0	0	2	0	2	0	.250	.250
2002	Greensboro (SAL)	A	.276	113	474	67	131	20	9	14	66	29	78	2	.445	.321
	Staten Island (NY-P)	A	.276	22	87	11	24	5	1	1	15	4	8	6	.391	.308
2003	Tampa (FSL)	A	.276	90	366	50	101	16	3	5	50	17	49	1	.377	.313
	Trenton (EL)	AA	.280	46	164	21	46	9	1	1	13	9	16	0	.366	.341
MINOR LEAGUE TOTALS			.269	330	1299	186	350	64	16	24	180	87	180	20	.399	.322

7 Ferdin Tejeda, ss

STEVE MOORE

Born: Sept. 15, 1982. **Ht.:** 5-11. **Wt.:** 170. **Bats:** R. **Throws:** R. **Career Transactions:** Signed out of Dominican Republic by Yankees, Feb. 12, 2000 . . . On disabled list, June 3-Sept. 29, 2000.

Signed for $35,000 in February 2000, Tejeda had his pro debut postponed for a year by an abdominal strain. He finished second in the Dominican Summer League with a .330 average in 2001. Last season, Tejeda was sidelined several times with hamstring injuries but recovered to hold his own in the Arizona Fall League. He's nicknamed Pescado because he eats only fish. A switch-hitter, Tejeda handles the bat well

from both sides and uses quick hands and an efficient line-drive swing. He puts the ball in play, though not with the same authority as Joaquin Arias. Defense is Tejeda's true calling card. He has one of the best arms in the system, athletic actions and soft, quick hands. While he stays back on breaking balls, Tejeda tends to be too aggressive early in the count. He has to gain more control of the strike zone to handle a jump to Double-A in 2004. Tejeda brings a lot of positive energy to the game, but remains coachable and willing to address his weaknesses. His AFL stint should help prepare him for the Eastern League.

Year	Club (League)	Class	AVG	G	AB	R	H	2B	3B	HR	RBI	BB	SO	SB	SLG	OBP
2000	Did not play-Injured															
2001	Yankees (DSL)	R	.330	46	188	41	62	7	7	1	19	26	30	13	.457	.411
2002	Yankees (GCL)	R	.300	16	60	13	18	3	0	0	2	10	9	3	.350	.394
	Staten Island (NY-P)	A	.276	47	181	29	50	7	2	0	18	11	33	11	.337	.316
2003	Tampa (FSL)	A	.295	51	217	33	64	9	5	0	20	6	38	4	.382	.320
	Yankees (GCL)	R	.393	8	28	4	11	2	0	0	3	2	4	1	.464	.433
MINOR LEAGUE TOTALS			.304	168	674	120	205	28	14	1	62	55	114	32	.392	.357

8 Jorge DePaula, rhp

Born: Nov. 10, 1978. **Ht.:** 6-1. **Wt.:** 160. **Bats:** R. **Throws:** R. **Career Transactions:** Signed out of Dominican Republic by Rockies, Jan. 13, 1997 . . . Traded by Rockies to Yankees, April 20, 2001; completing trade in which Yankees sent RHP Craig Dingman to Rockies for a player to be named (March 29, 2001).

DePaula was among the Latin American players to have his identity and date of birth corrected in the visa crackdown after Sept. 11. Formerly known as Julio DePaula, he's eight months older than previously reported. After spending five years in the lower minors, he made an impressive big league debut in September. Yankees catcher Jorge Posada's father signed DePaula for the Rockies. As he has gained experience, DePaula has made strides with his ability to vary his pitches. He sets hitters up with a deceptive changeup and runs his fastball between 88-93 mph. He wasn't fazed at all by pitching in the majors, but he doesn't possess a true out pitch. His fastball can get straight and he has a tendency to leave pitches up, leading to a career-high 23 home runs allowed. He throws a slurvy slider with inconsistent break. DePaula will vie for the final spot in the New York bullpen during spring training. The Yankees hope he can emerge as a Ramiro Mendoza type.

Year	Club (League)	Class	W	L	ERA	G	GS	CG	SV	IP	H	R	ER	HR	BB	SO	AVG
1997	Rockies (DSL)	R	3	6	4.75	15	11	1	0	66	77	46	35	4	28	59	.292
1998	Rockies (AZL)	R	5	5	3.81	17	9	0	2	54	54	30	23	1	18	62	.252
1999	Portland (NWL)	A	6	6	6.01	16	16	0	0	85	97	67	57	8	43	77	.290
2000	Asheville (SAL)	A	8	13	4.70	28	27	1	0	155	151	90	81	16	62	187	.260
2001	Asheville (SAL)	A	1	1	3.78	3	3	0	0	17	19	13	7	3	2	26	.268
	Greensboro (SAL)	A	6	1	2.75	8	8	0	0	56	35	19	17	2	21	67	.179
	Tampa (FSL)	A	9	5	3.58	16	13	0	0	83	65	43	33	3	53	77	.212
2002	Norwich (EL)	AA	14	6	3.45	27	26	6	0	175	141	74	67	11	52	152	.221
2003	Columbus (IL)	AAA	10	11	4.35	27	27	3	0	168	168	90	81	22	57	125	.262
	New York (AL)	MAJ	0	0	0.79	4	1	0	0	11	3	1	1	1	1	7	.083
MAJOR LEAGUE TOTALS			0	0	0.79	4	1	0	0	11	3	1	1	1	1	7	.083
MINOR LEAGUE TOTALS			62	54	4.20	157	140	11	2	859	807	472	401	70	336	832	.249

9 Estee Harris, of

Born: Jan. 8, 1985. **Ht.:** 5-11. **Wt.:** 170. **Bats:** L. **Throws:** R. **School:** Islip HS, Central Islip, N.Y. **Career Transactions:** Selected by Yankees in second round of 2003 draft; signed July 16, 2003.

Bronx-based Yankees scout Cesar Presbott netted the club's top two choices in 2003, Eric Duncan and Harris. With two premium picks in the New York area, Yankees scouts were able to get extended looks at both. Scouting director Lin Garrett measured one of Harris' high school home runs at 470 feet. The Yankees went against the consensus to snag Harris in the second round, but they love his bat. A good athlete with a light-ning-quick swing and plus power potential, Harris has drawn comparisons to a young Garret Anderson and could produce 30 home runs annually once he matures. He displays a natural feel for the barrel through the zone and has good pitch recognition. Harris has a funky throwing motion and a well-below-average arm that will limit him to left field. An inexperienced hitter, he'll need to become a more selective as he moves up. His pro debut was encouraging, as hitting six home runs in the Gulf Coast League isn't an easy feat, especially for a high school player. Harris will get his first full-season exposure at low Class A Battle Creek in 2004.

Year	Club (League)	Class	AVG	G	AB	R	H	2B	3B	HR	RBI	BB	SO	SB	SLG	OBP
2003	Yankees (GCL)	R	.277	27	101	18	28	7	1	6	18	14	28	4	.545	.368
MINOR LEAGUE TOTALS			.277	27	101	18	28	7	1	6	18	14	28	4	.545	.368

10 Bronson Sardinha, 3b

Born: April 6, 1983. **Ht.:** 6-1. **Wt.:** 195. **Bats:** L. **Throws:** R. **School:** Kamehameha HS, Honolulu. **Career Transactions:** Selected by Yankees in first round (34th overall) of 2001 draft; signed June 13, 2001.

Sardinha's brothers Dane (Reds) and Duke (Rockies) are also developing prospects. After showing signs of progress in 2002, when he hit 16 homers in his first full season, Bronson took a step in the wrong direction last season but regrouped after a demotion to Battle Creek. He worked with hitting coach Ty Hawkins and went back to an old stance. Sardinha displays good rhythm at the plate with a nice, fluid stroke. He's a pure hitter with more of a line-drive approach, but there's natural loft in his swing. He projects to hit lots of doubles and have above-average power. He's a plus baserunner with an innate feel for game situations. Drafted as a shortstop, Sardinha moved to left field late in 2002 and then to center to start last year. His hands and arm are fine, but his range and lack of first-step quickness are best suited for third base, where he'll move in 2004. After working year-round in Tampa in the past, Sardinha was given a break this offseason. The 2004 season will be critical in his development, as it's time for him to move forward.

Year	Club (League)	Class	AVG	G	AB	R	H	2B	3B	HR	RBI	BB	SO	SB	SLG	OBP
2001	Yankees (GCL)	R	.303	55	188	42	57	14	3	4	27	28	51	11	.473	.398
2002	Greensboro (SAL)	A	.263	93	342	49	90	13	0	12	44	34	78	15	.406	.334
	Staten Island (NY-P)	A	.323	36	124	25	40	8	0	4	16	24	36	4	.484	.433
2003	Tampa (FSL)	A	.193	59	212	23	41	8	2	1	17	24	57	0	.264	.279
	Battle Creek (Mid)	A	.275	71	269	54	74	16	0	8	41	40	40	5	.424	.374
MINOR LEAGUE TOTALS			.266	314	1135	193	302	59	5	29	145	150	262	43	.404	.356

11 Edwardo Sierra, rhp

Born: April 15, 1982. **Ht.:** 6-3. **Wt.:** 185. **Bats:** R. **Throws:** R. **Career Transactions:** Signed out of Dominican Republic by Athletics, Feb. 15, 1999 . . . Traded by Athletics with SS J.T. Stotts to Yankees for LHP Chris Hammond and cash, Dec. 18, 2003.

Five days after sending fireballer Yhency Brazoban to the Dodgers as part of the Kevin Brown trade, the Yankees acquired Sierra, another strong-armed righthander whom they believe has Brazoban's upside and better makeup. With a 95-mph fastball, Sierra has one of the best raw arms in the system. He pitches high in the zone with a power fastball. When his splitter is working and he can control his fastball, he can be virtually unhittable. However, command is the key to Sierra's success and it tends to waver. The Athletics moved him to the bullpen full-time last year and the Yankees plan on keeping him there. With two big weapons, he has closer potential as he matures and fills out his lanky frame. Likely to start 2004 in high Class A, he'll have an opportunity to advance to Double-A at midseason.

Year	Club (League)	Class	W	L	ERA	G	GS	CG	SV	IP	H	R	ER	HR	BB	SO	AVG
1999	Athletics East (DSL)	R	1	3	5.02	6	5	0	0	29	32	24	16	1	19	27	.288
	Athletics West (DSL)	R	1	1	3.18	8	1	0	1	28	26	18	10	1	13	27	.248
2000	Athletics West (DSL)	R	4	2	2.22	10	9	1	0	65	56	27	16	1	24	50	.230
	Athletics East (DSL)	R	1	2	3.57	4	4	0	0	23	21	9	9	0	9	19	.263
2001	Athletics (AZL)	R	2	1	3.02	12	6	0	1	45	45	19	15	1	9	41	.262
2002	Vancouver (NWL)	A	0	2	6.11	9	7	0	0	28	42	24	19	0	17	23	.336
	Athletics (AZL)	R	2	1	4.64	6	6	0	0	33	29	19	17	2	10	35	.240
2003	Kane County (Mid)	A	3	5	2.09	51	0	0	17	60	46	23	14	2	24	52	.204
MINOR LEAGUE TOTALS			14	17	3.36	106	38	1	19	311	297	163	116	8	125	274	.251

12 Chien-Ming Wang, rhp

Born: March 31, 1980. **Ht.:** 6-3. **Wt.:** 200. **Bats:** R. **Throws:** R. **Career Transactions:** Signed out of Taiwan by Yankees, May 5, 2000 . . . On disabled list, April 5-Sept. 15, 2001.

Less than a year after signing for $1.9 million out of Taiwan, Wang had reconstructive shoulder surgery and missed the entire 2001 season. He came back strong in 2002 and in the offseason was Taiwan's MVP at the Asian Games. Wang's successful return convinced the Yankees that he could go straight to Double-A in 2003. He proved to be up to the challenge early in the season but was inconsistent thereafter. His velocity fluctuated from 95 mph to just average. His health wasn't in question, other than one brief stint on the DL with a blister. Wang was trying to fool hitters instead of using his four-seam fastball and pitching to contact. His slider, forkball and changeup are all average pitches, but his command is his best asset. He has a good delivery with a long, easy arm action. Wang pitched for Taiwan again in the Asian Games, helping them earn a berth in the 2004 Olympics. He's ready to move up to Triple-A but still needs more refinement before contending for a big league job.

Year	Club (League)	Class	W	L	ERA	G	GS	CG	SV	IP	H	R	ER	HR	BB	SO	AVG
2000	Staten Island (NY-P)	A	4	4	2.48	14	14	2	0	87	77	34	24	2	21	75	.233
2001	Did not play—Injured																
2002	Staten Island (NY-P)	A	6	1	1.72	13	13	0	0	78	63	23	15	2	14	64	.219
2003	Trenton (EL)	AA	7	6	4.65	21	21	2	0	122	143	71	63	7	32	84	.294
	Yankees (GCL)	R	0	0	0.00	1	1	0	0	3	2	0	0	0	0	2	.182
MINOR LEAGUE TOTALS			17	11	3.16	49	49	4	0	290	285	128	102	11	67	225	.255

13 Scott Proctor, rhp

Born: Jan. 2, 1977. **Ht.:** 6-1. **Wt.:** 198. **Bats:** R. **Throws:** R. **School:** Florida State University. **Career Transactions:** Selected by Dodgers in fifth round of 1998 draft; signed June 6, 1998 . . . Traded by Dodgers with OF Bubba Crosby to Yankees for 3B Robin Ventura, July 31, 2003.

The Yankees didn't expect an aging Robin Ventura to command much of a return on the trade market, so they were ecstatic to get Proctor and Bubba Crosby from the Dodgers. Proctor was a middling prospect for the Dodgers as a starter. He won 10 games in 2002, but his average fastball/slider/changeup mix was less than intimidating, even for Double-A hitters. After he moved to the bullpen last spring, his velocity spiked to the high 90s in Double-A and hit 100 mph after the trade. Though he needs to add deception to his delivery and work on keeping the ball down, Proctor also improved his slider and still uses a changeup to keep hitters honest. He tends to finish his delivery in an upright position, which leads to mistakes up in the strike zone. He'll have an opportunity to win the final spot in the big league bullpen, but likely will return to Triple-A until an opportunity arises in the Bronx.

Year	Club (League)	Class	W	L	ERA	G	GS	CG	SV	IP	H	R	ER	HR	BB	SO	AVG
1998	Yakima (NWL)	A	0	1	10.80	3	1	0	2	5	9	8	6	1	1	4	.391
1999	Yakima (NWL)	A	4	2	7.20	16	6	0	0	50	57	45	40	4	26	41	.286
2000	Vero Beach (FSL)	A	3	7	5.16	35	5	0	1	89	93	65	51	13	54	70	.268
2001	Vero Beach (FSL)	A	6	4	2.48	15	15	0	0	91	73	30	25	8	30	79	.226
	Jacksonville (SL)	AA	4	3	4.17	10	9	0	0	50	39	26	23	6	31	48	.220
2002	Jacksonville (SL)	AA	7	9	3.51	26	25	0	0	133	111	63	52	10	85	131	.227
2003	Jacksonville (SL)	AA	1	2	1.00	17	0	0	0	27	20	6	3	0	7	24	.208
	Las Vegas (PCL)	AAA	4	2	3.66	24	0	0	1	39	35	17	16	2	13	35	.246
	Columbus (IL)	AAA	2	0	1.42	10	0	0	0	19	13	3	3	2	3	26	.197
MINOR LEAGUE TOTALS			31	30	3.92	156	61	0	4	503	450	263	219	46	250	458	.242

14 Danny Borrell, lhp

Born: Jan. 24, 1979. **Ht.:** 6-3. **Wt.:** 200. **Bats:** L. **Throws:** L. **School:** Wake Forest University. **Career Transactions:** Selected by Yankees in second round of 2000 draft; signed June 19, 2000.

Borrell has top 10 talent, but he tore a shoulder ligament early in 2003, casting doubt on his future. A two-way player at Wake Forest, he attracted more attention from scouts as a pitcher despite hitting 37 homers while posting a 6.21 ERA. He has made significant progress from a raw, strong-armed thrower to a pitcher who relies on command and changing speeds. Borrell's fastball has topped out at 94 mph, but he works effectively at 87-90 mph. He tends to pitch backward and has tremendous command of one of the best changeups in the organization. Borrell throws strikes and uses both sides of the plate. The Yankees were impressed with his work ethic during his rehab and expect him to be ready to go by the end of spring training. He was on the verge of competing for a big league job last spring before his velocity dropped to 83 mph. Given this setback, he'll spend most of 2004 getting back to where he was. He'll be 26 when he competes for a spot with the Yankees in 2005.

Year	Club (League)	Class	W	L	ERA	G	GS	CG	SV	IP	H	R	ER	HR	BB	SO	AVG
2000	Yankees (GCL)	R	0	1	0.00	1	1	0	0	3	2	1	0	0	0	2	.182
	Staten Island (NY-P)	A	4	2	3.20	10	10	0	0	56	39	21	20	2	19	44	.194
2001	Tampa (FSL)	A	7	9	3.97	22	20	0	0	111	109	58	49	6	38	84	.259
2002	Tampa (FSL)	A	4	1	2.33	7	6	0	0	39	33	11	10	0	10	44	.239
	Norwich (EL)	AA	9	4	2.31	21	20	1	0	128	116	44	33	5	39	91	.239
2003	Columbus (IL)	AAA	4	2	2.93	10	10	0	0	55	55	24	18	4	22	30	.259
MINOR LEAGUE TOTALS			28	19	2.98	71	67	1	0	393	354	159	130	17	128	295	.241

15 Matt DeSalvo, rhp

Born: Sept. 11, 1980. **Ht.:** 6-0. **Wt.:** 170. **Bats:** R. **Throws:** R. **School:** Marietta (Ohio) College. **Career Transactions:** Signed as nondrafted free agent by Yankees, May 15, 2003.

Despite recording a NCAA Division III record 205 strikeouts in 2001 and establishing NCAA all-division career marks for wins (53) and whiffs (603), DeSalvo went undrafted throughout his college career. He didn't go completely unnoticed by scouts. Yankees area scout Mike Gibbons signed him as a fifth-year senior before the 2003 draft. DeSalvo missed most of the 2002 season with a knee injury before coming back to win BA's Small College Player of the Year award with a 13-2, 1.31 record and 157 strikeouts in 96 innings. The injury, his size and herky-jerky delivery kept him from getting drafted. DeSalvo has legitimate stuff to support his gaudy numbers. His fastball ranges from 87-93 mph and maxed out at 94 in low Class A. He complements his heater with a good 12-to-6 curveball. His changeup is average, but he needs to incorporate it into his mix more often. His delivery includes a leg kick and his hip turn provides a deceptive look, as DeSalvo's pitches get on hitters in a hurry. He could jump all the way to Double-A to start his first full season.

Year	Club (League)	Class	W	L	ERA	G	GS	CG	SV	IP	H	R	ER	HR	BB	SO	AVG
2003	Staten Island (NY-P)	A	3	3	1.84	10	10	1	0	49	42	18	10	2	19	52	.232
	Battle Creek (Mid)	A	2	0	0.82	3	3	0	0	22	15	5	2	0	5	21	.195
MINOR LEAGUE TOTALS			5	3	1.52	13	13	1	0	71	57	23	12	2	24	73	.221

16 Hector Made, ss

Born: Dec. 18, 1984. **Ht.:** 6-1. **Wt.:** 155. **Bats:** R. **Throws:** R. **Career Transactions:** Signed out of Dominican Republic by Yankees, July 17, 2001.

The Yankees are excited about their up-and-coming shortstops. Made is a year behind Joaquin Arias and Ferdin Tejeda, and all three are being promoted aggressively. Made will make his full-season debut this year in low Class A as a teenager. He projects to have the best power of the threesome. Made has a unique approach at the plate. He swings out of a wide, spread-out stance and has a slight uppercut that he worked on making more level at the Yankees' Dominican academy during the offseason. He also needs to improve his plate coverage, which will help him use the whole field. He tends to be pull-oriented at this stage in his development. Another pure shortstop, he doesn't always play under control in the field. He has an above-average arm, and runs well with good range and flashy actions to make highlight-reel plays. While Made presents an intriguing package of plus tools, he is raw and will have to make a big leap from the Gulf Coast League to the Midwest League.

Year	Club (League)	Class	AVG	G	AB	R	H	2B	3B	HR	RBI	BB	SO	SB	SLG	OBP
2002	Yankees West (DSL)	R	.283	61	191	34	54	8	0	0	10	30	31	13	.325	.389
2003	Yankees (GCL)	R	.236	52	178	28	42	6	2	5	18	20	19	8	.376	.314
	Staten Island (NY-P)	A	.259	7	27	4	7	1	0	1	1	0	5	3	.407	.259
MINOR LEAGUE TOTALS			.260	120	396	66	103	15	2	6	29	50	55	24	.354	.348

17 Sean Henn, lhp

Born: April 23, 1981. **Ht.:** 6-5. **Wt.:** 200. **Bats:** R. **Throws:** L. **School:** McLennan (Texas) JC. **Career Transactions:** Selected by Yankees in 26th round of 2000 draft; signed May 25, 2001 . . . On disabled list, April 4-Sept. 11, 2002.

Signed to what was then a draft-and-follow record bonus of $1.701 million in 2001, Henn lasted just 42 innings before requiring Tommy John surgery. He missed the entire 2002 season and returned last year with lackluster results. His upper-90s velocity was the reason he got big money, but his velocity hasn't returned yet and he has been tagged as a one-pitch pitcher. The Yankees want him to raise his arm slot from a low three-quarters release to a traditional three-quarter slot. He primarily throws four-seam fastballs but wasn't able to overpower anyone at 91-92 mph. Henn's slider is better now than when he signed, but it's still inconsistent and not a reliable offering. His command and changeup are shaky. The Yankees were discouraged with Henn's work habits coming back from surgery. While some pitchers can race back, Henn's timetable will be slower. He will be more than two years post-op by spring training and should start to see his velocity increase. The development of his breaking ball likely won't be enough to save him from the bullpen, though.

Year	Club (League)	Class	W	L	ERA	G	GS	CG	SV	IP	H	R	ER	HR	BB	SO	AVG
2001	Staten Island (NY-P)	A	3	1	3.00	9	8	0	1	42	26	15	14	3	15	49	.178
2002	Did not play—Injured																
2003	Tampa (FSL)	A	4	3	3.61	16	16	0	0	72	69	31	29	3	37	52	.259
	Yankees (GCL)	R	1	1	2.25	2	1	0	0	8	5	3	2	1	3	10	.167
MINOR LEAGUE TOTALS			8	5	3.31	27	25	0	1	122	100	49	45	7	55	111	.226

18 Mark Phillips, lhp

Born: Dec. 30, 1981. **Ht.:** 6-3. **Wt.:** 200. **Bats:** L. **Throws:** L. **School:** Hanover (Pa.) HS. **Career Transactions:** Selected by Padres in first round (ninth overall) of 2000 draft; signed July 6, 2000 . . . Traded by Padres with OF Bubba Trammell to Yankees for OF Rondell White, March 19, 2003.

Getting Phillips last spring when they traded Rondell White to the Padres for Bubba Trammell looked like a coup at the time for the Yankees. The ninth overall pick in the 2000 draft, Phillips was one of the Padres' top prospects in each of his first three seasons. He reported to spring training out of shape in 2001 and 2002, though he was nearly untouchable by the end of each of those seasons. Phillips is in good shape after the trade, but the Yankees never saw the same power stuff they had scouted. When he's right he can run his fastball up to 97 mph and sit in the low 90s. Yet in 2003, he couldn't consistently break 90 mph. His curveball drops out of sky and is the best breaking ball in the system. There's speculation that Phillips' arm isn't sound, and he ended the season on the disabled with a nagging leg injury. His arm action was different and not as fluid as it had been with the Padres, and his delivery was out of sync all season. His command was already an issue, and mechanical concerns further hinder his ability to throw strikes. After an offseason of rest and conditioning, Phillips will look to bounce back in high Class A this year.

Year	Club (League)	Class	W	L	ERA	G	GS	CG	SV	IP	H	R	ER	HR	BB	SO	AVG
2000	Idaho Falls (Pio)	R	1	1	5.35	10	10	0	0	37	35	30	22	2	24	37	.254
2001	Eugene (NWL)	A	3	1	3.74	4	4	0	0	22	16	10	9	1	9	19	.208
	Fort Wayne (Mid)	A	4	1	2.64	5	5	0	0	31	19	11	9	1	14	27	.174
	Lake Elsinore (Cal)	A	2	1	2.57	5	5	0	0	28	19	8	8	0	14	34	.190
2002	Lake Elsinore (Cal)	A	10	8	4.19	28	26	0	0	148	123	81	69	9	94	156	.225
2003	Tampa (FSL)	A	6	6	5.76	16	13	0	0	70	63	48	45	2	51	50	.249
MINOR LEAGUE TOTALS			26	18	4.34	68	63	0	0	336	275	188	162	15	206	323	.225

19 Melky Cabrera, of

Born: Aug. 11, 1984. **Ht.:** 5-11. **Wt.:** 170. **Bats:** B. **Throws:** L. **Career Transactions:** Signed out of Dominican Republic by Yankees, Nov. 13, 2001.

The Yankees often get the equivalent of a No. 1 overall draft pick on the international market. This has worked in their favor (Jose Contreras, Orlando Hernandez, Hideki Matsui, Alfonso Soriano), as well as against them (Adrian Hernandez, Jackson Melian, Andy Morales, Wily Mo Pena). New York has the money to brush off mistakes, but hopes to prevent further big-money blunders. While the Yankees will continue to be players for top international free agents, they're concentrating on signing more players for less money. Dioner Navarro's $260,000 and Cabrera's $175,000 bonus represent significant signings, but they hardly dent New York's budget. Dominican scout/summer league hitting coach Freddy Tiburcio discovered Cabrera in 2001. His first three at-bats at the Dominican academy produced a line drive, a homer and a double. A gap hitter from both sides of the plate, Cabrera has a good foundation of plate discipline. He profiles as a No. 2 hitter, has a natural feel for the barrel of the bat and makes consistent contact to all fields. He shows occasional pop. A good athlete with 4.2-second speed down the first-base line, Cabrera is the system's best defensive outfielder and has a plus arm. He'll make his full-season debut in low Class A.

Year	Club (League)	Class	AVG	G	AB	R	H	2B	3B	HR	RBI	BB	SO	SB	SLG	OBP
2002	Yankees West (DSL)	R	.335	60	218	37	73	19	3	3	29	18	23	7	.491	.388
2003	Staten Island (NY-P)	A	.283	67	279	34	79	10	2	2	31	23	36	13	.355	.345
MINOR LEAGUE TOTALS			.306	127	497	71	152	29	5	5	60	41	59	20	.414	.364

20 Jose Garcia, rhp

Born: June 2, 1981. **Ht.:** 6-1. **Wt.:** 160. **Bats:** R. **Throws:** R. **Career Transactions:** Signed out of Venezuela by Yankees, Feb. 1, 1999.

Garcia emerged from a group of inexperienced young starters in Battle Creek last year. He exceeded expectations and was successful after a late-season promotion to high Class A. While he can't match the arm strength of his former Battle Creek rotation mates, Garcia is far more advanced in terms of his approach to pitching. His fastball sits at 90 mph with arm-side life and good sink, and he has the makings of a plus changeup. His slider projects as major league average, while his curveball is a touch below. He has solid-average command of his four pitches, allowing him to locate to both sides of the plate. Garcia's arm works well and his delivery is fine, though he could stand to limit his head jerk at release. His velocity shouldn't increase much and he profiles as a No. 4 starter. He'll return to Tampa as the Opening Day starter in 2004.

Year	Club (League)	Class	W	L	ERA	G	GS	CG	SV	IP	H	R	ER	HR	BB	SO	AVG
2000	La Pradera (VSL)	R	0	1	4.80	6	2	0	0	15	14	9	8	0	6	14	.259
2001	Yankees (DSL)	R	4	2	1.86	7	1	0	0	29	32	9	6	0	4	23	.267
2002	Yankees West (DSL)	R	4	2	1.35	10	8	1	0	47	34	13	7	0	15	51	.202
2003	Battle Creek (Mid)	A	9	8	2.64	21	21	4	0	136	111	46	40	10	33	90	.224
	Tampa (FSL)	A	1	0	1.74	4	4	0	0	21	13	4	4	0	4	14	.173
MINOR LEAGUE TOTALS			18	13	2.36	48	36	5	0	248	204	81	65	10	62	192	.223

21 Jose Valdez, rhp

Born: Jan. 22, 1983. **Ht.:** 6-4. **Wt.:** 185. **Bats:** R. **Throws:** R. **Career Transactions:** Signed out of Dominican Republic by Yankees, Oct. 5, 2000.

There's no question the Yankees system is depleted. But if it not for their Latin American scouting department, they would have no depth to speak of. Their willingness to spend freely in the international market certainly aids their efforts, though that shouldn't take away from the foundation set up by Latin American coordinator Carlos Rios. While New York has landed several projectable athletes such as Rudy Guillen, Joaquin Arias and Ferdin Tejeda and Rudy Guillen, they have netted only a few power arms. The most promising is Valdez, though his full-season debut last year was just pedestrian. He didn't register as many 96s on the radar guns and generally was ineffective after the second inning, which ultimately may lead him to the bullpen. His fastball sat at 90-94 mph, and the Yankees believe he could pitch at 96-97 in shorter stints. Valdez has developed a good feel for a splitter but he hasn't developed his slider, allowing hitters to sit dead-red fastball when he falls behind in the count. He has trouble repeating a complicated delivery at times, another indication that his future may be in relief. For now, Valdez will remain in the rotation in high Class A, where he'll try to build stamina and arm strength.

Year	Club (League)	Class	W	L	ERA	G	GS	CG	SV	IP	H	R	ER	HR	BB	SO	AVG
2001	Yankees (DSL)	R	3	4	1.94	15	10	0	1	70	60	21	15	1	11	50	.230
2002	Staten Island (NY-P)	A	1	3	5.40	4	4	0	0	20	19	14	12	0	9	21	.250
	Yankees (GCL)	R	1	4	3.35	8	7	0	0	40	45	19	15	2	10	28	.283
2003	Battle Creek (Mid)	A	11	7	3.64	22	22	0	0	134	132	67	54	14	42	76	.259
	Tampa (FSL)	A	1	1	4.02	3	3	0	0	16	11	7	7	2	4	9	.200
MINOR LEAGUE TOTALS			17	19	3.32	52	46	0	1	279	267	128	103	19	76	184	.252

22 Michael Vento, of

Born: May 25, 1978. **Ht.:** 6-0. **Wt.:** 195. **Bats:** R. **Throws:** R. **School:** Santa Ana (Calif.) JC. **Career Transactions:** Selected by Yankees in 40th round of 1997 draft; signed May 25, 1998.

Vento was drafted in the 10th round by the Reds out of a New Mexico high school, but opted for junior college instead. A draft-and-follow, he has had to prove himself at every level, battling injuries along the way. He even had a difficult time garnering attention after winning the high Class A Florida State League MVP award in 2001. Vento was limited to 64 games in 2002 after breaking his nose and suffering a second-degree concussion in a home-plate collision. In 2003, he took advantage of his first opportunity in Triple-A after Juan Rivera was promoted to New York. Vento continued to rake in the Arizona Fall League, though a shoulder injury relegated him to DH. Built along the lines of Shane Spencer, Vento makes consistent hard contact and shows above-average power. He has made strides to improve his plate coverage and is no longer as pull-happy, though he still doesn't draw many walks. Vento will spend a full season in Triple-A and be on call in case of emergency in New York. He's not a first-division corner outfielder, though he could fill a reserve role.

Year	Club (League)	Class	AVG	G	AB	R	H	2B	3B	HR	RBI	BB	SO	SB	SLG	OBP
1998	Oneonta (NY-P)	A	.304	43	148	25	45	9	3	1	23	14	28	8	.426	.379
1999	Tampa (FSL)	A	.259	70	255	37	66	10	1	7	28	17	69	2	.388	.310
	Greensboro (SAL)	A	.250	40	148	20	37	11	1	3	16	14	46	3	.399	.321
2000	Tampa (FSL)	A	.167	10	30	1	5	0	0	1	4	4	12	1	.267	.278
	Greensboro (SAL)	A	.261	84	318	49	83	15	2	6	52	47	66	13	.377	.372
2001	Tampa (FSL)	A	.300	130	457	71	137	20	10	20	87	45	88	13	.519	.372
2002	Norwich (EL)	AA	.238	64	227	29	54	16	2	4	26	25	49	3	.379	.314
2003	Trenton (EL)	AA	.303	81	314	46	95	19	3	9	56	22	52	4	.468	.354
	Columbus (IL)	AAA	.304	51	184	28	56	14	1	5	31	14	36	1	.473	.363
MINOR LEAGUE TOTALS			.278	573	2081	306	578	114	23	56	323	202	446	48	.435	.350

23 J.T. Stotts, ss/2b

Born: Jan. 21, 1980. **Ht.:** 5-11. **Wt.:** 185. **Bats:** R. **Throws:** R. **School:** Cal State Northridge. **Career Transactions:** Selected by Athletics in third round of 2001 draft; signed June 26, 2001 . . . Traded by Athletics with RHP Edwardo Sierra to Yankees for LHP Chris Hammond and cash, Dec. 18, 2003.

After embracing a utility role last year, Stotts impressed the Athletics with his versatility. The Yankees also were attracted to his plate discipline, which is why they sought him in the Chris Hammond trade. A well-rounded athlete who was a two-time league MVP as a 5-foot-10 point guard in high school, Stotts lacks natural middle-infield actions and is an average runner with an average arm. While he doesn't show enough range or footwork to play short-stop on a daily basis, his instincts are solid and he makes routine plays. After signing in 2001, he initially had trouble adjusting to wood bats. Now he profiles as a No. 2 hitter who can make consistent contact, advance runners and get on base. With the Yankees stacked at shortstop at the full-season level and Robinson Cano ticketed for second base in Trenton, Stotts will start at third base and hone his utilityman skills in Double-A this year.

Year	Club (League)	Class	AVG	G	AB	R	H	2B	3B	HR	RBI	BB	SO	SB	SLG	OBP
2001	Vancouver (NWL)	A	.270	62	241	35	65	5	2	0	17	26	34	19	.307	.348
2002	Visalia (Cal)	A	.275	133	483	66	133	20	3	2	64	65	75	13	.342	.363
2003	Modesto (Cal)	A	.284	75	292	34	83	16	1	2	37	31	37	11	.366	.363
	Midland (TL)	AA	.307	46	176	24	54	8	0	0	14	18	41	4	.352	.377
MINOR LEAGUE TOTALS			.281	316	1192	159	335	49	6	4	132	140	187	47	.342	.362

24 Brad Halsey, lhp

Born: Feb. 14, 1981. **Ht.:** 6-1. **Wt.:** 180. **Bats:** L. **Throws:** L. **School:** University of Texas. **Career Transactions:** Selected by Yankees in eighth round of 2002 draft; signed July 1, 2002.

The Yankees drafted Halsey in the 19th round as a junior college freshman in 2000 but didn't land him until two years later, after he won a College World Series at Texas. After a sparkling pro debut, he tied for the minor league lead with 17 victories in his first full season. Halsey has drawn comparisons to former Yankees pitching prospect Brandon Claussen because he primarily operates with a fastball and slider. He led the organization in strikeouts last year, but also surrendered 219 hits—the second-highest total in the minors—in 175 innings. Double-A hitters teed off to the tune of a .325 average. Halsey's fastball sits around 87-89 mph with cutting action, but he can touch 90-92. He tends to pitch backwards with his slider and changeup. Both are average offerings with plus potential, and they're enhanced by his ability to work the strike zone. He used a splitter in college but since has scrapped it. Halsey needs to learn how to exploit hitters' weaknesses more effectively with his movement to both sides of the plate. He'll return to Double-A and likely spend the year there before advancing. He projects as a back-of-the-rotation starter.

Year	Club (League)	Class	W	L	ERA	G	GS	CG	SV	IP	H	R	ER	HR	BB	SO	AVG
2002	Staten Island (NY-P)	A	6	1	1.93	11	10	0	0	56	39	15	12	0	17	53	.195
2003	Tampa (FSL)	A	10	4	3.43	14	13	1	0	84	96	36	32	3	14	56	.287
	Trenton (EL)	AA	7	5	4.93	15	15	0	0	91	123	51	50	4	22	78	.325
MINOR LEAGUE TOTALS			23	10	3.66	40	38	1	0	231	258	102	94	7	53	187	.283

25 Jason Stephens, rhp

Born: Oct. 10, 1984. **Ht.:** 6-4. **Wt.:** 190. **Bats:** R. **Throws:** R. **School:** Tallmadge (Ohio) HS. **Career Transactions:** Selected by Yankees in sixth round of 2003 draft; signed June 17, 2003.

The Yankees proved they care little about the commissioner's office bonus recommendations when they lured Stephens away from his Georgia Tech commitment for $500,000 bonus. It was the largest in the sixth round by far, and nearly five times the average bonus for that round. Area scout Mike Gibbons was intrigued with Stephens' projection, and most clubs didn't spend much time scouting him because they knew they couldn't afford him. At 6-foot-4 and 185 pounds, Stephens throws 87-90 mph with relative ease. The balls jumps out of his hand and he spins a solid curveball. While he was somewhat overwhelmed by the adjustment to pro ball, he displays a good feel for locating and mixing his pitches. In high school, he showed potential with a splitter, though the Yankees aren't likely to allow him to use that pitch in the early stages of his development. Stephens could make it to low Class A late this season, but likely will begin the year in extended spring training and head to Staten Island afterward.

Year	Club (League)	Class	W	L	ERA	G	GS	CG	SV	IP	H	R	ER	HR	BB	SO	AVG
2003	Yankees (GCL)	R	0	2	4.55	10	3	1	1	32	42	20	16	1	9	25	.333
MINOR LEAGUE TOTALS			0	2	4.55	10	3	1	1	32	42	20	16	1	9	25	.333

26 Jon-Mark Sprowl, c

Born: Aug. 1, 1980. **Ht.:** 6-1. **Wt.:** 200. **Bats:** L. **Throws:** R. **School:** Shelton State (Ala.) JC. **Career Transactions:** Selected by Cubs in 47th round of 1998 draft; signed May 25, 1999 . . . Contract purchased by Diamondbacks from Cubs, March 15, 2002 . . . Traded by Diamondbacks with OF David Dellucci and RHP Bret Prinz to Yankees for OF Raul Mondesi, July 30, 2003.

Sprowl's father Bobby pitched briefly in the majors and coached Jon-Mark at Shelton State. Sprowl moved behind the plate as a freshman and originally signed with the Cubs as a draft-and-follow. Traded to the Diamondbacks for future considerations, he came to New York in a deal for Raul Mondesi. Sprowl is an example of the increased emphasis the Yankees' pro scouting department is placing on performance. Because of his advanced plate discipline, Sprowl was targeted on a list of "stat guys" compiled by special assistant in pro scouting John Coppolella. He hits for average and does an excellent job of controlling the strike zone, leading the Midwest League with a .425 on-base percentage last year, though he hasn't hit for much power. The Yankees hope he'll take to catching and will give him every opportunity to develop behind the plate in high Class A. As shown by his 13 errors and 18 passed balls in 93 games behind the plate in 2003, he has much room for improvement. Sprowl has an average arm but threw out just 22 percent of basestealers. He's a hard-nosed competitor with above-average instincts for the game. If the catching experiment fails, he'll move to third base, where he could develop into a pre-2003 version of Bill Mueller.

Year	Club (League)	Class	AVG	G	AB	R	H	2B	3B	HR	RBI	BB	SO	SB	SLG	OBP
1999	Cubs (AZL)	R	.392	31	97	19	38	9	2	0	14	18	14	1	.526	.483
2000	Lansing (Mid)	A	.000	2	4	3	0	0	0	0	0	3	2	0	.000	.429
	Eugene (NWL)	A	.235	40	98	9	23	2	0	1	7	14	24	3	.286	.325
2001	Lansing (Mid)	A	.219	54	155	12	34	9	0	3	28	18	24	0	.335	.311
2002	Lancaster (Cal)	A	.278	76	230	39	64	12	1	6	27	43	42	2	.417	.404
2003	South Bend (Mid)	A	.296	95	321	56	95	22	3	4	42	54	31	5	.421	.402
	Battle Creek (Mid)	A	.402	29	97	21	39	8	0	1	20	17	8	0	.515	.500
MINOR LEAGUE TOTALS			.292	327	1002	159	293	62	6	15	138	167	145	11	.411	.399

27 Erick Almonte, ss

Born: Feb. 1, 1978. **Ht.:** 6-2. **Wt.:** 180. **Bats:** R. **Throws:** R. **Career Transactions:** Signed out of Dominican Republic by Yankees, Feb. 12, 1996.

The Yankees have compared Almonte to Derek Jeter, and his frustration at being stuck behind the perennial all-star has been evident. In 2002, Almonte demanded a trade after being demoted to Double-A. His big opportunity came last year on Opening Day when Jeter separated his shoulder. Almonte held his own as Jeter's replacement, homering in his first game, but his shortcomings were exposed. He struggles to recognize and lay off breaking stuff, and he swings and misses too often. His raw power never quite has translated to games. Defensively, Almonte's best attribute is a plus arm. But he has gotten thicker in his lower half and isn't the athlete he once was. He needs to get in better shape and is now a below-average runner. A knee injury in May kept Almonte on the shelf for more than a month, and he was sidelined briefly in September with a calf strain. He recovered in time to earn a spot on the League Championship Series roster, though he garnered no playing time. Designated for assignment after the Yankees' winter spending spree, he could be traded before spring training. He can't play shortstop every day, but his versatility and offensive potential as a utility infielder could help a team.

Year	Club (League)	Class	AVG	G	AB	R	H	2B	3B	HR	RBI	BB	SO	SB	SLG	OBP
1996	Yankees (DSL)	R	.282	58	216	37	61	7	0	8	36	15	30	3	.426	.333
1997	Yankees (GCL)	R	.283	52	180	32	51	4	4	3	31	21	27	8	.400	.355
1998	Greensboro (SAL)	A	.209	120	450	53	94	13	0	6	33	29	121	6	.278	.260
1999	Tampa (FSL)	A	.257	61	230	36	59	8	2	5	25	18	49	3	.374	.313
	Yankees (GCL)	R	.300	9	30	5	9	2	0	2	9	3	10	1	.567	.343
2000	Norwich (EL)	AA	.271	131	454	56	123	18	4	15	77	35	129	12	.427	.326
2001	Columbus (IL)	AAA	.287	97	345	55	99	19	3	12	55	44	90	4	.464	.369
	Norwich (EL)	AA	.250	3	12	2	3	0	0	0	0	1	6	1	.250	.308
	New York (AL)	MAJ	.500	8	4	0	2	1	0	0	0	0	1	2	.750	.500
2002	Columbus (IL)	AAA	.235	66	221	25	52	10	1	9	28	15	60	2	.412	.282
	Norwich (EL)	AA	.241	53	187	28	45	7	0	8	33	30	59	10	.406	.342
2003	New York (AL)	MAJ	.260	31	100	17	26	6	0	1	11	8	24	1	.350	.321
	Columbus (IL)	AAA	.240	48	179	26	43	11	1	4	26	17	46	4	.380	.310
	Yankees (GCL)	R	.286	6	21	4	6	0	0	0	0	5	9	0	.286	.423
MAJOR LEAGUE TOTALS			.269	39	104	17	28	7	0	1	11	8	25	3	.365	.327
MINOR LEAGUE TOTALS			.255	704	2525	359	645	99	15	72	353	233	636	54	.392	.320

28 Tyler Clippard, rhp

Born: Feb. 14, 1985. **Ht.:** 6-4. **Wt.:** 170. **Bats:** R. **Throws:** R. **School:** J.W. Mitchell HS, Trinity, Fla. **Career Transactions:** Selected by Yankees in ninth round of 2003 draft; signed June 6, 2003.

Clippard became the first athlete in Mitchell High history to receive a NCAA Division I scholarship when he committed to South Florida. But Clippard, who was also a standout prep golfer, was kicked off the baseball team. The Yankees drafted him in the ninth round and signed him for $75,000. Senior vice president for baseball operations Mark Newman calls Clippard one of the more impressive high school pitchers the Yankees have had since Zach Day. Clippard's fastball touches 92 mph and he pitches around 89-90 mph with good life. A sharp 76-78 mph curveball is his best and most advanced pitch. His changeup needs improvement, as does his stamina. He repeats his delivery and fills the strike zone with quality pitches. His eye-catching 56-5 strikeout-walk ratio in his pro debut speaks to his feel for pitching. The Yankees are more apt to take it easy with their young arms, which probably means Clippard will have to begin 2004 in extended spring training. He's more polished than Jason Stephens and another live-armed righthander, Mike Knox, and the three should rise slowly together.

Year	Club (League)	Class	W	L	ERA	G	GS	CG	SV	IP	H	R	ER	HR	BB	SO	AVG
2003	Yankees (GCL)	R	3	3	2.89	11	5	0	0	44	33	16	14	3	5	56	.212
MINOR LEAGUE TOTALS			3	3	2.89	11	5	0	0	44	33	16	14	3	5	56	.212

29 Ben Julianel, lhp

Born: Sept. 4, 1979. **Ht.:** 6-2. **Wt.:** 180. **Bats:** B. **Throws:** L. **School:** San Diego State University.
Career Transactions: Selected by Cardinals in 12th round of 2001 draft; signed June 8, 2001 . . . Traded by Cardinals with RHP Justin Pope to Yankees for LHP Sterling Hitchcock, Aug. 22, 2003.

While unloading the contracts of overpriced veterans in 2003, the Yankees were able to acquire some promising second- and third-tier prospects. They got Jon-Mark Sprowl in the Raul Mondesi trade, Scott Proctor and Bubba Crosby for Robin Ventura, and Julianel and Justin Pope for Sterling Hitchcock. A solid athlete, Julianel was an all-league performer in football (quarterback) and basketball (shooting guard) in high school. His nasty slider makes him a prototypical situational lefthander. Lefties batted just .232 with no homers in 82 at-bats against him last season. He operates with a deceptive delivery from a tough low-three quarters slot, making his slider and 85-89 mph fastball tough to recognize. Julianel will open 2004 in high Class A.

Year	Club (League)	Class	W	L	ERA	G	GS	CG	SV	IP	H	R	ER	HR	BB	SO	AVG
2001	New Jersey (NY-P)	A	6	6	3.48	15	15	0	0	85	88	38	33	1	26	86	.270
2002	Peoria (Mid)	A	8	3	3.50	38	8	0	1	100	106	49	39	9	32	96	.270
2003	Peoria (Mid)	A	4	2	1.05	51	0	0	9	52	41	11	6	1	25	78	.215
	Battle Creek (Mid)	A	0	0	1.69	4	0	0	0	5	6	1	1	0	2	10	.273
MINOR LEAGUE TOTALS			18	11	2.93	108	23	0	10	243	241	99	79	11	85	270	.259

30 Mike Knox, rhp

Born: Sept. 19, 1983. **Ht.:** 6-4. **Wt.:** 195. **Bats:** R. **Throws:** R. **School:** Navarro (Texas) JC.
Career Transactions: Selected by Yankees in 27th round of 2002 draft; signed May 26, 2003.

The Yankees have had a lot of success with the draft-and-follow rule. Texas-based area scout Mark Batchko has contributed mightily, identifying pitching prospects such as Brandon Claussen (traded for Aaron Boone last summer) and Sean Henn. Knox, Batchko's latest find, was drafted out of Dallas' Jesuit College Prep High in the 27th round in 2002 and signed after a season at Navarro (Texas) Junior College. Knox' father John hit .274 over parts of four seasons as a second baseman for the Tigers in 1972-75. At 6-foot-4 and 195 pounds, Mike towers over his father, who played at 6 feet and 170 pounds. The ball jumps out of Knox' hand and he has topped out at 96 mph while sitting at 91-93. He has an ideal pitcher's frame and his loose, easy arm action provides plenty of room for projection on his fastball. His curveball shows the makings of a quality major league pitch, though it tends to get slurvy at times, and he's working on a changeup. Though Knox received a promotion to high Class A within months of signing, he's scheduled to begin 2004 in extended spring training with a chance to jump into the low Class A rotation at some point.

Year	Club (League)	Class	W	L	ERA	G	GS	CG	SV	IP	H	R	ER	HR	BB	SO	AVG
2003	Yankees (GCL)	R	2	2	1.48	10	1	0	2	24	13	6	4	0	7	16	.155
	Tampa (FSL)	A	1	1	3.72	3	1	0	0	10	8	6	4	1	6	5	.235
MINOR LEAGUE TOTALS			3	3	2.12	13	2	0	2	34	21	12	8	1	13	21	.178

OAKLAND
ATHLETICS

Now that "Money-ball" has slipped off the best-seller lists, it's time to see just how the book's celebrated draft picks will develop for the Athletics.

Perhaps no draft in recent memory has been steeped in more controversy than Oakland's 2002 effort. The A's had seven picks before the second round and pulled some surprises, to say the least. In "Moneyball," author Michael Lewis portrayed the club as having established a superior method of talent evaluation, the key to success for a small-revenue team on a budget. The flaw in Lewis' thinking was that the A's had changed their methodology in 2002, passing from the guidance of former scouting director Grady Fuson to a more unorthodox, statistical-based manner of projection. Fuson had been sort of a renegade himself during his days in Oakland before he became assistant general manager for the Rangers. He sought polished picks with baseball instincts over raw tools players. He looked for performance over potential, and he valued hitting above all other skills.

When Fuson moved on to Texas, the A's took it a step further. Performance became even more important. The emphasis for hitters became more focused on power and patience, with less even regard to tools. College players went from being preferred to being the only ones considered.

TOP 30 PROSPECTS

1. Bobby Crosby, ss
2. Joe Blanton, rhp
3. Dan Johnson, 1b
4. Brad Sullivan, rhp
5. Graham Koonce, 1b
6. Nick Swisher, of
7. Omar Quintanilla, ss
8. Mike Rouse, ss
9. Andre Ethier, of
10. Justin Duchscherer, rhp
11. Chad Harville, rhp
12. Mike Wood, rhp
13. John Rheinecker, lhp
14. Jeremy Brown, c
15. Mark Teahen, 3b
16. Freddie Bynum, 2b
17. Ben Fritz, rhp
18. John Baker, c
19. John McCurdy, ss
20. Justin Lehr, rhp
21. Esteban German, 2b
22. Jason Grabowski, of/1b
23. Shane Komine, rhp
24. Mark Kiger, 2b/ss
25. Brian Snyder, 3b
26. Mario Ramos, lhp
27. Marcus McBeth, of
28. Javier Herrera, of
29. Dustin Majewski, of
30. Frank Brooks, lhp

By Casey Tefertiller

The two players most identified with the "Moneyball" draft are outfielder Nick Swisher and catcher Jeremy Brown. While Lewis wrote glowingly of both players and the A's are excited about their early progress, other teams said both were overdrafted in the first round and project neither as impact players.

After 2004, the "Money-ball" picks can be fairly evaluated and baseball will have a better view of the A's innovative approach. How well it works could shape the future of the organization. After years of producing quality players, Oakland's farm system needs another generation to replace the ones who are growing too expensive, and the talent supply is drying up. All-stars Jason Giambi, Ramon Hernandez and Miguel Tejada have left, and the A's may not be able to keep Eric Chavez, Tim Hudson, Mark Mulder and Barry Zito in the next few years.

While righthander Rich Harden reached the majors last summer and top prospect Bobby Crosby is ready to step in for Tejada, Oakland has replaced Giambi and Hernandez with retreads Scott Hatteberg and Damian Miller. Beyond righthander Joe Blanton, the system may not have another frontline player. The organization is optimistic about a pair of 2003 first-round picks, righty Brad Sullivan and infielder Omar Quintanilla, and that crop may prove more bountiful than the "Moneyball" group.

ORGANIZATION
OVERVIEW

General manager: Billy Beane. **Farm director:** Keith Lieppman. **Scouting director:** Eric Kubota.

2003 PERFORMANCE

Class	Team	League	W	L	Pct.	Finish*	Manager
Majors	Oakland	American	96	66	.593	2nd (14)	Ken Macha
Triple-A	Sacramento River Cats	Pacific Coast	92	52	.639	+1st (16)	Tony DeFrancesco
Double-A	Midland RockHounds	Texas	69	70	.496	6th (8)	Greg Sparks
High A	Modesto A's	California	74	66	.529	t-5th (10)	Rick Rodriguez
Low A	Kane County Cougars	Midwest	80	59	.576	1st (14)	Webster Garrison
Short-season	Vancouver Canadians	Northwest	35	41	.461	5th (8)	Dennis Rogers
Rookie	AZL Athletics	Arizona	15	33	.313	8th (9)	Ruben Escalera
OVERALL 2003 MINOR LEAGUE RECORD			365	321	.532	4th (30)	

*Finish in overall standings (No. of teams in league) +League champion

ORGANIZATION LEADERS

BATTING
*Minimum 250 At-Bats

*AVG	Bobby Crosby, Sacramento	.308
R	Gary Thomas, Modesto	95
	Mark Kiger, Modesto	95
H	Dan Johnson, Sacramento/Midland	157
TB	Dan Johnson, Sacramento/Midland	273
2B	Mark Kiger, Modesto	38
	Nick Swisher, Midland/Modesto	38
3B	Freddie Bynum, Midland	9
HR	Graham Koonce, Sacramento	34
RBI	Graham Koonce, Sacramento	115
BB	Graham Koonce, Sacramento	98
SO	Matt Allegra, Midland	156
SB	Esteban German, Sacramento	32
*SLG	Bobby Crosby, Sacramento	.544
*OBP	Graham Koonce, Sacramento	.403

PITCHING
#Minimum 75 Innings

W	Brad Weis, Modesto	15
L	Derell McCall, Modesto/Kane County	13
#ERA	Kyle Crowell, Midland/Modesto	2.19
G	Justin Lehr, Sacramento	53
CG	Drew Dickinson, Kane County	5
SV	Chad Harville, Sacramento	18
IP	Drew Dickinson, Kane County	191
BB	Brad Weis, Modesto	60
SO	Joe Blanton, Midland/Kane County	174

BEST TOOLS

Best Hitter for Average	Bobby Crosby
Best Power Hitter	Dan Johnson
Fastest Baserunner	Marcus McBeth
Best Athlete	Javier Herrera
Best Fastball	Joe Blanton
Best Curveball	Joe Blanton
Best Slider	Brad Sullivan
Best Changeup	Steve Obenchain
Best Control	Joe Blanton
Best Defensive Catcher	John Baker
Best Defensive Infielder	Bobby Crosby
Best Infield Arm	Francis Gomez
Best Defensive Outfielder	Marcus McBeth
Best Outfield Arm	Marcus McBeth

PROJECTED 2007 LINEUP

Catcher	Damian Miller
First Base	Dan Johnson
Second Base	Mark Ellis
Third Base	Bobby Crosby
Shortstop	Eric Chavez
Left Field	Steve Swisher
Center Field	Mark Kotsay
Right Field	Bobby Kielty
Designated Hitter	Erubiel Durazo
No. 1 Starter	Tim Hudson
No. 2 Starter	Mark Mulder
No. 3 Starter	Barry Zito
No. 4 Starter	Rich Harden
No. 5 Starter	Joe Blanton
Closer	Arthur Rhodes

LAST YEAR'S TOP 20 PROSPECTS

1. Rich Harden, rhp	11. Nick Swisher, of
2. John Rheinecker, lhp	12. Jason Grabowski, of/c
3. Bobby Crosby, ss	13. Chad Harville, rhp
4. Jeremy Brown, c	14. Matt Allegra, of
5. Mike Wood, rhp	15. Mark Teahen, 3b
6. Joe Valentine, rhp	16. Esteban German, 2b
7. Marcus McBeth, ss	17. Steve Obenchain, rhp
8. Freddie Bynum, 2b/ss	18. Adam Morrissey, 3b/2b
9. Joe Blanton, rhp	19. Dan Johnson, 1b
10. Ben Fritz, rhp	20. John McCurdy, ss

TOP PROSPECTS OF THE DECADE

1994	Steve Karsay, rhp
1995	Ben Grieve, of
1996	Ben Grieve, of
1997	Miguel Tejada, ss
1998	Ben Grieve, of
1999	Eric Chavez, 3b
2000	Mark Mulder, lhp
2001	Jose Ortiz, 2b
2002	Carlos Pena, 1b
2003	Rich Harden, rhp

TOP DRAFT PICKS OF THE DECADE

1994	Ben Grieve, of
1995	Ariel Prieto, rhp
1996	Eric Chavez, 3b
1997	Chris Enochs, rhp
1998	Mark Mulder, lhp
1999	Barry Zito, lhp
2000	Freddie Bynum, ss (2)
2001	Bobby Crosby, ss
2002	Nick Swisher, of
2003	Brad Sullivan, rhp

ALL-TIME LARGEST BONUSES

Mark Mulder, 1998	$3,200,000
Nick Swisher, 2002	$1,780,000
Barry Zito, 1999	$1,625,000
Joe Blanton, 2002	$1,400,000
John McCurdy, 2002	$1,375,000

MINOR LEAGUE
DEPTH CHART

OAKLAND ATHLETICS   RANK: 17

Impact potential (C): Bobby Crosby should be up to the task of replacing Miguel Tejada at shortstop. He won't completely make up for Tejada's offensive prowess, but he has solid tools across the board and has succeeded at every level. Joe Blanton could be ready to pitch in the big leagues by the second half of 2004. Dan Johnson and Graham Koonce put up big numbers in the upper levels of the minors, but not all scouts expect them to emerge as first-division regulars.

Depth (C): With nine extra draft picks in the first round over the last two years, the outlook in the minors should be more encouraging. The much-hyped 2002 "Moneyball" draft hasn't blown anyone away, and there are reports the A's are questioning last year's overdraft of first-rounder Brian Snyder. Trading prospects has helped them stay competitive in the American League West, but depleted the overall depth.

Sleeper: Mark Teahen, 3b.   —*Depth charts prepared by **Josh Boyd**. Numbers in parentheses indicate prospect rankings.*

LF
Nick Swisher (6)
Jason Grabowski (22)
Nelson Cruz
Jason Perry
Brian Sellier
Brian Stavisky
Matt Watson

CF
Marcus McBeth (27)
Javier Herrera (28)
Steve Stanley
Mike Lockwood

RF
Andre Ethier (9)
Dustin Majewski (29)
Matt Allegra
Alexi Ogando
Jon Weber

3B
Mark Teahen (15)
Brian Snyder (25)
Adam Morrissey

SS
Bobby Crosby (1)
Omar Quintanilla (7)
Mike Rouse (8)
Francis Gomez

2B
Freddie Bynum (16)
John McCurdy (19)
Esteban German (21)
Mark Kiger (24)
Jorge Mejia

1B
Dan Johnson (3)
Graham Koonce (5)
Don Sutton
Eddie Kim

SOURCE OF TALENT

Homegrown		Acquired	
College	21	Trades	3
Junior College	1	Rule 5 draft	2
Draft-and-follow	0	Independent	0
High school	0	Free agents/waivers	1
Nondrafted free agent	0		
Foreign	2		

C
Jeremy Brown (14)
John Baker (18)
Adam Melhuse
Casey Myers
Jed Morris

RHP

Starters	Relievers
Joe Blanton (2)	Chad Harville (11)
Brad Sullivan (4)	Mike Wood (12)
Justin Duchscherer (10)	Justin Lehr (20)
Ben Fritz (17)	Shane Bazzell
Shane Komine (23)	Steve Obenchain
Mike Ziegler	Jeff Meussig
Brad Knox	Jairo Garcia
Tomas Cabaniel	Chris Mowday
	Bert Snow

LHP

Starters	Relievers
John Rheinecker (13)	Frank Brooks (30)
Mario Ramos (26)	Ryan Cullen
Drew Dickinson	
Brad Weis	

DRAFT
ANALYSIS

Best Pro Debut: SS Omar Quintanilla (1) hit .358-2-20 between the short-season Northwest League and high Class A.

Best Athlete: RHP Brad Sullivan (1) is athletic for a pitcher and makes spectacular defensive plays off the mound. He also played first and second base for Houston during the NCAA regionals last spring. Among position players, OF Andre Ethier (2) stands out. His power is developing and his speed is nothing special.

Best Pure Hitter: 3B Brian Snyder (1) wasn't a first-rounder on most draft boards, but the Athletics believe he'll improve upon his .253-1-17 NWL debut when he's not fighting minor injuries. Ethier showed an advanced approach in instructional league.

Best Raw Power: Six-foot-4, 260-pound 1B Eddie Kim (4) used his strength to hit .305-4-39 in the NWL. 3B Vasili Spanos (11) has plenty of pop and a better approach. He didn't get to show much after breaking a hamate bone.

Fastest Runner: The A's value speed as little as any team. Quintanilla's average speed is the best in this draft.

Best Defensive Player: Most teams project Quintanilla as a second baseman, but the A's will give him a look at shortstop. He gets himself into position to make the routine plays, and his sure hands allow him to cut down on mistakes.

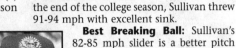

Snyder

JOHN SPEAR

Best Fastball: Before he wore down at the end of the college season, Sullivan threw 91-94 mph with excellent sink.

Best Breaking Ball: Sullivan's 82-85 mph slider is a better pitch than his fastball, though he falls in love with it. He also throws an effective curveball.

Most Intriguing Background: 3B Eric Macha's (33) father Ken manages the A's and spent parts of six seasons in the majors. Unsigned RHP Justin Cassel (30) has two brothers in sports: Jack pitches in the Padres system and Matt is a quarterback at Southern California.

Closest To The Majors: Sullivan or Quintanilla. Both should see Double-A action in 2004.

Best Late-Round Pick: RHP Jared Trout (28) spent more time as an outfielder than as a pitcher at Rhode Island. He touches 90-91 mph with his fastball.

The One Who Got Away: The A's signed their first 17 picks, but lost Cassel to UC Irvine. His command and mechanics are his strong suits, but his arm speed portends better stuff.

Assessment: Getting Sullivan at No. 25 overall was a coup. With him and Quintanilla among their three first-round picks, the A's may ultimately have more success than they did with seven first-rounders in their ballyhooed "Moneyball" draft of 2002.

2002 DRAFT   GRADE: **B**

The "Moneyball" draft looks just fair at this point, considering it contained seven first-round picks. RHP Joe Blanton (1) has the best chance of becoming a star, while OF Nick Swisher (1), C Jeremy Brown (1) and 3B Mark Teahen (1) might wind up as regulars—or merely role players. LHP Bill Murphy (3) is intriguing but was dealt for Mark Redman.

2001 DRAFT   GRADE: **A**

GM Billy Beane might have thrown a chair when his club took RHP Jeremy Bonderman (1), but the since-traded Bonderman has all-star potential. So does SS Bobby Crosby (1), who will step in for Miguel Tejada. LHP Neal Cotts (2) helped land Keith Foulke, and 1B Dan Johnson (7) could provide much-needed power.

2000 DRAFT   GRADE: **B+**

Oakland had no first-round choice and used its first pick on 2B Freddie Bynum (2), but more than made up for that slow start with draft-and-follow RHP Rich Harden (17).

1999 DRAFT   GRADE: **A**

LHP Barry Zito (1) alone makes this a terrific draft. If he can stay healthy, since-traded OF Ryan Ludwick (2) might make noise as well.

—Draft analysis prepared by **Jim Callis.** *Numbers in parentheses indicate draft rounds.*

Bobby Crosby

Born: Jan. 12, 1980.
Ht.: 6-3. **Wt.:** 195.
Bats: R. **Throws:** R.
School: Long Beach State University.
Career Transactions: Selected by Athletics in first round (25th overall) of 2001 draft; signed July 3, 2001.

With some pride, Crosby says, "I've never been the best player on any team I've played for." Crosby has the attitude that he always has to improve, and he has done just that at Long Beach State and in pro ball. He's the son of former big leaguer Ed Crosby, who signed Jason Giambi as an Athletics scout and now works for the Diamondbacks. The Big West Conference player of the year in 2001, he went 25th overall in that June's draft and earned then-scouting director Grady Fuson's highest compliment: "This guy's a baseball player." Crosby made an immediate impression by hitting .395 in 11 games at high Class A Modesto, then followed up with a solid first full season in 2002. He stunned the A's by being a much better player in 2003, a tribute to his aptitude and work ethic. He was the Triple-A Pacific Coast League's rookie of the year and will be a prime contender for the same award in the American League this year. If he hadn't been promoted in late August, he would have started at shortstop for Team USA in the Olympic qualifying tournament.

Crosby won't be the run producer that Miguel Tejada was for Oakland, but he'll be better than most shortstops. He has a solid approach, using the entire field and drawing walks, and should hit for average with 20-homer power. Though he's not a spectacular defender, he's a consistent, dependable shortstop who gets the job done. Crosby reads the ball well off the bat, which gives him satisfactory range, and he rarely makes mistakes. His hands are outstanding and his arm is strong. He made significant improvement last year by learning to cut off balls on his side, quickening his ability to make play. From the day Crosby signed, the A's have talked about his instincts for the game, and they seem to keep improving. His desire to keep getting better allows him to do so. The A's are more conscious of plate discipline than any organization, and they'd like Crosby to chase fewer pitches out of the strike zone and to improve his two-strike approach. Those adjustments should come with experience. His speed is below-average for a shortstop and he doesn't have classic range for the position. He has battled nagging injuries during his tenure as a pro and must prove his durability.

Having Crosby waiting in the wings eased Tejada's departure as a free agent. He won't quite fill his predecessor's shoes, but Oakland still will have a shortstop who's above-average offensive and defensively. "He's ready for the big leagues," Triple-A Sacramento manager Tony DeFrancesco says. "I think he will be in the class with the other great shortstops." That may be setting a high standard, but Crosby has lived up to every challenge he has faced.

Year	Club (League)	Class	AVG	G	AB	R	H	2B	3B	HR	RBI	BB	SO	SB	SLG	OBP
2001	Modesto (Cal)	A	.395	11	38	7	15	5	0	1	3	3	8	0	.605	.439
2002	Modesto (Cal)	A	.307	73	280	47	86	17	2	2	38	33	43	5	.404	.393
	Midland (TL)	AA	.281	59	228	31	64	16	0	7	31	19	41	9	.443	.335
2003	Sacramento (PCL)	AAA	.308	127	465	86	143	32	6	22	90	63	110	24	.544	.395
	Oakland (AL)	MAJ	.000	11	12	1	0	0	0	0	0	1	5	0	.000	.143
MAJOR LEAGUE TOTALS			.000	11	12	1	0	0	0	0	0	1	5	0	.000	.143
MINOR LEAGUE TOTALS			.305	270	1011	171	308	70	8	32	162	118	202	38	.485	.383

Joe Blanton, rhp

Born: Dec. 11, 1980. **Ht.:** 6-3. **Wt.:** 225. **Bats:** R. **Throws:** R. **School:** University of Kentucky. **Career Transactions:** Selected by Athletics in first round (24th overall) of 2002 draft; signed July 20, 2002.

Acquired with a first-round pick from the Yankees as compensation for Jason Giambi, Blanton is the best prospect from the A's 2002 "Moneyball" draft. He dominated the low Class A Midwest League last year, winning the strikeout crown despite being promoted in late July. Unlike Oakland's other 2002 draftees, he also made an easy transition to Double-A. Blanton has the makings of a classic power pitcher. He usually throws 93-94 mph and hits 96 with his fastball, and he has tremendous command of the pitch. MWL managers rated his slider as the league's best breaking ball, and his curveball also can buckle hitters' knees. Blanton is still learning the art of pitching. He sometimes relies on one or two pitches rather than using his full repertoire, and he must learn to sequence pitches to keep hitters off balance. His changeup is just beginning to develop. An intense competitor, he'll overthrow and lose control at times. There's some effort to his delivery. Blanton will return to Double-A Midland to start this season. He made dramatic progress during 2003, and similar improvement could land him in Oakland in 2005.

Year	Club (League)	Class	W	L	ERA	G	GS	CG	SV	IP	H	R	ER	HR	BB	SO	AVG
2002	Vancouver (NWL)	A	1	1	3.14	4	2	0	0	14	11	5	5	0	2	15	.216
	Modesto (Cal)	A	0	1	7.50	2	1	0	0	6	8	6	5	1	6	6	.296
2003	Kane County (Mid)	A	8	7	2.57	21	21	2	0	133	110	47	38	6	19	144	.219
	Midland (TL)	AA	3	1	1.26	7	5	1	1	36	21	6	5	1	7	30	.174
MINOR LEAGUE TOTALS			12	10	2.52	34	29	3	1	189	150	64	53	8	34	195	.214

Dan Johnson, 1b

Born: Aug. 10, 1979. **Ht.:** 6-2. **Wt.:** 220. **Bats:** L. **Throws:** R. **School:** University of Nebraska. **Career Transactions:** Selected by Athletics in seventh round of 2001 draft; signed June 18, 2001.

Undrafted out of high school and junior college, Johnson became a star at the University of Nebraska. He set school records for homers in a game (three) and season (25) and has continued to mash as a pro. He led the Double-A Texas League in homers, RBIs and total bases (271) last year. Power and patience are the organization's watchwords, and Johnson has both in abundance. He's a great fastball hitter with power to all fields and outstanding plate discipline for a slugger. After making major adjustments to shorten his stroke, he makes consistent, hard contact. Johnson is big and slow, limited to first base and DH. Though he has worked hard on his defense, he's only adequate. Some scouts remain skeptical whether his power will translate to the majors. The A's will send Johnson to Triple-A to see if he can continue producing as he has. If he does, he could be an upgrade for them at first base after they got just 16 homers and a .399 slugging percentage out of the position in 2003.

Year	Club (League)	Class	AVG	G	AB	R	H	2B	3B	HR	RBI	BB	SO	SB	SLG	OBP
2001	Vancouver (NWL)	A	.283	69	247	36	70	15	2	11	41	27	63	0	.494	.354
2002	Modesto (Cal)	A	.293	126	426	56	125	23	1	21	85	57	87	4	.500	.371
2003	Midland (TL)	AA	.290	139	538	90	156	26	4	27	114	68	82	7	.504	.365
	Sacramento (PCL)	AAA	.250	1	4	0	1	1	0	0	0	0	0	0	.500	.250
MINOR LEAGUE TOTALS			.290	335	1215	182	352	65	7	59	240	152	232	11	.500	.364

Brad Sullivan, rhp

Born: Sept. 12, 1981. **Ht.:** 6-0. **Wt.:** 195. **Bats:** R. **Throws:** R. **School:** University of Houston. **Career Transactions:** Selected by Athletics in first round (25th overall) of 2003 draft; signed July 21, 2003.

Sullivan came within 10 whiffs of becoming the first pitcher since the 1970s to successfully defend an NCAA Division I strikeout title, but he wore down late in the spring and slipped out of the top 10 picks. The A's were shocked when he was available with the 25th overall selection. After signing him for $1.36 million, Oakland handled him gingerly. Sullivan's darting fastball and hard slider are both plus offerings with excellent movement. His curveball also can serve as an out pitch at times. He's athletic, which allows him to repeat his delivery and field his position well. He has terrific feel for pitching and keeps hitters off balance by varying his arm slot, location and velocity. Sullivan also played first and second base for Houston in the NCAA playoffs, and he was exhausted when he joined the A's. The velocity on his fastball dipped from 91-93 mph to the high 80s, and his slider dropped from 82-85 mph to the high 70s. The hope is that he'll bounce back after a winter of rest. Oakland has revamped his mechanics to improve his durability. If he's 100 percent, Sullivan should be able to start this season at high Class A and reach the majors before most 2003 draftees. An optimistic ETA would be late 2005.

Year	Club (League)	Class	W	L	ERA	G	GS	CG	SV	IP	H	R	ER	HR	BB	SO	AVG
2003	Kane County (Mid)	A	1	0	3.18	6	0	0	0	11	9	4	4	1	7	9	.225
MINOR LEAGUE TOTALS			1	0	3.18	6	0	0	0	11	9	4	4	1	7	9	.225

5 Graham Koonce, 1b

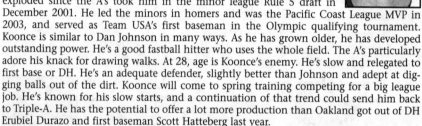

Born: May 15, 1975. **Ht.:** 6-4. **Wt.:** 220. **Bats:** L. **Throws:** L. **School:** Julian (Calif.) Union HS. **Career Transactions:** Selected by Tigers in 60th round of 1993 draft; signed Sept. 5, 1993 . . . Released by Tigers, March 26, 1997 . . . Signed by independent Tri-City (Western), May 1997 . . . Signed by independent Chico (Western), May 1998 . . . Signed by Padres, Dec. 5, 1998 . . . Selected by Athletics from Padres in Rule 5 minor league draft, Dec. 13, 2001.

Released by the Tigers in 1997, Koonce spent two years in the independent Western League. He signed with the Padres in 1998 and has exploded since the A's took him in the minor league Rule 5 draft in December 2001. He led the minors in homers and was the Pacific Coast League MVP in 2003, and served as Team USA's first baseman in the Olympic qualifying tournament. Koonce is similar to Dan Johnson in many ways. As he has grown older, he has developed outstanding power. He's a good fastball hitter who uses the whole field. The A's particularly adore his knack for drawing walks. At 28, age is Koonce's enemy. He's slow and relegated to first base or DH. He's an adequate defender, slightly better than Johnson and adept at digging balls out of the dirt. Koonce will come to spring training competing for a big league job. He's known for his slow starts, and a continuation of that trend could send him back to Triple-A. He has the potential to offer a lot more production than Oakland got out of DH Erubiel Durazo and first baseman Scott Hatteberg last year.

Year	Club (League)	Class	AVG	G	AB	R	H	2B	3B	HR	RBI	BB	SO	SB	SLG	OBP
1994	Bristol (Appy)	R	.217	43	115	14	25	4	0	0	15	28	22	3	.252	.372
1995	Jamestown (NY-P)	A	.280	73	289	37	81	16	1	3	34	35	63	8	.374	.361
1996	Fayetteville (SAL)	A	.239	133	486	61	116	22	3	8	59	58	97	7	.346	.323
1997	Tri-City (West)	IND	.287	89	286	46	82	15	3	3	34	67	55	13	.392	.422
1998	Chico (West)	IND	.331	69	242	50	80	15	0	10	41	38	41	0	.517	.426
1999	Rancho Cuca. (Cal)	A	.285	132	474	76	135	16	1	19	79	76	110	4	.443	.392
2000	Rancho Cuca. (Cal)	A	.295	137	475	92	140	40	3	18	93	107	105	0	.505	.425
2001	Mobile (SL)	AA	.266	109	320	52	85	18	0	13	48	89	83	0	.444	.429
	Portland (PCL)	AAA	.214	6	14	5	3	1	0	1	2	5	6	0	.500	.421
2002	Midland (TL)	AA	.274	140	470	86	129	28	0	24	96	133	117	2	.487	.440
2003	Sacramento (PCL)	AAA	.277	138	480	82	133	23	1	34	104	98	119	0	.542	.403
	Oakland (AL)	MAJ	.125	6	8	0	1	1	0	0	0	0	6	0	.250	.125
MAJOR LEAGUE TOTALS			.125	6	8	0	1	1	0	0	0	0	6	0	.250	.125
MINOR LEAGUE TOTALS			.271	911	3123	505	847	168	9	120	541	629	722	24	.446	.397

6 Nick Swisher, of

Born: Nov. 25, 1980. **Ht.:** 6-0. **Wt.:** 190. **Bats:** B. **Throws:** L. **School:** Ohio State University. **Career Transactions:** Selected by Athletics in first round (16th overall) of 2002 draft; signed June 14, 2002.

The A's made Swisher their No. 1 target in the 2002 draft and were ecstatic to get him 16th overall. His father Steve was a first-rounder in June 1973 and an all-star catcher in 1976. Nick's transition to pro ball has been erratic. He struggled in his pro debut and again after a promotion to Double-A last year. Swisher works deep counts and can hit once he gets there. He has plus power potential from both sides of the plate. He has excellent instincts and an average arm in the outfield, and could be a Gold Glover at first base. But he has struck out too much as a pro because pitchers have learned he'll chase off-speed pitches out of the zone. He's a below-average runner who may lack the speed for center field. Other teams don't like his power as much as the A's do. He's too hard on himself, which has hampered his ability to make adjustments. Swisher will return to Double-A in 2004. His supporters see him maturing into a player who combines patience, power and defense. His detractors see him as a player who doesn't profile as a standout at any position.

Year	Club (League)	Class	AVG	G	AB	R	H	2B	3B	HR	RBI	BB	SO	SB	SLG	OBP
2002	Vancouver (NWL)	A	.250	13	44	10	11	3	0	2	12	13	11	3	.455	.433
	Visalia (Cal)	A	.240	49	183	22	44	13	2	4	23	26	48	3	.399	.340

Year	Club (League)	Class	AVG	G	AB	R	H	2B	3B	HR	RBI	BB	SO	SB	SLG	OBP
2003	Modesto (Cal)	A	.296	51	189	38	56	14	2	10	43	41	49	0	.550	.418
	Midland (TL)	AA	.230	76	287	36	66	24	2	5	43	37	76	0	.380	.324
MINOR LEAGUE TOTALS			.252	189	703	106	177	54	6	21	121	117	184	6	.435	.362

7 Omar Quintanilla, ss

Born: Oct. 24, 1981. **Ht.:** 5-9. **Wt.:** 190. **Bats:** L. **Throws:** R. **School:** University of Texas. **Career Transactions:** Selected by Athletics in first round (33rd overall) of 2003 draft; signed July 13, 2003.

Quintanilla was somewhat of a surprise as a supplemental first-round pick, but his strong pro debut was not. He had established a sterling track record at Texas, where he was the Big 12 Conference freshman of the year in 2001 and a key player on a College World Series championship team the following year. Quintanilla has solid all-around tools and knows how to get the most out of them. He's capable of producing for average and gap power. He has average speed and good baserunning instincts. Defensively, he has excellent hands and consistently makes the routine plays. He entered pro ball with tendinitis in his throwing arm, so Quintanilla never showed what he could do at shortstop. He's thick-bodied and will have to work hard to maintain his quickness, and even then may have to move to second base. He often hits in early counts, contradicting the A's preference for their hitters to take pitches and draw walks. Quintanilla will return to high Class A and try to build on his early success. The A's say he can stay at shortstop, and he'd still be an above-average offensive player at second base if he has to move.

Year	Club (League)	Class	AVG	G	AB	R	H	2B	3B	HR	RBI	BB	SO	SB	SLG	OBP
2003	Vancouver (NWL)	A	.341	32	129	22	44	5	4	0	14	12	20	7	.442	.401
	Modesto (Cal)	A	.417	8	36	9	15	3	0	2	6	3	6	0	.667	.462
MINOR LEAGUE TOTALS			.358	40	165	31	59	8	4	2	20	15	26	7	.491	.414

8 Mike Rouse, ss

Born: April 25, 1980. **Ht.:** 5-11. **Wt.:** 185. **Bats:** L. **Throws:** R. **School:** Cal State Fullerton. **Career Transactions:** Selected by Blue Jays in fifth round of 2001 draft; signed July 2, 2001 . . . Traded by Blue Jays with RHP Chris Mowday to Athletics for RHP Cory Lidle, Nov. 16, 2002.

A Big West Conference rival of Bobby Crosby at Cal State Fullerton, Rouse came from the Blue Jays in a November 2002 trade for Cory Lidle. After missing half of 2002 with a broken hamate bone in his right wrist, Rouse returned to Double-A last year and hit with more authority. When Crosby was unavailable, Rouse took over at shortstop and starred for Team USA at the Olympic qualifying tournament. With great hands and exceptional ability to read the ball off the bat, Rouse is a solid defender at shortstop. He has excellent focus, which helped him lead Texas League shortstops with a .967 fielding percentage. He handles the bat well, gets on base and runs OK. The A's believe he can reach double figures in homers. Rouse doesn't have the arm or range to make plays in the hole, and he'll probably wind up at second base. Oakland also wanted him to get stronger over the offseason. Rouse is ready for Triple-A and may get time at second base. The A's envision him as an everyday middle infielder, though he'll have to fight off Mark Ellis ahead of him and Omar Quintanilla behind him to earn that status in Oakland.

Year	Club (League)	Class	AVG	G	AB	R	H	2B	3B	HR	RBI	BB	SO	SB	SLG	OBP
2001	Dunedin (FSL)	A	.272	48	180	27	49	17	2	5	24	13	45	3	.472	.327
2002	Tennessee (SL)	AA	.260	71	231	35	60	11	0	9	43	29	47	7	.424	.342
2003	Midland (TL)	AA	.300	129	457	75	137	33	3	3	53	63	83	7	.405	.392
	Sacramento (PCL)	AAA	.429	2	7	2	3	0	0	0	1	0	0	0	.429	.429
MINOR LEAGUE TOTALS			.285	250	875	139	249	61	5	17	121	105	175	17	.424	.366

9 Andre Ethier, of

Born: April 10, 1982. **Ht.:** 6-3. **Wt.:** 195. **Bats:** L. **Throws:** L. **School:** Arizona State University. **Career Transactions:** Selected by Athletics in second round of 2003 draft; signed July 1, 2003.

The A's drafted Ethier in the 37th round out of Chandler-Gilbert (Ariz.) Community College in 2001 and signed him out of Arizona State as a second-round pick two years later. In between, he earned all-Pacific-10 Conference honors in both years with the Sun Devils and finished his college career with a 23-game hitting streak. Ethier has tremendous hand-eye coordination, the basic natural ability that can make for a great hitter. Some scouts say he could compare with Shawn Green once he fills out. He has the patience at the plate that Oakland likes. He also has average speed and arm strength, and his excellent instincts allow him to play all three outfield positions. He's highly motivated. Ethier has a tendency to guide the ball with the bat, slightly pulling off rather than attacking it. He made outstanding progress learning to drive pitches in instructional league. He doesn't cover a lot of ground for a center fielder and might fit best in left. Ethier is ticketed for high Class A, and Oakland is eager to see what develops. Some club officials say he has the highest ceiling among their farmhands.

Year	Club (League)	Class	AVG	G	AB	R	H	2B	3B	HR	RBI	BB	SO	SB	SLG	OBP
2003	Vancouver (NWL)	A	.390	10	41	7	16	4	1	1	7	3	3	2	.610	.444
	Kane County (Mid)	A	.272	40	162	23	44	10	0	0	11	19	25	2	.333	.355
MINOR LEAGUE TOTALS			.296	50	203	30	60	14	1	1	18	22	28	4	.389	.373

10 Justin Duchscherer, rhp

Born: Nov. 19, 1977. **Ht.:** 6-3. **Wt.:** 190. **Bats:** R. **Throws:** R. **School:** Coronado HS, Lubbock, Texas. **Career Transactions:** Selected by Red Sox in eighth round of 1996 draft; signed June 14, 1996 . . . Traded by Red Sox to Rangers for C Doug Mirabelli, June 12, 2001 . . . Traded by Rangers to Athletics for RHP Luis Vizcaino, March 18, 2002.

A car crash after the 2001 season led to back problems that ruined Duchscherer's first year in the Oakland system. He bounced back in 2003 to become the Pacific Coast League's pitcher of the year and wins leader. He was at his best on Sept. 9, shutting out the Angels for seven innings to earn his first win for the A's. Duchscherer is a poised and crafty control pitcher. He upsets hitters' timing by changing speeds on his fastball and curveball. His curve is his best pitch, and his changeup is right behind. None of Duchscherer's pitches grades better than average, and his fastball doesn't even rate that high. He pitches at 85-87 mph and rarely breaks 90. He needs to improve his cutter so he can work inside to righthanders. He has little margin for error. While his total package was devastating against Triple-A hitters, how well it will translate to the majors remains a major question mark. The A's say Duchscherer could emerge as a successful big league starter after gaining a couple of years of experience at that level. Oakland's offseason trade for Mark Redman paves the way for Duchscherer to learn in a middle-relief role in 2004.

Year	Club (League)	Class	W	L	ERA	G	GS	CG	SV	IP	H	R	ER	HR	BB	SO	AVG
1996	Red Sox (GCL)	R	0	2	3.13	13	8	0	1	55	52	26	19	0	14	45	.249
1997	Red Sox (GCL)	R	2	3	1.81	10	8	0	0	45	34	18	9	0	17	59	.204
	Michigan (Mid)	A	1	1	5.63	4	4	0	0	24	26	17	15	1	10	19	.274
1998	Michigan (Mid)	A	7	12	4.79	30	26	0	0	143	166	87	76	9	47	106	.298
1999	Augusta (SAL)	A	4	0	0.22	6	6	0	0	41	21	1	1	0	8	39	.148
	Sarasota (FSL)	A	7	7	4.49	20	18	0	0	112	101	62	56	14	30	105	.237
2000	Trenton (EL)	AA	7	9	3.39	24	24	2	0	143	134	59	54	7	35	126	.246
2001	Trenton (EL)	AA	6	3	2.44	12	12	1	0	74	49	25	20	6	14	69	.179
	Tulsa (TL)	AA	4	0	2.08	6	6	1	0	43	39	14	10	3	10	55	.242
	Texas (AL)	MAJ	1	1	12.27	5	2	0	0	15	24	20	20	5	4	11	.353
	Oklahoma (PCL)	AAA	3	3	2.84	7	7	1	0	51	48	20	16	6	10	52	.255
2002	Sacramento (PCL)	AAA	2	4	5.57	14	11	0	0	63	73	45	39	7	17	52	.283
2003	Sacramento (PCL)	AAA	14	2	3.25	24	23	0	0	155	151	59	56	12	18	117	.254
	Oakland (AL)	MAJ	1	1	3.31	4	3	0	0	16	17	7	6	1	3	15	.262
MAJOR LEAGUE TOTALS			2	2	7.55	9	5	0	0	31	41	27	26	6	7	26	.308
MINOR LEAGUE TOTALS			57	46	3.52	170	153	5	1	948	894	433	371	65	230	844	.247

11 Chad Harville, rhp

Born: Sept. 16, 1976. **Ht.:** 5-9. **Wt.:** 180. **Bats:** R. **Throws:** R. **School:** University of Memphis. **Career Transactions:** Selected by Athletics in second round of 1997 draft; signed June 19, 1997.

A dominant Triple-A performance and promising outings in the majors last year have returned Harville to the A's bullpen mix for 2004. Because he's out of options, he'll either have to make the Oakland roster or risk being lost on waivers. With Chad Bradford the only established righthander in the A's relief corps, Harville has a good shot at earning a set-up job. When he first came to the A's, he was a young blazer with a fastball that hit 97 mph and a propensity to throw it thigh-high instead of at the knees. After seven years of experience, he has developed a sinker in the low 90s, and still occasionally busts a 95 mph four-seamer. He also has added a slow curve to mess with hitters' timing. Command has never been his strong suit, and he has had problems throwing strikes during his various stints with Oakland. Harville also has a history of injuries, including rotator-cuff tendinitis in 2001 and elbow inflammation in 2002.

Year	Club (League)	Class	W	L	ERA	G	GS	CG	SV	IP	H	R	ER	HR	BB	SO	AVG
1997	S. Oregon (NWL)	A	1	0	0.00	3	0	0	0	5	3	0	0	0	3	6	.176
	Visalia (Cal)	A	0	0	5.79	14	0	0	0	19	25	14	12	2	13	24	.325
1998	Visalia (Cal)	A	4	3	3.00	24	7	0	4	69	59	25	23	0	31	76	.230
	Huntsville (SL)	AA	0	0	2.45	12	0	0	8	15	6	4	4	0	13	24	.122
1999	Midland (TL)	AA	2	0	2.01	17	0	0	7	22	13	6	5	1	9	35	.165
	Vancouver (PCL)	AAA	1	0	1.75	22	0	0	11	26	24	5	5	0	11	36	.240
	Oakland (AL)	MAJ	0	2	6.91	15	0	0	0	14	18	11	11	2	10	15	.310
2000	Sacramento (PCL)	AAA	5	3	4.50	53	0	0	9	64	53	35	32	8	35	77	.222
2001	Modesto (Cal)	A	0	0	3.00	2	1	0	0	3	2	2	1	0	0	3	.182
	Visalia (Cal)	A	0	0	0.00	1	1	0	0	3	3	0	0	0	0	3	.250
	Sacramento (PCL)	AAA	5	2	3.98	33	0	0	8	41	35	20	18	5	12	55	.230
	Oakland (AL)	MAJ	0	0	0.00	3	0	0	0	3	2	0	0	0	0	2	.182
2002	Sacramento (PCL)	AAA	1	2	5.40	24	0	0	5	30	32	19	18	5	13	26	.274
2003	Sacramento (PCL)	AAA	3	5	2.05	48	0	0	18	57	42	16	13	5	21	57	.202
	Oakland (AL)	MAJ	1	0	5.82	21	0	0	1	22	25	15	14	3	17	18	.294
MAJOR LEAGUE TOTALS			1	2	5.77	39	0	0	1	39	45	26	25	5	27	35	.292
MINOR LEAGUE TOTALS			22	15	3.34	253	9	0	70	353	297	146	131	26	161	422	.226

12 Mike Wood, rhp

Born: April 26, 1980. **Ht.:** 6-3. **Wt.:** 180. **Bats:** R. **Throws:** R. **School:** University of North Florida. **Career Transactions:** Selected by Athletics in 10th round of 2001 draft; signed June 10, 2001.

Though Wood was undrafted out of high school and went to NCAA Division II North Florida as a walk-on infielder, he reached the majors little more than two years after turning pro. But after he succeeded at every stop in the minors, big league hitters were able to tee off on his mid-80s pitches. Wood has a devastating sinker that the A's have compared to Tim Hudson's, and the same scout (John Poloni) signed both pitchers. Oakland now believes his best role might be as a reliever who enters in double-play situations. Wood reached 91 mph as a college closer but his velocity has been down to 86-89 as a pro. He also throws a splitter and changeup, both highly effective pitches, and has good command of the strike zone. Wood probably will begin 2004 in the Triple-A rotation, waiting for an opening in the Oakland bullpen.

Year	Club (League)	Class	W	L	ERA	G	GS	CG	SV	IP	H	R	ER	HR	BB	SO	AVG
2001	Vancouver (NWL)	A	2	0	1.25	5	2	0	0	22	17	4	3	0	4	24	.210
	Modesto (Cal)	A	4	3	3.09	10	9	0	0	58	46	22	20	6	10	52	.211
2002	Modesto (Cal)	A	3	3	3.48	7	7	0	0	41	41	17	16	4	6	50	.265
	Midland (TL)	AA	11	3	3.15	17	17	0	0	106	103	41	37	8	29	63	.259
2003	Sacramento (PCL)	AAA	9	3	3.05	16	16	0	0	91	87	34	31	5	23	59	.257
	Oakland (AL)	MAJ	2	1	10.54	7	1	0	0	14	24	17	16	1	7	15	.387
MAJOR LEAGUE TOTALS			2	1	10.54	7	1	0	0	14	24	17	16	1	7	15	.387
MINOR LEAGUE TOTALS			29	12	3.03	55	51	0	0	318	294	118	107	23	72	248	.247

13 John Rheinecker, lhp

Born: May 29, 1979. **Ht.:** 6-2. **Wt.:** 215. **Bats:** L. **Throws:** L. **School:** Southwest Missouri State University. **Career Transactions:** Selected by Athletics in first round (37th overall) of 2001 draft; signed June 30, 2001.

Rheinecker ranked No. 2 on this list behind Rich Harden a year ago, and he won 11 games while reaching Triple-A in 2003. Yet his stock has slipped significantly. He allowed a minor league-high 233 hits in 180 innings, raising questions as to whether he can miss enough bats to be an effective big league starter. Rheinecker is a good battler who often fights his way out of trouble. When he commands his 88-89 fastball, he can dominate games, but he doesn't do that often enough. While he doesn't beat himself with walks, he leaves his pitches up in the strike zone too often. His slider is his best pitch, and he also uses a cutter and changeup. Like many of Oakland's top pitching prospects, Rheinecker is a fine athlete who was a two-way player in college. He would have been an early pick in the 2000 draft if he hadn't torn the anterior cruciate ligament in his right knee while playing the outfield. He'll pitch out of the Triple-A rotation in 2004, trying to improve his pitch sequencing and his ability to work down in the zone.

Year	Club (League)	Class	W	L	ERA	G	GS	CG	SV	IP	H	R	ER	HR	BB	SO	AVG
2001	Vancouver (NWL)	A	0	1	1.59	6	5	0	0	23	13	5	4	0	4	17	.160
	Modesto (Cal)	A	0	1	6.30	2	2	0	0	10	10	7	7	1	5	5	.256
2002	Visalia (Cal)	A	3	0	2.31	9	9	0	0	51	41	16	13	2	10	62	.216
	Midland (TL)	AA	7	7	3.38	20	20	1	0	128	137	63	48	7	24	100	.274
2003	Midland (TL)	AA	9	6	4.74	23	23	1	0	142	186	90	75	13	32	89	.313
	Sacramento (PCL)	AAA	2	0	3.79	6	6	0	0	38	47	19	16	1	12	26	.303
MINOR LEAGUE TOTALS			21	15	3.75	66	65	2	0	392	434	200	163	24	87	299	.278

14 Jeremy Brown, c

Born: Oct. 25, 1979. **Ht.:** 5-10. **Wt.:** 210. **Bats:** R. **Throws:** R. **School:** University of Alabama.
Career Transactions: Selected by Athletics in first round (35th overall) of 2002 draft; signed June 7, 2002.

Perhaps no player in baseball inspires more diversity of opinion than the squat catcher from Alabama. No other team evaluated him as an early-round pick in 2002, yet Oakland drafted him 35th overall. Saving money with seven first-round picks was a factor, as Brown's $350,000 bonus was the lowest in the top 66 choices. But the A's probably could have taken him five rounds later and signed him for $10,000. They say he'll be a top-flight big league catcher, putting up outstanding offensive numbers while functioning well on defense. Scouts outside the organization point to his lack of athleticism and fear he won't have the mobility to block pitches out of the strike zone, which would prevent him from becoming an everyday catcher. Those limitations became more apparent when he advanced to Double-A last year. The A's put Brown on an intense agility program over the winter, hoping to increase his flexibility. After a spectacular pro debut in 2002, Brown continued to pile up walks in Double-A, but his average slipped and his power fell off dramatically. He earns high marks for calling games and working with pitchers, but his sluggishness behind the plate also detracts from his slightly above-average arm. He threw out just 21 percent of basestealers in 2003. Brown missed the second half of the season and instructional league with a strained left thumb. He may need to return to Double-A at the start of this year.

Year	Club (League)	Class	AVG	G	AB	R	H	2B	3B	HR	RBI	BB	SO	SB	SLG	OBP
2002	Vancouver (NWL)	A	.286	10	28	7	8	1	0	0	1	10	5	1	.321	.487
	Visalia (Cal)	A	.310	55	187	36	58	14	0	10	40	44	49	1	.545	.444
2003	Midland (TL)	AA	.275	66	233	37	64	10	1	5	37	41	38	3	.391	.388
MINOR LEAGUE TOTALS			.290	131	448	80	130	25	1	15	78	95	92	5	.451	.419

15 Mark Teahen, 3b

Born: Sept. 6, 1981. **Ht.:** 6-3. **Wt.:** 210. **Bats:** L. **Throws:** R. **School:** St. Mary's (Calif.) College.
Career Transactions: Selected by Athletics in first round (39th overall) of 2002 draft; signed June 9, 2002.

In "Moneyball," scouting director Eric Kubota said, "I hate to say it, but if you want to talk about another Jason Giambi, this guy could be it." Teahen hasn't lived up to that assessment yet, but the biggest excitement generated in instructional league camp came when he began driving the ball. Suddenly the tall third baseman went from power-deprived to potentially powerful, a major leap forward. Teahen had shown line-drive hitting ability but not the pop required of a third baseman. In instructional league, the A's got him to incorporate his legs more in his swing and to pull pitches more often. He has good plate discipline and exceptional hand-eye coordination, though he needs to make more contact. Defensively, Teahen is a solid third baseman with averge speed and a plus arm for the position. The hope is that the lessons he learned in instructional league will carry over this year in Double-A.

Year	Club (League)	Class	AVG	G	AB	R	H	2B	3B	HR	RBI	BB	SO	SB	SLG	OBP
2002	Vancouver (NWL)	A	.404	13	57	10	23	5	1	0	6	5	9	4	.526	.444
	Modesto (Cal)	A	.239	59	234	25	56	9	1	1	26	21	53	1	.299	.307
2003	Modesto (Cal)	A	.283	121	453	68	128	27	4	3	71	66	113	4	.380	.377
MINOR LEAGUE TOTALS			.278	193	744	103	207	41	6	4	103	92	175	9	.366	.361

16 Freddie Bynum, 2b

Born: March 15, 1980. **Ht.:** 6-1. **Wt.:** 180. **Bats:** L. **Throws:** R. **School:** Pitt County (N.C.) CC.
Career Transactions: Selected by Athletics in second round of 2000 draft; signed June 19, 2000.

Oakland's surprise top pick (second round) in 2000, Bynum has made progress but at a slower pace than the A's would have hoped. After an encouraging performance at the plate in 2002, he regressed in Double-A last year. He still has the tools to develop into an exciting leadoff man and second baseman, but he still has a lot of work to do. Bynum has excellent speed and a line-drive approach. He won't ever hit for much power and has to tighten up his strike zone. Primarily a shortstop in his first two pro seasons, he has found a better fit at second base the last two years. He certainly has enough range and arm strength to play shortstop, but his hands and inconsistent throwing accuracy held him back there. Oakland is toying with moving him to center field, a weak spot in the system. He probably would benefit from repeating Double-A but may move to Triple-A in 2004.

Year	Club (League)	Class	AVG	G	AB	R	H	2B	3B	HR	RBI	BB	SO	SB	SLG	OBP
2000	Vancouver (NWL)	A	.256	72	281	52	72	10	1	1	26	31	58	22	.310	.341
2001	Modesto (Cal)	A	.261	120	440	59	115	19	7	2	46	41	95	28	.350	.325
2002	Visalia (Cal)	A	.306	135	539	83	165	26	5	3	56	64	116	41	.390	.385
2003	Midland (TL)	AA	.263	132	510	84	134	18	9	5	58	56	135	22	.363	.344
MINOR LEAGUE TOTALS			.275	459	1770	278	486	73	22	11	186	192	404	113	.359	.351

17 Ben Fritz, rhp

Born: March 29, 1981. **Ht.:** 6-4. **Wt.:** 225. **Bats:** R. **Throws:** R. **School:** Fresno State University.
Career Transactions: Selected by Athletics in first round (30th overall) of 2002 draft; signed June 28, 2002.

One A's official put it succinctly: "He had a crappy year. But there's something special about Ben that makes you think he'll get it eventually." Fritz battled shoulder tendinitis in 2003, his first full pro season, leading to erratic performances and getting him shut down after July 1. Another former two-way player among Oakland's best pitching prospects, Fritz also caught and played first base at Fresno State. His arm strength, power and agility made him a legitimate catching prospect, but teams liked him even better on the mound. When healthy, Fritz has a 92-94 mph fastball, a decent slider and two variations of a changeup. His fastball has good life, which combined with his easy delivery leads to a lot of late or checked swings. He'll need to improve his command and stay healthy in 2003, which he'll probably begin back in high Class A. Some club officials believe his best long-term role may be as a closer, because he has the makeup to thrive in that role.

Year	Club (League)	Class	W	L	ERA	G	GS	CG	SV	IP	H	R	ER	HR	BB	SO	AVG
2002	Vancouver (NWL)	A	1	4	2.95	9	9	0	0	40	29	16	13	1	14	33	.199
	Visalia (Cal)	A	1	0	3.71	3	3	0	0	17	15	7	7	1	6	16	.242
2003	Modesto (Cal)	A	4	7	4.91	15	15	0	0	77	83	49	42	3	34	77	.278
MINOR LEAGUE TOTALS			6	11	4.17	27	27	0	0	134	127	72	62	5	54	126	.250

18 John Baker, c

Born: Jan. 20, 1981. **Ht.:** 6-1. **Wt.:** 215. **Bats:** L. **Throws:** R. **School:** University of California.
Career Transactions: Selected by Athletics in fourth round of 2002 draft; signed June 28, 2002.

Baker ranks as the best defensive catcher among Oakland farmhands, though that's more a reflection of the state of the system than any Gold Glove prowess on his part. He's an offense-first player with power to both alleys and good plate discipline. He does a good job of putting the sweet spot of the bat on the ball, though he could make more consistent contact. Low Class A pitchers were no match for him, though he cooled off after a promotion to Double-A. Baker didn't begin to catch until his sophomore season at California, but he's highly intelligent and learns quickly. The A's have been pleased with his defensive progress, as his receiving skills are average and his blocking ability is adequate. The biggest question is his arm, which is fringe average at best. He threw out just 23 percent of basestealers in 2003 before straining his shoulder late in the season. He was limited to DH duty in instructional league. Baker likely will begin 2004 in Double-A, where he may split time behind the plate with Jeremy Brown.

Year	Club (League)	Class	AVG	G	AB	R	H	2B	3B	HR	RBI	BB	SO	SB	SLG	OBP
2002	Vancouver (NWL)	A	.235	39	115	15	27	5	0	1	22	22	37	2	.304	.389
2003	Kane County (Mid)	A	.309	82	304	42	94	23	2	6	49	47	77	1	.457	.414
	Midland (TL)	AA	.240	43	150	16	36	3	0	1	21	14	46	0	.280	.316
MINOR LEAGUE TOTALS			.276	164	569	73	157	31	2	8	83	83	160	3	.380	.384

19 John McCurdy, ss

Born: April 17, 1981. **Ht.:** 6-2. **Wt.:** 195. **Bats:** R. **Throws:** R. **School:** University of Maryland.
Career Transactions: Selected by Athletics in first round (26th overall) of 2002 draft; signed June 30, 2002.

McCurdy had one of the best offensive seasons ever for a college shortstop, hitting .443-19-77 at Maryland in 2002. Some scouts believed his breakthrough was an aberration, but the A's saw some Jeff Kent in him and took him with one of their seven first-round picks. McCurdy didn't do much offensively in his pro debut or for most of last season, but he hit .391 in the final month and continued to show improvement in instructional league. He finally started to prepare to play every day and learned to put mistakes behind him. At his best, McCurdy is a fierce hitter with power to all fields. At his worst, he loses the strike zone and hits routine groundouts. He doesn't walk as much as a typical Oakland prospect. McCurdy's defense always will be an issue, and several Midwest League observers couldn't figure out why he played shortstop and relegated Francis Gomez to second base at low Class A Kane County last year. McCurdy has arm strength and soft hands, but his range and footwork are ordinary and he lacks consistency. Second base might even be a stretch, and his best fit could come at third base. He could switch position this year in high Class A.

Year	Club (League)	Class	AVG	G	AB	R	H	2B	3B	HR	RBI	BB	SO	SB	SLG	OBP
2002	Vancouver (NWL)	A	.242	56	223	33	54	9	1	3	29	12	57	5	.332	.282
2003	Kane County (Mid)	A	.274	130	515	64	141	33	1	4	52	34	86	22	.365	.331
MINOR LEAGUE TOTALS			.264	186	738	97	195	42	2	7	81	46	143	27	.355	.316

20 Justin Lehr, rhp

Born: Aug. 3, 1977. **Ht.:** 6-1. **Wt.:** 200. **Bats:** R. **Throws:** R. **School:** University of Southern California. **Career Transactions:** Selected by Athletics in eighth round of 1999 draft; signed June 29, 1999.

Lehr spent his first three college seasons mostly catching at UC Santa Barbara, then transferred to Southern California and served as the No. 2 starter behind Barry Zito. After five years in the minors, Lehr is close to getting a major league shot. His fastball jumped from 91 mph previously to 94-95 in 2003. He also did a much better job of throwing quality strikes to the first batter he faced after entering a game. Lehr backs up his fastball with a slider, and also has a splitter and changeup from his days as a starter. He has found a home in the bullpen after moving there full-time in 2002. His calm demeanor serves him well in tense late-inning situations. After making major progress, Lehr will get a chance to win a job in Oakland this spring. He led the Puerto Rican League with eight saves this winter, helping his cause. In time, he could develop into a setup man.

Year	Club (League)	Class	W	L	ERA	G	GS	CG	SV	IP	H	R	ER	HR	BB	SO	AVG
1999	S. Oregon (NWL)	A	2	6	5.95	14	4	0	0	42	62	36	28	3	17	40	.341
2000	Modesto (Cal)	A	13	6	3.19	29	25	0	0	175	161	71	62	10	46	138	.249
	Sacramento (PCL)	AAA	0	0	11.25	1	1	0	0	4	7	5	5	1	3	3	.389
2001	Midland (TL)	AA	11	12	5.45	29	27	0	0	155	206	107	94	20	43	103	.318
2002	Midland (TL)	AA	8	3	4.05	58	0	0	4	80	88	39	36	7	31	59	.290
2003	Sacramento (PCL)	AAA	3	2	3.72	53	0	0	4	75	74	34	31	3	27	64	.259
MINOR LEAGUE TOTALS			37	29	4.33	184	57	0	8	532	598	292	256	44	167	407	.287

21 Esteban German, 2b

Born: Jan. 26, 1978. **Ht.:** 5-9. **Wt.:** 165. **Bats:** R. **Throws:** R. **Career Transactions:** Signed out of Dominican Republic by Athletics, July 4, 1996.

Just two years ago German was one of the premier prospects in the organization, considered the cream of a deep middle-infield crop that also included Bobby Crosby, Mark Ellis and Freddie Bynum. He was Oakland's minor league player of the year in 2001, but his stock slipped the following year, when it also was discovered that he was 11 months older than previously believed. German rebounded in 2003, but still will have trouble pushing Ellis or Crosby aside to earn regular big league playing time. German has the tools to become a solid leadoff man, with plus speed and on-base ability. He also has good bunting skills. He recognizes that he has little power and doesn't try to drive. Defensively, German has to play second base because he lacks the arm for shortstop. He doesn't read balls quickly off the bat and doesn't cover as much ground as might be expected for a player with his speed. He did make strides last year with his double-play pivot and range to his right side. German could claim a big league utility job if he performs well this spring.

Year	Club (League)	Class	AVG	G	AB	R	H	2B	3B	HR	RBI	BB	SO	SB	SLG	OBP
1997	Athletics East (DSL)	R	.317	69	249	69	79	17	1	2	29	73	30	58	.418	.474
1998	Athletics West (DSL)	R	.313	10	32	9	10	1	0	4	7	2	1	.406	.436
	Athletics (AZL)	R	.307	55	202	52	62	3	10	2	28	33	43	40	.450	.413
1999	Modesto (Cal)	A	.311	128	501	107	156	16	12	4	52	102	128	40	.415	.428
2000	Midland (TL)	AA	.213	24	75	13	16	1	0	1	6	18	21	5	.267	.379
	Visalia (Cal)	A	.264	109	428	82	113	14	10	2	35	61	86	78	.357	.361
2001	Midland (TL)	AA	.284	92	335	79	95	20	3	6	30	63	66	31	.415	.415
	Sacramento (PCL)	AAA	.373	38	150	40	56	8	0	4	14	18	20	17	.507	.457
2002	Sacramento (PCL)	AAA	.275	121	458	72	126	16	4	2	43	78	66	26	.341	.390
	Oakland (AL)	MAJ	.200	9	35	4	7	0	0	0	0	4	11	1	.200	.300
2003	Sacramento (PCL)	AAA	.306	115	467	86	143	20	8	3	51	56	64	32	.403	.379
MAJOR LEAGUE TOTALS			.200	9	35	4	7	0	0	0	0	4	11	1	.200	.300
MINOR LEAGUE TOTALS			.295	761	2897	609	856	116	49	26	292	509	526	328	.396	.407

22 Jason Grabowski, of/1b

Born: May 24, 1976. **Ht.:** 6-3. **Wt.:** 200. **Bats:** L. **Throws:** R. **School:** University of Connecticut. **Career Transactions:** Selected by Rangers in second round of 1997 draft; signed June 12, 1997 . . . Claimed on waivers by Mariners from Rangers, Dec. 18, 2000 . . . Selected by Athletics from Mariners in Rule 5 major league draft, Dec. 13, 2001 . . . Granted free agency, March 26, 2002; re-signed by Athletics, March 28, 2002.

At 27, Grabowski has done just about everything possible to prove he can play in the majors, but he never has gotten much of an opportunity. He has just 16 at-bats over the last two seasons in Oakland. Grabowski has hit for average and power and reached base consistently throughout his pro career. He doesn't project to have quite enough offense to hold down a regular job as a corner outfielder, but he's versatile enough to have played every position but second base and pitcher as a pro. He has an average arm and runs slightly below average. Grabowski's ability to produce at the plate and fill in at a variety of positions could make him a useful big league reserve. He's out of options, so the A's risk losing him on waivers if he doesn't make their club in spring training.

Year	Club (League)	Class	AVG	G	AB	R	H	2B	3B	HR	RBI	BB	SO	SB	SLG	OBP
1997	Pulaski (Appy)	R	.293	50	174	36	51	14	0	4	24	40	32	6	.443	.423
1998	Savannah (SAL)	A	.270	104	352	63	95	13	6	14	52	57	93	16	.460	.372
1999	Charlotte (FSL)	A	.313	123	434	68	136	31	6	12	87	65	66	13	.495	.407
	Tulsa (TL)	AA	.167	2	6	1	1	0	0	0	0	2	2	0	.167	.375
2000	Tulsa (TL)	AA	.274	135	493	93	135	33	5	19	90	88	106	8	.477	.383
2001	Tacoma (PCL)	AAA	.297	114	394	60	117	32	3	9	58	61	94	7	.462	.390
2002	Sacramento (PCL)	AAA	.294	73	265	50	78	22	3	12	52	39	56	6	.536	.387
	Oakland (AL)	MAJ	.375	4	8	3	3	1	1	0	1	3	1	0	.750	.545
2003	Sacramento (PCL)	AAA	.292	67	250	44	73	13	2	9	40	31	46	7	.468	.364
	Oakland (AL)	MAJ	.000	8	8	0	0	0	0	0	0	1	5	0	.000	.111
	Athletics (AZL)	R	.333	2	6	1	2	1	0	0	1	3	0	0	.500	.556
MAJOR LEAGUE TOTALS			.188	12	16	3	3	1	1	0	1	4	6	0	.375	.350
MINOR LEAGUE TOTALS			.290	670	2374	416	688	159	25	79	404	386	495	63	.478	.389

23 Shane Komine, rhp

Born: Oct. 18, 1980. **Ht.:** 5-9. **Wt.:** 175. **Bats:** R. **Throws:** R. **School:** University of Nebraska.
Career Transactions: Selected by Athletics in ninth round of 2002 draft; signed June 27, 2002.

A college star at Nebraska, Komine set a slew of school records, finished fifth on the all-time NCAA Division I strikeout list (510 in 431 innings) and twice was named Big 12 Conference pitcher of the year. But because he's 5-foot-9 and had a history of back problems, he lasted until the ninth round of the 2002 draft. Komine stayed healthy and pitched well in his first full pro season. His biggest asset is that he's a strike machine who can throw his fastball, curveball and changeup at any point in the count. Komine had an 89-94 mph fastball and a hard slider when he was at his best for the Cornhuskers, but he usually pitches at 88-89 mph these days and has dropped the slider. He wore down in the final month of last season, and given his past he just may not have the durability to be a starter. He'll stay in that role this year in Double-A, however.

Year	Club (League)	Class	W	L	ERA	G	GS	CG	SV	IP	H	R	ER	HR	BB	SO	AVG
2002	Visalia (Cal)	A	1	3	5.96	18	0	0	0	26	23	20	17	2	20	22	.240
2003	Kane County (Mid)	A	6	0	1.82	8	8	1	0	54	45	12	11	1	9	50	.223
	Midland (TL)	AA	4	6	3.75	19	18	1	0	103	108	51	43	6	30	75	.271
MINOR LEAGUE TOTALS			11	9	3.49	45	26	2	0	183	176	83	71	9	59	147	.253

24 Mark Kiger, 2b/ss

Born: May 30, 1980. **Ht.:** 5-11. **Wt.:** 180. **Bats:** R. **Throws:** R. **School:** University of Florida.
Career Transactions: Selected by Athletics in fifth round of 2002 draft; signed June 13, 2002.

Kiger has instincts and work ethic similar to David Eckstein and Mark Ellis, who preceded him as shortstops at the University of Florida. He also may have more pure talent than those two. Kiger had a 44-game hitting streak and hit .497 to win the California community college batting title as a Grossmont CC freshman, and he batted .403 as a Gators senior. Thus the A's were surprised when he didn't do much offensively in his pro debut, but Kiger shortened his stroke in instructional league and fared much better last year. He led Oakland minor leaguers in pitches seen while showing a propensity for drawing walks and hitting for gap power. He does need to cut down on his strikeouts, however. Kiger split time between second base and shortstop in 2003 and is better suited for the former. He's can play short adequately but doesn't quite have the arm for the position. His decent range and exceptional hands play well at second base. Kiger has a great chance of progressing as a utilityman, and the A's have a history of turning their utility players into regulars. He'll start in the middle infield at Double-A in 2004.

Year	Club (League)	Class	AVG	G	AB	R	H	2B	3B	HR	RBI	BB	SO	SB	SLG	OBP
2002	Vancouver (NWL)	A	.244	66	246	44	60	12	1	5	27	40	58	7	.362	.346
2003	Modesto (Cal)	A	.281	131	526	95	148	38	3	8	73	77	106	3	.411	.375
MINOR LEAGUE TOTALS			.269	197	772	139	208	50	4	13	100	117	164	10	.395	.366

25 Brian Snyder, 3b

Born: March 17, 1982. **Ht.:** 6-0. **Wt.:** 195. **Bats:** R. **Throws:** R. **School:** Stetson University.
Career Transactions: Selected by Athletics in first round (26th overall) of 2003 draft; signed July 1, 2003.

After an All-America season at Stetson, Snyder projected to go as high as 13th overall to the Blue Jays in the 2003 draft. The A's were happy to get him with the 26th choice, making him the fourth recent Wellington (Fla.) Community High alumnus to go in the first round, joining Bobby Bradley (1999), Sean Burnett (2000) and Justin Pope (2001 after attending Central Florida). Most teams considered Snyder a second- or third-round talent, but Oakland loved his Atlantic Sun Conference-leading .505 on-base percentage. Though he had difficulty adjusting to pro ball at short-season Vancouver, the A's weren't concerned and said minor injuries were partly to blame. He hit well with wood bats in the Cape Cod League in 2002, and he made major progress in instructional league. Snyder has an excellent eye for drawing walks and hits for gap power, though he'll need to make more consistent contact. There are questions as to whether he'll have enough pop for the hot corner and where he fits best on the diamond. Though he's stocky, he's more athletic than he looks and second base could be a possibility. He didn't play well there at Stetson last spring, however, and showed better instincts and reactions at third base. His hands are good and his arm is adequate for the position. Snyder should reach high Class A by the end of 2004.

Year	Club (League)	Class	AVG	G	AB	R	H	2B	3B	HR	RBI	BB	SO	SB	SLG	OBP
2003	Vancouver (NWL)	A	.253	44	146	14	37	6	0	1	17	39	36	9	.315	.409
MINOR LEAGUE TOTALS			.253	44	146	14	37	6	0	1	17	39	36	9	.315	.409

26 Mario Ramos, lhp

Born: Oct. 19, 1977. **Ht.:** 5-11. **Wt.:** 180. **Bats:** L. **Throws:** L. **School:** Rice University. **Career Transactions:** Selected by Athletics in sixth round of 1999 draft; signed Aug. 23, 1999 . . . Traded by Athletics with OF Ryan Ludwick, 1B Jason Hart and C Gerald Laird to Rangers for 1B Carlos Pena and LHP Mike Venafro, Jan. 14, 2002 . . . Claimed on waivers by Athletics from Rangers, Nov. 19, 2003.

Ramos was the A's top pitching prospect when they included him in the January 2002 Carlos Pena trade with the Rangers. But after going 30-9, 2.88 in the Oakland system, he was shellacked to the tune of a 12-19, 5.74 with Texas, including a brief stint in the majors last June. When the Rangers tried to remove Ramos from their 40-man roster this offseason, the A's reclaimed him on the waivers. They're hoping to resurrect his career by reuniting him with the pitching coaches who helped him rise. His changeup is his best pitch, but he foolishly tried to overpower hitters following the trade and never has regained his confidence. His fastball sits at 85-88 mph, so he must survive by varying speeds and throwing strikes. He also mixes in a curveball. The most likely scenario is that Ramos will begin 2004 in Triple-A, where he has struggled mightily the previous two years after pitching well there in 2001.

Year	Club (League)	Class	W	L	ERA	G	GS	CG	SV	IP	H	R	ER	HR	BB	SO	AVG
2000	Modesto (Cal)	A	12	5	2.90	26	24	1	0	152	131	63	49	6	50	134	.234
	Midland (TL)	AA	2	0	1.32	4	4	0	0	27	24	6	4	0	6	19	.242
2001	Midland (TL)	AA	8	1	3.07	15	15	0	0	94	71	37	32	7	28	68	.204
	Sacramento (PCL)	AAA	8	3	3.14	13	13	1	0	80	74	32	28	5	27	82	.241
2002	Oklahoma (PCL)	AAA	3	8	7.40	34	19	0	0	122	162	107	100	20	53	75	.321
2003	Frisco (TL)	AA	8	7	3.86	19	19	0	0	121	130	59	52	9	28	103	.277
	Oklahoma (PCL)	AAA	0	3	6.40	5	5	0	0	32	39	24	23	1	12	22	.305
	Texas (AL)	MAJ	1	1	6.23	3	3	0	0	13	11	9	9	3	13	8	.224
MAJOR LEAGUE TOTALS			1	1	6.23	3	3	0	0	13	11	9	9	3	13	8	.224
MINOR LEAGUE TOTALS			41	27	4.12	116	99	2	0	629	631	328	288	48	204	503	.261

27 Marcus McBeth, of

Born: Aug. 23, 1980. **Ht.:** 6-1. **Wt.:** 185. **Bats:** R. **Throws:** R. **School:** University of South Carolina. **Career Transactions:** Selected by Athletics in fourth round of 2001 draft; signed Aug. 16, 2001.

The 2003 season was an exercise in frustration for the most athletic player in the system. After a disastrous start in high Class A, McBeth reported to extended spring training for a hitting tutorial. It took him a while to find a groove at low Class A Kane County, and shortly after he did he broke his right index finger diving for a fly ball. A former kick returner at South Carolina, McBeth is an outstanding center fielder with tremendous arm strength and foot speed. His problem has been making hard contact at the plate. He showed dramatic improvement during instructional league in 2002, seeming to conquer his propensity for swinging at pitches out of the zone. However, once the 2003 season began, his control of the strike zone disintegrated. He has raw power potential but has been unable to tap into it. There's some thought that McBeth should be moved to the mound to utilize an arm that grades as an 80 on the 20-80 scouting scale. For now, he'll take a second crack at high Class A as an outfielder.

Year	Club (League)	Class	AVG	G	AB	R	H	2B	3B	HR	RBI	BB	SO	SB	SLG	OBP
2002	Visalia (Cal)	A	.227	76	255	45	58	7	3	10	39	29	73	14	.396	.318
	Athletics (AZL)	R	.333	4	9	5	3	0	0	0	0	3	0	3	.333	.500
2003	Modesto (Cal)	A	.130	15	54	7	7	0	0	0	5	5	20	2	.130	.210
	Kane County (Mid)	A	.256	68	234	30	60	9	3	4	26	28	57	8	.372	.349
MINOR LEAGUE TOTALS			.232	163	552	87	128	16	6	14	70	65	150	27	.359	.324

28 Javier Herrera, of

Born: April 9, 1985. **Ht.:** 5-10. **Wt.:** 160. **Bats:** R. **Throws:** R. **Career Transactions:** Signed out of Venezuela by Athletics, July 27, 2001.

Of the players on this list who signed their first pro contract with Oakland, Herrera and Esteban German are the only ones who aren't college products. Herrera has five-tool potential, but drew the most attention in 2003 when he ran into the center-field fence during a Rookie-level Arizona League game on July 1. He had to be airlifted to a Phoenix hospital after losing all feeling in his legs. Herrera made a complete recovery but wasn't as electric once he returned. He has center-field speed, a plus-plus arm and early signs of power. He's unpolished and will need a lot more experience and adjustments. He tends to play out of control and is overaggressive at the plate. He'll probably return to the AZL in 2004.

Year	Club (League)	Class	AVG	G	AB	R	H	2B	3B	HR	RBI	BB	SO	SB	SLG	OBP
2002	Athletics East (DSL)	R	.286	65	227	40	65	14	5	5	47	23	56	21	.458	.359
2003	Athletics (AZL)	R	.230	17	61	12	14	3	1	2	13	7	19	3	.410	.329
MINOR LEAGUE TOTALS			.274	82	288	52	79	17	6	7	60	30	75	24	.448	.353

29 Dustin Majewski, of

Born: Aug. 16, 1981. **Ht.:** 5-11. **Wt.:** 190. **Bats:** L. **Throws:** L. **School:** University of Texas. **Career Transactions:** Selected by Athletics in third round of 2003 draft; signed June 24, 2003.

In two seasons at Texas, Majewski led the Big 12 Conference in hitting (.401) in 2002 and in RBIs (85) in 2003. He and fellow A's draftee Omar Quintanilla were the offensive leaders as the Longhorns made back-to-back College World Series appearances and won the 2002 national title. They're similar in that they both work hard to get the most of solid but not great tools. Majewski's sound swing and approach and his ability to make adjustments will allow him to hit for average. He uses the entire field and has gap power. He doesn't have true center-field speed, but he runs well and gets good jumps. Majewski might be a tweener who lacks the defense for center and the home run power for the corners, but in that case he'd still make a good fourth outfielder. He could make the jump to high Class A in 2004.

Year	Club (League)	Class	AVG	G	AB	R	H	2B	3B	HR	RBI	BB	SO	SB	SLG	OBP
2003	Vancouver (NWL)	A	.291	46	175	33	51	13	2	3	19	28	35	6	.440	.390
	Kane County (Mid)	A	.167	4	18	2	3	1	0	0	2	1	9	0	.222	.211
MINOR LEAGUE TOTALS			.280	50	193	35	54	14	2	3	21	29	44	6	.420	.375

30 Frank Brooks, lhp

Born: Sept. 6, 1978. **Ht.:** 6-1. **Wt.:** 190. **Bats:** L. **Throws:** L. **School:** St. Peter's College. **Career Transactions:** Selected by Phillies in 13th round of 1999 draft; signed June 7, 1999 . . . Traded by Phillies to Pirates for RHP Mike Williams and cash, July 20, 2003 . . . Selected by Mets from Pirates in Rule 5 major league draft, Dec.15, 2003 . . . Traded from Mets to Athletics for a player to be named, Dec. 15, 2003.

Brooks emerged as a legitimate relief prospect in 2003, changing addresses three times in the process. The Phillies traded him to the Pirates in July for Mike Williams. The Mets took Brooks fourth overall in the major league Rule 5 draft at the Winter Meetings, then immediately sent him to the A's for a player to be named later. Brooks won't blow hitters away, but he has good command of an 88-91 mph fastball and curve. His deceptive delivery makes it tough to pick up his pitches, though he sometimes works high in the strike zone and becomes vulnerable to homers. A situational lefty, Brooks may find it tough to stick with Oakland after the club's subsequent moves to stockpile southpaws. The A's re-signed Ricardo Rincon, traded for Chris Hammond and signed Arthur Rhodes as a free agent. Before sending Brooks to the minors, Oakland would have to place him on waivers and offer him back to Philadelphia for half the $50,000 draft price.

Year	Club (League)	Class	W	L	ERA	G	GS	CG	SV	IP	H	R	ER	HR	BB	SO	AVG
1999	Batavia (NY-P)	A	7	3	2.91	16	12	1	0	77	64	26	25	2	33	58	.232
2000	Piedmont (SAL)	A	14	8	3.44	29	27	3	0	178	152	78	68	17	60	138	.236
2001	Clearwater (FSL)	A	5	10	4.71	37	15	0	1	113	113	70	59	18	58	92	.262
2002	Clearwater (FSL)	A	3	5	3.46	35	0	0	7	39	34	18	15	2	27	33	.233
	Reading (EL)	AA	1	1	3.10	17	1	0	2	29	29	11	10	1	12	23	.266
2003	Reading (EL)	AA	3	4	2.30	34	0	0	9	59	40	16	15	5	13	71	.194
	Altoona (EL)	AA	0	0	7.71	1	0	0	0	2	3	2	2	1	0	4	.300
	Nashville (PCL)	AAA	2	0	2.54	16	0	0	0	28	22	9	8	2	11	22	.218
MINOR LEAGUE TOTALS			35	31	3.46	185	55	4	19	525	457	230	202	48	214	441	.238

PHILADELPHIA
PHILLIES

Everything looked to be shaping up for the Phillies in 2003. The Braves were forced to cut costs and overhaul their pitching staff, while the other National League East teams all seemed to be rebuilding or revamping. After the offseason additions of Jim Thome and Kevin Millwood, most pundits rated the Phillies as sure a bet for the postseason as any NL club.

The season didn't play out that way. The new-look Braves won their 12th consecutive division title, while the upstart Marlins received a boost from their farm system and actually added salary as they captured the wild card and went on to win the World Series. Philadelphia led the wild-card race with nine days left, then dropped six straight games to ruin its season.

Nonetheless, the Phillies should enter 2004 with as much optimism as they did in 2003. While the Braves and Marlins have lost key players because of salary constraints, and the Expos and Mets continue to search for direction, the Phillies are moving into Citizens Bank Park and will generate considerably more revenue there.

The Phillies will bring back their entire 2003 nucleus and spent the offseason retooling the bullpen. They made a quick strike on the trade market to land closer Billy Wagner from the budget-conscious Astros. Righthander Tim Worrell, a free agent who spent the 2003 season as a closer

TOP 30 PROSPECTS

1. Cole Hamels, lhp
2. Gavin Floyd, rhp
3. Ryan Howard, 1b
4. Ryan Madson, rhp
5. Keith Bucktrot, rhp
6. Alfredo Simon, rhp
7. Michael Bourn, of
8. Elizardo Ramirez, rhp
9. Juan Richardson, 3b
10. Terry Jones, 3b
11. Anderson Machado, ss
12. Kiel Fisher, 3b
13. Kyle Kendrick, rhp
14. Scott Mathieson, rhp
15. Javon Moran, of
16. Francisco Butto, rhp
17. Chris Roberson, of
18. Josh Hancock, rhp
19. Danny Gonzalez, ss
20. Jake Blalock, of
21. Jorge Padilla, of
22. Tim Moss, 2b
23. Robinson Tejeda, rhp
24. Carlos Rodriguez, ss
25. Zach Segovia, rhp
26. Victor Alvarez, lhp
27. Seung Lee, rhp
28. Matt Squires, lhp
29. Welinson Baez, 3b
30. Joe Wilson, lhp

By Will Kimmey

for the Giants, was added as a set-up man. The Wagner deal cost the Phillies major league righthander Brandon Duckworth and two more righties who would have appeared near the top of their prospects list in Taylor Buchholz and Ezequiel Astacio.

All three pitchers came from the organization's recently productive farm system. It allowed the Phillies to make the deal and should provide a solid backbone as the they push to make their first playoff appearance since the 1993 World Series. It has produced everyday players Pat Burrell, Mike Lieberthal and Jimmy Rollins, and over the last year plugged in Marlon Byrd, Brett Myers and Chase Utley.

Because many of the system's top prospects have graduated to the majors, there isn't much high-end talent ready for Philadelphia in 2004. But there's plenty of help on the horizon with two of the game's top pitching prospects, Cole Hamels and Gavin Floyd, just a year or two away.

Hamels and Floyd are a testament to the system's greatest strength: pitching. Overall, the Phillies have decent prospects at multiple positions and at multiple levels, even though they've forfeited five of their 12 picks in the first three rounds over the past four drafts because of free-agent signings. Philadelphia has also implemented a newly proficient Latin American scouting program.

ORGANIZATION
OVERVIEW

General manager: Ed Wade. **Farm director:** Steve Noworyta. **Scouting director:** Marti Wolever.

2003 PERFORMANCE

Class	Team	League	W	L	Pct.	Finish*	Manager
Majors	Philadelphia	National	86	76	.531	6th (16)	Larry Bowa
Triple-A	Scranton/W-B Red Barons	International	73	70	.510	t-7th (14)	Marc Bombard
Double-A	Reading Phillies	Eastern	62	79	.440	t-10th (12)	Greg Legg
High A	Clearwater Phillies	Florida State	72	61	.541	4th (12)	Roly deArmas
Low A	Lakewood BlueClaws	South Atlantic	57	81	.413	14th (16)	Buddy Biancalana
Short-season	Batavia Muckdogs	New York-Penn	30	45	.400	12th (14)	Luis Melendez
Rookie	GCL Phillies	Gulf Coast	23	33	.411	12th (12)	Ruben Amaro Sr.
OVERALL 2003 MINOR LEAGUE RECORD			317	369	.462	27th (30)	

*Finish in overall standings (No. of teams in league)

ORGANIZATION LEADERS

BATTING *Minimum 250 At-Bats
*AVG	Chase Utley, Scranton	.323
R	Jeff Inglin, Reading	86
H	Jeff Inglin, Reading	153
TB	Jeff Inglin, Reading	254
2B	Travis Chapman, Scranton	36
3B	Jake Blalock, Batavia	7
HR	Jeff Inglin, Reading	24
RBI	Jeff Inglin, Reading	103
BB	Anderson Machado, Reading	108
SO	Ryan Howard, Clearwater	151
SB	Chris Roberson, Lakewood	59
*SLG	Chase Utley, Scranton	.517
*OBP	Chase Utley, Scranton	.390

PITCHING #Minimum 75 Innings
W	Ezequiel Astacio, Clearwater	15
L	Francisco Butto, Lakewood	12
	Matt Sweeney, Lakewood	12
#ERA	Cole Hamels, Clearwater/Lakewood	1.34
G	Jim Crowell, Scranton	54
CG	Amaury Telemaco, Scranton	3
	Layne Dawson, Reading/Clearwater	3
SV	Bobby Korecky, Clearwater	25
IP	Josh Hancock, Scranton	166
BB	Nick Bourgeois, Lakewood	62
SO	Cole Hamels, Clearwater/Lakewood	147
	Ryan Madson, Scranton/Clearwater	147

BEST TOOLS

Best Hitter for Average	Ryan Howard
Best Power Hitter	Ryan Howard
Fastest Baserunner	Michael Bourn
Best Athlete	Chris Roberson
Best Fastball	Alfredo Simon
Best Curveball	Gavin Floyd
Best Slider	Seung Lee
Best Changeup	Ryan Madson
Best Control	Cole Hamels
Best Defensive Catcher	Tim Gradoville
Best Defensive Infielder	Anderson Machado
Best Infield Arm	Anderson Machado
Best Defensive Outfielder	Chris Roberson
Best Outfield Arm	Chris Roberson

PROJECTED 2007 LINEUP

Catcher	Mike Lieberthal
First Base	Jim Thome
Second Base	Chase Utley
Third Base	Juan Richardson
Shortstop	Jimmy Rollins
Left Field	Pat Burrell
Center Field	Marlon Byrd
Right Field	Bobby Abreu
No. 1 Starter	Brett Myers
No. 2 Starter	Kevin Millwood
No. 3 Starter	Cole Hamels
No. 4 Starter	Gavin Floyd
No. 5 Starter	Randy Wolf
Closer	Billy Wagner

LAST YEAR'S TOP 20 PROSPECTS

1. Gavin Floyd, rhp
2. Chase Utley, 2b/3b
3. Marlon Byrd, of
4. Taylor Buchholz, rhp
5. Cole Hamels, lhp
6. Ryan Madson, rhp
7. Anderson Machado, ss
8. Ryan Howard, 1b
9. Elizardo Ramirez, rhp
10. Zach Segovia, rhp
11. Seung Lee, rhp
12. Jorge Padilla, of
13. Keith Bucktrot, rhp
14. Juan Richardson, 3b
15. Carlos Cabrera, rhp
16. Erick Arteaga, rhp
17. Carlos Rodriguez, ss
18. Brad Baisley, rhp
19. Eric Valent, of
20. Jake Blalock, of/3b

TOP PROSPECTS OF THE DECADE

1994	Tyler Green, rhp
1995	Scott Rolen, 3b
1996	Scott Rolen, 3b
1997	Scott Rolen, 3b
1998	Ryan Brannan, rhp
1999	Pat Burrell, 1b
2000	Pat Burrell, 1b/of
2001	Jimmy Rollins, ss
2002	Marlon Byrd, of
2003	Gavin Floyd, rhp

TOP DRAFT PICKS OF THE DECADE

1994	Carlton Loewer, rhp
1995	Reggie Taylor, of
1996	Adam Eaton, rhp
1997	*J.D. Drew, of
1998	Pat Burrell, 1b
1999	Brett Myers, rhp
2000	Chase Utley, 2b
2001	Gavin Floyd, rhp
2002	Cole Hamels, lhp
2003	Tim Moss, 2b (3)

*Did not sign

ALL-TIME LARGEST BONUSES

Gavin Floyd, 2001	$4,200,000
Pat Burrell, 1998	$3,150,000
Brett Myers, 1999	$2,050,000
Cole Hamels, 2002	$2,000,000
Chase Utley, 2000	$1,780,000

MINOR LEAGUE
DEPTH CHART

PHILADELPHIA PHILLIES RANK: 21

Impact potential (B): The system is in position to feed the parent club with two of the most promising pitching prospects in baseball a couple of years from now, but beyond that it's difficult to count any sure things.

Depth (D): To keep up in the National League East, the Phillies have brought in veteran talent. Free agents cost them their first two draft picks in 2003, and in the trade market it cost them power righthander Taylor Buchholz. The good news is they retained all their picks for the 2004 draft, and they continue to get a steady flow of talent from Latin America.

Sleeper: Francisco Butto, rhp. —*Depth charts prepared by **Josh Boyd**. Numbers in parentheses indicate prospect rankings.*

LF
Jake Blalock (20)
Jason Crosland

CF
Michael Bourn (7)
Javon Moran (15)
Chris Roberson (17)
Josue Perez

RF
Jorge Padilla (21)

3B
Juan Richardson (9)
Terry Jones (10)
Kiel Fisher (12)
Welinson Baez (29)
Sean Walsh

SS

Anderson Machado (11)
Danny Gonzalez (19)
Carlos Rodriguez (24)

2B
Tim Moss (22)
Nick Italiano

1B
Ryan Howard (3)
Bryan Hansen

SOURCE OF TALENT

Homegrown		Acquired	
College	6	Trade	1
Junior College	1	Rule 5 draft	0
Draft-and-follow	0	Independent	0
High school	12	Free agent/waivers	1
Nondrafted free agent	0		
Foreign	9		

C
Tim Gradoville
Russ Jacobson

RHP

Starters	Relievers
Gavin Floyd (2)	Eric Junge
Ryan Madson (4)	Geoff Geary
Keith Bucktrot (5)	Jean Machi
Alfredo Simon (6)	Jeremy Wedel
Elizardo Ramirez (8)	Lee Gwaltney
Kyle Kendrick (13)	Taft Cable
Scott Mathieson (14)	Darin Naatjes
Francisco Butto (16)	Dan Giese
Josh Hancock (18)	Brad Ziegler
Robinson Tejeda (23)	
Zach Segovia (25)	
Seung Lee (27)	
Clemente Doble	
Yoel Hernandez	

LHP

Starters	Relievers
Cole Hamels (1)	Matt Squires (28)
Kyle Parcus	Joe Wilson (30)
	Victor Alvarez (26)
	Nick Bourgeois
	Greg Kubes

DRAFT
ANALYSIS

2003 DRAFT

Best Pro Debut: OF Javon Moran (5) led the short-season New York-Penn League with 27 steals and hit .284-1-12. If he had signed quicker, OF Michael Bourn (4) would have grabbed that title because he swiped 23 bases and batted .280 in 25 fewer games. LHP Joe Wilson (13) went 5-3, 2.14 with 72 strikeouts in 64 innings between the Rookie-level Gulf Coast League and the NY-P. LHP Dan Hodges (26) went 2-0, 0.99 with four saves between the NY-P and low Class A.

Best Athlete: The Phillies used their top three picks on speedsters with 2B Tim Moss (3), Bourn and Moran. Bourn is the fastest but isn't as strong as the other two. RHP Kyle Kendrick (7) turned down a scholarship to play quarterback at Washington State and starred in basketball for his high school team.

Best Pure Hitter: Bourn accepts his role better than Moss and Moran do. He draws more walks and focuses on getting on base.

Best Raw Power: OF Jason Crosland (9), who finished third in the national junior college ranks with 23 homers in 2003, has more strength than 1B Matt Hopper (10).

Fastest Runner: Bourn goes from the left side to first in 3.8-3.9 seconds. Over a longer distance, Moss might catch him.

Best Defensive Player: Bourn and Moran both cover the gaps from center field and have fringe-average arms.

Moss

Best Fastball: RHP Nate Cabrera (16) reached 94 mph in the spring but didn't match that velocity after signing because he came down with a tender arm. RHP Matt Linder (8) hit 92-93 mph before the draft.

Best Breaking Ball: Hodges' screwball is so good that it allows him to succeed with a fastball that rarely breaks 80 mph.

Most Intriguing Background: C Jose Cortez (14) tied the NCAA Division III career record with 70 homers.

Closest To The Majors: Moran or Bourn. They're ahead of Moss, who hit .150 in the NY-P.

Best Late-Round Pick: Wilson surprised the Phillies with the quality of his stuff. LHP Derek Griffith (17) has a 6-foot-6 frame and would have gone 10 rounds earlier had he not had Tommy John surgery in April.

The One Who Got Away: A quarterback recruited by several NCAA Division I football programs, RHP Greg Reynolds (41) will play baseball only at Stanford. He could blossom into a 2006 first-rounder.

Assessment: The Phillies put a lot of faith in the speed of Moss, Bourn and Moran. If they don't drive the ball often enough to be effective offensive players, this draft could be thin. Surrendering their top two picks for free agents Jim Thome and David Bell also hurt their effort.

2002 DRAFT   GRADE: B

LHP Cole Hamels (1) was sensational in his 2003 pro debut. The rest of this crop has been slow to develop.

2001 DRAFT   GRADE: B+

RHP Gavin Floyd (1) has been everything he was advertised to be. 1B Ryan Howard (5) is easily the system's best hitting prospect.

2000 DRAFT   GRADE: C+

RHP Taylor Buchholz (6) ranked right behind Hamels and Floyd before the Phillies used him as the key prospect in the Billy Wagner trade. 2B Chase Utley (1) could start for Philadelphia this year.

1999 DRAFT   GRADE: A

RHP Brett Myers (1) and OF Marlon Byrd (10) are all-stars in the making. Myers is one of the best No. 4 starters in baseball and should move up in the rotation before too long, while Byrd already is the Phillies' best center fielder since Lenny Dykstra.

—Draft analysis prepared by Jim Callis. Numbers in parentheses indicate draft rounds.

DAVID SCHOFIELD

Cole
Hamels

Born: Dec. 27, 1983.
Ht.: 6-3. **Wt.:** 170.
Bats: L. **Throws:** L.
School: Rancho Bernardo HS, San Diego.
Career Transactions: Selected by Phillies in first round (17th overall) of 2002 draft; signed Aug. 28, 2002.

Hamels had nothing but question marks entering his pro career and has provided only exclamation points since signing. He ranked as one of the top pitchers in the 2002 draft, but a broken humerus in his left arm caused him to miss his junior season at Rancho Bernardo High and slip to the 17th overall pick. He originally injured his arm in an off-field accident and aggravated it by pitching. He had surgery performed by the Padres team doctor in his native San Diego and rehabbed with pitching guru Tom House before returning and impressing as a high school senior. Protracted contract negotiations kept Hamels away from baseball before he agreed to a $2 million bonus, and then he showed up out of shape from the long layoff. Because he got little done in instructional league, the Phillies sent him to extended spring training in 2003. Once they turned him loose, he dominated the low Class A South Atlantic and high Class A Florida State leagues. His combined 1.34 ERA would have led the minors had Hamels accumulated 11 more innings to qualify. He allowed just 15 earned runs and not a single home run all season. His command, stuff and feel for pitching allowed him to edge Gavin Floyd for the top spot, and being lefthanded also aided Hamels' cause.

Hamels should have three above-average pitches when he reaches the majors. He already shows plus command of a fastball that sits between 89-92 mph with plenty of movement. He can reach back for more when he needs it, topping out at 94. His best pitch might be his plus-plus changeup, which was neck-and-neck with Ryan Madson's as the best in the organization and possibly the minors. Hamels displays exceptional control of his changeup at such a young age, and it drops and fades away from hitters. Hamels shows a businesslike demeanor, with no great highs or lows. He's a great athlete, allowing him to repeat his delivery, hold runners and field his position well. Hamels' curveball should become a third plus pitch, and its movement is already there. He just needs to develop more consistency with the curve. His overall command and control are advanced for his age—and ahead of where Floyd and Brett Myers were at similar stages in their development—but he can continue to improve it as he progresses.

Hamels hasn't experienced any repercussions from his high school arm injury. A pulled muscle in his right shoulder blade caused the Phillies to remove him from the trials for Team USA's Olympic qualifying squad. The minor injury isn't a long-term concern, and he should begin 2004 on schedule by returning to high Class A Clearwater. He'll be challenged in Double-A Reading as soon as he proves he's ready.

Year	Club (League)	Class	W	L	ERA	G	GS	CG	SV	IP	H	R	ER	HR	BB	SO	AVG
2003	Lakewood (SAL)	A	6	1	0.84	13	13	1	0	75	32	8	7	0	25	115	.136
	Clearwater (FSL)	A	0	2	2.73	5	5	0	0	26	29	9	8	0	14	32	.299
MINOR LEAGUE TOTALS			6	3	1.34	18	18	1	0	101	61	17	15	0	39	147	.183

2 Gavin Floyd, rhp

Born: Jan. 27, 1983. **Ht.:** 6-5. **Wt.:** 210. **Bats:** R. **Throws:** R. **School:** Mount St. Joseph HS, Baltimore. **Career Transactions:** Selected by Phillies in first round (fourth overall) of 2001 draft; signed Aug. 24, 2001.

Floyd would rank as the top prospect in many other organizations. He signed for a club-record $4.2 million as the fourth overall pick in 2001—one spot before fellow Mount St. Joseph High product Mark Teixeira. Philadelphia signed Gavin's older brother Mike, an outfielder, as a 22nd-rounder out of the same draft. Floyd entered his pro career with two plus pitches, a 92-95 mph fastball with movement, and a shoulders-to-shoelaces hard curveball that rates 80 on the 20-80 scouting scale at times. His main focus since has been developing a changeup, which now rates average. Floyd works hard at improving his skills and shows above-average makeup. A longtime fan of Kevin Millwood, Floyd tried to emulate his idol's deliberate delivery after watching him in spring training. It cost Floyd his rhythm and deceptiveness, and it took a month to remedy the problem. He must continue to hone his location and ability to repeat pitches, but he's still ahead of most pitchers his age. Floyd's development is right on track. He'll move up to Double-A in 2004, and the pitching depth in the organization means the Phillies won't have to rush him.

Year	Club (League)	Class	W	L	ERA	G	GS	CG	SV	IP	H	R	ER	HR	BB	SO	AVG
2002	Lakewood (SAL)	A	11	10	2.77	27	27	3	0	166	119	59	51	13	64	140	.200
2003	Clearwater (FSL)	A	7	8	3.00	24	20	1	0	138	128	61	46	9	45	115	.247
MINOR LEAGUE TOTALS			18	18	2.87	51	47	4	0	304	247	120	97	22	109	255	.222

3 Ryan Howard, 1b

Born: Nov. 19, 1979. **Ht.:** 6-4. **Wt.:** 230. **Bats:** L. **Throws:** L. **School:** Southwest Missouri State University. **Career Transactions:** Selected by Phillies in fifth round of 2001 draft; signed July 2, 2001.

Howard was a potential first-round pick before a junior slump that included a school-record 74 strikeouts. He ended up being a nice prize in the fifth round, leading the Florida State League in batting and homers in 2003, and missing the triple crown by seven RBIs. Howard has legitimate power to all fields, especially on low pitches, and even launched a blast over the batter's eye behind the 400-foot center-field wall in Clearwater. He has made progress in his approach as an all-around hitter, opening his stance to better handle inside pitches. He has proven to be a surprisingly good defender for a big man, with average range and plus hands. Howard still has work to do in identifying pitches. As a power hitter, he'll always strike out some, but he needs to trim his lofty totals. As he matures as a hitter, Howard should learn to wait for specific pitches and to take or foul off those he can't drive. There's no reason Howard can't reach 35 homers a year in the majors. His power should play fine in Double-A in 2004. He won't be rushed because of Jim Thome's presence in Philadelphia, but likely will be ready before Thome's contract expires after 2008.

Year	Club (League)	Class	AVG	G	AB	R	H	2B	3B	HR	RBI	BB	SO	SB	SLG	OBP
2001	Batavia (NY-P)	A	.272	48	169	26	46	7	3	6	35	30	55	0	.456	.384
2002	Lakewood (SAL)	A	.280	135	493	56	138	20	6	19	87	66	145	5	.460	.367
2003	Clearwater (FSL)	A	.304	130	490	67	149	32	1	23	82	50	151	0	.514	.374
MINOR LEAGUE TOTALS			.289	313	1152	149	333	59	10	48	204	146	351	5	.483	.373

4 Ryan Madson, rhp

Born: Aug. 28, 1980. **Ht.:** 6-6. **Wt.:** 180. **Bats:** L. **Throws:** R. **School:** Valley View HS, Moreno Valley, Calif. **Career Transactions:** Selected by Phillies in ninth round of 1998 draft; signed June 10, 1998.

Madson has reached double-digits in wins three times since 2000, and rebounded from an off year in 2001 by becoming more aggressive and attacking hitters on the inside half of the plate. He started the 2003 Triple-A all-star game for the International League. Madson's father wouldn't let him throw a curveball in Little League, so he had to settle for a changeup. It has emerged as a plus-plus pitch, edging Cole Hamels' as the system's best. It has natural movement, and some hitters think it's a splitter or breaking ball. Madson's two-seam fastball sits at 90 mph and touches 92. It has sinking action and runs away from righthanded hitters. He junked his curveball for a slider, which improved over the season. Madson could stand to add muscle to his lanky frame, especially his lower half, to increase his velocity and durability. Madson will have a shot to win the fifth starter's role in Philadelphia this spring. He made a positive impression with pitching coach Joe Kerrigan during his September callup last year.

Year	Club (League)	Class	W	L	ERA	G	GS	CG	SV	IP	H	R	ER	HR	BB	SO	AVG
1998	Martinsville (Appy)	R	3	3	4.83	12	10	0	0	54	57	38	29	5	20	52	.265
1999	Batavia (NY-P)	A	5	5	4.72	15	15	0	0	88	80	51	46	5	43	75	.247
2000	Piedmont (SAL)	A	14	5	2.59	21	21	2	0	136	113	50	39	5	45	123	.225
2001	Clearwater (FSL)	A	9	9	3.90	22	21	1	0	118	137	68	51	4	49	101	.291
2002	Reading (EL)	AA	16	4	3.20	26	26	2	0	171	150	68	61	11	53	132	.242
2003	Clearwater (FSL)	A	0	0	5.63	2	2	0	0	8	11	5	5	0	2	9	.324
	Scranton/W-B (IL)	AAA	12	8	3.50	26	26	0	0	157	157	70	61	9	42	138	.262
	Philadelphia (NL)	MAJ	0	0	0.00	1	0	0	0	2	0	0	0	0	0	0	.000
MAJOR LEAGUE TOTALS			0	0	0.00	1	0	0	0	2	0	0	0	0	0	0	.000
MINOR LEAGUE TOTALS			59	34	3.59	124	121	5	0	731	705	350	292	39	254	630	.255

5 Keith Bucktrot, rhp

Born: Nov. 27, 1980. **Ht.:** 6-2. **Wt.:** 180. **Bats:** L. **Throws:** R. **School:** Claremore (Okla.) HS. **Career Transactions:** Selected by Phillies in third round of 2000 draft; signed June 26, 2000.

Bucktrot always had the makings of plus stuff, but his mechanics were so inconsistent that some teams liked him better as a hitter during his high school career. He improved his command and trimmed his walks per nine innings from 4.4 in 2002 to 2.5 in 2003. Bucktrot improved as much as anyone in the organization in 2003, and part of the credit goes to his makeup. Asked to repeat high Class A, he worked hard and improved the quality of his pitches after getting to Double-A. His heavy fastball sits in the 92-94 mph range with sinking action. It touched 95-96 more often in instructional league. His changeup is a solid-average pitch. Bucktrot switched from a curveball to a slurve, an intermediate step to a hard slider. It should be at least average but is still inconsistent. Despite his repertoire, he doesn't strike out many hitters. Bucktrot reported to the Arizona Fall League, but felt an elbow twinge and was pulled off the roster. He'll begin 2004 back in Double-A but once he's ready, the Phillies won't hesitate to make room for him in what could become a crowded Triple-A rotation.

Year	Club (League)	Class	W	L	ERA	G	GS	CG	SV	IP	H	R	ER	HR	BB	SO	AVG
2000	Phillies (GCL)	R	3	2	4.78	11	7	0	0	38	39	21	20	5	19	40	.267
2001	Lakewood (SAL)	A	6	11	5.28	24	24	3	0	135	139	93	79	16	58	97	.269
2002	Clearwater (FSL)	A	8	9	4.88	27	24	2	0	160	167	101	87	10	78	84	.276
2003	Clearwater (FSL)	A	7	7	3.33	19	17	0	0	111	104	50	41	8	29	68	.250
	Reading (EL)	AA	3	1	2.56	7	7	0	0	46	34	17	13	3	15	30	.217
MINOR LEAGUE TOTALS			27	30	4.42	88	79	5	0	489	483	282	240	42	199	319	.263

6 Alfredo Simon, rhp

Born: May 8, 1981. **Ht.:** 6-4. **Wt.:** 215. **Bats:** R. **Throws:** R. **Career Transactions:** Signed out of Dominican Republic by Phillies, July 2, 1999.

Simon posted three solid seasons in the organization while known as Carlos Cabrera, before visa problems revealed his true name and birthdate (21 months earlier than originally believed). Once he was allowed to re-enter the United States last June, he pitched well and continued to mature physically. His massive 6-foot-4 frame has grown from 174 pounds when he signed to 215. Simon runs his fastball into the 93-96 mph range and should reach 98 when he finishes filling out. His heater bores in on hitters, sawing off bats and making solid contact difficult. His physical size and arm strength give him plenty of durability. Simon must develop consistency with his secondary pitches. His changeup is too soft, allowing hitters to recognize it and tee off. He has gone from a curveball to a power slider while trying to find an effective breaking ball. Repeating his delivery better, and the mechanics on these two pitches specifically, would help. While he could still emerge as a middle-of-the-rotation starter, it's more likely Simon will become a late-inning reliever. He'll work on all of his pitches as a high Class A starter in 2004.

Year	Club (League)	Class	W	L	ERA	G	GS	CG	SV	IP	H	R	ER	HR	BB	SO	AVG
2000	Phillies (DSL)	R	0	0	1.46	4	4	0	0	12	6	3	2	0	9	10	.136
2001	Phillies (GCL)	R	2	2	2.91	10	8	0	0	43	35	23	14	2	23	40	.220
2002	Batavia (NY-P)	A	9	2	3.59	15	14	0	0	90	79	44	36	5	46	77	.237
2003	Lakewood (SAL)	A	5	0	3.79	14	7	0	2	71	59	32	30	4	25	66	.224
MINOR LEAGUE TOTALS			16	4	3.40	43	33	0	2	217	179	102	82	11	103	193	.224

7 Michael Bourn, of

Born: Dec. 27, 1982. **Ht.:** 5-11. **Wt.:** 180. **Bats:** L. **Throws:** R. **School:** University of Houston. **Career Transactions:** Selected by Phillies in fourth round of 2003 draft; signed July 24, 2003.

An excellent high school athlete and scholar, Bourn turned down the Astros as a 19th-round pick in 2000 in favor of a scholarship to Houston. Though hampered at times by a broken hamate bone and sore hamstring, Bourn stole 90 bases in three seasons with the Cougars and ranked fifth in the short-season New York-Penn League in his pro debut. Bourn is a Kenny Lofton type and he knows it. He doesn't try to do too much and is content to work a walk or lay down a bunt. His top-of-the-line speed comes with quick acceleration, making him play even faster. He's an obvious threat on the bases and tracks down everything in center field. Bourn's arm strength is fringe average, but his reads and instincts still make him an above-average defender. He's not a home run hitter by any means, but he can shoot balls into the gaps when he gets his pitch. Bourn and fellow 2003 draftee Javon Moran are similar players. They'll continue alternating between left and center field at low Class A Lakewood in 2004. The Phillies hope Bourn can become a leadoff hitter with game-changing skills.

Year	Club (League)	Class	AVG	G	AB	R	H	2B	3B	HR	RBI	BB	SO	SB	SLG	OBP
2003	Batavia (NY-P)	A	.280	35	125	12	35	0	1	0	4	23	28	23	.296	.404
MINOR LEAGUE TOTALS			.280	35	125	12	35	0	1	0	4	23	28	23	.296	.404

8 Elizardo Ramirez, rhp

Born: Jan. 28, 1983. **Ht.:** 6-0. **Wt.:** 140. **Bats:** R. **Throws:** R. **Career Transactions:** Signed out of Dominican Republic by Phillies, July 2, 1999.

Ramirez jumped from the Rookie-level Gulf Coast League to high Class A in 2003 and made the move look much like his nickname, "Easy." He didn't repeat his 73-2 strikeout-walk ratio from 2002, but still registered a 101-33 mark. His composure, command, desire and build recall a young Pedro Martinez, but Ramirez doesn't have that kind of stuff. Ramirez has a loose arm and an easy, compact delivery that should allow him to be a workhorse. His fastball sits at 90 mph and tops out at 91-92. He throws an average curveball and changeup. Ramirez succeeds because of his advanced feel for pitching and excellent location. While his command is impressive, Ramirez' strikeout and hit rates were troubling, owing to average stuff across the board. He must stay sharp and maintain a consistent delivery, being careful not to be too precise by working around batters he can retire. Ramirez also can become more consistent with his breaking ball. Ramirez could repeat high Class A because of his youth and a glut of pitchers ahead of him in the system. If there's an open spot in the Double-A rotation, however, he'll be ready for it.

Year	Club (League)	Class	W	L	ERA	G	GS	CG	SV	IP	H	R	ER	HR	BB	SO	AVG
2000	Phillies (DSL)	R	5	2	1.88	11	9	0	1	57	47	19	12	1	5	67	.216
2001	Phillies (DSL)	R	10	1	1.26	14	14	1	0	93	71	26	13	0	9	81	.208
2002	Phillies (GCL)	R	7	1	1.10	11	11	2	0	73	44	18	9	3	2	73	.165
2003	Clearwater (FSL)	A	13	9	3.78	27	25	1	0	157	181	85	66	4	33	101	.290
MINOR LEAGUE TOTALS			35	13	2.36	63	59	4	1	381	343	148	100	8	49	322	.237

9 Juan Richardson, 3b

Born: Jan. 27, 1979. **Ht.:** 6-1. **Wt.:** 170. **Bats:** R. **Throws:** R. **Career Transactions:** Signed out of Dominican Republic by Phillies, July 1, 1998.

Off-the-field developments have hampered Richardson's progress the last two years. He had two years added to his age, then in 2003 he slipped on the stairs at his home and badly sprained his ankle. The injury ended his season in June, just after he had been named to the Eastern League all-star team while leading the circuit in home runs. The injury problems continued in the offfseason, as Richardson had surgery to repair a torn labrum in his throwing shoulder. When healthy, Richardson ranks behind only Howard for pure power in the organization. He probably won't ever hit for much average, but he could produce 30-35 homers annually. He's an average third baseman with an average arm, and he improved his range in 2003. Plate discipline has been Richardson's undoing. Like many power hitters he's eager at the plate, and he must lay off breaking balls in the dirt. His defense often mimics his performance at the plate. Because he missed half the year in Double-A, Richardson will probably return there when he's ready to play. He'll likely miss the first month of the season. The best all-around third baseman in the system, Richardson could take over in Philadelphia by 2005 if he stays healthy.

Year	Club (League)	Class	AVG	G	AB	R	H	2B	3B	HR	RBI	BB	SO	SB	SLG	OBP
1999	Phillies (GCL)	R	.226	46	164	27	37	14	0	5	23	11	46	7	.402	.290
	Piedmont (SAL)	A	.167	4	12	0	2	1	0	0	2	1	5	0	.250	.231
	Batavia (NY-P)	A	.125	7	24	1	3	0	0	1	2	2	8	0	.250	.222
2000	Piedmont (SAL)	A	.242	43	149	19	36	11	0	2	15	17	43	0	.356	.327
	Batavia (NY-P)	A	.154	10	39	0	6	2	0	0	2	3	15	0	.205	.214
2001	Lakewood (SAL)	A	.240	137	505	68	121	31	2	22	83	51	147	7	.440	.325
2002	Clearwater (FSL)	A	.257	122	456	52	117	21	2	18	83	44	122	0	.430	.339
2003	Reading (EL)	AA	.270	65	248	37	67	9	0	15	34	17	69	2	.488	.327
MINOR LEAGUE TOTALS			.244	434	1597	204	389	89	4	63	244	146	455	16	.423	.321

10 Terry Jones, 3b

RODGER WOOD

Born: March 20, 1983. **Ht.:** 6-2. **Wt.:** 190. **Bats:** R. **Throws:** R. **School:** Upland (Calif.) HS. **Career Transactions:** Selected by Phillies in fourth round of 2001 draft; signed July 26, 2001.

The Phillies used a $500,000 bonus to buy Jones out of a University of California scholarship in 2001, and his skills finally are starting to catch up to the athleticism that turned scouts' eyes during his prep career. He's also a second cousin of NFL quarterback Rodney Peete. Jones has drawn comparisons to Chipper Jones, as both were high school shortstops with solid power. Having the same surname didn't hurt, either. He showed the ability to turn on, lift and drive balls better in 2003. Defensively, he's the best third baseman in the system, owing to his athleticism and average to plus arm. Looking at Jones' raw numbers, it's hard to see a lot of bat potential in a .233 career hitter. But he made strides in 2003, especially after a dreadful .192 average in April. Jones must develop more selectivity at the plate. He often gets overaggressive and tries to do too much. Phillies officials say Jones can be an above-average major league hitter capable of hitting .280 with 20-25 homers annually. He'll work on his patience in high Class A in 2004.

Year	Club (League)	Class	AVG	G	AB	R	H	2B	3B	HR	RBI	BB	SO	SB	SLG	OBP
2001	Phillies (GCL)	R	.194	9	36	3	7	0	0	0	4	2	5	0	.194	.237
2002	Batavia (NY-P)	A	.223	43	157	13	35	8	4	1	16	12	40	5	.344	.297
2003	Lakewood (SAL)	A	.240	129	454	57	109	27	4	11	66	43	111	11	.390	.306
MINOR LEAGUE TOTALS			.233	181	647	73	151	35	8	12	86	57	156	16	.368	.300

11 Anderson Machado, ss

Born: Jan. 25, 1981. **Ht.:** 5-11. **Wt.:** 160. **Bats:** B. **Throws:** R. **Career Transactions:** Signed out of Venezuela by Phillies, Jan. 14, 1998.

After hitting .251-12-77 in 2002, Machado looked ready to head to Triple-A. But the Phillies sent him back to Reading and his 2003 season didn't go as planned. Machado was beset by personal and family problems that led to a deep slump at the plate and culminated with a monthlong hiatus in Venezuela. After the dreadful season ended, Machado headed to instructional league and spent a week with hitting instructor Don Long reworking his swing before going to winter ball. He changed his set-up at the plate, which had created a loop in his swing, and worked to remove an uppercut from his stroke. That adjustment would allow him to hit more grounders and make better use of his above-average speed. While Machado always had nice pop for his size, he must focus on working counts and playing small ball. Defensively, he's without parallel in the system and could serve as a first-division shortstop immediately. He has above-average hands, range and arm strength. He committed 26 errors last year, but organization officials attribute those to his wide range and youth. He'll finally get that trip to Scranton this year, which should determine if he's an everyday major leaguer, utility player or slick-fielding shortstop without an offensive game.

Year	Club (League)	Class	AVG	G	AB	R	H	2B	3B	HR	RBI	BB	SO	SB	SLG	OBP
1998	Phillies (DSL)	R	.201	68	219	26	44	7	0	0	17	30	44	4	.233	.313
1999	Phillies (GCL)	R	.259	43	143	26	37	6	3	2	12	15	38	6	.385	.335
	Clearwater (FSL)	A	.000	1	2	0	0	0	0	0	0	0	1	0	.000	.000
	Piedmont (SAL)	A	.233	20	60	7	14	4	2	0	7	7	20	2	.367	.324
2000	Clearwater (FSL)	A	.245	117	417	55	102	19	7	1	35	54	103	32	.331	.330
	Reading (EL)	AA	.364	3	11	2	4	1	0	1	2	0	4	0	.727	.364
2001	Clearwater (FSL)	A	.261	82	272	49	71	5	8	5	36	31	66	23	.393	.342
	Reading (EL)	AA	.149	31	101	13	15	2	0	1	8	12	25	5	.198	.237
2002	Reading (EL)	AA	.251	126	450	71	113	24	3	12	77	72	118	40	.398	.353
2003	Reading (EL)	AA	.196	123	423	80	83	19	4	5	20	108	120	49	.296	.360
MINOR LEAGUE TOTALS			.230	614	2098	329	483	87	27	27	214	329	539	161	.336	.337

12 Kiel Fisher, 3b

Born: Sept. 29, 1983. **Ht.:** 6-4. **Wt.:** 190. **Bats:** L. **Throws:** R. **School:** Riverside Poly HS, Riverside, Calif. **Career Transactions:** Selected by Phillies in third round of 2002 draft; signed June 18, 2002.

After forgoing a scholarship to Cal Poly San Luis Obispo and signing with Philadelphia as a surprise third-round pick in 2002, Fisher had a mediocre pro debut. The system's depth at third base kept him in extended spring training to begin 2003, as the Phillies wanted Terry Jones to play every day in low Class A. Fisher continued to struggled during extending spring, so he went to the Gulf Coast League when short-season play started. His bat finally got going, and improved again after a promotion to short-season Batavia. The key to Fisher's success was eliminating a loop in his swing, allowing him to be quicker to the ball and make use of his natural bat speed and loft. He projects average to plus power and makes adjustments well enough to hit for a solid average. He draws a good amount of walks for a young player, stays back on breaking balls and crushes fastballs. Defensively, Fisher shows average range with suitable feet and hands at third. He's big and built well, so a switch to first base or the outfield might be necessary. There's no doubt his bat would play at a more power-driven position. He'll head to Lakewood in 2004.

Year	Club (League)	Class	AVG	G	AB	R	H	2B	3B	HR	RBI	BB	SO	SB	SLG	OBP
2002	Phillies (GCL)	R	.229	35	105	9	24	4	1	3	20	13	34	1	.371	.322
2003	Phillies (GCL)	R	.323	29	96	16	31	6	3	1	13	18	21	4	.479	.429
	Batavia (NY-P)	A	.340	26	97	12	33	4	2	1	11	13	26	3	.454	.420
MINOR LEAGUE TOTALS			.295	90	298	37	88	14	6	5	44	44	81	8	.433	.389

13 Kyle Kendrick, rhp

Born: Aug. 26, 1984. **Ht.:** 6-3. **Wt.:** 185. **Bats:** R. **Throws:** R. **School:** Mount Vernon (Wash.) HS. **Career Transactions:** Selected by Phillies in seventh round of 2003 draft; signed June 25, 2003.

Don't be fooled by Kendrick's 0-4, 5.46 pro debut. He has the makings of a special pitcher, and Phillies assistant GM Mike Arbuckle compares him to a young Jason Schmidt. Like Schmidt, he hails from Washington state, is athletic (he played three sports in high school) and shows the raw ingredients of three plus pitches. Kendrick would have gone earlier than the seventh round last June had teams not been scared off by a scholarship to play quarterback at Washington State. His two-seam fastball has good movement at 89-92 mph and projects to add velocity, while his overhand curveball shows signs of becoming a plus pitch. He also has made strides with his circle changeup, which fades away from lefthanders and is already an average pitch at times. During instructional league, Phillies pitching prospects watched film of Josh Beckett throwing his changeup in the postseason and it gave Kendrick more confidence in his. He fanned three hitters with his changeup in his next instructional league outing. He has shown the aptitude to pick up things quickly and the work ethic to master them. He used to get his head out of line in his delivery, causing him to fall off to the side of the mound. He fixed the problem through video work in instructional league. The key for Kendrick is to get his lanky limbs and quick arm working in unison as he becomes more consistent in repeating what is already a good basic delivery. He'll work on that in 2004 at either Batavia or Lakewood.

Year	Club (League)	Class	W	L	ERA	G	GS	CG	SV	IP	H	R	ER	HR	BB	SO	AVG
2003	Phillies (GCL)	R	0	4	5.46	9	5	0	0	31	40	24	19	3	12	26	.305
MINOR LEAGUE TOTALS			0	4	5.46	9	5	0	0	31	40	24	19	3	12	26	.305

14 Scott Mathieson, rhp

Born: Feb. 27, 1984. **Ht.:** 6-3. **Wt.:** 190. **Bats:** R. **Throws:** R. **School:** Aldergrove (B.C.) SS. **Career Transactions:** Selected by Phillies in 17th round of 2002 draft; signed July 3, 2002.

British Columbia made its presence felt atop the 2002 draft, with Adam Loewen going fourth overall and Jeff Francis following closely at No. 9. Mathieson was the third pitcher selected from B.C.'s lower mainland, though he lasted until the 17th round. The Phillies bought Mathieson, who pitched with Francis and Loewen on national and select teams, out of a scholarship to El Paso (Texas) Junior College. Though he has been hit hard in two Gulf Coast League stints, Mathieson has made significant strides. He even has a new nickname, "The Goose." He has filled out and packed on strength. He also worked several flaws out of his delivery and now has mechanics as smooth as any pitcher in the organization to go along with his loose, quick arm. The result: A fastball that reached 84 mph when he was a high school senior now touches 94 and sits at 90-91. Mathieson also works with a down-breaking curveball with depth and a changeup that sinks and tails. Both pitches are average to above-average. He still has room for more projection, and adding more muscle could result in more added velocity. He'll be tested in low Class A this year.

Year	Club (League)	Class	W	L	ERA	G	GS	CG	SV	IP	H	R	ER	HR	BB	SO	AVG
2002	Phillies (GCL)	R	0	2	5.40	7	2	0	0	17	24	11	10	0	6	14	.338
2003	Phillies (GCL)	R	2	7	5.52	11	11	0	0	59	59	42	36	5	13	51	.247
	Batavia (NY-P)	A	0	0	0.00	2	0	0	1	6	0	0	0	0	0	7	.000
MINOR LEAGUE TOTALS			2	9	5.09	20	13	0	1	81	83	53	46	5	19	72	.253

15 Javon Moran, of

Born: Sept. 30, 1982. **Ht.:** 5-11. **Wt.:** 175. **Bats:** R. **Throws:** R. **School:** Auburn University. **Career Transactions:** Selected by Phillies in fifth round of 2003 draft; signed June 24, 2003.

Speed was the overriding theme of the Phillies' 2003 draft, and Moran fits the bill. He's close to an 80 runner on the 20-80 scouting scale and led the New York-Penn League with 27 steals in his pro debut, though he was caught 11 times. He also uses his speed as a center fielder to outrun balls hit into the gaps. Moran split time between center and left field with fellow 2003 draft pick Michael Bourn as the Phillies wanted each to learn both slots. Moran followed Bourn (a fourth-round pick) in the draft and in the Batavia lineup, often in the No. 2 spot. Though he broke Tim Hudson's Auburn record with 18 multi-hit Southeastern Conference games and led the Tigers in runs for three straight years, he struggled some with the transition from aluminum to wood. Phillies instructors had to teach Moran to trigger with his hands to help add the extra sock he lost without aluminum. He's a singles hitter anyway, but still needs to generate a bit more power to smack balls to the fences and use his speed for extra bases. Moran's build and hitting style remind some of Pokey Reese. He's learning to incorporate more bunting into his game, and he needs to draw more walks as well. Moran will move up to high Class A as the Phillies look to see if there's any separation between him and Bourn.

Year	Club (League)	Class	AVG	G	AB	R	H	2B	3B	HR	RBI	BB	SO	SB	SLG	OBP
2003	Batavia (NY-P)	A	.284	60	250	33	71	9	3	1	12	16	32	27	.356	.326
MINOR LEAGUE TOTALS			.284	60	250	33	71	9	3	1	12	16	32	27	.356	.326

16 Francisco Butto, rhp

Born: May 11, 1980. **Ht.:** 6-1. **Wt.:** 200. **Bats:** R. **Throws:** R. **Career Transactions:** Signed out of Venezuela by Phillies, Feb. 9, 1999.

Butto and Yoel Hernandez are products of the Phillies' improving scouting and developmental efforts in Venezuela. The organizational glut of pitchers at the two Class A levels forced Butto to come out of the bullpen early in 2003 at Clearwater. Once he found a place in the rotation, Butto settled in nicely and reeled off the best year of his pro career. His fastball, which tops out at 93 mph, and breaking ball rate as average and can be a touch above at times. His changeup has a chance to be average. Like Hernandez, Butto has a good feel for pitching and solid command. Butto also spent the 2002 offseason pitching for Aragua in his native Venezuela, and the experience allowed him to grow mentally and emotionally, and made him more confident on the mound. He had another strong winter in the Venezuelan League after the 2003 season, which should further build his confidence. Butto will focus on consistently repeating his delivery and stuff in Double-A. He should fold into the back of a rotation or a middle-relief role in the long term.

Year	Club (League)	Class	W	L	ERA	G	GS	CG	SV	IP	H	R	ER	HR	BB	SO	AVG
1999	La Victoria (VSL)	R	5	2	4.37	15	4	0	1	47	42	24	23	1	32	43	.236
2000	La Victoria (VSL)	R	4	3	2.04	14	9	1	1	62	39	26	14	2	26	76	.182
2001	Phillies (GCL)	R	2	3	2.42	15	0	0	2	26	22	10	7	1	12	20	.232
2002	Phillies (GCL)	R	7	2	2.31	12	9	3	1	62	37	18	16	1	20	52	.176
2003	Lakewood (SAL)	A	10	12	3.03	27	25	2	0	149	134	65	50	8	59	104	.243
MINOR LEAGUE TOTALS			28	22	2.86	83	47	6	5	346	274	143	110	13	149	295	.220

17 Chris Roberson, of

Born: Aug. 23, 1979. **Ht.:** 6-2. **Wt.:** 180. **Bats:** R. **Throws:** R. **School:** Feather River (Calif.) JC. **Career Transactions:** Selected by Phillies in ninth round of 2001 draft; signed June 7, 2001.

Like his father Rick, who played seven seasons in the NBA, Roberson is athletically gifted. He showed signs of parlaying his tools into performance in 2003, especially in the last three months of the season. He started making contact more consistently, a must for a top-of-the-order hitter with plus speed. He stole an organization-high 59 bases and could have pushed into the 80s had he reached base more frequently. He was thrown out 16 times but is continuing to work on getting jumps and running in the right counts. Roberson's strength could produce 15 home runs per year at the major league level, but hitting instructors are discouraging him from loading up right now, stressing the importance of contact. Defensively, Roberson shows plus-plus range in center field, getting great jumps on balls and running everything down. His arm is fringe average. Roberson is less polished than fellow center fielders Michael Bourn and Javon Moran, both 2003 draftees, but has more room for projection as he's a year younger and didn't play in college. He'll move up to high Class A, staying a level ahead of his competition.

Year	Club (League)	Class	AVG	G	AB	R	H	2B	3B	HR	RBI	BB	SO	SB	SLG	OBP
2001	Phillies (GCL)	R	.248	38	133	17	33	8	1	0	13	16	30	6	.323	.336
2002	Batavia (NY-P)	A	.276	62	214	29	59	8	3	2	24	26	51	17	.369	.377
2003	Lakewood (SAL)	A	.234	132	470	64	110	19	5	2	32	57	108	59	.309	.331
MINOR LEAGUE TOTALS			.247	232	817	110	202	35	9	4	69	99	189	82	.327	.344

18 Josh Hancock, rhp

Born: April 11, 1978. **Ht.:** 6-3. **Wt.:** 210. **Bats:** R. **Throws:** R. **School:** Auburn University. **Career Transactions:** Selected by Red Sox in fifth round of 1998 draft; signed June 15, 1998 . . . Traded by Red Sox to Phillies for 1B Jeremy Giambi, Dec. 15, 2002.

The Red Sox wanted Jeremy Giambi and his high on-base percentage, so they sent Hancock to the Phillies at the 2002 Winter Meetings. But as he had in Philadelphia, Giambi fell out of favor quickly in Boston and never made any real impact. Hancock, on the other hand, enjoyed a solid Triple-A season and will compete for the Phillies' No. 5 starter's role this season. It appears to be Ryan Madson's job to lose, but Hancock is more than capable. He shows average stuff across the board, but can boost his fastball from 91 mph to 94 when he needs it. Hancock's curveball and changeup still lack consistency, but at his best, he locates all three pitches on both sides of the plate. He has shown his tough nature over the last two seasons as he's battled back from injury. He returned a month early after a line drive broke his jaw in June 2002, and also healed rapidly after surgery in December 2002 to repair a small tear in his pelvic wall. If the major league pitching staff shakes out the way Phillies executives hope, Hancock will spend his third straight season in Triple-A. But he'll be a nice insurance policy or trade bait.

Year	Club (League)	Class	W	L	ERA	G	GS	CG	SV	IP	H	R	ER	HR	BB	SO	AVG
1998	Red Sox (GCL)	R	1	1	3.38	5	1	0	0	13	9	5	5	1	3	21	.196
	Lowell (NY-P)	A	0	1	2.25	1	1	0	0	4	5	2	1	0	4	4	.333
1999	Augusta (SAL)	A	6	8	3.80	25	25	0	0	140	154	79	59	12	46	106	.279
2000	Sarasota (FSL)	A	5	10	4.45	26	24	1	0	144	164	89	71	9	37	95	.286
2001	Trenton (EL)	AA	8	6	3.65	24	24	0	0	131	138	60	53	8	37	119	.273
2002	Trenton (EL)	AA	3	4	3.61	15	14	2	1	85	82	40	34	9	18	69	.250
	Pawtucket (IL)	AAA	4	2	3.45	8	8	0	0	44	39	20	17	2	26	29	.235
	Boston (AL)	MAJ	0	1	3.68	3	1	0	0	7	5	3	3	1	2	6	.200
2003	Scranton/W-B (IL)	AAA	10	9	3.86	28	27	2	0	166	147	78	71	14	46	122	.238
	Philadelphia (NL)	MAJ	0	0	3.00	2	0	0	0	3	2	1	1	0	0	4	.182
MAJOR LEAGUE TOTALS			0	1	3.48	5	1	0	0	10	7	4	4	1	2	10	.194
MINOR LEAGUE TOTALS			37	41	3.86	132	124	5	1	726	738	373	311	55	217	565	.263

19 Danny Gonzalez, ss

Born: Nov. 20, 1981. **Ht.:** 6-0. **Wt.:** 180. **Bats:** B. **Throws:** R. **School:** Florida Air Academy, Melbourne, Fla. **Career Transactions:** Selected by Phillies in fourth round of 2000 draft; signed Aug. 25, 2000.

The Puerto Rican-born Gonzalez played high school baseball at the Florida Air Academy in Melbourne, where the Phillies found Jorge Padilla two years earlier. While off-field problems caused Anderson Machado and Carlos Rodriguez to regress in 2003, Gonzalez' work ethic made him one of the organization's few shortstops to show improvement last season. While his raw tools aren't as good as theirs, Gonzalez is average across the board and has an outstanding mental approach. He's reliable at shortstop and makes all the routine plays, though he doesn't have the athleticism to complete the exceptional ones. Gonzalez is adept at reading the ball off the bat, enabling him to get to more grounders than his average speed should allow. He's a slap hitter at the plate, where he doesn't try to do too much. Gonzalez did show more pop in 2003, cranking 22 doubles after hitting just 23 the previous two seasons. He'll need to continue getting stronger and enhancing his on-base skills this year in Double-A, because his bat ultimately will decide if he can play every day or serve as a utility infielder.

Year	Club (League)	Class	AVG	G	AB	R	H	2B	3B	HR	RBI	BB	SO	SB	SLG	OBP
2001	Batavia (NY-P)	A	.238	73	281	33	67	9	4	0	20	18	52	1	.299	.289
2002	Lakewood (SAL)	A	.270	131	493	58	133	14	4	4	43	55	88	11	.339	.349
2003	Clearwater (FSL)	A	.271	113	436	62	118	22	5	0	34	49	56	5	.344	.348
MINOR LEAGUE TOTALS			.263	317	1210	153	318	45	13	4	97	122	196	17	.331	.335

20 Jake Blalock, of

Born: Aug. 6, 1983. **Ht.:** 6-4. **Wt.:** 210. **Bats:** R. **Throws:** R. **School:** Rancho Bernardo HS, San Diego. **Career Transactions:** Selected by Phillies in fifth round of 2002 draft; signed July 25, 2002.

Blalock's surname immediately brings to mind his older brother Hank, but let the comparisons end there. Jake bats righthanded and projects to have more power and hit for less average than Hank, and his upside is more comparable to Pat Burrell. Blalock has the raw pop to hit 35 homers annually, and like Burrell has moved to the outfield after playing third base. Blalock, a high school shortstop, projects to be an adequate outfielder with limited range, and his arm strength plays fine in left or right field. He struggled at the plate some in his first full pro season, as he was too pull-conscious and his swing was too long. Blalock must focus on keeping his front shoulder in and using the entire field. He handles offspeed pitches as well as fastballs but gets too aggressive at the plate. He's a hard worker, though he sometimes is too hard on himself. His next stop is low Class A.

Year	Club (League)	Class	AVG	G	AB	R	H	2B	3B	HR	RBI	BB	SO	SB	SLG	OBP
2002	Phillies (GCL)	R	.250	25	88	13	22	6	0	1	13	10	15	3	.352	.317
2003	Batavia (NY-P)	A	.245	72	261	36	64	23	7	5	31	30	81	9	.444	.323
MINOR LEAGUE TOTALS			.246	97	349	49	86	29	7	6	44	40	96	12	.421	.322

21 Jorge Padilla, of

Born: Aug. 11, 1979. **Ht.:** 6-2. **Wt.:** 200. **Bats:** R. **Throws:** R. **School:** Florida Air Academy, Melbourne, Fla. **Career Transactions:** Selected by Phillies in third round of 1998 draft; signed July 19, 1998.

Padilla just can't stay healthy. A foot problem bothered him in 2000, and a hamstring injury cost him a chance at a 20-20 season in 2001. He avoided the disabled list in 2002, but wore down playing a full year. His 2003 season ended in June after he dove for a ball and sustained a stress fracture in his left hand. He returned to instructional league in good shape, and spent a week there to regain his timing before heading to Venezuela for winter ball. Padilla did show an improvement in his plate discipline but still hasn't developed the loft power expected of him. Though his basestealing speed remains, he gets thrown out too much to be a true threat. Padilla is an above-average right fielder and can play center in a pinch. He has an average arm. He was close to a Triple-A promotion when he got hurt, and will head there in 2004. The 30-30 projections and Bobby Abreu comparisons have ceased, and Padilla now seems most likely to end up as a fourth outfielder.

Year	Club (League)	Class	AVG	G	AB	R	H	2B	3B	HR	RBI	BB	SO	SB	SLG	OBP
1998	Martinsville (Appy)	R	.356	23	90	10	32	3	0	5	25	4	24	2	.556	.378
1999	Piedmont (SAL)	A	.208	44	168	13	35	10	1	3	17	5	44	0	.333	.247
	Batavia (NY-P)	A	.252	65	238	28	60	10	1	3	30	22	79	2	.340	.331
2000	Piedmont (SAL)	A	.305	108	413	62	126	24	8	11	67	26	89	8	.482	.346
2001	Clearwater (FSL)	A	.260	100	358	62	93	13	2	16	66	40	73	23	.441	.343
2002	Reading (EL)	AA	.256	127	484	71	124	30	2	7	65	40	77	32	.370	.322
2003	Reading (EL)	AA	.295	46	173	21	51	13	1	2	23	18	29	11	.416	.363
MINOR LEAGUE TOTALS			.271	513	1924	267	521	103	15	47	293	155	415	78	.413	.332

22 Tim Moss, 2b

Born: Jan. 26, 1982. **Ht.:** 5-9. **Wt.:** 150. **Bats:** B. **Throws:** R. **School:** University of Texas. **Career Transactions:** Selected by Phillies in third round of 2003 draft; signed July 10, 2003.

Moss was the first of the three speedsters the Phillies took at the top of their 2003 draft. He's also the least polished. Moss comes from an athletic family, as his father Harry played baseball at Tennessee State and his sister Lanette played tennis at Texas-Arlington. The Phillies say that Moss' superb athleticism allowed him to skate through college with poor fundamentals, which caught up to him as a pro. He has a raw swing that's more suited for an aluminum bat. He has trouble getting his hands started to provide the bat speed and pop that doesn't come as easily with wood. He needs to draw a lot more walks and make a lot more contact to be anything more than a No. 8 hitter. Defensively, Moss has soft hands but needs to significantly improve his footwork. Moss got a late start at Batavia and was tired when he arrived because of a long college season. He struggled at first and then pressed, which caused a further downward spiral. The Phillies believe Moss has the athleticism and work ethic to improve, and they've compared him to Mark McLemore, who plays a similar game and also developed slowly. If Moss makes enough improvement over the offseason, he could begin 2004 in low Class A.

Year	Club (League)	Class	AVG	G	AB	R	H	2B	3B	HR	RBI	BB	SO	SB	SLG	OBP
2003	Batavia (NY-P)	A	.150	43	160	10	24	5	2	1	11	11	47	5	.225	.220
MINOR LEAGUE TOTALS			.150	43	160	10	24	5	2	1	11	11	47	5	.225	.220

23 Robinson Tejeda, rhp

Born: March 24, 1982. **Ht.:** 6-3. **Wt.:** 180. **Bats:** R. **Throws:** R. **Career Transactions:** Signed out of Dominican Republic by Phillies, Nov. 24, 1998.

A typographical error by a Phillies player-development staffer raised a red flag on Tejeda's visa application, delaying his return from the Dominican Republic by four months. He returned to action in late May, but the lost time really ate into Tejeda's development as he missed spring training and had to return to Lakewood after ending 2002 in Clearwater. Whether it had anything to do with the visa process is uncertain, but Tejeda came back to the United States with added maturity, and he focused on playing hard and improving his skills. His delivery and breaking ball were more consistent in 2003 than ever before, and his fastball was clocking in at 93-94 mph. He also throws an average changeup. Tejeda profiles as a back-of-the-rotation starter or middle reliever, but could improve his stock with a solid year of development. Spring training will determine whether he heads to high Class A or Double-A this year.

Year	Club (League)	Class	W	L	ERA	G	GS	CG	SV	IP	H	R	ER	HR	BB	SO	AVG
1999	Phillies (GCL)	R	1	3	4.27	12	9	0	0	46	47	27	22	5	27	39	.273
2000	Phillies (GCL)	R	2	5	5.54	10	6	1	0	39	44	30	24	3	12	22	.273
2001	Lakewood (SAL)	A	8	9	3.40	26	24	1	0	151	128	74	57	10	58	152	.228
2002	Clearwater (FSL)	A	4	8	3.97	17	17	1	0	100	73	48	44	14	48	87	.204
2003	Lakewood (SAL)	A	0	3	5.30	5	4	0	0	19	17	11	11	4	16	20	.246
	Clearwater (FSL)	A	2	4	3.20	11	11	1	0	65	53	25	23	4	23	42	.221
MINOR LEAGUE TOTALS			17	32	3.89	81	71	4	0	419	362	215	181	40	184	362	.232

24 Carlos Rodriguez, ss

Born: Oct. 4, 1983. **Ht.:** 6-0. **Wt.:** 170. **Bats:** B. **Throws:** R. **Career Transactions:** Signed out of Dominican Republic by Phillies, Oct. 13, 2000.

Rodriguez tried the Phillies' patience in 2003. He refused to show focus or take accountability, and his immaturity got him sent home to the Dominican Republic for a month. Makeup questions aside, Rodriguez' tools and abilities rival those of any shortstop in the organization. He has plus arm strength, hands, range and agility. He entered the 2003 season a .293 career hitter before dropping off terribly, but still has the skills to become more than a defense-first shortstop. His above-average bat speed and potential to reach double figures in homers played a large role in the Phillies signing him for $700,000 after a showcase at the 2000 Area Code Games. If Rodriguez doesn't return to spring training in a better frame of mind, his time in the organization could be waning. If he grows up, however, he could develop into a big league regular. He'll give high Class A another try in 2004.

Year	Club (League)	Class	AVG	G	AB	R	H	2B	3B	HR	RBI	BB	SO	SB	SLG	OBP
2001	Phillies (GCL)	R	.297	35	128	22	38	10	1	3	23	11	25	6	.461	.368
2002	Batavia (NY-P)	A	.290	61	248	29	72	7	3	0	15	19	48	21	.343	.351
2003	Lakewood (SAL)	A	.196	93	322	27	63	10	3	0	24	30	63	18	.245	.270
MINOR LEAGUE TOTALS			.248	189	698	78	173	27	7	3	62	60	136	45	.319	.317

25 Zach Segovia, rhp

Born: April 11, 1983. **Ht.:** 6-2. **Wt.:** 220. **Bats:** R. **Throws:** R. **School:** Forney (Texas) HS. **Career Transactions:** Selected by Phillies in second round of 2002 draft; signed July 2, 2002.

Segovia debuted at No. 10 on this list a year ago, but fell after having Tommy John surgery in the fall. He had a solid showing in spring training, but came down with a tender elbow a few starts into his first full season. He didn't tell anyone and tried to continue pitching. The Phillies knew something was wrong when his velocity dipped from 92-93 mph to the mid-80s. Segovia eventually went on the disabled list to rest his arm and tried to rehab it. He saw several doctors and had a few MRIs, but it took until after the season to find out what was wrong. It's the first arm problem Segovia has experienced, and it left both him and the Phillies puzzled and frustrated. He lost a year of development already, and will now miss a significant portion of 2004 as well, if not the entire season. Before he was sidelined, Segovia used a tight-breaking slider and rapidly improving changeup along with his fastball to dominate hitters. He projected as a solid starter with the stuff and mindset to become a closer if needed in the bullpen. The prognosis remains the same if he can put his elbow woes behind him, though surgery sets his timetable back.

Year	Club (League)	Class	W	L	ERA	G	GS	CG	SV	IP	H	R	ER	HR	BB	SO	AVG
2002	Phillies (GCL)	R	3	2	2.10	8	8	0	0	34	21	11	8	0	3	30	.174
2003	Lakewood (SAL)	A	1	5	3.99	11	10	0	0	50	63	25	22	2	14	27	.307
	Phillies (GCL)	R	0	1	4.00	5	4	0	0	9	8	5	4	0	0	6	.235
MINOR LEAGUE TOTALS			4	8	3.29	24	22	0	0	93	92	41	34	2	17	63	.256

26 Victor Alvarez, lhp

Born: Nov. 8, 1976. **Ht.:** 5-10. **Wt.:** 155. **Bats:** L. **Throws:** L. **Career Transactions:** Signed out of Mexico by Dodgers, May 16, 1997 . . . Loaned by Dodgers to Mexico City Red Devils (Mexican), March 18-Oct. 28, 1998 . . . Loaned to Mexico City Red Devils, April 2-June 12, 2000 . . . Claimed off waivers by Phillies from Dodgers, Dec. 20, 2003.

Dan Plesac's retirement left an opening for a lefthanded reliever in the Philadelphia bullpen, and the Phillies found a candidate to replace him when they claimed Alvarez off waivers from the Dodgers. His two main pitches are a 90-91 mph fastball and a slurvy, low-70s breaking ball. He split time between the rotation and bullpen last year in Triple-A, with a 1.71 ERA as a reliever and a 3.69 ERA as a starter. He held lefthanders to a .203 average and projects as a specialist. Alvarez still has to prove he can pitch in the majors. His stuff and slight build haven't intimidated many big league hitters, and he looked a bit scared at times during two brief stints with Los Angeles. If Alvarez can't fill in for Plesac, he'll go to Triple-A.

Year	Club (League)	Class	W	L	ERA	G	GS	CG	SV	IP	H	R	ER	HR	BB	SO	AVG
1997	Dodgers (DSL)	R	2	0	0.90	3	0	0	1	10	4	1	1	1	5	18	.121
	Great Falls (Pio)	R	4	1	3.35	12	8	0	0	48	49	30	18	0	17	50	.261
1998	M.C. Reds (Mex)	AAA	3	4	3.62	22	12	0	2	80	93	39	32	3	49	36	.306
1999	Vero Beach (FSL)	A	4	4	1.97	12	12	1	0	73	56	21	16	4	16	57	.215
	San Antonio (TL)	AA	4	3	3.67	9	9	0	0	56	58	27	23	5	10	43	.266
2000	M.C. Reds (Mex)	AAA	0	2	6.33	7	6	0	0	21	30	15	15	3	14	14	.345
	San Antonio (TL)	AA	0	3	3.91	11	8	0	0	48	44	27	21	3	30	43	.254
	Vero Beach (FSL)	A	1	1	5.16	4	4	0	0	23	17	14	13	6	11	20	.205
2001	Jacksonville (SL)	AA	2	0	1.20	8	8	0	0	45	27	6	6	1	7	40	.176
	Las Vegas (PCL)	AAA	7	4	4.27	20	20	0	0	118	115	63	56	12	41	94	.256
2002	Las Vegas (PCL)	AAA	10	7	4.70	34	15	0	3	123	132	69	64	11	39	106	.278
	Los Angeles (NL)	MAJ	0	1	4.35	4	1	0	0	10	9	5	5	1	2	7	.237
2003	Las Vegas (PCL)	AAA	4	4	2.70	22	7	0	1	63	53	25	19	2	15	47	.255
	Los Angeles (NL)	MAJ	0	1	12.71	5	0	0	0	6	9	8	8	1	6	3	.391
MAJOR LEAGUE TOTALS			0	2	7.31	9	1	0	0	16	18	13	13	2	8	10	.295
MINOR LEAGUE TOTALS			41	33	3.61	164	109	1	7	709	678	337	284	51	254	568	.255

27 Seung Lee, rhp

Born: June 2, 1979. **Ht.:** 6-4. **Wt.:** 220. **Bats:** R. **Throws:** R. **Career Transactions:** Signed out of Korea by Phillies, March 6, 2001.

The Phillies spent $2 million on Lee and righthander Il Kim in March 2001, figuring they nabbed two first-round talents while announcing their Pacific Rim presence. They since have released Kim and fired Doug Takaragawa, the scout who signed the two pitchers. Meanwhile, Lee isn't reaching the 95 mph velocity he showed as a Korean amateur and hasn't developed into an upper-tier prospect. He struggled through his Phillies debut with a bulging disc in his back and has had trouble adjusting to the United States. His rising weight drew concerns a year ago, especially with the back troubles, but he reported in better shape in 2003. The Phillies still think they can get some return on their investment. They've pared down Lee's hands-over-head delivery. His best pitch is a backdoor slider, and his fastball sits right around 90 mph. He often pitches hitters backward, using the breaking ball to set up his fastball. He also has a decent changeup and occasionally mixes in a splitter, which might be his best pitch in the long run. Lee makes up for his lack of dominant stuff with a solid approach to pitching and setting up hitters. He'll return to Triple-A in 2004, trying to make-up for a couple of ugly outings late in 2003. He can still be a back-of-the-rotation starter, but more likely will end up in middle relief.

Year	Club (League)	Class	W	L	ERA	G	GS	CG	SV	IP	H	R	ER	HR	BB	SO	AVG
2001	Phillies (GCL)	R	1	0	3.00	3	3	0	0	9	12	7	3	0	0	4	.308
	Batavia (NY-P)	A	0	3	7.65	4	4	0	0	20	31	24	17	3	4	14	.341
2002	Lakewood (SAL)	A	7	10	3.24	23	22	5	1	147	132	64	53	8	46	112	.244
	Clearwater (FSL)	A	2	0	0.00	3	3	1	0	19	6	1	0	0	2	16	.095
	Reading (EL)	AA	0	1	0.00	1	1	0	0	6	5	2	0	1	0	6	.217
2003	Reading (EL)	AA	11	6	4.96	26	25	0	0	147	140	85	81	21	47	109	.248
	Scranton/W-B (IL)	AAA	0	2	23.63	2	1	0	0	5	18	15	14	2	0	5	.581
MINOR LEAGUE TOTALS			21	22	4.28	62	59	6	1	354	344	198	168	35	99	266	.254

28 Matt Squires, lhp

Born: Jan. 24, 1979. **Ht.:** 5-10. **Wt.:** 200. **Bats:** L. **Throws:** L. **School:** Whitworth (Wash.) College. **Career Transactions:** Selected by Phillies in 19th round of 2001 draft; signed June 7, 2001.

The Phillies found Squires, an Idaho native, at tiny Whitworth College, an NCAA Division III school in Spokane, Wash., with an enrollment around 2,000. Squires spent the early part of his college career as an outfielder, and continued to DH even as he threw a no-hitter and earned all-Northwest Conference honors on the mound as a senior. Squires uses an easy delivery and gets his fastball in the 89-91 mph range. He has a good feel for his changeup and also throws an 81 mph slider. While Squires doesn't have great stuff, his command, competitive nature and strong makeup allow him to succeed in his role as a lefthanded specialist. He held lefties to a .194 average in 2003. He's the kind of player who must prove himself at each level. He was a late addition to the Arizona Fall League, replacing Keith Bucktrot, who left with an elbow twinge. Squires made the most of his opportunity, opening his AFL campaign with 10 scoreless appearances. While he has a limited ceiling, Squires still could be a successful lefty in a big league bullpen. So could 2003 draftee Daniel Hodges, whose screwballing success at Lakewood should help him follow Squires up the organizational ladder.

Year	Club (League)	Class	W	L	ERA	G	GS	CG	SV	IP	H	R	ER	HR	BB	SO	AVG
2001	Phillies (GCL)	R	0	2	1.21	17	0	0	0	30	16	5	4	0	11	33	.165
	Clearwater (FSL)	A	0	1	6.75	4	0	0	0	5	5	4	4	1	7	8	.238
2002	Lakewood (SAL)	A	5	6	3.82	36	1	0	8	66	62	34	28	3	40	71	.256
2003	Clearwater (FSL)	A	4	2	1.86	41	0	0	2	63	61	14	13	1	23	52	.260
MINOR LEAGUE TOTALS			9	11	2.69	98	1	0	10	164	144	57	49	5	81	164	.242

29 Welinson Baez, 3b

Born: July 7, 1984. **Ht.:** 6-3. **Wt.:** 190. **Bats:** R. **Throws:** R. **Career Transactions:** Signed out of Dominican Republic by Phillies, Aug. 28, 2002.

Signed for $250,000 in the summer of 2002, Baez illustrates both the Phillies' efforts in Latin America and depth at third base. He's still raw, but his overall package of tools ranks among the best in the organization. He reminds some Phillies officials of Juan Richardson from a physical and mental standpoint. Richardson struggled in his first year in the United States. Once he made cultural adjustments, he gained confidence and improved rapidly on the field. Baez generates good bat speed and power. The ball really jumps when he makes contact, but that's the rub. He's a free swinger who must improve his ability to identify pitches and not chase poor ones. He also has a few holes in his swing. At third base, Baez gets good reads off the bat and displays average to plus hands and arm strength. His speed is fringe average. He has the skills and athleticism to play shortstop in a pinch, but will grow too big for the position as he fills out his 6-foot-4 frame. Baez didn't play much organized baseball until he signed and needs more experience to enhance his feel for the game. His spring performance will determine his destination in 2004, and a return to the Gulf Coast League wouldn't be viewed as a setback.

Year	Club (League)	Class	AVG	G	AB	R	H	2B	3B	HR	RBI	BB	SO	SB	SLG	OBP
2003	Phillies (GCL)	R	.246	41	142	20	35	6	1	3	17	12	37	3	.366	.319
MINOR LEAGUE TOTALS			.246	41	142	20	35	6	1	3	17	12	37	3	.366	.319

30 Joe Wilson, lhp

Born: Aug. 2, 1982. **Ht.:** 6-3. **Wt.:** 195. **Bats:** L. **Throws:** L. **School:** University of Maryland-Baltimore County. **Career Transactions:** Selected by Phillies in 13th round of 2003 draft; signed June 7, 2003.

The Phillies found an interesting prospect just 100 miles away from Citizens Bank Park at Maryland-Baltimore County. Wilson transferred there after spending his freshman season at St. John's. After going 9-3, 2.26 as sophomore, he tailed off to 4-6, 6.05 in 2003 and fell to the 13th round of the draft. Despite his slump, Wilson impressed the Phillies in his predraft workout in Philadelphia, where he showed his athleticism, a strong body and sound delivery. Wilson works with a loose, quick, strong arm, and shows the makings of three average pitches. He throws his fastball in the 89-93 mph range with good life. He'll need to improve his secondary offerings, which are inconsistent. Wilson gets a hard downward bite on his slider when it's working, and has shown an excellent feel for his changeup, which he focused on in his first pro summer. He'll continue his quest to join fellow Retrievers Jay Witasick and Wayne Franklin in the majors by working out of the rotation in low Class A this season. Philadelphia projects his ceiling as a No. 4 or 5 starter.

Year	Club (League)	Class	W	L	ERA	G	GS	CG	SV	IP	H	R	ER	HR	BB	SO	AVG
2003	Batavia (NYP)	A	1	1	2.40	3	2	0	0	15	11	4	4	1	7	14	.211
	Phillies (GCL)	R	4	2	2.24	11	9	0	0	52	44	20	13	0	17	58	.222
MINOR LEAGUE TOTALS			5	3	2.27	14	11	0	0	67	55	24	17	1	24	72	.220

PITTSBURGH PIRATES

By John Perrotto

Losing has become perpetual for the Pirates, who have finished below .500 for 11 straight seasons since their last playoff appearance in 1992. The 2004 season will mark the 25th anniversary of their last World Series berth. And Pittsburgh doesn't appear ready to win anytime soon. Claiming the team somehow has lost $30 million since moving into beautiful PNC Park in 2001, owner Kevin McClatchy plans to take the payroll down to at least $35 million in 2004 after it was at $54 million to start 2003.

The Pirates began slashing in the second half of the 2003 season. They gutted their roster by trading Brian Giles, Kenny Lofton, Aramis Ramirez, Scott Sauerbeck, Randall Simon, Jeff Suppan and Mike Williams. Pittsburgh did add interesting young players—including outfielder Jason Bay, middle infielders Bobby Hill and Freddy Sanchez, and left-handers Oliver Perez and Cory Stewart—but in some of the deals their only accomplishment was shedding salary. Compounding Pittsburgh's woes is its lack of impact prospects ready to step into the major leagues. Instead, most of the talent is at least a year away.

Things are looking up for the Pirates at the minor league level, however, and its player-development plan is more solid than it has been in years. General manager Dave Littlefield and farm director Brian Graham have emphasized winning. In Graham's two seasons overseeing the system, the Pirates have finished second and first in minor league winning percentage, topping all clubs with a .581 mark in 2003. Each of the six affiliates had winning seasons in both 2002 and 2003. All six reached the playoffs in 2003.

A steady flow of talent has come into the system thanks to solid drafts by scouting director Ed Creech and his predecessor, Mickey White. That was never more evident than when Pirates farmhands were five of the first six selections in the major league Rule 5 draft in December. It did seem odd, however, that the team didn't protect its full complement of 40 players, especially after losing Matt Guerrier, Duaner Sanchez and Walter Young on waivers while finalizing the roster.

The Pirates have put a strong emphasis on pitching, to the point that the system has a dearth of impact hitters. Their top picks in each of the last six drafts have been pitchers. It remains to be seen whether the plan will pay off. What is certain is that fans are restless, as a drop of nearly 800,000 in attendance at PNC Park from its inaugural 2001 season to 2003 attests.

"I think our farm system is real close to the point where it is ready to start supplying a lot of players at the major league level, and that's what we're going to need to be successful over the long haul," McClatchy said.

TOP 30 PROSPECTS

1. John VanBenschoten, rhp
2. Sean Burnett, lhp
3. Jason Bay, of
4. Bryan Bullington, rhp
5. Blair Johnson, rhp
6. Ian Snell, rhp
7. Freddy Sanchez, ss/2b
8. Paul Maholm, lhp
9. Cory Stewart, lhp
10. Ryan Doumit, c
11. Mike Johnston, lhp
12. Jose Castillo, 2b/ss
13. J.J. Davis, of
14. Matt Capps, rhp
15. Zach Duke, lhp
16. Nyjer Morgan, of
17. Jorge Cortes, of
18. Nate McLouth, of
19. Tom Gorzelanny, lhp
20. Mike Gonzalez, lhp
21. Tony Alvarez, of
22. Wardell Starling, rhp
23. Jonathan Albaladejo, rhp
24. Javier Guzman, ss
25. J.R. House, c
26. Mike Connolly, lhp
27. Brian Holliday, lhp
28. Bobby Bradley, lhp
29. Brad Eldred, 1b
30. Leo Nunez, rhp

ORGANIZATION
OVERVIEW

General manager: Dave Littlefield. **Farm director:** Brian Graham. **Scouting director:** Ed Creech.

2003 PERFORMANCE

Class	Team	League	W	L	Pct.	Finish*	Manager
Majors	Pittsburgh	National	75	87	.463	11th (16)	Lloyd McClendon
Triple-A	Nashville Sounds	Pacific Coast	81	62	.566	2nd (16)	Trent Jewett
Double-A	Altoona Curve	Eastern	78	63	.553	3rd (12)	Dale Sveum
High A	Lynchburg Hillcats	Carolina	76	59	.563	2nd (8)	Dave Clark
Low A	Hickory Crawdads	South Atlantic	82	54	.603	2nd (16)	Tony Beasley
Short-season	Williamsport Crosscutters	New York-Penn	46	30	.605	3rd (14)	Andy Stewart
Rookie	GCL Pirates	Gulf Coast	36	20	.643	2nd (12)	Woody Huyke
OVERALL 2003 MINOR LEAGUE RECORD			399	288	.581	1st (30)	

*Finish in overall standings (No. of teams in league)

ORGANIZATION LEADERS

BATTING
*Minimum 250 At-Bats

*AVG	Nyjer Morgan, Williamsport	.343
R	Chris Shelton, Altoona/Lynchburg	88
H	Chris Shelton, Altoona/Lynchburg	147
TB	Chris Shelton, Altoona/Lynchburg	248
2B	Ryan Doumit, Lynchburg	38
3B	Three tied at	7
HR	Brad Eldred, Hickory	28
RBI	Walter Young, Lynchburg	87
BB	Chris Shelton, Altoona/Lynchburg	76
SO	Brad Eldred, Hickory	142
SB	Tike Redman, Nashville	42
*SLG	Chris Shelton, Altoona/Lynchburg	.568
*OBP	Chris Shelton, Altoona/Lynchburg	.441

PITCHING
#Minimum 75 Innings

W	Sean Burnett, Altoona	14
	Ian Snell, Altoona/Lynchburg	14
L	Landon Jacobsen, Altoona	11
#ERA	Brady Borner, Altoona/Lynchburg	2.25
G	Three tied at	51
CG	Jonathan Albaladejo, Hickory	5
SV	Mark Corey, Nashville	30
IP	Landon Jacobsen, Altoona	163
BB	Alex Hart, Lynchburg/Hickory	62
SO	Ryan Vogelsong, Nashville	146

BEST TOOLS

Best Hitter for Average	Freddy Sanchez
Best Power Hitter	J.J. Davis
Fastest Baserunner	Rajai Davis
Best Athlete	Nyjer Morgan
Best Fastball	Jeremy Harts
Best Curveball	Ian Snell
Best Slider	Mike Johnston
Best Changeup	Sean Burnett
Best Control	Sean Burnett
Best Defensive Catcher	Ryan Doumit
Best Defensive Infielder	Jose Castillo
Best Infield Arm	Jose Castillo
Best Defensive Outfielder	Nyjer Morgan
Best Outfield Arm	J.J. Davis

PROJECTED 2007 LINEUP

Catcher	Jason Kendall
First Base	Craig Wilson
Second Base	Bobby Hill
Third Base	Jose Castillo
Shortstop	Freddy Sanchez
Left Field	Jason Bay
Center Field	Nyjer Morgan
Right Field	J.J. Davis
No. 1 Starter	Kip Wells
No. 2 Starter	Oliver Perez
No. 3 Starter	John VanBenschoten
No. 4 Starter	Sean Burnett
No. 5 Starter	Bryan Bullington
Closer	Ian Snell

LAST YEAR'S TOP 20 PROSPECTS

1. John VanBenschoten, rhp
2. Sean Burnett, lhp
3. Bryan Bullington, rhp
4. Jose Castillo, ss
5. Duaner Sanchez, rhp
6. Tony Alvarez, of
7. Jose Bautista, 3b
8. J.J. Davis, of
9. Mike Gonzalez, lhp
10. Ian Snell, rhp
11. Humberto Cota, c
12. Ryan Doumit, c
13. Ryan Vogelsong, rhp
14. Bobby Bradley, rhp
15. J.R. House, c
16. Zach Duke, lhp
17. Walter Young, 1b
18. Matt Guerrier, rhp
19. Blair Johnson, rhp
20. Alex Hart, rhp

TOP PROSPECTS OF THE DECADE

1994	Midre Cummings, of
1995	Trey Beamon, of
1996	Jason Kendall, c
1997	Kris Benson, rhp
1998	Kris Benson, rhp
1999	Chad Hermansen, of
2000	Chad Hermansen, of
2001	J.R. House, c
2002	J.R. House, c
2003	John VanBenschoten, rhp

TOP DRAFT PICKS OF THE DECADE

1994	Mark Farris, ss
1995	Chad Hermansen, ss
1996	Kris Benson, rhp
1997	J.J. Davis, of
1998	Clint Johnston, lhp/of
1999	Bobby Bradley, rhp
2000	Sean Burnett, lhp
2001	John VanBenschoten, rhp/of
2002	Bryan Bullington, rhp
2003	Paul Maholm, lhp

ALL-TIME LARGEST BONUSES

Bryan Bullington, 2002	$4,000,000
John VanBenschoten, 2001	$2,400,000
Bobby Bradley, 1999	$2,225,000
Paul Maholm, 2003	$2,200,000
Kris Benson, 1996	$2,000,000

PITTSBURGH **PIRATES**   RANK: **11**

Impact potential (B): John VanBenschoten, Sean Burnett and Jason Bay should enjoy productive careers and could be occasional all-stars. Considering the quality of the Pirates system, there are several prospects, including Blair Johnson and Zach Duke, on the verge of breaking out this season. They may, however, regret drafting Bryan Bullington over B.J. Upton with the first pick in 2002.

Depth (B): That the Pirates lost five players in the major league Rule 5 draft and two more significant prospects (Walter Young and Duaner Sanchez) on waiver claims, speaks volumes about the progress the system has made in recent years.

Sleeper: Tom Gorzelanny, lhp.   —*Depth charts prepared by* **Josh Boyd**. *Numbers in parentheses indicate prospect rankings.*

LF
Jorge Cortes (17)
Tony Alvarez (21)
Shawn Garrett

CF
Jason Bay (3)
Nyjer Morgan (16)
Nate McLouth (18)
Chris Duffy
Rajai Davis
Ray Sadler
Vic Buttler
Chaz Lytle

RF
J.J. Davis (13)
Luke Allen

3B
Craig Stansberry

SS
Jose Castillo (12)
Javier Guzman (24)
Taber Lee

2B
Freddy Sanchez (7)
Jeff Keppinger
Victor Mercedes

1B
Brad Eldred (29)
Carlos Rivera

SOURCE OF TALENT

Homegrown		Acquired	
College	4	Trades	4
Junior College	4	Rule 5 draft	0
Draft-and-follow	1	Independent leagues	0
High school	12	Free agents/waivers	0
Nondrafted free agent	0		
Foreign	5		

C
Ryan Doumit (10)
J.R. House (25)
Humberto Cota
Steve Lerud
Ronny Paulino

RHP

Starters	Relievers
John VanBenschoten (1)	Henry Owens
Bryan Bullington (4)	Ben Shaffar
Blair Johnson (5)	Justin Reid
Ian Snell (6)	Josh Sharpless
Matt Capps (14)	
Wardell Starling (22)	
Jonathan Albaladejo (23)	
Bobby Bradley (28)	
Leo Nunez (30)	
Alex Hart	
Jason Sharber	
Yoann Torrealba	
Landon Jacobsen	
Kyle Pearson	

LHP

Starters	Relievers
Sean Burnett (2)	Mike Johnston (11)
Paul Maholm (8)	Mike Gonzalez (20)
Cory Stewart (9)	Jeremy Harts
Zach Duke (15)	John Grabow
Tom Gorzelanny (19)	
Mike Connolly (26)	
Brian Holliday (27)	

DRAFT
ANALYSIS

Best Pro Debut: The Pirates' top two picks, LHPs Paul Maholm (1) and Tom Gorzelanny (2), both posted sub-2.00 ERAs in the short-season New York-Penn League. Five-foot-11 RHP Chris Hernandez (22) had a better ERA (1.64) and averaged more than a strikeout per inning (41 in 38) at the same level.

Best Athlete: A baseball/football/track star in high school, OF Adam Boeve (12) went to Northern Iowa on a football scholarship as a safety and started his baseball career as a catcher. The 2003 Missouri Valley Conference player of the year has solid all-around tools.

Best Pure Hitter: C Steve Lerud (3) missed the summer because the Pirates wanted a previous foot injury to heal correctly. He swung the bat well in instructional league.

Best Raw Power: Lerud owns the Nevada high school career home run record with 60. He has more offensive upside than most catchers.

Fastest Runner: OF Pedro Powell (18) is a little guy with big-time speed. He's 5-foot-7 and 150 pounds, and the Pirates have clocked him from the right side of the plate to first base in 3.7-3.8 seconds.

Best Defensive Player: 2B Craig Stansberry (5) was a shortstop in junior college and the most athletic third baseman in college baseball last season. His athleticism

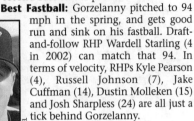

Gorzelanny

allowed him to make a seamless transition to second base in the pros.

Best Fastball: Gorzelanny pitched to 94 mph in the spring, and gets good run and sink on his fastball. Draft-and-follow RHP Wardell Starling (4 in 2002) can match that 94. In terms of velocity, RHPs Kyle Pearson (4), Russell Johnson (7), Jake Cuffman (14), Dustin Molleken (15) and Josh Sharpless (24) are all just a tick behind Gorzelanny.

Best Breaking Ball: RHP Sergio Silva (8) and Sharpless have equally effective sliders.

Most Intriguing Background: OF Brett Holmes (20) is the grandson of 1955 National League rookie of the year and former Pirates manager Bill Virdon.

Closest To The Majors: Owner Kevin McClatchy prefers nearly ready college players in the first round, and that's what he got in Maholm.

Best Late-Round Pick: Cuffman or Sharpless are two Pittsburgh-area products who got little predraft exposure.

The One Who Got Away: RHP Dallas Buck's (19) draft stock kept rising until he made it clear he wanted to play football at Oregon State.

Assessment: For a team that signed just 18 players, the Pirates got more than their share of intriguing pitchers. Lerud has the kind of power that's lacking in Pittsburgh.

2002 DRAFT — GRADE: B

RHP Bryan Bullington (1), the No. 1 overall pick, leveled off in his 2003 pro debut. But RHPs Blair Johnson (2) and Matt Capps (7) stepped forward, and OF Nyjer Morgan (33) and RHP Wardell Starling (4) did well in their debuts.

2001 DRAFT — GRADE: B

No one questions the Pirates' decision to keep RHP John VanBenschoten (1), a former NCAA Division I home run champ, on the mound these days. They also made three fine late-round picks in LHP Zach Duke (20), draft-and-follow third baseman Kody Kirkland (30) and 1B/C Chris Shelton (33).

2000 DRAFT — GRADE: C+

LHP Sean Burnett (1) is advancing steadily toward the majors. Mickey White, Pittsburgh's scouting director from 1999-2001, again showed his knack for late-round picks with draft-and-follow 3B Jose Bautista (20) and OF Nate McLouth (25).

1999 DRAFT — GRADE: C

Injuries have short-circuited the promise of C J.R. House (5) and RHP Bobby Bradley (1). C Ryan Doumit (2), who is finally staying healthy, has moved to the head of this class.

—Draft analysis prepared by Jim Callis. Numbers in parentheses indicate draft rounds.

John VanBenschoten

Born: April 14, 1980.
Ht.: 6-4. **Wt.:** 210.
Bats: R. **Throws:** R.
School: Kent State University.
Career Transactions: Selected by Pirates in first round (eighth overall) of 2001 draft; signed July 3, 2001.

Former Pirates scouting director Mickey White, always an unorthodox sort, stunned the scouting community in 2001 when he drafted VanBenschoten in the first round as a pitcher. While VanBenschoten was at Kent State, he also led NCAA Division I with 31 homers that spring and most teams saw him as a prototypical right fielder. He has certainly justified White's decision, however. VanBenschoten has gone 24-12, 3.02 in 62 pro starts and was a standout in the 2003 Futures Game. He also pitched for Team USA in the Olympic qualifying tournament, delivering three scoreless innings in a quarterfinal loss to Mexico. VanBenschoten went 26 consecutive starts at one point without losing: his last eight at low Class A Hickory in 2002, then all nine at high Class A Lynchburg and his first nine at Double-A Altoona in 2003. The Pirates used VanBenschoten as both a pitcher and DH in his debut season with short-season Williamsport in 2001, but he has stayed strictly on the mound the last two years. He showed he still had his hitting stroke last season by going 4-for-12 (.333) with two doubles for Altoona.

VanBenschoten has the makings of four average to plus pitches, the best of which is a 90-93 mph fastball that reaches 95 and has good movement down in the strike zone. His curveball is an above-average offering that he consistently throws for strikes. His slider and changeup continue to get better. VanBenschoten is athletic, which allows him to repeat his delivery and help himself in the field. In fact, his fluid mechanics make his heater look even faster. He's free-spirited with a terrific sense of humor, and he rarely gets rattled on the mound. He's confident without being cocky. VanBenschoten tired late in 2003, losing five straight decisions in the second half and getting knocked out in the first inning of his only playoff start against eventual Eastern League champion Akron. The Pirates say his stamina won't be a long-term problem and had no problem letting him pitch in the Olympic qualifying tourney. VanBenschoten has yet to gain full confidence in his changeup, a pitch he'll need to succeed in the majors. He's vulnerable when he leaves his pitches up in the strike zone. He still needs more experience pitching against high-caliber competition after concentrating on hitting in college.

After making great strides in his three pro seasons despite his inexperience, VanBenschoten looks like he can be a frontline pitcher in Pittsburgh's rotation. He has adapted to each level of the minors but is likely to return to Double-A to open the season. He could move up to Triple-A Nashville before getting a September callup, and regardless should join the Pirates for good in 2005.

Year	Club (League)	Class	AVG	G	AB	R	H	2B	3B	HR	RBI	BB	SO	SB	SLG	OBP
2001	Williamsport (NY-P)	A	.227	32	75	9	17	5	0	0	8	7	23	3	.293	.302
2003	Altoona (EL)	AA	.333	17	12	2	4	2	0	0	1	0	4	0	.500	.333
MINOR LEAGUE TOTALS			.241	49	87	11	21	7	0	0	9	7	27	3	.322	.306

Year	Club (League)	Class	W	L	ERA	G	GS	CG	SV	IP	H	R	ER	HR	BB	SO	AVG
2001	Williamsport (NY-P)	A	0	2	3.51	9	9	0	0	26	23	11	10	0	10	14	.247
2002	Hickory (SAL)	A	11	4	2.80	27	27	0	0	148	119	57	46	6	62	145	.219
2003	Lynchburg (Car)	A	6	0	2.22	9	9	0	0	49	33	14	12	1	18	49	.192
	Altoona (EL)	AA	7	6	3.69	17	17	1	0	90	95	46	37	5	34	78	.268
MINOR LEAGUE TOTALS			24	12	3.02	62	62	1	0	313	270	128	105	12	124	291	.232

2 Sean Burnett, lhp

RICH ABEL

Born: Sept. 17, 1982. **Ht.:** 6-1. **Wt.:** 170. **Bats:** L. **Throws:** L. **School:** Wellington (Fla.) Community HS. **Career Transactions:** Selected by Pirates in first round (19th overall) of 2000 draft; signed July 7, 2000.

The Pirates drafted Burnett a year after making his high school teammate Bobby Bradley a first-rounder. While Bradley has yet to get past Class A because of a variety of arm problems, Burnett has excelled. He was the Eastern League's 2003 pitcher of the year. More impressive than his stuff, Burnett has outstanding control and keeps the ball in the park. His best pitch is a changeup that falls off the table. He also throws a good curveball and a slider that he picked up in 2002. Burnett's other pitches offset that his fastball sits in the 85-88 mph range. His low strikeout rate hasn't hurt him yet, but it could be a factor when he reaches the majors. Because of his slight build, stamina will always be a question. Burnett missed the EL playoffs with a sore elbow but returned to pitch in instructional league. As a lefty who induces ground balls, Burnett seems to be a perfect fit for PNC Park. He figures to move into the rotation after spending 2004 in Triple-A.

Year	Club (League)	Class	W	L	ERA	G	GS	CG	SV	IP	H	R	ER	HR	BB	SO	AVG
2000	Pirates (GCL)	R	2	1	4.06	8	6	0	0	31	31	17	14	0	3	24	.250
2001	Hickory (SAL)	A	11	8	2.62	26	26	1	0	161	164	63	47	11	33	134	.265
2002	Lynchburg (Car)	A	13	4	1.80	26	26	2	0	155	118	46	31	4	33	96	.210
2003	Altoona (EL)	AA	14	6	3.21	27	27	2	0	160	158	60	57	2	29	86	.265
MINOR LEAGUE TOTALS			40	19	2.64	87	85	5	0	507	471	186	149	17	98	340	.248

3 Jason Bay, of

Born: Sept. 20, 1978. **Ht.:** 6-2. **Wt.:** 200. **Bats:** R. **Throws:** R. **School:** Gonzaga University. **Career Transactions:** Selected by Expos in 22nd round of 2000 draft; signed June 16, 2000 . . . Traded by Expos with RHP Jim Serrano to Mets for SS Lou Collier, March 27, 2002 . . . Traded by Mets with LHP Bobby Jones and RHP Josh Reynolds to Padres for RHP Steve Reed and RHP Jason Middlebrook, July 31, 2002 . . . Traded by Padres with LHP Oliver Perez and a player to be named to Pirates for OF Brian Giles, Aug. 26, 2003; Pirates acquired LHP Cory Stewart to complete trade (Oct. 2, 2003).

Bay has been a traveling man the last two years, and Pittsburgh acquired him as part of the Brian Giles trade. He finished the year as the Pirates' left fielder and drove in eight runs against the Cubs on Sept. 19. Bay doesn't have an overpowering tool but does most everything well. He hits for power and average while showing solid plate discipline. He also is a good runner and a high-percentage basestealer. He has enough athleticism for center field and has enough arm for right. He's a little older than most prospects, meaning he probably won't get much better. While he continued to walk in the major leagues, he expanded his strike zone and struck out far more often than he did in the minors. Bay had surgery to repair a torn labrum in December, but he is expected back by Opening Day. The Pirates hope he will be their starting left fielder, a more difficult position in PNC Park than right. The Pirates hope he fulfills comparisons to Jeff Conine.

Year	Club (League)	Class	AVG	G	AB	R	H	2B	3B	HR	RBI	BB	SO	SB	SLG	OBP
2000	Vermont (NY-P)	A	.304	35	135	17	41	5	0	2	12	11	25	17	.385	.358
2001	Jupiter (FSL)	A	.195	38	123	12	24	4	1	1	10	18	26	10	.268	.306
	Clinton (Mid)	A	.362	87	318	67	115	20	4	13	61	48	62	15	.572	.449
2002	St. Lucie (FSL)	A	.272	69	261	48	71	12	2	9	54	34	54	22	.437	.363
	Binghamton (EL)	AA	.290	34	107	17	31	4	2	4	19	15	23	13	.477	.383
	Mobile (SL)	AA	.309	23	81	16	25	5	2	4	12	13	22	4	.568	.411
2003	Portland (PCL)	AAA	.303	91	307	64	93	11	1	20	59	55	71	23	.541	.410
	San Diego (NL)	MAJ	.250	3	8	2	2	1	0	1	2	1	1	0	.750	.400
	Pittsburgh (NL)	MAJ	.291	27	79	13	23	6	1	3	12	18	28	3	.506	.423
MAJOR LEAGUE TOTALS			.287	30	87	15	25	7	1	4	14	19	29	3	.529	.421
MINOR LEAGUE TOTALS			.300	377	1332	241	400	61	12	53	227	194	283	104	.483	.393

4 Bryan Bullington, rhp

RODGER WOOD

Born: Sept. 30, 1980. **Ht.:** 6-5. **Wt.:** 220. **Bats:** R. **Throws:** R. **School:** Ball State University. **Career Transactions:** Selected by Pirates in first round (first overall) of 2002 draft; signed Oct. 30, 2002.

There was considerable debate within the organization, but owner Kevin McClatchy wanted to go the safe route with the No. 1 overall pick in 2002. So the Pirates chose Bullington, a college pitcher, over high school star B.J. Upton. Bullington didn't make his pro debut until 2003 because he didn't sign for a club-record $4 million until late October 2002. Bullington has a projectable pitcher's body and the makings of a power fastball/slider combination. He throws from a three-quarters arm slot, which gives his pitches more movement. His curveball improved and he got experience throwing his changeup, a pitch he didn't need often in college. Bullington's fastball topped out at 90 mph and sat between 87-89 last season, 3-4 mph below where it was in college, and his slider didn't have consistent bite. The Pirates attribute the lack of velocity to his long layoff between college and the start of his pro career. Bullington will get tested at Double-A Altoona in 2004. Despite the pedigree of the first overall pick, he projects as a No. 2 or 3 starter, likely reaching the majors sometime in 2005.

Year	Club (League)	Class	W	L	ERA	G	GS	CG	SV	IP	H	R	ER	HR	BB	SO	AVG
2003	Hickory (SAL)	A	5	1	1.39	8	7	0	0	45	25	10	7	3	11	46	.155
	Lynchburg (Car)	A	8	4	3.05	17	17	2	0	97	101	39	33	5	27	67	.270
MINOR LEAGUE TOTALS			13	5	2.52	25	24	2	0	143	126	49	40	8	38	113	.236

5 Blair Johnson, rhp

Born: March 25, 1984. **Ht.:** 6-4. **Wt.:** 210. **Bats:** R. **Throws:** R. **School:** Washburn HS, Topeka, Kan. **Career Transactions:** Selected by Pirates in second round of 2002 draft; signed June 24, 2002.

After getting Bryan Bullington, the Pirates used the first pick of the second round of the 2002 draft to take Johnson, a raw high school pitcher from Kansas. He pitched two innings that summer because of a sore shoulder. He started 2003 in extended spring training before breaking through in his second Rookie-level Gulf Coast League season. Johnson's fastball reaches 95 mph but shows more movement when he dials it down to 91-92. He complements his heater with a good curveball and a changeup that improved markedly in 2003. He likes to challenge hitters inside. Johnson needs to be more consistent with the arm speed on his changeup. He got hit hard in the South Atlantic League playoffs after moving up to low Class A, a sign he needs more innings against better competition. Johnson has the makings of a top-of-the-rotation starter. He's still young, and the Pirates aren't likely to rush him with plenty of other pitching prospects in the system. Look for Johnson to return to Hickory in 2004 and arrive in Pittsburgh in 2007.

Year	Club (League)	Class	W	L	ERA	G	GS	CG	SV	IP	H	R	ER	HR	BB	SO	AVG
2002	Pirates (GCL)	R	0	1	8.10	2	1	0	0	3	4	6	3	0	3	4	.286
2003	Pirates (GCL)	R	4	1	1.34	9	9	0	0	47	32	9	7	2	11	42	.188
	Hickory (SAL)	A	1	1	8.71	2	2	0	0	10	11	10	10	0	3	7	.282
MINOR LEAGUE TOTALS			5	3	2.97	13	12	0	0	61	47	25	20	2	17	53	.211

6 Ian Snell, rhp

Born: Oct. 30, 1981. **Ht.:** 5-11. **Wt.:** 160. **Bats:** R. **Throws:** R. **School:** Caesar Rodney HS, Camden, Del. **Career Transactions:** Selected by Pirates in 26th round of 2000 draft; signed June 21, 2000.

Snell was known as Ian Oquendo for three seasons, taking his wife's last name after the couple had a child in 2000. He changed back to Snell this offseason. A small Delaware high school righthander, he drew scant attention from scouts when the father of Pirates lefthander Dave Williams recommended him to the team. Snell has gone on to be almost unbeatable, going 36-9, 2.48 in 3½ pro seasons. He led the system with 14 wins and was Pittsburgh's minor league pitcher of the year in 2003. He has a lively fastball that reaches 95 mph and sits comfortably at 91-92. His best pitch is a hard curveball that has such late break that many confuse it for a slider. He's also an outstanding athlete who fields his position well. Snell's changeup needs work. He was suspended for two weeks in 2002 after an argument with Hickory pitching coach Scott Lovekamp but showed newfound maturity in 2003. He spent the final month of 2003 in Double-A and needs at least another half-season there. It's conceivable he could be ready for the major leagues late in 2004, but the following season seems more likely. With his slight stature and two above-average pitches, he could wind up as a closer in the big leagues.

Year	Club (League)	Class	W	L	ERA	G	GS	CG	SV	IP	H	R	ER	HR	BB	SO	AVG
2000	Pirates (GCL)	R	1	0	2.35	4	0	0	0	8	5	2	2	1	1	8	.200
2001	Pirates (GCL)	R	3	0	0.47	3	3	0	0	19	12	2	1	0	5	13	.185
	Williamsport (NY-P)	A	7	0	1.39	10	9	1	0	65	55	16	10	2	10	56	.230
2002	Hickory (SAL)	A	11	6	2.71	24	22	0	0	140	127	49	42	8	45	149	.243
2003	Lynchburg (Car)	A	10	3	3.33	20	20	1	0	116	105	46	43	3	33	122	.244
	Altoona (EL)	AA	4	0	1.96	6	6	0	0	37	36	13	8	2	10	23	.252
MINOR LEAGUE TOTALS			36	9	2.48	67	60	2	0	384	340	128	106	16	104	371	.239

7 Freddy Sanchez, ss/2b

Born: Dec. 21, 1977. **Ht.:** 5-11. **Wt.:** 180. **Bats:** R. **Throws:** R. **School:** Oklahoma City University. **Career Transactions:** Selected by Red Sox in 11th round of 2000 draft; signed June 14, 2000 . . . Traded by Red Sox with LHP Mike Gonzalez and cash to Pirates for RHP Jeff Suppan, RHP Brandon Lyon and RHP Anastacio Martinez, July 31, 2003.

Sanchez was the Red Sox' most advanced prospect until they parted with him to acquire Scott Sauerback and Jeff Suppan in July. The Pirates planned for Sanchez to take over at second base in September, but he played just one game at Triple-A Nashville before being shut down with a stress fracture in his right ankle. A career .323 hitter in the minors, Sanchez sprays line drives to all fields and has a good understanding of the strike zone. He has good pop for a middle infielder and drove the ball better than ever in 2003. He also wins high marks for his enthusiasm, hustle and instincts. Sanchez has played a lot of shortstop, but his below-average arm makes him better suited for second. His ankle problem may hurt his speed and range, which were average to begin with. Sanchez will battle Bobby Hill, another touted young infielder acquired in a midseason trade, for the starting job at second base. He could go back to shortstop, particularly if Jack Wilson, a former summer league teammate, doesn't improve offensively.

Year	Club (League)	Class	AVG	G	AB	R	H	2B	3B	HR	RBI	BB	SO	SB	SLG	OBP
2000	Lowell (NY-P)	A	.288	34	132	24	38	13	2	1	14	9	16	2	.439	.347
	Augusta (SAL)	A	.303	30	109	17	33	7	0	0	15	11	19	4	.367	.372
2001	Sarasota (FSL)	A	.339	69	280	40	95	19	4	1	24	22	30	5	.446	.388
	Trenton (EL)	AA	.326	44	178	25	58	20	0	2	19	9	21	3	.472	.363
2002	Trenton (EL)	AA	.328	80	311	60	102	23	1	3	38	37	45	19	.437	.403
	Pawtucket (IL)	AAA	.301	45	183	25	55	10	1	4	28	12	21	5	.432	.350
	Boston (AL)	MAJ	.188	12	16	3	3	0	0	0	2	2	3	0	.188	.278
2003	Pawtucket (IL)	AAA	.341	58	211	46	72	17	0	5	25	31	36	8	.493	.430
	Boston (AL)	MAJ	.235	20	34	6	8	2	0	0	2	0	8	0	.294	.235
	Nashville (PCL)	AAA	.400	1	5	1	2	1	0	0	0	0	1	0	.600	.400
MAJOR LEAGUE TOTALS			.220	32	50	9	11	2	0	0	4	2	11	0	.260	.250
MINOR LEAGUE TOTALS			.323	361	1409	238	455	110	8	16	163	131	189	46	.446	.385

8 Paul Maholm, lhp

Born: June 25, 1982. **Ht.:** 6-2. **Wt.:** 215. **Bats:** L. **Throws:** L. **School:** Mississippi State University. **Career Transactions:** Selected by Pirates in first round (eighth overall) of 2003 draft; signed July 9, 2003.

A 17th-round pick by the Twins out of high school in 2000, Maholm opted to attend Mississippi State. That proved to be a wise move as he went eighth overall in 2003. As with Bullington, McClatchy's desire for safer college talent played a role in Pittsburgh's decision. Maholm has an advanced feel for pitching as he changes speeds well, moves the ball around in the strike zone and does the little things like hold runners and field his position. Both his curveball and changeup are above-average pitches. His fastball rarely tops 90 mph and sits at 88 but is effective because of Maholm's ability to locate it. Maholm's lack of pure stuff did not hurt him in the short-season New York-Penn League, but it remains to be seen how he'll fare against higher-caliber hitters. He also needs to tighten his slider, though the Pirates may ask him to concentrate on his curve. Because Maholm faced strong competition in college, the Pirates are likely to challenge him and send him to high Class A in 2004. Maholm figures to be a middle-of-the-rotation starter in the majors, perhaps as early as 2006.

Year	Club (League)	Class	W	L	ERA	G	GS	CG	SV	IP	H	R	ER	HR	BB	SO	AVG
2003	Williamsport (NY-P)	A	2	1	1.83	8	8	0	0	34	25	11	7	1	10	32	.197
MINOR LEAGUE TOTALS			2	1	1.83	8	8	0	0	34	25	11	7	1	10	32	.197

9 Cory Stewart, lhp

Born: Nov. 14, 1979. **Ht.:** 6-4. **Wt.:** 180. **Bats:** L. **Throws:** L. **School:** Boerne (Texas) HS. **Career Transactions:** Selected by Reds in 27th round of 1998 draft, Aug. 17, 1998 . . . On disabled list, June 16-Sept. 27, 2000 . . . Released by Reds, March 24, 2001 . . . Signed by independent Amarillo (Texas-Louisiana), May 2001 . . . Signed by Padres, Oct. 15, 2001 . . . Traded by Padres to Pirates, Oct. 2, 2003, completing trade in which Pirates sent OF Brian Giles to Padres for LHP Oliver Perez, OF Jason Bay and a player to be named (Aug. 26, 2003).

The Pirates acquired Stewart in the trade that sent Brian Giles to the Padres. Drafted by Cincinnati in 1998 and released two years later after having shoulder surgery, he signed with San Diego in 2002 after one season in the independent Texas-Louisiana League. He was the Padres' best pitching prospect at the time of the trade. Stewart is a rare lefthanded starter who can overpower hitters with a fastball. It tops out at 94 mph and usually works at 88-92, and it has good movement. He complements his heater with a big-breaking curveball. He's mentally tough, shown by his rise from indy ball refugee to prospect. Stewart's changeup is below-average, and he tends to telegraph it. His curveballs can be erratic, and he must improve his secondary pitches in order to remain a starter. He also loses concentration at times. Stewart will go to Triple-A in 2004 and should get a chance to make his major league debut late in the season.

Year	Club (League)	Class	W	L	ERA	G	GS	CG	SV	IP	H	R	ER	HR	BB	SO	AVG
1999	Billings (Pio)	R	2	0	3.14	10	10	0	0	49	50	25	17	2	21	37	.263
2000	Did not play—Injured																
2001	Amarillo (T-L)	IND	6	6	5.39	22	20	3	0	120	132	87	72	9	67	107	.276
2002	Fort Wayne (Mid)	A	6	3	2.39	17	11	0	0	64	46	21	17	4	18	86	.198
	Lake Elsinore (Cal)	A	5	3	3.20	12	12	0	0	65	60	29	23	3	29	69	.251
2003	Mobile (SL)	AA	12	7	3.72	24	24	0	0	126	104	60	52	10	50	133	.222
MINOR LEAGUE TOTALS			25	13	3.24	63	57	0	0	303	260	135	109	19	118	325	.230

10 Ryan Doumit, c

RODGER WOOD

Born: April 3, 1981. **Ht.:** 6-0. **Wt.:** 190. **Bats:** B. **Throws:** R. **School:** Moses Lake (Wash.) HS. **Career Transactions:** Selected by Pirates in second round of 1999 draft; signed June 16, 1999.

Injuries to his back, knee and hand have dogged Doumit since he turned pro. He finally had the first healthy season of his career in 2003, and his 458 at-bats nearly doubled his career high. He led the high Class A Carolina League in doubles. Doumit has a lot of offensive upside for a catcher. He's a switch-hitter who can hit for average and has emerging power, especially from the left side. He improved his plate discipline when he got regular at-bats, though he still needs work in that area. He also moves well behind the plate and has a strong arm. Doumit is a streaky hitter and needs to be more consistent. Despite his good defensive tools, CL teams ran on him. He needs to become more accurate with his throws, and some question his game-calling and receiving ability. Doumit will catch in Double-A in 2004 and is on track to reach Pittsburgh in 2006. He has the stuff be a No. 1 catcher in the majors.

Year	Club (League)	Class	AVG	G	AB	R	H	2B	3B	HR	RBI	BB	SO	SB	SLG	OBP
1999	Pirates (GCL)	R	.282	29	85	17	24	5	0	1	7	15	14	4	.376	.410
2000	Williamsport (NY-P)	A	.313	66	246	25	77	15	5	2	40	23	33	2	.439	.371
2001	Hickory (SAL)	A	.270	39	148	14	40	6	0	2	14	10	32	2	.351	.333
	Pirates (GCL)	R	.235	7	17	2	4	2	0	0	3	2	0	0	.353	.316
	Altoona (EL)	AA	.250	2	4	0	1	0	0	0	2	1	1	0	.250	.400
2002	Hickory (SAL)	A	.322	68	258	46	83	14	1	6	47	18	40	3	.453	.377
2003	Lynchburg (Car)	A	.275	127	458	75	126	38	1	11	77	45	79	4	.434	.351
MINOR LEAGUE TOTALS			.292	338	1216	179	355	80	7	22	190	114	199	15	.424	.363

11 Mike Johnston, lhp

Born: March 30, 1979. **Ht.:** 6-3. **Wt.:** 200. **Bats:** L. **Throws:** L. **School:** Garrett (Md.) CC. **Career Transactions:** Selected by Pirates in 20th round of 1998 draft; signed June 4, 1998.

Johnston was raised in a tough section of Philadelphia and dropped out of high school because of problems related to Tourette Syndrome. He continued playing summer ball and went on to pitch in junior college, where the Pirates spotted him. Johnston is often overpowering, throwing a 96-mph fastball along with an outstanding slider that has good late bite and is his out pitch. He's aggressive on the mound and goes right after hitters with his plus stuff. Johnston is prone to bouts of wildness but improved his command last season after being made a full-time reliever. He can be emotional at times and broke his hand in 2002 when he punched the dugout wall following a poor start in high Class A. Johnston took a major step forward in 2003 and is now Pittsburgh's best relief prospect. He could see the major leagues at some point this season. Johnston has the makings of a top-flight set-up man and perhaps even a rare lefthanded closer.

Year	Club (League)	Class	W	L	ERA	G	GS	CG	SV	IP	H	R	ER	HR	BB	SO	AVG
1998	Pirates (GCL)	R	1	2	3.34	13	3	0	0	30	28	17	11	1	10	17	.248
	Erie (NY-P)	A	0	0	4.50	2	0	0	0	2	4	4	1	0	2	1	.364
1999	Williamsport (NY-P)	A	3	2	4.25	14	2	0	2	42	46	26	20	5	18	30	.267
2000	Hickory (SAL)	A	4	2	6.22	26	0	0	2	51	66	42	35	2	30	52	.320
2001	Hickory (SAL)	A	4	5	3.38	16	16	0	0	93	88	47	35	5	42	80	.249
	Lynchburg (Car)	A	4	4	3.34	11	10	1	0	62	66	27	23	2	24	44	.272

2002	Lynchburg (Car)	A	4	2	3.63	15	10	0	0	57	50	29	23	2	26	50	.230
2003	Altoona (EL)	AA	6	2	2.12	46	0	0	7	72	49	17	17	4	27	65	.199
MINOR LEAGUE TOTALS			26	19	3.63	143	41	1	11	409	397	209	165	21	178	340	.254

12 Jose Castillo, 2b/ss

Born: March 19, 1981. **Ht.:** 6-1. **Wt.:** 200. **Bats:** R. **Throws:** R. **Career Transactions:** Signed out of Venezuela by Pirates, July 2, 1997.

Castillo grew up in Venezuela idolizing countrymen such as Luis Aparicio, Dave Concepcion, Ozzie Guillen and Omar Vizquel. He played primarily at shortstop until last May, when he moved to second base when then-Pirates second baseman Pokey Reese suffered a season-ending thumb injury. After Pittsburgh traded for young middle infielders Freddy Sanchez and Bobby Hill, Castillo figures to play at short in Triple-A this year. Though he has a very strong arm and good range, some scouts believe he'll eventually outgrow the middle infield and move to third base or the outfield. Castillo has a line-drive stroke that has sporadically produced homers. He was able to hit for average in Double-A last season after a slow start, but his power and plate discipline dipped. He runs well and is a threat to steal. While Castillo has good defensive tools, he tends to get lazy with his throwing mechanics and sometimes loses his concentration on routine plays. If he performs well at Nashville, he'll be in line for a September callup and in position to challenge for a starting job in 2005.

Year	Club (League)	Class	AVG	G	AB	R	H	2B	3B	HR	RBI	BB	SO	SB	SLG	OBP
1998	Montalban (VSL)	R	.291	55	179	31	52	9	1	1	13	20	30	23	.369	.380
1999	Pirates (GCL)	R	.266	47	173	27	46	9	0	4	30	11	23	8	.387	.316
2000	Hickory (SAL)	A	.299	125	529	95	158	32	8	16	72	29	107	16	.480	.346
2001	Lynchburg (Car)	A	.245	125	485	57	119	20	7	7	49	21	94	23	.359	.288
2002	Lynchburg (Car)	A	.300	134	503	82	151	25	2	16	81	49	95	27	.453	.370
2003	Altoona (EL)	AA	.287	126	498	68	143	24	6	5	66	40	81	19	.390	.339
MINOR LEAGUE TOTALS			.283	612	2367	360	669	119	24	49	311	170	430	116	.415	.339

13 J.J. Davis, of

Born: Oct. 25, 1978. **Ht.:** 6-5. **Wt.:** 240. **Bats:** R. **Throws:** R. **School:** Baldwin Park (Calif.) HS. **Career Transactions:** Selected by Pirates in first round (eighth overall) of 1997 draft; signed June 3, 1997.

Just when his career had all but flamed out, Davis put together fine back-to-back seasons in 2002 and 2003. He led the Triple-A Pacific Coast League in slugging last year and would have played for Team USA in the Olympic qualifying tournament had he not injured his right hamstring. He had lobbied the Pirates to convert him into a pitcher in 2001, then changed his attitude and saw his production increase markedly. Davis has plenty of tools, most notably a power bat. He has learned to use the entire field the last two seasons and is now capable of hitting the ball out to any part of the park. Davis also has a strong arm and began learning how to turn his above-average speed into basestealing success in 2003. He's still averse to taking walks but is doing a better job of cutting down on his strikeouts. Despite his athleticism, Davis sometimes looks awkward in the field and doesn't always take good routes to fly balls. He's out of minor league options, so he'll almost certainly make the big league club in 2004. The Pirates want to ease Davis into the majors and figures to platoon in right field, playing him primarily against lefthanders.

Year	Club (League)	Class	AVG	G	AB	R	H	2B	3B	HR	RBI	BB	SO	SB	SLG	OBP
1997	Pirates (GCL)	R	.255	45	165	19	42	10	2	1	18	14	44	0	.358	.315
	Erie (NY-P)	A	.077	4	13	1	1	0	0	0	0	0	4	0	.077	.077
1998	Augusta (SAL)	A	.198	30	106	11	21	6	0	4	11	3	24	1	.368	.220
	Erie (NY-P)	A	.270	52	196	25	53	12	2	8	39	20	54	4	.474	.341
1999	Hickory (SAL)	A	.265	86	317	58	84	26	1	19	65	44	99	2	.533	.360
2000	Lynchburg (Car)	A	.243	130	485	77	118	36	1	20	80	52	171	9	.445	.319
2001	Altoona (EL)	AA	.250	67	228	21	57	13	3	4	26	21	79	2	.386	.317
	Pirates (GCL)	R	.471	4	17	3	8	1	0	2	6	1	2	0	.882	.500
2002	Altoona (EL)	AA	.287	101	348	51	100	17	3	20	62	33	101	7	.526	.351
	Pittsburgh (NL)	MAJ	.100	9	10	1	1	0	0	0	0	0	4	0	.100	.182
2003	Nashville (PCL)	AAA	.284	122	426	68	121	29	4	26	67	35	85	23	.554	.342
	Pittsburgh (NL)	MAJ	.200	19	35	1	7	0	0	1	4	3	13	0	.286	.263
MAJOR LEAGUE TOTALS			.178	28	45	2	8	0	0	1	4	3	17	0	.244	.245
MINOR LEAGUE TOTALS			.263	641	2301	334	605	150	16	104	374	223	663	48	.478	.331

14 Matt Capps, rhp

Born: Sept. 3, 1983. **Ht.:** 6-3. **Wt.:** 220. **Bats:** R. **Throws:** R. **School:** Alexander HS, Douglasville, Ga. **Career Transactions:** Selected by Pirates in seventh round of 2002 draft; signed July 8, 2002.

Capps was outstanding on both ends of the battery in high school, starring as a pitcher and catcher. While some teams projected him as a catcher, the Pirates drafted him as a pitcher and haven't been disappointed after signing him away from Louisiana State. Capps threw 95 mph in high school but has taken a little off his fastball as a pro, finding better control at 91-93. He has outstanding command for a young pitcher and consistently throws his curveball and changeup for strikes. He also uses an occasional slider. Capps is an outstanding competitor who never gives in and isn't averse to backing hitters off the plate. The next logical step for him would be Short-season Williamsport, but his poise and command will get him a ticket to Class A Hickory to start 2004. The Pirates won't rush Capps, but he could force his way into the major league picture by 2007 and be an innings-eating mainstay.

Year	Club (League)	Class	W	L	ERA	G	GS	CG	SV	IP	H	R	ER	HR	BB	SO	AVG
2002	Pirates (GCL)	R	1	0	0.69	7	0	0	1	13	13	2	1	0	6	8	.271
2003	Pirates (GCL)	R	5	1	1.87	10	10	1	0	63	40	16	13	1	9	54	.178
	Lynchburg (Car)	A	0	0	5.40	1	1	0	0	5	3	3	3	0	4	5	.167
MINOR LEAGUE TOTALS			6	1	1.90	18	11	1	1	81	56	21	17	1	19	67	.192

15 Zach Duke, lhp

Born: April 19, 1983. **Ht.:** 6-2. **Wt.:** 200. **Bats:** L. **Throws:** L. **School:** Midway HS, Clifton, Texas. **Career Transactions:** Selected by Pirates in 20th round of 2001 draft; signed July 31, 2001.

Duke signed too late to pitch in 2001 but made a good showing in instructional league that year. After an outstanding pro debut in the Gulf Coast League in 2002, he lost 20 pounds and made a smooth jump to low Class A last year. Duke makes up for a lack of overwhelming stuff with outstanding poise and command. He doesn't rattle and has the confidence to throw his outstanding curveball at any point in the count, even 3-0. His fastball rarely reaches 90 mph and is usually around 86-88, but it has excellent movement and he keeps it down in the strike zone. Duke struggles at times to throw his changeup for strikes and he'll need that pitch to have a long-term future as a starter. He tired out in the second half of 2003 and must improve his stamina. Duke has moved quickly in the system and will start this season in high Class A. He projects to be a solid a starter in the middle of a rotation, and he should be ready to challenge for a major league spot sometime late in 2006.

Year	Club (League)	Class	W	L	ERA	G	GS	CG	SV	IP	H	R	ER	HR	BB	SO	AVG
2002	Pirates (GCL)	R	8	1	1.95	11	11	1	0	60	38	15	13	2	18	48	.185
2003	Hickory (SAL)	A	8	7	3.11	26	26	1	0	142	124	66	49	7	46	113	.237
MINOR LEAGUE TOTALS			16	8	2.77	37	37	2	0	202	162	81	62	9	64	161	.222

16 Nyjer Morgan, of

Born: July 2, 1980. **Ht.:** 6-0. **Wt.:** 180. **Bats:** L. **Throws:** L. **School:** Walla Walla (Wash.) CC. **Career Transactions:** Selected by Pirates in 33rd round of 2002 draft; signed July 29, 2002.

Morgan is older than most junior college products because he spent four years playing junior hockey in Canada before committing to baseball. He signed too late to play in 2002 but made an immediate splash last season, leading the New York-Penn League with 92 hits and the Pirates system with a .343 average. Morgan has outstanding leadoff skills. He has the ability to hit for average and draw a fair amount of walks, and he's also a terrific bunter. All of that enhances his plus-plus speed. He doesn't have much power but Pittsburgh will be satisfied if he gets on base and wreaks havoc afterward. Like many inexperienced hitters, Morgan can be fooled by good breaking pitches and changeups. He needs to learn how to read pitchers' moves after getting caught 17 times in 43 steal attempts last year. Defensively, he's an above-average center fielder who chases down everything in the gaps while also showing a decent arm. The Pirates laud his makeup as well. Because of his age, Morgan has to move quickly. He likely will split this season between the two Class A affiliates.

Year	Club (League)	Class	AVG	G	AB	R	H	2B	3B	HR	RBI	BB	SO	SB	SLG	OBP
2003	Williamsport (NY-P)	A	.343	72	268	49	92	7	4	0	23	33	44	26	.399	.439
MINOR LEAGUE TOTALS			.343	72	268	49	92	7	4	0	23	33	44	26	.399	.439

17 Jorge Cortes, of

Born: Oct. 17, 1980. **Ht.:** 6-0. **Wt.:** 180. **Bats:** L. **Throws:** L. **Career Transactions:** Signed out of Colombia by Pirates, Oct. 24, 1997.

After spending three straight years at Williamsport, Cortes looked like an organizational player. Then everything clicked for him, and he was named South Atlantic League MVP and led the league in on-base percentage before being promoted to high Class A in July. Cortes' approach at the plate and his understanding of the strike zone are both solid. He began exhibiting good plate discipline in 2002 and it carried over to last year. Cortes doesn't have the ideal power one looks for in a corner outfielder, though his nine homers in 2003 exceeded his combined total from his four previous seasons in the United States. He has average speed and is not a factor on the bases. While he's a good defender who began seeing action in center field last year, his quickness is better suited for the corners. His arm is average. Cortes will start 2004 back in high Class A, and if he continues to progress as rapidly as he did last season, he'll finish the year in Double-A.

Year	Club (League)	Class	AVG	G	AB	R	H	2B	3B	HR	RBI	BB	SO	SB	SLG	OBP
1998	Montalban (VSL)	R	.298	57	171	32	51	14	0	5	36	45	37	3	.468	.462
1999	Pirates (GCL)	R	.301	32	93	14	28	4	1	0	14	14	19	2	.366	.385
2000	Williamsport (NY-P)	A	.202	51	173	18	35	11	0	4	22	20	48	0	.335	.289
2001	Williamsport (NY-P)	A	.254	51	189	23	48	17	1	2	31	20	25	2	.386	.329
2002	Hickory (SAL)	A	.254	17	59	13	15	3	1	1	11	7	11	1	.390	.343
	Williamsport (NY-P)	A	.328	70	253	38	83	14	4	1	35	44	20	7	.427	.426
2003	Hickory (SAL)	A	.325	98	345	55	112	24	2	8	66	56	47	9	.475	.427
	Lynchburg (Car)	A	.264	37	129	17	34	6	0	1	15	11	25	1	.333	.315
MINOR LEAGUE TOTALS			.288	413	1412	210	406	93	9	22	230	217	232	25	.413	.387

18 Nate McLouth, of

Born: Oct. 28, 1981. **Ht.:** 5-11. **Wt.:** 170. **Bats:** L. **Throws:** R. **School:** Whitehall (Mich.) HS. **Career Transactions:** Selected by Pirates in 25th round of 2000 draft; signed Aug. 29, 2000.

McLouth had a lifelong dream of playing at the University of Michigan before the Pirates dissuaded him with a $500,000 bonus. McLouth was thrown into a full-season league for his pro debut in 2001 and wound up repeating high Class A in 2003, where he led the Carolina League with 85 runs scored. Though he has pop, particularly to the gaps, the Pirates asked McLouth to concentrate on honing his leadoff skills last season. He responded by hitting for average, drawing walks and using his plus speed to steal 40 bases in 44 attempts. He has sacrificed power for average since his debut season and could stand to learn how to turn on some inside pitches. McLouth plays a solid center field with decent range and an adequate arm. There are durability questions about him because injuries have nagged him throughout his career. McLouth will go to Double-A this season. The Pirates suddenly have a number of leadoff prospects and he'll need to keep pace in order to hit his major league ETA of late 2005.

Year	Club (League)	Class	AVG	G	AB	R	H	2B	3B	HR	RBI	BB	SO	SB	SLG	OBP
2001	Hickory (SAL)	A	.285	96	351	59	100	17	5	12	54	43	54	21	.464	.371
2002	Lynchburg (Car)	A	.244	114	393	58	96	23	4	9	46	41	48	20	.392	.324
2003	Lynchburg (Car)	A	.300	117	440	85	132	27	2	6	33	55	68	40	.411	.386
MINOR LEAGUE TOTALS			.277	327	1184	202	328	67	11	27	133	139	170	81	.421	.361

19 Tom Gorzelanny, lhp

Born: July 12, 1982. **Ht.:** 6-2. **Wt.:** 200. **Bats:** B. **Throws:** L. **School:** Triton (Ill.) JC. **Career Transactions:** Selected by Pirates in second round of 2003 draft; signed July 1, 2003.

Gorzelanny began his collegiate career at the University of Kansas but encountered academic difficulties after his redshirt freshman season, causing him to transfer back home to Illinois and powerhouse Triton. The move paid off as he wound up being a second-round draft pick. Gorzelanny scared some scouts off because of his loss of velocity late in the junior college season but he made mechanical adjustments at Williamsport and got his fastball back to the 91-94 mph range. His heater also has nice run and sink, making it difficult to hit. Gorzelanny also has a good variety of complementary pitches with a splitter, changeup, curveball and slider. There were questions about Gorzelanny's maturity in college, but he showed great enthusiasm and aptitude in his first pro season. The Pirates plan to eventually ask him to drop a pitch, so can concentrate on honing a narrower repertoire. He'll get his first taste of full-season ball this year in low Class A. Based on his pro debut, Gorzelanny looks like he could move fast and challenge for a major league rotation spot by 2006.

Year	Club (League)	Class	W	L	ERA	G	GS	CG	SV	IP	H	R	ER	HR	BB	SO	AVG
2003	Williamsport (NY-P)	A	1	2	1.78	8	8	0	0	30	23	6	6	1	10	22	.215
MINOR LEAGUE TOTALS			1	2	1.78	8	8	0	0	30	23	6	6	1	10	22	.215

20 Mike Gonzalez, lhp

Born: May 23, 1978. **Ht.:** 6-2. **Wt.:** 210. **Bats:** R. **Throws:** L. **School:** San Jacinto (Texas) JC. **Career Transactions:** Selected by Pirates in 30th round of 1997 draft; signed June 24, 1997 . . . Traded by Pirates with LHP Scott Sauerbeck to Red Sox for RHP Brandon Lyon and RHP Anastacio Martinez, July 22, 2003 . . . Traded by Red Sox with SS Freddy Sanchez and cash to Pirates for RHP Jeff Suppan, RHP Brandon Lyon and RHP Anastacio Martinez, July 31, 2003.

Gonzalez had a nutty 2003 season. He was kept back at extended spring training because of back spasms before spending time with the top three clubs in the Pirates system. Then Pittsburgh shipped him to Boston with Scott Sauerbeck for righthanders Brandon Lyon and Anastacio Martinez in a July 22 trade that looked one-sided in the Red Sox' favor. After the

Pirates subsequently claimed Lyon had an injured elbow, they reworked the trade nine days later and reacquired Gonzalez. He has rare velocity for a lefthander, dialing his fastball up from 92 to 95 mph when the occasion merits. He also has a hard slider to complement his heater, giving him two plus pitches. Gonzalez has a history of injuries, including shoulder and knee surgeries. He also has a hard time harnessing his stuff and is prone to giving up walks and homers. Gonzalez hasn't developed a feel for a changeup. He didn't look ready for the majors when he joined Pittsburgh late last season. He could win a bullpen job with a good spring training, though more time in Triple-A seems likely.

Year	Club (League)	Class	W	L	ERA	G	GS	CG	SV	IP	H	R	ER	HR	BB	SO	AVG
1997	Pirates (GCL)	R	2	0	2.48	7	3	0	0	29	21	9	8	0	8	33	.200
	Augusta (SAL)	A	1	1	1.86	4	3	0	0	19	11	5	4	1	8	22	.164
1998	Augusta (SAL)	A	4	2	2.84	11	9	0	0	51	43	24	16	2	26	72	.231
	Lynchburg (Car)	A	0	3	6.67	7	7	0	0	28	40	21	21	5	13	22	.351
1999	Lynchburg (Car)	A	10	4	4.02	20	20	0	0	112	98	55	50	10	63	119	.240
	Altoona (EL)	AA	2	3	8.10	7	5	0	0	27	34	25	24	4	19	31	.312
2000	Pirates (GCL)	R	1	0	4.50	2	1	0	0	6	8	6	3	1	4	7	.267
	Lynchburg (Car)	A	4	3	4.66	12	10	0	0	56	57	34	29	6	34	53	.269
2001	Lynchburg (Car)	A	2	2	2.93	14	2	0	0	31	28	14	10	3	7	32	.241
	Altoona (EL)	AA	5	4	3.71	14	14	1	0	87	81	38	36	5	36	66	.251
2002	Altoona (EL)	AA	8	4	3.80	16	16	0	0	85	77	38	36	4	47	82	.244
	Pirates (GCL)	R	2	0	0.00	2	2	0	0	13	5	1	0	0	3	14	.114
2003	Lynchburg (Car)	A	0	1	5.14	5	0	0	0	7	7	9	4	0	5	9	.269
	Altoona (EL)	AA	0	0	1.23	5	0	0	1	7	4	1	1	1	2	10	.154
	Nashville (PCL)	AAA	0	0	4.50	7	0	0	2	10	9	5	5	0	4	10	.231
	Pawtucket (IL)	AAA	0	0	0.00	2	0	0	1	2	2	0	0	0	1	2	.286
	Pittsburgh (NL)	MAJ	0	1	7.56	16	0	0	0	8	7	7	7	4	6	6	.233
MAJOR LEAGUE TOTALS			0	1	7.56	16	0	0	0	8	7	7	7	4	6	6	.233
MINOR LEAGUE TOTALS			41	27	3.90	135	92	1	4	571	525	285	247	42	280	584	.247

21 Tony Alvarez, of

Born: May 10, 1978. **Ht.:** 6-1. **Wt.:** 200. **Bats:** R. **Throws:** R. **Career Transactions:** Signed out of Venezuela by Pirates, Sept. 27, 1995.

Alvarez burst onto the prospect scene in 1999 by winning MVP honors in the New York-Penn League. He made it to Pittsburgh for a September callup in 2002 but had an up-and-down Triple-A season last year. He was suspended for a week because of an undisclosed disciplinary problem and didn't get promoted in September. Alvarez is a high-average hitter who hits line drives and has gap power. His speed allows him to steal bases and play any of the three outfield positions. Alvarez is an aggressive player who's willing to dive for balls and take an extra base. His style also gets him into trouble, however, as he runs into too many outs on the bases and plays singles into triples when he gets reckless on defense. He also doesn't show enough patience at the plate. His hot-dog antics rankle opponents and, at times, the Pirates. Alvarez' star isn't nearly as bright as it was entering last season. He'll have to return to Triple-A and have a good year to win his way back into the organization's good graces.

Year	Club (League)	Class	AVG	G	AB	R	H	2B	3B	HR	RBI	BB	SO	SB	SLG	OBP
1996	Pirates (DSL)	R	.138	39	109	12	15	2	0	1	9	8	12	6	.183	.203
1997	Guacara 1 (VSL)	R	.220	38	91	15	20	3	0	0	6	9	10	3	.253	.282
1998	Pirates (GCL)	R	.247	50	190	27	47	13	1	4	29	13	24	19	.389	.299
1999	Williamsport (NY-P)	A	.321	58	196	44	63	14	1	7	45	21	36	38	.510	.418
2000	Hickory (SAL)	A	.285	118	442	75	126	25	4	15	77	39	93	52	.462	.357
2001	Lynchburg (Car)	A	.344	25	93	10	32	4	0	2	11	7	11	7	.452	.390
	Altoona (EL)	AA	.319	67	254	34	81	16	1	6	25	9	30	17	.461	.359
2002	Altoona (EL)	AA	.318	125	507	79	161	37	1	15	59	27	71	29	.483	.361
	Pittsburgh (NL)	MAJ	.308	14	26	6	8	2	0	1	2	3	5	1	.500	.379
2003	Nashville (PCL)	AAA	.298	106	349	50	104	27	3	9	53	28	69	22	.470	.361
MAJOR LEAGUE TOTALS			.308	14	26	6	8	2	0	1	2	3	5	1	.500	.379
MINOR LEAGUE TOTALS			.291	626	2231	346	649	141	11	59	314	161	356	193	.443	.351

22 Wardell Starling, rhp

Born: March 14, 1983. **Ht.:** 6-4. **Wt.:** 200. **Bats:** R. **Throws:** R. **School:** Lawrence E. Elkins HS, Missouri City, Texas. **Career Transactions:** Selected by Pirates in fourth round of 2002 draft; signed May 25, 2003.

Starling and Dodgers first-base prospect James Loney were two-way stars who led Elkins High (Missouri City, Texas) to the 2002 national championship. The Pirates took Starling in the fourth round, but he balked at signing and went to Odessa (Texas) JC. Starling continued to pull double duty, hitting .420-12-80 to rank among the national juco leaders in all three categories, but the consensus is that his future is greater on the mound. Odessa coach Rick Zimmerman, who has 1,030 juco victories to his credit, says Starling is as good as any player he's ever had with the exception of his former Trinidad State (Colo.) Junior College ace, Danny Jackson. Starling signed for $500,000 just before he would have re-entered the draft. He has a long, loose body and routinely throws his fastball at 92-94 mph. Starling also throws a slider, curveball and changeup. He's still learning the art of pitching after splitting his amateur career between the mound and outfield. He needs to hone his breaking pitches and changeup, which will come with experience, as well as work on keeping the ball in the park. Starling has a lot of unrefined talent and the Pirates will let him develop at his own pace. However, he's good enough to force himself into the low Class A rotation this season.

Year	Club (League)	Class	W	L	ERA	G	GS	CG	SV	IP	H	R	ER	HR	BB	SO	AVG
2003	Pirates (GCL)	R	4	1	3.94	11	11	0	0	48	47	23	21	5	13	52	.247
MINOR LEAGUE TOTALS			4	1	3.94	11	11	0	0	48	47	23	21	5	13	52	.247

23 Jonathan Albaladejo, rhp

Born: Oct. 30, 1982. **Ht.:** 6-5. **Wt.:** 230. **Bats:** R. **Throws:** R. **School:** Miami-Dade CC. **Career Transactions:** Selected by Pirates in 19th round of 2001 draft; signed June 6, 2001.

After spending his first two pro years in the Gulf Coast League, Albaladejo came out of nowhere to lead the Puerto Rican League in ERA following the 2002 season. He had another big offseason this year, beating Mexico and Panama as Puerto Rico finished fourth at the Olympic qualifying tournament in Panama. Big and strong, Albaladejo has the makings of a workhorse and led the South Atlantic League in complete games during his full-season debut. His best pitch is a fastball that reaches 95 mph, though he usually throws it in the 92-93 range. He has outstanding command for a hard-throwing youngster and is able to spot his fastball all around the strike zone. Albaladejo also throws a curveball, slider and changeup but needs to work on all of those pitches. He must find a consistent second pitch in order to put hitters away with two strikes. Albaladejo has made great progress in the last year and will begin 2004 in high Class A Lynchburg. If he doesn't refine his stuff enough to make the grade as a starter, he could make it to the majors as a set-up man or closer.

Year	Club (League)	Class	W	L	ERA	G	GS	CG	SV	IP	H	R	ER	HR	BB	SO	AVG
2001	Pirates (GCL)	R	0	3	4.74	10	2	0	1	19	22	13	10	1	2	24	.286
2002	Pirates (GCL)	R	3	2	2.40	12	10	0	0	60	71	20	16	2	6	37	.302
2003	Hickory (SAL)	A	12	5	3.11	29	20	5	1	139	114	53	48	14	19	110	.225
MINOR LEAGUE TOTALS			15	10	3.06	51	32	5	2	218	207	86	74	17	27	171	.253

24 Javier Guzman, ss

Born: May 4, 1984. **Ht.:** 5-11. **Wt.:** 160. **Bats:** R. **Throws:** R. **Career Transactions:** Signed out of Dominican Republic by Pirates, Aug. 19, 2000.

Guzman has been among the best shortstops in his league in each of his first two pro seasons. He cooled offensively after hot starts both years yet cracked BA's prospect lists in the Gulf Coast League in 2002 and the New York-Penn League in 2003. Guzman has a lot of raw athletic ability that he's still working to hone. He has a live bat with surprisingly good power for a smaller guy. He has plenty of defensive tools with good range, arm and hands. He also runs well and is a fine bunter. Guzman needs to develop skills to go with his tools. He is a free swinger who doesn't control the strike zone. He also needs to develop more consistency in the field to cut down on his careless errors. Guzman is still very much a work in progress and will likely climb the minor league ladder one level at time. That means he'll move to low Class A in 2004.

Year	Club (League)	Class	AVG	G	AB	R	H	2B	3B	HR	RBI	BB	SO	SB	SLG	OBP
2001	Pirates (DSL)	R	.209	57	206	30	43	4	3	0	15	27	49	23	.257	.311
2002	Pirates (GCL)	R	.307	50	199	42	61	6	6	5	20	12	25	13	.472	.347
2003	Williamsport (NY-P)	A	.243	47	173	19	42	9	2	2	24	10	26	4	.353	.283
MINOR LEAGUE TOTALS			.253	154	578	91	146	19	11	7	59	49	100	40	.360	.315

25 J.R. House, c

Born: Nov. 11, 1979. **Ht.:** 5-10. **Wt.:** 200. **Bats:** R. **Throws:** R. **School:** Seabreeze HS, Daytona Beach, Fla. **Career Transactions:** Selected by Pirates in fifth round of 1999 draft; signed June 12, 1999.

House was MVP of the low Class A South Atlantic League in 2000 and seemed on the fast track to stardom. He has lost much of the last two seasons to injuries, having two operations to repair a hernia in 2002 before Tommy John surgery that September. His elbow reconstruction ended speculation that he might try to play quarterback at West Virginia, which recruited him after he set since-broken national high school records for single-season and career passing yards. House returned to action in mid-July last year and played well, even getting a chance to make his major league debut with the Pirates in the final week of the season when injuries created an opening for him. He also helped his cause with a strong performance in the Arizona Fall League. The elbow injury certainly hasn't affected House's hitting stroke. In fact, he's much improved at the plate as he has learned to use the whole field and better handle breaking and offspeed pitches. House has the ability to hit for both average and power. House wasn't a good defensive catcher before the surgery, and basestealers went a perfect 16-for-16 against him in 2003. His future may not be behind the plate. He played a game at first base in the AFL and the Pirates plan to work him out in left field during spring training. Because of his missed time, House needs one more full season in the minors. He'll spend 2004 in Triple-A, rotating between catcher, first base and left field.

Year	Club (League)	Class	AVG	G	AB	R	H	2B	3B	HR	RBI	BB	SO	SB	SLG	OBP
1999	Pirates (GCL)	R	.327	33	113	13	37	9	3	5	23	11	23	1	.593	.394
	Williamsport (NY-P)	A	.300	26	100	11	30	6	0	1	13	9	21	0	.390	.358
	Hickory (SAL)	A	.273	4	11	1	3	0	0	0	0	0	3	0	.273	.273
2000	Hickory (SAL)	A	.348	110	420	78	146	29	1	23	90	46	91	1	.586	.414
2001	Altoona (EL)	AA	.258	112	426	51	110	25	1	11	56	37	103	1	.399	.323
2002	Altoona (EL)	AA	.264	30	91	9	24	6	0	2	11	13	21	0	.396	.349
	Pirates (GCL)	R	.313	5	16	3	5	2	0	1	2	3	1	0	.625	.421
2003	Pirates (GCL)	R	.400	20	65	16	26	9	0	4	23	12	5	0	.723	.476
	Altoona (EL)	AA	.333	20	63	12	21	6	0	2	11	5	11	0	.524	.382
	Pittsburgh (NL)	MAJ	1.000	1	1	0	1	0	0	0	0	0	0	0	1.000	1.000
MAJOR LEAGUE TOTALS			1.000	1	1	0	1	0	0	0	0	0	0	0	1.000	1.000
MINOR LEAGUE TOTALS			.308	360	1305	194	402	92	5	49	229	136	279	3	.499	.376

26 Mike Connolly, lhp

Born: June 2, 1982. **Ht.:** 6-0. **Wt.:** 180. **Bats:** L. **Throws:** L. **School:** Oneonta (N.Y.) HS. **Career Transactions:** Selected by Pirates in 19th round of 2000 draft; signed June 9, 2000.

Connolly didn't draw a whole lot of interest as a high school player because of his small stature. His younger brother Jon pitches in the Tigers system and has attracted more attention after leading the minors with a 1.41 ERA last year, but Mike has turned in four solid pro seasons and finished up strong last year in Double-A. Connolly's best pitch is an above-average curveball that is tough on lefthanders. His fastball rarely gets past 90 mph but he is able to survive at 86-87 mph because of his ability to spot the pitch. Connolly sometimes catches too much of the plate with his fastball, making him vulnerable to homers. He also needs to become more consistent with his changeup, and his stamina is another issue. Connolly will start in Double-A this year but should reach Triple-A at some point. If he doesn't get to the majors as a starter, his curveball gives him a good chance of making it as a reliever.

Year	Club (League)	Class	W	L	ERA	G	GS	CG	SV	IP	H	R	ER	HR	BB	SO	AVG
2000	Pirates (GCL)	R	1	2	2.29	11	0	0	2	20	20	6	5	0	6	25	.267
2001	Hickory (SAL)	A	11	7	3.94	33	15	2	0	121	116	59	53	10	41	107	.256
2002	Lynchburg (Car)	A	10	3	2.94	29	19	0	0	122	111	46	40	5	46	100	.251
2003	Altoona (EL)	AA	7	8	3.39	25	23	0	0	127	123	55	48	10	38	90	.253
MINOR LEAGUE TOTALS			29	20	3.37	98	57	2	2	390	370	166	146	25	131	322	.254

27 Brian Holliday, lhp

Born: June 1, 1984. **Ht.:** 6-2. **Wt.:** 180. **Bats:** L. **Throws:** L. **School:** Moon Area HS, Moon Township, Pa. **Career Transactions:** Selected by Pirates in 12th round of 2002 draft; signed June 20, 2002.

Holliday led Moon High, in the Pittsburgh suburbs, to the state title in Pennsylvania's highest classification in both his junior and senior years. He spent his first two pro seasons in the Gulf Coast League, not surprising because he had limited experience. Holliday has a big-breaking curveball and he's learning to change speeds with it. He has pumped up the volume with his fastball, jumping it from 84 to 90 mph after making some mechanical changes following his first pro season. Like many young pitchers, Holliday needs to improve his changeup in order to have a solid third pitch. He's still a project as the Pirates have completely rebuilt his delivery. He made strides last season as he became more serious about the game. Holliday will move slowly through the system and will begin 2004 in low Class A.

Year	Club (League)	Class	W	L	ERA	G	GS	CG	SV	IP	H	R	ER	HR	BB	SO	AVG
2002	Pirates (GCL)	R	1	1	4.91	10	5	0	1	33	35	22	18	2	18	26	.282
2003	Pirates (GCL)	R	3	2	3.83	10	10	1	0	52	50	24	22	1	22	52	.255
MINOR LEAGUE TOTALS			4	3	4.25	20	15	1	1	85	85	46	40	3	40	78	.266

28 Bobby Bradley, rhp

Born: Dec. 15, 1980. **Ht.:** 6-1. **Wt.:** 180. **Bats:** R. **Throws:** R. **School:** Wellington (Fla.) Community HS. **Career Transactions:** Selected by Pirates in first round (eighth overall) of 1999 draft; signed July 7, 1999 . . . On disabled list, April 5-Sept. 11, 2002.

Bradley appeared on the fast track to the major leagues after being the Pirates' first-round pick in 1999. However, he has been slowed by two operations on his elbow, including Tommy John surgery in 2001, and a third on his shoulder. Bradley has an outstanding curveball, a true 12-to-6 hammer he learned in Little League from his grandfather. It's virtually unhittable, but relying on it so much contributed to his arm problems. Bradley isn't a hard thrower, rarely touching 90 mph, but he has good life on his fastball. He also has a decent changeup. He must start using his changeup and fastball more often, and he needs to regain the command he showed before he started getting hurt. He no longer has the look of a potential ace but could be a No. 3 or 4 starter if everything works out. He'll return to low Class A and should move to Double-A at some point in 2004 if he stays healthy.

Year	Club (League)	Class	W	L	ERA	G	GS	CG	SV	IP	H	R	ER	HR	BB	SO	AVG
1999	Pirates (GCL)	R	1	1	2.90	6	6	0	0	31	31	13	10	2	4	31	.258
2000	Hickory (SAL)	A	8	2	2.29	14	14	3	0	83	62	31	21	3	21	118	.203
2001	Lynchburg (Car)	A	1	2	3.12	9	9	0	0	49	44	23	17	3	20	46	.238
2002	Did not play—Injured																
2003	Lynchburg (Car)	A	3	2	3.40	12	12	0	0	50	43	21	19	1	28	36	.232
	Pirates (GCL)	R	0	0	0.00	1	1	0	0	3	1	0	0	0	1	4	.111
MINOR LEAGUE TOTALS			13	7	2.79	42	42	3	0	216	181	88	67	9	74	235	.225

29 Brad Eldred, 1b

Born: July 12, 1980. **Ht.:** 6-6. **Wt.:** 240. **Bats:** R. **Throws:** R. **School:** Florida International University. **Career Transactions:** Selected by Pirates in sixth round of 2002 draft; signed June 5, 2002.

Eldred burst onto the scene as a senior at Florida International in 2002, finishing second in NCAA Division I with 29 homers. He has continued to hit for power in pro ball, making a rather seamless transition to wooden bats. Big and strong, Eldred can hit the ball a mile. His pop is intriguing in an organization lacking in that area, especially after losing first basemen Walter Young (to Baltimore on waivers) and Chris Shelton (to Detroit in the major league Rule 5 draft) during the offseason. The rest of Eldred's game isn't as solid. His lengthy swing makes him prone to strikeouts, and his long arms leave him vulnerable to being tied up by inside fastballs. He has decent speed and can steal a base if opponents forget about him. Eldred has gotten better defensively but still needs to improve his footwork at first base. The Pirates don't have a true first-base prospect ahead of him, but he'll have to develop better plate discipline in order to make it to the majors. Eldred will work on that this year in high Class A.

Year	Club (League)	Class	AVG	G	AB	R	H	2B	3B	HR	RBI	BB	SO	SB	SLG	OBP
2002	Williamsport (NY-P)	A	.283	72	276	43	78	22	3	10	48	18	74	10	.493	.338
2003	Hickory (SAL)	A	.250	115	420	62	105	22	0	28	80	38	142	7	.502	.326
MINOR LEAGUE TOTALS			.263	187	696	105	183	44	3	38	128	56	216	17	.499	.331

30 Leo Nunez, rhp

Born: Aug. 14, 1983. **Ht.:** 6-1. **Wt.:** 150. **Bats:** R. **Throws:** R. **Career Transactions:** Signed out of Dominican Republic by Pirates, Feb. 16, 2000.

After he showed a live arm and a plus-plus fastball in the Gulf Coast League in 2002, the Pirates jumped Nunez to low Class A last season. That proved more than he could handle, but he recovered nicely with a fine showing at Williamsport. Despite a lithe frame, Nunez routinely runs his fastball up to 95 mph. He's reminiscent of another smallish Dominican pitcher, Pedro Martinez. Nunez' other pitches are still in the rudimentary stages, though he made progress with his curveball and changeup in 2003. He felt some elbow pain late in the year and his slight build leads to concerns about his long-term stamina. Nunez will remain a starter for the foreseeable future because the Pirates want him to develop his secondary pitches. However, his long-term role may be as a reliever because of the durability concerns. With his lively fastball, Nunez looks like a pitcher who could close if he can command at least one other pitch. He'll get another crack at Hickory this season, but the Pirates see no need to rush him.

Year	Club (League)	Class	W	L	ERA	G	GS	CG	SV	IP	H	R	ER	HR	BB	SO	AVG
2000	Pirates (DSL)	R	5	3	2.19	14	14	1	0	86	69	26	21	0	27	82	—
2001	Pirates (GCL)	R	2	2	4.39	10	7	1	0	53	62	28	26	4	9	34	.284
2002	Pirates (GCL)	R	4	2	3.43	11	11	0	0	60	54	23	23	5	5	52	.238
	Hickory (SAL)	A	0	0	0.00	1	1	0	0	4	5	0	0	0	3	1	.333
2003	Hickory (SAL)	A	2	1	5.59	13	7	0	0	48	59	34	30	6	14	37	.304
	Williamsport (NY-P)	A	4	3	3.05	8	8	0	0	38	31	14	13	0	12	41	.211
MINOR LEAGUE TOTALS			17	11	3.50	57	48	2	0	290	280	125	113	15	70	247	.263

TOP 30 PROSPECTS

1. Blake Hawksworth, rhp
2. Adam Wainwright, rhp
3. Chris Narveson, lhp
4. Yadier Molina, c
5. Jimmy Journell, rhp
6. Travis Hanson, 3b
7. John Gall, 1b/of
8. Rhett Parrott, rhp
9. Hector Luna, ss
10. Daric Barton, c
11. Tyler Johnson, lhp
12. Shaun Boyd, of/2b
13. John Nelson, ss
14. Mark Michael, rhp
15. Stuart Pomeranz, rhp
16. Cody Haerther, of/3b
17. John Santor, 1b
18. Brendan Ryan, ss
19. Anthony Reyes, rhp
20. Josh Axelson, rhp
21. Josh Kinney, rhp
22. Reid Gorecki, of
23. Dee Haynes, of
24. Evan Rust, rhp
25. Brad Thompson, rhp
26. Calvin Hayes, ss
27. Nick Stocks, rhp
28. Josh Pearce, rhp
29. Skip Schumaker, of
30. Matt Lemanczyk, of

**By Will
Lingo**

After three straight years atop the National League Central and a 97-win season in 2002, the Cardinals fully expected to stay on top of their division and perhaps push into the World Series. But injuries and suspect pitching did in St. Louis, which finished third in the Central and was left with a lot of questions heading into 2004. While the offense and defense were statistically better than in 2002, the Cardinals' pitching was a patchwork operation again. This time, the patches didn't hold, as the bullpen blew 30 of 70 save opportunities.

The team went into the season with an $83 million payroll, slightly above what ownership had budgeted, so when the Cardinals needed a midseason deal to bolster the pitching staff they were unable to do anything major. They did get Mike DeJean and Sterling Hitchcock in August, but those two were unable to bail the team out. St. Louis gave up four pitching prospects in the two deals: 2001 first-round pick Justin Pope, plus Mike Crudale, Ben Julianel and John Novinsky. Though none of those arms were major parts of the franchise's future, the moves further weakened one of the game's thinnest minor league systems. To bolster the team's pitching and trim payroll in the offseason, the Cardinals traded J.D. Drew and Eli Marrero to the Braves for Jason Marquis and Ray King, as

well as premium prospect Adam Wainwright.

The system did provide a few pieces to the big league team. Last year's top prospect, righthander Dan Haren, got called up in June and pitched well before his workload of the last two years seemed to catch up with him. Overachieving 33rd-round pick Bo Hart provided a spark at second base when Fernando Vina went down, but he's not seen as a long-term answer.

The Cardinals have a lot of players like that in their system, guys who can contribute in the big leagues but won't have key roles on championship teams. St. Louis has done a good job of holding onto its premium prospects while making frequent deals for major leaguers in recent years—getting such stars as Edgar Renteria—but those premium prospects are getting fewer and farther between each year.

In a nod to that trend as well as to the best-selling book "Moneyball," the Cardinals restructured their scouting department. Scouting director Marty Maier was reassigned to special-assignment scout, and assistant general manager John Mozeliak took over the scouting department in addition to his duties as director of baseball operations. The Cardinals also hired Jeff Luhnow as an assistant vice president of baseball development to compile databases and try to improve the team's efficiency with the draft.

ORGANIZATION
OVERVIEW

General manager: Walt Jocketty. **Farm director:** Bruce Manno. **Scouting director:** John Mozeliak.

2003 PERFORMANCE

Class	Team	League	W	L	Pct.	Finish*	Manager
Majors	St. Louis	National	85	77	.525	t-7th (16)	Tony LaRussa
Triple-A	Memphis Redbirds	Pacific Coast	64	79	.448	15th (16)	Tom Spencer
Double-A	Tennessee Smokies	Southern	72	67	.518	4th (10)	Mark DeJohn
High A	Palm Beach Cardinals	Florida State	54	84	.391	12th (12)	Tom Nieto
Low A	Peoria Chiefs	Midwest	65	73	.471	11th (14)	Joe Cunningham
Short-season	New Jersey Cardinals	New York-Penn	31	42	.425	10th (14)	Tommy Shields
Rookie	Johnson City Cardinals	Appalachian	27	36	.429	7th (10)	Danny Sheaffer
OVERALL 2003 MINOR LEAGUE RECORD			313	381	.451	29th (30)	

*Finish in overall standings (No. of teams in league)

ORGANIZATION LEADERS

BATTING   *Minimum 250 At-Bats
*AVG	John Gall, Memphis/Tennessee	.314
R	Bucky Jacobsen, Tennessee	84
H	John Gall, Memphis/Tennessee	161
TB	Bucky Jacobsen, Tennessee	252
2B	Caonabo Cosme, Tennessee	35
3B	Reid Gorecki, Peoria	8
HR	Bucky Jacobsen, Tennessee	31
RBI	John Gall, Memphis/Tennessee	85
BB	Jon Nunnally, Memphis	98
SO	Jon Nunnally, Memphis	126
SB	Matt Lemanczyk, Tennessee /Peoria	57
*SLG	Bucky Jacobsen, Tennessee	.564
*OBP	Jon Nunnally, Memphis	.408

PITCHING   #Minimum 75 Innings
W	Jeremy Cummings, Memphis/Tennessee	15
L	Tyler Adamczyk, Peoria	12
	Rhett Parrott, Memphis/Tennessee	12
#ERA	Josh Kinney, Tennessee/Palm Beach	1.11
G	Carmen Cali, Palm Beach	62
CG	Don Graves, Palm Beach/Peoria	2
SV	Mike Lyons, Tennessee	31
IP	Jason Ryan, Memphis	190
BB	Chance Caple, Palm Beach	63
SO	Rhett Parrott, Memphis/Tennessee	137

BEST TOOLS

Best Hitter for Average	John Gall
Best Power Hitter	Dee Haynes
Fastest Baserunner	Matt Lemanczyk
Best Athlete	Brendan Ryan
Best Fastball	Blake Hawksworth
Best Curveball	Tyler Johnson
Best Slider	Brad Thompson
Best Changeup	Blake Hawksworth
Best Control	Adam Wainwright
Best Defensive Catcher	Yadier Molina
Best Defensive Infielder	Travis Hanson
Best Infield Arm	John Nelson
Best Defensive Outfielder	Skip Schumaker
Best Outfield Arm	Skip Schumaker

PROJECTED 2007 LINEUP

Catcher	Yadier Molina
First Base	John Gall
Second Base	Bo Hart
Third Base	Scott Rolen
Shortstop	Edgar Renteria
Left Field	Albert Pujols

Center Field	Jim Edmonds
Right Field	J.D. Drew
No. 1 Starter	Matt Morris
No. 2 Starter	Blake Hawksworth
No. 3 Starter	Dan Haren
No. 4 Starter	Adam Wainwright
No. 5 Starter	Chris Narveson
Closer	Jimmy Journell

LAST YEAR'S TOP 20 PROSPECTS

1. Dan Haren, rhp	11. Scotty Layfield, rhp
2. Jimmy Journell, rhp	12. Kyle Boyer, ss/2b
3. Chris Narveson, lhp	13. John Gall, 1b
4. Justin Pope, rhp	14. Travis Hanson, 3b
5. Blake Hawksworth, rhp	15. David Williamson, lhp
6. Shaun Boyd, 2b	16. Gabe Johnson, 3b
7. Rhett Parrott, rhp	17. Reid Gorecki, of
8. John Nelson, ss	18. Shane Reedy, rhp
9. Tyler Johnson, lhp	19. John Santor, 1b
10. Yadier Molina, c	20. John Novinsky, rhp

TOP PROSPECTS OF THE DECADE

1994	Brian Barber, rhp
1995	Alan Benes, rhp
1996	Alan Benes, rhp
1997	Matt Morris, rhp
1998	Rick Ankiel, lhp
1999	J.D. Drew, of
2000	Rick Ankiel, lhp
2001	Bud Smith, lhp
2002	Jimmy Journell, rhp
2003	Dan Haren, rhp

TOP DRAFT PICKS OF THE DECADE

1994	Bret Wagner, lhp
1995	Matt Morris, rhp
1996	Braden Looper, rhp
1997	Adam Kennedy, ss
1998	J.D. Drew, of
1999	Chance Caple, rhp
2000	Shaun Boyd, of
2001	Justin Pope, rhp
2002	Calvin Hayes, ss (3)
2003	Daric Barton, c

ALL-TIME LARGEST BONUSES

J.D. Drew, 1998	$3,000,000
Rick Ankiel, 1997	$2,500,000
Chad Hutchinson, 1998	$2,300,000
Shaun Boyd, 2000	$1,750,000
Braden Looper, 1996	$1,675,000

MINOR LEAGUE
DEPTH CHART

ST. LOUIS CARDINALS — RANK: 28

Impact potential (C): The addition of Adam Wainwright was a much-needed boost for a thin system. He and Blake Hawksworth represent the only hope for high-end potential in the future. The Cardinals lack position prospects with the raw tools or athleticism to make a difference in the majors.

Depth (F): The barren state of the Cardinals system was evident last summer when they didn't have the prospects on hand to execute a major deal at the trade deadline. They were forced to settle for lower-tier options in the trade market, such as first-round bust Justin Pope helping to bring in Sterling Hitchcock.

Sleeper: Cody Haerther, of. —*Depth charts prepared by Josh Boyd. Numbers in parentheses indicate prospect rankings.*

LF
Reid Gorecki (22)
Dee Haynes (23)
Matt Lemanczyk (30)

CF
Shaun Boyd (12)
Skip Schumaker (29)
Terry Evans
Jutt Hileman

RF
Cody Haerther (16)

3B
Travis Hanson (6)
Gabe Johnson

SS
Hector Luna (9)
John Nelson (13)
Brendan Ryan (18)
Calvin Hayes (26)
Kyle Boyer

2B
Kevin Estrada

1B
John Gall (7)
John Santor (17)
J.P. Davis
Chris Duncan

SOURCE OF TALENT

Homegrown		Acquired	
College	17	Trades	2
Junior College	0	Rule 5	1
Draft-and-follow	2	Independent	1
High school	6	Free agents	0
Nondrafted free agent	0		
Foreign	1		

C
Yadier Molina (4)
Daric Barton (10)
Tyler Parker

RHP

Starters	Relievers
Blake Hawksworth (1)	Josh Axelson (20)
Adam Wainwright (2)	Evan Rust (24)
Jimmy Journell (5)	Brad Thompson (25)
Rhett Parrott (8)	Brandon DeJaynes
Mark Michael (14)	Kiko Calero
Stuart Pomeranz (15)	Matt Duff
Anthony Reyes (19)	Scotty Layfield
Josh Kinney (21)	Jared Smith
Nick Stocks (27)	Andy Cavazos
Josh Pearce (28)	Roberto Batista
Tyler Adamczyk	
Dennis Dove	
Cristobal Correa	
Blake Williams	
Shane Reedy	
Josh Teekel	
Miguel Martinez	
Jordan Pals	
Erik Drown	

LHP

Starters	Relievers
Chris Narveson (3)	Tyler Johnson (11)
Tom Blair	Carmen Cali
	Josh Brey

DRAFT
ANALYSIS

Best Pro Debut: The Cardinals spent a late pick on OF Sal Frisella (37) because he had a quick bat and a right-field arm. He paid them back by hitting .315-8-37 and leading the Rookie-level Appalachian League in on-base percentage. SS Brendan Ryan (7) batted .311-0-13 with 11 steals in the short-season New York-Penn League. RHP Justin Garza (9) went 3-0, 1.53 between the two leagues.

Best Athlete: Ryan is a four-tool shortstop who lacks only power. RHPs Mark Michael (4) and Garza were two-way players in college.

Michael

RICH ABEL

Best Pure Hitter: C Daric Barton (1) is a gifted lefthanded hitter who batted .291-4-29 against more experienced Appy League pitchers.

Best Raw Power: OF Levi Webber (26) looks like a young Richie Sexson, though he does more damage in batting practice than in games (.188-4-23 in the Appy League). Barton isn't as strong but may have more usable power in the long run.

Fastest Runner: Ryan and 2B Temetric Thomas (24) have solid average speed.

Best Defensive Player: C Matt Pagnozzi (8) led NY-P catchers by throwing out 51 percent of basestealers. He can get the ball from home plate to second base (mitt to glove) in 1.8 seconds. He's so advanced defensively that he may jump to high Class A in 2004 despite batting .178 in his pro debut.

Best Fastball: RHP Dennis Dove (3) regularly throws in the mid-90s but is learning the importance of movement. RHP Stuart Pomeranz (2) works in the low 90s, and at 6-foot-7 he projects to catch up to Dove.

Best Breaking Ball: LHP Buddy Blair (10) has a sharp curveball.

Most Intriguing Background: Pagnozzi's uncle Tom was an all-star catcher for the Cardinals. OF Jose Virgil's (18) father Ozzie Jr. also was an all-star backstop, and his grandfather Ozzie Sr. was the first Dominican to play in the majors. SS Omar Pena's (16) brother Carlos is the Tigers' first baseman.

Closest To The Majors: RHP Anthony Reyes (15), if he can stay healthy and pitch like he did in instructional league. If not, Blair could get there first as a lefty specialist.

Best Late-Round Pick: At times, Reyes outpitched Mark Prior at Southern California as a freshman in 2000, but elbow trouble hampered the rest of his college career. In instructional league, he regained his low-90s fastball and good slider.

The One Who Got Away: RHP Ian Kennedy (14), now at USC, is advanced for his age and owns a solid fastball and slider.

Assessment: The Cardinals stocked up on young catchers and raw arms, two of the riskier demographics. Reyes has the potential to be the best pick in this draft.

2002 DRAFT   GRADE: **D**

The Cardinals didn't pick in the first two rounds, then may have reached for SS Calvin Hayes (3). Athletic 3B Travis Hanson (9) is the best player from this lackluster crop.

2001 DRAFT   GRADE: **B+**

St. Louis found 40 percent of its future rotation in RHPs Dan Haren (2) and Blake Hawksworth (28, draft-and-follow). RHP Rhett Parrott (9) may join them. RHP Justin Pope (1) had elbow issues before being dealt for Sterling Hitchcock.

2000 DRAFT   GRADE: **C**

LHP Chris Narveson (2) is back on track after Tommy John surgery in 2001, though RHP Blake Williams (1) never bounced back after the same operation. C Yadier Molina (4), 1B/OF John Gall (11), draft-and-follow LHP Tyler Johnson (34) and OF/2B Shaun Boyd (1) stand out somewhat in one of the game's thinnest systems.

1999 DRAFT   GRADE: **A**

OF Albert Pujols (13) erased the bad memories of three failed first-rounders: RHPs Chance Caple and Nick Stocks and 1B Chris Duncan. RHP Jim Journell (4) still has promise, and since-traded OF Coco Crisp (7) and 2B Bo Hart (33) had their moments in the majors in 2003.

—Draft analysis prepared by Jim Callis. Numbers in parentheses indicate draft rounds.

KEVIN MAY

Blake
Hawksworth

Born: March 1, 1983.
Ht.: 6-3. **Wt.:** 195.
Bats: R. **Throws:** R.
School: Bellevue (Wash.) CC.
Career Transactions: Selected by Cardinals in 28th round of 2001 draft; signed May 30, 2002.

He pitched just 87 innings in his first full professional season because of persistent ankle problems, but Hawksworth established himself as the organization's brightest light. He was a prominent prospect in high school, pitching on the same 2001 Eastlake High (Sammamish, Wash.) staff with Andy Sisco, a second-round pick that year who has emerged as one of the best prospects in the pitching-rich Cubs system. He fell to St. Louis in the 28th round because of a perceived strong commitment to Cal State Fullerton. At the last minute, though, he decided to enroll at nearby Bellevue CC, so the Cardinals retained his rights. They signed him the next May as a draft-and-follow for $1.475 million, making up for their lack of a first- or second-round pick that year. Hawksworth earned a promotion to high Class A Palm Beach last year after just 10 starts at low Class A Peoria, still enough to rank him as the Midwest League's top pitching prospect. He had a small spur in his ankle that bothered him all season and limited his running. He tried to pitch through it and did for the most part, but the Cardinals finally decided to shut him down at the end of July so he could have the spur removed. He should be at full strength for spring training.

Hawksworth has the highest ceiling of any St. Louis pitching prospect since Rick Ankiel. His fastball usually ranges from 90-92 mph, but it was clocked at 96 in the seventh inning of one start. He could pitch at 92-94 consistently as he fills out, and he has started pitching off his fastball consistently after relying too much on his offspeed stuff as an amateur. Both his curveball and changeup are potential above-average pitches. His curve has good rotation and his changeup has good fade. Hawksworth also has a good approach to pitching and admirable toughness. He makes pitches when he needs to, and when he gets ahead of hitters he puts them away. Fastball command is Hawksworth's biggest need, as it lags behind his control of the curve and changeup. Again, that's a function of his younger days, when he dominated hitters with his offspeed stuff and used his fastball sparingly. He can pitch to all four quadrants of the strike zone but doesn't always do so consistently. In part that's because, while his mechanics are smooth, his release point varies. Hawksworth needs to pitch a full season, not only to prove he's healthy but also to soak up the experience that only innings can bring.

Because the ankle injury slowed him down, Hawksworth could return to Palm Beach to start the 2004 season. But he'll likely spend a good portion of the season in Double-A Tennessee. One Midwest League manager said Hawksworth would be in St. Louis in no more than two years, and that's not an unreasonable prediction. He projects as a front-of-the-rotation starter in an organization that desperately needs pitching help.

Year	Club (League)	Class	W	L	ERA	G	GS	CG	SV	IP	H	R	ER	HR	BB	SO	AVG
2002	Johnson City (Appy)	R	2	4	3.14	13	12	0	0	66	58	31	23	8	18	61	.232
	New Jersey (NY-P)	A	1	0	0.00	2	2	0	0	10	6	0	0	0	2	8	.171
2003	Peoria (Mid)	A	5	1	2.30	10	10	0	0	55	37	16	14	0	12	57	.187
	Palm Beach (FSL)	A	1	3	3.94	6	6	0	0	32	28	14	14	2	11	32	.235
MINOR LEAGUE TOTALS			9	8	2.83	31	30	0	0	162	129	61	51	10	43	158	.214

2 Adam Wainwright, rhp

Born: Aug. 30, 1981. **Ht.:** 6-6. **Wt.:** 190. **Bats:** R. **Throws:** R. **School:** Glynn Academy, Brunswick, Ga. **Career Transactions:** Selected by Braves in first round (29th overall) of 2000 draft; signed June 12, 2000 . . . Traded by Braves with LHP Ray King and RHP Jason Marquis to Cardinals for OF J.D. Drew and OF Eli Marrero, Dec. 14, 2003.

Wainwright was the top pitching prospect in a deep Braves organization and provides a needed boost to the Cardinals after being the key player in the J.D. Drew trade. In his first season in Double-A, he overcame five straight losses at midseason to go 5-1, 2.14 in his final seven starts and rank 10th in the Southern League in ERA. Wainwright has an ideal combination of size, talent and makeup. He started working off his 92-93 mph fastball more often at midseason and the positive results were immediate. He also throws a hard curveball and a solid changeup, and he mixes his pitches and throws strikes well. He has a great work ethic and is one of the most intelligent pitchers in the minors. Wainwright needs to continue to gain confidence and trust his stuff. He tends to be too fine with his pitches instead of challenging hitters. He also needs to get his body stronger so he'll have better durability throughout the season and late into games. It was encouraging that Wainwright finished the season stronger than he started. He's still maturing and learning his craft and will continue to do so at Triple-A Memphis in 2004.

Year	Club (League)	Class	W	L	ERA	G	GS	CG	SV	IP	H	R	ER	HR	BB	SO	AVG
2000	Braves (GCL)	R	4	0	1.13	7	5	0	0	32	15	5	4	1	10	42	.136
	Danville (Appy)	R	2	2	3.68	6	6	0	0	29	28	13	12	3	2	39	.252
2001	Macon (SAL)	A	10	10	3.77	28	28	1	0	165	144	89	69	9	48	184	.230
2002	Myrtle Beach (Car)	A	9	6	3.31	28	28	1	0	163	149	67	60	7	66	167	.240
2003	Greenville (SL)	AA	10	8	3.37	27	27	1	0	150	133	59	56	9	37	128	.242
MINOR LEAGUE TOTALS			35	26	3.36	96	94	3	0	539	469	233	201	29	163	560	.233

3 Chris Narveson, lhp

Born: Dec. 20, 1981. **Ht.:** 6-3. **Wt.:** 180. **Bats:** L. **Throws:** L. **School:** T.C. Roberson HS, Skyland, N.C. **Career Transactions:** Selected by Cardinals in second round of 2000 draft; signed June 27, 2000.

Narveson returned to the mound in 2002 after Tommy John surgery in August 2001, but he didn't really regain his form until 2003. Named the organization's best minor league pitcher in spring training, he was selected for the high Class A Florida State League all-star game and retired both of the batters he faced in the Futures Game. Though he potentially has four pitches that could be major league average or better, Narveson's real strength is his intelligence and understanding of how to get hitters out. His changeup is a potential plus pitch. His fastball ranges from 86-90 mph, and his slider and curveball should be average pitches, with the slider more useful at this point. Narveson's command isn't what it needs to be yet, both in terms of throwing strikes and pitching effectively out of the strike zone. But the Cardinals liked the way he battled and stayed in games even when his control wasn't great. Narveson will probably go back to Double-A to start 2004. He profiles as a solid No. 3 starter who can be a workhorse.

Year	Club (League)	Class	W	L	ERA	G	GS	CG	SV	IP	H	R	ER	HR	BB	SO	AVG
2000	Johnson City (Appy)	R	2	4	3.27	12	12	0	0	55	57	33	20	7	25	63	.263
2001	Peoria (Mid)	A	3	3	1.98	8	8	0	0	50	32	14	11	3	11	53	.185
	Potomac (Car)	A	4	3	2.57	11	11	1	0	67	52	22	19	4	13	53	.212
2002	Johnson City (Appy)	R	0	2	4.91	6	6	0	0	18	23	12	10	2	6	16	.307
	Peoria (Mid)	A	2	1	4.46	9	9	0	0	42	49	24	21	5	8	36	.283
2003	Palm Beach (FSL)	A	7	7	2.86	15	14	1	0	91	83	34	29	4	19	65	.242
	Tennessee (SL)	AA	4	3	3.00	10	10	0	0	57	56	21	19	6	26	34	.262
MINOR LEAGUE TOTALS			22	23	3.05	71	70	2	0	381	352	160	129	31	108	320	.244

4 Yadier Molina, c

Born: July 13, 1982. **Ht.:** 5-11. **Wt.:** 185. **Bats:** R. **Throws:** R. **School:** Maestro Ladi HS, Vega Alta, P.R. **Career Transactions:** Selected by Cardinals in fourth round of 2000 draft; signed Sept. 6, 2000.

As the brother of Angels catchers Bengie and Jose Molina, Molina has terrific catching bloodlines, and he's on his way toward joining them in the majors. Skipping over high Class A, Molina held his own in Double-A in 2003. The only hiccup came when he missed a couple of weeks with a bruised ankle. As with his brothers, defense is Molina's calling card. He has a plus arm and soft hands, and led Southern League regulars by throwing out 40 percent of basestealers. He also is advanced for his age in working with pitchers and likes to take charge on the field. Speed is by far Molina's weakest tool, rating as low as 20 on the 20-80 scouting scale. It hurts him on offense, though he showed progress otherwise in 2003, staying on balls well and going the other way. He needs to do that more consistently and to improve his plate discipline. He never has hit for much power. Molina was batting third in the Tennessee order by the end of the season. He isn't expected to bat there as a big leaguer, but it showed he can handle the bat and continue to move quickly. He'll get a chance to be the starting catcher at Triple-A Memphis in 2004.

Year	Club (League)	Class	AVG	G	AB	R	H	2B	3B	HR	RBI	BB	SO	SB	SLG	OBP
2001	Johnson City (Appy)	R	.259	44	158	18	41	11	0	4	18	12	23	1	.405	.320
2002	Peoria (Mid)	A	.280	112	393	39	110	20	0	7	50	21	36	2	.384	.331
2003	Tennessee (SL)	AA	.275	104	364	32	100	13	1	2	51	25	45	0	.332	.327
MINOR LEAGUE TOTALS			.274	260	915	89	251	44	1	13	119	58	104	3	.367	.328

5 Jimmy Journell, rhp

STEVE MOORE

Born: Dec. 29, 1977. **Ht.:** 6-4. **Wt.:** 210. **Bats:** R. **Throws:** R. **School:** University of Illinois. **Career Transactions:** Selected by Cardinals in fourth round of 1999 draft; signed Aug. 12, 1999.

After two years as a starter, Journell went back to his college roots and returned to the bullpen in 2003. The results were dramatic, as his ERA was three runs lower as a reliever and batters hit .225 against him, as opposed to .311 as a starter. He made his big league debut in June. Journell has dynamic stuff when he's on, and that occurred much more regularly in relief. His fastball touched 96 mph out the pen, compared to 88-91 when he was starting, and his slider was much more effective. He likes relieving, and it's more comfortable for him physically as well. What ultimately drove Journell out of starting was his inconsistent mechanics, which affected his location and durability. He moves his arm slot and release point when he doesn't need to, which has been an issue throughout his career. Journell is at the age and stage of development where he needs to establish himself in the majors. The move to the bullpen gives him a good opportunity, and he'll get a long look in spring training.

Year	Club (League)	Class	W	L	ERA	G	GS	CG	SV	IP	H	R	ER	HR	BB	SO	AVG
2000	New Jersey (NY-P)	A	1	0	1.97	13	1	0	0	32	12	12	7	0	24	39	.111
2001	Potomac (Car)	A	14	6	2.50	26	26	0	0	151	121	54	42	8	42	156	.220
	New Haven (EL)	AA	1	0	0.00	1	1	1	0	7	0	0	0	0	3	6	.000
2002	New Haven (EL)	AA	3	3	2.70	10	10	2	0	67	50	22	20	3	18	66	.206
	Memphis (PCL)	AAA	2	4	3.68	7	7	0	0	37	38	16	15	3	18	32	.264
2003	Memphis (PCL)	AAA	6	6	3.92	40	7	0	5	78	80	38	34	3	32	70	.268
	St. Louis (NL)	MAJ	0	0	6.00	7	0	0	0	9	10	7	6	0	11	8	.278
MAJOR LEAGUE TOTALS			0	0	6.00	7	0	0	0	9	10	7	6	0	11	8	.278
MINOR LEAGUE TOTALS			27	19	2.86	97	52	3	5	371	301	142	118	17	137	369	.221

6 Travis Hanson, 3b

JOHN SPEAR

Born: Jan. 24, 1981. **Ht.:** 6-2. **Wt.:** 195. **Bats:** L. **Throws:** R. **School:** University of Portland. **Career Transactions:** Selected by Cardinals in ninth round of 2002 draft; signed June 9, 2002.

The valedictorian of his high school graduating class in suburban Seattle, Hanson was a late bloomer on the baseball field. He earned only a partial scholarship to Portland, where he was a three-year starter. He got off to a hot start at Peoria in his first full season, but a slow May and June left him with more pedestrian numbers. The organization already regards Hanson as its best defensive infielder. He shows athleticism, soft hands and a strong arm at third base, and some scouts think he should return to shortstop, his college position. He might fit better there offensively, because while he has gap power he could max out at 15 homers per year. Hanson does have a smooth, natural swing and uses the entire field. Hanson has good instincts at the plate but is still learning the strike zone and pitch recognition. He needs to get more selective and look for pitches he can drive. His speed is below-average. Hanson's age for his stage of development tempers excitement about him a bit, but he could remove questions with a midseason jump to Double-A. He'll open 2004 in high Class A.

Year	Club (League)	Class	AVG	G	AB	R	H	2B	3B	HR	RBI	BB	SO	SB	SLG	OBP
2002	New Jersey (NY-P)	A	.294	75	272	31	80	17	5	4	40	12	55	1	.438	.326
2003	Peoria (Mid)	A	.277	136	527	70	146	31	5	9	78	35	104	3	.406	.325
MINOR LEAGUE TOTALS			.283	211	799	101	226	48	10	13	118	47	159	4	.417	.325

7 John Gall, 1b/of

JOHN SPEAR

Born: April 2, 1978. **Ht.:** 6-0. **Wt.:** 195. **Bats:** R. **Throws:** R. **School:** Stanford University. **Career Transactions:** Selected by Cardinals in 11th round of 2000 draft; signed June 22, 2000.

Gall grew up 10 miles from the Stanford campus and played four years there, setting numerous school and Pacific-10 Conference offensive records. A cousin of Athletics outfielder Eric Byrnes, Gall flopped in his first Triple-A experience in 2003. He batted .179 in April, but got back on track in Double-A and raked when he returned to Memphis. His .314 combined average was best in the system. Gall has proven he'll hit no matter where he plays. He's patient, works counts and drives the ball to all fields. He's also an intelligent hitter, keeping a daily journal during the season with notes on virtually every at-bat. Gall's lack of atheticism works against him. He has toiled to improve his defense and footwork every offseason, but that part of his game remains far behind his offense. While his power has increased in the last couple of years, it may not be enough for first base. The Cardinals will give Gall time in left field in 2004 because his bat would fit better there. He'll get a shot at a big league job but is likely to return to Triple-A to start the season.

Year	Club (League)	Class	AVG	G	AB	R	H	2B	3B	HR	RBI	BB	SO	SB	SLG	OBP
2000	New Jersey (NY-P)	A	.239	71	259	28	62	10	0	2	27	25	37	16	.301	.304
2001	Peoria (Mid)	A	.302	57	205	27	62	23	0	4	44	16	18	0	.473	.353
	Potomac (Car)	A	.317	84	319	44	101	25	0	4	33	24	40	5	.433	.369
2002	New Haven (EL)	AA	.316	135	526	82	166	45	3	20	81	38	75	4	.527	.362
2003	Memphis (PCL)	AAA	.312	123	461	62	144	24	1	16	73	39	56	5	.473	.368
	Tennessee (SL)	AA	.327	12	52	6	17	1	0	3	12	3	4	0	.519	.357
MINOR LEAGUE TOTALS			.303	482	1822	249	552	128	4	49	270	145	230	30	.458	.355

8 Rhett Parrott, rhp

STEVE MOORE

Born: Nov. 12, 1979. **Ht.:** 6-2. **Wt.:** 190. **Bats:** R. **Throws:** R. **School:** Georgia Tech. **Career Transactions:** Selected by Cardinals in ninth round of 2001 draft; signed July 11, 2001.

Parrott built on his breakout 2002 season by getting to Triple-A in 2003, though it wasn't easy. He was called up on short notice at the end of July when Tennesee was on the road, so he spent a night in a Chicago airport and met Memphis in Omaha for a noon game the next day. Using all borrowed equipment, he gave up one run in five innings. The Cardinals like that story as an illustration of Parrott's mental toughness and thirst for competition. His stuff is also pretty good, with a fastball that registers 88-91 mph and an improving changeup. Parrott has struggled to develop a reliable breaking pitch. He threw a slider in college, abandoned it for a curveball as a pro and went back to it in 2003. It was an out pitch at times but still isn't consistent. His fastball command also took a step back, as he got quick to the plate and dropped his arm slot at times. Parrott will return to Triple-A to smooth out his remaining rough spots. He should make his big league debut in 2004 and profiles as a middle-of-the-rotation starter.

Year	Club (League)	Class	W	L	ERA	G	GS	CG	SV	IP	H	R	ER	HR	BB	SO	AVG
2001	New Jersey (NY-P)	A	1	3	4.93	11	11	0	0	46	45	27	25	3	28	58	.262
2002	Potomac (Car)	A	8	5	2.71	19	19	2	0	113	91	42	34	6	41	82	.221
	New Haven (EL)	AA	4	1	2.86	9	9	3	0	66	53	24	21	3	13	38	.223
2003	Tennessee (SL)	AA	8	9	3.27	21	21	1	0	124	122	52	45	11	40	112	.259
	Memphis (PCL)	AAA	2	3	3.54	7	7	0	0	41	39	16	16	2	19	25	.257
MINOR LEAGUE TOTALS			23	21	3.26	67	67	6	0	389	350	161	141	25	141	315	.242

9 Hector Luna, ss

JOHN SPEAR

Born: Feb. 1, 1980. **Ht.:** 6-1. **Wt.:** 170. **Bats:** R. **Throws:** R. **Career Transactions:** Signed out of Dominican Republic by Indians, Feb. 2, 1999 . . . Selected by Devil Rays from Indians in Rule 5 major league draft, Dec. 16, 2002 . . . Returned to Indians, April 2, 2003 . . . Selected by Cardinals from Indians in Rule 5 major league draft, Dec. 15, 2003.

The Indians lost Luna as a major league Rule 5 draft pick for the second straight year in December. After the Devil Rays picked him in 2002 and then returned him at the end of spring training, he went through a funk when he was returned to the Indians and assigned to Double-A. But he turned it around by the end of the season, hitting .313 in July and .407 in August. Luna is athletic and an above-average baserunner who can contribute offensively without driving the ball. He tends to drag the barrel of the bat through the zone, robbing him of power. He needs to use his strength more, and should be capable of hitting double figures in homers in the big leagues. Luna needs to play under control, particularly defensively, where his high error totals are a concern despite his arm, range and hands. He made 35 errors last year, mainly because he has poor footwork and fields the ball too close to his body. With improved consistency, Luna projects as a major league shortstop. If not, he could be a useful utilityman, and the role the Cardinals will use him in as they try to retain him. Rule 5 guidelines mandate that players selected have to be kept on the active major league roster, or else they have to be placed on waivers and then offered back to his original team for half the $50,000 draft price. Because Luna already has been through the process once and was outrighted last year, he'd become a free agent if he cleared waivers.

Year	Club (League)	Class	AVG	G	AB	R	H	2B	3B	HR	RBI	BB	SO	SB	SLG	OBP
1999	Indians (DSL)	R	.256	61	234	44	60	13	2	1	24	27	36	29	.342	.345
2000	Burlington (Appy)	R	.204	55	201	25	41	5	0	1	15	27	35	19	.244	.306
	Mahoning Valley (NY-P)	A	.316	5	19	2	6	2	0	0	4	1	3	0	.421	.350
2001	Columbus (SAL)	A	.266	66	241	36	64	8	3	3	23	23	48	15	.361	.339
2002	Kinston (Car)	A	.276	128	468	67	129	15	6	11	51	39	79	32	.404	.334
2003	Akron (EL)	AA	.297	127	462	87	137	19	2	2	38	48	64	17	.359	.368
MINOR LEAGUE TOTALS			.269	442	1625	261	437	62	13	18	155	165	265	112	.356	.342

10 Daric Barton, c

Born: Aug. 16, 1985. **Ht.:** 6-0. **Wt.:** 205. **Bats:** L. **Throws:** R. **School:** Marina HS, Huntington Beach, Calif. **Career Transactions:** Selected by Cardinals in first round (28th overall) of 2003 draft; signed June 10, 2003.

While Barton was one of three catchers picked by the Cardinals in the first eight rounds of the 2003 draft, it was his bat that intrigued them. He played third base as a high school senior because his coach's son did most of the catching, but spent most of his time behind the plate at Rookie-level Johnson City. Barton had one of the best lefthanded bats in the 2003 high school class. He's short to the ball and has a balanced swing. He already can hit for average and shows a good idea of the strike zone. He can pound the ball and will have power as he matures. The Cardinals said they were encouraged with Barton's defense, but he'll have to work to stay behind the plate, especially with Molina and eighth-rounder Matt Pagnozzi in the system. Barton has the potential to be a good receiver, but his arm is just average. He threw out 29 percent of Appalachian League basestealers. Barton is a baseball rat with the potential to be the impact bat the Cardinals system needs. He could blossom into a No. 3 hitter and would have tremendous value if he can catch. He'll stay behind the plate in low Class A in 2004.

Year	Club (League)	Class	AVG	G	AB	R	H	2B	3B	HR	RBI	BB	SO	SB	SLG	OBP
2003	Johnson City (Appy)	R	.294	54	170	29	50	10	0	4	29	37	48	0	.424	.420
MINOR LEAGUE TOTALS			.294	54	170	29	50	10	0	4	29	37	48	0	.424	.420

11 Tyler Johnson, lhp

Born: June 7, 1981. **Ht.:** 6-2. **Wt.:** 180. **Bats:** B. **Throws:** L. **School:** Moorpark (Calif.) JC. **Career Transactions:** Selected by Cardinals in 34th round of 2000 draft; signed May 15, 2001.

Johnson's amateur career stalled after high school, as he struggled to stay on the field because of academic difficulties. But he has moved quickly as a pro, leading the system with 15 wins in 2002 and jumping to Double-A in his second full season. His transition to the bullpen went as smoothly as could be expected. Johnson's curveball is the best breaking pitch in the organization, a true 12-to-6 bender that can be electric. He seemed happier and more confident in relief, and he likes knowing he could play every night. His fastball, which can touch 90-92 mph, and his improving changeup are solid-average pitches at times. Johnson is still maturing and learning how to pitch. He didn't show up in shape for spring training, and that resulted in nagging injuries and took away from his fastball, which was at 87-88 mph last season. Johnson's changeup is in the rudimentary stages. Johnson should move up to Triple-A to start 2004 and be ready to contribute to the big league bullpen later in the year. With his stuff, he should be able to be more than just a lefty specialist.

Year	Club (League)	Class	W	L	ERA	G	GS	CG	SV	IP	H	R	ER	HR	BB	SO	AVG
2001	Johnson City (Appy)	R	1	1	2.66	9	9	0	0	41	26	17	12	1	21	58	.181
	Peoria (Mid)	A	0	1	3.95	3	3	0	0	14	14	9	6	1	10	15	.255
2002	Peoria (Mid)	A	15	3	2.00	22	18	0	0	121	96	35	27	7	42	132	.218
2003	Palm Beach (FSL)	A	5	5	3.08	22	10	0	0	79	79	29	27	2	38	81	.262
	Tennessee (SL)	AA	1	0	1.65	20	0	0	0	27	16	7	5	1	15	39	.168
MINOR LEAGUE TOTALS			22	10	2.46	76	40	0	0	282	231	97	77	12	126	325	.223

12 Shaun Boyd, of/2b

Born: Aug. 15, 1981. **Ht.:** 5-10. **Wt.:** 175. **Bats:** R. **Throws:** R. **School:** Vista HS, Oceanside, Calif. **Career Transactions:** Selected by Cardinals in first round (13th overall) of 2000 draft; signed June 26, 2000.

Boyd's continuing search for a defensive home might finally end in the outfield. He has bounced between the outfield and second base since the Cardinals drafted him, but they finally put him back there for good after he committed 40 errors at second in 2002 and got off to a rough start there in high Class A last year. Boyd has the potential to be a dynamic offensive presence, and when his defensive struggles started to affect him at the plate, St. Louis decided a change was needed. He has a smooth swing and profiles as a No. 2 hitter with some pop in his bat. He draws walks and makes contact, but Boyd must start driving the ball with more consistent authority. Though he has taken to the outfield and can make up for many mistakes with his athleticism, Boyd still needs repetitions to improve his routes and other nuances of outfield play. He played left and center field in the Arizona Fall League, and the Cardinals hope he can handle center because he doesn't profile as well as a corner outfielder. His arm is OK and could get better with more outfield work. The move to the outfield may allow Boyd to move more quickly up the organizational ladder. He'll open 2004 back in Double-A.

Year	Club (League)	Class	AVG	G	AB	R	H	2B	3B	HR	RBI	BB	SO	SB	SLG	OBP
2000	Johnson City (Appy)	R	.263	43	152	15	40	9	0	2	15	10	22	6	.362	.315
2001	Peoria (Mid)	A	.282	81	277	42	78	12	2	5	27	33	42	20	.394	.357
2002	Peoria (Mid)	A	.313	129	520	91	163	36	5	12	60	54	78	32	.471	.379
2003	Palm Beach (FSL)	A	.257	110	416	59	107	17	2	5	35	54	70	28	.344	.343
	Tennessee (SL)	AA	.273	27	88	9	24	6	0	0	6	4	12	2	.341	.305
MINOR LEAGUE TOTALS			.284	390	1453	216	412	80	9	24	143	155	224	88	.401	.354

13 John Nelson, ss

Born: March 3, 1979. **Ht.:** 6-1. **Wt.:** 190. **Bats:** R. **Throws:** R. **School:** University of Kansas. **Career Transactions:** Selected by Cardinals in eighth round of 2001 draft; signed June 17, 2001.

Nelson started in the organization as an outfielder, but he got an opportunity at shortstop because of a temporary shortage of players in spring training 2002. He had a breakthrough season, but regressed significantly in 2003. Sent to the Arizona Fall League to try to turn things around, Nelson broke a bone in his hand trying to check his swing. Nelson has the makings of a big league shortstop, with a 70 arm on the 20-80 scouting scale as his best tool. He's a good athlete and above-average runner. He has the strength to put a charge in the ball. Nelson needs to learn plate discipline and change his approach. He gets anxious and overaggressive if he gets in a hole and thinks one swing can get him out of it. That thinking just gets him out. He needs to slow things down and shorten his swing. Nelson's struggles weren't a complete surprise to the Cardinals because he skipped high Class A, but the extent of them was. Because he didn't get to redeem himself in the AFL, he'll probably go back to Double-A to start the season.

Year	Club (League)	Class	AVG	G	AB	R	H	2B	3B	HR	RBI	BB	SO	SB	SLG	OBP
2001	New Jersey (NY-P)	A	.238	66	252	43	60	16	3	8	26	35	76	14	.421	.332
2002	Peoria (Mid)	A	.274	132	481	85	132	28	5	16	63	54	123	16	.453	.349
2003	Tennessee (SL)	AA	.237	136	506	60	120	22	1	5	42	44	117	10	.314	.301
MINOR LEAGUE TOTALS			.252	334	1239	188	312	66	9	29	131	133	316	40	.390	.326

14 Mark Michael, rhp

Born: Aug. 25, 1982. **Ht.:** 6-4. **Wt.:** 215. **Bats:** R. **Throws:** R. **School:** University of Delaware. **Career Transactions:** Selected by Cardinals in fourth round of 2003 draft; signed June 5, 2003.

Michael was a two-way standout for Gloucester (N.J.) Catholic High when it won the 2000 national high school championship, and the Twins made him a 21st-round pick. He went to Old Dominion instead and transferred to Delaware after his freshman year. He spent more time hitting than pitching before 2003, playing the corner infield positions and DH. The Blue Hens used him on the mound last spring and the results weren't pretty: 3-4, 6.96 with 27 walks, 12 wild pitches and 16 hit batters in 53 innings. The Cardinals liked his live arm, though, and think he could develop quickly after signing for $220,550 as a fourth-round pick. He made consecutive starts without a walk late in the season and looked very sharp in his lone victory. Pitching coordinator Mark Riggins and short-season New Jersey pitching coach Sid Monge worked on Michael's mechanics because he opened up too soon and his arm dragged, getting his delivery out of sync. The adjustments made an immediate difference. Michael throws 89-94 mph from a three-quarters arm angle, sitting at 91 most of the time. His curveball and changeup both show potential. He has a big, projectable body and could add velocity as he gains experience. He still has screws in his elbow from surgery he had in high school, but his health isn't a concern. While Michael is definitely a project, the early returns were promising. If he pitches well in low Class A to start the season, he could move quickly.

Year	Club (League)	Class	W	L	ERA	G	GS	CG	SV	IP	H	R	ER	HR	BB	SO	AVG
2003	New Jersey (NY-P)	A	1	2	3.17	11	10	0	0	54	50	23	19	0	20	56	.249
MINOR LEAGUE TOTALS			1	2	3.17	11	10	0	0	54	50	23	19	0	20	56	.249

15 Stuart Pomeranz, rhp

Born: Dec. 17, 1984. **Ht.:** 6-7. **Wt.:** 220. **Bats:** R. **Throws:** R. **School:** Houston HS, Collierville, Tenn. **Career Transactions:** Selected by Cardinals in second round of 2003 draft; signed July 23, 2003.

The top prospect in Tennessee for the 2003 draft, Pomeranz also earned High School All-America honors. He went 13-1, 0.52 with 165 strikeouts in 94 innings and had a 52-inning scoreless streak. The Cardinals signed him for $570,000 after making him a second-round pick, then gave him a light workload at Rookie-level Johnson City. They love his big body, which makes him projectable even though he already throws 88-92 mph. He also has an above-average curveball with good depth, and a changeup that's advanced for a prep pitcher. Pomeranz also has strong mound presence, a feel for pitching and the ability to throw strikes. He doesn't have a very quick arm, which may keep his velocity down a bit. Pomeranz' first real chance to prove himself as a pro will come in low Class A this season.

Year	Club (League)	Class	W	L	ERA	G	GS	CG	SV	IP	H	R	ER	HR	BB	SO	AVG
2003	Johnson City (Appy)	R	1	1	6.14	4	3	0	0	15	13	10	10	2	4	14	.236
MINOR LEAGUE TOTALS			1	1	6.14	4	3	0	0	15	13	10	10	2	4	14	.236

16 Cody Haerther, of/3b

Born: July 14, 1983. **Ht.:** 6-0. **Wt.:** 190. **Bats:** L. **Throws:** R. **School:** Chaminade Prep, Chatsworth, Calif. **Career Transactions:** Selected by Cardinals in sixth round of 2002 draft; signed July 31, 2002.

Haerther was a star at Chaminade Prep in Chatsworth, Calif., where his brother Casey was named the state's freshman baseball player of the year by one organization in 2003. Cody fell in the 2002 draft because of a perceived strong commitment to UC Irvine. The Cardinals signed him for $250,000, the largest bonus in the sixth round, and he didn't make his pro debut until last year. He topped the Rookie-level Appalachian League in hits and was among the leaders in several offensive categories, and he followed up with a strong instructional league performance. Haerther's bat is his calling card. He has bat speed, a sound approach and a good eye at the plate. He shows the ability to drive the ball and should hit for power down the road. He has decent speed. The Cardinals are trying to find a defensive home for Haerther. He has some arm strength and played third base in high school, but St. Louis moved him to left field last year. Though he has work to do in the outfield, he was more comfortable there and the Cards don't want his defense to get in the way of his bat. They'll move him to low Class A in 2004.

Year	Club (League)	Class	AVG	G	AB	R	H	2B	3B	HR	RBI	BB	SO	SB	SLG	OBP
2003	Johnson City (Appy)	R	.332	63	226	31	75	12	6	3	39	22	30	2	.478	.390
MINOR LEAGUE TOTALS			.332	63	226	31	75	12	6	3	39	22	30	2	.478	.390

17 John Santor, 1b

Born: Nov. 16, 1981. **Ht.:** 6-1. **Wt.:** 215. **Bats:** B. **Throws:** R. **School:** Highland HS, Palmdale, Calif. **Career Transactions:** Selected by Cardinals in 35th round of 2000 draft; signed June 16, 2000.

Santor continues to move methodically through the organization after the Cardinals took a 35th-round shot at him in the 2000 draft. After three seasons in short-season ball, Santor had a solid year in low Class A, making the Midwest League's midseason all-star team and tying a league record by going 4-for-4 with four doubles in one game. Santor is a strong switch-hitter with a smooth swing who uses his hands well. His approach started to come around at New Jersey in 2002 and continued last season, as he centered the ball well and sprayed the ball all over the field. The Cardinals expect him to add power but don't want him to change his approach to try to do so. He can turn on balls and handle breaking pitches, though St. Louis wants him to cut down his strikeouts. He should be an average first baseman with better mobility than might be expected for his size, and he led MWL first basemen in assists and double plays last season. In a system devoid of impact bats, the Cardinals' patience with Santor could pay off. They'll try to skip him over high Class A to Double-A in 2004.

Year	Club (League)	Class	AVG	G	AB	R	H	2B	3B	HR	RBI	BB	SO	SB	SLG	OBP
2000	Johnson City (Appy)	R	.174	14	46	3	8	3	0	0	4	2	13	1	.239	.208
2001	New Jersey (NY-P)	A	.227	54	185	17	42	12	2	2	26	22	64	3	.346	.308
2002	Peoria (Mid)	A	.000	1	4	0	0	0	0	0	0	0	1	0	.000	.000
	New Jersey (NY-P)	A	.293	68	239	44	70	24	1	13	62	32	62	4	.565	.380
2003	Peoria (Mid)	A	.268	133	474	57	127	28	2	9	71	54	105	4	.392	.348
MINOR LEAGUE TOTALS			.261	270	948	121	247	67	5	24	163	110	245	12	.418	.341

18 Brendan Ryan, ss

Born: March 26, 1982. **Ht.:** 6-2. **Wt.:** 195. **Bats:** R. **Throws:** R. **School:** Lewis-Clark State (Idaho) College. **Career Transactions:** Selected by Cardinals in seventh round of 2003 draft; signed June 14, 2003.

Ryan played for NAIA power Lewis-Clark State, winning a NAIA World Series championship in 2002 but getting dismissed from the program before the Warriors repeated in 2003. He also won a National Baseball Congress World Series title with the Alaska Goldpanners in 2002. Ryan had a promising pro debut, putting together 16 multihit games, including a five-hit contest. Ryan is a good athlete who brings a high-energy approach to the field and is always in motion. He has some strength and bat speed, uses his hands well and already has a decent idea of the strike zone. He also has some power potential and was occasionally impressive in the way he drove the ball, though he needs to fill out. Ryan also has promising defensive tools, including quickness, soft hands and arm strength, though he committed 14 errors in just 32 games in the field. Ryan's biggest need at this point is experience. The Cardinals were impressed with the way he adjusted to pro ball and will send him to low Class A to open 2004.

Year	Club (League)	Class	AVG	G	AB	R	H	2B	3B	HR	RBI	BB	SO	SB	SLG	OBP
2003	New Jersey (NY-P)	A	.311	53	193	20	60	14	4	0	13	14	25	11	.425	.363
MINOR LEAGUE TOTALS			.311	53	193	20	60	14	4	0	13	14	25	11	.425	.363

19 Anthony Reyes, rhp

Born: Oct. 16, 1981. **Ht.:** 6-2. **Wt.:** 215. **Bats:** R. **Throws:** R. **School:** University of Southern California. **Career Transactions:** Selected by Cardinals in 15th round of 2003 draft; signed Aug. 29, 2003.

Reyes gained national attention as a freshman at Southern California in 2000, pitching better than teammate Mark Prior at times as the Trojans advanced to the College World Series. But while Prior built on that experience, Reyes failed to live up to expectations and struggled with injuries. He had elbow tendinitis in 2002 and his velocity dropped, so he fell to the 13th round of the draft. He declined to sign with the Tigers and opted to return for his senior year to improve his stock, but he showed only flashes of his previous form and again struggled with elbow problems. The Cardinals took a chance on him in the 15th round, and he looked like he might be returning to form in instructional league. His fastball, which ranged from 89-94 mph in college, was back in the low 90s, and his slider was sharp again. Reyes never lost his effortless delivery, and if his stuff returns he could be the steal of the 2003 draft. His command also is expected to be strong, but that's of secondary concern at this point. The Cardinals are anxious to send Reyes to one of their Class A affiliate to see if he can keep up the encouraging results.

Year	Club (League)	Class	W	L	ERA	G	GS	CG	SV	IP	H	R	ER	HR	BB	SO	AVG
2003	Did not play—Signed 2004 contract																

20 Josh Axelson, rhp

Born: Dec. 4, 1978. **Ht.:** 6-1. **Wt.:** 200. **Bats:** R. **Throws:** R. **School:** Michigan State University. **Career Transactions:** Selected by Cardinals in fifth round of 2000 draft; signed June 14, 2000.

Axelson has been one of the organization's biggest enigmas since he was drafted, and he was just as puzzling at Michigan State. He has bounced back and forth between the bullpen and the rotation during the last two years, though he was the best starter on the Double-A staff in the final month of the 2003 season. The Cardinals sent him to the Arizona Fall League to get more work as a starter, but he was out of gas and got knocked around with a 7.36 ERA in 33 innings. Axelson has an average fastball that ranged from 88-92 mph last year, a good curveball and a slider he uses occasionally. His changeup showed progress last season. More important, though, Axelson started to understand how to pitch. He regarded himself as a power pitcher coming out of college, and his stubborn, bulldog approach often held him back. After a change to his mechanics got him going in 2002, the mental adjustment moved him further ahead last season. He'll have a chance to win a spot in the Triple-A rotation in 2004, though it won't be considered a disappointment if he opens the season back in Tennessee. The Cardinals think he can succeed either starting or relieving.

Year	Club (League)	Class	W	L	ERA	G	GS	CG	SV	IP	H	R	ER	HR	BB	SO	AVG
2000	New Jersey (NY-P)	A	3	9	5.13	15	14	0	0	74	79	53	42	2	34	63	.275
2001	Peoria (Mid)	A	5	7	4.61	18	18	1	0	109	112	62	56	12	28	77	.264
	Potomac (Car)	A	2	5	5.56	10	10	1	0	57	61	41	35	10	19	38	.275
2002	Potomac (Car)	A	6	7	4.09	32	20	2	0	136	135	72	62	12	40	82	.259
2003	Palm Beach (FSL)	A	0	2	3.12	9	1	0	0	26	21	9	9	1	4	23	.219
	Tennessee (SL)	AA	4	2	2.76	27	8	0	0	75	68	26	23	7	19	58	.247
MINOR LEAGUE TOTALS			20	32	4.28	111	71	4	0	477	476	263	227	44	144	341	.261

21 Josh Kinney, rhp

Born: March 31, 1979. **Ht.:** 6-1. **Wt.:** 195. **Bats:** R. **Throws:** R. **School:** Quincy (Ill.) University. **Career Transactions:** Signed by independent River City (Frontier), June 2001 . . . Contract purchased by Cardinals from River City, June 15, 2001.

Kinney had a 2.31 ERA as a senior at NCAA Division II Quincy (Ill.), but he was passed over in the draft and signed with River City in the independent Frontier League. It took just three starts there before the Cardinals snapped him up, and he has moved up quickly if quietly as a reliever. He dominated in high Class A and was even better after a promotion to Double-A in 2003, then went to the Arizona Fall League after the season. Injured in his second AFL appearance, he didn't feel pain but couldn't get anything on the ball. An MRI revealed a partial tear of his labrum and he had shoulder surgery, though he's supposed to be healthy for spring training. Kinney is a sinker/slider pitcher, throwing his fastball at 88-90 mph with hard dowward action. His slider is more sweeping than sharp. He's a groundball pitcher who can come in and get a double-play ball. He doesn't use a changeup very often but doesn't usually need to. His command improved significantly last season, but it needs further refinement for him to be successful against advanced hitters. He'll stay in the bullpen and probably go back to Double-A to open 2004, assuming he's healthy. He could figure into the Cardinals' bullpen plans for 2005.

Year	Club (League)	Class	W	L	ERA	G	GS	CG	SV	IP	H	R	ER	HR	BB	SO	AVG
2001	River City (Fron)	IND	1	0	1.71	3	3	0	0	21	18	7	4	1	7	18	.237
	New Jersey (NY-P)	A	2	0	0.00	3	0	0	0	6	2	0	0	0	0	5	.111
	Peoria (Mid)	A	1	4	4.39	27	0	0	0	41	47	24	20	1	15	35	.287
2002	Potomac (Car)	A	1	3	2.29	44	0	0	7	55	52	21	14	2	23	42	.248
2003	Palm Beach (FSL)	A	3	0	1.52	31	0	0	3	41	38	7	7	0	10	35	.245
	Tennessee (SL)	AA	2	1	0.68	29	0	0	2	40	19	4	3	2	12	48	.142
MINOR LEAGUE TOTALS			9	8	2.17	134	0	0	12	183	158	56	44	5	60	165	.232

22 Reid Gorecki, of

Born: Dec. 22, 1980. **Ht.:** 6-1. **Wt.:** 180. **Bats:** R. **Throws:** R. **School:** University of Delaware. **Career Transactions:** Selected by Cardinals in 13th round of 2002 draft; signed June 10, 2002.

Gorecki broke the short-season New York-Penn League's 30-year-old record for triples with 13 in his 2002 pro debut. He built on that success last year by leading a weak Peoria lineup in several offensive categories. Gorecki is a strong athlete with a nice all-around game. He has a solid swing and some power potential. His approach at the plate improved in 2003, though he still strikes out too much for someone who provides mainly gap power. Gorecki has good speed but struggles to use it judiciously on the basepaths, getting caught 11 times in 34 attempts last year. His speed plays well on defense, however, and makes him a strong center fielder. His hustle helps him on defense as well, and his outgoing personality makes him a favorite of Cardinals brass and fans. Gorecki offers no overwhelming tools but is solid in all aspects. He has been moved slowly so far, particularly for a college player, and the Cardinals are looking for big things when he moves up to high Class A this season.

Year	Club (League)	Class	AVG	G	AB	R	H	2B	3B	HR	RBI	BB	SO	SB	SLG	OBP
2002	New Jersey (NY-P)	A	.281	73	274	55	77	8	52	9	57	22	.493	.327
2003	Peoria (Mid)	A	.267	128	480	77	128	19	8	15	61	51	90	23	.433	.338
MINOR LEAGUE TOTALS			.272	201	754	132	205	27	21	23	113	71	147	45	.455	.334

23 Dee Haynes, of

Born: Feb. 22, 1978. **Ht.:** 6-0. **Wt.:** 205. **Bats:** R. **Throws:** R. **School:** Delta State (Miss.) University. **Career Transactions:** Selected by Cardinals in 14th round of 2000 draft; signed June 12, 2000.

It's no wonder that Haynes is a fan favorite. He grew up in Mississippi and now lives in Memphis, and he called the Memphis Redbirds' front office this offseason to see if he could help in any way. The Redbirds brought him in to help make season-ticket calls, so when he wasn't working out in the AutoZone Park weight room he was selling tickets to fans. On the field in Memphis last year, he had middling results on the heels of a breakout year in 2002. He had surgery to remove bone spurs from both big toes after the 2003 season, as well as laser-eye surgery. Haynes is a muscular specimen with above-average power potential, and he has a knack for getting the bat on the ball. He still needs to learn to lay off pitchers' pitches, though. He doesn't strike out a lot, but he rarely walks and gets himself out too often. Haynes should be average in left field, though he has to work to keep himself from getting too bulky. St. Louis' left-field situation is muddled, so it's conceivable Haynes could work his way into the picture with a hot spring. Realistically, though, he'll repeat Triple-A.

Year	Club (League)	Class	AVG	G	AB	R	H	2B	3B	HR	RBI	BB	SO	SB	SLG	OBP
2000	New Jersey (NY-P)	A	.255	64	243	31	62	18	4	7	37	16	53	4	.449	.300
2001	Potomac (Car)	A	.290	114	417	45	121	24	3	13	72	14	82	5	.456	.329
2002	New Haven (EL)	AA	.312	131	504	75	157	29	4	21	98	25	67	3	.510	.355
2003	Memphis (PCL)	AAA	.252	125	441	53	111	24	3	18	70	15	50	3	.442	.279
MINOR LEAGUE TOTALS			.281	434	1605	204	451	95	14	59	277	70	252	15	.468	.319

24 Evan Rust, rhp

Born: May 4, 1978. **Ht.:** 6-1. **Wt.:** 200. **Bats:** R. **Throws:** R. **School:** St. Mary's (Calif.) University. **Career Transactions:** Signed as nondrafted free agent by Devil Rays, June 15, 2000 . . . Traded by Devil Rays with a player to be named to Cardinals for 1B Tino Martinez, Nov. 21, 2003; Cardinals acquired 1B John-Paul Davis to complete trade (Dec. 16, 2003).

Rust was the key player the Cardinals acquired in the Tino Martinez deal, though the main thrust of the trade was simply to unload Martinez. Rust signed as a nondrafted free agent in 2000 after going 1-11 at St. Mary's (Calif.). Managers rated him the best reliever in the high Class A California League in 2002, and he encored with a solid performance last season. Rust's fastball sits in the low 90s and he complements it with a curveball. He does a good job of keeping his pitches down in the strike zone, allowing only one homer in 2003 and just eight as a pro. He's not overpowering but has proven himself at every step so far. With the St. Louis bullpen in flux, Rust figures to get a long look in the spring. If he doesn't make the big league club, he'll start the year in Triple-A.

Year	Club (League)	Class	W	L	ERA	G	GS	CG	SV	IP	H	R	ER	HR	BB	SO	AVG
2000	Princeton (Appy)	R	5	2	2.89	26	0	0	1	44	37	17	14	3	13	34	.226
2001	Charleston, SC (SAL)	A	7	6	3.06	35	11	0	12	97	88	47	33	3	27	88	.238
2002	Bakersfield (Cal)	A	0	1	2.18	28	0	0	23	33	28	8	8	1	10	45	.233
	Orlando (SL)	AA	1	3	3.70	26	0	0	8	24	30	10	10	0	14	25	.294
2003	Orlando (SL)	AA	1	3	2.65	30	0	0	11	34	28	13	10	0	15	35	.212
	Durham (IL)	AAA	2	2	3.25	26	0	0	1	36	32	13	13	1	10	26	.244
MINOR LEAGUE TOTALS			16	17	2.96	171	11	0	56	268	243	108	88	8	89	253	.239

25 Brad Thompson, rhp

Born: Jan. 31, 1982. **Ht.:** 6-1. **Wt.:** 190. **Bats:** R. **Throws:** R. **School:** Dixie (Utah) JC. **Career Transactions:** Selected by Cardinals in 16th round of 2002 draft; signed Aug. 3, 2002.

Thompson has been in the right place at the right time a lot recently. He was going to walk on at the CC of Southern Nevada after graduating from high school, but attended Dixie (Utah) JC. The Cardinals spotted him there while scouting his teammate, infielder Kyle Boyer, and drafted both of them in 2002. After a strong pro debut last year, Thompson was in instructional league when Josh Kinney hurt his shoulder in the Arizona Fall League. Chosen to replace Kinney, Thompson put up a 1.59 in nine AFL appearances. His main pitches are a low-90s sinker and the best slider in the system. He worked on adding a changeup in instructional league after never really using one before. Thompson throws strikes but has to locate his pitches better in the strike zone because he has been hittable. Though he has set up and closed so far as a pro, he projects as a middle reliever in the big leagues. He could open at Double-A with a good spring, though he's more likely to start 2004 back in high Class A.

Year	Club (League)	Class	W	L	ERA	G	GS	CG	SV	IP	H	R	ER	HR	BB	SO	AVG
2003	Peoria (Mid)	A	5	3	2.91	30	4	0	0	65	70	23	21	2	10	43	.273
	Palm Beach (FSL)	A	1	0	0.00	2	1	0	0	6	3	0	0	0	0	4	.158
MINOR LEAGUE TOTALS			6	3	2.66	32	5	0	0	71	73	23	21	2	10	47	.265

26 Calvin Hayes, ss

Born: March 21, 1984. **Ht.:** 5-9. **Wt.:** 190. **Bats:** R. **Throws:** R. **School:** East Rowan HS, Salisbury, N.C. **Career Transactions:** Selected by Cardinals in third round of 2002 draft; signed Aug. 20, 2002.

Hayes was the Cardinals' first pick in the 2002 draft, though he was the final selection of the third round. St. Louis lost its first two picks for signing free agents Tino Martinez and Jason Isringhausen. Hayes had committed to the University of North Carolina, but St. Louis signed him late in the summer for $400,000. He stood out more as a running back in high school and many teams didn't see him as a third-rounder, but the Cardinals zeroed in on him early. He missed a month of his pro debut last year with a strained left wrist. Hayes is an all-around athlete, and his speed and quickness stand out the most among his tools. He uses his wheels well on the basepaths, succeeding on 16 of his 18 steal attempts in 2003. He should have gap power and showed a better-than-expected approach at the plate. He jumps at the ball sometimes and will need to channel his aggressive approach. Hayes has the tools to be a solid defender, though he'll probably outgrow shortstop and struggled there in Rookie ball, making 19 errors in just 32 games. He's very much a work in progress. He'll spend this season in low Class A.

Year	Club (League)	Class	AVG	G	AB	R	H	2B	3B	HR	RBI	BB	SO	SB	SLG	OBP
2003	Johnson City (Appy)	R	.304	35	125	25	38	5	0	2	11	14	20	16	.392	.387
MINOR LEAGUE TOTALS			.304	35	125	25	38	5	0	2	11	14	20	16	.392	.387

27 Nick Stocks, rhp

Born: Aug. 27, 1978. **Ht.:** 6-2. **Wt.:** 185. **Bats:** R. **Throws:** R. **School:** Florida State University. **Career Transactions:** Selected by Cardinals in first round (36th overall) of 1999 draft; signed Aug. 29, 1999.

Stocks isn't the pitcher he was when the Cardinals made him a supplemental first-round pick in 1999, but that might turn out to be best for all involved. He had Tommy John surgery while at Florida State, and he has been bothered by persistent back and shoulder problems as a pro. He finally put together a full, healthy season at Double-A in 2003, and while he didn't have good numbers the organization still considered it a bounce-back year. His velocity came closer to his old mid-90s peak after he threw in the mid-80s in 2002, but he chose to focus on movement rather than pure velocity. He threw a two-seam fastball that's 3-4 mph slower than his four-seamer, so he sat at 87-88 mph and touched 92-93 when he needed something extra. His curveball and changeup were also effective at times, though he must get more consistent with them. His command wasn't good, but the Cardinals expect it to improve with more healthy innings. Stocks finally made the adjustments the organization wanted him to make several years ago, when he thought he could rely on power. He could get himself back into the big league picture with another healthy season and better results. He'll compete for a Triple-A job in spring training.

Year	Club (League)	Class	W	L	ERA	G	GS	CG	SV	IP	H	R	ER	HR	BB	SO	AVG
2000	Peoria (Mid)	A	10	10	3.78	25	24	1	0	150	133	88	63	4	52	118	.234
2001	New Haven (EL)	AA	2	12	5.16	16	15	1	0	82	89	52	47	10	33	63	.276
2002	New Jersey (NY-P)	A	0	2	5.73	7	7	0	0	22	28	14	14	0	13	24	.308
	Peoria (Mid)	A	1	0	2.25	1	1	0	0	8	6	2	2	0	1	3	.222
	Potomac (Car)	A	0	2	5.74	3	3	0	0	16	18	13	10	3	6	11	.277
2003	Tennessee (SL)	AA	10	8	4.77	27	26	0	0	151	160	86	80	17	58	109	.275
MINOR LEAGUE TOTALS			23	34	4.53	79	76	2	0	429	434	255	216	34	163	328	.262

28 Josh Pearce, rhp

Born: Aug. 20, 1977. **Ht.:** 6-3. **Wt.:** 220. **Bats:** R. **Throws:** R. **School:** University of Arizona. **Career Transactions:** Selected by Cardinals in second round of 1999 draft; signed June 18, 1999.

Pearce showed flashes of his old form last year in his return from shoulder surgery. He was worked hard in college at Arizona, then piled up 423 more innings in his first 2½ pro seasons. He finally broke down in May 2002 with a torn labrum. Pearce got called up to St. Louis briefly last July, then was told along with the rest of his Memphis teammates that none of them would be called up in September. The Cardinals changed their mind and promoted Pearce as an extra arm for their bullpen, and he pitched well in that role. Pearce mixed strong outings with bad ones throughout the season, but the Cardinals say it was to be expected. His velocity was back to its previous 88-91 mph level most of the time, and he also showed good command. His slurvy breaking ball and changeup should be at least average pitches. He has a bulldog mentality and competes hard, but he has no real out pitch and can get knocked around if he's not sharp. Pearce will compete for a bullpen job in spring training and return to Triple-A if he doesn't win one.

Year	Club (League)	Class	W	L	ERA	G	GS	CG	SV	IP	H	R	ER	HR	BB	SO	AVG
1999	New Jersey (NY-P)	A	3	7	4.98	14	14	1	0	78	78	45	43	8	20	78	.257
2000	Potomac (Car)	A	5	3	3.45	10	10	1	0	63	70	25	24	5	10	42	.283
	Arkansas (TL)	AA	5	6	5.46	17	17	0	0	97	117	68	59	13	35	63	.298
2001	New Haven (EL)	AA	6	8	3.75	18	18	0	0	115	111	55	48	11	34	96	.253
	Memphis (PCL)	AAA	4	4	4.26	10	10	0	0	70	72	43	33	11	12	36	.266
2002	Memphis (PCL)	AAA	0	4	7.65	4	4	0	0	20	28	18	17	8	3	17	.322
	St. Louis (NL)	MAJ	0	0	7.62	3	3	0	0	13	20	13	11	1	8	1	.377
2003	Palm Beach (FSL)	A	1	4	3.21	6	5	0	0	28	28	10	10	2	2	15	.275
	Tennessee (SL)	AA	2	1	4.09	5	5	0	0	33	34	15	15	3	3	20	.270
	Memphis (PCL)	AAA	3	3	4.08	10	9	0	0	46	51	22	21	8	8	27	.280

St. Louis (NL)	MAJ	0	0	3.00	7	0	0	0	9	11	3	3	0	2	4	.306
MAJOR LEAGUE TOTALS		0	0	5.73	10	3	0	0	22	31	16	14	1	10	5	.348
MINOR LEAGUE TOTALS		29	40	4.42	94	92	2	0	550	589	301	270	69	127	394	.274

29 Skip Schumaker, of

Born: Feb. 3, 1980. **Ht.:** 5-10. **Wt.:** 175. **Bats:** L. **Throws:** R. **School:** UC Santa Barbara. **Career Transactions:** Selected by Cardinals in fifth round of 2001 draft; signed June 26, 2001.

Schumaker was a two-way player at UC Santa Barbara, and some teams liked him better as a pitcher after seeing him touch 92 mph with his fastball. Because of his stature, he knew he had a better future as a hitter. He was hurt for much of his first Double-A exposure in 2003, missing time with a stress fracture in his leg and a hand injury. The Cardinals sent him to the Arizona Fall League to make up at-bats. Schumaker has the speed to be a leadoff hitter, though he was limited last year by his leg injury. He occasionally shows the plate discipline needed to bat at the top of the lineup, but he doesn't do so consistently enough. He recognizes that he's not a power hitter and has worked on his bunting to make better use of his speed. Schumaker played center field in 2003 and it should be his long-term position, though he has played both corners as well. He has the defensive tools to play anywhere, including a plus arm, but doesn't fit the offensive profile for a corner spot and prefers center. He'll probably return to Double-A to start the season.

Year	Club (League)	Class	AVG	G	AB	R	H	2B	3B	HR	RBI	BB	SO	SB	SLG	OBP
2001	New Jersey (NY-P)	A	.253	49	162	22	41	10	1	0	14	29	33	11	.327	.368
2002	Potomac (Car)	A	.287	136	551	71	158	22	4	2	44	45	84	26	.352	.342
2003	Tennessee (SL)	AA	.251	91	342	43	86	20	3	2	22	37	54	6	.345	.330
MINOR LEAGUE TOTALS			.270	276	1055	136	285	52	8	4	80	111	171	43	.346	.342

30 Matt Lemanczyk, of

Born: Oct. 5, 1980. **Ht.:** 6-2. **Wt.:** 195. **Bats:** R. **Throws:** R. **School:** Sacred Heart (Conn.) University. **Career Transactions:** Selected by Cardinals in 10th round of 2002 draft; signed June 9, 2002.

The son of former all-star pitcher Dave Lemanczyk, Matt set Northeast Conference records for steals in each of his last two years at Sacred Heart and has won stolen-base crowns in each of his first two seasons as a pro. Managers rated him the best baserunner and fastest baserunner in the Midwest League last year, when he swiped 56 bases in 69 tries. The Cardinals consider him a throwback to St. Louis players of days gone by, such as Vince Coleman. Lemanczyk makes fielders uneasy because he can reach base if they make the slightest hesitation or bobble. He's a slap hitter who hasn't shown much pop, so he's going to need to work counts better and draw more walks to find an offensive niche. Because he played at a small college and grew up in a cold-weather region, Lemanczyk still needs work to refine his game. Though he has the speed and arm to play center field, the Cardinals have used him in left because he's raw. He moved up to Double-A at the end of the season to provide speed off the bench as Tennessee went to the Southern League playoffs, but he'll open 2004 in high Class A.

Year	Club (League)	Class	AVG	G	AB	R	H	2B	3B	HR	RBI	BB	SO	SB	SLG	OBP
2002	Johnson City (Appy)	R	.239	60	209	38	50	5	2	1	15	15	42	31	.297	.310
2003	Peoria (Mid)	A	.273	125	477	74	130	12	1	1	32	41	83	56	.308	.333
	Tennessee (SL)	AA	.167	7	12	1	2	0	0	0	0	0	1	1	.167	.231
MINOR LEAGUE TOTALS			.261	192	698	113	182	17	3	2	47	56	126	88	.302	.324

SAN DIEGO
PADRES

TOP 30 PROSPECTS

1. Josh Barfield, 2b
2. Khalil Greene, ss
3. Freddy Guzman, of
4. Tim Stauffer, rhp
5. Akinori Otsuka, rhp
6. Ben Howard, rhp
7. Jon Knott, of/1b
8. David Pauley, rhp
9. Kennard Jones, of
10. Tagg Bozied, 1b
11. Chris Oxspring, rhp
12. Rusty Tucker, lhp
13. Jared Wells, rhp
14. Sean Thompson, lhp
15. Justin Germano, rhp
16. Javier Martinez, rhp
17. Edgar Huerta, lhp
18. Michael Johnson, 1b
19. Humberto Quintero, c
20. Wilmer Villatoro, rhp
21. Billy Hogan, 3b
22. Aaron Coonrod, rhp
23. Peter Stonard, 2b
24. Greg Sain, 3b/c
25. Bernie Castro, 2b
26. Henri Stanley, of
27. Jake Gautreau, 2b/3b
28. Jason Szuminski, rhp
29. George Kottaras, c
30. Brian Whitaker, rhp

**By Jim
Callis**

The Padres' outlook couldn't have been better at the end of the 1998 season, which they concluded by making the second World Series trip in franchise history. Shortly afterward, voters approved a referendum to help pay for a new ballpark.

The Padres said they couldn't afford to keep the National League champions intact but promised to have a winner in place when the park opened in 2002. Neither of those things happened. Ballpark construction fell into a quagmire of 16 separate lawsuits, denying the club the additional revenue it projected. Owner John Moores' dealings with city council member Valerie Stallings were investigated. One of Moores' companies, Peregrine Systems, became embroiled in a financial scandal.

As a result, San Diego peaked at 79 victories in the five seasons after it won the pennant. The Padres slid to 64-98 in 2003, their worst record in a decade. The silver lining is that they gained the No. 1 overall pick in the 2004 draft.

With Petco Park ready for 2004, the Padres hope it will mark the dawn of a new era for San Diego baseball. While teams like the Brewers, Pirates and Tigers have proven a new ballpark doesn't guarantee the revitalization of a franchise, the Padres have taken significant steps to improve their team.

San Diego is one of the few clubs that actually has expanded its payroll this season, moving into the neighborhood of $60 million. Last August, they brought San Diego native Brian Giles home in a trade with the Pirates. It was a tribute to the Padres' scouting and resourcefulness that they gave up three young players who were acquired inexpensively. Lefthander Oliver Perez was signed out of Mexico at a bargain price; outfielder Jason Bay was stolen from the Mets in a trade for Steve Reed; and lefthander Cory Stewart came from the independent Texas-Louisiana League.

During the offseason the Padres, who have had eight different regular catchers since Benito Santiago left after 1992, shored up the position by trading for Oakland's Ramon Hernandez. They also shored up their pitching staff by signing Japan's Akinori Otsuka and free agents Sterling Hitchcock, Ismael Valdes and David Wells, all at reasonable prices. They plugged their center-field hole by signing Jay Payton to a modest deal.

With Khalil Greene ready to step in at shortstop and Mark Loretta keeping second base warm for top prospect Josh Barfield, San Diego has a deep lineup. The Padres also are optimistic about a rotation built around Jake Peavy, Adam Eaton and Brian Lawrence. As soon as their pitching stabilizes, San Diego once again will be ready to contend in the NL West. It has been a longer wait than expected, but it's about to end.

ORGANIZATION
OVERVIEW

General manager: Kevin Towers. **Farm director:** Tye Waller. **Scouting director:** Bill Gayton.

2003 PERFORMANCE

Class	Team	League	W	L	Pct.	Finish*	Manager
Majors	San Diego	National	64	98	.395	16th (16)	Bruce Bochy
Triple-A	Portland Beavers	Pacific Coast	69	75	.479	12th (16)	Rick Sweet
Double-A	Mobile BayBears	Southern	61	77	.442	10th (10)	Craig Colbert
High A	Lake Elsinore Storm	California	75	65	.536	4th (10)	Jeff Gardner
Low A	Fort Wayne Wizards	Midwest	71	66	.518	5th (14)	Gary Jones
Short-season	Eugene Emeralds	Northwest	39	37	.513	4th (8)	Roy Howell
Rookie	Idaho Falls Padres	Pioneer	24	52	.316	8th (8)	Carlos Lezcano
OVERALL 2003 MINOR LEAGUE RECORD			339	372	.476	24th (30)	

*Finish in overall standings (No. of teams in league)

ORGANIZATION LEADERS

BATTING
*Minimum 250 At-Bats

*AVG	Josh Barfield, Lake Elsinore	.337
R	Josh Barfield, Lake Elsinore	99
H	Josh Barfield, Lake Elsinore	185
TB	Josh Barfield, Lake Elsinore	291
2B	Josh Barfield, Lake Elsinore	46
3B	J.J. Furmaniak, Mobile/Lake Elsinore	9
HR	Jon Knott, Portland/Mobile	28
RBI	Josh Barfield, Lake Elsinore	128
BB	Jon Knott, Portland/Mobile	86
SO	Jake Gautreau, Mobile	131
SB	Freddy Guzman, Port./Mobile/Lake Elsinore	90
*SLG	Jason Bay, Portland	.541
*OBP	Jason Bay, Portland	.410

PITCHING
#Minimum 75 Innings

W	Gabe Ribas, Lake Elsinore/Fort Wayne	17
L	Mike Bynum, Portland	12
#ERA	Brian Whitaker, Fort Wayne	2.09
G	Three tied at	64
CG	Brian Whitaker, Fort Wayne	3
SV	Rusty Tucker, Mobile	28
IP	Justin Germano, Mobile/Lake Elsinore	169
BB	Dennis Tankersley, Portland	67
SO	Gabe Ribas, Lake Elsinore/Fort Wayne	152

BEST TOOLS

Best Hitter for Average	Josh Barfield
Best Power Hitter	Jon Knott
Fastest Baserunner	Marcus Nettles
Best Athlete	Freddy Guzman
Best Fastball	Aaron Coonrod
Best Curveball	Sean Thompson
Best Slider	Chris Oxspring
Best Changeup	Brad Baker
Best Control	Brian Whitaker
Best Defensive Catcher	Humberto Quintero
Best Defensive Infielder	Khalil Greene
Best Infield Arm	Juan Ciriaco
Best Defensive Outfielder	Freddy Guzman
Best Outfield Arm	Yordany Ramirez

PROJECTED 2007 LINEUP

Catcher	Ramon Hernandez
First Base	Ryan Klesko
Second Base	Josh Barfield
Third Base	Sean Burroughs
Shortstop	Khalil Greene
Left Field	Xavier Nady
Center Field	Jay Payton

Right Field	Brian Giles
No. 1 Starter	Jake Peavy
No. 2 Starter	Adam Eaton
No. 3 Starter	Tim Stauffer
No. 4 Starter	Brian Lawrence
No. 5 Starter	David Pauley
Closer	Akinori Otsuka

LAST YEAR'S TOP 20 PROSPECTS

1. Xavier Nady, of
2. Khalil Greene, ss
3. Mark Phillips, lhp
4. Tagg Bozied, 1b
5. Jake Gautreau, 2b
6. Ben Howard, rhp
7. Josh Barfield, 2b
8. Mike Nicolas, rhp
9. Rusty Tucker, lhp
10. Cory Stewart, lhp
11. Javier Martinez, rhp
12. Jason Bay, of
13. Justin Germano, rhp
14. Mike Bynum, lhp
15. Ben Johnson, of
16. Eric Cyr, lhp
17. Kennard Jones, of
18. Vince Faison, of
19. Bernie Castro, 2b
20. David Pauley, rhp

TOP PROSPECTS OF THE DECADE

1994	Joey Hamilton, rhp
1995	Dustin Hermanson, rhp
1996	Ben Davis, c
1997	Derrek Lee, 1b
1998	Matt Clement, rhp
1999	Matt Clement, rhp
2000	Sean Burroughs, 3b
2001	Sean Burroughs, 3b
2002	Sean Burroughs, 3b
2003	Xavier Nady, of

TOP DRAFT PICKS OF THE DECADE

1994	Dustin Hermanson, rhp
1995	Ben Davis, c
1996	Matt Halloran, ss
1997	Kevin Nicholson, ss
1998	Sean Burroughs, 3b
1999	Vince Faison, of
2000	Mark Phillips, lhp
2001	Jake Gautreau, 3b
2002	Khalil Greene, ss
2003	Tim Stauffer, rhp

ALL-TIME LARGEST BONUSES

Mark Phillips, 2000	$2,200,000
Sean Burroughs, 1998	$2,100,000
Jake Gautreau, 2001	$1,875,000
Khalil Greene, 2002	$1,500,000
Vince Faison, 1999	$1,415,000

SAN DIEGO **PADRES**   RANK: 25

Impact potential (C): Josh Barfield has the tools, including power, to be an offensive weapon at second base. If Tim Stauffer can put his shoulder troubles behind him, he has a chance to move fast and the stuff and command to pitch in the front of a rotation.

Depth (D): The Padres' depth took a hit last year when they dealt Jason Bay, Cory Stewart and Oliver Perez to the Pirates for Brian Giles, but the dropoff in talent from just a couple of years ago is considerable. That's due in part to graduating Sean Burroughs, Jake Peavy and Xavier Nady to San Diego, but also because Dennis Tankersley and Jake Gautreau, among others, have been disappointments.

Sleeper: Jared Wells, rhp.   *—Depth charts prepared by Josh Boyd. Numbers in parentheses indicate prospect rankings.*

LF
Henri Stanley (26)

CF
Freddy Guzman (3)
Kennard Jones (9)
Drew Macias

RF
Jon Knott (7)
Alex Fernandez
Josh Carter
Ben Johnson

3B
Billy Hogan (21)

SS
Khalil Greene (2)
Ron Merrill
Luis Cruz
Juan Ciriaco

2B
Josh Barfield (1)
Peter Stonard (23)
Bernie Castro (25)
Jake Gautreau (27)
J.J. Furmaniak

1B
Tagg Bozied (10)
Michael Johnson (19)
Todd Sears

SOURCE OF **TALENT**			
Homegrown		**Acquired**	
College	12	Trades	3
Junior College	2	Rule 5 draft	1
Draft-and-follow	2	Independent leagues	1
High school	4	Free agents/Waivers	1
Non drafted free agent	0		
Foreign	4		

C
Humberto Quintero (19)
Greg Sain (25)
George Kottaras (29)
Colt Morton
Nick Trzesniak
Jose Lobaton

RHP

Starters	**Relievers**
Tim Stauffer (4)	Akinori Otsuka (5)
David Pauley (8)	Ben Howard (6)
Jared Wells (13)	Chris Oxspring (11)
Justin Germano (15)	Wilmer Villatoro (20)
Javier Martinez (16)	Aaron Coonrod (22)
Brian Whitaker (30)	Jason Szuminski (28)
Clark Girardeau	Eddie Bonine
Matt Bruback	Gabe Ribas
Clay Hensley	Bryan Sanches
Henry Perez	Dale Thayer
William Ponce	Bart Miadich
Joel Santo	Mike Wodnicki
Geivy Garcia	Brad Baker
	Cory Doyne

LHP

Starters	**Relievers**
Sean Thompson (14)	Rusty Tucker (12)
Daniel Moore	Edgar Huerta (17)
Fabian Jimenez	Roger Deago

DRAFT
ANALYSIS

Best Pro Debut: 3B Billy Hogan (5) hit .315-4-43 against older pitchers in the Rookie-level Pioneer League and the short-season Northwest League. RHP Ryan Klatt (38) was a dominant closer in the Pioneer League, recording 12 saves and a 2.12 ERA. RHP Eddie Bonine (23) was nearly as effective closing games in the NWL, with 14 saves and 33 whiffs in as many innings.

Best Athlete: The Padres made an effort to find bats, making athleticism a secondary concern. 2B Peter Stonard (4) has decent tools across the board but doesn't have an obvious defensive home.

Best Pure Hitter: Stonard won the 2002 Cape Cod League batting title with a .348 average. He has good bat control and hit .293 in low Class A.

Best Raw Power: C Colt Morton (3) may never hit for average, but his 6-foot-6, 227-pound frame generates a lot of leverage. He hit .231-9-27 in the NWL and low Class A.

Fastest Runner: OF Jeff Leise (12), who has 60 speed on the 20-80 scouting scale.

Best Defensive Player: Though C Matt Lauderdale (9) had a better reputation, the Padres say Morton is better behind the plate. He has soft hands and good instincts.

Best Fastball: RHP Tim Stauffer (1), more for his outstanding life than 91-92 mph velocity. Stauffer, LHP Daniel Moore (2) and

Hogan

JOHN SPEAR

RHPs Clark Girardeau (7) and Chuck Bechtel (15) all can hit 94.

Best Breaking Ball: Stauffer's curveball.

Most Intriguing Background: 1B Fernando Valenzuela Jr.'s (10) father made six all-star teams and spawned Fernandomania in Los Angeles during the 1980s. The Padres drafted but didn't sign OF Tommy Skipper (38), who's better known as the national high school record-holder in the pole vault at 18 feet, 3 inches. Lauderdale's sister Mandy was featured in the first edition of the Fox show "Temptation Island." 2B Brett Burnham's (21) brother Gary was a Triple-A first baseman in the Blue Jays system in 2003.

Closest To The Majors: Stauffer, if he's healthy, or Stonard. Bonine and Klatt could move quickly as relievers.

Best Late-Round Pick: Bonine and Klatt. Bonine pitches at 90-91 mph and can throw two types of knuckleballs. Klatt has a harder fastball and can flash a good slider.

The One Who Got Away: OF Cory Patton (6) showed no desire to play pro ball and returned to Texas A&M.

Assessment: The top of San Diego's draft looks shaky with Stauffer's shoulder problems, Moore's and Morton's inconsistency in college and the pros, and Stonard's off-field issues. They supplemented the draft with an impressive haul of 2002 draft-and-follows.

GRADE: **B**

SS Khalil Greene (1) started in the majors 15 months after being drafted. OF Kennard Jones (3) and LHP Sean Thompson (5) are developing nicely. San Diego signed several draft-and-follows from this crop, most notably RHP Jared Wells (31), first baseman Michael Johnson (2) and C George Kottaras (20).

GRADE: **B+**

2B Josh Barfield (4) should form the Padres' double-play combo with Greene in the near future. They signed another top infield prospect in SS Jason Bartlett (13), but traded him for Brian Buchanan. While 2B Jake Gautreau (1) is moving backward, RHP David Pauley (8), 1B Tagg Bozied (3) and LHP Rusty Tucker (21) are getting closer to the majors.

GRADE: **C**

OF Xavier Nady (2) is better than he showed in the majors last year. LHP Mark Phillips (1) nosedived after being traded for Rondell White in 2003.

GRADE: **B**

Of six first-round picks, only LHP Mike Bynum has appeared in the majors and only C Nick Trzesniak retains much promise. Stealing RHP Jake Peavy (15) helps to ease that pain.

—Draft analysis prepared by Jim Callis. Numbers in parentheses indicate draft rounds.

LARRY GOREN

Josh Barfield

Born: Dec. 17, 1982.
Ht.: 6-0. **Wt.:** 185.
Bats: R. **Throws:** R.
School: Klein HS, Spring, Texas.
Career Transactions: Selected by Padres in fourth round of 2001 draft; signed June 15, 2001.

Since Bill Gayton took over as scouting director in September 2000, the Padres have spent just three of their 30 choices in the first 10 rounds on high school players. Only the Athletics have made a stronger effort to avoid prep picks. Yet San Diego's three high school selections happen to be three of its top prospects: Barfield (fourth round, 2001), righthander David Pauley (eighth, 2001) and lefty Sean Thompson (fifth, 2002). The son of former American League home run champ Jesse Barfield, Josh turned down a Baylor scholarship to sign for $300,000. He didn't receive much hype coming out of high school, and little more when he hit better than .300 in his first two pro seasons. After a breakout 2003, Milwaukee's Rickie Weeks and Arizona's Scott Hairston are his only rivals as the top second-base prospects in the game. Barfield won MVP honors in the high Class A California League and led the minors in hits, doubles, RBIs and extra-base hits. The organization's minor league player of the year in 2003, Barfield did it all despite being bothered by a sore right wrist for much of the year. He had offseason surgery to repair ligament damage, which prevented him from playing in the Arizona Fall League.

Barfield is a rare second baseman who's capable of batting third in the order. He uses his quick stroke to smoke line drives all over the field. Not only is he the best hitter in the system, but he's also the best at making adjustments. Some of his doubles will carry over the fence once he gains more strength and experience, giving him 25-homer power. Barfield isn't a speedster or a future Gold Glover, but he's a better runner and defender than most people realize. He complements average speed with fine instincts, and he has succeeded on 77 percent of his basestealing attempts in the minors. The Padres say Barfield will be able to stay at second base, where his sure hands are his best asset. Nevertheless, Barfield isn't a surefire second baseman. He shows a solid-average arm when he only has time to react, but he often makes tentative throws on routine ground balls. He's still smoothing out his footwork and his double-play pivot. If he fills out like his father, who played at 6-foot-1 and 205 pounds, Barfield may have to move to the outfield. At the plate, he tends to dive into pitches and will have to learn to turn on balls when pitchers work him inside. He could stand to draw a few more walks, though he nearly doubled his total from 27 in 2002 to 50 last year.

In August, the Padres signed incumbent second baseman Mark Loretta to a two-year, $5.25 million contract extension with a vesting option for 2006. Unless Barfield's development slows considerably, however, he should be ready by mid-2005 at the latest. His wrist will be 100 percent for spring training, and he'll open 2004 at Double-A Mobile.

Year	Club (League)	Class	AVG	G	AB	R	H	2B	3B	HR	RBI	BB	SO	SB	SLG	OBP
2001	Idaho Falls (Pio)	R	.310	66	277	51	86	15	4	4	53	16	54	12	.437	.350
2002	Fort Wayne (Mid)	A	.306	129	536	73	164	22	3	8	57	26	105	26	.403	.340
	Lake Elsinore (Cal)	A	.087	6	23	2	2	0	0	0	4	1	4	0	.087	.120
2003	Lake Elsinore (Cal)	A	.337	135	549	99	185	46	6	16	128	50	122	16	.530	.389
MINOR LEAGUE TOTALS			.316	336	1385	225	437	83	13	28	242	93	285	54	.455	.358

2 Khalil Greene, ss

Born: Oct. 21, 1979. **Ht.:** 5-11. **Wt.:** 210. **Bats:** R. **Throws:** R. **School:** Clemson University. **Career Transactions:** Selected by Padres in first round (13th overall) of 2002 draft; signed June 30, 2002.

Undrafted out of high school and a 14th-round pick as a college junior, Greene became a first-round pick as well as BA's College Player of the Year and the Golden Spikes Award winner in 2002. He breezed through the minors and became the first position player from his draft class to reach the majors. Greene has more ability to hit for average with gap power than most middle infielders. He doesn't have the speed or arm strength of a classic shortstop, but he has enough to handle the position. Add in his tremendous hands, quick first step and uncanny instincts, and he's the system's best defensive infielder. During his September callup, Greene showed that he still faces several offensive adjustments. He must make more contact and draw more walks to realize his potential as a No. 2 hitter. The Padres are comfortable making Greene their starting shortstop in 2004. He will have growing pains, and the Padres will protect him by batting him low in the order.

Year	Club (League)	Class	AVG	G	AB	R	H	2B	3B	HR	RBI	BB	SO	SB	SLG	OBP
2002	Eugene (NWL)	A	.270	10	37	5	10	1	0	0	6	5	6	0	.297	.400
	Lake Elsinore (Cal)	A	.317	46	183	33	58	9	1	9	32	12	33	0	.525	.368
2003	Mobile (SL)	AA	.275	59	229	20	63	17	2	3	20	16	55	2	.406	.327
	Portland (PCL)	AAA	.288	76	319	42	92	19	0	10	47	20	52	5	.442	.346
	San Diego (NL)	MAJ	.215	20	65	8	14	4	1	2	6	4	19	0	.400	.271
MAJOR LEAGUE TOTALS			.215	20	65	8	14	4	1	2	6	4	19	0	.400	.271
MINOR LEAGUE TOTALS			.290	191	768	100	223	46	3	22	105	53	146	7	.444	.349

3 Freddy Guzman, of

Born: Jan. 20, 1981. **Ht.:** 5-10. **Wt.:** 165. **Bats:** B. **Throws:** R. **Career Transactions:** Signed out of Dominican Republic by Padres, March 21, 2000.

Guzman, previously known as Pedro de los Santos and thought to be 2½ years younger, was the most significant player uncovered in an organizational crackdown on falsified identities in the 2002-03 offseason. But his prospect status soared after he moved from high Class A Lake Elsinore to Triple-A and led the minors with 90 steals while getting caught just 17 times. Not the fastest of the organization's crop of speedsters, Guzman is the best player among them. He has a nice stroke from both sides of the plate and the patience required of a leadoff man. No one on the big league club can chase balls down in center field like him. Guzman chases pitches in the dirt and at times tries to drive the ball, which isn't his game. His arm is well below-average. He's not lazy but must learn the importance of playing hard every day. The Padres didn't have a viable center fielder until they signed Jay Payton to a two-year contract in January. His acquisition allows Guzman to spend the 2004 season in Triple-A and break into the majors as a reserve in 2005.

Year	Club (League)	Class	AVG	G	AB	R	H	2B	3B	HR	RBI	BB	SO	SB	SLG	OBP
2000	Padres (DSL)	R	.210	49	167	38	35	6	1	1	10	46	38	24	.275	.386
2001	Idaho Falls (Pio)	R	.348	12	46	11	16	4	1	0	5	2	10	5	.478	.388
2002	Lake Elsinore (Cal)	A	.259	21	81	13	21	3	0	1	6	8	12	14	.333	.326
	Fort Wayne (Mid)	A	.279	47	190	35	53	7	5	0	18	18	37	39	.368	.341
	Eugene (NWL)	A	.225	21	80	14	18	2	1	0	8	7	15	16	.275	.293
2003	Lake Elsinore (Cal)	A	.285	70	281	64	80	12	3	2	22	40	60	49	.370	.375
	Mobile (SL)	AA	.271	46	177	30	48	5	2	1	11	26	34	38	.339	.368
	Portland (PCL)	AAA	.300	2	10	1	3	0	0	0	0	0	1	3	.300	.300
MINOR LEAGUE TOTALS			.266	268	1032	206	274	39	13	5	80	147	207	188	.343	.360

4 Tim Stauffer, rhp

Born: June 2, 1982. **Ht.:** 6-2. **Wt.:** 205. **Bats:** R. **Throws:** R. **School:** University of Richmond. **Career Transactions:** Selected by Padres in first round (fourth overall) of 2003 draft; signed Aug. 11, 2003.

A two-time All-American at Richmond, Stauffer was considered the player closest to the big leagues in the 2003 draft crop. After the Padres took him fourth overall, an MRI revealed weakness in his shoulder. He admitted his condition to his team, which reduced its initial $2.6 million offer to $750,000. Stauffer's fastball usually sits no higher than 91-92 mph, but it's an out pitch because of its outstanding life. His curveball and changeup are plus pitches, and his cutter gives him another solid option. He commands all four offerings for strikes. His honesty reinforced the Padres' belief that he has special makeup. Stauffer's shoulder obviously is worrisome. The good news is that he hasn't required surgery and San Diego hoped to have him ready for spring training. But until he gets on a mound, shows his former stuff and proves he can stay healthy, he's a question mark. Before his shoulder problems, Stauffer might have gone from the draft to San Diego as quickly as Khalil Greene. Now it's impossible to set any kind of timetable. The Padres will monitor him closely this spring before determining a game plan for 2004.

Year	Club (League)	Class	W	L	ERA	G	GS	CG	SV	IP	H	R	ER	HR	BB	SO	AVG
2003	Did not play—Signed 2004 contract																

5 Akinori Otsuka, rhp

Born: Jan. 13, 1972. **Ht.:** 6-0. **Wt.:** 200. **Bats:** R. **Throws:** R. **Career Transactions:** Drafted by Kintetsu (Japan) in second round of 1997 Japanese draft . . . Signed by Padres, Dec. 9, 2003.

All-star Trevor Hoffman should be healthy after missing most of 2003 recovering from two shoulder surgeries, and Rod Beck filled in well in Hoffman's absence. Nevertheless, the Padres fortified their bullpen by adding another accomplished closer during the offseason. Otsuka became the fourth Japanese major leaguer to come to the United States via the posting process. San Diego bid $300,000 to win the rights to negotiate with Otsuka, then signed him for two years and $1.5 million, plus either a $1.75 million option or $200,000 buyout in 2006. The Osaka Kintetsu Buffaloes actually posted Otsuka following the 2002 season, but no U.S. teams bid for his rights and he suspected the Buffaloes front office sabotaged the process. He held out last spring until he was traded to the Chunichi Dragons, for whom he split closing duties with former Tiger and Devil Ray Eddie Gaillard. Otsuka's out pitch is a diving slider that Padres general manager Kevin Towers compared to Robb Nen's. His control is impeccable, as shown by his gaudy 56-5 strikeout-walk ratio in 2003. Otsuka throws a solid-average fastball that he locates with precision, though it lacks much movement. His changeup is an effective pitch and he also has a splitter. It will be a surprise if Otsuka doesn't succeed as a set-up man. With Hoffman and Beck getting up in years and battling injuries, Otsuka is the Padres' closer of the future.

Year	Club (League)	Class	W	L	ERA	G	GS	CG	SV	IP	H	R	ER	HR	BB	SO	AVG
1997	Kintetsu (PL)	JPN	4	5	2.07	52	0	0	7	83	44	22	19	2	46	127	—
1998	Kintetsu (PL)	JPN	3	2	2.11	49	0	0	35	55	43	19	13	5	25	74	—
1999	Kintetsu (PL)	JPN	1	4	2.73	25	0	0	6	30	24	12	9	1	10	32	—
2000	Kintetsu (PL)	JPN	1	3	2.38	39	0	0	24	42	31	11	11	3	13	49	—
2001	Kintetsu (PL)	JPN	2	5	4.02	48	0	0	26	56	42	25	25	7	15	82	—
2002	Kintetsu (PL)	JPN	2	1	1.28	41	0	0	22	42	22	7	6	4	3	54	—
2003	Chunichi (CL)	JPN	1	3	2.09	51	0	0	17	43	31	10	10	4	5	56	.199
JAPANESE LEAGUE TOTALS			14	23	2.39	305	0	0	137	351	237	106	93	26	117	474	—

6 Ben Howard, rhp

Born: Jan. 15, 1979. **Ht.:** 6-2. **Wt.:** 190. **Bats:** R. **Throws:** R. **School:** Central Merry HS, Jackson, Tenn. **Career Transactions:** Selected by Padres in second round of 1997 draft; signed June 25, 1997.

STEVE MOORE

Howard was the lone survivor of a February 2002 car crash that killed Padres outfielder Mike Darr and another passenger. He missed a month in 2003 after arthroscopic surgery on his left knee before pitching creditably after a late-August callup. Before he hurt his elbow in June 2002, Howard could touch 99 mph with his fastball. He now sits in the low 90s and tops out around 95. His slider has improved, and his changeup looked better than ever in the majors. He trusted it more under the guidance of pitching coach Darren Balsley, who turned his career around when they were in the minors together. Howard has trouble repeating his delivery, so his command fluctuates. He has dialed down his velocity to throw more strikes, but gives up too many walks and homers when he's off. In the minors, he threw his changeup too hard and didn't use it enough. Howard could make the Padres out of spring training as either a starter or middle reliever. If he regains his power fastball and never masters the changeup, he eventually could become a closer.

Year	Club (League)	Class	W	L	ERA	G	GS	CG	SV	IP	H	R	ER	HR	BB	SO	AVG
1997	Padres (AZL)	R	1	4	7.45	13	12	0	0	54	54	53	45	3	63	59	.255
1998	Idaho Falls (Pio)	R	4	5	6.03	15	15	0	0	69	67	61	46	2	87	79	.260
1999	Fort Wayne (Mid)	A	6	10	4.73	28	28	0	0	145	123	100	76	17	110	131	.226
2000	Rancho Cucamonga (Cal)	A	5	11	6.37	32	19	0	0	107	88	87	76	8	111	150	.227
2001	Lake Elsinore (Cal)	A	2	8	2.83	18	18	0	0	102	86	37	32	4	32	107	.229
	Mobile (SL)	AA	2	0	2.40	7	5	0	0	30	17	9	8	3	15	29	.167
2002	Mobile (SL)	AA	3	1	2.18	6	6	0	0	33	26	10	8	2	16	30	.222
	San Diego (NL)	MAJ	0	1	9.28	3	2	0	0	11	13	11	11	4	14	10	.302

	Portland (PCL)	AAA	0	4	6.20	11	7	0	0	45	47	34	31	10	15	25	.266
2003	Portland (PCL)	AAA	7	9	4.55	22	22	0	0	131	118	69	66	17	49	68	.243
	San Diego (NL)	MAJ	1	3	3.63	6	6	0	0	35	31	17	14	10	15	24	.235
MAJOR LEAGUE TOTALS			1	4	4.96	9	8	0	0	45	44	28	25	14	29	34	.251
MINOR LEAGUE TOTALS			36	46	4.88	152	132	0	0	715	626	460	388	66	498	678	.235

7 Jon Knott, of/1b

Born: Aug. 4, 1978. **Ht.:** 6-3. **Wt.:** 220. **Bats:** R. **Throws:** R. **School:** Mississippi State University. **Career Transactions:** Signed as nondrafted free agent by Padres, Sept. 28, 2001.

Undrafted after he strained a tendon in his right leg late in his senior season at Mississippi State, Knott won the Cal League batting title (.341) in his 2002 pro debut. Shifting his focus to hitting for more power in 2003, he increased his homer output from 11 to 28 (tops in the organization) and led the Double-A Southern League with 59 extra-base hits. Knott has the most usable game power in the system. He also has the potential to hit for average and draws lots of walks. He runs well and plays decent defense for a man his size, and he has enough arm to handle right field. He's an overachiever whose makeup can take him far. Knott ran hot and cold in 2003, sometimes falling into extended slumps when pitchers wouldn't challenge him. There's still a question about whether he's a long-term outfielder or merely a first baseman. Knott needs a full year in Triple-A before trying to break through a logjam of similar players in San Diego. Brian Giles, Ryan Klesko, Xavier Nady and Phil Nevin are entrenched ahead of him.

Year	Club (League)	Class	AVG	G	AB	R	H	2B	3B	HR	RBI	BB	SO	SB	SLG	OBP
2002	Fort Wayne (Mid)	A	.333	37	126	19	42	12	3	3	18	17	33	2	.548	.411
	Lake Elsinore (Cal)	A	.341	93	367	55	125	33	8	8	73	46	68	5	.540	.414
2003	Mobile (SL)	AA	.252	127	432	83	109	32	0	27	82	82	117	5	.514	.387
	Portland (PCL)	AAA	.346	7	26	5	9	1	0	1	5	4	3	0	.500	.433
MINOR LEAGUE TOTALS			.300	264	951	162	285	78	11	39	178	149	221	12	.528	.402

8 David Pauley, rhp

Born: June 17, 1983. **Ht.:** 6-2. **Wt.:** 170. **Bats:** R. **Throws:** R. **School:** Longmont (Colo.) HS. **Career Transactions:** Selected by Padres in eighth round of 2001 draft; signed June 7, 2001.

The Padres have been patient with Pauley, keeping him in short-season leagues for his first two years of pro ball. He held his own at low Class A Fort Wayne in 2003, with the only setback a month's stay on the disabled list with tendinitis. He went 4-2, 2.48 after he returned in July. Pauley's best offering is a curveball that can become a plus pitch. His fastball has solid-average velocity, sitting at 88-91 mph and reaching 94, and has good life. Though he's not big, he has a quick arm and throws hard without effort. His changeup is progressing nicely. Pauley has a good feel for pitching but is still learning to use all of his pitches in tandem. He tends to fall in love with his curveball, and he'll have to mix his stuff to keep more advanced hitters off balance. He showed signs of doing that in instructional league. San Diego will keep moving Pauley one step at a time, sending him to high Class A Lake Elsinore this year. He could reach the majors in the second half of 2006.

Year	Club (League)	Class	W	L	ERA	G	GS	CG	SV	IP	H	R	ER	HR	BB	SO	AVG
2001	Idaho Falls (Pio)	R	4	9	6.03	15	15	0	0	69	88	57	46	8	24	53	.308
2002	Eugene (NWL)	A	6	1	2.81	15	15	0	0	80	81	32	25	6	18	62	.266
2003	Fort Wayne (Mid)	A	7	7	3.29	22	21	0	1	118	109	51	43	9	38	117	.245
MINOR LEAGUE TOTALS			17	17	3.85	52	51	0	1	266	278	140	114	23	80	232	.269

9 Kennard Jones, of

Born: Sept. 8, 1981. **Ht.:** 5-11. **Wt.:** 180. **Bats:** L. **Throws:** L. **School:** University of Indiana. **Career Transactions:** Selected by Padres in third round of 2002 draft; signed July 18, 2002.

Ignored in the draft for three straight years in high school and junior college, Jones went in the third round after one season at Indiana. An all-star in the low Class A Midwest League in his first full year, he was promoted to high Class A but missed August after breaking his left hand in an off-field incident. Jones' trademark is his speed, just as it was for his cousin, basketball Hall of Famer Sam Jones. He should become an above-average center fielder and basestealer. He has a good offensive approach, with a short stroke designed for contact and an eye for walks. He has some strength and could develop power down the road. Jones plays out of control too often. He was caught stealing 21 times in 44 tries last year because he doesn't know how to read pitchers. He must improve his breaks and routes in center field. Jones is destined for a full season in high Class A. If he can develop better instincts, he'll challenge Freddy Guzman as the center fielder of the future.

Year	Club (League)	Class	AVG	G	AB	R	H	2B	3B	HR	RBI	BB	SO	SB	SLG	OBP
2002	Eugene (NWL)	A	.295	16	61	15	18	2	0	0	3	10	12	12	.328	.411
	Fort Wayne (Mid)	A	.286	20	77	15	22	4	0	0	5	11	21	3	.338	.382
2003	Fort Wayne (Mid)	A	.307	81	306	61	94	13	4	1	30	50	52	20	.386	.407
	Lake Elsinore (Cal)	A	.250	17	76	16	19	3	2	0	5	4	11	3	.342	.288
MINOR LEAGUE TOTALS			.294	134	520	107	153	22	6	1	43	75	96	38	.365	.388

10 Tagg Bozied, 1b

Born: July 24, 1979. **Ht.:** 6-3. **Wt.:** 210. **Bats:** R. **Throws:** R. **School:** University of San Francisco. **Career Transactions:** Signed by independent Sioux Falls (Northern), June 2001 . . . Selected by Padres in third round of 2001 draft; signed Nov. 9, 2001.

Bozied led the system with 24 homers and 92 RBIs in his 2002 pro debut, then set an Arizona Fall League record with 12 homers. He had trouble unleashing that power in Triple-A, where he received more attention for going after a Las Vegas fan who taunted him and threw a soft souvenir ball at him. Nineteen of his teammates followed him into the stands and all were suspended, including Bozied for eight games. Bozied is stronger and has more pure power than Jon Knott. He raised his average 13 points from 2002 by making adjustments to fight breaking balls and pitches on the outer half of the plate. He projects as a .260 hitter with 25-plus homers, along the lines of Eric Karros. His new approach cost him pop, and Bozied needs to regain aggressiveness at the plate. He won't ever hit for a high average or draw many walks. Though he has decent arm strength, his lack of speed relegates him to first base, where he's adequate. He'll return to Triple-A in 2004 and try to recapture his power. As with Knott, there are several players in Bozied's path to the major leagues.

Year	Club (League)	Class	AVG	G	AB	R	H	2B	3B	HR	RBI	BB	SO	SB	SLG	OBP
2001	Sioux Falls (NorC)	IND	.307	58	228	35	70	17	0	6	31	13	34	3	.461	.359
2002	Lake Elsinore (Cal)	A	.298	71	282	45	84	23	1	15	60	35	60	3	.546	.377
	Mobile (SL)	AA	.214	60	234	35	50	14	0	9	32	16	43	1	.389	.268
2003	Portland (PCL)	AAA	.273	119	450	59	123	25	2	14	59	38	80	1	.431	.331
MINOR LEAGUE TOTALS			.266	250	966	139	257	62	3	38	151	89	183	5	.454	.330

11 Chris Oxspring, rhp

Born: May 13, 1977. **Ht.:** 6-1. **Wt.:** 180. **Bats:** L. **Throws:** R. **Career Transactions:** Signed by independent Cook County (Frontier), June 2000 . . . Signed by Padres, Oct. 31, 2000.

The Padres have a knack for uncovering talent in independent leagues, and Oxspring has been one of their better finds since signing out of a rain-soaked tryout for Frontier Leaguers in 2000. An Australian who pitched in the 2001 World Cup, he took off after moving into Mobile's rotation in late May. He went 10-4, 2.47 and didn't give up more than three runs in an outing until his final start of 2003. Oxspring has the best slider in the system and a 91-93 mph fastball. He also throws a curveball and changeup, though those pitches aren't as advanced. After lacking confidence in the past—he preferred pitching in middle relief—he took to starting and began to believe in himself. Oxspring has to trust his stuff. He still needs to go after hitters more aggressively. His curveball, changeup and command all can improve. He made three trips to the disabled list with shoulder problems in 2002, but held up throughout last season. Added to the 40-man roster for the first time, Oxspring is headed for Triple-A. If he can maintain his confidence, he could be pitching for the Padres by the end of the season.

Year	Club (League)	Class	W	L	ERA	G	GS	CG	SV	IP	H	R	ER	HR	BB	SO	AVG
2000	Cook County (Fron)	IND	1	0	3.10	13	2	0	1	29	29	18	10	1	15	29	.257
2001	Fort Wayne (Mid)	A	4	1	4.15	41	2	0	0	56	66	29	26	5	25	54	.297
	Lake Elsinore (Cal)	A	0	0	0.64	7	0	0	0	14	10	2	1	1	6	17	.200
2002	Lake Elsinore (Cal)	A	0	1	4.78	15	1	0	0	26	24	16	14	2	8	30	.238
	Mobile (SL)	AA	0	0	1.26	6	1	0	0	14	13	3	2	0	8	21	.245
2003	Mobile (SL)	AA	10	6	2.92	40	18	1	0	136	106	47	44	6	62	129	.211
MINOR LEAGUE TOTALS			14	8	3.17	109	22	1	0	247	219	97	87	14	109	251	.236

12 Rusty Tucker, lhp

Born: July 15, 1980. **Ht.:** 6-1. **Wt.:** 190. **Bats:** R. **Throws:** L. **School:** University of Maine. **Career Transactions:** Selected by Padres in 21st round of 2001 draft; signed June 11, 2001.

After a breakthrough in velocity in 2002, Tucker continued to pitch well after a promotion to Double-A last season. He continued to throw in the mid-90s, an astounding fastball for a short lefthander, and blew away Southern League hitters. But he lost some velocity and started to get hit in July, then felt a pop in his elbow when he threw a pitch in early August. He had Tommy John surgery shortly thereafter and probably won't pitch during the 2004 regular season. The track record with that operation is very good, so Tucker should be able to regain his fastball after diligent rehabilitation. When he comes back, he'll need to continue to tighten a hard, slurvy breaking ball into a true slider. Tucker was starting to learn that there's more than pitching to sheer power, as he mixed in more two-seam fastballs and changeups than in the past. His four-seamer lacks much movement and he'll need to find something he can use to shutdown righthanders. They hit .256 and slugged .372 against him in 2003, compared to .188 and .250 by lefties. He'll also have to improve his control. The Padres won't rush Tucker back and would be happy to get him back on the mound after the season in instructional league or the Arizona Fall League.

Year	Club (League)	Class	W	L	ERA	G	GS	CG	SV	IP	H	R	ER	HR	BB	SO	AVG
2001	Idaho Falls (Pio)	R	0	2	7.13	30	0	0	0	35	41	41	28	4	50	43	.297
2002	Fort Wayne (Mid)	A	5	1	1.01	31	0	0	13	36	19	8	4	2	10	50	.150
	Lake Elsinore (Cal)	A	2	3	2.43	26	0	0	14	30	26	10	8	1	18	33	.226
2003	Mobile (SL)	AA	2	6	3.74	51	0	0	28	53	49	26	22	4	31	63	.240
MINOR LEAGUE TOTALS			9	12	3.63	138	0	0	55	154	135	85	62	11	109	189	.231

13 Jared Wells, rhp

Born: Oct. 31, 1981. **Ht.:** 6-4. **Wt.:** 200. **Bats:** R. **Throws:** R. **School:** San Jacinto (Texas) JC. **Career Transactions:** Selected by Padres in 31st round of 2002 draft; signed May 31, 2003.

The Padres invested more heavily in draft-and-follows than any team did before the 2003 draft, signing eight 2002 picks. Wells was the best of a group that also included four junior college players (catcher George Kottaras, lefthander Danny de la O and outfielders Drew Macias and Chad Etheridge) and two fifth-year seniors (first baseman Michael Johnson and outfielder Brian Wahlbrink). San Diego drafted Wells in the 31st round out of Tyler (Texas) Junior College in 2002 and he spent his sophomore season at San Jacinto, which finished second at the Junior College World Series. Wells has a projectable body and a quick arm that allowed him to reach 97 mph during the spring. He was worn out by the time he turned pro and his fastball sat at 87-92 mph during the summer, but his velocity should rebound after an offseason of rest. His control should be better as well, though he sometimes catches too much of the plate. Wells' slider and changeup both should become average pitches with more consistency. Headed for low Class A in 2004, he could blossom into a No. 2 or 3 starter.

Year	Club (League)	Class	W	L	ERA	G	GS	CG	SV	IP	H	R	ER	HR	BB	SO	AVG
2003	Eugene (NWL)	A	4	6	2.75	14	14	0	0	79	77	34	24	6	32	53	.256
MINOR LEAGUE TOTALS			4	6	2.75	14	14	0	0	79	77	34	24	6	32	53	.256

14 Sean Thompson, lhp

Born: Oct. 13, 1982. **Ht.:** 5-11. **Wt.:** 160. **Bats:** L. **Throws:** L. **School:** Thunder Ridge HS, Denver. **Career Transactions:** Selected by Padres in fifth round of 2002 draft; signed June 24, 2002.

The Padres have selected just two high school pitchers in the first 10 rounds of the last three drafts, and area scout Darryl Milne (now with the Red Sox) signed both David Pauley and Thompson, both Colorado products. His size and his fastball certainly aren't big, but Thompson was one of the toughest pitchers to hit in the short-season Northwest League last year. He works everything off the best curveball in the system, a knee-buckler that rates at least a 65 on the 20-80 scouting scale. His changeup is at least solid average and will be a plus pitch once he gains more experience. As for his fastball, Thompson usually works in the high 80s and gets some arm-side run. He can touch 92 mph but that's by overthrowing, which leaves his fastball vulnerable and up in the zone. He needs to throw more strikes, particularly with his fastball. He's a possible No. 4 starter who may wind up in the bullpen because he's short and lacks stamina. He'll get his first taste of full-season ball this year in low Class A.

Year	Club (League)	Class	W	L	ERA	G	GS	CG	SV	IP	H	R	ER	HR	BB	SO	AVG
2002	Idaho Falls (Pio)	R	4	3	3.83	13	11	0	0	56	51	34	24	4	38	69	.249
2003	Eugene (NWL)	A	7	1	2.48	15	15	0	0	80	58	28	22	5	39	97	.204
MINOR LEAGUE TOTALS			11	4	3.04	28	26	0	0	136	109	62	46	9	77	166	.222

15 Justin Germano, rhp

Born: Aug. 6, 1982. **Ht.:** 6-2. **Wt.:** 190. **Bats:** R. **Throws:** R. **School:** Claremont (Calif.) HS. **Career Transactions:** Selected by Padres in 13th round of 2000 draft; signed June 13, 2000.

Germano's pitching approach is so advanced that the Padres consistently have challenged him, sending him to low Class A at 18 and to Double-A at 20 last year. His best attribute is his ability to throw strikes, though at times he does that too much and becomes too hittable. His overhand curveball is occasionally a plus pitch, but Germano's arsenal is average across the board. San Diego hoped that his lanky build and quick arm were harbingers that he'd add velocity, but his fastball has stayed at 86-88 mph and tops out in the low 90s. He has a good feel for a changeup. The consensus is that Germano's stuff was more impressive in 2002, when he was the organization's minor league pitcher of the year. If he continues to locate his pitches, he could be a back-of-the-rotation starter in the majors. After being added to the 40-man roster in November, he'll open 2004 by returning to Double-A.

Year	Club (League)	Class	W	L	ERA	G	GS	CG	SV	IP	H	R	ER	HR	BB	SO	AVG
2000	Padres (AZL)	R	5	5	4.59	17	8	0	1	67	65	36	34	4	9	67	.249
2001	Fort Wayne (Mid)	A	2	6	4.98	13	13	0	0	65	80	47	36	7	16	55	.302
	Eugene (NWL)	A	6	5	3.49	13	13	2	0	80	77	35	31	5	11	74	.246
2002	Fort Wayne (Mid)	A	12	5	3.18	24	24	1	0	156	166	63	55	14	19	119	.269
	Lake Elsinore (Cal)	A	2	0	0.95	3	3	0	0	19	12	3	2	1	5	18	.174
2003	Lake Elsinore (Cal)	A	9	5	4.23	19	19	1	0	111	127	61	52	4	25	78	.287
	Mobile (SL)	AA	2	5	4.34	9	9	1	0	58	60	34	28	6	13	44	.268
MINOR LEAGUE TOTALS			38	31	3.86	98	89	5	1	555	587	279	238	41	98	455	.268

16 Javier Martinez, rhp

Born: Dec. 9, 1982. **Ht.:** 6-3. **Wt.:** 170. **Bats:** B. **Throws:** R. **Career Transactions:** Signed out of Mexico by Padres, March 26, 2000.

Few pitchers in the system have a higher ceiling than Martinez, but he was disappointing enough in 2003 that the Padres didn't protect him on the 40-man roster. A sore elbow shut him down for seven weeks starting in May and again for three weeks at the end of the season. He sometimes throws his splitter too much, and that may have been the culprit. After pitching at 90-95 in 2002, Martinez was down to 86-91 mph last year. He needs to add strength to his lanky frame, which could take his velocity up. His curveball and changeup both are solid pitches, so he doesn't need to mess with the splitter. He has good command and reminds scouts of fellow Mexican Ismael Valdes, who signed with the Padres during the offseason. Martinez' work habits have been questioned and he must show he can bounce back from adversity. He'll try to recapture his promise when he returns to high Class A.

Year	Club (League)	Class	W	L	ERA	G	GS	CG	SV	IP	H	R	ER	HR	BB	SO	AVG
2000	Padres (AZL)	R	0	0	0.00	3	0	0	1	3	0	0	0	0	3	2	.000
2001	Idaho Falls (Pio)	R	1	4	6.43	10	8	0	0	42	42	35	30	6	26	38	.261
2002	Eugene (NWL)	A	0	0	4.50	2	2	0	0	10	4	5	5	2	5	6	.121
	Fort Wayne (Mid)	A	6	4	3.38	12	12	0	0	69	55	28	26	5	19	69	.211
2003	Lake Elsinore (Cal)	A	6	3	3.23	16	16	0	0	84	76	35	30	7	23	70	.234
MINOR LEAGUE TOTALS			13	11	3.93	43	38	0	1	208	177	103	91	20	76	185	.224

17 Edgar Huerta, lhp

Born: Feb. 9, 1980. **Ht.:** 5-11. **Wt.:** 140. **Bats:** L. **Throws:** L. **Career Transactions:** Signed out of Mexico by Braves, Jan. 1, 1997 . . . Loaned by Braves to Mexico City Tigers (Mexican), May 17-Sept. 11, 1997 . . . Loaned by Braves to Mexico City Tigers, March 16-Sept. 23, 1998 . . . Released by Braves, Sept. 30, 1998 . . . Signed by Mexico City Tigers, Aug. 1999 . . . Signed by independent Mexico (Arizona), June 2000 . . . Signed by Mexico City Tigers, March 2001 . . . Signed by Puebla (Mexican), March 2001 . . . Signed by Mexico City Tigers, March 2002 . . . Signed by Padres, Jan. 6, 2004.

Akinori Otsuka isn't the only offseason international acquisition who could make the San Diego bullpen out of spring training. The Padres paid the Mexico Tigers $850,000 for the rights to Huerta. Though Huerta is just 5-foot-11, he generates 92-97 mph fastballs and backs them up with a plus slider. San Diego has a working agreement with the Mexico City Red Devils, whose president, Roberto Mansur, recommended Huerta. He signed with the Braves in 1997 and spent two years on loan to the Mexico City Tigers before Atlanta released him after the 1998 season. He spent the 1997 and '98 seasons in the Mexican minors. Huerta went to big league camp with the Devil Rays last spring, but looked timid and gave up eight runs in 2⅓ innings before being returned to Angelopolis. San Diego officials believe Huerta will be more comfortable in his second exposure to the United States. He'll need to improve his command. He doesn't have an offspeed pitch to fall back on, though that's less crucial because he's a reliever. The Padres say Huerta has closer potential, and they'll break him in by using him in a set-up role this year in either the majors or Triple-A.

Year	Club (League)	Class	W	L	ERA	G	GS	CG	SV	IP	H	R	ER	HR	BB	SO	AVG
1999	M.C. Tigers (Mex)	AAA	0	0	0.00	1	0	0	0	0	0	1	1	0	1	0	--
2000	Mexico (AZL)	R	4	2	3.33	9	8	3	0	54	54	23	20	0	25	78	.263

2001	M.C. Tigers (Mex)	AAA	0	0	0.00	1	0	0	0	1	0	0	0	0	1	1	.000
	Puebla (Mex)	AAA	1	0	3.16	19	1	0	0	26	21	10	9	1	14	25	.226
2002	M.C. Tigers (Mex)	AAA	7	4	4.47	29	15	1	2	103	98	55	51	7	56	84	.257
2003	M.C. Tigers (Mex)	AAA	4	2	3.70	31	5	0	0	56	53	28	23	1	38	69	.244
MINOR LEAGUE TOTALS			16	8	3.91	90	29	4	2	239	226	117	104	9	135	257	.251

18 Michael Johnson, 1b

Born: June 25, 1980. **Ht.:** 6-3. **Wt.:** 215. **Bats:** L. **Throws:** R. **School:** Clemson University.
Career Transactions: Selected by Padres in second round of 2002 draft; signed June 2, 2003.

Negotiations with Johnson deteriorated after the Padres drafted him in 2002, one round after they took Clemson teammate Khalil Greene. The two sides were roughly $300,000 apart when Johnson returned to college, where he dislocated his right ankle during fall practice. But San Diego retained his rights up until the 2003 draft because he was a fifth-year senior, and he signed for $500,000. Sent straight to high Class A, Johnson was a bit overmatched and struggled with a bruised left knee. Johnson is similar to former Padre Dave Magadan, a line-drive hitter who uses the whole field and controls the strike zone. The key is how much power Johnson will develop. Though he finished with 58 homers at Clemson, one shy of the school record, he doesn't turn on pitches and hasn't shown much home run pop with wood bats. He has to improve at first base, where he looked awkward in his pro debut, and San Diego has ruled out trying him as a left fielder, though he has below-average arm strength. Johnson would be best off returning to high Class A, at least to begin 2004. Now that he's acclimated and healthy, the Padres expect to see the player they thought they were getting.

Year	Club (League)	Class	AVG	G	AB	R	H	2B	3B	HR	RBI	BB	SO	SB	SLG	OBP
2003	Lake Elsinore (Cal)	A	.275	46	178	22	49	17	1	5	24	17	48	0	.466	.343
MINOR LEAGUE TOTALS			.275	46	178	22	49	17	1	5	24	17	48	0	.466	.343

19 Humberto Quintero, c

Born: Aug. 2, 1979. **Ht.:** 6-1. **Wt.:** 190. **Bats:** R. **Throws:** R. **Career Transactions:** Signed out of Venezuela by White Sox, Jan. 16, 1997 . . . Traded by White Sox with OF Alex Fernandez to Padres for 3B D'Angelo Jimenez, July 12, 2002.

Quintero was the organization's most improved player in 2003. He entered the year with little indication that he'd ever hit much. But after they acquired him in a July 2002 trade with the White Sox, the Padres got Quintero to abandon a dead-pull approach and try to use the whole field. He hit .309 in the final month of 2002, a prelude to the best year of his career. He focused on making contact and succeeded, showing gap power if not drawing many walks. Quintero doesn't have a pretty swing and never will be an offensive force, but now looks like he'll hit enough to at least be a big league backup. He long has had a reputation of having one of the best arms in the game, drawing comparisons to Pudge Rodriguez. Quintero is the best defensive catcher in the system, and he threw out 39 percent of basestealers last year in the Southern League. He sometimes loses his concentration as a receiver, but he has improved in that area as well as leadership. More troubling are rumors the last two years that Quintero has tipped pitches to Venezuelan hitters on other teams in exchange for getting the same information from them. The Padres investigated the situation and say they've found nothing. With San Diego trading for Ramon Hernandez, Quintero will get a full year in Triple-A. If he continues to hit, he'll back Hernandez up in 2005.

Year	Club (League)	Class	AVG	G	AB	R	H	2B	3B	HR	RBI	BB	SO	SB	SLG	OBP
1997	Guacara 1 (VSL)	R	.262	24	42	4	11	2	0	0	5	0	5	9	1	.310	.333
1998	Miranda (VSL)	R	.205	30	73	6	15	1	0	0	1	3	12	0	.219	.266
1999	Bristol (Appy)	R	.277	48	155	30	43	5	2	0	15	9	19	11	.335	.341
2000	Burlington (Mid)	A	.238	75	248	23	59	12	2	0	24	15	31	10	.302	.287
	White Sox (AZL)	R	.393	15	56	13	22	2	2	0	8	0	3	1	.500	.414
2001	Kannapolis (SAL)	A	.269	60	197	32	53	7	1	1	20	8	20	7	.330	.321
	Winston-Salem (Car)	A	.240	43	154	15	37	6	0	0	12	5	19	9	.279	.268
	Birmingham (SL)	AA	.211	5	19	0	4	0	0	0	2	0	2	0	.211	.250
2002	Winston-Salem (Car)	A	.194	52	160	15	31	1	1	0	12	8	23	2	.213	.247
	Birmingham (SL)	AA	.500	4	12	1	6	0	0	0	3	0	1	1	.500	.538
	Charlotte (IL)	AAA	.220	15	41	2	9	1	0	0	5	3	8	0	.244	.273
	Mobile (SL)	AA	.240	37	125	11	30	8	0	1	14	5	12	0	.328	.286
2003	Mobile (SL)	AA	.298	110	386	37	115	26	0	3	52	19	41	0	.389	.343
	San Diego (NL)	MAJ	.217	12	23	1	5	0	0	0	2	1	6	0	.217	.250
MAJOR LEAGUE TOTALS			.217	12	23	1	5	0	0	0	2	1	6	0	.217	.250
MINOR LEAGUE TOTALS			.261	518	1668	189	435	71	8	5	168	80	200	42	.322	.309

20 Wilmer Villatoro, rhp

Born: June 27, 1983. **Ht.:** 6-0. **Wt.:** 150. **Bats:** R. **Throws:** R. **Career Transactions:** Signed out of El Salvador by Padres, June 13, 2000.

Few scouts have more worldwide contacts than former Padres international supervisor Bill Clark, who was fired in September and replaced by former GM Randy Smith. Clark found righthanders Villatoro and William Ponce in El Salvador and made them the first two players ever signed from that nation. Ponce, who's similar to Justin Germano, made more strides than anyone in San Diego's instructional league camp after the 2003 season. Villatoro, who signed for $5,000, has better pure stuff. He was nearly unhittable as a set-up man in low Class A, where his stuff got better over the course of the season. Villatoro threw a 92 mph fastball and a loose slider early in the year, but was pitching with a 94 mph heater and a tighter slider by August. He'll have to throw more strikes at higher levels. Nevertheless, his first full season couldn't have been more encouraging. He'll step up to high Class A in 2004.

Year	Club (League)	Class	W	L	ERA	G	GS	CG	SV	IP	H	R	ER	HR	BB	SO	AVG
2000	Padres (AZL)	R	0	0	15.43	2	0	0	0	2	3	4	4	0	2	5	.375
2001	Idaho Falls (Pio)	R	0	3	5.26	30	0	0	3	38	39	24	22	7	21	35	.267
2002	Eugene (NWL)	A	3	7	5.13	22	7	0	2	53	50	36	30	8	19	69	.245
2003	Fort Wayne (Mid)	A	3	2	2.62	39	0	0	2	55	31	20	16	7	28	77	.164
MINOR LEAGUE TOTALS			6	12	4.39	93	7	0	7	148	123	84	72	22	70	186	.225

21 Billy Hogan, 3b

Born: May 20, 1983. **Ht.:** 6-3. **Wt.:** 210. **Bats:** R. **Throws:** R. **School:** Chandler-Gilbert (Ariz.) JC. **Career Transactions:** Selected by Padres in fifth round of 2003 draft; signed June 3, 2003.

Hogan starred as a high schooler in Texas and on the 1999 U.S. youth national team, but his commitment to Alabama caused teams to pass him by in the 2002 draft. After attending Alabama that fall, he had second thoughts and transferred to junior college to become eligible for the 2003 draft. He emerged as the top hitting prospect among Arizona juco players and signed for a $215,000 bonus. With his strong 6-foot-4 frame and quick bat, Hogan has a chance to hit for both average and power. He needs to shorten his swing, tighten his strike zone and learn to recognize breaking balls. A shortstop in high school, he was a DH in junior college and needs to work to stay at third base. He has the arm strength and footwork for the position but lacks the instincs and fundamentals. Some Padres officials were disappointed by Hogan's immaturity, saying he was too high on himself and full of excuses. If he can't handle the hot corner, he'll have to move to left field or first base. For now, San Diego will keep him at third base and challenge him with a promotion to low Class A.

Year	Club (League)	Class	AVG	G	AB	R	H	2B	3B	HR	RBI	BB	SO	SB	SLG	OBP
2003	Idaho Falls (Pio)	R	.344	45	163	22	56	17	1	3	33	15	36	3	.515	.419
	Eugene (NWL)	A	.256	22	78	6	20	7	0	1	10	8	21	0	.385	.333
MINOR LEAGUE TOTALS			.315	67	241	28	76	24	1	4	43	23	57	3	.473	.392

22 Aaron Coonrod, rhp

Born: May 17, 1980. **Ht.:** 6-4. **Wt.:** 210. **Bats:** R. **Throws:** R. **School:** John A. Logan (Ill.) JC. **Career Transactions:** Selected by Padres in fourth round of 2002 draft; signed June 9, 2002.

The Padres have their share of intriguing arms in the lower levels of their system. Coonrod is the most advanced, surfacing in low Class A at the end of 2003 for Fort Wayne's playoff run. Scouts backed off him coming out of high school in 1999 because of an ankle injury. Ohio State recruited him as a quarterback, but he failed to qualify academically and attended junior college instead. He pitched sparingly as a freshman and became academically ineligible, so he spent 2001 working in a factory. Coonrod rejoined Logan in 2002, finishing among the national leaders in strikeouts while leading the Volunteers to the Junior College World Series. For most of his first two pro seasons, San Diego used Coonrod as a starter to get him innings, but he took off when he moved to his long-term role in the bullpen. His fastball, the best in the system, moved up to the mid-90s and topped out at 97 mph. His breaking ball, which came and went when he was in the rotation, was a more consistent power slider. He also has an effective changeup, though he won't use it as much in relief. Coonrod has a maximum-effort delivery that makes it difficult for him to sustain his stuff, another reason he fits best in the bullpen. His focus, command and secondary pitches still need work. A potential closer, he'll pitch in Class A this season.

Year	Club (League)	Class	W	L	ERA	G	GS	CG	SV	IP	H	R	ER	HR	BB	SO	AVG
2002	Eugene (NWL)	A	3	3	5.54	15	12	0	0	65	75	48	40	2	24	45	.287
2003	Eugene (NWL)	A	3	3	5.37	13	10	0	0	52	48	32	31	3	33	45	.255
	Fort Wayne (Mid)	A	0	0	0.00	4	0	0	0	7	6	1	0	0	3	9	.214
MINOR LEAGUE TOTALS			6	6	5.15	32	22	0	0	124	129	81	71	5	60	99	.270

23 Peter Stonard, 2b

Born: Dec. 31, 1981. **Ht.:** 6-0. **Wt.:** 195. **Bats:** L. **Throws:** R. **School:** San Diego State University. **Career Transactions:** Selected by Padres in fourth round of 2003 draft; signed June 10, 2003.

In the fall of 2002, Stonard and Billy Hogan were teammates at Alabama. Neither played for the Crimson Tide last spring, however. Stonard twice tested positive for marijuana and was dismissed from the team in November 2002. He transferred to San Diego State and wrote a letter to major league teams, admitting he had made poor decisions and promising it wouldn't happen again. But it did, and the Aztecs kicked him off their team last April. That knocked Stonard, the 2002 Cape Cod League batting champ with a .348 average, to the fourth round, where the Padres signed him for $280,000. Stonard went straight to low Class A and did what he always does: make good, consistent line-drive contact. Stonard has decent tools across the board but still has a lot of questions. He's so good at putting the bat on the ball, even on pitches out of the strike zone, that he makes outs on balls others would miss. It also cuts down on his walk totals. He's an average runner with good hands at second base, but scouts aren't sure he can stick there. The outfield might become his home, and he'd have to hit for more power than he currently projects. Most of all, Stonard has to work harder and prove his dedication to the game after his college travails. He'll try to polish his all-around game in high Class A this year.

Year	Club (League)	Class	AVG	G	AB	R	H	2B	3B	HR	RBI	BB	SO	SB	SLG	OBP
2003	Lake Elsinore (Cal)	A	.200	1	5	1	1	0	0	0	1	0	2	0	.200	.200
	Fort Wayne (Mid)	A	.293	64	239	22	70	10	0	0	27	18	25	4	.335	.338
MINOR LEAGUE TOTALS			.291	65	244	23	71	10	0	0	28	18	27	4	.332	.336

24 Greg Sain, 3b/c

Born: Dec. 26, 1979. **Ht.:** 6-2. **Wt.:** 200. **Bats:** R. **Throws:** R. **School:** University of San Diego. **Career Transactions:** Selected by Padres in fifth round of 2001 draft; signed June 14, 2001.

The Padres drafted Sain as a catcher and are waiting to see if he can handle the position. He led both the West Coast Conference and Northwest League in homers in 2001, but needed surgery to repair tears in the labrum and rotator cuff in his right shoulder after the season. He has caught just 22 games as a pro. What is certain is that he's not a third baseman. Sain, whose father Tommy reached Triple-A in the 1970s, showed poor agility at the hot corner last year and led California League third baseman with 35 errors in just 94 games. He showed average arm strength before the surgery and his receiving skills are fine. While Sain has some of the best raw power in the system and drove in 100 runs last year, some say he has a slider-speed bat that won't catch up to quality fastballs at the upper levels. He'll also have to improve his plate discipline. San Diego should have a better idea of what Sain can offer after he spends a full year in Double-A. He may have to share the catching duties there with Nick Trzesniak, who has his share of backers within the organization.

Year	Club (League)	Class	AVG	G	AB	R	H	2B	3B	HR	RBI	BB	SO	SB	SLG	OBP
2001	Eugene (NWL)	A	.293	67	256	48	75	19	1	16	40	21	68	1	.563	.356
2002	Fort Wayne (Mid)	A	.245	105	387	54	95	29	0	13	57	35	77	2	.421	.323
2003	Lake Elsinore (Cal)	A	.274	123	467	74	128	35	0	19	100	43	119	3	.471	.336
MINOR LEAGUE TOTALS			.268	295	1110	176	298	83	1	48	197	99	264	6	.475	.336

25 Bernie Castro, 2b

Born: July 14, 1979. **Ht.:** 5-10. **Wt.:** 160. **Bats:** B. **Throws:** R. **Career Transactions:** Signed out of Dominican Republic by Yankees, Sept. 25, 1997 . . . On disabled list, June 5-Sept. 24, 1999 . . . Traded by Yankees to Padres for OF Kevin Reese, Dec. 18, 2001.

Castro won a minor league stolen base title in each of his five pro seasons, topping the Pacific Coast League last year with 49 in 62 attempts. He extended his streak despite spraining the anterior cruciate ligament in his left knee sliding into home plate in mid-August, ending his season five weeks early. The injury cost him the opportunity to chase his third straight Dominican League batting title, and Castro may not be ready for the start of spring training. Managers rated Castro the PCL's fastest baserunner, and he can get down the line from the plate to first base in 3.9-4.0 seconds. He does a good job of playing to his speed, making contact, keeping the ball on the ground, bunting skillfully and using the entire field. But while his average spiked in the hitter-friendly PCL, his walk rate declined. He'll need to get on base more to offset his lack of power. Defensively, Castro's arm presents a huge question mark. It's barely playable at second base, which is one of the deepest positions in the system. He does have the range, hands and double-play pivot for the position. The Padres eventually could give him a look in center field, though that's unlikely in 2004, when he'll again be Freddy Guzman's teammate in Triple-A.

Year	Club (League)	Class	AVG	G	AB	R	H	2B	3B	HR	RBI	BB	SO	SB	SLG	OBP
1998	Yankees (DSL)	R	.330	61	224	78	74	6	4	0	17	37	40	63	.393	.432
1999	Did not play—Injured															
2000	Yankees (DSL)	R	.348	55	210	69	73	9	2	2	13	36	24	56	.438	.450
	Yankees (GCL)	R	.441	9	34	7	15	4	1	0	6	6	4	3	.618	.525
2001	Greensboro (SAL)	A	.260	101	389	71	101	15	7	1	36	54	67	67	.342	.350
	Staten Island (NY-P)	A	.351	15	57	6	20	1	0	0	7	11	12	8	.368	.464
2002	Mobile (SL)	AA	.260	109	419	61	109	13	3	0	32	52	67	53	.305	.345
2003	Portland (PCL)	AAA	.311	105	425	57	132	17	5	2	24	25	43	49	.388	.349
MINOR LEAGUE TOTALS			.298	455	1758	349	524	65	22	5	135	221	257	299	.369	.380

26 Henri Stanley, of

Born: Dec. 15, 1977. **Ht.:** 5-10. **Wt.:** 185. **Bats:** L. **Throws:** L. **School:** Clemson University. **Career Transactions:** Signed as nondrafted free agent by Astros, June 15, 2000 . . . Claimed on waivers by Padres from Astros, Nov. 14, 2003.

Stanley endeared himself to the Astros, but they removed him from their 40-man roster in November, allowing the Padres to grab him with a waiver claim. He has hit line drives and shown on-base skills since turning pro. He has gap power and above-average speed. Stanley can be too passive early in the count and could drive the ball more often if he were more aggressive. He runs the bases well but doesn't get good reads and jumps to be a big bases-stealing threat. Defensively, he has the range but not the instincts for center field, and his well-below-average arm relegates him to left field. He's a classic tweener outfielder who can't handle the defense in center or provide enough offense to play on the corner. But Stanley would make a good fourth outfielder and could have a career like Troy O'Leary's. San Diego may not have an outfield opening on its roster, so Stanley may have to repeat Triple-A.

Year	Club (League)	Class	AVG	G	AB	R	H	2B	3B	HR	RBI	BB	SO	SB	SLG	OBP
2000	Martinsville (Appy)	R	.248	46	165	34	41	8	6	4	20	25	37	10	.442	.347
2001	Michigan (Mid)	A	.300	114	400	75	120	24	12	14	76	73	84	30	.525	.408
2002	Round Rock (TL)	AA	.314	127	456	90	143	36	10	16	72	72	85	14	.542	.408
2003	New Orleans (PCL)	AAA	.292	135	506	85	148	28	8	11	48	60	93	15	.445	.368
MINOR LEAGUE TOTALS			.296	422	1527	284	452	96	36	45	216	230	299	69	.494	.389

27 Jake Gautreau, 2b/3b

Born: Nov. 14, 1979. **Ht.:** 6-0. **Wt.:** 185. **Bats:** L. **Throws:** R. **School:** Tulane University. **Career Transactions:** Selected by Padres in first round (14th overall) of 2001 draft; signed June 21, 2001.

San Diego gave Gautreau $1.875 million as the 14th overall pick in 2001, but his career has been sidetracked by ulcerative colitis. After moving him from third to second base, the Padres envisioned Gautreau as another Jeff Kent, but his bat has been a disappointment. The colitis, diagnosed in July 2002, has sapped him of strength and bat speed. He's also pull-conscious and has holes in his swing, which prevent him from making consistent contact. Gautreau also puts too much pressure on himself, making it even harder to snap out of his doldrums. While he has stayed at second base for two years and has improved, he still is just adequate and doesn't make all of the routine plays. His double-play pivot needs work. Second base has become a position of strength in the organization, and Gautreau likely will return to the hot corner in 2004. That will require more offense, and his agility will be an issue at third. The Padres left Gautreau off their 40-man roster, something inconceivable when they drafted him, but he went unchosen in the major league Rule 5 draft.

Year	Club (League)	Class	AVG	G	AB	R	H	2B	3B	HR	RBI	BB	SO	SB	SLG	OBP
2001	Eugene (NWL)	A	.309	48	178	28	55	19	0	6	36	22	47	1	.517	.389
	Portland (PCL)	AAA	.286	2	7	2	2	0	0	1	2	2	2	0	.714	.444
2002	Lake Elsinore (Cal)	A	.286	93	371	43	106	20	1	10	62	42	86	2	.426	.358
2003	Mobile (SL)	AA	.242	122	438	48	106	24	0	14	55	50	131	1	.393	.324
MINOR LEAGUE TOTALS			.271	265	994	121	269	63	1	31	155	116	266	4	.430	.350

28 Jason Szuminski, rhp

Born: Dec. 11, 1978. **Ht.:** 6-5. **Wt.:** 220. **Bats:** R. **Throws:** R. **School:** Massachusetts Institute of Technology. **Career Transactions:** Selected by Cubs in 27th round of 2000 draft; signed June 9, 2000 . . . Selected by Royals from Cubs in Rule 5 major league draft, Dec. 15, 2003 . . . Traded by Royals with cash to Padres for OF Rich Thompson, Dec. 15, 2003.

Szuminski has had to overcome long odds just to have a professional baseball career. The second player ever drafted out of MIT, he attended college on an Air Force ROTC scholarship that mandated military service after he graduated with an aerospace engineering degree. He became the first baseball player to enter the Air Force's World Class Athlete Program, which allowed him to train with the goal of reaching the 2004 Olympics. Though that dream ended when Team USA failed to qualify for the Athens Games, his baseball career likely will be spared because he was taken in the major league Rule 5 draft. The Royals drafted him from the Cubs, who had too much pitching to protect Szuminski, and traded him to San Diego for fellow Rule 5 pick Rich Thompson. The Padres can't send Szuminski to the minors in 2004 without having him clear waivers and then offering him back to Chicago, and if he sticks it would be a public-relations boon for the Air Force. He made great progress in 2003, moving from high Class A to Triple-A after dropping his arm angle. He sacrificed velocity for better command and life on his fastball. Szuminski's fastball now sits at 88 mph and tops out at 91, but its improved sink gets lots of groundballs. He also scrapped his curveball and now throws a slider, which has been more effective. He also has a splitter that drops straight down, and all three of his pitches feature different types of movement. If Szuminski throws strikes, he should be able to make the Padres in spring training.

Year	Club (League)	Class	W	L	ERA	G	GS	CG	SV	IP	H	R	ER	HR	BB	SO	AVG
2000	Cubs (AZL)	R	2	1	2.43	10	4	0	0	41	39	15	11	0	13	31	.253
	Lansing (Mid)	A	3	1	3.38	4	4	0	0	21	19	8	8	0	10	7	.247
2001	Lansing (Mid)	A	4	3	6.44	14	4	0	0	36	56	27	26	2	17	22	.359
2002	Daytona (FSL)	A	5	2	5.12	39	7	0	1	91	95	61	52	7	41	53	.261
2003	Daytona (FSL)	A	2	1	3.65	13	0	0	0	25	29	12	10	0	9	23	.296
	West Tenn (SL)	AA	7	4	2.26	29	3	0	2	60	51	19	15	1	19	45	.233
	Iowa (PCL)	AAA	0	0	3.55	3	2	0	0	13	11	5	5	0	1	5	.234
MINOR LEAGUE TOTALS			23	12	3.99	112	24	0	3	287	300	147	127	10	110	186	.269

29 George Kottaras, c

Born: May 16, 1983. **Ht.:** 6-0. **Wt.:** 180. **Bats:** L. **Throws:** R. **School:** Connors State (Okla.) JC. **Career Transactions:** Selected by Padres in 20th round of 2002 draft; signed May 26, 2003.

The Padres bolstered their catching depth by drafting Colt Morton (third round) and Matt Lauderdale (ninth) in June, but their most significant acquisition was Kottaras in May. They signed him as a draft-and-follow from 2002, giving him a $375,000 bonus. A Canadian who played more fast-pitch softball than baseball while he was growing up, Kottaras spent most of July with the Greek national team. He was the starting catcher as Greece finished second at the European Championship, and he's a candidate to rejoin them for the Olympics. Though Kottaras is relatively inexperienced, his potential is obvious and draws him comparisons to Mike Lieberthal. He has a compact, fluid swing and the ball jumps off his bat. He exudes discipline at the plate, though he's sometimes too patient and falls behind in the count after letting hittable pitches go by. He's a below-average runner but above average for a catcher. Kottaras has solid arm strength and threw out 36 percent of basestealers in the Rookie-level Pioneer League. He needs work defensively but has potential as a receiver. The addition of former all-star Joe Ferguson as a roving catching instructor should help him. Kottaras could go to low Class A in 2004, but also could wind up in Eugene.

Year	Club (League)	Class	AVG	G	AB	R	H	2B	3B	HR	RBI	BB	SO	SB	SLG	OBP
2003	Idaho Falls (Pio)	R	.259	42	143	27	37	8	1	7	24	19	36	1	.476	.348
MINOR LEAGUE TOTALS			.259	42	143	27	37	8	1	7	24	19	36	1	.476	.348

30 Brian Whitaker, rhp

Born: Nov. 5, 1979. **Ht.:** 6-4. **Wt.:** 200. **Bats:** R. **Throws:** R. **School:** UNC Wilmington. **Career Transactions:** Selected by Padres in 27th round of 2002 draft; signed June 7, 2002.

The Padres named Gabe Ribas their minor league pitcher of the year in 2003 after he tied for the minor league lead with 17 victories, but with the exception of his changeup his stuff is very fringy. Whitaker, who like Ribas excelled in low Class A while being old for the level at 23, has a better chance to succeed. A 27th-round find by area scout Mike Rikard in 2002, Whitaker topped the system with a 2.09 ERA last year. He also paced the Midwest League in walks per nine innings (1.1), and the managers there rated his command as the best in the league. He never walked more than two batters in any of his 26 starts. With his 6-foot-4 frame, Whitaker is able to pitch to the bottom of the strike zone with a lively 86-89 mph sinker that touches the low 90s. That makes him a groundball machine, and his 2.2 ground/fly ratio in 2003 was one of the highest in the minors. He has traded in his curveball for a more effective slider and also uses a changeup. Whitaker has a great body, loose arm and easy delivery. He still needs to prove himself against lefthanders and against hitters his own age. San Diego will accelerate his development, meaning Whitaker should reach Double-A at some point in 2004.

Year	Club (League)	Class	W	L	ERA	G	GS	CG	SV	IP	H	R	ER	HR	BB	SO	AVG
2002	Eugene (NWL)	A	5	8	2.93	16	14	0	0	83	79	36	27	6	16	63	.250
2003	Fort Wayne (Mid)	A	7	6	2.09	26	26	3	0	164	149	60	38	5	20	121	.240
MINOR LEAGUE TOTALS			12	14	2.37	42	40	3	0	247	228	96	65	11	36	184	.243

SAN FRANCISCO GIANTS

The Giants proved they could win without manager Dusty Baker in 2003, claiming the National League West division title for the second time in four seasons. Since 1997, San Francisco has been in contention for a playoff berth every September. As long as 39-year-old Barry Bonds is around and playing anywhere near his MVP level, that should continue. The Giants' object is to surround Bonds with as much big league talent as the team can afford—and win now. To that end, general manager Brian Sabean and Dick Tidrow, who as vice president of player personnel oversees both the scouting and player-development operations, haven't been afraid to sign free agents and trade prospects to keep the Giants competitive.

It's in the eye of the beholder to judge the Giants' track record in player development. On one hand, they have consistently produced enough talent for trades to keep the team at or near the top of the NL West. On the other hand, most of the prospects they've traded haven't developed into legitimate major leaguers with other teams. The Giants' draft fortunes have picked up since 1998, when they had five of the first 41 picks yet produced no big leaguer of more substance than Nate Bump.

In 1999, San Francisco nabbed right-handers Kurt Ainsworth and Jerome Williams with its first two picks. Williams had

TOP 30 PROSPECTS

1. Merkin Valdez, rhp
2. Matt Cain, rhp
3. David Aardsma, rhp
4. Dan Ortmeier, of
5. Todd Linden, of
6. Kevin Correia, rhp
7. Travis Ishikawa, 1b
8. Craig Whitaker, rhp
9. Fred Lewis, of
10. Brian Buscher, 3b
11. Todd Jennings, c
12. Nate Schierholtz, 3b
13. Erick Threets, lhp
14. Lance Niekro, 1b
15. Noah Lowry, lhp
16. Brooks McNiven, rhp
17. Justin Knoedler, c
18. Jon Armitage, of
19. Jamie Athas, 2b/ss
20. Glenn Woolard, rhp
21. Pat Misch, lhp
22. Cody Ransom, ss
23. Josh Habel, lhp
24. Angel Chavez, ss
25. Jason Ellison, of
26. Carlos Valderrama, of
27. Tim Hutting, ss/2b
28. Kelyn Acosta, rhp
29. Jeremy Accardo, rhp
30. Brian Wilson, rhp

By John Manuel

an excellent rookie season in 2003, while Ainsworth was traded to the Orioles for Sidney Ponson. In 2000, the Giants nabbed power arms Boof Bonser and Ryan Hannaman, using them in separate deals this offseason to net Ponson (Hannaman) and all-star catcher A.J. Pierzynski (Bonser). In 2001, San Francisco found Jesse Foppert in the second round. While he appears to be a keeper, he had Tommy John surgery and may not pitch in 2004.

The Pierzynski trade provides graphic evidence of the strengths and weaknesses of the organization's player development. Its pitching-focused drafts have netted enough arms to provide the big league team with the likes of Foppert, Williams and Kevin Correia, while leaving enough spare parts to bolster the offense with trades. The lineup has needed all the help it can get, though, because the Giants haven't developed an everyday big leaguer since drafting Bill Mueller and Chris Singleton in 1993.

The Giants hope to turn that around, but there are few position players of note in the farm system. They attempted to address this with a 2003 draft that was more focused on position players than usual.

Tidrow has been better at finding power arms than he has quality bats. But as long as he finds players Sabean can trade to support the aging Bonds, the Giants' game plan will continue to work in the short term.

ORGANIZATION
OVERVIEW

General manager: Brian Sabean. **Farm director:** Jack Hiatt. **Scouting director:** Dick Tidrow.

2003 PERFORMANCE

Class	Team	League	W	L	Pct.	Finish*	Manager
Majors	San Francisco	National	100	61	.621	2nd (16)	Felipe Alou
Triple-A	Fresno Grizzlies	Pacific Coast	55	88	.385	16th (16)	Fred Stanley
Double-A	Norwich Navigators	Eastern	62	79	.440	t-10th (12)	Shane Turner
High A	San Jose Giants	California	58	82	.414	9th (10)	Bill Hayes
Low A	Hagerstown Suns	South Atlantic	68	67	.504	8th (16)	Mike Ramsey
Short-season	Salem-Keizer Volcanoes	Northwest	43	33	.566	3rd (8)	Jack Lind
Rookie	Scottsdale Giants	Arizona	25	24	.510	t-5th (9)	Bert Hunter

OVERALL 2003 MINOR LEAGUE RECORD   311   373   .454   28th (30)
*Finish in overall standings (No. of teams in league)

ORGANIZATION LEADERS

BATTING *Minimum 250 At-Bats
*AVG	Brian Dallimore, Fresno	.352
R	Todd Linden, Fresno	75
H	Alejandro Freire, Norwich	155
TB	Alejandro Freire, Norwich	242
2B	Dan Ortmeier, San Jose	32
3B	Fred Lewis, Hagerstown	8
	Jose Yens, AZL Giants	8
HR	Dan Trumble, San Jose	21
RBI	Mike Cervenak, Norwich	91
BB	Travis Ishikawa, Hagerstown/Salem-Keiser	77
SO	Travis Ishikawa, Hagerstown/Salem-Keiser	146
SB	Pat Hallmark, Norwich	31
*SLG	Alejandro Freire, Norwich	.486
*OBP	Brian Dallimore, Fresno	.427

PITCHING #Minimum 75 Innings
W	Greg Bruso, Norwich /San Jose	13
L	Mitch Walk, Norwich	13
#ERA	Merkin Valdez, Hagerstown	2.25
G	Joe Horgan, Fresno	55
CG	Greg Bruso, Norwich /San Jose	3
	Clay Hensley, Hagerstown	3
SV	Matt Palmer, Norwich/Hagerstown	25
IP	Greg Bruso, Norwich/San Jose	170
BB	Boof Bonser, Fresno/Norwich	75
SO	Merkin Valdez, Hagerstown	166

BEST TOOLS

Best Hitter for Average	Dan Ortmeier
Best Power Hitter	Nate Schierholtz
Fastest Baserunner	Fred Lewis
Best Athlete	Fred Lewis
Best Fastball	Merkin Valdez
Best Curveball	Matt Cain
Best Slider	Brad Hennessey
Best Changeup	Josh Habel
Best Control	Merkin Valdez
Best Defensive Catcher	Justin Knoedler
Best Defensive Infielder	Jake Wald
Best Infield Arm	Cody Ransom
Best Defensive Outfielder	Jon Coutlangus
Best Outfield Arm	Jon Coutlangus

PROJECTED 2007 LINEUP

Catcher	A.J. Pierzynski
First Base	Travis Ishikawa
Second Base	Ray Durham
Third Base	Edgardo Alfonzo
Shortstop	Cody Ransom
Left Field	Todd Linden
Center Field	Fred Lewis

Right Field	Dan Ortmeier
No. 1 Starter	Jason Schmidt
No. 2 Starter	Jesse Foppert
No. 3 Starter	Jerome Williams
No. 4 Starter	Merkin Valdez
No. 5 Starter	Matt Cain
Closer	David Aardsma

LAST YEAR'S TOP 20 PROSPECTS

1. Jesse Foppert, rhp	11. Matt Cain, rhp
2. Kurt Ainsworth, rhp	12. Deivis Santos, of/1b
3. Jerome Williams,rhp	13. Tony Torcato, of
4. Francisco Liriano, lhp	14. Travis Ishikawa, 1b
5. Todd Linden, of	15. Melvin Valdez, rhp
6. Boof Bonser, rhp	16. Noah Lowry, lhp
7. Fred Lewis, of	17. Jason Ellison, of
8. Ryan Hannaman, lhp	18. Carlos Valderrama, of
9. Lance Niekro, 1b/3b	19. David Cash, rhp
10. Erick Threets, lhp	20. Dan Ortmeier, of

TOP PROSPECTS OF THE DECADE

1994	Salomon Torres, rhp
1995	J.R. Phillips, 1b
1996	Shawn Estes, lhp
1997	Joe Fontenot, rhp
1998	Jason Grilli, rhp
1999	Jason Grilli, rhp
2000	Kurt Ainsworth, rhp
2001	Jerome Williams, rhp
2002	Jerome Williams, rhp
2003	Jesse Foppert, rhp

TOP DRAFT PICKS OF THE DECADE

1994	Dante Powell, of
1995	Joe Fontenot, rhp
1996	*Matt White, rhp
1997	Jason Grilli, rhp
1998	Tony Torcato, 3b
1999	Kurt Ainsworth, rhp
2000	Boof Bonser, rhp
2001	Brad Hennessey, rhp
2002	Matt Cain, rhp
2003	David Aardsma, rhp
*Did not sign.

ALL-TIME LARGEST BONUSES

Jason Grilli, 1997	$1,875,000
David Aardsma, 2003	$1,425,000
Brad Hennessey, 2001	$1,380,000
Matt Cain, 2002	$1,375,000
Osvaldo Fernandez, 1996	$1,300,000
Kurt Ainsworth, 2000	$1,300,000

MINOR LEAGUE
DEPTH CHART

SAN FRANCISCO GIANTS
RANK: 24

Impact potential (C): Merkin Valdez had only Rookie-level experience when the Giants acquired him from the Braves as part of the Russ Ortiz deal after the 2002 season. He managed to exceed expectations in his first full year, and could project as either a frontline starter or dominant closer. Matt Cain also has a high ceiling, but missed half of last season with an injury.

Depth (D): Perhaps no GM uses his farm system more efficiently to prop up the big league club more than Brian Sabean. Last year, he shipped out prospects Kurt Ainsworth, Ryan Hannaman, Boof Bonser and Francisco Liriano to acquire veteran talent, but he hung onto Jerome Williams and Jesse Foppert, who contributed in San Francisco. The trades depleted their system, but the Giants addressed an organizational weakness by adding several polished college bats in the draft.

Sleeper: Todd Jennings, c.   *—Depth charts prepared by Josh Boyd. Numbers in parentheses indicate prospect rankings.*

LF
Todd Linden (5)
Deivis Santos
Tony Torcato
Adam Shabala
Dan Trumble

CF
Fred Lewis (9)
Jason Ellison (25)
Carlos Valderrama (26)

3B
Brian Buscher (10)
Nate Schierholtz (12)

RF
Dan Ortmeier (4)
Jon Armitage (18)
Carlos Sosa
Mike Wagner

SS
Cody Ransom (22)
Angel Chavez (24)
Tim Hutting (27)
Jake Wald
Johany Abreu

2B
Jamie Athas (19)
Aaron Hornostaj
Ryan Strain

1B
Travis Ishikawa (7)
Lance Niekro (14)
Julian Benavidez

SOURCE OF TALENT

Homegrown		Acquired	
College	21	Trades	1
Junior College	2	Rule 5 draft	0
Draft-and-follow	0	Independent leagues	0
High school	3	Free agents/waivers	0
Non drafted free agent	0		
Foreign	3		

C
Todd Jennings (11)
Justin Knoedler (17)
Trey Lunsford
Dayton Buller

RHP

Starters	Relievers
Merkin Valdez (1)	David Aardsma (3)
Matt Cain (2)	Jeremy Accardo (29)
Kevin Correia (6)	Matt Palmer
Craig Whitaker (8)	Billy Sadler
Brooks McNiven (16)	James Garcia
Glenn Woolard (20)	
Kelyn Acosta (28)	
Brian Wilson (30)	
Brian Stirm	
Brad Hennessey	
Brion Treadway	
Mike Musgrave	
Ryan Sadowski	
Ben Thurmond	
Anthony Pannone	
Jeff Clark	

LHP

Starters	Relievers
Noah Lowry (15)	Erick Threets (13)
Pat Misch (21)	Travis NeSmith
Josh Habel (23)	Tim Alvarez
Jesse English	
Jeff Urban	

DRAFT
ANALYSIS

Best Pro Debut: RHP David Aardsma (1) had no problem going from the College World Series to high Class A. He had a 1.96 ERA and eight saves over 18 innings. RHP Ben Thurmond (15) went 5-0, 1.93 with a 45-9 strikeout-walk ratio in the short-season Northwest League. 3B Nate Schierholtz (2) hit .331-5-34 between the Rookie-level Arizona League and the NWL.

Best Athlete: C Todd Jennings (2) also played second base, third base and the outfield at Long Beach State. He hit .296-3-32 in the NWL. The Giants compare his athleticism to Jason Kendall's.

McNiven

Best Pure Hitter: Schierholtz didn't get much play before the draft, but scouting coordinator Matt Nerland found him at Chabot (Calif.) Junior College, vice president of player personnel Dick Tidrow's alma mater.

Best Raw Power: Schierholtz should hit for power and average. 3B Brian Buscher (3) also has some pop.

Fastest Runner: OF Jon Coutlangus (19) rates a 55 on the 20-80 scouting scale.

Best Defensive Player: Jennings led NWL catchers by erasing 39 percent of basestealers.

Best Fastball: Aardsma and RHP Craig Whitaker (1) both sit in the mid-90s and top out at 98 mph. RHPs Billy Sadler (6) and Kellen Ludwig (9) can push their fastballs to 95-96 mph.

Best Breaking Ball: Before he needed Tommy John surgery, RHP Brian Wilson's (24) curveball was easily the class of this crop. Until he returns, RHP Brooks McNiven's (4) slider and LHP Pat Misch's (7) curve are the best.

Most Intriguing Background: OF Patrick Dobson's (18) father Kevin was a regular on "Kojak" and "Knots Landing." C Nick Conte's (13) dad Stan is the Giants' head trainer. Unsigned LHP Tyler Coon (26) was tournament MVP after helping the Southern Nevada win the Junior College World Series.

Closest To The Majors: Aardsma will be ready once he develops consistency with his slider.

Best Late-Round Pick: Wilson might have been a supplemental first-rounder if he hadn't blown out his elbow. The Giants expect he'll eventually regain his curveball and 90-93 mph fastball.

The One Who Got Away: Florida Christian High (Miami) teammates C Raul Rodriguez (20) and RHP Sean Watson (21). Rodriguez is at Florida State. Watson, who has a nice assortment of pitches led by an 88-92 mph fastball, went to Tennessee.

Assessment: The Giants started off with two powerful arms in Aardsma and Whitaker, then did what they do best. They work hard and aren't afraid to buck the consensus, an approach that brought them Jennings, Schierholtz and Buscher.

In a major upset, RHP Kevin Correia (4) became the first 2002 draftee to reach the majors. He and RHP Matt Cain (1), OF Dan Ortmeier (3), 1B Travis Ishikawa (21) and OF Fred Lewis (2) all made the Giants top 10 list.

RHP Jesse Foppert (2) eclipsed all three first-rounders before having Tommy John surgery last summer. OF Todd Linden (1) and LHP Noah Lowry (1) still have upside, while RHP Brad Hennessey (1) has had to overcome two benign tumors on his back.

Four players from this draft have upside, but none is a sure thing. The Giants still have LHP Erick Threets (7) and 1B Lance Niekro (7), while they've traded RHP Boof Bonser (1) and LHP Ryan Hannaman (4).

San Francisco looked like it locked up 40 percent of its future rotation in the first round with RHPs Kurt Ainsworth (1) and Jerome Williams (1). Both pitched well for the Giants, but Ainsworth was dealt for Sidney Ponson last year.

—Draft analysis prepared by Jim Callis. Numbers in parentheses indicate draft rounds.

BILL MITCHELL

rhp

Merkin Valdez

Born: Nov. 5, 1981.
Ht.: 6-3. **Wt.:** 170.
Bats: R. **Throws:** R.
Career Transactions: Signed out of Dominican Republic by Braves, Nov. 18, 1999 . . . Traded by Braves with LHP Damian Moss to Giants for RHP Russ Ortiz, Dec. 17, 2002.

Though the Giants had developed Russ Ortiz from college middle reliever to big league frontline starter, they weren't afraid to deal him when he became too expensive. So they sent Ortiz to the Braves for lefthander Damian Moss and Valdez in December 2002. Valdez was known as Manuel Mateo and believed to be nine months younger than his true age when he signed for $7,500 in 1999. While he has a ways to go to match Ortiz as a big league 20-game winner, the trade worked out for the Giants. San Francisco used Moss to get Sidney Ponson from the Orioles for the 2003 stretch run, while Valdez established himself as the Giants' clear No. 1 prospect with a dominating year at Class A Hagerstown. He won the strikeout crown in the Rookie-level Gulf Coast League in 2002, then repeated the feat in the South Atlantic League in his Giants debut. Valdez has the rare ability to invite consistent weak contact with his fastball.

With his combination of velocity and command, the Giants say he compares favorably to last year's No. 1 prospect, Jesse Foppert. Valdez throws a two-seam heater that the Giants rate a 70 on the 20-80 scouting scale due to its excellent sink and consistent velocity. When he worked as a starter for Hagerstown, his fastball sat in the 92-95 mph range. In a late assignment to the Arizona Fall League, he ran it to 96-98 in short relief stints. He's not afraid to work inside and attacks lefthanders successfully. The Giants rate his slider as a 60 pitch, though it tends to be less consistent than his fastball. Valdez generally does a good job of staying tall, throwing downhill and keeping on top of his slider. His changeup remains in its developing stages, but the Giants were encouraged by the flashes he showed in instructional league, when he threw it for strikes. This was just Valdez' first full season, so he could use more innings of experience to refine his overall game, particularly his changeup and slider. He can be guilty of rushing his delivery and overthrowing. He missed a start in the spring when he was trying so hard to ramp up his velocity that he pulled his groin. He sometimes alters his delivery for his offspeed stuff, hurting his consistency. All of these are correctable flaws, however.

Added to the 40-man roster, Valdez will compete for a big league bullpen job in spring training, following Foppert's example. While Foppert was a college draftee, he wasn't a full-time pitcher until his junior season at the University of San Francisco, and Valdez' experience level is similar. If he's allowed to develop more in the minor leagues—likely at high Class A San Jose to start until the weather warms up at Double-A Norwich—Valdez still could jump to the majors sometime in 2004. With more refinement, Valdez profiles as a front-of-the-rotation starter.

Year	Club (League)	Class	W	L	ERA	G	GS	CG	SV	IP	H	R	ER	HR	BB	SO	AVG
2000	Braves (DSL)	R	1	5	1.57	14	7	0	0	57	52	27	10	2	14	32	.234
2001	Braves 2 (DSL)	R	6	7	2.93	15	14	1	0	92	93	41	30	0	18	48	.258
2002	Braves (GCL)	R	7	3	1.98	12	8	1	0	68	47	18	15	0	12	76	.193
2003	Hagerstown (SAL)	A	9	5	2.25	26	26	2	0	156	119	42	39	11	49	166	.213
MINOR LEAGUE TOTALS			23	20	2.26	67	55	4	0	374	311	128	94	13	93	322	.225

2 Matt Cain, rhp

Born: Oct. 1, 1984. **Ht.:** 6-3. **Wt.:** 180. **Bats:** R. **Throws:** R. **School:** Houston HS, Germantown, Tenn. **Career Transactions:** Selected by Giants in first round (25th overall) of 2002 draft; signed June 26, 2002.

Cain has blossomed from No. 2 pitcher on his high school team (behind Conor Lalor, now at South Carolina) to No. 2 prospect in the Giants organization, and he was pushing for No. 1 before a stress fracture in his elbow sidelined him midway through the 2003 season. Cain showed he had returned to health with seven dominant innings in instructional league. Cain might have a better arm than Merkin Valdez, and he profiles better as a starter. He starts with a 92-97 mph fastball that he throws on a good downhill plane. He also throws a power downer curveball with good velocity (77-80 mph). When it's on, it has late break and good depth and is a true strikeout pitch. The Giants laud his aptitude and maturity. Cain has shown a feel for a changeup with late movement but hasn't used it much. He also tends to get under the ball and rush his delivery, which puts stress on his elbow. The Giants are confident he'll grow out of that as he matures physically. One of the South Atlantic League's youngest players in 2003, Cain dominated at times anyway. If he can stay healthy, he'll be pushed and could reach Double-A sometime in 2004.

Year	Club (League)	Class	W	L	ERA	G	GS	CG	SV	IP	H	R	ER	HR	BB	SO	AVG
2002	Giants (AZL)	R	0	1	3.72	8	7	0	0	19	13	10	8	1	11	20	.197
2003	Hagerstown (SAL)	A	4	4	2.55	14	14	0	0	74	57	24	21	5	24	90	.209
MINOR LEAGUE TOTALS			4	5	2.80	22	21	0	0	93	70	34	29	6	35	110	.206

3 David Aardsma, rhp

Born: Dec. 27, 1981. **Ht.:** 6-5. **Wt.:** 200. **Bats:** R. **Throws:** R. **School:** Rice University. **Career Transactions:** Selected by Giants in first round (22nd overall) of 2003 draft; signed June 29, 2003.

The closer for Rice's 2003 College World Series championship team, Aardsma broke 1997 No. 1 overall pick Matt Anderson's career and season saves records in two seasons after transferring from Penn State. If he makes the big leagues, he'll move ahead of Hank Aaron in the all-time alphabetical listing of big leaguers. Aardsma throws his fastball anywhere from 93-98 mph, and it has explosive late life. He switched from a slider to a knuckle-curve that many Rice pitchers throw, and it's a plus pitch at times. His changeup is major league-ready. Aardsma's closing background has hindered the development of his breaking ball; he only recently ditched his slider. He started at Penn State, and some scouts think he has the stuff and size to succeed in a rotation. Others cite his "pie thrower" delivery, which puts a lot of strain on his elbow, as precluding him from having the needed durability. Aardsma showed big league closer stuff during his debut in high Class A. He should move quickly to San Francisco after a short apprenticeship in Double-A in 2004.

Year	Club (League)	Class	W	L	ERA	G	GS	CG	SV	IP	H	R	ER	HR	BB	SO	AVG
2003	San Jose (Cal)	A	1	1	1.96	18	0	0	8	18	14	4	4	2	7	28	.212
MINOR LEAGUE TOTALS			1	1	1.96	18	0	0	8	18	14	4	4	2	7	28	.212

4 Dan Ortmeier, of

Born: May 11, 1981. **Ht.:** 6-4. **Wt.:** 220. **Bats:** B. **Throws:** L. **School:** University of Texas-Arlington. **Career Transactions:** Selected by Giants in third round of 2002 draft; signed June 23, 2002.

Ortmeier has been on the radar for some time, but still ranks as somewhat of a sleeper. He was drafted out of high school in 1999 (27th round, White Sox) and was a two-time all-Southland Conference selection. He started 2003 as a DH primarily while recovering from left shoulder surgery. Ortmeier has the organization's best combination of tools and skills. His swing is consistent and smooth from both sides of the plate. He shows a quick enough bat to hit inside pitches and lashes line drives from gap-to-gap. He also made strides with his two-strike approach. He runs well enough to play center field, though he profiles best in right. Ortmeier's shoulder injury sapped some strength from what had been a plus arm, though it should bounce back. Some club officials fear his all-out playing style could work against him in the form of more injuries in the future. He hasn't learned to pull the ball yet for the power teams want from their corner outfielders. Ortmeier has the potential to hit .280-.300 with 20-homer power from both sides of the plate. He'll try to prove he's on track to that kind of future projection in 2004 at Double-A Norwich.

Year	Club (League)	Class	AVG	G	AB	R	H	2B	3B	HR	RBI	BB	SO	SB	SLG	OBP
2002	Salem-Keizer (NWL)	A	.292	49	195	32	57	9	1	5	31	18	37	3	.426	.352
2003	San Jose (Cal)	A	.304	115	408	62	124	32	6	8	56	39	89	13	.471	.378
MINOR LEAGUE TOTALS			.300	164	603	94	181	41	7	13	87	57	126	16	.456	.370

5 Todd Linden, of

Born: June 30, 1980. **Ht.:** 6-3. **Wt.:** 210. **Bats:** B. **Throws:** R. **School:** Louisiana State University. **Career Transactions:** Selected by Giants in first round (41st overall) of 2001 draft; signed Sept. 4, 2001.

Linden was the Pacific-10 Conference batting champion and the Cape Cod League's top prospect in 2000, then led Louisiana State in home runs after transferring in 2001. He has moved rapidly through the system since signing late in 2001, when he negotiated his own signing bonus after a needlessly protracted holdout. Linden has good raw power and projects to hit 30 homers in the major leagues. He generally holds his own against lefthanded pitching. Though he's a bit bulkier than when he signed, he still has good athletic ability, runs well for his size and has an average throwing arm. One club official summed up Linden's offensive plan thusly: "He swings very hard in case he hits it." That wild approach was exploited by Triple-A pitchers. His high leg-kick swing can get out of sync in a hurry, leading to slumps and strikeouts. The free-agent signing of Michael Tucker and the re-signing of Jeffrey Hammonds throw two more obstacles in Linden's way to San Francisco. He'll likely return to Triple-A Fresno for 2004.

Year	Club (League)	Class	AVG	G	AB	R	H	2B	3B	HR	RBI	BB	SO	SB	SLG	OBP
2002	Shreveport (TL)	AA	.314	111	392	64	123	26	2	12	52	61	101	9	.482	.419
	Fresno (PCL)	AAA	.250	29	100	18	25	2	1	3	10	20	35	2	.380	.380
2003	Fresno (PCL)	AAA	.278	125	471	75	131	24	3	11	56	40	105	14	.412	.356
	San Francisco (NL)	MAJ	.211	18	38	2	8	1	0	1	6	1	8	0	.316	.231
MAJOR LEAGUE TOTALS			.211	18	38	2	8	1	0	1	6	1	8	0	.316	.231
MINOR LEAGUE TOTALS			.290	265	963	157	279	52	6	26	118	121	241	25	.437	.385

6 Kevin Correia, rhp

Born: Aug. 24, 1980. **Ht.:** 6-3. **Wt.:** 200. **Bats:** R. **Throws:** R. **School:** Cal Poly. **Career Transactions:** Selected by Giants in fourth round of 2002 draft; signed July 9, 2002.

Big league injuries and his good command made Correia the first player from the 2002 draft to reach the majors. He didn't even play baseball while at Grossmont (Calif.) JC in 1999, but transferred to Cal Poly and was its top pitcher in 2001 and 2002. A good athlete, Correia throws strikes with three average pitches. His fastball usually sits in the 88-92 mph range, and he has good sink on his fastball and changeup when he's going right. His slider has fringe average movement, but he usually throws it where he wants it. He's aggressive and fearless. Correia doesn't have a plus pitch, and unless he develops one he's destined for the back of the rotation or the bullpen. His relative inexperience shows with inconsistent mechanics, which lead to him leaving his fastball and slider up in the zone. Correia went to spring training with a chance to become the No. 5 starter. If he doesn't, he could return to Fresno to start or stick in San Francisco as a middle reliever.

Year	Club (League)	Class	W	L	ERA	G	GS	CG	SV	IP	H	R	ER	HR	BB	SO	AVG
2002	Salem-Keizer (NWL)	A	2	2	4.54	10	8	0	0	38	37	20	19	1	14	31	.257
2003	Norwich (EL)	AA	6	6	3.65	16	14	0	0	86	80	38	35	3	30	73	.248
	San Francisco (NL)	MAJ	3	1	3.66	10	7	0	0	39	41	16	16	6	18	28	.275
	Fresno (PCL)	AAA	1	0	2.84	3	3	0	0	19	16	8	6	3	2	23	.222
MAJOR LEAGUE TOTALS			3	1	3.66	10	7	0	0	39	41	16	16	6	18	28	.275
MINOR LEAGUE TOTALS			9	8	3.78	29	25	0	0	143	133	66	60	7	46	127	.247

7 Travis Ishikawa, 1b

Born: Sept. 24, 1983. **Ht.:** 6-3. **Wt.:** 190. **Bats:** L. **Throws:** L. **School:** Federal Way (Wash.) HS. **Career Transactions:** Selected by Giants in 21st round of 2002 draft; signed July 11, 2002.

The Giants weren't sure if Ishikawa was ready for a full-season league in 2003 but decided to send him to low Class A rather than keep him in extended spring training. After many strikeouts and struggles, he matched his regular-season output with an organization-record six homers in 60 instructional league at-bats in the fall. Ishikawa received a $955,000 signing bonus because the Giants believe in his bat. He has a smooth lefthanded swing that remind some in the organization of John Olerud, and he has more raw power. A high school wide receiver, Ishikawa has good actions around the bag at first base. Ishikawa was overmatched in low Class A, leading to some confidence problems. He didn't have a consistent approach at the plate, leading to hot and cold streaks. He took some of his bad at-bats into the field, helping account for 16 errors. Ishikawa needs to re-establish his confidence back at Hagerstown. He's off the fast track, but not off the radar, with a San Francisco ETA of late 2006.

Year	Club (League)	Class	AVG	G	AB	R	H	2B	3B	HR	RBI	BB	SO	SB	SLG	OBP
2002	Giants (AZL)	R	.279	19	68	10	19	4	2	1	10	7	20	7	.441	.364
	Salem-Keizer (NWL)	A	.307	23	88	14	27	2	1	1	17	5	22	1	.386	.347
2003	Hagerstown (SAL)	A	.206	57	194	20	40	5	0	3	22	33	69	3	.278	.329
	Salem-Keizer (NWL)	A	.254	66	248	53	63	17	4	3	31	44	77	0	.391	.376
MINOR LEAGUE TOTALS			.249	165	598	97	149	28	7	8	80	89	188	11	.360	.355

8 Craig Whitaker, rhp

Born: Nov. 19, 1984. **Ht.:** 6-4. **Wt.:** 170. **Bats:** R. **Throws:** R. **School:** Lufkin (Texas) HS. **Career Transactions:** Selected by Giants in first round (34th overall) of 2003 draft; signed June 19, 2003.

Whitaker catapulted into the first round of the 2003 draft with an April no-hitter that featured 14 strikeouts and concluded with a mid-90s fastball. He signed for $975,000, eschewing a scholarship offer from Texas A&M. Whitaker isn't quite a classic Texas fireballer, but while he lacks the sturdy build of the Nolan Ryan/Roger Clemens/Kerry Wood/Josh Beckett lineage, he has the electric fastball. Long, lithe and lanky, he pumps easy mid-90s heat with a quick arm action. His curveball has as much potential as his fastball. When he stays on top of it, it's a potential 70 pitch on the 20-80 scouting scale, with excellent power and depth. "Raw as rain," in the words of one Giants staffer, Whitaker has a lot to learn about the craft of pitching. He has to be more consistent with his delivery to avoid the elbow pain that sidelined him after just five innings of Rookie ball. His changeup needs work. Whitaker is behind Matt Cain at a similar stage of their careers, but his ceiling is just as high. If he has a strong, healthy spring training, he could start 2004 in low Class A. More likely, he'll go to extended spring before heading to short-season Salem-Keizer.

Year	Club (League)	Class	W	L	ERA	G	GS	CG	SV	IP	H	R	ER	HR	BB	SO	AVG
2003	Giants (AZL)	R	0	1	1.69	3	1	0	0	5	2	2	1	0	4	8	.105
MINOR LEAGUE TOTALS			0	1	1.69	3	1	0	0	5	2	2	1	0	4	8	.105

9 Fred Lewis, of

Born: Dec. 9, 1980. **Ht.:** 6-2. **Wt.:** 190. **Bats:** L. **Throws:** R. **School:** Southern University. **Career Transactions:** Selected by Giants in second round of 2002 draft; signed June 20, 2002.

Lewis remains one of the organization's more raw players, owing to his playing more football than baseball at Mississippi Gulf Coast JC. He spent one year at Southern and made as much progress between instructional league in 2002 and 2003 as any Giants farmhand. The fastest runner in the system, Lewis' speed rates a 65 on the 20-80 scouting scale. He worked extensively with former Giants outfielder Darren Lewis (no relation) to improve his reads and jumps in the outfield and to become a better baserunner. Club officials say Lewis' 2003 numbers don't do justice to the juice in his bat and his good raw power. He earns comparisons to former all-star Devon White. Lewis drew a good number of walks in his first full season, but the Giants say that happened by accident. His inexperience leaves him with little feel for the strike zone, which is why his raw power hasn't translated into game power yet. He has work to do turning his speed into stolen bases and making more consistent contact. Lewis needs time to mature physically and emotionally. He'll move up to high Class A in 2004 and could be ready by mid-2006.

Year	Club (League)	Class	AVG	G	AB	R	H	2B	3B	HR	RBI	BB	SO	SB	SLG	OBP
2002	Salem-Keizer (NWL)	A	.322	58	239	43	77	9	3	1	23	26	58	9	.397	.396
2003	Hagerstown (SAL)	A	.250	114	420	61	105	17	8	1	27	68	112	30	.336	.361
MINOR LEAGUE TOTALS			.276	172	659	104	182	26	11	2	50	94	170	39	.358	.373

10 Brian Buscher, 3b

Born: April 18, 1981. **Ht.:** 6-0. **Wt.:** 201. **Bats:** L. **Throws:** R. **School:** University of South Carolina. **Career Transactions:** Selected by Giants in third round of 2003 draft; signed June 29, 2003.

Buscher comes from a baseball family, as his father, uncle and brother all played professionally. Brian was drafted twice and starred at Central Florida Community College before transferring to South Carolina. He helped lead the Gamecocks to back-to-back College World Series trips and won the 2003 Southeastern Conference batting title at .393. Buscher has a consistent approach at the plate, using a short swing to hit line drives from gap to gap. He doesn't give away at-bats, is hard to strike out and is always taking extra swings in the cage. Defensively, he's reliable at third base with an accurate arm. Buscher didn't hit for power in his pro debut because he doesn't pull the ball well right now. Down the line he projects to hit 10-15 homers annually. He doesn't run particularly well. Buscher could move quickly if he starts turning on balls and showing more pop. The Giants, who see him as a lefthanded-hitting Joe Randa, already have challenged him by starting his pro career in low Class A. He could begin 2004 in Double-A with a strong showing in spring training.

Year	Club (League)	Class	AVG	G	AB	R	H	2B	3B	HR	RBI	BB	SO	SB	SLG	OBP
2003	Hagerstown (SAL)	A	.275	54	200	19	55	7	1	0	26	10	25	0	.320	.318
MINOR LEAGUE TOTALS			.275	54	200	19	55	7	1	0	26	10	25	0	.320	.318

11 Todd Jennings, c

Born: Dec. 10, 1981. **Ht.:** 6-0. **Wt.:** 190. **Bats:** R. **Throws:** R. **School:** Long Beach State University. **Career Transactions:** Selected by Giants in second round of 2003 draft; signed June 20, 2003.

Jennings reminds some Giants officials of Craig Biggio, both with his facial resemblance and the positions he has played, though he doesn't have Biggio's offensive upside or power. The Giants plan to keep him at catcher, which Jennings first played as a freshman at Long Beach State. Jennings also played some second and third base as well as outfield for the 49ers. He produced a solid debut in the short-season Northwest League but missed instructional league after suffering a concussion in a plate collision during the playoffs. Wiry strong and athletic, Jennings has a strong arm and led the NWL by throwing out 39 percent of basestealers. He has to prove he can hold up under the daily grind of catching a full season while also showing more pop and on-base ability than he did at Salem-Keizer. Jennings is a line-drive hitter who tends to get too pull-conscious, but the Giants also feel his power was somewhat masked by cavernous Blair Field in college. He may skip a level and begin his first full pro season in high Class A.

Year	Club (League)	Class	AVG	G	AB	R	H	2B	3B	HR	RBI	BB	SO	SB	SLG	OBP
2003	Salem-Keizer (NWL)	A	.296	59	233	27	69	9	2	3	32	15	36	5	.391	.346
MINOR LEAGUE TOTALS			.296	59	233	27	69	9	2	3	32	15	36	5	.391	.346

12 Nate Schierholtz, 3b

Born: Feb. 15, 1984. **Ht.:** 6-2. **Wt.:** 215. **Bats:** L. **Throws:** R. **School:** Chabot (Calif.) JC. **Career Transactions:** Selected by Giants in second round of 2003 draft; signed June 25, 2003.

Schierholtz grew up in San Francisco's East Bay as a Giants fan. When he wasn't drafted in 2002, he seemed set to attend Utah before a strong summer with an American Legion team in Danville, Calif., convinced him to try the junior college route. The Giants found him at Chabot Junior College, where farm/scouting director Dick Tidrow pitched before signing with the Indians in 1967. While other clubs didn't project Schierholtz as an early pick, he wowed San Francisco officials with a .400-18-60 freshman season, ranking second among California juco players in homers. Schierholtz sealed their decision with a prodigious workout at Pac Bell Park prior to the draft. The Giants also popped him early to sway him from a commitment to Long Beach State. Schierholtz was drafted for his offense and has a quick bat that produces as much raw power as any Giants farmhand. He has shown good plate coverage and the ability to hit breaking balls. However, the speed of the pro game sometimes catches up with Schierholtz in the field, where he's raw. His hands are stiff at third base, and while he has arm strength, he needs polish with his footwork and other nuances of playing the position. One Giants official said Schierholtz reminded him most of former all-star slugger Larry Parrish, who started at third base and eventually moved to right field. Schierholtz will play in low Class A this year.

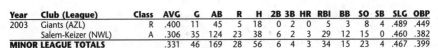

Year	Club (League)	Class	AVG	G	AB	R	H	2B	3B	HR	RBI	BB	SO	SB	SLG	OBP
2003	Giants (AZL)	R	.400	11	45	5	18	0	2	0	5	3	8	4	.489	.449
	Salem-Keizer (NWL)	A	.306	35	124	23	38	6	2	3	29	12	15	0	.460	.382
MINOR LEAGUE TOTALS			.331	46	169	28	56	6	4	3	34	15	23	4	.467	.399

13 Erick Threets, lhp

Born: Nov. 4, 1981. **Ht.:** 6-5. **Wt.:** 240. **Bats:** L. **Throws:** L. **School:** Modesto (Calif.) JC. **Career Transactions:** Selected by Giants in seventh round of 2000 draft; signed Aug. 1, 2000.

One of the most enigmatic prospects in baseball, Threets may be the game's hardest thrower. He reportedly has been clocked as high at 103 mph. But one San Francisco official compares him to Steve Dalkowski, a minor league legend in the 1950s and '60s. While Dalkowski also was a wild, flamethrowing lefty, that's not a flattering comparison—he never reached the majors. Threets has shown flashes of control in the past, and finally started to do so in games that count in the second half of 2003 at low Class A. In one August outing he needed just 54 pitches to work five innings, his longest stint of the season. He worked closely with Hagerstown pitching coach Bob Stanley, who lowered Threets' hands in his delivery and tried to get him to relax. Late in instructional league, Threets lowered his arm slot a bit, and the results continued to be encouraging. After signing him out of the Cape Cod League in 2000, the Giants immediately raised his angle from his natural slot, which was nearly sidearm. That jumped his fastball from the low 90s range to triple digits. If Threets ever throws consistent strikes, he could be the game's premier lefthanded reliever, combining intimidating size, unhittable heat with movement and a power slider. He'll try to put it all together at Double-A in 2004.

Year	Club (League)	Class	W	L	ERA	G	GS	CG	SV	IP	H	R	ER	HR	BB	SO	AVG
2001	San Jose (Cal)	A	2	10	4.25	14	14	0	0	59	49	34	28	2	40	60	.224
	Hagerstown (SAL)	A	2	0	0.75	12	0	0	1	24	13	3	2	1	9	32	.155
2002	San Jose (Cal)	A	0	1	6.67	26	0	0	0	28	23	24	21	2	28	43	.225
2003	Norwich (EL)	AA	0	0	15.88	11	0	0	0	11	15	20	20	1	21	16	.306
	Hagerstown (SAL)	A	2	3	3.26	22	0	0	0	50	26	20	18	2	42	47	.159
MINOR LEAGUE TOTALS			4	14	4.64	85	14	0	1	173	126	101	89	8	140	198	.204

14 Lance Niekro, 1b

Born: Jan. 29, 1979. **Ht.:** 6-3. **Wt.:** 210. **Bats:** R. **Throws:** R. **School:** Florida Southern College. **Career Transactions:** Selected by Giants in second round of 2000 draft; signed July 3, 2000.

Niekro carries a .313 career average as a minor leaguer, and his swing, offensive potential and big league bloodlines (his father Joe and uncle Phil won 539 big league games between them as knuckleballers) have the Giants encouraged that he'll help in the majors soon. The evidence, however, points toward him doing so as a role player rather than as a middle-of-the-lineup regular. Once touted as a power prospect, Niekro has just a .431 slugging percentage in the minors. He has gap power in his swing but isn't selective enough to hit home runs. While San Francisco lauds his aggressiveness, he doesn't do enough else of value beyond hitting for average. His speed and defense are below average, and a constant stream of injuries have pushed him from third base to first. Niekro has yet to play a full season, thanks to right shoulder surgery in 2001, a broken left hand in 2002 and a strained right hamstring in 2003. Added to the 40-man roster this offseason, Niekro could use more minor league time. The re-signing of J.T. Snow probably means Niekro will return to Fresno in 2004.

Year	Club (League)	Class	AVG	G	AB	R	H	2B	3B	HR	RBI	BB	SO	SB	SLG	OBP
2000	Salem-Keizer (NWL)	A	.362	49	196	27	71	14	4	5	44	11	25	2	.551	.404
2001	San Jose (Cal)	A	.288	42	163	18	47	11	0	3	34	4	14	4	.411	.298
2002	Shreveport (TL)	AA	.310	79	297	33	92	20	1	4	34	7	32	0	.424	.327
2003	Fresno (PCL)	AAA	.302	98	381	43	115	15	2	4	41	19	39	3	.383	.334
	San Francisco (NL)	MAJ	.200	5	5	2	1	1	0	0	2	0	1	0	.400	.200
MAJOR LEAGUE TOTALS			.200	5	5	2	1	1	0	0	2	0	1	0	.400	.200
MINOR LEAGUE TOTALS			.313	268	1037	121	325	60	7	16	153	41	110	9	.431	.340

15 Noah Lowry, lhp

Born: Oct. 10, 1980. **Ht.:** 6-2. **Wt.:** 190. **Bats:** L. **Throws:** L. **School:** Pepperdine University. **Career Transactions:** Selected by Giants in first round (30th overall) of 2001 draft; signed June 20, 2001.

Lowry reached the major leagues in a hurry, needing just 221 minor league innings before reaching Pac Bell Park. Even shoulder soreness in 2002 and a lackluster performance in Double-A last year didn't slow him down much. He didn't miss a start after being pushed to Norwich but didn't show the stuff he flashed in high Class A, perhaps a lingering affect of his shoulder problems. Lowry has shown a low-90s fastball and plus curveball in the past, but neither was in evidence in the first half of 2003 as the California native struggled with the New England weather and a poor defense behind him. He survived with a good change-up and good command, which stems from his ability to repeat his delivery and arm slot. Lowry didn't use his breaking ball as much last year and he seemed to suffer for it as lefties batted .299 against him. As the year went on, Lowry improved dramatically. Counting his six near-perfect big league innings, he posted a 1.85 ERA in his last 39 innings at three levels. He figures to start 2004 in Triple-A and needs to carry his late improvement over a full season.

Year	Club (League)	Class	W	L	ERA	G	GS	CG	SV	IP	H	R	ER	HR	BB	SO	AVG
2001	Salem-Keizer (NWL)	A	1	1	3.60	8	7	0	0	25	26	15	10	2	8	28	.265
2002	San Jose (Cal)	A	6	5	2.15	15	12	0	0	59	38	21	14	4	20	62	.186
2003	Norwich (EL)	AA	9	6	4.72	23	23	2	0	118	127	66	62	7	47	97	.285
	Fresno (PCL)	AAA	1	0	2.37	4	4	0	0	19	15	5	5	0	6	13	.227
	San Francisco (NL)	MAJ	0	0	0.00	4	0	0	0	6	1	0	0	0	2	5	.048
MAJOR LEAGUE TOTALS			0	0	0.00	4	0	0	0	6	1	0	0	0	2	5	.048
MINOR LEAGUE TOTALS			17	12	3.71	50	46	2	0	221	206	107	91	13	81	200	.253

16 Brooks McNiven, rhp

Born: June 19, 1981. **Ht.:** 6-5. **Wt.:** 180. **Bats:** R. **Throws:** R. **School:** University of British Columbia. **Career Transactions:** Selected by Giants in fourth round of 2003 draft; signed June 8, 2003.

McNiven got plenty of exposure in 2002 as a college teammate of Rockies first-round pick Jeff Francis. A veteran of Canadian junior national teams, he has projection remaining despite signing as a senior. The Giants see him developing into a power sinker/slider pitcher in the middle of their rotation. McNiven's pitcher's body is one source of their optimism. He has long arms and legs and plenty of room to fill out physically. He has a loose arm and throws an easy 88-92 mph fastball from a three-quarters delivery, getting good tailing and sinking action when he keeps it down. While his delivery is smooth, San Francisco believes some adjustments (such as getting better extension on his follow-through) and physical maturity will have McNiven throwing harder in 2004. His late-biting, low-80s slider has the potential to be an out pitch. He also throws a hard curveball that serves as his changeup. McNiven's strong instructional league peformance—eight scoreless innings with seven strikeouts—could springboard him to high Class A for his first full season.

Year	Club (League)	Class	W	L	ERA	G	GS	CG	SV	IP	H	R	ER	HR	BB	SO	AVG
2003	Salem-Keizer (NWL)	A	7	5	3.62	16	11	0	0	70	74	40	28	1	16	45	.273
MINOR LEAGUE TOTALS			7	5	3.62	16	11	0	0	70	74	40	28	1	16	45	.273

17 Justin Knoedler, c

Born: July 17, 1980. **Ht.:** 6-2. **Wt.:** 210. **Bats:** R. **Throws:** R. **School:** Miami (Ohio) University. **Career Transactions:** Selected by Giants in fifth round of 2001 draft; signed June 20, 2001.

Knoedler finally has settled behind the plate. He starred at catcher for Lincoln Land (Ill.) Community College in 1999-2000, winning the National Junior College Athletic Association championship and player-of-the-year award as a sophomore. He didn't sign as a Giants 13th-round pick in 2000, opting to transfer to Miami, where he played both ways and had much more success as a backstop. San Francisco signed Knoedler as fifth-rounder in 2001 and immediately made him a full-time pitcher. But the organization's dearth of catchers prompted the Giants to move him back behind the plate in 2002. Knoedler, whose twin brother Jason is an outfielder in the Tigers system, made great strides offensively last year to earn a spot on the 40-man roster. He overhauled his swing, straightening up his stance and showing the ability to catch up to inside pitches. His natural strength gives him average power, and he runs well and has good athleticism for his position. Arm strength is Knoedler's best tool—the Giants rate his an 80 on the 20-80 scouting scale—and he led Cal League regulars by throwing out 40 percent of basestealers. His receiving and blocking skills are average. Aside from his arm, Knoedler's greatest asset may be his throwback mentality and work ethic. If his bat develops more, the Giants see him as a starter in the big leagues. His big arm should make him at least a quality backup. He'll make the jump to Double-A in 2004.

Year	Club (League)	Class	W	L	ERA	G	GS	CG	SV	IP	H	R	ER	HR	BB	SO	AVG
2001	Salem-Keizer (NWL)	A	1	1	1.26	13	0	0	1	29	22	4	4	0	9	38	.211
MINOR LEAGUE TOTALS			1	1	1.26	13	0	0	1	29	22	4	4	0	9	38	.211

Year	Club (League)	Class	AVG	G	AB	R	H	2B	3B	HR	RBI	BB	SO	SB	SLG	OBP
2002	Hagerstown (SAL)	A	.257	86	280	32	72	16	2	5	33	37	56	6	.382	.349
2003	San Jose (Cal)	A	.257	101	354	48	91	25	2	10	43	35	78	13	.424	.326
MINOR LEAGUE TOTALS			.257	187	634	80	163	41	4	15	76	72	134	19	.405	.336

18 Jon Armitage, of

Born: Oct. 29, 1980. **Ht.:** 6-5. **Wt.:** 210. **Bats:** B. **Throws:** R. **School:** University of Georgia.
Career Transactions: Signed as nondrafted free agent by Giants, Aug. 6, 2003.

The Giants scored with several nondrafted free agents in 2003, including Alaska League star Jeremy Accardo, short-season Northwest League ERA leader Jesse Floyd and NWL co-home run champ Brad Vericker. The best of the group is Armitage, who signed out of the Cape Cod League for $25,000, enough money to cover his final year at the University of Georgia. He signed too late to make his pro debut but made his mark with a Giants instructional league club that went 22-0-2. Armitage redshirted as a college freshman and was the Bulldogs' starting shortstop in 2002 before moving to center field last spring. He has middle-of-the-field tools, grading out as average or above across the board, with the exception of his arm. Despite hitting just nine homers in his college career, Armitage has big raw power, especially from the left side, and he can put on batting-practice displays. He shortened his swing with wood bats on the Cape, which unleashed some of his power. He also showed a good plate approach on the Cape and runs well for his size, though he profiles better in right field than in center. Look for him to start 2004 in high Class A.

Year	Club (League)	Class	AVG	G	AB	R	H	2B	3B	HR	RBI	BB	SO	SB	SLG	OBP
2003	Did not play—Signed 2004 contract															

19 Jamie Athas, 2b/ss

Born: Oct. 14, 1979. **Ht.:** 6-2. **Wt.:** 190. **Bats:** L. **Throws:** R. **School:** Wake Forest University.
Career Transactions: Selected by Giants in seventh round of 2001 draft; signed June 16, 2001.

In an organization thin on middle-infield prospects, Athas had an encouraging, bounce-back season in 2003. He was the everyday shortstop in Double-A and really came on in the second half to claim a spot on the Giants' 40-man roster. Athas has solid athletic ability but doesn't have a tool that stands out in either a good or bad way. He has a smooth lefthanded swing with minimal power, but he found a groove and hit safely in 24 of his final 26 games. He crowds the plate and gets hit by pitches to boost his on-base percentage, though he lacks the speed to take advantage on the basepaths. Athas spent the regular season at shortstop and has smooth actions, but played second base in the Arizona Fall League and profiles better on the right side of the bag because of his footwork. On either side, he earns comparisons to Mike Bordick, a fellow New Englander who got the most out of his tools. He'll probably play second base in Triple-A this year, though he may see time at shortstop if Cody Ransom makes the big league club.

Year	Club (League)	Class	AVG	G	AB	R	H	2B	3B	HR	RBI	BB	SO	SB	SLG	OBP
2001	Hagerstown (SAL)	A	.274	65	234	44	64	10	3	2	28	31	55	17	.368	.370
2002	San Jose (Cal)	A	.251	123	466	65	117	15	7	1	40	48	124	14	.320	.328
2003	Norwich (EL)	AA	.275	128	444	59	122	14	2	3	41	47	82	12	.336	.363
MINOR LEAGUE TOTALS			.265	316	1144	168	303	39	12	6	109	126	261	43	.336	.350

20 Glenn Woolard, rhp

Born: April 18, 1981. **Ht.:** 6-1. **Wt.:** 200. **Bats:** R. **Throws:** R. **School:** Kutztown (Pa.) University.
Career Transactions: Selected by Giants in 10th round of 2002 draft; signed June 12, 2002.

Woolard has known nothing but success in baseball, and he finished strong after stumbled a bit for the first time in 2003. At Coatesville (Pa.) Area High, he went two years without losing a game. In college, he led Kutztown (Pa.) State to the NCAA Division II College World Series and was that level's best pitcher in 2002, when he was nation's national leader in wins (14-2, 2.81) and strikeouts (148 in 106 innings). The key for Woolard is a devastating knuckle-curve that he throws at varying speeds. He commands the pitch well and can throw it in or out of the strike zone. Woolard also has a good changeup and attacks lefthanders well, holding them to a .210 average in 2003. His fastball, however, will decide whether he can become the No. 4 starter the Giants project him as. He throws an average 89-91 mph four-seamer and needs to keep it down in the strike zone. He could use more strength and toughness. He wore down physically during his first full season and lost confidence during a midseason slump before rebounding in his last two starts, during which he struck out 16 in 15 scoreless innings. Woolard could skip a level to Double-A with a good spring.

Year	Club (League)	Class	W	L	ERA	G	GS	CG	SV	IP	H	R	ER	HR	BB	SO	AVG
2002	Salem-Keizer (NWL)	A	3	2	2.96	17	11	0	0	67	51	26	22	3	32	75	.207
2003	Hagerstown (SAL)	A	8	9	3.44	26	25	2	0	144	126	63	55	10	43	135	.236
MINOR LEAGUE TOTALS			11	11	3.28	43	36	2	0	211	177	89	77	13	75	210	.227

21 Pat Misch, lhp

Born: Aug. 18, 1981. **Ht.:** 6-2. **Wt.:** 170. **Bats:** R. **Throws:** L. **School:** Western Michigan University. **Career Transactions:** Selected by Giants in seventh round of 2003 draft; signed June 8, 2003.

Misch got caught in Houston's temporary draft embargo in 2002. Shortly after taking him in the fifth round, the Astros suspended negotiations with all their unsigned picks, and he decided to return to Western Michigan for his senior year after posting a 1.34 ERA in the Cape Cod League. Poised for a big year in 2003, Misch stumbled instead and went 3-4, 4.42. He's a lefthander who pounds the strike zone and pitches inside aggressively with average stuff, and his approach works much better against wood bats. He was a strikeout pitcher for Western Michigan, setting single-game (19), season (99) and career (265) school records for whiffs, but pitches more like Kirk Rueter. Misch throws an 86-89 mph fastball for strikes and moves it all over the zone. He also throws a slider, curveball and changeup. None stands out consistently, though he gets strikeouts with his breaking pitches. Misch may start his first full season in high Class A and could move quickly through a system starved for lefthanded pitching after trading Ryan Hannaman, Francisco Liriano, Damian Moss and John Thomas in 2003.

Year	Club (League)	Class	W	L	ERA	G	GS	CG	SV	IP	H	R	ER	HR	BB	SO	AVG
2003	Salem-Keizer (NWL)	A	7	5	2.18	14	14	0	0	87	78	33	21	3	20	61	.247
MINOR LEAGUE TOTALS			7	5	2.18	14	14	0	0	87	78	33	21	3	20	61	.247

22 Cody Ransom, ss

Born: Feb. 17, 1976. **Ht.:** 6-2. **Wt.:** 190. **Bats:** R. **Throws:** R. **School:** Grand Canyon (Ariz.) University. **Career Transactions:** Selected by Giants in ninth round of 1998 draft; signed June 4, 1998.

Ransom, whose younger brother Troy was a reliever at Hagerstown last season, has been a regular on Giants prospect lists throughout his career, owing more to his defense than offense. If he ever had hit with more consistency, he would have become a major league regular by now. That may never happen, but his glove is so good that he still merits mention as a prospect. One major league scout said Ransom would be the best defensive shortstop in the National League if the Giants were to give him the starting job for 2004. He's out of options and could compete with Neifi Perez to replace Rich Aurilia. Ransom has excellent range and a plus-plus arm that allows him to make plays in the hole with ease. He has spent the last three seasons at Triple-A Fresno, hitting 23 homers there in 2001, when the Grizzlies played at cozy Beiden Field, and 25 combined the last two seasons. He runs OK and draws a few walks. He did cut down on his strikeouts in 2003, but Ransom's best-case scenario is as a .240 hitter with modest power. Combine that with his offense, and he'd be more valuable than Perez.

Year	Club (League)	Class	AVG	G	AB	R	H	2B	3B	HR	RBI	BB	SO	SB	SLG	OBP
1998	Salem-Keizer (NWL)	A	.233	71	236	52	55	12	7	6	27	43	56	19	.419	.351
1999	Bakersfield (Cal)	A	.275	99	356	69	98	12	6	11	47	54	108	15	.435	.382
	Shreveport (TL)	AA	.122	14	41	6	5	0	0	2	4	4	22	0	.268	.208
2000	Shreveport (TL)	AA	.200	130	459	58	92	21	2	7	47	40	141	9	.301	.263
2001	Fresno (PCL)	AAA	.241	134	469	77	113	21	6	23	78	44	137	17	.458	.303
	San Francisco (NL)	MAJ	.000	9	7	1	0	0	0	0	0	0	5	0	.000	.000
2002	Fresno (PCL)	AAA	.207	135	449	53	93	18	4	13	46	47	151	6	.352	.283
	San Francisco (NL)	MAJ	.667	7	3	2	2	0	0	0	1	1	1	0	.667	.750
2003	Fresno (PCL)	AAA	.253	112	396	56	100	16	4	12	50	45	91	14	.404	.331
	San Francisco (NL)	MAJ	.222	20	27	7	6	1	0	1	1	1	11	0	.370	.250
MAJOR LEAGUE TOTALS			.216	36	37	10	8	1	0	1	2	2	17	0	.324	.256
MINOR LEAGUE TOTALS			.231	695	2406	371	556	100	29	74	299	277	706	80	.389	.312

23 Josh Habel, lhp

Born: Sept. 10, 1980. **Ht.:** 6-1. **Wt.:** 190. **Bats:** L. **Throws:** L. **School:** University of Northern Iowa. **Career Transactions:** Selected by Giants in 14th round of 2002 draft; signed June 7, 2002.

Habel is the 2003 version of Jeff Clark, a soft-tossing minor leaguer who earned a look as a prospect because of his performance. While Habel didn't have much success at Northern Iowa with a 6.69 ERA in four seasons, he did have two solid summers in the wood-bat Northwoods League. He doesn't have the power arm of the typical Giants prospect, but he's lefthanded and throws strikes. He pushed his way into Hagerstown's rotation last June and pitched scoreless ball in five of his final 13 starts to make the South Atlantic League all-star team. He emulates Jamie Moyer by commanding a high-80s fastball and a plus changeup. One San Francisco official rated Habel's changeup an 80 on the 20-80 scouting scale because of its deception, command and movement down in the zone. Habel will need to further develop his breaking ball to stay in the rotation. He'll advance to high Class A this year as the Giants hope he has more staying power than Clark, who faded after a breakout 2002.

Year	Club (League)	Class	W	L	ERA	G	GS	CG	SV	IP	H	R	ER	HR	BB	SO	AVG
2002	Salem-Keizer (NWL)	A	2	2	6.00	16	7	0	0	48	57	35	32	2	24	33	.318
2003	Hagerstown (SAL)	A	11	7	2.36	37	16	1	2	122	90	36	32	9	35	127	.203
MINOR LEAGUE TOTALS			13	9	3.39	53	23	1	2	170	147	71	64	11	59	160	.236

24 Angel Chavez, ss

Born: July 22, 1981. **Ht.:** 6-1. **Wt.:** 180. **Bats:** R. **Throws:** R. **Career Transactions:** Signed out of Panama by Giants, Oct. 30, 1998.

Chavez doesn't get anyone overly excited, but he showed steady progress while making the transition from third base to shortstop last year. He repeated high Class A and improved in nearly every statistical category. He has the physical ability to play shortstop, with good hands, solid range and a plus arm that ranks as his best tool. At times, Chavez lays back on balls and relies too much on his arm, but he started to correct that as the season wore on. The question will be his bat, as is the case with other Giants middle-infield prospects such as Jamie Athas, Cody Ransom, Tim Hutting and Jake Wald. Like Ransom, Chavez is a free swinger with some power. Nine of his 10 homers last year came away from San Jose's spacious Municipal Stadium. He might have shown even more power if not for a left thumb injury in June. Chavez reduced his strikeouts in 2003 but never will be a walk machine. The Giants will know more about Chavez' bat after he moves to Double-A this year.

Year	Club (League)	Class	AVG	G	AB	R	H	2B	3B	HR	RBI	BB	SO	SB	SLG	OBP
1999	La Victoria (VSL)	R	.344	52	186	40	64	12	1	14	49	15	32	11	.645	.392
2000	Giants (AZL)	R	.276	7	29	2	8	0	1	1	7	1	5	1	.448	.300
2001	Hagerstown (SAL)	A	.189	13	37	5	7	2	0	2	3	1	12	1	.405	.231
	San Jose (Cal)	A	.244	84	316	37	77	22	2	3	28	16	60	10	.354	.280
2002	San Jose (Cal)	A	.257	130	471	61	121	20	5	8	62	28	83	21	.372	.303
2003	San Jose (Cal)	A	.280	120	478	69	134	23	6	10	58	22	60	20	.416	.314
MINOR LEAGUE TOTALS			.271	406	1517	214	411	79	15	38	207	83	252	64	.418	.311

25 Jason Ellison, of

Born: April 4, 1978. **Ht.:** 5-10. **Wt.:** 180. **Bats:** R. **Throws:** R. **School:** Lewis-Clark State (Idaho) College. **Career Transactions:** Selected by Giants in 22nd round of 2000 draft; signed June 11, 2000.

Ellison made a big leap forward in 2002, skipping Double-A and having a solid Triple-A season. He leveled out last year, and the Giants are pretty sure he's going to be a steady fourth or fifth outfielder who works hard and is limited by his fringy offensive tools. Ellison is the latest big leaguer San Francisco found at NAIA powerhouse Lewis-Clark State, following Marvin Benard, Keith Foulke and Steve Reed, among others. Like Benard, Ellison can play all three outfield spots. His best tool is his strong arm. Ellison runs well enough to be a threat offensively, though he's not an efficient basestealer. Ellison would do well to take more walks and play the little man's game. He has some juice for a man his size, but he'll never hit for real power in the majors. He makes the Top 30 over 1998 first-round pick Tony Torcato, who has defensive shortcomings and has regressed offensively due to a lack of plate discipline and repeated shoulder injuries. With San Francisco's re-signing of Jeffrey Hammond and offseason acquisitions of Dustan Mohr and Michael Tucker, Ellison probably will spend most of 2004 in Triple-A.

Year	Club (League)	Class	AVG	G	AB	R	H	2B	3B	HR	RBI	BB	SO	SB	SLG	OBP
2000	Salem-Keizer (NWL)	A	.300	74	300	67	90	15	2	0	28	29	45	13	.363	.374
2001	Hagerstown (SAL)	A	.291	130	494	95	144	38	3	8	55	71	68	19	.429	.388
2002	San Jose (Cal)	A	.270	81	322	40	87	13	0	5	40	25	37	9	.357	.325
	Fresno (PCL)	AAA	.311	49	196	31	61	8	1	3	8	21	28	16	.408	.389
2003	Fresno (PCL)	AAA	.295	119	461	74	136	22	4	6	39	39	52	21	.399	.356
	San Francisco (NL)	MAJ	.100	7	10	1	1	0	0	0	0	0	1	0	.100	.100
MAJOR LEAGUE TOTALS			.100	7	10	1	1	0	0	0	0	0	1	0	.100	.100
MINOR LEAGUE TOTALS			.292	453	1773	307	518	96	10	22	170	185	230	78	.395	.366

26 Carlos Valderrama, of

Born: Nov. 30, 1977. **Ht.:** 5-11. **Wt.:** 175. **Bats:** R. **Throws:** R. **Career Transactions:** Signed out of Venezuela by Giants, Feb. 23, 1995.

Valderrama has been one of the Giants' better outfield prospects for years, and ranked in the top 10 before a rotator cuff injury to his right shoulder in 2001 stunted his progress. His arm is healthy, though its strength hasn't quite come back to where it used to be and now grades as average or a tick below. More important, the injury cost him a year of development time, and he had to spend much of 2002 in high Class A because he was limited to

DH. Ready for the outfield again in 2003, Valderrama showed tools that tease the Giants but continued to display maddening inconsistency. He isn't an efficient defender in center field, which is where he needs to play because he lacks the power for an outfield corner. However, he seems to think he is a power hitter and doesn't take full advantage of his plus speed. Valderrama had a strong winter in his native Venezuela, but must produce more in the United States before San Francisco considers him anything more than a fourth outfielder. He's ticketed for a full season in Triple-A this year.

Year	Club (League)	Class	AVG	G	AB	R	H	2B	3B	HR	RBI	BB	SO	SB	SLG	OBP
1995	Giants (DSL)	R	.228	22	57	7	13	1	0	0	4	6	10	1	.246	.302
1996	Giants (DSL)	R	.223	46	166	29	37	4	1	0	11	29	24	26	.259	.342
1997	Salem-Keizer (NWL)	A	.319	41	138	21	44	7	3	3	28	12	29	22	.478	.368
1998	Salem-Keizer (NWL)	A	.345	7	29	5	10	1	0	0	4	1	7	4	.379	.367
1999	San Jose (Cal)	A	.256	26	90	12	23	2	0	0	12	4	19	8	.278	.287
	Salem-Keizer (NWL)	A	.291	40	134	27	39	3	1	2	18	12	34	17	.373	.349
2000	Bakersfield (Cal)	A	.315	121	435	78	137	21	5	13	81	39	96	54	.476	.370
2001	Shreveport (TL)	AA	.308	41	159	29	49	12	2	1	8	18	29	11	.428	.379
2002	San Jose (Cal)	A	.314	74	299	65	94	19	6	15	45	34	60	14	.569	.384
	Shreveport (TL)	AA	.244	37	135	13	33	3	1	4	15	10	23	4	.370	.304
2003	Norwich (EL)	AA	.308	65	240	37	74	15	3	1	18	25	34	13	.408	.375
	Fresno (PCL)	AAA	.277	54	202	20	56	5	0	3	10	12	28	7	.347	.324
	San Francisco (NL)	MAJ	.143	7	7	0	1	0	0	0	0	0	3	1	.143	.143
MAJOR LEAGUE TOTALS			.143	7	7	0	1	0	0	0	0	0	3	1	.143	.143
MINOR LEAGUE TOTALS			.292	574	2084	343	609	93	22	42	254	202	393	181	.418	.356

27 Tim Hutting, ss/2b

Born: Oct. 29, 1981. **Ht.:** 6-0. **Wt.:** 190. **Bats:** R. **Throws:** R. **School:** Long Beach State University. **Career Transactions:** Selected by Giants in eighth round of 2003 draft; signed June 10, 2003.

A cousin of White Sox outfielder Aaron Rowand and Devil Rays minor league righthander Jamie Shields, Hutting is best described as a ballplayer. He's a scrappy, hard worker who doesn't look like a shortstop but makes all the plays. Hutting has quick feet and a good arm, and the Giants believe he can remain at shortstop if he can learn to stay wide on ground balls and keep his body low. They expect him to improve in 2004 once he's fully recovered from a right knee injury that caused him to miss a month of the college season. Offensively, Hutting made great strides at the plate in instructional league. His offensive approach in college, dictated by Long Beach's power-sapping Blair Field, was to dink and dunk balls the other way. He started to use his strong upper body to turn on pitches in the fall and profiles as a No. 2 hitter because of his bat control and ability to bunt. Hutting will play in low Class A in 2004.

Year	Club (League)	Class	AVG	G	AB	R	H	2B	3B	HR	RBI	BB	SO	SB	SLG	OBP
2003	Salem-Keizer (NWL)	A	.218	64	248	29	54	7	0	1	31	25	32	4	.258	.300
MINOR LEAGUE TOTALS			.218	64	248	29	54	7	0	1	31	25	32	4	.258	.300

28 Kelyn Acosta, rhp

Born: April 24, 1985. **Ht.:** 6-1. **Wt.:** 170. **Bats:** R. **Throws:** R. **Career Transactions:** Signed out of Dominican Republic by Giants, March 6, 2002.

The Giants' recent track record in Latin America hasn't been impressive. Just three of their signees are on the 40-man roster, and none of them (Angel Chavez, Yorvit Torrealba, Carlos Valderrama) looks like a future regular. Yet San Francisco hasn't given up. Acosta was one of several intriguing Dominican arms on its Rookie-level Arizona League club in 2003. He's understandably raw and primarily operates off his fastball. However, his heater could be special, as he touches 96-97 mph. Acosta also shows the makings of a power slider, which he throws in the upper 80s. He hasn't learned to change speed but has plenty of time to do so. His arm strength and age give him a slight edge over fellow righty Carlos Villanueva, who has an advanced feel for pitching for a 20-year-old Dominican and throws in the 89-92 mph range with good control. How Acosta performs this spring will determine if the Giants send him to low Class A.

Year	Club (League)	Class	W	L	ERA	G	GS	CG	SV	IP	H	R	ER	HR	BB	SO	AVG
2002	Giants (DSL)	R	5	7	3.40	17	16	2	0	85	80	52	32	9	22	64	.235
2003	Giants (AZL)	R	3	4	4.40	10	8	0	0	45	56	28	22	0	16	35	.315
MINOR LEAGUE TOTALS			8	11	3.75	27	24	2	0	130	136	80	54	9	38	99	.263

29 Jeremy Accardo, rhp

Born: Dec. 8, 1981. **Ht.:** 6-2. **Wt.:** 190. **Bats:** R. **Throws:** R. **School:** Illinois State University. **Career Transactions:** Signed as nondrafted free agent by Giants, Aug. 12, 2003.

After Jon Armitage, Accardo may have the most upside of the Giants' 2003 class of nondrafted college players. Accardo ranked eighth in the Alaska League in batting (.290-2-21) while playing shortstop and batting third for Athletics In Action. He also pitched in college and is Illinois State's career saves leader with 12. It was on the mound where he enticed the Giants. Pitching in Alaska's season-ending wood bat tournament in front of dozens of scouts, Accardo threw an easy 92-93 mph fastball and supplemented it with a plus slider. Suddenly in demand after going undrafted in June, Accardo signed with San Francisco after the National Baseball Congress World Series rather than return to Illinois State for his senior year. He touched some 95s during instructional league. He has to learn many of the nuances of pitching, and the Giants will give him innings to do so in the low Class A rotation this year. He profiles as a power bullpen arm down the line.

Year	Club (League)	Class	W	L	ERA	G	GS	CG	SV	IP	H	R	ER	HR	BB	SO	AVG
2003	Did not play—Signed 2004 contract																

30 Brian Wilson, rhp

Born: March 16, 1982. **Ht.:** 6-1. **Wt.:** 205. **Bats:** R. **Throws:** R. **School:** Louisiana State University. **Career Transactions:** Selected by Giants in 24th round of 2003 draft; signed Aug. 24, 2003.

The Giants have gone to the Louisiana State well for pitchers several times recently, with mixed results. Righty Jake Esteves had too many arm injuries to make it to the majors, but fellow righty Kurt Ainsworth overcame Tommy John surgery to reach San Francisco. Ainsworth went to the Orioles in the Sidney Ponson trade, leaving Wilson and reliever Billy Sadler, a 2003 draftee with plenty of arm strength but less pitchability, as the LSU representatives in the Giants system. Wilson might have been a supplemental first-round pick if he hadn't blown out his elbow and needed Tommy John surgery in April. LSU coaches were stunned when he signed as a 24th-round pick. When healthy, Wilson has shown a 90-93 mph fastball and a plus curveball. If his rehabilitation goes as scheduled, he'll work in extended spring training before reporting to Salem-Keizer in June.

Year	Club (League)	Class	W	L	ERA	G	GS	CG	SV	IP	H	R	ER	HR	BB	SO	AVG
2003	Did not play—Injured																

MARINERS

**By Jim
Callis**

TOP 30 PROSPECTS

1. Felix Hernandez, rhp
2. Clint Nageotte, rhp
3. Travis Blackley, lhp
4. Jose Lopez, ss/2b
5. Shin-Soo Choo, of
6. Chris Snelling, of
7. Rett Johnson, rhp
8. Cha Baek, rhp
9. Adam Jones, ss
10. Jamal Strong, of
11. Justin Leone, 3b
12. Bobby Madritsch, lhp
13. Greg Dobbs, 3b
14. Ryan Feierabend, lhp
15. Aaron Taylor, rhp
16. Wladimir Balentien, of
17. J.J. Putz, rhp
18. Ryan Ketchner, lhp
19. Matt Thornton, lhp
20. Rene Rivera, c
21. Aaron Jensen, rhp
22. Jeff Flaig, 3b
23. Aaron Looper, rhp
24. Josh Womack, of
25. Michael Garciaparra, ss
26. Troy Cate, lhp
27. Glenn Bott, lhp
28. Bobby Livingston, lhp
29. Ryan Christianson, c
30. Michael Wilson, of

Pat Gillick's four-year reign as Mariners general manager ended when he resigned following the 2003 season. Though he had little choice but to let franchise icons Ken Griffey Jr., Alex Rodriguez and Lou Piniella leave town during his tenure, Seattle averaged 98 wins under Gillick, including a record-tying 116 in 2001. The Mariners advanced to the American League Championship Series in Gillick's first two seasons, and fell just short of the playoffs in the last two. While Gillick extended his reputation as one of the more successful GMs in baseball history, he was unable to take the franchise to its first World Series.

That responsibility now falls to Bill Bavasi. The GM for the Angels in 1994-99 and most recently farm director for the Dodgers, Bavasi reshuffled Seattle's front office. Roger Jongewaard, vice president for scouting and player development since 1989, was moved to special assistant to the GM. Benny Looper, who along with Detroit assistant GM Al Avila was a finalist to replace Gillick, was promoted from farm director to Jongewaard's old job.

Frank Mattox, who ran the last six drafts for the Mariners, moved from scouting director to farm director. The new scouting director is Bob Fontaine Jr., Bavasi's scouting director in Anaheim and most recently the farm director for the White Sox. Bavasi resigned after the 1999 season rather than accede to demands to revamp the scouting department. Gillick will serve as a consultant to Bavasi.

Bavasi also has been busy reconstructing the big league team. He let Mike Cameron and Arthur Rhodes walk as free agents and replaced them by signing Eddie Guardado and Raul Ibanez. He reworked the left side of the infield by signing Rich Aurilia and Scott Spiezio, then traded Carlos Guillen to Detroit. Whether the Mariners improved themselves is debatable, but Bavasi did avoid blocking most of the young talent that's almost ready for the majors. Shortstop Jose Lopez and outfielder Chris Snelling could replace Aurilia and Edgar Martinez when their one-year contracts expire after 2004. Clint Nageotte, Travis Blackley and Rett Johnson, among others, should be able to pitch their way onto the big league staff in the next couple of years.

The Mariners' free-agent spree will cost them their first two picks in the 2004 draft, though they're accustomed to going without a first-rounder. They didn't have one in 2000, '01 and '03, and failed to sign John Mayberry Jr. in 2002. Seattle has compensated on the international market, where it has found four of its top five prospects. The Mariners signed Blackley (Australia), Lopez (Venezuela) and outfielder Shin-Soo Choo (South Korea) in 2000, and landed righty Felix Hernandez (Venezuela) in 2002.

ORGANIZATION
OVERVIEW

General manager: Bill Bavasi. **Farm director:** Frank Mattox. **Scouting director:** Bob Fontaine.

2003 PERFORMANCE

Class	Team	League	W	L	Pct.	Finish*	Manager
Majors	Seattle	American	93	69	.574	4th (14)	Bob Melvin
Triple-A	Tacoma Rainiers	Pacific Coast	66	78	.458	14th (16)	Dan Rohn
Double-A	San Antonio Missions	Texas	88	51	.633	+1st (8)	Dave Brundage
High A	Inland Empire 66ers	California	78	62	.557	+2nd (10)	Steve Roadcap
Low A	Wisconsin Timber Rattlers	Midwest	69	66	.511	t-6th (14)	Daren Brown
Short-season	Everett Aquasox	Northwest	32	44	.421	7th (8)	Pedro Grifol
Rookie	AZL Mariners	Arizona	29	19	.604	3rd (9)	Scott Steinmann
OVERALL 2003 MINOR LEAGUE RECORD			362	320	.531	6th (30)	

*Finish in overall standings (No. of teams in league). +League champion.

ORGANIZATION LEADERS

BATTING   *Minimum 250 At-Bats

*AVG	Greg Jacobs, San Antonio/Inland Empire	.345
R	Justin Leone, San Antonio	103
H	Greg Jacobs, San Antonio/Inland Empire	163
TB	A.J. Zapp, San Antonio	262
2B	Greg Jacobs, San Antonio/Inland Empire	42
3B	Shin-Soo Choo, Inland Empire	13
HR	A.J. Zapp, San Antonio	26
RBI	Justin Leone, San Antonio	92
	A.J. Zapp, San Antonio	92
BB	Justin Leone, San Antonio	92
SO	A.J. Zapp, San Antonio	178
SB	Mike Curry, San Antonio	58
*SLG	Justin Leone, San Antonio	.541
*OBP	Greg Jacobs, San Antonio/Inland Empire	.412

PITCHING   #Minimum 75 Innings

W	Travis Blackley, San Antonio	17
L	Jeff Heaverlo, Tacoma	12
	Chris Wright, Tacoma/San Antonio	12
#ERA	T.A. Fullmer, Wisconsin	2.58
G	Jared Hoerman, San Antonio	56
CG	T.A. Fullmer, Wisconsin	5
SV	Jared Hoerman, San Antonio	36
IP	Bobby Livingston, Wisconsin	178
BB	Bobby Madritsch, San Antonio	67
	Clint Nageotte, San Antonio	67
SO	Ryan Ketchner, Inland Empire	159
	Troy Cate, Tacoma/Inland Empire	159

BEST TOOLS

Best Hitter for Average	Chris Snelling
Best Power Hitter	Wladimir Balentien
Fastest Baserunner	Jamal Strong
Best Athlete	Shin-Soo Choo
Best Fastball	Felix Hernandez
Best Curveball	Felix Hernandez
Best Slider	Clint Nageotte
Best Changeup	Travis Blackley
Best Control	Ryan Ketchner
Best Defensive Catcher	Rene Rivera
Best Defensive Infielder	Jose Lopez
Best Infield Arm	Adam Jones
Best Defensive Outfielder	Shin-Soo Choo
Best Outfield Arm	Shin-Soo Choo

PROJECTED 2007 LINEUP

Catcher	Rene Rivera
First Base	John Olerud
Second Base	Bret Boone
Third Base	Justin Leone
Shortstop	Jose Lopez
Left Field	Raul Ibanez
Center Field	Shin-Soo Choo
Right Field	Ichiro Suzuki
Designated Hitter	Chris Snelling
No. 1 Starter	Felix Hernandez
No. 2 Starter	Joel Pineiro
No. 3 Starter	Clint Nageotte
No. 4 Starter	Travis Blackley
No. 5 Starter	Freddy Garcia
Closer	Rafael Soriano

LAST YEAR'S TOP 20 PROSPECTS

1. Rafael Soriano, rhp	11. Ryan Christianson, c
2. Chris Snelling, of	12. Luis Ugueto, ss
3. Jose Lopez, ss	13. Willie Bloomquist, inf/of
4. Shin-Soo Choo, of	14. Ismael Castro, 2b
5. Clint Nageotte, rhp	15. Kevin Olore, rhp
6. Aaron Taylor, rhp	16. Michael Garciaparra, ss
7. Travis Blackley, lhp	17. Kenny Kelly, of
8. Rett Johnson, rhp	18. Ryan Anderson, lhp
9. Greg Dobbs, 3b/of	19. Jeff Heaverlo, rhp
10. Jamal Strong, of	20. J.J. Putz, rhp

TOP PROSPECTS OF THE DECADE

1994	Alex Rodriguez, ss
1995	Alex Rodriguez, ss
1996	Jose Cruz Jr., of
1997	Jose Cruz Jr., of
1998	Ryan Anderson, lhp
1999	Ryan Anderson, lhp
2000	Ryan Anderson, lhp
2001	Ryan Anderson, lhp
2002	Ryan Anderson, lhp
2003	Rafael Soriano, rhp

TOP DRAFT PICKS OF THE DECADE

1994	Jason Varitek, c
1995	Jose Cruz Jr., of
1996	Gil Meche, rhp
1997	Ryan Anderson, lhp
1998	Matt Thornton, lhp
1999	Ryan Christianson, c
2000	Sam Hays, lhp (4)
2001	Michael Garciaparra, ss
2002	*John Mayberry Jr., of
2003	Adam Jones, ss/rhp

*Did not sign.

ALL-TIME LARGEST BONUSES

Ichiro Suzuki, 2000	$5,000,000
Ryan Anderson, 1997	$2,175,000
Ryan Christianson, 1999	$2,100,000
Kazuhiro Sasaki, 2000	$2,000,000
Michael Garciaparra, 2001	$2,000,000

MINOR LEAGUE
DEPTH CHART

SEATTLE MARINERS   RANK: 12

Impact potential (C+): Felix Hernandez signed out of Venezuela in July 2002 and jumped to the top of Seattle's prospect list after a dominant pro debut. Another righty with overpowering stuff, Clint Nageotte has two out pitches.

Depth (B-): Five of the Mariners' top six prospects come as a result of their foreign scouting efforts, but they either haven't had or signed a first-round pick in five years. The three prior to that (Ryan Anderson, Matt Thornton and Ryan Christianson) are fighting to keep their prospect status alive.

Sleeper: Ryan Feierabend, lhp.   *—Depth charts prepared by Josh Boyd. Numbers in parentheses indicate prospect rankings.*

LF
Chris Snelling (6)
Jaime Bubela
Greg Jacobs
Casey Craig

CF
Shin-Soo Choo (5)
Jamal Strong (10)
Josh Womack (24)
Michael Wilson (30)
Gary Harris
Chris Colton

RF
Wladimir Balentien (16)
T.J. Bohn

3B
Justin Leone (11)
Greg Dobbs (13)
Jeff Flaig (22)

SS
Jose Lopez (4)
Adam Jones (9)
Michael Garciaparra (25)
Luis Ugueto
Oswaldo Navarro
Asdrubal Cabrera
Rayon Lampe

2B
Ismael Castro
Nick Orlandos

1B
Jon Nelson

SOURCE OF TALENT

Homegrown		Acquired	
College	5	Trade	0
Junior College	1	Rule 5 draft	0
Draft-and-follow	1	Independent	1
High school	13	Free agent/waivers	0
Nondrafted free agent	2		
Foreign	7		

C
Rene Rivera (20)
Ryan Christianson (29)
Justin Ruchti

LHP

Starters	Relievers
Travis Blackley (3)	Bobby Madritsch (12)
Ryan Feierabend (14)	Matt Thornton (19)
Ryan Ketchner (18)	Jared Thomas
Troy Cate (26)	Justin Blood
Glenn Bott (27)	Miguel Martinez
Bobby Livingston (28)	
Erik O'Flaherty	
Casey Abrams	
Craig Anderson	
Tom Oldham	
Ryan Anderson	
Paul Fagan	

RHP

Starters	Relievers
Felix Hernandez (1)	Aaron Taylor (15)
Clint Nageotte (2)	J.J. Putz (17)
Rett Johnson (7)	Aaron Looper (23)
Cha Baek (8)	Emiliano Fruto
Aaron Jensen (21)	Jared Hoerman
Jeff Heaverlo	Rich Dorman
Elvis Perez	Chris Buglovsky
Juan Done	T.A. Fulmer

DRAFT
ANALYSIS

Best Pro Debut: Scouts questioned SS Adam Jones' (1) bat and thought he'd be better off as a hard-throwing righthander, but he hit .303-0-12 between the Rookie-level Arizona League and the short-season Northwest League. LHP Tom Oldham (8) went 5-3, 2.86 with 63 strikeouts in as many NWL innings.

Best Athlete: Jones could be a four-tooled shortstop if he continues to hit. OF Sam Bradford (22) isn't as strong as Jones, but he's faster and he's a switch-hitter with a quick bat, and has been clocked at 93 mph.

Best Pure Hitter: SS Jeff Flaig (2) was the best hitter on the 2001 U.S. youth national team that also included three 2002 first-round picks. Flaig tore his rotator cuff in 2002, which has affected his throwing, but the Mariners like his defensive instincts and will try to keep him at shortstop.

Best Raw Power: Jones has more pop than Flaig, though both are still growing into their bodies.

Fastest Runner: Bradford is a plus runner, but the Mariners didn't get any burners.

Best Defensive Player: C Justin Ruchti's (9) debut was cut short when he strained a hip. It hampered his ability to shut down the running game, his greatest strength.

Best Fastball: Jones hit 96 mph during the spring, creating the interest in making him a pitcher. Among the guys who will

Flaig

JOHN SPEAR

stay on the mound, RHP Aaron Jensen (19) has the top fastball. LHP Casey Abrams (5) and RHP Tim Dorn (14) also touch 94 mph, but Jensen does it consistently.

Best Breaking Ball: Jensen can throw his hard, biting 12-to-6 curveball for strikes. Abrams has the best slider.

Most Intriguing Background: Unsigned OF Trevor Heid's (39) father Ted is in charge of Pacific Rim operations for the Mariners' scouting department. They picked Ruchti's brother Aaron, a catcher, in both 2001 and 2002. Unsigned C Yusuf Carter (38) is the nephew of Joe Carter.

Closest To The Majors: There aren't any obvious candidates. A healthy Ruchti might arrive first, based on his defense alone.

Best Late-Round Pick: Jensen was considered the best Utah high school pitcher in several years. Signability was the only reason he didn't go in the first two rounds.

The One Who Got Away: LHP Scott Maine (15), the Mariners' highest unsigned pick, already throws 89-92 and is still filling out his 6-foot-3 frame. He could have been Miami's ace as a freshman, but he had Tommy John surgery and will miss a year.

Assessment: The Mariners had a rough draft in 2002, when they failed to sign two of their top three choices. They rebounded in 2003 with two multitooled infielders, Jensen and a host of lefthanders.

2002 DRAFT   GRADE: D

The Mariners failed to sign 1B John Mayberry Jr. (1) and OF Eddy Martinez-Esteve (3), two gifted hitters who could be first-round picks out of college. OF Josh Womack (2) and LHP Troy Cate (6) can't make up for that missed opportunity.

2001 DRAFT   GRADE: D

A surprise supplemental first-rounder, SS Michael Garciaparra has developed very slowly. No one from this draft is among the organization's top 15 prospects.

2000 DRAFT   GRADE: C+

The Mariners didn't have picks in the first three rounds and their top choice, LHP Sam Hays (4), has struggled and had shoulder surgery. RHP Rett Johnson (8), OF Jamal Strong (6) and LHP Ryan Ketchner (10) were nice finds in later rounds.

1999 DRAFT   GRADE: B

RHP Clint Nageotte (5) is just about ready to help the big league club. Willie Bloomquist (2) is a versatile utilityman, and RHP J.J. Putz (6) and 3B Justin Leone (13) will add depth in Seattle. OF Terrmel Sledge (10) could have had he not been traded for Chris Widger. Injuries have slowed both first-rounders, C Ryan Christianson and RHP Jeff Heaverlo.

—Draft analysis prepared by Jim Callis. Numbers in parentheses indicate draft rounds.

rhp

Felix Hernandez

Born: April 8, 1986.
Ht.: 6-3. **Wt.:** 170.
Bats: R. **Throws:** R.
Career Transactions: Signed out of Venezuela by Mariners, July 4, 2002.

T he Mariners expected Hernandez to be good when they signed him for $710,000 in July 2002. But they didn't expect him to be this good, this fast. Seattle never has been able to challenge precocious teenagers with an assignment to the short-season Northwest League, populated mostly by former college players. When he threw in the mid-90s last spring, he punched his ticket to Everett. The youngest player in the NWL by nearly eight months, Hernandez was dominant despite being kept on tight pitch counts. He pitched scoreless ball in five of his 11 outings and surrendered more than one earned run only twice. He was an easy choice as the NWL's No. 1 prospect. Promoted for the low Class A Midwest League stretch drive, he responded with two quality starts in as many tries. In the season finale, he shut out Kane County, one of the MWL's top offenses, with 10 strikeouts in seven innings. Hernandez succeeded against even more experienced hitters this winter, going 1-1, 4.23 in six starts for Lara in his native Venezuela. The Mariners shut him down in December so he wouldn't exceed 100 innings in 2003.

Hernandez has scary upside. He'll open this season as a 17-year-old and he doesn't need to develop any more stuff. The only guy in the organization with a comparable arm is big leaguer Rafael Soriano. Hernandez has the best fastball in the system and commands his mid-90s heat well. He regularly touches 97 and could reach triple digits as his skinny frame fills out. Hernandez' curveball is also unparalleled among Mariners farmhands and gives him the possibility for two 70 pitches on the 20-80 scouting scale. Though he's young and can easily overpower hitters at the lower levels, he understands the value of a changeup and is developing a good one. He can pitch down in the strike zone or blow the ball by hitters upstairs. He has poise and mound presence beyond his years. Hernandez just has to learn how to pitch. He needs to tweak his command and refine his pitches on the way to Seattle. Typical of a teenager with a lightning arm, he'll overthrow at times but should grow out of that. Arm problems would appear to be the only thing that could derail him from stardom, and Hernandez has been perfectly healthy so far. The Mariners will go to great lengths to make sure he isn't overworked in the minors.

Seattle wants to move Hernandez slowly, but he may not let that happen. He's not going to need to spend a full season at each level and might need just two more years in the minors. He'll probably start 2004 back at low Class A Wisconsin—the Mariners concede he could have spent all of last season there—and could be bucking for a promotion to high Class A Inland Empire by midseason. It's easy to get overexcited about young pitchers, but Hernandez has the legitimate potential to become the best pitcher ever developed by the Mariners.

Year	Club (League)	Class	W	L	ERA	G	GS	CG	SV	IP	H	R	ER	HR	BB	SO	AVG
2003	Everett (NWL)	A	7	2	2.29	11	7	0	0	55	43	17	14	2	24	73	.218
	Wisconsin (Mid)	A	0	0	1.93	2	2	0	0	14	9	4	3	1	3	18	.176
MINOR LEAGUE TOTALS			7	2	2.22	13	9	0	0	69	52	21	17	3	27	91	.210

2 Clint Nageotte, rhp

Born: Oct. 25, 1980. **Ht.:** 6-3. **Wt.:** 200. **Bats:** R. **Throws:** R. **School:** Brooklyn (Ohio) HS. **Career Transactions:** Selected by Mariners in fifth round of 1999 draft; signed Aug. 18, 1999.

Nageotte has succeeded from the day he entered pro ball. He won the Rookie-level Arizona League championship game in 2000, ranked as the Midwest League's No. 1 pitching prospect in 2001 and led the minors in strikeouts in 2002. Last year, he pitched in the Futures Game and topped the Double-A Texas League in whiffs. Nageotte's slider ranks with those of Francisco Rodriguez, John Smoltz and Ryan Wagner as the best anywhere. Nageotte throws his at 84-87mph with late, hard downward break. Sitting on his slider does hitters no good and just sets them up for his 90-95 mph fastball. Nageotte rarely throws his changeup, leading some scouts to project him as a reliever. But his changeup should be effective once he starts using it more. He throws his slider too much, which led to elbow tendinitis that prevented him from closing for Team USA at November's Olympic qualifying tournament. He can improve his command—he tied for the TL lead in walks—as well as his work habits. The Mariners want Nageotte to start 2004 at Triple-A Tacoma and make it to Seattle as a starter. He could help them as a K-Rodesque reliever if needed.

Year	Club (League)	Class	W	L	ERA	G	GS	CG	SV	IP	H	R	ER	HR	BB	SO	AVG
2000	Mariners (AZL)	R	4	1	2.16	12	7	0	1	50	29	15	12	0	28	59	.167
2001	Wisconsin (Mid)	A	11	8	3.13	28	26	0	0	152	141	65	53	10	50	187	.246
2002	San Bernardino (Cal)	A	9	6	4.54	29	29	1	0	165	154	101	83	10	68	214	.241
2003	San Antonio (TL)	AA	11	7	3.10	27	27	2	0	154	127	60	53	6	67	157	.224
MINOR LEAGUE TOTALS			35	22	3.47	96	89	3	1	521	450	241	201	26	213	617	.231

3 Travis Blackley, lhp

Born: Nov. 4, 1982. **Ht.:** 6-3. **Wt.:** 190. **Bats:** L. **Throws:** L. **Career Transactions:** Signed out of Australia by Mariners, Oct. 29, 2000.

Blackley sustained a small fracture in his elbow in instructional league in 2001, but made a quick recovery and stood out as the youngest pitcher in the high Class A California League the following year. He was even better in 2003, pitching in the Futures Game, winning the Texas League pitcher of the year award and tying for the minor league lead in wins. His brother Adam pitches in the Red Sox system. Blackley expertly mixes four average or better pitches, including the best changeup in the system. He also throws a fastball with natural cutting action, a curveball and a slider. Double-A San Antonio pitching coach Rafael Chaves made an adjustment to Blackley's release that allow him to boost his fastball up to 88-92 mph. Blackley has good command but sometimes gets too cute and winds up issuing more walks than he should. He tends to rush his delivery against lefthanders, which takes away from his stuff. Lefties hit .301 against him last year, compared to .188 by righties. Both of his breaking balls need a little refinement. The Mariners refer to him as Jamie Moyer with better stuff. After a year in Triple-A Tacoma, Blackley will be ready to join Moyer in Seattle's rotation.

Year	Club (League)	Class	W	L	ERA	G	GS	CG	SV	IP	H	R	ER	HR	BB	SO	AVG
2001	Everett (NWL)	A	6	1	3.32	14	14	0	0	79	60	34	29	7	29	90	.211
2002	San Bernardino (Cal)	A	5	9	3.49	21	20	1	0	121	102	52	47	11	44	152	.227
2003	San Antonio (TL)	AA	17	3	2.61	27	27	0	0	162	125	55	47	11	62	144	.215
MINOR LEAGUE TOTALS			28	13	3.06	62	61	1	0	362	287	141	123	29	135	386	.218

4 Jose Lopez, ss/2b

Born: Nov. 24, 1983. **Ht.:** 6-2. **Wt.:** 170. **Bats:** R. **Throws:** R. **Career Transactions:** Signed out of Venezuela by Mariners, July 2, 2000.

Lopez missed most of spring training last year recovering from surgery to remove a growth on a bone in his right foot, but that didn't stop him from making the Texas League all-star team as the circuit's youngest player. He led San Antonio to the championship by leading all playoff hitters with a .391 average and two homers in five games. While Lopez has an impressive array of tools, several Mariners officials say his greatest asset is his instincts. They rate him as the best defensive infielder in the system, while TL managers said he had the strongest infield arm in their league. He makes excellent contact and has well above-average pop for a middle infielder. He has slightly above-average speed and savvy on the bases. Lopez rarely swings and misses, but he draws few walks because he puts the ball in play so easily. He needs to work deeper counts and add a little consistency to all phases of his game. Lopez spent time at second and third base in 2003 so he'd be ready for whatever big league opening might come his way. His opportunity should come at shortstop after a season in Triple-A and Rich Aurilia's one-year contract expires.

Year	Club (League)	Class	AVG	G	AB	R	H	2B	3B	HR	RBI	BB	SO	SB	SLG	OBP
2001	Everett (NWL)	A	.256	70	289	42	74	15	0	2	20	13	44	13	.329	.309
2002	San Bernardino (Cal)	A	.324	123	522	82	169	39	5	8	60	27	45	31	.464	.360
2003	San Antonio (TL)	AA	.258	132	538	82	139	35	2	13	69	27	56	18	.403	.303
MINOR LEAGUE TOTALS			.283	325	1349	206	382	89	7	23	149	67	145	62	.411	.326

5 Shin-Soo Choo, of

Born: July 13, 1982. **Ht.:** 5-11. **Wt.:** 170. **Bats:** L. **Throws:** L. **Career Transactions:** Signed out of South Korea by Mariners, Aug. 14, 2000.

Choo signed for $1.335 million after the 2000 World Junior Championships, where he starred as a pitcher and faced off against Travis Blackley. An all-star in his first two pro seasons, Choo helped Inland Empire win the California League championship in 2003. He missed three weeks with a broken bone in his right foot yet still led the league in triples. Choo doesn't have a below-average tool. His arm, which delivered 95-mph fastballs during his amateur days, rates a 70 on the 20-80 scouting scale and is the best in the system. He's also the top athlete and defensive outfielder among Seattle farmhands. He drills line drives to all fields and has slightly above-average speed. Though Choo never has hit more than nine homers in a season, the Mariners say he has above-average pop. He's learning to be a sound hitter before looking for homers, which is fine, but he'll have to close his swing and adjust his Ichiro Suzuki-like approach before he can tap into his power. This offseason, Seattle signed Ichiro to a four-year extension and Raul Ibanez and Randy Winn to three-year deals. Choo, who's headed for Double-A, will be ready for the majors in two years, so something will have to give.

Year	Club (League)	Class	AVG	G	AB	R	H	2B	3B	HR	RBI	BB	SO	SB	SLG	OBP
2001	Mariners (AZL)	R	.302	51	199	51	60	10	10	4	35	34	49	12	.513	.420
	Wisconsin (Mid)	A	.462	3	13	1	6	0	0	0	3	1	3	2	.462	.533
2002	Wisconsin (Mid)	A	.302	119	420	69	127	24	8	6	48	70	98	34	.440	.417
	San Bernardino (Cal)	A	.308	11	39	14	12	5	1	1	9	9	9	3	.564	.460
2003	Inland Empire (Cal)	A	.286	110	412	62	118	18	13	9	55	44	84	18	.459	.365
MINOR LEAGUE TOTALS			.298	294	1083	197	323	57	32	20	150	158	243	69	.465	.401

6 Chris Snelling, of

Born: Dec. 3, 1981. **Ht.:** 5-10. **Wt.:** 160. **Bats:** L. **Throws:** L. **Career Transactions:** Signed out of Australia by Mariners, March 2, 1999.

As usual, Snelling produced at the plate and spent time on the disabled list in 2003. He hit .316, matching his previous career average. He missed April recovering from surgery on his left knee, another 2½ weeks in June with tendinitis in the knee and the final three weeks when he tore the meniscus in the knee. Snelling is such an obviously gifted hitter that former Mariners manager Lou Piniella wanted him on his Opening Day roster in 2001—when Snelling was 19. He has quick, explosive hands and makes hard contact to all fields. Tremendously instinctive and driven, he has an average arm and can play solid defense on either outfield corner. Snelling plays so aggressively that he can't stay in one piece. The knee injuries and natural physical maturation have knocked his speed down to a tick below average. His home run power is still developing and may not exceed 15-20 per year, which is fringy for a corner outfielder. After his second knee surgery, Snelling should be 100 percent for spring training. He'll probably go to Triple-A to get much-needed at-bats in 2004. Next year he could replace Edgar Martinez at DH.

Year	Club (League)	Class	AVG	G	AB	R	H	2B	3B	HR	RBI	BB	SO	SB	SLG	OBP
1999	Everett (NWL)	A	.306	69	265	46	81	15	3	10	50	33	24	8	.498	.388
2000	Wisconsin (Mid)	A	.305	72	259	44	79	9	5	9	56	34	34	7	.483	.386
2001	San Bernardino (Cal)	A	.336	114	450	90	151	29	10	7	73	45	63	12	.491	.418
2002	San Antonio (TL)	AA	.326	23	89	10	29	9	2	1	12	12	11	5	.506	.429
	Seattle (AL)	MAJ	.148	8	27	2	4	0	0	1	3	2	4	0	.259	.207
2003	San Antonio (TL)	AA	.333	47	186	24	62	12	2	3	25	8	30	1	.468	.371
	Tacoma (PCL)	AAA	.269	18	67	11	18	2	0	3	10	5	12	1	.433	.333
MAJOR LEAGUE TOTALS			.148	8	27	2	4	0	0	1	3	2	4	0	.259	.207
MINOR LEAGUE TOTALS			.319	343	1316	225	420	76	22	33	226	137	174	34	.486	.396

7 Rett Johnson, rhp

Born: July 6, 1979. **Ht.:** 6-2. **Wt.:** 210. **Bats:** L. **Throws:** R. **School:** Coastal Carolina University. **Career Transactions:** Selected by Mariners in eighth round of 2000 draft; signed June 13, 2000.

Brandon Webb and Dontrelle Willis weren't the only eighth-round steals in the 2000 draft. Johnson slipped that far because he wore down while setting Coastal Carolina records with 133 innings and 151 strikeouts that spring. He since has gone 40-20, 2.95 while reaching Triple-A. Johnson's out pitch is a hard slider that's a notch below Clint Nageotte's. He sets it up with a heavy 91-93 mph sinker. After minor league pitching coordinator Pat Rice shortened Johnson's stride in spring training, his command and ability to pitch down in the strike zone improved greatly. He's poised and competitive. Johnson's changeup has improved but still lags behind his two plus pitches. He needs it as a weapon against lefthanders, who hit .268 against him last year (righties batted .210). There's some effort to his delivery, which led to shoulder tendinitis at the end of last season. If they had nontendered Freddy Garcia, the Mariners would have let Johnson compete for their No. 5 starter job. Several scouts say he profiles better as a reliever along the lines of Jeff Nelson. Johnson could make the big league bullpen in spring training.

Year	Club (League)	Class	W	L	ERA	G	GS	CG	SV	IP	H	R	ER	HR	BB	SO	AVG
2000	Everett (NWL)	A	5	4	2.07	17	8	0	0	70	51	26	16	1	21	88	.198
2001	Wisconsin (Mid)	A	5	5	2.27	16	16	2	0	99	92	33	25	4	30	96	.248
	San Bernardino (Cal)	A	6	2	4.09	12	12	0	0	66	56	36	30	5	33	70	.230
2002	San Bernardino (Cal)	A	3	1	3.65	7	7	0	0	37	27	17	15	1	11	34	.199
	San Antonio (TL)	AA	10	4	3.62	21	21	1	0	117	107	63	47	5	53	104	.242
2003	San Antonio (TL)	AA	6	2	3.04	14	14	1	0	83	74	31	28	7	21	63	.237
	Tacoma (PCL)	AAA	5	2	2.15	11	10	1	0	71	63	26	17	2	18	49	.241
MINOR LEAGUE TOTALS			40	20	2.95	98	88	5	0	543	470	232	178	25	187	504	.232

8 Cha Baek, rhp

Born: May 29, 1980. **Ht.:** 6-4. **Wt.:** 190. **Bats:** R. **Throws:** R. **Career Transactions:** Signed out of South Korea by Mariners, Sept. 25, 1998 . . . On disabled list, April 4-Sept. 17, 2002.

Baek was Seattle's first big international signing, agreeing to a $1.3 million bonus in 1998. He and Choo were teammates at Pusan (South Korea) High. Baek blew out his elbow in 2001 and missed all of 2002 rehabbing from Tommy John surgery, then made a strong comeback last year. The only setback was a month off with elbow inflammation. Though Travis Blackley gets more notoriety, Baek has better command and feel for pitching. His delivery and arm action are smooth and consistent, allowing him to repeat pitches and throw strikes. He mixes four offerings: an 88-93 mph fastball with decent sink, a curveball he can vary speeds with, a slider and a changeup. Baek doesn't have a knockout pitch or even a plus one, leaving him little margin for error. He threw in the low 90s more often before he hurt his elbow, so it's possible he could regain a little more velocity as he gets stronger. Added to the 40-man roster, Baek probably will spend the first half of 2004 in Double-A. He projects as a No. 4 starter unless his stuff bounces back more.

Year	Club (League)	Class	W	L	ERA	G	GS	CG	SV	IP	H	R	ER	HR	BB	SO	AVG
1999	Mariners (AZL)	R	3	0	3.67	8	4	0	0	27	30	13	11	2	6	25	.283
2000	Wisconsin (Mid)	A	8	5	3.95	24	24	0	0	128	137	71	56	13	36	99	.275
2001	San Bernardino (Cal)	A	1	0	3.43	5	4	0	0	21	17	10	8	2	2	16	.224
2002	Did not play—Injured																
2003	Inland Empire (Cal)	A	5	1	3.65	13	10	0	1	57	55	27	23	3	9	50	.249
	San Antonio (TL)	AA	3	3	2.57	9	9	0	0	56	49	18	16	2	17	46	.238
MINOR LEAGUE TOTALS			20	9	3.56	59	51	0	1	288	288	139	114	22	70	236	.260

9 Adam Jones, ss

Born: Aug. 1, 1985. **Ht.:** 6-2. **Wt.:** 180. **Bats:** R. **Throws:** R. **School:** Morse HS, San Diego. **Career Transactions:** Selected by Mariners in first round (37th overall) of 2003 draft; signed July 18, 2003.

Scouts were tracking Jones as a shortstop when he hit 96 mph off the mound last spring, spurring many of them to prefer him as a pitcher. But Jones wants to play shortstop, and the Mariners acceded to his wishes when they signed him for $925,000. If that doesn't work out, Seattle always can convert him to the mound like it did with former position players Rafael Soriano and Jorge Sosa. Jones has a chance to be a five-tool

shortstop. Though he's tall for the position, he has a narrow waist and thus projects to retain his athleticism as he fills out. He has a cannon arm to go with good hands and actions. He has plus speed, and should hit for average with power. Though he hit .303 in his pro debut, there are still questions about Jones' bat. He's raw at the plate and will overswing at times. He also made 12 errors in 30 games at short, so he's still learning on defense as well. It will take time to turn Jones' tools into baseball skills. He'll move up to low Class A in 2004.

Year	Club (League)	Class	AVG	G	AB	R	H	2B	3B	HR	RBI	BB	SO	SB	SLG	OBP
2003	Mariners (AZL)	R	.284	28	109	18	31	5	1	0	8	5	19	5	.349	.368
	Everett (NWL)	A	.462	3	13	2	6	1	0	0	4	1	3	0	.538	.467
MINOR LEAGUE TOTALS			.303	31	122	20	37	6	1	0	12	6	22	5	.369	.379

10 Jamal Strong, of

Born: Aug. 5, 1978. **Ht.:** 5-10. **Wt.:** 180. **Bats:** R. **Throws:** R. **School:** University of Nebraska. **Career Transactions:** Selected by Mariners in sixth round of 2000 draft; signed June 14, 2000.

Strong won two stolen-base titles in his first three years as a pro, but his chances of adding a third last year ended when he tore his labrum and dislocated his left shoulder on a headfirst slide in spring training. The Mariners feared he would miss all of 2003, but he surprised them by returning in June. One of the fastest players in the minors, Strong has true 80 speed on the 20-80 scouting scale. He understands his role is to get on base and create havoc, so he draws walks and hits the ball on the ground. His speed gives him good range in center field. Strong's swing is a bit long and he can be pounded inside with fastballs. His approach isn't conducive to power. He doesn't always take the best routes on fly balls, though his speed covers up his mistakes. His arm is just playable. Ticketed for Triple-A, Strong is on the bubble between big league regular or fourth outfielder. His bat will determine his future, though he has little chance of cracking Seattle's starting lineup yet.

Year	Club (League)	Class	AVG	G	AB	R	H	2B	3B	HR	RBI	BB	SO	SB	SLG	OBP
2000	Everett (NWL)	A	.314	75	296	63	93	7	3	1	28	52	29	60	.368	.422
2001	Wisconsin (Mid)	A	.353	51	184	41	65	12	1	0	19	40	27	35	.429	.478
	San Bernardino (Cal)	A	.311	81	331	74	103	11	2	0	32	51	60	47	.356	.411
2002	San Antonio (TL)	AA	.278	127	503	63	140	16	5	1	31	62	87	46	.336	.366
2003	Mariners (AZL)	R	.714	2	7	5	5	0	1	0	4	3	1	3	1.000	.692
	Tacoma (PCL)	AAA	.305	56	210	38	64	6	1	2	19	25	38	26	.371	.390
	Seattle (AL)	MAJ	.000	12	2	2	0	0	0	0	0	0	0	0	.000	.000
MAJOR LEAGUE TOTALS			.000	12	2	2	0	0	0	0	0	0	0	0	.000	.000
MINOR LEAGUE TOTALS			.307	392	1531	284	470	52	13	4	133	233	242	217	.366	.406

11 Justin Leone, 3b

Born: March 9, 1977. **Ht.:** 6-1. **Wt.:** 210. **Bats:** R. **Throws:** R. **School:** St. Martin's (Wash.) College. **Career Transactions:** Selected by Mariners in 13th round of 1999 draft; signed June 8, 1999.

Leone opened last year treading close to the "organization player" label. He showed athleticism and power, but he also had a career .250 average and had less faith in himself than the Mariners did. Slated to be a utilityman in Double-A, he caught a break when Greg Dobbs ruptured his left Achilles tendon in the second game of the year. Leone took over at third base and became the Texas League MVP. He led the league in runs, doubles, extra-base hits and on-base percentage while finishing second in slugging. Managers rated him the best defensive third baseman in the TL, and he capped his year by leading Team USA with three homers at the Olympic qualifying tournament in November. One of the keys to Leone's breakthrough was letting Travis Blackley persuade him to play the previous winter in Australia, where he began to overcome his problems hitting breaking balls. Another was that he started to hit smarter, worked himself into better counts and drew more walks. He has power to all fields, good speed for his size and even better baserunning instincts. Defensively, Leone can handle second base and shortstop in addition to third. His hands, arm and actions fit at any of the positions, and he could be a Gold Glover at third base. He needs another good year to prove he's more than a 26-year-old who had his career year in Double-A. Seattle added him to the 40-man roster and will play him in Triple-A this year.

Year	Club (League)	Class	AVG	G	AB	R	H	2B	3B	HR	RBI	BB	SO	SB	SLG	OBP
1999	Everett (NWL)	A	.263	62	205	34	54	14	2	6	35	32	49	5	.439	.361
2000	Wisconsin (Mid)	A	.267	115	374	77	100	32	3	18	63	79	107	9	.513	.407
2001	San Bernardino (Cal)	A	.233	130	485	70	113	27	4	22	69	57	158	4	.441	.318
2002	San Bernardino (Cal)	A	.249	98	358	64	89	20	5	18	58	57	98	6	.483	.358
2003	San Antonio (TL)	AA	.288	135	455	103	131	38	7	21	92	92	104	20	.541	.405
MINOR LEAGUE TOTALS			.259	540	1877	348	487	131	21	85	317	317	516	44	.487	.370

12 Bobby Madritsch, lhp

Born: Feb. 28, 1976. **Ht.:** 6-2. **Wt.:** 190. **Bats:** L. **Throws:** L. **School:** Point Park (Pa.) College. **Career Transactions:** Selected by Reds in sixth round of 1998 draft; signed June 10, 1998 . . . On disabled list, July 1-Sept. 13, 1999 . . . Released by Reds, March 24, 2001 . . . Signed by independent Rio Grande (Texas-Louisiana), June 2001 . . . Signed by independent San Angelo (Texas-Louisiana), July 2001 . . . Signed by independent Chico (Western), Aug. 2001 . . . Signed by independent Winnipeg (Northern), May 2002 . . . Signed by Mariners, Sept. 23, 2002.

Baseball America's Independent League Player of the Year in 2002, when he set a Northern League record with 153 strikeouts in 125 innings, Madritsch made a triumphant return to Organized Baseball in 2003. A Native American who's a member of the Lakota Nation, he won the Rookie-level Pioneer League strikeout crown after signing with the Reds as a sixth-round pick in 1998. But he hurt his shoulder the following year, had surgery and got released by Cincinnati in the spring of 2001. He spent two years bouncing around three indy leagues before the Mariners outbid several teams to sign him. Madritsch's bread and butter is a 90-95 mph fastball that he'll bust inside on hitters or beat them with upstairs. Lefthanders can't get comfortable against him because of his arm angle and effective wildness, and he gets righties out just as easily. His changeup improved a lot last year, as did his confidence in throwing it. The key for Madritsch will be finding a usable breaking ball. His slider is below-average and he might be better off with more of a cutter. He also needs better command after tying Clint Nageotte for the Texas League high in walks. Madritsch held up well all season and through the TL playoffs, where he won both his starts, including the finale. The Mariners project him as a starter and will use him in the Triple-A rotation in 2004. If he can't come up with a reliable breaking pitch, he could make a tough reliever.

Year	Club (League)	Class	W	L	ERA	G	GS	CG	SV	IP	H	R	ER	HR	BB	SO	AVG
1998	Billings (Pio)	R	7	3	2.80	14	13	0	0	80	72	30	25	3	35	87	.240
1999	Did not play—Injured																
2000	Reds (GCL)	R	1	1	2.01	6	4	0	0	22	15	5	5	0	9	27	.192
	Dayton (Mid)	A	0	0	0.90	2	2	0	0	10	8	1	1	0	7	7	.222
2001	Rio Grande Valley (T-L)	IND	3	4	3.15	10	9	3	0	60	55	25	21	1	34	58	.239
	San Angelo (T-L)	IND	0	2	1.73	3	3	1	0	26	14	8	5	2	6	27	.159
	Chico (West)	IND	0	1	11.74	5	0	0	0	8	14	12	10	2	6	12	.359
2002	Winnipeg (NorC)	IND	11	4	2.30	19	18	2	0	125	94	35	32	6	36	153	.205
2003	San Antonio (TL)	AA	13	7	3.63	27	27	2	0	159	133	75	64	11	67	154	.226
MINOR LEAGUE TOTALS			21	11	3.15	49	46	2	0	271	228	111	95	14	118	275	.228

13 Greg Dobbs, 3b

Born: July 2, 1978. **Ht.:** 6-1. **Wt.:** 200. **Bats:** L. **Throws:** R. **School:** University of Oklahoma. **Career Transactions:** Signed as nondrafted free agent by Mariners, May 28, 2001.

The Mariners drafted Dobbs in the 53rd round out of high school in 1996 but didn't land him until signing him as a fifth-year senior just before the 2001 draft. In between, he went from Riverside (Calif.) Community College to Long Beach State to Oklahoma, earning all-league honors every season except for 2000, when he was academically ineligible. Dobbs has perhaps the prettiest swing in the system, a classic lefthanded stroke that has enabled him to hit everywhere he has played. The only thing that has slowed him as a pro has been a ruptured left Achilles tendon that ended his 2003 season after two games. The injury not only let Justin Leone move past him but it also left questions about whether Dobbs can handle third base unresolved. His hands, range and arm are adequate at the hot corner, but he needs to improve his footwork and throwing accuracy. The other options would be to move him to first base or left field, and Dobbs should have enough bat for those positions. He projects to hit .280-.300 with 20-25 homers while drawing a fair amount of walks. Expected to be 100 percent in spring training, Dobbs will again open as the Double-A third baseman.

Year	Club (League)	Class	AVG	G	AB	R	H	2B	3B	HR	RBI	BB	SO	SB	SLG	OBP
2001	Everett (NWL)	A	.321	65	249	37	80	17	2	6	41	30	39	5	.478	.396
	San Bernardino (Cal)	A	.385	3	13	2	5	1	0	1	3	0	4	0	.692	.357
2002	Wisconsin (Mid)	A	.275	86	320	43	88	16	2	10	48	31	50	13	.431	.338
	San Antonio (TL)	AA	.365	27	96	13	35	4	0	5	15	9	17	1	.542	.425
2003	San Antonio (TL)	AA	.333	2	6	0	2	2	0	0	0	0	1	0	.667	.333
MINOR LEAGUE TOTALS			.307	183	684	95	210	38	4	22	107	70	111	19	.471	.372

14 Ryan Feierabend, lhp

Born: Aug. 22, 1985. **Ht.:** 6-3. **Wt.:** 190. **Bats:** L. **Throws:** L. **School:** Midview HS, Grafton, Ohio. **Career Transactions:** Selected by Mariners in third round of 2003 draft; signed July 13, 2003.

Though the Marlins already had a deep stock of lefthanded pitching, they also thought that was one of the strengths of the 2003 draft crop. So they signed five southpaws from the first eight rounds, starting with Feierabend. He gave up a scholarship from Kent State for a $437,000 bonus. "You see Travis Blackley in this guy," one scout said, "with a touch more velocity and he's younger." Feierabend already throws 88-91 mph and should sit in the low 90s once he fills out his projectable frame. His smooth delivery and advanced feel for pitching let him put his pitches where he wants. His changeup already ranks among the best in the system. Feierabend throws two breaking balls and both need work. His slider is better than his curveball at this point. Adding strength is also on his priority list after he tired in his pro debut. Because he's so young—he didn't turn 18 until late in the season—the Mariners will handle him carefully. Feierabend likely will start the season in extended spring training before reporting to Everett in June.

Year	Club (League)	Class	W	L	ERA	G	GS	CG	SV	IP	H	R	ER	HR	BB	SO	AVG
2003	Mariners (AZL)	R	2	3	2.61	6	5	0	1	21	23	11	6	0	6	12	.288
MINOR LEAGUE TOTALS			2	3	2.61	6	5	0	1	21	23	11	6	0	6	12	.288

15 Aaron Taylor, rhp

Born: Aug. 20, 1977. **Ht.:** 6-8. **Wt.:** 240. **Bats:** R. **Throws:** R. **School:** Lowndes HS, Valdosta, Ga. **Career Transactions:** Selected by Braves in 11th round of 1996 draft; signed June 5, 1996 . . . Selected by Mariners from Braves in Rule 5 minor league draft, Dec. 13, 1999.

The Mariners stole a future all-star reliever when they plucked Jeff Nelson from the Dodgers in the 1986 minor league Rule 5 draft. They may have done the same again when they picked Taylor from the Braves in the 1999 minor league Rule 5 draft. Taylor didn't immediately pay off, posting a 7.43 ERA in his first year in the Seattle system and quitting baseball briefly in 2001. After returning, he shot from low Class A to the majors in 15 months. Taylor has the raw stuff to close games but needs more polish. He has a heavy 94-97 mph fastball, and his 6-foot-5 frame allows him to drive his heater down in the zone. He's similar to Braden Looper in that he has a big-time fastball but no consistent second pitch. Taylor's slider and splitter have their moments but aren't reliable. He started to have more success late last year when he went to a slurvier slider. He also could use better command and more finesse in his approach. Taylor's 2003 season ended in early August with a small tear in his rotator cuff. His recovery was progressing faster than expected, so he may be ready for spring training. Assuming he's healthy, he should get another shot in the majors in 2004.

Year	Club (League)	Class	W	L	ERA	G	GS	CG	SV	IP	H	R	ER	HR	BB	SO	AVG
1996	Braves (GCL)	R	0	9	7.74	13	9	0	0	52	68	54	45	0	28	33	.315
1997	Danville (Appy)	R	1	8	5.53	15	7	0	0	55	65	49	34	4	31	38	.288
1998	Danville (Appy)	R	3	6	6.25	14	14	1	0	72	87	60	50	9	36	55	.300
1999	Macon (SAL)	A	6	7	4.88	27	8	0	1	79	86	56	43	9	27	78	.270
2000	Everett (NWL)	A	1	4	7.43	15	14	0	0	63	76	54	52	5	37	57	.304
2001	Wisconsin (Mid)	A	3	1	2.45	28	0	0	9	29	19	9	8	1	11	50	.184
2002	San Antonio (TL)	AA	4	3	2.34	61	0	0	24	77	51	28	20	5	34	93	.184
	Seattle (AL)	MAJ	0	0	9.00	5	0	0	0	5	8	5	5	2	0	6	.348
2003	Tacoma (PCL)	AAA	1	3	2.45	33	0	0	16	40	30	11	11	3	13	34	.208
	Seattle (AL)	MAJ	0	0	8.53	10	0	0	0	13	17	12	12	0	6	9	.315
MAJOR LEAGUE TOTALS			0	0	8.66	15	0	0	0	18	25	17	17	2	6	15	.325
MINOR LEAGUE TOTALS			19	41	5.05	206	52	1	50	469	482	321	263	36	217	438	.264

16 Wladimir Balentien, of

Born: July 2, 1984. **Ht.:** 6-2. **Wt.:** 160. **Bats:** R. **Throws:** R. **Career Transactions:** Signed out of Curacao by Mariners, July 9, 2000.

Balentien won both the regular-season and playoff MVP awards and added the home run crown in the Rookie-level Venezuelan Summer League in 2002. His U.S. debut last season was even better. Balentien destroyed the Arizona League home run mark and led the AZL in extra-base hits and slugging percentage. He employs a grip-it-and-rip-it mentality, swinging hard at everything that comes his way and displaying well-above-average power to all fields. First baseman Jon Nelson has arguably more raw pop than Balentien but can't match him in terms of usable power. It's unlikely Balentien's approach will work against advanced pitching. He'll need to learn to wait on breaking balls and develop more discipline. He's not just a one-dimensional slugger, however. His speed and arm are average tools. A converted third baseman, he played all three outfield positions in the AZL and fits best in right field. The Mariners may be tempted to move Balentien to full-season ball this year in low Class A.

Year	Club (League)	Class	AVG	G	AB	R	H	2B	3B	HR	RBI	BB	SO	SB	SLG	OBP
2001	Aguirre (VSL)	R	.206	53	131	27	27	2	1	0	9	25	48	7	.237	.333
2002	Aguirre (VSL)	R	.279	59	197	41	55	13	4	10	39	34	52	6	.538	.390
2003	Mariners (AZL)	R	.283	50	187	42	53	12	5	16	52	22	55	4	.658	.363
MINOR LEAGUE TOTALS			.262	162	515	110	135	27	10	26	100	81	155	17	.505	.366

17 J.J. Putz, rhp

Born: Feb. 22, 1977. **Ht.:** 6-5. **Wt.:** 220. **Bats:** R. **Throws:** R. **School:** University of Michigan. **Career Transactions:** Selected by Mariners in sixth round of 1999 draft; signed June 17, 1999.

Putz had been a full-time starter in his three full seasons as a pro, but he was so impressive in relief last spring that he might have made the Mariners if he had more bullpen experience. They sent him back to Triple-A, and he got his first big league promotion in August. Putz showed promise as a starter, projecting as a workhorse with his strong frame and average four-pitch repertoire. His stuff works much better out of the bullpen, however. His low-90s fastball became an explosive 93-97 mph heater, and his curveball went from ordinary to a plus pitch that now falls off the table. He also has a slider and a changeup from his days in the rotation. Moved from middle relief to a late-inning role at midseason, Putz had nine saves and a 0.90 ERA in his final two months in Triple-A. His control improved after that change as well. He has an effortless, easy delivery with deception to it. The Mariners might have been tempted to let him compete for a starting job had they nontendered Freddy Garcia. Putz instead will be a leading candidate to claim a spot in the bullpen this spring, with his chances enhanced by Kazuhiro Sasaki's decision to stay home in Japan.

Year	Club (League)	Class	W	L	ERA	G	GS	CG	SV	IP	H	R	ER	HR	BB	SO	AVG
1999	Everett (NWL)	A	0	0	4.84	10	0	0	2	22	23	13	12	2	11	17	.288
2000	Wisconsin (Mid)	A	12	6	3.15	26	25	3	0	143	130	71	50	4	63	105	.247
2001	San Antonio (TL)	AA	7	9	3.83	27	26	0	0	148	145	80	63	11	59	135	.259
2002	San Antonio (TL)	AA	3	10	3.64	15	15	1	0	84	84	41	34	7	28	60	.264
	Tacoma (PCL)	AAA	2	4	3.83	9	9	0	0	54	51	23	23	4	21	39	.258
2003	Tacoma (PCL)	AAA	0	3	2.51	41	0	0	11	86	69	30	24	4	34	60	.225
	Seattle (AL)	MAJ	0	0	4.91	3	0	0	0	4	4	2	2	0	3	3	.267
MAJOR LEAGUE TOTALS			0	0	4.91	3	0	0	0	4	4	2	2	0	3	3	.267
MINOR LEAGUE TOTALS			24	32	3.45	128	75	4	13	537	502	258	206	32	216	416	.253

18 Ryan Ketchner, lhp

Born: April 19, 1982. **Ht.:** 6-1. **Wt.:** 190. **Bats:** L. **Throws:** L. **School:** John Leonard HS, Greenacres, Fla. **Career Transactions:** Selected by Mariners in 10th round of 2000 draft; signed June 19, 2000.

With a successful season in high Class A, Ketchner proved he's more than a human-interest story. He's a good pitching prospect, too. Born partially deaf, he has 40 percent of his hearing. He compensates by wearing hearing aids in both ears, which allow him to detect vibrations but not read words, and by reading lips. The USA Deaf Sports Federation named Ketchner its 2003 co-athlete of the year, making him the first baseball player honored in the 48-year history of the award. He led the California League in strikeouts, strikeout-walk ratio (4.8) and shutouts (two). He also was the playoff MVP, pitching Inland Empire to the championship with 13 scoreless innings. Ketchner throws an 85-88 mph fastball with good life, an ordinary slider and a solid average changeup. While he doesn't have a plus pitch, he has a lot going for him. He has the best command in the system and makes his stuff play much better than it is. He can put his pitches exactly where he wants when he wants, and his deceptive delivery has limited pro hitters to a .214 average. Ketchner deftly mixes his pitches and changes speeds, and he has an innate gift for sense a batter's weakness. He can watch his swing path and immediately figure out where the holes are. Ketchner opened 2003 in the bullpen but has earned the chance to start. He'll do that in Double-A this year.

Year	Club (League)	Class	W	L	ERA	G	GS	CG	SV	IP	H	R	ER	HR	BB	SO	AVG
2000	Mariners (AZL)	R	1	2	4.21	9	1	0	0	26	22	14	12	0	3	27	.227
2001	Everett (NWL)	A	3	3	2.92	20	5	0	2	52	38	19	17	3	18	58	.199
2002	Wisconsin (Mid)	A	3	6	2.59	31	12	0	1	111	75	39	32	3	39	118	.190
	Tacoma (PCL)	AAA	0	1	4.76	1	1	0	0	6	9	3	3	0	0	6	.360
2003	Inland Empire (Cal)	A	14	7	3.45	31	22	2	1	157	133	63	60	10	33	159	.228
MINOR LEAGUE TOTALS			21	19	3.18	92	41	2	4	351	277	138	124	16	93	368	.214

19 Matt Thornton, lhp

Born: Sept. 15, 1976. **Ht.:** 6-6. **Wt.:** 220. **Bats:** L. **Throws:** L. **School:** Grand Valley State (Mich.) University. **Career Transactions:** Selected by Mariners in first round (22nd overall) of 1998 draft; signed July 3, 1998.

A surprise 1998 first-round pick after making more of a name for himself as a basketball player, Thornton didn't win a game in college or in his first two years as a pro. He broke out in 2001 with a strikeout crown and pitcher-of-the-year honors in the California League, only to blow out his elbow and require Tommy John surgery the following season. Thornton returned to the mound within 11 months, but lasted just six weeks last season before going down with a herniated disc in his neck. His pitches weren't as crisp as they had been in the past, though that's typical for someone coming back so quickly from Tommy John surgery.

His fastball dipped from the low 90s to the high 80s. His slider, the key to his emergence in 2001, didn't have the same late, quick bite. Thornton's command and changeup remain works in progress. He tends to backdoor his slider rather than trust his changeup against righthanders. Given that he's a two-pitch pitcher with durability concerns, he'd probably be best off in relief. He worked out of the bullpen in the Arizona Fall League, where he got tattooed but did get back to 90-93 mph with his fastball. If Thornton's stuff comes the rest of the way back in 2004, the Mariners could give him a look as a long reliever.

Year	Club (League)	Class	W	L	ERA	G	GS	CG	SV	IP	H	R	ER	HR	BB	SO	AVG
1998	Everett (NWL)	A	0	0	27.00	2	0	0	0	1	1	4	4	0	3	0	.200
1999	Wisconsin (Mid)	A	0	0	4.91	25	1	0	1	29	39	19	16	1	25	34	.320
2000	Wisconsin (Mid)	A	6	9	4.01	26	17	0	0	103	94	59	46	2	72	88	.245
2001	San Bernardino (Cal)	A	14	7	2.52	27	27	0	0	157	126	56	44	9	60	192	.220
2002	San Antonio (TL)	AA	1	5	3.63	12	12	0	0	62	52	31	25	3	29	44	.237
2003	Inland Empire (Cal)	A	0	0	4.00	2	2	0	0	9	9	4	4	2	4	14	.265
	San Antonio (TL)	AA	3	0	0.36	4	4	0	0	25	8	3	1	0	9	18	.104
	Tacoma (PCL)	AAA	0	2	8.00	2	2	0	0	9	14	11	8	2	3	5	.359
MINOR LEAGUE TOTALS			24	23	3.36	100	65	0	1	396	343	187	148	19	205	395	.236

20 Rene Rivera, c

Born: July 31, 1983. **Ht.:** 5-10. **Wt.:** 190. **Bats:** R. **Throws:** R. **Career Transactions:** Selected by Mariners in second round of 2001 draft; signed June 14, 2001.

With Ryan Christianson continually snakebitten by injuries, Rivera has supplanted him as the organization's top catching prospect. The Mariners believe their 2003 Wisconsin team MVP can give them what they hoped for from Christianson: strong catch-and-throw skills and some pop in his bat. Rivera's defense is ahead of his offense at this point. Managers rated him the best defensive catcher in the Midwest League after he threw out 40 percent of basestealers. He has a strong arm with a quick release, and he enjoys running a pitching staff. As Rivera gets stronger and gets a better grasp of the strike zone, he'll have 15-20 home run power. Right now he's a free swinger who needs a more consistent approach. His stroke is sound, and he's starting to understand which pitches he can and can't hit. As with most catchers, he doesn't have much speed. Rivera will move up to high Class A for 2004.

Year	Club (League)	Class	AVG	G	AB	R	H	2B	3B	HR	RBI	BB	SO	SB	SLG	OBP
2001	Everett (NWL)	A	.089	15	45	3	4	1	0	2	3	1	19	0	.244	.106
	Mariners (AZL)	R	.338	21	71	13	24	4	0	2	12	2	11	0	.479	.360
2002	Everett (NWL)	A	.242	62	227	29	55	18	1	1	26	16	38	5	.344	.314
2003	Wisconsin (Mid)	A	.275	116	407	39	112	19	0	9	54	38	81	2	.388	.344
MINOR LEAGUE TOTALS			.260	214	750	84	195	42	1	14	95	57	149	7	.375	.323

21 Aaron Jensen, rhp

Born: June 11, 1984. **Ht.:** 6-2. **Wt.:** 180. **Bats:** R. **Throws:** R. **School:** Springville (Utah) HS. **Career Transactions:** Selected by Mariners in 19th round of 2003 draft; signed Aug. 25, 2003.

Jensen was a 19th-round steal in 2003. The top prospect in Utah, he led Springfield High to the state 4-A title and would have gone in the top three rounds if his commitment to Brigham Young hadn't worried clubs. The Mariners reeled him in with third-round money in late August. Jensen has a quick arm two plus pitches, a 90-94 mph fastball and a hard 12-6 curveball. With his strong 6-foot-2 frame, he's more developed than projectable. Like almost any young pitcher, he'll have to get acclimated to pro ball, improve the consistency of his pitches and refine his changeup and command. He's poised and mature, so Seattle expects that he'll be able to make those adjustments. The plan for 2004 is to start Jensen in extended spring training before he makes his pro debut in the Arizona or Northwest league.

Year	Club (League)	Class	W	L	ERA	G	GS	CG	SV	IP	H	R	ER	HR	BB	SO	AVG
2003			Did not play—Signed 2004 contract														

22 Jeff Flaig, 3b

Born: March 3, 1985. **Ht.:** 6-2. **Wt.:** 170. **Bats:** R. **Throws:** R. **School:** El Dorado HS, Placentia, Calif. **Career Transactions:** Selected by Mariners in second round of 2003 draft; signed Aug. 16, 2003.

Flaig led Team USA in all the triple-crown categories at the 2001 World Youth Championship, batting .536-3-12 in seven games on a squad that also included 2003 first-round picks Chris Lubanski, Lastings Milledge and Jarrod Saltalamacchia. Flaig played shortstop and also pitched, earning a save against Japan in the quarterfinals en route to a gold medal. But he tore the labrum and rotator cuff in his right shoulder in 2002, leading to surgery that still affects his throwing. After signing late in August for $710,000 he reported to instructional league, where he had further shoulder problems. Flaig required another labrum operation in November. He no longer has the 90 mph fastball he once flashed, and his arm may never be strong enough for him to play shortstop, his position as an amateur, in pro ball. He still has a sweet, pure stroke, however, and projects as a hitter in the same class as fellow El Dorado High (Placentia, Calif.) products Bret Boone and Phil Nevin. Flaig already has an advanced approach at the plate and should hit for power and average. He runs fine and has good all-around instincts. His footwork is better suited for third base than shortstop, though he'll have to prove he can make the throws from the hot corner. The best-case scenario for now is that Flaig will be able to DH in July or August, presumably making his pro debut in the Arizona or Northwest league.

Year	Club (League)	Class	AVG	G	AB	R	H	2B	3B	HR	RBI	BB	SO	SB	SLG	OBP
2003							Did not play—Signed 2004 contract									

23 Aaron Looper, rhp

Born: Sept. 7, 1976. **Ht.:** 6-2. **Wt.:** 180. **Bats:** R. **Throws:** R. **School:** Indian Hills (Iowa) CC. **Career Transactions:** Selected by Mariners in 30th round of 1997 draft; signed May 29, 1998.

When their pitchers hit a wall in their development, the Mariners often have them drop their arm angle to see if that will help. Switching to a very low three-quarters delivery in 2002 did wonders for Looper, who shared the organization's minor league pitcher of the year award that season and reached the majors last year. He no longer is known mainly for being the son of Seattle vice president Benny Looper and the cousin of big leaguer Braden Looper. Looper's new approach added a lot of sink and cost him just 1-2 mph in velocity on his fastball, which he now throws at 88-92 mph. It took him longer to adapt his slider, but he made it into a long, sweeping pitch that he throws at a crossfire angle that's tough on righthanders. They hit just .193 against him in Triple-A last year. Lefties batted .328 because he's still refining his changeup. He'll try to backdoor his slider against lefties, but an improved change would work better. Looper has a rubber arm and wants the ball every day. He handles pressure well and is a groundball machine against righties. He acquitted himself well in his first exposure to the majors last year and should get another opportunity in 2004.

Year	Club (League)	Class	W	L	ERA	G	GS	CG	SV	IP	H	R	ER	HR	BB	SO	AVG
1998	Everett (NWL)	A	4	5	6.86	14	14	0	0	59	72	52	45	8	31	40	.306
1999	Wisconsin (Mid)	A	9	6	4.10	38	7	0	3	90	89	47	41	8	26	73	.251
2000	Lancaster (Cal)	A	5	3	5.70	51	0	0	0	73	105	62	46	7	22	47	.329
2001	San Bernardino (Cal)	A	6	11	2.79	56	0	0	5	71	59	34	22	1	22	77	.224
2002	San Antonio (TL)	AA	6	1	2.28	57	0	0	0	91	76	33	23	4	30	73	.230
2003	Tacoma (PCL)	AAA	5	2	3.11	46	0	0	5	75	72	27	26	10	26	67	.247
	Seattle (AL)	MAJ	0	0	5.14	6	0	0	0	7	7	4	4	1	2	6	.269
MAJOR LEAGUE TOTALS			0	0	5.14	6	0	0	0	7	7	4	4	1	2	6	.269
MINOR LEAGUE TOTALS			35	28	3.98	262	21	0	13	459	473	255	203	38	157	377	.264

24 Josh Womack, of

Born: Jan. 5, 1984. **Ht.:** 6-1. **Wt.:** 190. **Bats:** L. **Throws:** L. **School:** Crawford HS, San Diego. **Career Transactions:** Selected by Mariners in second round of 2002 draft; signed June 12, 2002.

The Mariners' 2002 draft didn't exactly go as planned. They failed to sign first-rounder John Mayberry Jr. and third-rounder Eddy Martinez-Esteve, who project as possible first-round picks in 2005. Seattle may salvage something with Womack, whom they drafted in between those two. More of a football player in high school, Womack is an all-around athlete. His speed is his most noticeable tool, rating a 60 on the 20-80 scouting scale. He has some power in his bat, though some scouts worry about his stroke. He has a front arm bar, meaning he extends his right arm straight as he gets started. That makes his swing long and could allow him to get tied up by better fastballs. Womack's timing was OK in the Northwest League, but he'll have to make adjustments against higher quality pitching. He also needs to make better contact. Defensively, Womack has average range and arm strength for a center field. He'll advance to low Class A this year.

Year	Club (League)	Class	AVG	G	AB	R	H	2B	3B	HR	RBI	BB	SO	SB	SLG	OBP
2002	Mariners (AZL)	R	.269	43	160	20	43	10	5	1	12	13	25	8	.413	.337
2003	Everett (NWL)	A	.297	41	155	25	46	9	4	3	18	19	40	8	.465	.374
MINOR LEAGUE TOTALS			.283	84	315	45	89	19	9	4	30	32	65	16	.438	.355

25 Michael Garciaparra, ss

Born: April 2, 1983. **Ht.:** 6-1. **Wt.:** 160. **Bats:** R. **Throws:** R. **School:** Don Bosco Tech HS, Rosemead, Calif. **Career Transactions:** Selected by Mariners in first round (36th overall) of 2001 draft; signed Aug. 20, 2001.

Some teams didn't list Garciaparra on their draft boards in 2001 after he blew out the anterior cruciate ligament in his right knee while making a tackle as the kicker on his high school football team. He got just 12 at-bats that spring and might have flown completely under the prospect radar if he weren't the younger brother of Nomar Garciaparra. Michael had played on scout teams in California for the Mariners, piquing their interest, and they popped him 36th overall and signed him for $2 million. While Garciaparra's 2003 statistics are underwhelming, Seattle says he was the most improved player in the system, bettering himself in all phases of the game. He didn't cross the Mendoza Line for good until mid-May, but hit .269 and settled down defensively in the final few months of the season. He resembles his brother at the same age, though Nomar had better speed and has turned himself into a physical specimen. Michael shares Nomar's work ethic and has added 15 pounds since signing, but he's going to have to get a lot stronger to become an effective hitter. He has a good swing path, pitch-recognition skills and quick wrists. He has plate discipline but could use more. Garciaparra is a solid average runner and potentially a plus defender. His arm and range play well at shortstop, though he made 50 errors in 122 games last year. Most of those miscues came on rushed throws, and he settled down later in the season. He won't be the second coming of his brother, but he could turn into an Adam Everett. Garciaparra will play in high Class A this season.

Year	Club (League)	Class	AVG	G	AB	R	H	2B	3B	HR	RBI	BB	SO	SB	SLG	OBP
2002	Mariners (AZL)	R	.275	46	160	27	44	8	5	0	20	20	42	13	.388	.383
	Everett (NWL)	A	.161	9	31	3	5	2	0	0	3	4	15	0	.226	.257
2003	Wisconsin (Mid)	A	.243	122	440	55	107	12	1	2	38	38	80	14	.289	.314
MINOR LEAGUE TOTALS			.247	177	631	85	156	22	6	2	61	62	137	27	.311	.330

26 Troy Cate, lhp

Born: Oct. 21, 1980. **Ht.:** 6-1. **Wt.:** 200. **Bats:** L. **Throws:** L. **School:** Ricks (Idaho) JC. **Career Transactions:** Selected by Mariners in sixth round of 2002 draft; signed June 16, 2002.

Jamie Moyer's success in Seattle helps the cause of the many finesse lefthanders in the system. Inland Empire won the California League championship behind three of them: Ryan Ketchner, Cate and Glenn Bott. Cate, who put his career on hold for two years to go on a Mormon mission to England after high school, tossed seven-plus innings of shutout ball to win the postseason clincher 1-0. He excels at changing the speed on his fastballs, throwing both two- and four-seam varieties that range from 85-90 mph. His changeup grades out as slightly above average, while his slider is inconsistent but good at times. Cate's command and feel for pitching give him a chance to keep climbing the minor league ladder. The Mariners weren't sure exactly what they had when he finished second in the Northwest League in ERA and strikeouts during his pro debut. His first full season showed that he's for real, and he'll get a chance to prove himself in Double-A in 2004.

Year	Club (League)	Class	W	L	ERA	G	GS	CG	SV	IP	H	R	ER	HR	BB	SO	AVG
2002	Everett (NWL)	A	6	1	2.00	16	12	1	0	85	62	21	19	6	11	95	.203
2003	Inland Empire (Cal)	A	9	11	4.11	27	25	0	0	160	165	79	73	10	37	153	.264
	Tacoma (PCL)	AAA	1	0	1.69	1	1	0	0	5	4	3	1	2	2	6	.190
MINOR LEAGUE TOTALS			16	12	3.34	44	38	1	0	251	231	103	93	18	50	254	.243

27 Glenn Bott, lhp

Born: Sept. 17, 1981. **Ht.:** 6-0. **Wt.:** 170. **Bats:** L. **Throws:** L. **School:** San Jacinto (Texas) JC. **Career Transactions:** Signed as nondrafted free agent by Mariners, June 7, 2001.

San Jacinto gets more exposure than most junior college programs, thanks to an ever-flowing talent pipeline that has included Roger Clemens and Andy Pettitte. Yet Bott had to sign as a nondrafted free agent after two years with the Gators. He was overshadowed by fellow lefty Zach Parker (now with the Rockies) and didn't stand out because he's a short lefthander without an overwhelming pitch. Bott has fared well as a pro, averaging more than a strikeout per inning, because he mixes three pitches and has command. His 83-88 mph misses bats because it's lively and he locates it well. His best pitch is his changeup, and he's trying to improve the consistency of his slider. He seemed more confident in his second tour of the California League in 2003, going after hitters more aggressively and cutting down on his walks. Bott contributed to Inland Empire's title run by winning two of his three playoff starts. He'll move up to Double-A with the similar Ryan Ketchner and Troy Cate this year.

Year	Club (League)	Class	W	L	ERA	G	GS	CG	SV	IP	H	R	ER	HR	BB	SO	AVG
2001	Mariners (AZL)	R	0	0	6.00	2	0	0	1	3	5	2	2	0	0	4	.357
	Everett (NWL)	A	2	3	2.30	19	0	0	4	43	32	17	11	4	23	57	.196
2002	San Bernardino (Cal)	A	7	7	3.88	30	23	2	0	151	141	70	65	13	64	142	.246
2003	Inland Empire (Cal)	A	7	7	3.16	31	21	0	1	142	131	55	50	8	38	143	.241
MINOR LEAGUE TOTALS			16	17	3.40	82	44	2	6	339	309	144	128	25	125	346	.239

28 Bobby Livingston, lhp

Born: Sept. 3, 1982. **Ht.:** 6-3. **Wt.:** 190. **Bats:** L. **Throws:** L. **School:** Trinity Christian HS, Lubbock, Texas. **Career Transactions:** Selected by Mariners in fourth round of 2001 draft; signed Aug. 18, 2001.

Livingston threw in the low 90s early in his senior season of high school and had a chance to go late in the first round or early in the second. His velocity dipped to 86-87 before the draft, however, so the Mariners were able to take him in the fourth. While he's projectable at 6-foot-3 and 190 pounds, his fastball has inexplicably regressed. Livingston pitched anywhere from 81-87 mph in 2003. One Midwest League scout gave his fastball a 35 on the 20-80 scale for velocity, but 55 for sink and command. He's more concerned with location than radar guns. His changeup is a plus pitch, and between his curveball and slider he should come up with an average breaking ball. He's extremely poised and fearless. He doesn't miss as many bats as fellow finesse lefties Travis Blackley, Ryan Ketchner, Troy Cate and Glenn Bott, so Livingston probably will have to regain at least a little velocity to succeed at the upper levels. The hitter-friendly California League will test his pitchability in 2004.

Year	Club (League)	Class	W	L	ERA	G	GS	CG	SV	IP	H	R	ER	HR	BB	SO	AVG
2002	Everett (NWL)	A	6	5	3.02	15	14	0	0	80	80	33	27	2	14	76	.255
2003	Wisconsin (Mid)	A	15	7	2.73	26	26	1	0	178	176	72	54	10	28	105	.259
MINOR LEAGUE TOTALS			21	12	2.82	41	40	1	0	258	256	105	81	12	42	181	.258

29 Ryan Christianson, c

Born: April 21, 1981. **Ht.:** 6-2. **Wt.:** 210. **Bats:** R. **Throws:** R. **School:** Arlington HS, Riverside, Calif. **Career Transactions:** Selected by Mariners in first round (11th overall) of 1999 draft; signed July 18, 1999.

Yet another Mariners prospect felled by labrum surgery, Christianson hurt his shoulder in spring training and played in just four games last season. That was especially disappointing because it came on the heels of him missing two months in 2002 with a broken left foot. The 11th overall pick in 1999, Christianson has the potential to be an all-around catcher but has yet to deliver on it. Losing a year and a half of development time hasn't helped. He has natural power to all fields, but undermines himself by trying to pull and lift too many pitches. A more disciplined approach also would benefit him. Christianson has improved as a receiver and has a strong arm, but an inconsistent release affects his throws. He has below-average speed. Seattle expected Christianson to be ready for Opening Day and likely will send him to Double-A.

Year	Club (League)	Class	AVG	G	AB	R	H	2B	3B	HR	RBI	BB	SO	SB	SLG	OBP
1999	Mariners (AZL)	R	.263	11	38	3	10	8	0	0	7	2	12	2	.474	.300
	Everett (NWL)	A	.280	30	107	19	30	7	0	8	17	14	31	3	.570	.379
2000	Wisconsin (Mid)	A	.249	119	418	60	104	20	0	13	59	50	98	1	.390	.328
2001	San Bernardino (Cal)	A	.248	134	528	65	131	42	5	12	85	53	112	3	.415	.320
2002	San Antonio (TL)	AA	.253	52	190	20	48	11	0	5	17	16	36	0	.389	.317
	San Bernardino (Cal)	A	.282	21	71	12	20	5	1	1	8	4	17	1	.423	.346
2003	Mariners (AZL)	R	.200	4	10	0	2	0	0	0	2	2	3	0	.200	.333
MINOR LEAGUE TOTALS			.253	371	1362	179	345	93	6	39	195	141	309	10	.416	.328

30 Michael Wilson, of

Born: June 29, 1983. **Ht.:** 6-2. **Wt.:** 240. **Bats:** B. **Throws:** R. **School:** Booker T. Washington HS, Tulsa. **Career Transactions:** Selected by Mariners in second round of 2001 draft; signed July 16, 2001.

The Mariners signed two outfield/football prospects out of the 2001 draft. They gave Wilson $900,000 as a second-round pick, getting him to give up a scholarship to play linebacker at Oklahoma. Matthew Ware, a 21st-rounder, signed a deal that allowed him to play defensive back at UCLA. He'll likely be lost to the NFL as an early-round pick in April. Wilson is a classic high-risk, high-reward player. He's a switch-hitting center fielder with plus power and speed, but he's also raw. He had a disappointing pro debut in 2002 and had to repeat the Arizona League last year. His swing is a bit long and loopy, which makes it hard for him to make consistent contact. He feasts on mistakes and struggles against better pitching. Caught in half of his 12 steal attempts last year, Wilson will have to improve his reads and jumps to become a useful basestealer. He shows good range and an average arm in center. He did make strides in instructional league and should finally be ready for low Class A three years after being drafted.

Year	Club (League)	Class	AVG	G	AB	R	H	2B	3B	HR	RBI	BB	SO	SB	SLG	OBP
2002	Mariners (AZL)	R	.238	41	143	28	34	5	0	4	19	18	52	4	.357	.357
2003	Mariners (AZL)	R	.311	48	177	33	55	9	3	3	25	20	46	6	.446	.391
MINOR LEAGUE TOTALS			.278	89	320	61	89	14	3	7	44	38	98	10	.406	.375

TAMPA BAY
DEVIL RAYS

TOP 30 PROSPECTS

1. B.J. Upton, ss
2. Delmon Young, of
3. Doug Waechter, rhp
4. James Houser, lhp
5. Joey Gathright, of
6. Chad Gaudin, rhp
7. Wes Bankston, of
8. Seth McClung, rhp
9. Antonio Perez, 2b
10. Jonny Gomes, of
11. Pete LaForest, c
12. Elijah Dukes, of
13. Jason Pridie, of
14. Jon Switzer, lhp
15. Scott Autrey, rhp
16. Josh Hamilton, of
17. Chris Seddon, lhp
18. Jon Barratt, lhp
19. Shawn Riggans, c
20. Travis Schlichting, 3b
21. Chris Flinn, rhp
22. Carlos Hines, rhp
23. Jino Gonzalez, lhp
24. Brian Henderson, lhp
25. Alec Zumwalt, rhp
26. Shaun Cumberland, of
27. Matt Diaz, of
28. Nick DeBarr, rhp
29. Chad Orvella, rhp
30. Elliot Johnson, 2b

By Bill Ballew

If the future will ever come—and for many residents of St. Petersburg, the possibility is bleak—the Devil Rays could be on the verge of respectability, if not overwhelming success. While the franchise still seeks its first 70-win season, most of the moves the Rays have made after abandoning their ill-advised spending spree in the 1999-2000 offseason have been steps in the right direction.

Bringing Lou Piniella back home as manager gave the Rays a much-needed dose of credibility. Carl Crawford, Rocco Baldelli and Aubrey Huff survived on-the-job training in the major leagues to form the game's best young outfield. Despite being strapped for cash, Tampa Bay has signed the best prospect out of each of the last two drafts. In August, they made a huge addition to their front office by hiring former Blue Jays vice president of baseball operations Tim Wilken as a special assistant.

All the while, the team's administration has remained patient, laying the groundwork for future success even as last-place finishes continue to pile up. Losing at the major league level has had its rewards. Undaunted by high price tags, the Devil Rays used the No. 2 overall pick in 2002 on shortstop B.J. Upton and the No. 1 choice in 2003 on outfielder Delmon Young. They're among the best prospects in the game right now. Baldelli was the sixth overall selection

in 2000, while righthander Dewon Brazelton (No. 3 in 2001) seemed to have turned the corner at the end of the season and in the AFL.

The Rays have returned to the player-development roots that general manager Chuck LaMar pledged to plant nearly a decade ago. Tampa Bay already has developed at least one major league starter from every draft from 1997-2000 (Toby Hall, Huff, Crawford, Baldelli), a trend that should continue through each of the next three drafts (outfielders Joey Gathright, Jonny Gomes, Upton, Young). The result is a stocked organization that should continue to feed the big league club for the foreseeable future. The Devil Rays also are no longer living in the past, as they got rid of all their bad contracts by the end of the 2003 season.

And while Tampa Bay has yet to taste any big league success, its Triple-A Durham affiliate became the first International League team since 1991-92 to repeat as champions. That accomplishment, and those of Upton, Young and Co., helped make up for the disappointments of outfielder Josh Hamilton and righthander Matt White.

Hamilton, the No. 1 pick in the 1999 draft ahead of Josh Beckett, missed the entire season on personal leave. White, whose $10.2 million bonus in 1996 remains a baseball record for an amateur, had shoulder surgery for the second time in as many years and was removed from the 40-man roster.

ORGANIZATION
OVERVIEW

General manager: Chuck Lamar. **Farm and scouting director:** Cam Bonifay.

2003 PERFORMANCE

Class	Team	League	W	L	Pct.	Finish*	Manager
Majors	Tampa Bay	American	63	99	.389	13th (14)	Lou Piniella
Triple-A	Durham Bulls	International	73	67	.521	+5th (14)	Bill Evers
Double-A	Orlando Rays	Southern	65	72	.474	7th (10)	Charlie Montoyo
High A	Bakersfield Blaze	California	70	70	.500	8th (10)	Omer Munoz
Low A	Charleston RiverDogs	South Atlantic	77	62	.554	4th (16)	Mako Oliveras
Short-season	Hudson Valley Renegades	New York-Penn	37	37	.500	t-8th (14)	David Howard
Rookie	Princeton Devil Rays	Appalachian	23	41	.359	10th (10)	Jamie Nelson
OVERALL 2003 MINOR LEAGUE RECORD			345	349	.497	16th (30)	

*Finish in overall standings (No. of teams in league) + League champion

ORGANIZATIONAL LEADERS

BATTING
*Minimum 250 At-Bats

*AVG	Matt Diaz, Durham/Orlando	.391
R	John-Paul Davis, Orlando/Charleston	86
H	Matt Diaz, Durham/Orlando	170
TB	Matt Diaz, Durham/Orlando	254
2B	Ryan Jackson, Durham	45
3B	Jason Smith, Durham	14
HR	Vince Harrison, Charleston	19
RBI	Matt Diaz, Durham/Orlando	86
BB	B.J. Upton, Orlando/Charleston	73
SO	Jonny Gomes, Durham/Orlando	153
SB	Joey Gathright, Orlando/Bakersfield	69
*SLG	Pete LaForest, Durham/Orlando	.546
*OBP	Matt Diaz, Durham/Orlando	.419

PITCHING
#Minimum 75 Innings

W	Scott Autrey, Orlando/Charleston	14
L	Jason Cromer, Orlando/Charleston	14
#ERA	Chad Gaudin, Orlando/Bakersfield	1.81
G	Lee Gardner, Durham	57
	Carlos Hines, Orlando/Bakersfield/Charleston	57
CG	Five tied at	2
SV	Lee Gardner, Durham	30
IP	Scott Autrey, Orlando/Charleston	171
BB	Jim Magrane, Durham/Orlando	55
SO	Jose Veras, Durham/Orlando	121

BEST TOOLS

Best Hitter for Average	Delmon Young
Best Power Hitter	Delmon Young
Fastest Baserunner	Joey Gathright
Best Athlete	B.J. Upton
Best Fastball	Carlos Hines
Best Curveball	Seth McClung
Best Slider	Chad Gaudin
Best Changeup	Chris Seddon
Best Control	James Houser
Best Defensive Catcher	Dan Massiatte
Best Defensive Infielder	B.J. Upton
Best Infield Arm	B.J. Upton
Best Defensive Outfielder	Elijah Dukes
Best Outfield Arm	Delmon Young

PROJECTED 2007 LINEUP

Catcher	Toby Hall
First Base	Aubrey Huff
Second Base	Antonio Perez
Third Base	Travis Schlichting

Shortstop	B.J. Upton
Left Field	Carl Crawford
Center Field	Rocco Baldelli
Right Field	Delmon Young
Designated Hitter	Jose Cruz Jr.
No. 1 Starter	Doug Waechter
No. 2 Starter	Dewon Brazelton
No. 3 Starter	Victor Zambrano
No. 4 Starter	James Houser
No. 5 Starter	Seth McClung
Closer	Danys Baez

LAST YEAR'S TOP 20 PROSPECTS

1. Rocco Baldelli, of	11. Jason Standridge, rhp
2. Josh Hamilton, of	12. Jonny Gomes, of
3. B.J. Upton, ss	13. Chris Flinn, rhp
4. Dewon Brazelton, rhp	14. Chris Seddon, lhp
5. Seth McClung, rhp	15. Gerardo Garcia, rhp
6. Wes Bankston, of	16. Pete LaForest, c
7. Jon Switzer, lhp	17. Delvin James, rhp
8. Antonio Perez, ss/2b	18. Elijah Dukes, of
9. Jason Pridie, of	19. Shawn Riggans, c
10. Doug Waechter, rhp	20. Matt White, rhp

TOP PROSPECTS OF THE DECADE

1997	Matt White, rhp
1998	Matt White, rhp
1999	Matt White, rhp
2000	Josh Hamilton, of
2001	Josh Hamilton, of
2002	Josh Hamilton, of
2003	Rocco Baldelli, of

TOP DRAFT PICKS OF THE DECADE

1996	Paul Wilder, of
1997	Jason Standridge, rhp
1998	Josh Pressley, 1b (4)
1999	Rocco Baldelli, of
2000	Josh Hamilton, of
2001	Dewon Brazelton, rhp
2002	B.J. Upton, ss
2003	Delmon Young, of

ALL-TIME LARGEST BONUSES

Matt White, 1996	$10,200,000
Rolando Arrojo, 1997	$7,000,000
B.J. Upton, 2002	$4,600,000
Dewon Brazelton, 2001	$4,200,000
Josh Hamilton, 1999	$3,960,000

MINOR LEAGUE
DEPTH CHART

TAMPA BAY DEVIL RAYS   RANK: 9

Impact potential (A+): Rocco Baldelli injected life into the Rays' lineup as a rookie in 2003, and B.J. Upton and Delmon Young aren't too far from joining him as the franchise's nucleus. No organization can match Tampa Bay's 1-2 punch of elite position prospects.

Depth (C): While they've hit on recent premium picks to add frontline talent to the system, the Devil Rays' drafts have found depth by uncovering late-round gems (Joey Gathright, Chad Gaudin and Jonny Gomes). There is a shocking absence of international flavor, though.

Sleeper: Elijah Dukes, of.   *—Depth charts prepared by Josh Boyd. Numbers in parentheses indicate prospect rankings.*

LF
Jonny Gomes (10)
Elijah Dukes (12)
Shaun Cumberland (26)
Matt Diaz (27)
Joey Gomes
Matt Bowser
Blair Irvin

CF
Joey Gathright (5)
Jason Pridie (13)
Luis Mateo

RF
Delmon Young (2)
Wes Bankston (7)
Josh Hamilton (16)
Matt Rico

3B
Travis Schlichting (20)
Juan Salas
Vince Harrison

SS
B.J. Upton (1)
Jorge Cantu
Jace Brewer
Aneudi Cuevas
Matthew Maniscalo
Luis De Paula

2B
Antonio Perez (9)
Elliot Johnson (30)
Fernando Cortez

1B
Aaron Clark

SOURCE OF TALENT

Homegrown		Acquired	
College	6	Trade	1
Junior College	2	Rule 5 draft	1
Draft-and-follow	2	Independent	0
High school	15	Free agent/waivers	2
Nondrafted free agent	1		
Foreign	0		

C
Pete LaForest (11)
Shawn Riggans (19)
Dan Massiatte

RHP

Starters	Relievers
Doug Waechter (3)	Carlos Hines (22)
Chad Gaudin (6)	Alec Zumwalt (25)
Seth McClung (8)	Chad Orvella (29)
Scott Autrey (15)	Josh Parker
Chris Flinn (21)	Jose Veras
Nick DeBarr (28)	Bartolome Fortunato
Jamie Shields	Romelio Lopez
Brian Stokes	Austin Coose
Matt White	Mark Comolli
	Tim Corcoran

LHP

Starters	Relievers
James Houser (4)	Jon Barratt (18)
Jon Switzer (14)	Brian Henderson (24)
Chris Seddon (17)	Bobby Seay
Jino Gonzalez (23)	
Brandon Mann	
Joe Little	

DRAFT
ANALYSIS

Best Pro Debut: Primarily a shortstop at North Carolina State, RHP Chad Orvella (13) put up eight saves, 12 scoreless innings and a 15-1 strikeout-walk ratio in the short-season New York-Penn League. LHP Joe Little (26) went 4-0, 0.29 in five NY-P starts to earn a promotion to high Class A.

Best Athlete: OF Shaun Cumberland (10) is the purest athlete but is raw as a baseball player. 3B Travis Schlichting (4) has plus power and arm strength.

Best Pure Hitter: OF Delmon Young (1) went No. 1 overall because of his hitting prowess.

Best Raw Power: Young hits 450-foot bombs in batting practice and keeps the power turned on once the game starts.

Fastest Runner: Cooper and SS Brandon Rousseve (45) have 6.6-second speed in the 60-yard dash.

Best Defensive Player: The Devil Rays think they got several premium gloves in Schlichting, C Christian Lopez (6), SS Matthew Maniscalco (8) and Rousseve.

Best Fastball: Orvella already throws 94-95 mph and could add velocity now that he'll be given time to hone his craft. LHP Jon Barratt (5) may have the quickest arm in the entire draft and he reaches 93 mph.

Best Breaking Ball: LHP James Houser (2) and Barratt have good curveballs. Houser is more projectable at 6-foot-5 and shows three plus pitches at times.

Little

Most Intriguing Background: Young and his brother Dmitri, an all-star with the Tigers, are the highest-drafted siblings in draft history. Dmitri went fourth overall to the Cardinals in 1991. Unsigned OF Rod Allen Jr.'s (22) father got 50 big league at-bats and is the color analyst on Detroit telecasts. RHP Brent Speigner's (50) brother Levale, also a righty, was the Twins' 14th-rounder.

Closest To The Majors: Young's bat should get him to Tampa Bay by the end of 2005.

Best Late-Round Pick: Orvella has the chance to be a set-up man.

The One Who Got Away: LHP Andrew Miller (3) and RHP Jared Hughes (16) each ranked as the nation's top high school prospect at one point during the year leading up to the draft. Miller became the highest-drafted player not to sign and went to North Carolina, while Hughes went to Santa Clara. South Florida RHP Casey Hudspeth (21) and Alabama LHP Wade LeBlanc (36) also will be coveted picks in 2006.

Assessment: Young is a safer bet to produce than Tampa Bay's No. 1 overall pick in 1999, Josh Hamilton. The Devil Rays upgraded their lefthanded pitching significantly with Houser, Barratt, Brian Henderson (7), Gangi, Little and draft-and-follow Rejino Gonzalez (46 in 2002).

2002 DRAFT — GRADE: A

SS B.J. Upton (1) is "A" material all by himself, and OFs Wes Bankston (4), Elijah Dukes (3) and Jason Pridie (2) are prospects as well. Unsigned RHP Mike Pelfrey (15) and LHP Mark Romanczuk (5) look like 2005 first-rounders.

2001 DRAFT — GRADE: B

RHP Dewon Brazelton (1) showed signs of coming around at the end of 2003. Joey Gathright (32), RHP Chad Gaudin (34) and OF Jonny Gomes (18) were late-round steals. The Devil Rays also like LHP Jon Switzer (2), but would have helped themselves by signing RHPs David Bush (4), Thomas Diamond (38) and Eric Beattie (47).

2000 DRAFT — GRADE: A

OF Rocco Baldelli (1) went from high school in Rhode Island to center field in Tampa Bay in just over two years. The Rays didn't pick again until the fifth round and got little else.

1999 DRAFT — GRADE: B

Whether OF Josh Hamilton (1), the No. 1 overall pick, can conquer his personal demons and make good on his promise remains to be seen. OF Carl Crawford (2) beat him to the majors, as have RHPs Doug Waechter (3) and Seth McClung (5).

—Draft analysis prepared by Jim Callis. Numbers in parentheses indicate draft rounds.

B.J. Upton

Born: Aug. 21, 1984.
Ht.: 6-3. **Wt.:** 170.
Bats: R. **Throws:** R.
School: Greenbrier Christian Academy, Chesapeake, Va.
Career Transactions: Selected by Devil Rays in first round (second overall) of 2002 draft; signed Sept. 16, 2002.

The No. 2 overall pick in the 2002 draft, Upton may not even end up as the highest-drafted player in his family. Younger brother Justin, a high school junior, is a candidate to go first in the 2005 draft. By then, B.J. likely will be starting for the Devil Rays at shortstop—at age 20. After signing for a $4.6 million bonus in September 2002, Upton made his pro debut last year at low Class A Charleston. After looking overmatched in April, Upton made adjustments and hit .411 in July to earn a two-step promotion to Double-A Orlando. He showed the Devil Rays everything they could have hoped for and was named the top prospect in the low Class A South Atlantic League as well as the Arizona Fall League. You could make a case for Upton as the top prospect in the minor leagues.

Upton is one of the few players who truly possesses five plus tools. His arm strength and speed grade close to 80 on the 20-80 scouting scale, and his bat speed is easily a 70. He's a poised hitter with an excellent idea of what he wants to accomplish at the plate, and he's capable of driving the ball to all fields. He showed the ability to work counts, even after his jump to Double-A, drawing an organization-high 73 walks. Considering his wiry frame, he has surprising raw power. Upton has enough pop to eventually hit 30 homers on an annual basis. Within the organization, only blazer Joey Gathright can top his baserunning talents. Defensively, Upton's range and quickness are unparalleled, and his footwork is outstanding. He's aggressive in the field and on the basepaths, and considers virtually any ball he can reach to be an out. Upton led the minors with 56 errors. Many came when he either sat back too long on grounders or tried to make difficult plays with his cannon arm. He worked on his footwork and double-play feeds to the second baseman in the AFL. By charging more balls, Upton should improve his defense and become an all-around star. The only other thing he needs is experience. He should continue to improve because of his athleticism and work ethic.

Upton is cruising along the fast track to the majors. The Rays have been looking for a cornerstone shortstop since day one—remember when they traded Bobby Abreu for Kevin Stocker?—and haven't found one. Their wait should end in the near future with Upton. Tampa Bay hasn't been shy about giving such players as Carl Crawford and Rocco Baldelli jobs in the big leagues before they were completely ready, and that could be the case with Upton as well. Unless he struggles at Double-A Montgomery or Triple-A Durham, he should make his debut at Tropicana Field at some point in 2004. It's not unrealistic to pencil him in as the Rays' starting shortstop on Opening Day 2005.

Year	Club (League)	Class	AVG	G	AB	R	H	2B	3B	HR	RBI	BB	SO	SB	SLG	OBP
2003	Charleston, SC (SAL)	A	.302	101	384	70	116	22	6	7	46	57	80	38	.445	.394
	Orlando (SL)	AA	.276	29	105	14	29	8	0	1	16	16	25	2	.381	.376
MINOR LEAGUE TOTALS			.297	130	489	84	145	30	6	8	62	73	105	40	.431	.390

Delmon Young, of

Born: Sept. 14, 1985. **Ht.:** 6-3. **Wt.:** 205. **Bats:** R. **Throws:** R. **School:** Camarillo (Calif.) HS. **Career Transactions:** Selected by Devil Rays in first round (first overall) of 2003 draft; signed Sept. 8, 2003.

The first overall pick in the 2003 draft, Young received $3.7 million as part of a guaranteed major league contract worth at least $5.8 million. The younger brother of Dmitri Young, the fourth overall pick in 1991, Delmon signed too late to play in the regular season. He showed advanced skills in the Arizona Fall League, where he batted .417/.451/.625 in 15 games. Young has an impressive combination of natural baseball ability and an old-school work ethic. He had the most raw power in the 2003 draft, and was the best pure hitter among high school players. He's a good defender with a plus arm that will allow him to man right field in the majors. His speed is his worst tool, but it's average now and won't hold him back when he gets stronger and slows down. He was a bit overaggressive in the AFL, though it didn't hurt his performance and may just have been the result of being anxious to play. Upon signing, the ever-confident Young predicted he would be in the big leagues by 2005. He upped that projection to 2004 during his stint in the AFL. A September callup after strong showings in Class A and/or Double-A this summer is a strong possibility.

Year	Club (League)	Class	AVG	G	AB	R	H	2B	3B	HR	RBI	BB	SO	SB	SLG	OBP
2003	Did Not Play—Signed 2004 Contract															

Doug Waechter, rhp

Born: Jan. 28, 1981. **Ht.:** 6-4. **Wt.:** 200. **Bats:** R. **Throws:** R. **School:** Northeast HS, St. Petersburg, Fla. **Career Transactions:** Selected by Devil Rays in third round of 1999 draft; signed June 27, 1999.

One of the nation's top high school quarterbacks in 1999, Waechter gave up a football scholarship from South Florida to turn pro for $500,000. In his first big league start last year, he shut out the Mariners with a two-hitter. Waechter has matured into a quality pitcher. He has a fine arm, tremendous makeup and the durability to become a workhorse. His command has steadily improved over the past two years. He moves his 88-94 mph fastball around in the strike zone and has a good slider with a late break. His focus and even-keel approach to pitching are off the charts. An improved changeup would do wonders for Waechter's ability to succeed the second and third time he goes through a lineup. With his tall frame, he must keep his mechanics in check. The St. Petersburg product has a chance to make a major impact on the organization. He'll be a strong candidate for the Tampa Bay rotation this spring.

Year	Club (League)	Class	W	L	ERA	G	GS	CG	SV	IP	H	R	ER	HR	BB	SO	AVG
1999	Princeton (Appy)	R	0	5	9.77	11	7	0	0	35	46	45	38	2	35	38	.317
2000	Hudson Valley (NY-P)	A	4	4	2.35	14	14	2	0	73	53	23	19	2	37	58	.205
2001	Charleston, SC (SAL)	A	8	11	4.34	26	26	1	0	153	179	97	74	14	38	107	.285
2002	Charleston, SC (SAL)	A	3	3	3.47	7	7	0	0	36	39	20	14	2	16	36	.277
	Bakersfield (Cal)	A	6	3	2.66	17	17	0	0	108	114	43	32	9	29	101	.267
	Orlando (SL)	AA	1	3	9.00	4	4	1	0	18	27	20	18	4	13	18	.338
2003	Orlando (SL)	AA	5	3	4.13	13	12	0	0	76	74	39	35	6	19	45	.257
	Durham (IL)	AAA	3	3	3.33	10	10	0	0	51	51	25	19	9	12	35	.262
	Tampa Bay (AL)	MAJ	3	2	3.31	6	5	1	0	35	29	13	13	4	15	29	.225
MAJOR LEAGUE TOTALS			3	2	3.31	6	5	1	0	35	29	13	13	4	15	29	.225
MINOR LEAGUE TOTALS			30	35	4.06	102	97	4	0	551	583	312	249	48	199	438	.270

James Houser, lhp

Born: Dec. 15, 1984. **Ht.:** 6-4. **Wt.:** 185. **Bats:** L. **Throws:** L. **School:** Sarasota (Fla.) HS. **Career Transactions:** Selected by Devil Rays in second round of 2003 draft; signed June 17, 2003.

Houser was a potential first-rounder who slid to the top of the second round. His velocity was down during the spring, and he has a heart murmur that concerned some clubs. After signing for $900,000, he ranked as the No. 4 prospect in the Rookie-level Appalachian League. Houser lived in the strike zone last summer at Princeton. He throws from a three-quarters slot with the potential to have three plus pitches, including a low-90s fastball, changeup and two versions of a curveball. He throws one curve inside against left-handers, and another over-the-top curve that breaks straight down and back-doors righties.

Well-coached as an amateur, Houser takes instruction well, but he sometimes worries too much about the intricacies of pitching instead of letting his ability take over. He still needs better feel and more consistency with his curveballs. By signing Houser, the Rays were able to justify wasting a third-round pick on high school lefty Andrew Miller, who had first-round talent but was considered unsignable and chose to attend North Carolina. Houser should jump to low Class A in 2004.

Year	Club (League)	Class	W	L	ERA	G	GS	CG	SV	IP	H	R	ER	HR	BB	SO	AVG
2003	Princeton (Appy)	R	0	4	3.73	10	10	0	0	41	43	23	17	1	13	44	.262
MINOR LEAGUE TOTALS			0	4	3.73	10	10	0	0	41	43	23	17	1	13	44	.262

5 Joey Gathright, of

Born: April 27, 1981. **Ht.:** 5-10. **Wt.:** 170. **Bats:** L. **Throws:** R. **School:** Bonnabal HS, Metairie, La. **Career Transactions:** Selected by Devil Rays in 32nd round of 2001 draft; signed Aug. 29, 2001.

The Rays' 2003 minor league player of the year, Gathright topped the system in stolen bases and ranked second in batting before a dislocated left shoulder brought his season to an early end. The injury cost him a September callup and a possible spot on the U.S. Olympic qualifying team. Possibly the fastest player in the minors, Gathright is more polished than most burners. He's a disciplined hitter with solid strike-zone judgment, and he already shows on-base ability to go with his leadoff speed. With his athleticism, Gathright can leap cars, from front to end. Though he was successful on 69 of his 85 attempts, Gathright still is learning the nuances of stealing bases. His power is minimal, though he's adept at making hard contact. His first two pro seasons have been cut short by dislocated left shoulders. That's his non-throwing shoulder, but his arm is below-average. After surgery to repair a torn labrum, Gathright resumed workouts in December and should be fine in 2004. He'll open in Double-A or Triple-A, and should reach the majors by season's end.

Year	Club (League)	Class	AVG	G	AB	R	H	2B	3B	HR	RBI	BB	SO	SB	SLG	OBP
2002	Charleston, SC (SAL)	A	.264	59	208	30	55	1	0	0	14	21	36	22	.269	.360
2003	Bakersfield (Cal)	A	.324	89	340	65	110	6	3	0	23	41	54	57	.359	.406
	Orlando (SL)	AA	.376	22	85	12	32	1	0	0	5	5	15	12	.388	.419
MINOR LEAGUE TOTALS			.311	170	633	107	197	8	3	0	42	67	105	91	.333	.392

6 Chad Gaudin, rhp

Born: March 24, 1983. **Ht.:** 5-10. **Wt.:** 160. **Bats:** R. **Throws:** R. **School:** Crescent City Baptist HS, Metairie, La. **Career Transactions:** Selected by Devil Rays in 34th round of 2001 draft; signed Aug. 23, 2001.

Gaudin had a whirlwind season, starting at high Class A Bakersfield. Promoted to Double-A in mid-July, he tossed a perfect game in his first start and was in Tampa Bay by August. He was more aggressive pitching in relief, posting a 3.16 ERA in that role for the Rays. Gaudin shows no fear on the mound. He goes right after hitters and is willing to throw his cutting slider at any time in the count. Hitters have difficulty picking up the spin on his slider. His fastball has excellent movement, including good sinking action that runs away from righthanders. His changeup is average. Gaudin doesn't have ideal size and doesn't generate much downhill plane on his pitches. He is primarily a two-pitch pitcher, though he can vary speeds from 86-92 mph. He was more tentative and struggled with his command in his three big league starts. Based on his performance and the team's needs, Gaudin could be a mainstay in the Tampa Bay bullpen this season. He projects as a middle reliever.

Year	Club (League)	Class	W	L	ERA	G	GS	CG	SV	IP	H	R	ER	HR	BB	SO	AVG
2002	Charleston, SC (SAL)	A	4	6	2.26	26	17	0	1	119	106	43	30	5	37	106	.244
2003	Bakersfield (Cal)	A	5	3	2.13	14	14	1	0	80	63	23	19	2	23	70	.214
	Orlando (SL)	AA	2	0	0.47	3	3	1	0	19	8	1	1	0	3	23	.131
	Tampa Bay (AL)	MAJ	2	0	3.60	15	3	0	0	40	37	18	16	4	16	23	.240
MAJOR LEAGUE TOTALS			2	0	3.60	15	3	0	0	40	37	18	16	4	16	23	.240
MINOR LEAGUE TOTALS			11	9	2.06	43	34	2	1	219	177	67	50	7	63	199	.224

7 Wes Bankston, of

Born: Nov. 23, 1983. **Ht.:** 6-4. **Wt.:** 200. **Bats:** R. **Throws:** R. **School:** Plano East HS, Plano, Texas. **Career Transactions:** Selected by Devil Rays in fourth round of 2002 draft; signed June 17, 2002.

Bankston led the Appalachian League with 18 homers and 57 RBIs in his 2002 pro debut, but he battled a wrist injury and tailed off in the second half of 2003. Bankston is a prototype right fielder, with plus arm strength and budding power. He could blossom into a 30-homer, 100-RBI man in the majors. He's selectively aggressive at the plate and improved his discipline last year. He's an average runner with good mobility on the bases and in the outfield. His swing is a little long, and Bankston goes through stretches when he doesn't make consistent contact. After batting .192 with three homers in the last two months of the 2003 season, he'll have to get stronger. His biggest problem may be the logjam of outfielders in the organization. With so many good young players ahead of him on the depth chart, Bankston may not have a place to play in Tampa Bay. Bankston could move to first base, where he played five games last year, but Aubrey Huff may move there at the major league level. The Rays have no reason to rush Bankston. At 20, he'll be one of the high Class A California League's younger players in 2004.

Year	Club (League)	Class	AVG	G	AB	R	H	2B	3B	HR	RBI	BB	SO	SB	SLG	OBP
2002	Princeton (Appy)	R	.301	62	246	48	74	10	1	18	57	18	46	2	.569	.346
	Hudson Valley (NY-P)	A	.303	8	33	2	10	1	0	0	1	0	6	1	.333	.294
2003	Charleston, SC (SAL)	A	.256	103	375	46	96	18	1	12	60	53	94	2	.405	.346
MINOR LEAGUE TOTALS			.275	173	654	96	180	29	2	30	118	71	146	5	.463	.344

8 Seth McClung, rhp

Born: Feb. 7, 1981. **Ht.:** 6-6. **Wt.:** 230. **Bats:** R. **Throws:** R. **School:** Greenbrier East HS, Lewisburg, W.Va. **Career Transactions:** Selected by Devil Rays in fifth round of 1999 draft; signed June 21, 1999.

McClung opened the season in the Tampa Bay bullpen before moving into the rotation in late April. It was feast or famine as a starter, as he pitched well in three starts and got bombed in two others. His season ended in May when he tore an elbow ligament, and he had Tommy John surgery on June 26. McClung is a power pitcher with good command of his mid-90s fastball. He also throws a hard curveball with tight spin. Manager Lou Piniella liked McClung's aggressiveness. He was fined in early May for intentionally throwing at Bobby Kielty. In addition to making a comeback from ligament-replacement surgery, McClung must improve his control in order to have consistent success in the major leagues. The depth and fade of his changeup need to improve in order to give him a solid third pitch. If that doesn't happen, his future could be as a closer. The Rays hope McClung can resume pitching in the minor leagues by early June. He's determined not to rush his return, though that is contrary to his personality. If all goes well, he could be back in the big leagues during the second half of the 2004 season.

Year	Club (League)	Class	W	L	ERA	G	GS	CG	SV	IP	H	R	ER	HR	BB	SO	AVG
1999	Princeton (Appy)	R	2	4	7.69	13	10	0	0	46	53	47	39	3	48	46	.285
2000	Hudson Valley (NY-P)	A	2	2	1.85	8	8	0	0	44	37	18	9	0	17	38	.227
	Charleston, SC (SAL)	A	2	1	3.19	6	6	0	0	31	30	14	11	0	19	26	.246
2001	Charleston, SC (SAL)	A	10	11	2.79	28	28	2	0	164	142	72	51	6	53	165	.231
2002	Bakersfield (Cal)	A	3	2	2.92	7	7	0	0	37	35	16	12	1	11	48	.243
	Orlando (SL)	AA	5	7	5.37	20	19	0	0	114	138	74	68	12	53	64	.299
2003	Tampa Bay (AL)	MAJ	4	1	5.35	12	5	0	0	39	33	23	23	6	25	25	.241
MAJOR LEAGUE TOTALS			4	1	5.35	12	5	0	0	39	33	23	23	6	25	25	.241
MINOR LEAGUE TOTALS			24	27	3.93	82	78	2	0	436	435	241	190	22	201	387	.257

9 Antonio Perez, 2b

Born: Jan. 26, 1980. **Ht.:** 5-11. **Wt.:** 170. **Bats:** R. **Throws:** R. **Career Transactions:** Signed out of Dominican Republic by Reds, March 21, 1998 . . . Traded by Reds with RHP Jake Meyer, OF Mike Cameron and RHP Brett Tomko to Mariners for OF Ken Griffey, Jr., Feb. 10, 2000 . . . Traded by Mariners to Devil Rays for OF Randy Winn, Oct. 28, 2002.

Perez came from Seattle with manager Lou Piniella in a trade for Randy Winn in October 2002. His progress had been stalled by wrist injuries the previous two seasons, but Perez stayed healthy in 2003 and spent the second half of the year in the majors. He played regularly in July, then slumped in August and saw little time in September. Perez is a capable defensive shortstop who could be a star at second base. He has soft hands, a strong arm and good instincts. He has excellent range for the position. While his power is good for a middle infielder, he's best slapping the ball into the gaps and hitting for average. He has above-average speed. Perez doesn't get good jumps or show good instincts on the bases, which limits his running and basestealing ability. He'll have to make more contact to hit effectively in the majors. With Marlon Anderson gone to the Cardinals, Perez is the frontrunner for the starting second-base job in Tampa Bay. He has no long-term competition at the position.

Year	Club (League)	Class	AVG	G	AB	R	H	2B	3B	HR	RBI	BB	SO	SB	SLG	OBP
1998	Reds (DSL)	R	.255	63	212	57	54	11	0	2	24	53	33	58	.335	.408
1999	Rockford (Mid)	A	.288	119	385	69	111	20	3	7	41	43	80	35	.410	.376
2000	Lancaster (Cal)	A	.276	98	395	90	109	36	6	17	63	58	99	28	.527	.376
2001	San Antonio (TL)	AA	.143	5	21	3	3	0	0	0	0	0	7	0	.143	.143
2002	San Antonio (TL)	AA	.258	72	240	30	62	8	2	2	24	11	64	15	.333	.312
	Mariners (AZL)	R	.333	6	15	3	5	1	0	1	3	4	2	4	.600	.476
2003	Orlando (SL)	AA	.272	24	81	16	22	5	1	2	10	18	18	3	.432	.423
	Durham (IL)	AAA	.284	34	134	27	38	12	2	6	20	10	38	3	.537	.345
	Tampa Bay (AL)	MAJ	.248	48	125	19	31	6	1	2	12	18	34	4	.360	.345
MAJOR LEAGUE TOTALS			.248	48	125	19	31	6	1	2	12	18	34	4	.360	.345
MINOR LEAGUE TOTALS			.272	421	1483	295	404	93	14	37	185	197	341	146	.429	.370

10 Jonny Gomes, of

Born: Nov. 22, 1980. **Ht.:** 6-1. **Wt.:** 200. **Bats:** R. **Throws:** R. **School:** Santa Rosa (Calif.) CC. **Career Transactions:** Selected by Devil Rays in 18th round of 2001 draft; signed June 13, 2001.

After suffering a mild heart attack in December 2002, Gomes recovered to make his big league debut last September, doubling off David Wells in his first at-bat. He tied for second in the system with 17 homers and continued to slug in the Arizona Fall League, where he nearly earned a spot on the U.S. Olympic qualifying team. His brother Joey is also a power-hitting outfielder in the Rays organization. An aggressive hitter, Gomes hits the ball with authority. He has plus power from left field to right-center. He runs well in the outfield and on the bases. Gomes must continue to refine his approach in order to make more consistent contact. His defense is rough, but it's not from a lack of effort. If he played football, Gomes would be described as having a non-stop motor. His arm strength will keep him in left field. Gomes' strong AFL showing will help his chances of sticking in the big leagues in 2004. He may need time in Triple-A, but he could crack the Tampa Bay lineup as a DH at some point this year.

Year	Club (League)	Class	AVG	G	AB	R	H	2B	3B	HR	RBI	BB	SO	SB	SLG	OBP
2001	Princeton (Appy)	R	.291	62	206	58	60	11	2	16	44	33	73	15	.597	.442
2002	Bakersfield (Cal)	A	.278	134	446	102	124	24	9	30	72	91	173	15	.574	.432
2003	Orlando (SL)	AA	.249	120	442	68	110	28	3	17	56	53	148	23	.441	.348
	Durham (IL)	AAA	.316	5	19	2	6	2	1	0	1	2	5	0	.526	.435
	Tampa Bay (AL)	MAJ	.133	8	15	1	2	1	0	0	0	0	6	0	.200	.188
MAJOR LEAGUE TOTALS			.133	8	15	1	2	1	0	0	0	0	6	0	.200	.188
MINOR LEAGUE TOTALS			.270	321	1113	230	300	65	15	63	173	179	399	53	.525	.403

11 Pete LaForest, c

Born: Jan. 27, 1978. **Ht.:** 6-2. **Wt.:** 200. **Bats:** L. **Throws:** R. **School:** Gatineau (Quebec) HS. **Career Transactions:** Selected by Expos in 16th round of 1995 draft; signed June 5, 1995 . . . Contract voided, Aug. 15, 1995 . . . Signed by Devil Rays, May 10, 1997.

LaForest's season got off to a bad start when visa problems caused him to miss his first major league camp as well as the first six weeks of the regular season. He originally signed with the Expos as a 16th-round pick out of a Quebec high school in 1995, only to have the contract voided because of a pre-existing injury. The Devil Rays spotted him at Fort Scott, Kan., Community College and signed him two years later. But a Tampa Bay official told him to use his student visa rather than wait for a proper work visa, and U.S. immigration authorities caught LaForest. He was banned from entering the United States but has received a special-exemption waiver every year. However, the Immigration and Naturalization Service lost his paperwork before the 2003 season, leading to a lengthy delay. LaForest led the Double-A Southern League in homers in 2002 and his bat will determine how long he plays in the big leagues. He has good power from the left side and draws a good amount of walks. He hit .292 with three homers as Canada finished second at the Olympic qualifying tournament in November, earning a berth in the Athens Games. LaForest has a big swing and strikes out a lot, the main reason he never has hit better than .275 at any of his stops in the minors. LaForest is still developing behind the plate, where he moved from third base in 2000. He threw out just 15 percent of basestealers last year and also needs to improve his receiving and game-calling skills. He might be better suited to be a DH/first baseman/backup catcher than a regular backstop. With the Rays signing Brook Fordyce in the offseason, LaForest probably will return to Triple-A to begin 2004.

Year	Club (League)	Class	AVG	G	AB	R	H	2B	3B	HR	RBI	BB	SO	SB	SLG	OBP
1995	Expos (GCL)	R	.000	2	6	1	0	0	0	0	0	2	4	0	.000	.250
1996	Did not play															
1997	Devil Rays (GCL)	R	.262	34	107	21	28	7	2	3	21	10	18	4	.449	.328
1998	Princeton (Appy)	R	.275	25	91	18	25	7	1	2	14	12	18	4	.440	.365
1999	Charleston, SC (SAL)	A	.256	125	445	64	114	21	3	13	53	55	97	9	.404	.343
2000	St. Petersburg (FSL)	A	.270	129	474	85	128	28	7	14	70	56	108	7	.447	.351
2001	Orlando (SL)	AA	.095	7	21	3	2	0	0	1	1	5	9	0	.238	.269
2002	Orlando (SL)	AA	.270	106	359	57	97	18	1	20	64	60	94	9	.493	.374
	Durham (IL)	AAA	.258	17	66	7	17	3	0	3	15	3	28	0	.439	.290
2003	Orlando (SL)	AA	.250	21	72	9	18	8	0	3	15	16	17	0	.486	.385
	Durham (IL)	AAA	.269	61	201	40	54	14	2	14	38	36	56	2	.567	.382
	Tampa Bay (AL)	MAJ	.167	19	48	0	8	2	0	0	6	1	14	0	.208	.196
MAJOR LEAGUE TOTALS			.167	19	48	0	8	2	0	0	6	1	14	0	.208	.196
MINOR LEAGUE TOTALS			.262	527	1842	305	483	106	16	73	291	255	449	30	.456	.355

12 Elijah Dukes, of

Born: June 26, 1984. **Ht.:** 6-2. **Wt.:** 220. **Bats:** B. **Throws:** R. **School:** Hillsborough HS, Tampa. **Career Transactions:** Selected by Devil Rays in third round of 2002 draft; signed Aug. 21, 2002.

Dukes, who turned down a North Carolina State football scholarship to sign for $500,000, is as pure an athlete as there is in the minor leagues. To the surprise of many scouts, his baseball skills are catching up rapidly with his physical abilities. The Devil Rays pushed Dukes by sending him to low Class A for his initial taste of pro ball, and his lack of experience was evident early. Dukes was unable to sniff contact with a breaking ball until August and made several mistakes on line drives in the outfield. He started to settle down as he gained experience, and he made big impressions when he had success. His first home run was a Ruthian blast over the center-field wall at Hagerstown. Displaying his plus speed, he showed extreme aggressiveness on the basepaths by going from first to third on everything hit to the outfield. He also swiped 33 bases despite having virtually no idea of basestealing fundamentals. His arm strength is outstanding, and he has become the best defensive outfielder in the organization. While he has plus power and some idea of the strike zone, Dukes needs more discipline to cut down on his whiffs. His makeup, which was a concern when he was an amateur, still needs fine-tuning. He was ejected from more games and got into verbal confrontations with hecklers. There's a chance he could return to low Class A this year.

Year	Club (League)	Class	AVG	G	AB	R	H	2B	3B	HR	RBI	BB	SO	SB	SLG	OBP
2003	Charleston, SC (SAL)	A	.245	117	383	51	94	17	4	7	53	45	130	33	.366	.338
MINOR LEAGUE TOTALS			.245	117	383	51	94	17	4	7	53	45	130	33	.366	.338

13 Jason Pridie, of

Born: Oct. 9, 1983. **Ht.:** 6-1. **Wt.:** 180. **Bats:** L. **Throws:** R. **School:** Prescott (Ariz.) HS. **Career Transactions:** Selected by Devil Rays in second round of 2002 draft; signed June 12, 2002.

Pridie discovered how exhausting a first full pro season can be. After leading all short-season players in hits in his pro debut, he was dragging by the end of 2003 and saw his average drop 106 points. The younger brother of Twins minor league righthander Jon Pridie, Jason is a natural hitter with good balance at the plate and above-average power to the opposite field. He tinkered with his swing throughout last season before settling on the same smooth stroke that got him into pro ball. His speed is another plus, and he has excellent instincts and aggressivenss on the basepaths and in center field. His strong arm, which threw low-90s fastballs in high school, is yet another asset. In addition to adding some overall strength, much of which will come with maturity, Pridie needs to handle the ups and downs a little better. He's his own worst critic and tends to get down on himself, which can lead to extended slumps at the plate. Pridie also needs to make better contact against breaking balls and improve his overall plate discipline. He went 27 straight games without a walk, something a potential leadoff hitter can't do. That said, Pridie is making progress and will take the next step up the ladder to high Class A in 2004.

Year	Club (League)	Class	AVG	G	AB	R	H	2B	3B	HR	RBI	BB	SO	SB	SLG	OBP
2002	Princeton (Appy)	R	.368	67	285	60	105	12	9	7	33	19	35	13	.547	.410
	Hudson Valley (NY-P)	A	.344	8	32	4	11	1	1	1	1	3	6	0	.531	.400
2003	Charleston, SC (SAL)	A	.260	128	530	75	138	28	10	7	48	30	113	26	.391	.302
MINOR LEAGUE TOTALS			.300	203	847	139	254	41	20	15	82	52	154	39	.449	.342

14 Jon Switzer, lhp

Born: Aug. 13, 1979. **Ht.:** 6-3. **Wt.:** 190. **Bats:** L. **Throws:** L. **School:** Arizona State University. **Career Transactions:** Selected by Devil Rays in second round of 2001 draft; signed Aug. 13, 2001.

Switzer roomed with Dewon Brazelton while with Team USA in 2000 and could join him in the big league rotation at some point this year after impressing Devil Rays manager Lou Piniella last August. After finishing strong in Double-A to earn a brief taste of the majors, Switzer pitched well in Triple-A and fanned 11 while winning the opener of the International League finals. He has good mound presence and commands a lively 88-92 mph fastball. He threw with a stiff wrist at Arizona State but has developed a sharp, late-breaking slider as a pro. His changeup, which was his third pitch last year in spring training, also has shown considerable progress and now possesses excellent depth and fade. The change is a vital pitch for him against righthanders, who teed off on him for a .476 average in the majors. Tampa Bay acquired lefties John Halama and Mark Hendrickson this offseason, increasing the chances that Switzer will begin 2004 in Triple-A.

Year	Club (League)	Class	W	L	ERA	G	GS	CG	SV	IP	H	R	ER	HR	BB	SO	AVG
2001	Hudson Valley (NY-P)	A	2	0	0.63	5	0	0	0	14	9	3	1	0	2	20	.173
2002	Bakersfield (Cal)	A	7	5	4.27	20	20	0	0	103	108	55	49	8	26	129	.269
2003	Orlando (SL)	AA	8	8	3.43	22	22	2	0	126	117	63	48	10	32	100	.246
	Tampa Bay (AL)	MAJ	0	0	7.45	5	0	0	0	10	13	8	8	2	3	7	.342
	Durham (IL)	AAA	1	0	1.80	1	1	0	0	5	6	1	1	1	0	3	.316
MAJOR LEAGUE TOTALS			0	0	7.45	5	0	0	0	10	13	8	8	2	3	7	.342
MINOR LEAGUE TOTALS			18	13	3.58	48	43	2	0	249	240	122	99	19	60	252	.253

15 Scott Autrey, rhp

Born: Jan. 26, 1981. **Ht.:** 6-2. **Wt.:** 210. **Bats:** R. **Throws:** R. **School:** University of North Carolina. **Career Transactions:** Selected by Devil Rays in seventh round of 2002 draft; signed June 22, 2002.

Undrafted out of high school, Autrey has made rapid progress since signing out of North Carolina. The Devil Rays named him their minor league pitcher of the year after he set an organization record with 14 victories in his first full pro season. Autrey made significant improvements with his confidence last year, both in himself as well as with his pitches. He no longer tried to strike out every batter, as he did in his pro debut. He started getting ahead in the count with his low-90s fastball, then mixing in his slider and changeup. He throws all three pitches for strikes, moves his offerings inside and out, and does an excellent job of keeping his pitches down in the strike zone. The Rays also like Autrey's bulldog mentality and his work ethic. He hasn't missed many bats in the minors, which may mean he lacks a major league out pitch. With a good spring, Autrey will move up to Triple-A in 2004.

Year	Club (League)	Class	W	L	ERA	G	GS	CG	SV	IP	H	R	ER	HR	BB	SO	AVG
2002	Hudson Valley (NY-P)	A	2	3	3.57	11	11	0	0	58	55	24	23	3	14	36	.249
2003	Charleston, SC (SAL)	A	9	3	2.61	14	14	0	0	93	77	29	27	6	10	54	.219
	Orlando (SL)	AA	5	4	2.99	12	12	2	0	78	79	31	26	9	15	37	.257
MINOR LEAGUE TOTALS			16	10	2.98	37	37	2	0	229	211	84	76	18	39	127	.240

16 Josh Hamilton, of

Born: May 21, 1981. **Ht.:** 6-4. **Wt.:** 200. **Bats:** L. **Throws:** L. **School:** Athens Drive HS, Raleigh, N.C. **Career Transactions:** Selected by Devil Rays in first round (first overall) of 1999 draft; signed June 3, 1999 . . . On restricted list, May 15-Nov. 17, 2003.

Hamilton entered the 2001 season as the top prospect in baseball but has played just 83 games since. Back problems related to a spring-training car accident short-circuited his 2001 season, while shoulder and elbow surgery cut short his 2002. He left the team last March after being sent down in spring training and took a year of personal leave to overcome undisclosed off-field problems. The Devil Rays, who have been tight-lipped regarding Hamilton's demons, aren't sure what will become of his career. He has five-tool potential and the ability to dominate in the majors if he can get his life and his career in order. Hamilton possesses a classic lefthanded swing and the size, strength and loft to hit for average with at least 30 homers annually. He also runs well for his size, and his lone offensive weakness is a lack of walks. Hamilton's defensive instincts and range are impressive in center field. He'd move to right field alongside Rocco Baldelli in Tampa Bay, and Hamilton's arm strength and accuracy easily will fit there. He threw 94 mph in high school and could have been a first-round pick as a pitcher. Hamilton's talent is unquestioned, but the Rays are in a wait-and-see mode regarding his future.

Year	Club (League)	Class	AVG	G	AB	R	H	2B	3B	HR	RBI	BB	SO	SB	SLG	OBP
1999	Princeton (Appy)	R	.347	56	236	49	82	20	4	10	48	13	43	17	.593	.378
	Hudson Valley (NY-P)	A	.194	16	72	7	14	3	0	0	7	1	14	1	.236	.213

2000	Charleston, SC (SAL)	A	.302	96	391	62	118	23	3	13	61	27	71	14	.476	.348
2001	Orlando (SL)	AA	.180	23	89	5	16	5	0	0	4	5	22	2	.236	.221
	Charleston, SC (SAL)	A	.364	4	11	3	4	1	0	1	2	2	3	0	.727	.462
2002	Bakersfield (Cal)	A	.303	56	211	32	64	14	1	9	44	20	46	10	.507	.359
2003	Did not play															
MINOR LEAGUE TOTALS			.295	251	1010	158	298	66	8	33	166	68	199	44	.474	.338

17 Chris Seddon, lhp

Born: Oct. 13, 1983. **Ht.:** 6-3. **Wt.:** 170. **Bats:** L. **Throws:** L. **School:** Canyon HS, Santa Clarita, Calif. **Career Transactions:** Selected by Devil Rays in fifth round of 2001 draft; signed July 31, 2001.

Seddon got off to a strong start in high Class A last year, allowing a total of four earned runs in his first four starts. Though he slumped afterward, he still figures prominently in Tampa Bay's plans. Seddon brings a solid repertoire with heavy stuff to the table. His changeup and a hard slider that drives in on the hands of righthanders are among the best in the system. He also has a fastball with good movement that sits in the low 90s. The Rays are confident Seddon's growing, yet wiry frame will enable him to produce additional velocity in the near future, making him more difficult to hit. He needs some more strength, command and consistency, but the ingredients are there. He'll open this season in Double-A.

Year	Club (League)	Class	W	L	ERA	G	GS	CG	SV	IP	H	R	ER	HR	BB	SO	AVG
2001	Princeton (Appy)	R	1	2	5.11	4	2	0	0	12	15	7	7	2	6	18	.300
2002	Charleston, SC (SAL)	A	6	8	3.62	26	20	0	1	117	93	63	47	7	68	88	.218
2003	Bakersfield (Cal)	A	9	11	5.00	26	26	0	0	133	147	93	74	12	54	95	.279
MINOR LEAGUE TOTALS			16	21	4.39	56	48	0	1	263	255	163	128	21	128	201	.254

18 Jon Barratt, lhp

Born: March 19, 1985. **Ht.:** 5-9. **Wt.:** 165. **Bats:** R. **Throws:** L. **School:** Hillcrest HS, Springfield, Mo. **Career Transactions:** Selected by Devil Rays in fifth round of 2003 draft; signed Aug. 25, 2003.

Though the Devil Rays have limited money and already had spent most of their 2003 draft budget, they found $300,000 late last summer to sign Barratt, a fifth-rounder. Adding him to a draft class that started with Delmon Young, James Houser and Travis Schlichting makes it one of the strongest in Tampa Bay annals. He spent the summer as the ace of the U.S. junior national team that won the silver medal at the Pan American Cup in Curacao, winning twice while fanning 26 in 13 innings. Barratt had one of the quickest arms in the draft and has dominated amateur competition. If he were taller—he's listed at 5-foot-10 and scouts say that's being kind—he would have been a first-round pick. He generates low-90s velocity with arm speed rather than leverage, and his delivery is free and easy. Barratt's fastball is just one of four quality pitches he throws. His mid-80s splitter, hard curveball and changeup all are plus pitches at times. After a solid showing in instructional league, he'll probably make his pro debut in low Class A.

Year	Club (League)	Class	W	L	ERA	G	GS	CG	SV	IP	H	R	ER	HR	BB	SO	AVG
2003	Did not play—Signed 2004 contract																

19 Shawn Riggans, c

Born: July 25, 1980. **Ht.:** 6-2. **Wt.:** 190. **Bats:** R. **Throws:** R. **School:** Indian River (Fla.) JC. **Career Transactions:** Selected by Devil Rays in 24th round of 2000 draft; signed May 7, 2001.

After an elbow injury and subsequent Tommy John surgery prevented Riggans from catching much in his first two pro seasons, he returned to earn best-defensive-catcher honors in the South Atlantic League in 2003. One of the best receivers in the organization, Riggans has greatly improved his gamecalling ability. Charleston pitchers loved working with him, benefiting from his knowledge of hitters and feel for the game. His arm strength and accuracy are good but not great, with his surgery showing some residual effects. He threw out 26 percent of basestealers last year. His greatest needs from a defensive standpoint are improving his agility and his ability to block balls in the dirt. Offensively, he generates power with his quick bat. The Rays believe he can be a run producer while hitting in the bottom half of the lineup, and he didn't look overmatched following a late-season promotion to Double-A. With Pete LaForest likely ticketed for Triple-A, Riggans probably will start this season back in the Southern League.

Year	Club (League)	Class	AVG	G	AB	R	H	2B	3B	HR	RBI	BB	SO	SB	SLG	OBP
2001	Princeton (Appy)	R	.345	15	58	15	20	4	0	8	17	9	18	1	.828	.433
2002	Hudson Valley (NY-P)	A	.263	73	266	34	70	13	0	9	48	32	72	2	.414	.343
2003	Charleston, SC (SAL)	A	.280	68	232	33	65	17	0	3	34	19	35	3	.392	.340
	Orlando (SL)	AA	.274	22	62	7	17	6	0	1	11	4	14	0	.419	.319
MINOR LEAGUE TOTALS			.278	178	618	89	172	40	0	21	110	64	139	6	.445	.348

20 Travis Schlichting, 3b

Born: Oct. 19, 1984. **Ht.:** 6-4. **Wt.:** 190. **Bats:** R. **Throws:** R. **School:** Round Rock (Texas) HS. **Career Transactions:** Selected by Devil Rays in fourth round of 2003 draft; signed June 21, 2003.

Schlichting was a two-way star at Round Rock (Texas) High, which spent most of the spring ranked No.1 in the nation. He played shortstop and served as the No. 3 starter behind Rangers first-rounder John Danks and White Sox fifth-rounder Matt Nachreiner. Moved to third base after signing for $400,000, Schlichting has all the tools to become a premium performer at the hot corner. He struggled offensively in Rookie balls, revealing some flaws in his swing that carried over from using aluminum bats. But he has quick hands and should be able to adjust, becoming a solid average hitter with plus power. His bat speed is excellent and he hits the ball with authority. Scouts love Schlichting's lean body, which should fill out nicely once he adds muscle with maturity. He has good actions for the left side of the infield, and he possesses above-average arm strength with good accuracy. Schlichting will move up to low Class A in 2004.

Year	Club (League)	Class	AVG	G	AB	R	H	2B	3B	HR	RBI	BB	SO	SB	SLG	OBP
2003	Princeton (Appy)	R	.226	46	146	18	33	2	2	0	9	14	38	6	.267	.298
MINOR LEAGUE TOTALS			.226	46	146	18	33	2	2	0	9	14	38	6	.267	.298

21 Chris Flinn, rhp

Born: Aug. 18, 1980. **Ht.:** 6-2. **Wt.:** 180. **Bats:** R. **Throws:** R. **School:** University at Stony Brook. **Career Transactions:** Selected by Devil Rays in third round of 2001 draft; signed June 13, 2001.

The Devil Rays' greatest need is pitching, and Flinn is yet another arm they plucked from the 2001 draft. He was their third-round pick behind Dewon Brazelton and Jon Switzer, and other signees included Chris Seddon (fifth round) and Chad Gaudin (34th). Tampa Bay's haul would have been even more impressive had it been able to sign David Bush (fourth), now a top prospect in the Toronto system, and Thomas Diamond (38th) and Eric Beattie (47th), who project as possible first-round picks in 2004. Flinn has good stuff and knows how to pitch. He throws a low-90s fastball, a tough knuckle-curve, a solid splitter and a decent slider. He pitches to both sides of the plate and keeps the ball down in the strike zone. The Rays believe he'll be ready after he repeats his delivery more often, giving him better balance and more consistency. Flinn made 10 relief appearances in 2003 and could be a valuable swingman in Tampa. He'll return to Double-A, where he finished strong at the end of last year.

Year	Club (League)	Class	W	L	ERA	G	GS	CG	SV	IP	H	R	ER	HR	BB	SO	AVG
2001	Hudson Valley (NY-P)	A	3	4	2.36	15	10	0	2	69	54	33	18	3	21	72	.209
2002	Bakersfield (Cal)	A	0	4	8.64	7	7	0	0	33	52	36	32	9	17	22	.359
	Charleston, SC (SAL)	A	8	6	2.31	19	19	2	0	128	103	44	33	6	41	116	.222
2003	Bakersfield (Cal)	A	8	6	4.57	24	17	2	0	100	116	65	51	8	35	79	.290
	Orlando (SL)	AA	1	2	2.57	7	4	0	0	21	15	11	6	0	6	16	.195
MINOR LEAGUE TOTALS			20	22	3.58	72	57	4	2	352	340	189	140	26	120	305	.253

22 Carlos Hines, rhp

Born: Sept. 26, 1980. **Ht.:** 6-3. **Wt.:** 190. **Bats:** R. **Throws:** R. **School:** Smithfield-Selma HS, Smithfield, N.C. **Career Transactions:** Selected by Reds in 24th round of 1999 draft; signed June 9, 1999 . . . Released by Reds, Aug. 25, 1999 . . . Signed by Devil Rays, June 20, 2001.

Though Hines has won seven games since turning pro in 1999 and hasn't experienced any success above high Class A, the Devil Rays added him to their 40-man roster in the offseason. He has been a different pitcher since moving to the bullpen in mid-2002, and he showcased one of the best fastballs in the Arizona Fall League following the 2003 season. Hines pitches off a mid-90s fastball that regularly touches 97 mph. It only has modest movement. Hines' problems come when he must throw something other than his heater. He doesn't have confidence in his slider and he hangs it on occasion. His changeup has little depth or fade, and its lack of effectiveness was a major reason he couldn't remain a starter. There had been some questions regarding Hines' makeup in the past—the Reds released him for disciplinary reasons shortly after signing him in 1999—but the reserved pitcher produced no problems last year. If he can polish a second pitch, Hines could be a situational reliever in the major leagues, possibly as soon as late 2004.

Year	Club (League)	Class	W	L	ERA	G	GS	CG	SV	IP	H	R	ER	HR	BB	SO	AVG
1999	Reds (GCL)	R	0	0	8.10	5	0	0	0	10	15	12	9	0	8	7	.349
2000	Did not play																
2001	Princeton (Appy)	R	2	3	4.44	13	7	0	0	49	51	33	24	3	17	56	.260
2002	Charleston, SC (SAL)	A	1	3	5.21	24	7	0	2	48	54	29	28	1	15	26	.287
	Hudson Valley (NY-P)	A	2	2	3.96	5	5	0	0	25	28	13	11	3	7	12	.295

			W	L	ERA	G	GS	CG	SV	IP	H	R	ER	HR	BB	SO	AVG
	Orlando (SL)	AA	0	0	16.20	3	0	0	0	3	8	9	6	0	5	3	.400
2003	Charleston, SC (SAL)	A	1	0	1.46	30	0	0	16	37	25	6	6	2	9	25	.195
	Bakersfield (Cal)	A	1	1	2.77	25	0	0	8	26	22	10	8	0	13	23	.220
	Orlando (SL)	AA	0	1	9.00	2	0	0	0	3	5	3	3	0	1	2	.417
MINOR LEAGUE TOTALS			7	10	4.25	107	19	0	26	201	208	115	95	9	75	154	.266

23 Jino Gonzalez, lhp

Born: Sept. 5, 1982. **Ht.:** 6-2. **Wt.:** 210. **Bats:** L. **Throws:** L. **School:** CC of Southern Nevada. **Career Transactions:** Selected by Devil Rays in 46th round of 2002 draft; signed June 2, 2003.

After missing all of 2002 with a shoulder injury, Gonzalez came back to be the No. 1 starter for Junior College World Series champion Southern Nevada. He would have been drafted for the fourth straight year had he not signed with the Devil Rays as a draft-and-follow for a reported $200,000. Though Tampa Bay kept him on a tight pitch count and shut him down for a month as a precaution, his stuff jumped out during his limited pro debut and in instructional league. He has two plus pitches in his low-90s fastball and sharp-breaking slider. He also has a straight changeup and good overall command of his three pitches. The Rays believe Gonzalez can move quickly because of his solid foundation and his mature approach. He's expected to open his first full season in low Class A but could jump to high Class A by midseason.

Year	Club (League)	Class	W	L	ERA	G	GS	CG	SV	IP	H	R	ER	HR	BB	SO	AVG
2003	Princeton (Appy)	R	2	1	2.00	3	1	0	0	9	5	6	2	0	1	10	.143
	Hudson Valley (NY-P)	A	0	1	4.50	3	3	0	0	12	11	7	6	0	6	11	.244
MINOR LEAGUE TOTALS			2	2	3.43	6	4	0	0	21	16	13	8	0	7	21	.200

24 Brian Henderson, lhp

Born: May 19, 1982. **Ht.:** 5-11. **Wt.:** 195. **Bats:** L. **Throws:** L. **School:** University of Houston. **Career Transactions:** Selected by Devil Rays in seventh round of 2003 draft; signed June 10, 2003.

Henderson didn't get much fanfare as a swingman on a Houston staff that included 2003 first-rounders Ryan Wagner (Reds) and Brad Sullivan (Athletics), plus fifth-rounder Danny Zell (Tigers) and Garrett Mock, who will go early in 2004. But the Devil Rays took Henderson in the seventh round, sent him straight to low Class A and watched him have no trouble making the transition. That wasn't a surprise, considering that Henderson has overachieved since being cut from his high school team as a freshman. He possesses incredible determination and intelligence, as evidenced by his 1510 SAT score and pursuit of a chemical engineering degree at Houston. Henderson's best pitch is a big league curveball. He also has an average fastball, and is working on a straight change with plus potential. He throws strikes and though he's just 5-foot-11, he pitches down in the strike zone. Headed for high Class A to start 2004, he's on the fast track and could surface in Tampa Bay's bullpen as early as late 2005.

Year	Club (League)	Class	W	L	ERA	G	GS	CG	SV	IP	H	R	ER	HR	BB	SO	AVG
2003	Charleston, SC (SAL)	A	2	0	2.51	24	0	0	2	32	31	11	9	2	12	27	.250
MINOR LEAGUE TOTALS			2	0	2.51	24	0	0	2	32	31	11	9	2	12	27	.250

25 Alec Zumwalt, rhp

Born: Jan. 20, 1981. **Ht.:** 6-2. **Wt.:** 190. **Bats:** R. **Throws:** R. **School:** East Forsyth HS, Kernersville, N.C. **Career Transactions:** Selected by Braves in fourth round of 1999 draft; signed June 3, 1999 . . . Selected by Devil Rays from Braves in Rule 5 major league draft, Dec. 15, 2003.

Few pitchers in the Braves organization made more impressive progress during the 2003 season than Zumwalt. Atlanta didn't want to lose him, yet had too many pitching prospects to find room on their 40-man roster for him. The Devil Rays took him in the major league Rule 5 draft and will try to keep him in their big league bullpen throughout 2004. If they can't, he must clear waivers and be offered back to the Braves for half of the $50,000 Rule 5 price before Tampa Bay could send him to the minors. A two-way player in high school, Zumwalt was a 1999 fourth-round pick as an outfielder. He hit just .216 and struggled to make contact for three seasons before returning to the mound during instructional league in 2001. He's aggressive with his low-90s fastball and has retained a good feel for pitching despite his time away from the mound. His slider and changeup are average if inconsistent at this point, but Atlanta believe both had the potential to become plus pitches. His command requires the most improvement if he's to stick with the Devil Rays. He could develop into a solid setup man in the future.

Year	Club (League)	Class	AVG	G	AB	R	H	2B	3B	HR	RBI	BB	SO	SB	SLG	OBP
1999	Braves (GCL)	R	.207	51	188	19	39	3	1	3	22	15	48	1	.282	.284
2000	Danville (Appy)	R	.235	59	204	27	48	15	2	3	28	38	67	5	.373	.368
2001	Macon (SAL)	A	.209	101	349	43	73	20	2	6	38	34	101	8	.330	.286
2003	Greenville (SL)	AA	.500	11	2	0	1	0	0	0	0	1	0	0	.500	.667
MINOR LEAGUE TOTALS			.217	222	743	89	161	38	5	12	88	88	216	14	.330	.311

Year	Club (League)	Class	W	L	ERA	G	GS	CG	SV	IP	H	R	ER	HR	BB	SO	AVG
2002	Macon (SAL)	A	2	1	4.31	24	0	0	0	40	39	25	19	2	16	34	.250
	Myrtle Beach (Car)	A	0	3	8.63	21	0	0	1	24	33	25	23	2	13	21	.324
2003	Myrtle Beach (Car)	A	5	2	2.22	30	0	0	6	45	29	11	11	2	16	43	.191
	Greenville (SL)	AA	1	1	1.42	11	0	0	0	19	13	3	3	0	12	19	.191
MINOR LEAGUE TOTALS			8	7	3.96	86	0	0	7	127	114	64	56	6	57	117	.238

26 Shaun Cumberland, of

Born: Aug. 1, 1984. **Ht.:** 6-2. **Wt.:** 185. **Bats:** L. **Throws:** R. **School:** Pace HS, Milton, Fla.
Career Transactions: Selected by Devil Rays in 10th round of 2003 draft; signed June 8, 2003.

A 10th-round pick last June, Cumberland was the best athlete in the Devil Rays' 2003 draft class. His physical tools were evident during his pro debut, as was the fact that his baseball skills are raw and unpolished. The Rays are confident that he'll continue to mature physically and develop into a hitter who can produce for average and power at higher levels. He lacks significant pop right now, but his wiry frame should be able to add strength. He lost weight during his first pro summer, so getting on a workout program is a must. While only an average runner, Cumberland is a fine corner outfielder with good instincts. He also has above-average arm speed and should be able to stay in right field. The Rays also love Cumberland's makeup and intangibles, which should help him realize his ceiling. He'll play this year in low Class A.

Year	Club (League)	Class	AVG	G	AB	R	H	2B	3B	HR	RBI	BB	SO	SB	SLG	OBP
2003	Princeton (Appy)	R	.252	62	218	28	55	11	5	1	32	19	41	12	.362	.314
MINOR LEAGUE TOTALS			.252	62	218	28	55	11	5	1	32	19	41	12	.362	.314

27 Matt Diaz, of

Born: March 3, 1978. **Ht.:** 6-1. **Wt.:** 200. **Bats:** R. **Throws:** R. **School:** Florida State University.
Career Transactions: Selected by Devil Rays in 17th round of 1999 draft; signed June 24, 1999.

Diaz raked his way into prospect status in 2003 by hitting .354 (second in the minors) and leading Devil Rays farmhands with 86 RBIs. A Southern League all-star in his second stint in Double-A, he earned a brief callup in July. Diaz has a quick bat and is capable of hitting for average with 20 homers per season. He consistently makes hard contact, though because he rarely swings and misses, he also rarely walks. The problem for Diaz is that he doesn't have a defensive position. Tampa Bay's greatest strength by far is outfielders, and while he has an average arm he's a shaky defender. With his arm and frame, his best position might be catcher but he's just not consistent enough to move behind the plate. He worked on his defense in Puerto Rico this winter, and if he improves enough he could win a backup job with the Devil Rays this year. If not, he'll be a solid middle-of-the-order hitter in Triple-A.

Year	Club (League)	Class	AVG	G	AB	R	H	2B	3B	HR	RBI	BB	SO	SB	SLG	OBP
1999	Hudson Valley (NY-P)	A	.245	54	208	22	51	15	2	1	20	6	43	6	.351	.284
2000	St. Petersburg (FSL)	A	.270	106	392	37	106	21	3	6	53	11	54	2	.385	.305
2001	Bakersfield (Cal)	A	.328	131	524	79	172	40	2	17	81	24	73	11	.510	.370
2002	Orlando (SL)	AA	.274	122	449	71	123	28	1	10	50	34	72	31	.408	.337
2003	Orlando (SL)	AA	.383	60	227	32	87	21	0	5	41	19	24	9	.542	.444
	Durham (IL)	AAA	.328	67	253	35	83	18	3	8	45	16	45	6	.518	.382
	Tampa Bay (AL)	MAJ	.111	4	9	2	1	0	0	0	0	1	3	0	.111	.200
MAJOR LEAGUE TOTALS			.111	4	9	2	1	0	0	0	0	1	3	0	.111	.200
MINOR LEAGUE TOTALS			.303	540	2053	276	622	143	11	47	290	110	311	65	.452	.352

28 Nick DeBarr, rhp

Born: Aug. 24, 1983. **Ht.:** 6-4. **Wt.:** 220. **Bats:** R. **Throws:** R. **School:** Lassen (Calif.) JC. **Career Transactions:** Selected by Devil Rays in 14th round of 2002 draft; signed June 7, 2002.

Honing his splitter made all the difference for DeBarr. He started 2003 in the low Class A bullpen, and he initially tried to be too fine his pitches. Once he got more aggressive and gained the splitter as an effective second pitch, he moved to the rotation and emerged as Charleston's ace after Scott Autrey was promoted. DeBarr's fastball sits in the low 90s, and his strong frame suggests that there could be more velocity to come. His slider is average at best, which is why the splitter was so important for him. It looks exactly like his fastball until it drops off at the plate. The Rays worked incessantly with DeBarr last year to speed up his delivery. He was a tortoise-like 1.85 seconds to home plate, and basestealers succeded in 28 of 34 (83 percent) against him. He has developed a slide-step that shows some promise. DeBarr will pitch in high Class A in 2004.

Year	Club (League)	Class	W	L	ERA	G	GS	CG	SV	IP	H	R	ER	HR	BB	SO	AVG
2002	Princeton (Appy)	R	3	1	4.71	11	6	0	0	50	60	31	26	5	12	31	.305
	Hudson Valley (NY-P)	A	1	2	4.24	4	3	0	0	17	18	8	8	2	2	15	.273
2003	Charleston, SC (SAL)	A	11	7	4.15	27	20	2	0	139	149	77	64	8	40	105	.272
MINOR LEAGUE TOTALS			15	10	4.30	42	29	2	0	205	227	116	98	15	54	151	.280

29 Chad Orvella, rhp

Born: Oct. 1, 1980. **Ht.:** 5-11. **Wt.:** 190. **Bats:** R. **Throws:** R. **School:** North Carolina State University. **Career Transactions:** Selected by Devil Rays in 13th round of 2003 draft; signed June 9, 2003.

Orvella spent most of his time at North Carolina State as a light-hitting shortstop and had an 8.10 ERA in 13 innings as a senior last spring. But he showed a 94-95 mph while on the mound, so the Devil Rays moved him there full-time after signing him as a 13th-rounder. Orvella blew away hitters in the short-season New York-Penn League until he partially tore the meniscus in his left knee and required minor yet season-ending surgery. Tampa Bay believes his fastball could produce even more velocity now that he's devoting his efforts to pitching on a full-time basis for the first time. There's not much finesse to his game, but his ability to overpower hitters for short stretches could enable him to become a big league setup man. Orvella also throws a hard slider that's inconsistent, and he has a decent change-up for show. He'll open 2004 as the closer in low Class A.

Year	Club (League)	Class	W	L	ERA	G	GS	CG	SV	IP	H	R	ER	HR	BB	SO	AVG
2003	Hudson Valley (NY-P)	A	0	0	0.00	10	0	0	8	12	6	0	0	0	1	15	.140
MINOR LEAGUE TOTALS			0	0	0.00	10	0	0	8	12	6	0	0	0	1	15	.140

30 Elliot Johnson, 2b

Born: March 9, 1984. **Ht.:** 6-0. **Wt.:** 160. **Bats:** B. **Throws:** R. **School:** Thatcher HS, Thatcher, Ariz. **Career Transactions:** Signed as nondrafted free agent by Devil Rays, June 29, 2002.

Johnson is an underdog who could be on the verge of a breakthrough season. A non-drafted free agent signed out of a high school in a remote area of Arizona, he missed two months last year with a left hamstring injury. His strengths are his athleticism, plus speed and knack for drawing walks. He has excellent strike-zone judgment and tries to hit everything on the ground in order to take advantage of his wheels. He does have a long ways to go offensively, however, as he strikes out too much and exhibits little power. He'll have to get stronger. Defensively, he's solid at second base and turns double plays well. Though he remains a work in progress, Johnson could be a surprise. He'll start for one of Tampa Bay's Class A affiliates this year.

Year	Club (League)	Class	AVG	G	AB	R	H	2B	3B	HR	RBI	BB	SO	SB	SLG	OBP
2002	Princeton (Appy)	R	.263	42	152	21	40	10	1	1	13	18	48	14	.362	.345
2003	Charleston, SC (SAL)	A	.212	54	151	22	32	4	0	0	15	38	32	8	.238	.370
MINOR LEAGUE TOTALS			.238	96	303	43	72	14	1	1	28	56	80	22	.300	.358

TEXAS
RANGERS

For the Rangers, last year will be remembered not for what did happen, but what didn't. The prospective trade of Alex Rodriguez to the Red Sox turned into a circus fueled by media speculation, changing deadlines and intervention from the commissioner's office and the union.

Rodriguez' $252 million contract has become an albatross for the franchise. Trading him would have increased Texas' roster flexibility and allowed the club to be more aggressive in acquiring much-needed pitching. But in the midst of their fourth straight last-place finish in the American League West, the Rangers were able to unload pending free agents Carl Everett and Ugueth Urbina and replenish the farm system with prospects. Everett brought in righthanders Josh Rupe and Franklin Francisco and outfielder Anthony Webster from the White Sox. Urbina landed first baseman Adrian Gonzalez—who immediately became the Rangers' top prospect—lefthander Ryan Snare and outfielder Will Smith from the Marlins.

Dealing Rodriguez could have been a disaster, and it's impossible to argue the Rangers aren't better off from a talent standpoint with him instead of Manny Ramirez. The AL MVP will form the heart of a potent lineup along with recent homegrown products Hank Blalock and Mark Teixeira, whose

TOP 30 PROSPECTS

1. Adrian Gonzalez, 1b
2. John Danks, lhp
3. Ramon Nivar, of
4. Juan Dominguez, rhp
5. Vince Sinisi, of
6. Gerald Laird, c
7. Wes Littleton, rhp
8. Jason Bourgeois, 2b
9. Drew Meyer, ss/of
10. Josh Rupe, rhp
11. Kelvin Jimenez, rhp
12. Anthony Webster, of
13. Ben Kozlowski, lhp
14. Edwin Moreno, rhp
15. Erik Thompson, rhp
16. C.J. Wilson, lhp
17. Kameron Loe, rhp
18. Will Smith, of
19. Jason Botts, of
20. Ryan Snare, lhp
21. John Hudgins, rhp
22. A.J. Murray, lhp
23. Jeremy Cleveland, of
24. Patrick Boyd, of
25. Matt Lorenzo, rhp
26. Nick Regilio, rhp
27. Nate Gold, 1b/3b
28. Franklin Francisco, rhp
29. Justin Echols, rhp
30. Marc LaMacchia, rhp

By Josh Boyd

brightest days are ahead of them. Texas brass also is excited about the players on the verge of stepping in: Ramon Nivar, Laynce Nix and Gonzalez.

Many of the Rangers' positives came down on the farm in 2003. Nix would have rated No. 1 on this list had he not graduated to the big leagues ahead of schedule. Nivar and righthander Juan Dominguez emerged and made their major league debuts. In addition to all the trade acquisitions, Texas also had a deep draft that netted two first-round talents in lefty John Danks (the 10th overall pick) and outfielder Vince Sinisi (a second-rounder only because of signability concerns). Fourth-round righty Wes Littleton, who entered last spring with first-round aspirations, jumped on the fast track and could reach the majors as early as September. The Rangers also took a chance on righthander Marc LaMacchia in the 21st round though he was just a few months removed from Tommy John surgery.

Acquiring pitching depth has been a priority for assistant general manager/scouting director Grady Fuson. His emphasis on college prospects has filled the system with polished arms who could be knocking on the door to majors before long. Other than Danks, though, they don't have a frontline pitcher on the way. If they're going to climb out of the AL West cellar, they'll need more of them.

ORGANIZATION
OVERVIEW

General manager: John Hart. **Farm director:** Bob Miscik. **Scouting director:** Grady Fuson.

2003 PERFORMANCE

Class	Team	League	W	L	Pct.	Finish*	Manager
Majors	Texas	American	71	91	.438	t-10th (14)	Buck Showalter
Triple-A	Oklahoma RedHawks	Pacific Coast	70	72	.493	t-9th (16)	Bobby Jones
Double-A	Frisco RoughRiders	Texas	73	67	.521	3rd (8)	Tim Ireland
High A	Stockton Ports	California	77	63	.550	3rd (10)	Arnie Beyeler
Low A	Clinton LumberKings	Midwest	69	66	.511	t-6th (14)	Carlos Subero
Short-season	Spokane Indians	Northwest	50	26	.658	+1st (8)	Darryl Kennedy
Rookie	AZL Rangers	Arizona	35	14	.714	1st (9)	Pedro Lopez
OVERALL 2003 MINOR LEAGUE RECORD			374	308	.548	3rd (30)	

*Finish in overall standings (No. of teams in league). +League champion

ORGANIZATION LEADERS

BATTING *Minimum 250 At-Bats
*AVG	Ramon Nivar, Oklahoma/Frisco	.345
R	Jason Bourgeois, Frisco/Stockton	103
H	Drew Meyer, Frisco/Stockton	143
TB	Jason Hart, Oklahoma	214
2B	Nate Gold, Clinton	35
	G.J. Raymundo, Oklahoma/Stockton	35
3B	Drew Meyer, Frisco/Stockton	10
HR	Jason Hart, Oklahoma	21
RBI	Jason Botts, Frisco/Stockton	88
BB	Craig Ringe, Clinton	82
SO	Juan Senreiso, Clinton	117
SB	Cameron Coughlan, Clinton	47
*SLG	Ryan Ludwick, Oklahoma	.558
*OBP	Andrew Wishy, Spokane	.416

PITCHING #Minimum 75 Innings
W	Erik Thompson, Stockton/Clinton	13
L	John Barnett, Stockton	14
#ERA	Kameron Loe, Stockton/Clinton	1.67
G	Erick Burke, Frisco	64
CG	Robert Ellis, Oklahoma	2
	Tony Mounce, Oklahoma/Frisco	2
SV	Spike Lundberg, Oklahoma/Frisco	31
IP	Mario Ramos, Oklahoma/Frisco	154
BB	Justin Echols, Frisco/Stockton	69
SO	Juan Dominguez, Okla./Frisco/Stockton	140

BEST TOOLS

Best Hitter for Average	Adrian Gonzalez
Best Power Hitter	Vince Sinisi
Fastest Baserunner	Ramon Nivar
Best Athlete	Anthony Webster
Best Fastball	Wes Littleton
Best Curveball	John Danks
Best Slider	Josh Rupe
Best Changeup	Juan Dominguez
Best Control	Erik Thompson
Best Defensive Catcher	Gerald Laird
Best Defensive Infielder	Drew Meyer
Best Infield Arm	Drew Meyer
Best Defensive Outfielder	Rick Asadoorian
Best Outfield Arm	Juan Senreiso

PROJECTED 2007 LINEUP

Catcher	Gerald Laird
First Base	Adrian Gonzalez
Second Base	Michael Young
Third Base	Hank Blalock
Shortstop	Alex Rodriguez
Left Field	Laynce Nix

Center Field	Ramon Nivar
Right Field	Mark Teixeira
Designated Hitter	Vince Sinisi
No. 1 Starter	John Danks
No. 2 Starter	Colby Lewis
No. 3 Starter	Ricardo Rodriguez
No. 4 Starter	Joaquin Benoit
No. 5 Starter	Juan Dominguez
Closer	Francisco Cordero

LAST YEAR'S TOP 20 PROSPECTS

1. Mark Teixeira, 3b
2. Colby Lewis, rhp
3. Ben Kozlowski, lhp
4. Laynce Nix, of
5. Gerald Laird, c
6. Drew Meyer, ss/2b
7. Ryan Ludwick, of
8. C.J. Wilson, lhp
9. Travis Hughes, rhp
10. Jason Bourgeois, 2b/ss
11. Jason Hart, of/1b
12. Marshall McDougal, inf
13. Jose Dominguez, rhp
14. Kelvin Jimenez, rhp
15. A.J. Murray, lhp
16. Ryan Dittfurth, rhp
17. Nick Regilio, rhp
18. John Barnett, rhp
19. Jermaine Clark, of/2b
20. Mario Ramos, lhp

TOP PROSPECTS OF THE DECADE

1994	Benji Gil, ss
1995	Julio Santana, rhp
1996	Andrew Vessel, of
1997	Danny Kolb, rhp
1998	Ruben Mateo, of
1999	Ruben Mateo, of
2000	Ruben Mateo, of
2001	Carlos Pena, 1b
2002	Hank Blalock, 3b
2003	Mark Teixeira, 3b

TOP DRAFT PICKS OF THE DECADE

1994	Kevin Brown, c (2)
1995	Jonathan Johnson, rhp
1996	R.A. Dickey, rhp
1997	Jason Romano, 3b
1998	Carlos Pena, 1b
1999	Colby Lewis, rhp
2000	Scott Heard, c
2001	Mark Teixeira, 3b
2002	Drew Meyer, ss
2003	John Danks, lhp

ALL-TIME LARGEST BONUSES

Mark Teixeira, 2001	$4,500,000
John Danks, 2003	$2,100,000
Vince Sinisi, 2003	$2,070,000
Drew Meyer, 2002	$1,875,000
Carlos Pena, 1998	$1,850,000

MINOR LEAGUE
DEPTH CHART

TEXAS RANGERS
RANK: 16

Impact potential (C): The system has been busy churning out premium big league bats, and Adrian Gonzalez should follow Hank Blalock, Mark Teixeira and Laynce Nix to Arlington. Don't be fooled by his injury-induced dropoff in production last year; he still profiles as an all-star first baseman. John Danks won't be ready for a while, but has frontline starter potential.

Depth (C): The Rangers' primary objective is to develop pitching to complement an explosive offense, and they are loaded with polished pitching prospects. Most rely more on location than velocity, so it remains to be seen what their future roles will be.

Sleeper: Kelvin Jimenez, rhp. *—Depth charts prepared by Josh Boyd. Numbers in parentheses indicate prospect rankings.*

LF
Vince Sinisi (5)
Will Smith (18)
Jeremy Cleveland (23)
Jason Jones
Dane Bubela
Peter Zoccollilo

CF
Ramon Nivar (3)
Anthony Webster (12)
Patrick Boyd (24)
Larry Grayson

RF
Jason Botts (19)
Juan Senreiso
Andrew Wishy
Larry Charles
Lizahio Baez

3B
Marshall McDougall

SS
Drew Meyer (9)

2B
Jason Bourgeois (8)
Chris O'Riordan

1B
Adrian Gonzalez (1)
Nate Gold (27)
Jason Hart

SOURCE OF TALENT

Homegrown		Acquired	
College	13	Trades	8
Junior College	0	Rule 5	0
Draft-and-follow	2	Independent	0
High school	3	Free agents	0
Nondrafted free agent	0		
Foreign	4		

C
Gerald Laird (6)
Scott Heard
Dustin Smith

RHP

Starters	Relievers
Juan Dominguez (4)	Franklin Francisco (28)
Wes Littleton (7)	Williams Sarmiento
Josh Rupe (10)	Chris Mabeus
Kelvin Jimenez (11)	Edison Volquez
Edwin Moreno (14)	Travis Hughes
Erik Thompson (15)	Billy Sylvester
Kameron Loe (17)	Jason Andrew
John Hudgins (21)	
Matt Lorenzo (25)	
Nick Regilio (26)	
Justin Echols (29)	
Marc LaMacchia (30)	
Matt Farnum	
Jovanny Cedeno	
Cody Smith	
John Barnett	
Kiki Bengochea	
Omar Beltre	
Gary Hogan	

LHP

Starters	Relievers
John Danks (2)	Erick Burke
Ben Kozlowski (13)	Sam Narron
C.J. Wilson (16)	
Ryan Snare (20)	
A.J. Murray (22)	

DRAFT
ANALYSIS

Best Pro Debut: OF Jeremy Cleveland (8) hit .322-7-53 and led the short-season Northwest League with 64 runs. OF Dane Bubela (22) edged him for the batting title at .323-4-35 and led the NWL in on-base percentage (.436). RHP Wes Littleton (4) went 6-0, 1.56 with a 47-8 strikeout-walk ratio in 52 NWL innings.

Best Athlete: The Rangers didn't sign a classic power/speed combination, but OFs Vince Sinisi (2), Adam Bourassa (6), Cleveland and SS Ian Kinsler (17) are good athletes.

Bourassa

Best Pure Hitter: Sinisi was one of the best college bats available and would have gone in the top 15 picks if signability hadn't been an issue. Cleveland is another gifted hitter, and OF Andrew Wishy (12) has the skills to produce at the plate.

Best Raw Power: Six-foot-3, 210-pound 1B Ian Gac (26).

Fastest Runner: Bourassa has 4.0-4.1 second speed down the first-base line.

Best Defensive Player: Bourassa's speed and instincts serve him well in center field.

Best Fastball: RHPs Matt Lorenzo (5) and Matt Farnum (7) reached 95 mph in college, and Farnum did on a few occasions during the summer. LHP John Danks (1) and Littleton can both get to 94.

Best Breaking Ball: Danks' curveball is better than his fastball at times. Littleton has the top slider.

Most Intriguing Background: Unsigned 3B Josh Lansford's (39) father Carney won the 1981 American League batting title. RHP John Hudgins (3) was the Most Outstanding Player at the 2003 College World Series, where he won three times but saw his Stanford team lose to Rice in the finals. Wishy is an accomplished pianist. Bubela's brother Jaime is an outfielder in the Mariners system.

Closest To The Majors: Hudgins and Littleton, who fit the Rangers' philosophy of prizing savvy over unrefined pure stuff. Hudgins developed a nerve problem in his ribcage after pitching two innings as a pro.

Best Late-Round Pick: RHP Marc LaMacchia (21) had a 91-92 sinker before having Tommy John surgery in mid-May. Had he stayed healthy, he could have gone in the second or third round.

The One Who Got Away: The Rangers signed their first 17 selections. RHP Brad Lincoln (28) is just 6 feet tall, but he throws in the low 90s with little effort. He should crack the Houston rotation as a freshman.

Assessment: Getting Danks and Sinisi was the equivalent of having two picks in the upper half of the first round. After giving up their 2002 second- through fifth-round choices as free-agent compensation, the Rangers kept their selections this time and grabbed some much-needed pitching.

SS Drew Meyer (1) was considered a reach with the 10th overall pick and hasn't exactly dispelled that notion. Texas hampered its efforts by surrendering its second- through fifth-rounders for free agents, though RHP Erik Thompson (12) has been a strike-throwing machine.

Future draftologists will be amazed to learn that 1B/OF Mark Teixeira (1) lasted five picks. LHP C.J. Wilson (5) was moving quickly before he blew out his elbow last year.

The Rangers blew their three first-round choices on C Scott Heard, unsigned OF Tyrell Godwin and oft-injured RHP Chad Hawkins. But they did get OF Laynce Nix (4), 3B Edwin Encarnacion (9) and 2B Jason Bourgeois (2). They're lucky, however, that we don't deduct points for giving up Encarnacion in a trade for Rob Bell.

While RHP Colby Lewis (1) has frontline starter stuff if he figures out how to use it, the real gem is 3B Hank Blalock (3). OF Kevin Mench (4) has proven he can hit in the majors. RHP David Mead (1) went 3-20 in 2001-02 before having shoulder surgery.

—Draft analysis prepared by Jim Callis. Numbers in parentheses indicate draft rounds.

BILL MITCHELL

Adrian
Gonzalez

Born: May 8, 1982.
Ht.: 6-2. **Wt.:** 190.
Bats: L. **Throws:** L.
School: Eastlake HS, Chula Vista, Calif.
Career Transactions: Selected by
Marlins in first round (first overall) of
2000 draft; signed June 6, 2000 . . .
Traded by Marlins with OF Will Smith
and LHP Ryan Snare to Rangers for RHP
Ugueth Urbina, July 11, 2003.

More than any baseball draft, the 2000 edition was dictated more by signability than ability. Nine of the top 10 picks agreed to predraft deals, including Gonzalez, who received $3 million as the No. 1 pick from the Marlins. While he was regarded as the best pure high school hitter in the draft, he was projected as more of a mid-first-rounder. Gonzalez has outplayed most of 2000's first-rounders (save for Rocco Baldelli) and is a safer bet than the players who fell out of the first round because of signability (Xavier Nady, Dane Sardinha, Jason Young). He had surgery to repair torn cartilage in his right wrist following the 2002 season, a problem that seemed to hinder his ability to drive the ball throughout last season. The Marlins decided Gonzalez was expendable as Jason Stokes, their second-round pick in 2000, packs more power potential at first base. So Florida made him the centerpiece of a three-prospect package to acquire closer Ugueth Urbina from the Rangers last July. Gonzalez comes from good baseball lineage. His father David was a star first baseman for the Mexican national team, while his older brother Edgar is a third baseman whom Texas plucked from Tampa Bay in the minor league Rule 5 draft in December.

Gonzalez' pure hitting approach and sweet lefthanded stroke draw comparisons to Rafael Palmeiro. Gonzalez has great balance with a short, quick swing. He sprays line drives all over the field, hitting fastballs and offspeed pitches alike. Though he's geared to smoke balls into the gaps now, he projects to develop above-average longball power in time, much like Palmeiro did. Defensively, Gonzalez is a Gold Glover in the making. He has soft hands and demonstrates excellent footwork around the bag. He's already adept at making plays to his backhand and aggressive in making plays with his strong, accurate arm on relays or throws across the diamond. The lingering affects of his wrist surgery made it hard for Gonzalez to turn on pitches on the inner half of the plate. After consecutive 17-homer seasons, he tailed off to just five last year. Some scouts question just how much power he'll develop, though they say he'll be a doubles machine—maybe more along the lines of Mark Grace than Palmeiro. Gonzalez isn't a natural athlete and some scouts are concerned about his soft body. He's a 20 runner on the 20-80 scouting scale. He always had shown a fair amount of patience, but his walk rate dipped below an acceptable level in 2003.

After getting his swing together toward the end of the season and in the Arizona Fall League, Gonzalez spent the offseason working with the Rangers' strength and conditioning coach Fernando Montes in Arizona. Texas believes it will get its first look at a fully healthy Gonzalez this season at Triple-A Oklahoma. The Rangers are crowded on the corners in the upper levels. When Gonzalez is ready to jump to Arlington in 2005, Mark Teixeira likely will move to the outfield.

Year	Club (League)	Class	AVG	G	AB	R	H	2B	3B	HR	RBI	BB	SO	SB	SLG	OBP
2000	Marlins (GCL)	R	.295	53	193	24	57	10	1	0	30	32	35	0	.358	.397
	Utica (NY-P)	A	.310	8	29	7	9	3	0	0	3	7	6	0	.414	.444
2001	Kane County (Mid)	A	.312	127	516	86	161	37	1	17	103	57	83	5	.486	.382
2002	Portland (EL)	AA	.266	138	508	70	135	34	1	17	96	54	112	6	.437	.344
2003	Albuquerque (PCL)	AAA	.216	39	139	17	30	5	1	1	18	14	25	1	.288	.286
	Carolina (SL)	AA	.307	36	137	15	42	9	1	1	16	14	25	1	.409	.368
	Frisco (TL)	AA	.283	45	173	16	49	6	2	3	17	11	27	0	.393	.326
MINOR LEAGUE TOTALS			.285	446	1695	235	483	104	7	39	283	189	313	13	.424	.359

2 John Danks, lhp

Born: April 15, 1985. **Ht.:** 6-2. **Wt.:** 190. **Bats:** L. **Throws:** L. **School:** Round Rock (Texas) HS. **Career Transactions:** Selected by Rangers in first round (ninth overall) of 2003 draft; signed July 11, 2003.

Danks went 10-3, 1.61 with 173 strikeouts in 100 innings to lead Round Rock High to the nation's top prep ranking for much of last spring. His father John Sr. helped the University of Texas to the 1978 NIT basketball championship, and his younger brother Jordan is an outfielder at Round Rock and potential first-rounder in 2006. John signed for $2.1 million. He impresses scouts with his effortless and repeatable delivery, which allows him to work consistently around the strike zone with three pitches. His fastball sits in the 89-92 mph range and he touches 93-94 at times. He displays an advanced feel for his knee-buckling curveball. Danks put in extra work on his changeup in instructional league. He's learning to maintain his arm speed on the pitch and has the aptitude to develop it into an effective third offering. The Rangers prefer college prospects in the first round, but Danks' poise and polish made him irresistible. After a heavy workload last year, he'll be limited to 120 innings in 2004, starting in low Class A Clinton.

Year	Club (League)	Class	W	L	ERA	G	GS	CG	SV	IP	H	R	ER	HR	BB	SO	AVG
2003	Rangers (AZL)	R	1	0	0.69	5	3	0	0	13	6	3	1	0	4	22	.136
	Spokane (NWL)	A	0	2	8.53	5	5	0	0	13	12	12	12	0	7	13	.267
MINOR LEAGUE TOTALS			1	2	4.56	10	8	0	0	26	18	15	13	0	11	35	.202

3 Ramon Nivar, of

Born: Feb. 22, 1980. **Ht.:** 5-10. **Wt.:** 170. **Bats:** R. **Throws:** R. **Career Transactions:** Signed out of Dominican Republic by Rangers, Jan. 25, 1998.

Formerly known as Ramon Martinez, Nivar took on his mother's maiden name. Unlike more than 30 other Rangers prospects, his age was unchanged. He switched positions at midseason last year, moving from second base to center field. Nivar grades as a top-of-the-scale runner, getting down the line in as fast as 3.9 seconds, and has garnered Rafael Furcal comparisons for his explosiveness. His speed prompted the move to center, and he displayed more than enough range to make up for his inexperience on routes. His arm strength is above-average. Nivar understands his role at the plate, and he can surprise pitchers with a little sock in his bat. He needs to develop his strikezone judgment and improve his bunting to become a complete leadoff hitter. Scouts love the energy Nivar brings, though he can get out of control at times. He hit .381 in the Arizona Fall League and has taken to center field so well that he could compete for the big league job in spring training. When he's ready, he'll push Laynce Nix to an outfield corner.

Year	Club (League)	Class	AVG	G	AB	R	H	2B	3B	HR	RBI	BB	SO	SB	SLG	OBP
1998	Rangers (DSL)	R	.285	54	179	23	51	13	0	3	21	8	7	2	.408	.328
1999	Rangers (DSL)	R	.359	50	195	43	70	19	2	7	44	9	16	7	.585	.409
2000	Charlotte (FSL)	A	.289	42	152	12	44	7	1	1	20	5	28	8	.368	.310
	Savannah (SAL)	A	.311	39	164	19	51	9	0	1	17	2	29	6	.384	.331
2001	Charlotte (FSL)	A	.241	128	515	69	124	20	1	2	32	28	65	28	.295	.286
2002	Charlotte (FSL)	A	.305	114	472	98	144	21	8	3	41	32	44	39	.403	.353
2003	Frisco (TL)	AA	.347	79	317	53	110	17	4	4	37	20	23	9	.464	.387
	Oklahoma (PCL)	AAA	.337	23	89	11	30	2	2	2	12	5	5	6	.472	.368
	Texas (AL)	MAJ	.211	28	90	9	19	1	2	0	7	4	10	4	.267	.253
MAJOR LEAGUE TOTALS			.211	28	90	9	19	1	2	0	7	4	10	4	.267	.253
MINOR LEAGUE TOTALS			.300	529	2083	328	624	108	18	23	224	109	217	105	.402	.341

4 Juan Dominguez, rhp

Born: May 18, 1980. **Ht.:** 6-2. **Wt.:** 180. **Bats:** R. **Throws:** R. **Career Transactions:** Signed out of Dominican Republic by Rangers, Dec. 26, 1999.

Previously known as Jose, Dominguez bolted through three levels and into the majors. He compiled a perfect minor league record along the way but was hammered in his two losses with the Rangers. His breakthrough season became less impressive when it turned out he's two years older than previously believed. Dominguez overmatched minor leaguers with command and two pitches: a lively 89-94 mph fastball and the best changeup in the system. His changeup acts like a splitter and grades as a 70 on the 20-80 scouting scale. Dominguez needs a better slider to make it as a big league starter. He tends to get under it, causing it to flatten out in the strike zone. He also needs to improve his mound presence and awareness of game situations. If his slider doesn't come around, Dominguez could make a good set-up man. The plan is to keep him in the rotation for now and have him start the year in Triple-A.

Year	Club (League)	Class	W	L	ERA	G	GS	CG	SV	IP	H	R	ER	HR	BB	SO	AVG
2000	Rangers (DSL)	R	1	6	4.52	14	14	0	0	68	69	49	34	2	38	56	.253
2001	Rangers (GCL)	R	4	2	4.01	11	9	1	0	58	56	29	26	4	12	55	.250
	Charlotte (FSL)	A	1	0	3.60	2	0	0	0	5	4	2	2	1	1	5	.235
2002	Rangers (DSL)	R	0	0	0.00	1	1	0	0	1	1	0	0	0	0	0	.250
	Savannah (SAL)	A	1	3	2.16	16	9	0	1	67	50	23	16	4	21	70	.209
2003	Stockton (Cal)	A	4	0	2.84	16	9	0	1	63	55	27	20	3	16	72	.226
	Frisco (TL)	AA	5	0	2.60	9	9	0	0	55	35	17	16	2	21	54	.178
	Oklahoma (PCL)	AAA	1	0	3.50	3	3	0	0	18	15	7	7	1	3	14	.227
	Texas (AL)	MAJ	0	2	7.16	6	3	0	0	16	16	14	13	5	12	13	.271
MAJOR LEAGUE TOTALS			0	2	7.16	6	3	0	0	16	16	14	13	5	12	13	.271
MINOR LEAGUE TOTALS			17	11	3.25	72	54	1	2	335	285	154	121	17	112	326	.226

5 Vince Sinisi, of

Born: Nov. 7, 1981. **Ht.:** 6-0. **Wt.:** 195. **Bats:** L. **Throws:** L. **School:** Rice University. **Career Transactions:** Selected by Rangers in second round of 2003 draft; signed Aug. 11, 2003.

In two seasons at Rice after redshirting at Texas, Sinisi earned second-team All-America status in 2002 and a College World Series championship ring last season. Sinisi's signability was in doubt and prompted him slipping to the second round last June. He signed for $2.07 million, getting the 10th-highest draft bonus in 2003 as the 46th overall pick. Sinisi reminds scouting director Grady Fuson of Jason Giambi, who was drafted by the A's when Fuson was their national crosschecker in 1992, at the same stage. Sinisi has a balanced approach at the plate and uses quick hands to propel the ball into the gaps with a compact stroke. He recognizes pitches well and should respond quickly to the Rangers' plate- discipline program. Sinisi projects to develop above-average power but has yet to show it in games. He hit just 21 home runs in two seasons at Rice. He's an underrated athlete and possesses the instincts to help make a smooth transition from first base in college to left field as a pro. The Rangers were encouraged by Sinisi's instructional league performance and expect him to rake at Double-A Frisco this season.

Year	Club (League)	Class	AVG	G	AB	R	H	2B	3B	HR	RBI	BB	SO	SB	SLG	OBP
2003	Stockton (Cal)	A	.258	14	62	9	16	1	0	1	5	3	8	1	.323	.288
MINOR LEAGUE TOTALS			.258	14	62	9	16	1	0	1	5	3	8	1	.323	.288

6 Gerald Laird, c

Born: Nov. 13, 1979. **Ht.:** 6-2. **Wt.:** 190. **Bats:** R. **Throws:** R. **School:** Cypress (Calif.) JC. **Career Transactions:** Selected by Athletics in second round of 1998 draft; signed June 1, 1999 . . . Traded by Athletics with LHP Mario Ramos, OF Ryan Ludwick and 1B Jason Hart to Rangers for 1B Carlos Pena and LHP Mike Venafro, Jan. 14, 2002.

Scouting director Grady Fuson held the same position with the Athletics when they signed Laird for $1 million as a draft-and-follow in 1999, then targeted him in a six-player deal after joining Texas in 2001. He got a surprising start over Joe Mauer for Team USA in the quarterfinal loss to Mexico during the Olympic qualifying tournament in November. While Laird has come along with the bat, he's more advanced as a defender. He erased a Pacific Coast League-best 39 percent of basestealers last year, combining plus arm strength with accuracy. At the plate, he shows raw power and the ability to drive the ball by getting good extension through his loose swing. Laird tends to be overaggressive and needs to lay off fastballs up in the strike zone. He's working to shorten his stroke. He runs like a catcher. Coming off a brief but impressive stint in the big leagues, Laird heads into spring training as the No. 2 catcher behind Einar Diaz. He should be the starter by no later than 2005.

Year	Club (League)	Class	AVG	G	AB	R	H	2B	3B	HR	RBI	BB	SO	SB	SLG	OBP
1999	S. Oregon (NWL)	A	.285	60	228	45	65	7	2	2	39	28	43	10	.360	.361
2000	Visalia (Cal)	A	.243	33	103	14	25	3	0	0	13	14	27	7	.272	.333
	Athletics (AZL)	R	.300	14	50	10	15	2	1	0	9	6	7	2	.380	.379
2001	Modesto (Cal)	A	.255	119	443	71	113	13	5	5	46	48	101	10	.341	.337
2002	Tulsa (TL)	AA	.276	123	442	70	122	21	4	11	67	45	95	8	.416	.343
2003	Oklahoma (PCL)	AAA	.260	99	338	50	88	20	5	9	42	37	61	9	.429	.344
	Texas (AL)	MAJ	.273	19	44	9	12	2	1	1	4	5	11	0	.432	.360
MAJOR LEAGUE TOTALS			.273	19	44	9	12	2	1	1	4	5	11	0	.432	.360
MINOR LEAGUE TOTALS			.267	448	1604	260	428	66	17	27	216	178	334	46	.380	.345

7 Wes Littleton, rhp

Born: Sept. 2, 1982. **Ht.:** 6-3. **Wt.:** 200. **Bats:** R. **Throws:** R. **School:** Cal State Fullerton. **Career Transactions:** Selected by Rangers in fourth round of 2003 draft; signed June 29, 2003.

Drafted by the Expos in the seventh round out of high school, Littleton was a potential first-rounder heading into 2003. His junior season was tarnished by a six-week suspension, after allegations that he took a teammate's parking permit. He wasn't as sharp upon his return, but did turn in a strong effort in the College World Series. Littleton's fastball ranks as the best in the organization, for its combination of velocity (89-94 mph) and vicious run and sink. He creates that outstanding life with a quick, whip-like arm action from a low three-quarters slot. He also throws a sweeping slider with late bite and a change-up that could become a plus pitch. He's an aggressive strike-thrower. While his low release point generates electric movement, finding a consistent weapon to against lefthanders will be a challenge. The sooner he hones his changeup, the quicker he'll move. Rangers scout Steve Flores has known Littleton since high school, and the organization has no concerns about his suspension. Texas expects him to move quickly after starting 2004 in high Class A, moving to Double-A in the second half and possibly the majors in September.

Year	Club (League)	Class	W	L	ERA	G	GS	CG	SV	IP	H	R	ER	HR	BB	SO	AVG
2003	Spokane (NWL)	A	6	0	1.56	12	8	0	0	52	36	9	9	2	8	47	.198
MINOR LEAGUE TOTALS			6	0	1.56	12	8	0	0	52	36	9	9	2	8	47	.198

8 Jason Bourgeois, 2b

Born: Jan. 4, 1982. **Ht.:** 5-9. **Wt.:** 170. **Bats:** R. **Throws:** R. **School:** Forest Brook HS, Houston. **Career Transactions:** Selected by Rangers in second round of 2000 draft; signed June 19, 2000.

Bourgeois was among the top hitters in the high Class A California League when he was promoted to Double-A. He was sidelined briefly with a bruised hand, but that wasn't enough to prevent him posting career highs in most offensive categories. At 5-foot-9, Bourgeois draws comparisons to athletic sparkplugs such as Ray Durham and Eric Young. He packs surprising sock despite his stature and started finding the gaps more regularly last year. He turns in consistent quality at-bats and has improved his strike-zone judgment. He has the quickness and speed to steal bases with a high success rate. Drafted as a shortstop, Bourgeois made the full-time switch to second base last season. He shows good anticipation on grounders and has an average arm, but overall is just a fringe-average defender. After a strong Arizona Fall League performance, Bourgeois will return to Double-A to begin 2004. His profile mirrors Durham's through the same point of development, and Bourgeois has all the intangibles and passion to continue on the same path.

Year	Club (League)	Class	AVG	G	AB	R	H	2B	3B	HR	RBI	BB	SO	SB	SLG	OBP
2000	Rangers (GCL)	R	.239	24	88	18	21	4	0	0	6	14	15	9	.284	.356
2001	Pulaski (Appy)	R	.311	62	251	60	78	12	2	7	34	26	47	21	.458	.387
2002	Savannah (SAL)	A	.255	127	522	72	133	21	5	8	49	40	66	22	.360	.318
	Charlotte (FSL)	A	.185	9	27	5	5	1	0	0	4	2	4	1	.222	.233
2003	Stockton (Cal)	A	.329	69	277	75	91	22	3	4	34	36	33	16	.473	.416
	Frisco (TL)	AA	.252	55	202	28	51	5	4	4	21	16	45	3	.376	.308
MINOR LEAGUE TOTALS			.277	346	1367	258	379	65	14	23	148	134	210	72	.396	.351

9 Drew Meyer, ss/of

Born: Aug. 29, 1981. **Ht.:** 5-10. **Wt.:** 180. **Bats:** L. **Throws:** R. **School:** University of South Carolina. **Career Transactions:** Selected by Rangers in first round (10th overall) of 2002 draft; signed June 26, 2002.

A Dodgers second-round pick in 1999, Meyer led South Carolina to the College World Series and topped the Southeastern Conference in hits (120) and steals (39) in 2002. Though the Rangers needed pitching and already had Alex Rodriguez, they drafted Meyer 10th overall and drew plenty of criticism. He started slowly last year while trying to adapt to Texas' plate-discipline program but earned a promotion to Double-A in July. A good athlete, Meyer's tools play up because of his superior instincts. He has a strong, accurate arm and solid middle-of-the-diamond range. He possesses the first-step quickness to steal bases and has dangerous speed once he gets under way. In addition to reworking his approach, Meyer also has toying with adjusting his stroke. He has an unorthodox style—similar to Ichiro, moving out of the box as he swings—with a flat plane to his swing path.

He manages to make hard contact but is overaggressive and strikes out too often. Meyer's athleticism and versatility provide all kinds of defensive options, including the possibility of moving him to center field, where he played last spring and in instructional league, or catcher. He'll probably open this year as a Double-A shortstop.

Year	Club (League)	Class	AVG	G	AB	R	H	2B	3B	HR	RBI	BB	SO	SB	SLG	OBP
2002	Savannah (SAL)	A	.243	54	214	15	52	5	4	1	24	10	53	7	.318	.274
	Tulsa (TL)	AA	.214	4	14	0	3	0	0	0	0	1	5	0	.214	.267
2003	Stockton (Cal)	A	.281	94	398	59	112	16	9	5	53	32	92	24	.405	.330
	Frisco (TL)	AA	.316	26	98	14	31	1	1	0	6	11	23	9	.347	.385
MINOR LEAGUE TOTALS			.273	178	724	88	198	22	14	6	83	54	173	40	.367	.320

10 Josh Rupe, rhp

Born: Aug. 18, 1982. **Ht.:** 6-2. **Wt.:** 180. **Bats:** R. **Throws:** R. **School:** Louisburg (N.C.) JC. **Career Transactions:** Selected by White Sox in third round of 2002 draft; signed June 14, 2002 . . . Traded by White Sox with OF Anthony Webster and RHP Franklin Francisco to Rangers, July 24, 2003, completing trade in which Rangers sent OF Carl Everett and cash to White Sox for three players to be named (July 1, 2003).

The Rangers were allowed to choose three prospects from a pool of eight when they traded Carl Everett to the White Sox last summer, but Rupe was atop their list all along. Chicago brought him along slowly and didn't moved him into its low Class A rotation until mid-June. Rupe works with four pitches and a loose, live arm. His fastball sits at 91 mph and tops out at 95 with outstanding sink. His slider ranks among the best breaking balls in the organization. He also throws a good downward-breaking curveball. The Rangers were pleasantly surprised with Rupe's changeup, but he needs to build confidence in the pitch by throwing it more often. He wore down at the end of the season and has to improve his endurance. Armed with four pitches, command and projectability, Rupe has all the ingredients to develop into a solid middle-of-the-rotation starter. He'll move up to high Class A this season.

Year	Club (League)	Class	W	L	ERA	G	GS	CG	SV	IP	H	R	ER	HR	BB	SO	AVG
2002	Bristol (Appy)	R	3	3	5.26	17	2	0	0	38	38	23	22	4	22	40	.260
2003	Kannapolis (SAL)	A	5	5	3.02	26	7	2	6	66	50	27	22	0	36	69	.212
	Clinton (Mid)	A	4	1	3.90	6	5	0	0	28	29	14	12	1	7	23	.266
MINOR LEAGUE TOTALS			12	9	3.85	49	14	2	6	131	117	64	56	5	65	132	.238

11 Kelvin Jimenez, rhp

Born: Oct. 27, 1980. **Ht.:** 6-2. **Wt.:** 150. **Bats:** R. **Throws:** R. **Career Transactions:** Signed out of Dominican Republic by Rangers, May 7, 2000.

Jimenez never has been dominant, but the Rangers say he's on the verge of a breakout season. He aged two years after the crackdown on fraudulent birth certificates and is growing into his lean, athletic frame and adding velocity to his plus fastball. He pitches in the 89-93 mph neighborhood and will flash a 95 occasionally. Those readings could become more frequent as he continues to fill out. Jimenez already shows good, tight rotation on a plus slider, another good sign of pure arm strength. He throws strikes with both pitches. His changeup needs refinement. His future as a starter or reliever could be predicated on his ability to develop a third pitch. Coming out of the bullpen, Jimenez would be a quality eighth-inning setup man with two plus pitches, and he'd likely consistently fire his fastball in the mid-90s. Though he went 0-2 in the California League playoffs, he pitched well enough to win both games and impressed the Rangers with his composure. He'll move up to Double-A in 2004.

Year	Club (League)	Class	W	L	ERA	G	GS	CG	SV	IP	H	R	ER	HR	BB	SO	AVG
2000	Rangers (DSL)	R	3	6	4.62	17	9	0	0	64	70	47	33	1	32	60	.273
2001	Pulaski (Appy)	R	0	3	6.28	4	4	0	0	14	24	14	10	2	4	10	.353
	Rangers (GCL)	R	3	3	2.56	9	6	1	1	46	36	19	13	2	9	51	.214
2002	Savannah (SAL)	A	5	10	3.20	29	16	0	0	121	122	63	43	9	37	116	.259
2003	Stockton (Cal)	A	6	5	4.73	34	18	0	2	131	135	81	69	14	43	101	.266
MINOR LEAGUE TOTALS			17	27	4.01	93	53	1	3	377	387	224	168	28	125	338	.263

12 Anthony Webster, of

Born: April 10, 1983. **Ht.:** 6-0. **Wt.:** 190. **Bats:** L. **Throws:** R. **School:** Riverside HS, Parsons, Tenn. **Career Transactions:** Selected by White Sox in 15th round of 2001 draft; signed June 16, 2001 . . . Traded by White Sox with RHP Josh Rupe and RHP Franklin Francisco to Rangers, July 24, 2003, completing trade in which Rangers sent OF Carl Everett and cash to White Sox for three players to be named (July 1, 2003).

Webster was part of the payment for Carl Everett. An all-Tennessee running back in high school, he was recruited by Southeastern Conference football programs. The resulting signability concerns dropped him in the 2001 draft. After he hit .330 in two years of Rookie ball, his production dropped in his first full season but he still held his own. Webster has a good idea at the plate and puts the ball in play consistently. Rangers hitting instructors are working with him to improve his hand position and his pre-swing load to help him drive the ball more often. Webster is a 60 runner on the 20-80 scouting scale, with an above-average arm and solid instincts for center field. He's scheduled to play in high Class A this year.

Year	Club (League)	Class	AVG	G	AB	R	H	2B	3B	HR	RBI	BB	SO	SB	SLG	OBP
2001	White Sox (AZL)	R	.307	55	225	38	69	9	7	0	30	9	33	18	.409	.332
2002	Bristol (Appy)	R	.352	61	244	58	86	7	3	1	30	38	38	16	.418	.448
2003	Kannapolis (SAL)	A	.289	94	363	68	105	18	1	2	33	31	58	20	.361	.353
	Clinton (Mid)	A	.270	18	74	11	20	7	0	1	9	0	8	4	.405	.286
MINOR LEAGUE TOTALS			.309	228	906	175	280	41	11	4	102	78	137	58	.392	.370

13 Ben Kozlowski, lhp

Born: Aug. 16, 1980. **Ht.:** 6-6. **Wt.:** 220. **Bats:** L. **Throws:** L. **School:** Santa Fe (Fla.) CC. **Career Transactions:** Selected by Braves in 12th round of 1999 draft; signed June 12, 1999 . . . Traded by Braves to Rangers for LHP Andy Pratt, April 9, 2002.

Kozlowski and C.J. Wilson entered last season as the top southpaws in the system. Kozlowski blew out his elbow and had Tommy John surgery in June, and Wilson had the same operation two months later. The Rangers hope to get Kozlowski back on the mound in May, while Wilson will miss the 2004 season. The Rangers picked up Kozlowski after the 2002 season, when they needed to find a home for Andy Pratt to clear a spot on their 40-man roster. Kozlowski was expected to contend for a rotation spot last season, but his velocity and ability to locate his pitches were absent last spring. When he's healthy, he's a workhorse in the Andy Pettitte mold. Kozlowski's fastball sits in the low 90s with solid movement, while his curveball has hard downward bite. Though he shows a feel for his changeup and maintains fastball arm speed with it, he was working on commanding the pitch more effectively before he broke down. The Rangers have been encouraged by his work ethic during rehab.

Year	Club (League)	Class	W	L	ERA	G	GS	CG	SV	IP	H	R	ER	HR	BB	SO	AVG
1999	Braves (GCL)	R	1	1	1.87	15	0	0	3	34	28	9	7	0	6	29	.222
2000	Macon (SAL)	A	3	8	4.21	15	14	0	0	77	76	53	36	6	39	67	.252
2001	Macon (SAL)	A	10	7	2.48	26	23	1	0	145	134	60	40	8	27	147	.248
	Myrtle Beach (Car)	A	0	2	3.77	2	2	0	0	14	15	7	6	1	3	13	.283
2002	Myrtle Beach (Car)	A	0	1	4.50	1	1	0	0	4	4	5	2	0	3	3	.235
	Charlotte (FSL)	A	4	4	2.05	21	12	0	0	79	63	31	18	2	25	76	.219
	Tulsa (TL)	AA	4	2	1.90	8	8	0	0	52	28	12	11	3	22	41	.155
	Texas (AL)	MAJ	0	0	6.30	2	2	0	0	10	11	7	7	3	11	6	.289
2003	Frisco (TL)	AA	3	2	5.43	11	10	0	0	55	71	38	33	4	27	29	.313
MAJOR LEAGUE TOTALS			0	0	6.30	2	2	0	0	10	11	7	7	3	11	6	.289
MINOR LEAGUE TOTALS			25	27	2.99	99	70	1	3	460	419	215	153	24	152	405	.242

14 Edwin Moreno, rhp

Born: July 30, 1980. **Ht.:** 6-1. **Wt.:** 170. **Bats:** R. **Throws:** R. **Career Transactions:** Signed out of Venezuela by Rangers, Feb. 13, 1998.

Moreno's velocity has made it hard for him to garner attention, and he was left unprotected through two Rule 5 drafts and missed much of 2002 with a foot injury. He returned in Double-A last season but didn't get a shot at the rotation until the end of May. Moreno flourished as a starter, going 5-4, 2.86 with a .231 opponent average. He throws four pitches for strikes to both sides of the plate, working on a nice downhill plane thanks to his over-the-top delivery. Moreno's fastball is solid-average at 90-91 mph and features occasional sinking action. His sharp, 80-85 mph slider and changeup are plus pitches, and he mixes in a decent curveball. There's not a lot of deception to his delivery, which is why he doesn't miss a lot of bats. He has to rely on location and changing speeds. Moreno is his own pitching coach on the mound. When he loses his arm slot, he can make the correction on his own. Moreno was fatigued in August and was shut down the last two weeks of the season with a sore shoulder. The Rangers don't count it as a significant setback. They expect him to join the Triple-A rotation this spring and contribute in Texas later in the year.

Year	Club (League)	Class	W	L	ERA	G	GS	CG	SV	IP	H	R	ER	HR	BB	SO	AVG
1998	Guacara 2 (VSL)	R	3	6	3.84	14	13	0	0	68	68	41	29	1	29	63	.265
1999	Cabudare (VSL)	R	1	0	0.49	8	3	0	0	18	13	6	1	0	7	16	.194
2000	Savannah (SAL)	A	9	8	3.25	23	22	1	0	133	127	58	48	9	46	89	.251
2001	Charlotte (FSL)	A	8	9	4.03	28	28	1	0	152	142	83	68	10	51	92	.247
2002	Rangers (GCL)	R	2	2	3.38	9	7	0	0	37	30	18	14	2	10	23	.213
	Charlotte (FSL)	A	3	0	0.59	6	6	0	0	31	20	2	2	0	3	23	.180
2003	Frisco (TL)	AA	6	5	3.29	29	15	0	0	112	105	50	41	7	33	74	.248
MINOR LEAGUE TOTALS			31	31	3.31	117	94	2	0	551	505	258	203	29	179	380	.243

15 Erik Thompson, rhp

Born: June 23, 1982. **Ht.:** 5-11. **Wt.:** 180. **Bats:** R. **Throws:** R. **School:** Pensacola (Fla.) JC. **Career Transactions:** Selected by Rangers in 12th round of 2002 draft; signed June 21, 2002.

Drafted in the 43rd round out of high school by the Rangers in 2000, Thompson passed on his commitment to Florida to spend two years at Pensacola Junior College. His freshman season was wiped out by Tommy John surgery. He recovered in time to get drafted by the Rangers again in 2002, and shows no ill effects from the operation. Despite his lack of size, Thompson has a power arm. As a high school sophomore, he once recorded all 21 outs in a seven-inning complete game by strikeout. He fills the zone with three pitches, including a 90-95 mph sinking fastball. His slider is a solid pitch when he stays on top of it, but he drops his arm slot, costing the pitch depth and bite. He's working on improving his changeup as well. If there's a knock on Thompson's stuff, it's that it often arrives on a flat plane, making it more hittable. He finished his first full season with 13 scoreless frames and 16 strikeouts in the California League playoffs. Thompson's command and control are so good, that his pitches should improve with experience. He's slated to join the Double-A rotation.

Year	Club (League)	Class	W	L	ERA	G	GS	CG	SV	IP	H	R	ER	HR	BB	SO	AVG
2002	Rangers (GCL)	R	2	2	2.04	10	5	0	0	40	38	12	9	2	2	34	.250
	Pulaski (Appy)	R	1	1	3.18	3	3	0	0	17	19	6	6	0	2	16	.297
2003	Clinton (Mid)	A	5	2	2.81	14	7	0	2	58	49	24	18	6	5	52	.225
	Stockton (Cal)	A	8	3	2.91	19	9	0	0	80	74	28	26	6	13	62	.243
MINOR LEAGUE TOTALS			16	8	2.73	46	24	0	2	195	180	70	59	14	22	164	.244

16 C.J. Wilson, lhp

Born: Nov. 18, 1980. **Ht.:** 6-2. **Wt.:** 190. **Bats:** L. **Throws:** L. **School:** Loyola Marymount University. **Career Transactions:** Selected by Rangers in fifth round of 2001 draft; signed June 12, 2001.

Wilson likely won't log any meaningful time on a mound until the spring of 2005 thanks to Tommy John surgery last August, but he should regain his status as one of the Rangers' top lefthanders. Wilson is a good athlete with an outstanding work ethic. He went from a 5-foot-2, 103-pound high school freshman to Orange Empire Conference co-player of the year in 2000 at national junior college powerhouse Santa Ana (Calif.). When he's on, he works aggressively with an 88-92 mph fastball that has good natural movement. He battled elbow soreness for much of 2003, costing him velocity and effectiveness at times. Wilson tightened the rotation on his curveball, which shows the makings of a plus pitch, and also improved his control last year. His changeup can be a weapon. A student of the game, he studies hitters' weaknesses and has a natural feel for exploiting them. The Rangers have been pleased with his rehab work, so it's possible he could return sooner than expected.

Year	Club (League)	Class	W	L	ERA	G	GS	CG	SV	IP	H	R	ER	HR	BB	SO	AVG
2001	Pulaski (Appy)	R	1	0	0.96	8	8	0	0	38	24	6	4	2	9	49	.178
	Savannah (SAL)	A	1	2	3.18	5	5	2	0	34	30	13	12	2	9	26	.252
2002	Charlotte (FSL)	A	10	2	3.06	26	15	0	1	106	86	48	36	4	41	76	.215
	Tulsa (TL)	AA	1	0	1.80	5	5	0	0	30	23	6	6	0	12	17	.211
2003	Frisco (TL)	AA	6	9	5.05	22	21	0	0	123	135	79	69	11	38	89	.276
MINOR LEAGUE TOTALS			19	13	3.46	66	54	2	1	331	298	152	127	19	109	257	.238

17 Kameron Loe, rhp

Born: Sept. 10, 1981. **Ht.:** 6-8. **Wt.:** 220. **Bats:** R. **Throws:** R. **School:** Cal State Northridge. **Career Transactions:** Selected by Rangers in 20th round of 2002 draft; signed June 8, 2002.

Six-foot-8 pitchers with a track record of success pitching at a high-profile NCAA Division I program usually aren't overlooked in the draft, but Loe's below-average velocity was hardly enough for area scouts to give him a second look in the spring of 2002. His low three-quarters arm slot didn't help him attract attention, either. His knack for pitching is tailor-made for the Rangers, however, and they were able to wait until the 20th round for him. His 1.67 ERA in his first full season ranked second in the minors behind only Detroit's Jon Connolly (1.41) in 2003. Loe, who hit 90 mph more consistently in high school, dropped his arm slot at Cal State Northridge and traded velocity for movement. He works with a deceptive delivery that makes his 85-90 mph sinker appear harder than it is. He pounds the ball down in the strike zone and induces lots of groundballs. Loe has an effective changeup with good late action. He's working to tighten the spin on his big, sweeping breaking ball. He consistently repeats his delivery and his arm works tension-free, leading the Rangers to believe there's more velocity in his future. Power never will be his forte, so he'll be challenged by more advanced hitters as he moves up the ladder. Loe's makeup is outstanding, which along with his plus command and movement will aid him as he tries to make the move to Double-A.

Year	Club (League)	Class	W	L	ERA	G	GS	CG	SV	IP	H	R	ER	HR	BB	SO	AVG
2002	Pulaski (Appy)	R	4	4	4.47	14	11	0	1	58	64	34	29	3	17	55	.271
2003	Clinton (Mid)	A	4	3	1.95	23	11	0	2	97	78	34	21	3	19	94	.217
	Stockton (Cal)	A	3	0	0.96	9	4	0	1	38	26	7	4	1	6	31	.183
MINOR LEAGUE TOTALS			11	7	2.52	46	26	0	4	193	168	75	54	7	42	180	.228

18 Will Smith, of

Born: Oct. 23, 1981. **Ht.:** 6-1. **Wt.:** 180. **Bats:** L. **Throws:** R. **School:** Palo Verde HS, Tucson. **Career Transactions:** Selected by Marlins in sixth round of 2000 draft; signed June 9, 2000 . . . Traded by Marlins with 1B Adrian Gonzalez and LHP Ryan Snare to Rangers for RHP Ugueth Urbina, July 11, 2003.

Adrian Gonzalez drew most of the attention in the Ugueth Urbina deal, but Smith gave the Rangers a second potent bat. He set the Arizona high school record for homers and has shown a consistent ability to drive the ball as a pro. Some scouts question his power potential, however. That may be because of his slight build or his unorthodox wide-open hitting stance. He was bothered by a wrist injury early last season, though he still managed to hit .313 in April before finally requiring surgery. The operation kept him out for two months and affected him upon his return. Smith didn't endear himself to his new organization with his work habits. His power output would benefit from a more consistent conditioning program, and the Rangers want him to put more time into extra hitting. Smith has to learn to take pitches the other way and buy into Texas' plate-discipline philosophy. He also has room for improvement as a left fielder, though his arm is solid-average. He'll return to Double-A and could be a pleasant surprise after a disappointing start in the Rangers system.

Year	Club (League)	Class	AVG	G	AB	R	H	2B	3B	HR	RBI	BB	SO	SB	SLG	OBP
2000	Marlins (GCL)	R	.368	54	204	37	75	21	2	2	34	26	24	7	.520	.440
2001	Kane County (Mid)	A	.280	125	535	92	150	26	2	16	91	32	74	4	.426	.324
2002	Jupiter (FSL)	A	.299	133	549	84	164	30	12	14	73	31	75	8	.474	.336
2003	Carolina (SL)	AA	.293	34	123	23	36	5	1	1	13	11	23	1	.374	.346
	Jupiter (FSL)	A	.083	3	12	0	1	1	0	0	2	0	2	0	.167	.083
	Frisco (TL)	AA	.200	37	130	11	26	6	1	4	15	5	28	0	.354	.226
MINOR LEAGUE TOTALS			.291	386	1553	247	452	89	18	37	228	105	226	20	.443	.336

19 Jason Botts, of

Born: July 26, 1980. **Ht.:** 6-6. **Wt.:** 250. **Bats:** B. **Throws:** R. **School:** Glendale (Calif.) JC. **Career Transactions:** Selected by Rangers in 46th round of 1999 draft; signed May 15, 2000.

Thanks to the Rangers' depth on the corners and the addition of first baseman Adrian Gonzalez at midseason, Botts has bounced between first base, his natural position, and left and right field. At 6-foot-6 and 250 pounds, he's an Adonis in a baseball uniform. Even at his size he doesn't sacrifice any athleticism and he ran the best 60-yard dash (6.55 seconds) in the organization two years ago. Botts has a patient approach and is an on-base machine, though at times he is too selective. The Rangers asked him to be more aggressive in trying to target pitches he could attack last season. He's more comfortable from the right side of the plate and temporarily gave up switch-hitting in junior college. There's length and often too much strength to his swing, creating problems getting the bat head to the ball on a direct path, especially with inside pitches. He won't tap into his big-time raw power until he makes adjustments. Botts hasn't taken to the outfield as expected, looking tentative and showing a well-below-average arm. He often is asked about in trade talks, by organizations who covet tools and athleticism as well as by those who emphasize plate discipline. However, he wasn't added to the 40-man roster last winter and was available in the Rule 5 draft. Botts will return to Double-A and try to find a defensive home, most likely in left field.

Year	Club (League)	Class	AVG	G	AB	R	H	2B	3B	HR	RBI	BB	SO	SB	SLG	OBP
2000	Rangers (GCL)	R	.319	48	163	36	52	12	0	6	34	26	29	4	.503	.440
2001	Savannah (SAL)	A	.309	114	392	63	121	24	2	9	50	53	88	13	.449	.416
	Charlotte (FSL)	A	.167	4	12	1	2	1	0	0	0	4	4	0	.250	.375
2002	Charlotte (FSL)	A	.254	116	401	67	102	22	5	9	54	75	99	7	.401	.387
2003	Stockton (Cal)	A	.314	76	283	58	89	14	2	9	61	45	59	12	.473	.409
	Frisco (TL)	AA	.263	55	194	26	51	11	1	4	27	21	45	6	.392	.341
MINOR LEAGUE TOTALS			.289	413	1445	251	417	84	10	37	226	224	324	42	.437	.399

20 Ryan Snare, lhp

Born: Feb. 8, 1979. **Ht.:** 6-0. **Wt.:** 190. **Bats:** L. **Throws:** L. **School:** University of North Carolina. **Career Transactions:** Selected by Reds in second round of 2000 draft; signed Aug. 11, 2000 . . . Traded by Reds with OF Juan Encarnacion and 2B Wilton Guerrero to Marlins for RHP Ryan Dempster, July 11, 2002 . . . Traded by Marlins with 1B Adrian Gonzalez and OF Will Smith to Rangers for RHP Ugueth Urbina, July 11, 2003.

Snare came to the Rangers in the Ugueth Urbina trade last year, making it the second straight summer he switched organizations. The Rangers coveted Snare's piching instincts and greeted him with a promotion to Triple-A after acquiring him. He commands three solid pitches for strikes. His fastball consistently sits between 88-92 mph with average movement, and his big, knee-buckling curveball is one of the top breaking balls in the system. He's still trying to hone his changeup. At just 6 feet tall, he pitches uphill at times, but he's also able to correct that flaw when he stays tall through his delivery. Some scouts project Snare as a quality set-up man, though it was surprising to see lefties rip him for a .295 average last year. He struggled to maintain the sharpness on his curve against lefties and didn't throw his changeup to them. Snare is aggressive with his fastball on the inner half against righties. He's slated to begin the year in the Triple-A rotation, though the bullpen hasn't been ruled out. He could be among the first prospects summoned to Arlington in 2004.

Year	Club (League)	Class	W	L	ERA	G	GS	CG	SV	IP	H	R	ER	HR	BB	SO	AVG
2001	Dayton (Mid)	A	9	5	3.05	21	20	0	0	115	101	45	39	7	37	118	.238
2002	Stockton (Cal)	A	8	2	3.07	13	13	0	0	82	74	36	28	4	18	81	.238
	Chattanooga (SL)	AA	0	0	3.00	5	0	0	0	6	5	3	2	1	3	4	.263
	Portland (EL)	AA	4	2	3.44	11	9	0	0	55	46	25	21	6	19	52	.224
2003	Carolina (SL)	AA	5	4	3.67	18	18	0	0	103	98	46	42	4	37	77	.253
	Oklahoma (PCL)	AAA	4	5	3.46	9	9	0	0	55	59	26	21	7	13	28	.277
MINOR LEAGUE TOTALS			30	18	3.31	77	69	0	0	416	383	181	153	29	127	360	.246

21 John Hudgins, rhp

Born: Aug. 31, 1981. **Ht.:** 6-2. **Wt.:** 195. **Bats:** R. **Throws:** R. **School:** Stanford University. **Career Transactions:** Selected by Rangers in third round of 2003 draft; signed July 17, 2003.

Scouting director Grady Fuson selected Hudgins in the 20th round out of high school in 2000, when he held the same position in Oakland. The 2003 Pacific-10 Conference pitcher of the year, Hudgins was at his best in the College World Series. Though Rice won the national title, Hudgins dealt the Owls their only loss in the three-game finals and was named Most Outstanding Player after going 3-0, 1.88 in 24 innings. His workload, however, became a controversial topic. Hudgins piled up an NCAA Division I-high 165 innings and threw 350 pitches in 10 days at the CWS. While it's impossible to know how directly it was related to his use at Stanford, Hudgins reported shoulder soreness and worked just two innings after signing for $490,000. Doctors discovered that he has thoracic outlet syndrome, a condition that causes circulation problems in his right arm. Hudgins opted for a conservative rehabilitation program as opposed to surgery. The operation is a relatively minor procedure that Kenny Rogers recovered from in 2001, and he discussed it with Hudgins. When healthy, Hudgins can carve up the plate with command of four average pitches. His fastball, which topped out at 93 mph in high school, is regularly clocked at 88-89 mph. His changeup is his most advanced pitch and has plus potential, while his curveball and slider both have tight rotation and depth. Hudgins is intelligent and knows how to go after hitters. He took a risk by avoiding surgery, and the concern is that his condition won't heal on its own and will set him back further in 2004. He was throwing twice a week during the offseason in preparation for spring training and a potential assignment to high Class A.

Year	Club (League)	Class	W	L	ERA	G	GS	CG	SV	IP	H	R	ER	HR	BB	SO	AVG
2003	Clinton (Mid)	A	0	0	0.00	1	0	0	0	2	1	0	0	0	0	4	.143
MINOR LEAGUE TOTALS			0	0	0.00	1	0	0	0	2	1	0	0	0	0	4	.143

22 A.J. Murray, lhp

Born: March 17, 1982. **Ht.:** 6-3. **Wt.:** 200. **Bats:** B. **Throws:** L. **School:** Salt Lake CC. **Career Transactions:** Selected by Rangers in 19th round of 2000 draft; signed May 27, 2001.

Murray represents the Rangers' pitching blueprint. He has moved quickly since signing as a draft-and-follow in 2001, and spent last year as the second-youngest regular starter in the Texas League. He turned in the league's seventh-best ERA and was even better (0.77 ERA) in two playoff starts. Nicknamed "Pirate" because his given name is Arlington and his teammates took to calling him "Arrr" in 2001, he's similar to C.J. Wilson and Ryan Snare. Murray may rely even more on touch and feel than those fellow lefties. He borders on the soft-tosser ledge with a fastball that sits from 86-88 mph and ranges from 84-90. He has a solid four-pitch mix, though, and locates his stuff to both sides of the plate. Murray's changeup is his best pitch, and he throws a big-breaking though inconsistent curveball. He has a good shot at joining the Triple-A rotation this year and profiles as a fifth starter in the majors.

Year	Club (League)	Class	W	L	ERA	G	GS	CG	SV	IP	H	R	ER	HR	BB	SO	AVG
2001	Rangers (GCL)	R	3	3	1.86	12	8	0	0	53	48	15	11	1	10	45	.247
2002	Savannah (SAL)	A	5	3	2.87	14	8	0	0	63	63	22	20	0	14	51	.270
	Charlotte (FSL)	A	3	3	3.02	19	14	0	2	83	77	31	28	4	20	68	.243

2003	Frisco (TL)		AA	10	4	3.63	27	25	0	0	144	134	68	58	13	63	90	.254
MINOR LEAGUE TOTALS				21	13	3.07	72	55	0	2	343	322	136	117	18	107	254	.253

23 Jeremy Cleveland, of

Born: Sept. 10, 1981. **Ht.:** 6-2. **Wt.:** 185. **Bats:** R. **Throws:** R. **School:** University of North Carolina. **Career Transactions:** Selected by Rangers in eighth round of 2003 draft; signed June 16, 2003.

Cleveland wasn't a classic premium prospect, but with the greater emphasis on performance and on-base ability these days, it's surprising he lasted until the eighth round of the 2003 draft. Cleveland led the Atlantic Coast Conference with a .410 average and 103 hits while posting a .512 OBP and 37-34 walk-strikeout ratio. He continued to rake after signing for $85,000, finishing second in the short-season Northwest League batting race to Spokane teammate Dane Bubela. While Cleveland hit 19 home runs last spring for North Carolina, most scouts write that off as aluminum-bat pop and don't project him to have better than average power. He does everything else right at the plate, though. Cleveland has a level swing with solid bat speed, similar to 2002 ACC batting champ Khalil Greene. Cleveland keeps his hands back and demonstrates advanced pitch recognition. Primarily a first baseman for the Tar Heels, Cleveland has below-average speed and arm strength. There are questions about where he can play defensively, but the Rangers are hoping he'll take to left field and continue to produce. He's advanced enough at the plate to skip a level and handle a jump to high Class A in 2004.

Year	Club (League)	Class	AVG	G	AB	R	H	2B	3B	HR	RBI	BB	SO	SB	SLG	OBP
2003	Spokane (NWL)	A	.322	64	245	64	79	20	3	7	53	40	50	5	.514	.432
MINOR LEAGUE TOTALS			.322	64	245	64	79	20	3	7	53	40	50	5	.514	.432

24 Patrick Boyd, of

Born: Sept. 7, 1978. **Ht.:** 6-3. **Wt.:** 200. **Bats:** B. **Throws:** R. **School:** Clemson University. **Career Transactions:** Selected by Rangers in seventh round of 2001 draft; signed Jan. 16, 2002.

Boyd made an immediate impact in Clemson's outfield after spurning the Mariners as a second-round pick out of high school in 1998. He emerged as a second-team All-American as a sophomore, when he hit .390-17-70 with 20 steals. But as a junior he was hampered by a thumb injury and hit a career-low .293 in 2000. The Pirates drafted him in the fourth round but didn't come close to signing him. As a senior, Boyd cracked a vertebra and was limited to two at-bats. He nearly returned to Clemson as a redshirt senior before signing with the Rangers as a seventh-rounder for $600,000—the second-highest bonus ever given to a player in that round. Injuries dogged him during his 2002 pro debut before Boyd finally played pain-free for the first time in four years in 2003. He's the best defensive outfielder in the system, with plus range to cover the gaps and above-average arm strength. He gets outstanding jumps by reacting to pitches as they cross the plate. Boyd might reach the big leagues for his defensive tools and athleticism alone, but to become anything more than a reserve he needs to make offensive adjustments. He's a line-drive hitter from both sides of the plate, though he shows more power as a righty. He recognizes pitches better from that side and looks for fastballs to hammer, but scouts like his lefthanded stroke more. He doesn't have tremendous bat speed and has holes on the inner half of the plate. Boyd will be an everyday center fielder in Double-A this year.

Year	Club (League)	Class	AVG	G	AB	R	H	2B	3B	HR	RBI	BB	SO	SB	SLG	OBP
2002	Savannah (SAL)	A	.241	69	257	25	62	15	2	5	30	24	68	8	.374	.313
	Charlotte (FSL)	A	.250	4	12	0	3	1	0	0	3	1	3	0	.333	.308
2003	Stockton (Cal)	A	.294	58	221	48	65	17	0	13	50	29	68	11	.548	.381
	Frisco (TL)	AA	.194	46	160	21	31	5	3	3	9	16	39	9	.319	.278
MINOR LEAGUE TOTALS			.248	177	650	94	161	38	5	21	92	70	178	28	.418	.328

25 Matt Lorenzo, rhp

Born: June 21, 1982. **Ht.:** 6-3. **Wt.:** 205. **Bats:** L. **Throws:** R. **School:** Kent State University. **Career Transactions:** Selected by Rangers in fifth round of 2003 draft; signed June 10, 2003.

After going 4-0, 2.82 as a Georgia Tech freshman in 2001, Lorenzo transferred closer to home to Kent State, which had recruited him out of an Ohio high school. His stock improved as his velocity increased, and he turned in one of his best performances against Ohio ace Marc Cornell with a host of scouts and crosscheckers on hand last spring. Lorenzo led the Mid-American Conference by limiting opposing hitters to a .203 average. Strong and durable, Lorenzo is equipped with a power arm and a polished delivery. He touched 95 mph in college and sat between 88-92 last summer after signing for $210,000. Lorenzo has a feel for four offerings, and his curveball could become his put-away pitch. It shows good, late downward action out of his high three-quarters release point. His slider and changeup are less consistent but have the potential to at least be effective. Lorenzo probably will start 2004 in low Class A, where he'll work on adding movement to his fastball and improving his command.

Year	Club (League)	Class	W	L	ERA	G	GS	CG	SV	IP	H	R	ER	HR	BB	SO	AVG
2003	Spokane (NWL)	A	5	1	2.53	16	12	0	0	57	43	19	16	2	22	54	.216
MINOR LEAGUE TOTALS			5	1	2.53	16	12	0	0	57	43	19	16	2	22	54	.216

26 Nick Regilio, rhp

Born: Sept. 4, 1978. **Ht.:** 6-2. **Wt.:** 180. **Bats:** R. **Throws:** R. **School:** Jacksonville University.
Career Transactions: Selected by Rangers in second round of 1999 draft; signed June 11, 1999.

The perfect game Regilio threw for in the high Class A Florida State League in 2001 should have been a blessing, but he seemingly has been cursed since. He was bothered in the second half of that season by a ribcage injury and missed time in 2002 with biceps tendinitis. That was a prelude to rotator-cuff surgery last spring, all but wiping out his 2003 season. Regilio rebounded rather quickly from an injury of such magnitude and made good use of his Arizona Fall League assignment last year. He regained his 91-93 mph fastball, touched 94-95 on several occasions in Arizona and didn't sacrifice any of his sinking movement. Regilio's fastball command is average at best right now and is hindered by his tendency to overthrow, which causes him to get offline to the plate. Overall, he has a compact delivery with good arm speed and a clean arm action. Regilio's curveball has hard downward bite, as does his slider, though he needs to do a better job of distinguishing between the two pitches. His changeup is solid-average. He needs more experience in the upper levels, but if he stays healthy he could make a push for the majors by the second half of 2004.

Year	Club (League)	Class	W	L	ERA	G	GS	CG	SV	IP	H	R	ER	HR	BB	SO	AVG
1999	Pulaski (Appy)	R	4	2	1.63	11	8	1	0	50	30	12	9	2	16	58	.172
2000	Charlotte (FSL)	A	4	3	4.52	20	20	0	0	86	94	54	43	8	29	63	.286
2001	Charlotte (FSL)	A	6	2	1.55	11	11	1	0	64	47	16	11	5	16	60	.200
	Tulsa (TL)	AA	1	3	5.54	10	10	0	0	52	62	34	32	2	20	40	.297
2002	Tulsa (TL)	AA	6	8	3.44	19	19	2	0	105	97	46	40	8	47	59	.245
	Oklahoma (PCL)	AAA	1	0	10.80	1	1	0	0	5	9	6	6	1	5	4	.391
2003	Rangers (AZL)	R	0	0	0.00	2	2	0	0	5	4	2	0	0	1	7	.235
	Frisco (TL)	AA	0	1	21.60	1	0	0	0	2	5	4	4	0	1	2	.556
MINOR LEAGUE TOTALS			22	19	3.55	75	71	4	0	368	348	174	145	26	135	293	.250

27 Nate Gold, 1b/3b

Born: June 12, 1980. **Ht.:** 6-3. **Wt.:** 220. **Bats:** R. **Throws:** R. **School:** Gonzaga University.
Career Transactions: Selected by Rangers in 10th round of 2002 draft; signed June 15, 2002.

Gold led NCAA Division I with 33 homers and was the West Coast Conference player of the year in 2002. He has carried the label of a one-dimensional slugger dating since his days at Treasure Valley (Ore.) Community College, but he has one other quality the Rangers covet: plate discipline. He draws comparisons to Jason Botts and Triple-A first baseman Jason Hart for his approach at the plate. Gold has 70 raw power on the 20-80 scouting scale, but has produced more doubles than homers since he turned pro. He's working on becoming less pull-conscious and driving the ball up the middle. In college, he was easy prey for pitchers who worked him away, but he has learned to lay off those pitches or take them to the opposite field. In the field, Gold is average at first base and got sporadic work at third base in the second half of 2003. He has an average arm, good feet and decent instincts for the hot corner, though it remains to be seen if he can handle the position on a daily basis. Gold will play primarily first base and see some time at third in high Class A this year.

Year	Club (League)	Class	AVG	G	AB	R	H	2B	3B	HR	RBI	BB	SO	SB	SLG	OBP
2002	Pulaski (Appy)	R	.319	30	113	19	36	9	1	5	30	17	20	2	.549	.405
	Savannah (SAL)	A	.190	37	142	12	27	7	0	5	14	11	38	0	.345	.258
2003	Clinton (Mid)	A	.268	107	369	58	99	35	3	12	71	59	76	4	.477	.370
MINOR LEAGUE TOTALS			.260	174	624	89	162	51	4	22	115	87	134	6	.460	.353

28 Franklin Francisco, rhp

Born: Sept. 11, 1979. **Ht.:** 6-2. **Wt.:** 180. **Bats:** R. **Throws:** R. **Career Transactions:** Signed out of Dominican Republic by Red Sox, Dec. 15, 1996 . . . On disabled list, May 31-Sept. 2, 1997 . . . Traded by Red Sox with LHP Byeong An to White Sox for RHP Bobby Howry, July 31, 2002 . . . Traded by White Sox with OF Anthony Webster and RHP Josh Rupe to Rangers, July 24, 2003, completing trade in which Rangers sent OF Carl Everett and cash to White Sox for three players to be named (July 1, 2003).

Francisco ranked as the No. 10 prospect in a weak Red Sox system following his breakthrough 2001 season. Since then he has gone through a few changes, switching organizations twice through trades and having his age revised upward nine months. He also switched from relieving to starting in mid-2002. Part of the Carl Everett trade with the White Sox, Francisco continues to attract attention and tease scouts with his power arsenal. His inconsistency prompts scouts to compare his plus fastball/slider combination to Octavio Dotel's one day and turn him in as a fringe prospect the next. When Francisco is on he can be electric, lighting up radar guns with 93-96 mph readings while also showing a plus slider and an occasional good changeup. But too often he struggles with his fastball location, and his velocity will dip to 90 mph because he's unable to repeat his delivery and release point. He was wildly inconsistent after joining the Rangers, but his flaws are correctable and he has two big league pitches. He'll return to the bullpen this year in Double-A, where he has a career 7.54 ERA.

Year	Club (League)	Class	W	L	ERA	G	GS	CG	SV	IP	H	R	ER	HR	BB	SO	AVG
1997	Did not play—Injured																
1998	Co-Op (DSL)	R	0	5	10.31	16	13	0	0	48	44	66	55	4	76	53	.243
1999	Red Sox (GCL)	R	2	4	4.56	12	7	0	0	53	58	39	27	3	35	48	.275
2000	Red Sox (GCL)	R	0	0	18.00	1	0	0	0	1	2	3	2	0	2	1	.400
2001	Augusta (SAL)	A	4	3	2.91	37	0	0	2	68	40	25	22	3	30	90	.168
2002	Trenton (EL)	AA	2	2	5.63	9	0	0	0	16	10	13	10	0	16	18	.172
	Sarasota (FSL)	A	1	5	2.55	16	10	0	0	53	33	19	15	1	27	58	.185
	Winston-Salem (Car)	A	0	4	8.06	6	6	0	0	26	31	23	23	3	18	25	.310
2003	Winston-Salem (Car)	A	7	3	3.56	16	16	1	0	78	59	40	31	7	36	67	.207
	Frisco (TL)	AA	2	3	8.41	7	6	0	0	35	43	33	33	5	18	22	.305
MINOR LEAGUE TOTALS			18	29	5.18	120	58	1	2	379	320	261	218	26	258	382	.229

29 Justin Echols, rhp

Born: Oct. 6, 1980. **Ht.:** 6-3. **Wt.:** 180. **Bats:** R. **Throws:** R. **School:** Greenway HS, Phoenix.
Career Transactions: Selected by Rangers in 11th round of 1999 draft; signed June 2, 1999.

The Rangers don't have many power arms capable of blowing up radar guns, but they're rich in pitchers with a feel for their craft, and Echols fits that mold. He repeated high Class A to begin 2003, taking part in Stockton's eight-man tandem starter program. After a slow start in April, he heated up to earn a promotion to Double-A. Echols continued to miss bats at the next level, though his control eluded him when he walked 14 in back-to-back starts. He needs to improve the command of his fringe-average 87-90 mph fastball to set hitters up for his secondary pitches. He has the ability to put them away with a tight 76-80 mph curveball, and his decent splitter as an effective alternative to a changeup. Echols is a good athlete who repeats his delivery well, but he's not projectable and will have to live with his present velocity. He profiles as a back-end starter or middle reliever and could compete for a Triple-A job this year.

Year	Club (League)	Class	W	L	ERA	G	GS	CG	SV	IP	H	R	ER	HR	BB	SO	AVG
1999	Rangers (GCL)	R	2	2	2.60	14	4	0	0	35	27	14	10	1	21	32	.223
2000	Pulaski (Appy)	R	0	4	4.41	9	5	0	0	33	34	21	16	2	15	39	.266
2001	Savannah (SAL)	A	5	9	3.80	36	13	1	3	123	88	58	52	4	67	156	.201
2002	Charlotte (FSL)	A	7	5	3.93	46	11	0	4	112	94	57	49	6	54	117	.225
2003	Stockton (Cal)	A	4	6	2.85	25	13	0	0	98	74	42	31	4	43	98	.206
	Frisco (TL)	AA	1	3	4.91	8	8	0	0	44	32	25	24	5	26	33	.205
MINOR LEAGUE TOTALS			19	29	3.68	138	54	1	7	445	349	217	182	22	226	475	.215

30 Marc LaMacchia, rhp

Born: March 27, 1982. **Ht.:** 6-1. **Wt.:** 190. **Bats:** R. **Throws:** R. **School:** Florida State University.
Career Transactions: Selected by Rangers in 21st round of 2003 draft; signed Aug. 24, 2003.

The Cardinals picked LaMacchia one slot ahead of Kyle Sleeth in the 18th round of the 2000 draft. They both opted for college and established themselves as high-profile prospects by the end of their sophomore seasons. Sleeth was drafted third overall by the Tigers in 2003, while LaMacchia's draft stock plummeted after he had Tommy John surgery last May. He made two early season starts before blowing out his elbow, allowing just one hit and fanning 11 in nine innings. Tabbed as a second- or third-rounder before the injury, he fell to the 21st round. He appeared to be heading back to Florida State and didn't sign until the day classes started. The Rangers say he's similar to John Hudgins but with more natural arm strength. LaMacchia's fastball was impressive for its 91-92 mph velocity and heavy sinking movement, and he also was armed with an above-average curveball. He had good command and understands how to set up hitters. He should regain his previous form, though he's not expected to start pitching again before May at the earliest. The Rangers would like to get him on the mound in low Class A before the end of 2004.

Year	Club (League)	Class	W	L	ERA	G	GS	CG	SV	IP	H	R	ER	HR	BB	SO	AVG
2003	Did not play—Signed 2004 contract																

TORONTO
BLUE JAYS

TOP 30 PROSPECTS

1. Alexis Rios, of
2. Dustin McGowan, rhp
3. Guillermo Quiroz, c
4. Gabe Gross, of
5. Francisco Rosario, rhp
6. Aaron Hill, ss
7. David Bush, rhp
8. Vince Perkins, rhp
9. Russ Adams, ss
10. Brandon League, rhp
11. Josh Banks, rhp
12. Adam Peterson, rhp
13. Kevin Cash, c
14. D.J. Hanson, rhp
15. John-Ford Griffin, of
16. Jason Arnold, rhp
17. Jayson Werth, of
18. Jesse Harper, rhp
19. Tyrell Godwin, of
20. Kurt Isenberg, lhp
21. Shaun Marcum, rhp
22. Chad Pleiness, rhp
23. Vinnie Chulk, rhp
24. Cam Reimers, rhp
25. Justin James, rhp
26. Jamie Vermilyea, rhp
27. Miguel Negron, of
28. Edward Rodriguez, rhp
29. Simon Pond, 1b/3b
30. Chris Leonard, lhp

By John Manuel

It's not easy competing in the strong American League East, but that hasn't stopped Blue Jays general manager J.P. Ricciardi from trying. In two short years, Ricciardi has been busy remaking the Blue Jays in his image, one almost completely opposite from the organization's glory days of the 1980s and early '90s under former GM Pat Gillick. The Blue Jays now stress college players in the draft and rely heavily on statistical analysis as a way of measuring a player's performance. They also have replaced many veteran scouts and minor league coaches with younger ones who follow their new philosophical approach.

Under Gillick and his successor, Gord Ash, the Jays were a large-revenue team that wasn't afraid to gamble on young talent that was long on tools and short on experience. That approach provided the best current Jays: Cy Young Award winner Roy Halladay, major league RBIs leader Carlos Delgado and big league hits leader Vernon Wells. All were high school drafts or international signings as teenagers. Four of the team's top five prospects have similar backgrounds.

Ricciardi's task is to appreciate the talent he has on hand and complement it with the cheap, productive players he was so skilled at identifying and acquiring in his days with the Athletics organization. He has done an admirable job, as the Jays won 86 games in 2003 with a major league Rule 5 pick (Aquilino Lopez) as their top reliever and cheap yet productive corner outfielders (Frank Catalanotto, Reed Johnson).

This offseason, Ricciardi was even more aggressive, signing free-agent right-handers Miguel Batista and Pat Hentgen (another former Jays prep draftee) and dealing for lefty Ted Lilly to reshape the rotation behind Halladay. The shaky bullpen has new go-to guys in righties Kerry Ligtenberg and Justin Speier.

Whether the Jays can catch the free-spending Yankees and Red Sox depends as much on the organization's ability to develop from within as on Ricciardi's deal-making. He has pegged the Angels and Marlins as models in franchise-building, proof that the biggest payroll doesn't necessarily produce the best teams. He says Toronto will need a breakthrough rookie or two to take the kind of step those teams made. To that end, the Jays have the most balanced and deepest farm system in the division. No AL East team can match Toronto's stable of power arms in the minor leagues, and no Jays prospects are as important as right-handers Dustin McGowan and Francisco Rosario, who have front-of-the-rotation stuff. Outfielders Alexis Rios and Gabe Gross aren't far from contributing in Toronto.

The Blue Jays have championship-caliber talent, no matter how much the Red Sox and Yankees spend. Now all they need are a few championship-caliber breaks.

ORGANIZATION
OVERVIEW

General manager: J.P. Ricciardi. **Farm director:** Dick Scott. **Scouting director:** Jon Lalonde.

2003 PERFORMANCE

Class	Team	League	W	L	Pct.	Finish*	Manager
Majors	Toronto	American	86	76	.531	t-6th (14)	Carlos Tosca
Triple-A	Syracuse SkyChiefs	International	62	79	.440	14th (14)	Omar Malave
Double-A	New Haven Ravens	Eastern	79	63	.556	2nd (12)	Marty Pevey
High A	Dunedin Blue Jays	Florida State	78	62	.557	1st (12)	Mike Basso
Low A	Charleston Alley Cats	South Atlantic	57	76	.429	12th (16)	Mark Meleski
Short-season	Auburn Doubledays	New York-Penn	56	18	.757	1st (14)	Dennis Holmberg
Rookie	Pulaski Blue Jays	Appalachian	38	29	.567	3rd (10)	Paul Elliott
OVERALL 2003 MINOR LEAGUE RECORD			370	327	.531	5th (30)	

*Finish in overall standings (No. of teams in league).

ORGANIZATIONAL LEADERS

BATTING *Minimum 250 At-Bats
*AVG	Alexis Rios, New Haven	.352
R	Russ Adams, New Haven/Dunedin	92
H	Alexis Rios, New Haven	181
TB	Alexis Rios, New Haven	268
2B	Gabe Gross, Syracuse/New Haven	39
3B	Alexis Rios, New Haven	11
HR	Guillermo Quiroz, New Haven	20
RBI	Simon Pond, Syracuse/New Haven	85
BB	Gabe Gross, Syracuse/New Haven	83
SO	Raul Tablado, Dunedin/Charleston	116
SB	Rich Thompson, Syracuse/New Haven	26
	Tyrell Godwin, New Haven/Dunedin	26
*SLG	Alexis Rios, New Haven	.521
*OBP	Gabe Gross, Syracuse/New Haven	.422

PITCHING #Minimum 75 Innings
W	David Bush, New Haven/Dunedin	14
L	Three tied at	10
#ERA	Andy Torres, Dunedin	2.16
G	Scott Cassidy, Syracuse	57
CG	Three tied at	2
SV	Mark Comolli, Dunedin/Charleston	24
IP	Cameron Reimers, New Haven	164
BB	Vince Perkins, Dunedin/Charleston	75
SO	David Bush, New Haven/Dunedin	148

BEST TOOLS

Best Hitter for Average	Alexis Rios
Best Power Hitter	Alexis Rios
Fastest Baserunner	Tyrell Godwin
Best Athlete	Tyrell Godwin
Best Fastball	Dustin McGowan
Best Curveball	Justin Maureau
Best Slider	Shaun Marcum
Best Changeup	Francisco Rosario
Best Control	David Bush
Best Defensive Catcher	Guillermo Quiroz
Best Defensive Infielder	Emmanuel Sena
Best Infield Arm	Aaron Hill
Best Defensive Outfielder	Alexis Rios
Best Outfield Arm	Gabe Gross

PROJECTED 2007 LINEUP

Catcher	Guillermo Quiroz
First Base	Josh Phelps
Second Base	Aaron Hill
Third Base	Eric Hinske
Shortstop	Russ Adams
Left Field	Gabe Gross
Center Field	Vernon Wells

Right Field	Alexis Rios
Designated Hitter	Carlos Delgado
No. 1 Starter	Roy Halladay
No. 2 Starter	Dustin McGowan
No. 3 Starter	Francisco Rosario
No. 4 Starter	Ted Lilly
No. 5 Starter	David Bush
Closer	Adam Peterson

LAST YEAR'S TOP 20 PROSPECTS

1. Dustin McGowan, rhp
2. Jayson Werth, of/c
3. Kevin Cash, c
4. Francisco Rosario, rhp
5. Jason Arnold, rhp
6. Brandon League, rhp
7. Alexis Rios, of
8. Russ Adams, ss/2b
9. John-Ford Griffin, of
10. Vinny Chulk, rhp
11. Gabe Gross, of
12. Guillermo Quiroz, c
13. Mark Hendrickson, lhp
14. David Bush, rhp
15. Dominic Rich, 2b
16. Miguel Negron, of
17. Chad Pleiness, rhp
18. D.J. Hanson, rhp
19. Tyrell Godwin, of
20. Tracy Thorpe, rhp

TOP PROSPECTS OF THE DECADE

1994	Alex Gonzalez, ss
1995	Shawn Green, of
1996	Shannon Stewart, of
1997	Roy Halladay, rhp
1998	Roy Halladay, rhp
1999	Roy Halladay, rhp
2000	Vernon Wells, of
2001	Vernon Wells, of
2002	Josh Phelps, c
2003	Dustin McGowan, rhp

TOP DRAFT PICKS OF THE DECADE

1994	Kevin Witt, ss
1995	Roy Halladay, rhp
1996	Billy Koch, rhp
1997	Vernon Wells, of
1998	Felipe Lopez, ss
1999	Alexis Rios, of
2000	Miguel Negron, of
2001	Gabe Gross, of
2002	Russ Adams, ss
2003	Aaron Hill, ss

ALL-TIME LARGEST BONUSES

Felipe Lopez, 1998	$2,000,000
Gabe Gross, 2001	$1,865,000
Russ Adams, 2002	$1,785,000
Aaron Hill, 2003	$1,675,000
Vernon Wells, 1997	$1,600,000

MINOR LEAGUE
DEPTH CHART

TORONTO BLUE JAYS   RANK: 8

Impact potential (A): Bright days lie' ahead for the Blue Jays, with a budding five-tool slugger in Alexis Rios, a potential ace in Dustin McGowan and a defensive-minded catcher with emerging power in Guillermo Quiroz. Not only are they close, but they're also getting better as they move up. The power arms of Francisco Rosario, Vince Perkins and Brandon League are tough to match.

Depth (B): The Blue Jays have supplemented their high-end talent with consecutive strong drafts emphasizing strong college performance more than raw tools. This new philosophy has been effective in adding polished pitching prospects who should move quickly into the upper levels. The organization is thin in lefthanded pitching.

Sleeper: Kurt Isenberg, lhp.   —*Depth charts prepared by Josh Boyd. Numbers in parentheses indicate prospect rankings.*

LF
John-Ford Griffin (15)
Ron Davenport
Rodney Medina
Christian Snavely
Noah Hall

CF
Alexis Rios (1)
Tyrell Godwin (19)
Miguel Negron (27)
Jayce Tingler

RF
Gabe Gross (4)
Jayson Werth (17)
Jason Waugh

3B
Rob Cosby

SS
Aaron Hill (6)
Manuel Mayorson

2B
Russ Adams (9)
Jorge Sequea
Dominic Rich
Juan Peralta
Emmanuel Sena

1B
Simon Pond (29)
Mike Snyder
Vito Chiaravalloti

SOURCE OF TALENT

Homegrown		Acquired	
College	14	Trade	3
Junior College	1	Rule 5 draft	0
Draft-and-follow	2	Independent	0
High school	5	Free agent/waivers	1
Nondrafted free agent	1		
Foreign	3		

C
Guillermo Quiroz (3)
Kevin Cash (13)
Robinzon Diaz

RHP

Starters	Relievers
Dustin McGowan (2)	Adam Peterson (12)
Francisco Rosario (5)	Jason Arnold (16)
David Bush (7)	Shaun Marcum (21)
Vince Perkins (8)	Jamie Vermilyea (26)
Brandon League (10)	John Wesley
Josh Banks (11)	Talley Haines
D.J. Hanson (14)	Derek Nunley
Jesse Harper (18)	Ryan Houston
Chad Pleiness (22)	Kevin Frederick
Vinnie Chulk (23)	Bubbie Buzachero
Cam Reimers (24)	Ryan Speier
Justin James (25)	
Edward Rodriguez (28)	
Mike Smith	
Tom Mastny	
Neomar Flores	
Ismael Ramirez	

LHP

Starters	Relievers
Kurt Isenberg (20)	Justin Maureau
Chris Leonard (30)	Ryan Costello
Chi-Hung Cheng	

DRAFT
ANALYSIS

Best Pro Debut: 1B Vito Chiaravalloti (15) won the short-season New York-Penn League triple crown (.351-12-67) and MVP award. Auburn went 56-18 thanks to Chiaravalloti and several other draftees. SS Aaron Hill (1) hit .361-4-34 before he was promoted to high Class A. LHP Kurt Isenberg (4) won the ERA title at 7-2, 1.63, while RHP Tom Mastny (11) was top in victories at 8-0, 2.26. RHP Josh Banks (2) gave Auburn a third dominant starter, going 7-2, 2.43.

Tingler

RICH ABEL

Best Athlete: Hill is an offensive middle infielder with average arm strength, range and quickness. RHP Shaun Marcum (3) and Isenberg were two-way players in college, with Marcum serving as a rare shortstop/closer on Southwest Missouri State's College World Series team.

Best Pure Hitter: Hill likely would have wrested the NY-P batting crown from Chiaravalloti if he had enough at-bats to qualify.

Best Raw Power: Chiaravalotti slumped from 23 homers as a junior in 2002 to 13 last spring, but got his bat going after turning pro.

Fastest Runner: OF Jayce Tingler (10) has 55 speed on the 20-80 scouting scale.

Best Defensive Player: 3B Ryan Roberts (18). Hill gets the job done at shortstop, and he could be good at second or third base.

Best Fastball: Batters can't sit on Banks' 90-94 mph heater because he has a nasty

splitter. He slid out of the first round when blisters caused his performance to slip.

Best Breaking Ball: Marcum has a plus slider. He can get his fastball to 90-92 on a good day.

Most Intriguing Background: The Blue Jays believe in LHP Matt Foster's (14) potential and are optimistic he'll join them full-time after he completes his two-year commitment after attending the U.S. Naval Academy. Currently in submarine school, Foster has a live 90-92 mph sinker but needs time to work on his other pitches. While in high school, Chiaravalloti was a YMCA national champion in the 100-yard backstroke and the New Jersey swimmer of the year. C Jeremy Knicely's (42) father Alan caught for parts of eight big league seasons.

Closest To The Majors: Hill and Banks.

Best Late-Round Pick: Chiaravalloti continued to swing the bat well in instructional league.

The One Who Got Away: The Blue Jays hoped RHP Brad Depoy (20) would attend junior college, but they lost his rights when he went to Houston. He touched 94 and made progress with his slider last spring.

Assessment: The Blue Jays prefer college players with a record of success, so it's no shock to see many of their picks post strong numbers in short-season leagues. It's also hard not to be impressed by those numbers.

Toronto switched to a college emphasis and came up with RHP David Bush (2), SS Russ Adams (1) and RHP Adam Peterson (4). They all should surface in the majors in the near future.

OF Gabe Gross (1) and RHP Brandon League (2) are two of the organization's brightest prospects. SS Mike Rouse (5), traded for Cory Lidle, is one of the best in the Oakland system.

The Blue Jays' current philosophy would exclude a projectable high school arm like RHP Dustin McGowan (1), but he's their best mound prospect. Draft-and-follow RHP Vince Perkins (18) gives them another power pitcher. Their top choice, OF Miguel Negron (1), was a signability pick and hasn't refined his raw tools.

OF Alexis Rios (1) has gone from a raw, cheap signability choice to one of the most exciting athletes in the minors. Since-waived draft-and-follow RHP Brandon Lyon (14) reached the majors very quickly, while OF Reed Johnson (17) started for Toronto in 2003.

—Draft analysis prepared by Jim Callis. Numbers in parentheses indicate draft rounds.

Alexis
Rios

Born: Feb. 18, 1981.
Ht.: 6-5. **Wt.:** 180.
Bats: R. **Throws:** R.
School: San Pedro Martir HS,
Guaynabo, P.R.
Career Transactions: Selected by
Blue Jays in first round (19th overall) of
1999 draft; signed June 4, 1999.

The Blue Jays had a tight signing budget in 1999, and then-scouting director Tim Wilken and his staff narrowed the team's choice in the first round to three players. Toronto could go with Ball State outfielder Larry Bigbie, Mississippi State righthander Matt Ginter or Rios, a Puerto Rican outfielder whose swing path and physical tools intrigued the organization. They also knew he'd come cheaper. Rather than spend about $1.5 million of their signing budget on one college player, the Jays decided to sign Rios for $845,000 (the only sub-$1 million bonus in the first round that year) and used the savings to sign several draft-and-follow prospects. Rios has since blossomed into a stud prospect, particulary in 2003, when he won the Eastern League batting championship and was Baseball America's Double-A player of the year. He also played in the Futures Game, hitting an opposite-field homer that showed off his best attributes.

Rios has a smooth, easy swing that belies his long frame and helps him make consistent, hard contact to all fields. He had five hitting streaks of 10 games or more in 2003. His bat always has been his best tool, and his developing power has pushed him to elite-prospect status. He hit three homers in the EL playoffs and hit .348-12-37 in 40 games to win league MVP honors during winter ball in his native Puerto Rico. Credit his emerging home run power to him filling out physically and gaining strength. Jays officials also consider him an accomplished center fielder who takes good angles to the ball and has a strong arm. Rios makes such consistent, hard contact that he's never going to walk a lot. His 85 strikeouts last year were a career high, as were his 39 walks. His offensive profile looks a lot like that of Vernon Wells, which is good, but Rios isn't as good a center fielder as Wells. He's going to have to keep hitting for the kind of power he was showing in Puerto Rico if Wells' presence prompts Rios move to right field. He has had some durability issues in the past linked to nagging injuries, and he began 2003 in extended spring training while overcoming a pulled quadriceps. His strong play in winter ball, though, has quieted those concerns.

Rios is a prime example of the way the Jays used to do business, a high-risk high school pick, a hitter who doesn't draw walks but who oozes tools. If the organization keeps him, it could have another Juan Gonzalez or Dave Winfield on its hands, a perennial all-star right fielder who could hit .300 with 35 homers, or win batting championships with 20-homer power. However, Rios isn't quite a finished product and looks likely to begin 2004 at Triple-A Syracuse unless he has an overwhelming spring.

Year	Club (League)	Class	AVG	G	AB	R	H	2B	3B	HR	RBI	BB	SO	SB	SLG	OBP
1999	Medicine Hat (Pio)	R	.269	67	234	35	63	7	3	0	13	17	31	8	.325	.321
2000	Hagerstown (SAL)	A	.230	22	74	5	17	3	1	0	5	2	14	2	.297	.256
	Queens (NY-P)	A	.267	50	206	22	55	9	2	1	25	11	22	5	.345	.314
2001	Charleston, WV (SAL)	A	.263	130	480	40	126	20	9	2	58	25	59	22	.354	.296
2002	Dunedin (FSL)	A	.305	111	456	60	139	22	8	3	61	27	55	14	.408	.344
2003	New Haven (EL)	AA	.352	127	514	86	181	32	11	11	82	39	85	11	.521	.402
MINOR LEAGUE TOTALS			.296	507	1964	248	581	93	34	17	244	121	266	62	.404	.339

2 Dustin McGowan, rhp

RICH ABEL

Born: March 24, 1982. **Ht.:** 6-3. **Wt.:** 190. **Bats:** R. **Throws:** R. **School:** Long County HS, Ludowici, Ga. **Career Transactions:** Selected by Blue Jays in first round (33rd overall) of 2000 draft; signed June 20, 2000.

Several clubs debated McGowan versus fellow Georgia prep product Adam Wainwright in the 2000 draft; Wainwright went four spots ahead of McGowan to the Braves. An inflamed elbow almost caused the Jays to void his contract after he signed for $950,000, but he has proved healthy since then. McGowan has added 30 pounds to his sturdy frame and now has No. 1 starter stuff that he maintains deep into games. He pitches at 94-95 mph with his fastball and touches 97 consistently with above-average life down in the zone. McGowan's power downer curveball and mid-80s slider, which at times is a plus put-away pitch, are average big league pitches. He has good arm speed on his changeup, though his changeup can be too firm and he could stand to vary speeds better. Otherwise, he most-ly needs experience, a few more innings and consistency repeating his delivery. McGowan has better stuff than Roy Halladay, the Cy Young Award winner whom he could join in Toronto's rotation soon. He's in line for a big league promotion sometime in 2004.

Year	Club (League)	Class	W	L	ERA	G	GS	CG	SV	IP	H	R	ER	HR	BB	SO	AVG
2000	Medicine Hat (Pio)	R	0	3	6.48	8	8	0	0	25	26	21	18	2	25	19	.274
2001	Auburn (NY-P)	A	3	6	3.76	15	14	0	0	67	57	33	28	1	49	80	.234
2002	Charleston, WV (SAL)	A	11	10	4.19	28	28	1	0	148	143	77	69	10	59	163	.251
2003	Dunedin (FSL)	A	5	6	2.85	14	14	1	0	76	62	29	24	1	25	66	.223
	New Haven (EL)	AA	7	0	3.17	14	14	1	0	77	78	28	27	1	19	72	.261
MINOR LEAGUE TOTALS			26	25	3.80	79	78	3	0	393	366	188	166	15	177	400	.246

3 Guillermo Quiroz, c

Born: Nov. 29, 1981. **Ht.:** 6-1. **Wt.:** 200. **Bats:** R. **Throws:** R. **Career Transactions:** Signed out of Venezuela by Blue Jays, Sept. 25, 1998.

Quiroz signed as a free agent with the Jays for $1.2 million after his agent, Scott Boras, took him around the high school showcase circuit. He missed time late in 2003 with a partially collapsed lung but returned for three games in the Eastern League playoffs. Quiroz' plus arm and good throwing mechanics help him post consistent sub-2.0-second times on throws to second base. He threw out 44 percent of opposing baserunners last year. Toronto officials rave about his near-flawless English and his ability to steer pitchers through tough innings. He has a power bat to go with his power arm, and like Rios he punished winter league pitching, drilling 11 homes in 44 games in Venezuela. Quiroz' swing is at times long and mechanical. He's good at making adjustments, but he doesn't project as much more than a .270 hitter. He has made strides in his concen-tration and keeping a steady approach through an entire season. His performance at Double-A New Haven vaulted Quiroz past Kevin Cash on the organization depth chart. He should establish himself as the Jays' starting catcher no later than 2005.

Year	Club (League)	Class	AVG	G	AB	R	H	2B	3B	HR	RBI	BB	SO	SB	SLG	OBP
1999	Medicine Hat (Pio)	R	.221	63	208	25	46	7	0	9	28	18	55	0	.385	.296
2000	Hagerstown (SAL)	A	.162	43	136	14	22	4	0	1	12	16	44	0	.213	.269
	Queens (NY-P)	A	.224	55	196	29	44	9	0	5	29	27	48	1	.347	.329
2001	Charleston, WV (SAL)	A	.199	82	261	25	52	12	0	7	25	29	67	5	.326	.294
2002	Dunedin (FSL)	A	.260	111	411	50	107	28	1	12	68	35	91	1	.421	.330
	Syracuse (IL)	AAA	.222	13	45	7	10	4	0	1	6	3	14	0	.378	.271
2003	New Haven (EL)	AA	.282	108	369	63	104	27	0	20	79	45	83	0	.518	.372
MINOR LEAGUE TOTALS			.237	475	1626	211	385	91	1	55	247	173	402	7	.395	.323

4 Gabe Gross, of

RICH ABEL

Born: Oct. 21, 1979. **Ht.:** 6-3. **Wt.:** 200. **Bats:** L. **Throws:** R. **School:** Auburn University. **Career Transactions:** Selected by Blue Jays in first round (15th overall) of 2001 draft; signed July 1, 2001.

Auburn's starting quarterback as a freshman in 1998, Gross has made the decision to leave football behind look smart. He grinded out a pro-ductive 2003 season, which ended with him starting in right field for the ill-fated U.S. Olympic qualifying team. Gross is a good athlete with solid average or above-average tools across the board. He has at least average power, runs well for his size and his arm fits well in right field. He com-mands the strike zone well and is learning to be aggressive in hitter's counts. Gross struggled in 2002 because he couldn't get his hands in good position for his swing, but he seems to have made that adjustment. His football background means he has less experience than a typical college draftee, so his home run production hasn't approached his ceiling yet. He struggles with southpaws (.248 with four homers in 129 at-bats last year). Gross could resemble Paul O'Neill, a corner outfielder who hits for a good average and 15-20 homers, or he could become a 30-homer threat. He should start 2004 back in Triple-A.

Year	Club (League)	Class	AVG	G	AB	R	H	2B	3B	HR	RBI	BB	SO	SB	SLG	OBP
2001	Dunedin (FSL)	A	.302	35	126	23	38	9	2	4	15	26	29	4	.500	.426
	Tennessee (SL)	AA	.244	11	41	8	10	1	0	3	11	6	12	0	.488	.373
2002	Tennessee (SL)	AA	.238	112	403	57	96	17	5	10	54	53	71	8	.380	.333
2003	New Haven (EL)	AA	.319	84	310	52	99	23	3	7	51	52	53	3	.481	.423
	Syracuse (IL)	AAA	.264	53	182	22	48	16	2	5	23	31	56	1	.456	.380
MINOR LEAGUE TOTALS			.274	295	1062	162	291	66	12	29	154	168	221	16	.441	.380

5 Francisco Rosario, rhp

Born: Sept. 28, 1980. **Ht.:** 6-0. **Wt.:** 160. **Bats:** R. **Throws:** R. **Career Transactions:** Signed out of Dominican Republic by Blue Jays, Jan. 11, 1999 . . . On disabled list, April 3-Sept. 2, 2003.

Rosario was putting the finishing touches on a breakout 2002 season when he felt a pop in his elbow while in the Arizona Fall League. He required Tommy John surgery and missed the entire 2003 season. However, Toronto officials were impressed with his recent showing in instructional league. Before his injury, Rosario threw his fastball from 92-97 mph with exceptional command. While his control wasn't pinpoint after his layoff, club officials were encouraged. He hasn't thrown many changeups since his return, but the ones he has flashed were above-average. Rosario will need time to recover from his elbow reconstruction, as many pitchers struggle to regain their touch and feel in their first season after the surgery. His slurvy breaking ball was his third-best pitch before he got hurt and still needs tightening. Rosario would have been the Jays' No. 1 prospect last year if not for the surgery. He can put himself in position for that honor again if he has a healthy, strong 2004. He'll start at high Class A Dunedin and move to Double-A once the Eastern League's weather improves.

Year	Club (League)	Class	W	L	ERA	G	GS	CG	SV	IP	H	R	ER	HR	BB	SO	AVG
1999	Blue Jays (DSL)	R	1	0	3.06	18	0	0	3	32	26	16	11	0	11	38	.208
2000	Blue Jays (DSL)	R	2	0	1.21	26	0	0	16	37	21	5	5	0	7	51	.160
2001	Medicine Hat (Pio)	R	3	7	5.59	16	15	0	0	76	79	61	47	8	38	55	.271
2002	Charleston, WV (SAL)	A	6	1	2.57	13	13	1	0	67	50	22	19	5	14	78	.206
	Dunedin (FSL)	A	3	3	1.29	13	12	0	0	63	33	10	9	3	25	65	.151
2003	Did not play—Injured																
MINOR LEAGUE TOTALS			15	11	2.98	86	40	1	19	275	209	114	91	16	95	287	.207

6 Aaron Hill, ss

Born: March 21, 1982. **Ht.:** 5-11. **Wt.:** 195. **Bats:** R. **Throws:** R. **School:** Louisiana State University. **Career Transactions:** Selected by Blue Jays in first round (13th overall) of 2003 draft; signed June 17, 2003.

Hill was drafted in the seventh round out of high school by the Angels, and soon after the draft got a full scholarship offer from Louisiana State. He had a stellar college career, earning Southeastern Conference player-of-the-year honors in 2003. Hill has average to plus tools and the skills to match. His strong throwing arm helps him make plays from the hole at shortstop. He keeps his swing short, and has shown average power (with more to come) and running ability. His fine plate discipline and off-the-charts makeup sealed the deal for the Blue Jays. Hill doesn't quite have Russ Adams' range at shortstop, and probably doesn't have enough to cover ground at the position on artificial turf. He'll have to use his tremendous instincts and learn to position himself perfectly to make up for his lack of quickness. Some scouts see Hill becoming an offensive second baseman a la Bret Boone if he fully realizes his power potential. At worst, he should be a solid big leaguer at either second or third. Hill should reach Double-A at some point in 2004.

Year	Club (League)	Class	AVG	G	AB	R	H	2B	3B	HR	RBI	BB	SO	SB	SLG	OBP
2003	Auburn (NY-P)	A	.361	33	122	22	44	4	0	4	34	16	20	1	.492	.446
	Dunedin (FSL)	A	.286	32	119	26	34	7	0	0	11	11	10	1	.345	.343
MINOR LEAGUE TOTALS			.324	65	241	48	78	11	0	4	45	27	30	2	.419	.397

7 David Bush, rhp

RICH ABEL

Born: Nov. 9, 1979. **Ht.:** 6-2. **Wt.:** 210. **Bats:** R. **Throws:** R. **School:** Wake Forest University. **Career Transactions:** Selected by Blue Jays in second round of 2002 draft; signed June 17, 2002.

A high school catcher, Bush converted to pitching at Wake Forest. He quickly established himself as one of college baseball's top closers. After not signing as a Devil Rays fourth-round pick in 2001, he overcame blood clots in his left leg to have a big senior season. He made a successful conversion to starting in 2003, his first full pro season. Bush competes hard and pounds the strike zone with four pitches. He repeats his delivery well and has the best command of any pitcher in the organization. Bush throws an 88-92 mph fastball with average life and a solid curve with depth. He also has shown a good feel for his changeup and has developed a decent slider. Bush doesn't have a knockout pitch. At times, he catches too much of the plate and his average stuff gets hit hard. Bush looks like a good bet to be a solid third starter. If that doesn't work, he has the mentality and command to go back to the bullpen, where his stuff would pick up a notch. He should begin 2004 in Triple-A but could earn a trip to Toronto during the season.

Year	Club (League)	Class	W	L	ERA	G	GS	CG	SV	IP	H	R	ER	HR	BB	SO	AVG
2002	Auburn (NY-P)	A	1	1	2.82	18	0	0	10	22	13	9	7	1	7	39	.159
	Dunedin (FSL)	A	0	1	2.03	7	0	0	0	13	10	3	3	1	2	9	.222
2003	Dunedin (FSL)	A	7	3	2.81	14	14	0	0	77	64	29	24	6	9	75	.223
	New Haven (EL)	AA	7	3	2.78	14	14	1	0	81	73	26	25	4	19	73	.239
MINOR LEAGUE TOTALS			15	8	2.74	53	28	1	10	194	160	67	59	12	37	196	.223

8 Vince Perkins, rhp

RODGER WOOD

Born: Sept. 27, 1981. **Ht.:** 6-5. **Wt.:** 220. **Bats:** L. **Throws:** R. **School:** Lake City (Fla.) CC. **Career Transactions:** Selected by Blue Jays in 18th round of 2000 draft; signed May 24, 2001.

Perkins isn't as athletic or polished as other recent British Columbia exports such as Athletics righty Rich Harden, his former Little League and high school teammate. However, Perkins broke out in 2003 by ranking among the minor league leaders in ERA (2.24) and opponent average (.179). Perkins has a big frame and big stuff. His fastball ranks right with those of McGowan, Brandon League and reliever Adam Peterson for pure velocity. He throws it in the 92-95 mph range and touches some 96s and 97s. His power slider sits at 87-89 and scrapes the low 90s. When he's on, minor league hitters don't touch him. Perkins isn't a graceful athlete. That makes it harder for him to repeat his delivery, the root of his control troubles. He has progressed making his delivery less mechanical and more fluid, but it doesn't come easy to him. His changeup is just fair. Perkins has as much upside as any starter the Jays have besides McGowan and Rosario. If he harnesses his control, he'll be a middle-of-the-rotation power starter who eats innings.

Year	Club (League)	Class	W	L	ERA	G	GS	CG	SV	IP	H	R	ER	HR	BB	SO	AVG
2001	Auburn (NY-P)	A	1	4	3.27	14	14	0	0	52	41	23	19	1	37	67	.220
2002	Auburn (NY-P)	A	5	5	3.34	15	15	0	0	73	51	32	27	3	44	85	.198
2003	Charleston, WV (SAL)	A	3	1	1.83	8	8	0	0	44	19	9	9	1	22	60	.136
	Dunedin (FSL)	A	7	6	2.45	18	17	0	0	84	58	32	23	1	53	69	.201
MINOR LEAGUE TOTALS			16	16	2.77	55	54	0	0	254	169	96	78	6	156	281	.194

9 Russ Adams, ss

RICH ABEL

Born: Aug. 30, 1980. **Ht.:** 6-1. **Wt.:** 180. **Bats:** L. **Throws:** R. **School:** University of North Carolina. **Career Transactions:** Selected by Blue Jays in first round (14th overall) of 2002 draft; signed June 7, 2002.

Adams is a quintessential "baseball player," a description that shortchanges his athletic ability. He went from solid college player to first-round pick with an all-star performance in the Cape Cod League in 2001, and he rose quickly to Double-A in his first full pro season. Adams is an above-average runner, has good range on either side of the bag and shows a knack for making consistent contact. He commands the strike zone well, then takes advantage of his good on-base percentage by being an efficient basestealer. He has good hands and quick feet defensively. Adams made 45 errors in 2003 between the regular season and Arizona Fall League. His throwing arm is below-average, and the extra depth needed to play shortstop on artificial turf could expose this shortcoming even more, making a move to second base probable. Neither Adams nor the organization has given up on him at shortstop, and his work ethic, instincts and hands may yet carry the day. He'll return to Double-A at Toronto's new New Hampshire affiliate.

Year	Club (League)	Class	AVG	G	AB	R	H	2B	3B	HR	RBI	BB	SO	SB	SLG	OBP
2002	Auburn (NY-P)	A	.354	30	113	25	40	7	3	0	16	24	11	13	.469	.464
	Dunedin (FSL)	A	.231	37	147	23	34	4	2	1	12	18	17	5	.306	.321
2003	Dunedin (FSL)	A	.279	68	258	50	72	9	5	3	16	38	27	9	.388	.380
	New Haven (EL)	AA	.277	65	271	42	75	10	4	4	26	30	37	8	.387	.349
MINOR LEAGUE TOTALS			.280	200	789	140	221	30	14	8	70	110	92	35	.384	.372

10 Brandon League, rhp

Born: March 16, 1983. **Ht.:** 6-2. **Wt.:** 180. **Bats:** R. **Throws:** R. **School:** St. Louis HS, Honolulu. **Career Transactions:** Selected by Blue Jays in second round of 2001 draft; signed July 3, 2001.

League and Hawaiian prep rival Bronson Sardinha (now with the Yankees) both committed to Pepperdine, but League's power arm proved too tempting for the Blue Jays. League remains one of the hardest throwers in the minor leagues, regularly delivering his fastball in the high 90s, sitting at 93-96 and at times touching triple digits. He throws from a low three-quarters arm slot that gives his hard heater wicked sinking action. His sweeping 87-88 mph slider is at times a plus pitch. He has the makings of a decent changeup. League's stuff usually produces more strikeouts, even for a sinker-slider pitcher. He doesn't command his breaking ball as well as he needs to. He sometimes over-rotates in his delivery and drags his arm, which keeps him from staying on top of his slider. League made progress working on his delivery with Dunedin pitching coach Rick Langford. His upside as a starter remains huge, and his fastball makes relieving a legitimate option if starting doesn't work out. He'll rejoin Dunedin's rotation at the outset in 2004.

Year	Club (League)	Class	W	L	ERA	G	GS	CG	SV	IP	H	R	ER	HR	BB	SO	AVG
2001	Medicine Hat (Pio)	R	2	2	4.66	9	9	0	0	39	36	23	20	3	11	38	.245
2002	Auburn (NY-P)	A	7	2	3.15	16	16	0	0	86	80	42	30	2	23	72	.248
2003	Charleston, WV (SAL)	A	2	3	1.91	12	12	0	0	71	58	15	15	1	18	61	.230
	Dunedin (FSL)	A	4	3	4.75	13	12	0	0	66	76	40	35	3	20	34	.288
MINOR LEAGUE TOTALS			15	10	3.44	50	49	0	0	261	250	120	100	9	72	205	.254

11 Josh Banks, rhp

Born: July 18, 1982. **Ht.:** 6-3. **Wt.:** 195. **Bats:** R. **Throws:** R. **School:** Florida International University. **Career Transactions:** Selected by Blue Jays in second round of 2003 draft; signed June 4, 2003.

Banks helped Florida International reach a super-regional in 2001 and missed part of 2002 with a strained ligament in his throwing elbow. He broke out early in 2003, quickly establishing himself as the best player in a weak Florida college draft class. He went in the second round, becoming the highest drafted player in school history (18 rounds ahead of Mike Lowell) after shrugging off a blister to lead the Sun Belt Conference with 114 strikeouts in 105 innings. Primarily a reliever in his first two years of college, Banks added an effective slider to his repertoire last season, becoming a three-pitch pitcher. He sits at 89-93 mph with his fastball and touches 94, and commands it well enough to both sides of the plate to earn a 60 grade on the 20-80 scouting scale. He then attacks hitters with a plus splitter and his slider, another above-average pitch at times. Besides just having good stuff, Banks has a plan on the mound and a good feel for the game. Banks' ability to pound the strike zone with quality stuff should allow him to move quickly through the system if he stays healthy. He could earn a spot in high Class A with a strong spring training.

Year	Club (League)	Class	W	L	ERA	G	GS	CG	SV	IP	H	R	ER	HR	BB	SO	AVG
2003	Auburn (NY-P)	A	7	2	2.43	15	15	0	0	67	58	21	18	1	10	81	.233
MINOR LEAGUE TOTALS			7	2	2.43	15	15	0	0	67	58	21	18	1	10	81	.233

12 Adam Peterson, rhp

Born: May 18, 1979. **Ht.:** 6-3. **Wt.:** 220. **Bats:** R. **Throws:** R. **School:** Wichita State University. **Career Transactions:** Selected by Blue Jays in fourth round of 2002 draft; signed June 11, 2002.

Peterson has as much opportunity as any Jays prospect to jump to Toronto in 2004 and make an impact. His makeup and stuff scream "closer," and Toronto lacks an established player in that role, even after the acquisitions of Kerry Ligtenberg and Justin Speier. Peterson was a 13th-round pick of the Phillies out of high school in Wisconsin and an eighth-round pick of the Yankees in 2001 out of Wichita State but didn't sign either time. He missed most of 2001 with a back injury and returned to Wichita State, going 9-3, 3.55 as a junior. After signing with the Jays, he moved to the bullpen. That change and a slight lowering of his arm angle jumped his 91-92 mph fastball with good life into a 96-97 mph heater with excellent movement down in the strike zone. His health and the consistency of his slider will determine his success. Peterson tends to get around on his breaking ball too much, costing him command, though he made progress with it in instructional league. At times, it's a filthy pitch with big tilt. He also has a playable changeup, which he won't use much out of the bullpen. Peterson could get some save chances in Toronto sooner than later.

Year	Club (League)	Class	W	L	ERA	G	GS	CG	SV	IP	H	R	ER	HR	BB	SO	AVG
2002	Auburn (NY-P)	A	2	0	2.30	18	0	0	5	31	29	10	8	2	9	19	.246
2003	Charleston, WV (SAL)	A	2	4	2.19	10	0	0	1	25	15	8	6	1	13	19	.190
	Dunedin (FSL)	A	1	0	0.71	9	0	0	1	13	5	1	1	0	13	.116
	New Haven (EL)	AA	2	2	4.88	24	0	0	9	24	24	13	13	1	7	24	.261
MINOR LEAGUE TOTALS			7	6	2.72	61	0	0	16	93	73	32	28	5	29	75	.220

13 Kevin Cash, c

Born: Dec. 6, 1977. **Ht.:** 6-0. **Wt.:** 180. **Bats:** R. **Throws:** R. **School:** Florida State University. **Career Transactions:** Signed as nondrafted free agent by Blue Jays, Aug. 7, 1999.

Cash remains one of the best defensive backstops in the minors. The former corner infielder has natural actions and tools to thrive behind the plate: plus arm, good footwork, soft hands and leadership ability. He rivals Guillermo Quiroz as the organization's best defensive catcher, and he led Triple-A International League regulars by throwing out 50 percent of basestealers last year. However, Quiroz has passed him on the organization's depth chart because of the gains he made at the plate in 2003, progress Cash didn't match. His plate discipline and home run power slipped. His aggressive approach, which had served him well earlier in his career, was further exposed in a 34-game big league trial, when he failed to post even a .400 on-base plus slugging percentage. Pitchers realized they didn't have to throw him strikes to get him out, so they didn't. The Blue Jays say Cash pressured himself too much and was focused on learning to work with Toronto's pitchers. Cash projects as a .260 hitter with 10-15 homers at best, and he'll need to get stronger and improve his conditioning to avoid tiring late in the season, when his bat tends to slow.

Year	Club (League)	Class	AVG	G	AB	R	H	2B	3B	HR	RBI	BB	SO	SB	SLG	OBP
2000	Hagerstown (SAL)	A	.245	59	196	28	48	10	1	10	27	22	54	5	.459	.323
2001	Dunedin (FSL)	A	.283	105	371	55	105	27	0	12	66	43	80	4	.453	.369
2002	Tennessee (SL)	AA	.277	55	213	38	59	15	1	8	44	36	44	5	.469	.381
	Syracuse (IL)	AAA	.220	67	236	27	52	18	0	10	26	25	72	0	.424	.299
	Toronto (AL)	MAJ	.143	7	14	1	2	0	0	0	0	1	4	0	.143	.200
2003	Syracuse (IL)	AAA	.270	93	326	37	88	28	2	8	37	29	81	1	.442	.331
	Toronto (AL)	MAJ	.142	34	106	10	15	3	0	1	8	4	22	0	.198	.179
MAJOR LEAGUE TOTALS			.142	41	120	11	17	3	0	1	8	5	26	0	.192	.181
MINOR LEAGUE TOTALS			.262	379	1342	185	352	98	4	48	200	155	331	15	.449	.343

14 D.J. Hanson, rhp

Born: Aug. 7, 1980. **Ht.:** 5-11. **Wt.:** 170. **Bats:** R. **Throws:** R. **School:** Richland (Wash.) HS. **Career Transactions:** Selected by Blue Jays in sixth round of 1999 draft; signed June 14, 1999 . . . On disabled list, June 16-Sept. 10, 2001.

Added to the 40-man roster in the offseason, Hanson has the stuff to rival all the pitchers ranked ahead of him but doesn't have the tools of the likes of Dustin McGowan, Francisco Rosario, Vince Perkins or Brandon League. Besides being just 5-foot-11 and 170 pounds, Hanson has an injury history, having had knee surgery twice to repair damage stemming from a spring-training collision in 2001 with Alvin Morrow (now Toronto's area scout in Southern California). Hanson also has a quick arm and big-time stuff. His fastball sits in the 89-93 mph range, and he can run it up to 94 or 95 on occasion. One such occasion was an Aug. 12 start at low Class A Charleston. He struck out 14 in a complete-game seven-hitter, and his last pitch registered 95. Hanson also throws a hard power slider in the mid- to upper 80s and a curveball with surprising depth coming from a short righthander. He was dominant down the stretch, giving up just two earned runs in his last 50 innings, showing his small frame can handle a full season. His protection on the 40-man roster means he'll be pushed to Double-A in 2004, as the Jays want to see just what they have.

Year	Club (League)	Class	W	L	ERA	G	GS	CG	SV	IP	H	R	ER	HR	BB	SO	AVG
1999	Medicine Hat (Pio)	R	1	2	5.32	14	7	0	0	46	64	33	27	1	21	35	.335
2000	Medicine Hat (Pio)	R	7	3	5.81	15	15	0	0	79	82	55	51	6	29	79	.262
2001	Did not play—Injured																
2002	Auburn (NY-P)	A	5	2	1.68	9	9	0	0	48	35	11	9	4	11	51	.203
2003	Charleston, WV (SAL)	A	10	10	2.54	25	25	2	0	138	110	51	39	4	56	113	.225
MINOR LEAGUE TOTALS			23	17	3.64	63	56	2	0	311	291	150	126	15	117	278	.250

15 John-Ford Griffin, of

Born: Nov. 19, 1979. **Ht.:** 6-2. **Wt.:** 210. **Bats:** L. **Throws:** L. **School:** Florida State University. **Career Transactions:** Selected by Yankees in first round (23rd overall) of 2001 draft; signed June 14, 2001 . . . Traded by Yankees with LHP Ted Lilly and RHP Jason Arnold to Athletics as part of three-way trade in which Yankees received RHP Jeff Weaver from Tigers and Tigers received 1B Carlos Pena, RHP Franklyn German and a player to be named from Athletics, July 6, 2002; Tigers acquired RHP Jeremy Bonderman from Athletics to complete trade (Aug. 22, 2002) . . . Traded by Athletics to Blue Jays for a player to be named, Jan. 27, 2003; Athletics acquired OF Jason Perry to complete trade (June 23, 2003).

Griffin added to his offensive reputation in 2003, though a stress fracture in his foot ended his season in late July. It's the second straight year Griffin saw truncated by an injury, as a hand problem cost him the last two months of 2002. Florida State coach Mike Martin calls Griffin the best hitter his program ever has produced, and he projects to have an above-average big league bat. He has a smooth lefthanded swing that grew shorter, allowing him to take advantage of his bat speed and hit for better power than he had previously shown. He matched his previous career home run total with 13. Some in the organization envision him as a .300 hitter with 20 homers, while others say he's more of a .270 hitter with 30- or even 40-homer pop. But Griffin doesn't do much else well. He's not a good runner, base-stealer or fielder, ill-suited even for left field because of his lack of speed and poor arm. If the power projections don't play out, Griffin would be a Jeremy Giambi clone, a solid hitter without a position. And Toronto already has Josh Phelps as a young, power-hitting DH. Griffin needs to reverse his downward defensive trend when he heads to Triple-A.

Year	Club (League)	Class	AVG	G	AB	R	H	2B	3B	HR	RBI	BB	SO	SB	SLG	OBP
2001	Staten Island (NY-P)	A	.311	66	238	46	74	17	1	5	43	40	41	10	.454	.413
2002	Tampa (FSL)	A	.267	65	255	32	68	16	1	3	31	29	45	1	.373	.344
	Norwich (EL)	AA	.328	18	67	17	22	3	0	5	10	8	13	0	.597	.400
	Midland (TL)	AA	.143	2	7	0	1	0	0	0	0	0	3	0	.143	.250
2003	New Haven (EL)	AA	.279	104	373	48	104	23	3	13	75	49	85	2	.461	.361
MINOR LEAGUE TOTALS			.286	255	940	143	269	59	5	26	159	126	187	13	.443	.372

16 Jason Arnold, rhp

Born: May 2, 1979. **Ht.:** 6-3. **Wt.:** 210. **Bats:** R. **Throws:** R. **School:** University of Central Florida. **Career Transactions:** Selected by Yankees in second round of 2001 draft; signed June 15, 2001 . . . Traded by Yankees with LHP Ted Lilly and OF John-Ford Griffin to Athletics as part of three-way trade in which Yankees received RHP Jeff Weaver from Tigers and Tigers received 1B Carlos Pena, RHP Franklyn German and a player to be named from Athletics, July 6, 2002; Tigers acquired RHP Jeremy Bonderman from Athletics to complete trade (Aug. 22, 2002) . . . Traded by Athletics to Blue Jays, Dec. 16, 2002, completing four-way trade in which Athletics received 1B Erubiel Durazo from Diamondbacks, Diamondbacks received RHP Elmer Dessens from Reds and Reds received SS Felipe Lopez from Blue Jays (Dec. 15, 2002).

Arnold remains a bone of contention within the organization. Some Jays officials say he's one of their best prospects, while others never have considered him more than a back-of-the-rotation starter or set-up man. He hit his first speed bump as a pro in 2003, and his adjustment will determine which camp is correct. Arnold's fastball, which reached 94 mph as a college closer, sits in the 87-90 range as a pro starter, and it's fairly straight. He dominated Double-A to start the season, but Triple-A hitters learned to lay off his plus changeup, a palmball, and didn't respect his below-average slider. They sat on the fastball and punished it regularly, and Arnold didn't adapt. He must stay tall in his delivery, maintaining a release point that allows him to throw downhill with leverage to keep his fastball down in the strike zone. He clearly doesn't have the arm of the Jays' elite prospects, but has excellent makeup. Arnold is active in charity work and is a reporter's best friend in the locker room. Toronto officials on both sides of the argument want him to succeed.

Year	Club (League)	Class	W	L	ERA	G	GS	CG	SV	IP	H	R	ER	HR	BB	SO	AVG
2001	Staten Island (NY-P)	A	7	2	1.50	10	10	2	0	66	35	13	11	2	15	74	.158
2002	Tampa (FSL)	A	7	1	2.48	13	13	0	0	80	64	27	22	2	22	83	.217
	Norwich (EL)	AA	1	2	4.15	3	3	0	0	17	17	14	8	1	5	18	.254
	Midland (TL)	AA	5	1	2.33	10	10	0	0	58	42	22	15	2	24	53	.208
2003	New Haven (EL)	AA	3	1	1.53	6	6	0	0	35	18	7	6	2	11	33	.153
	Syracuse (IL)	AAA	4	8	4.33	21	20	1	0	121	121	69	58	16	46	82	.262
MINOR LEAGUE TOTALS			27	15	2.86	63	62	3	0	377	297	152	120	25	123	343	.217

17 Jayson Werth, of

Born: May 20, 1979. **Ht.:** 6-5. **Wt.:** 210. **Bats:** R. **Throws:** R. **School:** Glenwood HS, Chatham, Ill. **Career Transactions:** Selected by Orioles in first round (22nd overall) of 1997 draft; signed June 13, 1997 . . . Traded by Orioles to Blue Jays for LHP John Bale, Dec. 11, 2000.

After ranking second on this list a year ago, Werth's worth has slipped as the likes of Reed Johnson, Gabe Gross and Alexis Rios have passed him. Injuries played a part, as Werth got a late start to the season after straining his wrist in spring training. It forced him to the disabled list and a rehab assignment in high Class A, and he was playing catch-up all year. He no longer plays catcher, which also diminished his value. He played solely in the outfield in 2003, and one Jays official termed him an emergency catcher only. Toronto GM J.P. Ricciardi considers Werth too tall at 6-foot-6 to be a catcher. He has made a nice transition to full-time outfield, however. Werth runs well enough to play center field and has a plus arm in right. Offense is the bigger question. Werth swings and misses too much to be an everyday hitter at this point. His size has created a swing that's too long and has too many holes, sabotaging his plus power. If he makes adjustments, he could be an average corner outfielder, and his versatility makes him a valuable reserve. That's likely to be his role in 2004 in Toronto, and Werth could be trade bait for a National League team that covets his flexibility.

Year	Club (League)	Class	AVG	G	AB	R	H	2B	3B	HR	RBI	BB	SO	SB	SLG	OBP
1997	Orioles (GCL)	R	.295	32	88	16	26	6	0	1	8	22	22	7	.398	.432
1998	Delmarva (SAL)	A	.265	120	408	71	108	20	3	8	53	50	92	21	.387	.364
	Bowie (EL)	AA	.158	5	19	2	3	2	0	0	1	2	6	1	.263	.238
1999	Frederick (Car)	A	.305	66	236	41	72	10	1	3	30	37	37	16	.394	.403
	Bowie (EL)	AA	.273	35	121	18	33	5	1	1	11	17	26	7	.355	.364
2000	Bowie (EL)	AA	.228	85	276	47	63	16	2	5	26	54	50	9	.355	.361
	Frederick (Car)	A	.277	24	83	16	23	3	0	2	18	10	15	5	.386	.347
2001	Dunedin (FSL)	A	.200	21	70	9	14	3	0	2	14	17	19	1	.329	.356
	Tennessee (SL)	AA	.285	104	369	51	105	23	1	18	69	63	93	12	.499	.387
2002	Syracuse (IL)	AAA	.257	127	443	65	114	25	2	18	82	67	125	24	.445	.354
	Toronto (AL)	MAJ	.261	15	46	4	12	2	1	0	6	6	11	1	.348	.340
2003	Dunedin (FSL)	A	.371	18	62	10	23	5	0	4	18	3	14	1	.645	.388
	Toronto (AL)	MAJ	.208	26	48	7	10	4	0	2	10	3	22	1	.417	.255
	Syracuse (IL)	AAA	.237	64	236	37	56	19	1	9	34	15	68	11	.441	.285
MAJOR LEAGUE TOTALS			.234	41	94	11	22	6	1	2	16	9	33	2	.383	.298
MINOR LEAGUE TOTALS			.265	701	2411	383	640	137	11	71	364	357	567	115	.420	.364

18 Jesse Harper, rhp

Born: Nov. 11, 1980. **Ht.:** 6-4. **Wt.:** 200. **Bats:** R. **Throws:** R. **School:** Galveston (Texas) JC. **Career Transactions:** Selected by Blue Jays in 21st round of 2000 draft; signed Aug. 21, 2000.

Harper doesn't have the stuff of the pitchers ahead of him, but he knows how to pitch and established himself as a prospect with a consistent 2003 season. He ranked second in the low Class A South Atlantic League in ERA in 2002, then earned a spot on the 40-man roster after leading Dunedin in wins, innings and strikeouts while finishing fourth in the Florida State League in ERA. Tall with a projectable frame, Harper was a 13th-round pick out of high school by the Diamondbacks and signed for a six-figure signing bonus after a year of junior college. His velocity hasn't caught up with the projections, but he has a high-80s fastball that scrapes 90-91 mph at times. He commands his fastball well and uses his height to throw with a good angle to the plate. Harper uses his heater to set hitters up for his slider, changeup and splitter. None stands out as more than average, and he seems to prefer the slider. Harper has room to get stronger, and if one or two of his pitches pick up a grade, he could be a factor in the rotation. He'll try to maintain his success this year at Double-A.

Year	Club (League)	Class	W	L	ERA	G	GS	CG	SV	IP	H	R	ER	HR	BB	SO	AVG
2001	Auburn (NY-P)	A	3	4	4.79	14	14	0	0	68	79	40	36	3	20	58	.289
2002	Charleston, WV (SAL)	A	6	5	2.16	21	14	0	1	113	98	38	27	4	25	97	.236
2003	Dunedin (FSL)	A	13	4	2.54	26	24	1	0	131	112	41	37	4	31	100	.229
MINOR LEAGUE TOTALS			22	13	2.89	61	52	1	1	311	289	119	100	11	76	255	.245

19 Tyrell Godwin, of

Born: July 10, 1979. **Ht.:** 6-0. **Wt.:** 200. **Bats:** L. **Throws:** R. **School:** University of North Carolina. **Career Transactions:** Selected by Blue Jays in third round of 2001 draft; signed July 2, 2001.

Godwin still flashes the tools that got him drafted in the first round twice, out of high school in 1997 by the Yankees, and as a North Carolina junior in 2000 by the Rangers. The one-time Tar Heels kickoff returner remains a plus runner and is putting his speed to use more on the bases, stealing 26 bases in 34 tries last year. His power, projected to be above-average while he was an amateur, has yet to show up consistently in games. Godwin chafed when the Blue Jays altered his swing to try to take advantage of his speed, and he hit for better power down the stretch in Double-A after reverting to his old approach. He also backtracked in plate discipline, after showing improvement in high Class A. Godwin's bat speed allows him to catch up to the best fastballs. His greatest improvement as a pro has come in throwing. His arm graded as a 35 on the 20-80 scouting scale when he was an amateur, and the Jays now consider it major league average, though his release needs to be quicker. He has become an average defender in center field and can play either corner as well. He needs a breakout season in Double-A to emerge from the organization's deep group of outfielders.

Year	Club (League)	Class	AVG	G	AB	R	H	2B	3B	HR	RBI	BB	SO	SB	SLG	OBP
2001	Auburn (NY-P)	A	.368	33	117	26	43	8	2	2	15	19	27	9	.521	.464
2002	Charleston, WV (SAL)	A	.281	48	185	31	52	8	5	0	16	20	23	10	.378	.364
2003	Dunedin (FSL)	A	.273	97	322	52	88	16	0	1	33	29	39	20	.332	.348
	New Haven (EL)	AA	.309	33	123	20	38	6	3	1	13	3	27	6	.431	.328
MINOR LEAGUE TOTALS			.296	211	747	129	221	38	10	4	77	71	116	45	.390	.368

20 Kurt Isenberg, lhp

Born: Jan. 15, 1982. **Ht.:** 6-0. **Wt.:** 190. **Bats:** R. **Throws:** L. **School:** James Madison University. **Career Transactions:** Selected by Blue Jays in fourth round of 2003 draft; signed June 8, 2003.

Teams that focus on college players in the draft frequently use performance in college as an indicator of future success. Isenberg went 8-8, 5.85 as a junior, so he wouldn't seem to fit the profile. The Jays saw through his 2003 struggles with James Madison, where he began the year as the No. 1 starter for a disappointing club. They looked at the above-average athleticism that allowed him to play both ways, saw that he struck out a batter an inning after posting a 3.43 ERA the year before, and knew he had a clean delivery with good arm action. Isenberg rewarded the Jays with a stellar pro debut, falling one-third of an inning shy of qualifying for the New York-Penn League ERA title, which he would have won by nearly half a run. His fastball sat at 89-91 mph, and club officials think there's a bit more as he focuses on pitching. He has an advanced feel for a good changeup—a trademark of pitchers at James Madison, whose coach, Spanky McFarland, has a pitching textbook—and made strides with his curveball. If his curve improves, Isenberg could evoke comparisons to Jimmy Key, whom the Jays also drafted as a two-way player back in 1982. He'll pitch in Class A this year.

Year	Club (League)	Class	W	L	ERA	G	GS	CG	SV	IP	H	R	ER	HR	BB	SO	AVG
2003	Auburn (NY-P)	A	7	2	1.63	13	13	0	0	61	40	17	11	1	19	57	.183
MINOR LEAGUE TOTALS			7	2	1.63	13	13	0	0	61	40	17	11	1	19	57	.183

21 Shaun Marcum, rhp

Born: Dec. 14, 1981. **Ht.:** 6-0. **Wt.:** 180. **Bats:** R. **Throws:** R. **School:** Southwest Missouri State University. **Career Transactions:** Selected by Blue Jays in third round of 2003 draft; signed June 23, 2003.

Marcum began his college career at Missouri before transferring to Southwest Missouri State, which allowed him to play shortstop and pitch out of the bullpen. His steady and at times spectacular defense and 13 saves helped lead the Bears to their first-ever College World Series in 2003. Marcum's defense at shortstop was sufficient, but his bat was not. After his all-star turn in the Cape Cod League in 2002, when he was Harwich's MVP with 10 saves and a 1.48 ERA, most clubs considered him a better fit on the mound. Marcum's athleticism translates to good command of an 89-92 mph fastball and a plus slider, the organization's best. His physical skills also make him a tremendous fielder at pitcher, and he has a good pickoff move. He has shown a good feel for a curveball and changeup as well and will be used as a starter in 2004, likely in low Class A. Whether Marcum starts just to get innings and experience or whether develops into another David Bush remains to be seen.

Year	Club (League)	Class	W	L	ERA	G	GS	CG	SV	IP	H	R	ER	HR	BB	SO	AVG
2003	Auburn (NY-P)	A	1	0	1.32	21	0	0	8	34	15	6	5	1	7	47	.129
MINOR LEAGUE TOTALS			1	0	1.32	21	0	0	8	34	15	6	5	1	7	47	.129

22 Chad Pleiness, rhp

Born: March 5, 1980. **Ht.:** 6-6. **Wt.:** 230. **Bats:** R. **Throws:** R. **School:** Central Michigan University. **Career Transactions:** Selected by Blue Jays in fifth round of 2002 draft; signed June 8, 2002.

Pleiness looked primed to make a big leap in 2003, his first full year as a pitcher. A three-sport athlete at Central Michigan, he went to school on a football scholarship as a tight end before starring both in basketball and baseball. He led NCAA Division I pitchers with 13.2 strikeouts per nine innings in 2002 and missed plenty of bats in his pro debut. Pleiness' stuff didn't improve as had been expected, though, and he faltered late in 2003 because of his conditioning and lack of experience with a full season. Opponents hit .203 off him through June, then battered him for a .340 clip the rest of the season. Pleiness throws an 88-92 mph fastball, curve and changeup. He struggled with keeping his deliberate delivery consistent and lost some of the bite on his curve, his out pitch. Pleiness needs to make the necessary adjustments when he returns to high Class A to start 2004.

Year	Club (League)	Class	W	L	ERA	G	GS	CG	SV	IP	H	R	ER	HR	BB	SO	AVG
2002	Auburn (NY-P)	A	8	3	2.42	16	9	0	0	74	48	23	20	2	32	70	.182
2003	Dunedin (FSL)	A	7	8	3.41	25	24	0	0	129	124	60	49	9	60	89	.258
MINOR LEAGUE TOTALS			15	11	3.05	41	33	0	0	204	172	83	69	11	92	159	.231

23 Vinnie Chulk, rhp

Born: Dec. 19, 1978. **Ht.:** 6-2. **Wt.:** 180. **Bats:** R. **Throws:** R. **School:** St. Thomas (Fla.) University. **Career Transactions:** Selected by Blue Jays in 12th round of 2000 draft; signed June 12, 2000.

Chulk had his worst season as a pro in 2003 and probably will return to the relief role he inhabited earlier in his career. His first extended shot at Triple-A started poorly as Chulk, a sinker/slider pitcher, elevated his fastball and gave up six homers in his first 20 innings. He missed a month with a sore throwing elbow, then made an adjustment that worked well the rest of the season and earned him a September callup. Chulk stopped trying to muscle his average 88-91 mph fastball past hitters and stuck to spotting it down in the strike zone. He's comparable to Jason Arnold in results and track record. His fastball has better movement and his hard slider is an average pitch, but he lacks Arnold's plus changeup and needs to command his change better. He throws a slurvy curve as well. Chulk has a track record as an effective setup man in the lower minors and has a resilient arm, which could come in handy if the Jays return him to bullpen. He'll start 2004 in Triple-A.

Year	Club (League)	Class	W	L	ERA	G	GS	CG	SV	IP	H	R	ER	HR	BB	SO	AVG
2000	Medicine Hat (Pio)	R	2	4	3.80	14	13	0	0	69	75	36	29	5	20	51	.277
2001	Dunedin (FSL)	A	1	2	3.12	16	1	0	1	35	38	16	12	2	13	50	.271
	Syracuse (IL)	AAA	1	0	1.50	5	0	0	0	6	5	1	1	0	4	3	.238
	Tennessee (SL)	AA	2	5	3.14	24	1	0	2	43	34	15	15	5	8	43	.227
2002	Tennessee (SL)	AA	13	5	2.96	25	24	0	1	152	133	55	50	12	53	108	.236
	Syracuse (IL)	AAA	0	1	5.79	2	1	0	0	5	6	3	3	0	6	2	.316
2003	Syracuse (IL)	AAA	8	10	4.22	23	21	1	0	119	118	70	56	14	46	90	.256
	Toronto (AL)	MAJ	0	0	5.06	3	0	0	0	5	6	3	3	0	3	2	.273
MAJOR LEAGUE TOTALS			0	0	5.06	3	0	0	0	5	6	3	3	0	3	2	.273
MINOR LEAGUE TOTALS			27	27	3.49	109	61	1	4	428	409	199	166	38	150	347	.252

24 Cam Reimers, rhp

Born: Sept. 15, 1978. **Ht.:** 6-5. **Wt.:** 200. **Bats:** R. **Throws:** R. **School:** JC of Southern Idaho. **Career Transactions:** Selected by Blue Jays in 35th round of 1998 draft; signed May 25, 1999.

Reimers received some of the money the Blue Jays saved when they drafted Alexis Rios in the first round in 1999 and signed him for $845,000. Toronto signed draft-and-follow righthanders Reimers, Aaron Dean and Ryan Houston to six-figure bonuses. Only Reimers, a Montana native who was one of the few prospects ever happy to play with the Jays' old Rookie-level affiliate in Medicine Hat, Alberta, remains a decent prospect. Reimers finally got the hang of Double-A in his third trip there in 2003. The Jays are under no misconceptions that the big-boned righthander, who no longer hits the occasional 94 mph on the radar gun, is a power pitcher, and neither is Reimers. He must spot his average fastball down in the zone and work for grounders with his sinker/slider approach. His changeup is just average and he doesn't have a plus pitch. Reimers profiles as a fourth or fifth starter along the lines of Jeff Suppan and will report to Triple-A—where he started and faltered in 2002.

Year	Club (League)	Class	W	L	ERA	G	GS	CG	SV	IP	H	R	ER	HR	BB	SO	AVG
1999	Medicine Hat (Pio)	R	1	5	3.25	13	5	0	2	44	39	21	16	2	12	29	.235
2000	Hagerstown (SAL)	A	7	11	3.73	26	26	2	0	154	158	79	64	10	45	112	.265
2001	Dunedin (FSL)	A	10	6	4.40	22	22	3	0	141	150	81	69	13	24	88	.272
	Tennessee (SL)	AA	1	2	6.60	5	4	0	0	30	32	22	22	8	5	19	.274
2002	Syracuse (IL)	AAA	2	3	4.99	12	10	0	0	49	68	39	27	8	11	17	.324
	Tennessee (SL)	AA	3	6	5.59	13	11	1	0	68	99	48	42	9	19	32	.350
2003	New Haven (EL)	AA	10	5	3.08	28	26	0	0	164	170	68	56	10	38	96	.270
MINOR LEAGUE TOTALS			34	38	4.10	119	104	6	2	650	716	358	296	60	154	393	.280

25 Justin James, rhp

Born: Sept. 13, 1981. **Ht.:** 6-3. **Wt.:** 215. **Bats:** R. **Throws:** R. **School:** University of Missouri. **Career Transactions:** Selected by Blue Jays in fifth round of 2003 draft; signed June 18, 2003.

James was one of the more intriguing arms in the 2003 draft as a sophomore-eligible just beginning to blossom. A sixth-round pick of the Red Sox in 2001, James struggled mightily as a freshman, when he tried to throw his low-90s fastball by every hitter he faced. He commands his fastball well and used it much more effectively at Missouri in 2003, helping lead the Tigers to their first regional bid since 1996. He was their Friday starter and went 7-6, 4.03, becoming the highest-drafted Missouri player since 1988 (Dave Silvestri, second round) when the Jays took him in the fifth round. James pitches in the 89-90 range most often, though he has touched 94 in the past. His hard curveball remains inconsistent, though at times it has good rotation. James's best pitch is a plus changeup that he throws with a funky grip. One Jays official says he can't describe it "because he won't show it to me." James pitches aggressively, challenging hitters with his fastball, and Toronto likes his competitiveness. He should start 2004 in low Class A but could move quickly.

Year	Club (League)	Class	W	L	ERA	G	GS	CG	SV	IP	H	R	ER	HR	BB	SO	AVG
2003	Auburn (NY-P)	A	2	1	3.20	13	8	0	0	39	34	14	14	2	11	42	.238
MINOR LEAGUE TOTALS			2	1	3.20	13	8	0	0	39	34	14	14	2	11	42	.238

26 Jamie Vermilyea, rhp

Born: Feb. 10, 1982. **Ht.:** 6-4. **Wt.:** 195. **Bats:** R. **Throws:** R. **School:** University of New Mexico. **Career Transactions:** Selected by Blue Jays in ninth round of 2003 draft; signed June 5, 2003.

Vermilyea had one of the best debuts of any 2003 draftee, on the heels of one of the best careers in New Mexico history. Vermilyea set single-season marks for starts and innings as a sophomore and junior, sandwiched around a star turn (1.63 ERA) in the Cape Cod League in 2002. He led the Mountain West Conference in strikeouts and innings (112 in 126) in 2003, then posted a 78-7 strikeout-walk ratio in pro ball. Vermilyea was a workhorse in college, but the Jays project him as an effective middle reliever. He throws a fastball in the high 80s, topping out around 89. His heater plays much better than that thanks to exceptional late life, especially down and in to righthanders, generated by a low three-quarters arm slot. Vermilyea's slider is well-above-average and one of the best in the organization, featuring late live and two-plane action. He also throws a splitter and commands all three pitches well. If the Jays start him, Vermilyea will have to be precise with his fastball's fringy velocity. As a middle reliever, he could move quickly. He'll begin this year in high Class A.

Year	Club (League)	Class	W	L	ERA	G	GS	CG	SV	IP	H	R	ER	HR	BB	SO	AVG
2003	Auburn (NY-P)	A	5	1	2.37	9	2	0	0	30	22	10	8	0	5	53	.204
	Dunedin (FSL)	A	0	2	2.49	9	0	0	2	22	21	6	6	1	2	25	.253
MINOR LEAGUE TOTALS			5	3	2.42	18	2	0	2	52	43	16	14	1	7	78	.225

27 Miguel Negron, of

Born: Aug. 22, 1982. **Ht.:** 6-2. **Wt.:** 170. **Bats:** L. **Throws:** L. **School:** Manuela Toro HS, Caguas, P.R. **Career Transactions:** Selected by Blue Jays in first round (18th overall) of 2000 draft; signed June 12, 2000.

Negron wasn't protected on the 40-man roster this offseason and went through the major league Rule 5 draft unclaimed, two signs that his career has stalled. He still has the tools that caused the Jays to draft him in the first round. While Negron was picked with an eye on managing the budget, he offers above-average speed and defense. He's a true center fielder who has enough arm and instincts to play all three outfield positions. For now, though, Negron profiles as no more than a fourth outfielder because his bat lags behind. Part of the problem is his approach. He's just starting to realize he's not a power hitter, and was making some progress on that front in winter ball back in his native Puerto Rico. The other part of the problem is injuries. A strained hamstring sidelined him in early June last year, and an elbow strain ended his season shortly after he returned later that month. Negron hasn't taken to the organization's plate-discipline doctrine and must do so to parlay his first-round tools into a big league career. He should get his first shot at high Class A in 2004.

Year	Club (League)	Class	AVG	G	AB	R	H	2B	3B	HR	RBI	BB	SO	SB	SLG	OBP
2000	Medicine Hat (Pio)	R	.232	53	190	26	44	5	0	0	13	23	39	5	.258	.324
2001	Charleston, WV (SAL)	A	.192	25	99	11	19	1	0	0	2	6	21	5	.202	.238
	Auburn (NY-P)	A	.253	50	186	27	47	6	1	1	13	15	22	7	.312	.314
2002	Charleston, WV (SAL)	A	.255	118	420	56	107	15	2	5	41	35	77	20	.336	.312
2003	Charleston, WV (SAL)	A	.303	30	109	13	33	8	1	1	11	2	16	6	.422	.330
MINOR LEAGUE TOTALS			.249	276	1004	133	250	35	4	7	80	81	175	43	.313	.310

28 Edward Rodriguez, rhp

Born: Oct. 6, 1984. **Ht.:** 6-4. **Wt.:** 170. **Bats:** R. **Throws:** R. **Career Transactions:** Signed out of Dominican Republic by Blue Jays, July 31, 2002.

The Jays have had some hits and misses with Latin American pitching prospects in the last decade, and the misses (Diegomar Markwell, Jose Pett) have often been spectacular and expensive. Rodriguez is a long way away, and the Jays won't really know what they have until he makes his U.S. debut at Auburn. But his arm strength and coordination have some organization officials comparing him to Francisco Rosario. Latin American scout Tony Arias signed Rodriguez for $325,000 in 2002 because he liked Rodriguez' size, arm action and easy 90-93 mph fastball velocity. The Jays were even more encouraged after his performance in the Rookie-level Dominican Summer League last year, when he ranked third in ERA and averaged a strikeout an inning. Rodriguez, who throws a middling curveball and is learning a changeup, is still growing into his frame and has some command. He's at least four years away from being a contender for Toronto's rotation, but his upside is considerable and he's the organization's best Latin prospect outside of Alexis Rios or Guillermo Quiroz.

Year	Club (League)	Class	W	L	ERA	G	GS	CG	SV	IP	H	R	ER	HR	BB	SO	AVG
2003	Blue Jays (DSL)	R	9	2	0.82	13	12	0	0	77	60	18	7	0	29	76	.213
MINOR LEAGUE TOTALS			9	2	0.82	13	12	0	0	77	60	18	7	0	29	76	.213

29 Simon Pond, 1b/3b

Born: Oct. 27, 1976. **Ht.:** 6-1. **Wt.:** 190. **Bats:** L. **Throws:** R. **School:** Argyle Secondary School, North Vancouver, B.C. **Career Transactions:** Selected by Expos in eighth round of 1994 draft; signed June 8, 1994 . . . Traded by Expos to Indians for future considerations, May 1, 2000 . . . Granted free agency, Oct. 15, 2000; re-signed by Indians, Jan. 29, 2001 . . . Released by Indians, March 29, 2002 . . . Signed by Blue Jays, March 30, 2002.

Previously given away by the Expos and released by the Indians, the Canadian corner infielder impressed Jays officials at a 2002 tryout camp after calling on his own to set up the workout. He showed big-time power from the left side and a blue-collar work ethic to win a spot on the 40-man roster after 2003. Pond typifies the approach employed by the "new Jays": He works counts, hits for power and doesn't play great defense. Bigger than his listed 6-foot-1 and 190 pounds, Pond has proven stiff at third base, doesn't run well enough to play the outfield and looks like a better fit at first base. One club official compared him physically and performance-wise to former Yankees and White Sox slugger Dan Pasqua. Whether or not Pond has enough bat for first base remains to be seen. In New Haven's deep, powerful lineup, he showed excellent patience and was a run producer, hitting stinging line drives to the gaps and over the fence. He was a bit more susceptible to Triple-A pitching, as his strikeout-walk ratio plummeted and his power numbers dipped after a promotion. Considering his defensive troubles, Pond's protection on the 40-man roster was a curious decision, but the Jays say his kind of lefthanded power is hard to find. Pond will have to prove he has enough pop to have a big league future when he returns to Triple-A in 2004.

Year	Club (League)	Class	AVG	G	AB	R	H	2B	3B	HR	RBI	BB	SO	SB	SLG	OBP
1994	Expos (GCL)	R	.259	40	147	18	38	7	0	0	15	16	25	1	.306	.329
1995	Albany (SAL)	A	.213	23	80	4	17	5	0	0	7	4	25	1	.275	.267
	Expos (GCL)	R	.150	45	133	13	20	6	1	0	12	22	34	2	.211	.276
1996	Vermont (NY-P)	A	.300	69	253	37	76	16	1	3	40	26	26	9	.407	.368
1997	Cape Fear (SAL)	A	.270	118	444	48	120	11	0	3	47	37	46	12	.315	.326
1998	Jupiter (FSL)	A	.238	105	344	40	82	15	1	1	32	24	58	1	.297	.296
	Harrisburg (EL)	AA	.000	2	3	0	0	0	0	0	0	1	1	0	.000	.250
1999	Jupiter (FSL)	A	.256	127	434	47	111	25	1	10	77	48	83	4	.387	.341
2000	Jupiter (FSL)	A	.206	19	63	7	13	1	0	3	8	9	13	1	.365	.315
	Kinston (Car)	A	.321	64	237	40	76	18	0	6	37	22	49	14	.473	.383
2001	Kinston (Car)	A	.340	25	97	13	33	8	1	4	24	10	12	1	.567	.400
	Akron (EL)	AA	.268	114	388	46	104	29	3	11	46	30	70	2	.443	.320
2002	Dunedin (FSL)	A	.284	103	401	58	114	25	7	13	88	46	73	2	.479	.357
2003	New Haven (EL)	AA	.338	61	228	44	77	17	1	7	49	39	33	1	.513	.440
	Syracuse (IL)	AAA	.306	63	248	33	76	21	1	5	36	16	42	1	.460	.353
MINOR LEAGUE TOTALS			.273	978	3500	448	957	204	17	66	518	350	590	52	.398	.343

30 Chris Leonard, lhp

Born: Oct. 9, 1980. **Ht.:** 6-1. **Wt.:** 190. **Bats:** L. **Throws:** L. **School:** Miami (Ohio) University. **Career Transactions:** Selected by Blue Jays in eighth round of 2002 draft; signed Aug. 2, 2002 . . . On disabled list, June 13-Sept. 25, 2003.

An organization short on southpaws decided to take a chance on Leonard, and in 2004 the Jays will start to see if their gamble pays off. Leonard entered 2002 ranked as one of the top college pitchers available for that year's draft. He led the Mid-American Conference in wins in 2001 at 11-3, 3.36, then followed up by leading the Cape Cod League in ERA during a 6-0, 0.98 summer. He ranked as the Cape's No. 4 prospect (behind fellow Jays farmhands Russ Adams and David Bush) thanks to a high-80s mph fastball, a smooth yet deceptive delivery, a solid curveball and a good changeup. Leonard struggled in 2002, though, going just 2-4, 4.85 while pitching with a split fingernail and blister on the index finger of his left hand. Later in the spring, he was diagnosed with elbow damage that required Tommy John surgery that summer. His recovery from the operation has gone slower than Francisco Rosario's. The Jays didn't push Leonard to throw in instructional league, where they had hoped to see him. He threw on the side but not in games. If he comes back healthy from the surgery—and the track record with Tommy John surgery is pretty good—Leonard could be a solid middle-of-the-rotation starter.

Year	Club (League)	Class	W	L	ERA	G	GS	CG	SV	IP	H	R	ER	HR	BB	SO	AVG
2003	Did not play—Injured																

SIGNING BONUSES

EVOLUTION OF THE BONUS RECORD
Domestic players only
Pre-Draft Record

Year	Team	Player	Pos.	School	Bonus
1964	Angels	Rick Reichart	of	Wisconsin	$205,000

Draft Era Record

Year	Team	Round	Player	Pos.	School	Bonus
1965	Athletics	1	Rick Monday	of	Arizona State	$104,000
1966	Phillies	1/sec.	Steve Arlin	rhp	Ohio State	105,000
1973	Rangers	1	David Clyde	lhp	HS—Houston	125,000
1975	Angels	1	Danny Goodwin	c	Southern	125,000
1978	Braves	1	Bob Horner	3b	Arizona State	175,000
	Tigers	1	Kirk Gibson	of	Michigan State	200,000
1988	Padres	1	Andy Benes	rhp	Evansville	235,000
1989	Braves	1	Tyler Houston	c	HS—Las Vegas	241,000
	Orioles	1	#Ben McDonald	rhp	Louisiana State	350,000
	Blue Jays	3	John Olerud	1b	Washington State	575,000
1991	Braves	1	Mike Kelly	of	Arizona State	575,000
	Yankees	1	Brien Taylor	lhp	HS—Beaufort, N.C.	1,550,000
1994	Mets	1	Paul Wilson	rhp	Florida State	1,550,000
	Marlins	1	Josh Booty	3b	HS—Shreveport, La.	1,600,000
1996	Pirates	1	Kris Benson	rhp	Clemson	2,000,000
	*Diamondbacks	1	Travis Lee	1b	San Diego State U.	10,000,000
	*Devil Rays	1	Matt White	rhp	HS—Chambersburg, Pa.	10,200,000

*Declared free agent on contract tendering technicality.

#Signed major league contract (For players signed to major league contracts, the amount is only the stated bonus in the contract. For players signed to standard minor league contracts, the amount is the full compensation to be paid out over the life of the contract.).

LARGEST BONUSES IN DRAFT HISTORY
For players signing with the teams that drafted them

Rank	Club	Year	Player	Pos.	School	Bonus
1.	White Sox	2000	Joe Borchard	of	Stanford	$5,300,000
2.	Twins	2001	Joe Mauer	c	HS—St. Paul	5,150,000
3.	Devil Rays	2002	B.J. Upton	ss	HS—Chesapeake, Va.	4,600,000
4.	Rangers	2001	#Mark Teixeira	3b	Georgia Tech	4,500,000
5.	Devil Rays	2001	#Dewon Brazelton	rhp	Middle Tennessee State	4,200,000
	Phillies	2001	Gavin Floyd	rhp	HS—Severna Park, Md.	4,200,000
7.	Cubs	2001	#Mark Prior	rhp	Southern California	4,000,000
	Pirates	2002	Bryan Bullington	rhp	Ball State	4,000,000
9.	Devil Rays	1999	Josh Hamilton	of	HS—Raleigh, N.C.	3,960,000
10.	Cubs	1998	Corey Patterson	of	HS—Kennesaw, Ga.	3,700,000
	Devil Rays	2003	#Delmon Young	of	HS—Camarillo, Calif.	3,700,000
12.	Marlins	1999	#Josh Beckett	rhp	HS—Spring, Texas	3,625,000
13.	Brewers	2003	#Rickie Weeks	2b	Southern	3,600,000
14.	Tigers	1999	#Eric Munson	c	Southern California	3,500,000
15.	Tigers	2003	Kyle Sleeth	rhp	Wake Forest	3,350,000
16.	Athletics	1998	Mark Mulder	lhp	Michigan State	3,200,000
17.	Phillies	1998	#Pat Burrell	1b	Miami	3,150,000
18.	Cardinals	1998	#J.D. Drew	of	St. Paul/Northern	3,000,000
	Marlins	2000	Adrian Gonzalez	1b	HS—Chula Vista, Calif.	3,000,000
	Indians	2002	#Jeremy Guthrie	rhp	Stanford	3,000,000

#Signed major league contract (For players signed to major league contracts, the amount is only the stated bonus in the contract. For players signed to standard minor league contracts, the amount is the full compensation to be paid out over the life of the contract).

SIGNING
BONUSES
TOP 100 PICKS · 2003 DRAFT

FIRST ROUND

Order. Player, Pos.	Bonus
1. Devil Rays. Delmon Young, of	$3,700,000
2. Brewers. Rickie Weeks, 2b	3,600,000
3. Tigers. Kyle Sleeth, rhp	3,350,000
4. Padres. Tim Stauffer, rhp	750,000
5. Royals. Chris Lubanski, of	2,100,000
6. Cubs. Ryan Harvey, of	2,400,000
7. Orioles. Nick Markakis, of/lhp	1,850,000
8. Pirates. Paul Maholm, lhp	2,200,000
9. Rangers. John Danks, lhp	2,100,000
10. Rockies. Ian Stewart, 3b	1,950,000
11. Indians. Michael Aubrey, 1b	2,010,000
12. Mets. Lastings Milledge, of	2,075,000
13. Blue Jays. Aaron Hill, ss	1,675,000
14. Reds. Ryan Wagner, rhp	1,400,000
15. White Sox. Brian Anderson, of	1,600,000
16. Marlins. Jeff Allison, rhp	1,850,000
17. Red Sox. David Murphy, of	1,525,000
18. Indians. Brad Snyder, of	1,525,000
19. Diamondbacks. Conor Jackson, 3b	1,500,000
20. Expos. Chad Cordero, rhp	1,350,000
21. Twins. Matt Moses, 3b	1,450,000
22. Giants. David Aardsma, rhp	1,425,000
23. Angels. Brandon Wood, ss	1,300,000
24. Dodgers. Chad Billingsley, rhp	1,375,000
25. Athletics. Brad Sullivan, rhp	1,360,000
26. Athletics. Brian Snyder, 3b	1,325,000
27. Yankees. Eric Duncan, 3b	1,250,000
28. Cardinals. Daric Barton, c	975,000
29. Diamondbacks. Carlos Quentin, of	1,100,000
30. Royals. Mitch Maier, c	900,000

SUPPLEMENTAL FIRST-ROUND

31. Indians. Adam Miller, rhp	1,025,000
32. Red Sox. Matt Murton, of	1,010,000
33. Athletics. Omar Quintanilla, ss	992,500
34. Giants. Craig Whitaker, rhp	975,000
35. Braves. Luis Atilano, rhp	950,000
36. Braves. Jarrod Saltalamacchia, c	950,000
37. Mariners. Adam Jones, ss	925,000

SECOND ROUND

38. Devil Rays. James Houser, lhp	900,000
39. Brewers. Anthony Gwynn, of	875,000
40. Tigers. Jay Sborz, rhp	865,000
41. Padres. Daniel Moore, rhp	800,000
42. Royals. Shane Costa, of	775,000
43. Braves. Jo Jo Reyes, lhp	800,000
44. Orioles. Brian Finch, rhp	750,000
45. Pirates. Tom Gorzelanny, lhp	775,000
46. Rangers. Vince Sinisi, 1b	2,070,000
47. Rockies. Scott Beerer, rhp	725,000
48. Indians. Javi Herrera, c	710,000
49. Red Sox. Abe Alvarez, lhp	700,000

50. Blue Jays. Josh Banks, rhp	650,000
51. Reds. Thomas Pauly, rhp	660,000
52. White Sox. Ryan Sweeney, of	785,000
53. Marlins. Logan Kensing, rhp	675,000
54. Red Sox. Mickey Hall, of	800,000
55. Giants. Todd Jennings, c	620,000
56. Mariners. Jeff Flaig, 3b	710,000
57. Expos. Jerry Owens, of	600,000
58. Twins. Scott Baker, rhp	600,000
59. Astros. Jason Hirsh, rhp	625,000
60. Angels. Anthony Whittington, lhp	650,000
61. Dodgers. Chuck Tiffany, lhp	1,100,000
62. Athletics. Andre Ethier, of	580,000
63. Giants. Nate Schierholtz, 3b	572,000
64. Yankees. Estee Harris, of	725,000
65. Cardinals. Stuart Pomeranz, rhp	570,000
66. Diamondbacks. Jamie D'Antona, 3b	560,000
67. Braves. Paul Bacot, rhp	550,000

THIRD ROUND

68. Devil Rays. Andrew Miller, lhp	Did not sign
69. Brewers. Lou Palmisano, c	$500,000
70. Tigers. Tony Giarratano, ss	500,000
71. Padres. Colt Morton, c	500,000
72. Royals. Brian McFall, 1b	385,000
73. Cubs. Jake Fox, c	500,000
74. Orioles. Chris Ray, rhp	485,000
75. Pirates. Steve Lerud, c	512,500
76. Rangers. John Hudgins, rhp	490,000
77. Rockies. Aaron Marsden, lhp	462,500
78. Indians. Ryan Garko, c	270,000
79. Braves. Jake Stevens, lhp	475,000
80. Blue Jays. Shaun Marcum, rhp	449,000
81. Reds. Jose Ronda, ss	440,000
82. White Sox. Clint King, of	440,000
83. Marlins. Jonathan Fulton, ss	440,000
84. Red Sox. Beau Vaughan, rhp	250,000
85. Phillies. Tim Moss, 2b	440,000
86. Mariners. Ryan Feierabend, lhp	437,500
87. Expos. Kory Casto, of	410,000
88. Twins. John Woodard, 1b	425,000
89. Astros. Drew Stubbs, of	Did not sign
90. Angels. Sean Rodriguez, ss	400,000
91. Dodgers. Cory Van Allen, lhp	Did not sign
92. Athletics. Dustin Majewski, of	220,000
93. Giants. Brian Buscher, 3b	215,000
94. Yankees. Tim Battle, of	425,000
95. Cardinals. Dennis Dove, rhp	400,000
96. Diamondbacks. Matt Chico, lhp	365,000
97. Braves. Matt Harrison, lhp	395,000

FOURTH ROUND

98. Devil Rays. Travis Schlichting, ss	400,000
99. Brewers. Charlie Fermaint, of	295,000
100. Tigers. Josh Rainwater, rhp	300,000

SIGNING
BONUSES
TOP 100 PICKS • 2002 DRAFT

FIRST ROUND

Order, Player, Pos.	Bonus
1. Pirates. Bryan Bullington, rhp	$4,000,000
2. Devil Rays. B.J. Upton, ss	4,600,000
3. Reds. Chris Gruler, rhp	2,500,000
4. Orioles. Adam Loewen, lhp	*3,200,000
5. Expos. Clint Everts, rhp	2,500,000
6. Royals. Zack Greinke, rhp	2,475,000
7. Brewers. Prince Fielder, 1b	2,400,000
8. Tigers. Scott Moore, ss	2,300,000
9. Rockies. Jeff Francis, lhp	1,850,000
10. Rangers. Drew Meyer, ss	1,875,000
11. Marlins. Jeremy Hermida, of	2,012,500
12. Angels. Joe Saunders, lhp	1,825,000
13. Padres. Khalil Greene, ss	1,500,000
14. Blue Jays. Russ Adams, ss	1,785,000
15. Mets. Scott Kazmir, lhp	2,150,000
16. Athletics. Nick Swisher, of	1,780,000
17. Phillies. Cole Hamels, lhp	2,000,000
18. White Sox. Royce Ring, lhp	1,600,000
19. Dodgers. James Loney, 1b	1,500,000
20. Twins. Denard Span, of	1,700,000
21. Cubs. Bobby Brownlie, rhp	2,500,000
22. Indians. Jeremy Guthrie, rhp	3,000,000
23. Braves. Jeff Francoeur, of	2,200,000
24. Athletics. Joseph Blanton, rhp	1,400,000
25. Giants. Matt Cain, rhp	1,375,000
26. Athletics. John McCurdy, ss	1,375,000
27. Diamondbacks. Sergio Santos, ss	1,400,000
28. Mariners. John Mayberry Jr., of	Did not sign
29. Astros. Derick Grigsby, rhp	1,125,000
30. Athletics. Ben Fritz, rhp, Fresno State	1,200,000

SUPPLEMENTAL FIRST-ROUND

31. Dodgers. Greg Miller, lhp	1,200,000
32. Cubs. Luke Hagerty, lhp	1,150,000
33. Indians. Matt Whitney, 3b	1,125,000
34. Braves. Dan Meyer, lhp	1,000,000
35. Athletics. Jeremy Brown, c	350,000
36. Cubs. Chadd Blasko, rhp	1,050,000
37. Athletics. Steve Obenchain, rhp	750,000
38. Cubs. Matt Clanton, rhp	875,000
39. Athletics. Mark Teahen, 3b	725,000
40. Reds. Mark Schramek, 3b	200,000
41. Indians. Micah Schilling, 2b	915,000

SECOND ROUND

42. Pirates. Blair Johnson, rhp	885,000
43. Devil Rays. Jason Pridie, of	892,500
44. Reds. Joey Votto, c	600,000
45. Orioles. Corey Shafer, of	800,000
46. Expos. Darrell Rasner, rhp	800,000
47. Royals. Adam Donachie, c	800,000
48. Brewers. Josh Murray, ss	825,000
49. Tigers. Brent Clevlen, of	805,000
50. Rockies. Micah Owings, rhp	Did not sign

51. Dodgers. Zach Hammes, rhp	750,000
52. Marlins. Robert Andino, ss	750,000
53. Angels. Kevin Jepsen, rhp	745,000
54. Padres. Michael Johnson, 1b	*500,000
55. Blue Jays. David Bush, rhp	450,000
56. Cubs. Brian Dopirak, 1b	740,000
57. Red Sox. Jon Lester, lhp	1,000,000
58. Phillies. Zach Segovia, rhp	712,500
59. White Sox. Jeremy Reed, of	650,000
60. Dodgers. Jonathan Broxton, rhp	685,000
61. Twins. Jesse Crain, rhp	650,000
62. Cubs. Justin Jones, lhp	625,000
63. Indians. Brian Slocum, rhp	625,000
64. Braves. Brian McCann, c	750,000
65. Braves. Tyler Greene, ss	Did not sign
66. Giants. Fred Lewis, of	595,000
67. Athletics. Steve Stanley, of	200,000
68. Diamondbacks. Chris Snyder, c	567,000
69. Mariners. Josh Womack, of	550,000
70. Astros. Mitch Talbot, rhp	550,000
71. Yankees. Brandon Weeden, rhp	565,000

SUPPLEMENTAL SECOND-ROUND

72. Indians. Pat Osborn, 3b	547,500

THIRD ROUND

73. Pirates. Taber Lee, ss	525,000
74. Devil Rays. Elijah Dukes, of	500,000
75. Reds. Kyle Edens, rhp	300,000
76. Orioles. Val Majewski, of	400,000
77. Expos. Larry Broadway, 1b	450,000
78. Royals. David Jensen, 1b	472,500
79. Brewers. Eric Thomas, rhp	470,000
80. Tigers. Curtis Granderson, of	469,000
81. Rockies. Ben Crockett, rhp	345,000
82. Indians. Jason Cooper, of	472,500
83. Marlins. Trevor Hutchinson, rhp	375,000
84. Angels. Kyle Pawelczyk, rhp	465,000
85. Padres. Kennard Jones, of	465,000
86. Blue Jays. Justin Maureau, lhp	455,000
87. Tigers. Matt Pender, rhp	450,000
88. Red Sox. Scott White, 3b	825,000
89. Phillies. Kiel Fisher, 3b	450,000
90. White Sox. Josh Rupe, rhp	440,000
91. Dodgers. Mike Nixon, c	950,000
92. Twins. Mark Sauls, rhp	Did not sign
93. Cubs. Billy Petrick, rhp	459,500
94. Indians. Daniel Cevette, lhp	400,000
95. Braves. Charlie Morton, rhp	415,000
96. Cubs. Matt Craig, ss	399,000
97. Giants. Dan Ortmeier, of	396,000
98. Athletics. Bill Murphy, lhp	410,000
99. Diamondbacks. Jared Doyle, lhp	390,000
100. Mariners. Eddy Martinez-Esteve, of	Did not sign

*Signed in 2003 as draft-and-follow

SIGNING
BONUSES
TOP 100 PICKS · 2001 DRAFT

FIRST ROUND

Order. Player, Pos.	Bonus
1. Twins. Joe Mauer, c	$5,150,000
2. Cubs. Mark Prior, rhp	4,000,000
3. Devil Rays. Dewon Brazelton, rhp	4,000,000
4. Phillies. Gavin Floyd, rhp	4,200,000
5. Rangers. Mark Teixeira, 3b	4,500,000
6. Expos. Josh Karp, rhp	2,650,000
7. Orioles. Chris Smith, lhp	2,175,000
8. Pirates. John VanBenschoten, rhp/1b	2,400,000
9. Royals. Colt Griffin, rhp	2,400,000
10. Astros. Chris Burke, 2b/ss	2,100,000
11. Tigers. Kenny Baugh, rhp	1,800,000
12. Brewers. Mike Jones, rhp	2,075,000
13. Angels. Casey Kotchman, 1b	2,075,000
14. Padres. Jake Gautreau, 3b	1,875,000
15. Blue Jays. Gabe Gross, of	1,865,000
16. White Sox. Kris Honel, rhp	1,500,000
17. Indians. Dan Denham, rhp	1,860,000
18. Mets. Aaron Heilman, rhp	1,508,750
19. Orioles. Mike Fontenot, 2b	1,300,000
20. Reds. Jeremy Sowers, lhp	Did not sign
21. Giants. Brad Hennessey, rhp	1,382,500
22. Diamondbacks. Jason Bulger, rhp	938,600
23. Yankees. John-Ford Griffin, of	1,200,000
24. Braves. Macay McBride, lhp	1,340,000
25. Athletics. Bobby Crosby, ss	1,350,000
26. Athletics. Jeremy Bonderman, rhp	1,350,000
27. Indians. Alan Horne, rhp	Did not sign
28. Cardinals. Justin Pope, rhp	900,000
29. Braves. Josh Burrus, ss	1,250,000
30. Giants. Noah Lowry, lhp	1,175,000

SUPPLEMENTAL FIRST ROUND

31. Orioles. Bryan Bass, ss	1,150,000
32. Tigers. Michael Woods, 2b	1,100,000
33. Angels.Jeff Mathis, c	850,000
34. Yankees. Bronson Sardinha, ss	1,000,000
35. Indians. J.D. Martin, rhp	975,000
36. Mariners. Michael Garciaparra, ss	2,000,000
37. Athletics. John Rheinecker, lhp	600,000
38. Mets. David Wright, 3b	960,000
39. White Sox. Wyatt Allen, rhp	872,500
40. Braves. Richard Lewis, 2b	850,000
41. Giants. Todd Linden, of	750,000
42. Yankees. Jon Skaggs, rhp	600,000
43. Indians. Michael Conroy, of	870,000
44. Rockies. Jayson Nix, ss	925,000

SECOND ROUND

45. Twins. Scott Tyler, rhp	875,000
46. Cubs. Andy Sisco, lhp	1,000,000
47. Devil Rays. Jon Switzer, lhp	850,000
48. Red Sox. Kelly Shoppach, c	737,500
49. Mariners. Rene Rivera, c	688,000

50. Expos. Donald Levinski, rhp	825,000
51. Indians. Jake Dittler, rhp	750,000
52. Braves. J.P. Howell, lhp	Did not sign
53. Royals. Roscoe Crosby, of	1,750,000
54. Astros. Mike Rodriguez, of	675,000
55. Tigers. Preston Larrison, rhp	685,000
56. Brewers. J.J. Hardy, ss	735,000
57. Angels. Dallas McPherson, 3b	660,000
58. Padres. Matt Harrington, rhp	Did not sign
59. Blue Jays. Brandon League, rhp	660,000
60. Marlins. Garrett Berger, rhp	795,000
61. Red Sox. Matt Chico, lhp	Did not sign
62. Yankees. Shelley Duncan, of	655,000
63. Yankees. Jason Arnold, rhp	400,000
64. Reds. Justin Gillman, rhp	625,000
65. Tigers. Matt Coenen, lhp	620,000
66. Diamondbacks. Mike Gosling, lhp	2,000,000
67. Mariners. Michael Wilson, of	900,000
68. Dodgers. Brian Pilkington, rhp	600,000
69. Athletics. Neal Cotts, lhp	525,000
70. Mets. Alhaji Turay, of	517,500
71. White Sox. Ryan Wing, lhp	575,000
72. Cardinals. Dan Haren, rhp	530,000
73. Braves. Cole Barthel, 3b	475,000
74. Giants. Jesse Foppert, rhp	520,000

SUPPLEMENTAL SECOND ROUND

75. Rockies. Trey Taylor, lhp	Did not sign
76. Mets. Corey Ragsdale, ss	480,000

THIRD ROUND

77. Twins. Jose Morales, ss	490,000
78. Cubs. Ryan Theriot, ss	485,000
79. Devil Rays. Chris Flinn, rhp	466,000
80. Mariners. Lazaro Abreu, c	400,000
81. Angels. Steven Shell, rhp	460,000
82. Expos. Mike Hinckley, lhp	425,000
83. Orioles. Dave Crouthers, rhp	425,000
84. Pirates. Jeremy Guthrie, rhp	Did not sign
85. Royals. Matt Ferrara, 3b	450,000
86. Astros. Kirk Saarloos, rhp	300,000
87. Tigers. Jack Hannahan, 3b	435,000
88. Brewers. Jon Steitz, rhp	460,000
89. Angels. Jacob Woods, lhp	442,500
90. Padres. Taggert Bozeid, 1b-3b	700,000
91. Blue Jays. Tyrell Godwin, of	480,000
92. Marlins. Allen Baxter, rhp	450,000
93. Red Sox. Jonathan DeVries, c	450,000
94. Rockies. Jason Frome, of	420,000
95. Yankees. Chase Wright, lhp	400,000
96. Reds. Alan Moye, of	400,000
97. Indians. Nick Moran, rhp	400,000
98. Diamondbacks. Scott Hairston, 2b	400,000
99. Mariners. Tim Merritt, ss	400,000
100. Dodgers. David Taylor, rhp	385,000

COLLEGE TOP 100
DRAFT PROSPECTS
CLASS OF 2004

Rank	Player, Pos.	College	Hometown	Class	B-T	Ht.	Wt.	Last Drafted
1.	Jeff Niemann, rhp	Rice	Houston, Texas	Jr.	R-R	6-9	260	Never drafted
2.	Justin Verlander, rhp	Old Dominion	Goochland, Va.	Jr.	R-R	6-4	180	Never drafted
3.	Jered Weaver, rhp	Long Beach State	Simi Valley, Calif.	Jr.	R-R	6-6	200	Never drafted
4.	Jeff Larish, 1b	Arizona State	Tempe, Ariz.	Jr.	L-R	6-2	180	Cubs '01 (32)
5.	Stephen Drew, ss	Florida State	Valdosta, Ga.	Jr.	B-R	6-1	185	Pirates '01 (11)
6.	Wade Townsend, rhp	Rice	Dripping Springs, Texas	Jr.	R-R	6-4	225	Never drafted
7.	Jeremy Sowers, lhp	Vanderbilt	Louisville, Ky.	Jr.	L-L	6-1	170	Reds '01 (1)
8.	Phil Humber, rhp	Rice	Carthage, Texas	Jr.	R-R	6-4	210	Yankees '01 (29)
9.	Justin Orenduff, rhp	Va. Commonwealth	Chesapeake, Va.	Jr.	R-R	6-4	220	Never drafted
10.	Chris Lambert, rhp	Boston College	Manchester, N.H.	Jr.	R-R	6-0	195	Never drafted
11.	Huston Street, rhp	Texas	Round Rock, Texas	Jr.	R-R	6-0	179	Never drafted
12.	Micah Owings, rhp/dh	Georgia Tech	Gainesville, Ga.	So.	R-R	6-4	212	Rockies '02 (2)
13.	Thomas Diamond, rhp	New Orleans	Metairie, La.	Jr.	R-R	6-3	220	Devil Rays '01 (38)
14.	Seth Smith, of	Mississippi	Jackson, Miss.	Jr.	L-L	6-3	205	D'backs '01 (48)
15.	Eric Beattie, rhp	Tampa	Valrico, Fla.	Jr.	R-R	6-3	175	Devil Rays '01 (47)
16.	Eric Patterson, 2b	Georgia Tech	Kennesaw, Ga.	Jr.	L-R	5-10	160	Rockies '01 (22)
17.	Danny Putnam, of	Stanford	Escondido, Calif.	Jr.	L-L	5-10	195	Never drafted
18.	Matt Durkin, rhp	San Jose State	San Jose, Calif.	Jr.	R-R	6-4	210	D'backs '01 (10)
19.	Justin Maxwell, of	Maryland	Olney, Md.	Jr.	R-R	6-5	215	Orioles '01(43)
20.	Steve Register, rhp	Auburn	Columbus, Ga.	Jr.	R-R	6-1	162	Never drafted
21.	Jeff Frazier, of	Rutgers	Toms River, N.J.	Jr.	R-R	6-3	170	Never drafted
22.	Matt Campbell, lhp	South Carolina	Simpsonville, S.C.	Jr.	L-L	6-2	170	Braves '01 (39)
23.	Mike Nickeas, c	Georgia Tech	Westlake Village, Ca.	Jr.	R-R	6-1	205	Never drafted
24.	Tyler Lumsden, lhp	Clemson	Roanoke, Va.	Jr.	L-L	6-2	190	Marlins '01 (5)
25.	J.P. Howell, lhp	Texas	Sacramento, Calif.	Jr.	L-L	5-11	165	Braves '01 (2)
26.	Garrett Mock, rhp	Houston	Houston	Jr.	R-R	6-4	205	Twins '02 (14)
27.	Marc Cornell, rhp	Ohio	Columbus, Ohio	Sr.	L-R	6-2	215	Reds '03 (5)
28.	Jason Jaramillo, c	Oklahoma State	Franksville, Wis.	Jr.	B-R	6-1	195	Phillies '01 (39)
29.	Sam Fuld, of	Stanford	Durham, N.H.	Sr.	L-L	5-10	180	Cubs '03 (24)
30.	Jeremy Slayden, of	Georgia Tech	Murfreesboro, Tenn.	Jr.	L-R	6-0	190	Padres '01 (20)
31.	Landon Powell, c	South Carolina	Cary, N.C.	Sr.	B-R	6-4	225	Cubs '03 (25)
32.	Josh Fields, 3b/1b	Oklahoma State	Stillwater, Okla.	Jr.	R-R	6-2	210	Never drafted
33.	Jonathan Zeringue, of	Louisiana State	Thibodeaux, La.	Jr.	R-R	6-2	210	White Sox '01 (3)
34.	David Purcey, lhp	Oklahoma	Dallas	Jr.	L-L	6-5	240	Yankees '03 (17)
35.	Wes Whisler, lhp/1b	UCLA	Noblesville, Ind.	Jr.	L-L	6-5	227	Cubs '01 (42)
36.	Donny Lucy, c	Stanford	Fallbrook, Calif.	Jr.	R-R	6-3	210	Never drafted
37.	Eddy Martinez-Esteve, 3b	Florida State	Miami, Fla.	So.	R-R	6-2	200	Mariners '02 (3)
38.	Josh Baker, rhp	Rice	Houston	Jr.	R-R	6-5	210	Rangers '01 (4)
39.	Brad McCann, 3b	Clemson	Duluth, Ga.	Jr.	R-R	6-2	195	Phillies '02 (22)
40.	Ross Ohlendorf, rhp	Princeton	Austin, Texas	Jr.	R-R	6-4	220	Never drafted
41.	Dustin Pedroia, ss	Arizona State	Woodland, Calif.	Jr.	R-R	5-9	165	Never drafted
42.	Ben Harrison, of	Florida	Key West, Fla.	Sr.	R-R	6-3	190	Indians '03 (4)
43.	Scott Lewis, lhp	Ohio State	Wash. Court House, Ohio	Jr.	L-L	6-0	185	Angels '01 (33)
44.	Kyle Schmidt, rhp	South Florida	Palm Harbor, Fla.	Jr.	R-R	6-3	220	Orioles '01 (29)
45.	Will Fenton, rhp	Washington	Kingston, Wash.	Jr.	R-R	6-2	195	Never drafted
46.	Brett Smith, rhp	UC Irvine	La Habra, Calif.	Jr.	R-R	6-5	215	D'backs '01 (21)
47.	Justin Hoyman, rhp	Florida	Cocoa, Fla.	Jr.	R-R	6-2	200	Rockies '02 (43)
48.	Sean Gamble, of	Auburn	Montgomery, Ala.	Jr.	L-L	6-1	183	Blue Jays '01 (11)
49.	Glen Perkins, lhp	Minnesota	Stillwater, Minn.	So.	L-L	6-0	190	Never drafted
50.	Andrew Dobies, lhp	Virginia	Wexford, Pa.	Jr.	L-L	6-1	190	Never drafted

51.	Taylor Tankersley, lhp	Alabama	Vicksburg, Miss.	Jr.	L-L	6-1	200	Royals '01 (39)
52.	J.C. Holt, of	Louisiana State	Sleper, La.	Jr.	L-R	5-9	172	Never drafted
53.	Grant Johnson, rhp	Notre Dame	Burr Ridge, Ill.	So.	R-R	6-5	220	Never drafted
54.	Matt Macri, ss/3b	Notre Dame	Clive, Iowa	Jr.	R-R	6-3	205	Twins '01 (17)
55.	Eric Dworkis, rhp	Gonzaga	Bellevue, Wash.	Jr.	R-R	6-5	185	Never drafted
56.	Ryan Schroyer, rhp	San Diego State	Casa Grande, Ariz.	Sr.	R-R	6-1	205	Twins '03 (11)
57.	Joey Metropoulos, 1b	So. California	Jamul, Calif.	Jr.	R-R	6-1	230	Tigers '01 (16)
58.	Michael Griffin, 3b	Baylor	Dallas	Jr.	R-R	5-9	180	Never drafted
59.	Bill Bray, lhp	William & Mary	Virginia Beach, Va.	Jr.	L-L	6-3	215	Never drafted
60.	Jim Brauer, rhp	Michigan	Carmel, Ind.	Jr.	R-R	6-4	196	Rockies '03 (17)
61.	Steve Gendron, 3b	Mississippi State	Jacksonville	Sr.	R-R	6-3	199	Padres '03 (14)
62.	Adam Lind, 1b	South Alabama	Anderson, Ind.	So.	L-L	6-2	190	Twins '02 (8)
63.	Darryl Lawhorn, of	East Carolina	Wilmington, N.C.	Jr.	L-R	6-2	165	Never drafted
64.	Trey Taylor, lhp	Baylor	Mansfield, Texas	Jr.	R-L	6-2	185	Rockies '01 (2)
65.	Tony Sipp, lhp/of	Clemson	Moss Point, Miss.	Jr.	L-L	6-0	180	White Sox '02 (33)
66.	C.J. Smith, 1b/of	Florida	Tampa	Jr.	R-R	6-3	208	Pirates '03 (6)
87.	Brandon Boggs, of	Georgia Tech	Marietta, Ga.	Jr.	B-R	5-11	192	Yankees '01 (50)
68.	Zach Jackson, lhp	Texas A&M	Cranberry Township, Pa.	Jr.	L-L	6-5	215	White Sox '01 (50)
69.	Chris Carter, 1b/of	Stanford	Walnut Creek, Calif.	Jr.	L-L	6-0	215	Never drafted
70.	Chris Niesel, rhp	Notre Dame	Plantation, Fla.	Jr.	R-R	6-0	195	Cubs '01 (46)
71.	Devin Ivany, c	South Florida	Fort Lauderdale, Fla.	Jr.	R-R	6-1	178	Angels '01 (9)
72.	John Hardy, ss	Arizona	Boise, Idaho	Jr.	R-R	6-1	170	Orioles '01 (11)
73.	Cory Patton, of	Texas A&M	Owasso, Okla.	Sr.	L-L	5-9	210	Padres '03 (6)
74.	Paul Janish, ss/rhp	Rice	Cypress, Texas	Jr.	R-R	6-2	160	Never drafted
75.	Myron Leslie, 3b	South Florida	Valrico, Fla.	Sr.	B-R	6-3	200	Phillies '03 (11)
76.	Kevin Hart, rhp	Maryland	Dallas	Jr.	R-R	6-4	220	Never drafted
77.	Justin Keadle, rhp	Wake Forest	Huntington Beach, Calif.	Jr.	R-R	6-2	200	Yankees '02 (38)
78.	Brad Davis, c	Long Beach State	Mission Viejo, Calif.	Jr.	R-R	6-2	185	Devil Rays '01 (48)
79.	Mark Jurich, of	Louisville	Louisville	Sr.	L-L	5-10	185	Braves '03 (13)
80.	Steve Uhlmansiek, lhp	Wichita State	Albuquerque	So.	L-L	6-3	170	Never drafted
81.	Erick San Pedro, c	Miami (Fla.)	Hialeah, Fla.	Jr.	R-R	6-0	204	Never drafted
82.	Dustin Miller, rhp	Cal State Fullerton	Diamond Bar, Calif.	So.	R-R	6-5	200	Phillies '01 (41)
83.	Garry Bakker, rhp	North Carolina	Sloatsburg, N.Y.	Jr.	R-R	6-2	211	Mariners '01 (24)
84.	Rob Johnson, c	Houston	Butte, Mont.	Jr.	R-R	6-0	195	Phillies '03 (18)
85.	Kyle Larsen, 1b	Washington	Sammamish, Wash.	Jr.	L-L	6-5	215	Mets '01 (14)
86.	Billy Becher, 1b	New Mexico State	Chandler, Ariz.	Sr.	R-R	6-5	235	Athletics '03 (18)
87.	Danny Figueroa, of	Miami (Fla.)	Miami, Fla.	Jr.	R-R	5-11	175	Braves '01 (48)
88.	Mike Rogers, rhp	North Carolina State	Hamilton, N.J.	So.	R-R	6-0	195	Never drafted
89.	Steve Sollmann, 2b	Notre Dame	Cincinnati	Jr.	R-R	5-10	190	Athletics '03 (32)
90.	Ronnie Prettyman, 3b	Cal State Fullerton	Los Alamitos, Calif.	Jr.	L-R	6-2	190	Never drafted
91.	Dave Haehnel, lhp	Illinois-Chicago	Wheeling, Ill.	Jr.	L-L	6-3	170	Never drafted
92.	Josh Ford, c	Baylor	Baytown, Texas	Jr.	R-R	6-2	210	Never drafted
93.	Joe Pietro, of	New Orleans	Omaha	Jr.	L-R	6-0	198	Never drafted
94.	Jeff Fiorentino, of	Florida Atlantic	Hollywood, Fla.	Jr.	L-R	6-1	175	Blue Jays '01 (21)
95.	Lou Santangelo, c	Clemson	Colts Neck, N.J.	Jr.	R-R	6-1	195	Never drafted
96.	Mark Jecmen, rhp	Stanford	Diamond Bar, Calif.	Jr.	R-R	6-9	230	Cubs '01 (42)
97.	Anthony Raglani, of	Geo. Washington	Indiana, Pa.	Jr.	L-L	6-2	210	Never drafted
98.	Jim Fasano, 1b	Richmond	Horsham, Pa.	Jr.	L-R	6-5	220	Never drafted
99.	Wyatt Toregas, c	Virginia Tech	Ashburn, Va.	Jr.	R-R	5-11	190	Never drafted
100.	Cesar Nicolas, 1b	Vanderbilt	Miami	Sr.	R-R	6-4	225	Never drafted

Compiled by Allan Simpson.

NOTE: List does not include junior college players.

HIGH SCHOOL TOP 100
DRAFT PROSPECTS
CLASS OF 2004

Rank	Player, Pos.	High School	Hometown	B-T	Ht.	Wt.	Committment
1.	Nick Adenhart, rhp	Williamsport	Hagerstown, Md.	R-R	6-3	185	North Carolina
2.	Matt Bush, ss/rhp	Mission Bay	El Cajon, Calif.	R-R	6-0	170	San Diego State
3.	Greg Golson, of	John Connally	Austin, Texas	R-R	6-1	185	Texas
4.	Homer Bailey, rhp	LaGrange	LaGrange, Texas	R-R	6-4	185	Texas
5.	Michael Taylor, of	Apopka	Apopka, Fla.	R-L	6-6	233	Stanford
6.	Jay Rainville, rhp	Bishop Hendricken	Pawtucket, R.I.	R-R	6-3	220	Tennessee
7.	Chuck Lofgren, of/lhp	Serra	Burlingame, Calif.	L-L	6-3	190	Santa Clara
8.	Mark Rogers, rhp	Mt. Ararat	Orr's Island, Maine	R-R	6-2	200	Miami
9.	Andy Gale, rhp	Phillips Exeter Acad.	Durham, N.H.	R-R	6-6	220	North Carolina
10.	Chris Nelson, ss/rhp	Redan	Decatur, Ga.	R-R	5-11	165	Georgia
11.	Phil Hughes, rhp	Foothill	Santa Ana, Calif.	R-R	6-4	215	Santa Clara
12.	Scott Elbert, lhp	Seneca	Seneca, Mo.	L-L	6-2	175	Missouri
13.	Kenn Kasparek, rhp	Weimar	Weimar, Texas	R-R	6-8	197	Texas
14.	Trevor Plouffe, inf/rhp	Crespi	Northridge, Calif.	R-R	6-1	170	Southern California
15.	Erik Davis, rhp	Mountain View	Mountain View, Calif.	R-R	6-3	180	Stanford
16.	Giovani Gonzalez, lhp	Monsignor Pace	Miami	L-L	6-0	170	Miami
17.	Troy Patton, lhp	Tomball	Magnolia, Texas	L-L	6-1	170	Texas
18.	Eric Hurley, rhp	Wolfson	Jacksonville, Fla.	R-R	6-4	192	Florida
19.	Neil Walker, c	Pine Richland	Gibsonia, Pa.	B-R	6-2	205	Clemson
20.	Mike Rozier, lhp	Henry County	Stockbridge, Ga.	L-L	6-5	210	North Carolina (FB)
21.	Stephen Chapman, of	Marianna	Marianna, Fla.	L-L	6-0	180	Auburn
22.	Alex Garabedian, c	Columbus	Miami	R-R	6-2	210	Miami
23.	Josh Copeland, rhp	Northgate	Palmetto, Ga.	R-R	6-2	200	Alabama
24.	Yovani Gallardo, rhp	Trimble Tech	Fort Worth, Texas	R-R	6-2	180	Texas Christian
25.	Warren McFadden, of	Nova	Plantation, Fla.	R-R	6-0	185	Tulane
26.	Joseph Bauserman, rhp	Lincoln	Tallahassee, Fla.	R-R	6-2	220	Ohio State (FB)
27.	Blake Johnson, rhp	Parkview Baptist	Baton Rouge, La.	R-R	6-4	195	Louisiana State
28.	Dexter Fowler, of	Milton	Alpharetta, Ga.	R-R	6-3	160	Miami
29.	Blake DeWitt, ss	Sikeston	Sikeston, Mo.	R-R	6-0	175	Georgia Tech
30.	Tate Casey, rhp	Longview	Longview, Texas	R-R	6-6	220	Arizona (FB)
31.	Drew Bowman, lhp	Dakota Ridge	Morrison, Colo.	R-L	6-3	175	Arizona State
32.	Matt Wieters, c	Stratford	Goose Creek, S.C.	B-R	6-4	210	Georgia Tech
33.	Seth Garrison, 3b	Coppell	Coppell, Texas	B-R	6-4	200	Arizona State
34.	Erik Cordier, rhp	Southern Door	Sturgeon Bay, Wis.	R-R	6-3	190	North Carolina State
35.	Preston Clark, c	Rockwall	Rockwall, Texas	R-R	5-10	178	Texas
36.	Sam Demel, rhp	Spring	Spring, Texas	R-R	6-0	185	Texas Christian
37.	Andrew Romine, ss	Trabuco Hills	Lake Forest, Calif.	B-R	6-0	180	Arizona State
38.	Matt Tuiasosopo, of	Woodinville	Woodinville, Wash.	R-R	6-2	200	Washington (FB)
39.	Brian Johnson, rhp	East Islip	Islip Terrace, N.Y.	R-R	6-2	190	
40.	Steven Marquardt, 3b/rhp	Kennewick	Kennewick, Wash.	R-R	6-2	190	Washington
41.	Eddie Burns, rhp	Hiram	Hiram, Ga.	R-R	6-5	210	Georgia Tech
42.	Javier Guerra, rhp	Denton Ryan	Denton, Texas	R-R	6-2	180	Arizona
43.	Billy Butler, 1b/rhp	Wolfson	Jacksonville, Fla.	R-R	6-2	232	Florida
44.	Brad Chalk, of	Riverside	Greer, S.C.	L-L	6-1	170	Clemson
45.	David Coulon, lhp	Hanford	Hanford, Calif.	L-L	5-11	155	Arizona
46.	Mark Trumbo, rhp	Villa Park	Orange, Calif.	R-R	6-5	220	Southern California
47.	Brian Futral, rhp	Newnan	Newnan, Ga.	R-R	6-4	180	Georgia Tech
48.	Michael Schlact, rhp	Wheeler	Marietta, Ga.	R-R	6-7	205	South Carolina
49.	Todd Frazier, of	Toms River South	Toms River, N.J.	R-R	6-3	185	Rutgers
50.	Jason Corder, of/rhp	Capistrano Valley	Mission Viejo, Calif.	R-R	6-3	190	California

51.	Jared Kubin, of/1b	Oakton	Oakton, Va.	R-R	6-3	225	Florida
52.	Luke French, lhp/1b	Heritage	Littleton, Colo.	L-L	6-3	220	UNLV
53.	Joe Savery, of/lhp	Lamar	Bellaire, Texas	L-L	6-3	190	Rice
54.	Billy Killian, c	Chippewa Hills	Stanwood, Mich.	L-R	6-1	180	Kentucky
55.	Cale Iorg, ss	Karns	Knoxville, Tenn.	R-R	6-2	175	Alabama
56.	Barry Enright, rhp	St. Mary's	Stockton, Calif.	R-R	6-2	190	Pepperdine
57.	Josh Johnson, ss	Middleton	Tampa	B-R	5-11	170	Texas
58.	Eddie Morlan, rhp	Coral Park	Miami, Fla.	R-R	6-2	185	Miami
59.	Troy Grundy, rhp	Carbon	Helper, Utah	R-R	6-1	170	
60.	Sean Morgan, rhp	Fort Bend Clements	Sugar Land, Texas	R-R	6-3	218	Tulane
61.	Chase Fontaine, ss	Nease	St. Augustine, Fla.	L-R	6-1	175	Texas
62.	Will Jostock, rhp	Lapeer West	Lapeer, Mich.	R-R	6-6	192	Tennessee
63.	Walter Diaz, ss	Braddock	Miami	R-R	6-0	180	Miami
64.	Eric Campbell, 2b/3b	Gibson Southern	Owensville, Ind.	R-R	6-0	175	
65.	Matthew McGahey, lhp/1b	Science Hill	Kingsport, Tenn.	L-L	6-3	205	Virginia Tech
66.	Tim Ladd, lhp	Kell	Marietta, Ga.	L-L	5-11	165	Georgia Tech
67.	Josh Horton, ss	Orange	Hillsborough, N.C.	L-R	6-1	175	North Carolina
68.	Josh Fields, rhp	Prince Avenue Christian	Hull, Ga.	R-R	6-0	165	Georgia
69.	Tyler Beranek, 1b	Waukesha South	Waukesha, Wis.	R-R	6-5	215	UNLV
70.	Randy Molina, 3b	South Gate	South Gate, Calif.	L-R	6-3	210	Stanford
71.	Stephen Porlier, rhp	Elkins	Sugar Land, Texas	R-R	6-3	186	Tulane
72.	Raudel Alfonso, rhp	Hialeah	Hialeah, Fla.	R-R	6-2	200	Miami
73.	Ed Easley, c	Olive Branch	Olive Branch, Miss.	R-R	6-2	180	Mississippi State
74.	Willie Bowman, 3b	Carson	Carson City, Nev.	R-R	6-2	200	UNLV
75.	Jon Mark Owings, 3b/of	Gainesville	Gainesville, Ga.	R-R	6-4	185	Clemson
76.	David Kopp, rhp	Coral Springs	Coral Springs, Fla.	R-R	6-3	185	Clemson
77.	Christian Garcia, c	Gulliver Prep	Miami	B-R	6-4	175	South Carolina
78.	Danny Payne, of/lhp	Sequoyah	Woodstock, Ga.	L-L	5-10	180	Georgia Tech
79.	Andy Lentz, ss/of	Woodinville	Woodinville, Wash.	L-R	6-0	185	Washington
80.	Lucas Duda, 1b	Arlington	Riverside, Calif.	L-R	6-4	220	Southern California
81.	David Price, lhp	Blackman	Murfreesboro, Tenn.	L-L	6-4	195	Vanderbilt
82.	Brad Bergesen, rhp	Foothill	Pleasanton, Calif.	L-R	6-2	215	San Diego
83.	Andrew Brackman, rhp	Moeller	Cincinnati	R-R	6-9	200	N.C. State (BKB)
84.	D.T. McDowell, of/rhp	Tucker School	Atlanta, Ga.	R-R	6-0	185	Nebraska (FB)
85.	James Parr, rhp/1b	La Cueva	Alburquerque, N.M.	R-R	6-1	185	Hawaii
86.	John Lalor, rhp	Houston	Germantown, Tenn.	R-R	6-7	220	Mississippi State
87.	Jacob McGee, lhp	Edward C. Reed	Sparks, Nev.	L-L	6-2	190	UNLV
88.	Bobby Cassevah, rhp	Pace	Pace, Fla.	R-R	6-3	190	Louisiana State
89.	Stan Widmann, ss	L.D. Bell	Hurst, Texas	R-R	6-1	180	Clemson
90.	Luke Putkonen, rhp	Walton	Marietta, Ga.	R-R	6-5	180	North Carolina
91.	Ryan Strauss, of/rhp	Bloomingdale	Tampa	R-R	6-2	195	Florida State
92.	Matt Spencer, 1b/lhp	Morristown West	Morristown, Tenn.	L-L	6-4	220	North Carolina
93.	Juan Carlos Portes, ss	Malden	Malden, Mass.	R-R	5-10	180	
94.	Ryan Pond, 3b	Western Branch	Chesapeake, Va.	R-R	6-2	225	N.C. State (FB)
95.	Corey Brown, of	Plant	Tampa	L-L	6-2	185	Virginia
96.	Joseph Dunigan, of	St. Ignatius College Prep	Chicago, Ill.	L-L	6-1	210	Oklahoma
97.	Chris Davis, ss/rhp	Longview	Longview, Texas	L-R	6-3	205	Texas
98.	John Poterson, 1b/c	Chandler	Chandler, Ariz.	B-R	6-1	220	
99.	Angel Salome, c	George Washington	New York	R-R	5-10	188	
100.	Michael Fisher, ss	Montgomery Bell Acad.	Nashville, Tenn.	B-R	6-2	187	Georgia Tech

Compiled by Allan Simpson.

MINOR LEAGUE
TOP 20 PROSPECTS

As a complement to our organizational prospect rankings, Baseball America also ranks prospects in every minor league right after each season. Like the organizational lists, they place more weight on potential than present performance and should not be regarded as minor league all-star teams.

The league lists do differ a little bit from the organizational lists, which are taken more from a scouting perspective. The league lists are based on conversations with league managers. They are not strictly polls, though we do try to talk with every manager. Some players on these lists, such as Miguel Cabrera and Rich Harden, were not eligible for our organization prospect lists because they are no longer rookie-eligible. Such players are indicated with an asterisk (*). Players who have been traded from the organizations they are listed with are indicated with a pound sign (#).

Remember that managers and scouts tend to look at players differently. Managers give more weight to what a player does on the field, while scouts look at what a player might eventually do. We think both perspectives are useful, so we give you both even though they don't always jibe with each other.

For a player to qualify for a league prospect list, he much have spent at least one-third of the season in a league. Position players must have one plate appearance per league game. Pitchers must pitch ⅓ inning per league game. Relievers must make at least 20 appearances in a full-season league or 10 appearances in a short-season league.

TRIPLE-A
INTERNATIONAL LEAGUE
1. *Jose Reyes, ss, Norfolk (Mets)
2. Justin Morneau, 1b, Rochester (Twins)
3. *Victor Martinez, c, Buffalo (Indians)
4. *Chase Utley, 2b, Scranton/Wilkes-Barre (Phillies)
5. #Freddy Sanchez, ss/2b, Pawtucket (Red Sox)
6. Adam LaRoche, 1b, Richmond (Braves)
7. Brandon Claussen, lhp, Columbus (Yankees)/ Louisville (Reds)
8. *Cliff Lee, lhp, Buffalo (Indians)
9. Jeremy Guthrie, rhp, Buffalo (Indians)
10. *Coco Crisp, of, Buffalo (Indians)
11. Dustin Moseley, rhp, Louisville Bats (Reds)
12. Michael Restovich, of, Rochester (Twins)
13. Ryan Madson, rhp, Scranton/Wilkes-Barre (Phillies)
14. Jesse Crain, rhp, Rochester (Twins)
15. Kevin Cash, c, Syracuse (Blue Jays)
16. Gabe Gross, of, Syracuse (Blue Jays)
17. Alex Escobar, of, Buffalo (Indians)
18. Grant Balfour, rhp, Rochester (Twins)
19. Cody Ross, of, Toledo (Tigers)
20. Jason Arnold, rhp, Syracuse (Blue Jays)

PACIFIC COAST LEAGUE
1. *Rich Harden, rhp, Sacramento (Athletics)
2. *Rafael Soriano, rhp, Tacoma (Mariners)
3. Bobby Crosby, ss, Sacramento (Athletics)
4. *Jerome Williams, rhp, Fresno (Giants)
5. #Jason Bay, of, Portland (Padres)
6. Khalil Greene, ss, Portland (Padres)
7. Chad Tracy, 3b, Tucson (Diamondbacks)
8. Garrett Atkins, 3b, Colorado Springs (Rockies)
9. Jason Young, rhp, Colorado Springs (Rockies)
10. *#Ryan Ludwick, of, Oklahoma (Rangers)
11. David Kelton, of/3b, Iowa (Cubs)
12. Aaron Taylor, rhp, Tacoma (Mariners)
13. Rodrigo Rosario, rhp, New Orleans (Astros)
14. David DeJesus, of, Omaha (Royals)
15. J.J. Davis, of, Nashville (Pirates)
16. Rene Reyes, of, Colorado Springs (Rockies)
17. Alfredo Amezaga, ss, Salt Lake (Angels)
18. John Buck, c, New Orleans (Astros)

19. Todd Wellemeyer, rhp, Iowa (Cubs)
20. Rett Johnson, rhp, Tacoma (Mariners)

DOUBLE-A
EASTERN LEAGUE
1. Joe Mauer, c, New Britain (Twins)
2. Alexis Rios, of, New Haven (Blue Jays)
3. Grady Sizemore, of, Akron (Indians)
4. Guillermo Quiroz, c, New Haven (Blue Jays)
5. Dustin McGowan, rhp, New Haven (Blue Jays)
6. J.D. Durbin, rhp, New Britain (Twins)
7. Dioner Navarro, c, Trenton (Yankees)
8. #Taylor Buchholz, rhp, Reading (Phillies)
9. Jason Bartlett, ss, New Britain (Twins)
10. John VanBenschoten, rhp, Altoona (Pirates)
11. Jesse Crain, rhp, New Britain (Twins)
12. Sean Burnett, lhp, Altoona (Pirates)
13. Kelly Shoppach, c, Portland (Red Sox)
14. Craig Brazell, 1b, Binghamton (Mets)
15. Kevin Youkilis, 3b, Portland (Red Sox)
16. Jeremy Guthrie, rhp, Akron (Indians)
17. #Jorge de la Rosa, lhp, Portland (Red Sox)
18. Fernando Cabrera, rhp, Akron (Indians)
19. David Bush, rhp, New Haven (Blue Jays)
20. Francisco Cruceta, rhp, Akron (Indians)

SOUTHERN LEAGUE
1. *Miguel Cabrera, 3b, Carolina (Marlins)
2. Edwin Jackson, rhp, Jacksonville (Dodgers)
3. Jeremy Reed, of, Birmingham (White Sox)
4. J.J. Hardy, ss, Huntsville (Brewers)
5. David Krynzel, of, Huntsville (Brewers)
6. Joel Hanrahan, rhp, Jacksonville (Dodgers)
7. *Dan Haren, rhp, Tennessee (Cardinals)
8. Neal Cotts, lhp, Birmingham (White Sox)
9. Angel Guzman, rhp, West Tenn (Cubs)
10. Mike Jones, rhp, Huntsville (Brewers)
11. Khalil Greene, ss, Mobile (Padres)
12. Adam LaRoche, 1b, Greenville (Braves)
13. #Adam Wainwright, rhp, Greenville (Braves)
14. Stephen Smitherman, of, Chattanooga (Reds)
15. Corey Hart, 3b, Huntsville (Brewers)
16. #Denny Bautista, rhp, Carolina (Marlins)
17. Bubba Nelson, rhp, Greenville (Braves)

18. #Adrian Gonzalez, 1b, Carolina (Marlins)
19. Reggie Abercrombie, of, Jacksonville (Dodgers)
20. Humberto Quintero, c, Mobile (Padres)

TEXAS LEAGUE
1. Chin-Hui Tsao, rhp, Tulsa (Rockies)
2. Zack Greinke, rhp, Wichita (Royals)
3. *Laynce Nix, of, Frisco (Rangers)
4. Ramon Nivar, of/2b, Frisco (Rangers)
5. Jose Lopez, ss, San Antonio (Mariners)
6. Travis Blackley, lhp, San Antonio (Mariners)
7. Bobby Jenks, rhp, Arkansas (Angels)
8. Clint Nageotte, rhp, San Antonio (Mariners)
9. *Jimmy Gobble, lhp, Wichita (Royals)
10. Chris Snelling, of, San Antonio (Mariners)
11. Scott Hairston, 2b, El Paso (Diamondbacks)
12. Freddie Bynum, 2b, Midland (Athletics)
13. Cory Sullivan, of, Tulsa (Rockies)
14. Dan Johnson, 1b, Midland (Athletics)
15. Adrian Gonzalez, 1b, Frisco (Rangers)
16. Greg Aquino, rhp, El Paso (Diamondbacks)
17. Chris Burke, 2b/ss, Round Rock (Astros)
18. Juan Dominguez, rhp, Frisco (Rangers)
19. Byron Gettis, of, Wichita (Royals)
20. Rett Johnson, rhp, San Antonio (Mariners)

HIGH CLASS A
CALIFORNIA LEAGUE
1. Casey Kotchman, 1b, Rancho Cucamonga (Angels)
2. Ervin Santana, rhp, Rancho Cucamonga (Angels)
3. Jeff Mathis, c, Rancho Cucamonga (Angels)
4. Dallas McPherson, 3b, Rancho Cucamonga (Angels)
5. Josh Barfield, 2b, Lake Elsinore (Padres)
6. Brad Nelson, 1b/of, High Desert (Brewers)
7. Joey Gathright, of, Bakersfield (Devil Rays)
8. Sergio Santos, ss, Lancaster (Diamondbacks)
9. Juan Dominguez, rhp, Stockton (Rangers)
10. Jayson Nix, 2b, Visalia (Rockies)
11. Jeff Francis, lhp, Visalia (Rockies)
12. Nick Swisher, of, Modesto (Athletics)
13. Shin-Soo Choo, of, Inland Empire (Mariners)
14. Chad Gaudin, rhp, Bakersfield (Devil Rays)
15. Jason Bourgeois, 2b/ss, Stockton (Rangers)
16. Josh Kroeger, of, Lancaster (Diamondbacks)
17. Drew Meyer, ss, Stockton (Rangers)
18. Steven Shell, rhp, Rancho Cucamonga (Angels)
19. Jason Botts, 1b, Stockton (Rangers)
20. Freddy Guzman, of, Lake Elsinore (Padres)

CAROLINA LEAGUE
1. Zack Greinke, rhp, Wilmington (Royals)
2. Jeremy Reed, of, Winston-Salem (White Sox)
3. Andy Marte, 3b, Myrtle Beach (Braves)
4. John VanBenschoten, rhp, Lynchburg (Pirates)
5. Kris Honel, rhp, Winston-Salem (White Sox)
6. Edwin Encarnacion, 3b, Potomac (Reds)
7. John Maine, rhp, Frederick (Orioles)
8. Dan Meyer, lhp, Myrtle Beach (Braves)
9. Ian Oquendo, rhp, Lynchburg (Pirates)
10. Bryan Bullington, rhp, Lynchburg (Pirates)
11. Macay McBride, lhp, Myrtle Beach (Braves)
12. Ryan Doumit, c, Lynchburg (Pirates)
13. Ryan Wing, lhp, Winston-Salem (White Sox)
14. Rommie Lewis, lhp, Frederick (Orioles)
15. Ty Howington, lhp, Potomac (Reds)
16. Hector Gimenez, c, Salem (Astros)
17. ^Chris Shelton, 1b/c, Lynchburg (Pirates)
18. Jared Gothreaux, rhp, Salem (Astros)
19. ^Willy Taveras, of, Kinston (Indians)
20. Andres Blanco, ss, Wilmington (Royals)

FLORIDA STATE LEAGUE
1. Joe Mauer, c, Fort Myers (Twins)
2. Greg Miller, lhp, Vero Beach (Dodgers)
3. Gavin Floyd, rhp, Clearwater (Phillies)
4. Franklin Gutierrez, of, Vero Beach (Dodgers)
5. Dioner Navarro, c, Tampa (Yankees)
6. J.D. Durbin, rhp, Fort Myers (Twins)
7. James Loney, 1b, Vero Beach (Dodgers)
8. Dustin McGowan, rhp, Dunedin (Blue Jays)
9. #Denny Bautista, rhp, Jupiter (Marlins)
10. David Wright, 3b, St. Lucie (Mets)
11. Brandon League, rhp, Dunedin (Blue Jays)
12. Chadd Blasko, rhp, Daytona (Cubs)
13. Bobby Brownlie, rhp, Daytona (Cubs)
14. Jason Stokes, 1b, Jupiter (Marlins)
15. Ryan Howard, 1b, Clearwater (Phillies)
16. David Bush, rhp, Dunedin (Blue Jays)
17. Jason Kubel, of, Fort Myers (Twins)
18. Robinson Cano, 2b, Tampa (Yankees)
19. Matt Peterson, rhp, St. Lucie (Mets)
20. Justin Huber, c, St. Lucie (Mets)

LOW CLASS A
MIDWEST LEAGUE
1. Prince Fielder, 1b, Beloit (Brewers)
2. Blake Hawksworth, rhp, Peoria (Cardinals)
3. Justin Jones, lhp, Lansing (Cubs)
4. Manny Parra, lhp, Beloit (Brewers)
5. Joe Blanton, rhp, Kane County (Athletics)
6. Joel Zumaya, rhp, West Michigan (Tigers)
7. Andy Sisco, lhp, Lansing (Cubs)
8. Felix Pie, of, Lansing (Cubs)
9. Tom Wilhelmsen, rhp, Beloit (Brewers)
10. Brent Clevlen, of, West Michigan (Tigers)
11. Alberto Callaspo, 2b, Cedar Rapids (Angels)
12. Jae-Kuk Ryu, rhp, Lansing (Cubs)
13. Dennis Sarfate, rhp, Beloit (Brewers)
14. Rafael Rodriguez, rhp, Cedar Rapids (Angels)
15. Erick Aybar, ss, Cedar Rapids (Angels)
16. Donald Murphy, 2b, Burlington (Royals)
17. John Baker, c, Kane County (Athletics)
18. Rudy Guillen, of, Battle Creek (Yankees)
19. Jon Connolly, lhp, West Michigan (Tigers)
20. Colt Griffin, rhp, Burlington (Royals)

SOUTH ATLANTIC LEAGUE
1. B.J. Upton, ss, Charleston (Devil Rays)
2. Scott Kazmir, lhp, Capital City (Mets)
3. Cole Hamels, lhp, Lakewood (Phillies)
4. Jeff Francoeur, of, Rome (Braves)
5. Jeremy Hermida, of, Greensboro (Marlins)
6. Hanley Ramirez, ss, Augusta (Red Sox)
7. Fausto Carmona, rhp, Lake County (Indians)
8. Merkin Valdez, rhp, Hagerstown (Giants)
9. Scott Olsen, lhp, Greensboro (Marlins)
10. Mike Hinckley, lhp, Savannah (Expos)
11. John Maine, rhp, Delmarva (Orioles)
12. Larry Broadway, 1b, Savannah (Expos)
13. Brandon League, rhp, Charleston (Blue Jays)
14. Matt Cain, rhp, Hagerstown (Giants)
15. Fernando Nieve, rhp, Lexington (Astros)
16. Delwyn Young, 2b, South Georgia (Dodgers)
17. Anthony Lerew, rhp, Rome (Braves)
18. Dan Meyer, lhp, Rome (Braves)
19. Michael Aubrey, 1b, Lake County (Indians)
20. Brian McCann, c, Rome (Braves)

SHORT-SEASON
NEW YORK-PENN LEAGUE
1. Nick Markakis, of, Aberdeen (Orioles)
2. Aaron Hill, ss, Auburn (Blue Jays)
3. Tony Giarratano, ss, Oneonta (Tigers)
4. Kody Kirkland, 3b, Oneonta (Tigers)
5. Josh Banks, rhp, Auburn (Blue Jays)
6. David Murphy, of, Lowell (Red Sox)
7. Kurt Isenberg, lhp, Auburn (Blue Jays)
8. Nyjer Morgan, of, Williamsport (Pirates)
9. Clint Everts, rhp, Vermont (Expos)

10. Tom Gorzelanny, lhp, Williamsport (Pirates)
11. Brad Snyder, of, Mahoning Valley (Indians)
12. Chris Ray, rhp, Aberdeen (Orioles)
13. Matt Murton, of, Lowell (Red Sox)
14. Paul Maholm, lhp, Williamsport (Pirates)
15. Aneudi Cuevas, ss, Hudson Valley (Devil Rays)
16. Juan Peralta, ss/2b, Auburn (Blue Jays)
17. Claudio Arias, 3b, Lowell (Red Sox)
18. Vincent Blue, of, Oneonta (Tigers)
19. Vito Chiaravalloti, 1b, Auburn (Blue Jays)
20. Javier Guzman, ss, Williamsport (Pirates)

NORTHWEST LEAGUE
1. Felix Hernandez, rhp, Everett (Mariners)
2. Conor Jackson, of, Yakima (Diamondbacks)
3. Nate Schierholtz, 3b, Salem-Keizer (Giants)
4. Wes Littleton, rhp, Spokane (Rangers)
5. Todd Jennings, c, Salem-Keizer (Giants)
6. Jeremy Cleveland, of, Spokane (Rangers)
7. Sean Marshall, lhp, Boise (Cubs)
8. Sean Thompson, lhp, Eugene (Padres)
9. Billy Petrick, rhp, Boise (Cubs)
10. Ching-Lung Lo, rhp, Tri-City (Rockies)
11. Aaron Marsden, lhp, Tri-City (Rockies)
12. Jaime D'Antona, 3b, Yakima (Diamondbacks)
13. Omar Quintanilla, ss, Vancouver (Athletics)
14. Dustin Majewski, of, Vancouver (Athletics)
15. Brian Dopirak, 1b, Boise (Cubs)
16. Oswaldo Navarro, ss, Everett (Mariners)
17. Matt Chico, lhp, Yakima (Diamondbacks)
18. Travis Ishikawa, 1b, Salem-Keizer (Giants)
19. Colt Morton, c, Eugene (Padres)
20. Pat Misch, lhp, Salem-Keizer (Giants)

ROOKIE
APPALACHIAN LEAGUE
1. Adam Miller, rhp, Burlington (Indians)
2. Chris Young, of, Bristol (White Sox)
3. Robert Valido, ss, Bristol (White Sox)
4. James Houser, lhp, Princeton (Devil Rays)
5. Daric Barton, c, Johnson City (Cardinals)
6. Chuck James, lhp, Danville (Braves)
7. Carlos Perez, lhp, Bluefield (Orioles)
8. Matt Esquivel, of, Danville (Braves)
9. Denard Span, of, Elizabethton (Twins)
10. Rafael Perez, lhp, Burlington (Indians)
11. Evan Meek, rhp, Elizabethton (Twins)
12. Mitch Talbot, rhp, Martinsville (Astros)
13. Tim Tisch, lhp, Bristol (White Sox)
14. Charlie Morton, rhp, Danville (Braves)
15. Dusty Gomon, 1b, Elizabethton (Twins)
16. Felipe Paulino, rhp, Martinsville (Astros)
17. Orionny Lopez, rhp, Bristol (White Sox)
18. Robinzon Diaz, c, Pulaski (Blue Jays)
19. Kyle Phillips, c/lb, Elizabethton (Twins)
20. Tyler Davidson, dh/of, Kingsport (Mets)

ARIZONA LEAGUE
1. Chris Lubanski, of, Royals 1
2. Wladimir Balentien, of, Mariners
3. Ryan Harvey, of, Cubs

4. Mitch Maier, c, Royals 1
5. Alexi Ogando, of, Athletics
6. Ronald Bay, rhp, Cubs
7. Shane Costa, of, Royals 2
8. Adam Jones, ss, Mariners
9. Brandon Wood, ss, Angels
10. Charlie Fermaint, of, Brewers
11. Leslie Nacar, rhp, Giants
12. Lizahio Baez, of, Rangers
13. Mike Aviles, ss, Royals 1
14. Jorge Mejia, 2b, Athletics
15. Don Sutton, 1b, Athletics
16. Brett Martinez, c, Angels
17. Irving Falu, 2b/ss, Royals 2
18. Sean Rodriguez, ss/3b, Angels
19. Gilberto Acosta, ss, Brewers
20. Javier Herrera, of, Athletics

GULF COAST LEAGUE
1. Eric Duncan, 3b, Yankees
2. Jake Stevens, lhp, Braves
3. Jarrod Saltalamacchia, c, Braves
4. Hector Made, ss, Yankees
5. Lorenzo Scott, of, Orioles
6. Blair Johnson, rhp, Pirates
7. Matt Moses, 3b, Twins
8. Tyler Pelland, lhp, Red Sox/Reds
9. Jai Miller, of, Marlins
10. Steve Doetsch, of, Braves
11. Etanislao Abreu, 2b, Dodgers
12. Harvey Garcia, rhp, Red Sox
13. Jo Jo Reyes, lhp, Braves
14. Alexander Smit, lhp, Twins
15. Matt Capps, rhp, Pirates
16. Jay Sborz, rhp, Tigers
17. Estee Harris, of, Yankees
18. Kiel Fisher, 3b, Phillies
19. Paul Bacot, rhp, Braves
20. Kenny Lewis, of, Reds

PIONEER LEAGUE
1. Ian Stewart, 3b, Casper (Rockies)
2. Chad Billingsley, rhp, Ogden (Dodgers)
3. Lou Palmisano, c, Helena (Brewers)
4. Bobby Wilson, c, Provo (Angels)
5. Xavier Paul, of, Ogden (Dodgers)
6. Habelito Hernandez, 2b, Billings (Reds)
7. Warner Madrigal, of, Provo (Angels)
8. Mike Megrew, lhp, Ogden (Dodgers)
9. Dana Eveland, lhp, Helena (Brewers)
10. Joey Votto, 1b, Billings (Reds)
11. Abel Moreno, rhp, Provo (Angels)
12. Chin-Lung Hu, ss, Ogden (Dodgers)
13. Howie Kendrick, 2b, Provo (Angels)
14. Carlos Morban, rhp, Provo (Angels)
15. Miguel Perez, c, Billings (Reds)
16. Brandon McCarthy, rhp, Great Falls (White Sox)
17. Marcos Carvajal, rhp, Ogden (Dodgers)
18. Carlos Gonzalez, of, Missoula (Diamondbacks)
19. Ricardo Nanita, of, Great Falls (White Sox)
20. Juan Morillo, rhp, Casper (Rockies)

INDEX

A

Aardsma, David (Giants) 419
Abercrombie, Reggie (Dodgers) 246
Abruzzo, Jared (Angels) 27
Accardo, Jeremy (Giants) 429
Acosta, Gilberto (Brewers) 266
Acosta, Kelyn (Giants) 428
Adams, Mike (Brewers) 268
Adams, Russ (Blue Jays) 485
Aguila, Chris (Marlins) 201
Albaladejo, Jonathan (Pirates) 379
Albers, Matt (Astros) 213
Allison, Jeff (Marlins) 195
Almonte, Erick (Yankees) 332
Alvarez, Abe (Red Sox) 84
Alvarez, Tony (Pirates) 378
Alvarez, Victor (Phillies) 364
Ambres, Chip (Marlins) 205
Anderson, Brian (White Sox) 117
Anderson, Jason (Mets) 315
Anderson, Josh (Astros) 217
Andino, Robert (Marlins) 199
Andrade, Stephen (Angels) 29
Aquino, Greg (Diamondbacks) 42
Aramboles, Ricardo (Reds) 139
Arias, Joaquin (Yankees) 323
Armitage, Jon (Giants) 425
Arnold, Jason (Blue Jays) 488
Astacio, Ezequiel (Astros) 216
Athas, Jamie (Giants) 425
Atkins, Garrett (Rockies) 167
Aubrey, Michael (Indians) 148
Autrey, Scott (Devil Rays) 456
Aviles, Mike (Royals) 235
Axelson, Josh (Cardinals) 393
Aybar, Erick (Angels) 21
Aybar, Willy (Dodgers) 247

B

Bacot, Paul (Braves) 61
Baek, Cha (Mariners) 437
Baez, Edgardo (Expos) 299
Baez, Welinson (Phillies) 365
Baker, Jeff (Rockies) 166
Baker, John (Athletics) 345
Baker, Scott (Twins) 281
Baldiris, Aaron (Mets) 310
Balentien, Wladimir (Mariners) 440
Balfour, Grant (Twins) 277
Balkcom, Blake (Angels) 29
Ball, Jarred (Diamondbacks) 44
Banks, Josh (Blue Jays) 486
Bankston, Wes (Devil Rays) 453
Barden, Brian (Diamondbacks) 44
Barfield, Josh (Padres) 402
Barmes, Clint (Rockies) 170
Barratt, Jon (Devil Rays) 457
Barrett, Jimmy (Astros) 220
Barthmaier, Jimmy (Astros) 214
Bartlett, Jason (Twins) 276
Barton, Daric (Cardinals) 390
Basham, Bobby (Reds) 137
Bass, Brian (Royals) 229
Bass, Bryan (Orioles) 77
Baugh, Kenny (Tigers) 182
Bausher, Tim (Brewers) 265

Bautista, Denny (Orioles) 68
Bautista, Jose (Orioles) 71
Bay, Bear (Cubs) 109
Bay, Jason (Pirates) 371
Bayliss, Jonah (Royals) 231
Bazardo, Yorman (Marlins) 196
Bedard, Erik (Orioles) 69
Belcher, Jason (Brewers) 269
Belisle, Matt (Reds) 138
Belizario, Ronald (Marlins) 199
Beltran, Francis (Cubs) 104
Bennett, Jeff (Brewers) 267
Bentz, Chad (Expos) 299
Bergmann, Jason (Expos) 295
Bergolla, William (Reds) 135
Bernadina, Rogearvin (Expos) 294
Betemit, Wilson (Braves) 54
Bevis, P.J. (Mets) 316
Billingsley, Chad (Dodgers) 244
Bittner, Tim (Angels) 26
Blackley, Travis (Mariners) 435
Blalock, Jake (Phillies) 362
Blanco, Andres (Royals) 229
Blanco, Gregor (Braves) 55
Blanco, Tony (Reds) 138
Blanton, Joe (Athletics) 339
Blasko, Chadd (Cubs) 100
Bonser, Boof (Twins) 280
Bootcheck, Chris (Angels) 25
Borchard, Joe (White Sox) 116
Borrell, Danny (Yankees) 327
Bott, Glenn (Mariners) 444
Botts, Jason (Rangers) 473
Bourgeois, Jason (Rangers) 469
Bourn, Michael (Phillies) 357
Bowen, Rob (Twins) 283
Bowman, Shawn (Mets) 314
Boyd, Patrick (Rangers) 475
Boyd, Shaun (Cardinals) 391
Boyer, Blaine (Braves) 56
Bozied, Tagg (Padres) 406
Bradley, Bobby (Pirates) 380
Brazell, Craig (Mets) 310
Brazoban, Yhency (Dodgers) 250
Broadway, Larry (Expos) 291
Brooks, Frank (Athletics) 349
Brown, Andrew (Dodgers) 249
Brown, Dustin (Red Sox) 89
Brown, Jamie (Red Sox) 92
Brown, Jeremy (Athletics) 344
Brownlie, Bobby (Cubs) 100
Broxton, Jonathan (Dodgers) 247
Bruney, Brian (Diamondbacks) 37
Bruso, Greg (Brewers) 268
Buchholz, Taylor (Astros) 210
Buck, John (Astros) 211
Bucktrot, Keith (Phillies) 356
Bukvich, Ryan (Royals) 234
Bullington, Bryan (Pirates) 371
Bumatay, Mike (Tigers) 188
Burgos, Ambiorix (Royals) 237
Burke, Chris (Astros) 211
Burnett, Sean (Pirates) 371
Buscher, Brian (Giants) 422
Bush, David (Blue Jays) 485
Butto, Francisco (Phillies) 360
Bynum, Freddie (Athletics) 344

C

Cabrera, Daniel (Orioles) 72
Cabrera, Fernando (Orioles) 148
Cabrera, Melky (Yankees) 329
Cain, Matt (Giants) 419
Callaspo, Alberto (Angels) 20
Cano, Robinson (Yankees) 324
Capellan, Jose (Braves) 54
Capps, Matt (Pirates) 375
Capuano, Chris (Brewers) 264
Carlson, Jesse (Astros) 218
Carmona, Fausto (Indians) 147
Cash, Kevin (Blue Jays) 487
Castillo, Jose (Pirates) 375
Castro, Bernie (Padres) 411
Castro, Fabio (White Sox) 120
Cate, Troy (Mariners) 444
Cave, Kevin (Marlins) 200
Cedeno, Juan (Red Sox) 85
Chapman, Travis (Royals) 233
Chavez, Angel (Giants) 427
Chavez, Wilton (Expos) 301
Chen, Chin-Feng (Dodgers) 248
Chico, Matt (Diamondbacks) 40
Choo, Shin-Soo (Mariners) 436
Christensen, Danny (Royals) 237
Christianson, Ryan (Mariners) 445
Chulk, Vinnie (Blue Jays) 491
Church, Ryan (Expos) 294
Claussen, Brandon (Reds) 131
Cleveland, Jeremy (Rangers) 475
Clevlen, Brent (Tigers) 179
Clippard, Tyler (Yankees) 332
Closser, J.D. (Rockies) 169
Colyer, Steve (Dodgers) 246
Connolly, Jon (Tigers) 185
Connolly, Mike (Pirates) 380
Coonrod, Aaron (Padres) 410
Cooper, Jason (Indians) 149
Corcoran, Roy (Expos) 300
Cordero, Chad (Expos) 292
Cormier, Lance (Diamondbacks) 45
Corn, Jessie (Red Sox) 91
Correia, Kevin (Giants) 420
Cortes, Jorge (Pirates) 376
Cosby, Quan (Angels) 26
Costa, Shane (Royals) 229
Cota, Jesus (Diamondbacks) 44
Cotts, Neal (White Sox) 115
Craig, Matt (Cubs) 109
Crain, Jesse (Twins) 276
Crockett, Ben (Rockies) 172
Crosby, Bobby (Athletics) 338
Crouthers, Dave (Orioles) 70
Cruceta, Francisco (Indians) 151
Cumberland, Shaun (Devil Rays) 460

D

Danks, John (Rangers) 467
D'Antona, Jamie (Diamondbacks) 39
Davidson, Tyler (Mets) 316
Davies, Kyle (Braves) 53
Davis, Cliff (Astros) 216
Davis, J.J. (Pirates) 375
DeBarr, Nick (Devil Rays) 460
DeJesus, David (Royals) 227

De la Cruz, Eulogio (Tigers) 186
De la Rosa, Jorge (Brewers) 262
Delcarmen, Manny (Red Sox) 85
Denham, Dan (Indians) 154
DePaula, Jorge (Yankees) 325
DeSalvo, Matt (Yankees) 327
Diaz, Felix (White Sox) 121
Diaz, Frank (Expos) 299
Diaz, Joselo (Mets) 313
Diaz, Matt (Devil Rays) 460
Diaz, Raymar (Astros) 217
Diaz, Victor (Mets) 309
Diggins, Ben (Brewers) 266
Dittler, Jake (Indians) 147
Dobbs, Greg (Mariners) 439
Dohmann, Scott (Rockies) 167
Dominguez, Juan (Rangers) 467
Donachie, Adam (Royals) 231
Dopirak, Brian (Cubs) 104
Doumit, Ryan (Pirates) 374
Downs, Darin (Cubs) 108
Doyle, Jared (Diamondbacks) 40
Dubois, Jason (Cubs) 102
Duchscherer, Justin (Athletics) 342
Duke, Zach (Pirates) 376
Dukes, Elijah (Devil Rays) 455
Dumatrait, Phil (Reds) 132
Duncan, Eric (Yankees) 323
Duran, Carlos (Braves) 57
Durbin, J.D. (Twins) 275

E

Echols, Justin (Rangers) 477
Eckenstahler, Eric (Tigers) 187
Eldred, Brad (Pirates) 381
Ellison, Jason (Giants) 427
Encarnacion, Edwin (Reds) 131
Esposito, Mike (Rockies) 170
Esquivel, Matt (Braves) 60
Ethier, Andre (Athletics) 341
Eveland, Dana (Brewers) 264
Evert, Brett (Braves) 59
Everts, Clint (Expos) 290

F

Farfan, Alex (Reds) 139
Feierabend, Ryan (Mariners) 439
Feliz, Rainer (Reds) 136
Fermaint, Charlie (Brewers) 266
Fielder, Prince (Brewers) 259
Figueroa, Jonathan (Dodgers) 248
Finch, Brian (Orioles) 71
Fischer, Rich (Angels) 26
Fisher, Kiel (Phillies) 359
Flaig, Jeff (Mariners) 442
Flannery, Mike (Marlins) 203
Flinn, Chris (Devil Rays) 458
Floyd, Gavin (Phillies) 355
Foley, Travis (Indians) 153
Fontenot, Mike (Orioles) 69
Ford, Lew (Twins) 280
Forystek, Brian (Orioles) 73
Francis, Jeff (Rockies) 163
Francisco, Ben (Indians) 156
Francisco, Franklin (Rangers) 476
Francoeur, Jeff (Braves) 51
Freeman, Choo (Rockies) 168
Fritz, Ben (Athletics) 345
Fulton, Jonathan (Marlins) 204

G

Gall, John (Cardinals) 389
Gallo, Mike (Astros) 215
Galvez, Gary (Red Sox) 90
Gamble, Jerome (Red Sox) 88
Garcia, Anderson (Mets) 317
Garcia, Danny (Mets) 312
Garcia, Harvey (Red Sox) 93
Garcia, Jose (Yankees) 329
Garciaparra, Michael (Mariners) 443
Gardner, Richie (Reds) 136
Garthwaite, Jay (Diamondbacks) 41
Gathright, Joey (Devil Rays) 452
Gaudin, Chad (Devil Rays) 452
Gautreau, Jake (Padres) 412
German, Esteban (Athletics) 346
Germano, Justin (Padres) 408
Gettis, Byron (Royals) 230
Giarratano, Tony (Tigers) 180
Gimenez, Hector (Astros) 212
Glant, Dustin (Diamondbacks) 43
Godwin, Tyrell (Blue Jays) 489
Gold, Nate (Rangers) 476
Gomes, Jonny (Devil Rays) 454
Gomez, Alexis (Royals) 233
Gomez, Mariano (Indians) 152
Gonzalez, Adrian (Rangers) 466
Gonzalez, Andy (White Sox) 123
Gonzalez, Carlos (Diamondbacks) 43
Gonzalez, Danny (Phillies) 361
Gonzalez, Edgar (Diamondbacks) 37
Gonzalez, Jino (Devil Rays) 459
Gonzalez, Mike (Pirates) 377
Gorecki, Reid (Cardinals) 394
Gorneault, Nick (Angels) 25
Gorzelanny, Tom (Pirates) 377
Gosling, Mike (Diamondbacks) 38
Gotay, Ruben (Royals) 230
Gothreaux, Jared (Astros) 216
Grabowski, Jason (Athletics) 346
Gracesqui, Franklyn (Marlins) 201
Granderson, Curtis (Tigers) 181
Gray, Antoin (White Sox) 123
Greene, Khalil (Padres) 403
Greinke, Zack (Royals) 226
Griffin, Colt (Royals) 228
Griffin, John-Ford (Blue Jays) 488
Griffiths, Jeremy (Mets) 309
Grigsby, Derick (Astros) 221
Gross, Gabe (Blue Jays) 483
Gruler, Chris (Reds) 134
Guillen, Rudy (Yankees) 323
Guthrie, Jeremy (Indians) 147
Gutierrez, Franklin (Dodgers) 243
Guzman, Angel (Cubs) 98
Guzman, Freddy (Padres) 403
Guzman, Javier (Pirates) 379
Guzman, Joel (Dodgers) 246
Gwynn, Anthony (Brewers) 264

H

Habel, Josh (Giants) 426
Hagerty, Luke (Cubs) 102
Haerther, Cody (Cardinals) 392
Hairston, Scott (Diamondbacks) 34
Hall, Josh (Reds) 135
Hall, Mickey (Red Sox) 87
Halsey, Brad (Yankees) 331
Hamels, Cole (Phillies) 354
Hamilton, Josh (Devil Rays) 456
Hammes, Zach (Dodgers) 253
Hampson, Justin (Rockies) 172

Hamulack, Tim (Red Sox) 89
Hancock, Josh (Phillies) 361
Hannaman, Ryan (Orioles) 70
Hanrahan, Joel (Dodgers) 244
Hanson, D.J. (Blue Jays) 487
Hanson, Travis (Cardinals) 388
Harben, Adam (Twins) 278
Hardy, J.J. (Brewers) 259
Harper, Jesse (Blue Jays) 489
Harris, Brendan (Cubs) 101
Harris, Estee (Yankees) 325
Hart, Corey (Brewers) 261
Harvey, Ryan (Cubs) 99
Harville, Chad (Athletics) 342
Hawk, Tommy (Brewers) 268
Hawksworth, Blake (Cardinals) 386
Hawpe, Brad (Rockies) 166
Hayes, Calvin (Cardinals) 395
Haynes, Dee (Cardinals) 394
Henderson, Brian (Devil Rays) 459
Hendrickson, Ben (Brewers) 261
Henkel, Rob (Tigers) 179
Henn, Sean (Yankees) 328
Hermida, Jeremy (Marlins) 194
Hernandez, Anderson (Tigers) 187
Hernandez, Felix (Mariners) 434
Hernandez, Habelito (Reds) 138
Herrera, Javi (Indians) 155
Herrera, Javier (Athletics) 349
Hill, Aaron (Blue Jays) 484
Hill, Koyie (Dodgers) 245
Hill, Rich (Cubs) 108
Hill, Shawn (Expos) 292
Hinckley, Mike (Expos) 291
Hines, Carlos (Devil Rays) 458
Hiraldo, Nelson (Indians) 156
Hirsh, Jason (Astros) 213
Hodges, Scott (Expos) 295
Hogan, Billy (Padres) 410
Holdzkom, Lincoln (Marlins) 198
Holliday, Brian (Pirates) 380
Holliday, Matt (Rockies) 165
Honel, Kris (White Sox) 115
Houlton, D.J. (Astros) 220
House, J.R. (Pirates) 379
Houser, James (Devil Rays) 451
Housman, Jeff (Brewers) 266
Howard, Ben (Padres) 404
Howard, Ryan (Phillies) 355
Howington, Ty (Reds) 134
Hu, Ching-Lung (Dodgers) 250
Huber, Justin (Mets) 308
Hudgins, John (Rangers) 474
Huerta, Edgar (Padres) 408
Huggins, Mike (Orioles) 74
Hughes, Dustin (Royals) 237
Hughes, Luke (Twins) 284
Huisman, Justin (Rockies) 173
Hutchinson, Trevor (Marlins) 198
Hutting, Tim (Giants) 428

I

Isenberg, Kurt (Blue Jays) 490
Ishikawa, Travis (Giants) 420

J

Jackson, Conor (Diamondbacks) 36
Jackson, Edwin (Dodgers) 242
Jackson, Kyle (Red Sox) 92
Jackson, Nic (Cubs) 103
Jacobs, Mike (Mets) 312

James, Chuck (Braves)	58	Leonard, Chris (Blue Jays)	493	McDonald, Darnell (Orioles)	75
James, Justin (Blue Jays)	491	Leone, Justin (Mariners)	438	McDonald, James (Dodgers)	252
Jenks, Bobby (Angels)	20	Lerew, Anthony (Braves)	53	McFall, Brian (Royals)	236
Jennings, Todd (Giants)	422	Lester, Jon (Red Sox)	85	McGinley, Blake (Mets)	316
Jensen, Aaron (Mariners)	442	Levinski, Don (Orioles)	72	McGowan, Dustin (Blue Jays)	483
Jepsen, Kevin (Angels)	22	Lewis, Fred (Giants)	421	McKeller, Ryan (Astros)	220
Jimenez, Kelvin (Rangers)	470	Lewis, Kenny (Reds)	141	McLouth, Nate (Pirates)	377
Jimenez, Ubaldo (Rockies)	163	Lewis, Rommie (Orioles)	69	McNiven, Brooks (Giants)	424
Jimerson, Charlton (Astros)	219	Linden, Todd (Giants)	420	McPherson, Dallas (Angels)	19
Johnson, Blair (Pirates)	372	Lindstrom, Matt (Mets)	313	Meaux, Ryan (White Sox)	121
Johnson, Dan (Yankees)	339	Liriano, Francisco (Twins)	281	Medders, Brandon	
Johnson, Elliot (Devil Rays)	461	Liriano, Pedro (Brewers)	265	(Diamondbacks)	40
Johnson, Josh (Marlins)	203	Littleton, Wes (Rangers)	469	Meek, Evan (Twins)	279
Johnson, Kelly (Braves)	54	Livingston, Bobby (Mariners)	445	Megrew, Mike (Dodgers)	249
Johnson, Michael (Padres)	409	Lizarraga, Sergio (Diamondbacks)	45	Mejia, Gilberto (Tigers)	187
Johnson, Rett (Mariners)	437	Lo, Ching-Lung (Rockies)	166	Mendoza, Luis (Red Sox)	86
Johnson, Tripper (Orioles)	74	Lockwood, Luke (Expos)	298	Merricks, Matt (Braves)	56
Johnson, Tyler (Cardinals)	390	Loe, Kameron (Rangers)	472	Meyer, Dan (Braves)	51
Johnston, Mike (Pirates)	374	Loewen, Adam (Orioles)	66	Meyer, Drew (Rangers)	469
Jones, Adam (Mariners)	437	Logan, Nook (Tigers)	185	Michael, Mark (Cardinals)	391
Jones, Justin (Cubs)	99	Loney, James (Dodgers)	243	Middleton, Kyle (Royals)	231
Jones, Kennard (Padres)	405	Looper, Aaron (Mariners)	443	Miles, Aaron (Rockies)	171
Jones, Mike (Brewers)	260	Lopez, Jose (Mariners)	435	Milledge, Lastings (Mets)	308
Jones, Terry (Phillies)	358	Lopez, Orionny (White Sox)	125	Miller, Adam (Indians)	149
Joseph, Onil (Braves)	55	Lopez, Pedro (White Sox)	122	Miller, Brian (White Sox)	119
Journell, Jimmy (Cardinals)	388	Lorenzo, Matt (Rangers)	475	Miller, Colby (Twins)	282
Julianel, Ben (Yankees)	333	Lowery, Devon (Royals)	236	Miller, Greg (Dodgers)	243
		Lowry, Noah (Giants)	423	Miller, Jai (Marlins)	197
		Lubanski, Chris (Royals)	227	Miller, Tony (Rockies)	171
		Luellwitz, Sean (Diamondbacks)	43	Miner, Zach (Braves)	60
K		Luna, Hector (Cardinals)	389	Misch, Pat (Giants)	426
Kaaihue, Kila (Royals)	236	Lydon, Wayne (Mets)	317	Mitchell, Lee (Marlins)	199
Karp, Josh (Expos)	291			Mitre, Sergio (Cubs)	104
Kazmir, Scott (Mets)	307			Molina, Yadier (Cardinals)	387
Kelly, Donald (Tigers)	185			Moore, Scott (Tigers)	181
Kelton, David (Cubs)	101	**M**		Morales, Alexis (Expos)	300
Kendrick, Howie (Angels)	23	Machado, Anderson (Phillies)	358	Morales, Jose (Twins)	284
Kendrick, Kyle (Phillies)	359	Made, Hector (Yankees)	328	Moran, Javon (Phillies)	360
Kensing, Logan (Marlins)	203	Madrigal, Warner (Angels)	24	Morban, Carlos (Angels)	27
Keppel, Bob (Mets)	309	Madritsch, Bobby (Mariners)	439	Morban, Jose (Orioles)	75
Ketchner, Ryan (Mariners)	441	Madson, Ryan (Phillies)	355	Moreno, Edwin (Rangers)	471
Kiger, Mark (Athletics)	347	Maholm, Paul (Pirates)	373	Moreno, Orber (Mets)	314
Kinney, Josh (Cardinals)	394	Maier, Mitch (Royals)	227	Morgan, Nyjer (Pirates)	376
Kirkland, Kody (Tigers)	180	Maine, John (Orioles)	67	Morillo, Juan (Rockies)	169
Kloosterman, Greg (Brewers)	268	Majewski, Dustin (Athletics)	349	Morla, Carlos (Red Sox)	93
Knoedler, Justin (Giants)	424	Majewski, Val (Orioles)	67	Morneau, Justin (Twins)	275
Knott, Jon (Padres)	405	Malaska, Mark (Red Sox)	91	Morse, Mike (White Sox)	121
Knox, Mike (Yankees)	333	Malek, Bob (Mets)	314	Morton, Charlie (Braves)	60
Komine, Shane (Athletics)	347	Malone, Corwin (White Sox)	122	Moseley, Dustin (Reds)	132
Koonce, Graham (Athletics)	340	Manning, Charlie (Reds)	140	Moses, Matt (Twins)	275
Kotchman, Casey (Angels)	18	Marchbanks, David (Marlins)	204	Moss, Steve (Brewers)	267
Kottaras, George (Padres)	413	Marcum, Shaun (Blue Jays)	490	Moss, Tim (Phillies)	362
Kozlowski, Ben (Rangers)	471	Markakis, Nick (Orioles)	67	Munoz, Arnie (White Sox)	118
Kroeger, Josh (Diamondbacks)	38	Marsden, Aaron (Rockies)	173	Murphy, Bill (Marlins)	196
Krynzel, David (Brewers)	261	Marshall, Sean (Cubs)	107	Murphy, David (Red Sox)	83
Kubel, Jason (Twins)	277	Marte, Andy (Braves)	50	Murphy, Donald (Royals)	228
		Martin, J.D. (Indians)	154	Murray, A.J. (Rangers)	474
		Martin, Russell (Dodgers)	249	Murton, Matt (Red Sox)	84
L		Martinez, Anastacio (Red Sox)	86		
Labandeira, Josh (Expos)	301	Martinez, Javier (Padres)	408		
LaForest, Pete (Devil Rays)	454	Martinez, Luis (Brewers)	263	**N**	
Laffey, Aaron (Indians)	154	Mateo, Aneudis (Red Sox)	89	Nageotte, Clint (Mariners)	435
Laird, Gerald (Rangers)	468	Materano, Oscar (Rockies)	168	Nance, Shane (Diamondbacks)	42
LaMacchia, Marc (Rangers)	477	Mathieson, Scott (Phillies)	359	Nanita, Ricardo (White Sox)	123
Lane, Jason (Astros)	211	Mathis, Jeff (Angels)	19	Narveson, Chris (Cardinals)	387
Langerhans, Ryan (Braves)	59	Matsui, Kazuo (Mets)	306	Navarro, Dioner (Yankees)	322
LaRoche, Adam (Braves)	52	Mattox, David (Reds)	137	Negron, Miguel (Blue Jays)	492
LaRoche, Andy (Dodgers)	245	Mauer, Joe (Twins)	274	Nelson, Brad (Brewers)	260
Larrison, Preston (Tigers)	184	McBeth, Marcus (Athletics)	348	Nelson, Bubba (Braves)	51
League, Brandon (Blue Jays)	486	McBride, Macay (Braves)	52	Nelson, John (Cardinals)	391
Lee, Seung (Phillies)	364	McCann, Brian (Braves)	52	Nickerson, Jon-Michael (Marlins)	201
Lehr, Justin (Athletics)	346	McCarthy, Brandon (White Sox)	118	Niekro, Lance (Giants)	423
Leicester, Jon (Cubs)	106	McClung, Seth (Devil Rays)	453	Nieve, Fernando (Astros)	212
Lemanczyk, Matt (Cardinals)	397	McCurdy, John (Athletics)	345		

Nin, Sandy (Rockies) 172
Nippert, Dustin (Diamondbacks) 35
Nivar, Ramon (Rangers) 467
Nix, Jayson (Rockies) 164
Nixon, Mike (Dodgers) 252
Nolasco, Ricky (Cubs) 105
Novoa, Roberto (Tigers) 186
Nunez, Leo (Pirates) 381

O

Ochoa, Ivan (Indians) 155
Oeltjen, Trent (Twins) 285
Olsen, Scott (Marlins) 195
Ortmeier, Dan (Giants) 419
Orvella, Chad (Devil Rays) 461
Otsuka, Akinori (Padres) 404
Owens, Jerry (Expos) 296
Oxspring, Chris (Padres) 406

P

Pacheco, Enemencio (White Sox) 120
Padilla, Jorge (Phillies) 362
Paduch, Jim (Reds) 139
Palmisano, Lou (Brewers) 262
Panther, Nathan (Indians) 153
Papelbon, Jon (Red Sox) 87
Parker, Zach (Rockies) 165
Parra, Manny (Brewers) 259
Parrott, Rhett (Cardinals) 389
Pascucci, Val (Expos) 296
Paul, Xavier (Dodgers) 244
Pauley, David (Padres) 405
Paulino, Felipe (Astros) 221
Pauly, Thomas (Reds) 137
Pawelczyk, Kyle (Angels) 28
Pearce, Josh (Cardinals) 396
Pelland, Tyler (Reds) 133
Pena, Brayan (Braves) 58
Perez, Antonio (Devil Rays) 453
Perez, Carlos (Orioles) 74
Perez, Miguel (Reds) 134
Perez, Rafael (Indians) 152
Perkins, Vince (Blue Jays) 485
Pesco, Nick (Indians) 150
Peterson, Adam (Blue Jays) 486
Peterson, Matt (Mets) 307
Petit, Yusmeiro (Mets) 317
Petrick, Billy (Cubs) 105
Phillips, Mark (Yankees) 328
Pie, Felix (Cubs) 100
Pignatiello, Carmen (Cubs) 108
Pilkington, Brian (Dodgers) 253
Pinto, Renyel (Cubs) 107
Pleiness, Chad (Blue Jays) 490
Pluta, Tony (Astros) 221
Pomeranz, Stuart (Cardinals) 392
Pond, Simon (Blue Jays) 493
Pratt, Andy (Braves) 57
Pridie, Jason (Devil Rays) 455
Prieto, Victor (Marlins) 202
Proctor, Scott (Yankees) 327
Putz, J.J. (Mariners) 441

Q

Qualls, Chad (Astros) 213
Quentin, Carlos (Diamondbacks) 36
Quintanilla, Omar (Athletics) 341
Quintero, Humberto (Padres) 409
Quiroz, Guillermo (Blue Jays) 483

R

Raburn, Ryan (Tigers) 182
Raines Jr., Tim (Orioles) 76
Rainwater, Josh (Tigers) 186
Rakers, Aaron (Orioles) 77
Ramirez, Elizardo (Phillies) 357
Ramirez, Hanley (Red Sox) 82
Ramirez, Ramon (Yankees) 324
Ramirez, Wilkin (Tigers) 182
Ramos, Mario (Athletics) 348
Ransom, Cody (Giants) 426
Rasner, Darrell (Expos) 293
Rauch, Jon (White Sox) 119
Ray, Chris (Orioles) 71
Redman, Prentice (Mets) 313
Reed, Eric (Marlins) 197
Reed, Jeremy (White Sox) 114
Regilio, Nick (Rangers) 476
Reimers, Cam (Blue Jays) 491
Resop, Chris (Marlins) 205
Restovich, Michael (Twins) 278
Reyes, Anthony (Cardinals) 393
Reyes, Jo Jo (Braves) 58
Reyes, Rene (Rockies) 164
Rheinecker, John (Athletics) 343
Richardson, Juan (Phillies) 357
Riggans, Shawn (Devil Rays) 457
Riley, Matt (Orioles) 68
Ring, Royce (Mets) 311
Rios, Alexis (Blue Jays) 482
Rivera, Juan (Dodgers) 253
Rivera, Rene (Mariners) 442
Roberson, Chris (Phillies) 360
Robinson, Scott (Astros) 218
Rodney, Fernando (Tigers) 184
Rodriguez, Carlos (Phillies) 363
Rodriguez, Eddy (Orioles) 72
Rodriguez, Edward (Blue Jays) 492
Rodriguez, Orlando (Dodgers) 251
Rodriguez, Rafael (Angels) 21
Rodriguez, Sean (Angels) 27
Rogers, Michael (Twins) 284
Romero, Alex (Twins) 279
Ronda, Willy Jo (Reds) 141
Rooi, Vince (Expos) 298
Rosario, Adriano (Diamondbacks) 36
Rosario, Francisco (Blue Jays) 484
Rosario, Rodrigo (Astros) 218
Rosa, Carlos (Royals) 232
Ross, Cody (Tigers) 183
Rouse, Mike (Athletics) 341
Rueckel, Danny (Expos) 300
Rundles, Rich (Expos) 296
Rupe, Josh (Rangers) 470
Rust, Evan (Cardinals) 395
Ryan, Brendan (Cardinals) 393
Ryan, Michael (Twins) 283
Ryu, Jae-Kuk (Cubs) 102

S

Sain, Greg (Padres) 411
Salazar, Jeff (Rockies) 169
Saltalamacchia, Jarrod (Braves) 57
Sanchez, Felix (Cubs) 106
Sanchez, Freddy (Pirates) 373
Sanchez, Humberto (Tigers) 184
Santana, Ervin (Angels) 19
Santor, John (Cardinals) 392
Santos, Chad (Royals) 235
Santos, Sergio (Diamondbacks) 35
Sardinha, Bronson (Yankees) 326
Sardinha, Dane (Reds) 140

Sarfate, Dennis (Brewers) 263
Saunders, Joe (Angels) 22
Sborz, Jay (Tigers) 181
Schierholtz, Nate (Giants) 422
Schlichting, Travis (Devil Rays) 458
Schnurstein, Micah (White Sox) 122
Schumaker, Skip (Cardinals) 397
Scott, Lorenzo (Orioles) 73
Seddon, Chris (Devil Rays) 457
Segovia, Zach (Phillies) 363
Seifrig, Cole (Marlins) 198
Self, Todd (Astros) 219
Shackelford, Brian (Reds) 140
Shell, Steven (Angels) 22
Shelton, Chris (Tigers) 183
Shinskie, Dave (Twins) 281
Shoppach, Kelly (Red Sox) 83
Sierra, Edwardo (Yankees) 326
Simon, Alfredo (Phillies) 356
Simon, Billy (Red Sox) 91
Simonitsch, Errol (Twins) 280
Sinisi, Vince (Rangers) 468
Sisco, Andy (Cubs) 99
Sizemore, Grady (Indians) 146
Sledge, Terrmel (Expos) 293
Sleeth, Kyle (Tigers) 178
Slocum, Brian (Indians) 155
Smit, Alexander (Twins) 279
Smith, Corey (Indians) 151
Smith, Sean (Indians) 157
Smith, Will (Rangers) 473
Smitherman, Stephen (Reds) 133
Snare, Ryan (Rangers) 473
Snell, Ian (Pirates) 372
Snelling, Chris (Mariners) 436
Snyder, Brad (Indians) 149
Snyder, Brian (Athletics) 347
Snyder, Chris (Diamondbacks) 39
Song, Seung (Expos) 293
Sosa, Pablo (Marlins) 204
Soto, Luis (Red Sox) 90
Span, Denard (Twins) 277
Spann, Chad (Red Sox) 84
Springer, Kenard (Royals) 235
Sprowl, Jon-Mark (Yankees) 331
Squires, Matt (Phillies) 364
Stahl, Richard (Orioles) 76
Stanford, Jason (Indians) 152
Stanley, Henri (Padres) 412
Starling, Wardell (Pirates) 378
Stauffer, Tim (Padres) 403
Stephens, Jason (Yankees) 331
Stevens, Jake (Braves) 55
Stewart, Cory (Pirates) 373
Stewart, Ian (Rockies) 163
Stewart, Josh (White Sox) 124
Stockman, Phil (Diamondbacks) 41
Stocks, Nick (Cardinals) 396
Stokes, Jason (Marlins) 195
Stonard, Peter (Padres) 411
Stotts, J.T. (Yankees) 330
Strange, Pat (Mets) 315
Strayhorn, Kole (Mets) 311
Strong, Jamal (Mariners) 438
Stumm, Jason (White Sox) 125
Sucre, Antonio (Expos) 297
Sullivan, Brad (Athletics) 339
Sullivan, Cory (Rockies) 170
Sweeney, Ryan (White Sox) 116
Swisher, Nick (Athletics) 340
Switzer, Jon (Devil Rays) 456
Szuminski, Jason (Padres) 412

T

Tadano, Kazuhito (Indians)	150
Takatsu, Shingo (White Sox)	117
Talbot, Mitch (Astros)	214
Tallet, Brian (Indians)	153
Taveras, Willy (Astros)	214
Taylor, Aaron (Mariners)	440
Teahen, Mark (Athletics)	344
Tejeda, Ferdin (Yankees)	324
Tejeda, Juan (Tigers)	189
Tejeda, Robinson (Phillies)	363
Terrero, Luis (Diamondbacks)	38
Thompson, Brad (Cardinals)	395
Thompson, Daryl (Expos)	297
Thompson, Erik (Rangers)	472
Thompson, Rich (Royals)	232
Thompson, Richard (Angels)	28
Thompson, Sean (Padres)	407
Thorman, Scott (Braves)	56
Thornton, Matt (Mariners)	441
Threets, Erick (Giants)	423
Thurston, Joe (Dodgers)	251
Tiffee, Terry (Twins)	283
Tiffany, Chuck (Dodgers)	248
Tisch, Tim (White Sox)	124
Tonis, Mike (Royals)	234
Tracy, Chad (Diamondbacks)	35
Tsao, Chin-Hui (Rockies)	162
Tucker, Rusty (Padres)	407
Tyler, Scott (Twins)	282

U

Upton, B.J. (Devil Rays)	450
Urdaneta, Lino (Tigers)	188

V

Valderrama, Carlos (Giants)	427
Valdez, Jose (Yankees)	330
Valdez, Merkin (Giants)	418
Valdez, Wilson (Marlins)	200
Valentine, Joe (Reds)	136
Valido, Robert (White Sox)	119
VanBenschoten, John (Pirates)	370
Vaquedano, Jose (Red Sox)	93
Vasquez, Jorge (Royals)	232
Vaughan, Beau (Red Sox)	87
Vento, Michael (Yankees)	330
Vermilyea, Jamie (Blue Jays)	492
Villatoro, Wilmer (Mariners)	410
Votto, Joey (Reds)	132

W

Waechter, Doug (Devil Rays)	451
Wagner, Ryan (Reds)	130
Wainwright, Adam (Cardinals)	387
Wallace, David (Indians)	156
Wang, Chien-Ming (Yankees)	326
Watson, Brandon (Expos)	295
Webb, John (Cubs)	107
Webster, Anthony (Rangers)	470
Weeks, Rickie (Brewers)	258
Wellemeyer, Todd (Cubs)	103
Wells, Jared (Padres)	407
Werth, Jayson (Blue Jays)	488
Whitaker, Brian (Padres)	413
Whitaker, Craig (Giants)	421
Whiteman, Tommy (Astros)	215
Whiteside, Eli (Orioles)	75
Whitney, Matt (Indians)	150
Whittington, Anthony (Angels)	23
Wilhelmsen, Tom (Brewers)	263

Williams, Marland (Diamondbacks)	39
Willingham, Josh (Marlins)	196
Wilson, Bobby (Angels)	24
Wilson, Brian (Giants)	429
Wilson, C.J. (Rangers)	472
Wilson, Joe (Phillies)	365
Wilson, Josh (Marlins)	202
Wilson, Michael (Mariners)	445
Wilson, Neil (Rockies)	168
Wing, Ryan (White Sox)	116
Womack, Josh (Mariners)	443
Wood, Brandon (Angels)	21
Wood, Mike (Athletics)	343
Woodard, Johnny (Twins)	285
Woods, Jake (Angels)	23
Woods, Michael (Tigers)	189
Woolard, Glenn (Giants)	425
Wright, David (Mets)	307
Wylie, Jason (Cubs)	105

Y

Yan, Ruddy (White Sox)	124
Yates, Tyler (Mets)	311
Youkilis, Kevin (Red Sox)	83
Young, Chris (White Sox)	118
Young, Chris (Expos)	297
Young, Delmon (Devil Rays)	451
Young, Delwyn (Dodgers)	250
Young, Jason (Rockies)	164
Young, Walter (Orioles)	73

Z

Zimmermann, Bob (Angels)	28
Zink, Charlie (Red Sox)	88
Zumaya, Joel (Tigers)	179
Zumwalt, Alec (Devil Rays)	459